lonely planet

South Africa, Lesotho & Swaziland

THIS EDITION WRITTEN

James Bai

Jean-Bernard Carillet, Lucy Corne, Alan Murphy,

Matt Phillips, Simon Richmond

PLAN YOUR TRIP

GREATER KUDU, KRUGER NATIONAL PARK P384

PETE OXFORD/GETTY IMAGES ©

CAPE TOWN P44

LITTLEWORMY/SHUTTERSTOCK ©

ON THE ROAD

Contents

ON THE ROAD

MICHAEL HEFFERNAN/LONELY PLANET ©

EASTERN CAPE P166

Contents

UNDERSTAND

SURVIVAL GUIDE

SPECIAL FEATURES

Welcome to South Africa, Lesotho & Swaziland

Lions, township art, clouds pouring over Table Mountain, Kalahari dunes, Swazi and Zulu ceremonies: Southern Africa's famous trio is rich with adventures and experiences, culture and scenery.

Rainbow Nation

With people from Afrikaners to Zulus living side by side and speaking 11 official languages, South Africa is undoubtedly one of the world's most diverse countries. Pastel *rondavels* (round huts with a conical roof) dot the green ridges of the Drakensberg and the Wild Coast, Nelson Mandela's birthplace; Basotho shepherds clad in distinctive hats and blankets lead their sturdy ponies through Lesotho's Maluti Mountains; and at the traditional reed dances in Swaziland and Zululand, debutantes dance with swaying reeds for local royalty. Meeting these people and experiencing their diverse cultures, all coexisting thanks to Mandela's legacy of tolerance, will leave you with indelible memories.

Wildlife Watching

South Africa is one of the continent's best safari destinations, offering the Big Five (lion, leopard, buffalo, elephant and rhino) and more in accessible parks and reserves. You can drive your car right into the epic wilderness in Kruger, Kgalagadi and other parks, or join khaki-clad rangers on guided drives and walks. A few coastal parks boast the Big Seven, adding southern right whales and great white sharks to the mix, while wildlife-rich Swaziland has more than its share of black and white rhinos.

Dramatic Landscapes

South Africa's landscapes are stunning, from the burning Karoo and Kalahari semideserts to the misty heights of the Drakensberg range and the massive Blyde River Canyon. Even in urban Cape Town you need only look up to see the beautiful *fynbos* (indigenous flora) climbing the slopes of Table Mountain while, nearby, two of the world's most dramatic coastal roads lead to Cape Point and Hermanus. Add the vineyards carpeting the Winelands, old-growth forests along the Garden Route and Tsitsikamma, Indian Ocean beaches and Lesotho's inspiring mountains, and there is a staggering variety to enjoy.

Activities & Adventure

Numerous activities take advantage of South Africa, Lesotho and Swaziland's sheer geographic and cultural diversity. Action-packed adventures such as abseiling from Table Mountain, shark-cage diving, surfing and walking safaris are all offered; plus, at Bloukrans Bridge you can brave the world's highest bridge bungee jump (216m), and at Lesotho's Maletsunyane Falls, the world's longest abseil (204m). For cultural experiences, spend a few days hiking the Wild Coast or trekking Lesotho's mountain passes on a Basotho pony. In the space of just a few hours, you can learn to make Xhosa dishes or Cape Malay curries, taste Cape wines or catch live music in a township.

Why I Love South Africa, Lesotho & Swaziland

By James Bainbridge, Author

I've been living in South Africa for five years, and I would find it hard to move. What gets me is the intoxicating sense of space and freedom in areas such as the cobalt-skied Karoo and mountainous Lesotho – and their accessibility. Within an hour's drive of Cape Town, you can be tasting at several hundred wine farms; within three, you can be deep in the Cederberg mountains. For wilderness, wildlife and African culture mixed with excellent accommodation and *lekker* (tasty) cuisine, South Africa, Lesotho and Swaziland are unbeatable.

For more about our authors, see page 640

Above: Sandstone formations, Cederberg Wilderness Area (p162)

South Africa, Lesotho & Swaziland

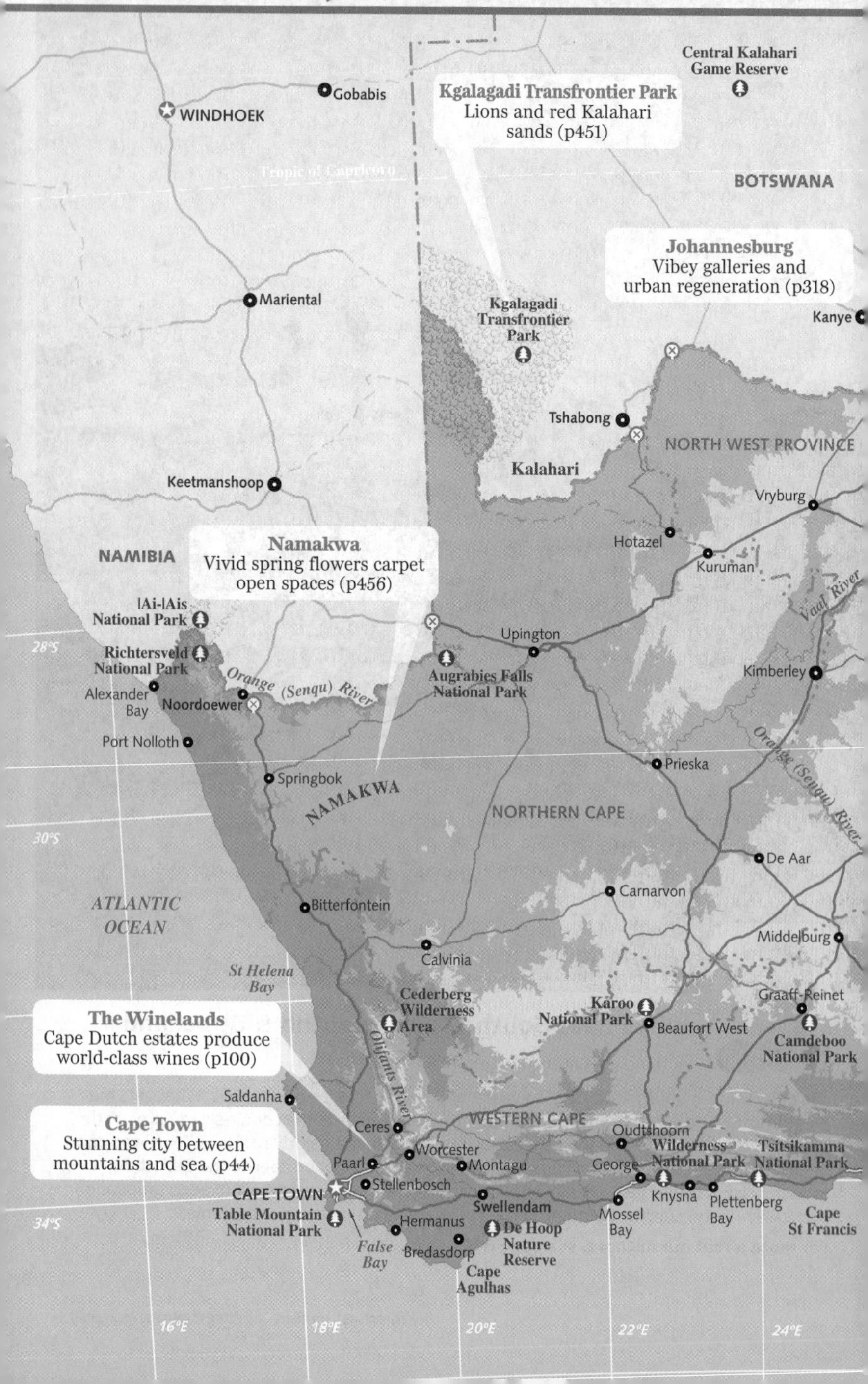

Kgalagadi Transfrontier Park
Lions and red Kalahari sands (p451)
Johannesburg
Vibey galleries and urban regeneration (p318)
Namakwa
Vivid spring flowers carpet open spaces (p456)
The Winelands
Cape Dutch estates produce world-class wines (p100)
Cape Town
Stunning city between mountains and sea (p44)
Central Kalahari Game Reserve
Gobabis
WINDHOEK
Tropic of Capricorn
BOTSWANA
Mariental
Kgalagadi Transfrontier Park
Kanye
Tshabong
NORTH WEST PROVINCE
Kalahari
Keetmanshoop
Vryburg
Hotazel
Kuruman
NAMIBIA
Vaal River
|Ai-|Ais National Park
Upington
28°S
Richtersveld National Park
Augrabies Falls National Park
Kimberley
Orange (Senqu) River
Alexander Bay
Noordoewer
Port Nolloth
Prieska
Springbok
NAMAKWA
NORTHERN CAPE
Orange (Senqu) River
30°S
De Aar
Carnarvon
ATLANTIC OCEAN
Bitterfontein
Middelburg
Calvinia
St Helena Bay
Cederberg Wilderness Area
Karoo National Park
Graaff-Reinet
Beaufort West
Camdeboo National Park
Olifants River
Saldanha
WESTERN CAPE
Ceres
Oudtshoorn
Wilderness National Park
Tsitsikamma National Park
Worcester
Paarl
Montagu
George
Stellenbosch
Knysna
CAPE TOWN
Swellendam
Plettenberg Bay
Mossel Bay
34°S
Table Mountain National Park
Hermanus
De Hoop Nature Reserve
Cape St Francis
False Bay
Bredasdorp
Cape Agulhas
16°E
18°E
20°E
22°E
24°E

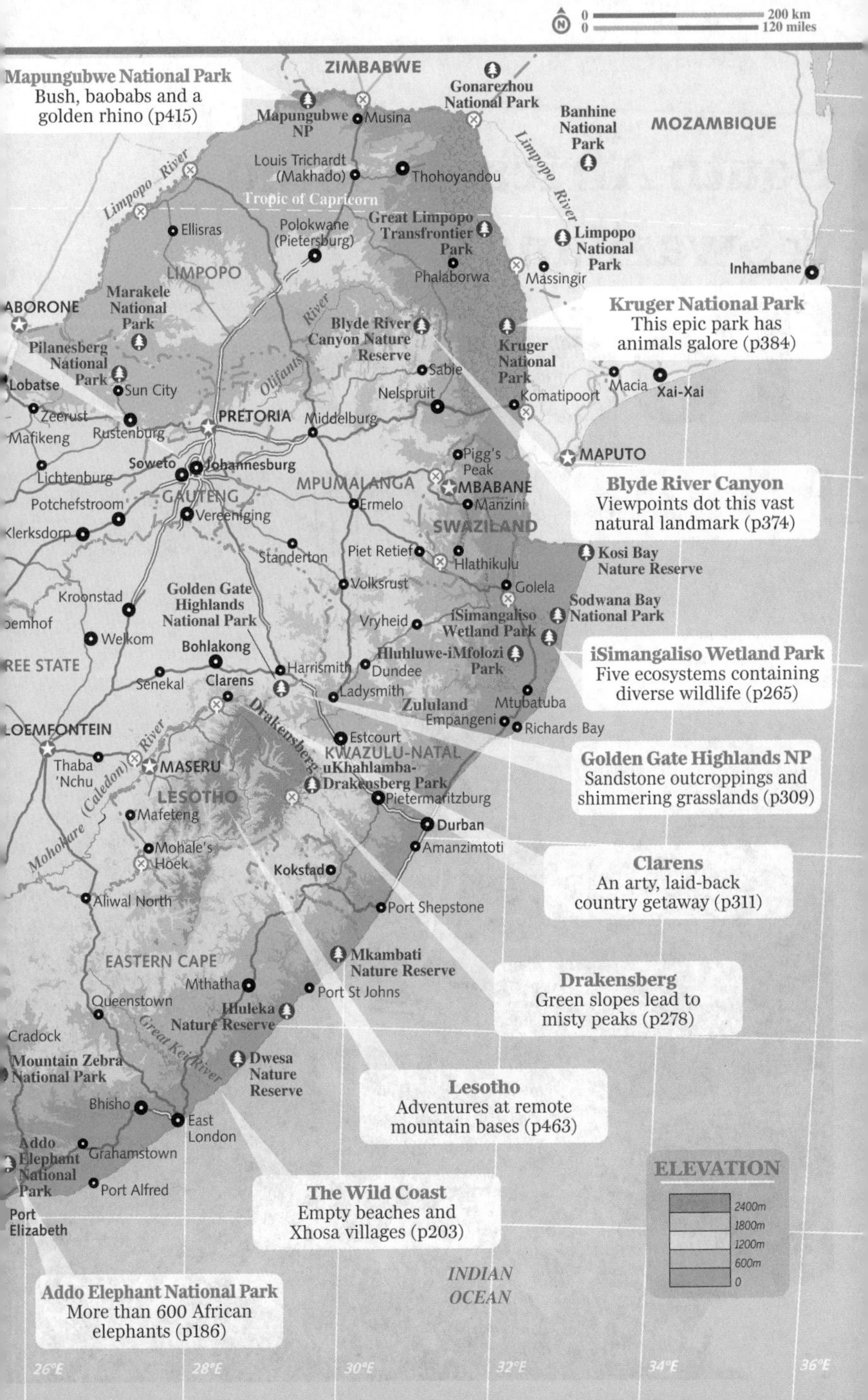

0 200 km
0 120 miles
Mapungubwe National Park
Bush, baobabs and a golden rhino (p415)
Kruger National Park
This epic park has animals galore (p384)
Blyde River Canyon
Viewpoints dot this vast natural landmark (p374)
iSimangaliso Wetland Park
Five ecosystems containing diverse wildlife (p265)
Golden Gate Highlands NP
Sandstone outcroppings and shimmering grasslands (p309)
Clarens
An arty, laid-back country getaway (p311)
Drakensberg
Green slopes lead to misty peaks (p278)
Lesotho
Adventures at remote mountain bases (p463)
The Wild Coast
Empty beaches and Xhosa villages (p203)
Addo Elephant National Park
More than 600 African elephants (p186)
ZIMBABWE
MOZAMBIQUE
Gonarezhou National Park
Banhine National Park
Mapungubwe NP
Musina
Louis Trichardt (Makhado)
Thohoyandou
Tropic of Capricorn
Limpopo River
Polokwane (Pietersburg)
Great Limpopo Transfrontier Park
Limpopo National Park
Phalaborwa
Massingir
Inhambane
Ellisras
LIMPOPO
Marakele National Park
GABORONE
Pilanesberg National Park
Sun City
Lobatse
Olifants River
Blyde River Canyon Nature Reserve
Sabie
Kruger National Park
Nelspruit
Komatipoort
Macia
Xai-Xai
Zeerust
Mafikeng
Rustenburg
PRETORIA
Middelburg
MAPUTO
Soweto
Johannesburg
Lichtenburg
Pigg's Peak
MPUMALANGA
MBABANE
Manzini
GAUTENG
Potchefstroom
Vereeniging
Ermelo
SWAZILAND
Klerksdorp
Standerton
Piet Retief
Hlathikulu
Kosi Bay Nature Reserve
Volksrust
Golela
Kroonstad
Golden Gate Highlands National Park
Sodwana Bay National Park
iSimangaliso Wetland Park
Vryheid
Welkom
Bohlakong
FREE STATE
Harrismith
Hluhluwe-iMfolozi Park
Dundee
Senekal
Clarens
Ladysmith
Zululand
Mtubatuba
Empangeni
Richards Bay
Drakensberg
BLOEMFONTEIN
Estcourt
KWAZULU-NATAL
Thaba 'Nchu
MASERU
uKhahlamba-Drakensberg Park
Mohokare (Caledon) River
LESOTHO
Pietermaritzburg
Durban
Mafeteng
Amanzimtoti
Mohale's Hoek
Kokstad
Aliwal North
Port Shepstone
EASTERN CAPE
Mkambati Nature Reserve
Mthatha
Port St Johns
Queenstown
Hluleka Nature Reserve
Great Kei River
Cradock
Dwesa Nature Reserve
Mountain Zebra National Park
Bhisho
East London
Addo Elephant National Park
Grahamstown
Port Alfred
Port Elizabeth
INDIAN OCEAN
ELEVATION
2400m
1800m
1200m
600m
0
26°E
28°E
30°E
32°E
34°E
36°E

South Africa, Lesotho & Swaziland's Top 25

1

Cape Town

1 Overlooked by flat-topped Table Mountain, with its cable car, walking trails and abseiling, Cape Town (p44) is one of the world's most beautiful cities. Days here are filled with visits to beaches and Constantia wine estates, wandering the V&A Waterfront, catching the ferry to Robben Island and, above all, meeting the easygoing Cape locals. In complement to its considerable natural charms, the city is benefiting from ongoing urban renewal, with gastronomic restaurants, food markets and design-savvy arcades opening in neighbourhoods such as Woodstock and East City. Below left: Table Mountain Cableway (p64)

Kruger National Park

2 Kruger National Park (p384) is one of Africa's great wilderness experiences and the mightiest of the country's national parks – a trip here will sear itself in your mind. Its accessibility, numbers and variety of wildlife, staggering size and range of activities make Kruger unique and compelling. From wilderness trails and bush walks to mountain biking and remote 4WD trails, there are myriad opportunities to enjoy both the wild and the wildlife. Kruger is simply one of the best places to see animals – big and small – in the world. Below right: Impala (p567)

NEIL AUSTEN / GETTY IMAGES ©

2

MICHAEL HEFFERNAN / LONELY PLANET ©

Drakensberg Region

3 Majestic, stunning and mysterious, the mountains and foothills of the World Heritage–listed uKhahlamba-Drakensberg Park (p278) are among the country's most awe-inspiring landscapes. Drakensberg means 'Dragon Mountains' in Afrikaans, and the Zulu named the range Quathlamba (Battlement of Spears); both convey beautifully the area's sublime backdrop of incredible peaks. With its Zulu villages, wilderness areas and wildflowers, good accommodation and eateries, the Drakensberg region is the perfect place for photographers, hikers and adventurous travellers.

The Winelands

4 Whitewashed Cape Dutch architecture dots an endlessly photogenic landscape of rolling hills and vines in neat rows. The Winelands (p100) is the quintessential Cape, where world-class wines are the icing on the proverbial cake. Stellenbosch, Franschhoek and Paarl, the area's holy trinity of wine-tasting towns, host some of the southern hemisphere's best wine estates. But this is not the only wine region – head to Tulbagh for sparkling wines, the heights of the Cederberg for crisp sauvignon blancs, and Route 62 for robust reds and port.

3

4

JAMES HAGER / GETTY IMAGES ©

TIER UND NATURFOTOGRAFIE J UND C SOHNS / GETTY IMAGES ©

Wild Coast Walks

5 With its rugged cliffs plunging into the sea, remote sandy beaches, rural Xhosa villages, and history of shipwrecks and stranded sailors, the aptly named Wild Coast (p203) is ideally explored on foot. From the Great Kei River to Port St Johns, pathways hug the shoreline, cutting through dense vegetation or snaking across denuded hillsides and gorges, and often overlook southern right whales and dolphins in the turquoise seas. Power down in rustic accommodation or overnight with families in traditionally designed *rondavels* (round huts with a conical roof). Above left: Coffee Bay (p208)

Kgalagadi Transfrontier Park

6 Kgalagadi (p451) covers almost 40,000 sq km of raw Kalahari in the Northern Cape and Botswana, an area roamed by some 2000 predators. But such statistics, albeit impressive, barely scrape the surface of this immense land of sizzling sunsets, velvety night skies and rolling red dunes. The park is one of the world's best places to spot big cats, and you might spy black-maned lions napping under thorn trees, or cheetahs and leopards tracking along the roadside. Best of all, you don't need a 4WD to access the park. Top right: Lioness (p562)

iSimangaliso Wetland Park

7 iSimangaliso Wetland Park (p265), which means 'miracle' or 'wonder' in Zulu, has a fitting name. This Unesco World Heritage site stretches for a glorious 220km, from the Mozambique border to Maphelane, at the southern end of Lake St Lucia. The 3280-sq-km park protects five distinct ecosystems, ranging from offshore reefs and beaches, to lakes, wetlands, woodlands and coastal forests. It's nature's playground, offering wildlife drives, kayak safaris, cycling and cruises, plus extraordinary animals. Bottom right: Hippopotamus (p568)

8

AFRIPICS.COM / ALAMY ©

9

Clarens

8 The odd international star popping in for a lungful of fresh mountain air gives this well-heeled town celebrity credentials. But with galleries, antiques, classy restaurants, a microbrewery and adventure activities in the surrounding countryside, there's something to appeal to most other visitors too. The laidback town is perfect for an evening stroll after a day exploring the nearby Golden Gate Highlands National Park. And with plenty of pubs to drop into and bookshops to browse in, Clarens (p311) is the best place in the Free State's Eastern Highlands to simply wind down.

Mapungubwe National Park

9 A real stand-out among South Africa's national parks, this transfrontier conservation area (p415) in the making has been declared a World Heritage Site for its important cultural heritage. The landscape is riveting, too: ancient terrain that is twisted and knotted, with rocky bluffs offering majestic views; and mighty rivers that intersect. The climate is harsh, but lions, leopards, cheetahs, elephants and white rhinos can be found here, as well as smaller species such as caracals. Getting around can be tough but the rewards are sublime.

Blyde River Canyon

10 This canyon (p374), the third largest in the world and possibly the greenest, is one of South Africa's great sights. The lack of foreign visitors to the canyon, where the Blyde snakes down from the Drakensberg Escarpment to the lowveld, is both perplexing and a real bonus for those who do make it here. On a clear day the viewpoints, with names like 'the Three Rondavels' and 'God's Window', will leave you breathless. This vast natural landmark scarring northern Mpumalanga can be appreciated on foot or by car.

10

11

GARY LATHAM / LONELY PLANET ©

Addo Elephant National Park

11 At Addo (p186) more than 600 African elephants roam through low bushes, tall grass and distant hills. The land (reclaimed after being decimated by farmers) and the park represent a conservation success story. Also roaming free are hyenas and lions, introduced in 2003 to bring the kudu, ostrich and warthog populations down. But it's all in the name – elephants are the show stoppers here, particularly when they burst from the undergrowth, flap their ears and dwarf all that is before them. Right: Elephants (p568)

Golden Gate Highlands National Park

12 Beneath the open skies of the Free State's Eastern Highlands, this park (p309) enjoys extraordinary sunsets, and hides plenty of antelope, zebras, jackals and birds among its grasslands and sandstone outcrops. Views of the Drakensberg and Maluti Mountains loom large and there's something almost fairytale-like about the wind sweeping patterns through the grass. If you don't have the chance to explore Lesotho, it's worth visiting the Basotho Cultural Village for tourists here.

Lesotho Trading Posts

13 Travel in high-altitude Lesotho has always been arduous. The ever-pragmatic British established trading posts to maintain commercial (nay, political) links with the isolated Basotho nation, and today's traveller benefits greatly from this spirit of endeavour – the former trading posts afford some of Southern Africa's most spectacular adventures. At Malealea (p484; above), Semonkong (p483), Ramabanta (p474) and Roma (p474), hikers, trekkers, pony riders, motorbikers and those seeking a village getaway gather at mealtimes to rejoice around the bonfire.

Namakwa Wildflowers

14 Namakwa is one of South Africa's forgotten corners, stretching up the west coast towards Namibia. Crossing the remote region, and reaching Port Nolloth's refreshing Atlantic vistas, is wonderful throughout the year. In spring, there's the wildflower bloom, which turns Namakwa's rocky expanses into a technicolour carpet. You could spend days travelling around the area, stopping at spots such as Namaqua National Park (p461) and Goegap Nature Reserve (p457), both of which are dedicated to wildflower watching.

Hiking & Stargazing in the Cederberg

15 By day the clear blue skies provide an arresting contrast to the craggy, fiery orange peaks of the Cederberg (p162); by night the Milky Way shines so brightly you can almost read by its light. But the Cederberg is the promised land for more than just stargazers – its otherworldly landscape is perfect for hikers, rock climbers and those simply in search of silent nights. Tackle challenging trails and hikes, visiting remote and forgotten mission villages.

16

DORI MORENO / GETTY IMAGES ©

17

18

Hluhluwe-iMfolozi Park

16 Sometimes overshadowed by Kruger National Park, Hluhluwe-iMfolozi (p263) in northern KwaZulu-Natal is nonetheless one of the country's best-known and most evocative parks. Stunningly beautiful, it features a variety of landscapes, from open savannah to mountains with wildflowers. And it teems with wildlife, including the Big Five and other amazing creatures. Hluhluwe-iMfolozi can be visited at any time – there's always plenty to see. Great wildlife drives, accommodation and hiking trails ensure a memorable experience. Above left: Impala (p567)

Venda Region

17 A lush region (p416) steeped in mystique and ancient custom, this is the Africa of mist-clad hills, dusty red tracks and mud huts. Sprinkled with lakes and forests containing enormous spiritual significance, and marking the primeval ties between indigenous culture and the land, the Limpopo province's former homeland is well worth exploring with a local guide. Stay in Elim or Louis Trichardt (Makhado) and begin with the Venda arts and crafts trail; the area is noted for its fine original artwork, with studios hidden throughout the landscape. Top right: Thohoyandou (p416)

Garden Route

18 The enduring popularity of this verdant coastal strip, where woodcutters once dodged elephants in the old-growth forests, lies not only in its undeniable scenic beauty. The Garden Route (p135) is also a magnet for those in search of a little outdoor adventure. Whether you're hiking the Knysna Forests, surfing in Victoria Bay, canoeing on Wilderness Lagoon or getting up close with great whites in a cage below Mossel Bay's waters, the Garden Route guarantees an adventure for every taste and budget. Bottom right: Surfers, Victoria Bay (p141)

Madikwe Game Reserve

19 One of the country's most exclusive reserves on such a large scale, Madikwe (p433) occupies 760 sq km of bushveld, savannah grassland and riverine forest. There's a good chance of spotting iconic African wildlife, and the lodges are experiences in themselves, from an ecolodge to five-star options offering creature comforts in the wilderness. Visits to Madikwe are on an all-inclusive basis, allowing you to relax once you're through the gates. Below: Jaci's Lodges (p434), Madikwe

Reed Dance

20 Africa has many colourful festivals that seem bizarre to outside eyes, but none stranger than Swaziland's Umhlanga dance (p490), which takes place in late August/early September. The week-long event is essentially a debutante ball for young Swazi maidens, who collect reeds to help repair the queen mother's house. The festivities climax with the debs dancing with tall swaying reeds in hand, hoping to catch King Mswati III's eye. A similar event happens in Zululand.

19

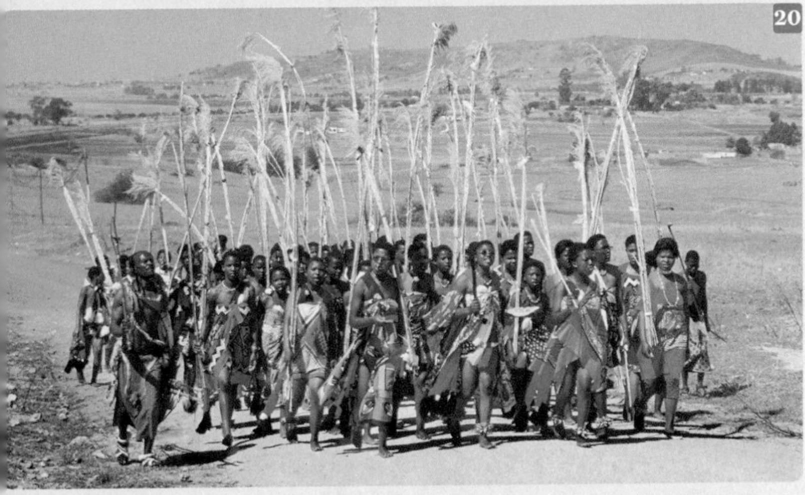
20

Johannesburg

21 With a grisly reputation, the City of Gold (p318) is a surprisingly vibey and inspiring place thanks to the regeneration uplifting its inner city. The cultural enclaves of Braamfontein, Newtown, 44 Stanley Avenue and the Maboneng Precinct are dynamic spots, with galleries, restaurants, bars and boutiques. Take a walking tour to understand the background of this urban transformation and try to time your visit to coincide with Braamfontein and Maboneng's weekly markets. Below: Market, Maboneng (p324)

Sani Top

22 The highest pub in Africa is a hell of a place to get to. From the west it's an endurance drive over Lesotho's awesome Central Highlands and huge dams that supply Gauteng. From KwaZulu-Natal, it's a vertiginous drive up the Sani Pass (2876m), which climbs 1300m through uncountable hairpin bends from the South African border post. At the top, raise a beer in the bar of Sani Mountain Lodge (p480) and celebrate being in the highest country (that is, the nation with the highest low point) in the world. Bottoms up!

21

22

CAY-UWE KULZER / GETTY IMAGES ©

ANDY NIXON / GETTY IMAGES ©

Mkhaya Game Reserve

23 You're more likely to meet rhinos here than anywhere else, thanks to Mkhaya's rhino protection program. Named after its *mkhaya* (knobthorn) trees, this private reserve (p505) in eastern Swaziland might also be one of Africa's best-value spots; accommodation rates include wildlife drives, walking safaris, park entry and meals. And as for the accommodation – where else can you sleep in luxurious semi-open stone and thatch cottages in a secluded bush zone? All that, plus a loo with a bush view. Above left: Rhinoceros

Pilanesberg National Park

24 Sprawling away from Sun City is this underrated park, where the Big Five and day-tripping Jo'burgers roam an extinct volcanic crater. With its tarred roads, Pilanesberg (p431) is sometimes dismissed as tame, yet the rhinos lapping at waterholes seem to disagree. To escape the other cars and score an up-close sighting, hit the gravel roads through the bush and stake out a dam. Guided drives and walks are available, as is a range of accommodation, making this a winner for families and those short on time.

Cradle of Humankind

25 As the Chemical Brothers sampled: 'it began in Afrika' (or Western Gauteng to be precise). Today, the Cradle of Humankind (p349) nurses hundreds of square kilometres of beautiful green and brown veld – and an increasing migration of tourists, descended from hominids, who sit with the fossils of their ancestors deep underground, before returning to civilisation at fine restaurants and day spas. There's wilderness, too; 50km northwest of Jo'burg are free-roaming elands, giraffes and gazelles. Bottom right: Maropeng (p350)

Need to Know

For more information, see Survival Guide (p577)

Currencies

South African rand (R), Lesothan loti (plural maloti, M), Swazi lilangeni (plural emalangeni, E)

Languages

Zulu, Xhosa, Afrikaans, English, Southern Sotho (Lesotho), Swati (Swaziland)

Visas

Not required for most Western nationals to stay for up to 90 days in South Africa, and 30 each in Lesotho and Swaziland.

Money

ATMs widespread and credit cards widely accepted in South Africa. ATMs common in Lesotho and Swaziland, but cards rarely accepted outside the capitals.

Mobile Phones

Most foreign phones can be used on roaming. Local SIM cards can be used in most unlocked foreign phones.

Time

South Africa Standard Time (GMT/UTC plus two hours)

When to Go

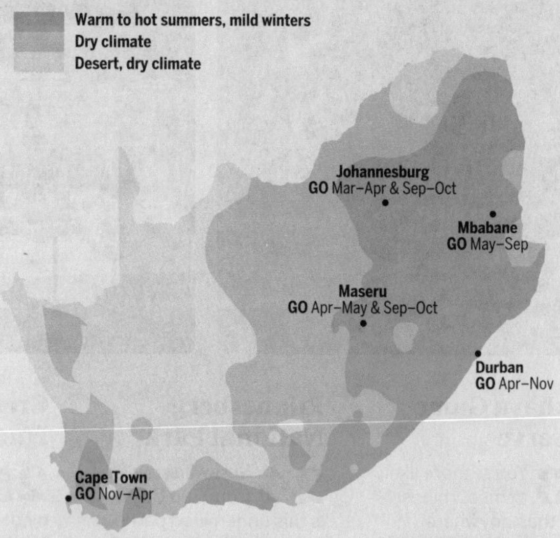

High Season (Nov–Mar)

- Peak times are early December to mid-January and around Easter.
- During peak times, accommodation in national parks and on the coast books up months in advance.

Shoulder (Apr–May, Sep, Oct)

- Sunny spring and autumn weather.
- Wildflower season late August to early September.
- School holiday late September to early October.
- Optimum wildlife-watching conditions autumn onwards.

Low Season (Jun–Aug)

- Winter is ideal for wildlife watching.
- Prices sometimes rise during the late June to mid-July school holiday; otherwise they are low, with discounts and packages offered.

Useful Websites

BBC (www.bbc.com/africa) Country profiles at bottom of page.

Fair Trade Tourism (www.fairtrade.travel) Accommodation, tours and itineraries.

Lonely Planet (www.lonelyplanet.com/south-africa) Information, bookings and forums.

South African National Parks (www.sanparks.org) Information, bookings and forums.

SouthAfrica.info (www.southafrica.info) News and information.

Travel Now Now (www.travelnownow.co.za) Backpacker guides and listings.

Important Numbers

Dial the local area code even if you are dialling from the same town or code area.

South Africa country code	☏27
Lesotho country code	☏266
Swaziland country code	☏268
International access code (all three countries)	☏00
South Africa police	☏10111

Exchange Rates

Australia	A$1	R9.32
Canada	C$1	R9.74
Europe	€1	R13.70
Japan	¥100	R9.32
Lesotho	M1	R1
New Zealand	NZ$1	R8.59
Swaziland	E1	R1
UK	£1	R17.26
USA	US$1	R11

For current exchange rates see www.xe.com.

Daily Costs

Budget: Under R1000

- Hostel dorm bed from R120
- Budget main dish under R75
- Two-week hop-on, hop-off Baz Bus pass R3480
- Free entry to some museums

Midrange: R1000–1800

- Double room R600–2500
- Midrange main dish R75–150
- Jo'burg–Cape Town tourist-class train R630
- Single room supplements common

Top End: Over R1800

- Double room over R1500
- Top-end main dish over R150
- Cape Town–Jo'burg flight from R750
- Wildlife drive from R300

Opening Hours

Banks 9am–3.30pm Mon–Fri, 9–11am Sat

Post offices 8.30am–4.30pm Mon–Fri, 8.30am–noon Sat

Government offices 8am–3pm Mon–Fri, 8am–noon Sat (Lesotho 8am–12.45pm & 2pm–4.30pm Mon–Fri; Swaziland 8am–4pm Mon–Fri)

Cafes 7am–5pm

Restaurants 11.30am–3pm & 7–10pm (last orders); many open 3–7pm

Bars 4pm–2am

Businesses and shopping 8.30am–5pm Mon–Fri, 8.30am–1pm Sat; many supermarkets also 9am–noon Sun; major shopping centres till 9pm daily

Arriving in South Africa

OR Tambo International Airport (p344) The Gautrain serves central Jo'burg (R145, 20 minutes) and Pretoria (R155, 45 minutes) every 12 to 30 minutes; shuttles and taxis take about one hour to Jo'burg (R400) and Pretoria (R450). There are car-hire companies at the airport; major roads lead to both Jo'burg and Pretoria.

Cape Town International Airport (p599) Shuttle (from R180), taxi (from R200) and MyCiTi bus (R70, every 30 minutes) to central Cape Town take about 30 minutes. There are car-hire companies at the airport; Cape Town is straight along the N2 highway. Shuttles also serve Stellenbosch (from R200, 45 minutes).

Getting Around

Car A great option in a country with a car-based lifestyle, with affordable rental rates and a good road network; the drawback is dangerous drivers.

Baz Bus The backpacker shuttle is a convenient and social option between Cape Town, Durban and Jo'burg/Pretoria.

Train Tourist class is an unsung secret, with sleeper coaches and dining car, linking Jo'burg to Cape Town and the coast. Economy class and commuter trains are not as safe.

Bus Lines including Greyhound, Intercape and Translux are useful, covering the country in comfortable vehicles at reasonable rates.

Shared minibus taxi Okay for short journeys but less practical over long distances; various safety and security issues.

For much more on **getting around**, see p604

If You Like...

Dramatic Landscapes

From the Cape's mix of coastline and mountains to expanses like Namakwa, the Kalahari and Karoo, South Africa and mountainous Lesotho feature some of Africa's most impressive landscapes.

Drakensberg The Dragon Mountains bristle with awesome peaks and formations such as the Ampitheatre. (p278)

Cape Peninsula A spine of mountains runs down the peninsula from Table Mountain to Cape Point. (p57)

Wild Coast Green hills dotted with pastel *rondavels* (round, conical-roofed huts), rugged cliffs and empty beaches. (p203)

Lesotho highlands Peaks climb over 3000m in the mountain kingdom's raw section of the Drakensberg. (p478)

Augrabies Falls National Park The world's sixth-tallest waterfall, created by the Orange River thundering into a ravine. (p454)

Wildlife

Diverse, accessible and swarming with wildlife, these parks and reserves are some of the world's best destinations to see the Big Five (lion, leopard, buffalo, elephant and rhino).

Kruger National Park South Africa's famous park has 12,000 elephants alone, in landscapes from woodland to savannah. (p384)

Kgalagadi Transfrontier Park Deep in the Kalahari, this is an unbeatable place to spot big cats, including black-maned lions. (p451)

Mkhaya Game Reserve Swaziland's stunning reserve has endangered species plus buffaloes, elephants and an impressive rhino population. (p505)

Elephant Coast KwaZulu-Natal's ecotourism destination offers sightings in tropical settings; highlights include Hluhluwe-iMfolozi Park. (p263)

Madikwe Game Reserve The exclusive reserve hosts the Big Five in bushveld, savannah grassland and riverine forest. (p433)

Addo Elephant National Park South Africa's third-largest national park offers some of the world's best elephant viewing. (p186)

Cultural Experiences

Escaping the comfortable, Westernised bubble of South Africa's tourist industry, and having hands-on experiences of the region's diverse traditions and beliefs, is hugely rewarding.

Townships From Soweto to Khayelitsha, take an interactive, themed tour or stay overnight in a homestay. (p345)

Umhlanga dance Swazi debutantes dance with reeds in hand at this annual festival. (p490)

Wild Coast The former Xhosa homeland offers community-run backpacking and activities at Bulungula, plus volunteering opportunities. (p210)

!Xaus Lodge Learn Khomani San tracking skills at one of a few locations offering culture alongside wildlife. (p453)

Venda region Meet the former homeland's artists and explore a sacred forest above Lake Fundudzi. (p417)

Trading posts Meet the friendly Basotho people at Lesotho's stunning Malealea Lodge, or the equally wonderful Semonkong, Ramabanta or Roma. (p484)

Zululand Learn about South Africa's largest ethnic group on visits to villages and ceremonies. (p253)

Activities & Adventures

Whether you want to cross vast wildernesses, search

Top: Zulu women in traditional dress, Zululand (p253)
Bottom: Augrabies Falls (p454)

for predators in the bushveld or just lounge on the beach, Africa's southernmost trio has it covered.

Garden Route The holiday strip offers surfing, canoeing, diving, kloofing (canyoning), horse riding, hiking and more. (p135)

Pony trekking Explore Lesotho's rugged highlands in the traditional way, on a Basotho pony. (p583)

Bloukrans Bridge Bungee The world's third-highest bungee jump is one of many thrills in the Tsitsikamma forests. (p170)

Multiday hikes Carry your equipment or take the easy 'slackpacking' option and have your bags transported. (p170)

Kalahari The semidesert makes use of the Orange River for rafting, canoeing and wine tasting. (p455)

Canopy tours Stroll Kirstenbosch's Boomslang walkway, and zip-line in the Drakensberg, Swaziland and beyond. (p55)

Lion's Head paragliding Take a tandem flight from Cape Town's sphinx-like mountain down to the beach. (p61)

Abseiling Shimmy down Table Mountain on the world's longest abseil (204m) at Lesotho's Maletsunyane Falls. (p483)

Cheetah tracking Get within 15m of Mountain Zebra National Park's collared but wild big cats. (p223)

History

Numerous sights remember South Africa's tumultuous history, and a strong sense of the past lingers in rural areas such as the Winelands and Karoo.

Cape Town Sights from the Castle of Good Hope to Robben

Island and historic walking tours. (p53)

Kimberley A Victorian diamond-mining settlement, historic pubs, ghost tours and Cecil Rhodes' club. (p439)

Liberation trail Spots from Jo'burg's Constitution Hill to Qunu's Nelson Mandela Museum celebrate the anti-apartheid struggle. (p324)

Apartheid Museum Entered through racial classification gates, Jo'burg's museum evokes the era of segregation. (p325)

Mapungubwe National Park The Unesco World Heritage Site was home to a significant Iron Age civilisation. (p415)

Oudtshoorn Mansions built by ostrich-farming 'feather barons', and pioneering engineer Thomas Bain's Swartberg Pass. (p153)

Cape Dutch Gabled museum houses in South Africa's oldest settlements: Cape Town (p44), Stellenbosch (p100), Swellendam (p133) and Graaff-Reinet (p218).

Food & Drink

From Cape Dutch wine estates to braais (barbecues) smoking away on township corners, sampling South Africa's *lekker* (tasty) produce is the best way to this agricultural country's heart.

Cooking safari Make Cape Malay curries in Cape Town's Bo-Kaap, and Xhosa dishes in the townships. (p541)

Food markets Try farm-fresh goodies at Cape Town and Jo'burg's Neighbourgoods Markets and rural events. (p93)

Wine tour Toast three centuries of local viticulture on stunning estates in Stellenbosch, Franschhoek and beyond. (p101)

Beer cruise Sample South Africa's burgeoning beer scene in microbreweries and bars such as Long Street's Beerhouse. (p82)

Altitudinous eats Africa's highest restaurant and pub, both in Lesotho, offer mountain views and novelty value. (p478)

Bunny chow Regional specialities include this creation from Durban: a hollow bread loaf filled with curry. (p241)

Wine on the River Quaff by the Breede River, Robertson; one of the Western Cape's many wine festivals. (p119)

Cooking wild A new spin on bush braais: Shamwari Game Reserve offers cookery classes on safari. (p188)

Art & Culture

Artworks reflecting South Africa's dramatic landscapes and social issues can be seen in galleries old and new, with vibrant cultural scenes in Jo'burg and Cape Town.

Cape Town The World Design Capital 2014 has private galleries galore, especially on Church St and in Woodstock. (p90)

Eastern Karoo Refined Graaff-Reinet has well-preserved architecture, and cement sculptures populate Nieu Bethesda's Owl House. (p222)

Clarens South Africa's foremost art town, this Free State gem has a dozen galleries. (p311)

Ecoshrine This ecological Stonehenge overlooks the Amathole Mountains in alternative, environmental Hogsback. (p201)

Jo'burg Cultural districts such as the Maboneng Precinct have galleries, street art and walking tours. (p323)

Craftwork Pick up tapestries in Teyateyaneng, Lesotho, and handicrafts in Swaziland's Ezulwini and Malkerns Valleys. (p475)

Venda region Down red tracks in Limpopo's former homeland, studios produce woodcarvings, pottery, batiks and textiles. (p417)

William Humphreys Art Gallery Artists in Kimberley's gallery range from prison inmates to Dutch and Flemish old masters. (p442)

Open Spaces

Whether you head inland or along the coast, the largely rural countryside offers an invigorating sense of freedom.

Namakwa The rocky hills and plains covering the country's western quarters fill with spring wildflowers. (p456)

Free State Discover golden sunflower and corn fields, and simmering grasslands in Golden Gate Highlands Natural Park. (p309)

Southern Lesotho This mountainous area has musk- and orange-coloured valleys, rivers and off-the-beaten-track villages. (p483)

Karoo The semiarid plateau experiences blazing summers and icy winters, stunning sunsets and starscapes. (p155)

Beaches Quiet beaches are common on South Africa's 2500km-plus coastline, from Cape Point upwards. (p552)

Kalahari Red dunes ripple all the way to the horizon, with added greenery by the Orange River. (p447)

Month by Month

TOP EVENTS

Wildlife-watching, July

Traditional festivals, September

Kirstenbosch Summer Sunset Concerts, November

Whale-watching, September

Cape Town Cycle Tour, March

January

South Africans descend on tourist areas, including the coast and major parks, during summer school holidays (early December to mid-January). Book accommodation and transport well in advance. High season for accommodation is November to March.

Cape Town Minstrel Carnival (Kaapse Klopse)

The Mother City's colourful new-year celebration begins with a carnival on 2 January and continues for a month. With satin- and sequin-clad minstrel troupes, ribald song-and-dance routines, floats and general revelry, it's the Cape's Mardi Gras. (p65)

February

Summer continues: smiles on southern beaches, half-price cable cars up Table Mountain for sunset, and rain in the north. Elephants munch marula trees and baby antelope, zebras and giraffes cavort in the parks.

Buganu (Marula) Festival

One of Swaziland's most popular 'first fruits' harvest festivals, Buganu celebrates the marvellous marula. Throughout February and March, women make *buganu* (marula wine), men drink it and everyone celebrates. Swazi royals attend the three-day ceremony. (p490)

Hands on Harvest

At the first of Robertson's four annual wine festivals, budding vintners can help with the harvest and sample the results. Activities include grape picking, bunch sorting, grape stomping, wine blending and vineyard tractor trips. (p119)

March

Summer rolls towards autumn, although days remain sunny, the lowveld steamy and landscapes green. Good for walking and beach bumming in the Western Cape; cultural and music festivals happen in Cape Town and Jo'burg.

Cape Town Cycle Tour

Held on the second Sunday in March, this 109km spin around the Cape Peninsula is the world's largest timed cycling event. More than 30,000 contestants, from serious racers to costumed Capetonians, tackle Table Mountain and Champman's Peak Drive. (p66)

April

There's a two-week school holiday around Easter, generally regarded as the beginning of autumn. Temperatures drop; wildlife-watching in the bushveld starts to look more attractive than beach bumming. Rutting season until May.

AfrikaBurn

Africa's entry in the global calendar of festivals inspired by America's Burning Man is a subcultural blowout and a survivalist challenge. Art installations and themed camps turn a corner of the Tankwa Karoo into a surreal paradise. (p461)

July

Winter brings rain to the Cape and cloud to Table Mountain. Northern areas experience fresh, sunny days and clear night skies. Low season is June to September, apart from mid-June to mid-July school holidays.

Oyster Festival

Knysna's 10-day oyster orgy is one of a few seafood-oriented events on the South African coastline. Fixtures include oyster-eating and -shucking competitions, wine tastings, cycle races and the Kynsna Forest Marathon. (p145)

Lesotho Ski Season

That's right, skiing in Southern Africa. Lesotho's peaks and passes receive snow in winter – particularly around Oxbow, where the season runs from June to August at the modern and well-equipped Afriski resort. (p478)

Wildlife-Watching

Cooler, drier winter weather is perfect for wildlife-watching. Thirsty animals congregate at waterholes and foliage is sparser, making spotting easier. The lower temperatures make toasty northern areas such as the bushveld and Kalahari more enjoyable. (p554)

Open of Surfing

The winter months bring big waves to the Eastern Cape, and Jeffrey's Bay holds its international Open of Surfing. Part of the surf-loving town's 10-day Winter Fest in mid-July, the contest attracts more than 10,000 spectators; accommodation fills and prices rise. (p175)

National Arts Festival

Feel Africa's creative pulse at the continent's largest arts festival, held over 10 days in early July in studenty Grahamstown. Performers from every conceivable discipline descend on the refined city, and Fingo Village township holds an associated festival. (p194)

September

Winter starts giving way to spring. Cherry trees bloom in the Free State Eastern Highlands in September and October, also the last dry months for wildlife viewing. School holidays are from late September to early October.

Namakwa Wildflowers

In late August and early September, nature plays a springtime trick and covers this barren area with wildflowers. Namakwa's parched terrain sprouts improbable meadows of flowers in rainbow hues. The spectacle also happens elsewhere in the Northern and Western Capes. (p457)

Whale-Watching

Watch southern right whales calve in Walker Bay throughout the second half of the year; the best time to spot them is the months around Hermanus Whale Festival in September/October. During this period, Hermanus is the world's best land-based whale-watching destination. (p124)

Traditional Festivals

Swaziland's *umhlanga* dance, in which Swazi women dance with reeds, takes place in late August/early September. A similar Zulu event (eshowe.com) happens around the same time, leading up to King Shaka Day, celebrating the Zulu hero. Lesotho's Morija Festival (www.morija.co.ls) showcases Basotho culture. (p490)

Jo'burg Festivals

Jozi's festival season (p324) between late August and late September starts with the multidisciplinary Arts Alive (p324) and continues with Joy of Jazz (p347). The Soweto Festival (p347) and Soweto Wine Festival take place at the University of Johannesburg's campus in the township.

November

Spring drifts into summer: wildflowers in the Drakensberg; beach potential before the worst humidity hits KwaZulu-Natal; all of the above in Cape Town and the Western Cape. Rain in the lowveld. High season begins.

Kirstenbosch Summer Sunset Concerts

Summer music festivals take place in stunning settings nationwide. In the Western Cape alone, the choice includes the Kirstenbosch Summer Sunset Concerts in Cape Town's botanic gardens (November to April); Rocking the Daisies (rockingthedaisies.com) and Up the Creek (www.upthecreek.co.za). (p66)

Itineraries

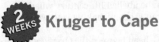

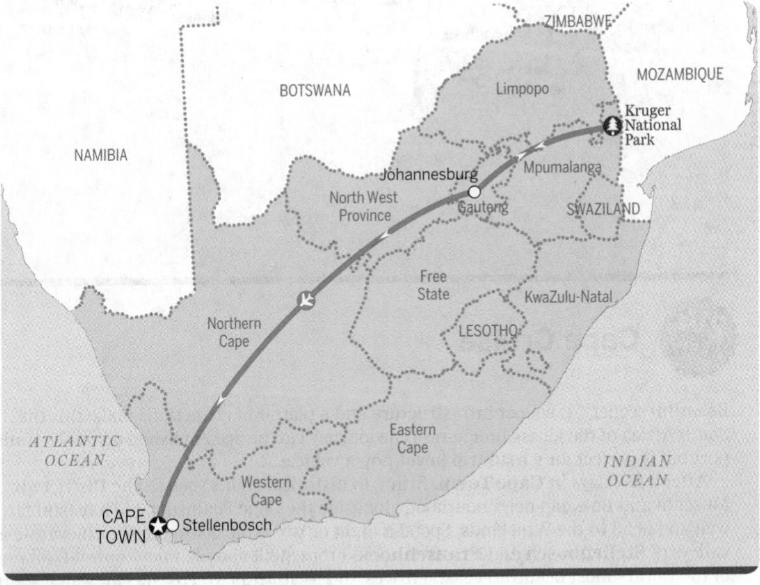

2 WEEKS Kruger to Cape

This trip combines wildlife-watching with the Cape's scenery and culture.

Head directly east from Johannesburg's OR Tambo International Airport to **Kruger National Park**, where more than 20,000 members of the Big Five (lion, leopard, buffalo, elephant and rhino) roam the bushveld. Staying in a bush camp or luxurious private reserve and going on self-drive safaris, guided drives and walks will keep you and your binoculars busy. From Kruger, head back to the bright lights of **Jo'burg**. Spend a night in the inner-city Maboneng Precinct's art hotel or a backpackers, experiencing Afro-globalisation and meeting local hipsters in the galleries and bars.

Next, pick up a flight to **Cape Town**; alternatively, take a scenic train ride in tourist class on the Trans-Karoo Express (or the Blue Train or Rovos Rail from Pretoria). Relax and enjoy one of the world's most beautiful cities, spending your days exploring the likes of Table Mountain and Kirstenbosch Botanical Garden, and your nights dining in world-class restaurants and drinking in the 'Tavern of the Seven Seas'. The Mother City is surrounded by beaches and vineyards; have lunch in wine-making **Stellenbosch** and wander the refined Cape Dutch town's lanes.

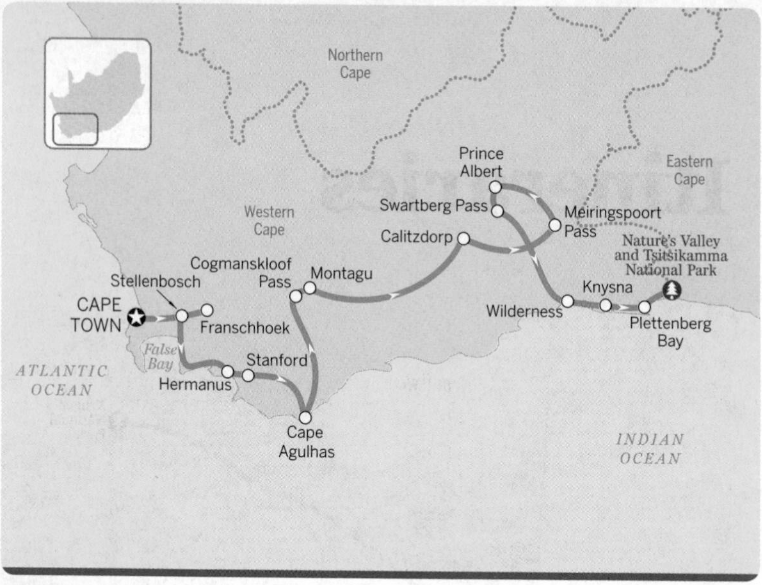

2½ WEEKS

Cape Cruise

Beautiful scenery, excellent infrastructure and a platter of attractions make this the South Africa of the glossy brochures. The journey can be accomplished on public transport but is perfect for a road trip in your own vehicle.

After a few days in **Cape Town**, fitting in historical sights such as the District Six Museum and Bo-Kaap neighbourhood alongside the Cape Peninsula, bid a tearful farewell and head to the Winelands. Spend a night or two wine tasting in the vineyard-clad valleys of **Stellenbosch** and **Franschhoek**. From Stellenbosch, take Route 44, for one of the world's most beautiful coastal drives, to **Hermanus**, where you can watch southern right whales (June to December). Overnight in the idyllic 19th-century village of **Stanford**, or stop for lunch in its gourmet restaurants, before making your way to **Cape Agulhas**, Africa's southernmost point.

Continuing the gastronomic Winelands activities, head between the Overberg region's green hills and along the **Cogmanskloof Pass** in the Langeberg range to countrified **Montagu**. With its whitewashed cottages and good restaurants, the quaint town is a great base for rock climbing and the Robertson Wine Valley. Montagu is considered the beginning of the Little Karoo: take Route 62 between rolling mountains dotted with farms and charming little towns such as port-making **Calitzdorp**. This is a *lekker* (tasty) area to slap some *boerewors* (farmer's sausage) on the braai (barbecue) at a farmstay.

At the far end of the Little Karoo, the **Meiringspoort Pass** crosses the Swartberg range from Oudtshoorn to the Great Karoo and **Prince Albert**. This pretty 18th-century village is green and fertile, with irrigation channels in the street. The nearby N1 highway leads back to Cape Town; alternatively, backtrack south, possibly via the untarred **Swartberg Pass**, to the ever-popular Garden Route, where **Wilderness'** beaches and lagoons are relatively undeveloped. East along the Indian Ocean, old-growth forests rise into the mountains above the resort towns of **Knysna** and **Plettenberg Bay**, both offering water sports and activities.

Shortly before the Eastern Cape border, descend a windy road to **Nature's Valley**, an aptly named beach village where happy hikers finishing the five-day Otter Trail hang their boots in a tree outside the pub. Shorter hikes also lead into the valleys of rainforest in the surrounding **Tsitsikamma National Park**.

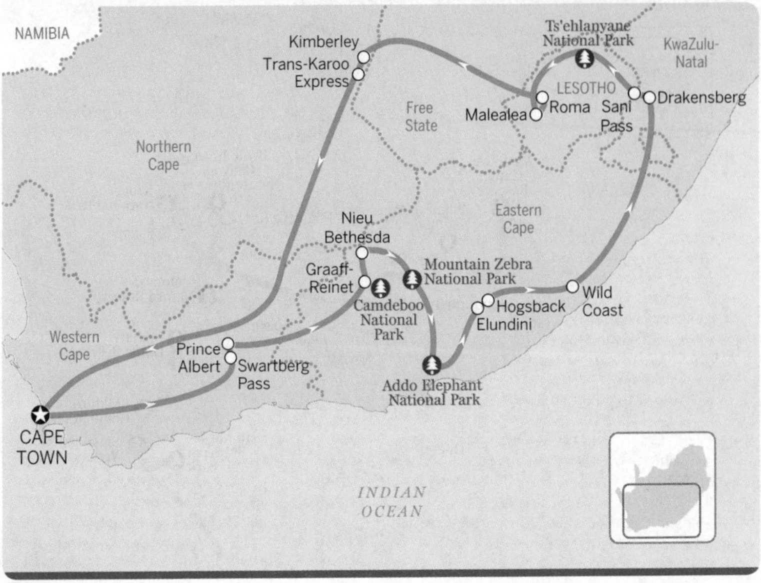

4 WEEKS Grand Circuit

This epic itinerary covers the bottom half of South Africa, including Wild Coast beaches, the Karoo semidesert and mountainous Lesotho.

From **Cape Town**, head along Route 62 and over the **Swartberg** to **Prince Albert**. Venture further into the Great Karoo's open spaces to reach the refined and gastronomic oasis of **Graaff-Reinet**, nicknamed the 'jewel of the Karoo' for its 220-plus national monuments and history stretching back to 1786. Also in this cultural corner of the Karoo are **Camdeboo National Park**, with Cape buffaloes and the Valley of Desolation's views over the plains, and arty **Nieu Bethesda**, home of the sculpture-adorned Owl House. Stop at **Mountain Zebra National Park** for cheetah tracking and more Karoo panoramas, or continue straight to **Addo Elephant National Park**, where great white sharks and southern right whales complete the 'Big Seven'.

Moving east, the Amathole Mountains are worth an inland detour for the eco-backpackers in **Elundini** and **Hogsback**. Staying in a *rondavel* (round hut with a conical roof) by an empty **Wild Coast** beach is likely to be a trip highlight when mixed with cultural experiences and community-run activities. Next, cross from the Eastern Cape to KwaZulu-Natal, and head north to the jagged green sweep of the iconic **Drakensberg** (Dragon Mountains). South Africa's highest pass, the **Sani Pass** (2876m), climbs over 1300m to Lesotho, where Africa's highest pub awaits.

Hiking and pony trekking in Lesotho, the world's highest country (judged by the elevation of the lowest point), you will meet Basotho people clad in their distinctive conical hats and patterned woollen blankets. Spend at least a few days crossing the mountain kingdom, stopping at beautiful lodges such as Maliba (pronounced 'Madiba' in Sesotho), in **Ts'ehlanyane National Park**, and **Malealea**. Pass your last Lesothan night among sandstone cliffs in **Roma**, a 19th-century mission station and now the country's seat of learning.

Over the international border, zip through the Free State's shimmering golden fields and cross another border to the Northern Cape capital, **Kimberley**. The city that witnessed the world's greatest diamond rush is a great place to get a feel for South African history, with Anglo-Boer battlefields, ghost tours, 150-year-old pubs and the world's largest hand-dug hole. From here, the **Trans-Karoo Express** will whisk you back to Cape Town (or up to Jo'burg).

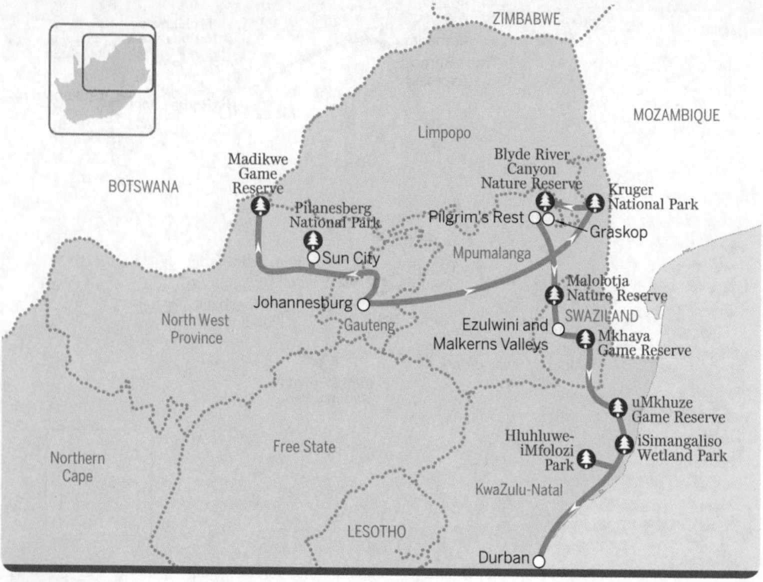

2 WEEKS

Safari Special

South Africa is one of the continent's best safari destinations – in a fortnight it's possible to cover several parks and reserves, plus a few extra stops such as the dramatic Blyde River Canyon. From Jo'burg's OR Tambo International Airport, head east to the country's 20,000-sq-km safari showpiece, **Kruger National Park**. The wildlife here and in the adjoining private wildlife reserves will hold you captivated on sunrise and sunset drives. **Blyde River Canyon Nature Reserve** is a scenic stopoff near Kruger's southern and central sections, with views of the river as it snakes from the Drakensberg Escarpment to the lowveld. Stay overnight in nearby **Graskop**, with gently sloping hills beyond its sleepy backstreets and craft shops; the town is a good base for **Pilgrim's Rest**, a perfectly preserved 19th-century gold-rush village, and outdoor activities.

If time is tight, you can hit the N4 west for accessible wildlife-watching on tar roads in **Pilanesberg National Park**, located within four hours' drive of OR Tambo International Airport. Stay at a lodge in the park, where the Big Five roam an extinct volcano crater, or in the glitzy surrounds of the adjoining **Sun City** casino complex. A little further, near the Botswana border, the 760-sq-km **Madikwe Game Reserve** is an exclusive destination with accommodation in five-star lodges (and one ecolodge with donkey boilers).

If you have a full two weeks, head south from the Kruger area to Swaziland's **Malolotja Nature Reserve**, where 200km of hiking trails cross grasslands and forests, and along the **Ezulwini and Malkerns Valleys** – stop to admire the woodlands and pick up local craftwork. Swaziland's highlight is the wildlife-rich **Mkhaya Game Reserve**, known for its unsurpassed black and white rhino populations. Explore the bushveld thickets and open veld on a guided walking safari, before returning to your camp in a bird-rich riverine forest to enjoy bush cuisine.

Leaving Swaziland, hit the N2 to KwaZulu-Natal's **uMkhuze Game Reserve**, where animals lap at waterholes in pans surrounded by fever trees. Nearby are the waterways and diverse ecosystems of the 200km-long **iSimangaliso Wetland Park**, and **Hluhluwe-iMfolozi Park**, where hiking the wilderness trails is a once-in-a-lifetime experience. From there, continue south along the Indian Ocean to **Durban's** well-connected airport and beaches, restaurants and bars, and toast all your wildlife sightings.

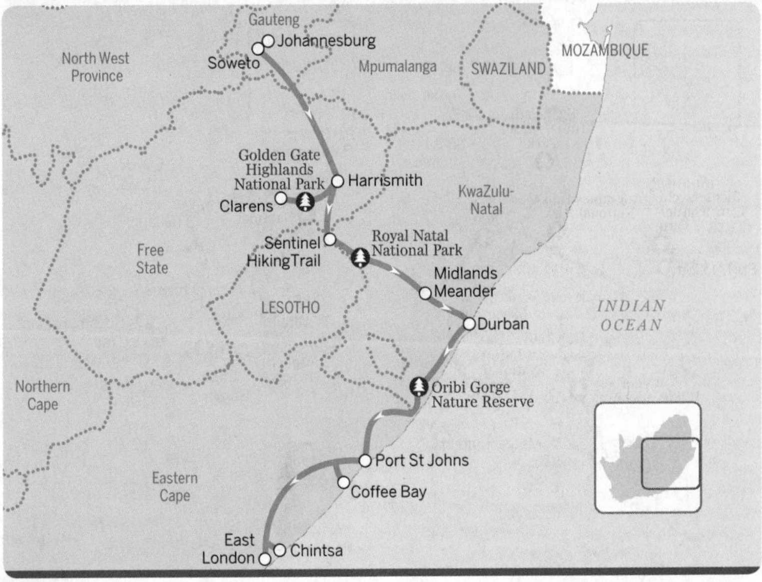

3 WEEKS Eastern Wander

This eastern jaunt mixes awesome mountain scenery with Xhosa and Zulu culture, and rural calm with urban vibes, giving a good look at the classic South Africa. After touching down at OR Tambo international Airport, linger a few days in the dynamic metropolis of **Jo'burg**, seeing how urban regeneration is transforming the inner city and creating hip enclaves of restaurants and bars. Go on a city walking tour or head out to South Africa's most famous township, **Soweto**. Visit a shebeen and see the street where Nobel Peace Prize winners Nelson Mandela and Archbishop Desmond Tutu lived.

Moving on from Jo'burg, cross the Free State and leave the N3 at Harrismith, to take scenic Rte 712 past Sterkfontein Dam to **Clarens**. The arty town, with its galleries and microbrewery, has surroundings worthy of an impressionist landscape. In the nearby **Golden Gate Highlands National Park**, stay in a riverside *rondavel* and hike between sandstone outcrops in the foothills of the Maluti Mountains bordering Lesotho; routes range from one-hour strolls to the overnight Rhebok Hiking Trail.

Just outside the park, past Phuthaditjhaba, the day-long **Sentinel Hiking Trail** climbs the iconic Ampitheatre to the top of the Drakensberg Escarpment. Now, feeling suitably inspired by the Northern Drakensberg, spend a couple of days enjoying the spectacular day walks, such as Tugela Gorge, in the **Royal Natal National Park**. Continuing across KwaZulu-Natal, declimatise from the Draks on the twee **Midlands Meander**, with its guesthouses and ceramic studios, before hitting **Durban**, a city of beaches and Indian cuisine that is slowly being revitalised by urban development.

Not far from the Eastern Cape border, **Oribi Gorge Nature Reserve** is an oft-overlooked reserve with its cliffs and forests above the Umzilkulwana River. From here, instead of taking the N2 to Mthatha, detour along the coast through Pondoland to **Port St Johns** – an appropriately laid-back introduction to the Wild Coast's pristine beaches and friendly Xhosa locals. Pastel *rondavels* dot the green hills overlooking the region's gravel roads, which lead to some stunning community-run backpackers around **Coffee Bay**.

At the southern end of the Wild Coast, spend a final night by the Indian Ocean in **Chintsa**, and pick up a plane, train or bus from nearby **East London** to Jo'burg or Cape Town.

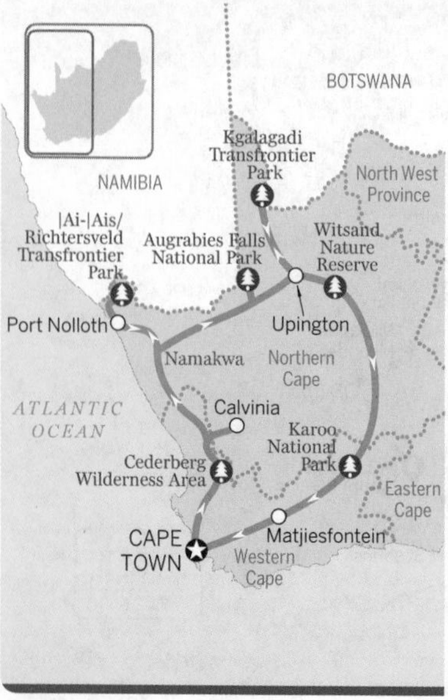

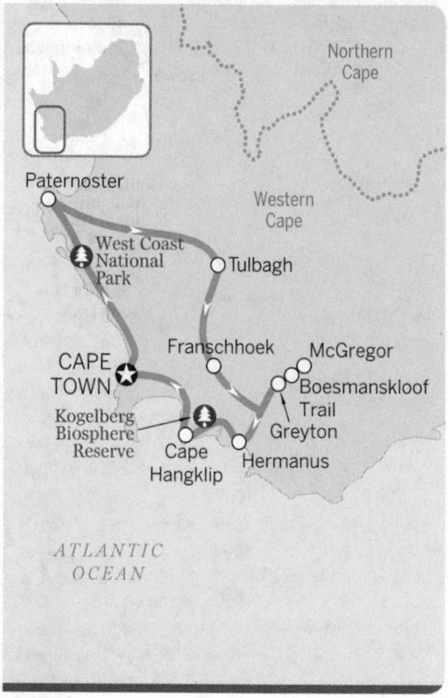

2½ WEEKS The Wild Northwest

Some of South Africa's gnarliest terrain is found in the vast Northern Cape province, which this itinerary tours in conjunction with the Western Cape's wilder corners.

From Cape Town, head north to the mountainous **Cederberg Wilderness Area**, with its sandstone formations, lodges and campsites. Continue over the Pakhuis or Vanrhyns Pass to the Hantam Karoo outpost of **Calvinia**, before hitting the N7 to Namakwa, its rocky expanses carpeted with wildflowers in spring. Almost at the end of the region's arrow-straight roads, between the Atlantic and the middle of nowhere, is **Port Nolloth**. If you have a 4WD, continue to the surreal mountain desert of **|Ai-|Ais/ Richtersveld Transfrontier Park**.

Head east to **Augrabies Falls National Park** for hiking, rafting and canoeing, and catch the Orange River in a mellow mood on a sunset cruise in **Upington**. Continue boldly north through the Kalahari to **Kgalagadi Transfrontier Park**, one of the world's best places to spot big cats, and back to see more of the thirsty semidesert at **Witsand Nature Reserve**. The route back to Cape Town crosses the Great Karoo, with stops en route including the **Karoo National Park** and historic, perfectly preserved **Matjiesfontein**.

1 WEEK Alternative Cape

This Western Cape itinerary suggests a few spots to escape the crowds.

From Cape Town, head north to the **West Coast National Park**, which offers an accessible, southern look at the spring wildflower bloom on the shores of the Langebaan Lagoon. Stay overnight in **Paternoster**.

Veer inland to **Tulbagh**, where there are some superb wineries overlooked by the Witsenberg mountains. Further into the Winelands, **Franschhoek** distils the area's refined, European charm, with its French Huguenot heritage, vineyards and restaurants. Cross the Franschhoek Pass and hit the N2 through the Overberg region to the delightful village of **Greyton**, with its thatched cottages, good restaurants, mountain views, and neighbouring 18th-century mission station. The 14km **Boesmanskloof Trail** leads hikers through the Riviersonderendberge range to **McGregor**, a New Age village in the Breede River Valley.

From Greyton, return to Cape Town via **Hermanus**, the world's best land-based whale-watching destination (June to December). Finish the journey on the stunning, coastal Rte 44, which winds around **Cape Hangklip** and skirts **Kogelberg Biosphere Reserve**.

Plan Your Trip

Travel with Children

South Africa is perhaps the continent's best destination for travelling with children, offering good facilities and family-friendly attractions. Swaziland is also a winner (although malaria is found in lower-lying areas) and mountainous Lesotho will be a memorable experience for adventurous older children.

South Africa

With its abundance of national parks, beaches, swimming pools and hiking trails suitable for a wide range of competencies, plus a good collection of museums and a handful of amusement parks, South Africa offers plenty for children of all ages in hazard-free settings.

Most South Africans are welcoming to children, and you will probably receive many offers of assistance. Get used to passing your child around like a curio; they will excite much interest and attention, particularly in rural and traditional parts of the country.

Lesotho

Lesotho is a welcoming destination for children. The rugged terrain and conditions are better suited to older children who would enjoy hiking or pony trekking. Most pony trekking centres arrange treks only for people over 12 years old.

There's no malaria, but everything is rougher around the edges than in many parts of South Africa. If you (and your children) are of an adventurous bent, you'll likely find travel here enjoyable. A little advance planning is recommended, because some accommodation options, such as the trading post lodges, are family friendly while others are less helpful and comfortable. Discounted accommodation rates for children are common.

Best Regions for Kids

Cape Town

Botanic gardens, an aquarium, the Table Mountain cable car, beaches, Greenmarket Sq market, harbour cruises, activities, good facilities and a relaxed atmosphere – the vibrant Mother City is a superb family destination.

Western Cape

Surrounding Cape Town, the Western Cape has good infrastructure as well as stunning scenery. Garden Route spots such as Mossel Bay and Nature's Valley are particularly well set up for family holidays, with beaches and activities galore.

KwaZulu-Natal

Durban has beaches, one of the world's largest aquariums and hot weather. The sandy fun continues along the surrounding Indian Ocean coastline, with activities from whale-watching to kayak safaris in iSimangaliso Wetland Park. Head inland for walking and camping opportunities in the stunning Drakensberg.

Swaziland

Swaziland in particular is a good family destination, with a child-friendly attitude and a relaxed pace. The main caveat is that malaria is a real risk in lower-lying areas of the country.

Many hotels in Swaziland offer family-friendly accommodation, and there are amusements such as minigolf to keep children occupied.

Children's Highlights

Wildlife

- Guided drives in large vehicles are excellent, with more chance of sightings and an expert to answer questions and take care of safety.
- Inhabited by the Big Five, Kruger National Park has easy accessibility and family-friendly rest camps.
- Also near Jo'burg, malaria-free Pilanesberg National Park, constructed with weekending families in mind, has tarred roads.
- Activities for children are offered in Kruger, Pilanesberg and other parks.
- There is a good chance of spotting elephants in malaria-free Addo Elephant National Park.
- Oudtshoorn has ostrich farms, a meerkat conservation project and a cheetah ranch.
- Penguin colonies and rehabilitation centres are found at Boulders Beach (Cape Peninsula), Cape St Francis and Port Elizabeth.

Walking

- Walking up Table Mountain will give older children a tremendous sense of achievement.
- Hiking and camping in the Drakensberg (including Lesotho) will also be a memorable experience for older children and teenagers.
- Hogsback is suitable for nature-loving parents with small children, with its fairy meander and easy trails through gardens and forests.

Beaches

- Sitting on a Cape Town beach such as Clifton No 4, among multicultural Capetonians, will be an interesting experience for all the family.
- Arniston, near Africa's southernmost point, has a sheltered beach with caves and rock pools.
- South Africa offers lots of watersports for older children to get stuck into, including surfing, diving, canoeing, kayaking, tubing and rafting.
- Jeffrey's Bay is one of the world's best surf spots.

Horse Riding

- Horse riding along Noordhoek beach is a breezy day out from Cape Town.
- Many operators offer horseback safaris and tours, in areas from Limpopo's Waterberg range to the Wild Coast.
- For older children, pony trekking in Lesotho is a wonderful way to see the mountainous country.

African Culture

- Teenagers will enjoy themed tours geared towards their interests, such as Cape Malay cooking, township jazz, Venda art or urban murals.
- On the Wild Coast, adventurous teenagers will enjoy glimpses of Xhosa culture at community-run backpackers such as Bulungula Lodge, which offers activities and cultural experiences.

Planning

Accommodation

- Family-oriented accommodation, such as triple or quadruple hotel rooms and four- to six-person self-catering cottages, is common throughout South Africa.
- Camping and self-catering are good options for families seeking affordability and privacy, with quality campsites and well-equipped cabins, cottages and chalets found nationwide.
- In KwaZulu-Natal, Ezemvelo KZN Wildlife offers good-value accommodation to groups and families – although animals roam freely in many of its parks.
- SAN (South Africa National) Parks accommodation is generally excellent, but pricey; it often works out cheaper to stay outside the park.
- Many wildlife lodges have restrictions on children under 12 years, so in parks and reserves the main accommodation options will sometimes be camping and self-catering.
- Many hotels and self-catering options can provide cots.

Childcare

- Many upscale hotels and resorts in tourist areas of South Africa can arrange childcare, and short-term day care may also be available.
- Especially during the high season, many South African coastal resorts have kids' clubs, offering daily children's activities.
- In Lesotho and Swaziland, informal childcare arrangements can be made; if you are staying in a good lodge or hotel, staff may be able to assist.

IMMIGRATION REGULATIONS

From 1 June 2015, all children under 18 years travelling to South Africa are required to show an unabridged birth certificate in addition to their passport. If you do not have one already, unabridged certificates are easy to apply for in most Western countries; unlike abridged birth certificates, they show both parents' details.

If both parents are accompanying the child, fine. If one or neither is travelling, the new immigration regulations ask for further paperwork including an affidavit giving permission for the child to travel, a court order in some cases and a death certificate if a parent is deceased. The controversial new regulations, which, according to the Department of Home Affairs, are designed to combat child trafficking, have received immense opposition and will possibly be relaxed. For further information and updates, check www.southafrica.info, www.home-affairs.gov.za, or with your government's travel advisory or your airline.

Discounts

➡ Children are usually admitted at discounted rates to national parks, museums and other sights (often free for babies and toddlers, and discounted for teenagers and younger).

➡ Many hotels offer children's discounts.

➡ Restaurants often have children's menus with dishes at good prices, or offer smaller portions of regular dishes at discounted prices.

Facilities

➡ Baby-changing rooms are not common in South Africa, but clean restrooms abound; in most, you should be able to find a makeshift spot to change a nappy (diaper).

➡ In Lesotho and Swaziland, most hotels and lodges have Western-style toilets, but on the road in rural areas, sometimes the only choice is a long-drop.

Health

South Africa

➡ See also the Health chapter (p615).

➡ Breastfeeding in public won't raise an eyebrow among many Africans, but in other circles it's best to be discreet.

➡ Overall, there are few health risks, and should your child become ill, good-quality medical care is available in the cities.

➡ Avoid government hospitals where possible and use private hospitals.

➡ Mediclinic (www.mediclinic.co.za) operates private hospitals from Cape Town to Limpopo.

➡ Seek medical advice about vaccinations months before your trip; not all are suitable for children or pregnant women.

➡ Specifically, seek medical advice on malaria prophylactics for children if you'll be in malarial areas (including Kruger National Park and the lowveld).

➡ Think twice before taking young children to malarial areas and try to visit in the winter, when the risk of mosquito bites is lower.

➡ Regardless of malaria, insect bites can be painful, so come prepared with nets, repellent and suitable clothing.

➡ Swimming in streams should generally be avoided, due to the risk of bilharzia (schistosomiasis) infection.

Lesotho & Swaziland

➡ There are reasonable medical facilities in Mbabane and Maseru, but for anything serious you'll need to head to South Africa. Malaria is present in lower-lying regions of Swaziland.

Resources

➡ The monthly magazine *Child* (www.childmag.co.za) has Cape Town, Durban, Jo'burg and Pretoria editions and a useful website.

➡ Lonely Planet's *Travel with Children* has tips for keeping children and parents happy on the road.

Supplies

South Africa

➡ Nappies, powdered milk and baby food are widely available, except in very rural areas.

➡ Outside supermarkets in major towns, it's difficult to find processed baby food without added sugar.

➡ Merry Pop Ins (www.merrypopins.co.za) in central Cape Town sells used clothes, furniture and equipment for children from newborns to 12-year-olds.

Lesotho & Swaziland

➡ Nappies, powdered milk and baby food are available in Mbabane, Manzini and Maseru, with only a limited selection in smaller towns.

Transport

➡ Most car-rental agencies can provide safety seats, but you'll need to book them in advance and usually pay extra.

Regions at a Glance

Cape Town and the Western Cape are refined, developed spots, where you can sip wine and enjoy activities on beaches and mountains. Head north to the Northern Cape and North West Province for rugged wildernesses and wildlife parks.

Surfers, hikers and lovers of African culture will enjoy the Eastern Cape, bordering the mountain kingdom of Lesotho and the Free State. The latter's golden fields and open spaces lead to the Drakensberg range, which stretches into KwaZulu-Natal, where beaches, wildlife parks and Zululand spread north from Durban.

Turning northwest, Swaziland has excellent reserves; Mpumalanga offers lowveld, the Drakensberg Escarpment and activities; and Gauteng is South Africa's urban heartbeat. The Big Five's hangout, Kruger National Park, crowns the region, alongside Limpopo's diverse landscapes and Venda culture.

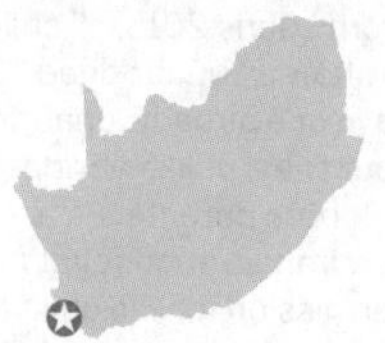

Cape Town

Outdoor Activities
Eating
Shopping

Mountain Walking

Its mountainous national park, beaches and ocean make Cape Town a scenic hiking location, with walking up Table Mountain at the top of many to-do lists. Even just strolling along Sea Point Promenade is a sheer pleasure beneath the Mother City's towering peaks, and kite-surfing, rock climbing and paragliding are also offered.

Diverse Cuisine

Cape Town's multiethnic peoples have bequeathed it a range of cuisines. Sample Cape Malay curries, Xhosa dishes and mouth-watering meats and fish from the braai (barbecue) in world-class restaurants.

Contemporary Craftwork

The 2014 World Design Capital is bursting with creativity: intricately beaded dolls, contemporary light fixtures made from recycled plastic, stylish buckskin and leather pillows – Cape Town's emporiums and artisan craft markets have it all.

p44

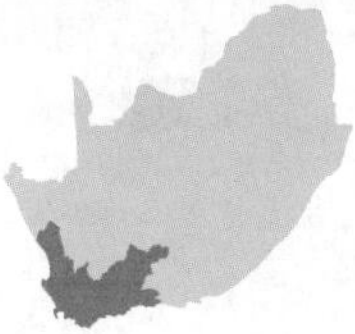

Western Cape

Food & Drink
Outdoor Activities
Adventure Sports

Wine Tasting

The Winelands around Stellenbosch, Franschhoek and Paarl are justifiably famous for their beautiful wine estates. Intrepid tasters should also explore other areas such as Wellington, Stanford, Tulbagh and Robertson. Pairing wines with chocolate or cheese adds an extra dimension to tastings.

Hiking

Longer hikes include the four-day Oystercatcher Trail, De Hoop Nature Reserve's five-day Whale Trail and the Greyton McGregor Trail. Hikes ranging in duration from hours to days lead into the bush around towns such as Swellendam and wildernesses including the Cederberg.

Water Sports

Among the many water sports and activities taking advantage of the Garden Route's beaches and lagoons are surfing, canoeing and diving. Gansbaai is the place to brave shark-cage diving.

p97

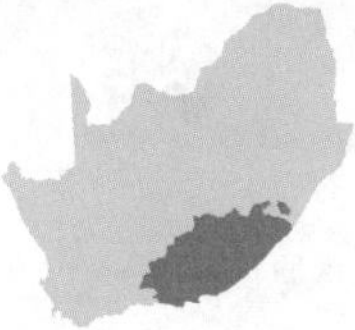

Eastern Cape

Hiking
Nature & Scenery
Wildlife

Multiday Hikes

In Tsitsikamma National Park are the Otter, Dolphin and Tsitsikamma Mountain Trails; overnight routes run the length of the Wild Coast; and the Amathole Trail climbs through waterfall-flecked forests.

Beaches

The Wild Coast is lined with empty beaches, which come with Xhosa culture at backpacker lodges such as Bulungula, Mdumbi and Buccaneers. The Jeffrey's Bay sands are dedicated to surfing, and forests overlook the dunes at Nature's Valley.

Diverse Sightings

Addo Elephant National Park boasts the 'Big Seven', including great white sharks and southern right whales. The nearby private wildlife reserves make the most of the Big Five with diverse programs of activities; and Mountain Zebra National Park offers Karoo panoramas, Cape mountain zebras and cheetah tracking.

p166

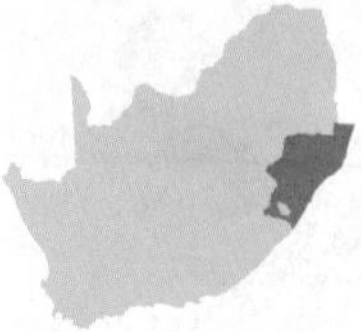

KwaZulu-Natal

Wildlife
Culture
Activities

Tropical Sightings

The steamy, tropical Elephant Coast in northern KwaZulu-Natal features three of South Africa's great wildlife parks, iSimangaliso Wetland Park, Mkhuze Game Reserve and Hluhluwe-iMfolozi Park, offering Big Five sightings with backdrops from savannah grasslands to Lake St Lucia.

Zulu Culture

Eshowe and Ulundi are capitals of Zulu culture, while Shakaland offers a Disneyfied look at the ethnic group. Three big events take place in Zululand in September and October, including a 'reed dance' akin to the famous Swazi Umhlanga festival. Durban's Campbell Collections hold documents and artworks relating to early Zulu culture.

Water Sports

Umkomaas and Scottburgh are diving centres, with the Aliwal Shoal and Protea Banks sites. Water-based activities in beachfront Durban include surfing, diving, fishing and ocean safaris.

p226

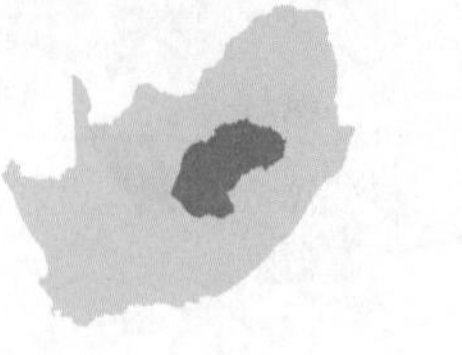

Free State

Landscape
Relaxed Travel
Hiking

Mountains & Foothills

The rugged Eastern Highlands offer views of the Drakensberg and Maluti Mountains. One of South Africa's most scenic drives crosses this region bordering mountainous Lesotho, taking in Clarens and the Golden Gate Highlands National Park.

Rustic Experiences

Mellow to the province's safe and rural pace: small towns such as Clarens promote their streets as safe to walk day and night; and as you travel dusty roads between golden fields and open skies, you will pass old *bakkies* (pick-up trucks) and tumbledown Sotho houses.

Mountain Trails

The Rhebok Hiking Trail and others cross the Golden Gate Highlands National Park, with views of the Drakensberg and Maluti Mountains. The nearby Sentinel Trail, one of South Africa's most impressive day walks, climbs the Drakensberg.

p297

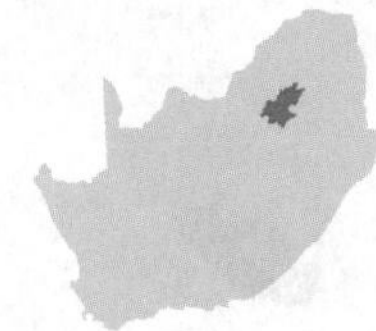

Johannesburg & Gauteng

History
Guided Tours
Culture

Mandela Trail

The Apartheid Museum powerfully evokes the dark era ended by Nelson Mandela et al. Also in Jo'burg, Constitution Hill covers both apartheid and today's democracy. Soweto is a hotbed of social history, and Pretoria's Freedom Park sits opposite the Voortrekker Monument.

Walking Tours

Jo'burg's inventive tours scratch the concrete surface of what can be a grimy Afro-Gotham. Inner-city walking tours showcase the urban regeneration transforming former no-go zones; in Soweto, meet the township locals on foot or bike.

Art & Design

Pick up a local artwork or some cool threads at galleries and shops in Jo'burg's Maboneng Precinct, Braamfontein and Newtown. Head to Maboneng's Market on Main (Sunday) for design and decor, and to 44 Stanley Ave for local fashion labels.

p315

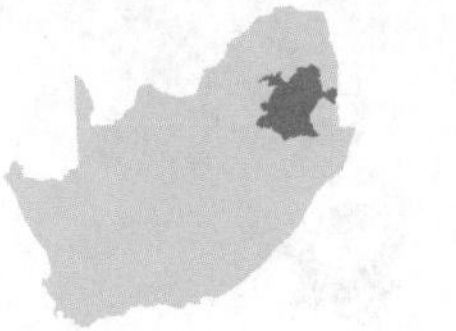

Mpumalanga

Landscape
Activities
Country Breaks

Natural Wonders

This province between Jo'burg and Mozambique covers both lowveld and the Drakensberg Escarpment. At the dramatic meeting of the two regions is the Blyde River Canyon, Mpumalanga's most scenic area and one of South Africa's most outstanding natural sights with its rock formations and viewpoints.

Adventure Sports

Graskop has one of the world's highest cable gorge swings. Sabie offers mountain bike trails, kloofing, candlelight caving, rafting and swimming holes. Head to Hazyview for hot-air ballooning, rafting, quad biking and zip lining.

Historic Towns

Pilgrim's Rest is a well-preserved gold-rush town. Also on the Drakensberg Escarpment, historic buildings stand on Lydenburg's wide streets. Barberton, another gold-rush town, was home to South Africa's first stock exchange.

p364

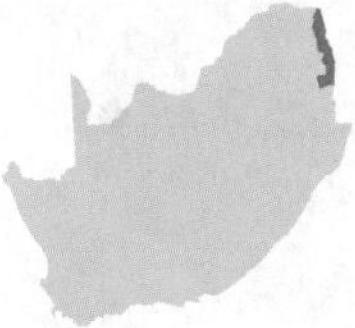

Kruger National Park

Wildlife
Landscape
Activities

Big Five

With 145 mammal species, including 1500 lions, 12,000 elephants, 2500 buffaloes, 1000 leopards and 5000 rhinos (black and white), Kruger is one of Africa's most epic places to see the Big Five acting out the daily drama of life and death.

Wilderness

Kruger is about the size of Belgium or Wales, with landscapes ranging from tropical riverine forest to mopaneveld. If you visit at a quiet time (such as late January to March) or go on a bush walk, nature will ring in your ears.

Walks

To access parts of the bush not glimpsed by vehicles, strike out with gun-toting rangers on a three-hour bush walk; or disappear into the wild on a four-day wilderness trail.

p384

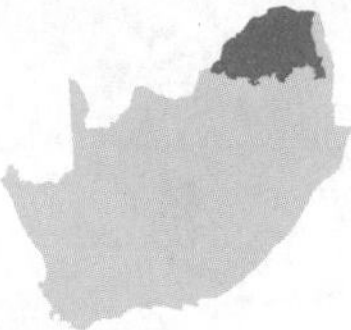

Limpopo

Arts & Crafts
Diverse Environments
African Culture

Studio Visits

The Venda region's artists, from woodcarvers to potters, are famous nationwide; tour their studios and pick up some distinctive work. Further south are Kaross, producing Shangaan embroidery, and the Mapusha Weavers Cooperative, where women make carpets and tapestries in Acornhoek township.

Mountain Escapes

Escape the heat by climbing to Haenertsburg and the Magoebaskloof Pass, where the pine plantations and waterfalls make a refreshing change from the steamy surrounds. In the Modjadji Nature Reserve, summer mists wrap around cycads and the Bolobedu Mountains.

Significant Sites

Mapungubwe National Park, declared a World Heritage Site for its cultural significance, contains an important Iron Age site. There's vivid African culture in the Modjadji area, mystic home of rain-summoning queens, and the Venda region.

p403

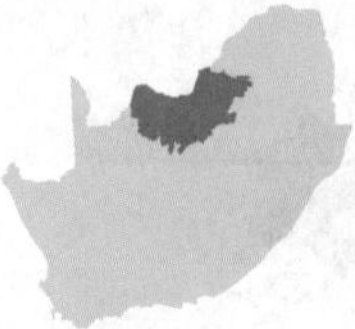

North West Province

Wildlife
Luxury
Activities

Accessible Animals

Collectively covering over 1000 sq km of Big Five-inhabited bushveld, Pilanesberg National Park has tarred roads near the Sun City casino complex, and Madikwe Game Reserve's lodges offer guided drives.

Accommodation

Sun City's hotels, particularly the Palace of the Lost City, are South Africa's last, Vegas-style word in glitz. Madikwe's five-star lodges offer wildlife-watching in the lap of luxury, with features such as spas and private decks.

Family Fun

The kitschy Sun City's endless swimming pools, wave pools, slides and flumes keep children happy on hot bushveld days. The outlandish theme of a lost African civilisation, with simulated volcanic eruptions and life-size fake elephants, entertains everyone, and the more active can explore neighbouring Pilanesberg. The Magaliesberg has an aerial cableway and zip-line canopy tours.

p426

Northern Cape

Wildernesses
Wildlife
Activities

Semideserts

The most epic province covers all of South Africa's cracked, arid wildernesses. Like a tumbleweed along a back road, the Karoo sweeps past attractive towns such as Sutherland; further north, nature is an untrammelled, awe-inspiring force in the sandy Kalahari and rocky Namakwa.

Big Cats

Kgalagadi Transfrontier Park is one of the world's best places to spot big cats, including cheetahs, lions and leopards. You might spy a black-maned lion snoozing under a thorn tree or purring down the road.

Adventure Sports

Raft and canoe down the Orange River; 4WD around Riemvasmaak and the transfrontier parks; go on wildlife drives and walks; sandboard and mountain bike in Witsand Nature Reserve.

p438

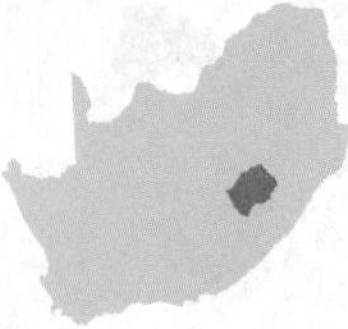

Lesotho

Adventure
Craftwork
Wilderness

Trading Posts

Malealea, Semonkong, Ramabanta and Roma lodges, former trading posts, are mountainside way stations that wow adventurers. Superb hiking and Basotho culture are offered alongside trekking on sturdy Basotho ponies, a classic Lesotho activity that literally takes travellers to another level. At Semonkong, abseilers descend Maletsunyane Falls.

Tapestries

The Basotho people have maintained cultural autonomy for centuries, resulting in distinctive craftwork. You can pick up tapestries in the lowland craft villages Teyateyaneng (TY), Leribe (Hlotse), Thaba-Bosiu and Morija.

National Parks

Lesotho's national parks are little-visited gems: Sehlathebethebe is an eerie green and grey moonscape; Ts'ehlanyane National Park, lush and rugged, is becoming the nation's poster child, with excellent accommodation at Maliba Mountain Lodge.

p463

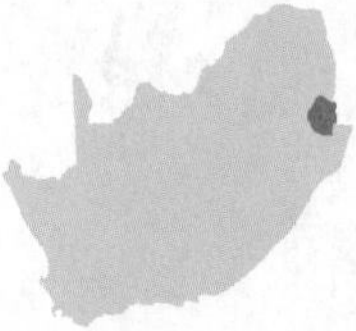

Swaziland

Craft Shopping
Parks & Reserves
Swazi Culture

Markets

Manzini Market's handicrafts and textiles are sold by a colourful mix of marketers, ranging from rural vendors to Mozambican traders. The neighbouring Ezulwini and Malkerns Valleys have a well-earned reputation for their craft markets, filled with surprises such as animal-shaped candles and zesty contemporary batiks.

Activities

In addition to African bush and wildlife, Swaziland's parks and reserves offer various activities. Options include hiking and canopy tours in Malolotja Nature Reserve; and walks, mountain biking and horse riding in Mlilwane Wildlife Sanctuary.

Festivals

Swaziland's traditional ceremonies are famous African festivals, among them the *umhlanga* (reed) dance, essentially a debutante ball for Swazi maidens, and the Buganu (Marula) Festival.

p487

On the Road

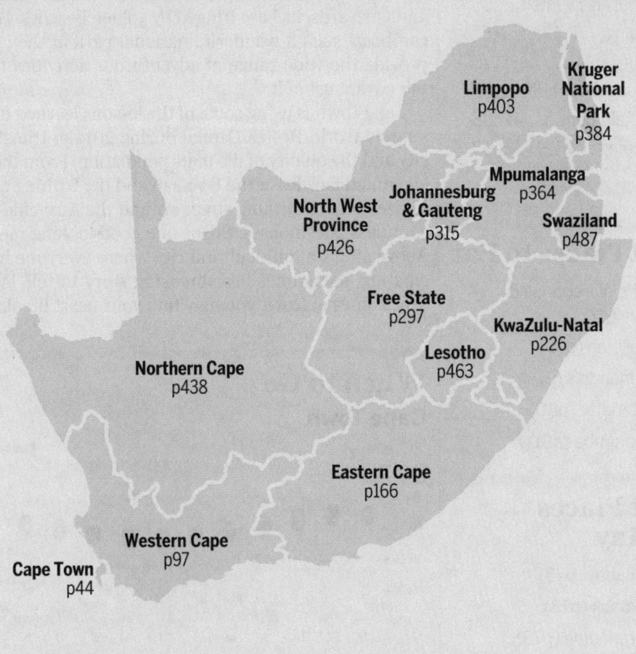

Limpopo
p403
Kruger
National
Park
p384
Mpumalanga
p364
North West
Province
p426
Johannesburg
& Gauteng
p315
Swaziland
p487
Free State
p297
KwaZulu-Natal
p226
Lesotho
p463
Northern Cape
p438
Eastern Cape
p166
Western Cape
p97
Cape Town
p44

Cape Town

POP 3.74 MILLION

Includes ➡

Best Places to Eat

- Chef's Warehouse & Canteen (p77)
- Hallellujah (p79)
- Ferdinando's (p79)
- La Mouette (p80)
- La Colombe (p81)

Best Places to Stay

- Mannabay (p73)
- Backpack (p73)
- La Grenadine (p73)
- Villa Zest (p74)
- Atlantic Point Backpackers (p74)

Why Go?

Known as the 'Mother City' for its historical role in the development of modern South Africa, Cape Town is dominated by magnificent Table Mountain, its summit draped with cascading clouds, its flanks coated with unique flora and vineyards, its base fringed by golden beaches. Few cities can boast such a wonderful national park at their heart or provide the wide range of adventurous activities that take full advantage of it.

Cape Town is using some of the lessons learned during its stint as World Design Capital during 2014 to transform the city and the quality of life of its population. From the brightly painted facades of the Bo-Kaap and the bathing chalets of Muizenberg to striking street art and the Afro-chic decor of countless guesthouses, this is one good-looking metropolis. Above all it's a multicultural city where everyone has a fascinating, sometimes heartbreaking story to tell. When the time comes to leave, you may find your heart breaking too.

When to Go

Cape Town

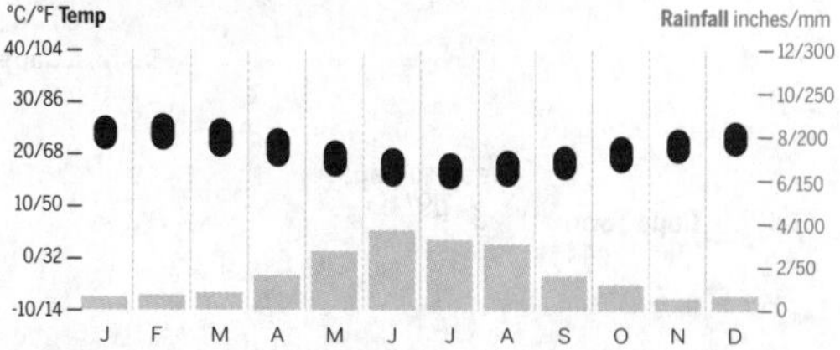

Jan Peak season but also a chance to see the Minstrel Carnival.

Mar Enjoy arts events such as Infecting the City and the International Jazz Festival.

Nov Spring sees beautiful flowers begin to bloom and the start of sunset concerts at Kirstenbosch.

History

Long before the Dutch East India Company (Vereenigde Oost-Indische Compagnie; VOC) established a base here in 1652, the Cape Town area was settled by the San and Khoekhoen nomadic tribes, collectively known as the Khoe-San. The indigenous peoples shunned the Dutch, so the VOC was forced to import slaves from Madagascar, India, Ceylon, Malaya and Indonesia to deal with the colony's chronic labour shortage. Women were in even shorter supply, so the Europeans exploited the female slaves and the local Khoe-San for both labour and sex. In time the slaves also intermixed with the Khoe-San. The offspring of these unions formed the basis of sections of today's coloured population and also helps explain the unique character of the city's Cape Muslim population.

Under the 150-odd years of Dutch rule, Kaapstad, as the Cape settlement became known, thrived and gained a wider reputation as the 'Tavern of the Seas', a riotous port used by every sailor travelling between Europe and the East. Following the British defeat of the Dutch in 1806 at Bloubergstrand, 25km north of Cape Town, the colony was ceded to the Crown on 13 August 1814. Cape Town continued to prosper after the slave trade was abolished in 1808, and all slaves were emancipated in 1833.

The discovery and exploitation of diamonds and gold in the centre of South Africa from the 1870s led to rapid changes. Cape Town was soon no longer the single dominant metropolis in the country, but as a major port it too was a beneficiary of the mineral wealth that laid the foundations for an industrial society. The same wealth led to imperialist dreams of grandeur on the part of Cecil John Rhodes (premier of the Cape Colony in 1890), who had made his millions at the head of De Beers Consolidated Mines.

An outbreak of bubonic plague in 1901 was blamed on the black African workers (although it actually came on boats from Argentina) and gave the government an excuse to introduce racial segregation: blacks were moved to two locations, one near the docks and the other at Ndabeni on the eastern flank of Table Mountain. This was the start of what would later develop into the townships of the Cape Flats.

Sights

Cape Town's commercial centre, known as the City Bowl, is bounded by Table Mountain and the suburbs of Bo-Kaap to the west, Gardens to the south, and East City, District Six and Woodstock to the east.

Moving west around the Atlantic Coast you'll first hit the Waterfront and Green Point. From Sea Point (which has an excellent outdoor swimming pavilion), you can head down to Clifton and Camps Bay. The road then hugs the coast for a thrilling drive to the fishing community of Hout Bay, which has a good beach and a harbour with boat trips.

The city sprawls quite a distance to the north and east across the Cape Flats. To the south, skirting the eastern flank of the mountains, are the leafy, wealthy Southern Suburbs. Apart from the large Cape of Good Hope section of Table Mountain National Park, the southern tip of the peninsula includes the small seaside communities of Muizenberg, Kalk Bay and Simon's Town, the main base for South Africa's navy.

City Bowl & Surrounds

★Castle of Good Hope MUSEUM

(Map p50; www.castleofgoodhope.co.za; cnr Castle & Darling Sts, City Bowl, entrance on Buitenkant St; Mon-Sat adult/child R30/15, Sun adult/child R25/10; 9am-4pm; P; Castle) Built by the Dutch between 1666 and 1679 to defend Cape Town, this stone-walled pentagonal castle remains the headquarters for the Western Cape military command. There are free guided **tours** of the site (11am, noon and 2pm Monday to Saturday), and don't miss climbing up to the bastions for an elevated view of the castle's layout and across to Grand Parade.

The **Military Museum** is interesting, as are the displays of antiques and decorative arts in the **William Fehr Collection** (Map p50; www.iziko.org.za; 9am-4pm; Castle).

★Company's Gardens GARDENS

(Map p50; City Bowl; 7am-7pm; Dorp/Leeuwen) These shady green gardens, which started as the vegetable patch for the Dutch East India Company, are a lovely place to relax. They are planted with a fine collection of botanical specimens from South Africa and the rest of the world, including frangipanis, African flame trees, aloes and roses.

Cape Town Highlights

1 Taking the cable car to the top of magnificent **Table Mountain** (p64) and looking down on the city.

2 Sailing out to the infamous prison **Robben Island** (p53), and pondering the country's past and present.

3 Exploring the **City Bowl** (p45), with its museums, the Company's Gardens and wonderful art-deco and Victorian architecture.

4 Heading to the **Cape of Good Hope** (p57) for wide open spaces, wildlife, empty beaches and the dramatic scenery of the peninsula's rugged tip.

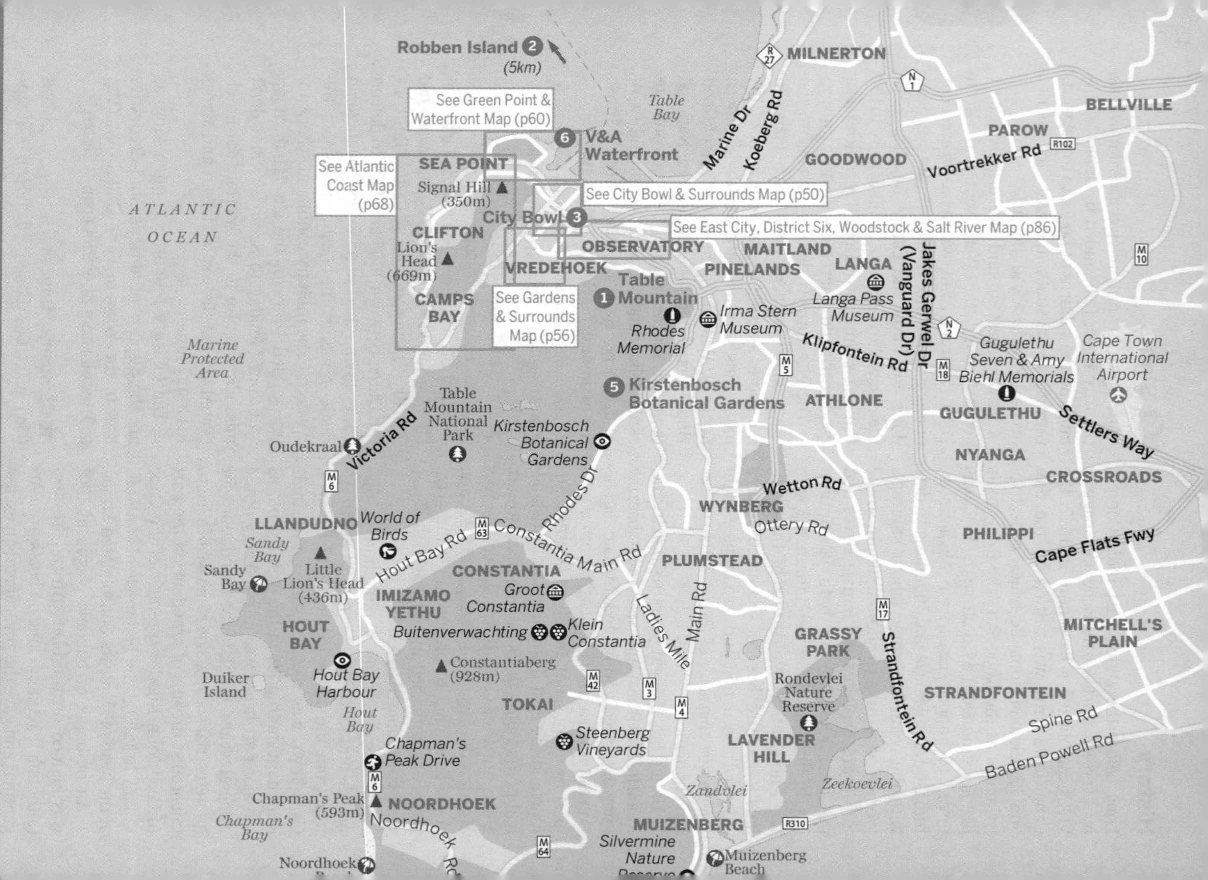

5 Wandering through the beautiful **Kirstenbosch Botanical Gardens** (p55), learning about the magnificent Cape floral kingdom.

6 Enjoying the shops, restaurants, harbour cruises and buzzing carnival atmosphere of the **V&A Waterfront** (p53).

7 Snapping photos of the superstar African penguins paddling along the beach at **Boulders** (p57).

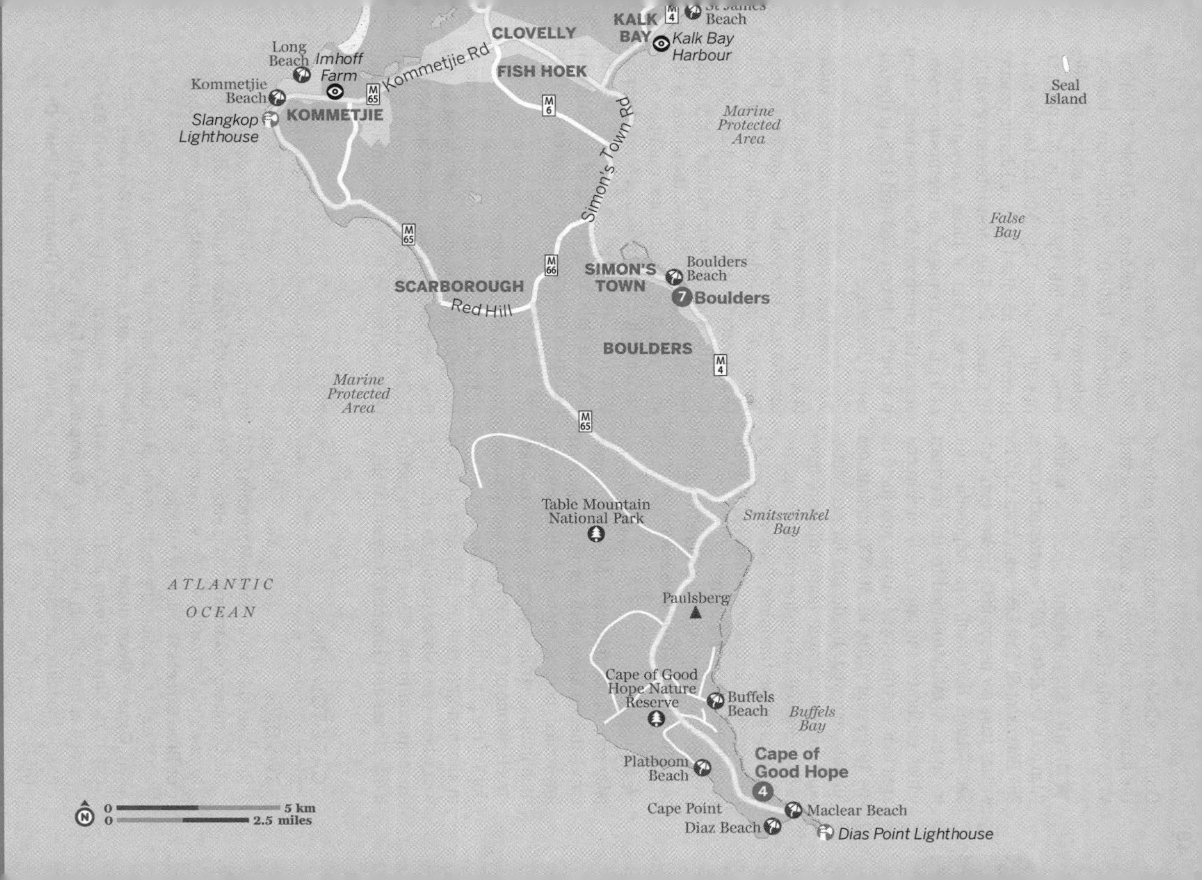

Cecil Rhodes' **statue** stands in the centre of the gardens, and there's a newly re-created VOC Vegetable Garden.

★District Six Museum MUSEUM
(Map p50; ☎021-466 7200; www.districtsix.co.za; 25A Buitenkant St, East City; adult/child R30/15, walking tours per person R60; ⏲9am-4pm Mon-Sat; 🚍Lower Buitenkant) It's impossible not to be emotionally touched by this museum which celebrates the once lively multiracial area that was destroyed during apartheid in the 1960s and 1970s, its 60,000 inhabitants forcibly removed. Inside the former Methodist Mission Church home interiors have been recreated, alongside photographs, recordings and testimonials, all of which build an evocative picture of a shattered but not entirely broken community.

Many township tours stop here first to explain the history of the pass laws.

★Bo-Kaap NEIGHBOURHOOD
(Map p50; 🚍Dorp/Leeuwen) Meaning 'Upper Cape', the Bo-Kaap with its vividly painted low-roofed houses, many of them historic monuments, strung along narrow cobbled streets, is one of the most photographed sections of the city. Initially a garrison for soldiers in the mid-18th century, this area of town was where freed slaves started to settle after emancipation in the 1830s. The most picturesque streets are Chiappini, Rose and Wale.

Bo-Kaap Museum MUSEUM
(Map p50; www.iziko.org.za; 71 Wale St, Bo-Kaap; adult/child R20/10; ⏲10am-5pm Mon-Sat; 🚍Leeuwen) This small museum provides some insight into the lifestyle of a prosperous 19th-century Cape Muslim family, and a somewhat idealised view of Islamic practice in Cape Town. The most interesting exhibit is the selection of black-and-white photos of local life displayed in the upstairs room, across the courtyard. The house itself, which was built between 1763 and 1768, is the oldest in the area.

Greenmarket Square ARCHITECTURE, MARKET
(Map p50; Greenmarket Sq, City Bowl; 🚍Church/Longmarket) This cobbled square is Cape Town's second-oldest public space after the Grand Parade. It hosts a lively and colourful crafts and souvenir market daily. Apart from the Old Town House, the square is also surrounded by some choice examples of art deco architecture, including **Market House** (Map p50; Greenmarket Sq, City Bowl; 🚍Groote Kerk), an elaborately decorated building with balconies and stone-carved eagles and flowers on its facade.

Michaelis Collection at the Old Town House MUSEUM
(Map p50; www.iziko.org.za; Greenmarket Sq, City Bowl; admission R20/10; ⏲10am-5pm Mon-Sat; 🚍Church/Longmarket) On the south side of Greenmarket Sq is the beautifully restored

CAPE TOWN IN...

Two Days

Ride the cable car up **Table Mountain** (p64), then return to the city and wander through the **Company's Gardens** (p45), nipping into the **South African National Gallery** (p53) to view its latest exhibition. Go souvenir shopping at the **Watershed** (p92) then hit **Long or Bree Streets** for late-night drinks.

On day two explore the southern end of the Cape Peninsula, starting at the magnificent **Cape of Good Hope** (p57). Move on to the cute penguin colony at **Boulders** (p57), charming **Simon's Town**, and the shops and picturesque fishing harbour at **Kalk Bay**. A good option for lunch is Kalk Bay's **Olympia Café & Deli** (p82) or **Live Bait** (p82) beside the harbour. Return to the city via the Atlantic Coast and **Chapman's Peak Drive** (p61).

Four Days

Drop by the **District Six Museum** (p48), then take a half-day **township tour** (p64). Sail out to **Robben Island** (p53) in the afternoon, hanging out at the **V&A Waterfront** (p53) afterwards for sunset drinks.

On day four head to **Groot Constantia** (p84) for a spot of wine tasting and the gorgeous grounds of the **Kirstenbosch Botanical Gardens** (p55). You could have afternoon tea here or at the tearoom beside the **Rhodes Memorial** (p56), with its sweeping view across the Cape Flats. Cap off your trip with a meal to remember at either **La Colombe** (p81) or **La Mouette** (p80).

Old Town House, a Cape rococo building dating from 1755 that was once City Hall. It now houses the impressive art collection of Sir Max Michaelis. Dutch and Flemish paintings and etchings from the 16th and 17th centuries (including works by Rembrandt, Frans Hals and Anthony van Dyck) hang side by side with contemporary works – the contrasts between old and new are fascinating.

Long Street ARCHITECTURE

(Map p50; Long St, City Bowl; Dorp/Leeuwen) A stroll along Long St is an essential element of a Cape Town visit. This busy commercial and nightlife thoroughfare, partly lined with Victorian-era buildings featuring lovely wrought-iron balconies, once formed the border of the Muslim Bo-Kaap. Along it you'll find the **Palm Tree Mosque** (Map p50; 185 Long St, City Bowl; closed to public; Dorp), dating from 1780; the **SA Mission Museum** (Map p50; 021-423 6755; 40 Long St, City Bowl; 9am-6pm Mon-Fri; Mid-Long) FREE, the oldest Mission church in South Africa; and the city's newest public art installation, Open House Cape Town.

Noon Gun VIEWPOINT

(Military Rd, Bo-Kaap) FREE At noon, Monday to Saturday, a cannon is fired from the lower slopes of 350m-high Signal Hill, which separates Sea Point from the City Bowl; you can hear it all over town. Traditionally, this allowed the burghers in the town below to check their watches. It's a stiff walk up here through the Bo-Kaap: take Longmarket St and keep going until it ends, just beneath the gun emplacement (which is off limits) – the view is phenomenal.

Iziko Slave Lodge MUSEUM

(Map p50; 021-467 7229; www.iziko.org.za; 49 Adderley St, City Bowl; adult/child R30/R15; 10am-5pm Mon-Sat; Groote Kerk) Dating back to 1660, the Slave Lodge is one of the oldest buildings in South Africa. Once home to as many as 1000 slaves, the lodge has a fascinating history; it has also been used as a brothel, a jail, a mental asylum, a post office, a library and the Cape Supreme Court in its time. Today, it's a museum mainly devoted to the history and experience of slaves and their descendants in the Cape.

Prestwich Memorial MEMORIAL

(Map p50; cnr Somerset & Buitengracht Sts, De Waterkant; 8am-6pm Mon-Fri, to 2pm Sat & Sun; Strand) FREE Construction in 2003 along nearby Prestwich St unearthed many skeletons. These were the unmarked graves of slaves and others executed by the Dutch in the 17th and 18th centuries on what was then known as Gallows Hill. The bones were exhumed and this memorial building, with an attractive facade of Robben Island slate, was created. It includes an ossuary and excellent interpretive displays, including a replica of the remarkable 360-degree panorama of Table Bay painted by Robert Gordon in 1778.

Prestwich Memorial Garden SCULPTURE

(Map p50; cnr Somerset & Buitengracht Sts, De Waterkant; Strand) Along the Walk of Remembrance (formerly known as the 2010 World Cup's Fan Walk) and one end of the proposed City Walk attraction is this attractive public space dotted with a collection of quirky sculptures and installations by Capetonian artists, including the rainbow arch *It's Beautiful Here* by Heath Nash, the *Full Cycle Tree* by KEAG and several Rock Girl benches (see p72).

Mutual Heights ARCHITECTURE

(Map p50; cnr Parliament & Darling Sts, City Bowl; Darling) Clad in rose- and gold-veined black marble, Mutual Heights is the most impressive of the City Bowl's collection of art deco structures. It's decorated with one of the longest continuous stone friezes in the world, designed by Ivan Mitford-Barberton and chiselled by master stonemasons the Lorenzi brothers. Much of the building's original detail and decoration have been preserved, including the impressive central banking space (sadly not open for general viewing).

Grand Parade ARCHITECTURE

(Map p50; Darling St, City Bowl; Darling) A prime location in Cape Town's history, the Grand Parade is where: the Dutch built their first fort in 1652; slaves were sold and punished; crowds gathered to watch Nelson Mandela's first address to the nation as a free man after 27 years in jail; and the official FIFA fan park for the 2010 World Cup was set up. A market is held on part of the square, which is also used for parking. The city has allotted R7 million for the renovation of the grand Edwardian **Cape Town City Hall**, which faces the parade and is now used occasionally for music and cultural events.

Gardens & Surrounds

South African Jewish Museum MUSEUM

(Map p56; www.sajewishmuseum.co.za; 88 Hatfield St, Gardens; adult/child R40/free;

City Bowl & Surrounds

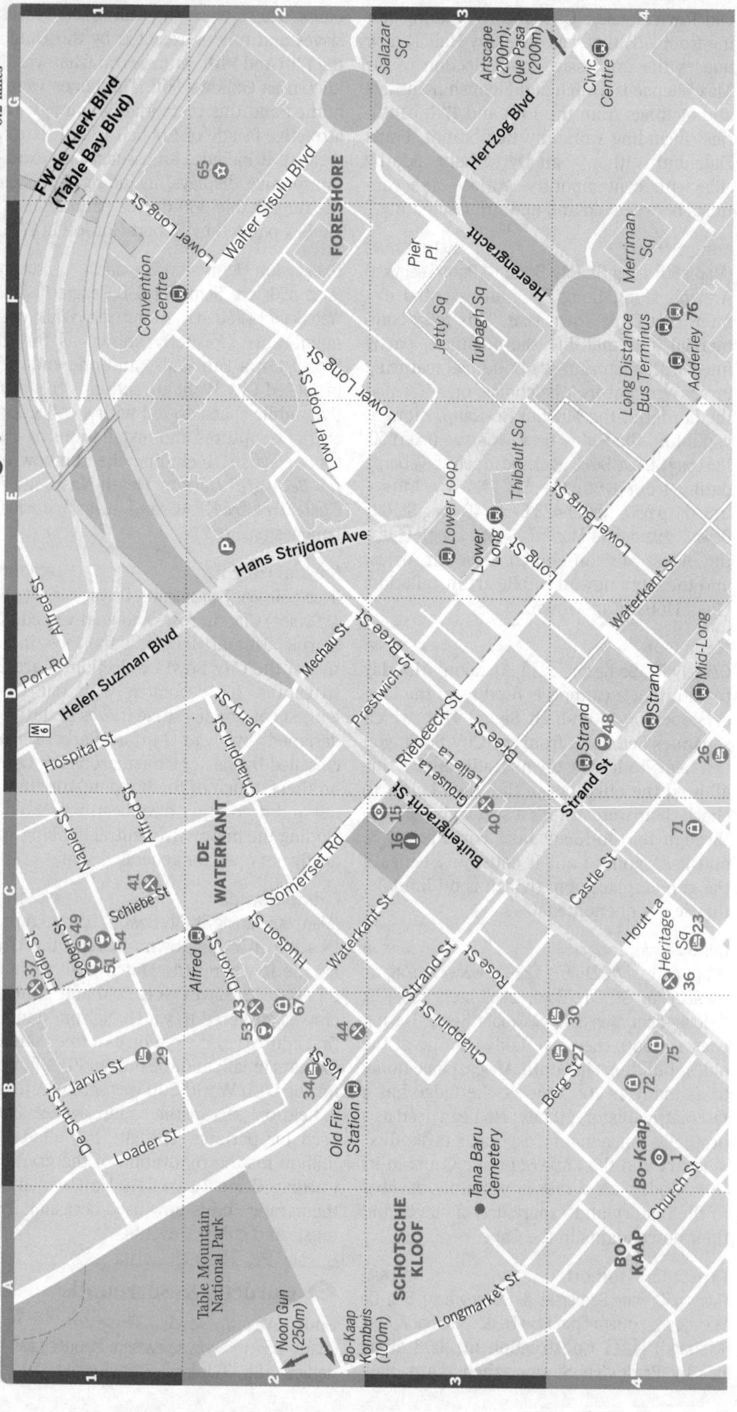

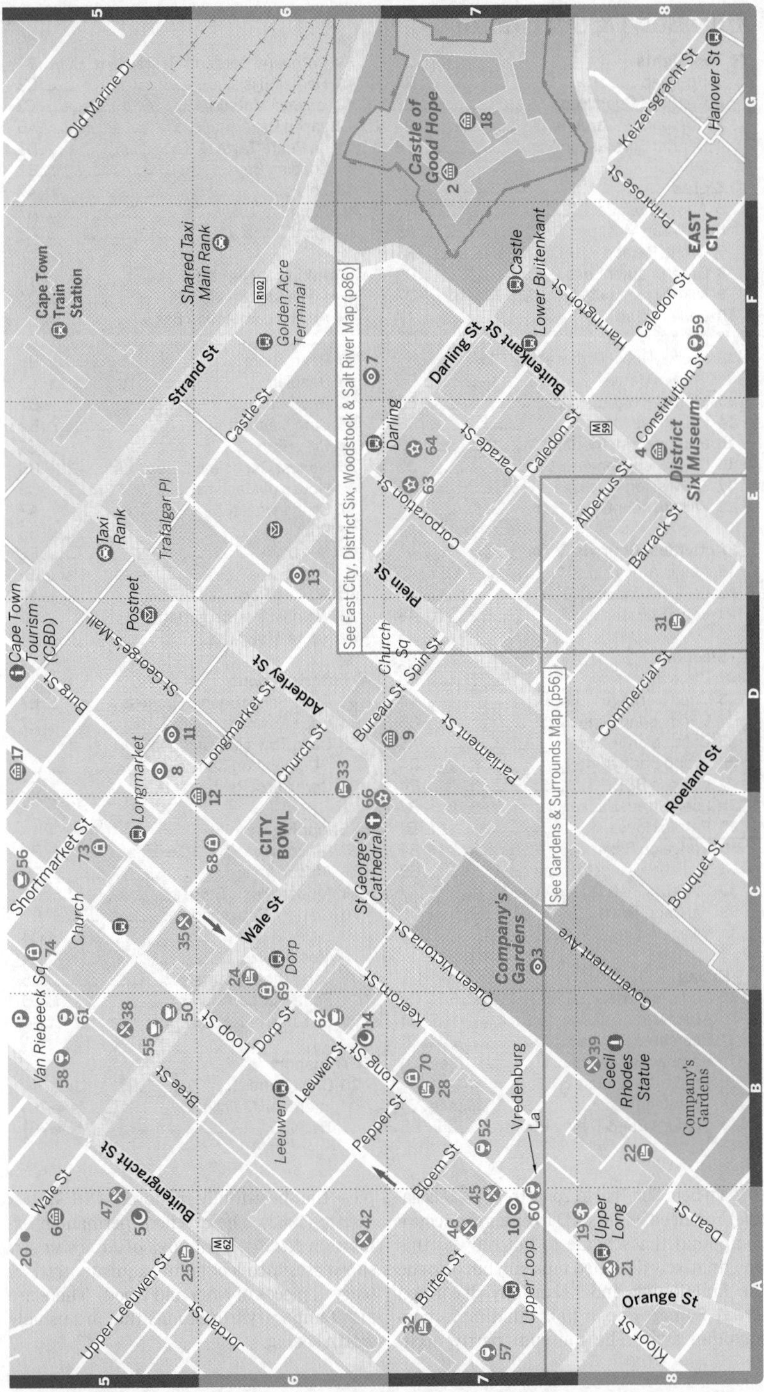
Cape Town Train Station
Old Marine Dr
Shared Taxi Main Rank
R102
Golden Acre Terminal
Strand St
Castle St
Castle of Good Hope
2
18
See East City, District Six, Woodstock & Salt River Map (p86)
7
Darling St
Darling
63
64
Corporation St
Buitenkant St
Lower Buitenkant
Castle
Harrington St
Primrose St
Keizersgracht St
Hanover St
EAST CITY
Caledon St
59
Parade St
Caledon St
M 59
4 Constitution St
District Six Museum
Albertus St
Barrack St
31
Commercial St
Roeland St
Bouquet St
Plein St
Spin St
Church Sq
Bureau St
9
Parliament St
13
Trafalgar Pl
Taxi Rank
Postnet
Cape Town Tourism (CBD)
Burg St
St George's Mall
Adderley St
Longmarket St
11
8
Longmarket
17
12
Church St
33
66
St George's Cathedral
CITY BOWL
Shortmarket St
56
73
68
Church
35
Wale St
Dorp
24
69
74
Van Riebeeck Sq
58
61
38
55
50
Loop St
Dorp St
62
14
Leeuwen St
Leeuwen
Long St
Keerom St
Queen Victoria St
Company's Gardens
3
Government Ave
See Gardens & Surrounds Map (p56)
70
28
Pepper St
Bree St
Buitengracht St
52
Vredenburg La
39
Cecil Rhodes Statue
Company's Gardens
22
Bloem St
45
10
60
42
46
Buiten St
Upper Loop
19
Upper Long
21
Dean St
Orange St
Kloof St
Wale St
6
20
47
5
M 62
25
Upper Leeuwen St
Jordan St
32
57

City Bowl & Surrounds

10am-5pm Sun-Thu, to 2pm Fri; P; Annandale) You need a photo ID to enter the secure compound that's home to not only to this imaginatively designed museum but also the the functioning and beautifully decorated **Great Synagogue**, a 1905 building in neo-Egyptian style. The museum partly occupies the beautifully restored **Old Synagogue** (1863). The excellent permanent exhibition *Hidden Treasures of Japanese Art* showcases a collection of exquisite *netsuke* (carved pieces of ivory and wood). There are also temporary exhibitions that are usually worth seeing.

South African National Gallery GALLERY
(Map p56; ☎021-481 3970; www.iziko.org.za/museums/south-african-national-gallery; Government Ave, Gardens; adult/child R30/15; ⏲10am-5pm; Annandale) The impressive permanent collection of the nation's premier art space harks back to Dutch times and includes some extraordinary pieces. But it's often contemporary works, such as the *Butcher Boys* sculpture by Jane Alexander – looking rather like a trio of Tolkienesque orcs who have stumbled into the gallery – that stand out the most.

Signal Hill VIEWPOINT
(Map p68; Kloof Nek) The early settlement's lookout point is so named because it was from here that flags were hoisted when a ship was spotted, giving the people below time to prepare goods for sale and dust off their tankards. Walk, cycle or drive to the summit, which is part of Table Mountain National Park, by taking the first turn-off to the right off Kloof Nek Rd onto Military Rd.

South African Museum MUSEUM
(Map p56; ☎021-481 3805; www.iziko.org.za/museums/south-african-museum; 25 Queen Victoria St, Gardens; adult/child R30/15; ⏲10am-5pm; Michaelis) South Africa's oldest museum may be showing its age, but it does contain a wide and often intriguing series of exhibitions, many on the country's natural history. The best galleries are the newest, showcasing the art and culture of the area's first peoples, the Khoekhoen and San, and including the famous Linton Panel, an amazing example of San rock art. There's an extraordinary delicacy to the paintings, particularly the ones of graceful elands.

Oranjezicht City Farm FARM
(Map p56; www.ozcf.co.za; Upper Orange St, Oranjezicht; ⏲farm 8am-4pm Mon-Sat, market 9am-2pm Sat; Upper Orange) FREE Local residents and volunteers have created this fantastic nonprofit venture on land where, in 1709, 'Oranje Zigt', the original farm in the Upper Table Valley, was founded. Grounds next to Homestead Park, recently occupied by a disused bowling green, have been crafted into a beautiful neighbourhood market garden. You are free to wander around, though guided tours can also be arranged: see the website for details.

Green Point & Waterfront

V&A Waterfront NEIGHBOURHOOD
(Map p60; www.waterfront.co.za; P; Nobel Square) This historic working harbour has a spectacular setting and many tourist-oriented attractions, including masses of shops, restaurants, bars, cinemas and cruises. The Alfred and Victoria Basins date from 1860 and are named after Queen Victoria and her son Alfred. Too small for modern container vessels and tankers, the Victoria Basin is still used by tugs, fishing boats and various other vessels. In the Alfred Basin you'll see ships under repair.

★ **Robben Island** LANDMARK
(☎021-413 4220; www.robben-island.org.za; adult/child R280/150; ⏲ferries depart at 9am, 11am, 1pm & 3pm, weather permitting; Nobel Square) Used as a prison from the early days of the VOC right up until 1996, this Unesco World Heritage Site is preserved as a memorial to those such as Nelson Mandela who spent many years incarcerated here. You can only go here on a tour, which last around four hours including ferry rides and depart from the **Nelson Mandela Gateway** (Map p60; Clock Tower Precinct, V&A Waterfront; ⏲9am-8.30pm; Nobel Square) FREE beside the Clock Tower at the Waterfront. Booking online well in advance is highly recommended as tours can sell out.

Two Oceans Aquarium AQUARIUM
(Map p60; www.aquarium.co.za; Dock Rd, V&A Waterfront; adult/child R125/60; ⏲9.30am-6pm; ; Aquarium) This excellent aquarium features denizens of the deep from the cold and the warm oceans that border the Cape Peninsula, including ragged-tooth sharks. There are penguins, turtles, an astounding kelp forest open to the sky, and pools in which kids can touch sea creatures. Qualified divers can get into the water for a closer look (R700, including dive gear).

Chavonnes Battery Museum MUSEUM
(Map p60; ☎021-416 6230; www.chavonnesmuseum.co.za; Clock Tower Precinct, V&A Waterfront; admission R35; ⏲9am-4pm) This museum houses the remains of an early-18th-century cannon battery, one of several fortifications the Dutch built around Table Bay. Although it had been partly demolished and covered over during the construction of the docks in 1860, an excavation of the site in 1999 revealed the remains. You can walk around the entire site and get a good feel for what it would have originally been like.

Zeitz MOCAA Pavilion MUSEUM
(Map p60; www.waterfront.co.za/activities/land-operators/zeitz-mocca-pavilion; North Wharf, V&A Waterfront; ⌚noon-8pm Wed-Sun; 🚌Nobel Square) FREE Until its Thomas Heatherwick-designed home in the Waterfront's old grain silo opens in 2017, a taster of the Zeitz MOCAA's collection of contemporary African art is displayed in this small pavilion next to the Bascule Bridge. Exhibits here change regularly, and several are put on in conjunction with the Chavonnes Battery Museum. Entrepreneur Jochen Zeitz's impressive art collection will provide the finished museum's permanent exhibition within some 80 proposed gallery spaces.

Nobel Square SQUARE
(Map p60; V&A Waterfront; 🚌Nobel Square) Here's your chance to have your photo taken with Desmond Tutu and Nelson Mandela. Larger-than-life statues of both men, designed by Claudette Schreuders, stand beside those of South Africa's two other Nobel Prize winners: Nkosi Albert Luthuli and FW de Klerk.

Green Point Urban Park PARK
(Map p60; www.gprra.co.za/green-point-urban-park.html; Bay Rd, Green Point; ⌚7am-7pm; P; 🚌Stadium) One of the best things to come out of the redevelopment of Green Point Common for the 2010 World Cup is this park and biodiversity garden. Streams fed by Table Mountain's springs and rivers water the park, which has three imaginatively designed areas – People & Plants, Wetlands, and Discovering Biodiversity – that, along with educational information boards, act as the best kind of outdoor museum. Guided tours (adult/child R35/11) can be arranged through the Cape Town Stadium.

Cape Town Stadium STADIUM
(Map p60; ☎021-417 0101; Granger Bay Blvd, Green Point; tours adult/child R45/17; ⌚tours 10am, noon & 2pm Tue-Sat; P; 🚌Stadium) Shaped like a giant, traditional African hat and wrapped with a Teflon-mesh membrane designed to catch and reflect natural light, this R4.5-billion stadium, built for the 2010 World Cup, is Cape Town's most striking piece of contemporary architecture. The hour-long tours will take you behind the scenes into the VIP and press boxes as well as the teams' dressing rooms.

Atlantic Coast

Sea Point Promenade OUTDOORS
(Map p68; Beach Rd, Sea Point; 🚌Promenade) Ambulating along Sea Point's wide, paved and grassy promenade is a pleasure shared by Capetonians from all walks of life – it's a great place to observe the city's multiculturalism. There are kids' playgrounds, a well-maintained outdoor gym, and several public artworks that are worth taking the time to see.

Clifton Beaches BEACH
(Map p68; Victoria Rd, Clifton; 🚌Clifton, Clifton 2nd, Clifton 3rd, Clifton 4th) Giant granite boulders break up the four beaches at Clifton, all accessible by steps from Victoria Rd. As they're almost always sheltered from the wind, they offer top sunbathing spots. Vendors hawk

MUSLIM CAPE TOWN

Islam first came to the Cape with the slaves brought by the Dutch from the Indian subcontinent and Indonesia (hence the term Cape Malays, although few of them actually hailed from what is today called Malaysia). Among them were educated political dissidents such as the exiled Islamic leader Tuan Guru from Tidore (Indonesia), who arrived in 1780. During his 13 years on Robben Island, Tuan Guru accurately copied the Quran from memory. In 1789 he helped establish the **Auwal Mosque** (Map p50; 34 Dorp St, Bo-Kaap; 🚌Leeuwen), the city's first mosque, in the Bo-Kaap, thus making this area the heart of the Islamic community in Cape Town.

Tuan Guru is buried in the Bo-Kaap's **Tana Baru cemetery** off the western end of Longmarket St. His grave is one of the 20 or so *karamats* (tombs of Muslim saints) encircling Cape Town and visited by the faithful on a mini pilgrimage. Islam is still widely practised in the city, predominantly among the coloured community.

Gamidah Jacobs grew up in the Bo-Kaap and lives in one of district's oldest houses, **Lekka Kombuis** (Map p50; ☎079-957 0226; lekkakombuis@mweb.co.za; 81 Wale St, Bo-Kaap; cooking class from R400, cooking class & tour from R600; 🚌Dorp/Leeuwen). Gamidah is a wonderful guide to the area and conducts hands-on Cape Malay cooking classes in her home.

CAPE TOWN FOR CHILDREN

Cape Town, with its beaches and fun attractions such as the **Two Oceans Aquarium** (p53), is a great place for a family vacation.

Among other animal-spotting opportunities are the seals at **Duiker Island**; those crowd pleasers – the penguins – at **Boulders** (p57); and thousands of birds and monkeys at **World of Birds**. Camel rides are on offer at **Imhoff Farm** (☎021-783 4545, camel rides 082 344 3163; www.imhofffarm.co.za; Kommetjie Rd, Kommetjie; admission free, snake & reptile park adult/child R35/30, camel rides adult/child R50/30; farm 9am-5pm, shop 8am-5pm, snake & reptile park 9am-5pm Mon-Fri, camel rides noon-4pm Tue-Sun; P), where you'll also find a snake and reptile park.

The **Planetarium** (Map p56; www.iziko.org.za/museums/planetarium; 25 Queen Victoria St, Gardens; adult/child R40/20; 10am-5pm; Michaelis) screens a kids' star show daily, and there are plenty of other displays to grab the attention of inquisitive children at the attached **South African Museum** (p53). Also educational and fun is the **Cape Town Science Centre** (☎021-300 3200; www.ctsc.org.za; 370B Main Rd, Observatory; admission R40; 9am-4.30pm Mon-Sat, 10am-4.30pm Sun; P; Observatory).

At the beach, parents should watch out for rough surf (not to mention hypothermia-inducing water temperatures!); **Muizenberg Beach** (p58) on a warm, calm day is the best bet, as is the rock pool at neighbouring **St James** (off Main Rd, St James; St James). The **Sea Point Pavilion** (p63) has a great family swimming pool that is significantly warmer than the surrounding ocean.

There are two inventively designed playgrounds at **Green Point Urban Park**, plus educational gardens of native plants. Nearby **Moullie Point** has a big play area, toy train, maze and golf putting course.

For other ideas, including kid-friendly cafes, restaurants and shops, check out **Cape Town Kids** (www.capetownkids.co.za).

drinks and ice creams along the beach and sun loungers and shades are available. However, there are no public toilets.

Camps Bay Beach BEACH

(Map p68; Victoria Rd, Camps Bay; Camps Bay) With soft white sand and a backdrop of the spectacular Twelve Apostles of Table Mountain, Camps Bay is one of the city's most popular beaches. However, it has drawbacks: it's one of the windiest beaches here; it gets crowded, particularly on weekends; there are no lifeguards on duty; and the surf is strong. So please take care if you do decide to swim.

World of Birds BIRD SANCTUARY

(www.worldofbirds.org.za; Valley Rd, Hout Bay; adult/child R85/40; 9am-5pm, monkey jungle 11.30am-1pm & 2-3.30pm; P; Valley) Barbets, weavers and flamingos are among the 3000 birds and small mammals – covering some 400 different species – that can be found here. A real effort has been made to make the aviaries, which are South Africa's largest, as natural-looking as possible, with the use of lots of tropical landscaping. In the **monkey jungle** you can interact with cheeky squirrel monkeys.

Hout Bay Harbour HARBOUR

(Harbour Rd, Hout Bay) Partly given over to tourism with complexes such as **Mariner's Wharf** (www.marinerswharf.co.za; Harbour Rd, Hout Bay; Northshore), Hout Bay's harbour still functions and the southern arm of the bay is a fishing port and processing centre. Cruises and snorkelling/diving trips to **Duiker Island** (Fishmarket) depart from here.

Southern Suburbs

Kirstenbosch Botanical Gardens GARDENS

(☎021-799 8782; www.sanbi.org/gardens/kirstenbosch; Rhodes Dr, Newlands; adult/child R55/15; 8am-7pm Sep-Mar, to 6pm Apr-Aug, conservatory 9am-5pm year-round) Location and unique flora combine to make these 52,800-sq-km botanical gardens among the most beautiful in the world. The main entrance at the Newlands end of the gardens is where you'll find the information centre, an excellent souvenir shop and the **conservatory**.

Added for garden's centenary in 2013, the **Tree Canopy Walkway** (informally known as the Boomslang, meaning 'tree snake') is a curvaceous steel and timber bridge that rises through the trees and provides amazing views.

Gardens & Surrounds

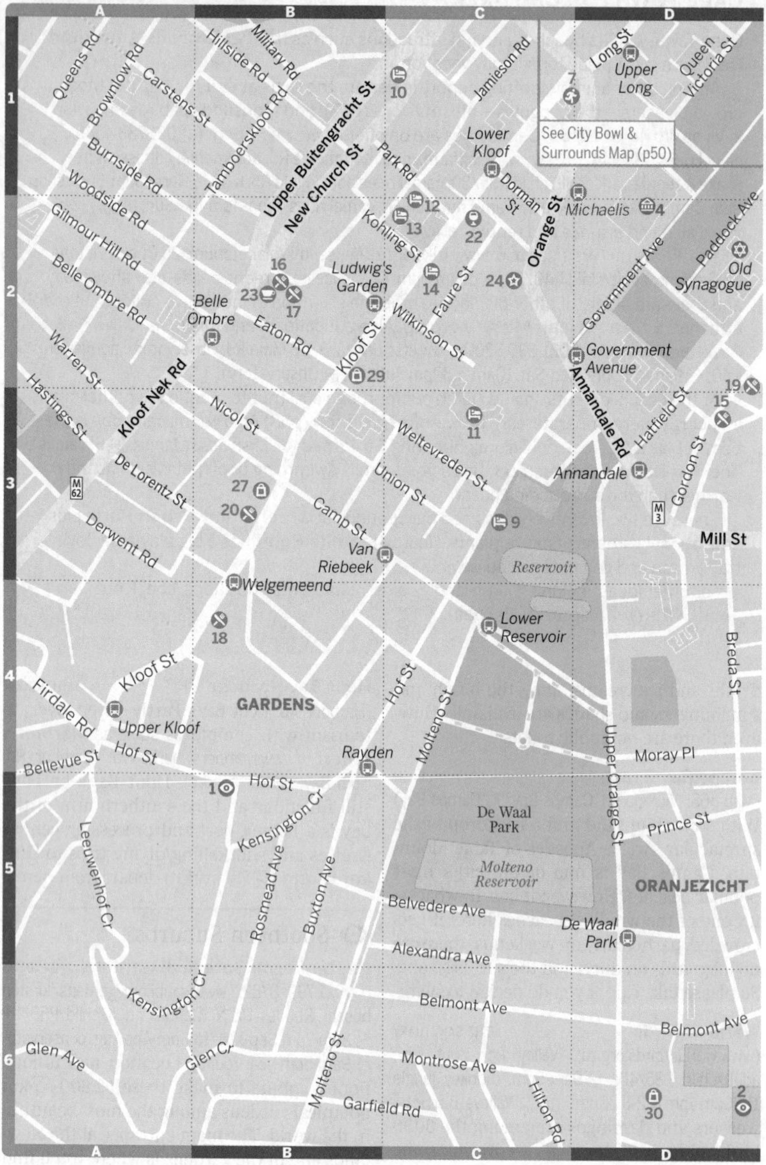

Rhodes Memorial MONUMENT

(www.rhodesmemorial.co.za; off M3, Groote Schuur Estate, Rondebosch; ⌚7am-7pm; P) FREE Partly modelled on the arch at London's Hyde Park Corner, this monumental granite memorial stands on the eastern slopes of Table Mountain, at a spot where the mining magnate and former prime minister used to admire the view. The 49 steps, one for each year of Rhodes' life, are flanked by pairs of proud lions; the top provides sweeping vistas to the Cape Flats and the mountain ranges beyond.

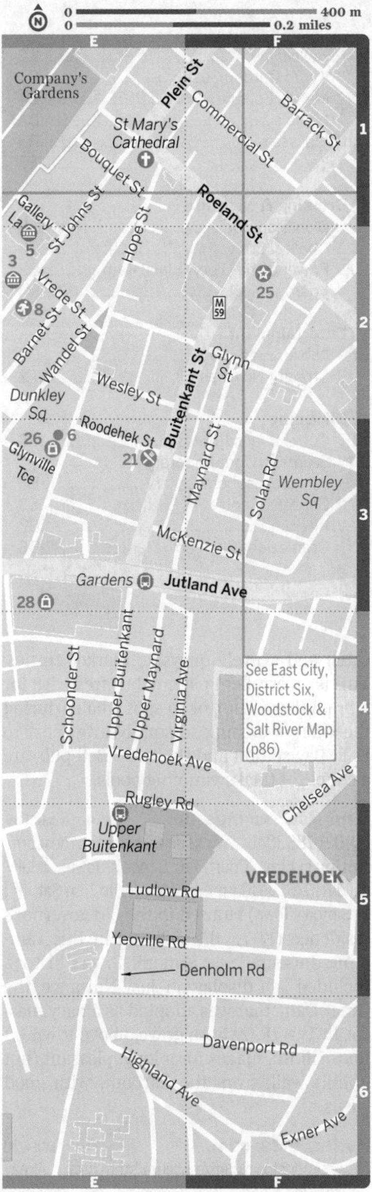

Irma Stern Museum MUSEUM

(☎021-685 5686; www.irmastern.co.za; Cecil Rd, Rosebank; adult/child R10/5; ⏰10am-5pm Tue-Sat; 🚆Rosebank) The pioneering 20th-century artist Irma Stern (1894–1966), whose works are some of the most sought-after among modern South African painters, lived here for almost 40 years; her studio has been left virtually intact, as if she'd just stepped out into the verdant garden for a breath of fresh air. Her ethnographic art-and-craft collection from around the world is as fascinating as her art, which was influenced by German expressionism and incorporates traditional African elements.

Southern Peninsula

Cape of Good Hope OUTDOORS

(www.tmnp.co.za; admission adult/child R110/55; ⏰6am-6pm Oct-Mar, 7am-5pm Apr-Sep; P) Commonly called Cape Point, this 77.50-sq-km section of Table Mountain National Park includes awesome scenery, fantastic walks, great birdwatching and often-deserted beaches. Bookings are required for the two-day **Cape of Good Hope Trail** (Sep-Apr R180, May-Aug R150, reserve entry fee separate), a spectacular 33.8km circular route with one night spent at the basic Protea and Restio huts. Contact the **Buffelsfontein Visitor Centre** (☎021-780 9204; Cape of Good Hope; ⏰9am-4pm Mon-Thu, to 3pm Fri) for further details.

Boulders Penguin Colony BIRD SANCTUARY

(www.tmnp.co.za; Simon's Town; adult/child R60/30; ⏰8am-5pm Apr-Sep, to 6.30pm Feb-Mar & Oct-Nov, 7am-7.30pm Dec & Jan; P; 🚆Simon's Town) Some 3km southeast of Simon's Town, this picturesque area, with enormous boulders dividing small, sandy coves, is home to a colony of 2100 delightful African penguins. A boardwalk runs from the Boulders Visitor Centre at the Foxy Beach end of the protected area (another part of Table Mountain National Park) to Boulders Beach, where you can get down on the sand and mingle with the waddling penguins. Don't, however, be tempted to pet them: they have sharp beaks that can cause serious injuries.

Silvermine Nature Reserve OUTDOORS

(☎021-715 0011; www.tmnp.co.za; Ou Kaapse Weg; adult/child R10/5; ⏰7am-6pm Oct-Mar, 8am-5pm Apr-Sep) This section of Table Mountain National Park is named after the fruitless attempts by the Dutch to prospect for silver in this area from 1675 to 1685. Today its focal point is the Silvermine Reservoir (built in 1898), which is a beautiful spot for a picnic or leisurely walk on a wheelchair-accessible boardwalk. The reservoir waters are tannin-stained and although there are signs forbidding swimming, you'll often find locals taking a dip here.

Gardens & Surrounds

Sights

1 Leeuwenhof B5
2 Oranjezicht City Farm D6
3 South African Jewish Museum E2
4 South African Museum D2
5 South African National Gallery E2
South African Planetarium ..... (see 4)

Activities, Courses & Tours

6 Coffeebeans Routes E3
7 Downhill Adventures C1
8 Mountain Club of South Africa E2

Sleeping

9 Ashanti Gardens C3
10 Backpack C1
11 Belmond Mount Nelson Hotel C3
12 Hippo Boutique Hotel C2
13 La Grenadine C2
14 Once in Cape Town C2

Eating

15 Aubergine D3
Chef's Table ..... (see 11)
Ferdinando's ..... (see 27)
16 Hallellujah B2
17 Kyoto Garden Sushi B2
18 Manna Epicure B4
19 Maria's D2
20 Melissa's B3
21 Yard E3

Drinking & Nightlife

Blah Blah Bar ..... (see 27)
22 Chalk & Cork C2
23 Power & the Glory/Black Ram B2
Yours Truly ..... (see 14)

Entertainment

24 Labia C2
25 Straight No Chaser F2

Shopping

26 Coffeebeans Routes E3
27 Erdmann Contemporary & Photographers Gallery B3
28 Gardens Centre E3
29 KIN B2
30 Oranjezicht City Farm Market D6

Casa Labia Cultural Centre ARTS CENTRE
(021-788 6068; www.casalabia.co.za; 192 Main Rd, Muizenberg; 10am-4pm Tue-Sun; Muizenberg) FREE This magnificent seaside villa built in 1930 was once the palatial home of Italian ambassador Count Natale Labia and his South African wife. It now hosts a program of concerts, lectures and events, as well as housing works from the Labia family's art collection (including paintings by Irma Stern and Gerald Sekoto) and regularly changing contemporary-art exhibitions. The building also houses an excellent cafe and the top-class arts and crafts shop **CasBah**.

Muizenberg Beach BEACH
(Beach Rd, Muizenberg; P; Muizenberg) Popular with families, this surf beach is famous for its row of colourfully painted Victorian bathing chalets. Surfboards can be hired and lessons booked at several shops along Beach Rd; lockers are available in the pavilions on the promenade. The beach shelves gently and the sea is generally safer here than elsewhere along the peninsula.

Kalk Bay Harbour HARBOUR
(Essex Rd, Kalk Bay; fish market 9am-5pm; P; Kalk Bay) This picturesque harbour is best visited in the morning, when the community's fishing boats pitch up with their daily catch and a lively quayside market ensues. This is an excellent place to buy fresh fish for a braai (barbecue), or to spot whales during the whale-watching season. Nearby, next to Kalk Bay station and the Brass Bell pub, are a couple of tidal swimming pools.

Simon's Town Museum MUSEUM
(021-786 3046; www.simonstown.com/museum/stm_main.htm; Court Rd, Simon's Town; adult/child R10/5; 10am-4pm Mon-Fri, to 1pm Sat; P; Simon's Town) Housed in the old governor's residence (1777), the exhibits in this rambling museum trace Simon's Town's history. Included is a display on Just Nuisance, the Great Dane that was adopted as a navy mascot in WWII – whose grave, above town off Red Hill Rd, makes for a long, pleasant (but uphill) walk from the harbour, with good views.

Heritage Museum MUSEUM
(www.simonstown.com/museum/sthm.htm; Almay House, King George Way, Simon's Town; admission R10; 11am-4pm Tue-Thu & Sun; P; Simon's Town) Simon's Town had a 7000-strong community of people of colour before apartheid forcibly removed most of them, mainly to the suburb of Ocean's View, across on the Atlantic side of the peninsula. This small but interesting museum, with a lovely front garden, is

WORTH A TRIP

EAST CITY TO SALT RIVER

East of the City Bowl are a series of working-class and industrial suburbs that are regenerating and partly gentrifying. The process is a patchy, controversial one and has long been so – this is where you'll find the empty lots of District Six, a multicultural area destroyed during apartheid.

Closest to the city, there are several creative businesses, cafes and restaurants in East City where you can check out the mural of Mandela on **Substation 13** (Map p86; Canterbury St, District Six; Lower Buitenkant) FREE; colourfully painted **Charly's Bakery** (p78); and **Land & Liberty** (Map p86; Keizersgracht, District Six; Hanover St), an eight-storey-tall painting by the prolific street artist Faith47 (www.faith47.com) depicting a mother with a baby strapped to her back.

Further east, Woodstock and Salt River continue their upward-mobility trajectory, with the **Woodstock Exchange** (p91) joining the phenomenal Old Biscuit Mill along Albert Rd. Also drop by the local art galleries including **Stevenson** (Map p86; www.stevenson.info; 160 Sir Lowry Rd, Woodstock; 9am-5pm Mon-Fri, 10am-1pm Sat; District Six), **Goodman Gallery Cape** (Map p86; 021-462 7573; www.goodman-gallery.com; 3rd fl, Fairweather House, 176 Sir Lowry Rd, Woodstock; 9.30am-5.30pm Tue-Fri, 10am-4pm Sat; District Six), **Southern Guild** (Map p86; 021-461 2856; www.southernguild.co.za; Unit 1, 10-16 Lewin St, Woodstock; 10am-5pm Tue-Fri, to 1pm Sat; District Six) and **What If the World** (Map p86; www.whatiftheworld.com; 1 Argyle St, Woodstock; 10am-4.30pm Tue-Fri, to 3pm Sat; Kent).

Street artists conducting tours around Woodstock include **Juma Mkwela** (073 400 4064; juma.mkwela@gmail.com; Woodstock/Khayelitsha tour R200/500), a friendly Zimbabwean and former resident, who also leads tours of the street art in Khayelitsha, where he now lives.

dedicated to the evictees and based in Almay House (1858). It's curated by Zainab Davidson, whose family was kicked out in 1975.

Activities

Abseiling & Kloofing

Abseil Africa EXTREME SPORTS
(Map p50; 021-424 4760; www.abseilafrica.co.za; 297 Long Street; abseiling R650) The 112m drop off the top of Table Mountain with this long-established outfit is a guaranteed adrenalin rush. Don't even think of tackling it unless you've got a head (and a stomach) for heights. Tag on a guided hike up Platteklip Gorge for R250.

Abseil Africa also offers kloofing (canyoning) trips around Cape Town. The sport of clambering into and out of kloofs (cliffs or gorges) also entails abseiling, climbing, hiking, swimming and jumping.

Cycling & Mountain Biking

City-tour outfits AWOL (p65) and **Day Trippers** (021-511 4766; www.daytrippers.co.za) also offer cycling itineraries.

Downhill Adventures CYCLING
(Map p56; 021-422 0388; www.downhilladventures.com; cnr Orange & Kloof Sts, Gardens; activities from R750; Upper Loop/Upper Long) Get the adrenalin pumping with Downhill's cycling trips, including a thrilling ride down from the lower cable station on Table Mountain, as well as more leisurely pedals in the Tokai Forest, or through the Constantia Winelands and the Cape of Good Hope. You can also hire bikes here (R300 per day) and arrange surf or sandboarding lessons.

Diving & Snorkelling

Into the Blue (Map p68; 021-434 3358; www.diveschoolcapetown.co.za; 88B Main Rd, Sea Point; open-water PADI courses from R4650, shore/boat dives R275/420, gear hire per day R520; Sea Point High) and **Table Bay Diving** (Map p60; 021-419 8822; www.tablebaydiving.com; Quay 5, Shop 7, V&A Waterfront; Breakwater) offer a number of excellent shore and boat dives.

★ **Animal Ocean** SNORKELLING, DIVING
(079 488 5053; www.animalocean.co.za; Hout Bay Harbour, Hout Bay; snorkelling/diving per person R650/850; ; Fishmarket) Although it's weather-dependent (and not for those who suffer seasickness), don't miss the chance to go snorkelling or diving with some of the thousands of playful, curious Cape fur seals that live on Duiker Island, and swim in the

Green Point & Waterfront

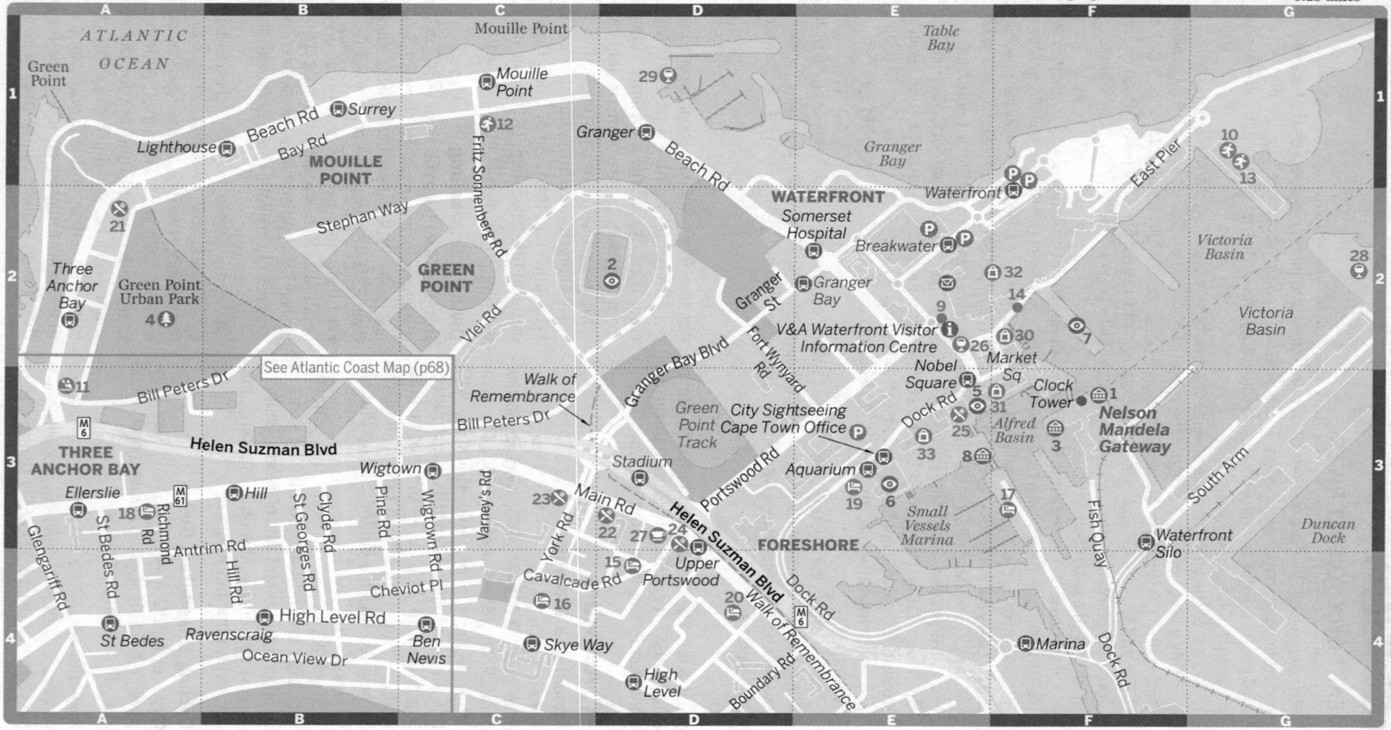

Green Point & Waterfront

shark-free waters around it. All necessary gear, including thick neoprene wetsuits, is provided. Trips run only from September to April.

Driving

Chapman's Peak Drive DRIVING, CYCLING
(www.chapmanspeakdrive.co.za; Chapman's Peak Drive; cars/motorcycles R38/25; Hout Bay) Take your time driving, cycling or walking along 'Chappies', a 5km toll road linking Hout Bay with Noordhoek – it's one of the most spectacular stretches of coastal highway in the world. There are picnic spots and viewpoints, and it's certainly worth taking the road at least one way en route to Cape Point. The toll booth is at the Hout Bay end of the road; you're free to walk up here and along the road.

Flying, Paragliding & Skydiving

Cape Town Tandem Paragliding PARAGLIDING
(076 892 2283; www.paraglide.co.za; flight R1150) Feel like James Bond as you paraglide off Lion's Head, land near the Glen Country Club and then sink a cocktail at Camps Bay. Novices can arrange a tandem paraglide, where you're strapped to an experienced flyer who takes care of the technicalities. Make enquiries on your first day in Cape Town as the weather conditions have to be right.

Cape Town Helicopters SCENIC FLIGHTS
(Map p60; 021-418 9462; www.helicopterscapetown.co.za; 220 East Pier, Breakwater Edge, V&A Waterfront; per person from R1300; Waterfront) Unforgettable views of the Cape Peninsula are guaranteed with these scenic flights. A variety of packages are available, from a 30-minute journey out to Robben

TABLE MOUNTAIN FRAMES

A legacy of Cape Town's World Design Capital program are these giant, bright-yellow metal frames sited at various locations around the city, all angled towards Table Mountain. Among other places, you'll find them on Signal Hill; the V&A Waterfront; beside Charly's Bakery in District Six; next to Cape Town Train Station; and at Lookout Hill in Khayelitsha. Sponsored by Table Mountain Aerial Cableway, they have proved to be popular, with many photos being uploaded to an online gallery (www.tablemountain.net/galleries).

Island and back to the hour-long journey down to Cape Point (R3500).

Sports Helicopters
SCENIC FLIGHTS

(Map p60; ☑ 021-419 5907; www.sport-helicopters. co.za/huey-combat-mission; East Pier Rd, V&A Waterfront; flights from R2700; 🖳 Waterfront) In this company's fleet is an ex–US Marine Corps Huey chopper from the Vietnam War era, which flies with open doors for that authentic *Apocalypse Now* experience. Standard tours last 30 minutes and take you towards Hout Bay and back; the hour-long tour gets you from the Waterfront to Cape Point.

Skydive Cape Town
EXTREME SPORTS

(☑ 082 800 6290; www.skydivecapetown.za.net; R1900) Based about 20km north of the city centre in Melkboshstrand, this experienced outfit offers tandem skydives. Needless to say, the views – once you stop screaming – are spectacular. Flights take off from the Delta 200 Airfield at Melkbosstrand; it doesn't offer Cape Town pick-ups, but can recommend transport operators if you don't have your own vehicle.

Golf
There are scores of superb courses on and around the Cape and many welcome visitors (but you should book). Contact the Western Province Golf Union (www.wpgu.co.za) for more information.

Metropolitan Golf Club
GOLF

(Map p60; ☑ 021-430 6012; www.metropolitan golfclub.co.za; Fritz Sonnenberg Rd, Mouille Point; caddie fees 9/18 holes R100/185, equipment hire 18/9 holes R200/300; 🖳 Mouille Point) As part of the revamp of the sports facilities on Green Point Common, this course also got an upgrade, with four species of local grasses planted to give it a more natural look. The wind-sheltered position – between Cape Town Stadium and Green Point Park, with Signal Hill in the background – can't be beat.

Mowbray Golf Club
GOLF

(☑ 021-685 3018; www.mowbraygolfclub.co.za; 1 Raapenberg Rd, Mowbray; 18 holes R350; ⊙ 7am-6pm; 🖳 Pinelands) Established in 1910, Mowbray is considered by some to be the best in-town course for its rural setting and abundant birdlife. It certainly has a lovely view of Devil's Peak.

Hiking & Rock Climbing
The mountainous spine of the Cape Peninsula is a hiker's and rock-climber's paradise, but it's not without its dangers, chief of

which is the capricious weather. Numerous books and maps give details, including Mike Lundy's *Best Walks in the Cape Peninsula* (www.hikecapetown.co.za), but to get the best out of the mountains hire a local guide.

Mountain Club of South Africa
ROCK CLIMBING

(Map p56; ☑ 021-465 3412; www.mcsacapetown. co.za; 97 Hatfield St; 🖳 Government Avenue) This club, which can recommend guides to serious climbers, also has a climbing wall (R5); call it to check on opening times for the public.

Venture Forth
HIKING

(☑ 086 617 3449, 021-510 3137; www.ventureforth. co.za; per person from R570) Excellent guided hikes and rock climbs with enthusiastic, savvy guides.

Walk in Africa
HIKING

(☑ 021-785 2264; www.walkinafrica.com) Steve Bolnick, an experienced and passionate safari and mountain guide, runs this company. The five-day, four-night Mountain in the Sea walk runs from Platteklip Gorge to Cape Point, partly following the Hoerikwaggo Trail.

Horse Riding

Sleepy Hollow Horse Riding
HORSE RIDING

(☑ 021-789 2341, 083 261 0104; www.sleepyhollow horseriding.com; Sleepy Hollow Lane, Noordhoek; per person R460) This reliable operation can arrange horse riding along the wide, sandy beach at Noordhoek, as well as in the mountainous hinterland. Two-hour rides leave at 9am, 1pm and 4.30pm.

Kayaking

Kaskazi Kayaks
KAYAKING, TOUR

(Map p60; ☑ 083 346 1146, 083 230 2726; www. kayak.co.za; Shell service station, 179 Beach Rd, Three Anchor Bay; per person R300; ⊙ 1-5.30pm Tue-Fri, 9am-1pm Sat; 🖳 Three Anchor Bay) This outfit runs two-hour guided kayak trips (weather dependent) from Three Anchor Bay to either Granger Bay or Clifton. There are astounding views of the mountains and coastline, as well as possible close encounters with dolphins, seals and penguins. Whale sightings in season are also on the cards. It can also arrange cycle tours and rental and tandem paraglides.

Sea Kayak Trips
KAYAKING

(☑ 082 501 8930; www.kayakcapetown.co.za; Simon's Town Jetty, Simon's Town; tours from R250; 🖳 Simon's Town) Paddle out to the African

SAFE HIKING TIPS

- Hike with long trousers. Much of the *fynbos* ('fine bush'; proteas, heaths and ericas) is tough and scratchy. There's also the seriously nasty blister bush (its leaves look like those of continental parsley); if you brush against this plant cover the spot immediately: exposure to sunlight activates the plant's toxins, which can leave blisters on your skin that may refuse to heal for years.
- Tell someone the route you're planning to climb and take a map (or, better still, a guide).
- Stick to well-used paths and don't be tempted to take shortcuts.
- Take plenty of water and some food.
- Take weatherproof clothing – the weather can change for the worse with lightning speed.
- Wear proper hiking boots or shoes and a sun hat.
- Take a fully charged mobile phone, if you have one.
- Don't climb alone – the park recommends going in groups of four.
- Don't leave litter on the mountain.
- Don't make a fire on the mountain – they're banned.

penguin colony at Boulders (R250) with this Simon's Town–based operation.

Surfing, Kitesurfing, Stand Up Paddle (SUP) Boarding

For the daily surf report check www.wavescape.co.za. If you don't want to get wet, there's sandboarding, which is like snowboarding except on sand dunes.

Surfstore Africa WATER SPORTS
(076 202 3703, 021-788 5055; www.surfstore.co.za; 48-50 Beach Rd, Muizenberg; kitesurfing/SUP/surfing lessons from R690/490/280; Muizenberg) You can take lessons in kitesurfing and SUP, as well as regular surfing, with these folks. Also here is a shop stocking a wide range of surf-related gear, and a cafe.

Gary's Surf School SURFING
(021-788 9839; www.garysurf.co.za; 34 Balmoral Bldg, Beach Rd, Muizenberg; 2hr lesson R380; 8.30am-5pm; Muizenberg) If genial surfing coach Gary Kleynhans can't get you standing on a board within a day, you don't pay for the lesson. His shop, the focus of Muizenberg's surf scene, hires out boards and wetsuits (per hour/day R100/300). It also runs sandboarding trips to the dunes at Kommetjie (R300).

Windswept WATER SPORTS
(082 961 3070; www.windswept.co.za; Bloubergstrand; 2hr group/individual lessons R495/990) Philip Baker runs windsurfing and kitesurfing camps out of his base in Bloubergstrand. Two-hour lessons are available for either groups or individuals, or if you already know the ropes you can hire a kite and board for R395. Packages including accommodation are also available.

Swimming & Sauna

If you want to swim safely in the sea, the False Bay side of the peninsula is usually a little warmer than the generally freezing Atlantic side; try the beaches and rock pools at Muizenberg, St James, Kalk Bay or Buffels Bay at Cape Point.

Sea Point Pavilion SWIMMING
(Map p68; Beach Rd, Sea Point; adult/child R20/10; 7am-7pm Oct-Apr, 9am-5pm May-Sep; Sea Point Pool) This huge outdoor pool complex, with its lovely art deco touches, is a Sea Point institution. It gets very busy on hot summer days – not surprisingly, since the pools are always at least 10°C warmer than the always-frigid ocean.

Long St Baths SWIMMING
(Map p50; www.capetown.gov.za/en/SportRecreation/Pages/LongStreetBaths.aspx; cnr Long & Buitensingel Sts, City Bowl; adult/child R5.50/1.50; 7am-7pm; Upper Loop/Upper Long) Dating from 1906, these nicely restored baths, featuring painted murals of city-centre life on the walls, are heated and very popular with the local community. The Turkish steam baths (R48) are a great way to sweat away some time, especially during the cooler months.

Women are admitted to the steam baths from 9am to 6pm Monday, Thursday and

DON'T MISS

TABLE MOUNTAIN NATIONAL PARK

Stretching from Signal Hill to Cape Point, this 220-sq-km **park** (☎021-712 2337; www.sanparks.org/parks/table_mountain) is a natural wonder, its range of environments including granite and sandstone mountains, giant-boulder-strewn beaches and shady forests.

For the vast majority of visitors the main attraction is the 1086m-high mountain itself, the top of which can easily be accessed by the **cableway** (☎021-424 0015; www.tablemountain.net; Tafelberg Rd, Table Mountain; adult 1-way/return from R115/225, child R58/110; ⏲8.30am-6pm Feb-Nov, 8am-9.30pm Dec & Jan; 🚌Lower Cable Car), which runs every 10/20 minutes in high/low season.

Concrete paths lead from the upper cableway station to the restaurant, shop and various terraces. Free volunteer-guided walks across Table Mountain's plateau run at 10am and noon daily from beside the upper cableway station.

To reach the mountain's 1088m summit you'll need to go a bit further along the track to **Maclear's Beacon**, a distance of around 5km, which should take one hour for the round trip. Don't attempt this route if there's low cloud or mist on the mountain, as it's very easy to lose your way.

The park is criss-crossed by myriad other hiking routes, ranging from easy strolls to extreme rock climbing. Entrance fees have to be paid for the Boulders, Cape of Good Hope, Oudekraal, Silvermine and Tokai sections of the park, but otherwise the routes are free. Signage is far from comprehensive and even with a map it's easy to get lost; follow our safety tips (p63) and consider hiring a guide.

Platteklip Gorge, the most straightforward route up the mountain, takes around two hours and is steep and fully exposed to the sun. Less of a slog is the **Pipe Track**, but following it takes roughly double the time. Climbing **Lion's Head** (Map p68; Signal Hill Rd, Tamboerskloof; Ⓟ; 🚌Kloof Nek), the giant, nipplelike outcrop that overlooks Sea Point and Camps Bay, takes about 45 minutes.

There are two popular routes up the mountain from Kirstenbosch Botanical Gardens along either **Skeleton Gorge** (which involves negotiating some sections with chains) or **Nursery Ravine**. Both can be done in three hours by someone of moderate fitness. The trails are well marked, and steep in places, but the way to the gardens from the cableway and vice versa is not signposted.

Possibilities for overnight hikes include the two-day/one-night, 33.8km **Cape of Good Hope Trail** (p57) and the five-day, four-night, 80km **Hoerikwaggo Trail** (☎021-465 8515) running the full length of the peninsula from Cape Point to the upper cableway station. The former has to be booked and includes accommodation; the latter can be done freely. Bookings for the beautifully designed tented camps along the trail can be made online (www.sanparks.org/parks/table_mountain/tourism/accommodation.php#tented) or by phone (☎021-712 7471) between 8am and 4pm Monday to Friday.

Saturday, and from 9am to 1pm on Tuesday; men from 1pm to 7pm on Tuesday, from 8am to 7pm on Wednesday and Friday, and from 8am to noon on Sunday.

☞ Tours

City Sightseeing Cape Town BUS TOUR
(☎021-511 6000; www.citysightseeing.co.za; adult/child 1 day R170/80, 2 days R270/170) These hop-on, hop-off buses, running two main routes, are perfect for a quick orientation, with commentary available in 16 languages. The open-top double-deckers also provide an elevated platform for photos. Buses run at roughly half-hourly intervals between 9am and 4.30pm, with extra services in peak season.

Coffeebeans Routes CULTURAL TOUR
(Map p56; ☎021-461 3572; www.coffeebeansroutes.com; 22 Hope St, Gardens; tours from R800; 🚌Roodehek) The concept – hooking up visitors with interesting local personalities, including musicians, artists, brewers and designers – is fantastic. Among innovative routes are ones focusing on South Africa's recent revolutionary history, creative enterprises and organic and natural wines.

Awol Tours CYCLING, TOUR
(Map p60; ☎021-418 3803; www.awoltours.co.za; Information Centre, Dock Rd, V&A Waterfront; Nobel Square) Discover Cape Town's cycle lanes on this superb city bike tour (three hours, R500, daily) from Awol's Waterfront base. Other pedalling itineraries include the Winelands, Cape Point and the township of Masiphumelele – a great alternative to traditional township tours. It also offers guided hikes on Table Mountain (from R1000).

Uthando CULTURAL TOUR
(☎021-683 8523; www.uthandosa.org; 9 Princes Rd, Harfield Village; R650) These township tours cost more because half of the money goes towards the social-upliftment projects that the tours visit and is specifically designed to support. Usually three or so projects are visited: they could be anything from an organic farm to an old folks' centre.

Run Cape Town TOUR
(☎072 920 7028; www.runcapetown.co.za; R450) Go sightseeing while you get a workout on this innovative company's variety of running routes across the city, both within Table Mountain National Park and further afield in Gugulethu and Darling (R550 with your own transport to Darling).

Good Hope Adventures WALKING TOUR
(☎021-510 7517; www.goodhopeadventures.com; 3-5hr tours from R250-500) Go underground on these fascinating walking tours as you explore the historic tunnels and canals that run beneath the city. You'll need to wear old shoes and clothes and have a torch. Not for the claustrophobic!

VoiceMaps WALKING TOUR
(www.voicemap.me) This locally developed website and app provides high-quality self-guided walking tours that you can download to your smartphone or listen to on your computer. Narrated by local experts, they provide insight into corners of the city sometimes overlooked by regular guided tours.

Simon's Town Boat Company BOAT TOUR
(☎083 257 7760; www.boatcompany.co.za; Town Pier, Simon's Town; harbour cruise adult/child R50/30; Simon's Town) Hop aboard the popular *Spirit of Just Nuisance* cruise around the harbour, as well as longer boat trips to Cape Point (adult/child R550/400) and Seal Island (adult/child R400/300). During the whale-watching season it also offers cruises that allow you to get up close to these magnificent animals.

Festivals & Events

For a full rundown of festivals and events, check Cape Town Tourism (p94).

January

Cape Town Minstrel Carnival CULTURAL
(www.capetown-minstrels.co.za) *Tweede Nuwe Jaar*, on 2 January, is when the satin- and sequin-clad minstrel troupes traditionally march through the city for the Kaapse Klopse (Cape Minstrel Festival) from Keizergracht St, along Adderley and Wale Sts to the Bo-Kaap. Throughout January into early February there are Saturday competitions between troupes at Athlone Stadium. See also p66.

J&B Met SPORT
(www.jbscotch.co.za/home) At Kenilworth Race Course, South Africa's richest horse race, with a jackpot of R1.5 million, is a time for big bets and even bigger hats. Generally held on the last Saturday in January.

February & March

Design Indaba DESIGN
(www.designindaba.com) This creative convention, bringing together the varied worlds of fashion, architecture, visual arts, crafts and media, is held at the end of February and early March, usually at the Cape Town International Convention Centre.

Infecting the City ARTS
(http://infectingthecity.com) Cape Town's wonderful squares, fountains, museums and theatres are the venues for this innovative end-of-February performing-arts festival featuring artists from across the continent.

GETTING AROUND THE SOUTHERN PENINSULA

A car is essential for getting the most out of the scattered sights of the southern peninsula, although the train will also do for many False Bay destinations, including Muizenberg, Kalk Bay and Simon's Town; a R30 day ticket allows unlimited travel between Cape Town and Simon's Town and all stations in between from 8am to 4.30pm.

The **Mellow Yellow Water Taxi** (☎073-473 7684; www.watertaxi.co.za; single/return R100/150) shuttles between Kalk Bay and Simon's Town – it's recommended to take the train to Simon's Town and the water taxi back to Kalk Bay rather than the other way around.

JOIN THE MERRY MINSTRELS

The riotous Cape Town Minstrel Carnival, also known in Afrikaans as the Kaapse Klopse, is the Mother City's equivalent of Rio's Mardi Gras parade – a noisy, joyous and disorganised affair with practically every colour of satin, sequin and glitter used in the costumes of the marching troupes, which can number more than 1000 members.

Although the festival dates back to early colonial times when slaves enjoyed a day of freedom the day after New Year, the look of today's carnival was inspired by visiting American minstrels in the late 19th century, hence the make-up, colourful costumes and ribald song-and-dance routines. The vast majority of participants come from the coloured communities of the Cape Flats.

Despite the carnival being a fixture on Cape Town's calendar, it has been subject to controversy, with problems over funding and clashes between rival carnival organisations. It has also always been something of a demonstration of coloured people power and remains so.

Cape Town Cycle Tour SPORT
(www.cycletour.co.za) Held on a Saturday in the middle of March, this is the world's largest timed cycling event, attracting more than 30,000 contestants. The route circles Table Mountain, heading down the Atlantic Coast and along Chapman's Peak Dr.

Cape Town Carnival CULTURAL
(http://capetowncarnival.com) Held in the middle of April along the Walk of Remembrance (the former Fan Walk) in Green Point, this is a city-sponsored parade and street party that celebrates the many facets of South African identity.

Cape Town International Jazz Festival MUSIC
(www.capetownjazzfest.com) Cape Town's biggest jazz event, attracting big names from both South Africa and overseas, is usually held at the Cape Town International Convention Centre at the end of March. It includes a free concert in Greenmarket Sq.

April & May

Old Mutual Two Oceans Marathon SPORT
(www.twooceansmarathon.org.za) This 56km marathon follows a similar route to the Pick 'n' Pay Cycle Tour around Table Mountain. It generally attracts about 9000 competitors.

Good Food & Wine Show FOOD, WINE
(www.goodfoodandwineshow.co.za) Cape Town goes gourmet with this four-day event held at the Cape Town International Convention Centre.

July

Cape Town World Music Festival MUSIC
(http://capetownworldmusicfestival.com) Held over Mandela Day weekend (around 18 July), this celebration of global beats and rythmns takes over old City Hall and parts of the Grand Parade.

September & October

Cape Town Fringe ARTS
(www.capetownfringe.co.za) A jamboree of the performing arts, organised in conjuctinon with the respected Grahamstown Festival, that peppers the Mother City with interesting happenings for 11 days at the end of September and into October

Outsurance Gun Run SPORT
(www.outsurance.co.za/gunrun) This popular half-marathon (21km) is the only time that the Noon Gun on Signal Hill gets fired on a Sunday – competitors try to finish the race before the gun goes off.

November & December

Kirstenbosch Summer Sunset Concerts MUSIC
(www.sanbi.org/gardens/kirstenbosch/summer-concerts) The start of the Sunday-afternoon outdoor concerts at Kirstenbosch Botanical Gardens, which run through until April. Bring a blanket and a picnic and join the crowds enjoying anything from arias performed by local divas to a funky jazz combo. There's always a special concert for New Year's Eve, too.

Adderely Street Christmas Lights MUSIC
Join the tens of thousands who turn out for the concert in front of Cape Town Railway station followed by a parade along festively illuminated Adderley St. The same street is pedestrianised each night from around 17 to 30 December for a night market also with live music.

Sleeping

Lively backpacker hostels, characterful guesthouses or unfettered luxury: Cape Town's accommodation choices tick all boxes. If beaches are your thing, then choose accommodation along the Atlantic or False Bay Coast. If you have transport, then anywhere is OK, but do enquire about the parking options when making a booking and check whether there's a charge (it could be anything up to R100 per day for city-centre hotels).

Apartment & House Rentals

For longer-term stays or self-catering options a serviced apartment or villa can work out as a good deal.

Cape Breaks ACCOMMODATION SERVICES
(Map p50; ☎083 383 4888; www.capebreaks.co.za) Offers studios and apartments in St Martini Gardens, beside the Company's Gardens.

Cape Stay ACCOMMODATION SERVICES
(www.capestay.co.za) Accommodation across the Cape.

In Awe Stays ACCOMMODATION SERVICES
(☎083 658 6975; www.inawestays.co.za) Stylish studios and cottages in Gardens and Fresnaye, from R850 a double.

Village & Life ACCOMMODATION SERVICES
(Map p50; ☎021-437 9700; www.villageandlife.com; Old Fire Station) Mainly has properties in De Waterkant and Camps Bay.

City Bowl & Bo-Kaap

St Paul's B&B Guesthouse B&B $
(Map p50; ☎021-423 4420; www.stpaulschurch.co.za/theguesthouse.htm; 182 Bree St, City Bowl; s/d with shared bathroom R450/750, with private bathroom R550/900; P; Upper Long/Upper Loop) This spotless B&B in a very handy location is a quiet alternative to the noise-plagued Long St backpackers. The simply furnished and spacious rooms have high ceilings, and there's a vine-shaded courtyard where you can relax or eat breakfast.

Scalabrini Guest House HOSTEL $
(Map p50; ☎021-465 6433; www.scalabrini.org.za; 47 Commercial St, City Bowl; dm/s/d or tw R240/420/600; @; Roeland) The Italian monastic order Scalabrini Fathers have provided welfare service to Cape Town's poor and to refugees since 1994. Housed in a former textile factory, it runs several social programs, and a pleasant guesthouse with 11 immaculately clean en suite rooms – plus a great kitchen for self-catering where you can watch satellite TV.

Long Street Backpackers HOSTEL $
(Map p50; ☎021-423 0615; www.longstreetbackpackers.co.za; 209 Long St, City Bowl; dm/s/d R140/260/370; ; Dorp/Leeuwen) Little has changed at this backpackers since it opened in 1993 (making it the longest-running of the many that dot Long St). In a block of 14 small flats, with four to eight beds and a bathroom in each, accommodation is arranged around a leafy courtyard decorated with funky mosaics, in which the resident cat, Bubbles, pads around.

Cape Heritage Hotel BOUTIQUE HOTEL $$
(Map p50; ☎021-424 4646; www.capeheritage.co.za; Heritage Sq, 90 Bree St, City Bowl; d/ste from R2250/3490, parking per day R75; P@; Church/Longmarket) Each room at this elegant boutique hotel, part of the Heritage Sq redevelopment of 18th-century buildings, has its own character. Some have four-poster beds and all have modern conveniences such

HARBOUR CRUISES

See Table Mountain as mariners of yore did on a cruise into Table Bay. The Waterfront has a host of operators.

Waterfront Charters (Map p60; ☎021-418 3168; www.waterfrontcharters.co.za; Shop 5, Quay 5, V&A Waterfront; Breakwater) Offers a variety of cruises, including highly recommended 1½-hour sunset cruises (R220), on its handsome wood-and brass-fitted schooner *Esperance*. A 30-minute jet-boat ride is R330.

Yacoob Tourism (Map p60; ☎021-421 0909; www.ytourism.co.za; Shop 8, Quay 5, V&A Waterfront; ; Breakwater) Among the several trips that this company runs are those on the *Jolly Roger Pirate Boat* (adult/child from R120/60) and *Tommy the Tugboat* (adult/child R50/25), both perfect for families. Adults may prefer its *Adrenalin* speed-boat jaunts or a cruise on the catamarans *Ameera* and *Tigress*.

Atlantic Coast

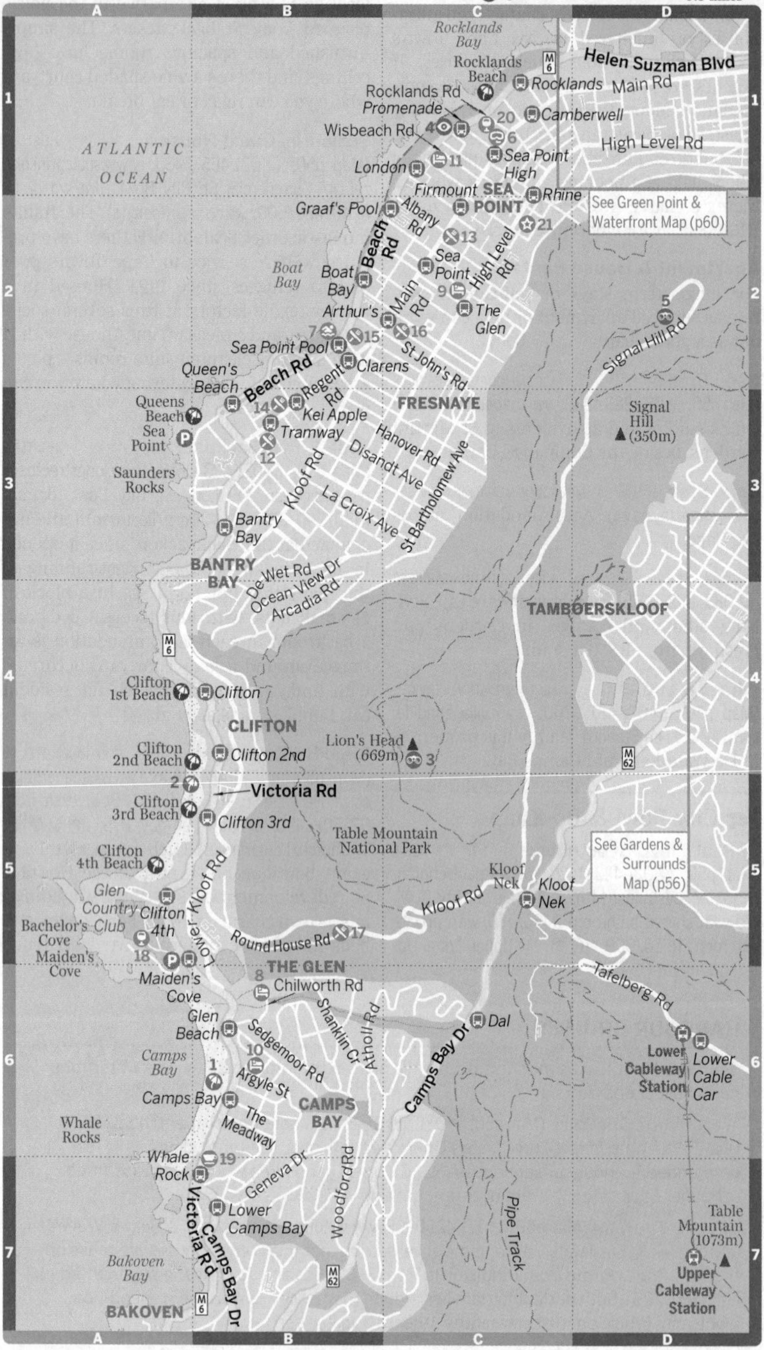
0 1 km
0 0.5 miles
ATLANTIC OCEAN
Rocklands Bay
Rocklands Beach
Helen Suzman Blvd
Rocklands
Main Rd
Rocklands Rd
Promenade
Camberwell
Wisbeach Rd
High Level Rd
Sea Point High
London
Firmount
SEA POINT
Rhine
See Green Point & Waterfront Map (p60)
Graaf's Pool
Albany Rd
Beach Rd
Boat Bay
Sea Point
High Level Rd
The Glen
Arthur's
Main Rd
Signal Hill Rd
Sea Point Pool
Clarens
St John's Rd
Queen's Beach
Regent Rd
Queens Beach
Kei Apple
FRESNAYE
Sea Point
Tramway
Hanover Rd
Signal Hill (350m)
Saunders Rocks
Kloof Rd
Disandt Ave
La Croix Ave
St Bartholomew Ave
Bantry Bay
BANTRY BAY
De Wet Rd
Ocean View Dr
Arcadia Rd
TAMBOERSKLOOF
Clifton 1st Beach
Clifton
CLIFTON
Lion's Head (669m)
Clifton 2nd Beach
Clifton 2nd
Victoria Rd
Clifton 3rd Beach
Clifton 3rd
Table Mountain National Park
Clifton 4th Beach
See Gardens & Surrounds Map (p56)
Kloof Nek
Kloof Rd
Glen Country Club
Clifton 4th
Lower Kloof Rd
Bachelor's Cove
Round House Rd
Maiden's Cove
Tafelberg Rd
Maiden's Cove
THE GLEN
Chilworth Rd
Glen Beach
Sedgemoor Rd
Shanklin Cr
Atholl Rd
Dal
Camps Bay
Argyle St
Camps Bay Dr
Lower Cableway Station
Lower Cable Car
Camps Bay
The Meadway
CAMPS BAY
Whale Rocks
Whale Rock
Geneva Dr
Woodford Rd
Pipe Track
Lower Camps Bay
Victoria Rd
Camps Bay Dr
Table Mountain (1073m)
Bakoven Bay
Upper Cableway Station
BAKOVEN

Atlantic Coast

Sights

1	Camps Bay Beach	B6
2	Clifton Beaches	A5
3	Lion's Head	C4
4	Sea Point Promenade	C1
5	Signal Hill	D2

Activities, Courses & Tours

6	Into the Blue	C1
7	Sea Point Pavilion	B2

Sleeping

8	Camps Bay Retreat	B6
9	Glen Boutique Hotel	C2
10	POD	B6
11	Winchester Mansions Hotel	C1

Eating

12	Kleinsky's Delicatessen	B3
13	La Boheme	C2
14	La Mouette	B3
15	La Perla	B2
16	Nü	C2
17	Roundhouse	B5

Drinking & Nightlife

18	Bungalow	A5
19	La Belle	B7
20	La Vie	C1

Entertainment

21	Studio 7	C2

as satellite TV and clothes presses. There's a roof terrace and a Jacuzzi pool.

Dutch Manor HISTORIC HOTEL **$$**
(Map p50; 021-422 4767; www.dutchmanor.co.za; 158 Buitengracht St, Bo-Kaap; s/d R1400/1900, parking per day R60; Dorp/Leeuwen) Four-poster beds, giant armoires and creaking floorboards lend terrific atmosphere to this six-room property crafted from an 1812 building. Although it overlooks busy Buitengracht, the noise is largely kept at bay thanks to modern renovations. On request, dinners can be prepared by the staff, who can also arrange Bo-Kaap walking tours for R70 (nonguests R100) with a local guide.

La Rose B&B B&B **$$**
(Map p50; 021-422 5883; www.larosecapetown.com; 32 Rose St, Bo-Kaap; s/d from R600/800; Old Fire Station) Adheena and Yoann are the very welcoming South African–French couple running this charming B&B, which has been so successful it's expanded into nearby properties. It's beautifully decorated and has a rooftop garden with the best views of the area. Yoann's speciality is making authentic crêpes for the guests.

Rouge on Rose BOUTIQUE HOTEL **$$**
(Map p50; 021-426 0298; www.rougeonrose.co.za; 25 Rose St, Bo-Kaap; s/d R1000/1500; Old Fire Station) This great Bo-Kaap option offers nine rustic-chic suites with kitchenettes, lounges and lots of workspace. The fun wall paintings are by a resident artist and all rooms have luxurious, open bath spaces with stand-alone tubs.

Purple House B&B, APARTMENT **$$**
(Map p50; 021-418 2508; www.purplehouse.co.za; 23 Jarvis St, De Waterkant; s/d/apt from R950/1050/1500; @; Alfred) Apart from their stylish and cosy B&B, set in the eponymous purple-painted house, the personable Dutch owners Hank and Guido also offer a self-catering cottage on the same street and a two-bed apartment on Loader St.

Daddy Long Legs Hotel BOUTIQUE HOTEL **$$**
(Map p50; 021-422 3074; www.daddylonglegs.co.za; 134 Long St, City Bowl; r/apt from R1175/1275; @; Dorp/Leeuwen) A stay at this boutique hotel–cum–art installation is anything but boring. Thirteen artists were given free rein to design the boudoirs of their dreams; the results range from a bohemian garret to a hospital ward! Our favourites include the karaoke room (with a mic in the shower) and the room decorated with cartoons of the South African pop group Freshlyground. Breakfast is extra.

Grand Daddy Hotel BOUTIQUE HOTEL **$$**
(Map p50; 021-424 7247; www.granddaddy.co.za; 38 Long St, City Bowl; r or trailer from R1910, parking per day R40; P@; Mid-Long/Church) The Grand Daddy's star attraction is its rooftop 'trailer park' of penthouse suites, made from seven vintage, artistically renovated Airstream trailers. The hotel's regular rooms are also stylish and incorporate playful references to South African culture. Its Daddy Cool bar has been blinged to the max with gold paint and trinkets.

Taj Cape Town LUXURY HOTEL **$$$**
(Map p50; 021-819 2000; www.tajhotels.com; Wale St, City Bowl; r/ste R7000/10,000; P@; Groote Kerk) India's luxury hotel group has breathed new life into the old Board of Executors building, set at the corner of Wale and Adderley. There's plenty

1

4

MICHAL KRAKOWIAK / GETTY IMAGES ©

3

PAUL THOMPSON / GETTY IMAGES ©

1. V&A Waterfront (p53)
Full of shops, bars and restaurants, this historic Cape Town area was named after Queen Victoria and her son Alfred. Table Mountain can be seen in the background.

2. Boulders Penguin Colony (p57)
African penguins.waddle around this protected area that's just 3km from Simon's Town.

3. Bo-Kaap (p48)
Brightly painted houses line narrow streets in this much-photographed neighbourhood.

4. Camps Bay Beach (p55)
The Twelve Apostles of Table Mountain form the stunning backdrop to this beach.

2

MICHAL KRAKOWIAK / GETTY IMAGES ©

WORTH A TRIP

VISITING THE TOWNSHIPS OF THE CAPE FLATS

The down-at-heel coloured communities and informal settlements (ie shacks) of the largely black townships would seem to be unlikely as tourist destinations. However, a visit to the Cape Flats might end up providing your fondest memories of Cape Town, particularly if you choose to spend a night in one of the B&Bs that are found there or to have a meal in one of the lively braai (grilled meat) joints.

Close to the city, Langa, founded in 1927, is the oldest planned township in South Africa and has areas of affluence as well as poverty – a pattern repeated in the other main townships of Guguletu and Khayelitsha (the largest, with an estimated population of over 1.5 million). It's not all one-note misery. The infrastructure in the townships has improved greatly since 1994 (though it could hardly have got any worse).

Langa

Don't miss the brilliantly decorated **Guga S'Thebe Arts & Cultural Centre** (☑ 021-695 3493; cnr Washington & Church Sts; ☺ 8am-4.30pm Mon-Fri, 8.30am-2pm Sat & Sun; P ☎; ▣ Langa) FREE, which has a new theatre, creatively constructed largely from recycled materials; the interesting **Langa Pass Museum** (☑ 084 863 3427; cnr Washington St & Lerotholi Ave; admission by donation; ☺ by appointment; P; ▣ Langa), detailing the apartheid history of the township; and the ambitious social-upliftment program **Langa Quarter** (iKhaya Le Langa; www.facebook.com/IKhayaLeLanga/timeline; cnr N'Dabeni & Bittenhout Sts; ☺ 8am-5pm; ☎; ▣ Langa) FREE, which also has a cafe.

A good place to eat is the butcher and braai shop **Nomzamo** (☑ 021-695 4250; 15 Washington St, Langa; meals R50-100; ☺ 9am-7pm; ▣ Langa).

Guguletu

The **Gugulethu Seven Memorial** (cnr Steve Biko St/NY1 & NY111; ▣ Nyanga) commemorates seven young black activists who were killed by the police here in 1986. Nearby is the **Amy Biehl Memorial**, celebrating the life of the US anti-apartheid activist who died under tragic circumstances in Guguletu in 1993, and a mosaic-covered bench, one in a series around Cape Town installed by **Rock Girl** (www.rockgirlsa.org) as part of a project to create refuges for both boys and girls from gangs.

The busy butchery **Mzoli's** (☑ 021-638 1355; 150 NY111; meals R50-100; ☺ 9am-6pm; ▣ Nyanga), serving some of Cape Town's tastiest grilled meats, has become something of an international sensation.

Khayelitsha

There are panoramic views of this massive township, as well as of Table Mountain, from **Lookout Hill** (☑ 021-367 7087; cnr Mew Way & Spine Rd; P; ▣ Khayelitsha) FREE.

A great place to eat is **Clifford & Sandra's** (Khayelisha market, off Ntlazane Rd; meals R20; ☺ 8am-6.30pm; ▣ Khayelitsha), a shack cafe next to Khayelitsha station.

Transport

If you take public transport into the townships, make sure you have a local meet you at the other end. More convenient for most visitors are township tours – good walking or cycling ones are run by **Vamos** (☑ 072 499 7866; www.vamos.co.za; walking/cycling tours R270/350) in Langa, **Laura Ndukwana** (☑ 082 979 5831; www.laurastownshiptours.co.za; tours from R400) in Guguletu and **Juma Mkwela** (p59) in Khayelitsha.

The half-day itineraries of most bus tours are similar, often including a visit to the District Six Museum, then a drive to visit some of the main townships. Tour guides are generally flexible in where they go, and respond to the wishes of the group.

of heritage here but a new tower also houses the chic contemporary-styled rooms, many offering spectacular views of Table Mountain. Service and facilities, including the excellent restaurant **Bombay Brasserie**, are top grade.

Salt River & Observatory

★ **Wish U Were Here** BACKPACKERS $
(021-447 0522; www.wishuwereherecapetown.com; 445 Albert Rd, Salt River; dm/s/d with shared bathroom R200/450/600, d with private bathroom R700; ; Kent) The designers clearly had a lot of fun with this place just a short stroll from the Old Biscuit Mill. One dorm is Barbie-doll pink; a romantic double has a bed made from a suspended fishing boat; another is styled after an intensive care unit! The building's wraparound balcony overlooks the Salt River roundabout (which is noisy in daytime).

Observatory Backpackers BACKPACKERS $
(021-447 0861; www.observatorybackpackers.com; 235 Lower Main Rd, Observatory; dm/s/d with shared bathroom from R160/360/460, r with private bathroom R530; ; Observatory) There's a funky African theme to this very appealing backpackers, just a short walk away from the heart of the Obs action further down Lower Main Rd. The spacious, shady backyard and lounges are a plus. No breakfast but Dolce Bakery is right next door.

Gardens & Surrounds

★ **Backpack** BACKPACKERS $
(Map p56; 021-423 4530; www.backpackers.co.za; 74 New Church St, Tamboerskloof; dm/s/d with shared bathroom from R270/720/1060, s/d/apt with private bathroom from R780/1320/1600; P@; Upper Long/Upper Loop) This Fair Trade in Tourism–accredited operation offers affordable style, a buzzy vibe and fantastic staff. Its dorms may not be Cape Town's cheapest but they're among its nicest, while the private rooms and self-catering apartments are charmingly decorated. There's a lovely mosaic-decorated pool and relaxing gardens with Table Mountain views to chill out in.

Ashanti Gardens BACKPACKERS $
(Map p56; 021-423 8721; www.ashanti.co.za; 11 Hof St, Gardens; dm/s/d with shared bathroom from R190/450/650, d with private bathroom R990; P@; Government Avenue) This is one of Cape Town's slickest backpackers, with much of the action focused on the lively bar and deck that overlook Table Mountain. The beautiful old house, decorated with a tasteful collection of contemporary art, holds the dorms; there's also a lawn where you can camp (R110 per person).

Once in Cape Town BACKPACKERS $
(Map p56; 021-424 6169; www.onceincapetown.co.za; 73 Kloof St, Gardens; dm/s/d or tw inc breakfast R235/850/910; P@; Ludwig's Garden) Great vibe and location for this new backpackers, where every room has its own bathroom. Breakfast is served in the hip cafe that fronts the building. There's a courtyard to chill in and a big kitchen for self-catering.

★ **La Grenadine** GUESTHOUSE $$
(Map p56; 021-424 1358; www.lagrenadine.co.za; 15 Park Rd, Gardens; r/2-bed cottage from R1300/2500; @; Ludwig's Garden) Expat couple Maxime and Mélodie ladle on the Gallic charm at this imaginatively renovated former stables, where the ancient stone walls are a feature of the rooms. The garden planted with fruit trees is a magical oasis, the lounge is stacked with books and vinyl LPs, and breakfast is served on actress Mélodie's prize collection of china.

Hippo Boutique Hotel BOUTIQUE HOTEL $$
(Map p56; 021-423 2500; www.hippotique.co.za; 5-9 Park Rd, Gardens; d/ste R1550/2200; P@; Lower Kloof) A brilliantly located and appealing boutique property that offers spacious, stylish rooms, each with a small kitchen for self-catering. Larger, arty suites, with mezzanine-level bedrooms and themes such as Red Bull and Mini Cooper, are worth the extra spend.

★ **Mannabay** BOUTIQUE HOTEL $$$
(021-461 1094; www.mannabay.com; 8 Bridle Rd, Oranjezicht; r/ste from R5000/6000; P@; Upper Orange) Nothing seems too much bother for the staff at this knockout property decorated with stunning pieces of contemporary art by local artists. The seven guest rooms are decorated in different themes: Versailles, world explorer, Japan etc. Its high hillside location on the edge of the national park provides amazing views. Rates include high tea, which is served in the library lounge.

Belmond Mount Nelson Hotel HOTEL $$$
(Map p56; 021-483 1000; www.mountnelson.co.za; 76 Orange St, Gardens; r/ste from R5000/7465; P@; Government Ave) The sugar-pink-painted 'Nellie' is a colonial charmer with its chintz decor and doormen in pith helmets. Rooms sport elegant silver and moss-green decorations. It's great for families since it pushes the boat out for the little ones, with kid-sized robes and

bedtime cookies and milk – not to mention the large pool and three hectares of gardens, including tennis courts.

Green Point & Waterfront

Atlantic Point Backpackers BACKPACKERS **$**
(Map p60; 021-433 1663; www.atlanticpoint.co.za; 2 Cavalcade Rd, Green Point; dm/d with shared bathroom from R225/820, d with private bathroom R940; ; Upper Portswood) This playfully designed and well-run place is steps away from Green Point's main drag. Features include a big balcony and bar, loft lounge covered in AstroTurf, a tiny pool to cool off in and bicycle rental (R70 per day).

B.I.G. Backpackers BACKPACKERS **$**
(Map p60; 021-434 0688; www.bigbackpackers.co.za; 18 Thornhill Rd, Green Point; dm/s/d/tr R300/705/965/1400; ; Skye Way) Tucked away on the slopes of Green Point, this new backpackers has a fun, laid-back atmosphere with decently decorated rooms, chill areas and a big kitchen (with an honesty bar). They also bake their own bread for breakfast and have a guitar and bicycles handy should you require either.

★ **Villa Zest** BOUTIQUE HOTEL **$$**
(Map p60; 021-433 1246; www.villazest.co.za; 2 Braemar Rd, Green Point; s/d from R1490/1590; ; Upper Portswood) This Bauhaus-style villa has been converted into a quirkily decorated boutique hotel. The lobby is lined with an impressive collection of '60s and '70s groovy electronic goods, including radios, phones, Polaroid cameras and eight-track cassette players. The seven guest rooms have bold, retro-design furniture and papered walls accented with furry pillows and shag rugs.

Head South Lodge BOUTIQUE HOTEL **$$**
(Map p60; 021-434 8777; www.headsouth.co.za; 215 Main Rd, Three Anchor Bay; d from R995; ; Ellerslie) A homage to the 1950s, with retro furnishings and collection of Tretchikoff prints hung en masse in the bar. Its big rooms, decorated in cool white and grey, are hung with equally striking modern art by Philip Briel.

Cape Grace LUXURY HOTEL **$$$**
(Map p60; 021-410 7100; www.capegrace.com; West Quay Rd, V&A Waterfront; r/ste from R6700/13,200; ; Nobel Square) One of the Waterfront's most appealing hotels, the Cape Grace sports an arty combination of antiques and crafts decoration – including hand-painted bed covers and curtains – providing a unique sense of place and Cape Town's history.

One & Only Cape Town HOTEL **$$$**
(Map p60; 021-431 5888; www.oneandonlycapetown.com; Dock Rd, V&A Waterfront; r/ste from R6495/12,595; ; Aquarium) Little expense seems to have been spared creating this luxury resort. Choose between enormous, plush rooms in the main building (with panoramic views of Table Mountain) or the even more exclusive island, beside the pool and spa. Its bar turns out inventive cocktails and is a nice place to plonk yourself before a meal at celeb-chef restaurants Nobu or Reuben's.

Atlantic Coast & Hout Bay

Glen Boutique Hotel BOUTIQUE HOTEL **$$**
(Map p68; 021-439 0086; www.glenhotel.co.za; 3 The Glen, Sea Point; d/ste from R1950/4900; ; The Glen) This gorgeous 'straight-friendly' boutique hotel occupies an elegant old house and a newer block behind. Spacious rooms are decorated in natural tones of stone and wood. In the middle is a fabulous pool and spa and outdoor dining for its restaurant.

Thulani River Lodge B&B **$$**
(021-790 7662; www.thulani.eu; 14 Riverside Tce, Hout Bay; s/d from R1150/1300; ; Imizamo Yethu) *Thulani* is Zulu for 'peace and tranquillity' – the perfect description for this treasure, an African-thatched mansion tucked away in a lush valley through which the Disa River flows towards Hout Bay. Lie in the four-poster bed in the honeymoon suite and you'll be treated to a sweeping panorama of the back of Table Mountain.

Winchester Mansions Hotel HOTEL **$$**
(Map p68; 021-434 2351; www.winchester.co.za; 221 Beach Rd, Sea Point; s/d from R2007/2397, ste s/d from R2521/2911; ; London) Offering a seaside location (you'll pay extra for rooms with views), old-fashioned style and even some corridors lined with putting greens for a spot of golf practice. The pool is a decent size and there's a lovely courtyard with a central fountain – a romantic place to dine.

★ **Tintswalo Atlantic** LUXURY HOTEL **$$$**
(021-201 0025; www.tintswalo.com; Chapman's Peak Dr, Hout Bay; s/d/ste from

R5070/7800/25,000; P❄@📶🏊; 🚌Hout Bay) Destroyed in a disastrous fire in March 2015, this heralded hotel should be back to its best by the time you read this. The only luxury lodge within Table Mountain National Park, Tintswalo hugs the edge of a beautiful rocky bay, a favourite resting ground for whales. Expect sublime views and rooms rich with natural materials. Rack rates include dinner and breakfast.

The complex will again be built on raised platforms to keep environmental impact to a minimum.

★POD BOUTIQUE HOTEL **$$$**
(Map p68; ☎021-438 8550; www.pod.co.za; 3 Argyle Rd, Camps Bay; r/ste incl breakfast from R3950/12,120; P❄@📶🏊; 🚌Camps Bay) Offering clean, contemporary design, POD is perfectly angled to catch the Camps Bay action from its bar and spacious pool and deck area. The cheapest rooms have mountain rather than sea views; luxury rooms have their own private plunge pools.

Camps Bay Retreat LUXURY HOTEL **$$$**
(Map p68; ☎021-437 8300; www.campsbayretreat.com; 7 Chilworth Rd, The Glen; d/ste from R5050/7850; P❄@📶🏊; 🚌Glen Beach) Based in the grand Earl's Dyke Manor (dating from 1929), this splendid option is set in a secluded nature reserve. Choose between rooms in either the main house or the contemporary Deck House, reached by a rope bridge over a ravine. There are also four pools, including some fed by a stream from Table Mountain.

Southern Suburbs

Off the Wall BACKPACKERS **$**
(☎076 322 4053, 021-671 6958; www.offthewallbackpackers.com; 117 Roscommon St, Claremont; dm/s/d with shared bathrooms R175/450/570; 📶; 🚆Claremont) In the thick of Claremont's shopping strip, this is a handy and appealing hostel should you wish to be based close to this area's sights. It's colourfully painted inside and out and has a great communal kitchen.

Vineyard Hotel & Spa LUXURY HOTEL **$$$**
(☎021-657 4500; www.vineyard.co.za; Colinton Rd, Newlands; s/d from R2150/2600, ste s/d from R4500/5040; P❄@📶🏊; 🚆Claremont) Built around the 1799 home of Lady Anne Barnard, the rooms at this delightful hotel have a contemporary look and are decorated in soothing natural tones. It's surrounded by lush gardens with views onto Table Mountain. Friendly staff, the fabulous **Angsana Spa**, a great gym and pool, and top gourmet restaurant **Myoga** complete the picture.

Southern Peninsula

African Soul Surfer BACKPACKERS **$**
(☎021-788 1771; www.africansoulsurfer.co.za; 13-19 York Rd, Muizenberg; dm/s/tw/d with shared bathroom R150/300/400/450; 📶; 🚆Muizenberg) Set in a heritage-listed building with splendid sea views, this backpackers is ideal for those who don't want to be more than 30 seconds from the sand. As well as nicely designed rooms, there's a huge kitchen, comfy lounge and ping-pong table. Rates exclude breakfast.

Simon's Town Boutique Backpackers BACKPACKERS **$**
(☎021-786 1964; www.capepax.co.za; 66 St George's St, Simon's Town; dm/s/d with shared bathroom R190/450/550, d with private bathroom R625; 📶; 🚆Simon's Town) Best-value place to stay in Simon's Town, with spacious, ship-shape rooms – several overlooking the harbour. Friendly staff can help you arrange a host of activities in the area, and there's bike hire for R200 per day.

Bella Ev GUESTHOUSE **$$**
(☎021-788 1293; www.bellaevguesthouse.co.za; 8 Camp Rd, Muizenberg; s/d from R700/1000; P@; 🚆Muizenberg) This charming guesthouse, with a delightful courtyard garden, could be the setting for an Agatha Christie mystery, one in which the home's owner has a penchant for all things Turkish – hence the Ottoman slippers for guests' use.

Chartfield Guest House B&B **$$**
(☎021-788 3793; www.chartfield.co.za; 30 Gatesville Rd, Kalk Bay; r from R900; P@📶🏊; 🚆Kalk Bay) This rambling, wooden-floored 1920s guesthouse is decorated with choice pieces of contemporary local arts and crafts. There's a variety of rooms, each with crisp linen, and bathrooms with a rain-style shower. There's also a lovely terrace and garden overlooking the harbour, where you can eat breakfast. Wi-fi access is R35 per day.

Boulders Beach Lodge B&B **$$**
(☎021-786 1758; www.bouldersbeach.co.za; 4 Boulders Pl, Simon's Town; s/d/apt incl breakfast from R650/1100/2400; P@📶; 🚆Simon's Town) Penguins waddle right up to the doors of this smart guesthouse, with rooms decorated in

wicker and wood and a range of self-catering units, where the rates also include breakfast. Its excellent restaurant has an outdoor deck. Note: penguins are not the quietest of creatures so you may want bring earplugs.

🛏 Cape Flats

Apart from the B&Bs, which are all run in people's homes, it's possible to do homestays in the townships. These can be arranged in Langa by Vamos (p72) and Langa Quarter (p72), and in Khayelitsha by Kopanong (p76) and **Khayelitsha Travel** (☑021-361 4505; www.khayelitshatravel.com; Lookout Hill complex, cnr Mew Way & Spine Rd, Ilitha Park, Khayelitsha; ᴿ Khayelitsha).

Liziwe Guest House B&B $
(☑021-633 7406; www.sa-venues.com/visit/ liziwesguesthouse; 121 NY 111, Gugulethu; r from R500; P @; ᴿ Nyanga) Liziwe has made her mansion into a palace, with four delightful en suite rooms all sporting TVs and African-themed decor. She was featured on a BBC cooking show, so you can be sure her food is delicious; breakfast is R70 extra, dinner R80. Plus her place is walking distance to Mzoli's (p72).

Kopanong B&B $
(☑082 476 1278, 021-361 2084; www.kopanong -township.co.za; 329 Velani Cres, Section C, Khayelitsha; s/d R390/780; P; ᴿ Khayelitsha) Thope Lekau, called 'Mama Africa' for obvious reasons, runs this excellent B&B with her equally ebullient daughter, Mpho. Her substantial brick home offers two stylishly decorated guest rooms, each with their own bathroom. Dinner (R120) is delicious. If they're already booked, Thope can assist with finding homestays in the area.

🍴 Eating

Dining in the Mother City is a pleasure, offering everything from fresh seafood to traditional African and Cape Malay cuisine and with places to suit practically everyone's taste and budget. Most restaurants are licensed, but some allow you to bring your own wine for little or no corkage. Call ahead to check the restaurant's policy. Several bars and pubs serve good food, too.

There are many great places in the city to buy provisions for a picnic or to self-cater. Stock up at the major supermarkets Pick 'n' Pay and Woolworths; there are branches located all over the city, usually at the major malls. For specialist products there are excellent delis, such as Giovanni's Deli World (p80) and Melissa's (p79).

🍴 City Bowl

Upper Long St has many inexpensive places to eat, plus interesting street life. Head to the Bo-Kaap to sample authentic Cape Malay dishes in unpretentious surroundings.

★ Plant VEGAN $
(Map p50; www.plantcafe.co.za; 8 Buiten St, City Bowl; mains R39-65; ⊙7am-7pm Mon & Tue, 7am-10pm Wed-Fri, 8.30am-11.30pm Sat, 9am-3pm Sun; 🍴; 🚃 Upper Loop/Upper Long) As its name suggests, Plant serves only vegan food, and it's so tasty that you may become converted to the cause. Mock cheese and egg substitutes are incorporated in sandwiches and salads, and giant portobello mushrooms or a mix of flaked potato and seaweed do service as alternative burgers. Its vegan cupcakes and brownies are delicious.

There's also a smaller branch in the **Bo-Kaap** (Map p50; www.plantcafe.co.za; Urban Hub, 142 Buitengracht Service St, Bo-Kaap; mains R39-65; ⊙9am-5pm Mon-Fri, to 3pm Sat; 🚃 Dorp/ Leeuwen), but the City Bowl branch keeps longer hours and serves wine and beer.

Jason Bakery BAKERY, CAFE $
(Map p50; ☑021-424 5644; www.jasonbakery.com; 185 Bree St, City Bowl; mains R50; ⊙7am-3.30pm Mon-Fri, 8am-2pm Sat; 🚃 Upper Loop/Upper Long) Move fast to secure a seat at this super-popular street-corner cafe that makes splendid breakfasts and sandwiches. It also serves decent coffee, And Union beers and MCC bubbles by the glass and bottle. Good job that it also has a take-away counter.

Clarke's Bar & Dining Room AMERICAN $
(Map p50; ☑021-422 7648; www.clarkesdining. co.za; 133 Bree St, City Bowl; mains R55; ⊙7am-5pm Mon, 7am-10.30pm Tue-Sat, 8am-3pm Sun; 🚃 Dorp/Leeuwen) A focus of the Bree St hipster scene is this convivial spot with counter seating that pays homage to the US diner tradition. All-day breakfast dishes include grilled cheese sandwiches and huevos rancheros. There are reubens and pork belly sandwiches from lunchtime, as well as burgers and mac and cheese.

Lola's INTERNATIONAL $
(Map p50; www.lolas.co.za; 228 Long St, City Bowl; mains R40-50; ⊙8am-4.30pm Sat-Wed, to 10.30pm Thu & Fri; 📶; 🚃 Upper Loop/Upper Long)

This old dame of the Long St scene has kept her looks and the vibe remains relaxed. The breakfasts, including sweetcorn fritters and eggs Benedict, are still good. Linger over a drink and watch Long St's passing parade, or drop by on Thursday and Friday evenings when she offers up a short and sweet menu of street-food dishes.

★Chef's Warehouse & Canteen TAPAS $$
(Map p50; ☎021-422 0128; www.chefswarehouse.co.za; Heritage Sq, 92 Bree St, City Bowl; tapas set for 2 R350; ⌚noon-3pm & 4-8pm Mon-Fri, noon-2.30pm Sat; 🚌Church/Longmarket) Hurry here for a delicious and very generous spread of small plates from chef Liam Tomlin and his talented crew. Flavours zip around the world, from a squid with a tangy Vietnamese salad to comforting coq au vin. If you can't get a seat (there are no bookings) then there's the take-away hatch **Street Food** in the space under the stoop.

★Hemelhuijs INTERNATIONAL $$
(Map p50; ☎021-418 2042; www.hemelhuijs.co.za; 71 Waterkant St, Foreshore; mains R60-120; ⌚9am-4pm Mon-Fri, to 3pm Sat; 📶; 🚌Strand) A quirky yet elegantly decorated space – think deer heads with broken crockery and contemporary art – showcases the art and culinary creations of Jacques Erasmus. The inventive food is delicious and includes lovely fresh juices, daily bakes, and signature dishes such as sandveld potato and saffron gnocchi with blackened quail breast and smoked aubergine.

Addis in Cape ETHIOPIAN $$
(Map p50; ☎021-424 5722; www.addisincape.co.za; 41 Church St, City Bowl; mains R95-125; ⌚noon-10.30pm Mon-Sat; 📶🌿; 🚌Church/Longmarket) Sit at a low basket-weave table and enjoy tasty Ethiopian cuisine served traditionally on plate-sized *injera* (sourdough pancakes), which you rip up and eat with in place of cutlery. It has a good selection of vegetarian and vegan dishes. Also try its home-made *tej* (honey wine) and authentic Ethiopian coffee.

Company Garden's Restaurant INTERNATIONAL $$
(Map p50; ☎021-423 2919; Company's Garden, Queen Victoria St, City Bowl; mains R50-85; ⌚7am-6pm; 📶👪; 🚌Dorp/Leeuwen) Restaurant wizards Madame Zingara have sprinkled their magic on the old Company's Garden cafe, transforming it into a chic contemporary space with charming outdoor features such as a giant chess set and wickerwork nests to play in. Menu items run from excellent breakfasts (try the French toast) to a lunch buffet table (R85).

Africa Café AFRICAN $$
(Map p50; ☎021-422 0221; www.africacafe.co.za; 108 Shortmarket St, City Bowl; set banquets R250; ⌚6-11pm Mon-Sat; 🚌Church/Longmarket) Touristy, yes, but still one of the best places to sample African food. Come with a hearty appetite as the set feast comprises some 15 dishes from across the continent, of which you can eat as much as you like. The talented staff go on song-and-dance walkabout around the tables midmeal.

Bombay Brasserie INDIAN $$$
(Map p50; ☎021-819 2000; www.tajhotels.com; Wale St, City Bowl; mains R70-110, tasting menus from R325; ⌚6-10.30pm Mon-Sat; 🚌Groote Kerk) Far from your average curry house, the Taj Hotel's main restaurant, hung with glittering chandeliers and mirrors, is darkly luxurious. Chef Harpreet Longani's cooking is creative and delicious, and the presentation spot on, as is the service. Go on a spice journey with one of the tasting menus.

Bo-Kaap & De Waterkant

La Petite Tarte CAFE $
(Map p50; ☎021-425 9077; Shop A11, Cape Quarter, 72 Waterkant St, De Waterkant; mains R50-80; ⌚8.30am-4pm Mon-Fri, to 2.30pm Sat; 🚌Alfred) Fancy teas by Mariage Frères and delicious homemade, sweet and savoury French-style tarts are served at this adorable cafe with streetside tables.

Loading Bay LEBANESE $
(Map p50; ☎021-425 6320; www.loadingbay.co.za; 30 Hudson St, De Waterkant; mains R50-75; ⌚8am-5pm Mon-Fri, 9am-4pm Sat, 9am-2pm Sun; 🚌Old Fire Station) Hang with the De Waterkant style set at this spiffy cafe serving coffee with 'microtextured milk' (it's heated only to 70°C) and bistro-style dishes such as crispy bacon and avocado on toast. Book for its Thursday-evening burger nights – the patties, both premium beef and vegetarian, are top grade.

★Izakaya Matsuri JAPANESE $$
(Map p50; ☎021-421 4520; www.izakayamatsuri.com; Shop 6, The Rockwell, Schiebe St, De Waterkant; mains R40-110; 🚌Alfred) Genial Arata-san serves some of the best sushi and rolls to be found in Cape Town, along with other

MORE DINING REVIEWS

For up-to-date online reviews of the Capetonian dining scene consult Eat Out (www.eatout.co.za) or Rossouw's Restaurants (www.rossouwsrestaurants.com).

Japanese *izakaya* pub-grub including noodles and tempura. When the weather's warm tables shift from the attractive interior hung with giant white and red paper lanterns out to the courtyard area.

Bo-Kaap Kombuis CAPE MALAY $$
(☎ 021-422 5446; www.bokaapkombuis.co.za; 7 Aug St, Bo-kaap; mains R75-95; ⏰ noon-4pm & 6-9.30pm Tue-Sat, noon-4pm Sun) You'll receive a hospitable welcome from Yusuf and Nazli and their staff at this spectacularly located restaurant, high up in the Bo-kaap. The panoramic views of Table Mountain and Devil's Peak alone make it worth visiting. There are all the traditional Cape Malay dishes on the menu plus vegetarian options such as sugar bean curry.

East City, Woodstock & Observatory

Also mark your calendar with a big red cross for Saturday's brunch fest at the Neighbourgoods Market (p93) in the Old Biscuit Mill.

★Kitchen SANDWICHES, SALADS $
(Map p86; www.lovethekitchen.co.za; 111 Sir Lowry Rd, Woodstock; sandwiches & salads R60-70; ⏰ 8am-3.30pm Mon-Fri; 🌿; 🚌 District Six) Over all the swanky restaurants in town, it was this little charmer that Michelle Obama chose for lunch, proving the First Lady has excellent taste. Tuck into plates of divine salads, rustic sandwiches made with love, and sweet treats with tea served from china teapots.

★Ocean Jewels SEAFOOD $
(Map p86; ☎ 083 582 0829; www.oceanjewels.co.za; Woodstock Exchange, 66 Albert Rd, Woodstock; mains R45-50; ⏰ 9.30am-5pm Mon-Fri, 10am-2pm Sat; 🚆 Woodstock) Fish straight from Kalk Bay harbour is served at this Southern African Sustainable Seafood Initiative–supporting cafe (see p539) that does a mean tuna burger with wedge fries. Despite being in the industrial chic Woodstock Exchange, the vibe is as relaxed as the seaside, with white-washed wooden tables and food served on rustic enamel plates.

Hello Sailor BISTRO $
(☎ 021-447 0707; www.hellosailorbistro.co.za; 86 Lower Main Rd, Observatory; mains R50; ⏰ 8am-10pm; 🚆 Observatory) A tattooed mermaid in a round portrait on the wall looks down on the tattooed patrons of this slick bistro serving price-friendly comfort food – burgers, salads, pastas – all done well. The restaurant closes at 10pm, but the bar here can kick on until 2am on the weekend.

Downtown Ramen JAPANESE $
(Map p86; 105 Harrington St, East City; noodles R65; ⏰ 11am-3pm & 5.30-10pm Mon-Sat; 🚌 Roeland) Although slightly different items are available at lunch and dinners, its two types of ramen – one with a slice of *char sui* pork, the other a veg version with tofu – are served at both times and should be sampled. Ask for the chilli on the side if you don't like your noodles so spicy. It's upstairs at Lefty's.

Café Ganesh AFRICAN, INDIAN $
(☎ 021-448 3435; www.cafeganesh.wozaonline.co.za; 38B Trill Rd, Observatory; mains R50-80; ⏰ 6-11.30pm Mon-Sat; 🚆 Observatory) Sample *pap* (maize porridge) and veg, grilled springbok or lamb curry at this funky hangout, squeezed into an alley between two buildings. Junkyard decor and matchbox-label wallpaper create that chic-shack look.

Charly's Bakery BAKERY, CAFE $
(Map p86; www.charlysbakery.co.za; 38 Canterbury St, East City; baked goods R17-35; ⏰ 8am-5pm Tue-Fri, 8.30am-2pm Sat; 🚌 Lower Buitenkant) The fabulous female team here, stars of the reality TV series *Charly's Cake Angels,* make – as they say – 'mucking afazing' cupcakes and other baked goods. Their heritage building is as colourfully decorated as their cakes.

Raw and Roxy VEGAN $
(Map p86; 302 Albert Rd, Woodstock; mains R70-90; ⏰ 9am-5pm Mon-Sat; 🌿; 🚌 Kent) Beatrice Holst has seduced meat-loving Capetonians with her delicious raw and vegan repasts and drinks, including super vitamin-charged juices, a raw lasagne that has foodies reaching for superlatives, and a silky smooth and super-rich avocado chocolate ganache cake.

★Pot Luck Club INTERNATIONAL $$
(Map p86; ☎ 021-447 0804; www.thepotluckclub.co.za; Silo Top Floor, Old Biscuit Mill, 373-375 Albert Rd, Woodstock; dishes R75-99; ⏰ 12.30-2.30pm & 6-8.30pm Mon-Sat, 11am-12.30pm Sun; 🚌 Kent) The more affordable of Luke Dale-Roberts' operations at the Old Biscuit Mill may offer

panoramic views of the surrounding area, but it's what's on the plate that tends to take the breath away. The dishes are designed to be shared; we defy you not to order a second plate of the smoked beef with truffle-café-au-lait sauce.

✕ Gardens & Surrounds

★Ferdinando's
PIZZA $

(Map p56; ☑084 771 0485; www.facebook.com/pages/Ferdinandos-pizza/418463764843892; 84 Kloof St, Gardens; pizzas R80-110; ⊙Wed-Sat 6-11pm; ⋒Welgemeend) Bookings are required for this charming 'secret pizza parla' that shares premises with the Blah Blah Bar. Diego is the pizza maestro and Kikki the bubbly host and creative artist, while their adorable mutt Ferdinando keeps them all in line. Toppings for their fantastic, crispy, thin-crust pizzas change with the season.

Yard
BURGERS, SANDWICHES $

(Map p56; www.facebook.com/YARDCT; 6 Roodehek St, Gardens; mains R70-110; ⊙7am-10.30pm Mon-Sat; ⋒Roodehek) The Dog's Bollocks' blockbuster burgers (only 50 served per night, from 5pm) got this hip grunge spot going a few years ago; it's now expanded to all-day dining, with Mucky Mary's for breakfast fry-ups and sandwiches, Bitch's Tits Tacos and Deluxe Coffeeworks, which also roasts its beans here. Great street art decorates the building.

Melissa's
INTERNATIONAL, DELI $

(Map p56; www.melissas.co.za; 94 Kloof St, Gardens; mains R50-70; ⊙7.30am-7pm Mon-Fri, 8am-7pm Sat & Sun; ⋒Welgemeend) Pay by weight for the delicious breakfast and lunch buffets, then browse the grocery shelves for picnic fare or gourmet gifts.

★Hallellujah
INTERNATIONAL $$

(Map p56; ☑079 839 2505; www.hallelujahhallelujah.co.za; 11 Kloof Nek Rd, Tamboerskloof; mains R88-128; ⊙6.30-11pm Wed-Sat; ⋒Ludwig's Garden) Emma Hoffmans is the talented young chef of this compact kitchen and its flamingo-decorated dining space (booking only for tables of four to six; counter seats available for walk-ins). Work your way through her short but very sweet menu of small plates, including grilled prawns in steamed buns, duck and cold soba noodles, and a zingy green-papaya tom yam salad.

Maria's
GREEK $$

(Map p56; ☑021-461 3333; 31 Barnet St, Dunkley Sq, Gardens; mains R75-135; ⊙8am-10.30pm Tue-Fri, 9am-10.30pm Sat; ☑; ⋒Annandale) There are few places more romantic or relaxing for a meal than Maria's on a warm night, when you can tuck into classic Greek mezze and dishes such as moussaka on rustic tables beneath the trees in the square. There are tons of vegetarian options on the menu, too.

Kyoto Garden Sushi
JAPANESE $$

(Map p56; ☑021-422 2001; 11 Lower Kloofnek Rd, Tamboerskloof; mains R80-195; ⊙5.30-11pm Mon-Sat; ⋒Ludwig's Garden) Beechwood furnishings and subtle lighting lend a calm, Zen-like air to this superior Japanese restaurant, owned by an LA expat but with an expert chef turning out sushi and sashimi. Its prawn noodle salad is excellent, as is its Asian Mary cocktail.

Manna Epicure
BAKERY $$

(Map p56; ☑021-426 2413; www.mannaepicure.com; 151 Kloof St, Gardens; mains R40-110; ⊙8am-5pm Tue-Sat, to 4pm Sun; ⋒Welgemeend) Come for a deliciously simple breakfast or lunch, or for late-afternoon cocktails and tapas on the verandah of this white-box cafe. The freshly baked breads alone – coconut or pecan and raisin – are worth dragging yourself up the hill for.

★Chef's Table
INTERNATIONAL $$$

(Map p56; ☑021-483 1864; www.belmond.com/mountnelsonhotel; Belmond Mount Nelson Hotel, 76 Orange St, Gardens; lunch R500, dinner without/with wines R595/995; ⊙noon-3pm Fri, 6.30-9pm Mon-Sat; ☑; ⋒Government Ave) The Nellie's swanky Planet restaurant and bar are worth a visit, but for a real treat book one of the four tables with a front-row view onto the drama and culinary magic unfolding inside the kitchen. The food is superb (vegetarians are catered for) and presented by the chefs who will take you on a behind-the-scenes tour.

Aubergine
INTERNATIONAL $$$

(Map p56; ☑021-465 0000; www.aubergine.co.za; 39 Barnet St, Gardens; 2-/3-course lunch R240/320, 3-/4-/5-course dinner R465/565/675; ⊙noon-2pm Wed-Fri, 5-10pm Mon-Sat; ☑; ⋒Annandale) German-born Harald Bresselschmidt is one of Cape Town's most consistent chefs, producing creative, hearty dishes that are served with some of the Cape's best wines. Don't overorder, as portions are large. Vegetarian menus are available and the service and ambiance are impeccable.

Green Point & Waterfront

The Waterfront's plethora of restaurants and cafes provide ocean views and open long hours daily, but choose carefully as this is real tourist-trap territory.

★V&A Market on the Wharf FOOD COURT $
(Map p60; www.marketonthewharf.co.za; Pump House, Dock Rd, V&A Waterfront; mains from R50; 10am-5.30pm Jun-Oct, to 7pm Nov-May; ; Nobel Square) There's no need to spend big to eat well (and healthily) at the Waterfront, thanks to this colourful, market-style food court in the old Pump House. Grab a coffee or freshly squeezed juice to go with a wrap or muffin, or opt for a larger meal such as fish and chips.

Café Neo GREEK, CAFE $
(Map p60; 129 Beach Rd, Mouille Point; mains R50-70; 7am-7pm; ; Three Anchor Bay) This favourite seaside cafe has a pleasingly contemporary design and atmosphere that sways from buzzy (at meal times) to more laid-back – great for a late-afternoon drink. Check out the big blackboard menu while sitting at the long communal table inside, or grab a seat on the deck overlooking the red-and-white lighthouse.

Giovanni's Deli World CAFE, DELI $
(Map p60; 103 Main Rd, Green Point; mains R30-60; 7.30am-8.30pm; Stadium) Its menu bursting with flavourful food, Giovanni's can make any sandwich you fancy, which is ideal for a picnic if you're on your way to the beach. The pavement cafe is a popular hangout.

Nü VEGETARIAN $
(Map p60; www.nufood.co.za; Shop 4 Portside, Main Rd, Green Point; mains R50-60; 7am-7pm Mon-Fri, 7.30am-7pm Sat, 7.30am-6pm Sun; ; Upper Portswood) A great place for a healthy veggie breakfast or lunch, with freshly squeezed juices, smoothies and nutritional salads and multigrain wraps packing out the menu. Order at the counter and enjoy in a bright, unfussy space. There's also a branch in **Sea Point** (Map p68; 021-439 7269; www.nufood.co.za; Shop 3, Piazza St. John, 395 Main Rd, Sea Point; 7.30am-7pm Mon-Sat, to 6pm Sun; ; Arthur's).

El Burro MEXICAN $$
(Map p60; 021-433 2364; www.elburro.co.za; 81 Main Rd, Green Point; mains R90-175; noon-10.30pm; Stadium) With a balcony providing views of Cape Town Stadium, this is one stylish donkey: the decor a bit more chic than your average Mexican joint, the menu more inventive. Supplementing the usual tacos and enchiladas are traditional dishes such as chicken mole poblano. Booking is advised, as it's popular.

Harbour House SEAFOOD $$$
(Map p60; 021-418 4744; Quay 4, V&A Waterfront; mains R95-260; noon-10pm; Nobel Square) The Kalk Bay institution has set up shop at the Waterfront with a good, white-tablecloth restaurant on the ground floor (ask for a table on the deck outside). It has an even better sushi and lounge bar on the upper deck – just the spot for a chilled glass of wine at sunset.

Atlantic Coast

★Kleinsky's Delicatessen DELI $
(Map p68; www.facebook.com/Kleinskys; 95 Regent Rd, Sea Point; mains R22-62; 8.30am-8.30pm; ; Tramway) An homage to classic, Jewish-style delis, Kleinsky's is a great addition to Sea Point's casual dining scene, serving dishes such as toasted bagels with smoked salmon or house-made chopped liver, chicken soup with matzo balls, and *latkes* (potato pancakes). It serves good coffee, too. The walls act as a gallery for local artists.

★La Boheme SPANISH $$
(Map p68; 021-434 8797; www.labohemebistro.co.za; 341 Main Rd, Sea Point; 2-/3-course dinner R125/160; noon-10.15pm Mon-Fri; ; Firmount) Although you can stoke up on espresso and its delicious tapas and light meals during the day, La Boheme is best visited in the evening, when candles twinkle on the tables and you can take advantage of its superb-value two- or three-course menus.

La Perla ITALIAN $$
(Map p68; 021-439 9538; www.laperla.co.za; cnr Church & Beach Rds, Sea Point; mains R95-160; 10am-midnight; Sea Point Pool) This eternally stylish restaurant, with its waiters in white jackets, has been a fixture of Sea Point's promenade for decades. Enjoy something from the menu of pasta, fish and meat dishes on the terrace shaded by stout palms, or retreat to the intimate bar.

★La Mouette FRENCH $$$
(Map p68; 021-433 0856; www.lamouette-restaurant.co.za; 78 Regent Rd, Sea Point; mains R125-180, tasting menu R295; noon-3pm Tue-Sun, 6-10.30pm daily; Kei Apple) Well-executed

classics (such as bouillabaisse and linefish Niçoise) and inventive new dishes (like salt-and-pepper prawns with chorizo popcorn) make this a standout culinary experience. The tasting menu is a great deal. It's delightful to dine in its lush, outdoor courtyard beside the bubbling fountain.

Roundhouse INTERNATIONAL **$$$**
(Map p68; ☎021-438 4347; www.theroundhouserestaurant.com; The Glen, Camps Bay; 4-course menu R665; ⏰6-10pm Tue-Sat year-round, noon-4pm Wed-Sat & noon-3pm Sun May-Sep; ☑; 🚌Kloof Nek) Overlooking Camps Bay, this heritage-listed 18th-century building, set in wooded grounds, is perfect for the elegant restaurant it now houses. Its menu can also be configured to provide a delicious vegetarian meal.

Southern Suburbs

Gardener's Cottage CAFE **$**
(☎021-689 3158; Montebello Craft Studios, 31 Newlands Ave, Newlands; mains R45-70; ⏰9.30am-2.30pm Tue-Fri, 8.30am-4.30pm Sat & Sun; 🚆Newlands) After exploring the Montebello craft studios, relax at this lovely cafe and tea garden in the grounds. It serves simple, hearty meals in the shade of leafy trees.

O'ways Teacafe VEGETARIAN **$**
(☎021-617 2850; www.oways.co.za; 20 Dreyer St, Claremont; mains R55-169; ⏰7.30am-5pm Mon-Fri, 9am-2pm Sat; ☑; 🚆Claremont) Pronounced 'always', this stylish, relaxing place is fully vegetarian, and includes tasty dishes such as dim sum dumplings and portobello mushrooms filled with couscous. It's also one of the best places in Cape Town to come for tea, with 60-odd loose-leaf teas and infusions on offer.

Bistro Sixteen82 TAPAS, INTERNATIONAL **$$**
(☎021-713 2211; www.steenberg-vineyards.co.za; Steenberg Vineyard, Tokai; mains R98-185; ⏰9am-8pm) Perfectly complementing the slick and contemporary wine-tasting lounge at Steenberg Vineyard is this highly appealing bistro, serving everything from breakfast with a glass of bubbly to an early supper of tapas with its quaffable merlot. Seating is both indoor and outdoor, with beguiling views of the gardens and mountain.

Jonkershuis CAPE MALAY **$$**
(☎021-794 6255; www.jonkershuisconstantia.co.za; Groot Constantia Rd, Constantia; mains R88-148; ⏰9am-10pm Mon-Sat, to 5pm Sun) This casual brasserie-style restaurant in the grounds of Groot Constantia has a pleasant, vine-shaded courtyard and tables looking onto the manor house. Sample Cape Malay dishes (including a tasting plate for R148) or cured meats with a glass or two of the local wines, or satisfy your sweet tooth with the desserts.

Rhodes Memorial Restaurant CAPE MALAY **$$**
(www.rhodesmemorial.co.za; Rhodes Memorial, off M3, Groote Schuur Estate, Rondebosch; mains R70-125; ⏰7am-5pm) Behind the memorial is a pleasant restaurant and alfresco tearoom in a 1920 thatched-roof cottage. It's family-run and specialises in Cape Malay dishes, such as curries, *bredies* (pot stews of meat or fish and vegetables) and *bobotie* (delicately flavoured ostrich-meat curry with a topping of beaten egg baked to a crust).

Bookings are advised on the weekends – especially on Sunday, when there's live jazz from 1pm to 4pm.

★**La Colombe** FRENCH **$$$**
(☎021-794 2390; www.lacolombe.co.za; Silvermist, Main Rd, Constantia; lunch mains R135-210, 4-/6-course dinner R465/685; ⏰12.30-2.30pm & 7.30-9.30pm) There's a new location on the Silvermist estate for this storied Constantia restaurant, but little else has changed. British chef Scot Kirton rustles up skilful dishes combining French and Asian techniques and flavours, such as smoked tomato risotto and miso-seared scallops. The coolly elegant setting and personable service couldn't be better.

Southern Peninsula

C'est La Vie BAKERY, FRENCH **$**
(20 Main Rd, Kalk Bay; mains R50; ⏰7am-3pm Wed-Sun; 🚆Kalk Bay) Serving coffee that everyone in Kalk Bay raves about, this compact, French-style artisan bakery and cafe is a good spot for breakfast and light lunches. It also serves freshly squeezed juices.

Empire Café INTERNATIONAL **$**
(☎021-788 1250; www.empirecafe.co.za; 11 York Rd, Muizenberg; mains R50-95; ⏰7am-4pm Mon-Tue & Thu-Sat, Wed to 9pm, 8am-4pm Sun; 📶; 🚆Muizenberg) The local surfers' favourite hang-out is a great place for a hearty 'eggs on toast' type of breakfast or lunch. Local art exhibitions enliven the walls and a dramatic chandelier dangles from the ceiling. On Wednesday it stays open later and serve gourmet burgers (R70).

★Lighthouse Cafe INTERNATIONAL $$
(☎021-786 9000; www.thelighthousecafe.co.za; 90 St Georges St, Simon's Town; mains R75-140; ⊙8.30am-4pm Sun-Tue, to 9.30pm Wed-Sat; 🚆Simon's Town) Relaxed, beachcomber-chic cafe, with a menu big on seafood – there's a delicious and filling Mauritian bouillabaisse and fish and chips made to Jamie Oliver's recipe. It also does burgers, pizza and mezze platters.

Casa Labia INTERNATIONAL $$
(☎021-788 6068; www.casalabia.co.za; 192 Main Rd, Muizenberg; mains R70-145; ⊙10am-4pm Tue-Thu, 9am-4pm Fri-Sun; 🌿; 🚆Muizenberg) Some of the ingredients at this pleasant cafe in this gorgeously decorated arts and cultural centre come from the adjoining garden. It has plans to make wine and olive oil from the vines and olive trees that grow on the slopes, too. Enjoy home-baked treats and delicious breakfasts, open sandwiches and plenty of vegetarian options.

Olympia Café & Deli BAKERY, INTERNATIONAL $$
(☎021-788 6396; www.facebook.com/OlympiaCafeKalkBay; 134 Main Rd, Kalk Bay; mains R60-100; ⊙7am-9pm; 🚆Kalk Bay) Setting a high standard for relaxed rustic cafes by the sea, Olympia bakes its own breads and pastries. It's great for breakfast, and its Mediterranean-influenced lunch dishes are delicious, too – particularly the heaped bowls of mussels.

Live Bait SEAFOOD $$
(☎021-788 5755; www.harbourhousegroup.co.za/livebait; Kalk Bay harbour, Kalk Bay; mains R75-200; ⊙noon-4pm & 6-10pm; 🚆Kalk Bay) Sit within arm's reach of the crashing waves and the bustle of Kalk Bay harbour at this breezy, Greek-island-style fish restaurant; it's one of the best options around for a relaxed seafood meal. The same company runs the fancy Harbour House restaurant upstairs, and the cheap-as-chips Lucky Fish takeaway next door.

Meeting Place INTERNATIONAL $$
(☎021-786 5678; www.themeetingplaceupstairs.co.za; 98 St George's St, Simon's Town; mains R75-120; ⊙9am-9pm Mon-Sat, to 3pm Sun; 🚆Simon's Town) Offering a busy deli-cafe on the ground floor, and an arty restaurant upstairs with a balcony overlooking Simon Town's main drag. Sample gourmet sandwiches or its homemade ice creams.

Drinking & Nightlife

The 'Tavern of the Seven Seas' is awash with watering holes; its hostelries range from well-stocked wine bars to microbrew pubs.

City Bowl

★Orphanage COCKTAIL BAR
(Map p50; ☎021-424 2004; www.theorphanage.co.za; cnr Orphange & Bree Sts, City Bowl; ⊙5pm-2am Mon-Thu & Sat, to 3am Fri; 🚌Upper Loop/Upper Long) Named after the nearby lane, the mixologists here prepare some tempting artisan libations with curious names including Knicker-Dropper Glory, Dollymop and Daylight Daisy, using ingredients as varied as peanut butter, kumquat compote and 'goldfish'! It's dark, sophisticated and stylish, with outdoor seating beneath the trees on Bree.

★Publik WINE BAR
(Map p50; www.publik.co.za; 81 Church St, City Bowl; ⊙4-10pm Mon & Tue, to midnight Wed-Fri; 🚌Church/Longmarket) By night, gourmet butchers Frankie Fenner Meat Merchants morphs into this relaxed, unpretentious bar, where the owners do a brilliant job at digging out hidden gems of the Cape's wine scene. Taste drops from sustainably farmed vineyards, interesting and unusual varietals and rare vintages. The tasting flight of five wines is a great deal at R100.

★Beerhouse BAR
(Map p50; www.beerhouse.co.za; 223 Long St, City Bowl; 🚌Upper Loop/Upper Long) With 99 brands of ale, both local and international, and several more local craft beers on tap, beer lovers will think they've died and gone to heaven at this brightly designed and spacious joint in the heart of Long St. The balcony is a great spot from which to watch the world go by.

★Honest Chocolate Cafe CAFE, BAR
(Map p50; www.honestchocolate.co.za; 64 Wale St, City Bowl; ⊙8am-4pm Mon-Fri, 9am-2pm Sat; 🚌Dorp/Leeuwen) Following a successful crowdfunding campaign, Honest Chocolate, which makes its artisan sweet treats at the Woodstock Exchange (p91), have launched this homage to fine dark chocolate in liquid, solid, ice-cream and cake form. It's a chocoholic's dream come true, with even vegan and gluten-free options.

★Weinhaus + Biergarten BEER HALL
(Map p50; www.biergartencpt.tumblr.com; 110 Bree St, City Bowl; noon-midnight; ; Church/Longmarket) To the rear of St Stephen's Church, this cool hang-out specialises in imported craft beers by Brewers & Union and, in summer, has ping pong and fairly frequent live gigs in the courtyard outside; check its Facebook page for details. Ethically sourced meats are used in tasty sandwiches, hot dogs and braais (barbequed meats).

Alexander Bar & Café GAY, COCKTAIL BAR
(Map p50; www.alexanderbar.co.za; 76 Strand St, City Bowl; 11am-1am Mon-Sat; Strand) Playwright Nicholas Spagnoletti and software engineer Edward van Kuik are the driving duo behind this fun, eccentric space in a gorgeous heritage building. Use antique telephones on the tables to chat with fellow patrons, place an order at the bar or send a telegram to someone you might have your eye on.

See the website for details of shows in the **studio theatre** upstairs.

House of Machines CAFE, BAR
(Map p50; www.thehouseofmachines.com; 84 Shortmarket St, City Bowl; 7am-4pm Mon, to midnight Tue-Sat; Church/Mid-Long) Combining a motorbike workshop with barbers, a boutique and a live-music/DJ space, this is a homage to Americana, with tasty, inventive bourbon cocktails, US craft beers and Evil Twin Coffee from NYC.

Bean There COFFEE
(Map p50; www.beanthere.co.za; 58 Wale St, City Bowl; 7.30am-4pm Mon-Fri, 9am-2pm Sat; Dorp/Leeuwen) Not much other than Fair Trade coffees from across Africa and a few sweet snacks are served in this chic cafe, which has space to spread out and a relaxed vibe despite all the caffeine.

Waiting Room BAR
(Map p50; 021-422 4536; 273 Long St, City Bowl; cover Fri & Sat R30; 7pm-2am Mon-Sat; Upper Loop/Upper Long) Climb the narrow stairway beside the Royale Eatery to find this hip bar decorated in retro furniture with DJs spinning funky tunes. Climb even further and you'll eventually reach the roof deck, the perfect spot from which to admire the city's glittering night lights.

East City, Woodstock & Salt River

★Taproom MICROBREWERY
(www.devilspeakbrewing.co.za; 95 Durham Ave, Salt River; 8am-4pm Mon, to 11pm Tue-Sat; Upper Salt River) Devil's Peak Brewing Company makes some of South Africa's best craft beers. Its taproom and restaurant provide a panoramic view up to Devil's Peak itself. The food is hearty fare (think burgers and fried chicken), designed to balance its stellar selection of on-tap beers. There are also barrel-aged brews and the new Explorer series of bottled ales.

★Truth COFFEE
(Map p86; www.truthcoffee.com; 36 Buitenkant St, East City; 7.30am-6pm Mon-Sat, to 2pm Sun; ; Lower Buitenkant) This self-described 'steampunk roastery and coffee bar', with pressed-tin ceilings, naked hanging bulbs and mad-inventor style metalwork, is an awe-inspiring space in which to mingle with city slickers. Apart from coffee, craft beers, baked goods and various sandwiches, burgers and hot dogs are on the menu.

There's also a branch in the **Prestwich Memorial** (Map p50; www.truthcoffee.com; Prestwich Memorial, cnr Somerset & Buitengracht Sts, De Waterkant; 8am-6pm Mon-Fri, to 2pm Sat & Sun; Strand).

Espressolab Microroasters COFFEE
(Map p86; http://espressolabmicroroasters.com; Old Biscuit Mill, 375 Albert Rd, Woodstock; 8am-4pm Mon-Fri, to 2pm Sat; Kent) Geek out about coffee at this lab staffed with passionate roasters and baristas. Their beans, which come from single farms, estates and co-ops from around the world, are packaged with tasting notes such as those for fine wines.

Lady Bonin's Tea TEAHOUSE
(Map p86; www.ladybonin.com; Shop AG11b, Woodstock Exchange, 66 Albert Rd, Woodstock; 9am-5pm Mon-Fri, to 3pm Sat; Woodstock) A charmingly decorated, relaxing place in which to sample organic and sustainable artisan teas, fruity and herbal brews, and vegan baked treats.

aMadoda Braai BAR, BRAAI
(Map p86; www.amadoda.co.za; 1-4 Strand St, Woodstock; noon-9pm Mon-Thu, to 2am Fri-Sun; Woodstock) Pulling off a township braai (barbecue; menus start at R50) and shebeen atmosphere, this slickly decorated

DON'T MISS

CONSTANTIA WINE ROUTE

South Africa's wine-farming industry began here back in 1685 when Governor Simon van der Stel chose the area for its wine-growing potential and named his farm Constantia. After Van der Stel's death in 1712 his 763-hectare estate was split up and the area is now the location for the **Constantia Wine Route** (www.constantiawineroute.com) covering 10 vineyards. The key ones to visit are listed below.

Groot Constantia (☎021-794 5128; www.grootconstantia.co.za; Groot Constantia Rd, Constantia; tastings R30, museum adult/child R20/free, cellar tours incl tasting R40; ⏲9am-5.30pm; P) Simon van der Stel's manor house, a superb example of Cape Dutch architecture, is maintained as a museum at Groot Constantia. Set in beautiful grounds, the estate can become busy with tour groups, but is big enough for you to escape the crowds. The large tasting room is first on your right as you enter the estate. Further on is the free orientation centre, which provides an overview of the estate's history, and the beautifully restored homestead.

Klein Constantia (www.kleinconstantia.com; Klein Constantia Rd, Constantia; tastings R30; ⏲tastings 10am-5pm Mon-Fri, to 4.30pm Sat, to 4pm Sun; P) Part of the original Constantia estate, Klein Constantia is famous for its Vin de Constance, a deliciously sweet muscat wine. It was Napoleon's solace on St Helena, and Jane Austen had one of her heroines recommend it for having the power to heal 'a disappointed heart'. It's worth visiting for its excellent tasting room and informative displays.

Buitenverwachting (☎021-794 5190; www.buitenverwachting.co.za; Klein Constantia Rd, Constantia; tastings R40; ⏲9am-5pm Mon-Fri, 10am-3pm Sat; P) Meaning 'beyond expectation', Buitenverwachting is known for offering good working and living conditions to its employees. Order ahead to enjoy a blissful **picnic lunch** (☎083 257 6083; lunch R145; ⏲noon-4pm Mon-Sat Nov-Apr) in front of the 1796 manor house. There's also a casual cafe and a fancier restaurant with a sweeping view of the vineyards.

Steenberg Vineyards (www.steenberg-vineyards.co.za; Steenberg Estate, Steenberg Rd, Tokai; tastings R20 & R40; ⏲10am-6pm; P) Enjoy the gorgeous contemporary tasting bar and lounge at Steenberg Vineyards, in which you can sample its great merlot, sauvignon blanc, semillon and Méthode Cap Classique sparkler. The farm estate is the oldest on the Cape, dating back to 1682 when it was known as Swaane-weide (Feeding Place of the Swans).

venue, tucked away down a side road beside the railway tracks, attracts a racially mixed crowd. The juke box is stacked with African, jazz and house-music tracks; it's worth checking out late on a weekend evening when patrons start to boogie.

Gardens & Surrounds

★Chalk & Cork WINE BAR

(Map p56; ☎021-422 5822; www.chalkandcork.co.za; 51 Kloof St, Gardens; ⏲9am-6pm Mon-Wed, to 10pm Thu-Sat; 🚌Lower Kloof) This wine bar and restaurant has a pleasant courtyard fronting Kloof St. The menu runs the gamut from breakfast dishes to tapas and sharing platters, but you're welcome to drop in for just the wines, plenty of which are served by the glass and are sourced from some of the region's best estates.

Power & the Glory/Black Ram CAFE, BAR

(Map p56; ☎021-422 2108; 13B Kloof Nek Rd, Tamboerskloof; ⏲cafe 8am-10pm Mon-Sat, bar 5pm-late Mon-Sat; 🚌Ludwig's Garden) The coffee and food (pretzel hot dogs, crusty pies and other artisan munchies) are good, but it's the smoky, cosy bar that packs the trendsters in, particularly on Thursday to Saturday nights.

Blah Blah Bar BAR

(Map p56; ☎082 349 8849; www.facebook.com/BlahBlahBarCPT; 84 Kloof St, Gardens; ⏲5pm-2am; 🚌Welgemeend) Working in conjunction with **Erdmann Contemporary** (Map p56; ☎021-422 2762; www.erdmanncontemporary.co.za; 84 Kloof St, Gardens; ⏲10am-9pm Wed-Sat; 🚌Welgemeend), which allows its upstairs gallery to be used for some of the bar's concerts, and with pizza supremos Ferdinando's (p79), Blah Blah is anything but blah. Check its Facebook page for live music and DJ events that are staged here; some have a cover charge.

★ Yours Truly
CAFE, BAR

(Map p56; www.yourstrulycafe.co.za; 73 Kloof St, Gardens; ⊙6am-11pm; ☒Ludwig's Garden) Fronting the backpackers Once in Cape Town, this place is hopping from early morning to late nights. Travellers mingle with hipster locals, who come for the excellent coffee, craft beer, gourmet sandwiches, thin-crust pizzas and the occasional DJ event.

The original, smaller branch is on **Long St** (Map p50; www.yourstrulycafe.co.za; 175 Long St, City Bowl; ⊙7am-5pm Mon-Fri, 8am-3pm Sat; ☒Dorp/Leeuwen).

🍷 Green Point & Waterfront

Shift
COFFEE

(Map p60; 47 Main Rd, Green Point; ⊙7am-7pm; 🛜; ☒Upper Portswood) Sporting an industrial-chic look with a cosy library corner inside and sheltered, spacious front courtyard outside, this is one of the area's most inviting cafes. Owner Luigi Vigliotti works hard to please customers, and he's come up with a few intriguing signature brews, including the 'Hashtag', which blends espresso with vanilla gelato and Oreo cookies.

Shimmy Beach Club
CLUB

(Map p60; ☎021-200 7778; www.shimmybeach club.com; South Arm Rd, V&A Waterfront; admission before/after 3pm free/R150; ⊙11am-2am Mon-Fri, 9am-2am Sat, 11am-6pm Sun; ☒Waterfront Silo) Drive past the smelly fish-processing factories to discover this glitzy megaclub and restaurant, arranged around a small fake beach studded with a glass-sided pool. Perhaps unsurprisingly, it has pool parties with scantily clad dancers shimmying to grooves by top DJs, including the electro-jazz group Goldfish, who have a summer Sunday residency here (bookings advised).

Bascule
BAR

(Map p60; ☎021-410 7100; www.capegrace.com; Cape Grace Hotel, West Quay Rd, V&A Waterfront; ⊙noon-2am; ☒Nobel Square) Over 450 varieties of whisky are served at the Grace's sophisticated bar, with a few slugs of the 50-year-old Glenfiddich still available (at just R18,000 a tot). Outdoor tables facing the marina are a superb spot for drinks and tasty tapas. Make a booking for one of its whisky tastings (from R240), in which you can sample various drams paired with food.

Tobago's Bar & Terrace
COCKTAIL BAR

(Map p60; ☎021-441 3000; Radisson Blu Hotel Waterfront, Beach Rd, Granger Bay; ⊙11am-midnight; ☒Granger Bay) Walk through the hotel to the spacious deck bar with a prime Table Bay position. It's a great place to enjoy a sunset cocktail; you can take a stroll along the breakwater afterwards.

Mitchell's Scottish Ale House & Brewery
PUB

(Map p60; ☎021-418 5074; www.mitchells-ale-house.com; cnr East Pier & Dock Rd, V&A Waterfront; ⊙10am-2am; ☒Nobel Square) Check all airs and graces at the door of South Africa's oldest microbrewery (established in 1983 in Knysna), which serves a variety of freshly brewed ales and good-value meals. Its 'Old Wobbly' packs an alcoholic punch.

🍷 Atlantic Coast

Hout Bay Coffee
CAFE

(www.facebook.com/HoutbayCoffee; Mainstream Shopping Centre, Main Rd, Hout Bay; ⊙9am-5pm Mon-Fri, to 3pm Sat & Sun; ☒Military) Sip excellent coffee at this rustic cafe, set in an 18th-century add-on to the original 17th-century woodcutters' cottage at Hout Bay. The outdoor area is shaded by a 150-year-old Norfolk Pine, with tables and chairs made from an old fishing boat. It also bakes filo-pastry chicken pies, luscious chocolate cakes and wheat-free quiche with free-range eggs.

Bungalow
BAR

(Map p68; ☎021-438 2018; www.thebungalow. co.za; Glen Country Club, 3 Victoria Rd, Clifton; ⊙noon-2am; ☒Maiden's Cove) This restaurant and lounge bar with a Euro-chic vibe is a great place for beers, cocktails or a boozy meal, after which you can crash on a daybed under a billowing white awning, or dangle your feet in the tiny barside splash pool. A DJ creates a more clubby atmosphere by night. Bookings are advised.

La Belle
CAFE, BAKERY

(Map p68; ☎021-437 1278; www.labellecampsbay. co.za; 201 The Promenade, Camps Bay; ⊙7am-11pm; ☒Whale Rock) This *belle* is one of the loveliest along the Camps Bay dining strip, and a whole lot more relaxed and less pretentious than some of its neighbours. Coffees, speciality teas, smoothies, shakes and a good range of cocktails are on offer – plus some extremely tempting baked goods, cakes and other light meals.

East City, District Six, Woodstock & Salt River

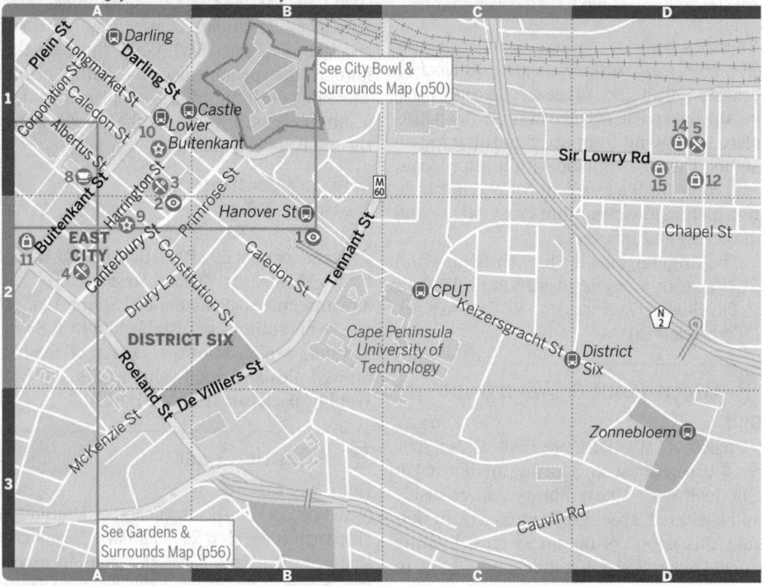

East City, District Six, Woodstock & Salt River

Sights

1 Land & Liberty B2
2 Substation 13 .... A2

Eating

3 Charly's Bakery A1
4 Downtown Ramen A2
5 Kitchen D1
Ocean Jewels .... (see 17)
Pot Luck Club .... (see 13)
6 Raw and Roxy H1

Drinking & Nightlife

7 aMadoda Braai G1
Espressolab Microroasters .... (see 13)
Lady Bonin's Tea .... (see 17)
8 Truth A1

Entertainment

9 Assembly A2
10 Fugard Theatre A1

Shopping

11 Book Lounge A2
Chapel .... (see 17)
Clementina Ceramics .... (see 13)
Cocofair .... (see 13)
12 Goodman Gallery Cape D1
Grandt Mason Originals .... (see 17)
Imiso Ceramics .... (see 13)
Mü & Me .... (see 13)
Neighbourgoods Market .... (see 13)
13 Old Biscuit Mill H1
14 Southern Guild D1
15 Stevenson D1
16 What If The World H1
17 Woodstock Exchange F1

La Vie BAR

(Map p68; ☎021-433 1530; www.lavie.co.za; 205 Beach Rd, Sea Point; ⌚9am-11.30pm; 📶; 🚌Promenade) Next to the South African Broadcasting Company's studios, this is one of the very few places where you can have anything from breakfast to late-night cocktails within sight of the Sea Point Promenade. Lounge on the outdoor terrace and enjoy the thin-crust pizza (R50 to R100).

Dunes BAR

(www.dunesrestaurant.co.za; 1 Beach Rd, Hout Bay; ⌚9am-11pm; 👪; 🚌Hout Bay) You can hardly get closer to the beach than this – in fact, the front courtyard *is* the beach. Up on the terrace or from inside the restaurant-bar you'll get a great view of Hout Bay, along with some decent pub grub and tapas. There's also a safe play area for kids.

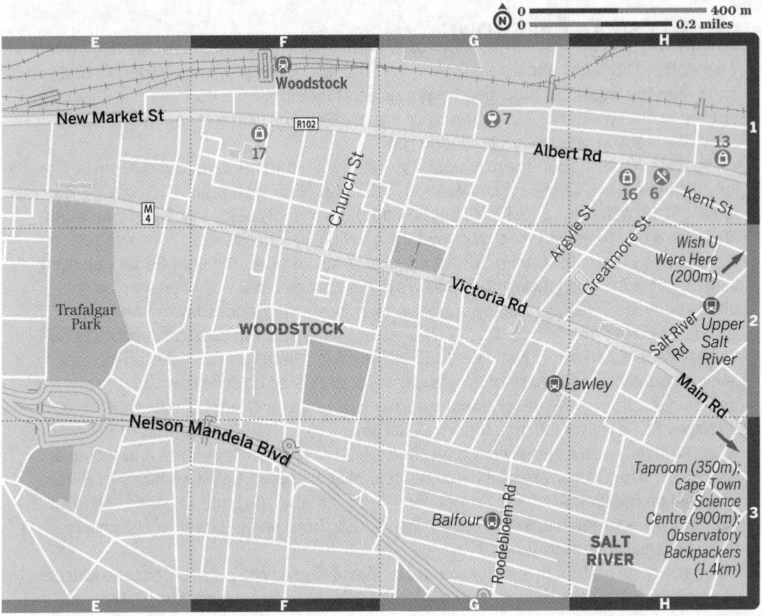

Southern Suburbs

Banana Jam BEER HALL

(www.bananajamcafe.co.za; 157 2nd Ave, Harfield Village, Kenilworth; 11am-11pm Mon-Sat, 5-10pm Sun; ; Kenilworth) Real beer lovers rejoice – this convivial Caribbean restaurant and bar is like manna from heaven, with over 30 beers on tap (including its own brews) and bottled ales from all the top local microbrewers, including Jack Black, Darling Brew and CBC.

Forrester's Arms PUB

(www.forries.co.za; 52 Newlands Ave, Newlands; 9am-11pm Mon-Thu & Sat, to midnight Fri, to 9pm Sun; ; Newlands) 'Forries' has been around for well over a century. This English-style pub offers a convivial atmosphere in which to enjoy a great range of local ales (both large-brewery and craft), good pub meals (including wood-fired pizza) and a very pleasant beer garden with a play area for the kids.

Southern Peninsula

★ **Brass Bell** BAR, RESTAURANT

(www.brassbell.co.za; Kalk Bay station, Main Rd, Kalk Bay; 11am-10pm; Kalk Bay) Follow the tunnel beneath the train tracks to reach this institution, lapped by the waves of False Bay. On a sunny day there are few better places to drink and eat (mains R50 to R100) by the sea. You can also take a dip in the adjacent tidal pools before or after.

★ **Cape Point Vineyards** WINERY

(021-789 0900; www.cpv.co.za; 1 Chapmans Peak Dr, Noordhoek; tastings R45; tastings 10am-6pm, restaurant noon-3pm & 6.30-8.30pm Mon-Wed, Fri & Sat, picnics 11am-6pm, market 4.30-8.30pm Thu;) Known for its fine sauvignon blanc, this small vineyard has a spectacular setting overlooking Noordhoek Beach. Enjoy the wines with a picnic (R395 for two, bookings essential) in the grounds, or at its restaurant. Its Thursday-evening community market (selling mainly food) is a weekly highlight for locals and great for kids, who can play on the lawns.

Slow Life CAFE

(www.facebook.com/slowlifesouthafrica; 152 Main Rd, Muizenberg; cover charge R50-120; 9am-10pm Tue-Sat; ; Muizenberg) Life in Muizenberg can feel pretty laid-back: this concept cafe gets the groove just right with an relaxed, arty atmosphere, long hours, a decent drinks and food menu and live music or comedy gigs often held on Friday and Saturday nights.

GAY & LESBIAN CAPE TOWN

The Mother City's gay and lesbian scene isn't the world's largest, but it's friendly and you can't fault the location's drop-dead glamour. Start by topping up your tan and checking out the talent on **Clifton No 3 beach** or **Sandy Bay**, the clothing-optional stretch of sand discreetly located near Llandudno Bay.

De Waterkant is ground zero for GLBT guesthouses, bars, clubs and restaurants. The long-running **Cafe Manhattan** (Map p50; 021-421 6666; www.manhattan.co.za; 74 Waterkant St, De Waterkant; 9.30am-2am; Alfred) is a friendly place to kick off your night and grab a bite to eat. A broad balcony allows a wide view of passersby. Also popular is **Beefcakes** (Map p50; 021-425 9019; www.beefcakes.co.za; 40 Somerset Rd, De Waterkant; burgers R55-85; noon-midnight; Gallow's Hill), a camp burger bar where you can play bitchy bingo on Tuesday or enjoy professional drag shows Wednesday to Saturday.

The **Amsterdam Action Bar & Backstage** (Map p50; www.amsterdambar.co.za; 10-12 Cobern St, De Waterkant; 5pm-late; Alfred) has dark rooms and cubicles on its upper level, a pool table in the nonsmoking area, and a streetside balcony to watch the comings and goings. Later, move on around the corner to **Crew Bar** (Map p50; www.crewbar.co.za; 30 Napier St, De Waterkant; from 10pm Fri & Sat cover R20; 7pm-2am Sun-Thu, to 3.30pm Fri & Sat; Alfred) with its hunky bar dancers dressed only in skimpy shorts and glitter, or **Beaulah** (Map p50; www.beaulahbar.co.za; 1st fl, 24 Somerset Rd, De Waterkant; cover R20; 9pm-4am Fri & Sat; Alfred). Pronounced 'byoo-lah', this fun bar and dance venue, up a floor from the street, has a devoted crowd of young boys and girls who are always ready to bop to the DJ's poppy tunes.

On the edge of the City Bowl, **Alexander Bar & Café** (p83) is a fun, eccentric space in a gorgeous heritage building and has a 50-seater studio theatre hosting a top-class range of shows.

Cape Town's lesbian community has been striking out with women-only parties **M.I.S.S.** (www.facebook.com/MISSmakeitsexysisters) and the **Unofficial Pink Parties** (www.facebook.com/pinkpartyza), which are lesbian-run but welcoming to everyone – the latter are usually hosted at **Sugarhut** (Map p50; www.sugarhutclub.co.za; 44 Constitution St, East City; cover R40; Lower Buitenkant).

For the latest openings and events check the annually updated **Pink Map** (http://mapmyway.co.za/printed-maps); **Gaynet Cape Town** (www.gaynetcapetown.co.za); and the monthly free newspaper **Pink Tongue** (www.pinktongue.co.za). Also mark your travel calendar for the city's two main GLBT events: **Cape Town Pride** (www.capetownpride.org) in early March and the **Mother City Queer Project** (p586), a fabulous fancy-dress dance party every December.

Tiger's Milk BAR, RESTAURANT
(021-788 1869; www.tigersmilk.co.za; cnr Beach & Sidmouth Rds, Muizenberg; kitchen 9am-10pm, bar to 2am; ; Muizenberg) There's a panoramic view of Muizenberg beach through the floor-to-ceiling window of this hangar-like bar and restaurant. Although it's open all day for food (good pizza and steaks), the vibe – with its long bar counter, comfy sofas and quirky decor (a BMW bike and a giant golden cow's head hanging on exposed-brick walls) – is more nightclub.

☆ Entertainment

Live music is a particular highlight, with jazz being prominent at venues across the Cape. There are several theatres, and multiplexes for mainstream movies can be found in Victoria Wharf at the Waterfront, Cavendish Sq and Canal Walk.

With tickets costing from around R30, attending the footy (soccer) in Cape Town is not only cheap but also a hugely fun and loud night out, with supporters taking every opportunity to blow their *vuvuzelas* (plastic trumpets). The season runs from August to May. **Ajax Cape Town** (www.ajaxct.com) plays at Cape Town Stadium, while **Athlone Stadium** (021-637 6607; Cross Blvd, Athlone; Athlone) is home to the team **Santos** (www.santosfc.co.za).

Tickets for many events can be booked with **Webtickets** (www.webtickets.co.za) or **Computicket** (http://online.computicket.com/web), which has outlets in Cape Town Tourism's main office on Burg St and at the Waterfront.

☆ City Bowl & Foreshore

Artscape THEATRE

(☎021-410 9800; www.artscape.co.za; 1-10 DF Malan St, Foreshore; Civic Centre) Consisting of three different-sized auditoriums, this behemoth is the city's main arts complex. Theatre, classical music, ballet, opera and cabaret shows – Artscape offers it all. If you're into swing and salsa, **Que Pasa** (www.quepasa.co.za; Jazzart Studios, Artscape, classes per hour from R70; Civic Centre) also runs regular classes at the Jazzart Studio here.

The desolate area means it's not recommended to walk around here at night; there's plenty of secure parking though.

Cape Town City Hall LIVE MUSIC

(Map p50; Darling St, City Bowl; Darling) One of the several venues where the **Cape Philharmonic Orchestra** (CPO; Map p50; www.cpo.org.za; tickets from R130; Darling), South Africa's 'orchestra for all seasons', plays concerts. The CPO has been working hard to ensure its musicians reflect the ethnic breakdown of the Western Cape more closely. To this end it has formed the Cape Philharmonic Youth Orchestra and the Cape Philharmonic Youth Wind Ensemble, with around 80% of members coming from disadvantaged communities.

Cape Town International Convention Centre CONCERT VENUE

(CTICC; Map p50; ☎021-410 5000; www.cticc.co.za; 1 Lower Long St, Foreshore; Convention Centre) Since opening in 2003, the CTICC has barely paused for breath, packing in a busy annual program of musical performances, exhibitions, conferences and other events, such as the Cape Town International Jazz Festival and Design Indaba. An extension to the complex is currently rising up on the plot between the current building and Artscape, almost doubling its size.

Crypt Jazz Restaurant JAZZ

(Map p50; ☎079 683 4658; www.thecryptjazz.com; 1 Wale St, City Bowl; cover R65; 6.30am-midnight Tue-Sat; Groote Kerk) Occupying part of the St George's Cathedral's vaulted stone crypt, this restaurant, which serves a continent-hopping menu of dishes, is best visited for its live jazz. Concerts start at either 7pm or 8pm and last most of the evening. Some very accomplished performers take to the stage here; for some concerts booking ahead is advisable.

ONLINE ENTERTAINMENT GUIDES

- What's On! (www.whatson.co.za/cityselect.php)
- Next 48 Hours (www.48hours.co.za)
- Tonight (www.iol.co.za/tonight)
- Cape Town Magazine (www.capetownmagazine.co.za)

☆ East City

Assembly LIVE MUSIC

(Map p86; www.theassembly.co.za; 61 Harrington St, East City; cover R30-50; Lower Buitenkant) In an old furniture-assembly factory, this live-music and DJ performance space has made its mark with an exciting, eclectic line-up of both local and international artists. It also holds the audio-visual event **Pecha Kucha** (www.pechakucha-capetown.co.za), generally once a month.

Fugard Theatre THEATRE

(Map p86; ☎021-461 4554; www.thefugard.com; Caledon St, East City; Lower Buitenkant) Named in honour of Athol Fugard, South Africa's best-known living playwright, this very impressive arts centre was created from the former Congregational Church Hall. There are two stages, the largest theatre also doubling up as a 'bioscope' – a fancy word for a digital cinema where top international dance and opera performances are screened.

☆ Gardens & Surrounds

Labia CINEMA

(Map p56; ☎021-424 5927; www.thelabia.co.za; 68 Orange St, Gardens; tickets R40; Michaelis) A Capetonian treasure and lifeline to the independent movie fan, the Labia is named after the old Italian ambassador and local philanthropist Count Labia. The African Screen program is one of the rare opportunities you'll have to see locally made films; check the website for session times.

Straight No Chaser JAZZ

(Map p56; ☎076-679 2697; www.straightnochaserclub.wordpress.com; 79 Buitenkant St, Gardens; 1/2 sets R60/100; 7pm-2am Wed-Sat; Roeland) Next to Diva's Pizza, this tiny jazz club aims to re-create the atmosphere of Ronnie Scott's and Village Vanguard. It's run by hard-core jazz cats who take their music

DON'T MISS

FIRST THURSDAYS

The hit **First Thursdays** (www.first-thursdays.co.za; ⌚5-9pm, 1st Thu of month) event is centred on the galleries and design shops clustered around Church and Bree Sts – it's a chance to dip into the local art scene, and a roving street party.

Church Sq is the open canvas for anything from debates to giant Scrabble games. Food trucks gather around Van Riebeek Sq and in Upper Bree St, where you're also likely to encounter buskers on Orphan Lane.

The sister event Thursday Late, held usually on the third Thursday of the month, focuses on the East City and Woodstock areas.

seriously – and who also have the connections to get top-class talent on the stage. Bookings are essential for the two sets per night, starting at 8.30pm and 10.30pm.

☆ Waterfront & Sea Point

★Studio 7 LIVE MUSIC

(Map p68; www.facebook.com/Studio7Sessions; 8 Calais Rd, Sea Point; Rhine) A few years ago, local musician Patrick Craig set up a members-only music club in his living room. Top local and international musicians play acoustic gigs here in very relaxed, intimate surroundings. Usually no more than 40 tickets are sold (online) – check the Facebook page for details, as it's a fantastic venue for true music lovers.

Jou Ma Se Comedy Club COMEDY

(Map p60; V&A Waterfront; tickets R80; Nobel Square) The title means 'Your mother's ***!' but you don't need to understand Afrikaans slang to get the jokes at this laugh-a-minute comedy club.

☆ Southern Suburbs

★Baxter Theatre THEATRE

(021-685 7880; www.baxter.co.za; Main Rd, Rondebosch; tickets from R120; Rosebank) Since the 1970s the Baxter has been the focus of Capetonian theatre. There are three venues – the main theatre, the concert hall and the studio – and between them they cover everything from kids' shows to African dance spectaculars. The theatre has an ongoing relationship with the Royal Shakespeare Company thanks to Capetonian Sir Anthony Sher, who has performed here.

Sahara Park Newlands SPECTATOR SPORT

(021-657 2043; www.wpca.org.za; 146 Campground Rd, Newlands; tickets R30-250; Newlands) If it weren't for a nearby brewery messing up the view towards the back of Table Mountain, Newlands would be a shoo-in for the title of world's prettiest cricket ground. With room for 25,000, it's used for all international matches. Local team the Nashua Mobile Cape Cobras play here during the season, which runs from September to March.

Newlands Rugby Stadium SPECTATOR SPORT

(021-659 4600; www.wprugby.com; 8 Boundary Rd, Newlands; Newlands) This hallowed ground of South African rugby is home to the Stormers (www.thestormers.com). Super-12 games and international matches are played here.

Shopping

Bring a big empty bag because chances are that you'll be leaving Cape Town laden with local booty.

City Bowl

★South African Market FASHION, CRAFTS

(SAM; Map p50; www.ilovesam.co.za; Bree St, City Bowl; ⌚9am-5pm Mon-Fri, 10am-2pm Sat; Church/Longmarket) A spacious loft space above La Parada is a showcase for local design talent across fashion, jewellery, homewares, stationery and artworks. There's a great selection of menswear, womenswear and clothing for kids here including the cute graphic T-shirts of Mingo Lamberti.

★African Music Store MUSIC

(Map p50; 021-426 0857; 134 Long St, City Bowl; ⌚9am-6pm Mon-Fri, to 2pm Sat; Dorp/Leeuwen) The range of local music here, including jazz, kwaito (a form of township music), dance and trance recordings, can't be surpassed; and the staff are knowledgable about the music scene. You'll also find DVDs and other souvenirs.

Luvey 'n Rose ARTS & CRAFTS

(Map p50; 083 557 7156; www.luveynrose.co.za; 66 Loop St, City Bowl; ⌚9am-5pm Mon-Fri, to 2pm Sat; Church/Longmarket) This smashing gallery, next to Prins & Prins but something of a hidden gem, mashes up collectable antiques and works by key South African and African artists such as Walter Battiss with more contemporary stuff from emerging talents. It doubles as a cafe and cigar lounge, a smart move to encourage visitors to linger and browse the eclectic art and design.

African Image ARTS & CRAFTS
(Map p50; www.african-image.co.za; cnr Church & Burg Sts, City Bowl; ⌚9am-5pm Mon-Fri, to 2pm Sat; 🚌Church/Longmarket) African Image has a fab range of new and old crafts and artefacts at reasonable prices, including the funky, colourful pillow covers and aprons of Shine Shine. You'll find a lot of township crafts here, as well as wildly patterned shirts.

Pan African Market ARTS & CRAFTS
(Map p50; 76 Long St, City Bowl; ⌚8.30am-5.30pm Mon-Fri, to 3.30pm Sat; 🚌Church/Longmarket) A microcosm of the continent, with a bewildering range of arts and crafts (which you should certainly bargain over). There's also the cheap cafe **Timbuktu**, with seating on the balcony overlooking Long St, a tailor and music shop, and the publishers of the pan-African newspaper *Chronic Chimurenga* (www.chimurenga.co.za), packed into three floors.

Clarke's Bookshop BOOKS
(Map p50; ☎021-423 5739; www.clarkesbooks.co.za; 199 Long St, City Bowl; ⌚9am-5pm Mon-Fri, 9.30am-1pm Sat; 🚌Dorp/Leeuwen) Take your time leafing through the best range of books on South Africa and the continent, with a great secondhand section upstairs. If you can't find what you're looking for here, it's unlikely to be in any of the other many bookshops along Long St (although there's no harm in browsing).

Bo-Kaap & De Waterkant

★**Streetwires** ARTS & CRAFTS
(Map p50; www.streetwires.co.za; 77 Shortmarket St, Bo-Kaap; ⌚8.30am-5pm Mon-Fri, 9am-1pm Sat; 🚌Church/Longmarket) The motto is 'anything you can dream up in wire we will build'. And if you visit this social project, designed to create sustainable employment, and see the wire sculptors at work, you'll see what that means! It stocks an amazing range, including working radios and chandeliers, life-sized animals and artier products such as the Nguni Cow range.

★**Africa Nova** ARTS & CRAFTS
(Map p50; www.africanova.co.za; Cape Quarter, 72 Waterkant St, De Waterkant; ⌚9am-5pm Mon-Fri, 10am-5pm Sat, 10am-2pm Sun; 🚌Alfred) One of the most stylish and desirable collections of contemporary African textiles, arts and crafts. You'll find potato-print fabrics made by women in Hout Bay, Karin Dando's mosaic trophy heads, Ronel Jordaan's handmade felt rock cushions (which look like giant pebbles) and a wonderful range of ceramics and jewellery.

Monkeybiz ARTS & CRAFTS
(Map p50; www.monkeybiz.co.za; 43 Rose St, Bo-Kaap; ⌚9am-5pm Mon-Thu, to 4pm Fri, 10am-1pm Sat; 🚌Church/Longmarket) Colourful beadwork crafts, made by local township women, are Monkeybiz's super-successful stock in trade – you'll find its products around the world but the largest selection is here. Profits are reinvested back into community services such as soup kitchens and a burial fund for artists and their families.

East City & Woodstock

Old Biscuit Mill SHOPPING CENTRE
(Map p86; www.theoldbiscuitmill.co.za; 373-375 Albert Rd, Woodstock; ⌚9am-5pm Mon-Fri, to 3pm Sat; 🚌Kent) This former biscuit factory houses an ace collection of arts, craft, fashion and design shops, as well as places to eat and drink. Favourites include **Clementina Ceramics** (Map p86; www.clementina.co.za) and **Imiso Ceramics** (Map p86; ☎021-447 7668; www.imisoceramics.co.za) for ceramics; the organic bean-to-shop chocolate factory **Cocofair** (Map p86; www.cocoafair.com); and **Mü & Me** (Map p86; www.muandme.net) for super-cute graphic art for cards, wrapping paper, stationery and kids' T-shirts.

Woodstock Exchange SHOPPING CENTRE
(Map p86; www.woodstockexchange.co.za; 66 Albert Rd, Woodstock; ⌚9am-5pm Mon-Fri, to 2pm Sat; 🚆Woodstock) There's a fair amount of original retail at the Exchange, including the atelier and showroom of **Grandt Mason Originals** (Map p86; www.g-mo.co.za; Shop 13, Woodstock Exchange, 66 Albert Rd, Woodstock; 🚆Woodstock), which uses luxurious fabrics from ends of rolls and swatch books to make one-off footwear; **Chapel** (Map p86; www.store.chapelgoods.co.za; Woodstock Exchange, 66 Albert Rd, Woodstock; 🚆Woodstock) leather goods; **Charlie. H**, who crafts kimonos, halter dresses, and skirts from printed fabrics; and boutique **Kingdom**, which mixes fashion and accessories with interior design.

Book Lounge BOOKS
(Map p86; ☎021-462 2425; www.booklounge.co.za; 71 Roeland St, East City; ⏰9.30am-7.30pm Mon-Fri, 8.30am-6pm Sat, 10am-4pm Sun; 🚌Roeland) The hub of Cape Town's literary scene, thanks to its great selection of titles, comfy chairs, simple cafe and busy program of events. There are up to three talks or book launches a week, generally with free drinks and nibbles, and readings for kids on the weekend.

Gardens

★KIN ART, CRAFTS
(Map p56; www.kinshop.co.za; 99B Kloof St, Gardens; ⏰9.30am-5.30pm Mon-Sat; 🚌Ludwig's Garden) You're sure to find a unique gift or item for yourself at this creative boutique representing over a hundred South African artists and designers, ranging from ceramics and jewellery to prints and bags. It also has a branch at the **Waterfront** (Map p60; www.kinshop.co.za; Shop 11B, Alfred Mall, V&A Waterfront; ⏰9am-9pm; 🚌V&A Waterfront), which stocks more African-themed designs.

Coffeebeans Routes ARTS & CRAFTS
(Map p56; www.coffeebeansroutes.com; 22 Hope St, Gardens; ⏰9am-5pm Mon-Fri; 🚌Roodehek) As well as running some of the best guided tours you can take in Cape Town, Coffeebean Routes are championing local creatives with this boutique that stocks an eclectic range of goods. Find great CDs and books by Capetonian musicians and writers, as well as fashion, accessories, art and various crafts.

Green Point & Waterfront

★Watershed SHOPPING CENTRE
(Map p60; www.waterfront.co.za/Shop/Pages/Watershed-Overview.aspx; Dock Rd, V&A Waterfront; ⏰10am-7pm; 🚌Nobel Square) The best place to shop for souvenirs in Cape Town, this exciting revamped retail market gathers together over hundreds of top Capetonian and South African brands in fashion, arts, crafts and design – there's something here for every pocket. On the upper level is an exhibition space, and a wellness centre offering holistic products and massages.

Victoria Wharf SHOPPING CENTRE
(Map p60; www.waterfront.co.za; Breakwater Blv, V&A Waterfront; ⏰9am-9pm; 🚌Breakwater) All the big names of South African retail (including Woolworths, CNA, Pick 'n' Pay, Exclusive Books and Musica), as well as international luxury brands, are represented at this appealing mall – one of Cape Town's best.

Cape Union Mart Adventure Centre OUTDOOR EQUIPMENT
(Map p60; www.capeunionmart.co.za; Quay 4, V&A Waterfront; ⏰9am-9pm; 🚌Nobel Square) This emporium is packed with backpacks, boots, clothing and practically everything else you might need for outdoor adventures, from a hike up Table Mountain to a Cape-to-Cairo safari. There's also a smaller branch in Victoria Wharf (p92), as well as in the **Gardens Centre** (Map p56; ☎021-465 1842; www.gardensshoppingcentre.co.za; cnr Mill & Buitenkant Sts, Gardens; ⏰9am-7pm Mon-Fri, to 5pm Sat, to 2pm Sun; 🚌Gardens) and Cavendish Square (p92) malls.

Atlantic Coast

Hout Bay Craft Market MARKET
(Baviaanskloof Rd, Hout Bay; ⏰10am-5pm Sun; 🚌Military) Browsing the stalls at this little village-green market, a fundraiser for the Lions Club of Hout Bay, is a lovely way to while away an hour or so on a Sunday. You'll find crafts made by locals, including impressive beadwork, colourfully printed cloths and cute guinea fowl made from pine cones.

Southern Suburbs

★Montebello ARTS & CRAFTS
(www.montebello.co.za; 31 Newlands Ave, Newlands; ⏰9am-5pm Mon-Fri, to 4pm Sat, to 3pm Sun; 🚆Newlands) This development project has helped several great craftspeople and designers along the way. In the leafy compound, artists studios are scattered around the central craft shop, where you can buy a great range of gifts, including some made from recycled materials. There's also a plant nursery, the excellent cafe **Gardener's Cottage** and car-washers.

Cavendish Square MALL
(☎021-657 5620; www.cavendish.co.za; Dreyer St, Claremont; ⏰9am-7pm Mon-Sat, 10am-5pm Sun; 🚆Claremont) The focal point of Claremont's shopping scene, this top-class mall has outlets of many of Cape Town's premier fashion designers, as well as supermarkets, department stores and multiplex cinemas.

WEEKLY ARTISAN FOOD & GOODS MARKETS

Capetonians love their weekly markets; the pick are listed below.

Neighbourgoods Market (Map p86; www.neighbourgoodsmarket.co.za; Old Biscuit Mill, 373-375 Albert Rd, Woodstock; 9am-2pm Sat; Kent) The first and still the best of the artisan goods markets that are now common across the Cape. Food and drinks are gathered in the main area where you can pick up groceries and gourmet goodies or just graze, while the separate Designergoods area hosts a must-buy selection of local fashions and accessories. Come early unless you enjoy jostling with crowds.

Oranjezicht City Farm Market (Map p56; www.ozcf.co.za; Homestead Park, Upper Orange St, Oranjezicht; 9am-2pm Sat; Upper Orange) Produce grown on the Oranjezicht City Farm and other local farms is sold every Saturday here. At the time of research it was temporarily being held at **Leeuwenhof** (Map p56; Hof St, Tamboerskloof; Upper Kloof), the official residence of the Western Cape Premier. It's a great event to attend with plenty of food stalls for brunching.

Bay Harbour Market (www.bayharbour.co.za; 31 Harbour Rd, Hout Bay; 5-9pm Fri, 9am-4pm Sat & Sun; Atlantic Skipper) At the far western end of the harbour is this imaginatively designed indoor market, one of Cape Town's best. There's a good range of things to buy, as well as very tempting food and drink. Live music gives it a relaxed, party-like atmosphere.

Blue Bird Garage Food & Goods Market (082 331 2471; www.bluebirdmarket.co.za; 39 Albertyn Rd, Muizenberg; 4-10pm Fri; Valsbaai) This hit artisan food-and-goods market is based in a 1940s hangar, once the base for the southern hemisphere's first airmail delivery service, and then a garage in the 1950s. It's a fun place to shop and graze, particularly on Friday nights, when there's live music.

Southern Peninsula

★Kalk Bay Modern ARTS & CRAFTS
(021-788 6571; www.kalkbaymodern.co.za; 136 Main Rd, Kalk Bay; 9.30am-5pm; Kalk Bay) This wonderful gallery is stocked with an eclectic and appealing range of arts and crafts, and there are often exhibitions by local artists showing here. Check out the Art-i-San collection of printed cloth, a fair-trade product made by the !Kung Bushmen in Namibia.

Artvark ARTS & CRAFTS
(021-788 5584; www.artvark.org; 48 Main Rd, Kalk Bay; 9am-6pm; Kalk Bay) This contemporary folk-art gallery is a great place to find attractive souvenirs. It stocks a wide range of interesting arts and crafts by local artists, including paintings, pottery and jewellery, as well as goods from India and Central America.

Information

DANGERS & ANNOYANCES

Cape Town's relaxed vibe can instil a false sense of security. Thefts are most likely to happen when visitors do something foolish such as leaving their gear on a beach while they go swimming.

Paranoia is not required, but common sense is. There is tremendous poverty on the peninsula and 'informal redistribution of wealth' is reasonably common. While the city centre is generally safe to walk around, always listen to local advice on where and where not to go. There is safety in numbers.

Swimming at any of the Cape beaches is potentially hazardous, especially for those inexperienced in the surf. Check for warning signs about rips and rocks, and only swim in patrolled areas.

EMERGENCY

In any emergency call 107, or 021-480 7700 if using a mobile phone. Other useful phone numbers are listed below.

Police (10111)

Sea Rescue (021-449 3500)

Table Mountain National Park (0861-106 417)

INTERNET ACCESS

Practically all hotels and hostels, as well as several cafes and restaurants, have internet facilities and/or wi-fi; we list places where it is available (). At some it will be free (ask for the password); at others you'll have to pay. Internet cafes (charging around R30 per hour) are fairly common in the City Bowl.

MEDIA

Cape Town's morning newspaper, the *Cape Times*, and the afternoon *Cape Argus* print practically the same news. *Cape Etc* is a decent bimonthly arts and listings magazine dedicated to what's going on around town. The online Cape Town Magazine (www.capetownmagazine.co.za) is also a useful source of information with up-to-date listings of places and events.

MEDICAL SERVICES

Medical services are of a high standard in Cape Town. Hotels and most other accommodation places can arrange a visit from a doctor if required.

Groote Schuur Hospital (☎021-404 9111; www.westerncape.gov.za/your_gov/163; Main Rd, Observatory; Observatory) In an emergency, you can go directly to the casualty (emergency) department.

Netcare Christiaan Barnard Memorial Hospital (☎021-480 6111; https://www.netcare.co.za/139/netcare-christiaan-barnard-memorial-hospital; 181 Longmarket St, City Bowl; Church/Longmarket) The best private hospital. Reception is on the 8th floor.

Netcare Travel Clinic (☎021-419 3172; www.travelclinic.co.za; 11th fl, Picbal Arcade, 58 Strand St, City Bowl; ⊙8am-4pm Mon-Fri; Adderely) For vaccinations and travel health advice.

MONEY

Money can be changed at the airport and there are ATMs all over town.

POST

See www.sapo.co.za to find the nearest post office. The post is reliable but slow. If you're mailing anything of value, consider using a private mail service such as **Postnet** (Map p50; www.postnet.co.za), which uses DHL for international deliveries.

General Post Office (Map p50; www.postoffice.co.za; Parliament St, City Bowl; ⊙8am-4.30pm Mon-Fri, to noon Sat) The General Post Office, located upstairs above the shopping centre, has a poste restante counter.

TELEPHONE

You can get a pay-as-you-go SIM card from the MTM and Vodacom desks at the airport or in town, where you'll also find Cell-C shops. Top-up cards are available all over town.

TOURIST INFORMATION

At the head office of **Cape Town Tourism** (Map p50; ☎021-487 6800; www.capetown.travel; Pinnacle Bldg, cnr Castle & Burg Sts, City Bowl; ⊙8am-5.30pm Mon-Fri, 8.30am-2pm Sat, 9am-1pm Sun; Church/Mid-Long) there are advisers who can book accommodation, tours and car hire. You can also get information on national parks and reserves.

There are several other Cape Town Tourism offices around the city.

Kirstenbosch Visitor Information Centre (☎021-762 0687; www.capetown.travel; Rhodes Dr, Kirstenbosch Botanical Gardens, Main Entrance, Newlands; ⊙8am-5pm)

Muizenberg Visitor Information Centre (☎021-787 9140; The Pavilion, Beach Rd; ⊙8am-5pm Mon-Fri, 9am-1pm Sat & Sun; Muizenberg)

Simon's Town Visitor Information Centre (☎021-786 8440; 111 St George's St, Simon's Town; ⊙8am-5pm Mon-Fri, 9am-1pm Sat & Sun; Simon's Town)

V&A Waterfront Visitor Information Centre (Map p60; ☎021-408 7600; Dock Rd, V&A Waterfront; ⊙9am-6pm; Nobel Square)

Getting There & Away

AIR

Cape Town International Airport (CPT; ☎021-937 1200; www.airports.co.za), 22km east of the city centre, has a tourist information office.

BUS

Interstate buses arrive at the bus terminus next to Cape Town Train Station, where you'll find the booking offices for the following bus companies, all open 6am to 6.30pm daily.

Baz Bus (☎0861 229 287, 021-422 5202; www.bazbus.com) Offers hop-on, hop-off fares and door-to-door service between Cape Town and Johannesburg/Pretoria via the Northern Drakensberg, Durban and the Garden Route.

Greyhound (Map p50; ☎021-418 4326; www.greyhound.co.za)

Intercape Mainliner (Map p50; ☎0861 287 287; www.intercape.co.za)

Translux (Map p50; ☎0861 589 282, 021-449 6209; www.translux.co.za)

TRAIN

Long-distance trains arrive at **Cape Town Train Station** (cnr Adderley & Strand Sts). There are services Wednesday, Friday and Sunday to and from Jo'burg via Kimberley on the **Shosholoza Meyl** (☎086 000 8888; www.shosholozameyl.co.za). These sleeper trains offer comfortable accommodation and dining cars, but if you require something more luxurious opt either for the elegant **Blue Train** (☎021-449 2672; www.bluetrain.co.za), which stops at Matjiesfontein on its way to Pretoria and Kimberley on the way back to Cape Town, or **Rovos Rail** (☎021-421 4020; www.rovos.com).

Getting Around

A listing in this chapter includes details of the nearest Cape Metro Rail station or MyCiTi bus stop when it is within 100m or so of the station or stop.

TO/FROM THE AIRPORT

MyCiTi buses run every 20 minutes between 5am and 10pm to Civic Centre station. The fare (adult/child aged four to 11/child aged under four R53.50/26.50/free) can be paid in cash or by using a myconnect card. **Backpacker Bus** (☎082 809 9185; www.backpackerbus.co.za) picks up from hostels and hotels in the city and offers airport transfers from R160 per person (R180 between 5pm and 8am).

Expect to pay around R200 for a nonshared taxi; the officially authorised airport taxi company is **Touch Down Taxis** (☎021-919 4659).

All the major car-hire companies have desks at the airport. Driving along the N2 into the city centre from the airport usually takes 15 to 20 minutes, although during rush hours (7am to 9am and 4.30pm to 6.30pm) this can extend up to an hour. There is a petrol station just outside the airport, handy for refilling before drop-off.

BICYCLE

If you're prepared for the many hills and long distances between sights, the Cape Peninsula is a terrific place to explore by bicycle. Dedicated cycle lanes are a legacy of the World Cup: there's a good one north out of the city towards Table View, and another runs alongside the Fan Walk from Cape Town Train Station to Green Point. Unfortunately, bicycles are banned on suburban trains.

The following offer bicycle hire:

Bike & Saddle (☎021-813 6433; www.bikeandsaddle.com)

Cape Town Cycle Hire (☎084 400 1604, 021-434 1270; www.capetowncyclehire.co.za; per day from R250) Delivers and collects bikes free of charge to the City Bowl and down the Atlantic seaboard to Llandudno.

Downhill Adventures (☎021-422 0388; www.downhilladventures.com; cnr Orange & Kloof Sts, Gardens; ⏲8am-6pm Mon-Fri, to 1pm Sat)

Up Cycles (☎076 135 2223; www.upcycles.co.za; 1hr/half-day/full day R50/150/200; ⏲8.30am-6.30pm May-Oct, 8am-9pm Nov-Apr) Pick up or drop off bikes at any of three stations: Sea Point Pavilion, Clock Tower Square at the Waterfront and Hotel Rhodes Mandela Place in the City Bowl.

BUS

MyCiTi

The **MyCiTi** (☎0800 656 463; www.myciti.org.za) network of commuter buses run daily between 5am and 10pm, with the the most frequent services between 8am and 5pm. Routes cover the city centre up to Gardens and out to the Waterfront; along the Atlantic seaboard to Camps Bay and Hout Bay; up to Tamboerskloof along Kloof Nek Rd, with a shuttle service to the cableway; Woodstock and Salt River; Khayelitsha; and the airport.

Fares have to be paid with a stored-value myconnect card (a non-refundable R35), which can be purchased from MyCiTi station kiosks and participating retailers. It's also possible to buy single-trip tickets (R30 or R75 to or from the airport). A bank fee of 2.5% of the value loaded (with a minimum of R1.50) will be charged, so if you load the card with R200 you will have R195 in credit. The card, issued by ABSA (a national bank), can also be used to pay for low-value transactions at shops and businesses displaying the MasterCard sign.

Fares charged depend on the time of day (peak-hour fares are charged between 6:30am and 8:30am and 4pm and 6pm) and whether you have pre-loaded the card with MyCiTi Mover package (amounts between R50 and R1000), which can cut the standard fares by 30%.

For journeys of under 5km (ie from Civic Centre to Gardens or the Waterfront) standard fares are R8.90 at peak times (6.30am to 8.30am and 4pm to 6pm Monday to Friday) and R6.80 at all other times; city centre to Table View is R12.50/9.40 peak/off-peak; city centre to airport is R68.70/65.60 peak/off-peak; city centre to Hout Bay is R12.50/9.40 peak/off-peak.

Golden Arrow

Golden Arrow (☎0800 656 463; www.gabs.co.za) buses run from the **Golden Acre Bus Terminal** (Map p50; Grand Pde), with most services stopping early in the evening. You might find them handy for journeys into the Cape Flats, the Northern Suburbs and even as far south as Simon's Town. Fares start at R5.

CAR & MOTORCYCLE

Cape Town has an excellent road and freeway system that, outside the early-morning and late-afternoon rush hour, carries surprisingly little traffic. The downside is getting used to the erratic, sometimes dangerous driving by fellow drivers.

The following places hire out cars and two-wheeled motors:

Around About Cars (☎021-422 4022; www.aroundaboutcars.com; 20 Bloem St; ⏲7.30am-7pm Mon-Fri, to 4pm Sat, 8am-1pm Sun; 🚌Upper Long/Upper Loop) Friendly local operation offering one of the best independent deals in town, with rates starting at R230 per day.

Avis (☎021-424 1177; www.avis.co.za; 123 Strand St, City Bowl; ⏲7.30am-6pm Mon-Fri, 8am-noon Sat & Sun; 🚌Strand)

Budget (☎021-418-5232; www.budget.co.za; 120 Strand St)

Hertz (☎021-410 6800; www.hertz.co.za; 40 Loop St, City Bowl; ⏱7am-6pm Mon-Fri, 8am-4pm Sat & Sun; 🚌Strand)

Harley Davidson Cape Town (☎021-401 4260; www.harley-davidson-capetown.com; 9 Somerset Rd, De Waterkant; ⏱8.30am-5.30pm Mon-Fri, 8am-2pm Sat; 🚌Alfred)

Scoot Dr (☎021-418-5995; www.scootdr.com; 61 Waterkant St, Foreshore; ⏱8am-5pm Mon-Fri, to 1pm Sat; 🚌Strand) Rents out Vespa and Yamaha scooters.

SHARED TAXI

In Cape Town (and South Africa in general) a shared taxi means a minibus. These private services, which cover most of the city with an informal network of routes, are a cheap and fast way of getting around. On the downside, they're usually crowded and some drivers can be reckless.

The main rank is on the upper deck of Cape Town Train Station and is accessible from a walkway in the Golden Acre Centre or from stairways on Strand St. It's well organised, and finding the right rank is easy. Anywhere else, you just hail shared taxis from the side of the road and ask the driver where they're going.

TAXI

Consider taking a nonshared taxi at night or if you're in a group. Rates are about R10 per kilometre. **Uber** (www.uber.com) is very popular and works well.

Excite Taxis (☎021-448 4444; www.excitetaxis.co.za)

Marine Taxi (☎0861 434 0434, 021-447 0329; www.marinetaxis.co.za)

SA Cab (☎0861 172 222; www.sacab.co.za)

Telecab (☎082 222 0282, 021-788 2717) For transfers from Simon's Town to Boulders and Cape Point.

TRAIN

Cape Metro Rail (p613) trains are a handy way to get around, although there are few (or no) trains after 6pm on weekdays and after noon on Saturday.

The difference between MetroPlus (first-class) and Metro (economy-class) carriages in price and comfort is negligible. The most important line for visitors is the Simon's Town line, which runs through Observatory and around the back of Table Mountain through upper-income suburbs such as Newlands, on to Muizenberg and the False Bay coast. These trains run at least every hour from 6am to 9pm, and during peak times (6am to 9pm and 3pm to 6pm) as often as every 15 minutes.

Metro trains also run out to Strand on the eastern side of False Bay, and into the Winelands to Stellenbosch and Paarl. They are the cheapest and easiest means of transport to these areas; security is best at peak times.

Some MetroPlus/Metro fares: Observatory (R9.50/7), Muizenberg (R12.50/8.50), Simon's Town (R15.50/9.50), Paarl (R18.50/12) and Stellenbosch (R18.50/12). A tourist ticket (R30) allows unlimited one-day travel between Cape Town and Simon's Town and all stations in between.

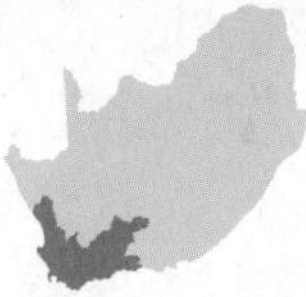

Western Cape

Includes ➜

Best Places to Eat

- ➜ Le Quartier Français: Tasting Room (p111)
- ➜ Die Strandloper (p161)
- ➜ Karoux (p121)
- ➜ Schoon de Companje (p104)
- ➜ Gallery (p156)

Best Places to Stay

- ➜ Vindoux Treehouses (p117)
- ➜ Brenton Cottages (p146)
- ➜ Nothando Backpackers Hostel (p148)
- ➜ Oudebosch Eco Cabins (p122)
- ➜ Arniston Spa Hotel (p132)

Why Go?

The splendours of the Western Cape lie not only in its world-class vineyards, stunning beaches and mountains, but also in lesser-known regions, such as the wide-open spaces of the Karoo, the nature reserves and the wilderness areas. Make sure you get out into these wild, less-visited areas for bird-watching and wildlife adventure as well as pure relaxation under vast skies.

The Western Cape offers a huge range of activities, from sedate endeavours such as wine tasting and scenic drives to more hair-raising encounters such as skydiving and rock climbing.

The melting pot of cultures in the region also begs to be explored. Khoe-San rock art is at its best in the Cederberg mountains and there are some fine opportunities to visit black townships and be entranced by the fascinating culture of the Xhosa people.

When to Go

Knysna

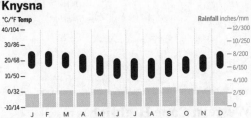

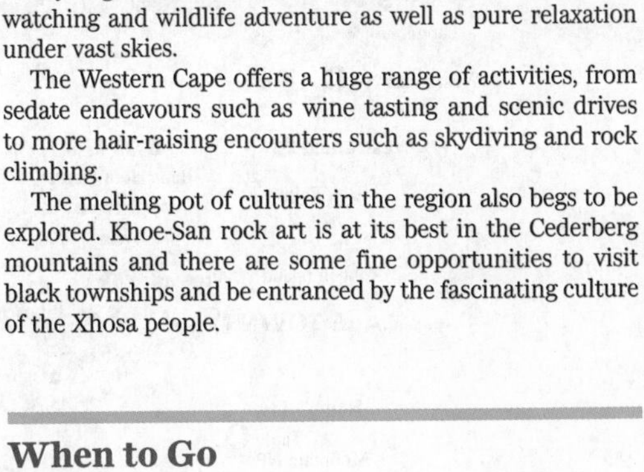

Feb, Mar & Nov Temperatures are perfect: not too hot to hike but still beach weather.

Jun–Aug Whale-watching season begins; flowers bloom on the West Coast.

Dec–Jan Prices rise and visitor numbers increase. Hot days and abundant festivals.

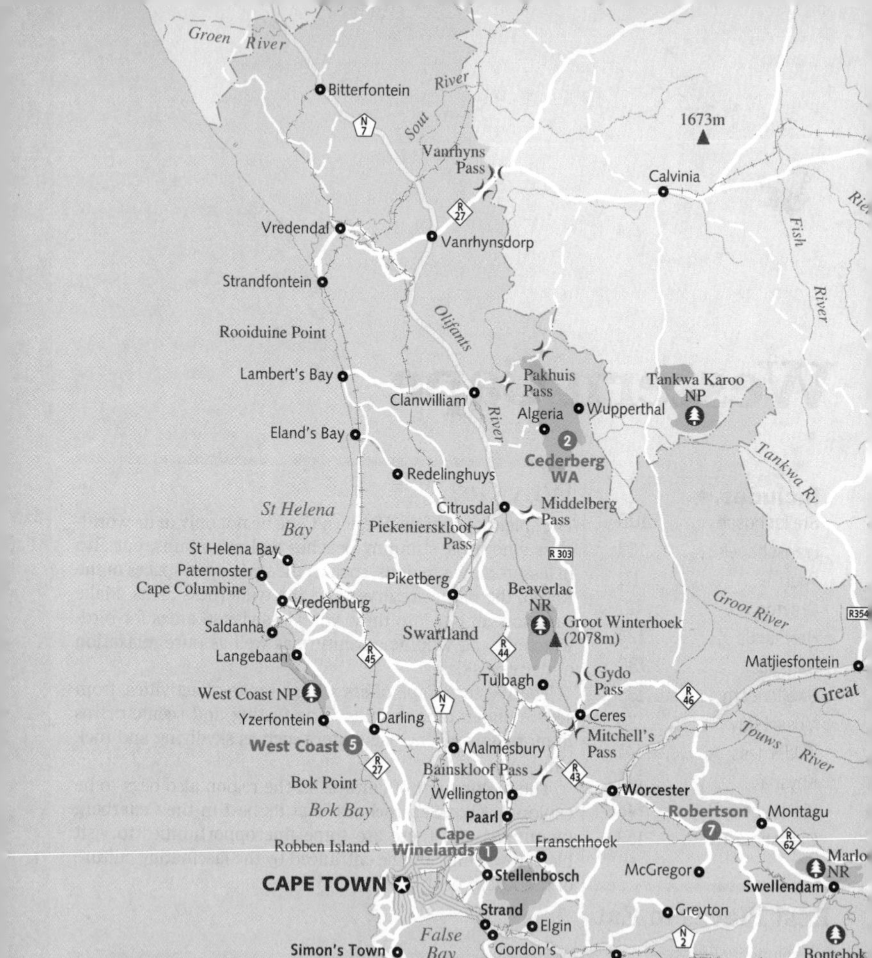

Western Cape Highlights

1. Sampling magnificent wines – and food – in the historic towns of the **Cape Winelands** (p100).
2. Exploring Khoe-San culture and hiking past bizarre rock formations in the **Cederberg Wilderness Area** (p162).
3. Taking the spectacularly scenic coastal drive through Betty's Bay to **Hermanus** (p124), then walking the cliff path to watch for whales.
4. Hiking the **Knysna** (p143) forests or feasting on oysters from the lagoon.

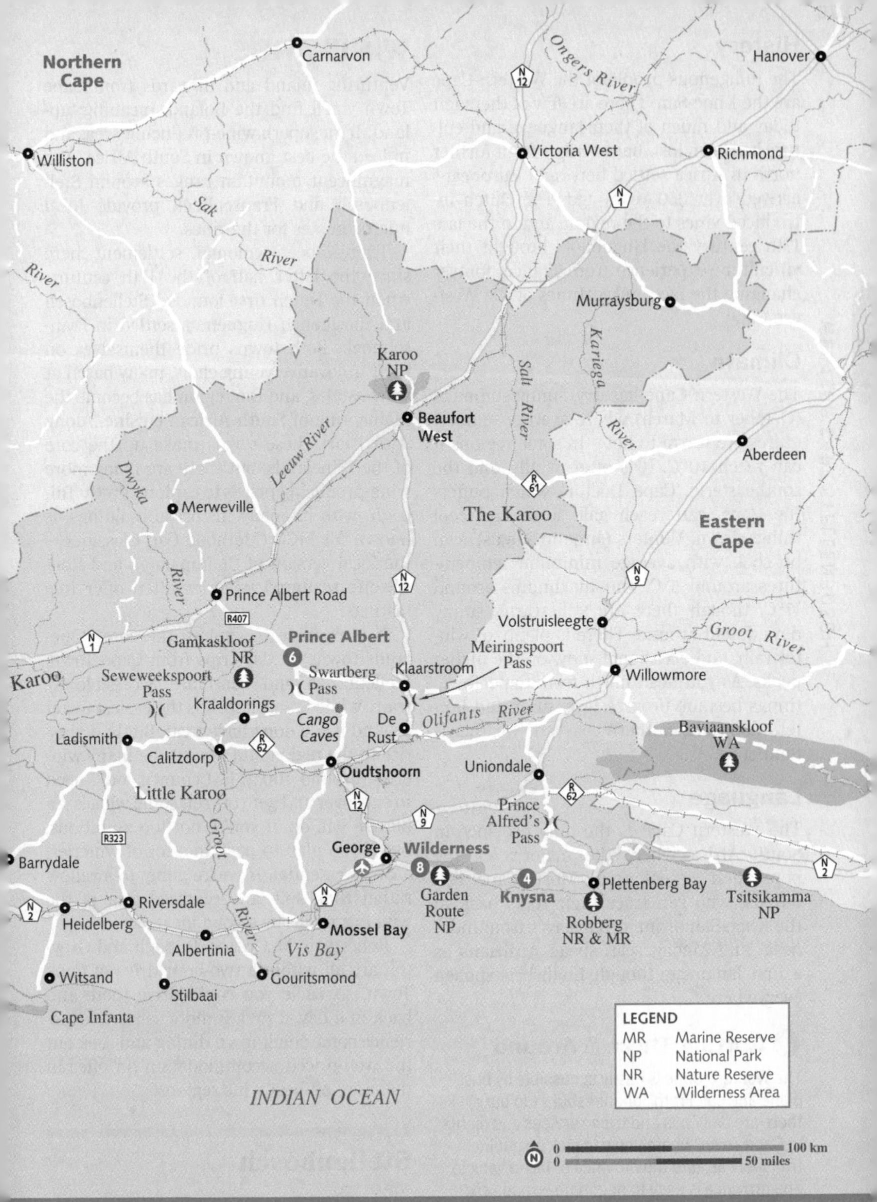

5 Learning to kite-surf on the **West Coast** (p158) and rewarding yourself with a beachside seafood extravaganza.

6 Feasting on fine food and enjoying Karoo hospitality in **Prince Albert** (p156).

7 Getting away from the sipping crowds in the lesser-visited wine region around **Robertson** (p118).

8 Walking along the windswept beach and kayaking the lagoons of **Wilderness** (p141).

History

The indigenous people of the Western Cape are the Khoe-San. There are few of them left today and much of their language and culture has been lost. Bantu tribes from further north in Africa settled here, and Europeans arrived over 350 years ago. The Dutch introduced vines to the region, and in the late 17th century the Huguenots brought their viticulture experience from France, forever changing the face and fortunes of the Western Cape.

Climate

The Western Cape has dry, sunny summers (October to March) where average temperatures are warm to hot – in some regions it can reach 40°C. It is often windy, and the southeasterly 'Cape Doctor', which buffets the Cape, can reach gale force and cool things down. Winters (June to August) can be cool, with average minimum temperatures around 5°C, and maximums around 17°C, though there are still warm, sunny days dotted around. There is plenty of winter rain, and occasional snow on the higher peaks. As you head north from Cape Town, things become progressively drier and hotter. Along the southern coast the weather is temperate.

Language

The Western Cape is the only province in South Africa where the majority of the population is coloured. Most 'Cape coloureds', who can trace their roots back to the Khoe-San or imported slaves from Indonesia and Madagascar, speak Afrikaans as a first language, though English is spoken everywhere.

ℹ Getting There & Around

The Western Cape is easily accessible by bus, plane and car. From Johannesburg (Jo'burg) there are daily bus and train services and flights to Cape Town, where you can pick up public transport around the province or hire a vehicle. The province is easy to negotiate – roads are good and distances are not too long. **Baz Bus** (☎0861 229 287; www.bazbus.com; 14-day pass R3400) offers a hop-on/hop-off shuttle service through the major towns of the Winelands, Overberg and Garden Route.

WINELANDS

Venturing inland and upwards from Cape Town you'll find the Boland, meaning 'upland'. It's a superb wine-producing area, and indeed the best known in South Africa. The magnificent mountain ranges around Stellenbosch and Franschhoek provide ideal microclimates for the vines.

There's been colonial settlement here since the latter half of the 17th century, when the Dutch first founded Stellenbosch and the French Huguenots settled in Franschhoek. Both towns pride themselves on their innovative young chefs, many based at wine estates, and the region has become the mainspring of South African cuisine. Along with Paarl, these towns make up the core of the Winelands, but there are many more wine-producing places to explore. Pretty Tulbagh, with its many historical buildings, is known for MCC (Méthode Cap Classique – the local version of Champagne), and Robertson's scattered wineries often offer free tastings.

It is possible to explore the core Winelands towns on day trips from Cape Town. Stellenbosch and Paarl are accessible by train, while Franschhoek is the easiest to get around if you don't have a car. But to do justice to the region and to visit the many wineries (around 400 at last count), you'll need to stay over and get yourself some wheels – a bicycle will do, if you're not too ambitious, but if you plan to pack in a lot of wineries, a car is essential. If you're going to swallow rather than spit, an organised tour of the wineries might be a good idea.

Robertson, McGregor, Tulbagh and Greyton are all within a two-hour drive of Cape Town, so while you could drive there and back in a day, it makes more sense to experience some small-town dining and seek out the well-priced accommodation on offer in the more off-beat wine regions.

Stellenbosch

POP 55,000

Stellenbosch is an elegant, historical town with stately Cape Dutch, Georgian and Victorian architecture along its oak-lined streets – and it is so much more than that. Full of interesting museums, quality hotels and a selection of bars, clubs and restaurants, it is constantly abuzz with locals, students, Capetonians and tourists.

Established by the governor of the Cape in 1679 on the banks of the Eerste River, Stellenbosch was – and still is – famed for its rich soil, just what was needed to produce vegetables and wine for ships stopping off at the Cape.

Sights & Activities

In Stellenbosch

Village Museum MUSEUM
(Map p102; www.stelmus.co.za; 18 Ryneveld St; adult/child R35/15; 9am-5pm Mon-Sat, 10am-4pm Sun) A group of exquisitely restored and period-furnished houses dating from 1709 to 1850 make up this museum, which occupies the entire city block bounded by Ryneveld, Plein, Drostdy and Church Sts and is a must-see. Also included are charming gardens and, on the other side of Drostdy St, stately **Grosvenor House** (Map p102).

Toy & Miniature Museum MUSEUM
(Map p102; 42 Market St, Rhenish Parsonage; adult/child R20/10; 9am-4pm Mon-Fri, 9am-2pm Sat) This delightful museum features a remarkable collection of detailed toys ranging from railway sets to dollhouses. The real highlight, though, is a chat with curator Philip Kleynhans, who is as passionate about local history and architecture as he is about the charming museum exhibits.

Braak PARK
(Map p102; Town Sq) At the north end of the Braak, an open stretch of grass, you'll find the neo-Gothic **St Mary's on the Braak Church** (Map p102; 021-887 6913; Braak; by appt 9am-4pm Mon-Fri) FREE, completed in 1852. West of the church is the **VOC Kruithuis** (Powder House; Map p102; adult/child R5/2; 9am-2pm Mon-Fri Sep-May), built in 1777 to store the town's weapons and gunpowder – it now houses a small military museum. On the northwest corner of the square is **Fick House** (Burgerhuis; Map p102), a fine example of Cape Dutch architecture from the late 18th century.

Bergkelder WINERY
(Map p102; 021-809 8025; www.bergkelder.co.za; tastings R40; 8am-5pm Mon-Fri, 9am-2pm Sat) For wine lovers without wheels, this cellar a short walk from the town centre is ideal. Hour-long tours are followed by an atmospheric candle-lit tasting in the cellar. The tours run at 10am, 11am, 2pm and 3pm Monday to Friday, and at 10am, 11am and noon Saturday. A wine and salt pairing (R75) is also on offer. Bookings are required for all activities.

> **WALKING STELLENBOSCH**
>
> If you need to walk off all those wine tastings, you could take a **guided walk** (per person R100; 11am & 3pm Mon-Fri, 9.30am Sat & Sun) from **Stellenbosch Tourism** (p107). Bookings are essential for weekend walks.

University Museum MUSEUM
(Map p102; 52 Ryneveld St; admission by donation; 10am-4.30pm Mon, 9am-4.30pm Tue-Sat) This fabulous Flemish Renaissance-style building houses an interesting and varied collection of local art, an array of African anthropological treasures and exhibits on South African culture and history.

Around Stellenbosch

There is an abundance of good wineries in the Stellenbosch area. Get the free booklet *Stellenbosch and its Wine Routes* from Stellenbosch Tourism for a more complete picture.

★**Villiera** WINERY
(Map p106; 021-865 2002; www.villiera.com; tastings free; 9am-5pm Mon-Fri, 9am-3pm Sat) Villiera produces several excellent Méthode Cap Classique wines and a highly rated and very well-priced shiraz. Excellent two-hour wildlife drives (R150 per person) with knowledgeable guides take in the various antelope, zebras and bird species on the farm.

Warwick Estate WINERY
(Map p106; 021-884 4410; www.warwickwine.com; tastings R25, wine safari R50; 10am-5pm;) Warwick's red wines are legendary, particularly its bordeaux blends. The winery offers an informative 'Big Five' wine safari (referring to grape varieties, not large mammals) through the vineyards and picnics to enjoy on the lawns.

Spier WINERY
(Map p106; 021-809 1100; www.spier.co.za; tastings from R38; 10am-5pm;) Spier has some excellent shiraz, cabernet and red blends, though a visit to this vast winery is less about wine and more about the other activities available. There are bird of prey displays, Segway tours through the vines,

Stellenbosch

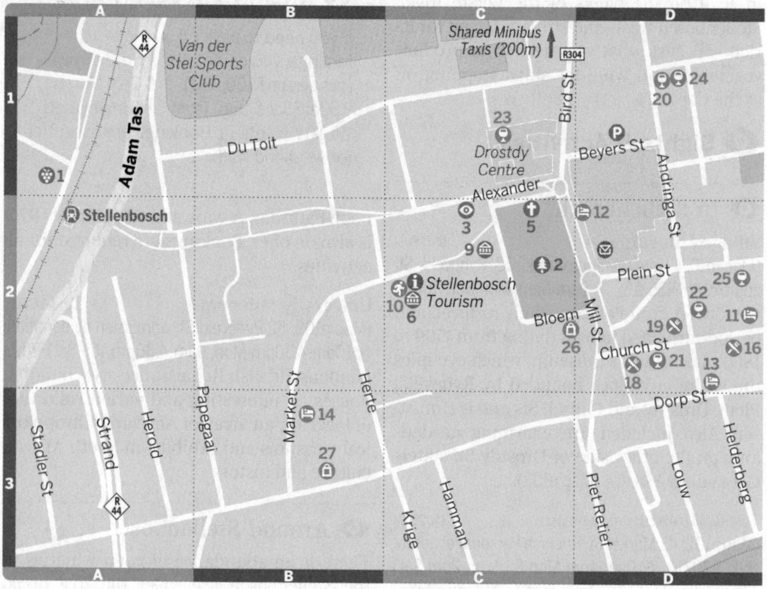

Stellenbosch

Sights
1 Bergkelder ... A1
2 Braak ... C2
3 Fick House ... C2
4 Grosvenor House ... E2
5 St Mary's on the Braak Church ... C2
6 Toy & Miniature Museum ... C2
7 University Museum ... E1
8 Village Museum ... E2
9 VOC Kruithuis ... C2

Activities, Courses & Tours
10 Adventure Shop ... C2
Easy Rider Wine Tours ... (see 14)

Sleeping
11 D'Ouwe Werf ... D2
12 Ikhaya Backpackers ... D2
13 Stellenbosch Hotel ... D2
14 Stumble Inn ... B3

Eating
15 Decameron ... E2
16 Helena's ... D2
17 Katjiepiering Restaurant ... F1
18 Schoon de Companje ... D2
19 Wijnhuis ... D2

Drinking & Nightlife
20 Bohemia ... D1
21 Brampton Wine Studio ... D2
22 Craft Wheat & Hops ... D2
23 Drostdy Centre ... C1
24 Mystic Boer ... D1
25 Nu Bar ... D2

Shopping
26 Craft Market ... C2
27 Oom Samie se Winkel ... B3

two restaurants, and picnics to enjoy in the grounds. Look out for special events, particularly the Spier Winelands Express, a train trip running from Cape Town in the summer months.

Hartenberg Estate WINERY
(Map p106; ☎021-865 2541; www.hartenbergestate.com; Bottelary Rd; tastings R25; ⏲9am-5pm Mon-Fri, 9am-4pm Sat year-round, 10am-4pm Sun Oct-Apr) Thanks to a favourable microclimate, Hartenberg produces superlative red wines, particularly cabernet, merlot and shiraz. Lunch is available (bookings essential) and from October to April picnics (R175) can be arranged to take on a wetland walk through the estate.

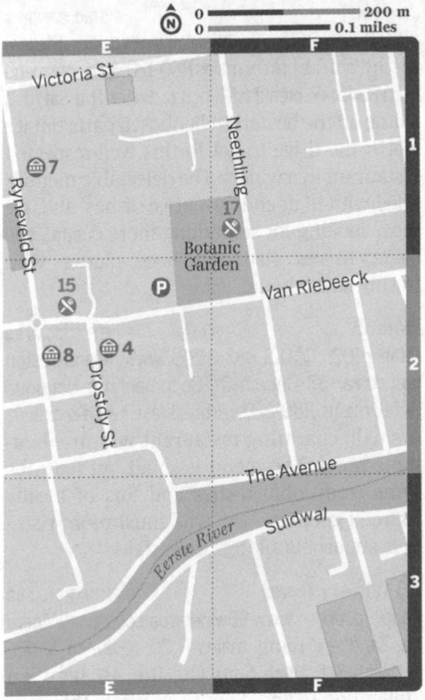

Van Ryn Brandy Cellar DISTILLERY
(Map p106; ☎021-881 3875; www.vanryn.co.za; tour & tastings from R50; ⏰9am-5.30pm Mon-Fri, to 3.30pm Sat year-round, 11am-3pm Sun Oct-Apr) This brandy distillery runs superb tours, which include a barrel-making display and end with your choice of tasting. Options include pairing brandy with chocolate or charcuterie and sampling brandy cocktails.

Jonkershoek Nature Reserve NATURE RESERVE
(www.capenature.co.za; Jonkershoek Rd; adult/child R40/20; ⏰7.30am-4pm) This small nature reserve is 8km southeast of town and set within a timber plantation. There is a 10km scenic drive, plus hiking trails ranging from 5km to 18km. A hiking map is available at the entrance.

Tours

★Bikes 'n Wines TOUR
(Map p106; ☎021-823 8790; www.bikesnwines.com; per person R550-790) This carbon-negative company comes highly recommended. Cycling routes range from 9km to 21km and take in three or four local wineries.

Easy Rider Wine Tours TOUR
(Map p102; ☎021-886 4651; www.winetour.co.za; 12 Market St) This long-established company operates from the Stumble Inn and offers good value for a full-day trip at R500 including lunch and all tastings.

Vine Hopper TOUR
(☎021-882 8112; www.vinehopper.co.za; 1-day pass R240) A hop-on/hop-off bus with two routes each covering six estates. There are five tours per day, departing from Stellenbosch Tourism (p107), where you can buy tickets.

Festivals & Events

Wine Festival WINE
(www.wineroute.co.za) This event in late January and early February offers visitors the chance to sample up to 400 different drops in one spot as well as attend talks and tutorials on wine.

Sleeping

Contact Stellenbosch Tourism (p107) for sleeping options if your initial choices are booked up.

★Banghoek Place BACKPACKERS $
(Map p106; ☎021-887 0048; www.banghoek.co.za; 193 Banghoek Rd; dm/r R150/600;) This stylish suburban hostel is a quieter budget alternative, away from the town centre. The recreation area has satellite TV and a pool table and there's a nice swimming pool in the garden.

Ikhaya Backpackers BACKPACKERS $
(Map p102; ☎021-883 8550; www.stellenboschbackpackers.co.za; 56 Bird St; dm/d without bathroom R130/370;) The superb, central location means you're within easy stumbling distance of the bars. Rooms are in converted apartments, so each dorm comes with its own kitchen and bathroom, shared with the adjoining double rooms.

Stumble Inn BACKPACKERS $
(Map p102; ☎021-887 4049; www.stumbleinnbackpackers.co.za; 12 Market St; camping R50, dm R130, d without bathroom R370;) Stellenbosch's undisputed party hostel is split over two old houses – the second building is the quieter option, away from the bar. Travellers have expressed concerns about security so take extra care with your belongings.

Stellenbosch Hotel HISTORIC HOTEL $$
(Map p102; ☎021-887 3644; www.stellenboschhotel.co.za; 162 Dorp St, cnr Andringa St; s/d incl breakfast from R880/1100;) A comfortable country-style hotel with a variety of rooms, including some with self-catering facilities and others with four-poster beds. A section

dating from 1743 houses the Jan Cats Brasserie, a good spot for a drink. The hotel and restaurant were undergoing rennovations when we visited.

Summerwood Guesthouse GUESTHOUSE $$$
(Map p106; ☎021-887 4112; www.summerwood.co.za; 28 Jonkershoek Rd; s/d incl breakfast R1310/2150; ❄📶🏊) In a suburban neighbourhood bordering a small nature reserve east of the town centre is this elegant guesthouse. The immaculate rooms are bright and spacious, with excellent amenities. Rates drop dramatically between April and September.

D'Ouwe Werf HISTORIC HOTEL $$$
(Map p102; ☎021-887 4608; www.ouwewerf.co.za; 30 Church St; d incl breakfast from R2000; ❄📶🏊) This appealing, old-style hotel dates back to 1802, though it had just undergone major refurbishments when we visited. The more expensive luxury rooms are furnished with antiques and brass beds, while the standard rooms are bright and modern.

Lanzerac Hotel & Spa LUXURY HOTEL $$$
(Map p106; ☎021-887 1132; www.lanzerac.co.za; Lanzerac Rd, Jonkershoek Valley; s/d/ste incl breakfast from R2960/3950/6500; ❄📶🏊) This opulent place consists of a 300-year-old manor house and winery set in grassy grounds with awesome mountain views. One suite even has a private pool.

Eating

Stellenbosch is a gourmet's delight, with a plethora of restaurants and bars. The surrounding wineries have some of the most interesting and innovative options in the country.

★Schoon de Companje DELI $
(Map p102; www.decompanje.co.za; 7 Church St; mains R50-100; ⏲breakfast & lunch Tue-Sun, pizzas served until 6pm) A vibrant bakery and deli priding itself on locally sourced ingredients. The menu features salads, sandwiches and mezze-style platters, as well as fresh cakes and pastries and local craft beer. There are tables on the pavement, while inside has a market-hall feel, with plenty of seating and some shops to browse.

Katjiepiering Restaurant CAFE $
(Map p102; Van Riebeeck St; mains R50-120; ⏲9am-5pm) Tucked away in the corner of the botanic garden and surrounded by exotic plants, this is a lovely spot for coffee, cake or a light lunch. Some traditional meals are served.

Jordan BISTRO, BAKERY $
(☎021-881 3612; www.jordanwines.com; Stellenbosch Kloof Rd; bakery mains R60-120, 3-course menu from R345; ⏲breakfast, lunch & dinner Thu-Sat) It's a little off the beaten Stellenbosch path, but it's worth the drive to get to this well-respected restaurant in a winery. The delectable menu is filled with high-end, inventive dishes, and, for those looking for something more casual, the bakery serves salads and cheese platters with freshly baked bread.

Helena's SOUTH AFRICAN $$
(Map p102; ☎021-883 3132; www.helenasrestaurant.co.za; 33 Church St, Coopmanhuijs Boutique Hotel; mains R80-220; ⏲breakfast, lunch & dinner) A small, charming restaurant within a boutique hotel. The menu is small but features some traditional dishes and lots of locally sourced goodies – the wild mushroom risotto is superb. Bookings essential.

96 Winery Road INTERNATIONAL $$
(Map p106; www.96wineryroad.co.za; Winery Rd, Zandberg Farm; mains R120; ⏲lunch & dinner Mon-Sat, lunch Sun) Off Rte 44 between Stellenbosch and Somerset West, this is a long-established restaurant, known for its dry aged beef.

Wijnhuis ITALIAN $$
(Map p102; www.wijnhuis.co.za; Andringa St, cnr Church St; mains R100-210; ⏲lunch & dinner) There's an interesting menu and an extensive wine list stretching to more than 500 labels. Around 20 wines are available by the glass and tastings are available (R50).

Decameron ITALIAN $$
(Map p102; 50 Plein St; mains R70-190; ⏲lunch & dinner Mon-Sat, lunch Sun) This Italian-food stalwart of Stellenbosch's dining scene has a shady patio next to the botanic gardens.

★Rust en Vrede FUSION $$$
(Map p106; ☎021-881 3757; www.rustenvrede.com; Annandale Rd; 4-course menu R620, 6-course menu with/without wines R1150/750; ⏲dinner Tue-Sat) Chef John Shuttleworth prepares contemporary takes on the classics at this winery restaurant.

Overture Restaurant FUSION $$$
(Map p106; ☎021-880 2721; Hidden Valley Wine Estate, off Annandale Rd; 3 courses R375, 6-course menu R540; ⏲lunch Wed-Sun, dinner Thu-Sat) A very modern wine estate and restaurant where TV chef Bertus Basson focuses on local, seasonal produce paired with Hidden Valley wines.

LOCAL KNOWLEDGE

THE ELGIN VALLEY

After you reach the top of Sir Lowry's Pass in the Hottentots Holland mountains east of Somerset West, you will begin to descend into apple country. The region around Elgin and Grabouw is close enough to visit on a day trip from Cape Town but is little known to travellers – its wineries (known for sauvignon blanc, chardonnay and pinot noir), hiking trails and other activities remain uncrowded.

Paul Cluver Wines (www.cluver.com; N2, Grabouw; ⏲9am-5pm Mon-Fri, 10am-2pm Sat & Sun) A worthy stop on the Elgin wine route, offering fine wine, a pleasant country-style restaurant and mountain-bike trails.

Green Mountain Trail (www.greenmountaintrail.co.za) A four-day 'slackpacking' hike through the mountains, where your bags are transported as you hike in relative luxury – think white-tableclothed picnics with fine wines and, at the end of the day, a handsome country manor to stay in.

Canopy Tour (www.canopytour.co.za; per person R595) If you are after an exhilarating way to experience the mountains, explore the Hottentots Holland Nature Reserve from above, sliding along a network of cables and resting in the trees as your guide gives punchy ecology lessons.

Peregrine Farmstall (N2; ⏲7.30am-6pm) Locals love to stop for a freshly baked pie and some just-pressed apple juice before heading off on a road trip.

Drinking & Nightlife

Stellenbosch's nightlife scene is geared largely towards the interests of the university students, but there are classier options. It's safe to walk around the centre at night, so a pub crawl could certainly be on the cards (if you're staying at the Stumble Inn one will probably be organised for you).

★Brampton Wine Studio WINE BAR
(Map p102; ☎021-883 9097; www.brampton.co.za; 11 Church St; ⏲9am-7.30pm Mon-Fri, from 10am Sat) Play games and scribble on tables while sipping shiraz at this trendy pavement cafe that also serves as Brampton winery's tasting room. Sandwiches and wraps (R50 to R70) are served throughout the day.

Drostdy Centre BAR
(Map p102; off Bird St) Dros, the Terrace and Tollies, clustered in this complex just north of the Braak, are among Stellenbosch's liveliest bars. There's a nightclub here too.

Craft Wheat & Hops BEER
(Map p102; Andringa St; ⏲11am-9.30pm Mon-Sat) This place has 15 local microbrewed beers on tap and another dozen in bottles. There's also a decent wine list and a great selection of spirits. Open sandwiches (R40 to R60) are served and there's a nice tapas menu available after 4pm.

Bohemia BAR
(Map p102; Victoria St, cnr Andringa St) A chilled, student-filled place that also serves lunch – opt for the pizza. There's often live music as well as regular drinks specials.

Mystic Boer BAR
(Map p102; www.diemysticboer.co.za; 3 Victoria St) This funky bar is a Stellenbosch institution. There's regular live music and decent bar food.

Nu Bar CLUB
(Map p102; www.nubar.co.za; 51 Plein St) This club has a small dance floor beyond the long bar where DJs pump out hip-hop and house.

Entertainment

★Oude Libertas Amphitheatre ARTS
(Map p106; www.oudelibertas.co.za; Oude Libertas Rd) Open-air performances of theatre, music and dance are held here from November to March.

Shopping

Craft Market MARKET
(Map p102; Braak; ⏲9am-5pm Mon-Sat) This open-air market is a great place to haggle for African carvings, paintings and costume jewellery.

Oom Samie se Winkel SOUVENIRS
(Uncle Sammy's Shop; Map p102; 84 Dorp St; ⏲8.30am-6pm Mon-Fri, 9am-5pm Sat & Sun)

Around Stellenbosch

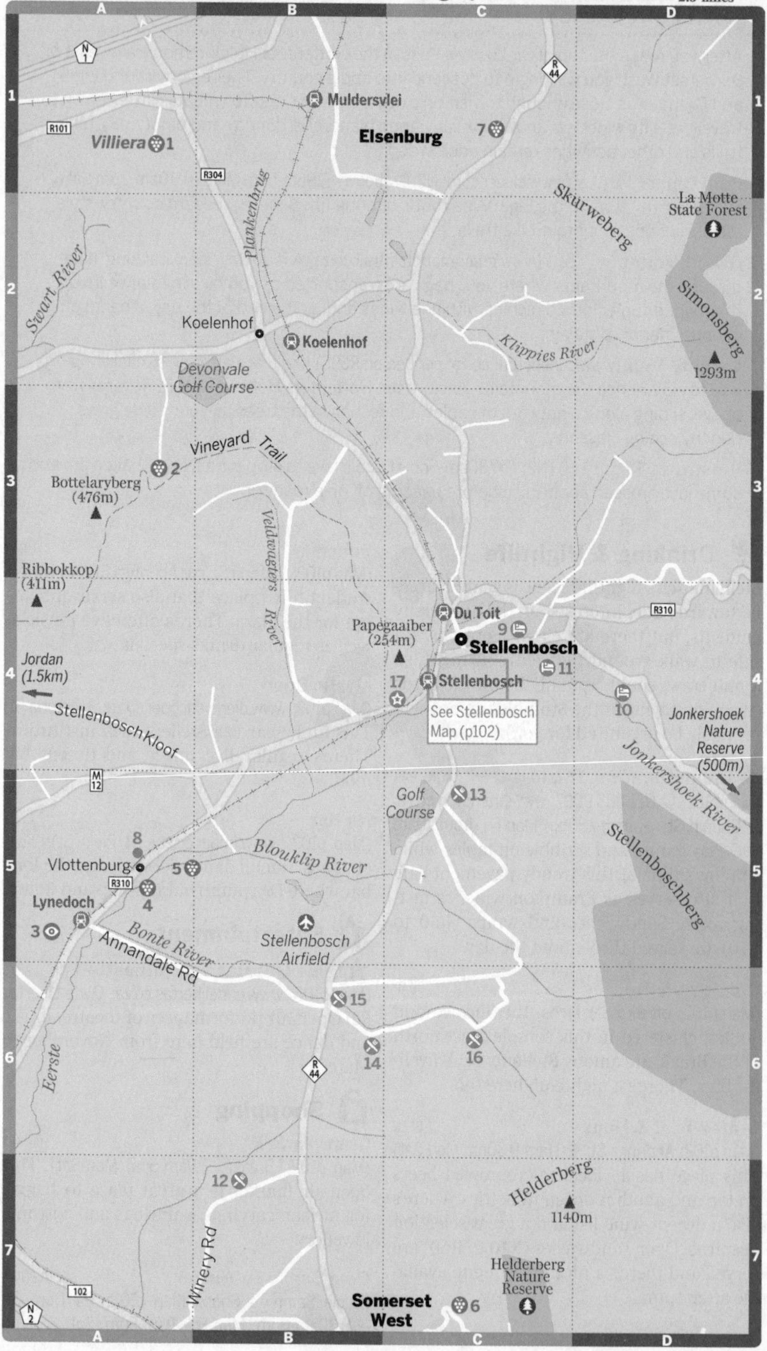
0 5 km
0 2.5 miles
A
B
C
D
1
2
3
4
5
6
7
N1
R44
R101
R304
R310
M12
102
N2
Muldersvlei
Elsenburg
Villiera 1
7
Plankenbrug
Skurweberg
La Motte State Forest
Swart River
Simonsberg
Koelenhof
Koelenhof
Klippies River
1293m
Devonvale Golf Course
Vineyard Trail
2
Bottelaryberg (476m)
Veldwagters River
Ribbokkop (411m)
Du Toit
9
Papegaaiber (254m)
Stellenbosch
11
Jordan (1.5km)
17
Stellenbosch
10
Stellenbosch Kloof
See Stellenbosch Map (p102)
Jonkershoek Nature Reserve (500m)
Jonkershoek River
Golf Course
13
8
Stellenboschberg
Vlottenburg
5
Blouklip River
4
Lynedoch
3
Stellenbosch Airfield
Bonte River
Annandale Rd
15
14
16
Eerste
12
Helderberg
1140m
Winery Rd
Helderberg Nature Reserve
Somerset West
6

Around Stellenbosch

Top Sights

1	Villiera	A1

Sights

2	Hartenberg Estate	A3
3	Lynedoch EcoVillage	A5
4	Spier	A5
5	Van Ryn Brandy Cellar	A5
6	Vergelegen	C7
7	Warwick Estate	C1

Activities, Courses & Tours

8	Bikes 'n Wines	A5

Sleeping

9	Banghoek Place	C4
10	Lanzerac Hotel & Spa	D4
11	Summerwood Guesthouse	C4

Eating

12	96 Winery Road	B7
13	Blaauwklippen Market	C5
14	Overture Restaurant	B6
15	Root 44 Market	B6
16	Rust en Vrede	C6

Entertainment

17	Oude Libertas Amphitheatre	C4

This place was on the Stellenbosch map before Stellenbosch was on the map. It's an unashamedly touristy general dealer but still worth visiting for its curious range of goods – everything from joke-shop tat to African crafts and local foodstuffs.

Information

Stellenbosch Tourism (Map p102; 021-883 3584; www.stellenboschtourism.co.za; 36 Market St; 8am-5pm Mon-Fri, 9am-2pm Sat & Sun;) The staff are extremely helpful. Pick up the excellent brochure *Historical Stellenbosch on Foot* (R5), with a walking-tour map and information on many of the historic buildings (also available in French and German).

Getting There & Away

Long-distance bus services charge high prices for the short sector to Cape Town and do not take bookings. The **Baz Bus** (0861 229 287; www.bazbus.com) runs daily to and from Cape Town (R260, 30 minutes).

Shared taxis to Paarl leave from the stand on Bird St (about R50, 45 minutes).

Metro trains run the 46km between Cape Town and Stellenbosch (1st/economy class R18.50/12, about one hour). For inquiries, call **Metrorail** (021-449 6478; www.metrorail.co.za). To be safe, travel in the middle of the day. If coming from Jo'burg, change to a metro train at Wellington.

Getting Around

Stellenbosch is navigable on foot and, being largely flat, is good cycling territory. Bikes can be hired from the **Adventure Shop** (Map p102; 021-882 8112; www.adventureshop.co.za; cnr Dorp & Mark Sts; per day R150), next to Stellenbosch Tourism.

For an economical way to get about town, try **Tuk Tuk Stellies** (076 011 3016; corne@tuktukstellies.co.za).

Franschhoek

POP 17,500

French Huguenots settled in this spectacular valley over 300 years ago, bringing their vines with them. Ever since, the town has clung to its French roots, and July visitors will find Bastille Day celebrated with boules matches, berets and brie. Franschhoek bills itself as the country's gastronomic capital, and you'll certainly have a tough time deciding where to eat. Plus, with a clutch of art galleries, wine farms and stylish guesthouses thrown in, it really is one of the loveliest towns in the Cape.

Sights & Activities

In Franschhoek

Huguenot Memorial Museum MUSEUM
(Map p108; www.museum.co.za; Lambrecht St; adult/child R10/2; 9am-5pm Mon-Sat, 2-5pm Sun) This museum celebrates South Africa's Huguenots and houses the genealogical records of their descendants. Behind the main complex is a pleasant cafe, in front is the **Huguenot Monument** (Map p108; 9am-5pm) FREE, opened in 1948, and across the road is the **annexe** (Map p108), which offers displays on the Anglo-Boer War and natural history.

Huguenot Fine Chocolates FOOD
(Map p108; 021-876 4096; www.huguenotchocolates.com; 62 Huguenot St; 8am-5.30pm Mon-Fri, 9am-5.30pm Sat & Sun) An empowerment program gave the two local guys who run this chocolatier a leg up and now people are raving about their confections. There are daily chocolate-making demonstrations including a tasting (R40) at 11am and 3pm – advance bookings recommended.

Franschhoek

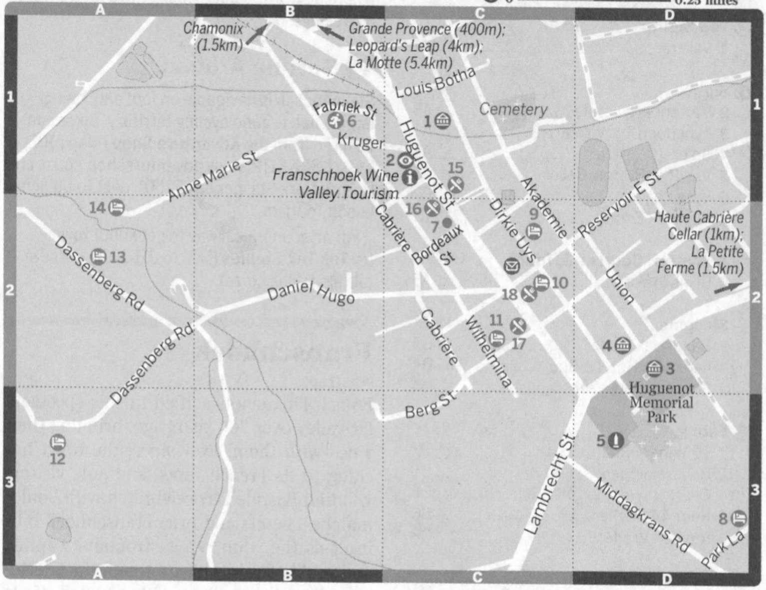

Franschhoek

Sights
1 Ceramics Gallery C1
2 Huguenot Fine Chocolates C1
3 Huguenot Memorial Museum D2
4 Huguenot Memorial Museum Annexe D2
5 Huguenot Monument D3

Activities, Courses & Tours
6 Franschhoek Cycles B1
7 Franschhoek Wine Tram C2

Sleeping
8 La Cabrière Country House D3
9 La Fontaine C2
10 Le Ballon Rouge C2
11 Le Quartier Français C2
12 Mont Rochelle Hotel A3
13 Otter's Bend Lodge A2
14 Reeden Lodge A2

Eating
15 Franschhoek Market C1
16 French Connection C2
17 Le Quartier Français: Living Room C2
Le Quartier Français: Tasting Room .... (see 17)
18 Reuben's C2

Ceramics Gallery GALLERY
(Map p108; ☎021-876 4304; www.davidwalters.co.za; 24 Dirkie Uys St; ⏲10am-6pm) Franschhoek boasts many fine galleries, mostly along Huguenot St. At the Ceramics Gallery you can watch David Walters, one of South Africa's most distinguished potters, at work in the beautifully restored home of Franschhoek's first teacher. There are also exhibits of work by other artists.

Franschhoek Wine Tram TOUR
(Map p108; ☎021-300 0338; www.winetram.co.za; 32 Huguenot Rd; adult/child R200/85) If you'd rather ditch the car and properly enjoy the tasting rooms, this is a fun alternative to the usual Winelands tour. The actual tram line is short and only two wineries have a tram stop. The rest of the hop-on, hop-off service makes use of an open-sided bus to shuttle passengers between the wine farms. There are two routes, each visiting up to seven wineries. Bookings advisable and dress warmly – the bus in particular can get pretty chilly.

Paradise Stables HORSE RIDING
(☎021-876 2160; www.paradisestables.co.za; per hr R200; ⏲Mon-Sat) As well as hourly rides

through Franschhoek's surrounds, there are four-hour trips taking in two vineyards (R750 including tastings).

Franschhoek Cycles CYCLING
(Map p108; www.franschhoekcycles.co.za; Fabriek St; half/full day R190/290) Rent bikes or have staff arrange a guided cycling tour of surrounding wineries (R385).

Around Franschhoek

There are some wineries within walking distance of the town centre, but you need your own wheels or to join a tour to really experience Franschhoek's wines.

★Boschendal WINERY
(Map p114; ☎021-870 4210; www.boschendal.com; Rte 310, Groot Drakenstein; tastings R35, manor house R20; ⏲9am-5.30pm) This is a quintessential Winelands estate, with lovely architecture, food and wine. There are excellent vineyard (R35) and cellar tours (R25); booking is essential. For a dose of history with your wine, take the self-guided tour of the manor house. Boschendal has three eating options: the huge buffet lunch (R240) in the main restaurant, light lunches in Le Café, or a 'Le Pique Nique' hamper (adult/child R175/75; bookings essential) served under parasols on the lawn from September to May.

★La Motte WINERY
(Map p114; ☎021-876 8000; www.la-motte.com; Main Rd; tastings R50; ⏲9am-5pm Mon-Sat) There's enough to keep you occupied for a full day at this vast estate just west of Franschhoek. As well as tastings on offer of the superb shiraz range, wine-pairing lunches and dinners are served at the **Pierneef à la Motte** (R100-200; ⏲breakfast Sat & Sun, lunch Tue-Sun, dinner Thu-Sat) restaurant. The restaurant is named for South African artist Jacob Hendrik Pierneef and a collection of his work is on show at the on-site museum.

This is also the starting point for historical walks (R50) through the estate, taking in four national monuments and a milling demonstration and ending with a bread tasting (Wednesday 10am, bookings essential). If you've over-indulged, walk off a few calories on the 5km circular hike that starts at the farm.

Leopard's Leap WINERY
(Map p114; ☎021-876 8002; www.leopardsleap.co.za; Rte 45; tastings from R25, restaurant mains R60-120; ⏲9am-5pm Tue-Sat, 11am-5pm Sun; 👪) The bright, modern, barn-like tasting room has comfy couches strewn around – you can either take your tasters to enjoy at leisure or sit at the bar for a slightly more formal affair. The large lawns have a jungle gym for kids, while the rotisserie restaurant (lunch Wednesday to Sunday) offers a very affordable way to eat in the Winelands. Cooking classes are available once a month – booking ahead is essential.

> **DON'T MISS**
>
> **VERGELEGEN**
>
> **Vergelegen** (Map p106; ☎021-847 1334; www.vergelegen.co.za; Lourensford Rd, Somerset West; adult/child R10/5, tastings R30; ⏲9.30am-4pm) Simon van der Stel's son Willem first planted vines here in 1700. The buildings and elegant grounds have ravishing mountain views and a 'stately home' feel to them. You can take a tour of the gardens (R20), a cellar tour (R20) or just enjoy a tasting of four of the estate's wines. Tasting the flagship Vergelegen Red costs an extra R10.There are also two restaurants.
>
> The bistro-style **Stables** (mains R70–175) overlooks the Rose Garden. For a more upmarket meal, try **Camphors** (lunch Wed to Sun, lunch & dinner Fri & Sat). **Picnic hampers** (November to April only; R150 per person) are also available – bookings are essential for these and Camphors.

Solms-Delta WINERY
(Map p114; ☎021-874 3937; www.solms-delta.com; Delta Rd, off Rte 45; tastings R10; ⏲9am-5pm Sun & Mon, to 6pm Tue-Sat) In addition to tastings and sales, various heritage tours are available at this excellent winery. The museum covers Cape history and tells the Solms-Delta story from the perspective of farm workers throughout the years. On the culinary side, there's **Fyndraai Restaurant** (Map p114; ☎021-874 3937; www.solms-delta.com; Delta Rd, off R45; mains R130-155; ⏲lunch), serving original dishes inspired by the Cape's varied cultures and using herbs from the on-site indigenous garden. You can also opt for a picnic, to be enjoyed along an enchanting riverside trail.

Grande Provence WINERY
(www.grandeprovence.co.za; Main Rd; tastings from R40, cellar tours R25; ⏲10am-7pm, cellar tours

11am & 3pm Mon-Fri) A beautifully revamped, 18th-century manor house that is home to a stylish restaurant and a splendid gallery showcasing contemporary South African art. There is a range of tasting options, including grape-juice tasting for the kids (R20). It's within walking distance of the town centre.

Chamonix
WINERY

(☑ 021-876 8426; www.chamonix.co.za; Uitkyk St; tastings R35; ⊙9.30am-5pm) Chamonix has cellar tours at 11am and 3pm by appointment (R10). The tasting room is in a converted blacksmith's workshop; there's also a range of schnapps and grappa to sample. The restaurant, Racine (☑021-876 8426; www.chamonix.co.za; Uitkyk St; mains R100-150; ⊙lunch Tue-Sun, dinner Thu-Sat), has a lovely deck overhanging a stream. It's uphill but you can walk from the town.

🛏 Sleeping

Otter's Bend Lodge
BACKPACKERS $

(Map p108; ☑021-876 3200; Dassenberg Rd; camping per site R150, dm/d R150/450; ⚏) A delightful budget option in a town not known for affordable accommodation. Basic double rooms lead to a shared deck shaded by poplar trees, and there's space for a couple of tents on the lawn. It's a 15-minute walk from town and close to a winery.

Chamonix Guest Cottages
CHALET $

(☑021-876 8406; www.chamonix.co.za; Uitkyk St; 2-person cottage from R500) Great value, with cute, basic self-catering cottages nestled in the vineyards. There are also slightly fancier options with a forest or mountain setting.

You can walk to town (though it's a long slog uphill to get back).

★ Reeden Lodge
CHALET $$

(Map p108; ☑021-876 3174; www.reedenlodge.co.za; Anne Marie St; cottage for 2 people from R750; ⊛⚏) A good-value, terrific option for families, with well-equipped, self-catering cottages sleeping up to 10 people, situated on a farm about 10 minutes' walk from town. Parents will love the peace and quiet and their kids will love the sheep, treehouse and open space.

Le Ballon Rouge
GUESTHOUSE $$

(Map p108; ☑021-876 2651; www.ballonrouge.co.za; 7 Reservoir East St; s/d from R800/110; ⚏⊛⚏) A small guesthouse with good-quality rooms and stylish suites with stunning bathrooms.

La Cabrière Country House
GUESTHOUSE $$$

(Map p108; ☑021-876 4780; www.lacabriere.co.za; Park Lane; d incl breakfast from R1980; ⚏⊛⚏) Under new ownership and having undergone major renovations, this modern boutique guesthouse is better than ever. The sumptuously decorated rooms have underfloor heating and sweeping views to the mountains. Also available is a two-bedroom self-catering cottage in the town centre with a private pool (R2500).

La Fontaine
GUESTHOUSE $$$

(Map p108; ☑021-876 2112; www.lafontaine franschhoek.co.za; 21 Dirkie Uys St; s/d from R1200/1700; ⚏⊛⚏) A stylishly appointed, very comfortable family home featuring 14 spacious rooms with wooden floors and mountain views.

FOOD MARKETS IN THE WINELANDS
· ·

Farmers markets are South Africa's favourite foodie craze, and the Winelands has a particularly good selection. Rather than places to do your shopping, these tend to be spots for meals in situ – expect to find anything from freshly baked bread and artisanal cheese to paella, Thai snacks and spicy curries, plus piles of cake, local wine and plenty of craft beer. Here are a few of our favourites:

Blaauwklippen Market (Map p106; www.blaauwklippen.com; Rte 44, Blaauwklippen Vineyards; ⊙10am-3pm Sun; 🚸) A particularly family-friendly market with carriage and pony rides on offer.

Franschhoek Market (Map p108; www.franschhoekmarket.wozaonline.co.za; 29 Huguenot Rd; ⊙9am-2pm Sat) Based in the grounds of the church, this market has a real country fete vibe.

Root 44 Market (Map p106; www.root44.co.za; Rte 44, Audacia Winery; ⊙10am-4pm Sat & Sun) A large indoor-outdoor market with plenty of crafts and clothing as well as the usual food and drink offerings.

Mont Rochelle Hotel BOUTIQUE HOTEL **$$$**
(Map p108; ☑ 011-325 4405; www.montrochelle.
co.za; Dassenberg Rd; d incl breakfast from R4500;
❄️🛜🏊) Along with the winery of the same
name, this boutique hotel and restaurant
were bought by Richard Branson in 2014. As
you would expect, it offers gilt-edged luxury
as well as magnificent views across the valley.

Le Quartier Français BOUTIQUE HOTEL **$$$**
(Map p108; ☑ 021-876 2151; www.lqf.co.za; Wil-
helmina St, cnr Berg St; d/ste incl breakfast from
R4300/5700; ❄️🛜🏊) Set around a leafy
courtyard and pool, the guest rooms at this
fabulous hotel are very large with fireplaces,
huge beds and stylish decor. If you're feeling flush, the Four Quarters suites (R8500)
come with private pools and a butler service.

✖️ Eating

Franschhoek's compactness means it's possible to stroll around and let your nose tell you
where to eat. Many places are well established, though, and advance booking is best.

Le Quartier Français: Living Room BISTRO **$$**
(Map p108; ☑ 021-876 2151; www.lqf.co.za; 16
Huguenot St; tapas R40-95; ⊙ breakfast, lunch &
dinner) Great for breakfast, light-ish lunch-
es and delectable dinners that won't break
the bank. The menu includes Asian-inspired
tapas using African ingredients like wilde-
beest and springbok.

Lust Bistro & Bakery BISTRO **$$**
(Map p114; www.lustbistro.com; Rte 45, cnr Simon-
dium Rd; mains R75-130; ⊙ breakfast & lunch) At
Vrede en Lust winery, this is a refreshingly
unfussy place to eat in a region known for
haute cuisine. The focus is on sandwiches
and pizzas, with all bread baked freshly. Try
the sourdough pizza base. On Sunday there's
a buffet lunch where you pay by the weight
of your plate – bookings essential.

French Connection INTERNATIONAL **$$**
(Map p108; 48 Huguenot St; mains R80-165;
⊙ lunch & dinner) No-nonsense bistro-style
food using only fresh ingredients is dished
up at this deservedly popular place.

La Petite Ferme SOUTH AFRICAN **$$**
(Franschhoek Pass Rd; mains R100-180; ⊙ lunch; 🛜)
In a stupendous setting overlooking the valley,
this quaint country bistro-style restaurant has
a small menu. Sample the boutique wines and
smoked, deboned salmon trout, its delicately
flavoured signature dish. There are some luxurious rooms if you can't bear to leave.

⭐**Le Quartier Français:
Tasting Room** FUSION **$$$**
(Map p108; ☑ 021-876 2151; www.lqf.co.za; 16 Hu-
guenot St; 5-course meal with wine R750; ⊙ dinner
Tue-Sat) Tasting Room is consistently rated
as one of the world's 50 top restaurants by
Restaurant Magazine UK. If you're really
serious about food, chef Margot Janse will
whip up the gourmet, eight-course menu at
R1350 with wines.

Haute Cabrière Cellar FUSION **$$$**
(☑ 021-876 3688; Franschhoek Pass Rd; mains
R140-180; ⊙ lunch Tue-Sun, dinner Tue-Sat) As
well as the delectable and imaginative à
la carte offerings, there is a six-course set
menu with accompanying wines (R750).
Tastings (from R30) are also available at the
cellar and on Saturdays the proprietor performs the *sabrage:* slicing open a bottle of
bubbly with a sabre.

Reuben's FUSION **$$$**
(Map p108; ☑ 021-876 3772; www.reubens.co.za; 19
Huguenot St; mains R125-200; ⊙ lunch & dinner)
The flagship restaurant for this local celebri-
ty chef is a relaxed place offering fusion cui-
sine with plenty of Asian influence.

ℹ️ Information

Franschhoek Wine Valley Tourism (Map p108;
☑ 021-876 2861; www.franschhoek.org.za; 62
Huguenot St; ⊙ 8am-6pm Mon-Fri, 9am-6pm
Sat, 9am-4pm Sun) Staff can provide you
with a map of the area's scenic walks (R15)
and issue permits (R30) for hikes in the Mont
Rochelle Nature Reserve, as well as book
accommodation.

ℹ️ Getting There & Away

Franschhoek is 32km east of Stellenbosch and
32km south of Paarl. The best way to reach Fran-
schhoek is in your own vehicle. Some visitors
choose to cycle from Stellenbosch, but roads are
winding and can be treacherous. Normal out-of-
shape souls can take a shared taxi from Stellen-
bosch (R20) or Paarl station (R22). A private taxi
is an option: try **Call a Cab** (☑ 082 256 6784).

Paarl

POP 112,000

Surrounded by mountains and vineyards,
and set on the banks of the Berg River, Paarl
is the Winelands' largest town. It's often
overlooked by people heading for Stellen-
bosch and Franschhoek, but it does have
its own charm, including interesting Cape

Paarl

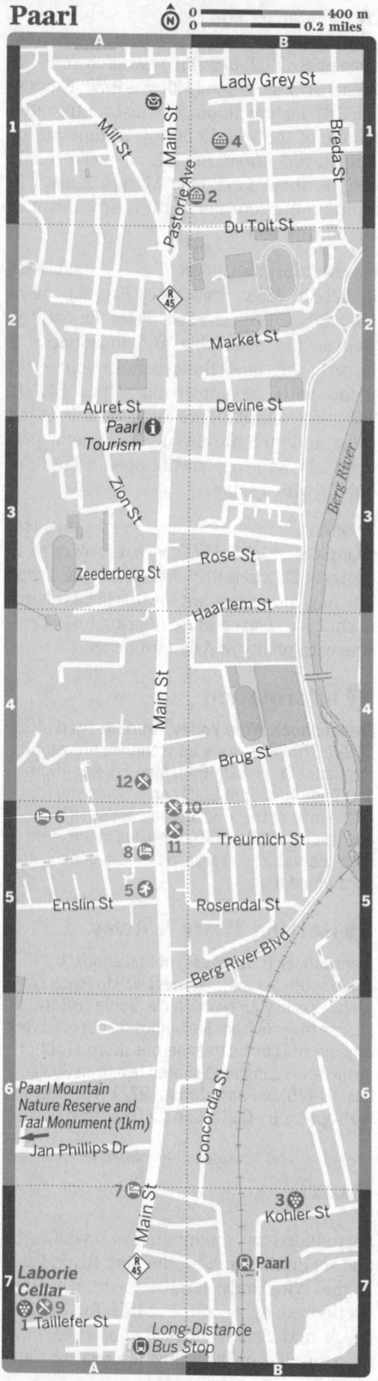

Paarl

Top Sights

1 Laborie Cellar A7

Sights

2 Afrikaans Language Museum B1
3 KWV Emporium B7
4 Paarl Museum B1

Activities, Courses & Tours

5 Wineland Ballooning A5

Sleeping

6 Grande Roche Hotel A5
7 Oak Tree Lodge A7
8 Rodeberg Lodge A5

Eating

Bosman's Restaurant .... (see 6)
9 Harvest at Laborie A7
10 Marc's Mediterranean Cuisine & Garden A5
11 Noop A5
12 Terra Mare A4

Dutch architecture and gracious homesteads, a good range of places to stay and some decent restaurants.

The main road is over 11km long, so not exactly walkable, but there are a couple of wineries an easy stroll from the train station.

Sights & Activities

In Paarl

★ Laborie Cellar WINERY

(Map p112; www.laboriewines.co.za; Taillefer St; tastings from R25; ⏲9am-5pm Mon-Sat, 11am-5pm Sun) Best known for its award-winning shiraz, Laborie also produces good Méthode Cap Classique and dessert wines. Tasting options include wine and olives (R30) or chocolate (R35).

KWV Emporium WINERY

(Map p112; www.kwvwineemporium.co.za; Kohler St; tastings R50; ⏲9am-4.30pm Mon-Sat, 11am-4pm Sun, cellar tours 10am, 10.30am & 2.15pm) This winery is a short walk from the train station. Its fortified wines and brandies are award-winning. Cellar tours (R40) are available and there is a range of tasting options, including chocolate and brandy, biltong and wine, and a tea and chocolate pairing for nondrinkers (R45).

Paarl Mountain Nature Reserve NATURE RESERVE
(Map p114; per vehicle R40, per person R15; ⏲7am-7pm) The three giant granite domes that dominate this reserve glisten like pearls when washed by rain – hence the name 'Paarl'. The reserve has mountain *fynbos* (literally 'fine bush'; primarily proteas, heaths and ericas), a cultivated wildflower garden that's a delightful picnic spot, and numerous walks with excellent views over the valley. You could also visit the rather phallic **Taal Monument** (Map p114; www.taalmuseum.co.za; adult/child R20/5; ⏲8am-5pm Apr-Nov, 8am-8pm Dec-Mar), a giant needlelike edifice that commemorates the Afrikaans language (*taal* is Afrikaans for 'language').

On a clear day there are stunning views as far as Cape Town.

Paarl Museum MUSEUM
(Map p112; 303 Main St; admission R5; ⏲9am-4pm Mon-Fri) Housed in the Oude Pastorie (Old Parsonage), built in 1714, this museum has an interesting collection of Cape Dutch antiques and relics of Huguenot and early Afrikaner culture.

Afrikaans Language Museum MUSEUM
(Map p112; www.taalmuseum.co.za; 11 Pastorie Ave; adult/child R20/5; ⏲9.30am-4.30pm Mon-Fri) Paarl is considered the wellspring of the Afrikaans language, a fact covered by this interesting museum. It also shows, thanks to a multimedia exhibition, how three continents contributed to the formation of the language.

Wineland Ballooning SCENIC FLIGHTS
(Map p112; ☎021-863 3192; www.kapinfo.com; 64 Main St; per person R3300) You'll need to get up very early in the morning, but a hot-air balloon trip over the Winelands will be unforgettable. Trips run between November and April when the weather conditions are right.

Around Paarl

★Spice Route WINERY
(Map p114; ☎021-863 5200; www.spiceroute.co.za; Suid-Agter-Paarl Rd; tastings from R25; ⏲9am-5pm) Spice Route is known for its complex red wines, particularly the Flagship syrah. Aside from wine there is a lot going on, including glass-blowing demonstrations, wine and chocolate pairings (R75), a chocolatier (tutored tasting R25), grappa distillery (tastings R30) and a superlative microbrewery (tastings R25). As well as the upmarket Spice Route restaurant (mains R95 to R170), there is a pizzeria (mains R50 to R90).

Fairview WINERY
(Map p114; ☎021-863 2450; www.fairview.co.za; Suid-Agter-Paarl Rd; wine & cheese tastings R25; ⏲9am-5pm) This hugely popular estate off Rte 101, 6km south of Paarl, is a wonderful winery but not the place to come for a tranquil tasting. It is great value, since tastings include six wines *and* a wide range of cheeses. The well-respected restaurant (mains R70 to R160) is open for breakfast and lunch.

Backsberg WINERY
(Map p114; ☎021-875 5141; www.backsberg.co.za; tastings R15; ⏲8am-5pm Mon-Fri, 9.30am-4.30pm Sat, 10.30am-4.30pm Sun) Backsberg is a hugely popular estate thanks to its reliable label and lavish outdoor lunches – book ahead for the Sunday lamb spit braai (R225). This was South Africa's first carbon-neutral wine farm and its wines include the easy-drinking Tread Lightly range, packaged in lightweight, environmentally friendly bottles.

Nederburg Wines WINERY
(Map p114; ☎021-862 3104; www.nederburg.co.za; tastings R25-70; ⏲8am-6pm Mon-Fri, 10am-4pm Sat & Sun) This is one of South Africa's best-known labels, a big but professional and welcoming operation featuring a vast range of wines. Look out for inventive tasting options such as blind food matching, burger pairings and a kids' grape juice and snack pairing experience.

Glen Carlou WINERY
(Map p114; ☎021-875 5528; www.glencarlou.co.za; Simondium Rd, Klapmuts; tastings R25-35; ⏲9am-5pm Mon-Fri, 10am-4pm Sat & Sun) Sitting south of the N1, the tasting room has a panoramic view of Tortoise Hill. Enjoy a glass of the sumptuous chardonnay or renowned bordeaux blend, Grand Classique, over lunch (three-course meal R340). There's an art gallery too.

Drakenstein Prison HISTORIC SITE
(Map p114) On 11 February 1990, when Nelson Mandela walked free from incarceration for the first time in over 27 years, the jail he left was not on Robben Island, but here. Then called the Victor Verster, this was where Mandela spent his last two years of captivity in the warders' cottage, negotiating the end of apartheid. It's still a working prison so

Around Paarl

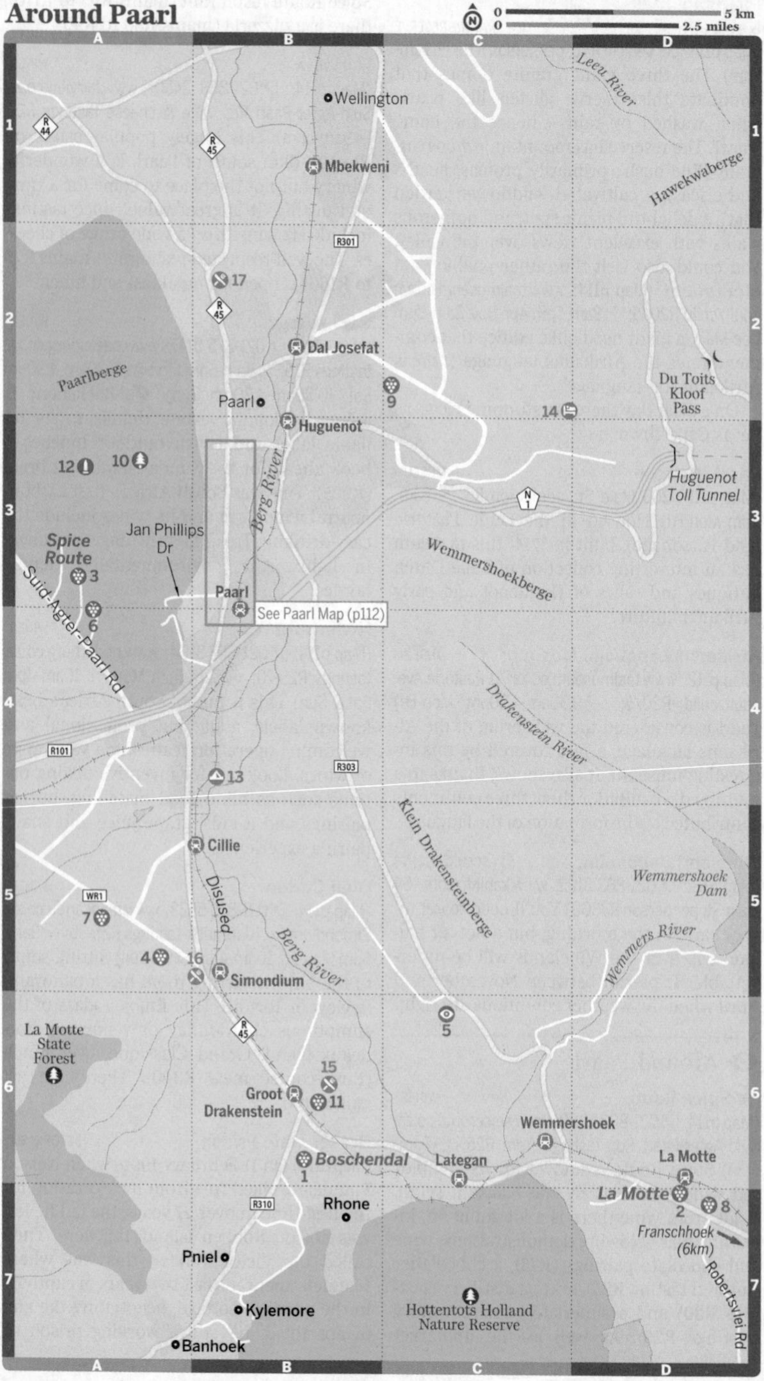
Wellington
Mbekweni
Leeu River
Hawekwaberge
R301
17
Dal Josefat
Paarlberge
9
Paarl
Huguenot
Du Toits
Kloof
Pass
14
12
10
Berg River
Huguenot
Toll Tunnel
N1
Spice
Route
3
Jan Phillips
Dr
Wemmershoekberge
Paarl
See Paarl Map (p112)
6
Suid-Agter-Paarl Rd
Drakenstein River
R101
R303
13
Klein Drakensteinberge
Cillie
WR1
Disused
Wemmershoek
Dam
7
Berg River
Wemmers River
4
16
Simondium
La Motte
State
Forest
5
15
Groot
Drakenstein
11
Wemmershoek
Boschendal
1
Lategan
La Motte
La Motte
2
8
R310
Rhone
Franschhoek
(6km)
Pniel
Robertsvlei Rd
Kylemore
Hottentots Holland
Nature Reserve
Banhoek

Around Paarl

Top Sights

1	Boschendal	B6
2	La Motte	D7
3	Spice Route	A3

Sights

4	Backsberg	A5
5	Drakenstein Prison	C6
6	Fairview	A4
7	Glen Carlou	A5
8	Leopard's Leap	D7
9	Nederburg Wines	C2
10	Paarl Mountain Nature Reserve	A3
11	Solms-Delta	B6
12	Taal Monument	A3

Sleeping

13	Berg River Resort	B4
14	Cascade Country Manor	C2

Eating

15	Fyndraai Restaurant	B6
16	Lust Bistro & Bakery	B5
17	Tea Under the Trees	B2

there are no tours but there's a superb statue of Mandela, fist raised in *viva* position.

Sleeping

Berg River Resort CAMPGROUND $
(Map p114; ☎021-863 1650; www.bergriverresort.co.za; camping per site from R350, d chalets from R715;) An attractive camping ground beside the Berg River, 5km from Paarl on Rte 45 towards Franschhoek. Facilities include canoes, trampolines and a cafe. It gets very crowded during school holidays and is best avoided then.

Oak Tree Lodge GUESTHOUSE $$
(Map p112; ☎021-863 2631; www.oaktreelodge.co.za; 32 Main St; s/d incl breakfast from R630/840;) Centrally located, this old house has comfortable, well-appointed rooms, some with balconies. The larger garden rooms are quieter, being off the main road.

Rodeberg Lodge GUESTHOUSE $$
(Map p112; ☎021-863 3202; www.rodeberglodge.co.za; 74 Main St; s/d incl breakfast R550/850;) Good rooms, some with air-con and TV. There's also a family room (R350 per person) in the attic. The hosts are friendly and travellers love the breakfasts taken in the conservatory.

★**Cascade Country Manor** BOUTIQUE HOTEL $$$
(Map p114; ☎021-813 6220; www.cascademanor.co.za; Waterfall Rd; s/d incl breakfast R1200/1870;) Tucked away along a dirt road 10km east of the centre, this place will make you feel like you're miles from anywhere, though it's an easy drive back to town. Rooms are just what you'd expect but it's the grounds that wow, with vast lawns, a large pool, olive groves and a short walk to a pretty waterfall.

Grande Roche Hotel LUXURY HOTEL $$$
(Map p112; ☎021-863 2727; www.granderoche.co.za; Plantasie St; ste from R3960;) A superluxurious hotel set in a Cape Dutch manor house, offering wonderful mountain views, a heated swimming pool and the award-winning Bosman's Restaurant (p116). It's a short walk to Paarl's main road.

Eating & Drinking

Many wineries have excellent restaurants or do picnic lunches.

★**Tea Under the Trees** TEA ROOM $
(Map p114; ☎082 825 5666; www.teaunderthetrees.co.za; Main Rd, Northern Paarl; mains R40-50; 9am-4pm Mon-Fri Oct-Apr) The only downside to this fabulous tea garden is that it's only open for half the year. Based on an organic fruit farm, it's a wonderful place to sit under century-old oak trees and enjoy an al fresco cuppa, a light lunch or a large slice of home-baked cake. There's no indoor seating.

Harvest at Laborie SOUTH AFRICAN $$
(Map p112; ☎021-807 3095; www.harvestatlaborie.co.za; Taillefer St; mains R90-140; lunch Mon-Sun, dinner Thu-Sat;) Eat on a patio overlooking vines at this elegant wine estate a short walk from Main St. Local produce dominates the menu, including West Coast mussels, Karoo lamb and seasonal game steaks. Bookings recommended for dinner and weekend lunches.

Marc's Mediterranean Cuisine & Garden MEDITERRANEAN $$
(Map p112; 129 Main St; mains R65-140; lunch & dinner Tue-Sat) This laidback spot is a long-standing Paarl favourite. Patron Marc Friedrich has created a light and bright place with food to match and a Provence-style garden to dine in.

Terra Mare FUSION $$
(Map p112; ☎021-863 4805; 90A Main St; mains R90-190; lunch & dinner Mon-Sat) The menu is fairly small but superb, offering intricate takes on the classics. Tables inside can be

WORTH A TRIP

WELLINGTON

This sedate and reasonably pretty town is 10km north of Paarl. Like surrounding towns, the main draw card is the range of wineries, which offer a less touristy experience than those in Paarl. Ask at the **tourism bureau** (☎021-864 1378; www.wellington.co.za; Malherbe St, cnr Burger St; ⏰8am-5pm Mon-Fri, 10am-1pm Sat & Sun) for a list of local wineries and information on the **Wellington Wine Walk**. If you're looking for something stronger than wine, visit the superb **Jorgensen's Distillery** (☎021-864 1777; www.jd7.co.za; Regent St; ⏰by appt), which produces handmade gin, brandy and absinthe.

While in the area, don't miss the chance to drive the spectacular **Bainskloof Pass**, one of South Africa's finest. It was built between 1848 and 1852 by legendary pass builder Thomas Bain, and other than having its surface tarred, the road has not been altered since.

There are several walks from the pass, including the 8km **Bobbejaans River Walk** to a waterfall. This walk starts at Eerste Tol and you need to buy a **permit** (adult/child R40/20), available from the tourism bureau.

a little noisy due to the proximity to busy Main St, but there's a delightful garden at the back.

★**Bosman's Restaurant** INTERNATIONAL $$$
(Map p112; ☎021-863 5100; www.granderoche.co.za; Plantasie St; 3 courses R420; ⏰lunch & dinner) This elegant spot within the Grande Roche Hotel is one of the country's top restaurants, serving multicourse dinners and more casual bistro-style lunches (mains from R90). Bookings highly recommended.

Noop FUSION $$$
(Map p112; www.noop.co.za; 127 Main St; mains R95-200; ⏰lunch & dinner Mon-Sat) Recommended by locals all over the Winelands, this restaurant and wine bar has a comprehensive menu of upmarket dishes.

Information

Paarl Tourism (Map p112; ☎073 708 2835; www.paarlonline.com; 216 Main St; ⏰8am-5pm Mon-Fri, 10am-1pm Sat & Sun) This office has an excellent supply of information on the whole region.

Getting There & Away

BUS

All the major long-distance bus companies offer services going through Paarl, making it easy to build the town into your itinerary. The bus segment between Paarl and Cape Town is R160, so consider taking the cheaper train to Paarl and then linking with the buses.

The **long-distance bus stop** (Map p112) is opposite the Shell petrol station on Main St as you enter town from the N1.

TRAIN

Metro trains run roughly every hour between Cape Town and Paarl (1st/economy class R19/12, 1¼ hours). Services are less frequent on weekends. Take care to travel on trains during the busy part of the day, for safety reasons.

You can travel by train from Paarl to Stellenbosch; take a Cape Town–bound train and change at Muldersvlei. If coming from Jo'burg, change to a metro train at Worcester.

Getting Around

If you don't have your own transport, your only option for getting around Paarl, apart from walking and cycling, is to call a taxi; try **Paarl Taxis** (☎021-872 5671).

Tulbagh

POP 9000

Beneath the dramatic backdrop of the Witsenberg range, Tulbagh (established in 1699) is a pretty town with historic buildings and delightful places to stay and eat. Church St, lined with trees and flowering shrubs, is a near-perfect example of an 18th- and 19th-century Cape Dutch village street. It was badly damaged in an earthquake in 1969, but the painstaking restoration has paid off.

Sights & Activities

Wandering down Church St is a pleasant way to spend a morning. Afterwards, take in a few wine tastings.

Oude Kerk Volksmuseum MUSEUM
(Old Church Folk Museum; 1 Church St; adult/child R15/5; ⏰9am-5pm Mon-Fri, 9am-3pm Sat, 11am-3pm Sun) This museum made up of four

buildings is worth a pause. Start at No 4, which has a photographic history of Church St, covering the earthquake and reconstruction; visit the beautiful Oude Kerk itself (1743); move to No 14, featuring Victorian furnishings; and end at No 22, a reconstructed town dwelling from the 18th century.

Saronsberg Cellar
WINERY

(www.saronsberg.com; Waveren Rd; tastings R50; ⊙8am-5pm Mon-Fri, 10am-2pm Sat) Sip superlative red blends while admiring the contemporary art that lines the walls of this smart cellar 6km north of town.

Drostdy Wines
WINERY

(www.drostdyhof.com; Van der Stel St; museum R10, tastings R20; ⊙10am-5pm Mon-Fri, 10am-2pm Sat) Built in 1806 and almost destroyed in an earthquake but completely restored, Drostdy is worth a visit. Informal help-yourself tastings take place by candlelight in the atmospheric former jail.

Twee Jonge Gezellen
WINERY

(Waveren Rd; tastings free; ⊙10.30am-4pm Mon-Fri, 9.30am-2pm Sat, cellar tours 11am) This long-established winery was under new management when we visited and the place was in need of a bit of a revamp. There are tours explaining the Méthode Cap Classique-making process (sparkling wine made in the Champagne style). Ask if you can attempt the *sabrage* (opening a bottle of bubbly with a sword).

🛏 Sleeping

Rijk's Country House
BOUTIQUE HOTEL $$

(☑023-230 1006; www.rijkscountryhouse.co.za; Van der Stel St; r incl breakfast R950; ❄⌂≋) Rijk's provides pleasant accommodation in thatched cottages on a beautiful wine estate with manicured lawns. There are tours and tastings at the winery and a good restaurant (mains R95 to R195) in the main building. The hotel is 2km north of the town centre.

De Oude Herberg
HISTORIC HOTEL $$

(☑023-230 0260; www.deoudeherberg.co.za; 6 Church St; s/d incl breakfast R715/1030; ❄⌂≋) A guesthouse since 1885, this is a very friendly place with traditional country furniture and a lovely patio. The **restaurant** (☑023-230 0260; 6 Church St; mains R90-155; ⊙dinner Mon-Sat) has a small menu featuring mostly local produce. It's open to nonguests but reservations are essential.

Cape Dutch Quarter
BACKPACKERS, GUESTHOUSE $$

(☑023-230 1171; www.cdq.co.za; 24 Church St; r R1200; ❄⌂≋) There is a variety of accommodation on offer, from basic backpacker-style rooms (s/d R400/600) to self-catering houses (four people R1350) and smart doubles with four-poster beds. The owner is a mine of information on the area and can arrange hiking and mountain biking permits and maps.

★Vindoux Treehouses
CABIN $$$

(☑023-230 0635; www.vindoux.com; Waveren Rd, Vindoux Farm; d incl breakfast R1700; ❄⌂≋) A definite for the romantically inclined, these luxury treehouses each have a spa bath and views of a small wildlife area with zebras, wildebeest and springbok. Hire bikes for a self-guided vineyard cycle then revive with a *fynbos* body wrap at the day spa (R500). There are also simpler cottages (R650 for two people).

🍴 Eating & Drinking

★Readers Restaurant
SOUTH AFRICAN $$

(12 Church St; mains R75-135; ⊙lunch & dinner Wed-Mon) The menu changes regularly, but always features a few traditional South African dishes and plenty of local ingredients. The attached gift shop is aimed at feline lovers, with an array of catty collectibles.

Olive Terrace
INTERNATIONAL $$

(22 Van der Stel St; mains R70-170; ⊙breakfast, lunch & dinner) Based in the Tulbagh Hotel, this restaurant serves a range of dishes including a few vegetarian options. The shady terrace is a delight in the Tulbagh summer heat.

Things I Love
CAFE $$

(61 Van de Stel St; mains R70-120; ⊙breakfast, lunch & dinner; ⌂) A friendly spot serving decent coffee and a little bit of everything, food-wise. There's also a shop selling crafts, clothing and foodstuffs.

ℹ Information

Tulbagh Tourism (☑023-230 1348; www.tulbaghtourism.co.za; 4 Church St; ⊙9am-5pm Mon-Fri, 9am-3pm Sat & Sun) The helpful staff provide information and maps about the area, including the Tulbagh Wine Route.

ℹ Getting There & Away

Tulbagh is reached either via Rte 44 from Wellington or Rte 43 from Worcester, a more scenic route. There is one train a day to and from Cape

Town, though the timings aren't too convenient. The train station is 4km south of town.

To get to Rte 46 (from where you can head east to Ceres or west towards Piketberg, which is on the N7), head south down Van der Stel St. Halfway up the hill leading away from the town, turn right. There's a small, faded sign to Kaapstad (Cape Town) and Gouda on Rte 46.

Ceres

POP 11,000

Named after the Roman goddess of agriculture, the small town of Ceres is nestled in a magnificent valley. It's the most important deciduous fruit- and juice-producing district in South Africa. The valley is beautiful in spring and even more so in autumn, when the fruit trees change colour.

The mountain passes around town are its greatest assets, offering some stupendous scenery. The Gydo Pass rises steeply as you head north from Ceres towards Citrusdal and the Cederberg mountains. On the southern side of town is Mitchell's Pass. Completed in 1848, this became the main route onto the South African plateau to the north, remaining so until the Hex River Pass was opened in 1875. Stop for tea and cake at the cafe situated in the old tollhouse.

Ceres is on Rte 46, 53km north of Wellington. As with many destinations, having your own vehicle is best, but there are shared taxis running between Voortrekker St and Worcester (R65, 35 minutes).

Togryers' Museum MUSEUM
(Transport Riders' Museum; 8 Oranje St; adult/child R5/0.50; ◷8am-5pm Mon-Fri) Ceres was once a famous centre for making horse-drawn vehicles. Consequently, the museum has an interesting collection of original wagons and carriages alongside exhibits on local history.

★**Ceres Zipline Adventures** ADVENTURE TOUR
(☑079 245 0354; www.ceresadventures.co.za; 1 Voortrekker St; tours R400; ◷8am-4pm) This 1.4km, 90-minute tour sees participants dangling from cables stretched across ravines, giving an unusual view of the surrounding Skurweberg mountains.

Ceres Inn HOTEL $$
(☑023-312 2325; www.ceresinn.co.za; 125 Voortrekker St; s/d R475/720; ❀☀❀) The smart decor at this hotel provides a fine contrast with the 19th-century building. The adjoining Witherley's Bistro (☑023-312 2325; www.ceresinn.co.za; 125 Voortrekker St; mains R60-115) dishes up reliable fare covering all tastes, which can be served in the shady garden.

Baba's Jem CAPE MALAY $
(☑023-312 3545; 13 Bester St; mains R60-95; ◷7am-9pm) You can buy homebaked goodies and swig on fresh ginger beer in this eatery based in a family home. Meals must be booked ahead; they always include traditional treats such as Cape Malay curry, tripe and *vetkoek* (deep-fried doughy bread).

ⓘ Information

Ceres Tourism Bureau (☑023-316 1287; www.ceres.org.za; Voortrekker St, cnr Owen St; ◷9am-5pm Mon-Fri, 9am-noon Sat) In the town's library.

Robertson

POP 22,000

In a valley located between the Langeberge and Riviersonderendberge, Robertson is the prosperous centre of one of the largest wine-growing areas in the country. It offers an excellent wine route encompassing the neighbouring villages of Ashton, Bonnievale and McGregor, as well as a wider range of outdoor activities than other towns on Rte 62. There's hiking in the mountains, gentle rafting on the river and horse riding – the town is famous for its horse studs.

⊙ Sights & Activities

★**Viljoensdrift** WINERY
(www.viljoensdrift.co.za; tastings free; ◷9am-5pm Mon-Fri, 10am-4pm Sat; ☑) One of Robertson's most popular places to sip, especially on weekends. Put together a picnic from the deli, buy a bottle from the cellar door and taste on an hour-long boat trip along the Breede River (adult/child R50/20). Boats leave on the hour from noon. Bookings essential.

Excelsior WINERY
(www.excelsior.co.za; Rte 317; tastings free; ◷10am-4pm Mon-Fri, 10am-3pm Sat) Tastings take place on a wooden deck overlooking a reservoir – it's a delightful spot. The real draw, though, is the 'blend your own' experience, where you can mix three wine varieties to your liking and take home a bottle of your own creation, complete with your own label (R60).

Springfield WINERY
(www.springfieldestate.com; ◷8am-5pm Mon-Fri, 9am-4pm Sat) Some of the wines here are un-

filtered – try the uncrushed Whole Berry for something different. Bring your own picnic to enjoy in the peaceful grounds, overlooking a lake.

Van Loveren WINERY
(www.vanloveren.co.za; tastings R45; ⏲8.30am-5pm Mon-Fri, 9.30am-3pm Sat, 11am-2pm Sun, bistro closed Tue; 👪) Wine-tasting options include pairings with cheese, chocolate and charcuterie as well as a grape juice tasting for kids (R25). Each of the trees in the tropical garden tells a story – grab the information pamphlet from reception or join a guided tour (R40). The low-key bistro (mains R55 to R110) serves excellent burgers and pizzas.

Graham Beck WINERY
(www.grahambeckwines.co.za; standard/other tastings free/from R50; ⏲9am-5pm Mon-Fri, 10am-4pm Sat & Sun) Tastings of award-winning syrah and the world-class bubblies (R75) are in a striking modern building with huge plate-glass windows. The winery comes as a breath of fresh air after all those Cape Dutch estates.

Nerina Guest Farm HORSE RIDING
(☎082 744 2580; www.nerinaguestfarm.com; Goree Rd) This outfit offers horse trails along the river or through the vineyards with an option to swim with the horses afterwards. Trails last from one hour (R150) to half a day (R600).

Festivals & Events

There are a number of wine-related events, including the **Hands on Harvest** in February, the **Wacky Wine Weekend** in June and the **Wine on the River Festival** (☎023-626 3167; www.robertsonwinevalley.com) in October. Accommodation in the town is scarce at these times, so book well in advance.

Sleeping & Eating

Robertson Backpackers BACKPACKERS $
(☎023-626 1280; www.robertsonbackpackers.co.za; 4 Dordrecht Ave; dm/s/d without bathroom R130/250/350, d R450; 📶) A terrific hostel, with spacious dorms and pleasant en suite doubles in the garden. There's a big grassy backyard, a shisha lounge, and wine and activity tours can be arranged. Camping for R70.

Pat Busch Mountain Reserve CHALET $
(☎023-626 2033; www.patbusch.co.za; r per person from R280; 🏊) Simple but well-equipped cottages based on the edge of a nature reserve 15km northeast of Robertson off Rte 60. Hiking, mountain biking, fishing and birdwatching are available. There are discounts midweek.

> **WORTH A TRIP**
>
> ### KAGGA KAMMA PRIVATE GAME RESERVE
>
> **Kagga Kamma** (☎021-872 4343; www.kaggakamma.co.za; full board s/d from R2580/3500, camping R60) Far from towns and paved roads, this is the perfect place to recharge. There are wildlife drives exploring the Karoo landscape, hikes to see San rock art and evening 'sky safaris' at the mini-observatory. Rooms are in mock-caves that blend seamlessly with the rugged surrounds. The reserve is 92km northeast of Ceres.
>
> For the ultimate in 'glamping', there's the Outcrop room – an entire luxury suite transported into the desert.

★ **Ballinderry** GUESTHOUSE $$
(☎023-626 5365; www.ballinderryguesthouse.com; 8 Le Roux St; s/d incl breakfast from R850/1100; ❄📶🏊) This colourful boutique guesthouse is impeccable, thanks to hosts Luc and Hilde. A champagne breakfast is served, as are superb dinners on request, and Dutch, French and German are spoken. Try to get one of the rooms that opens into the garden.

Gubas De Hoek GUESTHOUSE $$
(☎023-626 6218; www.gubas-dehoek.com; 45 Reitz St; s/d from R600/970; 📶🏊) 🍃 Highly recommended by readers is this comfortable home with well-appointed rooms. Owner-chef Gunther Huerttlen will cook you dinner (three courses R270) and there's a shared self-catering kitchen for preparing light meals. The owners are working to produce all of their own electricity.

★ **Strictly Coffee** CAFE $
(www.strictlycoffee.co.za; 5 Voortrekker St; mains R40-70; ⏲breakfast & lunch) As well as excellent coffee roasted on-site, you'll find simply wonderful sandwiches with incredibly fresh ingredients. Locals rave about the eggs benedict for breakfast.

Bourbon Street INTERNATIONAL $$
(☎023-626 5934; 22 Voortrekker St; mains R60-140; ⏲lunch & dinner Mon Sat, lunch Sun; 📶) A firm favourite with both locals and

visitors, this New Orleans–feel restaurant has a menu offering a little of everything. It's also about the only place you'll find night-time action in Robertson.

Information

Robertson Tourism Bureau (023-626 4437; www.robertsontourism.co.za; Voortrekker St, cnr Reitz St; 8am-5pm Mon-Fri, 9am-2pm Sat, 10am-2pm Sun) A friendly office with information about the wine region, Rte 62 and hiking trails in the mountains.

Getting There & Away

Translux (0861 589 282; www.translux.co.za) buses stop opposite the police station on Voortrekker St. Routes include Knysna (R270, five hours), Cape Town (R200, two hours, daily) and Port Elizabeth (R350, nine hours, daily).

Shared taxis running between Cape Town (R130, 1½ hours), Oudtshoorn (R200, three hours) and Montagu (R80, 30 minutes) stop opposite the **Shell petrol station** (John St, cnr Voortrekker St). These are not necessarily daily services; check with the taxi drivers about when they're leaving.

McGregor

POP 3100

Dreaming away at the end of a road going nowhere, quiet and sleepy McGregor makes for a delightful retreat with good accommodation, an arts route and plenty of spa treatments on offer. The main thoroughfare, Voortrekker St, has pretty whitewashed cottages dating from the mid-19th century, and the village is surrounded by farmland. It's a good base for hiking in the nearby Riviersonderendberge and is also one end of the excellent Boesmanskloof Trail. There are half a dozen wineries in the McGregor area, which are encompassed in the Robertson Wine Valley route.

Sights & Activities

Eseltjiesrus Donkey Sanctuary SANCTUARY
(023-625 1593; www.donkeysanctuary.co.za; entry by donation; Thu-Sun 10am-4pm) This long-running donkey sanctuary has new premises just off the main road from Robertson. It's a peaceful spot with a couple of dams offering good birdwatching, a tearoom serving homemade goodies and, of course, the chance to meet the donkeys, many of which were neglected in their former homes.

Tanagra Private Cellar WINERY
(023-625 1780; www.tanagra-wines.co.za; tastings free; by appt) Tanagra is a family-run farm offering tastings of its range of reds as well as the grappa distilled on-site. There's self-catering accommodation (two-person cottage from R750) and a range of short hikes on the farm, which can be extended to explore the adjoining Vrolijkheid Nature Reserve.

★ **Boesmanskloof Trail** HIKING
(Greyton McGregor Trail; day permit adult/child R40/20) One of the best reasons for coming to McGregor is to hike the trail to Greyton, roughly 14km through the spectacular *fynbos*-clad Riviersonderendberge mountains. The hike actually starts at Die Galg, about 15km south of McGregor; you'll need your own transport to get there. The McGregor-to-Greyton direction is easier. During peak times you must book in advance at Cape Nature; only 50 people per day are allowed on the trail. Permits are available from the tourism bureau.

Oakes Falls HIKING
(day permit adult/child R40/20) If you don't fancy hiking the full Boesmanskloof Trail, it's feasible to do a six-hour round-trip to these lovely waterfalls, roughly 6km from Die Galg, where you can cool off with a swim in the tannin-stained waters. You'll still need to get a permit from the tourism bureau before you set off.

Sleeping & Eating

★ **Lord's Guest Lodge** GUESTHOUSE $$
(023-625 1881; www.lordsguestlodge.co.za; cottage from R1200;) If McGregor isn't quiet enough for you, head to this luxury lodge south of the town. The thatched, stone cottages sit atop a hill and have wow vistas across the region. There's also a quaint pub and the **Lady Grey Restaurant** (mains R90-140), which is open to the public (bookings essential). Look out for the turn-off 10km before McGregor, from where it's a further 3km along a gravel road.

Green Gables Country Inn GUESTHOUSE $$
(023-625 1626; www.greengablescountryinn.co.za; Mill St, cnr Smith St; s/d incl breakfast R420/800;) Sitting on the southern border of town, this is a family-friendly place with well-kept grounds, affable hosts and a nice pool. A self-catering cottage with its own splash pool (two people R700) is also available.

Temenos Retreat CABIN $$
(023-625 1871; www.temenos.org.za; Voortrekker Rd, cnr Bree St; s/d R550/795;) These cottages set in spacious gardens aren't just for those on retreat. It's a peaceful place, with a decent lap pool, health treatments and a popular restaurant (mains R70 to R130) serving light lunches and daily dinner specials. Accommodation prices drop considerably during the week. No children under 12 years.

★ **Karoux** SOUTH AFRICAN $$
(023-625 1421; www.karoux.co.za; 42 Voortrekker Rd; mains R70-140; dinner Fri-Tue) Well known for its gourmet cuisine, this is one of the Western Cape's best small-town restaurants. The menu changes regularly but always features dishes that somehow manage to be both upmarket and rustic.

Information

Cape Nature (023-625 1621; www.capenature.org.za; McGregor Rd; 7.30am-4pm Mon-Fri) Administers the Greyton McGregor Trail. Its offices are about 15km south of Robertson.

McGregor Tourism Bureau (023-625 1954; www.tourismmcgregor.co.za; 53 Voortrekker St; 9am-4pm Mon-Fri, 9am-1pm Sat & Sun) Based at the museum, the tourism office arranges hiking permits. There's also a self-guided walking tour brochure for sale (R25).

Getting There & Away

Apart from the option of hiking in from Greyton, your own transport is essential: there's only one road in and out of McGregor (the 20km road north to Robertson).

Greyton

POP 2800

Although officially part of the Overberg region, Greyton and the neighbouring village of Genadendal are linked to McGregor because both are on the Boesmanskloof Trail.

Greyton is much more twee than McGregor; even locals admit its whitewashed, thatched-roof cottages are a bit artificial. It is a pleasant village but is best seen in conjunction with the old Moravian Mission of neighbouring Genadendal, with its well-preserved historic buildings that couldn't be more authentic.

Sights & Activities

★ **Genadendal Mission Station** HISTORIC SITE
Some 5km west of Greyton is Genadendal, the oldest mission station in South Africa, founded in 1738 and for a brief time the largest settlement in the colony after Cape Town. It now has a population of around 5000. The **Moravian Church** is a handsome, simply decorated building. The village's fascinating history is documented in the excellent **Mission Museum** (028-251 8582; adult/child R10/5; 8.30am-5pm Mon-Thu, 8.30am-3.30pm Fri, 10am-2pm Sat), situated in what was South Africa's first teacher-training college.

The village has a 'living museum' feel. As you wander you'll find one of the oldest printing presses in the country, a pottery workshop and a watermill among the many restored historical buildings. In 1995 Nelson Mandela renamed his official residence in Cape Town after this mission station. To get to the cluster of national monuments from Rte 406, keep driving through the rather scruffy outskirts until you arrive at Church Sq.

Genadendal Trail HIKING
Greyton is a perfect base for hiking in the Riviersonderendberge mountains, which rise dramatically to the village's north. As well as several shorter walks, there is this two-day trail for the serious hiker. It's a 25.3km circular route that begins and ends at Genadendal's Moravian Church, though you have to come equipped with a map because none of the locals knows much about the trail. Contact **Cape Nature** (023-625 1621; www.capenature.co.za) to book accommodation and hiking permits.

Sleeping & Eating

Greyton Ecolodge BACKPACKERS $
(072 626 7052; www.ecolodgegreyton.co.za; 2 Park St; dm R140, s/d without bathroom R200/360; @) Once the hostel for Greyton's boarding school, this cavernous place has a rather insitutional feel. It is part of a larger environmental project and all proceeds from accommodation go towards funding its work. Views of the Sonderend Mountains are awesome and it's a perfect base for hiking.

★ **Post House** HISTORIC HOTEL $$
(028-254 9995; www.theposthouse.co.za; 22 Main Rd; s/d incl breakfast from R945/1400;) Based in the town's historic former post house, with rooms set around a pretty garden and named after Beatrix Potter characters (yes, Greyton is a twee place). Its English-style pub is an atmospheric spot for a drink.

High Hopes B&B $$
(☎028-254 9898; www.highhopes.co.za; 89 Main Rd; s/d incl breakfast from R825/1100;) This delightful place has tastefully furnished rooms and a small pool in the rambling gardens. It's close to the start of the Greyton–McGregor trail, and if you've overdone it, you can book a treatment – reiki, reflexology and massages are offered. Fully catered retreats are also available, featuring activities such as yoga, art and gardening.

Oak & Vigne Café CAFE $
(DS Botha St; mains R60-90; breakfast & lunch;) This trendy deli/cafe/art gallery is a pleasant place to grab a light lunch or a good cup of coffee and relax in the garden.

Peccadillos FUSION $$
(☎028-254 9066; 23 Main Rd; mains R75-115; lunch & dinner Thu-Mon) Traditional dishes are given a new twist at this popular spot with minimalist decor and a creative menu featuring local, organic produce.

Information

Tourist Information Office (☎028-254 9414; www.greytontourism.com; 29 Main Rd; 8am-5pm Mon-Fri, 9am-2pm Sat) Staff can provide information on short hikes in the area.

Getting There & Away

If you're not hiking in from McGregor, the only way to Greyton is by your own transport. Rte 406 leads into town from the N2 from east and west, but note that the eastern section is a gravel road.

THE OVERBERG

Literally meaning 'over the mountain', Overberg refers to the region east of the Hottentots Holland range, where rolling wheat fields are bordered by the Breede River, the coast and the peaks of the Franschhoekberge, Wemmershoekberge and Riviersonderendberge.

There are no unattractive routes leading to the Overberg; the N2 snakes up Sir Lowry's Pass, which has magnificent views from the top, while Rte 44 stays at sea level and winds its way round Cape Hangklip, skirting the Kogelberg Biosphere Reserve and eventually reaching Hermanus. It's a breathtaking coastal drive, on a par with Chapman's Peak Dr in Cape Town, but without the toll.

Hermanus is a major draw for whales in the calving season (June to December) and for people wanting to watch them from easily accessed points throughout the town. If you're keen to escape the throngs that gather here, head for the less-crowded whale-watching spots around Gansbaai, Arniston and the magical De Hoop Nature Reserve. Further inland is the elegant town of Swellendam, which offers plenty for hikers and history buffs.

Kogelberg Biosphere Reserve

Kogelberg Biosphere Reserve NATURE RESERVE
(☎028-271 5138; www.capenature.co.za; adult/child R40/20) Proclaimed in 1988 as South Africa's first Unesco Biosphere Reserve, the Kogelberg biosphere lies 60km east of Cape Town and encompasses 1000 sq km.

The reserve has incredibly complex biodiversity, including more than 1880 plant species. Birdlife is prolific, wild horses live in the wetlands, and whales can be seen offshore. There are day hikes and overnight trails, and the reserve is used by mountain bikers; permits are required for all activities.

Bounded by the Kogelberg in the east and projecting 7.5km into the sea, the reserve abuts the villages of Rooi Els, Pringle Bay, Hangklip, Betty's Bay and Kleinmond. The entrance sits between Betty's Bay and Kleinmond on Rte 44. You'll need your own vehicle to visit.

Kogel Bay Resort CAMPGROUND $
(☎021-856 9622; Rte 44; camping per site R170) This campground has reasonable facilities on a fantastic surf beach (although it's unsafe for swimming and often windy). Bring all your own food.

★**Oudebosch Eco Cabins** CABIN $$
(☎021-483 0190; www.capenature.co.za; 2 people from R1060;) These modern, glass-fronted cabins were designed to meld with the natural surrounds and be as ecofriendly as possible. Delightful and well equipped, they are highly sought after so book ahead.

Betty's Bay

POP 1400

The small, scattered holiday village of Betty's Bay, on Rte 44, is worth a pause.

Stony Point African Penguin Colony WILDLIFE RESERVE
(admission R10; 8am-5pm) This is a much quieter place to watch the diminutive penguins

The Overberg & Route 62

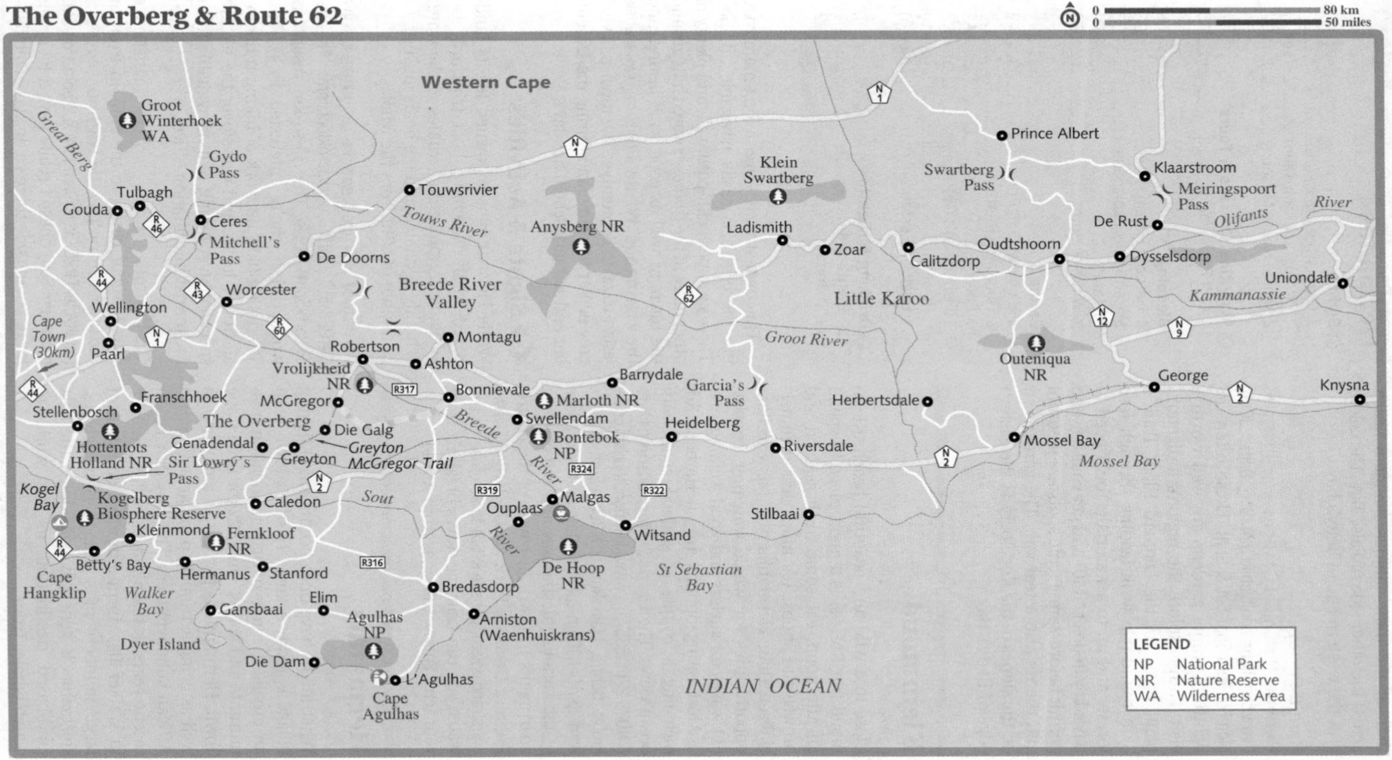

than at the more famous Boulders Beach, across the other side of False Bay. The colony is at the western end of Betty's Bay.

Harold Porter National Botanical Gardens GARDENS
(www.sanbi.org; adult/child R24/8; 8am-4.30pm Mon-Fri, 8am-5pm Sat & Sun) These often delightfully empty gardens are well worth a visit. Paths explore the region's indigenous plant life – try the Leopard Kloof Trail, a 3km round-trip walk leading through fern forests and up to a waterfall. You'll need to pay a key deposit (R50) and get your key and permit before 2pm. Picnic spots are plentiful and there's also a tearoom. The gardens sit on the slopes of the Kogelberg at the eastern edge of Betty's Bay.

Kleinmond

POP 6600

Close to a wild and beautiful beach, Kleinmond (on Rte 44) is a great place to spend an afternoon, eat some fresh seafood and browse the shops. It's much less commercialised than Hermanus and has excellent opportunities for whale watching, consistent waves for surfers and good walking.

Most eating options are on Harbour Rd, including a couple of seafood spots with ocean views. The **tourist information office** (028-271 5657; www.kleinmondtourism.co.za; Protea Centre, Main Rd; 8.30am-5pm Mon-Fri, 9am-2pm Sat, 10am-2pm Sun) has up-to-date lists of the various guesthouses and self-catering apartments in town. Just west of the centre, **Palmiet Caravan Park** (028-271 8400; www.overstrand.gov.za; per site R165) is so close to the water, you can hear the waves breaking from your tent. Follow the signs from Rte 44.

Hermanus

028 / POP 10,500

What might have once been a small fishing village is today a large, bustling town with an excellent range of accommodation, restaurants and shops. Only 122km from Cape Town, Hermanus is perfect for a day trip as well as being extremely popular with South African holidaymakers. The growth surge in recent years is mainly due to the presence in Walker Bay, from June to December, of large numbers of southern right whales. Hermanus is generally considered the best land-based destination in the world to watch whales from.

Hermanus

Sights
1 Old Harbour Museum C2
Photographic Museum .... (see 2)
2 Whale House Museum C2

Activities, Courses & Tours
3 Cliff Path Walking Trail A3

Sleeping
4 Harbour House Hotel C3
5 Hermanus Esplanade C3
6 Marine D1
7 Windsor Hotel B3

Eating
8 Bistro at Just Pure A3
9 Burgundy Restaurant C3
10 Eatery A2
11 Fisherman's Cottage C3
Pavilion .... (see 6)
Seafood Restaurant .... (see 6)

Drinking & Nightlife
12 Bientang's Cave D2
13 Shimmi C2

The town stretches over a long main road but the centre is easily navigable on foot. There's a superb cliff-path walk and plenty of other hikes in the *fynbos*-covered hills around the town, as well as good wine tasting, and the **Hermanus Whale Festival** (www.whalefestival.co.za) in September. The town gets very crowded at this time and during the December and January school holidays.

Sights & Activities

While Hermanus is renowned for its land-based whale watching, boat trips are also available. Approaching whales in the water is highly regulated and the boats must stay a minimum of 50m from the whales.

Fernkloof Nature Reserve NATURE RESERVE
(028-313 0819; www.fernkloof.com; Fir Ave; 9am-5pm) FREE This 15-sq-km reserve is wonderful if you're interested in *fynbos*. There's a 60km network of hiking trails for all fitness levels, and views over the sea are spectacular. A hiking map is available from the tourist information office.

Old Harbour HISTORIC SITE
This harbour clings to the cliffs in front of the town centre. The **Old Harbour Museum** (adult/child R20/5; 9am-1pm & 2-5pm Mon-Sat, noon-4pm Sun) doesn't really have a lot going for it, but outside there's a display of old fish-

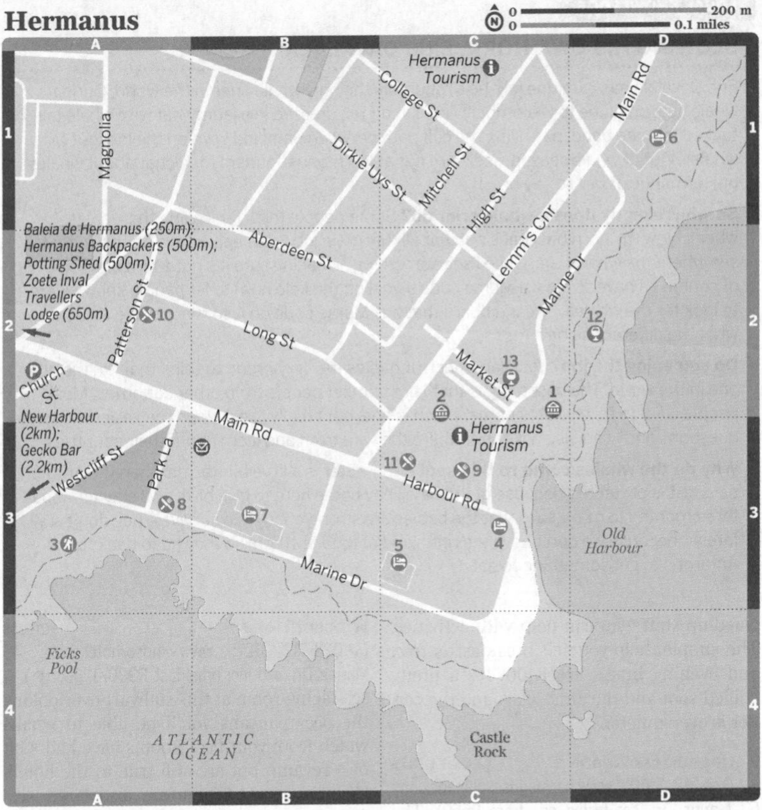

ing boats and the admission fee includes entrance to the more interesting **Whale House Museum** (Market Sq; ⏲9am-4.30pm Mon-Sat, 12pm-4pm Sun) and **Photographic Museum** (Market Sq; ⏲9am-4.30pm Mon-Sat, noon-4pm Sun). There's a permanent craft market in the square as well.

★Cliff Path Walking Trail HIKING

This scenic path meanders for 10km from New Harbour, 2km west of town, along the sea to the mouth of the Klein River; you can join it anywhere along the cliffs. It's simply the finest thing to do in Hermanus, whales or not. Along the way you pass Grotto Beach, the most popular beach; Kwaaiwater, a good whale-watching lookout; as well as Langbaai and Voelklip Beaches. The tourism office has a pamphlet with more details on the trail.

Southern Right Charters BOAT TOUR

(☎082 353 0550; www.southernrightcharters.co.za; 2hr trip adult/child R650/350) One of four licensed boat operators that run whale-watching trips from New Harbour.

Walker Bay Adventures WATER SPORTS

(☎082 739 0159; www.walkerbayadventures.co.za; kayaking R350, canoeing R450, boat-based whale watching R650) Watching whales from a sea kayak is a gobsmacking, if at times rather nervewracking, experience. Other activities on offer include sand-boarding, horse riding and boat trips.

Sleeping

There is a huge amount of accommodation in Hermanus but you might still find yourself searching in vain for a bed in the holiday season, so take care to book ahead.

Hermanus Backpackers BACKPACKERS $

(☎028-312 4293; www.hermanusbackpackers.co.za; 26 Flower St; dm R140, d with/without bathroom R410/380; 📶🏊) This is a great place with upbeat decor, good facilities and

LOCAL KNOWLEDGE

BLOWING HIS OWN HORN: ERIC DAVALALA

Eric Davalala has a unique job: he's reputedly the only whale crier in the world. During whale season (June to December) you'll find Eric, dressed in a jaunty hat with whale tail tucked into the band, patrolling the cliff path between 9am and 5pm on the lookout for whales. Out of whale season, seek him out at Hermanus Tourism for a chat about whales or Hermanus or just to say hi.

So what exactly does a whale crier do? Some people think I'm calling the whales when I blow my horn but that's not it at all! My main job is to keep an eye on the water to see where the whales are. Once I see something – making sure it's not a bird or a rock, of course – I have to blow a Morse code signal on the kelp horn to let people know where to look for the whales. I wear a board that has Morse code on it so that people will know what the different signals mean.

Do you enjoy the job? Yes! Very much. It makes me very proud to think that I'm the only one in the world. The best thing is that I get to meet people from other countries. Most people want to take photos of me, which is fine, but I really like it when they ask me a few questions and I can also ask them where they are from and learn about their countries.

Why do the whales come to this spot? The water is a little bit warmer than the Antarctic and it is protected because of the bay. They come here to give birth and stay for about three months to make sure that the babies are strong enough to survive. They don't stay forever because we don't have the right kind of food for them so they head back to the Antarctic to get something to eat.

clued-up staff who can help with activities. The simple, help-yourself breakfast is free, and evening braais are R100. It's a pretty chilled spot and the annexe around the corner is even quieter.

Hermanus Esplanade APARTMENT **$**
(☎028-312 3610; www.hermanusesplanade.com; 63 Marine Dr; sea-facing apt from R550) The furnishings are a bit worn and the slightly shabby apartments could do with an overhaul but they're right on the seafront and offer good value for money.

Zoete Inval Travellers Lodge BACKPACKERS **$**
(☎028-312 1242; www.zoeteinval.co.za; 23 Main Rd; dm from R130, d with/without bathroom R550/450;) A budget option in suburbia, this is a quiet place with good amenities (including a spa bath) and neatly furnished rooms.

★ **Potting Shed** GUESTHOUSE **$$**
(☎028-312 1712; www.thepottingshedaccommodation.co.za; 28 Albertyn St; s/d incl breakfast R715/920;) This friendly guesthouse offers delightful personal touches, including homemade whale-shaped biscuits on arrival. The neat rooms are comfortable and have bright, imaginative decor. There's a spacious loft studio and the owners also operate stylish self-catering apartments (four people R1150) closer to the sea.

Windsor Hotel HOTEL **$$**
(☎028-312 3727; www.windsorhotel.co.za; 49 Marine Dr; s/d incl breakfast R900/1250;) A sea-facing room at this stalwart overlooking the ocean means you'll be able to whale-watch from your bed. Rooms have had a bit of a revamp but are still true to the hotel's Victorian roots. There are also large, sea-facing apartments (four people R1500).

Baleia de Hermanus GUESTHOUSE **$$**
(☎028-312 2513; www.baleia.co.za; 57 Main Rd; s/d incl breakfast R520/960;) The smart, comfortable rooms are set around a swimming pool. Owner-run, it's a friendly and welcoming spot.

Harbour House Hotel HOTEL **$$$**
(☎028-312 1799; www.harbourhousehotel.co.za; 22 Harbour Rd; d incl breakfast from R2100;) Some of the bright, modern rooms have kitchenettes and all have a balcony or terrace. It's a delightful seaside hotel and the ocean views from the infinity pool are phenomenal.

Marine LUXURY HOTEL **$$$**
(☎028-313 1000; www.themarine.co.za; Marine Dr; r incl breakfast from R5000;) Right on the sea with immaculate grounds and amenities, including two sea-facing restaurants. The **Pavilion** (www.themarine.co.za; Marine Dr; mains R130-180; ⌚breakfast & dinner)

serves contemporary South African cuisine while the **Seafood Restaurant** (www.themarine.co.za; Marine Dr; mains R100-195; ⊙lunch & dinner) offers more range than its name would suggest.

Eating & Drinking

Eatery CAFE $
(Long St Arcade, Long St; mains R50-90; ⊙breakfast & lunch Mon-Fri, breakfast & brunch Sat) Tucked away in an arcade, this is a local hangout, lauded for its excellent coffee, fresh salads and sandwiches plus a range of tasty cakes baked on-site.

★**Burgundy Restaurant** SEAFOOD $$
(☎028-312 2800; www.burgundyrestaurant.co.za; Marine Dr; mains R70-175; ⊙breakfast, lunch & dinner) This long-standing restaurant is still going strong, popular with both locals and tourists as much for its superb sea view as for its menu. Seafood is the star, though vegetarians and carnivores are also well served.

Bistro at Just Pure CAFE $$
(www.justpurebistro.co.za; Park Ln, cnr Marine Dr; mains R55-95; ⊙breakfast & lunch; 📶) Adjoining a shop selling natural cosmetics, this seafront bistro is all about fresh, local, organic ingredients. Try the 'famous' cheesecake and watch whales from the patio as you eat.

Fisherman's Cottage SEAFOOD $$
(Lemm's Cnr; mains R70-140; ⊙dinner Mon, lunch & dinner Tue-Sat, lunch Sun) The emphasis is on seafood at this 1860s thatched cottage draped with fishing nets, though it also serves steaks and traditional meals.

Bientang's Cave BAR
(www.bientangscave.com; Marine Dr; ⊙lunch) This cave, occupied by the last Strandlopers (coastal indigenous people) at the turn of the 19th century, has a truly remarkable setting and is definitely worth a stop for a drink. Consider moving elsewhere for lunch. Access is only via a steep flight of cliff-side stairs.

Gecko Bar BAR
(New Harbour; ⊙11am-2am) The decor is a bit shabby but the ocean views make up for it. There's sushi and pizza on the menu (mains R45 to R75), local beer on tap and live music on weekends.

Shimmi BAR
(☎083 235 0881; Village Sq, Marine Dr; ⊙2pm-2am Wed-Sun) A chilled-out bar with good cocktails and DJs most nights.

Information

Hermanus Tourism (☎028-313 1602; www.hermanustourism.info; Market Sq; ⊙9am-6pm

WINE TASTING AROUND HERMANUS

The area is best known for whales but there are also some superb wineries just outside Hermanus. The **Hemel-en-Aarde** (Heaven on Earth) valley starts 5km west of the town and follows a winding route north for 15km.

If you don't have a nondrinker in your party, the highly recommended **Tuk-Tuk Transporter** (p130) provides transport between three wine farms, a stop for lunch and return to your accommodation for R250.

For an alternative way to see the wineries, join a quad-biking tour with **SA Forest Adventures** (☎083 517 3635; www.saforestadventures.co.za; tours R600).

Bouchard Finlayson (☎028-312 3515; www.bouchardfinlayson.co.za; tastings R140; ⊙9am-5pm Mon-Fri, 10am-1pm Sat) A traditional cellar known for its superlative pinot noir.

La Vierge (www.lavierge.co.za; Hemel en Aarde Road; tastings R30; ⊙tastings 9am-5pm, lunch Wed-Sun) Offers tastings and lunch (mains R75 to R150) in its ubermodern winery decked out in hot pink and glass.

Newton Johnson (☎021-200 2148; www.newtonjohnson.com; tastings free; ⊙9am-4pm Mon Fri, 10am-2pm Sat; restaurant lunch Wed-Sun, dinner Fri & Sat) Has a superb restaurant (mains R120 to R160).

Creation (www.creationwines.com; Hemel en Aarde Rd; pairing experiences from R75, restaurant mains R135; ⊙10am-5pm) Best known for its various wine-pairing options, which include a superb wine-and-canape pairing (R125) as well as tea pairings for designated drivers and even a juice pairing for kids. The restaurant menu lists the local butchers, bakers, cheesemakers and the like who supply the ingredients. Guided walks of the estate are also offered (R295).

1

FRASER HALL / GETTY IMAGES ©

2

4

HOUGAARD MALAN / GETTY IMAGES ©

ARIADNE VAN ZANDBERGEN / GETTY IMAGES ©

ROGER DE LA HARPE / GETTY IMAGES ©

1. Stellenbosch (p100)
Cape Dutch architecture adds an air of elegance to this lively town.

2. Cederberg Wilderness Area (p162)
Spectacular rock formations abound in this hiker's heaven.

3. Knysna oysters
Knysna (p143), a popular town on the Garden Route, is home to a thriving oyster industry.

4. Hermanus (p124)
Southern right whales swim in Walker Bay from June to December.

GETTING AROUND HERMANUS

Hermanus town centre is compact but if you're staying in the 'burbs you will find the handy **Tuk-Tuk Transporter** (084 688 5885; www.hermanustaxi.com) a cheap way to get around. A standard fare is R40 for two people.

Mon-Fri, 9am-5pm Sat, 11am-3pm Sun) Although this is not the main tourism office, it's in a much more convenient location. Staff are exceptionally helpful and the whale crier works here when there are no whales in the bay.

The larger tourism office (028-312 2629; www.hermanustourism.info; Mitchell St, Old Station Bldg; 8am-6pm Mon-Fri, 9am-5pm Sat, 11am-3pm Sun) is just north of the town.

Getting There & Away

Bernardus Tours (028-316 1093; bniehaus@vodamail.co.za) offers shuttles to Gansbaai (R400, 30 minutes) and Cape Town (R800, 1½ hours).

The hostels run a shuttle service (R75 one-way, 30 minutes) to the Baz Bus drop-off point in Botrivier, 50km west of town. There are no regular bus services to Hermanus from Cape Town.

Gansbaai

POP 11,600

Gansbaai's star has risen in recent years thanks to shark-cage diving, though most people just visit on a day trip from Cape Town. The unspoilt coastline is perfect for those wishing to explore more out-of-the-way Overberg nature spots.

The road from Hermanus leads you past the village of De Kelders – a great spot for secluded whale watching – straight into Main Rd, which runs parallel to the coastline. Kleinbaai, 7km further east along the coast, is the launch point for shark-cage diving tours.

Sights & Activities

A number of shark-cage diving operators are clustered around Kleinbaai's harbour, including **Marine Dynamics** (079 930 9694; www.sharkwatchsa.com; adult/child R1500/900) and **White Shark Projects** (028-007 0001; www.whitesharkprojects.co.za; dives R1500), which both have Fairtrade accreditation.

Walker Bay Reserve PARK

(adult/child R40/20; 7am-7pm) There are good walks here, and birdwatching, along with the impressive Klipgat Caves, site of an archaeological discovery of Khoe-San artefacts. Dyer Island, a breeding colony for African penguins, is 7km off the Danger Point coast.

Danger Point Lighthouse LIGHTHOUSE

(028-384 0530; adult/child R16/8; 10am-3pm Mon-Fri) Dating from 1895, the lighthouse is set in pretty grounds and has some information on the 1852 HMS *Birkenhead* shipwreck. The lighthouse is privately owned and opening times are not always observed.

Sleeping & Eating

Gansbaai Backpackers BACKPACKERS $

(083 626 4150; www.gansbaybackpackers.com; 6 Strand St; dm R140, d with/without bathroom R450/400;) Efficient and friendly, this is a great place for budget accommodation and activity bookings.

Aire del Mar GUESTHOUSE $$

(028-384 2848; www.airedelmar.co.za; 7 Van Dyk St, Kleinbaai; s/d incl breakfast R550/920;) A friendly place offering a good range of prices, including basic self-catering units (two people R680). Rooms have panoramic sea views out to Dyer Island.

★**Grootbos Private Nature Reserve** LODGE $$$

(028-384 8008; www.grootbos.com; Rte 43; s/d full board R6300/8400;) This superb luxury choice set on 17 sq km includes horse riding, hiking and local excursions in the price. Each of the free-standing cottages has an outdoor shower on the deck. The Grootbos Foundation runs a number of environmental and community projects – ask about the Social Responsibility Tour.

★**Coffee on the Rocks** CAFE $$

(028-384 2017; Cliff St, De Kelders; mains R50-110; 10am-5pm Wed-Sun) All breads are baked daily on-site and everything else is homemade too. The ocean-facing deck is a great place for a sandwich, a salad or just a coffee while you look out for whales in season.

Blue Goose SOUTH AFRICAN $$

(079 310 1770; 12 Franken St; mains R80-135; dinner Mon-Sun, lunch Fri-Sun) Based in an old fishing cottage, this local favourite has a menu that showcases local, seasonal ingredients. It's best known for seafood, though the lamb shank is also very good.

SHARK-CAGE DIVING CONTROVERSY

There has been much controversy over the last few years regarding shark-cage diving. Detractors believe that operators use bait to attract sharks to the cages in which people dive, thereby teaching these killers that boats and humans are associated with food. Attacks on swimmers and surfers are said to have increased as a direct result.

But the activity has many supporters, including marine scientists and even some environmentalists. Their argument is that shark-cage diving is a positive education tool that helps to remove fear and alleviate the bad rep these fish have had since the *Jaws* movie back in 1975.

Licensed operators are not allowed to use bait but throw 'chum' – blood and guts from other fish – into the water. The sharks are attracted by the smell but there's nothing for them to eat. Once the sharks come close, participants clad in wetsuits and snorkel masks take a deep breath and submerge themselves in the water for a close encounter with the great whites. No scuba experience is necessary and underwater visibility is best from May to September.

If you want to experience this close encounter with a wild animal, make sure you use a licensed operator who is fully insured.

If you prefer to avoid shark-cage diving, get in touch with an operator such as **Simon's Town Boat Company** (☎083 257 7760; www.boatcompany.co.za), which offers boat trips to view sharks feasting at Seal Island (a shark's diet consists of penguins and seals).

Great White House SEAFOOD $$
(☎028-384 3273; www.thegreatwhitehouse.co.za; 5 Geelbek St, Kleinbaai; mains R50-140; ⌚breakfast, lunch & dinner Wed-Mon, breakfast & lunch Tue) A multifarious place that dishes up fresh seafood (including hard-to-find abalone), clothing and curios, helps with tourist information and offers accommodation in pleasant thatched cottages (single/double including breakfast R560/840).

ℹ Information

Gansbaai Tourism (☎028-384 1439; www.gansbaaiinfo.com; Main Rd, Great White Junction; ⌚9am-5pm Mon-Fri, 9am-4pm Sat, 10am-2pm Sun)

ℹ Getting There & Away

Bernardus Tours (☎028-316 1093; bniehaus@vodamail.co.za) Runs shuttles to Hermanus (R400, 30 minutes) and Cape Town (R1000, two hours).

Cape Agulhas

Cape Agulhas is the southernmost tip of Africa, where the Atlantic and Indian Oceans collide. It's a rugged, windswept coastline and the graveyard for many a ship. Most people head straight for a photo with the sign marking where the oceans meet.

If you don't have your own wheels, contact the backpacker hostels in Hermanus or Robertson to arrange a tour.

Cape Agulhas Lighthouse LIGHTHOUSE
(adult/child R22/11; ⌚9am-5pm) It's worth climbing the 71 steps to the top. There's an interesting museum inside, as well as the **tourism bureau** (☎028-435 7185; www.discovercapeagulhas.co.za).

Agulhas National Park NATIONAL PARK
(☎028-435 6078; www.sanparks.org; adult/child R128/64) There is a range of hikes from 3km to 10km in length. Recommended is the 5.5km Rasperpunt Trail, which takes in the *Meisho Maru* shipwreck. An information booklet for each hike is available at the park office for R10. Also has charming self-catering **accommodation** (cottage/chalet R770/1075) by the sea.

Cape Agulhas Backpackers BACKPACKERS $
(☎082 372 3354; www.capeagulhasbackpackers.com; Duiker St, cnr Main St; dm R120, d with/without bathroom R400/350) Along the coast in Struisbaai, this is a good base for exploring the area. It's in a prime kite-surfing spot, and offers lessons as well as surfboard rentals.

Arniston (Waenhuiskrans)

POP 1300

One of the Western Cape's gems, Arniston is a charming village in a dramatic, windswept setting. It has a bit of an identity crisis – it's named after both the vessel wrecked off its treacherous coast in 1815 and the sea cave large enough to turn an ox-wagon

WORTH A TRIP

STANFORD

This picture-perfect village on the banks of the Klein River is a popular spot with Capetonians on weekends, and for good reason. The surrounding area boasts a handful of uncrowded wineries – try **Robert Stanford Estate** (☎028-341 0647; www.robertstanfordestate.co.za; Rte 43; tastings free; ⏲8am-4pm Thu-Sun) for its excellent sauvignon blanc and charming country restaurant. In Stanford itself you'll find trips on the river, kayaks for hire and a picturesque **brewery** (☎028-341 0013; www.birkenhead.co.za; Rte 326; tours incl tasting R40; ⏲10am-5pm, tours 10am & 3pm Wed-Fri) offering tastings on the lawn in summer or by a log fire in winter.

(Waenhuiskrans means 'ox-wagon crag'); not that a wagon could have got inside the cave as the small entrance is down a cliff.

Colourful boats, warm blue-green waters and the backdrop of **Kassiesbaai**, the 200-year-old hamlet of whitewashed cottages that forms the core of the town, make a pretty picture. South of Kassiesbaai is **Roman Beach** with white sand and gentle waves. It's a good place to bring the children as there are caves, coves and rock pools filled with sea urchins and colourful anemones at both ends. Be careful not to touch the sea urchins, because they can cause nasty cuts.

To visit the large sea **cave**, follow the signs marked 'Grot' (cave) south of Roman Beach, along the sandy road and down the cliffside to the sea. Note that the cave is only accessible at low tide.

Arniston Resort CAMPGROUND, CHALETS $
(Waenhuiskrans Oord; ☎028-445 9620; arniston@capeagulhas.com; Main Rd; camping/chalets from R130/450) This decent budget option has campsites and basic chalets a short walk from the beach. Bring your own bedding and provisions.

Arniston Seaside Cottages CABIN $$
(☎028-445 9772; www.arnistonseasidecottages.co.za; s/d self-catering R480/640) There are 22 whitewashed, thatched cottages dotted around the town. All are well equipped and comfortable, with some offering ocean views. Breakfast (R160) is served at the Arniston Spa Hotel.

★**Arniston Spa Hotel** HOTEL $$$
(☎028-445 9000; www.arnistonhotel.com; Beach Rd; s/d sea-facing incl breakfast from R1410/1880; 📶❄) The Arniston is a light-filled luxury hotel with a nautical theme and its own spa. Sea-facing rooms have floor-to-ceiling windows. The ocean-view restaurant serves lunch (R50 to R110) and dinner (R80 to R235) and has an extensive wine list.

★**Willeen's Restaurant** SOUTH AFRICAN $$
(☎028-445 9995; House C26, Kassiesbaai; mains from R85; ⏲lunch & dinner) You can sample true local cooking at this restaurant, based in a Kassiesbaai home. Willeen will rustle up a traditional fisherperson's meal. You'll need to book in advance, and bring your own wine.

De Hoop Nature Reserve

De Hoop Nature Reserve NATURE RESERVE
(☎028-542 1114; www.capenature.co.za; adult/child R40/20; ⏲7.30am-4pm) Covering 340 sq km and extending 5km out to sea, this reserve has a magnificent coastline, with long stretches of pristine beach and huge dunes. It's an important breeding and calving area for the southern right whale. You'll find exceptional coastal *fynbos* and animals such as endangered Cape mountain zebras and bonteboks. There is also prolific birdlife, including the only remaining breeding colony of the rare Cape vultures.

The reserve is about 260km from Cape Town, and the final 57km from either Bredasdorp or Swellendam is untarred. The only access to the reserve is via Wydgeleë on the Bredasdorp-to-Malgas road. Note that if you approach via Malgas, you'll have to take the manually operated pont (river ferry) over the Breede River (between dawn and dusk). The village of Ouplaas, 15km from the reserve entrance, is the nearest place to buy fuel and supplies. If you don't have your own car, try Swellencab in Swellendam, who offer days tours.

Whale Trail HIKING
(☎021-483 0190; per person R1540) Although there are numerous day walks, an overnight mountain-bike trail and good snorkelling along the coast, the De Hoop Nature Reserve's most interesting feature is the five-day Whale Trail. The 55km hike offers excellent opportunities to see whales between June and December. Accommodation is in modern, fully equipped self-catering cottages.

De Hoop Collection CAMPGROUND, CABIN **$$**
(☎021-422 4522; www.dehoopcollection.co.za; camping per site R325, rondavel without bathroom from R840, cottage from R1325) There's a staggering range of accommodation and something for every budget, from campsites and *rondavels* (huts) with shared ablutions, to elegant guesthouse rooms in the old stables (double including breakfast and dinner from R1900). You can self-cater or try the restaurant.

Swellendam

POP 17,500

Surrounded by the undulating wheat lands of the Overberg and protected by the Langeberge mountain range, Swellendam is perfectly positioned for exploring the Little Karoo and makes a good stopover on the way further east to the Garden Route. One of the oldest towns in South Africa (it dates back to 1745), it has beautiful Cape Dutch architecture and a worthwhile museum.

Sights & Activities

Drostdy Museum MUSEUM
(www.drostdymuseum.com; 18 Swellengrebel St; adult/child R25/5; ⏲9am-4.45pm Mon-Fri, 10am-3pm Sat & Sun) The centrepiece of this excellent museum is the beautiful *drostdy* (residence of an official) itself, which dates from 1747. The museum ticket also covers entrance to the nearby **Old Gaol**, where you'll find part of the original administrative buildings and a watermill; and **Mayville** (Hermanus Steyn St), another residence dating back to 1853, with a formal Victorian garden.

Marloth Nature Reserve NATURE RESERVE
(☎028-514 1410; www.capenature.co.za; adult/child R40/20) Perched in the Langeberge, 1.5km north of town, this reserve is particularly pretty in October and November when the ericas are in flower. If the day hikes don't hit the spot, try the demanding Swellendam Hiking Trail, regarded as one of South Africa's top 10 hikes. You can choose to walk any duration from two to six days. There are two basic overnight huts, and you'll need to be self-sufficient. Entrance to the reserve is via Andrew Whyte St.

Dutch Reformed Church CHURCH
(Voortrek St) Swellendam residents swear every visitor takes a photograph of this enormous church in the centre of town.

OFF THE BEATEN TRACK

ELIM

Even in a province awash with pretty villages, Elim stands out. This Moravian mission village lies some 30km from anywhere, and while one paved road now reaches the sprinkling of thatched cottages, it's still a remote and largely unvisited part of the Western Cape. Seek out local guide **Emile Richter** (☎074 544 7733) for a fascinating tour of the outsize church, slave monument and fully functioning watermill dating back to the mid-19th century. These days the watermill houses a pleasant tearoom, certainly the best place to get a snack. In an interesting juxtaposition, there is a trio of **wineries** on the tarred road from Bredasdorp. Elim itself is a dry town.

Two Feathers Horse Trails HORSE RIDING
(☎082 494 8279; 5 Lichtenstein St, Swellendam Backpackers Adventure Lodge; per hr R300) There are horse rides in the mountains lasting anything from an hour to a couple of days. Both inexperienced and experienced riders are catered for. Advance booking is essential.

Sleeping

Swellendam Backpackers Adventure Lodge BACKPACKERS **$**
(☎028-514 2648; www.swellendambackpackers.co.za; 5 Lichtenstein St; s/d without bathroom R250/300, s/d R350/410; ⓦ) This excellent hostel is set on a huge plot of land bordering the Marloth Nature Reserve. Horse riding, permits to the reserve and day trips to Cape Agulhas (R650) can all be arranged. The Baz Bus stops right outside. The dorms were being renovated when we visited, and the garden cabins with shared bathrooms are great value.

★**Cypress Cottage** GUESTHOUSE **$$**
(☎028-514 3296; www.cypress-cottage.co.za; 3 Voortrek St; s/d R495/770; ❄ⓦ≋) There are six individually decorated rooms in this 200-year-old house with a gorgeous garden and a refreshing pool. It's within walking distance of the church, museum and a handful of restaurants.

Braeside B&B B&B **$$**
(☎028-514 3325; www.braeside.co.za; 13 Van Oudtshoorn Rd; s/d incl breakfast from R700/1100; ❄ⓦ≋) This quiet, gracious Cape Edwardian

Swellendam

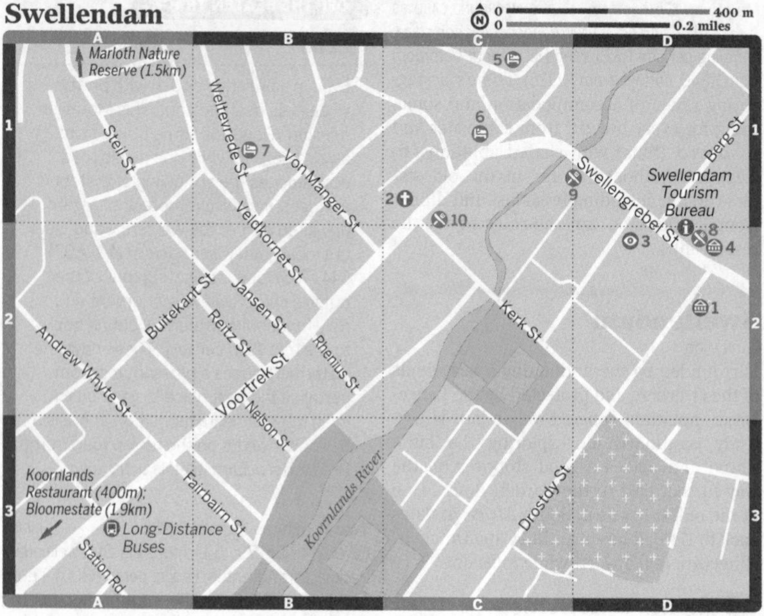

Swellendam

Sights

1 Drostdy Museum D2
2 Dutch Reformed Church C1
3 Mayville D2
4 Old Gaol D2

Sleeping

5 Braeside B&B C1
6 Cypress Cottage C1
7 De Kloof B1

Eating

8 Field & Fork D2
9 La Belle Alliance D1
10 Old Gaol on Church Square C1

home boasts a lovely garden, fantastic views and knowledgeable, gay-friendly hosts.

Bloomestate GUESTHOUSE $$$
(☎028-514 2984; www.bloomestate.com; 276 Voortrek St; s/d incl breakfast from R1485/1980; ❄📶🏊) A modern, friendly guesthouse set on a beautiful property, which offers Zenlike privacy to go with the luxurious, colourful rooms. Health and beauty treatments are available and, if relaxing around the pool isn't enough, you can hop in the spa bath that's sitting on a deck under the trees.

De Kloof GUESTHOUSE $$$
(☎028-514 1303; www.dekloof.co.za; 8 Weltevrede St; s/d incl breakfast from R1835/2750; ❄📶🏊) One of Swellendam's swankiest options, this is a supremely stylish guesthouse with a surprisingly personal touch. It's on a large estate dating back to 1801; the luxurious rooms are set around lawns where ducks wander. A couple of the suites come with spa bath and king-size heated waterbed.

Eating

La Belle Alliance SOUTH AFRICAN $
(1 Swellengrebel St; mains R50-100; ⏲breakfast & lunch) This appealing tearoom had the honour of serving Nelson Mandela in 1999. In an old Masonic lodge with shaded outdoor tables beside the Koornlands River, it's a good spot for lunch.

★Old Gaol on Church Square SOUTH AFRICAN $$
(www.oldgaolrestaurant.co.za; 8A Voortrek St; light meals R50-120; ⏲breakfast & lunch daily, dinner Wed-Fri; 👪) It might not be in the Old Gaol anymore, but the food at this empowerment venture is still just as good. There's lots of seating outside under the trees where you can enjoy delicious cakes, traditional breads and Cape Malay dishes.

Koornlands Restaurant SOUTH AFRICAN $$
(☎082 430 8188; www.koornlandsrestaurant.co.za; 192 Voortrek St; mains R85-160; ⊙dinner Wed-Mon) An eclectic menu of mostly African meat is served in an intimate candlelit setting. Among the more unusual offerings are crocodile sashimi and warthog samosas.

Field & Fork FUSION $$$
(☎028-514 3430; 26 Swellengrebel St; mains R110-185; ⊙dinner Mon-Sat) Locals rave about this stylish place based in the Old Gaol building. The small menu features intricate dishes that use local ingredients such as springbok, Karoo lamb and Franschhoek trout. There's also a three-course set menu (R265).

Information

Swellendam Tourism Bureau (☎028-514 2770; www.swellendamtourism.co.za; 22 Swellengrebel St; ⊙9am-5pm Mon-Fri, 9am-2pm Sat & Sun) A helpful office based in the Old Gaoler's Cottage. It rents mountain bikes (R150 per day) and staff can advise on biking routes.

Getting There & Away

All three major bus companies pass through Swellendam on their runs between Cape Town and Port Elizabeth, stopping opposite the Swellengrebel Hotel on Voortrek St. The Baz Bus stops at Swellendam Backpackers Adventure Lodge.

Bontebok National Park

Bontebok National Park NATIONAL PARK
(☎028-514 2735; adult/child R60/30; ⊙7am-7pm Oct-Apr, 7am-6pm May-Sep) Some 6km south of Swellendam is this national park, proclaimed in 1931 to save the remaining 30 bontebok. The project was successful, and bontebok as well as other antelopes and mountain zebras can be found in this smallest of South Africa's national parks. The *fynbos* that flowers in late winter and spring, rare renosterveld and an abundance of birdlife are features of the park. Swimming is possible in the Breede River.

A lot of thought has gone into the park's accommodation. Basic commodities, as well as curios, are available at the entrance shop but otherwise, stock up in Swellendam. To reach the park, take the N2 east of Swellendam. The entrance is signposted and is 5km along a gravel road to the south.

Campsites CAMPING $
(from R180) There are pleasant campsites close to the Breede River, some with electricity.

DON'T MISS

SEDGEFIELD FARMERS MARKET

Wild Oats Community Farmers' Market (www.wildoatsmarket.co.za; ⊙7.30am-noon Sat) A Garden Route institution, this farmers market has been operating for over a decade. Get there early to get your pick of the pies, biltong, cheese, cakes, bread, beer, fudge – all from small, local producers. The market is just off the N2, 1.5km east of Sedgefield's town centre.

Lang Elsie's Kraal CHALET $$
(chalet from R900) These 10 chalets have decks overlooking the river. Two of the chalets are adapted for people with special needs.

GARDEN ROUTE

High on the must-see lists of most visitors to South Africa is the Garden Route, and with good reason: you can't help but be seduced by the glorious natural beauty. The distance from Mossel Bay in the west to just beyond Plettenberg Bay in the east is under 300km, yet the range of topography, vegetation, wildlife and outdoor activities is remarkable.

The coast is dotted with excellent beaches, while inland you'll find picturesque lagoons and lakes, rolling hills and eventually the mountains of the Outeniqua and Tsitsikamma ranges that divide the Garden Route from the arid Little Karoo. The ancient indigenous forests that line the coast from Wilderness to Knysna offer adventure trails and hiking, birdwatching, canoeing on the rivers, sliding through the tree canopy or simply taking an easy walk through the forest to gasp at the size of a yellowwood tree that's over 600 years old. Wildlife enthusiasts will enjoy spotting brilliant green and red Knysna loeries or maybe even catching sight of one of the near-mythical elephants said to inhabit the forest.

With such a diverse range of things to do in this renowned region, it's not surprising that the scope of accommodation comes up trumps. The downside is the high volume of people in the most popular towns, Knysna and Plettenberg Bay. While they make good bases for exploring the area, these two spots can get very crowded during December and January, and prices rise significantly. This

Garden Route

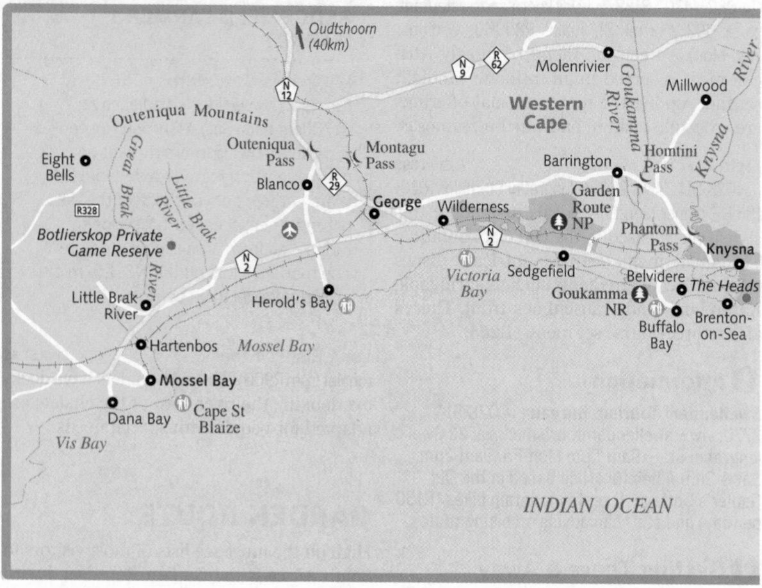

makes it important to book ahead if you're travelling at these times, or head for less crowded Wilderness.

Mossel Bay

POP 30,000

At first glance Mossel Bay is the ugly sister of the Garden Route. It was a hugely popular destination until the 1980s, when the building of the world's largest gas-to-oil refinery and concomitant industrial sprawl uglified it, and it fell into a slump. But if you can see beyond the unimpressive approach road, you'll find some fine beaches, gnarly surf spots, a wealth of activities and good places to stay. It has a way to go to catch up with its more glamorous neighbours, but it's trying hard to grab back some of its former glory.

The Portuguese explorers Bartholomeu Dias and Vasco da Gama were the first Europeans to visit the bay, late in the 15th century. It became a useful place for ships to stop because there was fresh water available and deals could be struck with the local Khoekhoen people. A large milkwood tree beside the spring was used as a postal collection point – expeditions heading east would leave mail to be picked up by ships returning home. The spring and the tree still exist, and you can post letters (they receive a special postmark) from a letterbox within the museum.

Sights

★Dias Museum Complex MUSEUM

(www.diasmuseum.co.za; Market St; adult/child R20/5; 9am-4.45pm Mon-Fri, 9am-3.45pm Sat & Sun; P) This excellent museum includes the spring from which Bartholomeu Dias watered the postal tree, the 1786 Dutch East India Company (Vereenigde Oost-Indische Compagnie; VOC) granary, a shell museum (with some interesting aquarium tanks) and a local history museum. The highlight of the complex is the replica of the caravel that Dias used on his 1488 voyage of discovery (adult/child R20/5). Its small size brings home the extraordinary skill and courage of the early explorers.

The replica was built in Portugal and sailed to Mossel Bay in 1988 to commemorate the 500th anniversary of Dias' trip.

Botlierskop Private Game Reserve WILDLIFE RESERVE

(044-696 6055; www.botlierskop.co.za; Little Brak River) This reserve contains a vast range of wildlife, including lions, elephants, rhinos, buffaloes and giraffes. Day visitors are

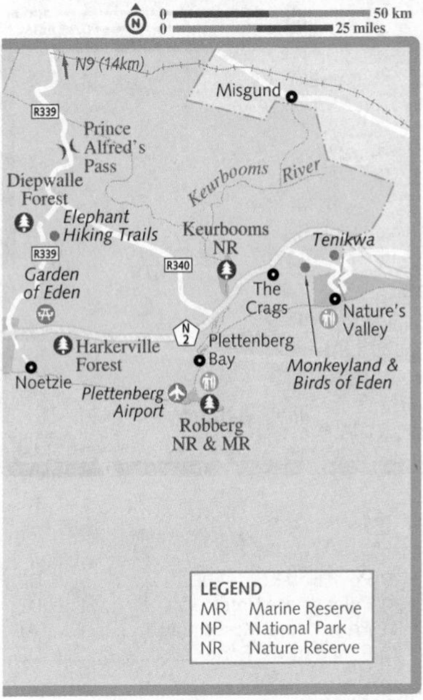

welcome for a variety of activities including three-hour wildlife drives (adult/child R420/210), horse riding (per hour R270) and elephant rides (R820). The reserve is about 20km northeast of Mossel Bay along the N2 (take the Little Brak River turn-off and follow the signs towards Sorgfontein). Bookings essential.

Cape St Blaize Lighthouse LIGHTHOUSE
(adult/child R16/8; 10am-3pm) There are wonderful views from the lighthouse. Sadly, the St Blaize Cave, dating back to the Stone Age era, is rather neglected and frequented by vandals.

Activities

It's easy to see where Mossel Bay's tourism slogan comes from. 'Do stuff', the authorities tell you, and the town is chock-full of activities.

Oystercatcher Trail HIKING
(www.oystercatchertrail.co.za; full board/self-catering from R3200/5400) Hikers can tackle this fabulous coastal trail in three or four days. It follows the coastline from Mossel Bay to Dana Bay via Cape St Blaize, where you're likely to see the endangered black oystercatcher.

Billeon SURFING
(www.billeon.com; 2hr lesson R350) Mossel Bay is well known for its surf and this company offers lessons for beginners. It also runs three-hour sandboarding experiences (R380).

Point of Human Origins CULTURAL TOUR
(044-691 0051; www.humanorigin.co.za; tours R395) Led by an archaeology professor, this fascinating four-hour tour includes a hike to the Pinnacle Point Caves, where discoveries have shed light on human life from 162,000 years ago.

Romonza BOAT TOUR
(044-690 3101; 1hr boat trips R140) Regular boat trips head out to Seal Island to see the seals, birds and dolphins that frequent these waters. In late winter and spring this outfit also runs whale-watching trips (R640, 2½ hours).

Skydive Mossel Bay ADVENTURE SPORTS
(082 824 8599; www.skydivemosselbay.com; Mossel Bay Airfield; skydives from R2000) Tandem skydives start from 3000m and when the weather and tides cooperate you get to land on Diaz Beach.

White Shark Africa DIVING
(044-691 3796; www.whitesharkafrica.com; 7 Church St; dives R1350) Full-day cage-diving trips to view great white sharks, including lunch, drinks and snacks.

Electrodive DIVING
(082 561 1259; www.electrodive.co.za; Mossel Bay Harbour; PADI open-water course R3600, boat-based dives from R225) While diving in Mossel Bay offers the opportunity to see quite a lot of coral, fish and other sea creatures, these aren't tropical waters and you're not going to have perfect visibility.

Sleeping

There are three municipal caravan parks in town. **Bakke** (044-690 3501, 044-691 2915; Santos Beach; camping per site from R210, chalet from R520) and **Santos** (044-690 3501, 044-691 2915; Santos Beach; camping per site from R210) are next to each other on pretty Santos Beach. **Punt** (044-690 3501, 044-691 2915; camping per site R210) is on the Point and very close to the surf. Prices rise steeply in December and January.

Mossel Bay Backpackers BACKPACKERS $
(044-691 3182; www.mosselbayhostel.co.za; 1 Marsh St; dm R140-160, d with/without bathroom R450/380;) This well-run and

Mossel Bay

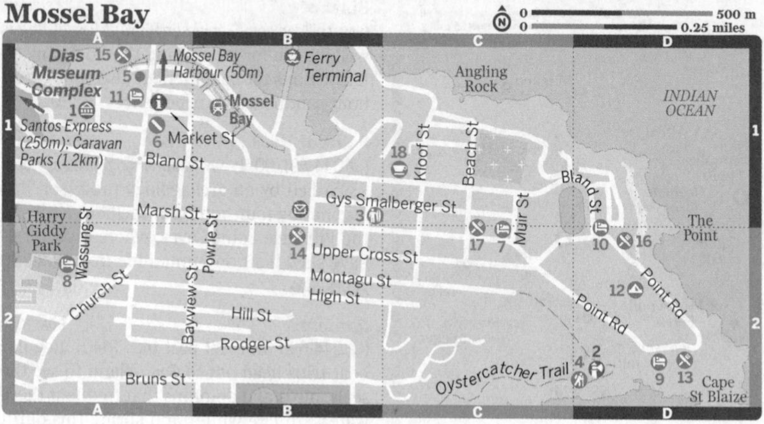

Mossel Bay

Top Sights
1 Dias Museum Complex ... A1

Sights
2 Cape St Blaize Lighthouse ... D2

Activities, Courses & Tours
3 Billeon ... B1
Electrodive ... (see 15)
4 Oystercatcher Trail ... D2
5 Romonza ... A1
6 White Shark Africa ... A1

Sleeping
7 Mossel Bay Backpackers ... C2
8 Park House Lodge & Travel Centre ... A2
9 Point Hotel ... D2
10 Point Village Hotel ... D2
11 Protea Hotel Mossel Bay ... A1
12 Punt Caravan Park ... D2

Eating
13 Big Blu ... D2
Café Gannet ... (see 11)
14 Café Havana ... B2
15 Kaai 4 ... A1
16 Kingfisher ... D2
17 Villa Point ... C2

Drinking & Nightlife
18 Blue Shed Coffee Roastery ... C1

long-established backpackers has swallowed the adjoining guesthouse, meaning there are some excellent en suite rooms on offer alongside dorms and basic doubles. There's even a honeymoon suite, complete with spa bath. Staff can arrange all sorts of activities.

Park House Lodge & Travel Centre BACKPACKERS $
(044-691 1937; www.park-house.co.za; 121 High St; camping/dm R110/170, d with/without bathroom R780/460;) This place, in a gracious old sandstone house next to the park, is friendly, smartly decorated and has beautiful gardens. Breakfast is R50, and staff can organise activities.

Santos Express BACKPACKERS $
(083 900 7797; www.santosexpress.co.za; Santos Beach; dm R120, s/d without bathroom R225/430) The position of this converted train, right beside the beach, can't be beaten, but the compartments are undeniably cramped. There's an attached bar-restaurant, with a very large menu (mains R50 to R140).

★**Point Village Hotel** HOTEL $$
(044-690 3156; www.pointvillagehotel.co.za; 5 Point Rd; s/d R500/840) The quirky, fake lighthouse on this exceptionally well-priced hotel's exterior is a sign of what's inside: a range of fun, funky, bright rooms and friendly service. Rooms have a kitchenette and some have balconies. There are also two- and three-bedroom apartments with good sea views (R1800).

Protea Hotel Mossel Bay HOTEL $$
(044-691 3738; www.proteahotels.com/mosselbay; Market St; r from R1375;) Part of the Protea chain, this is a classy hotel set in

the old post office building. Its restaurant, **Café Gannet** (www.proteahotels.com/mosselbay; Market St; mains R40-170; ⏲breakfast, lunch & dinner), has a large seafood, meat and pizza menu.

Point Hotel HOTEL $$$
(☎044-691 3512; www.pointhotel.co.za; Point Rd; s/d R1285/1710; 📶) This modern hotel boasts a spectacular location, right above the wave-pounded rocks at the Point. There's a decent restaurant (mains R60 to R120) and the spacious rooms have balconies with ocean views – request a south-facing room for the best vistas.

Eating & Drinking

Marsh St and the Point are where all the restaurant and nightlife action happens in Mossel Bay.

★**Kaai 4** BRAAI $$
(www.kaai4.co.za; Mossel Bay Harbour; mains R30-95; ⏲lunch & dinner) Boasting one of Mossel Bay's best locations, this low-key restaurant has picnic tables on the sand overlooking the ocean. Most of the dishes – including stews, burgers, boerewors (sausages) and some seafood – are cooked on massive fire pits and there's local beer on tap.

Café Havana INTERNATIONAL $$
(www.cafehavana.co.za; 38 Marsh St; mains R50-110; ⏲breakfast, lunch & dinner; 📶) A long-running Cuban-themed restaurant that's as popular as ever. Stews, steaks and seafood all make it on to the menu and there's a good cocktail list. It stays open late and is the best place for some after-hours action.

Big Blu INTERNATIONAL $$
(Point Rd; mains R50-95) This ramshackle place right on the rocks at the Point is great for a sundowner and serves burgers, seafood and steaks.

Kingfisher SEAFOOD $$
(Point Rd; mains R75-135; ⏲lunch & dinner) Locals love the seafood dishes and ocean views. It also serves salads, meat, and has a children's menu.

Villa Point SOUTH AFRICAN $$$
(☎044-691 1923; 11 Marsh St; mains R105-180; ⏲lunch & dinner Mon-Sat) A well-respected restaurant based in an old house. The menu is small and includes plenty of South African meat, including rack of lamb, kudu osso bucco and the very popular springbok shank.

★**Blue Shed Coffee Roastery** CAFE
(33 Bland St; ⏲6.30am-8pm; 📶) Enjoy great coffee and homemade cakes at this funky

SURFING ALONG THE GARDEN ROUTE

With the water warming up as you round Cape Agulhas, where the Indian Ocean takes over, you can be happy surfing in just boardshorts or a short suit during summer. You'll need a full suit in winter. There are good waves along the coast but Mossel Bay and Victoria Bay are considered the best spots.

In **Mossel Bay**, the main surf spot is Outer Pool (left of the tidal pool) – a great reef and point break. There's also a soft wave called Inner Pool to the right of the tidal pool. Elsewhere there's a good right in a big swell called Ding Dangs that's best at a lowish tide, especially in a southwesterly or easterly wind. If might be a bit of a hassle paddling out, but the right is better than the left.

You might find something at Grootbrak and Kleinbrak, but better is **Herold's Bay**. When it's on, there's a left-hand wedge along the beach, and it's unusual in that it works in a northwesterly wind.

Best of all is **Victoria Bay**, which has the most consistent breaks along this coast. It's perfect when the swell is about 1m to 2m and you get a great right-hander.

A little further along is **Buffalo Bay** (Buffel's Bay) where there's another right-hand point. Buffalo Bay is at one end of Brenton Beach; at the northern end, you'll find some good peaks but watch out for sharks.

On to **Plettenberg Bay**: avoid Robberg Peninsula, which is home to a seal colony. But the swimming area at Robberg Beach (where lifeguards are stationed) can have some good waves if the swell isn't too big. Central Beach has one of the best-known waves, the Wedge, which is perfect for goofy-footers. Lookout Beach can have some sandbanks and the Point can be good, but there's a lot of erosion here and the beach is slowly disappearing. Watch out for rip currents, especially when there are no lifeguards on duty.

WORTH A TRIP

EIGHT BELLS MOUNTAIN INN

Eight Bells Mountain Inn (044-631 0000; www.eightbells.co.za; s/d from R750/1200;) This country inn is 35km north of Mossel Bay on Rte 328 to Oudtshoorn (50km). It's in a lovely mountain setting at the foot of the Robinson Pass and its large grounds have something for everyone from children to squash players. You'll find a variety of rooms; the *rondavels* are fun. There's a tea garden, restaurant, and opportunities to hike and ride horses on the property. Prices rise sharply during school holidays.

cafe with eclectic decor and ocean views from the deck. It's an awesome spot to spend a couple of hours chilling or playing vinyl on the old-school jukebox.

Information

Tourism Bureau (044-691 2202; www.visitmosselbay.co.za; Market St; 8am-6pm Mon-Fri, 9am-4pm Sat & Sun) Staff are very friendly and can help with accommodation bookings. Pick up a brochure detailing a self-guided walking tour of historic Mossel Bay.

Getting There & Away

Mossel Bay is off the highway, so the long-distance buses don't come into town; they drop passengers at the Voorbaai Shell petrol station, 8km away. The hostels can usually collect you if you give notice, but private taxis (R80) are often waiting for bus passengers who need onward travel. If none are there call 082 932 5809, or during the day take a shared taxi (R10). The Baz Bus will drop you in town.

Translux (www.translux.co.za), Greyhound (www.greyhound.co.za) and Intercape (www.intercape.co.za) buses stop here on their Cape Town–Port Elizabeth runs. Intercape fares from Mossel Bay include Knysna (R310, two hours, twice daily), Plettenberg Bay (R310, 2½ hours, twice daily), Cape Town (R380, six hours, twice daily) and Port Elizabeth (R380, 6½ hours, twice daily).

George

POP 114,000

George, founded in 1811, is the largest town on the Garden Route yet remains little more than a commercial centre and transport hub with not much to keep visitors for long. It has some attractive old buildings, including the tiny St Mark's Cathedral and the more imposing Dutch Reformed Mother Church, but it's 8km from the coast and for most of its visitors its chief draw is the range of championship golf courses.

Sights & Activities

George Museum MUSEUM
(Courtenay St; admission by donation; 9am-4.30pm Mon-Fri, 9am-12.30pm Sat) George was the hub of the indigenous timber industry and, thus, this museum contains a wealth of related artefacts.

Outeniqua Transport Museum MUSEUM
(York St, cnr Courtenay St; adult/child R20/10; 8am-4.30pm Mon-Fri, 8am-2pm Sat) The starting point and terminus for journeys on the Outeniqua Power Van, this museum is worth a visit if you're interested in trains. A dozen locomotives and 15 carriages, as well as many detailed models, have found a retirement home here, including a carriage used by the British royal family in the 1940s.

Sleeping & Eating

Outeniqua Travel Lodge BACKPACKERS $
(082 316 7720; www.outeniqualodge.com; 70 Langenhoven St; dm/s/d R130/350/480;) It's a way from the centre, but this is a great budget option with en suite rooms in a quiet, residential area. Staff are friendly and can arrange activities.

★**French Lodge International** GUESTHOUSE $$
(044-874 0345; www.frenchlodge.co.za; 29 York St; s/d incl breakfast from R650/800;) Rooms are in luxurious thatched-roof *rondavels* set around the pool, with satellite TV and bathrooms with spa baths.

Fancourt Hotel LUXURY HOTEL $$$
(044-804 0000; www.fancourt.co.za; Montagu St, Blanco; d from R3400;) This is the area's most luxurious option, about 10km from the town centre, and has three 18-hole golf courses designed by Gary Player. There's a health spa and four restaurants.

Old Townhouse STEAKHOUSE $$
(044-874 3663; Market St; mains R50-130; lunch & dinner Mon-Fri, dinner Sat) In the one-time town administration building dating back to 1848, this longstanding restau-

rant is known for its excellent steaks and ever-changing game-meat options.

Robertson Brewery BREWERY

(www.robertsonbrewery.com; 1 Memoriam St; tastings R35, light meals R60; ⏲10am-7pm Mon-Sat) There's not a lot to keep you occupied in George, so this family-run microbrewery is a welcome addition. Sip a taster tray of the six staple beers brewed on-site and munch on simple platters while admiring the quirky mural detailing the brewing process.

Information

George Tourism (☎044-801 9295; www.georgetourism.org.za; 124 York St; ⏲7.45am-4.30pm Mon-Fri, 9am-1pm Sat) Information for George and the surrounding area.

Getting There & Away

Kulula (☎0861 585 852; www.kulula.com), **Airlink** (☎0861 606 606; www.flyairlink.com) and **SA Express** (☎0861 729 227; www.flyexpress.aero) fly to **George airport** (☎044-876 9310), which is 7km west of town.

Buses stop in George on their route between Cape Town and Port Elizabeth and between Jo'burg and the Garden Route. Greyhound (www.greyhound.co.za) services stop at the Caltex petrol station on York St, while Translux (www.translux.co.za) and Intercape (www.intercape.co.za) stop at the main station at the end of Hibernia St. Intercape fares include Knysna (R310, 1½ hours, twice daily), Plettenberg Bay (R310, two hours), Port Elizabeth (R380, 5½ hours, twice daily), Cape Town (R380, seven hours, twice daily), Bloemfontein (R540, 10 hours, daily) and Jo'burg (R700, 16 hours, daily).

The Baz Bus drops off passengers in town.

Montagu & Outeniqua Passes

Leaving the town of George, Montagu Pass is a quiet dirt road that winds its way through the mountains; it was opened in 1847 and is now a national monument. Head back on the Outeniqua Pass, a tarred road that is also north of George but where views are even better.

Alternatively, you could opt for the **Outeniqua Power Van** (☎082 490 5627; adult/child R130/110; ⏲Mon-Sat), a motorised trolley van that will take you from the Outeniqua Transport Museum on a 2½-hour trip into the Outeniqua mountains. You can even take a bike and cycle back down the Montagu Pass.

Herold's Bay

On a beautiful stretch of beach with decent surf is this tiny village. It's generally quiet, although it can become crowded on summer weekends. The town is 16km southwest of George. If you fancy staying the night, try **Makarios** (☎044-872 9019; www.makariosonsea.co.za; 4 Gericke's Cnr; ste from R1030), a stone's throw from the sand. The luxury apartments have full kitchens and sea views or there is a smaller room (from R550) without the view. There are no restaurants on the beachfront, though you can choose from a variety of ice-cream kiosks. Those looking for lunch should try **Dutton's Cove** (21 Rooidraai Rd; mains R60-110; ⏲lunch & dinner Mon-Sat, lunch Sun), a popular local hangout sitting high above the beach.

Victoria Bay

Victoria Bay is tiny and picturesque, and sits at the foot of steep cliffs, around 8km south of George. It's considered one of the Western Cape's top surfing spots and also has a tidal pool for children. There are apartments available by the beach – check out www.vicbay.com – and a **caravan park** (☎044-889 0081; camping per site from R172) sitting just above the sand.

Surfari Backpackers BACKPACKERS $$

(☎044-889 0113; www.vicbaysurfari.co.za; dm/s/d R180/325/550) It might not be close enough to smell the ocean, but Surfari is highly recommended. A family-run boutique backpackers, it has bright, beautifully decorated rooms with breathtaking views of the coastal forest and ocean beyond. The enormous lounge has a bar, large TV and pool table, plus the owners rent out surfboards (R150 per day) and can arrange lessons.

Wilderness

POP 6200

The name says it all: dense old-growth forests and steep hills run down to a beautiful stretch of coastline of rolling breakers, kilometres of white sand, bird-rich estuaries and sheltered lagoons. All this has made Wilderness very popular, but thankfully it doesn't show – the myriad holiday homes blend into the verdant green hills, and the town centre is compact and unobtrusive. Beach bums be aware, the beach here is beautiful, but a strong riptide means swimming is not advised. The only other drawback is that everything is quite widely scattered, making life very difficult if you don't have a vehicle.

Activities

Eden Adventures ADVENTURE SPORTS
(☎044-877 0179; www.eden.co.za; Fairy Knowe Hotel) Offers canoe rental (R250 per day), abseiling (R550), kloofing (canyoning, R550), and tours of the area.

Timberlake Organic Village ADVENTURE SPORTS
(www.timberlakeorganic.co.za; ⏲9am-5pm) This complex off the N2 between Wilderness and Sedgefield has a number of activities on offer, such as quad biking and zip-line tours. There are also small shops selling organically grown fresh produce and crafts.

Sleeping

Fairy Knowe Backpackers BACKPACKERS $
(☎044-877 1285; www.wildernessbackpackers.com; Dumbleton Rd; camping R80, dm/d without bathroom R130/400, d R500; 📶) Set in leafy grounds overlooking the Touws River, this long-running hostel is based in a 1874 farmhouse. The bar and cafe are in another building some distance away, so boozers won't keep you awake. Staff can arrange all manner of activities. If you're driving, head into Wilderness town and follow the main road for 2km to the Fairy Knowe turn-off.

Wilderness Beach House Backpackers BACKPACKERS $
(☎044-877 0549; www.wildernessbeachhouse.com; Wilderness Beach; dm/d without bathroom R150/350, d from R450; 📶) Southwest of town, this breezy hostel provides awesome ocean views, simple rooms, and a *lapa* bar and cafe (serving breakfast and dinner).

★**Interlaken** GUESTHOUSE $$
(☎044-877 1374; www.interlaken.co.za; 713 North St; s/d incl breakfast R695/1100; 📶🏊) It gets rave reviews from readers, and we can't argue: this is a well-run and very friendly guesthouse offering magnificent lagoon views. Delicious dinners are available on request.

★**Views Boutique Hotel** BOUTIQUE HOTEL $$$
(☎044-877 8000; www.viewshotel.co.za; South St; s/d incl breakfast R3200/4200; ❄📶🏊) With bright, modern, glass-fronted rooms looking on to the glorious beach, this hotel makes the most of its awesome location. It's worth paying the premium for an ocean-facing room if you can, though the mountain-view rooms are also delightful. The hotel has a rooftop pool, spa and steps leading straight to the sand.

Eating

Beejuice CAFE $
(Sands Rd; light meals R45-85; ⏲breakfast & lunch year-round, dinner Nov-Apr) Although no trains ply the tracks any more, this cafe filling the old station building is still a nice spot for salads and sandwiches. In the evenings, traditional South African fare is served.

★**Girls Restaurant** INTERNATIONAL $$
(1 George Rd; mains R100-285; ⏲dinner Tue-Sun) It doesn't look much from afar – a restaurant tucked down the side of a petrol station – but Girls gets rave reviews. Try the fresh prawns in a range of divine sauces or the venison fillet.

Zucchini EUROPEAN $$
(www.zucchini.co.za; Timberlake Organic Village; mains R60-130; ⏲breakfast & lunch daily, dinner Fri & Sat; ✎) 🍃 Stylish decor combines with home-grown organic produce, free-range meats and lots of vegetarian options at this delightful place.

Serendipity SOUTH AFRICAN $$$
(☎044-877 0433; Freesia Ave; 5-course menu R415; ⏲dinner Mon-Sat) Readers and locals recommend this elegant restaurant with a deck overlooking the lagoon. The South African-inspired menu changes monthly but always features original takes on old classics. It's the town's fine dining option. Bookings essential.

Information

Wilderness Tourism Bureau (☎044-877 0045; George Rd; ⏲7.45am-4.30pm Mon-Fri, 9am-1pm Sat) Just past the cluster of restaurants on the right as you enter the village.

Garden Route National Park (Wilderness Section)

Formerly the Wilderness National Park, this section has been incorporated into the vast and scattered **Garden Route National Park** (☎044-877 1197; www.sanparks.org; adult/child R106/53; ⏲7am-6pm) along with the Knysna Forests and Tsitsikamma. The park covers a unique system of lakes, rivers, wetlands and estuaries that are vital for the survival of many species.

GARDEN ROUTE NATIONAL PARK

Why Go Mountain-meets-forest-meets-lake vistas; shady hikes; spotting smaller wildlife species; superlative birdwatching; a host of outdoor activities including kayaking and kloofing.

When to Go By September the rains have passed, and the park is at its most gorgeous; December and January are the busiest times; June to August are the wetter months.

Practicalities The park is tricky to access by public transport – if you don't have your own car, hiking in or joining a tour are your only options. By car, access is via the N2, 2km east of Wilderness village. Gates are open 7am to 6pm.

Budget Tips You don't have to enter the park proper for some hiking trails, meaning you can just pay hiking permit fees and not the park entrance fee.

There are several nature trails in the national park for all levels of fitness, taking in the lakes, the beach and the indigenous forest. The **Kingfisher Trail** is a day walk that traverses the region and includes a boardwalk across the intertidal zone of the Touws River. The lakes offer anglers, canoeists, windsurfers and sailors an ideal venue. Canoes can be hired at Eden Adventures in Wilderness.

There are two similar camping grounds in the park with basic but comfortable accommodation: **Ebb & Flow North** (camping per site from R170, d with/without bathroom from R510/320), which is the smaller, and **Ebb & Flow South** (camping per site from R170, cabins from R625).

Buffalo Bay

Buffalo Bay is a blissful place with an almost deserted surf beach, a nature reserve and only a tiny enclave of holiday homes. That's about it, and it's all you need. It's 17km west of Knysna; signposts also read Buffel's Bay or Buffelsbaai.

Goukamma Nature Reserve (www.capenature.co.za; adult/child R40/20; ⌚8am-6pm), which is accessible for explorations from the Buffalo Bay road, protects 14km of rocky coastline, sandstone cliffs, dunes covered with coastal *fynbos* and forest, and Groenvlei, a large freshwater lake. The nature reserve also extends 1.8km out to sea and you can often see dolphins (and whales, in season) along the coast. There are day trails ranging from a two-hour forest walk to a 15km hike that takes you through the sand dunes. Permits can be obtained on arrival from the reserve's reception. Canoeing and fishing are great, and canoes can be hired (R30 per day).

In town, **Buffelsbaai Waterfront** (☎044-383 0038; www.buffelsbaai.co.za; apt from R750) is a one-stop shop for accommodation, meals and information on the area. It's a vast building behind the beach – you can't miss it. Accommodation in the reserve is fairly snazzy and ranges from the **Fish Eagle Loft** (per 2 people R705) and a range of **chalets** (per 4 people R960) to the more luxurious **Otter's Rest Lodge** (per 4 people R1150) and **Mbuvu Bush Camp** (4-person cottage R1210). Prices increase vastly during school holidays.

Knysna

POP 51,000

Embracing an exquisitely beautiful lagoon and surrounded by ancient forests, Knysna (pronounced ny-znah) is probably the most famous town on the Garden Route. Formerly the centre of the timber industry, supplying yellowwood and stinkwood for railway lines, shipping and house-building, it still has several shops specialising in woodwork and traditional furniture. The lagoon has always been popular with sailing enthusiasts, and there's a thriving oyster industry.

With its serene setting, arty and gay-friendly vibe, excellent places to stay, eat and drink, and wide range of activities, Knysna has plenty going for it. But if you're after something quiet and undeveloped, you might like to look elsewhere, particularly in high season, when the numbers of visitors threaten to overwhelm the town.

Sights

Knysna Lagoon PARK

The Knysna Lagoon opens between two sandstone cliffs known as the Heads – once proclaimed by the British Royal Navy to be the most dangerous harbour entrance in the world. There are good views from the eastern head, and from the Featherbed Nature Reserve on the western head.

The best way to appreciate the lagoon is by boat. The **Featherbed Company** (Map

Knysna

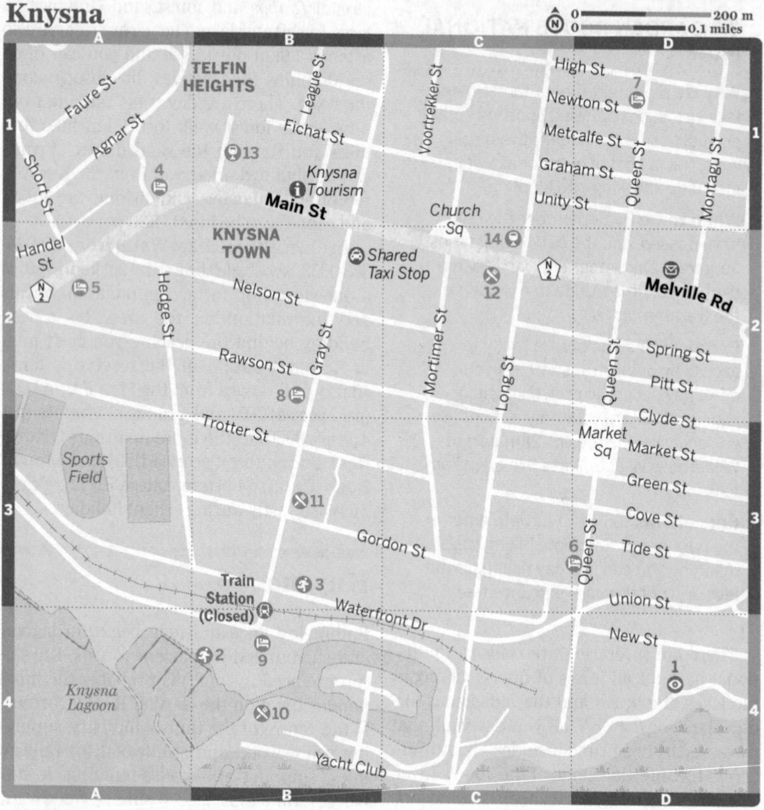

Knysna

Sights
1 Mitchell's Brewery D4

Activities, Courses & Tours
2 Featherbed Company B4
3 Knysna Cycle Works B3

Sleeping
4 Inyathi Guest Lodge A1
5 Island Vibe A2
6 Jembjo's Knysna Lodge D3
7 Knysna Backpackers D1
8 Knysna Log Inn B2
9 Protea Hotel Knysna Quays B4

Eating
10 Caffé Mario B4
11 Chatters Bistro B3
12 Olive Tree C2

Drinking & Nightlife
13 King's B1
14 Zanzibar Lounge C2

p144; ☎044-382 1693; www.featherbed.co.za; Remembrance Dr, off Waterfront Dr; boat trips adult/child from R100/55) operates various vessels and also runs a trip that allows you to explore the nature reserve on foot (adult/child R380/130).

Although regulated by SANParks, Knysna Lagoon is not a national park or wilderness area. Much is still privately owned, and the lagoon is used by industry and for recreation. The protected area starts just to the east of Buffalo Bay and follows the coastline to the mouth of the Noetzie River.

Mitchell's Brewery BREWERY
(Map p144; ☎044-382 4685; www.mitchellsbrewing.com; 10 New St; tastings R75, tours & tastings R150; ⏲10am-6pm Mon-Sat, tours 11am, 12.30pm & 2.30pm) South Africa's oldest microbrewery has moved to bright, new premises on the edge of the lagoon. You can join a tour, or just taste their range of English-style beers in the beer garden. Pub meals (R45 to R70) are also served. Bookings essential for tours.

DON'T MISS

HIKING THE KNYSNA FORESTS

Now part of the Garden Route National Park, the Knysna Forests are the perfect place for hikers of all levels. At the easy end of the scale is the **Garden of Eden** (adult/child R36/18), where there are lovely forest picnic spots and a wheelchair-friendly path. The **Millwood Gold Mine Walk** is also a gentle hike, while the **Elephant Trails** (adult/child R60/30) at Diepwalle offer varying degrees of difficulty.

More challenging is the **Harkerville Coast Trail** (per person R210), a two-day hike that leads to the popular Outeniqua Trail. The **Outeniqua Trail** (☎044-302 5606; adult/child R72/38) is 108km long and takes a week to walk, although you can do two- or three-day sections. It costs R76 per night to stay in a basic hut along the trail; bring your own bedding. For permits, maps and further information, contact **SANParks** (☎044-302 5600; www.sanparks.org; Long St, Thesen's Island; ⏲7.30am-4pm Mon-Fri).

There are also plenty of mountain-biking trails – contact Knysna Cycle Works for rentals and maps.

Belvidere VILLAGE

Belvidere, 10km from Knysna, is so immaculate it's positively creepy. But it's worth a quick look for the beautiful Norman-style **Belvidere church** (Map p147) that was built in the 1850s by homesick English expats. Further on is the **Featherbed Nature Reserve** (Map p147) and, on the seaward side, Brenton-on-Sea.

Activities

Township Tours & Homestays

The tourism office has an up-to-date list of the numerous operators offering tours to Knysna's hilltop townships. If you want to stay overnight in the townships, contact Knysna Tourism and ask for its brochure, *Living Local*.

Emzini Tours CULTURAL TOUR

(☎044-382 1087; www.emzinitours.co.za; adult/child R350/100) Led by township resident Ella, the three-hour trip visits some of Emzini's community projects. Tours can be tailored to suit your interests but generally end at Ella's home for tea, drumming and a group giggle as you try to wrap your tongue around the clicks of the Xhosa language.

Mad About Art CULTURAL TOUR

(☎044-375 0242; www.madaboutart.org; suggested donation R180) A nonprofit organisation that offers 90-minute walking tours visiting various art and education projects.

Outdoor Activities

The Garden Route is known for its adventure sports and outdoor activities. In and around Knysna you can hike, bike, surf, kloof, kayak, horse-ride and more.

Knysna Cycle Works CYCLING

(Map p144; ☎044-382 5152; www.knysnacycles.co.za; 20 Waterfront Dr; per day R200; ⏲8.30am-5pm Mon-Fri, 9am-1pm Sat) Long-running agency that rents out mountain bikes and supplies maps of the region's trails.

Trip Out WATER SPORTS

(☎083 306 3587; www.tripout.co.za; 2hr surfing class R350) Offers surfing classes for beginners, snorkelling around the Heads (R300) and boat cruises, as well as a full-on kloofing day trip (R850).

Festivals & Events

Pink Loerie Festival GAY

(www.pinkloerie.co.za) Knysna celebrates its gay-friendliness with a flamboyant Mardi Gras at the end of April and beginning of May.

Oyster Festival FOOD

(www.oysterfestival.co.za) There's an homage to the oyster in July; one event is the Knysna Marathon.

Sleeping

Low-season competition between the several backpackers and many guesthouses in town keeps prices down, but in high season expect steep rate hikes (except at the backpackers) – book ahead.

Island Vibe BACKPACKERS $

(Map p144; ☎044-382 1728; www.islandvibe.co.za; 67 Main St; dm R150, d with/without bathroom R550/480; 📶🏊) A funky backpackers with excellent communal areas, cheery staff and nicely decorated rooms. There's a lively bar and a small pool on the deck.

DON'T MISS

KNYSNA'S RASTAFARIANS

Knysna is home to South Africa's largest Rastafarian Community, **Judah Square**. You can take an impassioned walking tour of the community, which is within the township, with **Brother Zeb** (☎076 649 1034; tours from R70), an unforgettable local character.

Jembjo's Knysna Lodge BACKPACKERS $
(Map p144; ☎044-382 2658; www.jembjosknysnalodge.co.za; 4 Queen St; dm R130, s/d without bathroom R290/340, s/d R390/460;) A small, friendly hostel run by two former overland truck drivers. There's lots of info on activities in the area, mountain bikes to rent (R75 per day) and a free DIY breakfast.

Knysna Backpackers BACKPACKERS $
(Map p144; ☎044-382 2554; www.knysnabackpackers.co.za; 42 Queen St; dm R130, d with/without bathroom R480/380;) You'll find mainly double rooms at this large Victorian house a few blocks up from Main St. It's a fairly quiet, family-run hostel.

★ **Brenton Cottages** CHALET $$
(Map p147; ☎044-381 0082; www.brentononsea.net; 242 CR Swart Drive, Brenton-on-Sea; 2-person cabin R680, 6-person chalet R1380;) On the seaward side of the lagoon, the hills drop to Brenton-on-Sea, overlooking a magnificent 8km beach. The cottages have a full kitchen while cabins have a kitchenette; many have ocean views. There are plenty of braai areas dotted around the manicured lawns.

Inyathi Guest Lodge GUESTHOUSE $$
(Map p144; ☎044-382 7768; www.inyathiguestlodge.co.za; 52 Main St; s/d from R400/700;) This is an imaginatively designed guesthouse, with a real African flair that avoids the kitsch. Accommodation is in decorated timber lodges – delightful but rather lacking in soundproofing. It's a great budget option offering room-only rates and good prices for solo travellers.

Under Milk Wood CHALET $$$
(Map p147; ☎044-384 0745; www.milkwood.co.za; George Rex Dr; cabin from R1200) Perched on the shores of Knysna Lagoon are these highly impressive self-catering log cabins, each with its own deck and braai area. There's no pool but there is a small beach.

Protea Hotel Knysna Quays HOTEL $$$
(Map p144; ☎044-382 5005; www.proteahotels.com; Waterfront Dr; s/d R1550/1900;) Rooms are tastefully decorated at this stylish hotel. It has an inviting, heated pool and is moments away from shopping and eating options at the Waterfront. You'll want a lagoon-facing room.

Knysna Log Inn HOTEL $$$
(Map p144; ☎044-382 5835; www.log-inn.co.za; 16 Gray St; s/d incl breakfast R1320/1940;) This inn is said to be the largest log structure in the southern hemisphere. The rooms are comfortable, many with balconies, and there's a lovely pool in the garden.

Belvidere Manor HOTEL $$$
(Map p147; ☎044-387 1055; www.belvidere.co.za; Duthie Dr; cottage incl breakfast from R2180;) A tremendously peaceful place to stay, with luxury cottages around an immaculate lawn, some with lagoon views. There is a restaurant (mains R75 to R160) in the historical main house serving regional and international dishes, and an atmospheric pub, open to nonguests.

Phantom Forest Eco-Reserve LODGE $$$
(☎044-386 0046; www.phantomforest.com; Phantom Pass Rd; s/d from R2935/4275;) This small private ecoreserve, 6km west of Knysna, comprises 14 elegantly decorated treehouses built with sustainable materials. Various activities, including nature walks, are available. If nothing else, visit for the lavish six-course African dinner (R400) served in the Forest Boma daily; booking is essential.

Eating

There are plenty of good snack and coffee places along Main St.

★ **Ile de Pain** CAFE, BAKERY $
(Map p147; www.iledepain.co.za; Thesen's Island; mains R50-90; breakfast & lunch Tue-Sun;) A wildly popular bakery and cafe that's as much a hit with locals as it is with tourists. There's an excellent breakfast menu, lots of fresh salads, some inventive lunch specials and quite a bit for vegetarians.

Caffé Mario ITALIAN $
(Map p144; mains R50-100; breakfast, lunch & dinner) At the Waterfront, this is a good place for breakfast or coffee and cake. It also serves pizza and pasta.

Olive Tree BISTRO $$
(Map p144; ☎044-382 5867; 21 Main St; mains R90-170; dinner Mon-Sat) One of Knysna's

Around Knysna

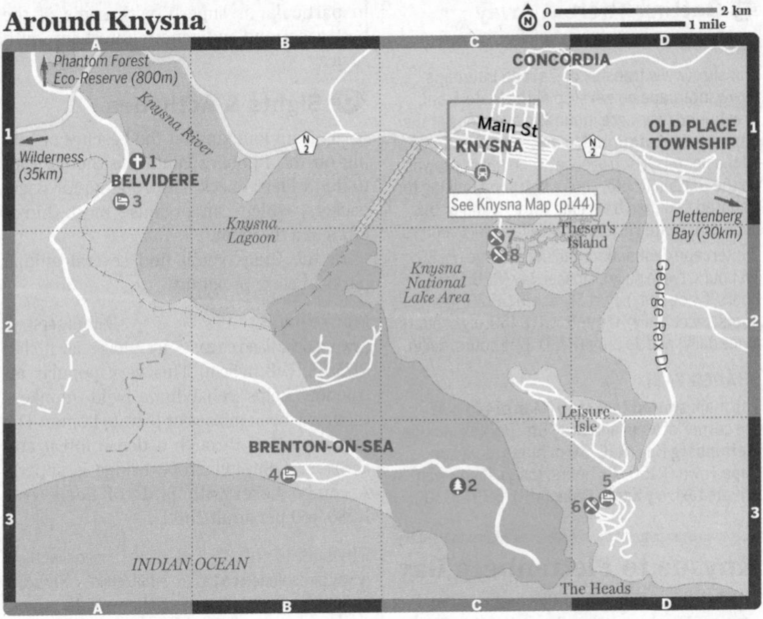

more upmarket restaurants is a romantic spot with a blackboard menu that changes regularly. Bookings advisable.

East Head Café CAFE $$
(Map p147; ☎044-384 0933; www.eastheadcafe.co.za; 25 George Rex Dr, Eastern Head; mains R75-145; ⊙breakfast & lunch;) There's an outdoor deck overlooking the lagoon and ocean, lots of fish and seafood, plus a few vegetarian dishes. It's a very popular spot so expect to wait for a table in high season.

Sirocco INTERNATIONAL $$
(Map p147; ☎044-382 4874; www.sirocco.co.za; Main Rd, Thesen's Island; mains R50-130; ⊙lunch & dinner) Inside, it's a stylish place to dine on steak and seafood; outside, it's a laid-back bar with wood-fired pizzas and the full range of Mitchell's beers.

Chatters Bistro PIZZA $$
(Map p144; www.chattersbistro.co.za; 9A Gray St; mains R60-130; ⊙lunch & dinner Tue-Sun) Restaurants seem to come and go in Knysna, but this pizza joint has been around a while. You'll also find burgers, pasta and some salads, plus a pleasant garden to enjoy them in.

Drinking & Nightlife

Head along Main St and check out the local bars, many of which are seasonal.

Around Knysna

Sights
1 Belvidere Church ... A1
2 Featherbed Nature Reserve ... C3

Sleeping
3 Belvidere Manor ... A1
4 Brenton Cottages ... B3
5 Under Milk Wood ... D3

Eating
6 East Head Café ... D3
7 Ile de Pain ... C2
8 Sirocco ... C2

King's PUB
(Map p144; Main St; ⊙11am-2am) A slightly grungy but popular pub with draught beer and pool tables.

Zanzibar Lounge CLUB
(Map p144; Main St; ⊙Tue-Sat) Knysna's top spot for late-night dancing offers a relaxed vibe and a balcony area for lounging.

Information

Knysna Tourism (Map p144; ☎044-382 5510; www.visitknysna.co.za; 40 Main St; ⊙8am-5pm Mon-Fri, 8.30am-1pm Sat year-round, plus 9am-1pm Sun Dec, Jan & Jul) An excellent office, with very knowledgeable staff.

Getting There & Away

BUS

Translux (www.translux.co.za) and Intercape (www.intercape.co.za) stop at the Waterfront; Greyhound (www.greyhound.co.za) stops at the **Engen petrol station** (Main St); Baz Bus drops at all the hostels. For travel between nearby towns on the Garden Route, you're better off looking for a shared taxi than travelling with the major bus lines, which are very expensive for short sectors.

Intercape destinations include George (R280, 1½ hours, twice daily), Mossel Bay (R280, two hours, twice daily), Port Elizabeth (R320, 4½ hours, twice daily), Cape Town (R450, eight hours, twice daily) and Jo'burg (R720, 17½ hours, daily).

SHARED TAXI

The main **shared taxi stop** (Map p144) is at the corner of Main and Gray Sts. Routes include Plettenberg Bay (R20, 30 minutes, daily) and Cape Town (R150, 7½ hours, daily). If you want a private taxi, try **Eagle Cabs** (☎076 797 3110).

Knysna to Plettenberg Bay

The N2 from Knysna to Plettenberg Bay has turn-offs both north and south that offer interesting detours.

The Knysna–Avontour road, Rte 339, climbs through the Outeniqua range via the beautiful **Prince Alfred's Pass**, regarded by some as even better than the Swartberg Pass. Be warned that the road is a bit on the rough side and it's slow going. The road has few really steep sections but the pass reaches a height of over 1000m, and there are great views to the north before the road winds its way into the Langkloof Valley.

Reached by a turn-off along the N2 10km east of Knysna, **Noetzie** is a quirky little place with holiday homes in mock-castle style. There's a lovely surf beach (spacious but dangerous) and a sheltered lagoon running through a forested gorge. The trail between the car park and beach is steep.

Plettenberg Bay

POP 6500

Plettenberg Bay, or 'Plett' as it's more commonly known, is a resort town through and through, with mountains, white sand and crystal-blue water making it one of the country's top local tourist spots. As a result, things can get very busy and somewhat overpriced, but the town retains a relaxed, friendly atmosphere and does have very good-value hostels. The scenery to the east in particular is superb, with some of the best coast and indigenous forest in South Africa.

Sights & Activities

Apart from lounging on the beaches or hiking on the Robberg Peninsula there's a lot to do in Plett; check with Albergo for Backpackers, which can organise most things, often at a discount.

At the Crags you'll find several animal parks in close proximity.

Monkeyland WILDLIFE RESERVE
(www.monkeyland.co.za; 1hr tour adult/child R175/88; ⏲8am-5pm) This very popular attraction helps rehabilitate wild monkeys that have been in zoos or private homes. The walking safari through a dense forest and across a 128m-long rope bridge is superb. A combo ticket with Birds of Eden costs R280/140 per adult/child.

Birds of Eden BIRD SANCTUARY
(www.birdsofeden.co.za; adult/child R175/88; ⏲8am-5pm) This is one of the world's largest free-flight aviaries with a 200-sq-m dome over the forest.

Ocean Blue Adventures BOAT TOUR
(☎044-533 5083; www.oceanadventures.co.za; Hopewood St, Milkwood Centre; dolphin/whale watching R440/700) Trips on 30-person boats to view dolphins and whales in season.

Sky Dive Plettenberg Bay ADVENTURE SPORTS
(☎082 905 7440; www.skydiveplett.com; Plettenberg Airport; tandem jump R1850) This recommended operator offers dives with outstanding views on the way down.

Learn to Surf Plett SURFING
(☎082 436 6410; www.learntosurfplett.co.za; 2hr group lesson incl equipment R350) A long-running surfing outfit that also offers stand-up paddle-boarding lessons (R150 per hour).

Sleeping

The tourism bureau has a full list of accommodation and can tell you about the many camping options, all in nearby Keurboomstrand. In low season there are bargains to be found.

★**Nothando Backpackers Hostel** BACKPACKERS $
(☎044-533 0220; www.nothando.com; 5 Wilder St; dm R160, d with/without bathroom R500/420; 📶) This excellent, five-star budget option is

Plettenberg Bay

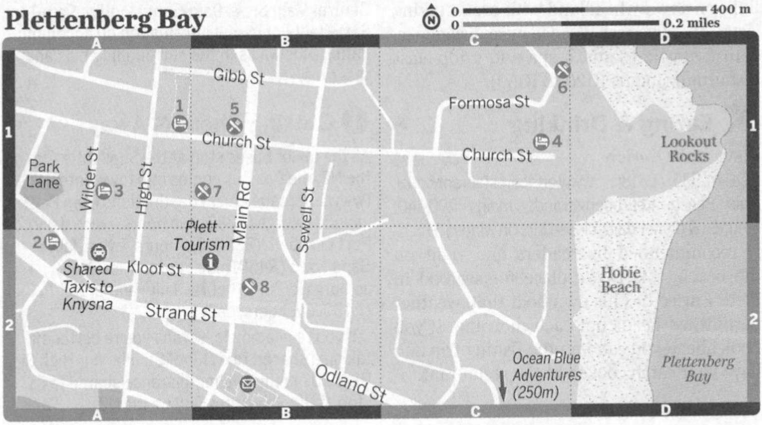

owner-run and it shows. There's a great bar area with satellite TV, yet you can still find peace and quiet in the large grounds. Rooms are worthy of a budget guesthouse.

Abalone Beach House BACKPACKERS $
(☎044-535 9602; www.abalonebeachhouse.co.za; 50 Milkwood Glen, Keurboomstrand; d with/without bathroom R600/500; 📶) This upmarket and extremely friendly backpackers is two minutes' walk from a magnificent beach; surf and body boards are provided free. To reach the house follow the Keurboomstrand signs from the N2 (about 6km east of Plett), then turn into Milkwood Glen.

Albergo for Backpackers BACKPACKERS $
(☎044-533 4434; www.albergo.co.za; 8 Church St; camping R100, dm R175, d without bathroom R500; 📶) Well-run and friendly, Albergo can organise just about any activity in the area and there are free body boards to use. The upstairs dorm has huge windows and a spacious balcony.

Amakaya Backpackers BACKPACKERS $
(☎044-533 4010; www.amakaya.co.za; 15 Park Lane; dm R140-175, d with/without bathroom R500/450) The focal point is the bar and deck with views of the Tsitsikamma Mountains. There are two 'private dorms' – basically a twin room with bunks, offering a cheaper alternative for two people travelling together. Rates include a DIY breakfast.

★**Hog Hollow** LODGE $$$
(☎044-534 8879; www.hog-hollow.com; Askop Rd, The Crags; s/d incl breakfast R2170/3100; ❄📶🏊) Hog Hollow, 18km east of Plett along the N2, provides delightful accommodation in

Plettenberg Bay

Sleeping

1	Albergo for Backpackers	A1
2	Amakaya Backpackers	A2
3	Nothando Backpackers Hostel	A1
4	Plettenberg	C1

Eating

5	Le Fournil de Plett	B1
6	Lookout	C1
7	Nguni	B1
8	Table	B2

African-art-decorated units overlooking the forest. Each unit comes with a private wooden deck and hammock. You can walk to Monkeyland from here; staff will collect you if you don't fancy the walk back.

Milkwood Manor HOTEL $$$
(☎044-533 0420; www.milkwoodmanor.co.za; Salmack Rd, Lookout Beach; d from R1520; 📶) A remarkable location, right on the beach and overlooking the lagoon. Rooms have had a revamp and their bright new look has a beachy feel. There's a restaurant on-site and kayaks are free for guests.

Periwinkle Guest Lodge GUESTHOUSE $$$
(☎044-533 1345; www.periwinkle.co.za; 75 Beachy Head Dr; s/d incl breakfast from R1365/1820; 📶) This bright, colourful beachfront guesthouse offers individually decorated rooms, all with great views – you might even be able to spot whales and dolphins.

Plettenberg LUXURY HOTEL $$$
(☎044-533 2030; www.plettenberg.com; 40 Church St; r incl breakfast from R5000; ❄📶🏊)

Built on a rocky headland with breathtaking vistas, this five-star place is pure decadence, with fantastic rooms, a spa and a top-class restaurant (mains R120 to R150).

Eating & Drinking

Ristorante Enrico SEAFOOD $$
(☎044-535 9818; www.enricorestaurant.co.za; Main Beach, Keurboomstrand; mains R90-140; ⊙lunch & dinner daily, closed Mon in winter) Highly recommended by readers and right on the beach, this is *the* place for seafood in Plett. Enrico has his own boat that, weather permitting, heads out each morning. If you book ahead you can join the fishing trip and have your catch cooked at the restaurant.

Le Fournil de Plett CAFE $$
(Church St, cnr Main St; mains R70-85; ⊙breakfast & lunch; 📶) Enjoy a good cup of coffee and a freshly baked pastry in the courtyard or on the balcony overlooking Plett's main road. There's also a small lunch menu, largely focusing on salads and sandwiches.

Table ITALIAN $$
(www.thetable.co.za; 9 Main St; mains R70-130; ⊙lunch & dinner Mon-Sat, lunch Sun) A funky, minimalist venue with pizzas featuring an array of inventive toppings.

Lookout SEAFOOD $$
(☎044-533 1379; www.lookout.co.za; Lookout Rocks; mains R70-130; ⊙breakfast, lunch & dinner) With a deck overlooking the beach, this is a great place for a simple meal and perhaps views of dolphins surfing the waves.

★Nguni STEAKHOUSE $$$
(☎044-533 6710; www.nguni-restaurant.co.za; 6 Crescent St; mains R115-240; ⊙lunch Mon-Fri, dinner Mon-Sat) Tucked away in a quiet courtyard, this is one of Plett's most upscale eateries. The speciality is Chalmar beef, though you'll also find lots of South African favourites including ostrich, Karoo lamb and traditional dishes such as bobotie. Reservations recommended.

Shopping

Old Nick Village ARTS & CRAFTS
(www.oldnickvillage.co.za) For a bit of retail therapy, head for this complex 3km east of town, with resident artists, a weaving museum, antiques and a restaurant.

Information

Plett Tourism (☎044-533 4065; www.plett-tourism.co.za; Melville's Corner Shopping Centre, Main St; ⊙9am-5pm Mon-Fri, 9am-1pm Sat) Plenty of useful information on accommodation plus walks in the surrounding hills and reserves.

Getting There & Away

All the major buses stop at the Shell Ultra City on the N2; the Baz Bus comes into town. Intercape (www.intercape.co.za) destinations from Plett include George (R280, two hours, twice daily), Port Elizabeth (R320, 3½ hours, twice daily), Cape Town (R450, nine hours, twice daily), Jo'burg (R720, 18 hours, daily) and Graaff-Reinet (R460, 6½ hours, daily).

If you're heading to Knysna you're better off taking a **shared taxi** (Kloof St, near cnr High St; R20; 30 minutes). Long-distance shared taxis stop at the Shell Ultra City on the N2.

Robberg Nature & Marine Reserve

This **reserve** (☎044-483 0190; www.capenature.org.za; adult/child R40/20; ⊙8am-6pm May-Sep, 7am-8pm Oct-Apr), 9km southeast of Plettenberg Bay, protects a 4km-long peninsula with a rugged coastline of cliffs and rocks. There are three circular walks of increasing difficulty, with rich intertidal marine life and coastal-dune *fynbos,* but it's very rocky and not for the unfit or anyone with knee problems! Basic accommodation is available at the spectacularly located **Fountain Shack** (4 people R875), which is reachable only by a two-hour hike; bookings are essential, through **Cape Nature** (☎021-483 0190; www.capenature.org.za). To get to the reserve head along Robberg Rd, off Piesang Valley Rd, until you see the signs.

You can also take a boat to view the peninsula – and its colony of Cape fur seals – from the water. You can even swim with the seals. Contact **Offshore Adventures** (www.offshoreadventures.co.za; boat trip R250, swimming with seals R500) to book.

ROUTE 62

Following Rte 62 will take you through some spectacular scenery changes, from the rugged mountain passes between Montagu and Calitzdorp, to the arid semi-desert of the Little Karoo region around Oudtshoorn. It's touted as the longest wine route in the world and is a great alternative to the N2 if you're travelling from Cape Town towards the Garden Route.

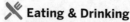

Montagu

POP 15,000

Coming into Montagu along Rte 62 from Robertson, the road passes through a narrow arch in the Langeberg mountains, and suddenly the town appears before you. Its wide streets are bordered by 24 restored national monuments, including some fine art deco architecture. There's a wide range of activities, including hot springs, a number of walks and superlative rock climbing, as well as excellent accommodation and some good restaurants.

◉ Sights & Activities

Montagu Museum MUSEUM
(41 Long St; adult/child R5/2; ⊙9am-5pm Mon-Fri, 10.30am-12.30pm Sat & Sun) Interesting displays and some good examples of antique furniture can be found at this museum in the old mission church.

Joubert House BUILDING
(☑023-614 1774; 25 Long St; adult/child R5/2; ⊙9am-4.30pm Mon-Fri, 10.30am-12.30pm Sat & Sun) Joubert House, a short walk from the Montagu Museum, is the oldest house in Montagu (built in 1853) and has been restored to its Victorian glory.

★Protea Farm ECOTOUR
(☑023-614 3012; www.proteafarm.co.za; adult/child R110/45; ⊙tours 10am Wed & Sat) Wonderful three-hour tractor rides explore Protea Farm, 29km from Montagu. There are sweeping views of the Breede River Valley and the trip includes snacks and drinks. Extend the day with a traditional lunch of *potjiekos* (pot stew) with homemade bread for R110/45 per adult/child. There's also farm accommodation (four-person cottage from R750).

Avalon Springs SWIMMING
(www.avalonsprings.co.za; entrance R50; ⊙8am-10pm) Water from these mineral springs finds its way into the swimming pools of the Avalon Springs Hotel, just north of town. The water gushes from a rock face underground at 43°C, and is renowned for its healing properties. The pools are commercialised and can get unpleasantly busy on weekends and in school holidays. Try to visit during off-peak times.

A great way to get there is to hike 2.4km along the Badskloof trail (R15) from the car park at the end of Tanner St.

Hiking

The **Bloupunt Trail** (admission R30) is 15.6km long and can be walked in six to eight hours; it traverses ravines and mountain streams, and climbs to 1000m. The **Cogmanskloof Trail** (admission R30) is 12.1km and can be completed in four to six hours; it's not as steep as the Bloupunt Trail but is still fairly strenuous. Both trails start from the car park at the northern end of Tanner St.

You can book the overnight huts (per person R120) near the start of the trails through the tourism bureau; they are basic (wood stoves, showers and toilet facilities) but cheap.

Climbing

Montagu is one of the Western Cape's top spots for rock climbing. Justin Lawson at **Montagu Rock Climbing** (☑023-614 3193; www.montaguclimbing.com; 45 Mount St; 2hr climbing trip R550) offers gear rental as well as guided climbing and abseiling for beginners.

🛏 Sleeping

Cottage on Long CABIN $
(☑023-614 2398; www.cottageonlong.co.za; 16 Long St; 2 people R450) Perched on the edge of town but within easy walking distance of many restaurants, this is a cute and well-equipped cottage with great views from the garden.

De Bos BACKPACKERS, CAMPGROUND $
(☑023-614 2532; www.debos.co.za; Bath St; camping R60, dm/s/d R90/190/360; 🛜🏊) A genuine farmstay for backpackers – there's a river, chickens and pecan trees on this 500-sq-m property with basic self-catering cottages (from R360). It's an easy walk into town.

★7 Church Street GUESTHOUSE $$
(☑023-614 1186; www.7churchstreet.co.za; 7 Church St; d incl breakfast from R1350; ❄🛜🏊) A friendly, upmarket guesthouse in a charming Karoo building. Affable owners Mike and May offer large, well-appointed rooms, manicured gardens in which to relax and a particularly memorable breakfast. They also supply honest tourist info on the region.

Mimosa Lodge HOTEL $$
(☑023-614 2351; www.mimosa.co.za; Church St; s/d incl breakfast from R770/1130; 🛜🏊) A delightful, upmarket lodge in a restored Edwardian landmark building with lovely gardens and a pool with a thatched-roof gazebo for shade. The menu at the attached restaurant serves four-course dinners (R360) and is open to nonguests. Wines from the owner's vineyard are served.

WORTH A TRIP

BARRYDALE

Often overshadowed by its better-known neighbour, Montagu, Barrydale is one of Rte 62's most underrated treats. Venture off the main road and you'll find stylish accommodation, craft shops and quirky restaurants with a bohemian feel. **Hiking** and **birdwatching** are on offer in surrounding nature reserves and there's the luxury **Sanbona Wildlife Reserve** (www.sanbona.com; off Rte 62, 18km west of Barrydale; r incl meals & game drives R10,500) boasting the Big Five nearby. This is brandy country and the **Barrydale Cellar** (☎028-572 1012; 1 Van Riebeeck St; ⏲9am-5pm Mon-Fri, 9am-3pm Sat) offers tours and tastings.

West of town, **Joubert-Tradauw** (www.joubert-tradauw.co.za; ⏲9am-5pm Mon-Fri, 9am-3pm Sat) is a charming spot for some boutique wine tasting and a light lunch from its small but sublime menu. And of course, there's the inimitable **Ronnie's Sex Shop** (Rte 62; mains R50-90; ⏲8.30am-9pm), towards Ladismith, whose bra-adorned and fairly dingy bar draws a constant stream of bikers and curious passersby.

Airlies Guest House GUESTHOUSE **$$**
(☎023-614 2943; www.airlies.co.za; Bath St; s/d incl breakfast R475/950;) This quaint, thatched guesthouse is well located, within walking distance of plenty of restaurants. The wood-floored rooms are simple but spacious. Opt for one of the more modern garden rooms overlooking the pool for a little more privacy.

Avalon Springs Hotel HOTEL **$$**
(☎023-614 1150; www.avalonsprings.co.za; Warmbronne Hot Springs; d from R900, 4-person apt from R1200;) This colossal place has smart rooms in the main building and enormous apartments on stilts. Features include the outdoor hot-spring pools, massages, a gym and plenty of kid-friendly activities. There's a shuttle bus into Montagu.

Eating

★ **Jessica's** TAPAS **$$**
(☎023-614 1805; www.jessicasrestaurant.co.za; 47 Bath St; tapas R20-50, mains R80-120; ⏲dinner Mon-Sat) Cosy Jessica's has had a menu overhaul, now serving fairly authentic and very tasty tapas, instead of the Karoo-fusion fare they've long been known for. Service is friendly and the excellent dessert menu remains.

Rambling Rose FARM STALL **$$**
(36 Long St; mains R60-120; ⏲breakfast & lunch Wed-Mon;) Great for brunch, lunch or cake, this shop-cum-restaurant serves local fodder on its shady patio. The shop sells all manner of local produce. It's an ideal stop if you're just passing through.

Ye Olde Tavern INTERNATIONAL **$$**
(☎023-614 2398; 22 Church St; mains R70-130; ⏲dinner) It's a Jack-of-all-trades menu, but locals love this long-running restaurant just off the main road.

Information

Tourism Bureau (☎023-614 2471; www.montagu-ashton.info; 24 Bath St; ⏲8.30am-5.30pm Mon-Fri, 9am-5pm Sat, 9.30am-5pm Sun) An extremely efficient and helpful office. Opening hours are slightly shorter between May and October.

Getting There & Around

Buses stop at Ashton, 9km from Montagu. Translux (www.translux.co.za) buses stop here on the run between Cape Town (R210, three hours, daily) and Port Elizabeth (R240, eight hours, daily).

Most accommodation establishments in town offer (prebooked) shuttles from Ashton to Montagu but you can also jump in a shared taxi (R20), which stops at **Foodzone** (Bath St).

Calitzdorp

POP 4300

Behind the nondescript main road lies a charming little town with architecture typical of the Little Karoo. Calitzdorp has a stunning setting on rolling farmland overlooked by the Groot Swartberge range to the north and the Rooiberge to the southwest.

Of the seven **wineries** in the area, four are within walking distance of the town centre – they all specialise in port (Calitzdorp is known for its excellent port-style wines) though there are table wines as well. There's also a **port festival** (www.portwinefestival.co.za) held in Calitzdorp each year in June.

Port-Wine Guest House GUESTHOUSE $$
(044-213 3131; www.portwine.net; 7 Queen St; s/d incl breakfast R525/850;) A beautifully appointed, thatched Cape cottage with four-poster beds. It's a short walk from three of the wineries.

Porto Deli PORTUGUESE $$
(Calitz St, cnr Voortrekker St; mains R70-130; lunch & dinner Mon-Sat, lunch Sun) An authentic Portuguese restaurant on the main road serving spicy seafood and meat.

Information

Tourism Bureau (044-213 3775; www.calitzdorp.org.za; 8am-5pm Mon-Fri, 10am-1pm Sat) Provides details on accommodation and the local wineries. It's in a building at the side of the Shell petrol station.

Oudtshoorn

POP 29,000

In the late 1860s, no self-respecting society lady in the Western world would be seen dead without an ostrich plume adorning her headgear. The fashion boom in ostrich feathers lasted until the slump of 1914 and during this time the 'feather barons' of Oudtshoorn made their fortunes.

You can still see their gracious homes, along with other architectural pointers to Oudtshoorn's former wealth such as the CP Nel Museum (formerly a school). The town remains the 'ostrich capital of the world' and is now the prosperous tourist centre of the Little Karoo. Ostrich leather is much sought after (and expensive), feathers, eggs and biltong are available everywhere, and the meat is always on the menu (a healthy option, low in cholesterol).

Oudtshoorn has much more to offer than ostriches, though. It makes a great base for exploring the different environments of the Little Karoo, the Garden Route (it's 55km to George along the N12) and the Great Karoo to the north.

Sights

Many of Oudtshoorn's sights are outside the town limits. Some hostels and B&Bs offer their guests discounts on attractions.

Cango Caves CAVE
(044-272 7410; www.cango-caves.co.za; adult/child R80/45; 9am-4pm) Named after the Khoe-San word for 'a wet place', the Cango Caves are heavily commercialised but impressive. The one-hour tour gives you just a glimpse, while the 90-minute Adventure Tour (adult/child R100/60) lets you explore deeper into the caves. It does involve crawling through tight and damp places, so is not recommended for the claustrophobic or unfit. Advance booking for both tours is essential. The caves are 30km north of Oudtshoorn.

CP Nel Museum MUSEUM
(www.cpnelmuseum.co.za; 3 Baron van Rheede St; adult/child R20/5; 8am-5pm Mon-Fri, 9am-1pm Sat) Extensive displays about ostriches and Karoo history make up this large and interesting museum, housed in a striking sandstone building completed in 1906 at the height of ostrich fever.

Included in the ticket price is admission to **Le Roux Townhouse** (High St, cnr Loop St; 9am-5pm Mon-Fri), decorated in authentic period furniture and as good an example of a 'feather palace' as you're likely to see.

Activities

There are four show farms that offer guided tours of 45 minutes to 1½ hours. There's little to choose between them; we found the staff at **Highgate Ostrich Show Farm** (www.highgate.co.za; adult/child 110/60; 8am-5pm) very knowledgeable – it's 10km from Oudtshoorn en route to Mossel Bay. Nearby is **Safari Ostrich Show Farm** (www.safariostrich.co.za; adult/child R100/50; 8am-4pm). **Cango Ostrich Show Farm** (www.cangoostrich.co.za; Cango Caves Rd; adult/child R80/45; 8am-4.30pm) is on the way to the Cango Caves, while **Chandelier Ostrich Show Farm** (www.chandelier.co.za; N12; adult/child R80/50; 9am-4pm) is south of Oudtshoorn on the road to George.

★ **Meerkat Adventures** WILDLIFE WATCHING
(084 772 9678; www.meerkatadventures.co.za; per person R550) This unique wildlife encounter sees you sitting around at sunrise, coffee in hand, as curious meerkats emerge from their burrows to warm up in the morning sun. It's considered a trip highlight by many. Passionate conservationist Devey Glinister operates the experience on De Zeekoe Farm, 9km west of Oudtshoorn. No children under 10 years.

Trips don't go ahead in inclement weather but once you're at the meeting point

Oudtshoorn

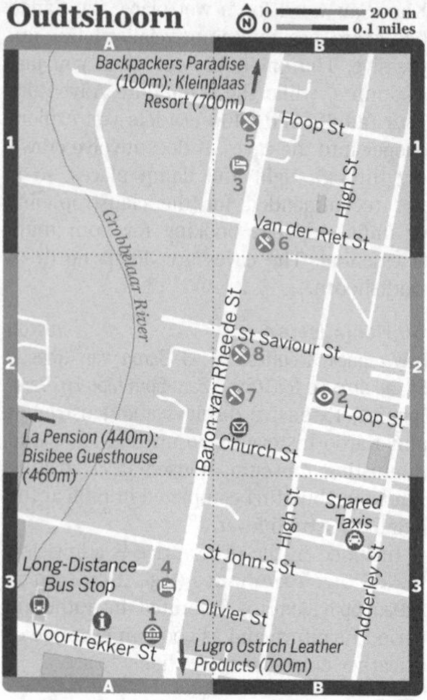

(where Rte 62 and Rte 328 meet), sightings are basically guaranteed.

Two Passes Route SCENIC DRIVE

A wonderful day's excursion is the round-trip from Oudtshoorn to Prince Albert taking in two magnificent passes. Head up the untarred **Swartberg Pass** and all the way down to Prince Albert, then return via the **Meiringspoort Pass**. Halfway down the latter is a waterfall and small visitor centre. Both passes are engineering masterpieces. Ask at your accommodation or the tourism bureau for a route map.

If driving isn't challenging enough, then hop on a mountain bike and ride from the top of Swartberg Pass down into Oudtshoorn. Book with **Backpackers Paradise** (☎044-272 3436; 148 Baron van Rheede St; tours R390) to be driven up. Be warned: it's not all downhill and it's a long ride.

Festivals & Events

ABSA Klein Karoo Nationale Kunstefees ARTS

(Little Karoo National Arts Festival; www.kknk.co.za) This April festival dedicates itself to the 'renaissance of Afrikaans' and showcases local artists, poets, thespians and musicians in a riotous week-long festival of creativity.

Oudtshoorn

Sights

1 CP Nel Museum ... A3
2 Le Roux Townhouse ... B2

Sleeping

3 Oakdene Guesthouse ... B1
4 Queen's Hotel ... A3

Eating

5 Black Swan ... B1
Café Brulé ... (see 4)
Die Kolonie Restaurant ... (see 4)
6 Jemima's ... B1
7 La Dolce Vita ... B2
8 Nostalgie ... B2

Sleeping

Karoo Soul Travel Lodge BACKPACKERS $

(☎044-272 0330; www.karoosoul.com; 1 Adderley St; dm R150, d with/without bathroom R420/350;) The gracious old house is more about doubles than dorms, though there is one small dorm. Try to get one of the west-facing doubles for a romantic sundowner from your bed, or ask about the garden cottages with en suite (R450).

Bisibee Guesthouse GUESTHOUSE $

(☎044-272 4784; www.bisibee.co.za; 171 Church St; s/d from R360/520;) These simple rooms offer excellent value. An optional continental breakfast costs R50 per person.

Backpackers Paradise HOSTEL $

(☎044-272 3436; www.backpackersparadise.net; 148 Baron van Rheede St; camping R80, dm R130, d with/without bathroom R450/400;) In a large old house, this lively hostel has a bar, ostrich braais and free ostrich-egg breakfasts (in season, you'll be given an egg – cook it any way you please). It also offers discounts to attractions in the area and can set you up with a host of activities.

Kleinplaas Resort CAMPGROUND $

(☎044-272 5811; www.kleinplaas.co.za; North St, near cnr Baron van Rheede St; camping per site R240, 4-person chalet R690;) A superb caravan park, with a big pool and decent, if slightly dated, chalets. The restaurant is only open for breakfast.

★ **Oakdene Guesthouse** GUESTHOUSE $$

(☎044-272 3018; www.oakdene.co.za; 99 Baron van Rheede St; s/d R790/1300;) The new owners have totally refurbished the rooms, which are fitted out with modern decor largely made of recycled wine crates. The rooms perfectly marry the modern with the classic – in keeping with the house's status as one of Oudtshoorn's oldest buildings.

La Pension GUESTHOUSE **$$**
(044-279 2445; www.lapension.co.za; 169 Church St; s/d incl breakfast R650/1000;) A reliable choice with spacious, stylish rooms and superb bathrooms, La Pension also has one self-catering cottage, plus a good-size pool and a large, immaculate garden.

Queen's Hotel HOTEL **$$$**
(044-272 2101; www.queenshotel.co.za; 11 Baron van Rheede St; s/d R950/1550;) Bang in the middle of town, this attractive old-style country hotel with spacious, understated rooms is refreshingly cool inside and has an inviting appeal. The attached **Die Kolonie Restaurant** (www.queenshotel.co.za; 11 Baron van Rheede St; mains R85-140) serves a range of local and international dishes.

Eating

As you'd expect, most places serve ostrich in one form or another.

Café Brulé CAFE **$**
(The Queen's Hotel, 11 Baron van Rheede St; mains R55-100; breakfast & lunch) A popular cafe, recommended for its freshly baked bread and cakes. There's a 'dish up and weigh' buffet on Wednesdays.

Nostalgie TEA ROOM **$$**
(74 Baron van Rheede St; mains R50-90; breakfast, lunch & dinner) This quaint tea garden, complete with lace tablecloths, is best as a place for breakfast, or coffee with a slice of home-baked cake. That said, there are no fewer than 10 ostrich dishes on the lunch and dinner menu, including carpaccio, burger and pie.

Black Swan INTERNATIONAL **$$**
(109 Baron van Rheede St; mains R75-125; dinner Mon-Sat, lunch Fri-Sun;) There are tables outside and in the atmospheric dining room at this large restaurant at the northern end of town. The menu is small but fairly varied and of course includes the requisite ostrich steaks.

La Dolce Vita INTERNATIONAL **$$**
(60 Baron van Rheede St; mains R50-100; breakfast, lunch & dinner Mon-Sat) Recommended by readers, this is a great spot to enjoy large portions of pizza, pasta, fish or steak on the shady patio.

★ **Jemima's** SOUTH AFRICAN **$$$**
(044-272 0808; www.jemimas.com; 94 Baron van Rheede St; mains R95-180; lunch & dinner) With a small menu specialising in traditional South African fare, this long-running restaurant is set in an attractive old house and garden. After your meal try a *swepie*, a mix of brandy and *jerepigo* (a dessert wine).

Shopping

Ostrich goods are naturally in demand, particularly items made from ostrich leather. The leather is pricey because of the low yield per bird, so it's worth shopping around, including at show ranches and in hotels.

Lugro Ostrich Leather Products ACCESSORIES
(133 Langenhoven Rd; 9am-5pm Mon-Sat) Lugro is independent of local ranches, so offers a shopping experience that avoids the tacky tourist vibe that usually accompanies the search for ostrich goods.

Information

Oudtshoorn Tourism Bureau (044-279 2532; www.oudtshoorn.com; Voortrekker St, cnr Baron van Rheede St; 8.30am-5pm Mon-Fri, 9.30am-12.30pm Sat) Behind the CP Nel Museum.

Getting There & Around

Buses stop in the Riverside Centre off Voortrekker St. Intercape (www.intercape.co.za) has services to Johannesburg (R700, 14½ hours, daily), Cape Town (R520, eight hours) and Mossel Bay (R390, two hours, daily).

The Baz Bus stops at George, from where you can arrange a transfer to Oudtshoorn with Backpackers Paradise (R150 one-way).

Shared taxis leave from behind the Spar supermarket on Adderley St en route to George (R60, 30 minutes) or Cape Town (R300, three hours). Bookings are required for the latter – contact the tourism bureau.

CENTRAL KAROO

The seemingly endless Karoo has a truly magical feel. It's a vast, semi-arid plateau (its name is a Khoe-San word meaning 'land of thirst') that features stunning sunsets and starscapes. Inhabited for over half a million years, the region is rich in archaeological sites, fossils, San paintings, wildlife and some 9000 plant species.

The Karoo covers almost one-third of South Africa's total area and is demarcated in the south and west by the coastal mountain ranges, and to the east and north by the mighty Senqu (Orange) River. It's often split into the Great Karoo (north) and the Little Karoo (south), but it doesn't respect provincial boundaries and sprawls into three provinces.

Prince Albert

POP 7000

To many urban South African people, Prince Albert – a charming village dating back to 1762 – represents an idyllic life in the Karoo. If you have your own transport, you can easily visit on a day trip from Oudtshoorn or even from the coast. Alternatively, stay in Prince Albert and make a day trip to Oudtshoorn via the spectacular Swartberg and Meiringspoort Passes, or – if the weather isn't too hot – consider going on a hike.

Despite being surrounded by very harsh country, the town is green and fertile (producing peaches, apricots, grapes and olives), thanks to the run-off from the mountain springs. There's an Olive Festival each April.

Sights & Activities

Many people drive the circular route to Oudtshoorn, taking the Meiringspoort Pass one way and returning by the Swartberg Pass (p154).

Swartberg Nature Reserve NATURE RESERVE
(www.capenature.co.za; adult/child R40/20) Many of Prince Albert's best attractions are outside the town, including the russet peaks of this reserve. There are over 100km of hiking trails, all administered by Cape Nature (☑044-203 6325; www.capenature.org.za) – check with them for updates on which trails are open and to book overnight walks. For guides, contact Prince Albert Tourism.

CULINARY PRINCE ALBERT

Prince Albert is popular with hikers, but in recent years the pretty town has also become known as a foodie destination. The 'culinary capital of the Karoo' offers olive tasting, fruit farms specialising in dried fruit production, fresh yoghurt, cream, milk and cheese from the local dairy, wine farms to visit and a well-established cooking school, as well as a few superb restaurants. There's also a market (☺8am-noon Sat) showcasing local foodstuffs and crafts next to the museum.

Sleeping & Eating

Bushman Valley CAMPGROUND $
(☑044-382 6805; www.bushmanvalley.com; Rte 407; camping R80, cottages per person R300; ☲) Prince Albert's only real budget option is 3km south of town and a fantastic base for hiking in the Swartberg mountains. Hiking permits are R20, and a guide (not essential) is R30 per person. The thatched cottages have decent kitchen facilities or you can camp in the grounds (hire tents for R50).

**Prince Albert
of Saxe-Coburg Lodge** GUESTHOUSE $$
(☑023-541 1267; www.saxecoburg.co.za; 60 Church St; r incl breakfast from R900; ❋☞☲) This place offers quality accommodation in lovely garden rooms. Owners Dick and Regina are a great source of information and offer guided hikes in the area.

Karoo Lodge GUESTHOUSE $$
(☑023-541 1467; www.karoolodge.com; 66 Church St; r from R1050; ❋☞☲) This owner-run guesthouse has an enormous garden with plenty of shady spots. The restaurant (mains R85 to R140) largely showcases Karoo fare. It's open to nonguests (dinner Wednesday to Sunday) but bookings are essential.

Lazy Lizard CAFE $
(9 Church St; mains R50-90; ☺7am-6pm; ☞) This bright, cosy house offers the best coffee in town and stocks home-baked goodies and crafts. The menu offers a little of everything. Try its legendary apple pie.

★**Gallery** FUSION $$
(☑023-541 1197; 57 Church St; mains R85-165; ☺dinner) Prince Albert's smartest dining option has an ever-changing menu featuring modern takes on local classics such as Karoo lamb and game steaks. There's also a couple of imaginative vegetarian choices.

Karoo Kombuis SOUTH AFRICAN $$
(Karoo Kitchen; ☑023-541 1110; 18 Deurdrift St; mains R80-110; ☺dinner Mon-Sat) After serving the same three traditional dishes since 1998, this homely restaurant has added two new options – but the bobotie, chicken pie and lamb, of course, remain. Bring your own drinks and make sure you book ahead.

Information

Prince Albert Tourism (☑023-541 1366; www.patourism.co.za; 21 Church St; ☺9am-5pm Mon-Fri)

Getting There & Away

Most people visit by driving over one of the area's passes from Oudtshoorn, or from the N1 between Cape Town and Jo'burg. There is no direct bus or train service to Prince Albert; the closest drop-off point is at Prince Albert Rd, 45km northwest of town. The **train** (☎0860 008 888; www.shosholozameyl.co.za) is cheaper than the bus, and private taxis from the station cost upwards of R200, or you could arrange a pick up with your accommodation.

Gamkaskloof Nature Reserve (Die Hel)

In a narrow valley in the Swartberg range is **Gamkaskloof**, better known as Die Hel. The first citizens of Die Hel were early Trekboers, who developed their own dialect. There was no road into Die Hel until the 1960s, and donkeys carried in the few goods the mostly self-sufficient community needed from Prince Albert.

Now the area is part of the Swartberg Nature Reserve, and there is self-catering **accommodation** (☎021-483 0190; www.capenature.co.za; cottage from R700) in restored farm cottages, as well as various trails and overnight huts.

The dirt road to Die Hel turns off the Swartberg Pass 18km from Prince Albert and extends for another 50km or so before hitting a dead end. Be warned: this short distance takes at least two hours to drive *each way*. The road is in terrible condition so you might want to leave your car in Prince Albert and opt for a guided tour. Lindsay Steyn from **Dennehof Tours** (☎023-5411 227; www.dennehof.co.za; day tour R850) is a mine of information on the region and offers superb full-day tours taking in the Swartberg Pass before descending the vertiginous road to Die Hel for lunch.

Beaufort West

POP 20,000

A transit town if ever there was one, Beaufort West is not a place most people linger, though it has a strange faded charm if you know where to look. Established in 1818, it's the oldest and largest town in the Karoo and in summer becomes a sluice gate for the torrent of South Africans heading for the coast – book ahead and expect higher prices at this time of year.

The town **museum** (☎023-415 2308; Church St, cnr Donkin St; adult/child R15/8; ⏲8.30am-12.45pm & 13.45-4.45pm Mon-Fri, 9am-noon Sat) is spread over three buildings, and is largely devoted to local hero Dr Christiaan Barnard, who performed the world's first human heart transplant.

The town is lined with guesthouses, many of which come and go. **Olive Grove** (☎023-414 3397; www.olivegrove.co.za; s/d R550/880) is a long-standing guest farm with pleasant rooms and self-catering cottages set on a vast farm featuring hiking trails and olive trees. It's 20km out of town, on the N12 to Oudtshoorn, but worth the drive. There's also a small **backpackers** (☎023-415 3226; www.karoobackpackers.com; 25 Donkin St; dm/s/d R140/230/330) above the tourism office, which can arrange donkey cart trails in the area.

Information

Tourist Information (☎023-415 1488; www.beaufortwest.net; 25 Donkin St; ⏲8am-5pm Mon-Fri)

WORTH A TRIP

MATJIESFONTEIN

One of the most curious and fascinating places in the Karoo, Matjiesfontein (pronounced 'mikeys-fontein') is an almost entirely privately owned railway siding around a grand hotel that has remained virtually unchanged for 100 years. It has a slight theme-park feel, but visiting the Victorian buildings, staffed by folks in period costume, is a lot of fun. There are two museums, one looking at **transport** (admission R5; ⏲8am-1pm & 2pm-5pm), the other a right old **jumble sale** (admission R5; ⏲8am-1pm & 2pm-5pm), containing everything from trophy heads to a collection of commodes. There's one **hotel** (☎023-561 3011; www.matjiesfontein.com; s/d from R800/1400; ❄) offering evening meals, an atmospheric pub and a **cafe** (mains R55-85; ⏲9am-5pm) serving light lunches.

Matjiesfontein is just off the N1, 240km from Cape Town and 230km from Beaufort West. Trains running between Cape Town and Jo'burg stop here and the Blue Train also pauses for an hour, with travellers given a tour of town on the double-decker London bus that stands outside the station.

Getting There & Away

Beaufort West is a junction for many bus services. Translux (www.translux.co.za) stops at the **Total petrol station** (Donkin St) in the centre of town. Greyhound (www.greyhound.co.za) and Intercape (www.intercape.co.za) stop at the Engen petrol station north of town. Long-distance **shared taxis** (083 756 8414) stop at the **BP petrol station** (Donkin St) en route to Cape Town and George.

The Shosholoza Meyl and the Blue Train stop at the station on Church St on their journeys between Cape Town and Jo'burg.

Karoo National Park

Karoo National Park NATIONAL PARK

(023-415 2828; www.sanparks.org; adult/child R152/76; 7am-7pm) The Karoo National Park covers 330 sq km of impressive Karoo landscapes and representative flora. Lions have been reintroduced and you might also spot black rhinos. More commonly sighted are dassies (agile, rodentlike mammals, also called hyraxes) and bat-eared foxes. Larger mammals include zebras, springboks, kudus and red hartebeests. There are many reptiles and birds, including black eagles.

Free guided walks are available and there's a 400m fossil trail that's accessible by wheelchair.

Accommodation is either at pleasant **campsites** (camping per site from R205) or in Cape Dutch–style **cottages** (2 people from R1200). The cottages are fully equipped with kitchens, towels and bedding; two have wheelchair access.

You cannot get out of your vehicle in the park, except at designated spots, so hiking the 10km from the gate to the rest camp is definitely not an option. You'll need your own transport. The park is 5km north of Beaufort West.

WEST COAST & SWARTLAND

The windswept coastline and desolate mountains on the western side of Western Cape are a peaceful, undeveloped paradise. Head north of Cape Town and you'll find whitewashed fishing villages, fascinating country towns, unspoilt beaches, a lagoon and wetlands teeming with birds, plus one of the best hiking regions in the country.

The West Coast National Park is a must for birdwatchers and lovers of seascapes, while inland lies the richly fertile Olifants River Valley, where citrus orchards and vineyards sit at the foot of the Cederberg mountains – a hiker's heaven. This remote area has spectacular rock formations and a wealth of San rock paintings.

Between the coast and the mountains lies the Swartland, undulating hills of wheat and yet more vineyards. Swartland (black land) gets its name from the threatened indigenous vegetation, *renosterveld,* that turns a dark grey in summer. This entire area is ablaze with colour in early spring (August and September) when the veld is carpeted with wildflowers. In season, you can check where the flowers are at their best on a daily basis by calling the **Flower Hotline** (072 938 8186).

Most public transport through this area travels from Cape Town north along the N7, either going all the way to Springbok and Namibia or leaving the N7 and heading through Calvinia to Upington. Getting to the coastal towns west of the N7 isn't easy if you don't have a car.

Darling

POP 1100

A quiet country town, Darling used to be famous just for its good-quality milk – that is, until the actor and satirist Pieter-Dirk Uys set up home here.

Don't forget to ask tourist information or your guesthouse about the underrated **Darling Wine Experience** (www.darlingtourism.co.za), the collective name for the five estates in the vicinity.

Sights

★ **Evita se Perron** THEATRE

(022-492 2851; www.evita.co.za; Darling Station; tickets R90; 2pm & 7pm Sat & Sun) This uniquely South African cabaret, featuring Pieter-Dirk Uys as his alter ego Evita Bezuidenhout, touches on everything from South African politics to history to ecology. Nothing is off limits – including the country's racially charged past and the AIDS epidemic. Although the shows include a smattering of Afrikaans, they're largely in English and always hilarious and thought-provoking.

Even if you're not seeing a show, a visit to the complex is well worth it. There's a politically themed sculpture garden and some fascinating apartheid memorabilia on show. The splendidly kitsch **restaurant** (Darling

DON'T MISS

GROOTE POST WINERY

Groote Post (022-492 2825; www.grootepost.com; tastings free, 2hr wildlife drives per person R130; 9am-5pm Mon-Fri, 10am-4pm Sat & Sun) Of all the Darling wineries, Groote Post has the most to offer the visitor, with wildlife drives, self-guided nature walks, a superb **restaurant** (022-492 2825; www.grootepost.com; Groote Post Winery; mains R110-130; lunch Wed-Sun) and, of course, free tastings of its excellent chardonnays and sauvignon blancs. It's 7km along a dirt road, off Rte 307; bookings are essential.

Station; mains R50-75; lunch Tue-Sun) serves traditional Afrikaner food. Uys also set up the Darling Trust (www.thedarlingtrust.org) to assist Swartland communities to empower themselves through participation in education and health programs. The A en C Shop at the complex stocks beading, clothes, wire-art and paintings.

Sleeping & Eating

Trinity GUESTHOUSE $$
(022-492 3430; www.trinitylodge.co.za; 19 Long St; s/d incl breakfast from R500/800;) A painstakingly renovated Victorian homestead with cosy country-style bedrooms and a beautiful garden.

Darling Lodge GUESTHOUSE $$
(022-492 3062; www.darlinglodge.co.za; 22 Pastorie St; s/d incl breakfast from R550/800;) An elegant and imaginatively decorated place. Rooms are named after local artists, whose work is displayed on the walls.

★**Marmalade Cat** CAFE $
(022-492 2515; 19 Main Rd; mains R50-95; breakfast & lunch daily, dinner Fri & Sat) For an afternoon coffee or all-day breakfast, this is the place. It also serves sandwiches, delicious cheeses and homemade sweet treats. Friday night is pizza night – bookings essential.

Drinking

Slow Quarter BAR
(5 Main Rd; Tue-Sat 10am-6pm) The tap room of the popular local beer, Darling Brew, is a chic place to munch on platters of locally sourced goodies and sip one of its five flagship beers. Light meals R55 to R85.

Information

Tourist Information (022-492 3361; www.darlingtourism.co.za; Pastorie St, cnr Hill Rd; 9am-1pm & 2-4pm Mon-Thu, 9am-3.30pm Fri, 10am-3pm Sat & Sun) In the museum.

Getting There & Away

Drive up Rte 27 from Cape Town and look out for the signs to Darling. An alternative route back to Cape Town is to head east out of the town and turn south down Rte 307. Turn right just before the town of Mamre to rejoin Rte 27. Do not follow Rte 304 past Atlantis.

West Coast National Park

West Coast National Park NATIONAL PARK
(www.sanparks.org; adult/child Oct-Jul R64/32, Aug & Sep R128/64; 7am-7pm) This park encompasses the clear, blue waters of the Langebaan Lagoon and is home to an enormous number of birds. The park covers around 310 sq km and protects wetlands of international significance and important seabird breeding colonies. Wading birds flock here by the thousands in summer. The most numerically dominant species is the curlew sandpiper, which migrates north from the sub-Antarctic in huge flocks. The offshore islands are home to colonies of African penguins.

The park is famous for its wildflower display, which is usually between August

WEST COAST NATIONAL PARK

Why Go Easy access from Cape Town; magnificent coastal views; year-round birdwatching; kayaking on the lagoon; largely uncrowded drives to seek out small wildlife species; spectacular spring wildflowers.

When to Go The park is at its finest from August to September when the flowers are in bloom, though this is also the busiest time. The rainy season is between May and August.

Practicalities Drive from Cape Town (120km) or Langebaan (7km). Gates are open 7am to 7pm (to 6pm April to August). Entry fees double in flower season (August and September).

Budget Tips If visiting a number of national parks, consider buying a Wild Card (p584).

DON'T MISS

!KHWA TTU

!Khwa ttu (www.khwattu.org; Rte 27, Yzerfontein; tours R150; ⏰9am-5pm, tours 10am & 2pm; 📶) !Khwa ttu is the only San-owned and -operated culture centre in the Western Cape. It is based on an 8.5-sq-km nature reserve within the ancestral lands of the San. Tours involve a nature walk in which you learn about San culture, and a wildlife drive – you'll likely see various antelopes, zebras and ostriches.

There is a restaurant open for lunch and a range of **accommodation** (bush camp/cottage per person R250/480, d R1360) available on the reserve. It's off Rte 27, 70km from Cape Town.

and September – it can get fairly crowded during this time. Aside from the white-sand beaches and turquoise waters of the ocean and lagoon, the park's greatest allure is that it is under-visited. If you visit midweek (and outside school holidays) you might find that you're sharing the roads only with zebras, ostriches and the occasional leopard tortoise ambling across your path.

★**Duinepos** CHALET $$
(☎022-707 9900; www.duinepos.co.za; s/d chalet from R540/800; 🚭) Bright, modern and well-equipped chalets in the heart of the park. It's an excellent birdwatching spot.

SANPark Cottages CABIN $$
(www.sanparks.org; cottage from R1200) Abrahamskraal Cottage is the plusher of the two, but Jo Anne's Beach Cottage has the better location, an easy walk from the lagoon. Both come with a decent kitchen and a large dose of tranquility.

Geelbek Visitor's Centre & Restaurant SOUTH AFRICAN $$
(☎022-772 2134; mains R85-135; ⏰breakfast & lunch) There's a wide menu, focusing on traditional fare. It's also an information centre for the park and can help with accommodation.

Langebaan

POP 8300

Its beautiful location overlooking the Langebaan Lagoon has made this seaside resort a favourite holiday destination with locals. But, though it's popular, it's fairly spread out so you can still easily find solitude. The town boasts some excellent hotels, a wonderful open-air seafood restaurant, phenomenal sunset views, windsurfing on the lagoon and a few good beaches, the best of which is **Langebaan Beach** – in town and popular with swimmers. The town is also a good base for exploring the West Coast National Park.

Sights & Activities

★**West Coast Fossil Park** ARCHAEOLOGICAL SITE
(☎022-766 1606; www.fossilpark.org.za; adult/child R20/15; ⏰8am-4pm Mon-Fri, 10am-1pm Sat & Sun) The first bear discovered south of the Sahara, lion-size sabre-toothed cats, three-toed horses and short-necked giraffes are all on display at this excellent fossil park on Rte 45 about 16km outside Langebaan. Fascinating tours depart hourly from 10am to 3pm (until 1pm on weekends) and take you to the excavation sites – among the richest fossil sites in the world. There are also mountain-biking and walking trails, and a coffee shop.

Cape Sports Centre WATER SPORTS
(☎022-772 1114; www.capesport.co.za; 98 Main Rd) Langebaan is a water sports mecca, particularly for windsurfing and kite-surfing. This cheery office offers kite-surfing courses (three-day course R2650), windsurfing lessons (two hours R700) and rents out surfboards, SUPs and kayaks (R295/345/385 per day).

Sleeping & Eating

Many of the sleeping options double as restaurants. There is also a cluster of restaurants on Bree St, some with beach views.

★**Friday Island** B&B $$
(☎022-772 2506; www.fridayisland.co.za; Main Rd; s/d R580/880; 📶) There are bright rooms and cheery staff at this popular beachfront B&B. You're going to want one of the two-level sea-facing rooms, each with its own deck. The restaurant (mains R70 to R130) is very popular.

Farmhouse Hotel HOTEL $$$
(☎022-772 2062; www.thefarmhousehotel.com; 5 Egret St; d incl breakfast R1850; ❄) Langebaan's oldest hotel sits on a hill overlooking the bay with lovely sunset views. Rooms are large, with country decor and their own fireplaces. The restaurant is reasonably priced (mains R85 to R185) with a creative menu. The hotel also has some self-catering **cottages** (www.kitequarters.co.za; r from R325, cottage from R1100) aimed at kite-surfers.

WORTH A TRIP

ELAND'S BAY

While much of the peninsula north of Paternoster is marred by smelly fish processing factories and rampant housing developments wherever there's a beach, past Veldrif the coast is undeveloped and the beaches beautiful. Eland's Bay is a particularly pretty spot oozing rustic charm and with a supreme setting: mountains run to the sea past a large lagoon frequented by waterbirds – it's a bird-lover's mecca.

The **Eland's Bay Hotel** (☎022-972 1640; www.elandsbayhotel.co.za; Hunter St; camping per site R200, dm R150, r incl breakfast from R550), which acts as the tourist information office, also has a restaurant serving average food with awesome views.

Eland's Bay is primarily a surf spot and is known as a goofy-footer's paradise, with extremely fast left-point waves working at a range of swell sizes. Body boards are available for hire in the town but surfers will need their own gear.

The gravel road to Lambert's Bay is in poor condition and was closed when we visited. The tarred road via Leipoldtville is recommended.

Club Mykonos RESTAURANT **$$**
(☎0800 226 770; www.clubmykonos.co.za) This Greek-themed, pseudo-Mediterranean resort might not appeal as a place to stay over, but it is a fun spot to spend an evening. There are eight restaurants to choose from as well as numerous bars and a casino, all open to nonguests.

★ **Die Strandloper** SEAFOOD **$$$**
(☎022-772 2490; www.strandloper.com; buffet R260; ⏲lunch Sat & Sun, dinner Fri & Sat Feb-Nov, lunch & dinner daily Dec-Jan) The West Coast life exemplified – a *10*-course fish and seafood braai right on the beach. There's also freshly made bread, bottomless *moerkoffie* (freshly ground coffee) and a local crooner who wanders the tables strumming his guitar. You can BYO (corkage free) or get drinks from the rustic bar, whose view is sensational. Bookings highly recommended.

Information

Tourist Information Centre (☎022-772 1515; www.capewestcoastpeninsula.co.za; Bree St; ⏲9am-5pm Mon-Fri, 9am-2pm Sat) In the municipal building.

Getting There & Away

Langebaan is an hour's drive north of Cape Town. Shared taxis run from the 7-Eleven car park to Cape Town (R95, two hours). **Elwierda** (☎0861 001 094; www.elwierda.co.za) also operates regular buses to Cape Town (R100, two to three hours), but bookings a day in advance are essential.

Paternoster

POP 2000

Not so many years ago, Paternoster was the West Coast's last traditional fishing village, little more than a clutch of simple whitewashed homes set against the blue sea. Then wealthy Capetonians and foreigners became captivated by its charms and property is now a hot commodity.

It remains a lovely town to visit. It's busiest during crayfish season, which, to a certain extent, is a moveable feast (sometime from mid-November to mid-April). Be aware that *kreef* (Afrikaans for this delicacy) sold from roadside vendors may have been illegally caught. Buy directly from fishingfolk at the harbour. If you want to try your hand at catching your own (or collect any other shellfish), make sure you get a permit from any post office and that you know the bag limits – rules are stringently applied.

Further north along the coast is the similar village of **St Helena Bay**, with a lovely sheltered stretch of water but no real beach.

Cape Columbine Nature Reserve NATURE RESERVE
(☎022-752 2718; admission adult/child R13/9, lighthouse tower R16/8; ⏲7am-7pm daily, lighthouse tower 10am-3pm Mon-Fri) Three kilometres south of Paternoster lies this windswept but stunningly beautiful reserve. It has campsites with basic facilities at Tieties Bay (R108 per site). The lighthouse tower is worth a climb and you can also stay here in renovated keepers' cottages (from R600).

Sleeping & Eating

Paternoster is rather lacking in street signs; instead look out for individual guesthouse signs. There are many B&Bs so it may be worth checking out a few places.

Beach Camp CAMPGROUND **$**
(☎082 926 2267; www.beachcamp.co.za; Cape Columbine Nature Reserve; camping R150, tent per person R315, hut per person R415) Beach

Camp is an ecofriendly place with a blissful setting right on the beach. Accommodation is in A-frame huts and pre-pitched dome tents equipped with single beds. It's a rustic, slightly ramshackle place that's all about the surroundings. There's no electricity but there is a cool bar. Bedding is an extra R50 per person.

Paternoster Lodge GUESTHOUSE $$
(022-752 2023; www.paternosterlodge.co.za; s/d R790/1100;) This is a snazzy place, with seven minimalist rooms, all with a sea view, and a breezy restaurant (mains R75 to R190) that's open all day. From the sun deck you can watch the fisherfolk bringing in their catch.

Abalone House GUESTHOUSE $$$
(022-752 2044; www.abalonehouse.co.za; 3 Kriedoring St; d R4200;) A five-star guesthouse with artsy rooms, a rooftop hot tub and plunge pool and a health spa. The restaurant (mains from R115), also open to nonguests, is part of a small chain of swanky eateries started by local celebrity chef Reuben Riffel.

Voorstrandt Restaurant SEAFOOD $$
(Strandloperweg; mains R70-175; lunch & dinner) A better location you couldn't wish for – you can hop from your table right onto the sand. Specialising in seafood, this is also an excellent spot to watch the sunset over a beer.

Information

Tourist Information (022-752 2323; www.capewestcoastpeninsula.co.za; Fish Market, Seeduiker St; 9am-5pm Mon-Fri, 10am-3pm Sat)

Lambert's Bay

POP 6100

The refreshing sea breezes of Lambert's Bay offer respite from the West Coast sun, but the ubiquitous fish-processing factories mean you'd be advised to stay upwind. Head south of the stinky centre for long stretches of largely unvisited beaches.

Lambert's Bay is a little-known whale-watching spot – look out for southern right whales in the spring and humpback whales in winter. The waters are also home to Heaviside's dolphin, an endemic species.

In March the **Crayfish Festival** brings cheap seafood and plenty of entertainment.

Sights & Activities

Bird Island PARK
(027-432 1672; www.capenature.co.za; adult/child R40/20; 7am-6pm) Sitting just 100m from the mainland, Bird Island is an important breeding site for the Cape gannet. You'll likely spot Cape fur seals too. The island is accessible on foot via a breakwater. There's a bird hide and plenty of informative signage.

Eco Adventure Boat Trips BOAT TOUR
(027-432 1774; Weskus Kombuis restaurant, Voortrekker St; 1hr trip R350, minimum 3 people) Boat trips take in Seal Island, Bird Island and in season, whale and dolphin watching. Sundowner cruises are also available.

Sleeping & Eating

Lambert's Bay Hotel HOTEL $$
(027-432 1126; Voortrekker St; s/d incl breakfast from R550/750;) The largest place to stay in town is a friendly spot with decent rooms and a bar/restaurant open to nonguests for lunch and dinner. Request a room with a view of the ocean.

Funky Tastebuds DELI $
(Voortrekker St; mains R45-80;) A surprisingly cool cafe tucked away behind the harbour. Light lunches, creative salads and good coffee are on offer, as well as a build-your-own picnic option if you'd rather take your lunch to the beach.

★ **Muisbosskerm** SEAFOOD $$$
(027-432 1017; www.muisbosskerm.co.za; buffet R195, crayfish extra; lunch & dinner) This open-air restaurant offers a multicourse seafood buffet featuring traditional stews, salads and a range of smoked, baked and braaied fish. Allow three hours to complete the banquet. It's 4km south of town on the Eland's Bay road. Bookings are essential.

Cederberg Wilderness Area

Some of the Western Cape's finest scenery is found in the desolate **Cederberg Wilderness Area** (www.capenature.co.za; adult/child R60/35). As you drive, bike or hike through the bizarre-shaped, weathered-sandstone formations, glowing ochre in the fabulous Cederberg light, you'd be forgiven for whistling the soundtrack to an old Western movie. The 830-sq-km wilderness area boasts San rock art, craggy mountains and clear streams. The peaks and valleys extend roughly north–south for 100km, between Vanrhynsdorp and Citrusdal. The highest peaks are Sneeuberg (2027m) and Tafelberg (1969m).

The region is famous for its plant life, which is predominantly mountain *fynbos*. Spring is the best time to see the wildflowers, although there's plenty of other things to see at other times of the year. The vegetation varies with altitude but includes the Clanwilliam cedar (which gives the region its name). The cedar survives only in relatively small numbers, growing between 1000m and 1500m.

There are small populations of baboons, rheboks, klipspringers and grysboks; and predators such as caracals, Cape foxes, honey badgers and the elusive leopard. There are also farms dotted about, many of which have been inhabited by the same families for generations. Almost all these farms offer accommodation.

As well as hiking, the Cederberg is popular with rock climbers, star-gazers and photographers, keen to capture the endlessly impressive landscapes.

CEDERBERG WILDERNESS AREA

Why Go Spectacular scenery; mountain hikes ranging from a few hours to a few days; ancient rock paintings; secluded farmstays; star-gazing.

When to Go Spring (August to October) is the best time, when temperatures are ideal and the wildflowers are in bloom. Summer (November to February) days can be scorching, while nights in winter (May to July) often plummet below zero.

Practicalities There are only gravel roads within the park. The main route is a public road and there is no fee to drive through. Entrance fees generally only apply to those undertaking activities.

Budget Tips With campsites and braai areas galore, this is a well-priced region to travel.

Sights & Activities

There is a vast network of hiking trails in the mountains. Two of the most popular hikes take in some of the region's more famous rock formations, the **Maltese Cross** and the **Wolfberg Arch**. The former is a relatively easy three-hour hike, the latter an all-day slog with some steep sections. Other hikes take in waterfalls, natural pools and rock art.

Permits are required for all hikes. At quiet times you can pick up a permit on the spot at **Algeria** or **Dwarsrivier** but during school holidays it's best to book ahead (☎021-483 0190) because hiker numbers are limited. The maximum group size is 12 and, for safety, the minimum is two adults.

Stadsaal Caves HISTORIC SITE

(adult/child R40/20) Once occupied by the San, these sandstone caves are glorious at sunset. First visit the rock art site, on the right as you drive through the gate, then explore the network of caves with their marvellous views. Permits are available from Dwarsrivier Farm.

Sleeping

Gecko Creek Wilderness Lodge LODGE $

(☎027-482 1300; www.geckocreek.com; camping R130, tent/cabin per person R200/290; @) There are magnificent views, San rock art and hiking trails on this 10-sq-km property on the outskirts of the Cederberg. Accommodation is in pre-erected tents or cabins (or bring your own tent), all sharing one set of ablutions. To find it, take the Algeria turn-off on the N7 and look out for the sign on the right.

Algeria CAMPGROUND $$

(☎027-482 2403; www.capenature.co.za; camping per site R315, 2-person cottage from R665) The main camping spot in the area has exceptional grounds in a shaded site alongside the Rondegat River. There is a swimming hole and lovely picnic spots. It gets busy at weekends and school holidays. Entrance to the camping ground closes at 4.30pm (9pm on Friday).

Getting There & Away

The Cederberg range is about 200km from Cape Town, accessible from Citrusdal, Clanwilliam and the N7. You can also drive from Rte 303 via Ceres on the eastern side.

It takes about an hour to get to Algeria from Clanwilliam by car. Algeria is not signposted from Clanwilliam, just follow the gravel road above the dam to the south – it's fairly rough going. Algeria *is* signposted from the N7 and is about 30 minutes from the main road; it's also a gravel road, but in good condition.

Unfortunately, public transport into the mountains is nonexistent.

Citrusdal & Around

POP 7200

The small town of Citrusdal is a good base for exploring the Cederberg. August to

DON'T MISS

DWARSRIVIER FARM

Deep in the Cederberg, this is an excellent base for **hiking** – both the Wolfberg Arch and Maltese Cross hikes start nearby. At **Sanddrif** (027-482 2825; www.cederbergwine.com/sanddrif; camping per site R180, 4-person cottage R800) there are shady campsites by the river or well-equipped cottages with patios gazing out at the mountains. Don't miss the **Cederberg Winery**, also on the premises – all of its wines are stupendous and the makings of a brewery was in progress when we visited. There's an excellent **astronomical observatory** (www.cederbergobs.org.za; entry by donation; 8pm Sat) nearby.

To get to Dwarsrivier, follow the Algeria turnoff from the N7. From here a gravel road winds into the mountains; it's 46km to Dwarsrivier.

September is wildflower season, which can be spectacular. This is also one of the best times for hiking. Although the town itself is quaint, some of the most interesting and beautiful places to stay are in the surrounding mountains. Make sure to explore beyond the town limits – the scenery is stupendous.

Sleeping & Eating

Ukholo Lodge BACKPACKERS $
(022-921 3988; www.ukholo-lodge.co.za; camping R90, dm R130, d with/without bathroom R400/350;) The rooms are stylish, there's plenty of space to pitch a tent and there are bathrooms all over the place. Activities include tubing on the adjacent river or mountain hiking. It's 21km from Citrusdal on the N7 towards Clanwilliam.

Burton's Farm at Steelwater CHALET $
(022-9213337; www.burtonsfarm.co.za; 2-person cottage R400, d incl breakfast R500;) A twisty dirt road leading off Rte 303 to Citrusdal climbs past groves of citrus trees before ending at Steelwater, with its chalet sleeping up to seven people. The hosts are exceptionally friendly and there are decent walks on the grounds. It's 12km from town on the way to the Baths.

★**Baths** RESORT $$
(022-921 8026; www.thebaths.co.za; camping R110, 2-person chalet from R650;) In a glorious location thick with trees and right up against craggy peaks is this hot-spring resort with outdoor pools and a range of private baths filled with spring water at 43°C. It's well signposted from Citrusdal – 18km on a tarred road. Booking is essential both for day visits (adult/child R80/40) and overnight stays.

Lovely Grapevine CAFE $
(mains R50-85; 8am-4pm Mon-Fri, 8am-1pm Sat) In a town with a dearth of eating options, Grapevine is a pleasant place for a light lunch in the pretty garden. It serves decent coffee and a range of cakes as well as sandwiches and a small selection of daily specials.

Information

Tourism Bureau (022-921 3210; www.citrusdal.info; 39 Voortrekker St; 8.30am-5pm Mon-Fri, 9am-noon Sat)

Getting There & Around

Intercape (www.intercape.co.za) buses stop at the Caltex petrol station 6km out of town on the N7. Destinations include Cape Town (R400, three hours) and Springbok (R430, five hours).

There's an excellent scenic road (Rte 303) over Middelberg Pass into the Koue Bokkeveld and a beautiful valley on the other side, which is topped by the Gydo Pass. The back road into the wilderness area is also excellent.

Clanwilliam & Around

POP 7700

The adjacent dam and some adventurous dirt roads into the Cederberg make the compact town of Clanwilliam a popular weekend resort. The dam is a favourite with waterskiers, though if current plans to raise the dam are fulfilled, this and the landscape of the region will change somewhat.

Clanwilliam is the centre of the **rooibos** (red bush) tea industry. It's made from the leaves of the *Aspalathus linearis* plant, which only grows in the Cederberg region. Rooibos contains no caffeine and much less tannin than normal tea and is said to have health benefits. Tours of the **Elandsberg Rooibos Estate** (027-482 2022; www.elandsberg.co.za; tour per person R125), 22km west of Clanwilliam, are an excellent way to follow the process from planting to packaging. The owners of Rooibos Teahouse in town have also set up the **Rooibos Route** (www.rooibos-route.co.za), which takes in restaurants, tea producers and accommodation highlighting the region's most famous export.

SAN ROCK-ART SITES

The nomadic San, South Africa's indigenous people, inhabited the area north of Clanwilliam for millennia. While as a people they have been decimated and assimilated, thankfully the area is still home to some of the finest examples of their rock art in the country. Indeed, archaeologists consider some of these sites the most well preserved of their kind in the world.

If you're interested in learning more or visiting sites, contact the highly reputable **Living Landscape Project** (027-482 1911; www.cllp.uct.ac.za; 16 Park St, Clanwilliam; permits R30, tours from R85), which arranges visits and runs a community development program. Contact the Clanwilliam information centre for other tour operators.

An accessible spot with a cluster of rock-art sites is the **Sevilla Rock Art Trail** (permits R40) at the Traveller's Rest, 36km from Clanwilliam on the way to Bushmans Kloof. There are nine sites along a relatively easy self-guided 3km hike.

Sleeping & Eating

Lebanon Citrus CAMPGROUND $
(027-482 2508; www.lebanon.co.za; camping per site R200, 2-person cabin R350) There are campsites and cute wooden cabins at this gorgeous spot on the edge of the dam, with stupendous views of the Cederberg. It's 28km from Clanwilliam, mostly along a rutted gravel road. When the dam is raised, the campsite will be flooded, but the owners plan to move to a similarly spectacular location.

Daisy Cottage COTTAGE $
(027-482 1603; Foster St; r per person R300) In a quiet street close to the town centre, this adorable thatched cottage has a beautiful garden. There are two bedrooms plus a sleeper couch.

Saint du Barrys Country Lodge GUESTHOUSE $$
(027-482 1537; www.saintdubarrys.com; 13 Augsburg Dr; s/d incl breakfast R850/1400) A 150-year-old banyan tree looms over this pleasing guesthouse with five en suite rooms and a pint-size pool in the charming garden. Dinner is by arrangement.

Bushmans Kloof LUXURY HOTEL $$$
(021-481 1860; www.bushmanskloof.co.za; s/d incl full board from R5650/8000) This upmarket private reserve, 46km east of Clanwilliam along the Pakhuis Pass, is known for excellent San rock-art sites and extensive animal- and birdlife. Guests are assigned a guide and can partake in all manner of retreat-type activities or just gorge on excellent food.

Nancy's Tearoom CAFE $
(Main St; mains R45-100; breakfast & lunch Mon-Sat) Enjoy light meals on the shady patio at this friendly spot. Locals rave about the scones – try one with a rooibos cappuccino. Nancy's is a stop on the Rooibos Route and you'll find the tea in a number of dishes including bobotie, cheesecake and even rooibos lemon meringue.

Reinhold's SOUTH AFRICAN $$
(083 389 3040; Main St; mains from R85; dinner Tue-Sat) The music and the menu at this à la carte restaurant will take you back 50 years, but it's a long-standing favourite and there are few other places to eat in town. It specialises in fish and grills.

Drinking

★**Rooibos Teahouse** TEAHOUSE
(www.rooibosteahouse.co.za; 4 Voortrekker St; 8am-5pm Mon-Fri, 8am-2pm Sat) An absolute must for tea enthusiasts. There are more than 100 blends and flavours of rooibos available. The tea tasting (R70) is highly recommended – choose seven teas to taste, perhaps with a slice of cake. Tutored tastings can be arranged for groups of four or more (bookings essential). There's also a shop selling all the teas on the menu.

Information

Information Centre (027-482 2024; Main St; 8.30am-5pm Mon-Fri, 8.30am-12.30pm Sat) Opposite the old jail, dating from 1808, which doubles as the town's **museum**. Ask about the historical walkabout (R50), a one-hour guided tour of South Africa's seventh-oldest town.

Getting There & Away

Buses that go through Citrusdal also pass Clanwilliam, stopping at the Cedar Inn petrol station out of town – you'll need to arrange for your accommodation to collect you. Shared taxis running between Springbok (R320, five hours) and Cape Town (R160, three hours) go through Clanwilliam – the tourism office can help with bookings.

Eastern Cape

Includes ➡

Best Places to Eat

- Veld to Fork (p220)
- Hazel's Organic Restaurant (p189)
- Stanley St (p184)
- Haricot's Deli & Bistro (p194)

Best Places to Stay

- Bulungula Lodge (p210)
- Buccaneers Lodge (p206)
- Mdumbi Backpackers (p210)
- Die Tuishuise & Victoria Manor (p225)
- Edge Mountain Retreat (p202)
- Terra-Khaya (p202)

Why Go?

From lush tropical forests to uninhabited desert expanses, from easygoing hammock time to adrenaline-pumping adventures, the Eastern Cape offers a wide range of topography and experiences. Compared with the wealthier and more developed Western Cape, it can feel like a different country and provides opportunities to learn about Xhosa culture. Some of South Africa's finest hiking (and slackpacking) trails wind along the province's stunning coastline and through its mountainous, waterfall-filled landscapes.

Private wildlife reserves and national and regional parks abound; see the Big Five (lion, leopard, buffalo, elephant and rhino) or migrating whale and dolphins. You'll find tranquillity and culture in the towns of the semiarid Karoo; the imposing Drakensberg peaks and little-known valleys in the Highlands; good surfing in the Indian Ocean, coupled with amazing cultural experiences on the Wild Coast; and history throughout, including the legacy of some famous local sons – Nelson Mandela, Oliver Tambo and Steve Biko.

When to Go

Port Elizabeth

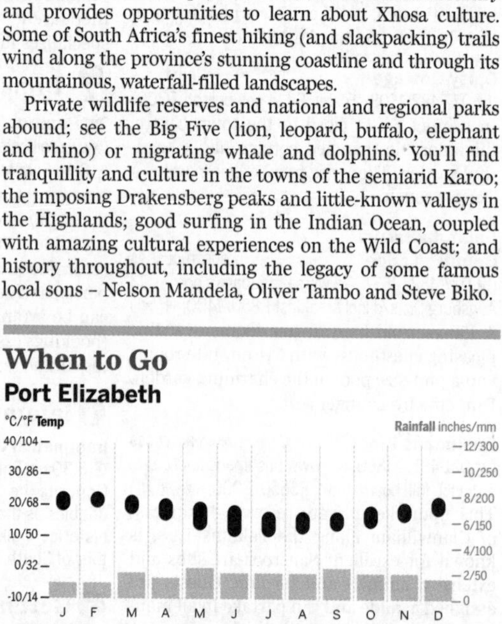

Apr Between the summer rains and the winter chill; good wildlife watching and quiet beaches.

Jul Africa's largest arts festival in Grahamstown and a world surfing competition in Jeffrey's Bay.

Sep–Oct Spring wild flowers and bearable presummer heat in the Karoo, and Hogsback's Spring Festival.

Language

Start practising those tongue clicks – Xhosa is the predominant language in the Eastern Cape. Local whites speak English and Afrikaans.

Getting There & Around

The easiest way to explore the province is by car, but backpacker shuttle the **Baz Bus** (☎0861 229 287; www.bazbus.com) is a good option for touring the coast. It runs between Cape Town and Port Elizabeth (R2020 one way hop-on, hop-off; 15 hours) five days a week in both directions, stopping at backpackers in the Crags (near Nature's Valley), Bloukrans Bridge, Storms River and Jeffrey's Bay. Baz Bus also runs between Port Elizabeth and Durban (R1830 one way hop-on, hop-off; 15¼ hours) four days a week, stopping in Port Alfred, East London, Chintsa and Mthatha. Seven- to 21-day passes are also available. Backpackers run shuttles from East London to Hogsback, and from Mthatha to Coffee Bay and Port St Johns.

The major bus companies, including **Greyhound** (☎in Jo'burg 011-611 8000; www.greyhound.co.za), **Translux** (City to City; ☎0861 589 282; www.translux.co.za), **Intercape** (☎in Cape Town 021-380 4400; www.intercape.co.za) and **City to City** (☎0861 589 282; www.citytocity.co.za), ply the same coastal route and also serve the hinterland, linking the Eastern Cape with Bloemfontein, Johannesburg (Jo'burg) and Pretoria. **Shosholoza Meyl** (☎0860 008 888; www.shosholozameyl.co.za) trains connect Port Elizabeth and East London with Jo'burg via Bloemfontein. Port Elizabeth, East London and Mthatha have airports.

Further off the beaten track, notably on the Wild Coast and in the Highlands, travellers on public transport will have to take shared taxis to reach more-obscure spots. Roads can be impassable after heavy rains. Some places on the Wild Coast are only accessible on foot or horseback.

GARDEN ROUTE EAST

This region includes the western edge of the Eastern Cape coast, an extension of the well-travelled Garden Route and, for that reason, is probably the most visited part of the province. Tsitsikamma National Park is deservedly well known but other lesser-known destinations such as Baviaanskloof Wilderness Area (p173) are also worthy of attention.

Nature's Valley

Nature's Valley is nestled in yellow-wood forest next to a magnificent beach and lagoon in the west of Tsitsikamma National Park. This is where the 46km Otter Trail (p170) ends and the 60km Tsitsikamma Mountain Trail (p171) begins. There are also plenty of shorter hikes in this part of the park, which is referred to as the De Vasselot Section.

A range of accommodation options and eateries are found above the village, signposted from Rte 102 as it runs 9km down to Nature's Valley from the N2 near Kurland Village. After passing Nature's Valley, Rte 102 loops back to the N2, crossing it at the Tsitsikamma toll plaza, 14km east of Kurland Village.

Sleeping

Nature's Valley Properties (☎082 772 2972; www.naturesvalleyproperties.co.za/accommodation) lists self-catering accommodation on its website.

Rocky Road BACKPACKERS $
(☎044-534 8148; www.rockyroadbackpackers.com; Loredo South; dm R120, safari tent s/d R190/280; P 📶 ♿) Rocky Road is like an enchanted clearing in the wood. Swing chairs, a donkey-boiler Jacuzzi (fired up on Fridays) and magical bathrooms are scattered on the fringes of indigenous forest. Walking trails lead through the trees, and accommodation options include comfortable safari tents and cabins with adjoining bathrooms. It is signposted from Rte 102 about 1km from the N2.

Nature's Valley Guesthouse & Hikers Haven GUESTHOUSE $
(☎044-531 6805; www.hikershaven.co.za; 411 St Patrick's Ave; s/d incl breakfast R450/740, without bathroom R350/600; closed Dec; P 📶) This thatched brick building has a big lawn, a self-catering kitchen, a lounge, and small, tidy rooms with outdated bathrooms. Transport to the start of the Otter Trail is offered (R480 for up to four people).

Tranquility Lodge LODGE $$
(☎044-531 6663; www.tranquilitylodge.co.za; 130 St Michael's Ave; s/d incl breakfast from R590/980; 📶) Soundtracked by a trickling fountain and the roaring waves, Tranquility has seven rooms decked out with beach-house furniture, African art and surf trimmings. Guests get free kayaks for the lagoon and discounts on local activities.

Nature's Valley Rest Camp CAMPGROUND $$
(☎044-531 6700; www.sanparks.org; camping R190, chalets R900) The national park campsite is a lovely spot at the edge of the river east of

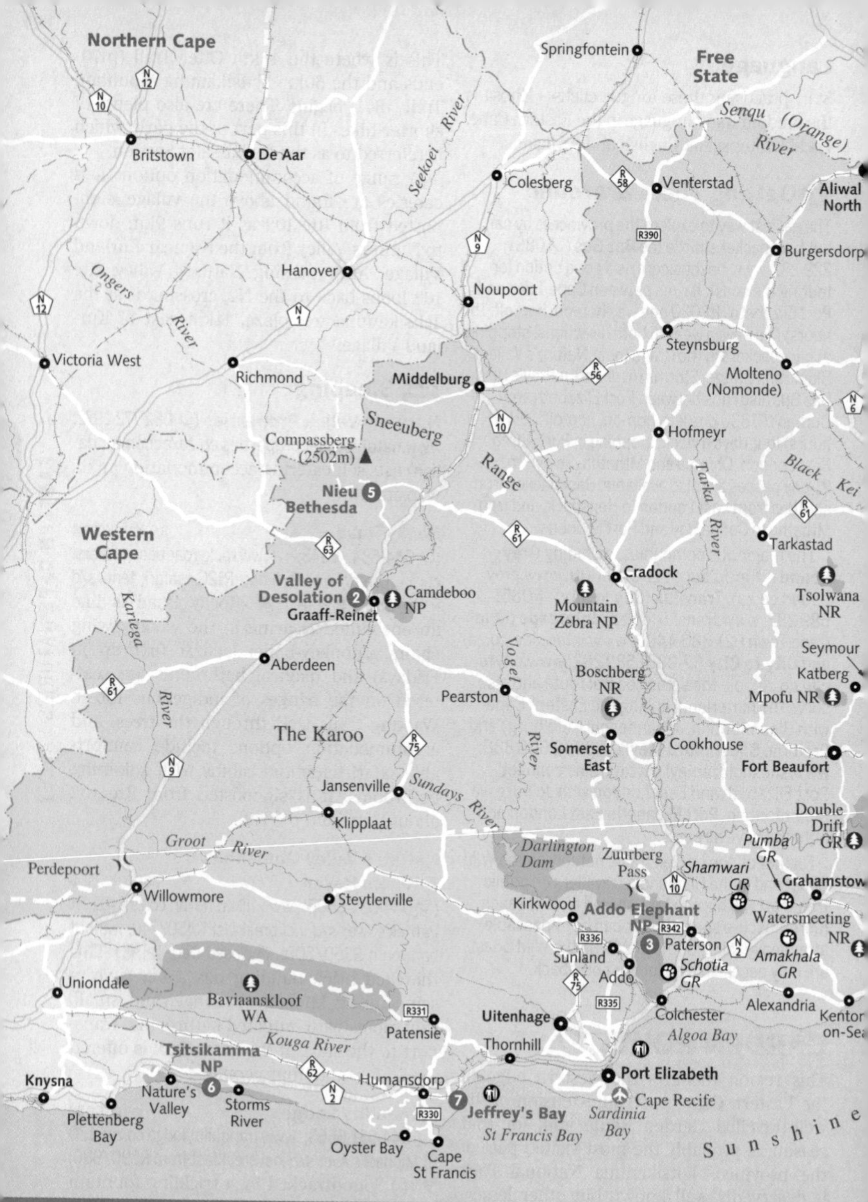

Eastern Cape Highlights

1. Walking the **Wild Coast's** (p209) coastal pathways and secluded beaches.
2. Taking in a Karoo sunset with views of Graaff-Reinet below in the **Valley of Desolation** (p221).
3. Observing African elephants up close at **Addo Elephant National Park** (p186) and the nearby reserves.
4. Hiking forested trails to waterfalls around **Hogsback** (p201).
5. Gazing at star-filled skies in the artistic Karoo outpost of **Nieu Bethesda** (p222).
6. Enjoying hiking, bungee jumping, tubing and zip-lining among **Tsitsikamma National**

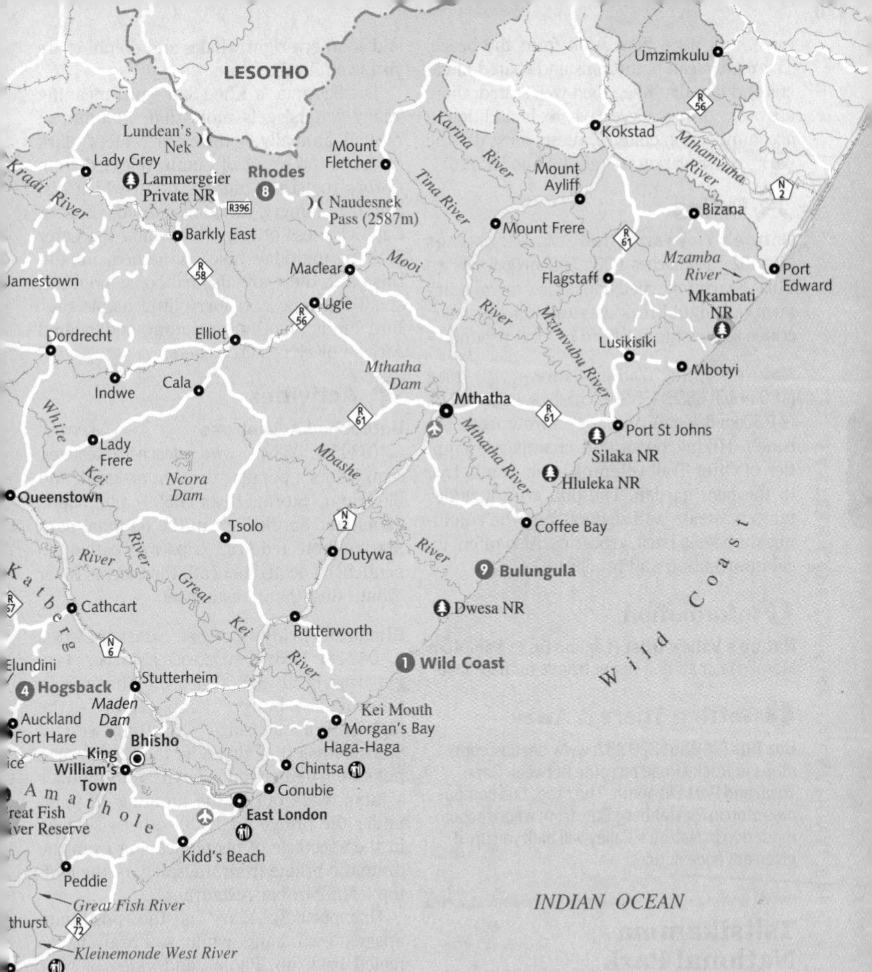

Park's (p170) churning rivers and ancient trees.

7 Surfing **Jeffrey's Bay** (p175) or simply marvelling at **Supertubes** (p178), one of the world's top-ranked waves.

8 Finding mountain solitude in the southern Drakensberg hamlet of **Rhodes** (p217).

9 Staying in a *rondavel* and meeting the Xhosa people at Wild Coast and Amathole backpackers, such as **Bulungula Lodge** (p210) and **Elundini Backpackers** (p203).

town, and it's a 2km walk from the beach. There are clean bathrooms and shared kitchens and laundry. Keep food well stored; there are pesky primates everywhere. In addition to accommodation charges, guests must pay the park's conservation fee (adult/child R72/36).

 Eating

Nature's Way Farm Stall CAFÉ, SELF-CATERING $
(Rte 102; sandwiches R30; ⊘9am-5pm; 🛜🅿) This charming roadside store on a dairy farm sells light breakfasts and lunches, cake, coffee and a smorgasbord of local produce.

Nature's Valley Trading Store PUB $
(☑044-531 6835; 135 St Michael's Ave; mains R70; ⊘9.30am-8.45pm) A spade's throw from the beach. Hiking boots and champagne empties of Otter Trail veterans hang from a tree in the beer garden. The pub grub includes burgers, steaks and seafood, and the adjoining shop sells basic groceries. Also offers local information and brochures.

ℹ Information

Nature's Valley Trust (Lagoon Dr; ⊘8am-4pm Mon-Fri) Located at the entrance to the village.

ℹ Getting There & Away

Baz Bus (☑0861 229 287; www.bazbus.com) stops at Rocky Road en route between Cape Town and Port Elizabeth. The other bus companies stop in Plettenberg Bay, from where accommodation in Nature's Valley will pick you up, if given advance notice.

Tsitsikamma National Park

Cut through by dark, coffee-coloured churning rivers, deep ravines and dense forests, Tsitsikamma National Park (☑042-281 1607; www.sanparks.org; 2hr adult/child R40/20, 4hr R80/40; ⊘gate 7am-7pm) encompasses 650 sq km between Plettenberg Bay and Humansdorp, as well a Marine Protected Area covering 80km of coastline and stretching 5km out to sea. A 77m-long suspension bridge spans the Storms River Mouth near the rest camp of the same name (not to be confused with the village of Storms River), where several walking trails pass thickets of ferns, lilies, orchids, coastal and mountain *fynbos* (fine bush), and yellow-wood and milkwood trees, some hundreds of years old. Millennia-old sandstone and quartz rock formations line the gorges and rocky shoreline,

and southern right whales and dolphins are visible out in the ocean.

Tsitsikamma, a Khoe-San word meaning 'many waters', gets more than 1200mm of rainfall annually – the river waters' dark colour is the result of tannin released from *fynbos* roots, the bitter taste of which discourages hungry, foraging animals. Elusive Cape clawless otters, after which the Otter Trail (a multiday hike) is named, inhabit this park; there are also baboons, monkeys, small antelope and furry little dassie rats. Bird life is plentiful, including endangered African black oystercatchers.

🏃 Activities

Untouched Adventures KAYAKING
(☑073-130 0689; www.untouchedadventures. com) Offers a popular three-hour kayak and lilo trip up Storms River (R399), plus scuba diving and snorkelling in the national park Marine Protected Area (trips are weather dependent). Located beneath the Storms River Mouth Rest Camp restaurant.

Bloukrans Bridge Bungee ADVENTURE SPORTS
(☑042-281 1458; www.faceadrenalin.com; bungee jumps R850; ⊘8.30am-5pm) The world's third-highest bungee jump (216m) – the highest from a bridge – is 21km west of Storms River directly under the N2. If you're not sure whether you have the gumption for a jump, walk out to the jumping-off point under the bridge for R100; otherwise, take in the spectacle of people leaping from the dramatic bridge from the safety of the clifftop terrace or bar-restaurant.

Unexpectedly scary is the post-jump upside-down hang while you wait to be reeled back up. Photos and video of your glorious lapse of judgement are available.

Hiking

If you don't have time for the long, overnight trails, don't worry; shorter walks are plentiful.

Otter Trail HIKING
(☑in Pretoria 012-426 5111; www.sanparks.org; per person R1000) The 46km Otter Trail is one of South Africa's most acclaimed hikes, hugging the coastline from Storms River Mouth to Nature's Valley. The walk, which lasts five days and four nights, involves fording a number of rivers and gives access to some superb stretches of coast. A good level of fitness is required for the walk, as it goes up-and downhill quite steeply in many places.

Book at least nine months ahead (six months if you are flexible about dates).

TSITSIKAMMA NATIONAL PARK

Why Go Mountainous landscape covered with indigenous forest, rolling down to rocky coastline. Activities include kayaking, tubing, horse riding and bungee jumping; walking trails range from short strolls to famous multiday hikes.

When to Go June and July are the driest months, and their relatively mild temperatures continue into August and September.

Practicalities The park's main information centre is at Storms River Mouth Rest Camp. You can also pay park entrance fees and get information at Nature's Valley Rest Camp.

Budget Tips Accommodation in Storms River and Nature's Valley is cheaper than at the park's rest camps; in Storms River, you can walk from accommodation to companies offering activities in the park. If you don't have a car, stay at accommodation on the Baz Bus route and organise shuttles into the park, rather than taking taxis. Get your second bungee jump at Bloukrans Bridge for R650!

There are often cancellations, however, so it's always worth trying, especially if you are in a group of only two or three people. Single hikers are permitted; you'll be tagged onto a group so you do not walk by yourself.

Accommodation is in six-bed rest huts with mattresses (without bedding), rainwater tanks, braais and firewood. Camping is not allowed.

Tsitsikamma Mountain Trail HIKING
(☎042-281 1712; www.mtoecotourism.co.za; per night R135) This 60km trail begins at Nature's Valley and ends at Storms River, taking you inland through the forests and mountains. It takes up to six days, but you can also opt to hike for two, three, four or five days, because each overnight hut has its own access route. Porterage is also available, as are day hikes (R30) and mountain bike trails.

Dolphin Trail HIKING
(☎042-280 3588; www.dolphintrail.co.za; s/d R5940/9980) Ideal for slackpackers who don't want to hoist a rucksack or sleep in huts, this two-day, 17km hike runs from Storms River Mouth Rest Camp to Misty Mountain (p173), and then onto the Fernery Lodge & Chalets (p173) for the last night. Book through the trail's website at least a year in advance.

Luggage is transported by vehicle between the overnight stops, and the price also includes three nights of accommodation, all meals, guides and a 4WD trip back to Storms River Mouth.

Sleeping

Storms River Mouth Rest Camp CAMPGROUND, CHALET $$
(☎042-281 1607; www.sanparks.org; camping R300) This campsite offers accommodation ranging from rustic forest huts (from R485) to chalets (from R945), family cottages with four single beds (R1545), and waterfront 'oceanette' cottages (from R885). Most have single beds with bedding and, apart from the forest huts, kitchens (including utensils) and bathrooms. Rates do not include the park's conservation fee (adult/child R150/75).

There is also a restaurant (open 8.30am to 10pm) and small shop here. The turn-off for the camp is between Bloukrans Bridge and Storms River on the N2. From here, the park gate is 4km, and the camp is 10km.

Getting There & Away

There is no public transport to either Nature's Valley Rest Camp or Storms River Mouth. Greyhound, Intercape, Translux and City to City stop in Plettenberg Bay and Storms River Bridge. Baz Bus gets you closer to the rest camps, stopping in the Crags (near Nature's Valley), at Bloukrans Bridge and at Storms River en route between Cape Town and Port Elizabeth.

Hiking Trail Transfers (☎082 696 5335; www.ottertrailtransfers.co.za) Offers transfers to walkers on the Otter and Tsitsikamma Mountain Trails.

Storms River

Tree-lined Storms River is a little hamlet with an excellent selection of accommodation options and a well-developed tourist industry, in large part because of its location in Tsitsikamma National Park near Bloukrans Bridge. Don't confuse Storms River with the turn-off 4km to the west for Storms River Mouth (Stormsriviermond in Afrikaans), located in the park.

Sights & Activities

Big Tree FOREST
(adult/child R12/8; 8am-5pm, to 6pm Sep-Apr; P) Just east of Storms River on the other side of the N2 is the Big Tree, a 36m-high yellow-wood that's over 1000 years old, and a forest with many fine examples of candle-wood, stinkwood and assegai. The 4.2km **Ratel Trail** begins here, with signs describing the trees in this forest, one of the best preserved in South Africa.

Mild 2 Wild OUTDOORS
(042-281 1842; www.mild2wildadventures.com; Darnell St) Runs horse-riding trips (two hours R350) and rents out mountain bikes (four hours R160) for the recommended 22km cycle through the national park to the Storms River Mouth. Adjoins Papa Africa pizzeria, and is affiliated with Dijembe Backpackers.

Blackwater Tubing ADVENTURE TOUR
(079 636 8008; tubenaxe.co.za/stormsriver-tubing; cnr Darnell & Saffron Sts) Tubing trips on the Storms River (half/full day from R450/750), run out of Tube 'n Axe backpackers. Because the river is susceptible to flooding, there may be no departures for several days after rains of any significance. It's worth asking how the river is flowing; with lower water levels you'll be doing almost as much walking as floating.

Tsitsikamma Falls Adventure ADVENTURE TOUR
(042-280 3770; www.tsitsikammaadventure.co.za; Witelsbos) Abseil (R100) 36m down a beautiful waterfall or explore the Kruis River gorge on eight zip-lines up to 211m long (R375). Around 12km east of the Storms River on the N2.

Tsitsikamma Canopy Tours ECOTOUR
(042-281 1836; www.stormsriver.com; Darnell St) This massive operation is the oldest branch in a nationwide network of canopy tours. Ten zip-lines up to 100m long cut through the forest covering between 10 platforms; it's more relaxing than thrilling. The three-hour guided tour (R495 including lunch and park entrance) departs every half-hour from 8.30am to 3.30pm. Guided forest drives and hikes are also offered.

Sleeping

In the Village

★**Dijembe Backpackers** BACKPACKERS $
(042-281 1842; www.dijembebackpackers.com; cnr Formosa & Assegai Sts; camping/dm/s/d R70/130/320/380; P) Reflecting the spirit of its nature-loving owner – who might arrive with a rescued horse, hang from the rafters and lead a drum circle, all in the space of a typical evening – much of this intimate backpackers is made from recycled wood. There's a Jacuzzi on the upper deck, free pancake breakfasts and township tavern visits, plus nightly bonfires and dinners (R70).

Accommodation includes safari tents and a cottage in the back garden.

Tsitsikamma Backpackers BACKPACKERS $
(042-281 1868; www.tsitsikammabackpackers.co.za; 54 Formosa St; dm/d/tr/q R170/500/750/900; P@) The faux log-cabin facade aside, a stay here feels like bedding down in a clean suburban home. Spick-and-span rooms are decorated with colourful flourishes in the bedding and artwork, while twin tents (R400) stand on covered platforms. Breakfast (R50) and dinner (R70) are available, and the lounge, well-equipped kitchen, and bar with pool and foosball sweeten the deal.

Tube 'n Axe BACKPACKERS $
(042-281 1757; tubenaxe.co.za; cnr Darnell & Saffron Sts; camping/dm/r R85/140/440; P) The social centre of this party hostel is the large bar and restaurant area that opens onto a large fire pit. A range of accommodation is available, including six- and 14-bed dorms, nicely decorated private rooms, log cabins and elevated two-person safari tents (R300).

When it's busy, noise can be an issue in some of the rooms in and around the main building.

At the Woods GUESTHOUSE $$
(042-281 1446; www.atthewoods.co.za; 43 Formosa St; s/d/tr/q R825/1100/1650/2000; P) This stylish guesthouse has an arty feel, with ceramics on the walls, colourful cushions on the beds and turquoise garden furniture. Rooms upstairs have wooden balconies; number six is particularly spacious and has some fetching wooden fish.

Tsitsikamma Village Inn INN $$
(042-281 1711; www.tsitsikammahotel.co.za; Darnell St; r incl breakfast R525-1390; P@) In this handsome minivillage, the majority of rooms are in old-fashioned low-slung cottages with four-poster beds and private porches surrounding a manicured lawn. A restaurant, bar, brewery, hair stylist and playground are on the premises.

Armagh Country Lodge & Spa LODGE $$
(☎042-281 1512; www.thearmagh.com; 24 Fynbos Ave; s incl breakfast R400-600, d incl breakfast R590-1500; P 📶) Just off the main access road into the village from the N2, Armagh is practically hidden from view by a lush and leafy garden. The rooms are spacious and warm and most have individual patios. There's a spa, and the on-site restaurant, Rafters, is one of the best places to eat in town.

Andelomi Forest Lodge LODGE $$
(☎042-281 1726; www.andelomi.com; 31 Formosa St; s incl breakfast R450-500, d incl breakfast R700-800; P 📶 👪) Andelomi offers no-frills accommodation, a restaurant and a pub in leafy grounds with views of Tsitsikamma's forested slopes. A four-person self-catering unit (R700 for one or two people, then R350 per adult) is also available.

Outside the Village

There are a couple of worthy accommodation options outside of Storms River village. From the N2, look out for the Blueliliesbush and Nompumelelo turning, between the Storms River Bridge and Tsitsikamma Falls Adventure; the accommodation is about 8km down that road.

★ **Fernery Lodge & Chalets** RESORT $$
(☎042-280 3588; www.forestferns.co.za/accommodation-all; s/d from R930/1860; P 📶 🏊) Hugging the edge of a cliff overlooking the Sandrift River gorge with falls and pools, the Fernery takes full advantage of its dramatic setting. Luxurious chalets and suites are scattered throughout; a Jacuzzi hovers over the void; and the restaurant is a cosy nook with floor-to-ceiling windows.

Misty Mountain Reserve CHALET $$
(☎042-280 3699; www.mistymountainreserve.co.za; s/d/f from R900/1440/2350) A string of large, individual A-frame cottages set back from a bluff over the ocean, each with a large Jacuzzi bath and some with a separate lounge. Meals are available, and on-site activities include walking and mountain-biking on trails through the indigenous forest.

Eating & Drinking

Papa Africa PIZZERIA $
(Darnell St; pizzas R70) With its oil-drum counters, coffee-sack tablecloths, corrugated-iron walls and fairy lights, Papa Africa has the feel of a barn expecting a dance. Choose five toppings from the blackboard and the personable pizza wizard Arthur will work his magic with the wood-fired oven.

Rafters SOUTH AFRICAN $$
(24 Fynbos Ave; mains R90; 📶) The Armagh Country Lodge's restaurant has a cosy dining room with an open fire and patio seating. Cape Malay specialities, including ostrich *bobotie* (delicately flavoured curry with a topping of beaten egg baked to a crust) and *bredie* (pot stew), are offered alongside less-local dishes such as Moroccan lamb shank and light lunches.

Marilyn's 60's Diner THEME BAR
(Darnell St; mains R70; ⏲10am-late) This wonderfully incongruous Elvis-, Marilyn Monroe– and Americana-inspired diner dominates the village centre. The menu mixes South African and American classics; dishes of varying quality range from hot dogs, curry and calamari to the 'A Little Less Conversation' sarmie (sandwich). Our advice is to just grab a beer and ogle the restored Cadillacs.

The **Elvis Festival Africa** (www.elvisfestival.co.za) takes place here over the last weekend in May.

Information

Just off the N2 is **Storms River Information Centre** (☎042-281 1098; Gamassi St; ⏲9am-5.30pm), which has a wall of brochures and can help with accommodation, including self-catering options. Across from Marilyn's 60's Diner is a small supermarket and liquor store with an ATM.

Getting There & Away

Baz Bus stops at the backpackers in Storms River en route between Cape Town and Port Elizabeth,

OFF THE BEATEN TRACK

BAVIAANSKLOOF

Baviaanskloof Wilderness Area
(Baviaanskloof Mega Reserve; ☎044-272 9908; www.travelbaviaans.co.za) One of South Africa's largest conservation areas, Baviaanskloof Wilderness Area is a World Heritage Site with leopards, antelope, buffaloes and Cape mountain zebras between the Kouga and Baviaanskloof Mountains. Stretching between the towns of Patensie and Willowmore, the region is best explored in your own vehicle (with high clearance) or on a tour. For more information, visit www.baviaanskloof.net and www.baviaans.net.

and your accommodation can organise shuttles to Tsitsikamma National Park and local activities. The main bus companies stop at Storms River Bridge, 5km east of town on the N2; arrange a pick-up with your accommodation from there.

SUNSHINE COAST

The Sunshine Coast covers a significant chunk of the Eastern Cape coastline, including Port Elizabeth, the seaside towns of Jeffrey's Bay and Port Alfred, and numerous sandy beaches. In the hinterland are the best wildlife-watching areas within easy reach of the coastline between Cape Town and Durban: Addo Elephant National Park and the nearby private reserves.

The region has an English heritage and flavour, thanks to the influence of the 1820 Settlers. These hardy Brits landed at Algoa Bay and, having tried to farm in the midst of internecine clashes between the Boers and the Xhosa, they ultimately ended up in Grahamstown, Port Elizabeth and beyond.

Cape St Francis & Around

Cape St Francis, 25km south of Humansdorp, is a small and unpretentious town with a wind-whipped beach and the Seal Point surf break. Southern right and humpback whales can be seen offshore between July and November; dolphins are seen throughout the year.

St Francis Bay, 8km north of Cape St Francis, is an upmarket resort partially constructed around a network of canals. It has a uniform building code that calls for black thatched roofs and white stucco walls. The beach here is narrower than at Cape St Francis, but pleasant nonetheless, and the surf is good for beginners. Off season, it's pretty much deserted, and its golf course and twee crescents create an air of immaculate sterility. However it does come to life in the high season, and is a safe and tranquil spot for a night or two throughout the year. You will find most facilities you might need here, including two malls, an ATM, a few restaurants and a brewery.

Accessed from St Francis Bay to the north, **Port St Francis** is a working port surrounded by a high-end condominium development. The port is one of the centres of the calamari fishing industry; catches include Cape Hope squid, known as *chokka* and often used as bait. At night you can see these ships floating offshore, lit by lamps meant to attract the calamari. A few yachts and motorboats are docked in the marina and the small mall has some good restaurants.

◉ Sights & Activities

Seal Point Lighthouse LIGHTHOUSE
(Seal Point Reserve, Cape St Francis; **P**) Built in 1878, this lighthouse is the tallest masonry tower on the South African coast, and marks the second-most-southern tip of Africa.

Penguin Rehabilitation Centre BIRD SANCTUARY
(www.penguin-rescue.org.za; Seal Point Reserve, Cape St Francis; admission free, guided tour adult/ child R50/30; ⊙9am-5pm; **P**) **FREE** Next to Seal Point Lighthouse, this haven for endangered African penguins is funded entirely by donations. You can adopt a starving penguin (R600) that will be cared for and released when healthy.

Irma Booysen Flora Reserve WALKING
(Da Gama Way, Cape St Francis) This small nature reserve, set up to preserve the area's coastal *fynbos*, has several footpaths.

River Break CRUISE
(☑042-298 0054; www.capestfrancis.co.za; St Francis Bay) Canal cruises (per person R200) and day-long trips upriver to a farm for kayaking and a braai (R450).

Chokka Trail HIKING
(☑073 825 0835; www.chokkatrail.co.za; s/d R4000/6800) This 56km slackpacking trail meanders around the headland's beaches, *fynbos*, forests and golf courses. The fourday package includes three nights of fullboard guesthouse accommodation, a canal cruise and calamari tasting.

🛏 Sleeping & Eating

Oasis Lodge GUESTHOUSE $$
(☑042-294 0456; www.oasislodge.biz; cnr Grand Comore St & Poivre Cres, St Francis Bay; s incl breakfast R450-495, d incl breakfast R720-750; **P🛜❄**) Close to the town centre and golf course, this canal-side idyll has thatched units opening onto a flowery garden, plus fantastic views of the canal's docks and decks from the lounge, dining room and patio.

Cape St Francis Resort RESORT $$
(☑042-298 0054; www.capestfrancis.co.za; Da Gama Way, Cape St Francis; camping R100-150, s/d from R360/480; **P🛜❄♿**) The various chalets and units at this oceanfront resort are attractive and well-equipped, with self-catering

and B&B options available. In the thatched and whitewashed village are Cape Dutch-style houses, beachfront luxury villas (with their own small pools), backpacker rooms with shower, kitchenette and a communal braai, apartments and more. There's also a spa, restaurant, small shop and bar on site.

Christy's Catch SEAFOOD, ASIAN **$$**
(165 St Francis Dr, St Francis Bay; mains R90) Christy's is all about seafood, including calamari burgers, tuna steaks and sushi; the thatched bar and decor of a boat and fishing tackle in the trees add nautical flavour to the courtyard. There is also an Asian counter offering stir-fries, curries and spring rolls.

Chokka Block SEAFOOD, STEAKHOUSE **$$**
(Triton Ave, Port St Francis Mall; mains R100; 11am-9pm Mon-Wed, Fri & Sat, to 4.30pm Sun) Seafood and grills, available on hefty platters, are served alongside sweeping harbour views and arty, nautical-themed decor.

Chez Patrick FRENCH **$$**
(Triton Ave, Port St Francis Mall; mains R85; 5-10pm Mon-Fri, 9am-3pm & 5-10pm Sat;) Floor-to-ceiling windows with views of the marina below and a stylish contemporary decor complement the inventively presented light and locally sourced fusion fare. Nightly specials are offered.

Getting There & Away

AdventureNow runs shuttles to St Francis Bay from Jeffrey's Bay (per person R150) and Port Elizabeth Airport (per vehicle from R650).

Jeffrey's Bay

POP 27,107

Once just a sleepy seaside town, 'J-Bay' is now one of the world's top surfing destinations. It's certainly South Africa's foremost centre of surfing and surf culture. Boardies from all over the planet flock here to ride waves such as the famous Supertubes, generally rated as one of the world's most perfect waves. June to September are the best months for experienced surfers, but novices can learn at any time of year.

Activities

Surfing

Wavecrest Surf School SURFING
(073 509 0400; www.wavecrestsurfschool.co.za; Drommedaris St; 2hr lessons incl board & wetsuit R250) This long-running operation offers daily lessons. Good for children and beginners.

Son Surf School SURFING
(076 501 6191; www.surfschools.co.za; 1½hr lessons R230) Good for intermediate surfers who want a refresher or to improve their technique. Owner Kelvin Zehmke also offers surf guiding to show experienced surfers the best local spots.

Rip Curl SURFING
(31 Da Gama Rd; board & wetsuit each per hr/half-/full-day R20/70/100; 9am-4.30pm Mon-Fri, to noon Sat) Hires out boards and wetsuits.

Other Activities

For nonsurfers, there's windsurfing, kitesurfing, stand-up paddle boarding, sandboarding, horse riding, dolphin- and whale-watching from the beaches, and birdwatching at Kabeljous Estuary, which makes a pleasant 6km **coastal walk** from town (for security reasons, don't go by yourself). Alternatively, wander down the boardwalk to Supertubes (p178) to watch impressive displays of surf skill.

AdventureNow ADVENTURE SPORTS
(079 490 2389; www.adventurenow.co.za; Da Gama Rd) Offers most of the possible activities and day trips in the region.

Festivals & Events

Winter Fest SPORTS
(www.jbaywinterfest.com) The biggest surf crowd comes to town every July for the Open of Surfing competition, part of this 10-day festival of sports, live music and entertainment. Demand for accommodation skyrockets during the festivals, and most places charge high-season rates.

Sleeping

Like many places in this part of Eastern Cape, J-Bay is chock-a-block with holidaymakers between mid-December and mid-January, so you'll have to book way ahead for accommodation at this time. With the notable exception of Island Vibe, most accommodation options are clustered around Supertubes.

A warning: there have been cases of people making online bookings for accommodation that turn out to be bogus. Confirm before paying that your chosen accommodation does actually exist in the offline world.

Stay in J-Bay (www.stayinjbay.co.za) is a useful and reputable resource for accommodation.

Island Vibe BACKPACKERS **$**
(042-293 1625; www.islandvibe.co.za; 10 Dageraad St; dm R150-170, r R400-650; P) Eighteen

Jeffrey's Bay

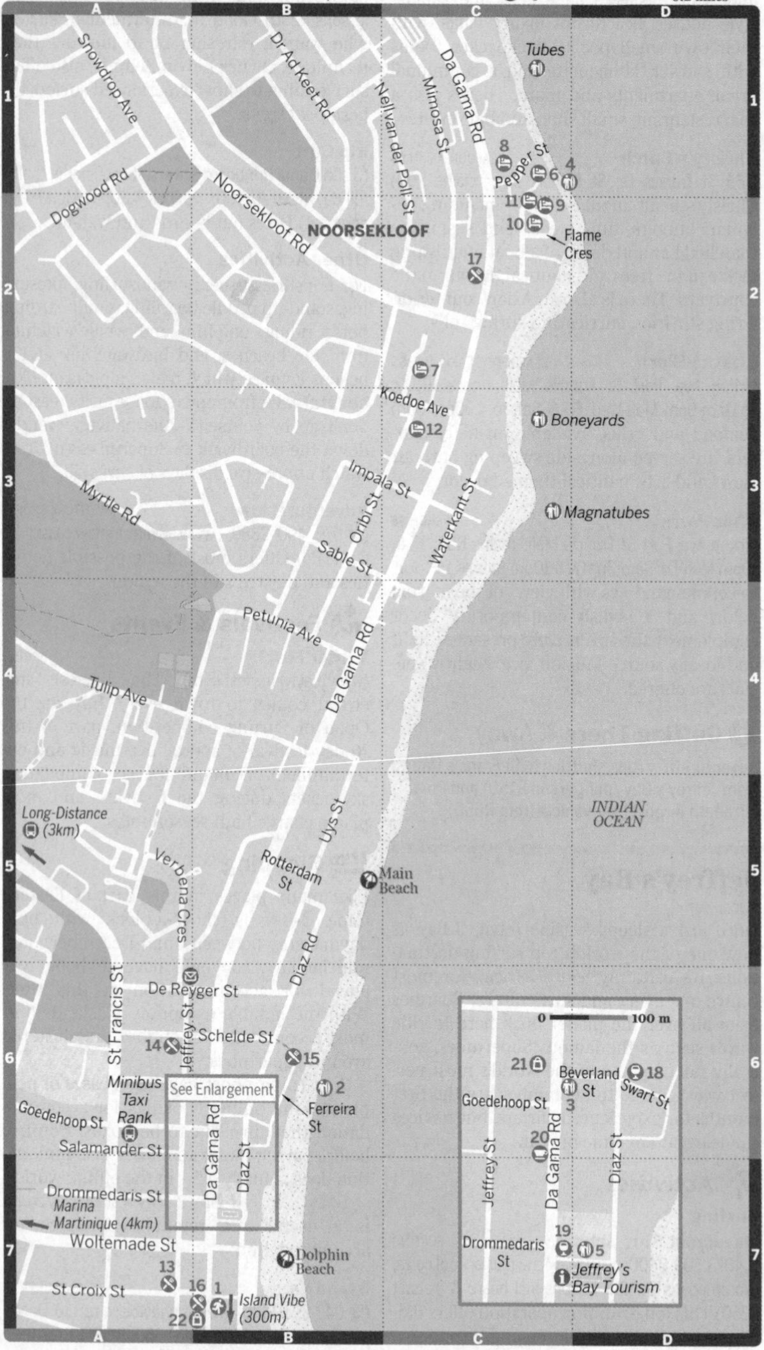

Jeffrey's Bay

Activities, Courses & Tours

1	AdventureNow	B7
2	Kitchen Windows	B6
3	Rip Curl	C6
4	Supertubes	C1
5	Wavecrest Surf School	D7

Sleeping

6	African Perfection	C1
7	African Ubuntu	C2
8	Aloe Again	C1
9	Beach Music	C2
10	Cristal Cove	C2
11	Dreamland	C2
12	Hard Rock	C3

Eating

13	Bay Pasta Co	A7
14	InFood Deli	A6
15	Kitchen Windows	B6
16	Love Food Cafe	B7
17	Nina's	C2

Drinking & Nightlife

18	Je'Vista Social Cafe	D6
19	Mexican	C7
20	Sunflower	C6

Shopping

21	Quiksilver	C6
22	Surf Village	B7

years young and still partying hard, Island Vibe is 500m south of the city centre, and the attendant raft of surfers attests to its prime beachfront location. Accommodation ranges from four- to 12-bed dorms and wooden cabins (numbers one and two have private balconies overlooking the beach), to a beach house and a flashpackers, both with ensuite rooms.

Surf-camp packages (three, five and seven days), daily lessons and board hire are offered, as are activities including horse riding, sandboarding and, of course, hanging out in the pirate-themed bar. The restaurant serves pizzas and set-menu dinners (R40 to R80).

African Ubuntu BACKPACKERS $
(042-296 0376; www.jaybay.co.za; 8 Cherry St; camping/dm/r incl breakfast R100/140/450; @ wi-fi) A suburban home transformed into an intimate and friendly backpackers by its passionate surfer owner. Some of the two dorms (six- and ten-bed) and five doubles and twins are slightly dark and dingy, but the garden, braai area and bar are good places to chill.

You can see Magnatubes and Boneyards from the balcony, and surfboard rental and activities can be organised.

Cristal Cove BACKPACKERS $
(042-293 2101; www.cristalcove.co.za; 49 Flame Cres; dm/r/f from R110/300/450; P wi-fi) This two-storey brick home has five carpeted and clean units – essentially miniapartments with lounge area, kitchen and several bedrooms. The reception has a bar and pool table.

Aloe Again BACKPACKERS $
(042-293 1401; www.aloeagainbackpackers.co.za; Pepper St; r R350-400, f R450-550; P wi-fi) Run out of African Perfection across the street, Aloe Again has small, clean rooms and a large open-plan lounge and kitchen with pool and foosball tables. The courtyard, garden and braai area offer plenty of space to chill and to hang your wetsuit out to dry.

Hard Rock BACKPACKERS $
(042-293 3140; hardrockbackpackers.co.za; 29 Oribi St; camping/dm/s/d/q incl breakfast R85/120/180/350/520; P wi-fi) Photos of hard rockers overlook the bar and pool table, but otherwise this is a sedate, clean spot in a suburban house.

Beach Music GUESTHOUSE $$
(042-293 2291; www.beachmusic.co.za; 33 Flame Cres; s R230-430, d R350-700; wi-fi) This burnt-umber-coloured building overlooking Supertubes resembles a Mexican villa. The wonderfully airy 1st-floor lounge and kitchen have superb ocean views, and the tastefully decorated rooms have small private patios.

Dreamland GUESTHOUSE $$
(042-293 3677; www.jbaylocal.com; 29 Flame Cres; r R300-1000; wi-fi) This thatch-roofed hand-crafted home has four individually designed units with Oregon pine wooden floors, private decks and direct access to Supertubes. The units all have a kitchen or kitchenette, and organic food is served upon request.

African Perfection B&B $$
(042-293 1401; www.africanperfection.co.za; 20 Pepper St; s incl breakfast R490-700, d incl breakfast R700-1200; P wi-fi) Occupying prime real estate in front of Supertubes, this luxury option is perfect for surfing voyeurs. Every room comes with a private balcony offering stunning sea views; the fabulous four-sleeper penthouse suite (R2300) has a fully equipped kitchen.

Eating

★InFood Deli INTERNATIONAL $

(cnr Schelde & Jeffrey Sts; mains R60; ⏰7am-5pm Mon-Sat; 📶) The sandwiches, burgers and other fare at this cafe, bakery and deli are far from ordinary. This is not surprising, considering the owner-chef's impressive CV – including once having cooked for Prince William. The mix of organic, locally sourced ingredients (such as Karoo *fynbos* honey) and wide-ranging culinary tastes (quesadillas, handmade pasta and Thai chicken curry) makes this a worthy foodie destination.

Love Food Cafe CAFE, DELI $

(4 Da Gama Rd; mains R70; 📶🖉) Love Food's owners also run an artisan bakery and chef academy; their culinary credentials show in the freshly baked breads and cakes, sarmies, salads and larger meals. The cheese burger and the honey mustard chicken wrap are popular choices.

★Nina's INTERNATIONAL $$

(16 Wavecrest Centre; mains R85) Most locals recommend Nina's, with its stylish decor of surfboards and coastal scenes around a paper-disc chandelier. Service can be slow, but the food is worth the wait. Seafood abounds on the wide-ranging menu, which also features burgers, curries, pizza, pasta, Thai food and nachos; the specials menu is a winner, offering dishes such as ostrich fillet and grilled tuna.

Kitchen Windows SEAFOOD $$

(80 Ferreira St; mains R60-140; ⏰11am-late Mon-Sat, to 3pm Sun) Sea views and white stucco

SURFING THE EASTERN CAPE

Surfing on the Eastern Cape coast is legendary. While Supertubes at Jeffrey's Bay is world class, and Bruce's Beauties at St Francis Bay inspired the movie *Endless Summer,* you can generally check out breaks anywhere along the coast, from Jeffrey's Bay to Port Edward.

The water temperature ranges from 16°C to 22°C, so you can get away with a short wetsuit (or even baggies) in summer, but you'll need a full wetsuit in winter.

Starting in the south, **Cape St Francis** (p174) is home to legendary Seal Point, one of the most consistent right-handed breaks. Nearby **St Francis Bay** has Bruce's Beauties and Hullets, the perfect longboard wave.

Jeffrey's Bay (p175) is one of the planet's 10 best surf spots, and ranks high on most people's list of 'waves I must surf before I die'. In July it hosts the Open of Surfing competition. Consequently, it can become crowded when the surf's up: remember your manners and say 'howzit' to the locals. **Supertubes** is a perfect right-hand point break, and once you've caught this, you'll be spoilt rotten. If you're a beginner, head to the softer **Kitchen Windows**.

In the rush to J-Bay, many surfers overlook nearby **Port Elizabeth** (PE). While the predominant southwesterly winds can blow everything away, Pipe in Summerstrand is PE's most popular break, and on a good day the Fence is another favourite.

Further north in **Port Alfred** (p195) there are excellent right-handers at East Pier, while West Pier has a more sheltered left.

East London (p198), home to some well-known surfing pros such as Greg Emslie and Rosy Hodge, is best known for the consistent Nahoon Reef; Gonubie Point and Gonubie Lefts can also come up with the goods. Nursery 'grommets' will find what they need at Nahoon Beach and Corner. There can be some dirty water in the area, which encourages shark activity, so keep an eye out and don't surf at dusk.

Heading north from East London, there are good waves in the coastal spots collectively known as East Coast Resorts and at the beginning of the Wild Coast. Look out for **Queensberry Bay** (where Hodge learnt her tricks), **Glen Eden**, **Yellow Sands** and **Chintsa** (p205).

Now you're on the **Wild Coast** – and wild, it is: a spectacular, often dangerous coastline that hasn't really been explored or exploited. Be careful at polluted river mouths: sharks are common, and in general you're a long way from medical attention. There's **Whacky Point** at **Kei Mouth** (p207), and **Coffee Bay** (p208) has a couple of waves. **Mdumbi** (p210) has a long, right-hand point break with a nice sandy bottom, **Whale Rock** is just around the corner, and then there are those secret spots that no one's ever going to tell you about...

walls give this airy restaurant a Mediterranean island feel. Less-expensive fare such as the calamari burger, beef *tramezzini* (Italian toasted sandwiches) and salads complement a sophisticated menu of creatively prepared fish, prawns, steaks and organic chicken.

Bay Pasta Co ITALIAN $$
(34 Jeffrey St; mains R85; 🖼) Adjoining a surf shop, this restaurant's surfy decor continues the theme. The deck is a popular hang-out, with live music on Sunday. More than a dozen varieties of pizza and pasta, as well as *tramezzini*, are on the menu.

InFood Blu BISTRO, SEAFOOD $$
(☑042-940 0053; mains R85; ⊘5-10pm Tue-Fri, from 10am Sat, 10am-4pm Sun) Under the same ownership as the town's best deli cafe, InFood Blu serves dishes such as red masala prawn curry, sticky ribs, sushi and steak, with a good selection of seafood. It's one of a few good restaurants at Marina Martinique, a short drive south of town on Clapton's Beach. To get here from the centre, bear left on Dolphin Dr from Woltemade St.

🍷 Drinking

Je'Vista Social Cafe COCKTAIL BAR
(1st fl, 33 Diaz St) This loungey spot with big, sea-facing windows is popular for cocktails. The rose petal mojito, Baileys banana colada and potent California iced tea are all hits.

Mexican THEME BAR
(Da Gama Rd; mains R65) A popular local hangout, this 1st-floor Latino bar-restaurant has a long balcony overlooking Da Gama Rd. Mexican classics such as enchiladas, fajitas, burritos and tacos are on the menu.

Sunflower CAFE
(20 Da Gama Rd) With Jack Black, Hansa and Castle on tap, this come-as-you-are hangout attracts backpackers and surfers to its deck. Sushi, wraps and coffee (R10) are on the menu.

🛍 Shopping

Surf Village SPORTS, FASHION
(Da Gama Rd) This cluster of surf shops, factory outlets and fashion shops offers pleasant browsing in modern, thatched buildings. Stores line Da Gama Rd south of St Croix St, with a few also found one block further inland on Jeffrey St. On Da Gama are the local labels Country Feeling (surf and fashion) and In Step (leather products), as well as Billabong, Rip Curl and RVCA.

Quiksilver SPORTS, FASHION
(☑042-293 2273; 24 Da Gama Rd) Has a 'museum' upstairs tracing the development of local surf culture, as well as surfboards, bodyboards, wetsuits and so on.

ℹ Information

Most ATMs are on Da Gama Rd, the main thoroughfare.

Jeffrey's Bay Tourism (☑042-293 2923; www.jeffreysbaytourism.org; Da Gama Rd; ⊘9am-5pm Mon-Fri, to noon Sat) Friendly and helpful, and can make bookings for accommodation and activities.

ℹ Getting There & Around

Baz Bus stops at several J-Bay backpackers en route between Cape Town and Port Elizabeth.

AdventureNow (p175) runs shuttles to/from destinations including Storms River (per person R270), Bloukrans Bridge (R320) and Port Elizabeth Airport (per vehicle from R500), with hop-on, hop-off tickets available.

Long-distance buses (Mentors Plaza, St Francis St) plying the Cape Town–Port Elizabeth–Durban route stop at the Mentors Plaza Caltex garage, at the junction of St Francis St and the N2.

Shared taxis depart when full, generally on the hour, from the corner of Goedehoop and St Francis Sts; it's R30 to Humansdorp (25 minutes) and R60 to Port Elizabeth (1¼ hours).

Local taxis, including **J-Bay Cabs** (☑083 611 1003), charge about R10 per kilometre.

Port Elizabeth

POP 1.2 MILLION

Port Elizabeth (PE for short) fringes Algoa Bay at the western end of the Sunshine Coast, and offers many good bathing beaches and surf spots. It's also a convenient gateway to worthy destinations in either direction along the coast, as well as to the eastern Karoo. Sadly, with the notable exception of vibrant Richmond Hill and a few other urban regeneration projects, the city centre remains rather rundown. Many of the more upmarket shops, restaurants and bars are found in the suburban shopping centres.

PE, its industrial satellite towns of Uitenhage and Despatch, and the massive surrounding townships, are collectively referred to as Nelson Mandela Bay.

🔘 Sights

Port Elizabeth's major attraction as a holiday destination is its wide sandy beaches

Port Elizabeth

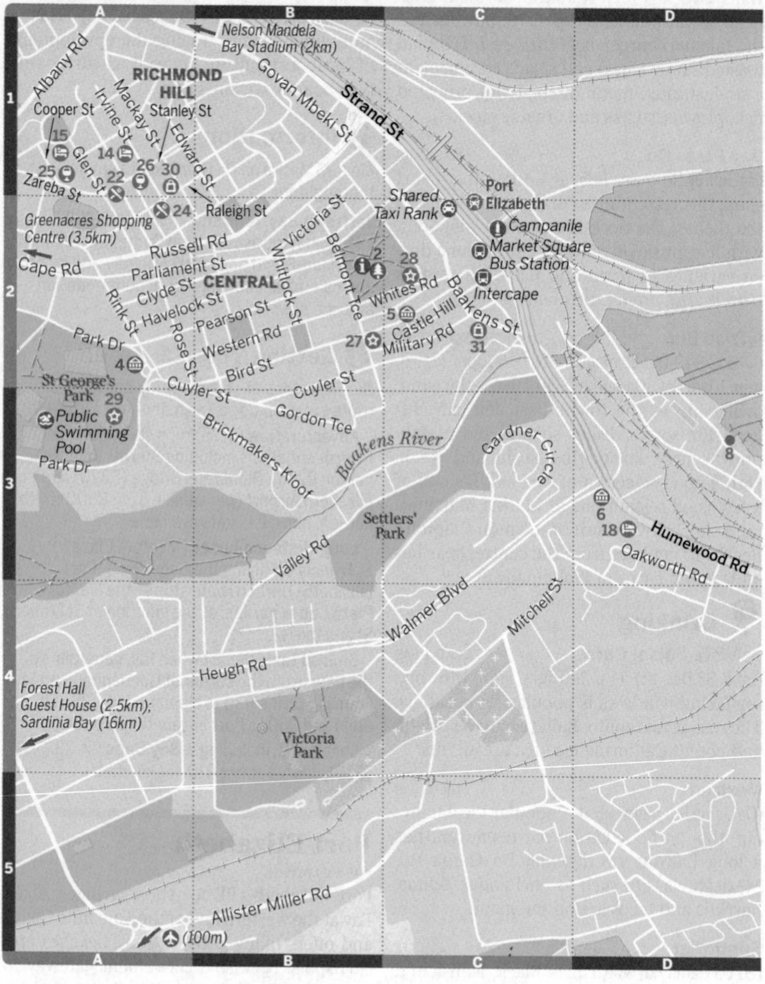

and the warm waters of the Indian Ocean. **Sardinia Bay**, 20km south of downtown past the airport, is easily the nicest in the area; to reach the 10km-long beach you walk over large sand dunes. However, strong currents mean it's best to play in the shallows and not venture out far from shore. There are broad beaches south of Central; **Kings Beach** stretches from the harbour to Humewood, and there are more beaches at Summerstrand, which are all fairly sheltered.

Donkin Reserve PARK

(Central; lighthouse adult/child R5/3; lighthouse 8.15am-4pm Mon-Fri, 9.30am-3pm Sat) This hilltop park is a good place to get your bearings, particularly if you climb up inside the **lighthouse**. The **pyramid** is a memorial to Elizabeth Donkin, wife of Sir Rufane Donkin, governor of the Cape Colony in the 1820s, who named PE after his beloved spouse. A **heritage trail** leads between the park's monuments and artworks, which narrate the important periods of the city's history, and form part of the wider **Route 67** trail through the centre. Ask at the tourist office here for more information.

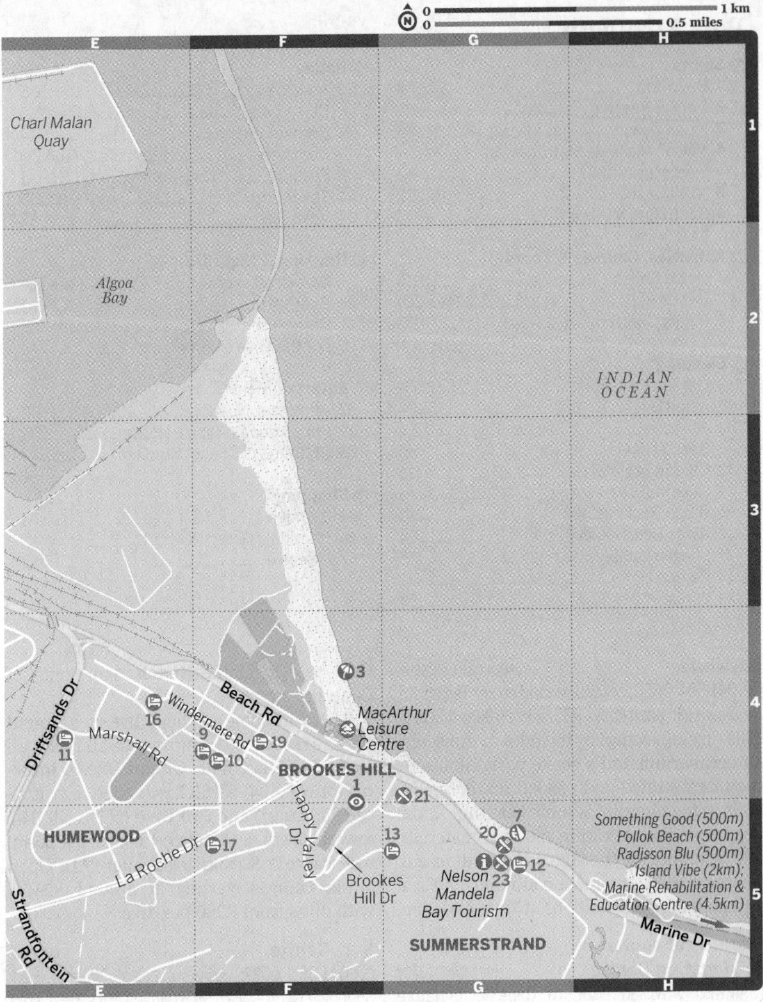

Nelson Mandela Metropolitan Art Museum GALLERY
(☎041-506 2000; www.artmuseum.co.za; 1 Park Dr, St George's Park; ⏲9am-5pm Mon & Wed-Fri, 1-5pm Tue, Sat & Sun) The museum, housed in two handsome buildings at the entrance to St George's Park, has a small gallery of paintings and sculpture by contemporary South African artists, some older British and Eastern Cape works, plus temporary exhibitions and graduate shows.

No. 7 Castle Hill HISTORIC BUILDING
(7 Castle Hill, Central; adult/child R10/5; ⏲10am-1pm & 2-4.30pm Mon-Thu, to 4pm Fri) This museum-house, occupying a picturesque cottage dating to 1827, evokes a settler family's life during the mid-Victorian period.

South End Museum MUSEUM
(☎041-582 3325; www.southendmuseum.co.za; cnr Walmer Blvd & Humewood Rd, South End; admission by donation; ⏲9am-4pm Mon-Fri, 10am-3pm Sat & Sun; P) FREE Multimedia exhibits relate the history of South End, a vibrant multicultural district destroyed by apartheid bulldozers during forced removals between 1965 and 1975 (under the infamous Group Areas Act). The inhabitants were relocated to other parts of the city, designated by race. Book ahead for a one-hour guided walking tour of the area (R40).

Port Elizabeth

Sights
1 Bayworld....F4
2 Donkin Reserve....B2
3 Kings Beach....F4
4 Nelson Mandela Metropolitan Art Museum....A2
5 No. 7 Castle Hill....C2
6 South End Museum....D3

Activities, Courses & Tours
7 Hobie Beach....G5
Pro Dive....(see 20)
8 Raggy Charters....D3

Sleeping
9 @9 Ferndale Road....F4
10 Algoa Bay....F4
11 Aristotle....E4
12 Beach Hotel....G5
13 Chapman Hotel....G5
14 Guesthouse on Irvine....A1
15 Hippo Backpackers....A1
16 Kings Beach Backpackers....E4
17 Lungile Lodge....F5
18 Paxton Hotel....D3
19 Windermere....F4

Eating
20 Angelo's....G5
Blue Waters Café....(see 20)
21 Brookes on the Bay....G4
Coachman....(see 21)
22 Fushin....A1
23 The Boardwalk....G5
24 Vovo Telo....A2

Drinking & Nightlife
Barney's Tavern....(see 20)
25 Beer Yard....A1
Coffee Cafe....(see 23)
26 For the Love of Wine....A1

Entertainment
27 Athenæum....B2
28 Port Elizabeth Opera House....C2
29 St George's Cricket Stadium....A3

Shopping
30 Camden....A1
31 Wezandla Gallery & Craft Centre....C2

Bayworld AQUARIUM, MUSEUM
(☎041-584 0650; www.bayworld.co.za; Beach Rd, Brookes Hill; adult/child R35/25; ⏲9am-4.30pm) This ageing complex includes a museum, an oceanarium and a snake park. Alongside the many stuffed and pickled marine mammals in the museum is some beautiful Xhosa beadwork incorporating modern materials, and a replica of the Algoasaurus dinosaur. There's a snake interaction at noon, and seal and penguin presentations at 11am and 3pm.

Marine Rehabilitation & Education Centre BIRD SANCTUARY
(SAMREC; www.samrec.org.za; Cape Recife Nature Reserve; adult/child R25/15; ⏲9.30am-3.30pm) Most of the world's remaining 25,000 breeding pairs of endangered African penguins are found around Algoa Bay; they are threatened by currents pushing their food far out to sea, causing them to digest much of it before they get back to their chicks. At this centre, learn more from volunteers and watch the penguins chilling by the pool, or having a feed at 2.30pm. There is a cafe here and coastal walking trails in the area.

Activities

PE is not known as the 'windy city' for nothing; windsurfers and sailors will find what they need at **Hobie Beach**, 5km south of Central.

There are some excellent dive sites around Port Elizabeth, with shipwrecks and reefs all over Algoa Bay. Both **Ocean Divers International** (☎041-581 5121; www.odipe.co.za; 10 Albert Rd, Walmer) and **Pro Dive** (☎041-581 1144; www.prodive.co.za; Watersport Centre, the Boardwalk, Marine Dr, Summerstrand) offer PADI Open Water courses starting at around R2450, with dives from R280 per dive.

Surf Centre SURFING
(☎041-585 6027; www.surf.co.za; Walmer Park Shopping Centre, Main Rd, Walmer) PE's best surf breaks are found between the harbour wall and Summerstrand, and at Pollok beach. The Surf Centre sells and hires out surfboards and bodyboards. Its surf school will teach you how to use them (1½-hour lesson R200).

Tours

Calabash Tours CULTURAL TOUR
(☎041-585 6162; www.calabashtours.co.za) Runs local trips, ranging from Addo Elephant National Park safaris (R1000) to several township tours (R550 to R695), including visits to shebeens (unlicensed drinking establishments) and story-telling residents' homes. The guides are locals who are proud of the Port Elizabeth

townships' part in the anti-apartheid struggle, and they highlight places of historical and political interest along the way.

Raggy Charters BOAT TOUR
(☎073 152 2277; www.raggycharters.co.za; Algoa Bay Yacht Club) Half-day tours (R900) with a qualified marine biologist to St Croix, Jahleel and Benton Islands, variously focused on penguins, whale and dolphins. Also sunset cruises (R450) to Cape Recife Lighthouse, with opportunities to spot birds and marine life.

Sleeping

Most of Port Elizabeth's choicest hotels and dozens of self-catering flats are lined up along the beachfront.

Humewood & Summerstrand

Lungile Lodge BACKPACKERS $
(☎041-582 2042; www.lungilebackpackers.co.za; 12 La Roche Dr, Humewood; dm R130-140, s/d/f from R330/460/720; P W S) Uphill from Kings Beach in a suburban neighbourhood, this well-run A-frame home's large entertainment area rocks most nights, and the dorms and tiny campsite can get full when the Baz Bus arrives. The private rooms in the rear annexe are more modern, with hefty wooden beds, African masks and shared balconies. Transfers and activities are offered, including township and Addo tours and sandboarding.

Kings Beach Backpackers BACKPACKERS $
(☎041-585 8113; kingsbeachbackpackers.wozaonline.co.za; 41 Windermere Rd, Humewood; camping/dm/d R65/130/380; W) A small, lived-in house on a quiet street a short walk from the beach. There are cabins in the back garden, including an ensuite family room, plus a lounge and outdoor bar and braai area. The travel desk can organise local activities and transport.

Island Vibe BACKPACKERS $
(☎041-583 1256; www.islandvibe.co.za; 4 Jenvey Rd, Summerstrand; dm/s/d/f R150/350/500/700; P @ W S) This 'flashpackers' in a nondescript suburban house is less characterful than its sister in Jeffrey's Bay, but makes a comfortable base with numerous facilities. The bar, pool table, foosball and outdoor Jacuzzi liven up the 'burbs, while the well-equipped kitchen, secure parking and ensuite rooms are welcome. Pollok Beach and the Pipe surf break are within walking distance.

Paxton Hotel HOTEL $$
(☎041-585 9655; www.paxton.co.za; Carnarvon Pl, Humewood; s/d/ste R1079/1358/3165; P A W S) A first-class option, although not beachfront; it's tucked behind a minimall and requires a short drive to the beach. Rooms have contemporary furnishings, DSTV and all mod-cons. The lobby and bar are smooth, business-hotel environments.

Algoa Bay GUESTHOUSE $$
(☎041-582 5134; www.algoabay.com; 13 Ferndale Rd, Humewood; s/d incl breakfast R550/700; P W S) Rooms at this modern B&B are tastefully furnished and come with DSTV; you can see Kings Beach from the top-floor rooms. There's an outdoor deck and solar-heated swimming pool. The owners run three other guesthouses in the area, including the equally recommended **@9 Ferndale Road** (☎041-582 5134; www.atnine.co.za; 9 Ferndale Rd, Humewood; s/d incl breakfast R650/850; P W S) and **Aristotle** (☎041-582 5134; www.aristotleguesthouse.com; 1 Chalmers Rd, Humewood; s/d incl breakfast R550/650; P W S).

Chapman Hotel HOTEL $$
(☎041-584 0678; www.chapman.co.za; Brookes Hill Dr, Brookes Hill; s/d/tr/q incl breakfast from R680/880/1130/1330; P W S F) The friendly, family-run Chapman, overlooking Kings Beach near Bayworld and Brookes on the Bay mall, is a good midrange option with a seafood restaurant and pool. Modern rooms have private balconies with sea views.

★ **Windermere** BOUTIQUE HOTEL $$$
(☎041-582 2245; www.thewindermere.co.za; 35 Humewood Rd; d incl breakfast R2090; P A W S) Located on a quiet street, only a block from the beach, is this oasis of design-savvy luxury. There are plush and contemporary furnishings throughout the nine palatial rooms, which glimpse the sea from their balconies. Additional attractions include a bar, a garden plunge pool overlooked by creeper-covered walls, and African art books scattered throughout.

Radisson Blu HOTEL $$$
(☎041-509 5000; www.radissonblu.com; cnr Marine Dr & 9th Ave, Summerstrand; r R1700; P A W S) This shining tower overlooking the beach has some of the most contemporary and stylish rooms in the city, and all the facilities of an international business-class hotel.

Beach Hotel HOTEL $$$
(☎041-583 2161; www.thebeachhotel.co.za; Marine Dr, Summerstrand; s incl breakfast R1100-1300, d incl breakfast R1760-2190; P A W S) This friendly four-star hotel is well positioned opposite

Hobie Beach and next to the Boardwalk. The exquisite 1920s building is worth a visit if only to take a look at the breakfast room with its stained-glass windows and chandelier. Ginger restaurant (mains R110), one of three restaurants in the hotel, serves steak and seafood with views of the sea and pier.

Richmond Hill & Inland

Guesthouse on Irvine GUESTHOUSE $
(041-582 1486; guesthouseonirvine.co.za; 40 Irvine St, Richmond Hill; s/d R380/500; P) A refurbished Victorian house a few doors from the Stanley St restaurants, with a kitchenette, a dining area, a garden and six tidy wood-floored rooms. The friendly owner, Tanya, is a fount of local recommendations.

Hippo Backpackers BACKPACKERS $
(041-585 6350; www.thehippo.co.za; 14 Glen St, Richmond Hill; dm/r R120/450, s/d without bathroom from R190/350; P) Near the Stanley St restaurants, the Hippo is a convenient and comfortable option. It has an inviting backyard pool and braai area, a bar and pool table, two attractive lounges, two kitchens and nicely furnished rooms.

Forest Hall Guest House GUESTHOUSE $$
(041-581 3356; www.foresthall.co.za; 84 River Rd, btwn 9th & 10th Aves, Walmer; s/d incl breakfast from R675/950; P) At this gracious suburban property, huge rooms with lots of natural light and private patios open onto a beautiful garden with an Italianate swimming pool.

Eating

Stanley St is the centrepiece of the up-and-coming Richmond Hill neighbourhood, a piece of urban regeneration echoing similar areas in Jo'burg and Cape Town. On Stanley between Glen and Mackay Sts is a vibey string of a dozen restaurants, serving cuisine ranging from Indian to Mediterranean. Most offer outdoor tables and lunch specials. There's a **night market** here on the first Wednesday of the month.

The **Boardwalk** (041-507 7777; Marine Dr, Summerstrand) and **Brookes on the Bay** (Beach Rd, Brookes Hill) malls have numerous chain restaurants.

★ **Something Good** CAFE $$
(off Marine Dr, Pollok Beach; mains R75; 8am-10.30pm) This roadhouse-cum-beach bar is an excellent spot for a sundowner, with a breezy interior, beachfront decks and a children's playground. Dishes include gourmet pizzas, burgers, seafood, steaks and, on the 'get fit' menu, bunless burgers, protein shakes and healthy breakfasts.

Vovo Telo CAFE, BAKERY $$
(cnr Raleigh & Irvine Sts, Richmond Hill; mains R75; 7.15am-3.15pm Mon-Fri, to 2.30pm Sat) The original branch of a now nationwide chain, Vovo Telo kicked off the regeneration of Richmond Hill. In a characterful old house with a wraparound stoep, locals catch up over artisan-bread sarmies, thin-crust pizza made with ciabatta dough, bruschetta and antipasto boards, and numerous breakfast choices.

Coachman STEAKHOUSE $$
(041-584 0087; Brookes on the Bay, Beach Rd, Brookes Hill; mains R100) Unreconstructed men will be in heaven: buxom waitresses in low-cut, electric-blue dresses serve steaks cooked to perfection. The Coachman is PE's best steakhouse and female carnivores will also appreciate the menu, an orgy of meat with burgers, steaks, poultry, seafood and umpteen sauces. The setting is fine dining, the service attentive and you should book ahead.

Fushin JAPANESE, ASIAN $$
(041-811 7874; www.fushin.co.za; Shop 5, Stanley on Bain, 15 Stanley St, Richmond Hill; mains R70-100; noon-10pm) This restaurant's experienced owner and chef creates high-quality sushi and handmade Singapore-inspired noodle dishes as well as creative fare like stuffed giant squid.

Angelo's BURGERS, STEAKHOUSE $$
(Beachfront Boardwalk, Marine Dr, Summerstrand; mains R60-95) With low lighting, stacked logs and straw baskets, this inviting Afro-rustic restaurant attracts a sophisticated multicultural crowd. Gourmet burgers, grills, stir-fries, pasta, salads, cocktails and milkshakes all feature.

In the same complex are the old favourites **Blue Waters Café** (Beachfront Boardwalk, Marine Dr, Summerstrand; mains R95; 7.30am-10pm), which is reasonable for a quick bite or a drink on the beachfront balcony, and **Barney's Tavern** (Beachfront Boardwalk, Marine Dr, Summerstrand), with a terrace and an open kitchen producing pizzas.

Drinking

With outside tables, the Stanley St restaurants are great for a drink.

★ **For the Love of Wine** WINE BAR
(1st fl, 20 Stanley St, Richmond Hill; noon-10pm Mon-Sat) At this excellent wine bar and bou-

tique, you can sample the output of Stellenbosch and beyond (tastings and wine by the glass start at R25), with craft beer and cheese platters also offered. If the wrapa-round porch feels too inviting to leave, you can order from a few local restaurants to eat here.

Beer Yard BAR
(1 Cooper St, Richmond Hill; ⏲noon-10pm Mon-Sat) With a Bedouin tent in the backyard, this craft-beer and cider bar encapsulates Richmond Hill's urban buzz. Handmade burgers (R60 to R75) and thin-crust pizzas (R50 to R85) are on the menu.

Coffee Cafe COFFEE
(Beachfront Boardwalk, Marine Dr, Summerstrand) Cookies, cakes, tea and chai are available at this rustic cafe, but the focus is overwhelmingly on cups of black gold, using beans from local roaster Mastertons.

☆ Entertainment

Port Elizabeth Opera House OPERA, THEATRE
(☎041-586 2256; www.peoperahouse.co.za; Whites Rd, Central) The oldest theatre in both Africa and the southern hemisphere, the PE Opera House hosts a wide range of performances, including plays, poetry, concerts and comedy.

Athenæum PERFORMING ARTS
(☎041-585 1041; www.theathenaeum.co.za; 7 Belmont Tce, Richmond Hill) This cultural centre in a renovated Victorian building hosts plays, performances and live music including jazz.

Nelson Mandela Bay Stadium STADIUM
(☎041-408 8900; www.nmbstadium.com; 70 Prince Alfred Rd, North End) Built for the 2010 football (soccer) World Cup, this futuristic stadium in the rundown North End area hosts sports matches and concerts. Call or email to arrange a 30-minute stadium tour (available between 11am and 3pm Monday, Wednesday and Friday).

St George's Cricket Stadium STADIUM
(☎041-585 1646; www.stgeorgespark.co.za; St George's Park) Home of Eastern Province Cricket, famous for its band-playing supporters who turn one-day internationals into tub-thumping affairs.

Shopping

There are craft shops at the Boardwalk mall. Head to the Kings Beach flea market on Sunday mornings for curios.

Wezandla Gallery & Craft Centre HANDICRAFTS
(27 Baakens St, Central) This brightly coloured arts and crafts centre has a huge array of items made by local groups, plus a small coffee shop.

Camden HOMEWARES, ACCESSORIES
(7 Raleigh St, Richmond Hill) Sells a range of design items and fashion accessories, from handbags to fridge magnets.

ℹ Information

Nelson Mandela Bay Tourism (☎041-585 8884; www.nmbt.co.za; Donkin Reserve; ⏲8am-4.30pm Mon-Fri, 9.30am-3.30pm Sat) Has an excellent supply of information and maps, and a cafe with city views. There are also branches at the Boardwalk (☎041-583 2030; Marine Dr, Summerstrand; ⏲8am-7pm), a good stop for infomation about the whole province, and the airport (☎041-581 0456; Port Elizabeth Airport; ⏲7am-9.30pm), while Wezandla (p185) craft shop also dispenses information.

ℹ Getting There & Away

AIR

South African Airways (☎041-507 7220; www.flysaa.com), its subsidiaries Airlink, SA Express and Mango, **FlySafair** (☎0871 351 351; www.flysafair.co.za), **Kulula** (☎0861 585 852; www.kulula.com) and **British Airways** (☎in Jo'burg 011-441 8600; www.ba.com) all fly daily to/from cities including Cape Town (from R500 with FlySafair, 1½ hours), Durban (from R1640 with Kulula, 1¼ hours) and Jo'burg (from R1200 with British Airways, 1¾ hours).

BUS

Greyhound, Translux and City to City depart from the **Greenacres Shopping Centre**, about 4km inland from the city centre. **Intercape** (cnr Fleming & North Union Sts) departs from its office behind the old post office.

To Cape Town

Greyhound, Translux, Intercape and City to City have daily buses to/from Cape Town (R400, 12 hours) via the Garden Route.

Baz Bus (p167) runs five days a week in both directions between Port Elizabeth and Cape Town (R2020 one way, hop-on, hop-off; 15 hours).

To Durban

Greyhound, Translux, Intercape and City to City have daily buses to/from Grahamstown (R230, two hours), East London (R300, 4½ hours), Mthatha (R350, eight hours) and Durban (R450, 14½ hours).

Baz Bus runs four days a week in both directions between Port Elizabeth and Durban (R1830 one way, hop-on, hop-off; 15¼ hours).

To Jo'burg

Greyhound, Translux, Intercape and City to City have daily buses to/from Jo'burg (R520, 15 hours) via Bloemfontein.

CAR

All the big car-rental operators have offices in Port Elizabeth or at the airport.

SHARED TAXI

Vehicles run to local destinations from the **shared taxi rank** (Strand St, Central) beneath the flyover.

TRAIN

Shosholoza Meyl runs to/from Jo'burg (20 hours, Wed, Fri & Sun) via Cradock and Bloemfontein. Choose between tourist class (sleeper R450), less-recommended economy class (seat only R290), and luxurious **Premier Classe** (in Jo'burg 011-773 9247; www.premierclasse.co.za; R2090).

Getting Around

Port Elizabeth Airport (www.airports.co.za; Allister Miller Rd, Walmer) is about 5km from the city centre. A taxi to the centre costs about R100.

Algoa Bus Company runs most routes (R8.50 one way) around the city and to the surrounding suburbs every 25 minutes, leaving from the **Market Square bus station** (Strand St).

Addo Elephant National Park

Located 70km north of Port Elizabeth, and encompassing both the Zuurberg mountains and the Sundays River Valley, South Africa's third-largest **national park** (042-233 8600; www.sanparks.org; adult/child R216/108; 7am-6pm) protects the remnants of the huge elephant herds that once roamed the Eastern Cape. When Addo was proclaimed a national park in 1931, there were only 11 elephants left; today there are more than 600 in the park, and you'd be unlucky not to see some. Addo, which was once farmland, now encompasses five biomes and about 1800 sq km, and extends to the coastline between the mouths of the Sundays and Bushman's Rivers. The coastal section includes Alexandria Dunefield, the southern hemisphere's largest and least degraded coastal dunefield, and islands with significant breeding colonies of African penguins, Cape gannets and Cape fur seals.

A day or two at Addo is a highlight of any visit to this part of the Eastern Cape, not only for the elephants but for the lions, zebras, black rhinos, Cape buffaloes, spotted hyenas and myriad birds. The park is one of few which boasts the 'Big Seven', thanks to sightings of great white sharks and southern right whales (in season) in Algoa Bay. Look out, too, for the rare flightless dung beetle, endemic to Addo. Female beetles bury elephant dung underground to eat, which both fertilises the soil and encourages the growth of the bright-green spekboom plants – the leaves of which are the main source of moisture for elephants and are nicknamed 'elephant's food'.

Activities

Book in advance for all activities, especially during the high season (October to March). Also bear in mind that for most SANParks activities and accommodation, you must pay the park's daily conservation fee on top of SANParks' quoted price.

Self-Drive Safaris

During summer it's best to arrive at the park by midmorning and stake out one of the waterholes, where the elephants tend to gather during the heat of the day. In winter, early mornings are the best time to see animals.

The elephants of Addo were once addicted to – and even fought violently over – the oranges and grapefruits fed to them by the park's first rangers to encourage them to stay within the park's boundaries. A fruit ban has been in place since the late 1970s; however, as the old adage goes, 'elephants have good memories' and the smell alone could provoke an old-timer. And, of course, do not get out of your car except at designated climb-out points.

As at most parks in southern Africa, it's not compulsory to hire a guide to explore Addo in your own vehicle. You can just turn up, pay the entrance fee and try your luck spotting elephants between the trees (and the other cars). For novice wildlife watchers, hiring a hop-on SANParks guide (R180 plus park entry fee; available 8am to 5pm) to ride along can be a helpful way of picking up a few tips for spotting animals.

Guided Wildlife Drives

SANParks Guided Wildlife Drives SAFARIS (042-233 8657; addogamedrives@sanparks.org; per person R280-395) Two-hour guided wildlife drives in large 4WDs with good viewing angles, departing every few hours between sunrise and evening. Fee doesn't cover park entry.

ADDO ELEPHANT NATIONAL PARK

Why Go More than 600 elephants offer almost guaranteed pachyderm sightings. The rest of the Big Five can also been seen on good roads in malaria-free territory.

When to Go Wildlife watching is good year-round, but autumn (around April) and spring (around September) offer mild weather, avoiding the winter chill and stiflingly hot summer. There should also be a few oranges on the trees; the main citrus season is winter. (Peak rainfall periods are February to March and October to November.)

Practicalities The main gate gives access from Rte 335 to the park reception at Addo Rest Camp, about 10km north of the small town of Addo. There is also a southern gate, Matyholweni, located 40km from Addo Rest Camp near Colchester. It is possible to drive between the two.

Budget Tips Winter is low season; between May and June the park offers discounts on accommodation.

Canoeing

Criss Cross Adventures CANOEING, OUTDOORS
(☎072 125 9152; www.crisscrossadventures.co.za; Chrislin Lodge) When in flood, the Sundays River is the fastest flowing river in South Africa, but at other times it's perfect for a guided canoe trip (half-day R450). Tunnels of river grass give way to wider vistas, and kingfishers and spotted eagle owls nest in the riverbanks. Guide Chris Pickels grew up on the river and knows it intimately. He also offers Addo safaris (half/full day R750/1300), mountain biking, sandboarding and hiking tours. Prices include park fees.

Horse Trails

Morning and afternoon rides are offered by SANParks in the park's Nyathi section (two hours R290). For mountainous scenery but not wildlife, rides are also offered in the Zuurberg section: there are one- (R195), three- (R270) and five-hour (R295) rides and an overnight trail to Narina Bush Camp. Prices do not include park fees.

Hiking

Alexandria Hiking Trail HIKING
(☎041-468 0916; matyholweni@sanparks.org; Woody Cape section, Addo Elephant National Park; per person per night R150, plus park fee) A 32km, two-day loop taking in endemic Eastern Cape forestry and rolling dunes in the park's coastal section. Minimum three hikers. The shorter Tree Dassie Trail covers the same area.

Sleeping

There's a string of convenient sleeping and eating options located just off Rte *335* as it makes its way through the small town of Addo and continues to the park's main gate, 10km north. If you have some time to play with and would like to see more of the Zuurberg mountains, there are also good options around Kirkwood and Sunland on Rte *336* and on the Zuurberg Pass road.

Park accommodation can get booked up in busy periods, so always reserve in advance, if possible. SANParks offers various accommodation throughout the park. The smaller **Camp Matyholweni** (☎041-468 0916; www.sanparks.org; cottages 1-2 people R1070) is just inside the southern gate, while various camps offer seclusion and immersion in the bush, including the recommended **Narina Bush Camp** (☎in Pretoria 012-428 9111; www.sanparks.org; Zuurberg section, Addo Elephant National Park; tents up to 4 people R1050), with four safari tents 27km north of the main rest camp.

Aardvark Guesthouse GUESTHOUSE, BACKPACKERS $
(☎042-233 1244; theaardvarkguesthouse.co.za; off Rte 335; camping/dm/s/d R60/140/350/550, f from R810; P @ 📶 👪) This handsome guesthouse is set around a manicured lawn down a tree-shaded country lane, next to Hazel's Organic Restaurant. Rooms in the main building have solid wood floors and artistic flourishes, and there are en-suite *rondavels* in the garden. In the backpacker section, choose between four-bed safari tents (from R300) and the contemporary dormitory with a massive Ikea-style kitchen. German and French are spoken.

Orange Elephant Backpackers BACKPACKERS $
(☎042-233 0023; www.addobackpackers.com; off Rte 335; camping/dm/r/tr incl breakfast R60/120/440/590; P 📶) Slightly ramshackle but clean and shipshape, the Orange Elephant is a good budget base for Addo, offering a shuttle from Port Elizabeth (R200 return) and tours of the park (half-/full-day R650/1000) and elsewhere. Accommodation ranges from rooms in the main house to the

10-bed dorm in a *rondavel* with bush showers. The on-site Thirsty Herd pub does pizzas and a house ale.

★Chrislin African Lodge LODGE **$$**
(☎042-233 0022; www.chrislin.co.za; off Rte 335; s incl breakfast R950-1150, d incl breakfast R1160-1370; P ❄ 📶 🏊 👪) 🍃 Chrislin is set among lawns, trees and aloes on a former citrus farm. The lodge offers thatched huts with stylish African decor and heat-banishing walls of cow dung and mud, and luxurious units. Activities including open-vehicle Addo safaris (half/full day R750/1250) are offered, as are three-course dinners (R195) featuring home-grown fruit, veg and herbs.

It's a refreshingly cool and rustic spot after a day spotting elephants.

Rosedale FARMSTAY **$$**
(☎042-233 0404; www.rosedalebnb.co.za; off Rte 335; s/d incl breakfast R550/800; P 📶 🏊) 🍃 On

PRIVATE EASTERN CAPE WILDLIFE RESERVES

With over a 10,000 sq km of malaria-free wildlife watching, the Eastern Cape's private reserves are a major attraction. Along with Addo Elephant National Park, a wildlife drive on one of these properties, possibly accompanied by a night in the bush, makes an exciting and memorable finale for people travelling along the Garden Route from Cape Town. There's a significant cluster of reserves between Addo and Grahamstown, including Pumba, Kwantu and Lalibela, as well as the following. Most of the reserves are dedicated to restocking large tracts of reclaimed land with animals that were common in the region before the advent of farmers and big-game hunters.

Many reserves offer a range of accommodation, varying in terms of comforts and price, from over-the-top honeymoon-level luxury at the private lodges to more-modest tent camps. Rates are generally all inclusive and significant winter discounts are offered between May and September.

A great way to experience a little of the reserves' magic is on a guided day safari. Most have the Big Five, and can be reached by travelling along the N2 between Addo and Grahamstown.

Schotia Game Reserve (☎042-235 1436; www.schotiasafaris.co.za) Schotia Game Reserve is contiguous with Addo (accessed from the N10 south of Paterson). Aiming to evoke the bush before humans arrived, Schotia was the first local reserve to introduce lions that hunt for themselves; their numbers have since been reduced from 18 to seven, to give their prey a fighting chance.

Its full-day Addo-Schotia tour (R2000 including lunch, dinner and return transfer from Port Elizabeth) is a good way to see the area; the late-afternoon Schotia tour (R1000) includes a bonfire and dinner in the *lapa* (South African English for an outdoor entertainment area). Tour operators and accommodation around Addo also offer Schotia excursions. The reserve has various lodges and tented camps, and offers packages including accommodation and several wildlife drives (one/two nights from R2000/5000).

Shamwari Game Reserve (☎in Port Elizabeth 041-509 3000; www.shamwari.com) Shamwari Game Reserve, roughly 40km east of Addo, is one of the most exclusive, luxurious and internationally renowned reserves. Accommodation here ranges from palatial bush tents to an Edwardian manor house; prices start from R4725 for an all-inclusive double. Activities include wildlife drives (one incorporating cookery classes), field-guide courses, and visits to a rhino awareness centre, a big-cat sanctuary and a wildlife rehabilitation centre with conservation volunteering opportunities.

Amakhala Game Reserve (☎041-581 0993; www.amakhala.co.za) A group of local landowners, descendants of the 1820 Settlers, combined their properties to create Amakhala, 75 sq km of rolling hills, bushveld and savannah. Named after the Xhosa for aloes, Amakhala, roughly 70km from PE and east of Addo, offers a morning wildlife drive (R750 including lunch) and an afternoon safari (R980) including a cruise on the Bushman's River.

Amakhala also offers conservation activities and volunteering opportunities. There are 11 different accommodation options, including the five-star Bukela, Bush and Hlosi lodges, Woodbury Tented Camp and Quatermain's 1920s-style safari camp. All-inclusive singles start at R3510, doubles at R5400.

an organic citrus farm, Rosedale offers eight modern cabins with stoeps overlooking the natural swimming pool and tropical trees. Organic breakfasts feature home-baked bread, free-range eggs and of course fresh-from-the-branch orange juice. Owner Keith will show you round the farm.

Addo Rest Camp CAMPGROUND, LODGE **$$**
(in Pretoria 012-428 9111; www.sanparks.org; camping 1-2 people R230, cabins R720;) Addo's main rest camp, at the park headquarters, has myriad cottages, chalets, safari tents and *rondavels,* some overlooking the floodlit waterhole where elephants slake their thirst. Options range from camping, to four-person forest cabins with shower and shared kitchen (from R720), to luxurious houses (from R3360) with two en-suite bedrooms, air-conditioning and DSTV.

Eating

Addo Rest Camp has a shady picnic site overlooking the waterhole, a **Cattle Baron** (042-233 8674; Addo Rest Camp; mains R55-180; 7am–9pm) steakhouse and a **shop** (8am-6pm) selling basic supplies.

★**Hazel's Organic Restaurant** ORGANIC **$$**
(082 573 1994; permaculturesouthafrica.com; off Rte 335; lunch/dinner mains R55/110;) Eating lunch on a sunny day at Hazel's, among birdsong and green goodies in the permaculture kitchen garden, is a pleasure indeed. Kudu burgers, wraps, springbok carpaccio and pizzas are on the lunch menu, while meatier fare such as kudu, ostrich and blue wildebeest are offered for dinner.

Information

The 'town' of Addo is nothing more than a few shops, a petrol station and a bank with ATMs sharing a dusty car park on Rte 335. Addo Rest Camp also has a shop and petrol station.

Getting There & Around

Orange Elephant Backpackers (p187) allows nonguests to join its shuttle from Port Elizabeth (R300), but will not make the trip unless it has guests to collect. Otherwise, hire a car in PE or book a tour.

The park's tar and gravel roads are mostly passable in a 2WD vehicle. The gravel roads can become impassable, so sections may close if there has been heavy rain – if in doubt, call the park headquarters.

Grahamstown

POP 50,217

Grahamstown is referred to as GOG (Good Old Grahamstown) or, more commonly, as the City of Saints because of its 40 or so religious buildings (mostly churches). The historic capital of Settler Country, Grahamstown is also one of South Africa's liveliest university towns, and hosts several annual festivals, including one of the world's largest arts festivals. With its dreaming spires, weathered edifices and beautiful pastel shopfronts, the town centre has some fine examples of Georgian, Victorian and early Edwardian architecture.

The academic town's genteel conservatism and English prettiness belie a bloody history; the Cape Frontier Wars, fought locally between European settlers and the Xhosa, continued for most of the 19th century. Once rulers of the region, the Xhosa were defeated by British and Boer forces after a fierce struggle – visit the nearby townships for a glimpse of their descendants' culture.

Socially, the students from Rhodes University dominate the town, packing out pubs and bars during term time. But, as artists and alternative spirits settle here and the population ages, a more sophisticated side to Grahamstown is developing.

Sights

The tourist office has booklets and information on self-guided walking tours.

Church Square HISTORIC SITE
Grand colonial edifices, university buildings, the 19th-century Anglican cathedral and colourful Victorian and Edwardian shopfronts all overlook this square. Good examples of the latter are the **Grocott's Mail** building, the original home of South Africa's oldest independent newspaper, and the neighbouring **Clicks** pharmacy.

Birch's (High St) has a marvellously old-fashioned 'slider' (a pulley system that sends money across the ceiling to and from the central till) and a vacuum pipe system used to send notes between floors. Staff will demonstrate the slider if you ask nicely.

Observatory Museum MUSEUM
(www.ru.ac.za/albanymuseum; Bathurst St; adult/child R10/5; 8am-4.30pm Mon-Fri) In this house dating to 1850 are: several rooms of Victorian furniture and memorabilia; the refurbished Meridian Room (which shows that Grahamstown is 14 minutes behind

South African standard time, because standard time is set in Durban); and the wonderful camera obscura. Sadly, the latter two attractions were closed at the time of writing, but will hopefully reopen.

Built in 1882, and the only one of its kind in the world outside of the UK, the camera obscura is a series of lenses that reflects a perfect panoramic image of Grahamstown onto a flat, white disc in a tower in the roof. It was built as a communication tool – people climbing up to the roof could see, for example, where the doctor was.

Albany History Museum MUSEUM
(www.ru.ac.za/albanymuseum; Somerset St; adult/child R10/5; ⏲9am-4.30pm Mon-Fri) Details the history and art of the peoples of the Eastern Cape, including the Xhosa and 1820 Settlers, with some beautiful beadwork and embroidery on display.

Albany Natural Science Museum MUSEUM
(Somerset St; adult/child R10/5; ⏲9am-4.30pm Mon-Fri) Covers a mishmash of subjects, from early human history to astronomy. The collection includes some impressive taxidermy and skeletons.

International Library of African Music MUSEUM
(ILAM; ☎046-603 8557; www.ru.ac.za/ilam; Rhodes University, Prince Alfred St; ⏲8am-5pm Mon-Fri) FREE There are 200 or so instruments to examine here – you can listen to field recordings and try to emulate what you've heard on *nyanga* (pan) pipes from Mozambique, a *kora* (stringed instrument) from West Africa or a Ugandan *kalimba* (thumb piano). Call ahead for an appointment.

South African Institute for Aquatic Biodiversity MUSEUM
(☎046-603 5800; www.saiab.ac.za; Rhodes University, Somerset St; ⏲8am-5pm Mon-Fri) FREE The second coelacanth (a marine fish with limblike pectoral fins) ever caught is exhibited here; until 1938 this primitive fish was thought to have been extinct.

1820 Settlers National Monument MONUMENT
(www.foundation.org.za; Gunfire Hill; ⏲8am-4.30pm Mon-Thu, to 4pm Fri) FREE This monument to the hardy British settlers and their contributions to South Africa has stupendous views of the surrounding countryside, and contains artworks and a large theatre.

National English Literary Museum LIBRARY, MUSEUM
(☎046-622 7042; www.ru.ac.za/static/institutes/nelm; 87 Beaufort St; ⏲8.30am-1pm & 2-4.30pm Mon-Fri) FREE The collection here contains South African manuscripts, first editions and works going back to 1797, with all the famous writers represented. The collection is in storage; phone ahead if there is something specific you would like to see. In February 2016 the museum should be moving

THE 1820 SETTLERS

In 1819, 90,000 applications were received by the British government in reply to their offer of free land in South Africa. Most applicants were very poor and unemployed. Only 4000 were approved, and the following year the settlers (now referred to as the '1820 Settlers') arrived in Algoa Bay. Duped by their government into believing they were migrating to a peaceful land of plenty, they were, in fact, used as a buffer between the Boers on one side of the Great Fish River and the Xhosa on the other, who battled interminably over the cattle-rich country known as the Zuurveld.

Life on the frontier was harsh. Beset by war, inexperience, crop disease, hostile neighbours, floods and droughts, many of the families retreated to the towns, particularly Port Elizabeth, East London and Grahamstown. There they pursued the trades and businesses they had followed in England. Grahamstown, in particular, developed into a trading and manufacturing centre, where axes, knives and blankets were exchanged for ivory and skins. Tradespeople among the settlers produced metal implements, wagons and clothes. Port Elizabeth and Port Alfred initially developed to service Grahamstown, which had quickly become the Cape Colony's second-largest city.

The settlers made a significant contribution to South African society. They insisted on a free press, which they'd enjoyed in England, and this was reluctantly granted in 1825. They also played an important part in establishing the Council of Advice, which advised the governor on matters of importance. Some who remained on the frontier became successful farmers and initiated wool farming, which became very lucrative.

Grahamstown

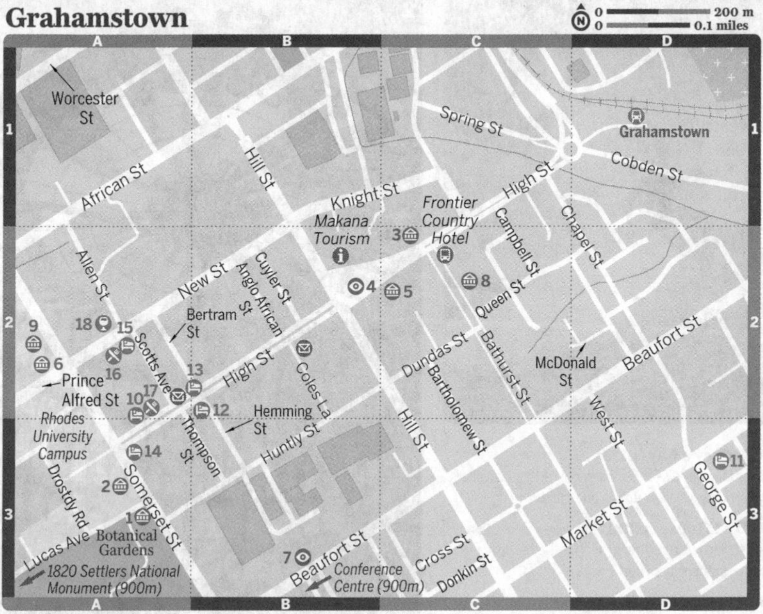

Grahamstown

Sights

1 Albany History Museum ... A3
2 Albany Natural Science Museum ... A3
3 Birch's Gentlemen's Outfitters ... C2
4 Church Square ... B2
5 Grocott's Mail ... C2
6 International Library of African Music ... A2
7 National English Literary Museum ... B3
8 Observatory Museum ... C2
9 South African Institute for Aquatic Biodiversity ... A2
11 Cock House ... D3
12 Evelyn House ... B2
13 Graham Hotel ... B2
14 High Corner ... A3
15 Historic Cottages ... A2

Sleeping

10 137 High Street ... A2

Eating

137 High Street ... (see 10)
Calabash ... (see 13)
16 Haricot's Deli & Bistro ... A2
Norden's ... (see 11)
17 Saint's Bistro ... A2

Drinking & Nightlife

Champs Action Bar ... (see 13)
18 Rat & Parrot ... A2

to a custom-built building on the corner of Worcester and Jacques Sts, where it will become a cultural centre with two theatres and exhibitions on South African literature.

Tours

A few guides offer tours of historic Fingo Village, one of South Africa's oldest townships. It was built on land given to the Mfengu people by the British, in exchange for their support in the Cape Frontier Wars. Accredited guide **Otto Ntshebe** (082 214 4242; ottours@webmail.co.za) runs tours by foot (three hours R250) or donkey cart (half-day R550), including visits to a local home, gallery and shebeen.

For spooky thrills, **Brian Jackson's ghost tours** (083 768 0193; info@whethu.com) explore the city's haunted sites, where the phantom residents include nuns, Jesuit brothers, and a typesetter in the Grocott's Mail newspaper building. The tour is paid by donation and should be booked 24 hours in advance.

PAUL KENNEDY / GETTY IMAGES ©

1. Jeffrey's Bay (p175)
One of the world's top surfing spots, 'J-Bay' also offers windsurfing, whale-watching and sandboarding.

2. Owl House (p222)
Artist Helen Martins turned her Nieu Bethesda home into this stunning, colourful work of art.

3. Xhosa woman
Clothing and beaded jewellery indicate a Xhosa's subgroup (p208).

4. Valley of Desolation (p221)
This area filled with dolerite columns is Camdeboo National Park's most popular sight.

SHAEN ADEY / GETTY IMAGES ©

Festivals & Events

National Arts Festival ARTS
(☎046-603 1103; www.nafest.co.za) Africa's largest arts festival runs for 10 days at the beginning of July. Remember two things: book ahead, as accommodation at this time can be booked out a year in advance; and nights can be freezing, so bring something warm. The associated Fringe and Fingo Festivals, the latter showcasing art, music and theatre from the townships, offer hundreds more performances.

Sleeping

At the time of writing, **Hill Street Manor** (☎082 333 8730, www.hillstreetmanor.co.za) was setting up a new backpackers on High St.

Bon Tempo BACKPACKERS, FARMSTAY $
(Penis Farm; ☎046-637 0880; www.bontempo.co.za; off Rte 67, Manley Flats; s/d/tr from R200/300/450; P) On a farm 20km from town en route to Bathurst, whimsical Bon Tempo offers rustic cottages and a gallery of penis sculptures. Meals are available.

Kwam eMakana HOMESTAY $
(☎072 448 0520; www.kwamemakana.co.za; s/d incl breakfast R350/500) Over 30 homestays offered by Xhosa mamas in Grahamstown's townships. Meals are available.

High Corner GUESTHOUSE $$
(☎046-622 8284; www.highcorner.co.za; 122 High St; s/d incl breakfast R680/1040, cottages R520/800; P) Appropriately, an account of this gracious house's 200-year history is the first thing you see you see upon entering. Rooms are split between the main building, with its antique furniture and elegant, high-ceilinged lounge and breakfast room, and modern self-catering cottages at the back.

Evelyn House GUESTHOUSE $$
(☎046-622 2366; www.evelynguesthouse.com; 115a High St; s/d incl breakfast R1030/1350; P) This beautifully renovated 19th-century house has spacious and comfortable rooms behind a tranquil garden.

Cock House GUESTHOUSE $$
(☎046-636 1287; www.cockhouse.co.za; 10 Market St; s/d incl breakfast R590/980; P) Named after William Cock, an enterprising 1820 Settler, and once home to author André Brink, this historic residence has nine double rooms in the main house and converted stables. There are also two-bedroom self-catering apartments.

Its restaurant, **Norden's** (☎046-636 1287; www.cockhouse.co.za; 10 Market St; lunch/dinner mains R70/95), offers fine dining overlooked by paintings of 19th-century South Africa. Traditionally a favourite of students when parents are treating, it has recently received mixed reviews.

Historic Cottages GUESTHOUSE $$
(☎046-622 8936; www.historiccottages.co.za; 1 Scotts Ave; s/d incl breakfast R550/900; P) Four quaint rooms and suites with private lounges and self-catering facilities, set among flowery gardens and courtyards in an historic 1820s British military barracks.

Graham Hotel HOTEL $$
(☎046-622 2324; www.grahamhotel.com; 123 High St; s/d incl breakfast R950/1230; P) This modern hotel is recommended less for its standard rooms than for its many facilities, including African restaurant **Calabash** (☎046-622 2324; 123 High St; mains R95;) and **Champs Action Bar** (☎046-622 2324; 123 High St).

The hotel's owners, Afri Temba, operate three midrange guesthouses in town.

137 High Street GUESTHOUSE $$
(☎046-622 3242; www.137highstreet.co.za; 137 High St; s/d incl breakfast R600/990; P) Offers seven small but comfortable rooms in a 200-year-old house built by Piet Retief, with thick walls and honey-coloured yellow-wood floors. The inhouse restaurant is recommended.

Eating & Drinking

Grahamstown's culinary scene is divided between pubs, cafes and fast-food joints catering to students on tight budgets, and swanky eateries for when the parents come to town. A few budget cafes at the university end of High St serve burgers and so on to students.

★**Haricot's Deli & Bistro** DELI, MEDITERRANEAN $$
(☎046-622 2150; www.haricots.co.za; 32 New St; mains R60-130; bistro noon-3pm & 6-9.30pm, deli 9am-5pm Mon-Fri, to 2pm Sat;) Eavesdrop on faculty gossip at Grahamstown's best eatery, which is simultaneously a relaxed courtyard cafe, foodie haven and refined restaurant. The menu has a strong Mediterranean influence with Asian and Moroccan twists, resulting in gourmet dishes such as pork loin in milk and braised lamb with white wine.

Its deli heaves with wholesome goodies including quiches, pastries, gluten-free muffins and flourless chocolate cake.

137 High Street INTERNATIONAL **$$**
(137 High St; mains R90; ⊘ 7.30am-9.30pm Mon-Fri, 8am-2pm & 5-9.30pm Sat, 8am-2pm Sun) With contemporary daubs on its green walls, this stylish restaurant serves steaks, burgers and light meals (R50) such as savoury pancakes. Venison and cups of local Mastertons coffee are its specialities.

Saint's Bistro INTERNATIONAL **$$**
(www.saintsbistro.com; 131 High St; mains R100; ☑) In its sunny rear courtyard and roomy interior with exposed beams, Saint's serves a good range of steaks, seafood, pasta and salads.

Rat & Parrot BAR
(59 New St) The centre of the student party scene, the Parrot's downstairs bar is wood panelled and cosy, while the upper floor has big windows and a veranda overlooking the street. It offers popular pizzas and, like a few pubs in this area, rugby on the TV.

❶ Information

Makana Tourism (☑ 046-622 3241; www.grahamstown.co.za; 63 High St; ⊘ 8.30am-5pm Mon-Fri, 8am-noon Sat; 🛜) Has accommodation information and sells Translux and City to City bus tickets. Offers free wi-fi and a computer with internet access.

❶ Getting There & Away

Greyhound, Translux, Intercape and City to City buses depart from the **Frontier Hotel** (cnr High & Bathurst Sts) and the **Conference Centre** (Grey St) on their daily runs to Cape Town (R450, 14 hours), Port Elizabeth (R230, two hours), Durban (R450, 12 hours) and Jo'burg (R480, 13 hours).

Shared taxis depart from Jacob Zuma Dr (previously Raglan Rd), the eastern continuation of Beaufort St.

Bathurst

The small, quaint village of Bathurst lies on Rte 67 between Port Alfred and Grahamstown. It's a famous Eastern Cape drinking spot, particularly during the annual **Ox Braai**, a huge party for the local farming community and students that takes place at the end of December. A few curio shops, galleries and restaurants cluster around the village's only intersection.

◉ Sights

Bathurst Agricultural Museum MUSEUM
(☑ 079 987 9507; www.bathurst.co.za; adult/child R15/10; ⊘ 9am-4pm Mon, Tue & Thu, to noon Wed, Sat & Sun) Displays a large collection of ox wagons, tractors and other farm equipment.

Big Pineapple MONUMENT
(☑ 046-625 0515; Summerhill Farm, off Rte 67; adult/child R10/5; ⊘ by appointment) Local farmers own the Big Pineapple, a few kilometres from the village en route to Port Alfred. It stands 16.7m high – you can climb to the top for great vistas of the surrounding countryside, and learn all about the pineapple industry. There are also tractor farm tours that include a pineapple tasting.

🛏 Sleeping & Eating

Summerhill Inn HOTEL **$**
(☑ 046-625 0833; www.summerhillinn.com; off Rte 67; s/d R390/520; 🅿 🛜 ⊠) Out of town, en route to Port Alfred, is Summerhill Inn, with comfortable rooms, extensive grounds and an atmospheric stone-walled bar-restaurant (snacks R45, mains R90).

Pig & Whistle Inn INN **$$**
(☑ 046-625 0673; www.pigandwhistle.co.za; s/d R356/624, without bathroom 276/450; 🅿 🛜) The characterful building, dating to 1832, offers renovated rooms with four-poster beds, free-standing baths and period furniture, and simpler rooms with shared bathrooms. The on-site pub (mains R70) does homemade burgers, seafood, pies and a Sunday roast.

Pic-Kwick's Restaurant ITALIAN **$**
(Village Green Complex; mains R60; ⊘ 10am-9pm Tue-Sat, to 4pm Sun) Across the road from the Pig & Whistle Inn, Pic-Kwick's serves two dozen varieties of pizza.

❶ Getting There & Away

About 45km from Grahamstown and 17km from Port Alfred, Bathurst is best visited in your own vehicle, although shared taxis do ply Rte 67 daily.

Port Alfred

POP 9747

Known as 'the Kowie' for the picturesque canal-like river that flows through its centre, Port Alfred is blessed with beautiful beaches,

Port Alfred

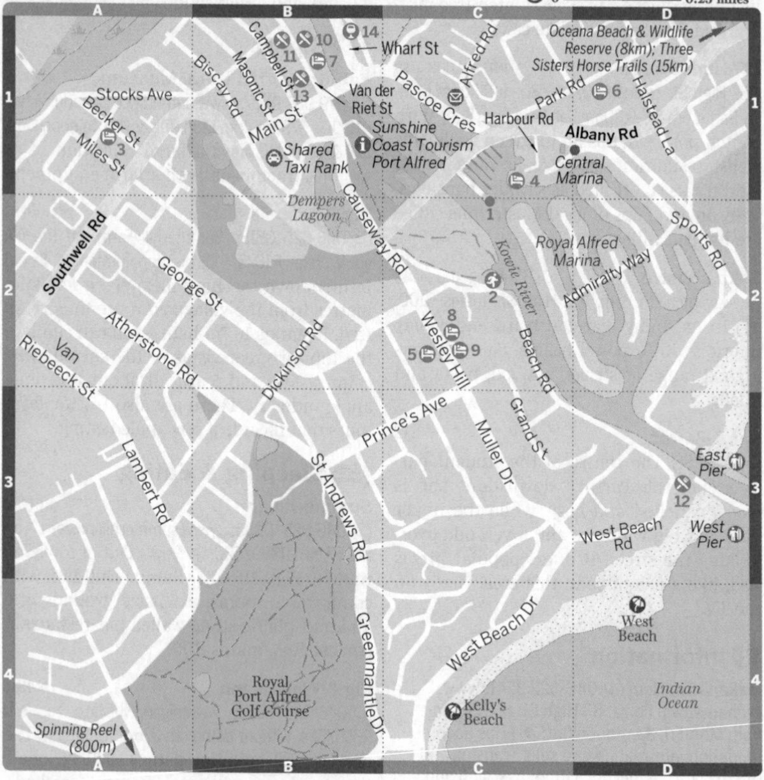

Port Alfred

Activities, Courses & Tours
1 Kowie River Cruises C2
2 Outdoor Focus C2

Sleeping
3 Dijembe Backpackers A1
4 Halyards Hotel & Spa C1
5 Links Coastal Inn C2
6 Lookout D1
7 My Pond Hotel B1
8 Panorama C2
9 Richmond House C2

Eating
10 Barmuda B1
11 Graze by the River B1
12 Guido's Restaurant D3
Lily .... (see 7)
13 Zest Café B1

Drinking & Nightlife
14 Wharf Street Brew Pub B1

with some to the north backed by massive sand dunes. Upscale, contemporary vacation homes line the marina and the hills surrounding town. It's generally a quiet place, except for visiting Grahamstown students. Things get busier during the intervarsity rowing regatta in late September, and from mid-December to January, when the town bustles with South African holidaymakers.

Sights & Activities

Apart from the pristine **beaches**, there are good right- and left-hand **surf** breaks at the river mouth. Drifting up the **Kowie River** also makes for a relaxing few hours; riverine euphorbia and private wildlife reserves meet the shore, African fish eagles circle overhead, and fishers dig for mud prawns to use as bait. Halyards Hotel & Spa rents out canoes (one hour R15) and organises boat cruises (one hour R80; minimum six people).

Oceana Beach & Wildlife Reserve WILDLIFE WATCHING
(083 616 0605; www.oceanareserve.com; Rietriver; drive R300, incl 3-course lunch R450) This five-star reserve, inhabited by antelope, zebras and giraffes, among other animals, offers a two-hour wildlife drive. Book ahead to join the drive, which starts at 10am. Oceana is located 8km from town on Rte 72 towards East London.

Outdoor Focus BOATING, DIVING
(046-624 4432; www.outdoorfocus.co.za; Beach Rd) A one-stop shop for activities, Outdoor Focus rents out canoes (one hour/day R50/220), and organises river cruises (adult/child R70/30) and sea trips (from R220). It can book the two-day **Kowie Canoe Trail** (per person R150), which is a fairly easy 21km canoe trip upriver from Port Alfred, with a night in a hut at Horseshoe Bend in the Watersmeeting Nature Reserve and an optional 12km hike.

Diving is best between May and August. Visibility is not outstanding (5m to 8m) but there are plenty of big fish, soft corals and raggy sharks.

Kowie River Cruises BOAT TOUR
(073 162 1611; www.kowierivercruises.co.za; Royal Alfred Marina; adult/child R75/50) Cruises in the *Lady Biscay*, an enclosed 13m-long barge.

Three Sisters Horse Trails HORSE RIDING
(082 645 6345; www.threesistershorsetrails.co.za; hour/half-day R250/550) Offers rides taking in beach and forest, and overnight trips along a river valley. Located 15km from town on Rte 72 towards East London.

Kowie Hiking Trail HIKING
(076 557 1324) An 8km trail through Kowie Nature Reserve – maps are available from the tourist office.

Sleeping

Panorama B&B $
(046-624 5853; www.portalfredpanorama.com; 15 Wesley Hill; s/d incl breakfast R370/620; P) Dutch–South African couple Rob and Marianne are gracious hosts at this well-priced hilltop guesthouse with winning views. Rob, a pilot and speed-boat owner, is full of suggestions for local activities.

Spinning Reel CABIN $
(046-624 4281; www.spinningreel.co.za; Freshwater Rd; cottages/chalets/r from R380/570/500; P) Basic self-catering beach cottages and newer Vermont-style pine chalets surrounded by indigenous dune forest, plus two rooms in the main house.

Dijembe Backpackers BACKPACKERS $
(072 226 4385; www.dijembebackpackers.com; 18 Becker St; dm/d R150/450, d without bathroom R350; P) The younger sibling of Storms River's eccentric Dijembe, this backpackers was being set up when we visited. Its huge deck overlooks the Kowie and accommodation ranges from dorms to an en-suite double with Jacuzzi bath. The managers' plans include a conservatory bar, lounge with woodburner, South African cuisine, and the Dijembe trademark – free pancakes for breakfast.

Lookout GUESTHOUSE $$
(046-624 4564; www.thelookout.co.za; 24 Park Rd; s/d/tr/q from R440/800/1000/1200; P) Perched on a hill, this contemporary whitewashed home has three units with kitchenettes and wonderful views.

Halyards Hotel & Spa HOTEL $$
(046-604 3300; www.riverhotels.com; Harbour Rd, Royal Alfred Marina; s/d incl breakfast from R660/860; P) This comfy riverfront hotel with attractive Cape Cod–style architecture has large well-equipped rooms overlooking the marina, two restaurants and a poolside bar. Inquire here about houseboats.

My Pond Hotel HOTEL $$
(046-624 4626; mypondhotel.com; Van der Riet St; s/d/ste incl breakfast from R850/1050/1530; P) This sleek boutique-style hotel on the Kowie River is operated and staffed by a hotel management school, so service is especially conscientious. The restaurant, **Lily** (046-624 4626; mypondhotel.com; Van der Riet St; mains R80), serves contemporary South African cuisine, including recommended lamb and mint spring rolls, and lamb shank.

Links Coastal Inn INN $$
(046-624 4533; www.thelinks.co.za; 14 Wesley Hill; s/d R400/600, cottages R450/650; P) A decorative African theme pervades this friendly inn's rooms and self-catering garden cottages. The **bar-restaurant** (mains R45 to R90) has an excellent deck for sundowners with a river view, and serves South African specialities such as *bobotie* and oxtail.

★ **Richmond House** CHALET $$$
(046-624 4878; www.richmondhousecottages.com; Wesley Hill; s R756-936, d R1260-1560; P)

WORTH A TRIP

SHIPWRECK HIKING & CANOE TRAIL

Shipwreck Hiking & Canoe Trail (☎082 391 0647; www.shipwreckhiking.co.za) As the graveyard for many errant ships, the coast between the Great Fish River and East London is deservedly known as the Shipwreck Coast. The 69km, six-day, five-night Shipwreck Hiking & Canoe Trail leads from Port Alfred to the Great Fish River Mouth and includes canoeing. You are rewarded with wild, unspoiled sections of surf beach, rich coastal vegetation and beautiful estuaries. Call for prices and more info.

A four-night, five-day trip excluding canoeing, and an overnight canoe trail on the Kleinemonde West River are other options.

Three luxury self-catering cottages among lawns and coral trees on the site of a historic homestead atop Wesley Hill. Offers seclusion and tranquillity in the town centre.

Eating & Drinking

★Zest Café MEDITERRANEAN $

(Van der Riet St; mains R70; ⏲8am-5pm Mon-Fri, to 3pm Sat; 📶) This friendly Mediterranean-style refuge occupies a flowery courtyard scattered with pastel furniture. Besides good ol' pizzas, try one of the more inventive dishes like spicy seafood, red pepper and almond tagine or vegetable rösti stack.

Graze by the River ORGANIC $$

(☎046-624 8095; 38 Van der Riet St; mains R85; ⏲9.30am-4pm Mon, Tue & Thu-Sun, dinner by appointment) This eccentric spot at the back of a curio shop serves slow food, organic veg and ethically produced meat, fish and dairy products. They also roast coffee beans and smoke meat and fish. Daily dinner specials include line-caught cob, fresh tuna steaks and 30-day matured rump steaks.

Phone to make a dinner booking; homemade cakes and toasted sandwiches are served during the day.

Guido's Restaurant ITALIAN $$

(West Beach Rd; mains R48-150) Guido's decks are perfect for a sundowner, with stunning views up the river and along the beach. It does wood-fired pizzas, and is popular with families and Grahamstown students on weekends.

Barmuda SOUTH AFRICAN $$

(Van der Riet St; mains R80) With a lovely riverside setting, this popular watering hole's pub-grub menu features gourmet burgers and beer-battered fish. Two-for-one cocktails on Sundays and, in season, daily live music and DJs attract the crowds.

Wharf Street Brew Pub BREWERY

(☎046-624 4947; 18 Wharf St; mains R70-110) Try beers from the neighbouring Little Brewery on the River in this 19th-century building on the old wharf, with a handsome dining room of exposed stone and brick, wood floors and poster-sized photos. The menu features steaks, crumbed calamari, prawn curry, schnitzel and prego rolls.

ℹ Information

Sunshine Coast Tourism Port Alfred (☎046-624 1235; www.sunshinecoasttourism.co.za; Causeway Rd; ⏲8am-4.30pm Mon-Fri, 8.30-11.30am Sat) Has brochures and maps, plus information about accommodation and activities including boat cruises and fishing charters.

ℹ Getting There & Away

Baz Bus passes through four days a week en route between Port Elizabeth (R250, two hours) and Durban (R1580, 13 hours). It stops at Dijembe Backpackers (p197).

From the **shared taxi rank** (Biscay Rd) outside the Heritage Mall, there are daily services to Port Elizabeth (R85), Grahamstown (R30) via Bathurst (R15), and East London (R85).

Avis and Budget car hire have offices here.

AMATHOLE

Running inland from East London, the Amathole region (pronounced 'ama-*tawl*-eh', from the Xhosa for 'calves') includes the eponymous mountain range, home to the enchanting village of Hogsback, and some wild and little-visited nature reserves. A good part of this area was the apartheid-era Xhosa homeland of Ciskei. If meeting the Xhosa people against a mountain backdrop sounds appealing, a few backpackers accommodations offer cultural experiences on a par with the Wild Coast.

East London

POP 267,007

In terms of population, geography and economy, this industrial and manufacturing centre (and the country's only river port) is an important Eastern Cape city. However, despite East London's bay-front location, which curves round to huge sand hills, stopping in this grey and rundown city is not recommended, especially when more appealing destinations lie nearby. You may pass through though; with its airport and location at the meeting of the Sunshine and Wild Coasts, East London is a transport hub. Much of the downtown area is dilapidated, dotted with falling-to-pieces Victorian buildings and 1960s and '70s monstrosities. Wealthy neighbourhoods with sizeable homes and neatly clipped lawns and gardens extend north of Eastern Beach.

Rte 72 runs through central East London from the airport and Port Alfred, then turns inland and crosses the northern suburbs to meet the N2 on the Chintsa side of town. Shortly after Rte 72 crosses the Buffalo River, Oxford St leads north (left) towards sights and eventually the N2. Rte 72 now passes through the Quigney Beach area, where many guesthouses and restaurants are located; turn right onto Currie or Moore Sts for the Esplanade and Eastern Beach.

Sights

The best **surfing** is at Nahoon Reef at the southern end of Nahoon Beach.

Ann Bryant Art Gallery MUSEUM
(☎043-722 4044; 9 St Marks Rd; admission free; ⏲9am-5pm Mon-Fri, to noon Sat) FREE This mixed late Victorian and early Edwardian mansion has a good collection of South African paintings from landscapes to city scenes, featuring the likes of Pierneef and Cecil Skotnes plus contemporary local work. Pick up a catalogue on the way in. There's a small coffee shop in the coach house.

East London Museum MUSEUM
(☎043-743 0686; www.elmuseum.za.org; 319 Oxford St; adult/child R15/5; ⏲9am-4.30pm Mon-Thu, to 4pm Fri) One of the first coelacanths, a type of fish thought to have become extinct over 50 million years ago, was discovered nearby in 1938; the stuffed original is on display here. Given the Eastern Cape's rich past the museum is worth a visit, with an excellent natural history collection, and exhibits on subjects from trace-fossil human footprints to maritime history.

Tours

Imonti Tours CULTURAL TOUR
(☎083 487 8975; www.imontitours.co.za) Owner Velile Ndlumbini runs a variety of tours in the area including to Mdantsane (half-day R280), South Africa's largest township after Soweto; a visit to a typical Xhosa village (half-day R390); and a Nelson Mandela-themed day trip to Qunu and Mthatha (R650). He also offers airport transfers and shuttles to Chintsa.

Sleeping

There isn't much reason to overnight in East London when a range of more appealing accommodation is available in nearby Chintsa.

City Centre

Sugarshack Backpackers BACKPACKERS $
(☎043-722 8240; www.sugarshack.co.za; Eastern Esplanade; camping/dm from R75/100) Just steps from Eastern Beach, this faux log-cabin complex has three- to 12-bed dorms and minicabins – all have seen better days. The upstairs deck and self-catering kitchen have great ocean views, and guests get free beer with meals at the equally raucous neighbouring Buccanners Pub & Grill.

On the downside, there's no parking, although a car guard does keep watch at night.

Garden Court BUSINESS HOTEL $$
(☎043-722 7260; www.tsogosunhotels.com; cnr John Bailie Rd & Moore St; r incl breakfast R1049; P ❄ @ 令 ≈) This 173-room chain hotel next to the Windmill Park centre has a full bouquet of facilities, including a bar, a restaurant and secure parking.

Northern Suburbs

If you get stuck here overnight, the best options are the many midrange and top-end B&Bs in the suburbs, only a few kilometres north of Eastern Beach. There is a good selection on and around John Bailie Rd, which runs north from the eastern end of Moore St.

John Bailie Guest Lodge GUESTHOUSE $$
(☎043-735 1058; www.johnbailieguestlodge.co.za; 9 John Bailie Rd, Bunkers Hill; s/d/tr from R450/600/750; P ≈) This restful guesthouse near the golf course has comfy carpeted rooms, ocean views and a pool and braai area, all surrounded by a manicured garden. Breakfast and dinner are offered, as is a 'backpacker' room with external bathroom. Walk-ins get lower rates.

Eating

Windmill Roadhouse FAST FOOD $
(Windmill Park, Moore St; mains R50) An American drive-in-style eatery complete with a big screen, where burgers and sandwiches are delivered to your car or to outdoor picnic tables. In the adjoining convenience store **Windmill Pizza** (Windmill Park, Moore St; pizza R45-69) does pizza to take away or to eat beneath the fluorescent lights.

Café Neo MEDITERRANEAN $$
(Windmill Park, Moore St; mains R85; wi-fi) Views from the outdoor balcony of this stylish 1st-floor restaurant and cocktail bar extend from the car park to the ocean. The large menu covers the gamut from wraps and linefish to steaks and decadent desserts.

Grazia Fine Food & Wine MEDITERRANEAN $$
(☎ 043-722 2009; www.graziafinefood.co.za; Upper Esplanade; mains R100) This stylish, centrally located restaurant has large windows with sea views as well as an outdoor deck for dining. The Italian-born owner has helped create a sophisticated menu with a variety of European influences; the menu includes pasta, pizza, meat and seafood. Reservations recommended.

Getting There & Away

AIR

East London Airport (☎ 043-706 0306; www.airports.co.za; Rte 72) is 10km southeast of the centre.

South African Airways (☎ 043-706 0203; www.flysaa.com), **SA Express** (☎ 0861 729 227; www.flyexpress.aero) and **Kulula** (☎ 0861 585 852; www.kulula.com) fly daily to Jo'burg (from R900 with Kulula, 1½ hours). SA Express also serves Cape Town (from R1800, two hours) and Durban (from R1650, one hour) daily; **Airlink** (☎ 043-706 0276; www.flyairlink.com) flies to Port Elizabeth (from R1700, 50 minutes, weekdays).

BUS

Baz Bus stops at Sugarshack en route between Port Elizabeth and Durban.

All the major bus lines serve the central **bus station** (Windmill Park, Moore St), near Eastern Beach.

Greyhound, Translux, Intercape and City to City offer daily services to Mthatha (R300, three hours), Port Elizabeth (R300, 4½ hours), Durban (R400, 9½ hours), Cape Town (R550, 16 hours) and Jo'burg (R500, 14 hours).

SHARED TAXI

Shared taxis leave from Oxford St and the surrounding streets. On the corner of Buffalo and College Sts (near East London Zoo) are long-distance taxis to destinations north of East London, including Mthatha (R85, four hours). A few blocks south, on the corner of Caxton and Gillwell Sts, are taxis for local destinations including King William's Town (R25, one hour).

TRAIN

On Wednesdays, Fridays and Sundays, **Shosholoza Meyl** runs a tourist-class (with sleepers) train both to and from Jo'burg (R440, 20 hours) via Queenstown (R140, 4½ hours) and Bloemfontein (R280, 13 hours). Less-recommended economy class (seat only) is also available on this route (R100/180/270 to Queenstown/Bloemfontein/Jo'burg).

Hogsback

POP 1029

There's something about Hogsback that inspires people. An Edenic little village 1300m up in the beautiful Amathole Mountains above Alice, the village's name is derived from the 'bristles' (known geologically as a 'hogsback') that cover peaks of the surrounding hills – but the name doesn't evoke the tranquillity the village is famous for.

For years now, artists, poets, alternative therapists and other like-minded folk have helped create an environmentally inclined community here – an easy sensibility to adopt with fabulous views of mountains and forested valleys from your window. The town's climate and history of green-fingered English settlers mean it's blessed with gorgeous (though seasonal) market garden estates. Locals will tell you that JRR Tolkien, who lived in Bloemfontein until he was three, visited Hogsback, sowing the seed of his fantastical novels. That is extremely unlikely, but the area may well have inspired him via his son Christopher, who came here while stationed in South Africa with the Royal Air Force.

The highest of the three hogs peaks in the distance is 1937m. The steepest slopes around Hogsback are still covered in beautiful rainforest: yellow-wood, assegai and tree fuchsia can be found. There are also extensive pine plantations on land that was once indigenous forest.

The weather is unpredictable and rainy, with misty days and even snow occuring any time of year. Winter (June to August) sees occasional snowfall, though it's generally dry with night-time temperatures dropping as low as -2°C. Spring (September to November) brings stunning sunshine and blooming flowers, while summer (December to February) days can be extremely warm and sunny with occasional short but heavy thunderstorms. Trees change colour in autumn (March to May).

Sights

Ecoshrine GARDENS

(www.ecoshrine.co.za; 22 Summerton Dr; adult/child R20/free; 9am-5pm Wed, Sat & Sun) Well-known mixed-media artist Diana Graham, a passionate environmental advocate, has created a cement sculpture garden dedicated to the forces of nature. The images, which Graham will explain, cover the origins of the earth, and ecological and scientific themes. The property has beautiful views (when the haze in the valley has cleared off) and can be reached from the village centre by road or a forest walking trail.

Starways Art Centre GALLERY

(082 953 7840; www.starways.org; Booysens Cres; by appointment) FREE Award-winning artist Anton van der Merwe exhibits pottery and paintings at this community arts centre. The atmospheric little theatre between the trees periodically hosts poetry readings and performances.

Mirrors Gallery & Crystal Corner GALLERY, GARDENS

(www.kenharvey.smugmug.com; admission by donation; 10am-5pm) Mirrors has a magical 180-sq-m garden with a stone circle and labyrinth, a gallery of owner Ken's landscape photography, and a crystal shop.

Prayer Trail GARDENS

(Main Rd) This meditative path meanders through the garden of St Patrick on the Hill chapel.

Fairy Realm Garden GARDEN

(045-962 1098; Main Rd; adult/child R30/15; 9.30am-4.30pm) A 400m path winds past the garden's ponds, cascading water and over 80 fairy sculptures.

Activities

There are some great walks, bike rides and drives through the area's indigenous forests and pine plantations; the tourist office has a map. A recommended hike (three to five hours) leaves from behind Away with the Fairies backpackers and takes in a massive 800-year-old yellow-wood tree, Swallow Tail Falls, Bridal Veil Falls and the Madonna & Child Falls before ending at Wolfbridge Rd, which takes you back to the village. Purchase a R10 hiking permit at Away with the Fairies or the tourist office.

True to Hogsback's alternative leanings, various invigorating and energy-balancing massages and treatments are available. The tourist office has details.

Hogsback Adventures ADVENTURE SPORTS

(Cycle Roots; 074 721 4885; hogsbackadventures.co.za; 9 Main Rd) Opposite the tourist office, this one-stop activities shop offers an 18km, four-hour guided mountain-bike adventure through the forest (R350 per person), plus bike rental (half-day R200), archery, and abseiling 35m down the Madonna & Child Falls (R250). They also offer tours by bike or car of Hogsback's galleries and gardens (R50 per person per hour).

Amathole Horse Trails HORSE RIDING

(082 897 7503; www.terrakhaya.co.za; off Plaatjieskraal Rd) Shane offers rides at all levels of experience, and practises 'natural horsemanship'. Outings last from 1½ hours (R250) to four days (R3150), with accommodation on the latter in a Xhosa homestay and dairy farm.

WORTH A TRIP

AMATHOLE TRAIL

Amathole Trail (per person per night incl accommodation R182) The 120km, six-day Amathole Trail starts at the Maden Dam, 23km north of King William's Town, and ends at the Tyumie River near Hogsback. It ranks as one of South Africa's top mountain walks, but it's pretty tough and in poor condition. Only attempt the walk if you are reasonably experienced and fit, and seek local advice before doing so.

Accommodation is in huts and it is possible to walk a section of the trail. Permits can be purchased through the **Department of Agriculture, Forestry & Fisheries** (DWAF; 084 308 6890, in King William's Town 043-604 5448; www.daff.gov.za; 2 Hargreaves Ave, King William's Town).

Walkers are rewarded with great views. About a third of the route crosses dense forest and numerous streams with waterfalls and swimming holes.

✨ Festivals & Events

Events from trail runs to a mind, body and spirit festival take place throughout the year; check www.hogsbackinfo.co.za/events for upcoming events.

Spring Festival CULTURE
(www.hogsbackgardens.blogspot.com; ☉ late Sep–late Oct) Hogsback's biggest annual event throws opens the green-fingered town's lovingly tended gardens and, in early October, prompts a weekend of fire dancing, drum circles, children's events and general merriment.

🛏 Sleeping

Numerous self-catering cottages are tucked away in the forests surrounding the village; visit www.hogsback.com, www.hogsback.co.za and www.hogsbackinfo.co.za for listings.

⭐ **Terra-Khaya** BACKPACKERS, FARMSTAY $
(☑ 082 8977 503; www.terrakhaya.co.za; off Plaatjieskraal Rd; dm incl breakfast R70, r incl breakfast without bathroom R285; P) 🍴 Get way off the grid at this unique and inspiring mountainside farm retreat at 1350m. The DIY aesthetic and philosophy of the owner (bareback-riding Shane of Amathole Horse Trails) is suffused throughout: everything is made from wattle, daub and recycled materials; electrical plug points are only found in the lounge; and ablutions consist of donkey-boiler showers and composting toilets.

With its sweeping views, this wonderfully tranquil place is difficult to leave; for longer stays, volunteering opportunities are offered.

Away with the Fairies BACKPACKERS $
(☑ 045-962 1031; www.awaywiththefairies.co.za; Ambleside Close; camping/dm/r/cottage from R90/145/360/500; P🛜🏊) 🍴 Terrific views abound at this magical, mystical clifftop backpackers: take an al fresco bath in the cliff-side tub, or climb 15m to the treehouse perched in the forest among parrots and monkeys. Activities including Xhosa lessons, picnics in the forest, pancakes at sunrise, fishing, hiking, tree hugging and creative writing workshops are offered.

The Wizard's Sleeve Bar, a colourful spot to down a few beers and swap tales, serves meals including made-to-order pizzas.

⭐ **Edge Mountain Retreat** LODGE $$
(☑ 045-962 1159; www.theedge-hogsback.co.za; Perry Bar Lane; s/d incl breakfast R450/790, self-catering cottages R600-1800; P🛜) The Edge's tastefully decorated cottages and garden rooms are strung out along a dramatic plateau edge, which once marked the border between the apartheid-era Ciskei homeland and South Africa proper. The cottages all have one big bedroom with a log fire and TV, plus separate bathroom and kitchen.

The vibe here is peace, quiet and relaxation. It's an unbeatable place for a healthy rest or a romantic weekend.

Granny Mouse House GUESTHOUSE $$
(☑ 045-962 1259; www.grannymousehouse.co.za; Nutwoods Dr; s/d from R400/550; P🛜🏊) Occupies a thatch, wattle and daub settler house dating to 1910, set in a lovely garden and orchard where two self-catering units stand and the resident Rhodesian Ridgebacks bound. Meals are available and the friendly owner Ingrid speaks German.

Hogsback Inn INN $$
(☑ 045-962 1006; www.hogsbackinn.co.za; Wolfridge Rd; d R620-1650, self-catering cottages R660-880; P🛜🏊) In a flowery garden, this late 19th-century country lodge has updated rooms and an old-fashioned English tavern.

🍴 Eating

Butterfly's Bistro VEGETARIAN, DELI $
(Main Rd; mains R65; ☉ 9am-6pm Tue, Wed & Sun, to 8pm Thu-Sat; 🛜🍴) This popular eatery, in a quaint, A-frame house next to the tourist office, serves veggie dishes, breakfasts, pizzas, burgers, wraps and weekly specials.

⭐ **Tea Thyme** INTERNATIONAL $$
(Perry Bar Lane; mains R80; ☉ 7.30am-8.30pm) The Edge's charming garden restaurant serves French toast with local berries and Hogsback's best coffee for breakfast; recommended tapas boards and wood-fired pizzas for lunch; and stuffed pork loin, pan-fried hake and slow-cooked lamb shank for dinner. Throw in homemade bread, fresh, organic local produce, a cosy dining room, and paths leading to the nearby labyrinth and viewpoint.

🔒 Shopping

Saturday Market MARKET
(off Main Rd; ☉ 9am-noon) Stretching from the back of the tourist office to Butterfly's Bistro, the market showcases the products and projects of the local community, including craftwork, clothing, crystals and the odd bio-farming demo.

OFF THE BEATEN TRACK

ELUNDINI BACKPACKERS

Elundini Backpackers (☎078 357 3285; www.elundinibackpackers.com; Elundini; camping/dm R60/120, r/tr/q without bathroom R290/390/490; Ⓟ) About 15km south of Hogsback, look out for the sign to Elundini Backpackers, located in Elundini village on the gravel road to Seymour. The backpackers, 8km from the turnoff, offers total immersion in this Xhosa village nestling in the Amathole countryside. Accommodation is in *rondavels* with shared rainwater showers and composting toilets, all gazing at the forested hills, and meals are served in the living area.

What really makes this Xhosa–Belgian backpackers special is the community-run activities, ranging from guided hikes and village tours to bread making and Xhosa lessons. Pick-ups are offered from Hogsback and Alice (R50); you can also hike here in four hours from Hogsback, and shared taxis run from Alice (R20). You can access Elundini by 2WD car from both Hogsback and Seymour.

Information

There's an ATM in the small supermarket, just off the main road, and a petrol station.

Hogsback Information Centre (☎045-962 1245; www.hogsback.com; Main Rd; ⏲9am-3pm Mon-Sat, to 1pm Sun) The helpful centre can provide accommodation advice and maps for walks.

Getting There & Away

The way up to Hogsback on Rte 345 (the turnoff is 4km east of Alice) is tarred, but try to arrive in daylight due to mountain bends and occasional itinerant livestock. Coming from Queenstown and the north, take Rte 67 towards Fort Beaufort and turn off in Seymour, following the good gravel road to Elundini and the backpackers there; after 22km, this road meets Rte 345 south of Hogsback. Do not attempt the more direct dirt road to/from Cathcart in a 2WD car.

The easiest way to get to Hogsback without a car is in the shuttle run by Away with the Fairies on Tuesday, Wednesday, Friday and Sunday. It picks up at Sugarshack Backpackers in East London (R150, two hours), Buccaneers Lodge in Chintsa (R180, 2½ hours), East London Airport and King William's Town.

By shared taxi, you can get to Hogsback from Alice (R30), but you must change in in Auckland.

City to City stops in Alice daily en route between East London (R140, two hours) and Pretoria via Queenstown, Bloemfontein and Jo'burg.

THE WILD COAST

This shipwreck-strewn coastline rivals any in the country in terms of beauty, stretching over 350km from just east of East London to Port Edward. Often referred to as the 'Transkei' (the name of the apartheid-era homeland that once covered most of this area), the Wild Coast region also stretches inland, covering pastoral landscapes where clusters of *rondavels* scatter the rolling hills covered in short grass.

The local Xhosa people are some of the friendliest you'll meet anywhere in South Africa, and chances are you'll be invited inside a home or, at the very least, a shebeen. South of the Mbashe River lives the Gcaleka tribe; the Mpondomise live to the north. In this land of far-flung river estuaries and backpackers resembling Xhosa settlements, numerous outdoor activities and cultural tours are on offer. Birdlife is abundant, especially in the parks; you can also buy seafood such as shad, cob, musselcrackers, crayfish, oysters and sardines from subsistence fishers, or try your luck with a rod.

This is the place to forgo the bus or your car for a while and make use of the walking paths that connect the coastal villages. There are a number of trails, some making use of hotels along the way and offering porterage, and some where you can stay with locals. It's likely you'll enjoy yourself more when you're off the road, so pick one of the out-of-the-way backpacker lodges – Bulungula, Mdumbi, Wild Lubanzi, the Kraal or Mtentu – and spend several days there. Port St Johns and Coffee Bay are good bases for day trips and explorations, while Chintsa and Morgan Bay have good access to the N2.

Tours

Even if guided tours aren't your usual style, the following outfits can help immeasurably with your understanding of the rich and complex culture of the Xhosa and Mpondo peoples who live on the Wild Coast. Check out www.wildcoastbookings.com to make accommodation bookings all along the coast.

The Wild Coast

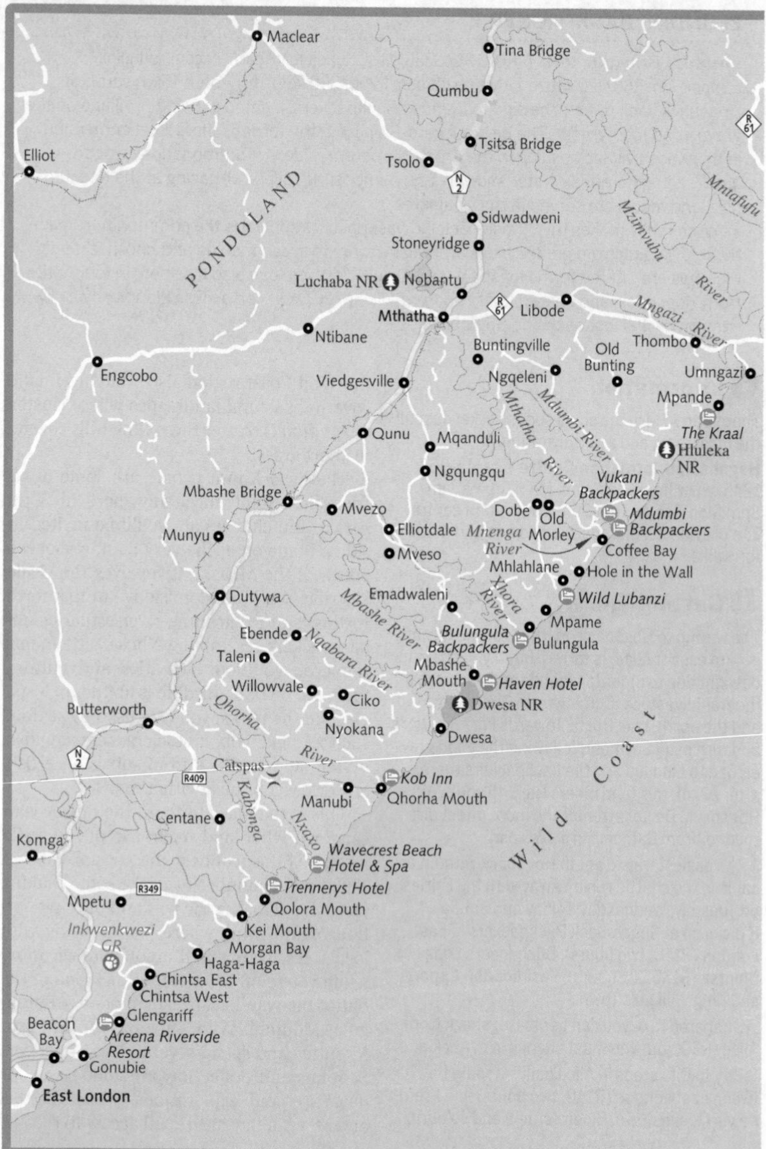

African Heartland Journeys ADVENTURE TOUR (☎ in Chintsa 043-738 5523; www.ahj.co.za; Chintsa West) A well-regarded tour company affiliated with Buccaneers Lodge. Their intrepid tours venture deep into the Wild Coast's rural corners, encompassing travel by foot, canoe, 4WD and mountain bike, with accommodation options ranging from hotels to villages. They also have a surf school, and offer two- to 12-week volunteering opportunities through Volunteer Africa 32° South (www.volunteerafrica.co.za) and Friends of Chintsa (www.friendsofchintsa.org).

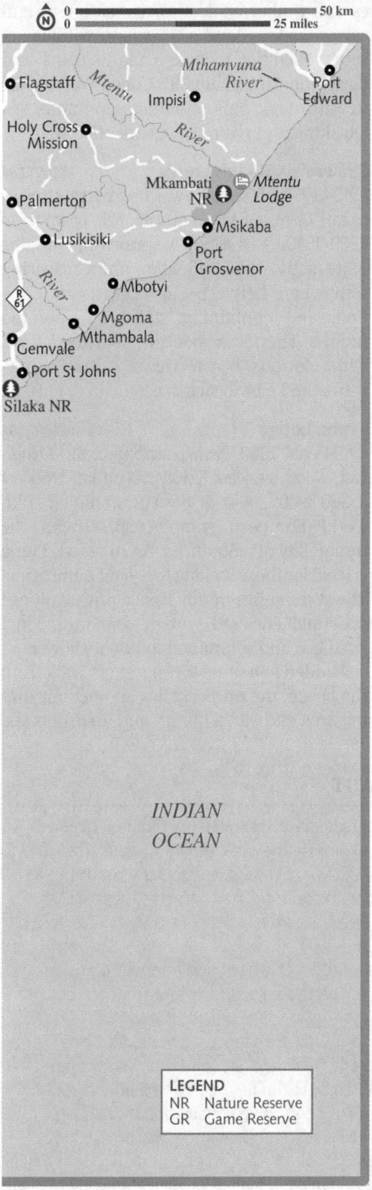

Wild Coast Holiday Reservations WALKING TOUR
(☎in East London 043-743 6181; www.wildcoastholidays.co.za) Organises five multiday hikes along the length of the coast, with accommodation in the area's great resorts and hotels, including the classic six-day, five-night Wild Coast Meander from Kob Inn resort to Morgan Bay Hotel. Local guides are employed. Accommodation and transfers can also be booked through this outfit.

WESSA Wild Walk WALKING TOUR
(☎in Chintsa 043-738 5523; www.wessa.org.za) This annual long-distance slackpacking trail, highlighting the rich and fragile coastal environment protected by WESSA (Wildlife and Environment Society of South Africa), runs from Port Edward to Bulungula in November. Groups of at least two can tackle two-, five- and seven-day sections.

Chintsa

POP 1803

Less than an hour's drive north of East London, Chintsa feels worlds away from the big city. It comprises two small villages – Chintsa East and Chintsa West, on either side of the Chintsa River Mouth – fronted by a spectacular white-sand beach with good, swimmable surf. It's a great place to hang out for a few days (or weeks) on this part of the coast.

Sights & Activities

Buccaneers (p206) offers numerous activities, including a **township and brewery tour** (R375 per person), with a visit to to the home of Mama Tofu, reputedly South Africa's oldest tour guide, in Ngxingxolo village; **horse riding** (R350), **surf lessons** (R205), **mountain biking** (R220); and visits to the primary school partly supported by Buccs' associated foundation.

Emerald Vale BREWERY
(☎073 078 9688; www.emeraldvalebrewery.co.za; Chintsa East; R60; ⏲tours by appointment noon & 4pm Mon-Sat) Half-hour tours of this brewery in a converted barn on a working farm include tasters of the four ales and an iced tea. The **bar-restaurant** (mains R65) serves food to complement the beer, including burgers and jalapeño poppers.

Inkwenkwezi Game Reserve WILDLIFE RESERVE
(☎043-734 3234; www.inkwenkwezi.com; s/d tented bush camp incl meals & activities from R1800/2200) Between the Chintsa East and West turnoffs, the private, upmarket Inkwenkwezi features the Big Five (although the elephants and lions are kept separately) and five biomes. In addition to wildlife drives (from R695 per person), the reserve offers guided mountain biking, hiking and canoeing.

🛏 Sleeping

The Chintsa area offers excellent accommodation for all budgets, making it an excellent alternative to East London.

★ Buccaneers Lodge BACKPACKERS $

(☑ 043-734 3012; www.cintsa.com; Chintsa West; camping/dm/r from R100/142/546; ⓟ@⬆☎) Offering an accessible taste of the Wild Coast, 'Buccs' is a sort of all-inclusive holiday resort for backpackers, beach bums and travellers interested in Xhosa culture. Sleeping options cover the spectrum between comfortable four- to 12-bed dorms, safari tents, self-catering cottages and gorgeous suites with sea-facing decks.

A mind-boggling range of activities, tours and cultural experiences is offered, while on-site entertainments include free use of canoes and boogie boards, complimentary wine and Sunday breakfast, beach volleyball, yoga and spa treatments. Meals are served, family-style, in the charming candlelit dining room and outdoor deck.

Areena Riverside Resort RESORT $$

(☑ 043-734 3055; www.areenaresort.com; Glengariff; camping/s/d/q from R145/385/650/795; ⓟ☎) Hugging the tree-shaded shore of the Kwelera River, Areena has everything from self-catering *rondavels*, thatched cottages and timber chalets to riverside tent and caravan sites – and a 3.5-sq-km wildlife reserve. Facilities include a tennis court and bar-restaurant (mains R70, open Wednesday to Saturday), plus abseiling, zip-lining, sea kayaking and river cruises are offered.

Crawfords Beach Lodge RESORT $$$

(☑ 043-738 5000; www.crawfordsbeachlodge.co.za; Chintsa East; s/d with half board from R920/1540; ⓟ✳⬆☎) A sprawling complex of attractive thatched white units, wavering somewhere between Cape Dutch and Cape Cod, and containing stylishly appointed rooms. There's a poolside bar-restaurant with glorious beach views, a spa, tennis courts and easy beach access.

Prana Lodge RESORT $$$

(☑ 043-704 5100; www.pranalodge.co.za; Chintsa East; s incl breakfast R2100-2500, d incl breakfast R3300-3900; ⓟ✳@⬆☎) Combining old-world European sumptuousness with the tranquillity of a Southeast Asian resort, Prana is ideal for those seeking top-flight pampering. The seven suites mostly have a private plunge pool and enclosed garden courtyard, king-sized bed and voluminous outdoor shower.

Hidden in a dune forest a short walk from the beach, the property has an open-air dining area and bar, a library and luxurious spa

ⓘ SAFE TRAVEL ON THE WILD COAST

Access to the coast from the N2 (which connects East London with KwaZulu-Natal via Mthatha) is limited by the rugged terrain, and exploring the area inevitably leads travellers down more than one bone-jarring road. Even tar roads here, such as the road linking Coffee Bay with the N2, should be approached with caution. They can be dangerously potholed, and the potholes may be difficult to see, so it's best to drive slowly unless you want to lose a hubcap – or worse.

Don't drive after dark; remember that many of the roads here don't appear on maps; and expect that signposts will be few and far between. It's also important to watch out for animals and people in the middle of the roads.

In general, whether you are travelling by car or public transport, do make advance contact with the accommodation option you are travelling to. Despite their remoteness, the Wild Coast's hotels, lodges, backpackers and resorts do fill up; phoning ahead could save you a long journey back to the N2 in search of alternative accommodation. Even if you have a booking, making advance contact will let your hosts know you are making your way through their section of the Wild Coast.

Many of the gravel roads can often be navigated in a 2WD hire car, provided you are a reasonably confident driver and you don't have a sentimental attachment to your vehicle. Tarring and upgrading are also slowly improving the local road network. However, unsealed roads often become impassable after rain. Again, phone ahead or seek local advice about the current state of the roads you plan to tackle.

Allow much longer travel times here than you would in other parts of South Africa, even on the tar roads. This applies to both drivers and travellers taking shared taxis, which only leave when they are full and make multiple stops along the way.

WORTH A TRIP

STRANDLOPER & SUNDOWNER TRAILS

Strandloper Trail (043-841 1046; www.strandlopertrails.org.za; per person R500) The 57km, four-day Strandloper Hiking Trail runs from Kei Mouth to Gonubie, just outside East London. The trail is named after the Strandlopers (meaning 'Beach Walkers'), a Khoe-San tribe who lived on the coast but disappeared as a distinct group after white settlement. It is fairly easy, but good fitness is required.

Nights are spent in cabins and the Haga-Haga Hotel, and accommodation is included in the trail fee, with a two-night option (R180) also available. Profits are channelled into environmental education for local children.

Sundowner Trail (043-841 1046; www.strandlopertrails.org.za; per person R6300) A slackpacker option for those looking to end their vigorous days of hiking with a little luxury, the five-day, four-night Sundowner Trail runs from Trennerys Hotel to Chintsa East. A six-day, five-night option leads from Kob Inn to Morgan Bay. All meals and transfers are included.

facilities. Half and full board are available, and nonguests can visit the spa (treatments R550 to R2200).

Eating

Chintsation SOUTH AFRICAN $
(www.chintsation.co.za; Adelsicht Farm; mains R60; 9am-4pm;) Just off the N2 en route to Chintsa East, this farm stall, cafe and craft shop serves homemade pies, burgers, salads and platters, with views of its kitchen garden and dam.

Barefoot Café PUB $
(Chintsa East; mains R65; noon-late Mon & Wed-Fri, from 10am Sat & Sun) What nightlife there is in Chintsa centres on this casual bar-restaurant where foreign volunteers, backpackers and locals mix. Blesbok (antelope) skewers, peri peri chicken, pizzas and beer-battered fish are on the menu. Kitchen closes at 8.30pm.

Information

Chintsa East has a shop, liquor store, ATM and petrol station.

Getting There & Away

Baz Bus stops at Buccaneers en route between Port Elizabeth and Durban. Many accommodation options at this end of the Wild Coast will arrange a transfer from East London with prior notice.

Driving, follow the brown signpost to Chintsa from the N2, about 30km north of East London. Chintsa East and West are both about 15km further on.

Morgan Bay & Kei Mouth

POP 612

Accessed from the N2 on the tarred Rte 349, Morgan Bay is a good place for some peace and quiet, and for beachcombing and surfing. A few kilometres further on, the tar ends in the somewhat ramshackle Kei Mouth, where taking the **pontoon ferry** (Vehicle Ferry; pedestrian/car R0.50/70; 7am-5.30pm) across the Great Kei River feels a little like crossing into the Wild Coast proper. Indeed, the river was once the southern border of the Xhosa homeland of Transkei.

Yellowwood Forest CAMPGROUND $
(043-841 1598; www.yellowwoodforest.co.za; Morgan Bay; camping R115, r from R300;) Yellowwood Forest, about 1km from Morgan Bay beach, is a tranquil riverside campsite surrounded by indigenous forest and frequented by louries and hornbills. There is a charming tea garden and a craft shop, wood-fired pizzas on offer, and loft rooms and cabins.

Morgan Bay Hotel HOTEL $$
(043-841 1062; www.morganbayhotel.com; Beach Rd, Morgan Bay; s/d incl breakfast & dinner from R930/1430, camping R210;) Light and airy Morgan Bay Hotel is perched directly over the beachfront. The attached bar and restaurant (mains R50) has a menu of seafood and pub grub, and great outside deck seating.

Dwesa Nature Reserve

One of South Africa's most remote and beautiful reserves, **Dwesa Nature Reserve** (043-705 4400; www.visiteasterncape.co.za; adult/child R20/10; 6am-6pm) blends lush forests, winding rivers, open grassland and rugged coastline, with walking trails and wildlife including buffaloes, zebras, antelope, warthogs, and crocodiles in the rivers.

THE XHOSA

Travelling along the Wild Coast is an excellent way to get to know Xhosa culture. You may hear the term 'red people', which refers to the red clothes and red-clay face paint worn by some Xhosa adults.

Clothing, colours and beaded jewellery all indicate a Xhosa's subgroup. The Tembu and Bomvana, for example, favour red and orange ochres in the dyeing of their clothing, while the Pondo and Mpondomise use light blue. The *isi-danga* – a long, turquoise necklace that identifies the wearer to their ancestors – is also still seen today.

Belief in witches (male and female) among the Xhosa is strong, and witch burning is not unknown. Most witchcraft is considered evil, with possession by depraved spirits a major fear. The *igqirha* (spiritual healer) is empowered to deal with both the forces of nature and the trouble caused by witches, and so holds an important place in traditional society. The *ixhwele* (herbalist) performs some magic, but is more concerned with health. Both are healers, and are often referred to as *sangomas*, though this is a Zulu word.

Many Xhosa have the top of their left little finger removed during childhood to prevent misfortune. Puberty and marriage rituals also play a central role. Males must not be seen by women during the three-month initiation period following circumcision at the age of 18; during this time the initiates disguise themselves with white clay, or in intricate costumes made of dried palm leaves.

In the female puberty ritual, a girl is confined in a darkened hut while her friends tour the area singing for gifts. Unmarried girls wear short skirts, which are lengthened as marriage approaches. Married women wear long skirts and cover their breasts. They often put white clay on their faces and wear large, turbanlike cloth hats and may smoke long-stemmed pipes. The length of the pipe denotes the woman's status in the clan.

Most villages comprise a series of *rondavels*, many of them painted a bright turquoise, grouped around the cattle kraal. The roofs are thatched and often sport an old tyre at the apex, filled with earth for stabilisation. The earth can be planted with cacti or shards of glass: sharp objects dissuade bad omens such as owls from alighting. On the death of the owner, the hut is abandoned and left to collapse.

Some 290 bird species have been identified, including the rare Narina trogon and mangrove kingfisher. Community-run activities include guided nature walks and boat trips over the Mbashe River.

There is self-catering accommodation (1-/2-bedroom chalets R300/600) and camping (R220) in Dwesa near the beach, accessed via a 47km gravel road from Willowvale. You need a high-clearance vehicle to get here.

Haven Hotel HOTEL **$$**
(☎047-576 8904; www.havenhotel.co.za; Mbashe Mouth; s/d with half board from R445/890; P ≋) This rustic resort is a good base for exploring Dwesa Nature Reserve, whether hiking in the forest, canoeing on the Mbashe River or horse riding on the beach. Accommodation is in cottages and *rondavels*.

Coffee Bay

POP 258

Because of its beautiful kilometre-long beach and easy access to dramatic surrounding scenery, this once-remote village has become something of a de rigueur Wild Coast stop for backpackers and South African hippies. No one is sure how tiny Coffee Bay got its name, but there is a theory that a ship, wrecked here in 1863, deposited its cargo of coffee beans on the beach. The village today is a scruffy nondescript place, where locals hover around the backpackers enclave, trying to sell *dagga* (marijuana), curios and day trips.

Popular activities such as guided hikes, horse riding, cultural visits and surfing trips can be organised through town's various accommodation options.

Sleeping & Eating

Most of the town's sleeping and eating options are clustered in the village centre, where a grocery store sells basic provisions.

White Clay CABINS **$**
(☎083 979 4499; www.whiteclayresort.co.za; camping/s/d/q R100/275/450/780; P ⓦ) Around the headland en route to Hole in

the Wall, White Clay's self-catering chalets climb the hillside above its simple seafood restaurant (mains R65 to R90, open 11am to 7pm) overlooking a pebble beach.

Sugarloaf Backpackers Lodge BACKPACKERS $
(☑047-575 2175; www.sugarloafbackpackers.com; dm/r from R120/400, r without bathroom R350; ℗🛜) On the main drag, Sugarloaf is a relaxed and relatively orderly budget choice, with a full complement of facilities and hang-out areas in leafy grounds atop a river bank. Safari tents (single/double R200/300) stand on decks overlooking the Mnenga River and the beach, which is a short walk or swim away.

Coffee Shack BACKPACKERS $
(☑047-575 2048; www.coffeeshack.co.za; camping/ dm/r/q R75/120/380/640, r without bathroom R320; ℗🛜) An enduringly popular beachfront option for travellers looking to surf and party, Coffee Shack doesn't let standards slip among the merrymaking. The complex is rather labyrinthine, with bright paint masking its sometimes-institutional feel, but there are *rondavels* across the river with more privacy. Camping is out back with ocean views.

The beach-shack bar and garden get lively and numerous activities are offered, including surfing lessons and guided hikes.

Bomvu Paradise BACKPACKERS $
(☑047-575 2073; www.bomvubackpackers.com; camping/dm/r/q R60/100/300/600, r without bathroom R250; ℗🛜) Mixing party credentials and alternative vibes, Bomvu is a rambling complex of small buildings – the double ensuite cabins are a good option for comfort and privacy – in a patch of riverine forest. There's a permaculture garden and natural ampitheatre, where festivals take place.

The brightly patterned restaurant resembles a Xhosa *rondavel,* and the horse riding, surfing lessons, cultural tours, yoga workshops and mesmerising in-house band drumming sessions ensure there is never a dull moment.

Jah Drums BACKPACKERS $
(☑081 297 0698; tent per person R120) Fifteen safari tents and a six-bed dorm (R120), drum-making courses and jams, and some very relaxed people in the bar.

Ocean View Hotel HOTEL $$
(☑047-575 2005; www.oceanview.co.za; s/d with half board from R859/1518; ℗🛜❄) This 45-year-old hotel offers a great mix of old-fashioned charm and modern elements, with generous buffet meals, a lovely thatched beach bar and chalet-style rooms with private patio overlooking the sea or garden. Located at the far end of the main beach from the Coffee Bay melee, it offers activities including guided hikes, horse riding and cultural tours.

Papazela's PIZZA $
(pizzas R75; ⏱4-9pm Tue-Sat) This popular shack serves wood-fired pizzas with predictably wacky names, eaten with fingers and accompanied by sweeping beach views.

❶ Getting There & Away

A tarred road runs to Coffee Bay from the N2 at Viedgesville. Backpacker shuttles (R70) meet the Baz Bus at the Shell Ultra City garage, 4km south of Mthatha. Shared taxis also run from from Mthatha (R25, one hour).

Around Coffee Bay

The walks around Coffee Bay are spectacular – one of the best and most popular is to Hole in the Wall, an offshore rock formation featuring a large, photogenic natural arch created by the pounding of the ocean waves. A gravel road also leads there from Coffee Bay (about 9km). At the time of writing, the road was passable in a 2WD car as far as Hole in the Wall, after which it disintegrated.

The three-hour walk to Hole in the Wall is doable without a guide (though not alone), but safer and easier with one, partly because you will get a lift back to Coffee Bay at the end. Coffee Shack and Bomvu Paradise charge about R80 per person for the guide and transfer back.

Further south, Wild Lubanzi (p211) can be reached in a day. Overnight guided hikes can also be arranged to Bulungula (two days, one night) and, to the north, Port St Johns (five days, four nights) via Hluleka and Silaka Nature Reserves; prices are typically about R250 per person, per day (including river crossings) plus accommodation and food. Nights on the hikes are generally spent in comfortable community-run hikers' huts and Xhosa *rondavels* in the villages en route (typically R250 including dinner and breakfast). Book guides through local backpackers or Wild Coast Hikes (p213).

Adventurous sorts can jump into the ocean from the rocks above the Mapuzi Caves, around 7km north of Coffee Bay, and

WILD COAST STAYS: KEI MOUTH TO DWESA NATURE RESERVE

There are a few accommodation options strung along the coast between Kei Mouth and Dwesa, catering to South African families and anglers, and offering numerous activities, home-style hotel meals, and weekend braais and seafood feasts. Prices skyrocket around Christmas and Easter, when you will be lucky to find a room, while the hotels are often pleasingly quiet out of season (especially during the week), when specials are offered.

Locals take shared taxis to get around the area, but the best way to explore is with your own vehicle. Hotels can organise transfers if requested in advance. Reaching most of the hotels involves a significant drive on gravel roads, but they should be accessible in a hire car.

Wavecrest Beach Hotel & Spa (☑ 047-498 0022; www.wavecrest.co.za; s/d incl full board & activities R905/1390; P ☎ ≋) This smart hotel overlooks an amazing coastal ecosystem, in which two rivers share a mouth and dune forest meets the world's southernmost mangroves. Dolphins and whales can be spotted from the wooden deck, while birders and anglers will also be happy. Accommodation is in comfortable *rondavels* and the many activities include lagoon cruises and canoeing, hiking and cultural visits.

Kob Inn (☑ 047-499 0011; www.kobinn.co.za; Qhorha Mouth; per person with full board from R830; P ☎ ≋) At the Qhorha River mouth, this family-focused resort offers accommodation in thatched units. There are activities to keep everyone busy, including fishing, mountain biking, hiking, horse riding and tennis, and babysitters are also available.

Trennerys Hotel (☑ 047-498 0095; www.trennerys.co.za; Qolora Mouth; s/d with half board R690/1380, camping R80; P ☎ ≋) Trennerys has large thatched bungalows with private, sea-facing balconies, and a poolside bar-restaurant (mains R60). It's all a bit run-down but still comfortable. Numerous activities are offered, including canoeing on the lagoon, sundowner cruises, hiking trails and fishing. It's a 16km drive from the Kei Mouth after taking the pontoon ferry crossing.

the grass-covered **cliffs** there are an ideal sundowner spot. Guides will take you there for about R80 per person, including transport back. If you go without a guide, find out when high tide is to avoid getting trapped.

🛏 Sleeping

★**Bulungula Lodge** BACKPACKERS $
(☑ 047-577 8900; www.bulungula.com; Bulungula; camping/dm R85/160, r/tr without bathroom R395/515; P @) ✦ Bulungula has legendary status on the Wild Coast for its stunning location, community-based activities and ecofriendly ethos. It's 100% owned by the local Xhosa community (founder Dave Martin donated his share in 2015), which runs tours including horse riding, hiking, canoeing, starwatching, cultural visits and pancakes at sunrise on the beach. Creatively painted, Xhosa-style *rondavels* serve as quarters.

Beats liven up the shipping container–like reception and lounge, but tranquillity is as close as the bonfire; the overall vibe will make you want to linger indefinitely. Ablution blocks include ecofriendly composting loos and paraffin-rocket showers. All meals

are offered; self-caterers should bring their own supplies because there isn't much available nearby.

Bulungula is around two hours' drive from Coffee Bay, via a gravel road; it's doable with a 2WD. If you're driving, visit Bulungula's website, phone or ask in Coffee Bay backpackers for a map. Shuttles run from Coffee Bay (R60) and Mthatha (R90), and should be booked in advance. It's also possible to get here by shared taxi.

★**Mdumbi Backpackers** BACKPACKERS $
(☑ 083 461 1834; www.mdumbi.co.za; Mdumbi; camping/dm R70/140, r without bathroom R300; P) ✦ Marvellous Mdumbi, a 23km drive north of Coffee Bay (the gravel road is normally passable in a 2WD car), is a rural retreat set in rolling hills above a wide white-sand beach. A collection of simply furnished *rondavels* shares the grounds with a kindergarten, former chapel and cafe.

There are lots of water-based activities (the surf can be phenomenal) and outdoorsy fun, plus numerous opportunities to meet the local Xhosa people in a genuine setting.

Volunteers looking to stay longer can also get involved in various community projects undertaken by Mdumbi's affiliated nonprofit organisation, **Transcape** (www.transcape.org). Book a day ahead for the shuttle here from Coffee Bay (R50). Otherwise, you can catch shared taxis from Mthatha (R60), but you have to change in Ngqeleni and the journey can take all day.

Wild Lubanzi BACKPACKERS **$**
(078 530 8997; www.lubanzi.co.za; Lubanzi; dm/r from R120/390, r without bathroom R320; P) Partly owned by the local community, Wild Lubanzi focuses on sustainable living and sociable evenings at the long dinner table in its cosy lounge. Accommodation includes two en-suite dorms, one with a loft reached by driftwood stairs, plus an enchanting room fit for a Hobbit, and another with an elevated shower open to the elements.

The rooftop deck overlooks a wild and woolly stretch of coastline, where surfing, chilling and hiking opportunities abound (Hole in the Wall is 1½ hours away, Bulungula five hours). If you don't fancy inflicting the bumpy gravel road on your car, a shuttle is available from the end of the tar road (R20 per person, plus R15 per night for secure parking).

Hole in the Wall Hotel HOTEL, BACKPACKERS **$$**
(0871 506 095; www.holeinthewall.co.za; Hole in the Wall; camping/dm R60/100, r R250-640; P) The fenced-in Hole in the Wall Hotel has plain, slightly tired self-catering chalets and cottages. The en-suite backpacker rooms and dorm are good value, giving you access to the hotel's facilities, which include a volleyball court, a spa and two bars (pool and sports).

The restaurant is distinctly average, but the food will taste good anyway after walking from Coffee Bay or Wild Lubanzi.

Qunu

Nelson Mandela Museum MUSEUM, MEMORIAL
(047-538 0217; www.mandelamuseum.org.za; entry by donation; 9am-4pm) The roadside village of Qunu is the home town of one Nelson Rolihlahla Mandela, who grew up here in the 1920s. The area has yet to fully capitalise on its famous son, but the Nelson Mandela Museum is worth a stop to get a sense of the great man's early life. The museum's two halls have information panels covering his childhood and later achievements. Also here are the remains of the primary school where a teacher gave the future president his Christian name.

Guides offer free tours; a highlight of the visit is when they point out spots in the undulating veld where, almost a century ago, the young Mandela herded cattle and swam in the river. You can also see his distant burial ground and his birthplace in the nearby village of Mvezo; in coming years these will hopefully open to the public, along with a museum in Mthatha's Bhunga Building. Phone the Nelson Mandela Museum in advance to organise a guided tour of the area.

The complex has worn but comfortable rooms (per person R137.50) with TV and a self-catering kitchen.

The museum is signposted on the N2 about 30km from Mthatha (and 500m across the village from there). Shared taxis running along the N2 can drop you at the turn-off for the museum.

Mthatha

POP 96,114

Busy and bustling and clogged with traffic, Mthatha (formerly Umtata) is chaotic, noisy, dusty and growing. There are some elegant, historic buildings in among the modern blocks. *Muti* (traditional medicine) sellers trade outside Western doctors' rooms, and rural people mingle with urban dwellers in this cultural melting pot.

The town was originally founded in 1882, when Europeans settled on the Mthatha River at the request of the Thembu tribe, to act as a buffer against Pondo raiders. During the apartheid era it became the capital of the Transkei, the largest of the black homelands, and it remains a regional centre.

Most travellers will pass through or stop here briefly, either en route along the N2 highway or while transferring to a shuttle to Coffee Bay or Port St Johns. The town also makes a convenient stop-off and base for visiting the Nelson Mandela Museum in nearby Qunu.

Sleeping & Eating

Most accommodation is aimed at visiting businesspeople and there's little reason to spend the night. The **Savoy Centre** mall and **Shell Ultra City** garage, both on the N2 on the Qunu side of town, have chain restaurants and shops.

Mthatha Backpackers
BACKPACKERS $

(☑ 047-531 3654; www.mthathabackpackers.co.za; 12 Aloe St, off Sisson Rd; dm/r R150/350; P 🛜 🖭) This suburban compound has rooms and small dorms in the house, plus wooden cabins. Owner Angus is full of local recommendations and can help with booking bus tickets, catching shared taxis and so on. He offers free pick-ups from Shell Ultra City, transfers to Coffee Bay, and day trips to spots such as waterfalls and Qunu.

Ebony Lodge
GUESTHOUSE $$

(☑ 047-531 3933; ebonylodge@telkomsa.net; 22 Park Rd; s/d incl breakfast R700/775; P 🛜 🖭) This early 20th-century mansion in a leafy garden has stylish rooms with African decor. The **restaurant** (mains R100; ⊙ 7am-9.30pm Mon-Fri, to 9.30am Sat & Sun) is one of Mthatha's best, serving cottage pie, Thai seafood pot and the usual steaks, salads and wraps to young black professionals.

La Piazza
INTERNATIONAL $$

(Delville Rd; mains R95; ⊙ 10am-10pm Mon-Fri, noon-10pm Sat) In a thatched *lapa* (semi-open entertainment area) with views across the golf course and town, Mthatha Country Club's restaurant serves a varied menu featuring pizzas, pasta, seafood and daily specials.

ⓘ Information

The Savoy Centre and Shell Ultra City have ATMs and shops. Take care in the latter, as there have been cases of ATM scams there.

ⓘ Getting There & Away

The N2 and Rte 61 (for Port St Johns) cross in the town centre. The intersection can be a gridlocked mess, so try to avoid weekday rush hours.

AIR

Mthatha Airport is 17km north of the centre on Rte 61. **Airlink** (☑ 047-536 0024; www.flyairlink.com) has daily flights to/from Jo'burg (from R2000).

BUS

Baz Bus stops at Shell Ultra City, 4km south of town, en route between Port Elizabeth and Durban.

Greyhound, Translux, Intercape and City to City stop at Shell Ultra City on their daily runs between Cape Town (R560, 20 hours) and Durban (R300, six hours).

CAR

The major car-rental companies have desks at the airport.

SHARED TAXI

Shared taxis in Mthatha depart from both Shell Ultra City and the main bus stop and taxi rank near Bridge St. Destinations include Port St Johns (R60; get out at Thombo for a shared taxi to the Kraal backpackers), Coffee Bay (R60) and East London (R110).

Mthatha to Port St Johns

The road between Mthatha and Port St Johns provides access to a great section of coast, including the **Hluleka Nature Reserve** (☑ bookings 043-705 4400; www.visiteasterncape.co.za; adult/child R20/10; ⊙ 8am-5pm), which conserves a spectacular coastline of rocky seashores, pristine beaches and lagoons, as well as indigenous forests and rolling grasslands. Wildlife includes zebras, several antelope species and abundant bird life.

A 47km gravel road leads to the reserve from near Libode on Rte 61. You need a high-clearance vehicle to get there.

🛏 Sleeping

Within Hluleka Nature Reserve there are seven beautiful two-bedroom, self-catering chalets (from R500) which overlook the ocean and a small secluded cove with a sandy beach.

Kraal
BACKPACKERS $

(☑ 082 871 4964; www.thekraal.co.za; Mpande; camping/dm R100/130, r without bathroom R350; P) 🌿 Power down and disconnect at this ecologically minded coastal retreat, which offers accommodation in traditionally designed *rondavels* illuminated by candlelight. A rustically cosy lounge, dining area and fully stocked kitchen open onto a back porch where the ocean view is framed by a V in the hillside.

Hiking, surfing, dolphin- and whale-watching are possibilities, as are visiting the preschool or lunching with a Xhosa family. Meals are available in the nearby village restaurant, but it's best to bring supplies. The turnoff to the Kraal is about 80km from Mthatha and 20km from Port St Johns. It is another 20km (around a 50-minute drive) on a rough road; do not attempt after rains in anything other than a 4WD vehicle.

★Umngazi River Bungalows & Spa
RESORT $$$

(☑ 047-564 1115; www.umngazi.co.za; Umngazi; s/d with full board from R1246/1780; P 🛜 🖭) Overlooking a large estuary and a deserted beach, this popular resort at the mouth of the Umngazi River is good for honeymooners and families. Activities, many provided by the local community, include canoeing, fishing, mountain biking, horse riding and sunset cruises; there's also a babysitting service and kids' club for when you want to hit the spa.

To get here in your own car from Port St Johns, take Rte 61 towards Mthatha for 14km to the signposted turn-off on your left, from where it is another 11km.

Port St Johns

POP 6441

Dramatically located at the mouth of the Mzimvubu (or Umzimvubu) River and framed by towering cliffs covered with tropical vegetation, the laid-back town of Port St Johns is the original Wild Coast journey's end. These days, there's something of a rundown quality to the town, which is the largest between East London and Port Edward. It feels less out of the ordinary than more-remotely situated spots elsewhere in the area, although Second Beach retains its escapist appeal.

Bull Zambezi sharks calve upriver and there have been several fatal attacks in recent years. Until shark nets are installed, it's recommended that you do nothing more than wade off the town's beaches.

Sights & Activities

Walk to the **Gap blowhole**, between First and Second Beach, at high tide. Several steep pathways from near Second Beach lead uphill to **Bulolo Waterfall**; there's a small pool at the bottom.

Second Beach BEACH

Second Beach is Port St Johns's heart and soul. Locals come to this idyllic stretch of sand to while away the hot days and party as the sun goes down. Wandering down to the shallows for a paddle and spotting Nguni cows lounging on the sand are classic Port St Johns experiences.

Mt Thesiger VIEWPOINT

Just north of the town centre on the banks of the Mzimvubu River, a sealed road (Concrete Rd) climbs to this favourite sunset spot – a flat-topped hill with a disused airstrip and one of the more spectacular views on the Wild Coast.

Museum MUSEUM

(Main St; 8am-4.30pm Mon-Fri) FREE A funky building with exhibits chronicling local history, including stories of close to a dozen nearby shipwrecks (the earliest is from 1847).

Silaka Nature Reserve NATURE RESERVE

(047-564 1177; www.visiteasterncape.co.za; adult/child R20/10; 6am-6pm) This small reserve, 6km south of Port St Johns, runs from Second Beach past Third Beach to Sugarloaf Rock, near the estuary where the Gxwaleni River flows into the sea and aloes grow down almost to the water. Clawless otters are often seen on the beach, white-breasted cormorants clamber up onto Bird Island, and you might spot zebras, blesboks and vervet monkeys.

The overgrown 2km pathway (wear long pants) from Second Beach to Third Beach, which is cleaner, quieter and normally untroubled by sharks, leaves from near Lodge on the Beach. Alternatively, follow the hilly road. Well-equipped, self-catering double and quadruple **chalets** (from R419) have stoeps and braais overlooking Third Beach.

Offshore Africa Port St Johns DIVING, BOAT TOUR

(084 951 1325; www.offshoreportstjohns.com; 1565 Ferry Point Rd) Diving trips, and dolphin- and whale-watching. The best of time of year to hit the water is during the sardine run (June to August).

Wild Coast Hikes HIKING

(082 507 2256; www.wildcoasthikes.com; per person per day R190) Jimmy and Mbuyi lead hikes from Port St John to destinations ranging from Silaka (five hours) to Coffee Bay (five days), with accommodation in Xhosa villages on the overnight trails. Accommodation is an extra R250 per person per night.

Sleeping

Amapondo Backpackers BACKPACKERS $

(047-564 1344; www.amapondo.co.za; Second Beach Rd; dm from R110, s/d without bathroom from R250/300; P) A mellow place where several low-slung buildings line a hillside with excellent views of Second Beach. A rambling network of stoeps, leafy walkways and chill spaces leads to the simple rooms, while smarter cottages stand on the hill above. An excellent range of activities is offered, include horse riding, cultural tours, canoeing,

Port St Johns

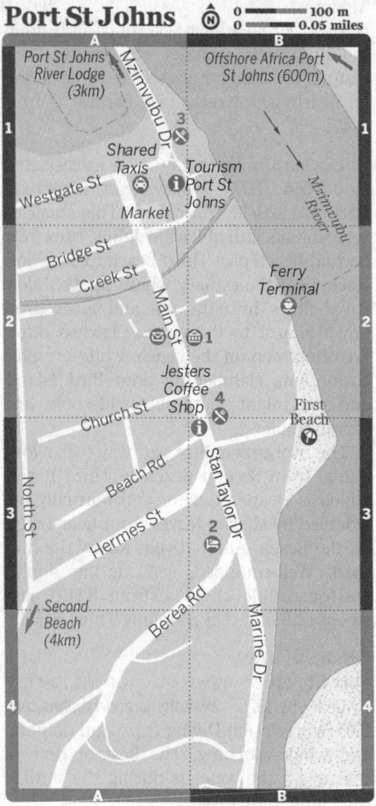

Port St Johns

Sights
1 Museum B2

Sleeping
2 Jungle Monkey B3

Eating
3 Fish Eagle Restaurant A1
4 Steve's Pub & Restaurant B2

hiking to Silaka and sundowners at the airstrip.

The bar-restaurant, where driftwood hangs from the beams, gets lively with a mix of locals and travellers.

Lodge on the Beach LODGE $
(083 374 9669; www.lodgeonthebeach.co.za; Second Beach; r R490; P @) Perched on a slight rise with unobstructed views of Second Beach, this well-kept thatch-roofed retreat has three rooms, each with its own small deck and an individual bathroom in the hallway. Breakfast and dinner can be provided.

Delicious Monster COTTAGE $
(083 997 9856; www.deliciousmonsterpsj.co.za; Second Beach; s/d/tr/q from R350/500/600/700; P) Just steps from the restaurant of the same name you'll find this airy loft-style cottage with ocean views from its front porch. With a well-equipped kitchen and cosy lounge, the three-bedroomed house can be hired for R1400.

Jungle Monkey BACKPACKERS $
(047-564 1517; www.junglemonkey.co.za; 3 Berea Rd; camping/dm R80/120, r without bathroom R350; P @) Music booms through the trees as you approach this casual hang-out, with its desert-island bar-restaurant overlooking the pool. Rooms are reasonably comfortable and distant from any party noise, while dorms are more basic. Hiking, activities and day trips are on offer. Jungle Monkey is located between town and Second Beach.

Port St Johns River Lodge LODGE $$
(047-564 0005; www.portstjohnsriverlodge.co.za; Mzimvubu Dr; s/d R485/880; P) One of a few riverside lodges north of town, this well-run complex has comfortable rooms, and a restaurant (mains R85) gazing across a lawn at the river cliffs.

Eating & Drinking

Outside the large grocery stores on Main St is a small street market where you might be able to buy fresh seafood – mussels, crayfish and fish – to cook your own meal.

Delicious Monster INTERNATIONAL, SEAFOOD $
(Second Beach; mains R70; 9am-3pm & 6-9pm Mon-Sat;) This restaurant has a fabulous view of Second Beach and the sea, and an eclectic menu that includes a recommended meze platter, *shwarma,* line fish and steaks.

Fish Eagle Restaurant INTERNATIONAL $
(cnr Mzimvubu Dr & Westgate St; mains R65) Grab a table on the rear deck with views of the river and Mt Sullivan, then choose from a large selection of chicken dishes, burgers, wood-fired pizzas and seafood.

Steve's Pub & Restaurant SOUTH AFRICAN $$
(Main Rd; lunch/dinner mains R55/90) An inviting spot with a covered stoep and cosy bar,

Steve's does a mix of pub grub and South African specialities, including bunny chow (hollowed-out bread filled with curry), wood-fired pizzas and steaks.

Information

There are ATMs in town.

Jesters Coffee Shop (Main St) This cafe is a better source of information than the tourist office, which is rarely staffed.

Getting There & Away

The R61 from Mthatha to Port St Johns is sealed, but it involves switchbacks and sharp curves. Amapondo and Jungle Monkey will pick you up from the Shell Ultra City, 4km south of Mthatha (where Baz Bus stops) for around R95, but it's essential to book ahead (and turn up when you've booked).

There are regular shared taxis to Port St Johns from Mthatha (R40, two hours) and Durban (R170, five hours).

Pondoland

On the 100km stretch of coast between Port St Johns and the Mthamvuna River lies some of the most biologically rich landscape of the whole region. Currently unspoiled, there are velvety hills dotted with brightly painted houses, serene tea plantations and waterfalls galore. With proposals such as the Xolobeni mine and N2 toll highway threatening the area's environment and communities, tourism is the key to insuring Pondoland's economic future, while maintaining its unspoilt state. Check out www.wildcoast.co.za for up-to-date information on environmental issues and tourism.

Mbotyi

You'll soon realise that the journey to Mbotyi (Place of Beans) is worth the effort when the road drops down through indigenous subtropical forest to a pristine river mouth and beach.

Mbotyi is roughly two hours' drive from Port St Johns. Just before Lusikisiki, 45km north of Port St Johns on Rte 61, turn right at the Mbotyi River Lodge sign; if you reach the Total garage, you've gone too far. Concrete and gravel roads (passable in a 2WD car) now lead 25km through the Magwa Tea plantations to Mbotyi. Shared taxis travel to/from Lusikisiki (with connections to Port St Johns and elsewhere).

Sleeping

Dingezwene Backpackers Village BACKPACKERS $
(☎071 253 4469; dm/s/d R100/150/300, dinner R75; P) This family compound, on a windswept stretch of coast with a small beach and cows dotting the grassy slopes, has *rondavels*, cabins, a well-equipped kitchen and a thatched dining room. The welcoming Xhosa family can organise horse riding and village visits.

Mbotyi Campsite CAMPGROUND $
(☎039-253 7200; www.mbotyi.co.za; camping R95, r without bathroom R375; P) Mbotyi Campsite, a joint venture between the neighbouring Mbotyi River Lodge and the local community, is the place for total relaxation and long walks on the beach. You'll need to be self-sufficient with food.

Mbotyi River Lodge RESORT $$
(☎039-253 7200; www.mbotyi.co.za; s/d with half board from R875/1250; P ❄ 🏊) Mbotyi River Lodge, an upmarket resort at the river mouth, has *rondavels* and more luxurious log cabins overlooking the beach and lagoon. Numerous activities can be arranged, including horse riding, hiking trails, canoeing and visits to the area's many waterfalls. The lodge is involved in local community projects.

Mkambati Nature Reserve

Breathtaking **Mkambati Nature Reserve** (☎bookings 043-705 4400; www.visiteasterncape.co.za; adult/child R20/10; ⏲6am-6pm) covers 77 sq km with some spectacular waterfalls, the deep Msikaba and Mtentu River gorges, rock pools, swamp forests and several hundred thousand square metres of grassland, where antelope species including red hartebeests and blue wildebeest graze. The magnificent coastal scenery is a haven for birds, including trumpeter hornbills and African fish eagles, while dolphins and whales can be seen.

Activities include canoe and walking trails, and self-drive wildlife viewing.

From Flagstaff on Rte 61, a tar road leads 32km east past Holy Cross Mission. From the end of the tar, a gravel road runs 40km to the reserve, requiring a 4WD or *bakkie* (pick-up truck).

🛏 Sleeping

There are twin self-catering *rondavels* (R360) near the Gwe Gwe River Mouth.

Mtentu Lodge BACKPACKERS $
(☑083 805 3356; www.mtentulodge.co.za; dm/r R150/700) On the isolated northern bank of the beautiful Mtentu Estuary, just across from Mkambati, is Mtentu Lodge. Six comfortable wood cabins with ocean views are linked by a boardwalk running through the naturally landscaped property. Toilets are communal and there's a choice of gas or solar powered showers. Three meals a day can be provided for R250 per person.

A range of activities are on tap, including hiking, horse riding, canoeing and experiencing a traditional healing ceremony – as is good ol' fashioned chilling out on the surrounding beaches. In dry weather, Mtentu can be reached in a 2WD car with high clearance, and there are other options including shuttles, guided shared taxi rides and guided hikes. In all cases, contact the lodge in advance to arrange your visit. By public transport, the closest Baz Bus stops are Kokstad and Port Shepstone, from where you will have to catch a shared taxi to Bizana. From there, a daily service leaves around 1pm for Mtentu.

NORTHEASTERN HIGHLANDS

The Northeastern Highlands, climbing up from the lush valleys of the Wild Coast to the south and bordered by the sharply ascending peaks of Lesotho to the north, has some of South Africa's most beautiful mountain scenery. There are tranquil towns little visited by tourists; rushing streams and rivers where trout and other fish abound; day hikes through bucolic landscapes; and even snow-covered mountain passes north of Rhodes in the winter.

It's worth approaching this region as a scenic road trip because, while the towns are appealing stop offs, you will likely find the journey more satisfying. Drive cautiously, as weather and road conditions can be harsh.

If you have covered the Wild Coast and you have a little time, Rte 56 makes a scenic alternative to the N2 for crossing the province. It runs east from Middelburg in the Karoo to Kokstad in KwaZulu-Natal, and is particularly scenic in the Highlands between Elliot and Maclear. A dramatic route linking the area with the Wild Coast is the Langeni Pass (1505m), one of South Africa's newest passes, which climbs 720m from Mthatha to Ugie.

Queenstown

POP 43,971

Queenstown is a rather nondescript bustling and dusty commercial centre. It was laid out in the shape of a hexagon for defence purposes when it was established in 1847; this pattern enabled defenders to shoot down the streets from a central point.

The town is a transport hub so you may pass through. If you get caught overnight, accommodation and meals are available at the comfortable and welcoming **Meerlin Guesthouse** (☑045-838 3125; meerlin@telkomsa.net; 4 Frost St; s/d incl breakfast R550/750, dinner R150; P⊛) and the altogether glitzier **Queens Casino Hotel** (☑045-807 9700; www.queenscasino.co.za; Cathcart Rd; s/d incl breakfast R1295/1620; P⊛⊛⊛).

Greyhound, Translux, Intercape and City to City have daily services to destinations including Cape Town (R500, 12 to 17 hours) via Graaff-Reinet or the Garden Route; Port Elizabeth (R320, 5½ hours) via Grahamstown, East London (R280, 3¼ hours), and Jo'burg (R410, 10 hours) via Bloemfontein. City to City also serves Mthatha (R160, 3½ hours), stopping at the Shell Ultra City or Sasol garage.

A seats-only economy **Shosholoza Meyl** train runs from Cape Town on Thursday (R300, 24 hours), returning on Friday. The train (p200) linking Jo'burg and East London via Bloemfontein also stops here.

Lady Grey

POP 1395

Backed by the imposingly steep and sun-baked cliffs of the Witteberge mountain range, Lady Grey is a sleepy agricultural community at the foot of Joubert's Pass (2236m). Accommodation is stretched to capacity at Easter, when the town's arts academy and Dutch Reformed Church stage a three-day **Passion Play**.

Delightful guesthouse **Comfrey Cottage** (☑051-603 0407; www.comfreycottage.co.za; 51-59 Stephenson St; s/d R550/900; ⊛) has four upmarket cottages with alpacas grazing the lawns of its beautiful garden. One cottage is self-catering and a half-board option is available. Geological and botanical tours can be arranged, as well as visits to the nearby Cape vulture restaurant, where the eponymous birds are fed.

If you have a 4WD, there are a few remote and beautiful lodges on the mountainous gravel roads leading off the main route from Lady Grey to Rhodes. For an accessible and affordable blast of country air, **Karnmelkspruit River Resort** (☎051-603 7036; krr@gmail.com; off Rte 58; camping R110, cottages R200; P) is located on a farm 20km towards Barkly East, with a Cape vulture breeding colony and 10km of fishing in its gorge.

The **tourist office** (www.ladygreytourism.co.za; cnr Joubert & Murray Sts) has an accommodation list plus brochures and a guide to fly-fishing in the Highlands.

Shared taxis pass on Rte 58 between Aliwal North and Barkly East.

Rhodes

POP 73

Deep in the southern Drakensberg, in a spectacular valley setting alongside the Bell River, the little village of Rhodes is a bucolic escape. The architecture remains as it was when the town was established in 1891 as a base for agriculture and commerce. In this mountain outpost, all four seasons can be experienced in a single day, and extremes are not uncommon – temperatures have reached -15°C in winter and 35°C in summer.

Trout fishing is extremely popular throughout the whole district; the **Wild Trout Association** (☎045-974 9290; www.wildtrout.co.za) is based at Walkerbouts Inn.

Sleeping

Walkerbouts Inn INN $$
(☎045-974 9290; www.walkerbouts.co.za; s/d with half board R735/1270) Oozing character, Walkerbouts has polished wood floors and cosy rooms with all-important panel heaters and electric blankets. The dining room serves wholesome country fare, while the beckoning pub does build-your-own pizzas. The lovely garden has magnificent views, and genial host Dave 'Walkabout' Walker knows just about everything there is to know about Rhodes and fly-fishing.

Tenahead Mountain Lodge LODGE $$$
(☎0861 748 374; www.riverhotels.co.za/en; Naudesnek Pass; s/d incl breakfast R1520/1880; P) This spectacular five-star lodge, perched at 2500m and surrounded by the Drakensberg, Witteberg and Maluti ranges, has seven luxurious rooms with fireplaces. Wooden decks make the most of the view and, if bad weather closes in, the library has 2000 books.

Self-Catering Cottages

There are several self-catering **cottages** in the village and surrounding farms; rates start at R390 for single or dual occupancy. You can book cottages online at www.highlandsinfo.co.za, www.rhodesvillage.co.za, and www.linecasters.co.za, or ☎045-974 9290. Book early for high season (there are three brief high seasons: 1 December to 15 January, 15 March to 30 April, and 25 May to 31 August) and bring warm clothes and blankets in winter; heating in some cottages is minimal and one lacks electricity.

Getting There & Away

Fuel is sometimes available here, but it's not unusual for the supply to run out, so fill up before driving to Rhodes. The gravel road from Barkly East (60km, 1½ hours) is fine for 2WD cars. The road on to Maclear (110km, three hours) cuts through the imposing Naudesnek Pass (2587m), the country's highest, and is best undertaken in a 4WD vehicle. Cars with good clearance can manage if it hasn't rained recently, but check locally for the latest road and weather conditions. There is no public transport here.

EASTERN KAROO

The Karoo is the vast and beautiful semi-desert stretching across the great South African plateau inland from the Cape coast; its southeastern section covers a chunk of the Eastern Cape. The dry region, with its variety of grasses, hardy shrubs, *tolbos* (tumbleweed in Afrikaans) and succulents, including the trademark red aloe, is a surprisingly rich cultural and historic destination. Graaff-Reinet, the architectural 'jewel of the Karoo', is complemented by artistic Nieu Bethesda and literary Cradock, while Camdeboo and Mountain Zebra National Parks offer stunning scenery and rare Cape mountain zebras. Throughout, the overwhelming sense of space, peace and freedom stand in sharp contrast to the busier coastline – and make the region pefect road-trip territory.

Between December and February temperatures in Karoo towns can reach 45°C, and things barely cool down in March and April. June and July see the thermometer plummet to -5°C, with snow in the mountain passes and frosts.

Graaff-Reinet

POP 26,585

Cradled in a curve of the Sundays River and encircled by the Camdeboo National Park, Graaff-Reinet is often referred to as the 'jewel of the Karoo'. South Africa's fourth-oldest town, the 'far-off colony of Graaff-Reinet', as the Dutch East India Company called the remote spot when they established it in 1786, has a superb architectural heritage. More than 220 buildings designated as national monuments include gabled Cape Dutch houses, flat-roofed Karoo cottages and ornate Victorian villas. Add in small-town charm, some excellent accommodation and restaurants, plus a handful of museums, and you'll begin to understand why Graaff-Reinet aquired its nickname.

History

In the 18th century, the interior of the Cape was wild and dangerous, with Boers clashing with the Khoe-San in the Sneeuberg Range, and the Xhosa to the east around the Great Fish River. Graaff-Reinet was named after former Cape governor Van der Graaff and his wife (whose maiden name was Reinet), and became an outpost in the harsh countryside. It was the fourth district in the Cape Colony to be granted a *drostdy* – the residence of a *landdrost* (local official) and seat of local government. This resulted from British attempts to establish law and order; they failed, and the town's citizens threw out the *landdrost* and established an independent republic. The British regained a semblance of control soon afterwards, but were constantly harried by both disgruntled Boers and a joint force of Khoe-San and Xhosa warriors.

In the mid-19th century, Graaff-Reinet became an important staging post for Voortrekkers heading north and escaping the control of the Cape Town administration.

Sights

You can buy a combined **pass** (☎049-892 3801; www.graaffreinetmuseums.co.za; adult 2/3/4/5 museums R30/45/60/75, child 2/3/4/5 museums R15/20/30/40) that gives access to any of the town's museums, apart from the Hester Rupert Art Museum.

Hester Rupert Art Museum MUSEUM
(☎049-807 5700; www.rupertartmuseum.co.za; Church St; adult/family R10/20; ⏲9am-12.30pm & 2-5pm Mon-Fri, to noon Sat & Sun) Located in one of South Africa's oldest churches, a Dutch Reformed Mission church consecrated in 1821, this collection of South African paintings (and a few sculptures) from the 1950s and '60s includes the likes of Irma Stern.

Old Library MUSEUM
(cnr Church & Somerset Sts; adult/child R20/10; ⏲8am-1pm & 1.45-4pm Mon-Fri, 9am-1pm Sat & Sun) This former library, built in 1847, houses a wide-ranging collection of historical artefacts. There's fossils from the Karoo, displays on Khoe-San rock paintings and slavery, and an exhibition about local son Robert Sobukwe, founder of the Pan African Congress (PAC).

Drostdy HISTORIC BUILDING
(Church St) A *drostdy* was the *landdrost's* (local administrator's) residence and included his office and courtroom as well as his family's living quarters. The Graaff-Reinet *drostdy,* built in 1806, is now a hotel, but you can still see the freed slaves' cottages on Stretcher's Court at the rear. The old slave bell was restored and then, in an awful piece of irony, unveiled by apartheid-era prime minister BJ Vorster.

Reinet House MUSEUM
(Murray St; adult/child R20/10; ⏲8am-4pm Mon-Fri, 9am-1pm Sat & Sun) This Dutch Reformed parsonage, built between 1806 and 1812, is a beautiful example of Cape Dutch architecture. The cobblestoned rear courtyard has a grapevine that was planted in 1870 and is one of the largest in the world.

Museum Houses
The wonderfully preserved Cape Dutch **Old Residency** (Parsonage St; adult/child R20/10; ⏲8am-1pm & 1.45-4pm Mon-Fri, 9am-noon Sat & Sun) and **Urquhart House** (Somerset St; adult/child R20/10; ⏲8am-1pm & 1.45-4pm Mon-Fri) show how well-to-do 19th-century families lived with their creaking wooden floors and period furniture. The **Military History Museum** (Somerset St; adult/child R20/10; ⏲8am-1pm & 1.45-4pm Mon-Fri) is accessed through the latter.

Tours

Camdeboo Adventure Tours ADVENTURE TOUR
(☎049-892 3410; www.karoopark.co.za; 81 Caledon St) Buks and Chantelle Marais of Camdeboo Cottages and Karoopark Guest House organise Camdeboo National Park tours, guided walks and wildlife-viewing drives. They also do trips further afield to Mountain Zebra National Park and Baviaanskloof Wilderness Area.

Graaff-Reinet

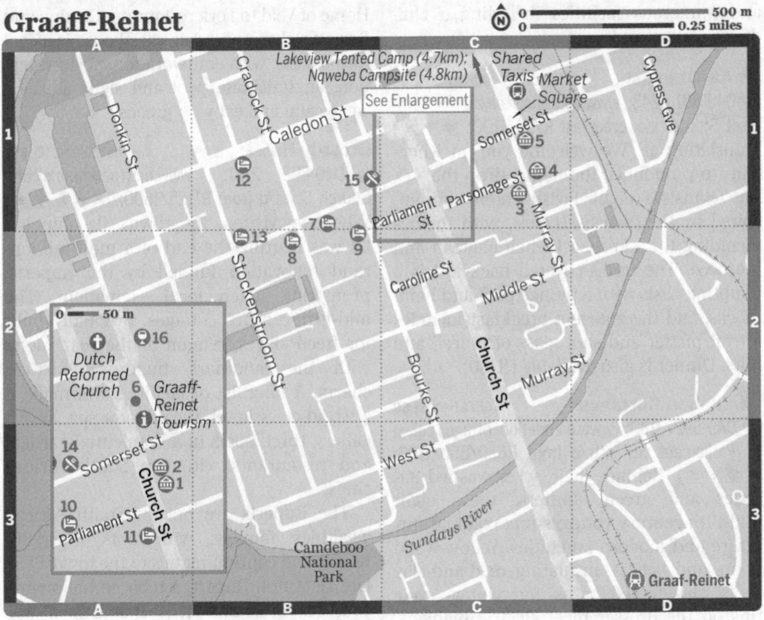

Graaff-Reinet

Sights
Drostdy (see 11)
1 Hester Rupert Art Museum A3
Military History Museum (see 5)
2 Old Library A3
3 Old Residency C1
4 Reinet House C1
5 Urquhart House C1

Activities, Courses & Tours
Camdeboo Adventure Tours (see 12)
6 Karoo Connections A2

Sleeping
7 Aa 'Qtansisi B1
8 Andries Stockenström Guesthouse B2
9 Buiten Verwagten B2
10 Camdeboo Cottages A3
11 Drostdy Hotel A3
12 Karoopark Guest House B1
13 Profcon Resort B2

Eating
14 Our Yard A3
15 Polka Cafe B1
Veld to Fork (see 8)

Drinking & Nightlife
16 Graaff-Reinet Club A2

Shopping
African Adventure (see 1)

Karoo Connections TOUR
(☎049-892 3978; www.karooconnections.co.za; 7 Church St) Based at McNaughton's Bookshop, David McNaughton organises a range of tours and transfers, including a sundowner tour of the Valley of Desolation by open Land Rover (R440 per person), a half-day trip to Nieu Bethesda (R660; full day including Bushman rock art and fossils R990), and wildlife-watching drives to Camdeboo (R400) and Mountain Zebra National Parks.

Ingomso Tours CULTURAL TOUR
(☎083 559 1207; 3hr tour R330) Ntombi Mashoeng's tours of Umasizakhe, one of the country's oldest townships and the birthplace of Robert Sobukwe, provide insight into Xhosa culture and history, and modern township life.

Sleeping

Profcon Resort COTTAGES, CAMPGROUND $
(☎049-892 2887; www.profconresort.co.za; 82 Somerset St; camping/s/d R150/400/550, cottages from R850; P❄📶🏊👪) A well-run complex with modern rooms, garden cottages

and numerous facilities including a children's playground.

★ Aa 'Qtansisi
GUESTHOUSE $$

(☑049-891 0243; www.aaqtansisi.co.za; 69 Somerset St; s/d incl breakfast R750/1100; ✳ ⧦ ⊠)
Translating as 'We welcome you' in Khoe-San (to pronounce the name, drop the 'Q'), Aa 'Qtansisi's eight lavish rooms are inspired by the owner's travels, with themes including the Karoo, a French chateau and Morocco. The trellis-covered backyard is a tempting oasis with a plunge pool and hammocks, and the gourmet breakfast includes a fruit platter and shot glass of muesli and nuts. Dinner is also available (R150).

Camdeboo Cottages
GUESTHOUSE $$

(☑049-892 3180; www.camdeboocottages.co.za; 16 Parliament St; r/tr/q from R650/850/1100; P ✳ ⧦ ⊠) Behind their whitewashed facades and green shutters, these eight mid-19th-century cottages mix colonial furniture and modern amenities. Yellow-wood floors and beams, insulating reed-and-clay roofs, claw-footed baths and vintage cake tins on the dresser meet electric blankets, radiators and DSTV.

The one- to three-bedroom cottages have kitchens. There's also a restaurant and poolside braai area, where owner Buks leads stargazing sessions.

Karoopark Guest House
GUESTHOUSE $$

(☑049-892 2557; www.karoopark.co.za; 81 Caledon St; s/tw/d from R600/650/700; P ✳ @ ⧦ ⊠)
This family-owned and -run complex is a good base, with a restaurant serving South African specialities (mains R90), a bar and a tour company, all in a garden environment. Various accommodation options, including rooms and self-catering units, occupy the historic main house and blocks in the leafy grounds.

Buiten Verwagten
GUESTHOUSE $$

(☑049-892 4504; www.buitenverwagten.co.za; 58 Bourke St; s/d incl breakfast from R750/1000; ✳ ⧦ ⊠) Every aspect of this Victorian-era home is tastefully curated by its friendly and professional owners. Inside are high ceilings, cedar and pine floors, and elegant antiques; outside are a trellis-covered stoep, a perfectly manicured lawn and a courtyard pool. There are two self-catering rooms at the back.

Andries Stockenström Guesthouse
GUESTHOUSE $$$

(☑049-892 4575; www.asghouse.co.za; 100 Cradock St; s/d incl breakfast from R950/1400; P ✳ ⧦ ⊠)
Home of Veld to Fork restaurant, Gordon and Rose Wright's upmarket guesthouse is a cool Karoo oasis, with craftwork for sale in reception, an Italianate pool and signs advising 'keep calm and eat your greens'.

Drostdy Hotel
HISTORIC HOTEL $$$

(☑049-892 2161; www.newmarkhotels.com; Church St; s/d from R1125/1500; P ✳ @ ⧦ ⊠)
When we visited, the town's flagship hotel was nearing the end of a multimillion-rand renovation funded by the Ruperts, prompting much local excitement. The mid-19th-century cottages, originally built for freed slaves, remain at the rear, along with the landmark building's historic charm. A long list of facilities will make it a world-class hotel, including a spa, an art gallery, three pools in a manicured garden, and restaurants with top South African chefs.

The Ruperts are one of South Africa's wealthiest families, with roots in Graaff-Reinet and continuing ties to the town. (The late Dr Anton Rupert, a tobacco billionaire, conservationist and critic of apartheid, was born here in 1916.)

✖ Eating & Drinking

Our Yard
CAFE $

(50 Somerset St; mains R55; ⊘8am-5pm Mon-Fri, to 2pm Sat; ☑) This 'roastery and culture stop' serves coffees from all over the world, light meals, scones and cakes in a shady courtyard. Also here are a gallery and T-shirt shop.

★ Polka Cafe
SOUTH AFRICAN $$

(☑087 550 1363; www.polkacafe.co.za; 52 Somerset St; lunch/dinner mains R75/110; ⊘7.30am-9pm Mon-Sat) Polka's nouvelle cuisine improves upon conventional fare and South African classics with subtle twists, beautiful presentation and taste upgrades. Karoo lamb, matured steaks and *bobotie* are on the dinner menu; lighter lunches include savoury pancakes and thin-crust pizzas.

The candlelit stoep and rear courtyard turn romantic at night, while the nouveau-rustic dining room has a bakery selling homemade cookies, cupcakes and pastries.

★ Veld to Fork
SOUTH AFRICAN $$$

(☑049-892 4575; www.asghouse.co.za; 100 Cradock St; dinner R300; ☑) ✹ Book before 2pm (and well ahead in high season) for dinner and a lesson in gastronomy from chef Gordon Wright and his local team, at South Africa's original Slow Food restaurant. Ingredients are mostly organic and sourced within 40km of Graaff-Reinet, and the style is classic, countrified Karoo with a modern twist. The creme nougat dessert is extremely special.

Graaff-Reinet Club CLUB
(English Club; Church St; ⊙1-9pm Mon-Thu, until late Fri & Sat, 11am-2pm Sun) This atmospheric one-time 'men only' club, one of South Africa's oldest, has walls and halls adorned with hunting trophies and a bar pocked with bullet holes. The Coldstream Guards, billeted in Graaff-Reinet during the Anglo-Boer War, celebrated on being recalled to Blighty by firing eight bullets into the counter. Visitors are welcome to have a drink with locals.

Shopping

Graaff-Reinet has a handful of stores selling antiques, homewares and Karoo crafts, to say nothing of the healthy business done by the town's taxidermy shops.

African Adventure ARTS, CRAFTS
(25 Church St) A good selection of quality African handicrafts.

Information

Graaff-Reinet Tourism (☎049-892 4248; www.graaffreinet.co.za; 13A Church St; ⊙8am-5pm Mon-Fri, 9am-noon Sat) This helpful office has accommodation information and an abundance of maps.

Getting There & Away

Intercape and **Translux** serve Cape Town (R360, 8½ hours) and Jo'burg (R450, 11 hours) daily; the latter also runs to East London (R300, five hours) and Port Elizabeth (R250, three hours). Tickets and info are available at the tourist office.

Shared taxis leave from Market Sq. Major destinations are Port Elizabeth (R200) and Cape Town (R400).

Avis has an office opposite Karoopark Guest House.

Camdeboo National Park

Covering an area of 194 sq km, **Camdeboo National Park** (☎049-892 3453; www.camdeboopark.com; adult/child R84/42; ⊙Lakeview Gate 6am-7pm Oct-Mar, 7am-5.30pm May-Aug, 6.30am-6.30pm Apr & Sep; P) has plenty of animals, but the real attractions are the spectacular geological formations, and great views of Graaff-Reinet and the sun-baked Karoo plains. The park's name comes from the Khoekhoen for 'green valleys' – probably a reference to the spekboom growing here, which remains verdant throughout the winter.

Sights

Valley of Desolation VIEWPOINT
(off Rte 63; ⊙6am-7.30pm Oct-Mar, 7am-6pm May-Aug, 6.30am-7pm Apr & Sep) The Valley of Desolation is the park's most popular sight. It's a hauntingly beautiful valley with an outstanding view – the rugged, piled dolerite columns here are set against the backdrop of the endless Karoo plains. Graaff-Reinet is also visible, nestled in a bend of the Sundays River. The valley viewpoint, 14km from town, can be reached by car on a steep but sealed road, and there's a 1.5km circuit walk. The best times to visit are sunrise and sunset.

➡ **Giant Flag** LANDMARK
(www.giantflag.co.za) A viewing deck at the Valley of Desolation viewpoint looks down on this 6600-sq-m flag, which is being created from millions of coloured desert plants.

CAMDEBOO NATIONAL PARK

Why Go Dramatic landscapes, rock formations and an unlikely ecological feat in the Valley of Desolation; animals including Cape mountain zebras; and day hikes.

When to Go The park is quiet in April, when the Karoo produces autumn colours and you can enjoy amazing sunsets in crisp weather. The vegetation is also thin, making wildlife easier to spot.

Practicalities Camdeboo is divided into three main sections: the wildlife-watching area north of the Nqweba Dam; the western section with the Valley of Desolation; and the eastern section with various 4WD trails. The park reception and accommodation are at Lakeview Gate, which is located on the N9 4km north of Graaff-Reinet. You'll need your own vehicle to visit the wildlife-watching area; otherwise, book a tour in Graaff-Reinet.

Budget Tips Camp and prepare your own food in the self-catering kitchen and braai.

When completed, it will be the world's largest flag – visible from space.

Activities

Wildlife-Watching

In the wildlife-watching area, accessed through Lakeview Gate, there are buffaloes, elands, kudus, red hartebeests, black wildebeest and springboks – to name a few of the park's 40-plus mammal species. Rare Cape mountain zebras may be spotted, but they prefer mountainous terrain. Good gravel roads lead 19km around the wildlife-watching area; visitors must stay in their vehicles except at the picnic sites.

There are also animals in the Valley of Desolation section of the park, while 200-plus bird species in the skies above include black eagles, African fish eagles and falcons.

Hiking

The Eerstefontein Day Trail runs through the park's western section past the Valley of Desolation; there are three route options with distances of 5km, 11km and 14km. Park reception has a map.

Sleeping

You can camp in the park near Nqweba Dam at **Lakeview Tented Camp** (tent R570; P), which has twin safari tents, and at **Nqweba Campsite** (camping R205; P).

Nieu Bethesda

POP 1540

Hidden in the deep Karoo, the tiny village of Nieu Bethesda has gained some attention for its extraordinary Owl House – the fantastically and unnervingly decorated home of 'outsider' artist, Helen Martins. These days, the village is a minor artistic colony, with creative cred added by *The Road to Mecca,* Athol Fugard's play about Martins. The Fugard Festival in March sees events all over town and rooms can be hard to come by.

With its dirt roads, water furrows, pretty cottages and endless stars, Nieu Bethesda is a great place to experience life in a Karoo village and unwind for a few days. Bethesda is about 55km from Graaff-Reinet – the drive is very scenic, with the Sneeuberg range dominating the region.

Sights & Activities

Owl House HISTORIC BUILDING
(☎049-841 1642; River St; admission R50; ⊙9am-5pm) The idiosyncratic vision that inspired artist Helen Martins (1897–1976) to turn her home and studio into a singular work of outsider art is the bedrock of Bethesda's bohemian identity. Martins and her assistant Koos Malgas worked for years designing and constructing the menagerie of concrete owls and myriad other figures in the backyard. Nearly every inch of the shadowy interior is covered with colorful painted glass shards, textiles and tchotchkes, recalling the troubled figure who eventually took her own life.

Outside, local craftspeople sell replica owls; they will soon be housed nearby in a new curio shop.

Bethesda Arts Centre GALLERY
(nieubethesda.org; Muller St; ⊙9am-4pm Mon-Fri, to noon Sat) This community arts centre exhibits huge tapestries made locally. Julia Malgas, the granddaughter of Helen Martins' assistant Koos, or another artist can explain the myths and beliefs of the San people portayed in the tapestries' designs.

Kitching Fossil Exploration Centre MUSEUM
(☎082 387 9224; Martin St; admission R20; ⊙9am-5pm) The models and fossil casts here depict prehistoric animals (gorgonopsians, dicynodonts and the like) around 253 million years old – 50 million years before the age of dinosaurs. Staff will take you to see the real thing, untouched and embedded in rocks in the nearby dry riverbed.

Compassberg HIKING
The biggest peak in the region at 2502m, Compassberg is about four hours each way from the start of the trail at Compassberg farm, 35km from Nieu Bethesda. There is also the **Canyon Hike**, a fairly flat 3km walk that follows a water furrow towards Ganora Guest Farm. You need permission to walk both trails; ask your accommodation to contact the landowner.

Ganora Guest Farm CULTURAL TOUR
(☎049-841 1302; www.ganora.co.za) Ganora Guest Farm, 7km east of Nieu Bethesda, offers numerous activities, including a guided walk around the on-site museum of fossils and Bushman artefacts, continuing into the veld for more discoveries. Another tour focuses on medicinal plants. Groups can even enjoy a sheep-shearing demonstration. Ganora rehabilitates meerkats so you might see one or two scurrying around. They also host periodic courses in photography, stargazing, art and cookery.

Sleeping

Owl House Backpackers BACKPACKERS $
(☎049-841 1642; www.owlhouse.info; Martin St; camping/dm/s/d R75/125/290/460;) The whitewashed Karoo facade conceals a home with old-fashioned character, funky nooks and crannies, and a sizeable back garden. For more privacy, try the loftlike backyard water tower with circular bedroom, composting toilet and kitchenette, or the self-catering garden cottage. En-suite rooms are across the street in Outsiders B&B. The owners can organise tours including visits to Bushman painting sites.

Bethesda Tower GUESTHOUSE $
(☎073 028 8887; bethesdatower.co.za; Muller St; s/d without bathroom R250/350) Climbing this three-storey castellated tower is like stepping into a fairy tale. The top room has a round double bed, covered with a quilt made at the adjoining Bethesda Arts Centre, while downstairs is a twin room and a cafe offering half board. Two rooms are also available in the neighbouring Priory, decorated with quilts, artwork and stained-glass windows.

★**Ganora Guest Farm** FARMSTAY $$
(☎049-841 1302; www.ganora.co.za; s/d incl breakfast from R550/790; P) If you'd rather be out of town under the soaring skies of the Karoo, this 18th-century farmstead is an excellent option. The stone kraal wall now forms part of the luxurious boutique-style rooms, with further options in whitewashed former workshops and sheds. The self-catering Khoe-San Cottage, which sleeps up to six, goes for R950. All meals are available, served in a rustic pioneer-style dining room.

Four Seasons Country House GUESTHOUSE $$
(☎084 862 8280; www.fourseasonscountryhouse.co.za; Martin St; s/d incl breakfast R500/900;) This guesthouse at the back of the popular Alfresco Pizzeria has three cool and tranquil rooms opening onto a patio and garden.

Eating

Karoo Lamb Restaurant SOUTH AFRICAN $$
(mains R80; 7am-9pm;) When all the elements of breakfast at this large eatery-cum-deli-cum-gift shop are laid out, half a picnic table is occupied. For lunch or dinner, hearty dishes such as lamb chops and *potjiekos* (stew cooked in a cast-iron pot) satsify after a long drive through the Karoo.

Two Goats DELI $$
(thebrewery.wozaonline.co.za; Pienaar St; mains R80; 10am-5pm Mon-Sat, to 3pm Sun) Across a bridge from the main part of the village is this charmingly rustic farmhouse on a working dairy farm, where you can sit under the trees sampling the house cheeses, salami, ales and coffee.

Information

Karoo Lamb Restaurant is the unofficial tourist office. There are no petrol stations or ATMS here, and credit cards are generally not accepted by accommodation.

Getting There & Away

There is no public transport to Nieu Bethesda. Owl House Backpackers can pick up guests from Graaff-Reinet (R150 per person), but it must be arranged in advance.

Mountain Zebra National Park

This **national park** (☎048-881 2427; www.sanparks.org; off Rte 61; adult/child R144/72; 7am-7pm Oct-Mar, to 6pm Apr-Sep; P), 20km west of Cradock on the northern slopes of the Bankberg range (2000m), encompasses 280 sq km with some superb Karoo vistas. The park was established to protect one of the world's rarest mammals: the Cape mountain zebra. There are now almost 800 in the park; they're distinguished from other zebra species by their small stature, reddish-brown nose, darker stripes and dewlap (a loose fold of skin hanging beneath the throat).

Activities

With your own vehicle, it's possible to get a taste of the park in a few hours. The road that loops from the main gate across to the rest camp and back can take under two hours, depending on how often you stop. There are two **swimming pools** near the rest camp.

Wildlife-Watching

In addition to Cape mountain zebras, the park supports many antelope species, buffaloes and black rhinos; two lions, eight cheetahs and several species of small cat; genets, aardwolves, bat-eared foxes, black-backed jackals, and more than 200 bird species. The park offers two-hour **wildlife drives** (adult/child from R175/85) and a unique **cheetah-tracking tour** (per person R310),

MOUNTAIN ZEBRA NATIONAL PARK

Why Go Cape mountain zebras, lions, buffaloes and many other mammals; Karoo landscapes on the slopes of the Bankberg range; and numerous activities, including cheetah tracking.

When to Go Anytime outside summer (November to February), to avoid extreme heat in the Karoo's semidesert environment.

Practicalities The roads are mostly good gravel and tar, suitable for 2WD cars, plus three 4WD trails. There's no public transport to the park so bring your own vehicle or come on a tour.

Budget Tips If you don't want to camp, stay in cheaper accommodation in nearby Cradock and visit the park on a day trip. If you do stay in the park, your conservation (entrance) fee will be calculated on a nightly, rather than daily, basis; if you stay one night, you will only pay for one day despite being in the park for two.

which takes you as close as 15m from the big cats.

Hiking

Hiking trails range from free 1km and 2.5km saunters around the rest camp, to longer guided walks including the 25km, three-day Impofu Hike (per person R415).

Sleeping

Mountain Zebra National Park Rest Camp CAMPGROUND $

The park rest camp offers campsites (from R205) and comfortable and well-equipped cottages (from R850).

The rest camp is 10km from the gate, and has the park reception, a shop (7am to 7pm) selling basic items and a bar-restaurant (lunch R70, dinner R85, open 7am to 9pm).

Mountain Cottages COTTAGES $

(from R700) The park's two mountain cottages, accessible in high-clearance vehicles, provide a secluded rustic experience with no electricity. Each has a braai, a fireplace, a gas-powered shower, a kitchen with gas stove and solar-powered fridge, two bedrooms and a hikers' dorm.

Doornhoek COTTAGE $$

(1-4 people R2435) A restored historic farmhouse, built in 1837 and hidden in a secluded valley. It can sleep six people in two doubles and two singles; additional adults pay R360 each, and additional kids pay R180 each.

Cradock

POP 36,671

Originally established as a military outpost in 1813 to stop the Xhosa from crossing the Great Fish River, Cradock became a bustling agricultural and commercial settlement in later decades. Market St was home to the artisans who served the ox-wagons passing through. It's still an important farming district and although it may appear slightly shabby at first, it's worth taking a closer look at the beautiful old buildings and tree-lined avenues. Stroll down lovely Dundas and Bree Sts, the latter the oldest in Cradock, past fine well-preserved 19th-century gabled homes.

The town's most famous sons were the Cradock Four, struggle activists who were abducted, assaulted and killed by members of the security police in 1985.

Sights & Activities

Olive Schreiner House MUSEUM

(☎048-881 5251; 9 Cross St; admission R5; ⏰8am-12.45pm & 2-4.30pm Mon-Fri) Schreiner is best known for her classic Karoo novel, *Story of an African Farm*. Published in 1883 under the pseudonym Ralph Iron, the provocative *plaasroman* and *bildungsroman* advocated views considered radical well into the 20th century. She lived in this typical Karoo house for only three years; however, several of its small rooms are now dedicated to a chronicle of her life, career and local history seen through the writer's eyes.

The bookshop has an excellent collection of South African novels and a booklet detailing a literary walking tour of Cradock.

Great Fish River Museum MUSEUM

(☎048-881 4509; 87 High St; by donation; ⏰8am-1pm & 2-4pm Mon-Fri) Housed in the former Dutch Reformed Church parsonage (1849), the museum's exhibits cover local topics including 19th-century pioneer life. Find it behind the Municipal Building.

Karoo River Rafting RAFTING, CANOEING

(☎084 429 9944; www.karoo-river-rafting.co.za) Rafting and canoeing trips down the Great Fish River and its tributaries.

Township Tours CULTURAL TOUR
(048-881 1650; admission by donation) Amos, who works at the Victoria Manor hotel, offers tours of the local township.

Sleeping

There are loads of B&Bs; check with the tourist office for a list.

★Die Tuishuise & Victoria Manor HISTORIC HOTEL $$
(048-881 1322, 048-881 1650; www.tuishuise.co.za; cnr Market & Voortrekker Sts; cottages s/d R470/780, hotel s/d R445/615; P❄📶🏊) The 'homely home' consists of 31 beautifully restored and handsomely furnished Karoo houses, their stoeps opening onto one of Cradock's oldest streets, and garden cottages. The neighbouring Victoria Manor is an atmospheric small-town inn with a spa, a splash pool, a wood-panelled bar-restaurant, and antiques in the charming rooms.

The picture-perfect self-catering houses, which each accommodate up to eight, are split between light and modern interpretations of Karoo rusticity and more historic decor, redolent of the Brits and Boers who once trod their floorboards. All offer a precious opportunity to step into a sepia-tinted Karoo scene for a night or two.

Heritage House B&B B&B $$
(048-881 3210; 45 Bree St; s/d incl breakfast R500/900; @📶🏊) This historic house dating to 1815 has rooms in the main building and garden cottages overlooking a fish pond. Owner Meyrick is full of local information.

Eating & Drinking

★Victoria Manor SOUTH AFRICAN $$
(cnr Market & Voortrekker Sts; mains R70, breakfast/dinner buffet R90/160) This atmospheric hotel dining room has dark-wood panelling and richly upholstered furnishings in 19th-century English style. Service is attentive, and the Karoo cuisine hearty and delicious. Karoo lamb chops, burgers and biltong salad are on the lunch menu.

True Living SOUTH AFRICAN $$
(44 JA Calata St; mains R75;) Cafes cluster around the corner of JA Calata and Albert Sts, mostly combined with nurseries or decor shops. In the latter category, this courtyard cafe sells plates and platters of farm-kitchen food, including *bobotie, sosaties* (curried skewered meat), Cradock lamb chops, quiches, steaks and burgers.

Information

Cradock Tourism (048-801 5000; http://cradockmiddelburg.co.za; JA Calata St) In the municipal building opposite the Spar Centre.

Getting There & Away

Translux, **Intercape** and **City to City** run daily to Cape Town (R430, 10 to 15 hours) via Graaff-Reinet (R250, 1½ hours) or Port Elizabeth (R300, four hours), and to East London (R250, 4½ hours) and Jo'burg (R550, 11 hours).

Tourist-class sleeper **trains** stop here en route between Port Elizabeth (R150, 4½ hours) and Jo'burg (R340, 15½ hours) via Bloemfontein on Wednesday, Friday and Sunday. Less-recommended economy class (seat only) is also available.

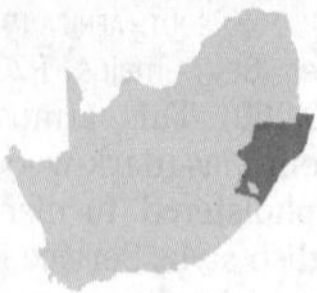

KwaZulu-Natal

Includes ➡

Best Places to Eat

- Cafe 1999 (p242)
- Zanj (p255)
- Tally's Corner Cafe (p257)
- Rosehurst (p277)
- Pucketty Farm (p283)

Best Places to Stay

- Napier House (p239)
- Hilltop Camp (p264)
- George Hotel (p257)
- Kosi Forest Lodge (p272)
- Hlalanathi (p289)

Why Go?

Rough and ready, smart and sophisticated, rural and rustic: there's no doubt that KwaZulu-Natal (KZN) is eclectic. It's a region where glassy malls touch shabby suburbs, and action-packed adventurers ooze adrenalin while laid-back beach bods drip with suntan lotion. Mountainscapes contrast with flat, dry savannahs, while the towns' central streets, teeming with African life, markets and noise, are in stark contrast to the sedate tribal settlements in rural areas. Here, too, is traditional Zululand, whose people are fiercely proud of their culture.

Throw in the wildlife – the Big Five (lion, leopard, buffalo, elephant and rhino) and rare marine species – and the historic intrigue of the Battlefields, fabulous hiking opportunities, and the sand, sea and surf of coastal resort towns, and you get a tantalising taste of local heritage and authentic African highlights that should be on every 'must-do' list.

When to Go

Durban

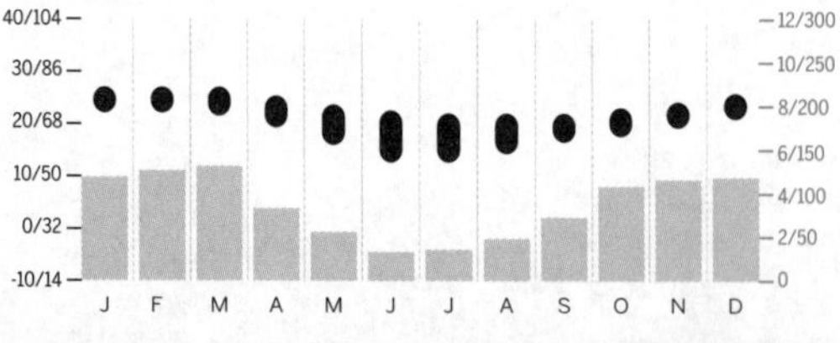

May–Oct Dry season brings cooler days but savannah conditions, perfect for wildlife-viewing.

Oct & Nov Pleasant beach weather and wildflowers cover the uKhahlamba-Drakensberg.

Nov–Feb Brings hot weather but also the results of mating season – baby animals rule!

History

Battled over by Boers, Brits and Zulus, Natal was named by Portuguese explorer Vasco da Gama, who sighted the coastline on Christmas Day 1497, and named it for the natal day of Jesus. It took the British Empire more than 300 years to set its sights on the region, proclaiming it a colony in 1843. Briefly linked to the Cape Colony in 1845, Natal again became a separate colony in 1856, when its European population numbered less than 5000.

The introduction of Indian indentured labour in the 1860s – sections of the province still retain a subcontinental feel – and the subsequent development of commercial agriculture (mainly sugar) boosted growth. The colony thrived from 1895, when train lines linked Durban's port (dredged to accommodate big ships) with the booming Witwatersrand.

The recorded history of the province up until the Union of South Africa is full of conflict: the *mfeqane* (the forced migration of South African tribes; Zulu for 'the crushing'), the Boer-Zulu and Anglo-Zulu Wars, which saw the Zulu kingdom subjugated, and the two wars between the British and the Boers.

Just after the 1994 elections, Natal Province was renamed KwaZulu-Natal, acknowledging that the Zulu homeland of KwaZulu comprises a large part of the province. From that time, Ulundi (the former KwaZulu capital) and Pietermaritzburg (the former Natal homeland capital) enjoyed joint status as capital of KwaZulu-Natal until 2005, when Pietermaritzburg was named the province's official capital.

Climate

The weather (and the water, thanks to the Agulhas current) stays warm year-round along much of the coast, with Durbanites claiming to lap up a heady 230 sunny days a year. In summer the heat and humidity, combined with the crowds that flood to the coast to enjoy it, can be exhausting, with temperatures regularly in the mid-30s (degrees Celsius). Most of the interior enjoys similarly balmy conditions, but sudden and explosive electrical storms, especially in the Drakensberg mountains and northern KwaZulu-Natal, often roll in during the afternoon. Winter brings a dusting of snow to the higher peaks.

Language

Eleven official languages are spoken in South Africa, but English, Zulu, Xhosa and Afrikaans are most widely used in KwaZulu-Natal.

Getting There & Around

With flights, buses and trains to destinations across the country, Durban is KwaZulu-Natal's undisputed transport hub, and, at least nationally, the city is well connected. However, getting around the province itself is a different story. While long-distance buses run to Port Shepstone, Margate and Kokstad in the south, Richards Bay and Vryheid in the north and a string of towns including Estcourt, Ladysmith and Newcastle in the west, many of the more remote locations are a headache to get to by public transport. Shared taxis provide a useful backup, but relying on minibuses as your sole means of getting about will mean many long hours in the back of a cramped van.

Baz Bus (www.bazbus.com) links many of the province's hostels.

DURBAN

POP 600,000

Cosmopolitan Durban, South Africa's third-largest city (known as eThekweni in Zulu), is sometimes unfairly passed over for her 'cooler' Capetonian cousin. But this isn't fair; there's a lot more to fun-loving Durbs (as she's affectionately known) than meets the eye.

The city had a major makeover leading up to the 2010 World Cup, with a sleek new stadium and a revamped waterfront. The renewal of the waterfront area and the sweeping away of the old sleaze has given municipal authorities new confidence and ambition – there are plans to extend the waterfront promenade right down the south coast.

Durban's downtown area – a buzzing, gritty grid comprising grandiose colonial buildings and fascinating art deco architecture – throbs to a distinctly African beat (but loses its shimmer when the sun goes down). The beachfront remains a daytime locus for beach lovers.

Home to the largest concentration of people of Indian descent outside of India, Durban also boasts an unmistakably Asian feel, with the marketplaces and streets of the Indian area replete with the sights, sounds and scents of the subcontinent.

KwaZulu-Natal Highlights

1. Wildlife-spotting through the Big Five stomping ground of **Hluhluwe-iMfolozi Park** (p263) or sitting near a pan at dawn at **uMkhuze Game Reserve** (p270).
2. Exploring the beauty of the extraordinary **iSimangaliso Wetland Park** (p265).
3. Walking in the mountainous wonderland of **uKhahlamba-Drakensberg Park** (p278).
4. Driving through the clouds over **Sani Pass** (p284) to Lesotho.

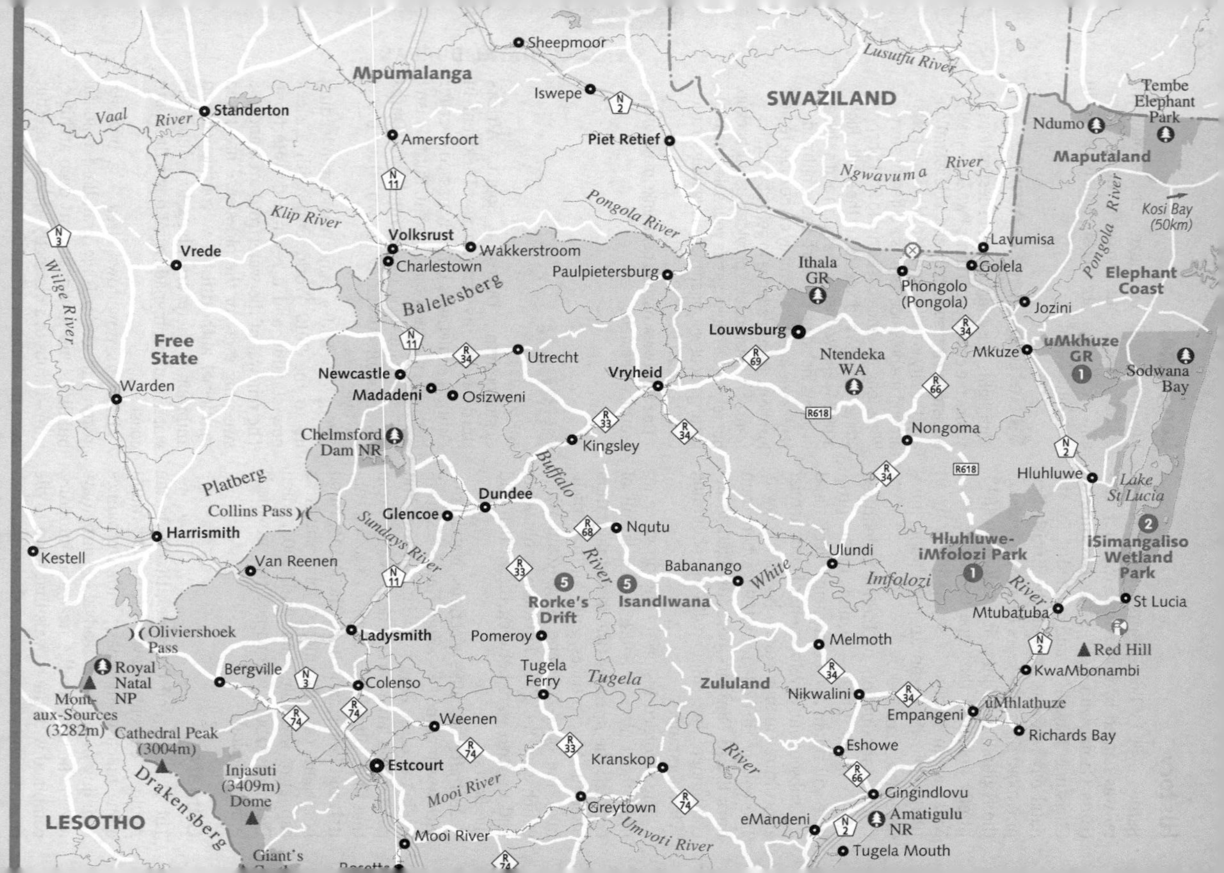

5 Reliving the clashes of the Anglo-Zulu War at **Isandlwana and Rorke's Drift** (p295).

6 Sniffing out the funky new cafes and eateries in fast-changing **Durban** (p227).

7 Working on the tan or just enjoying the waves along the **South Coast** (p247) and **North Coast** (p250).

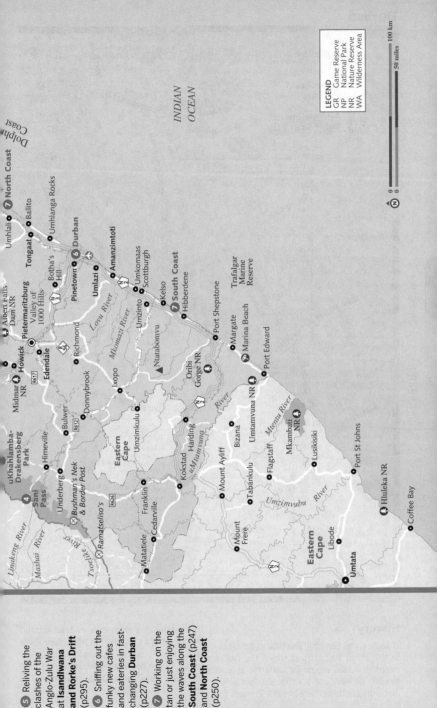

Durban

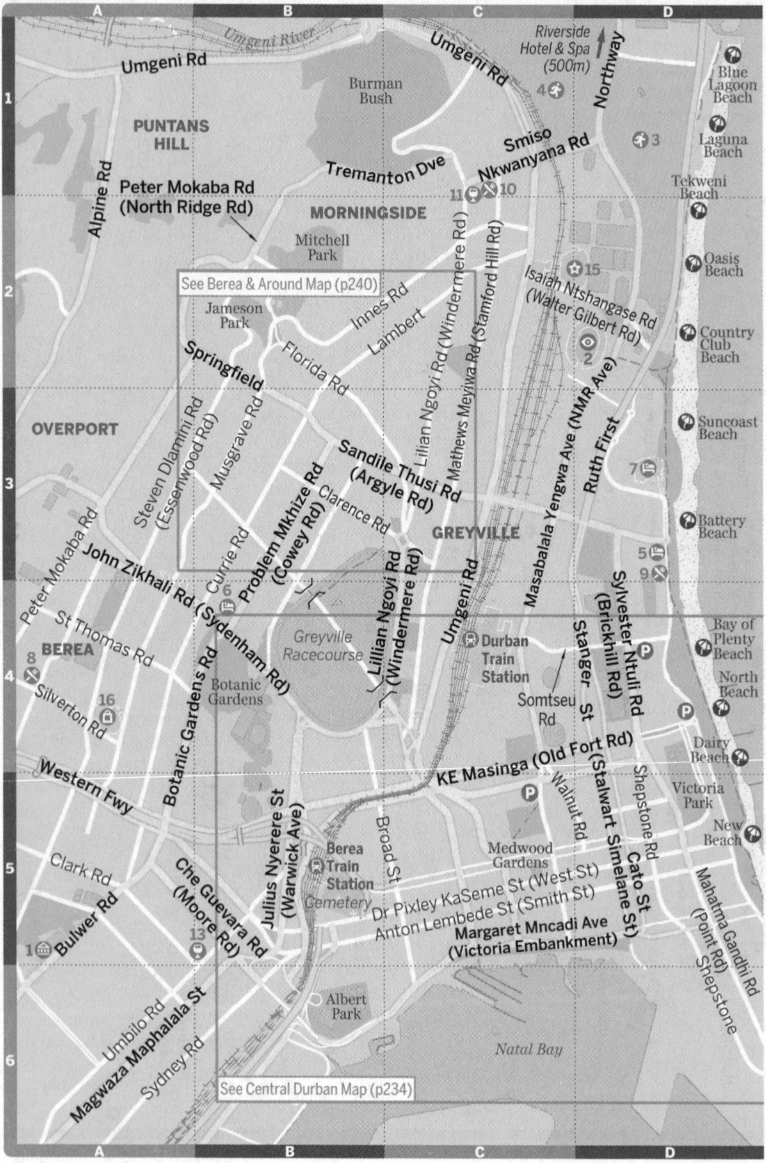

History

It took some time for Durban to be established. Natal Bay, around which the city is based, provided refuge for seafarers at least as early as 1685, and it's thought that Vasco da Gama anchored here in 1497. Though the Dutch bought a large area of land around the bay from a local chief in 1690, their ships didn't make it across the sand bar at the entrance to the bay until 1705, by which time the chief had died, and his son refused to acknowledge the deal.

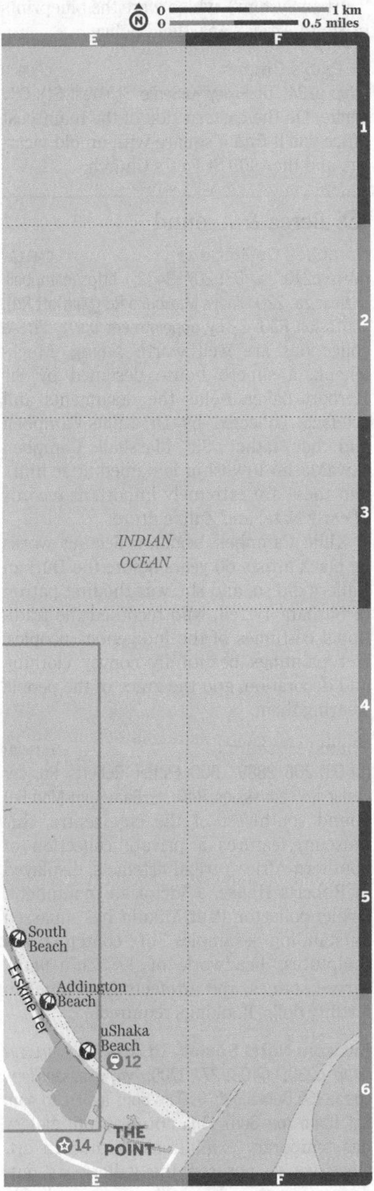

Durban

Sights

1 Kwazulu Natal Society of Arts............A5
2 Moses Mabhida Stadium....................D2

Activities, Courses & Tours

3 Durban Country Club D1
STS Sport ....(see 2)
4 Windsor Park Municipal Golf
Course C1

Sleeping

5 Blue Waters D3
6 Napier House.....................................B4
7 Southern Sun Suncoast Hotel
& Towers D3

Eating

8 Cafe 1999...A4
9 Cafe Jiran D3
10 Mali's Indian Restaurant C1

Drinking & Nightlife

11 Billy the Bum's C1
12 Moyo uShaka Pier Bar..........................E6
13 Origin B5
Unity Brasserie & Bar..................(see 8)

Entertainment

14 Chairman E6
15 Kings Park Stadium.............................D2

Shopping

16 Musgrave Centre A4

Natal Bay attracted little attention from Europeans until 1824, when Englishmen Henry Fynn and Francis Farewell set up a base here to trade for ivory with the Zulu. Shaka, a powerful Zulu chief, granted land around the bay to the trading company and it was accepted in the name of King George IV.

The settlement was slow to prosper, partly because of the chaos Shaka was causing in the area. By 1835 it had become a small town with a mission station, and that year it took the name D'Urban, after the Cape Colony governor.

In 1837 the Voortrekkers crossed the Drakensberg and founded Pietermaritzburg, 80km northwest of Durban. The next year, after Durban was evacuated during a raid by the Zulu, the Boers claimed control. It was reoccupied by a British force later that year, but the Boers stuck by their claim. The British sent troops to Durban to secure the settlement but were defeated by the Boers at the Battle of Congella in 1842.

The Boers retained control for a month until a British frigate arrived (fetched by Dick King, who rode the 1000km of wild country between Durban and Grahamstown in Eastern Cape in 10 days) and dislodged them. The next year Natal was annexed by the British, and Durban began its growth as an important colonial port city. In 1860 the first indentured Indian labourers arrived to work the cane fields. Despite the unjust system – slave labour by another name – many free Indian settlers arrived in 1893, including Mohandas Gandhi.

Sights

City Centre

City Hall NOTABLE BUILDING
(Map p234; Anton Lembede St (Smith St), City Centre) Dominating the city centre is the opulent 1910 Edwardian neobaroque City Hall. In front of the hall is **Francis Farewell Square**, where Fynn and Farewell made their camp in 1824.

Art Gallery GALLERY
(Map p234; ☎031-311 2262; Anton Lembede St (Smith St), City Centre; ⏰8.30am-4pm Mon-Sat, 11am-4pm Sun) FREE Under City Hall's impressive dome is this gallery with a small but interesting collection of South African artworks, including paintings, mixed media and ceramics. It also has temporary and rotating exhibitions.

Natural Science Museum MUSEUM
(Map p234; ☎031-311 2256; Anton Lembede St (Smith St), City Centre; ⏰8.30am-4pm Mon-Sat, 11am-4pm Sun) FREE This museum at City Hall boasts an impressive, if pleasantly retro, display of stuffed birds and insects, plus African animals. Check out the cockroach and dung-beetle displays, the reconstructed dodo and the life-size dinosaur model.

Old Courthouse Museum MUSEUM
(Map p234; ☎031-311 2229; 77 Samora Machel St (Aliwal St), City Centre; ⏰8.30am-4pm Mon-Sat) FREE Found in the beautiful 1866 courthouse behind City Hall, this museum offers a worthwhile insight into the highs and lows of colonial living. There's also a moving exhibit on the sadly brief life of journalist Nathaniel (Nat) Wakasa, as well as a collection of model ships that kids (and more than a few adults) will enjoy.

KwaMuhle Museum MUSEUM
(Map p234; ☎031-311 2233; 130 Bram Fischer Rd (Ordnance Rd), City Centre; ⏰8.30am-4pm Mon-Sat) FREE This was formerly the Bantu Administration headquarters, where Durban's colonial authorities formulated the structures of urban racial segregation (the 'Durban System'), which were the blueprints of South Africa's apartheid policy.

St Paul's Church CHURCH
(Map p234; Dr Pixley KaSeme St (West St), City Centre) On the eastern side of the main post office you'll find a square with an old vicarage and the 1909 St Paul's Church.

Berea & Around

Campbell Collections GALLERY
(Map p240; ☎031-207 3432; http://campbell.ukzn.ac.za; 220 Gladys Mazibuko Rd (Marriott Rd); admission R20; ⏰by appointment only) These collections are well worth seeing. Muckleneuk, a superb house designed by Sir Herbert Baker, holds the documents and artefacts collected by Dr Killie Campbell and her father Sir Marshall Campbell (KwaMashu township is named after him), and these are extremely important records of early Natal and Zulu culture.

Killie Campbell began collecting works by black artists 60 years before the Durban Gallery did so, and she was the first patron of Barbara Tyrrell, who recorded the traditional costumes of the indigenous peoples. Her paintings beautifully convey clothing and decoration, and the grace of the people wearing them.

Phansi Museum MUSEUM
(☎031-206 2889; 500 Esther Roberts Rd, cnr Cedar Rd; admission R40; ⏰8am-4pm Mon-Fri) Found southwest of the city centre, this museum features a private collection of Southern African tribal artefacts, displayed in Roberts House, a Victorian monument. Owner-collector Paul Mikula has amassed outstanding examples of contemporary sculptures, beadwork of KwaZulu-Natal, carved statues, and artefacts from pipes to fertility dolls. Bookings required.

Kwazulu Natal Society of Arts GALLERY
(Map p230; ☎031-277 1705; www.kznsagallery.co.za; 166 Bulwer Rd; ⏰9am-5pm Tue-Fri, to 4pm Sat, 10am-3pm Sun) This not-for-profit gallery has temporary exhibitions of modern art. Once you've perused the gallery, its outdoor cafe, set under shady trees, is a lovely place to visit. A gift shop is also within the complex.

Durban Botanic Gardens GARDENS
(Map p234; ☎031-309 9240; www.durbanbotanicgardens.org.za; John Zikhali Rd (Sydenham Rd); ⏰7.30am-5.30pm 16 Apr-15 Sep, to 5.15pm 16 Sep-

15 Apr) FREE A 2000-sq-metre garden featuring one of the rarest cycads *(Encephalartos woodii),* as well as many species of bromeliad, this is a lovely place to wander. On weekends bridal parties galore pose with their petals for photographers. The gardens play host to an annual concert series featuring the KwaZulu-Natal Philharmonic Orchestra and other concerts.

Moses Mabhida Stadium STADIUM

(Map p230; ☎031-582 8242; www.mmstadium.com; 44 Isaiah Ntshangase Rd (Walter Gilbert Rd), Stamford Hill; SkyCar adult/child R55/30, Adventure Walk per person R90, Big Swing per person R695; ⏲SkyCar 9am-5pm, Adventure Walk 10am, 1pm & 3pm Sat & Sun, Big Swing 10am-4pm, closed Tue & Thu) Durbanites are proud of their state-of-the-art stadium, constructed for the 2010 World Cup. Resembling a giant basket, it seats 56,000 people, and its arch was inspired by the 'Y' in the country's flag. Visitors can head up to the arch in a **SkyCar**, puff up on foot (550 steps) on an **Adventure Walk** or plunge off the 106m arch on the giant **Big Swing**. All options offer great views of Durban.

Cafes line a section of the stadium base; from here, too, you can hire a bike or walk to the beachfront on the pedestrian promenade.

North & West Durban

Umgeni River Bird Park WILDLIFE RESERVE

(☎031-579 4601; www.umgeniriverbirdpark.co.za; Riverside Rd; adult/child R50/30; ⏲9am-5pm) Found on the Umgeni River, north of the centre, this bird park makes for a relaxing escape from the throng. You can see many African bird species in lush vegetation and aviaries. Don't miss the free-flight bird show at 11am and 2pm Tuesday to Sunday, featuring birds from around the world.

Temple of Understanding RELIGIOUS

(☎031-403 3328; Bhaktieedanta Sami Circle; ⏲10am-1pm & 4-8pm) Situated in Durban's west, this is the biggest Hare Krishna temple in the southern hemisphere. The unusual building, designed in the shape of a lotus flower, also houses a vegetarian restaurant. Follow the N3 towards Pietermaritzburg and then branch off to the N2 south. Take the Chatsworth turnoff and turn right towards the centre of Chatsworth.

Margaret Mncadi Avenue (Victoria Embankment)

Sugar Terminal BUILDING

(Map p234; ☎031-365 8100; 25 Leuchars Rd; adult/concession R16/8; ⏲tours 8.30am, 10am, 11.30am & 2pm Mon-Thu) Maydon Wharf, which runs along the southwestern side of the harbour and south of Margaret Mncadi Ave, is home to the Sugar Terminal, which offers an insight into the sugar trade. The trade was the backbone of Durban's early economy.

Wilson's Wharf WATERFRONT

(Map p234) This once-hip waterside development is now a little tired, but it's the best place to get a view of Durban's harbour and its activities. The harbour is the busiest in Southern Africa (and the ninth busiest in the world). The wharf has a clutch of eateries, boat-charter outfits, shops and a theatre. By car, enter opposite Hermitage St.

Port Natal Maritime Museum MUSEUM

(Map p234; ☎031-311 2231; Maritime Dr; adult/child R5/3; ⏲8.30am-4pm Mon-Sat, 11am-4pm Sun) On a service road running parallel to Margaret Mncadi Ave you can explore two former steam tugs and see the huge wicker basket once used for hoisting passengers onto ocean liners.

Vasco da Gama Clock MONUMENT

(Map p234; Stanger St (Stalwart Simelane St)) This florid Victorian monument on the embankment, just east of Stalwart Simelane St, was presented by the Portuguese government in 1897 to mark the 400th anniversary of Vasco da Gama's sighting of Natal.

Indian Area

Juma Mosque MOSQUE

(Map p234; ☎031-304 1518; cnr Denis Hurley St (Queen St) & Dr Yusuf Dadoo St (Grey St); ⏲9am-4pm Mon-Fri, to 11am Sat) The largest mosque in the southern hemisphere; call ahead for a guided tour. Next to the mosque between Dr AB Xuma St and Cathedral Rd, and near the Catholic Emmanuel Cathedral, is the 1927 Madrassa Arcade, a bazaarlike shopping space with a distinctly Indian flavour.

Beachfront

The beachfront has experienced a resurgence thanks to the massive revamp that was completed prior to the World Cup. The

Central Durban

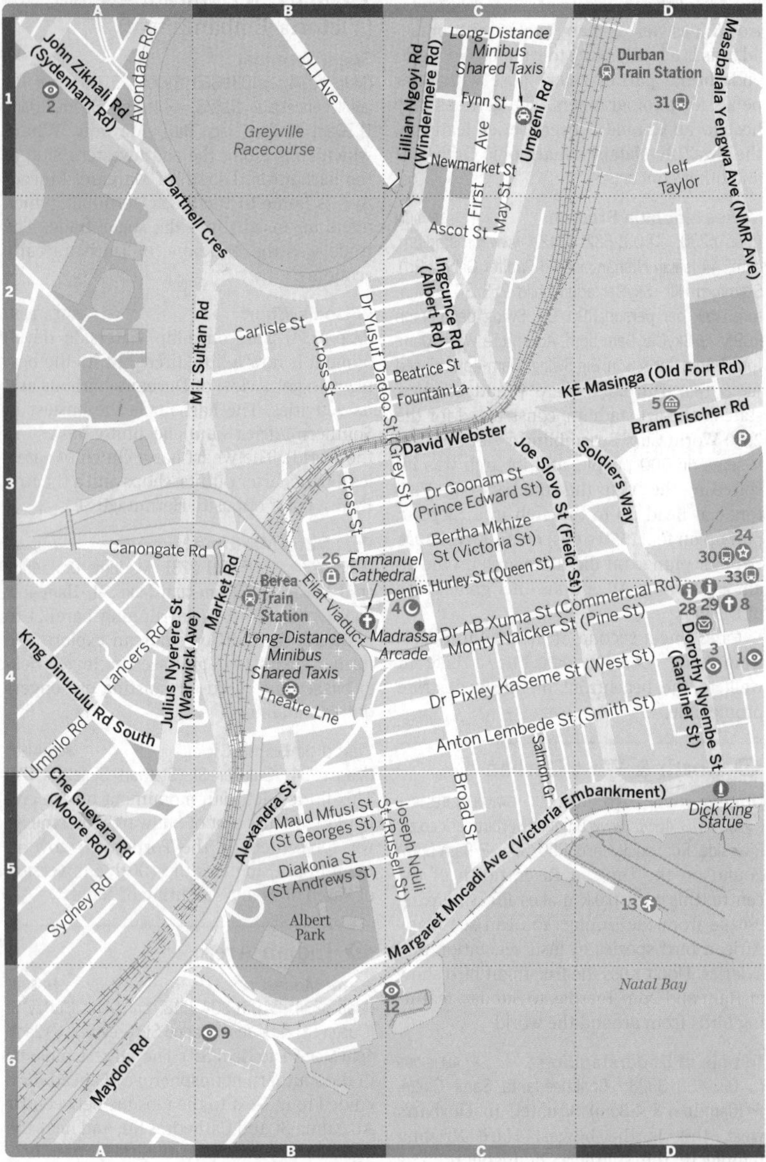

new promenade – a pedestrian superhighway – runs behind the beaches but offers little shade. Both the beaches and promenade extend from the Blue Lagoon (at the mouth of the Umgeni River) to uShaka Marine World on the Point, an area known as the 'Golden Mile', although it's much longer. The road behind this is OR Tambo Pde (Marine Pde), and it's lined with high-rise hotels and a sprinkling of cafes.

Excellent signage at the beaches provides maps and names of the different beach-

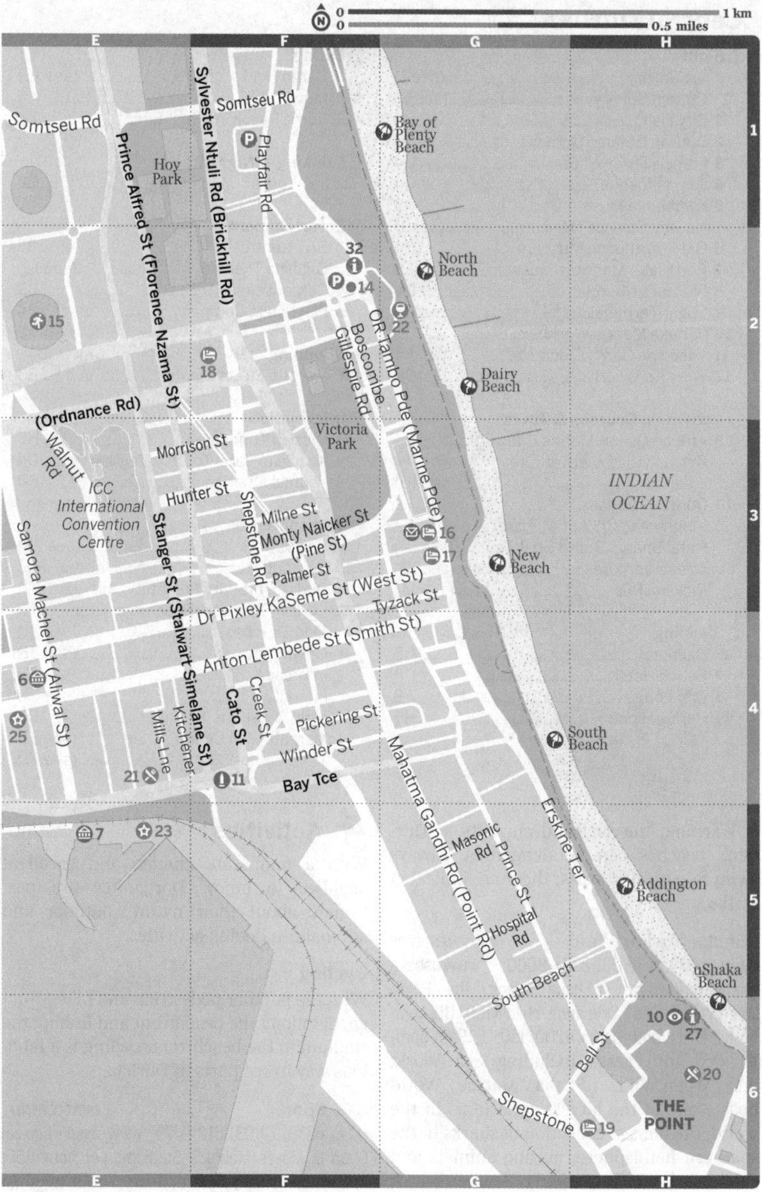

es, although it's really one stretch of sand with different names. At Suncoast Beach, in front of the casino, brollies and chairs are available on a first-come, first-served basis. Due to its location at the strip's southern end, uShaka Beach is often slightly more sheltered and is close to cafes and a small car park. Keep an eye out for the incredible sand sculptures done by locals, depicting anything from mermaids to lions. The uShaka Beach has activities including surfing lessons and kayaking.

Central Durban

Sights

	Art Gallery	(see 1)
	Church Square	(see 8)
1	City Hall	D4
2	Durban Botanic Gardens	A1
3	Francis Farewell Square	D4
4	Juma Mosque	C4
5	KwaMuhle Museum	D3
	Natural Science Museum	(see 1)
6	Old Courthouse Museum	E4
7	Port Natal Maritime Museum	E5
8	St Paul's Church	D4
9	Sugar Terminal	B6
10	uShaka Marine World	H6
11	Vasco da Gama Clock	F4
12	Wilson's Wharf	C6

Activities, Courses & Tours

13	African Queen Marine Charters	D5
	Calypso Dive & Adventure Centre	(see 10)
14	Durban Tourism	F2
15	Kingsmead Cricket Stadium	E2
	Natal Sharks Board Boat Tour	(see 12)
	Ocean Ventures	(see 10)
	Ricksha Bus	(see 14)

Sleeping

16	Balmoral	G3
17	Beach Hotel	G3
18	City Lodge	F2
19	Happy Hippo	H6

Eating

	Cargo Hold	(see 10)
20	Moyo	H6
21	Roma Revolving Restaurant	E4

Drinking & Nightlife

22	Joe Kool's	G2

Entertainment

23	BAT Centre	E5
	Catalina Theatre	(see 12)
24	Computicket	D3
25	Playhouse Company	E4

Shopping

26	Victoria Street Market	B3

Information

27	Durban Tourism	H6
28	KwaZulu-Natal Tourism Authority	D4
29	Tourist Junction	D4

Transport

	Baz Bus	(see 28)
30	Computicket	D3
31	Durban Intercity Bus Station	D1
32	Durban Tourism (Beachfront)	F2
	Eldo Coaches	(see 31)
	Greyhound	(see 31)
	Intercape	(see 31)
	Intercity	(see 31)
33	Main Local Bus Terminal	D3
	Margate Mini Coach	(see 31)
	Translux	(see 31)

Warning: the surf and currents at Durban's beaches can be dangerous. Always swim in patrolled areas; these are indicated by flags.

uShaka Marine World AMUSEMENT PARK

(Map p234; ☎031-328 8000; www.ushakamarineworld.co.za; uShaka Beach, the Point; Wet'n'Wild or Sea World adult/child R150/115, combo ticket for both parks R200/150; ⏰9am-5pm) Divided into areas including Sea World and Wet'n'Wild, uShaka Marine World boasts one of the largest aquariums in the world, the biggest collection of sharks in the southern hemisphere, marine animals and exhibits, a mock-up 1940s steamer wreck featuring two classy restaurants, a shopping centre, and enough freshwater rides to make you seasick. There are various options to 'meet' dolphins, seals and rays, but animal-welfare groups suggest such interactions create stress for these creatures.

Activities

With a temperate climate and excellent facilities to enjoy, Durbanites are passionate about their nature, outdoor and adrenalin-inducing activities.

Cycling

With the popular pedestrian and bike promenades along the beachfront and linking the stadium to the beachfront, cycling is a fabulous way to see parts of Durban.

STS Sport BICYCLE RENTAL

(Map p230; ☎031-312 9479; www.stssport.co.za; Shop 6, Moses Mabhida Stadium; per hour R50; ⏰8am-6pm) Bicycles for hire. You'll need to leave identification and R100 as a deposit; unfortunately, you can't lock up the bikes along the way.

Cruises

Several boat and charter trips can be arranged from Wilson's Wharf.

African Queen Marine Charters CRUISE
(Map p234; ☎076 812 7107; www.african-queen.co.za; Durban Yacht Harbour) The luxury yacht *African Queen* cruises dolphin waters for three hours.

Diving & Fishing

Calypso Dive & Adventure Centre DIVING
(Map p234; ☎031-332 0905; www.calypsoushaka.co.za; uShaka Marine World; ⏰9am-6pm) PADI-qualified operator Calypso Diving offers open-water diving courses (from R3500), and advanced courses and dives in nearby wrecks and elsewhere. Beginners' practice dives take place in uShaka's lagoon aquarium. Certified divers can also dive in uShaka's ocean aquarium (R495).

Casea Charters FISHING
(☎031-561 7381; www.caseacharters.co.za; Grannies Pool, Main Beach, Umhlanga; 3/4hr trip R500/600) Casea Charters is a family-run fishing-charter business operating from Umhlanga. Rods, tackle and bait are supplied, and you can keep your catch at no additional fee. Whale and dolphin sightings are often a bonus.

Golf

Durban has an array of decent golf courses. **Windsor Park Municipal Golf Course** (Map p230; fax 031-312 2245; Masabalala Yengwa Ave (NMR Ave); green fee R47) is a popular option. On another level is **Durban Country Club** (Map p230; ☎031-313 1777; www.dcclub.co.za; Walter Gilbert Rd; green fee R275), considered by some to be the best golf course in South Africa.

Indoor Extreme Activities

Besides the Big Swing (R695) inside Moses Mabhida Stadium (p233), try your surfing prowess at the artificial wave house (rides R25 to R85) at giant Gateway Mall (p244) – the water shots will have you performing tricks left, right and centre (your feet are secured into the board, so nonsurfers can have a go).

Skydiving

Skydive KZN EXTREME SPORTS
(☎072 2146 040; www.skydivekzn.co.za; tandem jumps R1800) Skydive KZN offers a seagull's view of Durban and surrounds.

Surfing

Durban has a multitude of good surfing beaches.

Ocean Ventures SURFING, KAYAKING
(Map p234; ☎086-100 1138; www.oceanventures.co.za; uShaka Marine World; lessons R150, soft/hard board hire per hour R100/150; ⏰8am-4pm) On uShaka Beach; also hires out kayaks.

Tours

A good way to experience Durban is in the company of a professional tour guide. Many hostels also arrange backpacker-oriented tours and activities in the Durban area and around KwaZulu-Natal.

Durban Tourism CULTURAL TOUR
(Map p234; ☎031-322 4173; www.durbanexperience.co.za; Old Pavilion Site, OR Tambo Pde (Marine Pde), North Beach) Runs a range of interesting three-hour walking tours of the oriental and

> **FREEDOM TO EXPLORE**
>
> To discover the region's true highlights (the uKhahlamba-Drakensberg region, the national parks and wildlife reserves and the Battlefields), you're better off hiring a car. Durban has a reasonable choice of operators. Most roads are good, but a few locations, such as Sani Pass (to which you can easily take a tour from Underberg), Tembe Elephant Park and many parts of iSimangaliso Wetland Park, require a 4WD.

> **DURBAN'S STREET NAMES**
>
> During 2007 and 2008 Durban's municipal council took a controversial step when it renamed many of Durban's city and suburban streets to reflect a 'new South Africa'. Debate continues to rage over the changes. Many locals are annoyed about the huge cost involved in altering street signs (saying the money would have been better spent on public services) and about the identities of some of the names – mostly former African National Congress (ANC) members and freedom fighters who, some believe, are inappropriate choices. There are also wider repercussions regarding familiarity and orientation.
>
> Confusingly, most locals (including businesses) often refer to the original street names. We have provided the new street names, plus the former street names (in brackets).

DON'T MISS

KWAZULU-NATAL'S PARKS & RESERVES

For those planning to spend time in the province's excellent parks and reserves, **Ezemvelo KZN Wildlife** (p277) is an essential first stop. Accommodation within the parks ranges from humble campsites to comfortable safari tents and luxurious lodges; the free *Fees & Charges* booklet lists accommodation options and prices, as well as entrance charges, for all Ezemvelo KZN Wildlife reserves. Maps of the parks are also available here.

All accommodation must be booked in advance by phone, online, or in person through the Pietermaritzburg office. Last-minute bookings (ie those within 48 hours) must be made directly with the camps.

Officially, the gate entry times of all parks are 5am to 7pm (1 October to 31 March) and 6am to 6pm (1 April to 30 September).

While many of the parks are a must-see for animal-lovers and outdoorsy types, their camps – many of which have high-quality bungalows or safari tents – are also excellent for families and those touring South Africa on a budget.

Tip: if you only have time to visit one or two reserves, highlights include Royal Natal National Park for some uKhahlamba-Drakensberg vistas; Hluhluwe-iMfolozi Park for the wildlife and wilderness accommodation options; Ithala Game Reserve and uMkhuze Game Reserve for its wonderful bird hides and waterholes; and iSimangaliso Wetland Park for its diverse scenery and ecological environments.

historical regions of the city (minimum two people, adult R100), as well as township tours. It can also provide a list of tour guides and operators.

Ricksha Bus BUS TOUR
(Map p234; Durban Tourism, Old Pavilion Site, OR Tambo Pde (Marine Pde), North Beach; adult/child R100/50) A three-hour tour in a rickshaw bus is a novel way to see the city. It covers some city highlights and heads to suburbs including Morningside (Florida Rd). Buses depart twice daily at 9am and 1pm from the beach branch of Durban Tourism.

Natal Sharks Board Boat Tour BOAT TOUR
(Map p234; ☎031-566 0400; www.shark.co.za; Wilson's Wharf; 2hr boat trip R300; ⊙departs 6.30am) A fascinating trip is to accompany Natal Sharks Board personnel in their boat when they tag and release trapped sharks and other fish from the shark nets that protect Durban's beachfront. Boats depart from Wilson's Wharf, which is not to be confused with the head office, which is located in Umhlanga Rocks.

Festivals & Events

Durban International Film Festival FILM
(www.cca.ukzn.ac.za) A cinematic showcase of 200-plus films, held in July.

Awesome Africa Music Festival MUSIC
Highlighting music and theatre from across the continent; held late September/early October.

Diwali RELIGIOUS
The three-day Diwali (in December) is also known as the Festival of Lights.

Sleeping

Despite what you may think when you see the hotel-lined beachfront promenade, much of Durban's best accommodation for all budgets is in the suburbs, where there are upmarket B&Bs and hostels for the budget traveller. Unless you are set on sleeping by the sea, accommodation in the suburbs is better value than the beachfront options. Some hostels will collect you from the airport, and may arrange trips to the beach and other places of interest. Many top-end options are in the suburbs and towards Umhlanga Rocks, with a few in and around the city centre.

City Centre

Note that the city centre shuts down (and is less safe) at night.

Happy Hippo BACKPACKERS $
(Map p234; ☎031-368 7181; www.happy-hippo.info; 222 Mahatma Gandhi Rd (Point Rd); dm R160, d R400-500; 📶) Close to the beach is this spacious, well-run, warehouse-style accommodation choice. There are bright colours, vast spaces and a rooftop bar, which make for a laid-back stay, though some travellers report it's noisy; rooms are off communal areas.

Berea & Around

Gibela Backpackers Lodge BACKPACKERS $
(Map p240; ☎031-303 6291; www.gibelabackpackers.co.za; 119 Ninth Ave, Morningside; dm/s/d R230/460/630; P @ 🛜 ≋) This hostel (a tastefully converted 1950s Tuscan-style home) gets lots of good reports from travellers, including those travelling by themselves. It even provides a continental breakfast – to be enjoyed in an attractive indoor-outdoor dining area. It definitely suits those looking to get away from the hostel party scene. The staff is helpful and there is a craft shop.

Tekweni Backpackers BACKPACKERS $
(Map p240; ☎031-303 1433; www.tekwenibackpackers.co.za; 169 Ninth Ave, Morningside; dm R140, s/d/tr without bathroom from R400/470/570; P 🛜 ≋) The motto of this place says it all: 'Tekweni goes off'. Its courtyard, complete with pool and bar, gets jammed with socialising backpackers on Friday and Saturday nights, as well as on the regular braai (barbecue) nights. The techno beats and general whooping reach all corners of the complex, which includes a couple of well-maintained and artfully decorated lodges.

If peace and quiet is your thing, try somewhere else.

★ **Napier House** B&B $$
(Map p230; ☎031-207 6779; www.napierhouse.co.za; 31 Napier Rd, Berea; s/d incl breakfast R620/900; P ❄ ≋) On a poky little street near the Botanic Gardens, this is an excellent, homey B&B that is terrific value. The former colonial residence has five en-suite rooms that are spacious, light and tastefully organised and have large bathrooms. Breakfast is a highlight, as are the friendly hosts.

Rosetta House GUESTHOUSE $$
(Map p240; ☎031-303 6180; www.rosettahouse.com; 126 Rosetta Rd, Morningside; s/d incl breakfast R725/1000; P ❄ 🛜) This place is very popular with visitors, and for good reason. An elegant place, it has a country-chic feel – and there's not a thing out of place. One of the rooms has a pleasant deck area from where you can glimpse the stadium and sea. It's perfect for mature travellers who seek comfort in a central location.

Benjamin BOUTIQUE HOTEL $$
(Map p240; ☎031-303 4233; www.benjamin.co.za; 141 Florida Rd, Morningside; s/d incl breakfast R975/1255; P ❄ 🛜 ≋) This upmarket boutique hotel is filled with clipped accents and smart rooms of the 'heavy drapes and floral furnishing' variety, around a pretty paved and green courtyard area. It's in a terrific location at the bottom of Florida Rd and with eating and drinking places galore a short walk away.

Concierge BOUTIQUE HOTEL $$$
(Map p240; ☎031-309 4434; www.the-concierge.co.za; 36-42 St Mary's Ave, Greyville; s/d incl breakfast R1000/1700; P ❄ 🛜) One of Durbs' most cutting-edge sleeping options, this cleverly conceived spot – 12 cosy rooms in four pods – is more about the design (urban, funky, shape-oriented) than the spaces (smallish but adequate). For breakfast, roll out of bed and head to Freedom Cafe, also on the premises.

Quarters BOUTIQUE HOTEL $$$
(Map p240; ☎031-303 5246; www.quarters.co.za; 101 Florida Rd, Morningside; s/d incl breakfast from R1500/2100; P ❄) Right in the throbbing heart of Durban's most fashionable eating and drinking quarter, this attractive boutique hotel – at two neighboring locations – balances colonial glamour with small-scale home comforts. A restaurant is on-site at both.

Brown's Bed & Breakfast B&B $$$
(Map p240; ☎031-208 7630; www.brownsguesthouse.co.za; 132 Gladys Mazibuko Rd (Marriott Rd), Essenwood; s/d incl breakfast R850/1500; P ❄) In short, the chic interior attracts even chicer guests who enjoy the 'suites' – a choice of four spacious rooms, each with a small kitchen and smart living space.

North Durban

The area north of Umgeni River comprises many suburbs, including Durban North and Umgeni Heights. Leafy, quiet and sedate, Durban North is one of Durban's wealthier areas and is still easily accessible to the city and the North Coast.

★ **Smith's Cottage** BACKPACKERS $
(☎031-564 6313; www.smithscottage.8m.com; 5 Mount Argus Rd, Umgeni Heights; dm/d R150/400, self-catering cottages R950; P 🛜 ≋) This is an excellent budget option within chirping distance of the Umgeni River Bird Park. It's set around a suburban garden and has a couple of freestanding (smallish) cabins, a large 12-bed dorm with attached kitchen and a smaller four-bed dorm inside the house. The whole place has a great feel and the hosts couldn't be friendlier.

Berea & Around

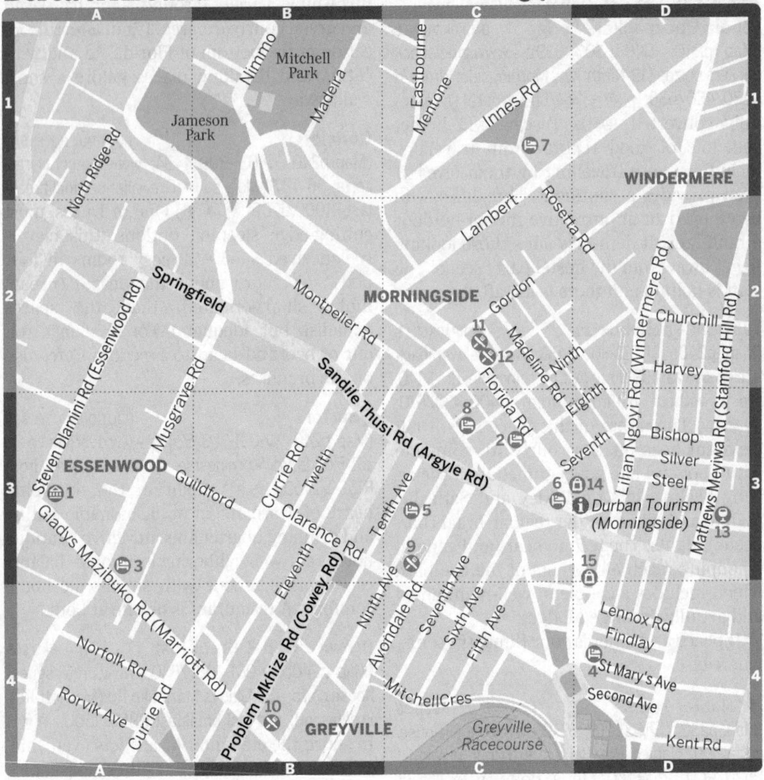

Riverside Hotel & Spa HOTEL $$
(☎031-563 0600; www.riversidehotel.co.za; 10 Kenneth Kaunda Rd (Northway), Durban North; r from R1000; P) It's hard to miss this white behemoth just over the Umgeni River on the right-hand side. The corridors have a touch of bling (LA-style neon-lit colonnades), but the rooms offer all the comforts of an upmarket place. It's readily accessible from the city and Durban's North Coast.

Beachfront

★Balmoral HOTEL $$
(Map p234; ☎031-368 8220; www.raya-hotels.com; 125 OR Tambo Pde (Marine Pde); s/d from R900/1000; P@) The only low-rise hotel on the beachfront, the Balmoral has a faded grandeur born of its former life as a colonial residence. It's in a great location on Durban's waterfront, with the promenade a short stroll away. Old-world charm meets new-age facilities in the well-laid-out rooms.

Beach Hotel HOTEL $$
(Map p234; ☎031-337 5511; www.beachhotel.co.za; 107 OR Tambo Pde; r incl breakfast from R650; P) Wake up to the sound, sight and smell of the ocean in a beachfront room at the ageing Beach Hotel. In the thick of Durban's watery action, the place could do with an upgrade but is handy to the informal weekend markets and the many promenade pools. Spacious rooms (some with bathtub) have a great view from the 6th floor.

Blue Waters HOTEL $$
(Map p230; ☎031-327 7000; www.bluewatershotel.co.za; 175 Snell Pde; s/d incl breakfast from R800/900; P) At the northern end of the beachfront, away from the promenade crowd, Blue Waters is a classic hotel that has recently undergone an extensive renovation. Rooms have brilliant ocean views, soft bedding and stylish furnishings. It also has a complicated pricing structure depending

Berea & Around

◉ **Sights**
1 Campbell CollectionsA3

🛏 **Sleeping**
2 Benjamin...C3
3 Brown's Bed & Breakfast....................A3
4 Concierge.. D4
5 Gibela Backpackers Lodge.................C3
6 Quarters...C3
7 Rosetta House.....................................C1
8 Tekweni BackpackersC3

🍴 **Eating**
9th Avenue Bistro(see 9)
Freedom Cafe...............................(see 4)
9 Joop's Place...C3
10 Market...B4
11 Mozambik ...C2
12 Spiga D'oro ..C2

🍷 **Drinking & Nightlife**
13 Lounge..D3
Spiga Bar...................................... (see 12)

🛍 **Shopping**
14 African Art Centre................................D3
15 Ike's Books & CollectablesD3

on the day of the week you stay – the rate displayed here is an average only.

Southern Sun
Suncoast Hotel & Towers HOTEL **$$$**
(Map p230; ☑031-314 7878; www.tsogosun hotels.com; 20 Battery Beach Rd; r from R1900; 🅿🌊🛜🏊) This hotel, adjacent to the casino, is a safe if businesslike bet. It has over 100 sleek and contemporary rooms with flash trimmings. Be aware that the 'Philadelphia suite' design means that the bathrooms are incorporated into the bedrooms themselves (read: little privacy among friends). Awesome vista from the top floor.

🍴 Eating

Indian and Asian flavours abound in Durban, as do healthy meat and salad dishes (although these can become a little repetitive). Look out for the Indian snack (representing a thick slice of Durban history) the bunny chow. It's a half or quarter loaf of bread hollowed out and filled with beans or curry stew.

🍴 City Centre

Around Dr Yusuf Dadoo St (Grey St) you'll find Indian takeaways (ask around). Otherwise, there are limited options in the centre.

Roma Revolving Restaurant ITALIAN **$$**
(Map p234; ☑031-337 6707; www.roma.co.za; 32nd fl, John Ross House, Margaret Mncadi Ave (Victoria Embankment), City Centre; mains R80-170; ⏰noon-2.30pm Fri & Sat, 6-10.30pm Mon-Sat; ❇) One of only a few revolving restaurants worldwide, and one of the handful of central restaurants surviving in Durban, Roma offers stunning views over Durban in its own leaning House of John Ross. Beautifully prepared dishes are mainly Italian, and include pasta any way you want it and lots of seafood variations.

🍴 Beachfront

On the beachfront, you'll be hard pressed to find much more than eateries serving the usual spread of burgers, pizza and candy floss. You are better off heading to the uShaka Marina or the casino, both of which have some excellent choices.

African Peninsula
Restaurant INTERNATIONAL **$$**
(☑031-467 1045; 599 Marine Dr, Brighton Beach; mains R90-120; ⏰lunch noon-4.30pm, dinner 5-10pm) Basically huge balcony overlooking the ocean, this coastal spot gets rave reviews from travellers. Offerings include smokey spare ribs, Moroccan lamb shank, tempura calamari and grilled line-caught fish of the day. While the food is good, it's the location that makes this place special. Brighton Beach is south of Durban harbour, reached via the M4.

Cafe Jiran CAFE **$$**
(Map p230; ☑031-332 4485; 151 Snell Pde; mains R40-130; ⏰6.30am-10pm) Next to Bel-Aire Suites Hotel, this funky space is the spot for a post-dip coffee, fruit crush or breakfast, or just to watch the beautiful people walk (run, cycle, skate) by. There are evening fine-dining options from Tuesday to Saturday – tapas dishes include chilli salt calamari, lamb koftas and grilled haloumi.

Cargo Hold SEAFOOD **$$**
(Map p234; ☑031-328 8065; uShaka Marine World, the Point; mains R150; ⏰noon-2.30pm & 6-9.30pm Mon-Sat, noon-5pm Sun) A seafood encounter of the most novel kind. On the *Phantom Ship* in uShaka Marina, your dining companions are fish with very large teeth – the glass tank forms one of the walls to a shark aquarium. Well known for casting some high-quality fish dishes with Spanish flavours.

Moyo INTERNATIONAL $$
(Map p234; ☎031-332 0606; uShaka Marina, the Point; mains R80-130; ⏰11am-11pm) Housed in the uShaka complex, Moyo is more novelty than quality cuisine, and makes for a fun (if noisy) night out. The concept is great – the decor features sculptures and decorations from recycled materials, and there's face painting, fabulous tableside serenades and bands of a high quality. Food includes ostrich salad and Knysna oysters.

Berea & Around

Florida Rd is chock-a-block with lively eateries, cafes and bars, and nearby Lilian Ngoyi Rd (Windermere Rd) has some good options, too. There is a wonderful cafe hub opposite Mitchell Park on Innes Rd.

Freedom Cafe CAFE $
(Map p240; ☎073 104 2866; www.tastefreedom.co.za; 37-43 St Mary's Ave; mains R60-80; ⏰7am-4pm, to 9pm Fri) An upmarket, colourful, funky place in an imaginatively converted space with a pebble-strewn courtyard. Asian-influenced food includes Vietnamese pulled pork; there are also vegetarian options and a kids' menu. It's behind Concierge Boutique Bungalows.

★**Cafe 1999** INTERNATIONAL $$
(Map p230; ☎031-202 3406; www.cafe1999.co.za; Silverton Rd, Silvervause Centre, Berea; tapas R50, mains R120; ⏰lunch 12.30-2.30pm Mon-Fri, dinner 6.30-10.30pm Mon-Sat) This classy restaurant looks unassuming inside, but assume that you will get seriously good modern Mediterranean fusion food here. Tapas including stuffed and deep-fried olives, kudu carpaccio and chilli prawns all hit the spot. There are always lots of daily specials, and friendly wait staff to run you through them.

9th Avenue Bistro INTERNATIONAL $$
(Map p240; ☎031-312 9134; Ninth Ave, Avonmore Centre, Morningside; mains R150; ⏰12-2.30pm Tue-Fri, 6-9.30pm Mon-Sat) The setting, in the car park of the Avonmore Centre, isn't anything to rave about, but the fine-dining experience is. This smart, modern spot serves up fabulously reliable international fare. The feature menu changes (often with venison, and the likes of smoked ostrich fillet), while the bistro standards include braised lamb shoulder and line-caught fish of the day.

Mali's Indian Restaurant INDIAN $$
(Map p230; ☎031-312 8535; 77 Smiso Nkwanya Rd (Goble Rd), Morningside; mains R90; ⏰lunch 11am-3pm Tue-Sun, dinner 6-10pm Tue-Thu, to 10.30pm Fri-Sun) In a city that boasts a huge Indian population, this place is about as good as Indian food gets in Durban's restaurant scene. North and South Indian dishes are available at fairly inconspicuous, family-run Mali's.

Market INTERNATIONAL $$
(Map p240; ☎031-309 8581; www.marketrestaurant.co.za; 40 Gladys Mazibuko Rd (Marriott Rd), Greyville; mains R80-160; ⏰breakfast & lunch Mon-Sun, dinner Tue-Sat) Both food and crowd are 'gourmet' here – smart, fashionable and very nice. The breakfasts, casual lunches and more formal dinners are delectable. Imaginative dishes include the likes of calamari, quinoa, feta, red pesto and macadamia salad; produce is locally sourced, free range and organic, where possible. The cafe's tree-lined courtyard and fountain are the perfect antidote to the hot weather.

Spiga D'oro ITALIAN $$
(Map p240; ☎031-303 9511; 200 Florida Rd; mains R50-90; ⏰breakfast, lunch & dinner) It looks like a typical cafe along this very popular strip, but Spiga serves up hearty helpings of Italian food, including delicious pasta dishes. On the weekends, this place is packed with locals enjoying some people-watching along Florida Rd. A dining section in the rear requires reservations.

Mozambik PORTUGUESE $$
(Map p240; ☎031-303 2135; 198C Florida Rd; mains R90-150; ⏰noon-10pm) Set in a courtyared just off Florida Rd, Mozambik has a very pleasant upstairs dining area that's a great place to put away some Portuguese-influenced fish, prawn, poultry or steak dishes. The grilled steak in particular is a highlight.

Joop's Place STEAKHOUSE $$
(Map p240; ☎031-312 9135; Ninth Ave, Avonmore Centre, Morningside; mains R80-170; ⏰dinner Mon-Thu & Sat, lunch & dinner Fri) In a most unlikely location at the rear of a shopping centre, unpretentious Joop's Place has Durbanites flocking in for high-quality steaks – each cooked by Joop himself. Rare, indeed.

Drinking & Nightlife

The best drinking and dancing dens are found in the suburbs along Florida Rd; the casino also has some good spots. Nightclubs seem to set up and close down to their own very fast beat; it's best to ask around for the latest offerings.

Moyo uShaka Pier Bar BAR
(Map p230; ☎031-332 0662; www.moyo.co.za; uShaka Marine World, the Point; ⊙11am-late) Perched out on the edge of a pier in front of uShaka Marine World, this is a top spot to go for a South African sundowner with fabulous views of the harbour on one side, the Indian Ocean on the other, and the stadium and cityscape beyond. It's laid-back, exotic Durban at its chic best.

Spiga Bar BAR
(Map p240; 200 Florida Rd; ⊙closed Mon) This brand-new bar attached to Spiga D'oro is an excellent spot for a relaxing drink, and it could be the start of something completely new in the Durban nightlife scene. It's cosy and intimate and has a long bar featuring Cape Town–brewed beer on tap. Refined but unpretentious, it reminded us of bars in Melbourne, Australia.

Unity Brasserie & Bar BREWERY
(Map p230; www.unitybar.co.za; 117 Silverton Rd; ⊙noon-10.30pm Mon-Thu & Sun, to midnight Fri & Sat) This cosy bar has quality craft beer on tap from That Brewing Co. The Irish Red goes down particularly well. It's a very friendly place, with families welcome during the day and early evening.

Billy the Bum's CLUB
(Map p230; ☎031-303 1988; www.billythebums.co.za; 504 Lilian Ngoyi Rd (Windermere Rd), Morningside; ⊙noon-late Mon-Sat) Attracting a crowd of Durban's upwardly mobile (a sign even says 'elegantly wasted'), this suburban cocktail bar is reliably raucous.

Joe Kool's CLUB
(Map p234; ☎082 378 8068; Lower OR Tambo Pde (Marine Pde), North Beach) The inevitable finish line for any day on the beach, this venerable nightspot cooks up a cocktail of cold beer, big-screen TV, dance music and feisty crowds.

Lounge GAY & LESBIAN
(Map p240; ☎031-303 9023; www.thelounge.za.org; 226 Mathews Meyiwa Rd (Stamford Hill Rd)) With a range of different bars, this is a good place to hook up, and it caters to both gay and lesbian crowds.

Origin CLUB
(Map p230; ☎031-201 9959; www.theorigin.co.za; 9 Clark Rd, Lower Glenwood; ⊙9pm-late Sat) Covering a range of music from deep house to electro, soul and funk (and much more), this stylish spot remains at the forefront of Durban's club scene. Sometimes open Friday night – check before going.

☆ Entertainment

Durban is a lively city with a vibrant cultural scene. Hundreds of events, from Natal Sharks games and cricket matches to film festivals and theatre performances, can be booked through **Computicket** (Map p234; ☎083 915 8000; www.computicket.co.za). There are outlets at the Playhouse Company, and at MTN shops at Pavilion and Gateway malls.

Live Music

KwaZulu-Natal Philharmonic Orchestra CLASSICAL MUSIC
(☎031-369 9438; http://kznphil.org.za) The orchestra has an interesting spring concert program with regular performances in City Hall. Check the calendar and events listings on the website.

Chairman LIVE MUSIC
(Map p230; 146 Mahatma Gandhi Rd (Point Rd); ⊙7pm-2am Thu-Sat, to midnight Sun-Wed) This classy lounge-bar is in a seedy part of Durban, so grab a cab to get here. A very classy joint that's both old-style and new-age, it challenges convention. It's essentially a jazz lounge, but it's well worth going just to taste one of the excellent cocktails.

BAT Centre LIVE MUSIC
(Map p234; ☎031-332 0451; www.batcentre.co.za; 45 Maritime Pl) One of Durban's more interesting, if unreliable, arty haunts, this venue features semiregular jazz performances – check what's on before heading down. Note that the area is isolated, so it can be dodgy at night. It's off Margaret Mncadi Ave (Victoria Embankment).

Rainbow Restaurant & Jazz Club JAZZ
(☎031-702 9161; www.therainbow.co.za; 23 Stanfield Lane, Pinetown) In Pinetown, 15km west of the centre, this was the first place in Natal to cater to blacks in a so-called 'white area' in the 1980s. With a reputation as the centre of the jazz scene and still the preferred local haunt, it features gigs on the first or last Sunday of the month. See the website for info.

Centre for Jazz JAZZ
(http://music.ukzn.ac.za; South Ridge Rd, Durban Campus, University of KwaZulu-Natal) The University of KwaZulu-Natal has contemporary music and jazz performances every Wednesday afternoon at 5pm during university

RIDE A 'RICKSHA'

Rickshaws – known locally as 'rickshas' – ply their trade along OR Tambo Pde (Marine Pde), many sporting exotic Zulu regalia. In 1904 there were about 2000 registered rickshaw-pullers, and it was an important means of transport. A 15-minute ride costs about R60 (plus R10 for a happy snap).

terms. Performers vary from township jazz players and professional performers (the likes of Jimmy Dludlu and Sipho 'Hotstix' Mabuse) to student performers.

Theatre

Playhouse Company THEATRE
(Map p234; ☎031-369 9555; www.playhousecompany.com; 29 Anton Lembede St (Smith St)) Opposite City Hall, Durban's central theatre is a stunning venue. The Zulu mosaics and beadwork in the foyer are alone worth seeing, as are the dance, drama and music performances.

Barnyard Theatre THEATRE
(☎031-566 3045; www.barnyardtheatre.co.za; Gateway Mall, Umhlanga Ridge) This unique and popular place is a reconstructed barnyard and houses mainstream theatre productions. Audience members can take their own food (and buy drinks at the bar) or buy food at the takeaway outlets.

Catalina Theatre THEATRE
(Map p234; ☎031-837 5999; www.catalinatheatre.co.za; 18 Boatman's Rd, Wilson's Wharf) This is a not-for-profit venture that brings new artistic works to the stage. Boatman's Rd runs parallel to Margaret Mncadi Ave (Victoria Embankment).

Sport

Cricket, football and rugby are played in KwaZulu-Natal. Professional teams such as AmaZulu and Manning Rangers play in town, and international teams also visit.

Moses Mabhida Stadium (p233) was built to host the 2010 World Cup. With 60,000 seats, **Kings Park Stadium** (Map p230; ☎031-312 5022; Jacko Jackson Dr) is currently home to the **Natal Sharks** (www.sharksrugby.co.za) rugby team. Cricket fever is cured at **Kingsmead Cricket Stadium** (Sahara Stadium; Map p234; ☎031-335 4200; 2 Kingsmead Cl), where the international knockabouts are hosted.

Shopping

Durban is known for its factory outlets, which stock everything from surfing items to footwear at reasonable prices. For necessities, major shopping centres include the **Musgrave Centre** (Map p230; ☎031-201 5129; Musgrave Rd) and **Pavilion** (☎031-265 0558; ⏲9am-6pm Mon-Fri, to 5pm Sat, 10am-5pm Sun); the latter is in Westville, just an 8km drive from the centre on the N3 towards Pietermaritzburg.

Victoria Street Market MARKET
(Map p234; ☎031-306 4021; www.indianmarket.co.za; 151-55 Bertha Mkhize St (Victoria St), City Centre; ⏲6am-6pm Mon-Fri, 8am-2pm Sat & Sun) At the western end of Bertha Mkhize St, this is the hub of the Indian community. It offers a typically rip-roaring subcontinental shopping experience, with more than 160 stalls selling wares from across Asia. Watch your wallet and don't take valuables. Note: most shops run by Muslims close between noon and 2pm on Friday.

African Art Centre ARTS & CRAFTS
(Map p240; ☎031-312 3084; www.afriart.org.za; Florida Rd; ⏲8.30am-5pm Mon-Fri, 9am-3pm Sat) This not-for-profit gallery has an excellent selection of high-quality work by rural craftspeople and artists.

Gateway Theatre of Shopping (Gateway Mall) MALL
(☎031-566 2332; www.gatewayworld.co.za; 1 Palm Blvd, Umhlanga Ridge; ⏲9am-7pm Mon-Thu, to 9pm Fri & Sat, to 6pm Sun) The mother of all shopping malls is popular with Durbanites. It's reached via the N2 just north of Uhmlanga Rocks.

Ike's Books & Collectables BOOKS
(Map p240; ☎031-303 9214; 48A Florida Rd; ⏲10am-5pm Mon-Fri, 9am-2pm Sat) More like a museum than a bookshop, this antique-filled delight is chock-a-block with first editions and is everything an antiquarian bookshop should be.

Information

DANGERS & ANNOYANCES

As with elsewhere in South Africa, crime against tourists and locals can and does occur in Durban. You should be aware and careful but not paranoid. Muggings and pickpocketing, once a problem around the beach esplanade, have declined since that area's upgrade, but be careful here at night. Extra care should also be taken around the Umgeni Rd side of the train station and the Warwick Triangle markets.

At night, with the exception of the casino and around the Playhouse theatre (if something is on), central Durban becomes a ghost town as people head to the suburbs for entertainment. Always catch a cab to and from nightspots, as well as uShaka Marine World (and ride with others, if possible).

If you have a car, parking is generally OK outside suburban restaurants, but don't leave your car in the street all night: use off-street parking (note that most accommodation options offer this). Never leave valuables exposed on your car seats, even while driving.

The best advice is from locals, so ask around when you get here. The security situation, although greatly improved in the city, is still 'fluid', so don't be shy about prompting locals for advice.

EMERGENCY

Ambulance (☎10177)

General Emergency (☎031-361 0000)

Main Police Station (☎10111; Stanger St (Stalwart Simelane St)) North of the city centre. There's another station on OR Tambo Pde, near Funworld on the beach.

INTERNET ACCESS

Wi-fi access is available at most cafes, and in some restaurants. Most hostels, guesthouses and hotels offer internet access. Charges start at about R30 per hour.

MEDICAL SERVICES

Entabeni Hospital (☎031-204 1300, 24hr trauma centre 031-204 1377; 148 Mazisi Kunene Rd (South Ridge Rd), Berea) The trauma centre charges around R700 per consultation, the balance of which is refunded if the full amount is not utilised.

St Augustines (☎031-268 5000; 107 Chelmsford Rd, Berea) KwaZulu-Natal's largest private hospital has a good emergency department.

Travel Doctor (☎031-360 1122; www.durbantraveldoctor.co.za; International Convention Centre, 45 Bram Fischer Rd (Old Ordanance Rd); ⌚8.30am-4pm Mon-Fri, to 11am Sat) For travel-related advice.

MONEY

There are banks with ATMs and change facilities across the city. These include Standard Bank, FNB, Nedbank and ABSA.

American Express Musgrave Centre (☎031-202 8733; FNB House, 151 Musgrave Rd, Musgrave)

Bidvest Bank (☎031-202 7833; Shop 311, Level 3, Musgrave Centre, Musgrave Rd, Berea; ⌚9am-5pm Mon-Fri, to 1pm Sat)

POST

There are post offices in the major shopping centres, including the Musgrave and Windermere Centres.

Main Post Office (Map p234; cnr Dr Pixley KaSeme St (West St) & Dorothy Nyembe St (Gardiner St); ⌚8am-5pm Mon-Fri, to 1pm Sat) Near City Hall.

TOURIST INFORMATION

You can pick up a free copy of the *Events Calendar* or the half-yearly *Destination Durban*.

Durban Tourism (Map p234; ☎031-337 8099; www.durbanexperience.co.za; uShaka Marine World, the Point) A useful information service on Durban and surrounds. It can help with general accommodation and arranges tours of Durban and beyond. There are also branches at the beachfront (Map p234; ☎031-322 4205; www.durbanexperience.co.za; Old Pavilion Site, OR Tambo Pde (Marine Pde); ⌚8am-5pm) and another at Morningside (Map p240; ☎031-322 4164; www.durbanexperience.co.za; 90 Florida Rd, Morningside; ⌚8am-4.30pm Mon-Fri), the latter of which can take reservations for South African national parks.

King Shaka Airport Tourist Information Office (☎031-322 6046; international arrivals hall; ⌚7am-9pm) Durban Tourism, KwaZulu-Natal Tourism Authority and Ezemvelo KZN Wildlife all share a desk (the latter open 8am to 4.30pm Monday to Friday only) at the airport.

KwaZulu-Natal Tourism Authority (KZN Tourism; Map p234; ☎031-366 7500; www.zulu.org.za; ground fl, Tourist Junction Bldg, 160 Monty Naicker St (Pine St), City Centre; ⌚8.30am-4.30pm Mon-Fri) Has lots of glossy brochures, but the assistance stops there.

Getting There & Away

AIR

Several airlines link Durban with South Africa's other main centres. Internet fares vary greatly depending on the day of the week, the month and even the time of day.

King Shaka International Airport (DUR; ☎032-436 6585; http://kingshakainternational.co.za) Opened in 2010, the airport is at La Mercy, 40km north of the city.

AIRPORT SHUTTLE

King Shaka Airport Shuttle Bus (☎031-465 5573; shuttle.airportbustransport.co.za; per person R80; ⌚to airport 4.30am-8pm, from airport 7.30am-10.30pm) The King Shaka Airport Shuttle Bus runs hourly between hotels and key locations in Durban and the beachfront via Umhlanga Rocks. Buy your ticket on board the bus.

SHARED TAXI

Some long-distance minibus taxis leave from stops in the streets opposite the Umgeni Rd entrance to the Durban train station. Others running mainly to the South Coast and the Wild Coast region of Eastern Cape leave from around the Berea train station. Check with your cab driver; they usually know the departure points. Be alert in and around the minibus taxi ranks.

Kulula.com (☎ 0861 585 852; www.kulula.com) A budget airline linking Durban with Jo'burg and Cape Town.

Mango (☎ 0861 001 234; www.flymango.com) A no-frills airline that is a subsidiary of SAA, with flights to Jo'burg and Cape Town.

South African Airlink (SAAirlink; ☎ 032-436 2602; www.flyairlink.co.za) Flies daily to Nelspruit, Bloemfontein and George.

South African Airways (SAA; www.flysaa.com) Flies at least once daily to most major regional airports in South Africa.

BUS

Long-distance buses leave from the bus stations near the Durban train station (p246). Enter the station from Masabalala Yengwa Ave (NMR Ave), not Umgeni Rd. Long-distance bus companies have their offices here.

Note: tickets for all long-distance buses can be bought from Shoprite/Checkers shops and online from **Computicket** (Map p234; www.computicket.com).

Baz Bus (Map p234; ☎ 0861 229 287; www.bazbus.com) Baz Bus is based in Cape Town. You can hop on and off as often as you like along the route for a given price, and can be picked up and dropped off at selected hostels. The seven-/14-/21-day pass (R2100/3400/4200) allows you to travel in any direction and as often as you like within the period. See the website for routes.

Eldo Coaches (Map p234; ☎ 031-307 3363; www.eldocoaches.co.za) Has three buses daily to Jo'burg (R210 to R280, eight hours).

Greyhound (Map p234; ☎ 083 915 9000; www.greyhound.co.za) Has daily buses to Jo'burg (R350, eight hours), Cape Town (R700, 22 to 27 hours), Port Elizabeth (R485, 15 hours) and Port Shepstone (R130, 1¾ hours). Within KZN, Greyhound buses run daily to Pietermaritzburg (R230, one hour) and Ladysmith (R310, four hours), among other destinations.

Intercape (Map p234; ☎ 0861 287 287; www.intercape.co.za) Has several daily buses to Jo'burg (R400, eight hours). For connections to Mozambique, buses head to Maputo (via Jo'burg; R550, 15 hours).

Intercity (Map p234; ☎ 031-305 9090; www.intercity.co.za) Operates daily services from Durban to Margate (R110, 2½ hours), Jo'burg's international airport (R390, 8½ hours), Jo'burg's Park Station Bus Terminal (R280, 8½ hours) and Pretoria (R300, nine hours).

Margate Mini Coach (Map p234; ☎ 039-312 1406; www.margatecoach.co.za) Head to Durban station or King Shaka International Airport to hop on this bus, which links Durban and Margate three times a day (R180, 2½ hours), and also Port Edward (R230, three hours).

Translux (Map p234; ☎ 0861 589 282; www.translux.co.za) Runs daily buses to Jo'burg (R350, eight hours) and Cape Town (R850, 27 hours).

CAR

Hiring a car is one of the best options in KZN; car travel is by far the easiest way of getting around. Most major car-rental companies have offices at the airport and in the city.

Aroundabout Cars (☎ 086 0422 4022; www.aroundaboutcars.com) This company's rates are competitive and it has options including unlimited mileage and full insurance.

TRAIN

Durban train station (Masabalala Yengwa Ave/NMR Ave) is huge. The local inner-city or suburban trains are not recommended for travellers; these are not commonly used and even hardy travellers report feeling unsafe.

However, mainline passenger long-distance services are another matter – they are efficient and arranged into separate male and female sleeper compartments. These are run by **Shosholoza Meyl** (☎ 086 000 8888, 031-361 7167; www.shosholozameyl.co.za) and include the Trans Natal, which leaves Durban several times a week for Jo'burg (R330, 12½ hours) via Pietermaritzburg and Ladysmith.

Premier Classe (☎ 086 000 8888, 031-361 7167; www.premierclasse.co.za) The fully serviced luxury Premier Classe has Jo'burg to Durban departures on the last Friday of the month, returning Durban to Jo'burg the following Sunday. Tickets should be booked in advance (R1120, about 14 hours).

Rovos Rail (☎ 012-315 8242; www.rovosrail.co.za) The Rovos is a luxury steam train on which, from a mere R16,230, you can enjoy old-world luxury on a three-day choof from Durban to Pretoria via the Battlefields and nature reserves.

Getting Around

TO/FROM THE AIRPORT

Some hostels run their own taxi shuttle services for clients at competitive prices. By taxi, the same trip costs around R450.

BUS

Durban People Mover (☎031-309 2731; www.durban.gov.za/City_Services/ethekwini_transport_authority/Pages/People_Mover.aspx; ⏰5am-10pm) The useful Durban People Mover shuttle bus operates along several routes. Tickets (R16) can be purchased on board and allow you to get on and off as many times as you like within a day. Single-leg tickets cost R5.50. The service runs daily between 5am and 10pm.

The bus links the beachfront to the city centre and runs the length of the beachfront from uShaka Marine World to Suncoast Casino, with designated stops (including the Victoria Street Market and City Hall) along the way.

Durban Transport (☎031-309 3250) runs the bus services Mynah and Aqualine. Mynah covers most of the city and local residential areas. Trips cost around R5 and you get a slight discount if you prepurchase 10 tickets. Stops include North Beach, South Beach, Musgrave Rd/Mitchell Park Circle, Peter Mokaba Ridge/Vause, Botanic Gardens and Kensington Rd. The larger Aqualine buses run through the greater metropolitan area.

TAXI

Always use metered cabs. A taxi between the beach and Florida Rd, Morningside, usually costs about R60. Companies running a reliable 24-hour service include **Mozzie Cabs** (☎031-303 5787; www.mozziecabs.mobi), **Zippy Cabs** (☎031-202 7067, 031-202 7068; www.zippycabs.co.za) and **Eagle** (☎0800 330 336; www.eagletaxicabs.co.za).

SOUTH COAST

South of Durban is a 160km-long string of seaside resorts and suburbs running from Amanzimtoti to Port Edward, near the Eastern Cape border. There's a bit of a *Groundhog Day* feel about this mass of shoulder-to-shoulder getaways that are spread out along two routes – the N2 and Rte 102. However, the coastal region's sandy beaches are interspersed with some pretty gardens and grassy areas, especially in the southern section. The region is a surfers' and divers' delight (the latter because of Aliwal Shoal dive site), and in summer there ain't much room to swing a brolly. Inland, the sugar cane, bananas and palms provide a pleasant, lush, green contrast to the beach culture. The attractive **Oribi Gorge Nature Reserve**, near Port Shepstone, provides beautiful forest walks, eating and accommodation options.

Pick up the useful brochure *Southern Explorer* (www.southernexplorer.co.za).

Warner Beach & Around

Warner Beach is the first place along the strip that offers a bit of breathing space. Further south, Umkomaas and Scottburgh are good diving-off points for Aliwal Shoal.

The best budget accommodation along this strip is **Blue Sky Mining Backpackers & Lodge** (☎031-916 5394; www.blueskymining.co.za; 5 Nelson Palmer Rd, Warner Beach; dm R150, d from R400; P@🛜≋), an ever-expanding designer-recycler's delight with a range of sleeping spaces, including a choice of two main houses and a brilliant outlook over the water below.

Information is available from **Tourism Umdoni** (☎039-976 1364; www.tourismsouthcoast.co.za; Scott St, Scottburgh; ⏰8am-5pm), next to the Scottburgh Memorial Library.

Umzumbe & Umtentweni

On the coast north of Port Shepstone, Umzumbe and Umtentweni make for pleasant stopovers.

Sleeping

Spot Backpackers BACKPACKERS $
(☎039-695 1318; www.spotbackpackers.com; 23 Ambleside Rd, Umtentweni; camping R100, dm/d without bathroom R150/360, cabin d R500; 🛜≋) Close to Port Shepstone, this is spot-on for position (a right-on-the-beach deal for sand, sun and surf) and is a justifiably popular, albeit slightly jaded, place. Offers use of kayaks and a host of other activities.

Mantis & Moon Backpacker Lodge BACKPACKERS $
(☎039-684 6256; www.mantisandmoon.net; 7/178 Station Rd, Umzumbe; dm R140, d with/without bathroom R480/380; ≋) This place has more accommodation options than subtropical tree varieties in its compact jungle garden: a giant teepee, small rustic cabins and tree houses. It's not five star, but there's a Jacuzzi, a rock pool, a bar and a laid-back atmosphere. You'll hear the words 'chilled' and 'vibe' mentioned a lot; travellers regularly give it the thumbs up.

Umdlalo Lodge LODGE $$
(☎039-695 0224; www.umdlalolodge.co.za; 5 Rethman Dr, Umtentweni; s/d incl breakfast from R700/1200; ❄🛜) With eight luxurious rooms, and even a honeymoon suite, this place makes a seriously good coastal chill

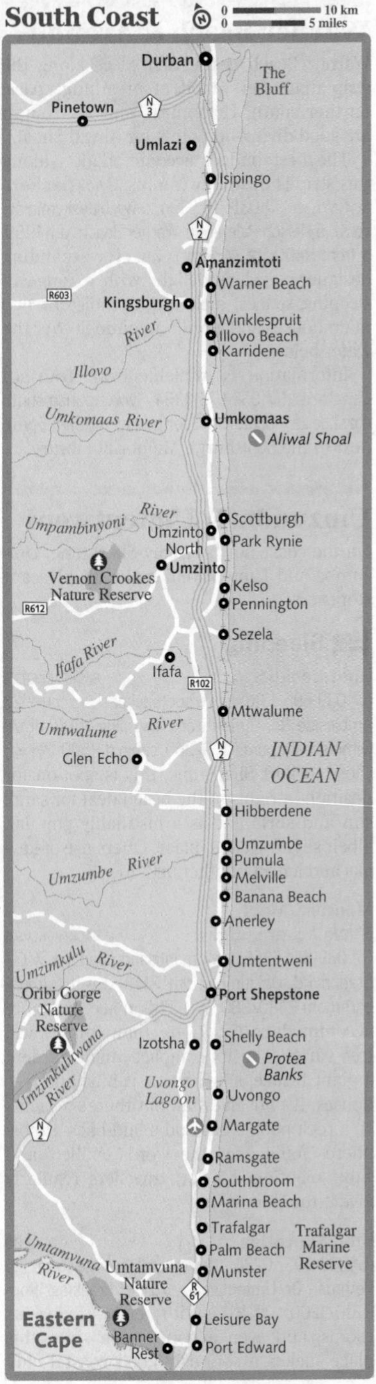

spot. Each bedroom suite leads onto a charming central courtyard. Zizi's Restaurant, on site, with its meat-driven menu is a great place for a relaxed meal.

Getting There & Away

Greyhound (083 915 9000; www.greyhound.co.za) has daily buses between Port Shepstone and Durban (R260, 1¾ hours). If you are staying at one of the backpackers, ask the driver to drop you in Umzumbe or Umtentweni. The Baz Bus (p246) also runs here.

Oribi Gorge Nature Reserve & Around

Oribi Gorge Nature Reserve NATURE RESERVE
(039-679 1644; www.kznwildlife.com; admission R10, camping R70, 2-bed huts R330; 6am-6pm summer, 7.30am-4.30pm winter) The Oribi Gorge Nature Reserve is inland from Port Shepstone, off the N2. The spectacular gorge, on the Umzimkulwana River, is one of the highlights of the South Coast with beautiful scenery, animals and birds, plus walking trails and pretty picnic spots. The reception office is accessed via the N2 on the southern side of the gorge. Here, too, are some delightful wooden chalets, nestled in the forest – the perfect base for those who wish to spend time in this area.

Lake Eland Game Reserve WILDLIFE RESERVE
(039-687 0395; www.lakeeland.co.za; day visitors adult/child R50/30, camping/dm R100/250, 2-person cabins R500-800; 7am-5.30pm) The reserve has over 40 animal species, and 200 bird species. You can head off on a self-drive (R50 per person) or a wildlife drive (R250 per person, minimum four). A 4.7km zip-line includes the zip-extreme, which reaches speeds of 160km/h (R410 to R510, including gate entry). A short gorge walk crosses a 130m-high suspension bridge, and fishing and canoeing are available. You'll find the reserve 40km from Port Shepstone; drive 26km along Oribi Flats Rd off the N2.

There are well-maintained log cabins overlooking a small lake; fisher cottages; camping; and dorm beds in a massive pipe! A restaurant is open from 8am to 4pm.

Wild 5 Adventures ADVENTURE SPORTS
(082 566 7424; www.wild5adventures.co.za; Oribi Gorge Hotel) Organises activities within the Oribi Gorge Nature Reserve, including a 100m Wild Swing (free-fall jump and swing) off Lehr's Falls (R400), abseiling (R300),

white-water rafting (R525), horse riding (R220 per 1½ hours) and a zip-line across the gorge (R250). It's located 11km off the N2 along the Oribi Flats Rd.

Leopard Rock Lookout Chalets CHALET $$
(☎039-687 0303; www.leopardrockc.co.za; Main Oribi Gorge Rd; s/d incl breakfast R800/1400) Accommodation here is in four pleasant chalets, although it's the vista that's the winner. The dining deck boasts a superb view of the uMzumkulu Gorge. Thoughtful touches include a sherry bottle and glasses, and two massive chairs in the lounge room for kicking back and letting Africa come to you. The coffee shop's open 9am to 4pm Wednesday to Sunday.

It's likely you'll find the appetising meals here more tasteful than the sign that reads 'children found unattended in this garden will be sold into slavery'.

Ramsgate, Southbroom & Around

The tourist hub of Margate is a claustrophobic concrete jungle with a string of loud and lively bars. You're better off heading to nearby Ramsgate, with a nice little beach, or to the lush green confines of Southbroom, the posh neck of the woods but delightful for the fact that it's within a bushbuck (large antelope) conservancy.

Sights & Activities

Umtamvuna Nature Reserve NATURE RESERVE
(www.kznwildlife.com; adult/concession R15/5; ⌚6am-6pm Apr-Sep, 7am-5pm Oct-Mar) The reserve is on a gorge on the Umtamvuna River (which forms part of the border with Eastern Cape). This beautiful dense forest has great nature walks, with wildflowers in spring, plus mammals and many species of bird. To get there from Port Edward, follow the signs off R61 to Izingolweni and continue for 8km. Pick up a brochure at the reserve's entrance.

Sleeping

Vuna Valley Lodge BACKPACKERS $
(☎039-311 3602; www.vunavalleyventureskzn.co.za; 9 Mitchell Rd, Banners Rest; s/d R300/500; ❄) By the entrance to the Umtamvuna Nature Reserve (inland from Port Edward), Vuna Valley has stylish double cabins and more budget (but very pleasant) rooms in the main house with separate entrances and spectacular gorge views. Walking, cycling and canoeing opportunities are nearby.

SOUTH COAST DIVING

The highlight of this beach strip is **Aliwal Shoal**, touted as one of the best dive sites in the world. The shoal was created from dune rock around 30,000 years ago. A mere 6500 years ago the sea level rose, creating a reef. This reef was named after a ship, the *Aliwal*, which ran aground here in 1849. Other ships have since met a similar fate. Today, the shoal's ledges, caves and pinnacles are home to everything from wrecks to rays, turtles, 'raggies' (ragged-mouth sharks), tropical fish and soft corals.

Further down the coast, near Shelly Beach, the extraordinary **Protea Banks** dive site is restricted to advanced divers and is the place to see sharks.

Numerous operators along the South Coast offer dive charters, PADI courses and accommodation packages. Packages vary enormously in terms of accommodation and equipment. (In some cases, equipment hire may cost extra.) To give you an idea, at the time of writing, a three-night, five-dive package cost around R4000.

Always speak to other travellers about their experiences because safety briefings vary among the operators – incidents can, and do, occur.

2nd Breath (☎039-317 2326; www.2ndbreath.co.za; cnr Bank St & Berea Rd, Margate) Highly qualified PADI professional who takes classes and safety issues very seriously.

Aliwal Dive Centre (☎039-973 2233; www.aliwalshoal.co.za; 2 Moodie St, Umkomaas) Also has pleasant rooms available.

Shoal (☎039-973 1777; www.theshoal.co.za; 21 Harvey St, Umkomaas) A recommended diving outfit.

Oceanworx (☎039-973 2578; www.oceanworx.co.za; 1 Reynolds St, Umkomaas) Two respected diving companies have merged to create this company, based in Umkomaas.

Southbroom Traveller's Lodge BACKPACKERS $
(039-316 8448; www.southbroomtravellerslodge.co.za; 11 Cliff Rd, Southbroom; r incl breakfast R400-500;) Joy, oh joy – a good-value place in this upmarket area, a beautiful neck of the (subtropical) woods and a 10-minute walk from the beach. This comfortable, laid-back place resembles a large holiday home with light and airy rooms, a massive lounge, a pool and a lovely garden.

Sunbirds B&B $$
(039-316 8202; www.sunbirds.co.za; 643 Outlook Rd, Southbroom; s/d R750/1200;) Welcoming hosts, wonderful breakfasts on the verandah (with good views), a smart, spacious lounge and a homey ambience keep the guests coming here. The patios with table and chair and the private entrance are also big ticks.

Treetops Lodge B&B $$
(039-317 2060; www.treetopslodge.co.za; 3 Poplar Rd, Margate; d from R1000;) This pleasant pebble-dashed place has neat, if dated, double rooms with breakfast, plus a self-catering unit. The rooms overlook green foliage, and there's a massive shared balcony with your own table and chairs. Rates outside the Christmas season are significantly lower.

Eating

Burlesque Cafe INTERNATIONAL $
(957 Marine Dr, Ramsgate; mains R50-100; 9am-4pm, to 6pm Wed-Sat) A quirky little retro treat with a chic vintage interior and cheeky menu items featuring organic produce.

Waffle House VEGETARIAN $
(039-314 9424; Marine Dr, Ramsgate; mains R50-75; 8am-5pm;) People flock to this pleasant spot on the edge of a lagoon for fresh Belgian-style waffles with every sweet and savoury filling under the sun. There are queues in the holiday season.

Trattoria La Terrazza ITALIAN $$
(039-316 6162; www.trattoria.co.za; Southbroom; mains R80-130; lunch Fri-Sun, dinner Tue-Sat) Ask for a restaurant recommendation in the area and the answer is overwhelmingly this Italian option. It has a popular meaty menu, including the likes of tender, grain-fed beef fillet and seafood such as west coast mussels and seared baby squid. The setting, on an estuary, is gorgeous. Reservations recommended.

Information

South Coast Tourism (039-312 2322; Panorama Pde, Main Beach, Margate; 8am-5pm Mon-Fri, to 1pm Sat & Sun) Information is available from here.

Getting There & Away

Margate Mini Coach (031-312 1406; www.margate.co.za) Margate Mini Coach links Durban and Margate three times daily (one way R200).

Intercity Express (031-305 9090; www.intercity.co.za) Intercity Express runs regular buses between Margate and Jo'burg (R415, 10 hours).

NORTH COAST

The North Coast, the coastal strip from Umhlanga Rocks north to Tugela River, is a profusion of upmarket time-share apartments and retirement villages with some pleasant beaches. The section from Zimbali, slightly north of Umhlanga, to the Tugela is known as the Dolphin Coast. The coast gets its name from the bottlenose dolphins that favour the area, attracted by the continental shelf and warm water.

The North Coast and its surrounds are home to a fascinating mix of peoples: descendants of former colonialists, Indians, French-Mauritian sugar-cane growers and indentured labourers from the Indian subcontinent, plus colourful Zulu cultures.

King Shaka is said to have established a military camp on the coast; royal handmaidens gathered salt from tidal pools, a practice since immortalised in the name Salt Rock. A memorial to King Shaka can be found at KwaDukuza (Stanger), slightly inland.

Metropolitan buses run between Durban and Umhlanga Rocks, and buses and minibus shared taxis also run between Durban and KwaDukuza (Stanger) and other inland towns.

Umhlanga Rocks & uMdloti Beach

The buckle of Durban's chichi commuter belt, Umhlanga is a cosmopolitan mix of upmarket beach resort, moneyed suburbia and small malls. Umhlanga means 'Place of Reeds' (the 'h' is pronounced something like 'sh'). Further north, uMdloti Beach has some good restaurants. Both locations are convenient to the airport.

Umhlanga Tourism Information Centre (p252) offers advice, and metro buses 716 and 706 run between Umhlanga and Durban.

Sights & Activities

Natal Sharks Board MUSEUM
(☎031-566 0400; www.shark.co.za; 1A Herrwood Dr, Umhlanga Rocks; audiovisual & dissection adult/child R45/25; ⏲8am-4pm Mon-Fri) This research institute is dedicated to studying sharks, specifically in relation to their danger to humans. There are audiovisual presentations and shark dissections at 9am and 2pm Tuesday, Wednesday and Thursday. The Natal Sharks Board is signposted; it's about 2km out of town, up steep Umhlanga Rocks Dr (the M12 leading to the N3).

The public can also accompany Sharks Board personnel on their boat trips from Durban.

Umhlanga Lagoon Nature Reserve NATURE RESERVE
(self-guided access free, guide per person R30; ⏲8am-6pm) Found on a river mouth just north of town, the reserve is home to many bird species (despite its small size: 2600 sq metres). Trails lead through stunning dune forest, across the lagoon and onto the beach.

Sleeping

Umhlanga is crowded with holiday apartments and B&Bs, most of which are close to the beach. Hotel prices are seasonal and vary enormously; expect fluctuations between seasons.

On the Beach Backpackers BACKPACKERS $
(☎031-562 1591; www.durbanbackpackers.com; 17 The Promenade, Glenashley; dm/s/d R180/570/850; P 📶 🏊) There are million-rand views from the double rooms here that overlook the water. Or you can slum it in a dorm for a much more reasonable price. A great spot for lazing on the coast, this light and airy house-turned-backpackers is 4km south of Umhlanga in Glenashley. It's on the Baz Bus route.

Fairlight Beach House GUESTHOUSE $$
(☎031-568 1835; www.fairlight.co.za; 1 Margaret Bacon Ave, uMdloti; r incl breakfast from R1200) A sprawling, smart guesthouse, Fairlight overlooks the beach and offers 10 rooms (not all with views). Rooms are spacious, furnishings are stylish and a stay here is memorable. It attracts a business crowd. Prices are lower outside the high season.

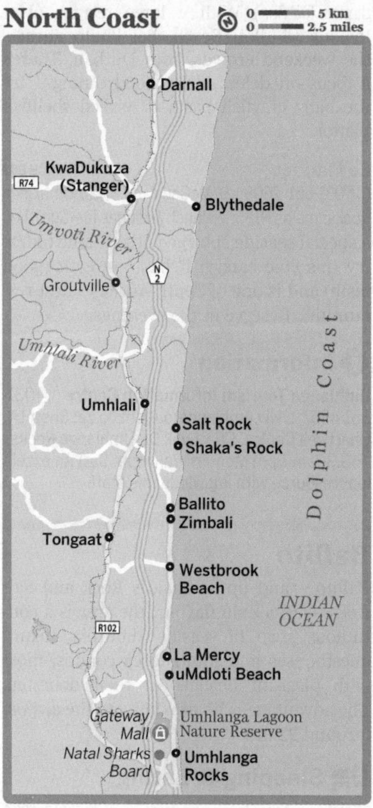

Beverley Hills Sun Intercontinental HOTEL $$$
(☎031-561 2211; www.southernsun.com; Lighthouse Rd; r incl breakfast from R3300; P ❄ 📶 🏊) They didn't pull out all the stops on the exterior, but this top-notch classic is deliciously stylish on the inside. It's the perfect place for a platinum-card splurge.

Eating

★**Mundo Vida** INTERNATIONAL $$
(☎031-568 2286; www.mundovida.co.za; uMdloti Beach; mains R140) Enjoy seafood and bistro fare in unpretentious surroundings at this excellent coastal restaurant, where traditional recipes have a modern twist. For a taste of everything fishy try the seafood medley or, if your pockets are deep, tuck into the deluxe version. Excellent wine list.

Bel Punto INTERNATIONAL $$
(☎031-568 2407; www.belpunto.co.za; uMdloti Beach; mains R150; ⏲lunch Wed-Sun,

dinner Tue-Sun) With a large terrace overlooking uMdloti Beach, Bel Punto attracts the weekend crowds from Durban. There's a focus on delectable seafood dining – try the baby crayfish pasta or grilled shellfish platter.

Ile Maurice FRENCH **$$$**
(☎031-561 7609; 9 McCausland Cres, Umhlanga Rocks; mains R185; ⏰lunch & dinner Tue-Sun) For a special seaside splurge with a Gallic touch, try this chic eatery; it has *bon goût* (good taste) and is one of South Africa's finest restaurants. Reserve in the evenings.

Information

Umhlanga Tourism Information Centre (☎031-561 4257; www.umhlangatourism.co.za; Shop 1A, Chartwell Centre, Chartwell Dr, Umhlanga Rocks; ⏰8.30am-5pm Mon-Fri, 9am-1pm Sat) An excellent resource with knowledgable staff.

Ballito

Ballito – and up to Shaka's Rock and Salt Rock – lacks Zulu flavour; the area is a continuous strip of seaside suburbia, luxury guesthouses and multistorey condos, most with pleasant beaches at their doorstep. The advantage is its proximity to the airport (around 22km).

Sleeping & Eating

Monkey Bay Backpackers BACKPACKERS **$**
(☎071 348 1278; www.monkeybaybackpackers.co.za; 9 Jack Powell Rd; dm/d R150/450) Calling all surf-rats. This casual place – made from recycled materials, and painted in funky colours inside – has a pleasantly hippie vibe and a friendly owner. Bathrooms are slightly limited, but it's handy to the sea and is one of the few budget options in the area.

Guesthouse GUESTHOUSE **$$**
(☎032-525 5683; www.theguesthouse.co.za; Ipahla Lane, Shaka's Rock; s/d incl breakfast from R600/1000; P 📶) Five rooms in a pleasant, neat-as-a-pin, slightly dated house (the owner's home). Best is the garden-facing room with private entrance.

Boathouse GUESTHOUSE **$$$**
(☎032-946 0300; www.boathouse.co.za; 33 Compensation Beach Rd; s/d R1250/2100; @) Taken over by new management in 2014, this upmarket choice is for those who'd like to treat themselves to a luxury coastal base.

Waterberry Coffee Shoppe DELI, CAFE **$**
(☎032-946 2797; www.thewaterberry.co.za; cnr Dolphin Cres & Leonora Dr; mains R50-80; ⏰8.30am-4pm) The perfect place to eat your way through a hot afternoon, under a canopy of lush coastal forest. Feast on fabulous home-made cakes or a range of healthy salads.

Information

Sangweni Tourism Centre (☎032-946 1997; www.thedolphincoast.co.za; cnr Ballito & Link Drs; ⏰8.30am-5pm Mon-Fri, 9am-1pm Sat) Houses the Dolphin Coast Publicity Association, which lists accommodation in the area. It's located near the BP station, where you leave the N2 to enter Ballito.

KwaDukuza (Stanger) & Around

POP 13,500

In July 1825, Shaka established KwaDukuza as his capital and royal residence. It was here that he was killed in 1828 by his half-brothers Mhlangane and Dingaan; Dingaan then took power. Each year Zulus don their traditional gear and gather in the Recreational Grounds for the **King Shaka Day Celebration**.

Also known as Stanger, KwaDukuza is a busy, rough-and-ready town with a large Indian population and an African buzz. The town has no accommodation, but it's an important stop for those undertaking a Shaka pilgrimage or those interested in Zulu culture.

Minibus shared taxis link KwaDukuza, servicing Durban (one hour) and towns along the coast.

Sights

Head to King Shaka Rd to visit the **Shaka Memorial Gardens**, where a memorial stone was erected in 1932 over Shaka's burial chamber, which was originally a grain pit. There is a rock featuring a well-worn groove where it's believed Shaka sharpened his spears.

King Shaka Visitor Centre CULTURAL CENTRE
(☎032-552 7210; 5 King Shaka Rd; ⏰8am-4pm Mon-Fri, 9am-4pm Sat & Sun) FREE The King Shaka Visitor Centre is worth visiting for limited but clear historical and chronological information about Shaka and his kingdom.

Dukuza Museum MUSEUM
(☎032-437 5075; King Shaka Rd; admission by donation; ⏰8.30am-4pm Mon-Fri) Opposite the King Shaka Visitor Centre, the museum has related historical exhibits.

LEGENDARY KING SHAKA

Despite all that is written about him, King Shaka was an enigmatic and controversial figure. Whether fact or mythology, Shaka is frequently portrayed as either a vicious and bloodthirsty tyrant or a military genius.

Shaka was the illegitimate son of Queen Nandi, to whom he was very close. By the 1820s he had created one of the most powerful kingdoms in the subcontinent. Violence was one of his weapons, both against his enemy and his own warriors. (On the death of his mother it is said that he killed many Zulus whom he believed weren't grieving enough.)

He is probably best known for his fighting tactics: he devised the ingenious 'bull formation' where groups of warriors – the 'head and chest' – penetrated the enemy front on, while the 'horns' encircled the enemy from behind. He shortened the throwing spear to a short-shafted, close-range stabbing spear and lengthened the shield.

In 1828 Shaka's life came to an unpleasant end – he was murdered by his half-brothers Dingaan and Mhlangane (who was later toppled by Dingaan). Contemporary Zulus are incredibly proud of their 'warrior king'. **Shaka Day** is celebrated annually on 24 September at the Shaka Memorial Gardens in KwaDukuza. Thousands of Zulus wearing traditional dress and carrying shields, spears and dancing sticks descend upon the gardens. The current king and the former chief minister, Dr Buthelezi, usually lead the celebration.

Luthuli Museum MUSEUM
(☎032-559-6822; www.luthulimuseum.org.za; Nokukhanya Luthuli St, Groutville; ⌚8.30am-4pm Mon-Sat, 11am-3pm Sun) FREE This museum is a tribute to Chief Albert John Mvumbi Luthuli – president of the African National Congress (ANC) from 1952 and Africa's first recipient of the Nobel Prize for Peace (1960) for his efforts to end apartheid in South Africa - and is located in Luthuli's house, where he lived all his life and which was his 'site of struggle'. Luthuli met with former US senator Robert Kennedy here in 1966. The house is surrounded by gardens and hosts changing exhibitions.

Luthuli died in 1967 in suspicious circumstances.

ZULULAND

Evoking images of wild landscapes and tribal rhythms, this beautiful swath of KwaZulu-Natal offers a different face of South Africa, where fine coastline, mist-clad hills and traditional settlements are in contrast to the ordered suburban developments around Durban. Dominated by the Zulu tribal group, the region offers fascinating historical and contemporary insights into one of the country's most enigmatic cultures. However, while the name Zulu (which means 'Heaven') aptly describes the rolling expanses that dominate the landscape here, it doesn't tell the whole story. Intense poverty and all the social problems that come with that are still commonplace, and much of the population struggles in a hand-to-mouth existence. If you head off the main roads this becomes glaringly obvious.

Zululand extends roughly from the mouth of the Tugela River up to St Lucia and inland west of the N2 to Vryheid. The region is most visited for the spectacular Hluhluwe-iMfolozi Park and its many traditional Zulu villages. Here you can learn about Zulu history and the legendary King Shaka.

Since 1971, Goodwill Zwelithini kaBhekuzulu has been ruling the Zulu nation.

Mtunzini

POP 2200

A little thatch of neatly tended lawns surrounded by the wild, rolling hills of Zululand, Mtunzini is an outpost of Europe in the heart of Africa. But there's more to this pretty village than herbaceous borders. Sitting above a lush sweep of rare raffia palms, and bordering the Umlalazi Nature Reserve, Mtunzini makes an excellent base for exploring this beautiful slice of Zululand.

The town had a colourful beginning. John Dunn, the first European to settle in the area, was granted land by King Cetshwayo. Dunn became something of a chief himself, taking 49 wives and siring 117 children. He held court here under a tree, hence the town's name (*mtunzini* is Zulu for 'a place in the shade'). After the British defeated Cetshwayo and divided the kingdom, Dunn was one of the chiefs granted power.

The town was declared a conservancy in 1995. Visitors can enjoy its network of nature trails, as well as sight some antelope and bird species.

Zululand & Elephant Coast

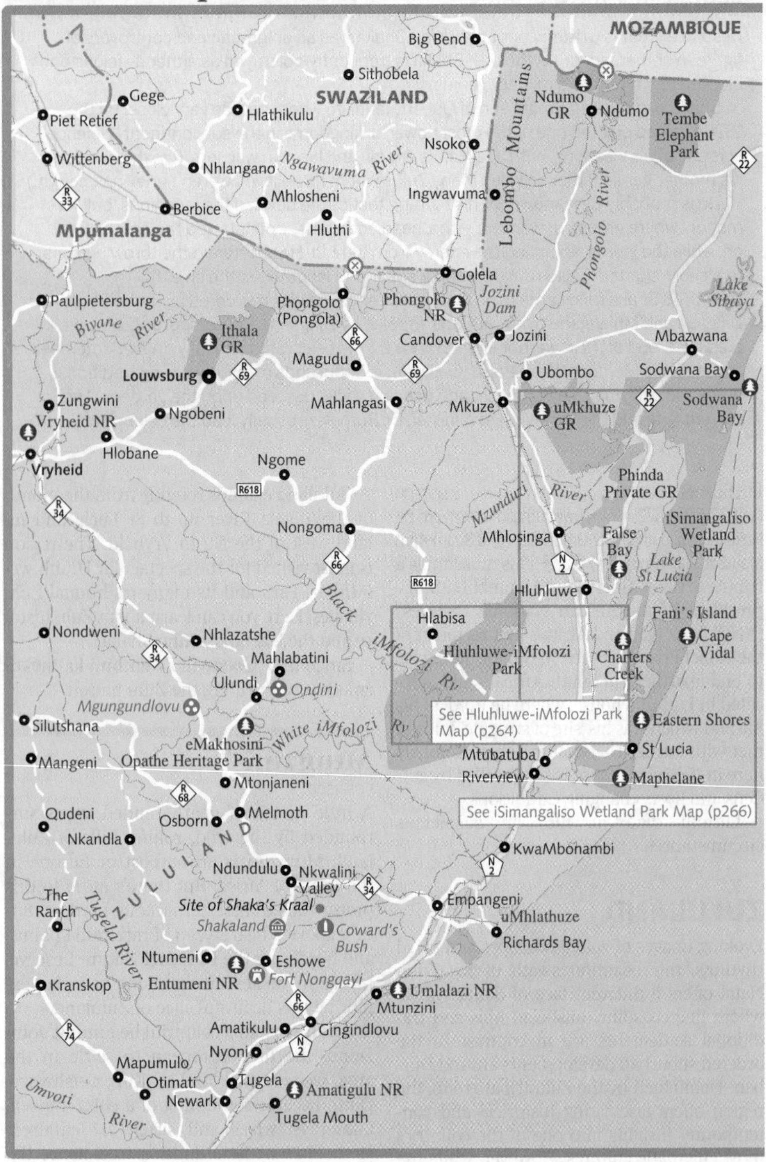

Sights & Activities

Raffia Palm Monument PARK

(24hr) FREE *Raphia Australis* palms were first planted here in 1916 from seeds. The idea was to use the palm fibres to make brooms for the prison service, but, as the fibres were too short, the commercial enterprise soon ended. However, the palms (the leaves of which are among the largest in the plant kingdom) flourished and by 1942 had been declared a national monument. The palms are home to the palmnut vulture *(Gypohierax angolensis)*, South Africa's rarest breeding bird of prey.

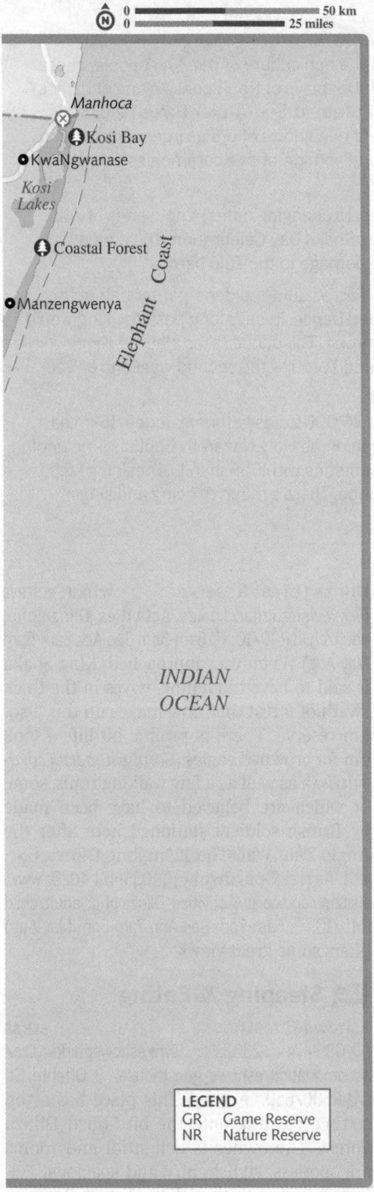

Umlalazi Nature Reserve NATURE RESERVE
(☎035-340 1836; www.kznwildlife.com; admission R20; ⊙5am-10pm) This reserve has walking trails through the pretty dune and forest ecosystems and is great for birders. Visit the Indaba Tree, where John Dunn held his court gatherings, and the remains of John Dunn's Pool, which he built so his wives could swim safely, well away from hippos and crocs. The entrance is 1.5km east of town, on the coast.

Sleeping & Eating

Umlalazi Nature Reserve Chalets & Campground CAMPGROUND $
(☎035-340 1836; www.kznwildlife.com; camping R90, chalets R300) Two well-organised camping areas (Inkwazi and Indaba) are set in gorgeous forest, close to the beach. Chalets are spacious, have great decks and are well organised inside.

Mtunzini B&B B&B $$
(☎035-340 1600; 5 Barker St; s/d incl breakfast R460/620;) A no-nonsense, friendly place with beautiful spaces, set around a beautiful garden. There's a range of rooms from doubles inside the main house to separate cabin, attic and self-catering options. Only some have private bathrooms.

One-on-Hely BOUTIQUE HOTEL $$
(☎035-340 2498; www.oneonhely.co.za; 1 Hely Hutchinson St; d without/with breakfast R1200/1400;) The village's flashest place, with enormous decks, forest views over Umlalazi Nature Reserve and the ocean, and luxury trimmings. It's popular, so book ahead.

★Zanj INTERNATIONAL $$
(☎035-340 1288; Hely Hutchinson St, Golden Penny Complex; mains R80-130; ⊙lunch Tue-Sun, dinner Tue-Sat) The outdoor decking is the place to eat a meal at this fine restaurant. There are lots of seafood options including curry prawns, crab pasta and fish pancake. It's all exceedingly well prepared and the use of fresh, quality ingredients really lifts the dishes. The weekly specials board displays a long list of international options.

Fat Cat Coffee Shop CAFE $$
(☎035-340 2897; 2 Station Rd; mains R50-100; ⊙8am-8pm Mon-Sat, to 2pm Sun) Casual, friendly Fat Cat is a nice, open spot tucked away off the main drag. Breakfast is recommended, especially the Mediterranean Surprise.

Eshowe

POP 14,800

Situated amid a beautiful indigenous forest and surrounded by green rolling hills, Eshowe has its own particular character. The

ZULU FESTIVALS

Throughout the year major festivals celebrate the rich culture of the Zulu people. These peaceful and joyous occasions involve colourful displays of traditional singing and dancing. See www.kzn.org.za for a sneak preview. **Zululand Eco-Adventures** (☎035-474 2298; www.zululandeco-adventures.com; 36 Main St) in Eshowe offers a large range of genuine Zulu adventure activities, from weddings and coming-of-age ceremonies to visits to witch doctors.

King Shaka Day Celebration In September (to changing dates), thousands of Zulus converge on KwaDukuza (Stanger) for the King Shaka Day Celebration. The annual event, attended by the current Zulu king, pays homage to the Zulu hero.

Reed Dance Every year thousands of bare-breasted Zulu 'maidens' gather before their king, honouring the ancient tradition of the Reed Dance. In days long past, the king would select a new bride from among the beautiful throng. The dance takes place at King Enyokeni's Palace (between Nongoma and Ulundi) around the second weekend of September, before the King Shaka Day Celebration.

Shembe Festival During October more than 30,000 Zulus gather at Judea, 15km east of Eshowe, to celebrate the Shembe, the Church of the Holy Nazareth Baptists – an unofficial religion that manages to combine Zulu traditions with Christianity. Presiding is the church's saviour, Prophet Mbusi Vimbeni Shembe. There's much dancing and singing and blowing of the horns of Jericho.

centre has a rural, rough-and-tumble atmosphere, but the suburbs are leafy and quiet. It is well placed for exploring the wider region and there are decent attractions and accommodation options.

Eshowe has been home to four Zulu Kings (Shaka, Mpande, Cetshwayo and Dinuzulu). It was Cetshwayo's stronghold before he moved to Ondini and, like Ondini, it was destroyed during the Anglo-Zulu War. The British occupied the site and built Fort Nongqayi in 1883, establishing Eshowe as the administrative centre of their newly captured territory.

Sights

Fort Nongqayi Museum Village MUSEUM
(www.eshowemuseums.org.za; Nongqayi Rd; adult/child R35/10; 7.30am-4pm Mon-Fri, 9am-4pm Sat & Sun) Based around three-turreted Fort Nongqayi, the museum village also includes the Zululand Historical Museum, with artefacts and Victoriana; the excellent Vukani Museum with its Zulu basketry collection; and a missionary chapel. Well worth a look is the small but delightful butterfly house: a walk-in greenhouse where visitors can enjoy indigenous vegetation and hundreds of (mostly local) African butterfly species.

You can walk from here to Mpushini Falls (40 minutes return), but note that bilharzia (snail fever) has been reported here.

Dlinza Forest Reserve WILDLIFE RESERVE
(www.visitzululand.co.za/Activities_Dlinza.php; adult/child R40/10; 6am-5pm Sep-Apr, 8am-5pm May-Aug) When war approached, King Shaka is said to have hidden his wives in the thick swath of forest that now makes up this 2-sq-km reserve. There is prolific birdlife – look out for crowned eagles *(Stephanoaetus coronatus)* – as well as a few walking trails, some of which are believed to have been made by British soldiers stationed here after the Anglo-Zulu War. The 125m-long **Dlinza Forest Aerial Boardwalk** (☎035-474 4029; www.visitzululand.co.za/Activities_Dlinza.php; adult/child R40/10; 6am-5pm Sep-Apr, 7am-5pm May-Aug) offers some great views.

Sleeping & Eating

Eshowe Guesthouse B&B $$
(☎035-474 2362; www.eshoweguide.co.za/accomodation/eshowe_guesthouse; 3 Oftebro St; s/d R500/650; P) This place has a top setting, backing onto the bird-filled Dlinza Forest. The owner is delightful and rooms are spotless, stylish, airy and spacious. Follow the signs to the Dlinza Forest Reserve; the guesthouse is just beyond the entrance. It gets busy; reserve ahead.

Dlinza Forest Accommodation CABIN $$
(☎035-474 2377; www.dlinzaforestaccommodation.co.za; 2 Oftebro St; s/d R450/600;) These four self-catering log cabins are neat, mod-

ern, clean and spacious. Follow the signs to the Dlinza Forest Reserve; the guesthouse is just beyond the entrance.

★George Hotel HOTEL, BACKPACKERS **$$**
(☎035-474 4919; www.eshowe.com; 38 Main St; dm R350, s/d incl breakfast R595/795; P 📶 🏊) Dripping with character, this grand old hotel (1902) is a good budget and midrange option. Rooms are a bit old and rickety (and water pressure can be hit-and-miss), but the huge beds are very comfy. The backpacker wing has been completely renovated and offers possibly the best value. The menu is limited, but the food is well prepared.

Two of the hotel's best features are its verandah, perfect for a sunset drink, and its lounge, with ancient reading material and a cosy vibe.

★Tally's Corner Cafe CAFE **$**
(Main St; mains R30-60; ⏲7.30am-2pm Mon-Fri) A real cafe in Zululand! This is the place to come if you're in need of a coffee. Just opening when we passed through town, Tally's had a limited menu but an impressive set-up. Tuck into American-style flapjacks, a bagel or a croissant for breakfast.

Adam's Outpost INTERNATIONAL **$**
(mains R60; ⏲9am-4pm) Find refuge in the garden cafe and cosy, corrugated-iron restaurant, complete with real fireplaces and candles – easily the standout in Eshowe's culinary roll call. Try a chicken mango salad or beef curry for lunch.

ℹ Information

ABSA (Osborne Rd, Miku Bldg) Changes money and has an ATM.

ℹ Getting There & Away

Minibus shared taxis leave from the bus and taxi rank (downhill from KFC near the Osborne and Main Sts roundabout; go across the bridge and to the right) to Empangeni (R50, one hour), which is the best place from which to catch taxis deeper into Zululand, and Durban (R90, 1½ hours).

Ulundi

POP 20,000

Once the hub of the powerful Zulu empire and until 2004 a joint capital of KZN (with Pietermaritzburg, which gained preeminence), Ulundi today is an unattractive, merely functional place that resembles a temporary settlement rather than an important Zulu centre. Brightly coloured boxlike houses have replaced traditional huts, and its small, central shopping mall has a transitory feel. However, there are historic Zulu sites, including the interesting Ondini, to explore in the immediate area. Ulundi offers alternative access to Hluhluwe-iMfolozi Park.

Sights

City Centre

KwaNodwengu HISTORIC SITE
Opposite the large former Legislative Assembly building is the site of King Mpande's

NKWALINI VALLEY & SHAKALAND

Shaka's kraal (fortified village), KwaBulawayo, once loomed over this beautiful valley, but today **Nkwalini Valley** is regimented with citrus orchards and cane fields rather than Zulu warriors. From Eshowe head north for 6km on R66, and turn right onto R230 (a dirt road that will eventually get you to R34).

Across the road from the KwaBulawayo marker is Coward's Bush, now just another marker, where warriors who returned from battle without their spears, or who had received wounds in the back, were executed.

Further west, a few kilometres before R230 meets R66, the Mandawe Cross was erected in the 1930s, against the wishes of the Zulu. There are excellent views from the hill.

Created as a set for the telemovie *Shaka Zulu*, the Disney-fied **Shakaland** (☎035-460 0912; www.shakaland.com; Nandi Experience R300; ⏲display 11am & 12.30pm) beats up a touristy blend of perma-grin performance and informative authenticity. The Nandi Experience (Queen Nandi was Shaka's mother) is a display of Zulu culture and customs (including lunch); the Zulu dance performance is said to be the best in the country. You can also stay overnight in luxury beehives at the four-star **hotel** (Shaka Experience cultural program & s/d with full board R1200/1800).

Shakaland is at Norman Hurst Farm, Nkwalini, 3km off R66 and 14km north of Eshowe.

PAL TERAVAGIMOV / GETTY IMAGES ©

1. Hluhluwe-iMfolozi Park (p263)
Jaw-dropping views and a variety of wildlife, including black and white rhinos, make this park a must-see.

2. Drakensberg Range (p278)
Striking landscapes and outdoor adventures await in this popular destination.

3. Isandlwana (p295)
White cairns mark the places where British soldiers fell during the Anglo-Zulu War.

4. Durban (p227)
Durban's recent revamp includes a beachfront promenade known as the Golden Mile (p234).

iKhanda (palace), KwaNodwengu. Mpande won control from Dingaan after the Zulus' disastrous loss at Blood River. He seized power with assistance from the Boers, but Zululand declined during his reign. The king's grave is here, but there's little else to see.

Ondini

Ondini HISTORIC SITE
(High Place; ☎035-870 2050; www.heritagekzn.co.za; adult/child R30/15; ⏲8am-4pm Mon-Fri, 9am-4pm Sat & Sun) Established as Cetshwayo's capital in 1873, Ondini was razed by British troops after the Battle of Ulundi (July 1879), the final engagement of the 1879 Anglo-Zulu War. The royal kraal section of the Ondini site has been rebuilt and you can see where archaeological digs have uncovered the floors of identifiable buildings. The floors, made of mud and cow dung, were preserved by the heat of the fires, which destroyed the huts above. The huge area is enclosed in a defensive perimeter of gnarled branches.

It took the British nearly six months to defeat the Zulu army, but the Battle of Ulundi went the same way as most of the campaign, with 10 to 15 times more Zulus than British killed. Part of the reason for the British victory at Ulundi was the adoption of the Boer *laager* tactic, with troops forming a hollow square to protect the cavalry, which attacked only after the Zulu army had exhausted itself trying to penetrate the walls.

To get to Ondini, take the 'Cultural Museum' turn-off from the highway just south of Ulundi centre and keep going for about 5km. Minibus shared taxis occasionally pass Ondini. This road continues on to Hluhluwe-iMfolozi Park (tarred for 30km). En route here from Ulundi you'll pass the Ulundi Battlefield Memorial, a stone structure commemorating the Battle of Ulundi and the final defeat of the Zulus.

KwaZulu Cultural-Historical Museum MUSEUM
(with Ondini admission free; ⏲8am-4pm Mon-Fri, 9am-4pm Sat & Sun) At Ondini is the KwaZulu Cultural-Historical Museum, with excellent exhibits on Zulu history and culture. It also has one of the country's best collections of beadwork on display. There's a good selection of books for sale.

Emakhosini Ophathe Heritage Park

Ulundi lies within the Valley of the Kings, the name of which is officially promoted as Emakhosini Ophathe Heritage Park. The area is of great significance to the Zulu. The great *makhosi* (chiefs) Nkhosinkulu, Senzangakhona (father of Shaka, Dingaan and Mpande) and Dinizulu are buried here. Signage for the park can be confusing as some sites are advertised but aren't fully functioning. However, a couple of the area's sites are open to the public.

Mgungundlovu HISTORIC SITE
The military settlement of Mgungundlovu (Ungungundhlovu), Dingaan's capital from 1829 to 1838, is southwest of Ulundi on Rte 34 (the road linking Vryheid and Melmoth). It was here that Pieter Retief and the other Voortrekkers were killed by their host in 1838, the event that precipitated the Boer-Zulu War. Signs point to the Piet Retief memorial marking the spot. In 1990 excavations revealed the site of Dingaan's *indlu* (great hut) nearby. A **multimedia information centre** (☎035-450 0916; www.heritagekzn.co.za; adult/child R30/15; ⏲8am-4pm Mon-Fri, 9am-4pm Sat & Sun) has high-tech displays and information.

From Ulundi head southwest along Rte 66 to Rte 34, turn right and continue on Rte 34 for several kilometres. Mgungundlovu is signed off Rte 34 to the west; it's another 5km to the site.

Spirit of eMakhosini Monument MONUMENT
(⏲8am-4pm Mon-Fri, 9am-4pm Sat & Sun) On Rte 34 and 2km north of Mgungundlovu, signs point west to Spirit of eMakhosini monument, which is perched on a hill. It comprises a massive bronze Zulu beer pot, surrounded by 18 bronze reliefs depicting Zulu life, and seven large horns symbolising the seven kings buried in the valley. Guides will explain the site's significance.

Sleeping

uMuzi Bushcamp HUT $$
(☎082 825 6896, 035-870 2500; www.umuzibushcamp.co.za; s/d with half-board R645/940) Inside the Ondini complex are these traditional beehive huts in pleasant surrounds, near marula trees. Admission includes entry to the Ondini cultural site.

Southern Sun Garden Court BUSINESS HOTEL $$$
(☎035-870 1012; www.southernsun.com; Princess Magogo St; r incl breakfast R1600;) Rooms here are spacious, with attention to detail and no-nonsense comforts. The hotel's restaurant serves meals throughout the day.

Getting There & Away

The minibus shared taxi park is opposite Southern Sun Garden Court, with services to destinations including Vryheid (R80, 1½ hours) and Eshowe (R75, 1½ hours).

Ithala Game Reserve

Ezemvelo KZN Wildlife's **Ithala Game Reserve** (☎034-983 2540, 033-845 1000; www.kznwildlife.com; adult/child R60/30) is severely underrated. It has all the assets of a private wildlife reserve but at much lower prices. It also doesn't get the crowds that flock into Hluhluwe-iMfolozi, as it's slightly off the main routes, but it's captivating in its own way.

Most of the 300 sq km are taken up by the steep valleys of six rivers (winding tributaries of the Phongolo), with some open grassland on the heights, rugged outcrops and bushveld. Some of the world's oldest rock formations are found here, as are Stone Age spear and axe heads.

Animals include black and white rhinos, elephants, tsessebis, buffaloes and giraffes (the park's emblem, as they are believed to be indigenous to Ithala Game Reserve) and rare bird species.

Guided walks (R200 per person) and wildlife and night drives (R200 per person) are available.

Sleeping

Ntshondwe CABIN $$
(☎033-845 1000; www.kznwildlife.com; 2-bed chalets per person R840;) This is the park's main resort, located at the foot of Ngotshe Mountain, with superb views of the reserve below. It's warthog heaven, and home to the red Pride of De Kaap flower and redbilled oxpeckers. Facilities include restaurant, shop and swimming pool. There's a full-board option for the units, on request.

Doornkraal CAMPGROUND $
(☎033-845 1000; www.kznwildlife.com; camping R130) This is one of a range of fabulous bush camps; the others have heftier minimum charges. Note, this is your 'real Africa' camping experience – it's cold-water showers only.

ITHALA GAME RESERVE

Why Go Panoramic views from the mountainous thornveld, the oldest rock formations in the world and a plethora of wildlife make Ithala unique. It is one of KwaZulu-Natal's most spectacular wildlife reserves. Giraffes are indigenous to the reserve; and black and white rhinos are both here.

When to Go Ithala is a year-round destination, although it can get chilly in the evening betweeen May and August, with frosts not uncommon.

Practicalities Gates are open from 5am to 7pm November to February, 6am to 6pm March to October. The nearest town with supplies is Vryheid, 70km away.

Budget Tips Bring your own food, and a tent; campsites are R130 per person. Take a self-guided walk.

Getting There & Away

Ithala is reached from Louwsburg, about 55km northeast of Vryheid on Rte 69, and about the same distance southwest of Phongolo via Rte 66 and Rte 69. Louwsburg is much smaller than many maps indicate.

THE ELEPHANT COAST

Up there on the podium with the world's great ecotourist destinations, and not far from the top of the scribbled list marked 'Places I Must See in South Africa', the Elephant Coast (formerly 'Maputaland') is a phenomenal stretch of natural beauty, with a fabulously diverse mix of environments and wildlife. The Elephant Coast is bounded in the south by the iMfolozi River just below the St Lucia Estuary, and to the northwest by the Lebombo Mountains.

This large stretch of coastline includes some of the country's true highlights, including the wonderfully diverse and perennially photogenic iSimangaliso Wetland Park that runs from Lake St Lucia in the south to Kosi Bay in the north. Uncompromisingly untamed, this region, away from the scattered resort towns, offers a glimpse of precolonial Africa. Slightly further inland, the incredible Hluhluwe-iMfolozi Park is KZN's answer to Kruger National Park. Indeed, it rivals its northern neighbour in beauty, and many prefer it for its accessibility (it's less than a 20th of Kruger's size).

The climate becomes steadily hotter as you go north and, thanks to the warm Indian Ocean, summers are steamy and tropical. The humid coastal air causes frequent dense mists on the inland hills, reducing visibility to a few metres. If driving, be careful of pedestrians and animals that may suddenly appear around a corner.

There is a good network of roads connecting the regions. Minibus shared taxis and local bus companies cover the coast. Self-drivers have a world open to them; while a 2WD will get you many places, a 4WD is required for the spectacular sandy road along the coast from Kosi Bay to Sodwana Bay.

Hluhluwe

POP 1100

Hluhluwe village (roughly pronounced shloo-*shloo*-wee) is northeast of Hluhluwe-iMfolozi Park. There's not much to the village – it spans a wide main road that joins the N2 – but it's the main gateway to the beautiful park itself.

Sleeping & Eating

Hluhluwe Backpackers BACKPACKERS $

(☎076 375 3831; d per person R150) Just outside Hluhluwe-iMfolozi memorial gate, this converted house has a great location. It's a bit dark and dingy inside, but friendly dogs, clean rooms and a very informal approach make it fine for a night or two. And it's a heck of a lot cheaper than staying in the park.

Orchard Farm Cottages BUNGALOW $

(☎082 494 1047; www.theorchardfarm.co.za; 1 Ngweni Rd; s/d from R400/550; ❄) These self-catering cottages, in a wildlife sanctuary that is part of a larger farm, are a comfy set-up. Rooms are fairly old-fashioned and they definitely have a lived-in feel, but its a good spot just out of town.

HLUHLUWE SIGNS

Signs to Hluhluwe and surrounds often confuse travellers. Useful to know when exiting the N2 is that Hluhluwe, the village, is on the eastern side of the N2, while Hluhluwe-iMfolozi Park is 12km west of the N2 (14km west of the town).

Isinkwe Backpackers Bushcamp BACKPACKERS $$

(☎083 338 3494; www.isinkwe.co.za; Bushlands; s/d/tr R525/700/840, dm/d without bathroom R180/500; @ 🏊) Located in a sweep of virgin bush 14km south of Hluhluwe, this budget place has a variety of accommodation options, from huts to rooms with bathrooms, a plethora of bush-focused (and other) activities, and a poolside bar where you can exchange tall-as-a-giraffe stories. The owners take safaris into Hluhluwe-iMfolozi and have half-board and accommodation-activity packages (see the website). Ring for directions.

★ **Hluhluwe River Lodge** LODGE $$$

(☎035-562 0246; www.hluhluwe.co.za; s/d with half board R1675/2400) About 11km from Hluhluwe, on the D540 (off Rte 22 and near False Bay), is this luxurious base from which to explore the park (the lodge offers tours). Set in its own piece of bush, each chalet is stylish, airy and spacious. The communal area features a stunning indoor-outdoor living room with terrace, and the lodge's chef serves up top-notch fare.

The indigenous forest has a delightful 'duiker walk', and a range of other activities are on offer.

Zululand Tree Lodge LODGE $$$

(☎035-562 1020; http://ubizane.co.za; s/d incl breakfast R1050/1700; ❄ 🏊) Like to wake up to the sound of birdsong? Seven kilometres outside Hluhluwe, and set in the Ubizane wildlife reserve amid fever trees, this romantic spot offers thatched tree houses set on stilts. Each room has its own viewing deck. There are excellent specials that include half board and safari drives; prices are flexible, depending on the package.

Bushwillow GUESTHOUSE $$$

(☎035-562 0473; www.bushwillow.com; Kuleni Game Park; s/d incl breakfast from R1375/1800) Within the privately owned Kuleni Game Park and surrounded by superb forest – flat crown, albizia and, of course, bush willows – is this romantic, relaxing hideaway. Soft wildlife (the likes of zebra, giraffe and duikers) surround the property and there are walking trails. It's 20km from Hluhluwe village on the Sodwana Bay road; look for the Kuleni sign. Half-board available.

Two units are linked by a common area with a kitchen for private use. Watch birds from the plunge pool or laze in the bathroom's claw-foot bath – it, too, has a green outlook.

Shopping

About 20km south of Hluhluwe on the N2 is the great-value Zamimpilo market, a women's cooperative that sells a variety of local crafts.

Ilala Weavers HANDICRAFTS
(☎087 802 1792; www.ilala.co.za; 1 Ngweni Rd; ⏲8am-5pm Mon-Fri, 9am-4pm Sat & Sat) Sells a large range of Zulu handicrafts, plus there's a **museum** and a local, slightly contrived 'village'. It's a good place to pick up souvenirs, but you may be fighting through the coach crowds.

Hluhluwe-iMfolozi Park

Rivalling Kruger National Park in its beauty and variety of landscapes, **Hluhluwe-iMfolozi Park** (☎035-550 8476; www.kznwildlife.com; adult/child R145/75) is one of South Africa's best-known, most evocative parks. Indeed, some say it's better than Kruger for its accessibility – it covers 960 sq km and there's plenty of wildlife including lions, elephants, rhinos (black and white), leopards, giraffes, buffaloes and African wild dogs.

Stunning Hluhluwe-iMfolozi has a mountainous landscape providing jaw-dropping views in all directions. The lack of thick vegetation in parts of the park, such as the drive from Memorial gate to Hilltop Camp, makes for excellent wildlife-spotting. You are almost certain to see white rhinos here.

Hluhluwe-iMfolozi can be visited at any time; there's always something happening and plenty to see. In summer (wet season) it's beautifully lush and animals range widely. Winter (dry season) visits can also be very rewarding, especially in the open savannah country areas, and animals often congregate at water sources (the White iMfolozi and Black iMfolozi Rivers flow here). Specific months bring their own rewards: from November to January it's baby time for impalas, zebras, wildebeest and giraffes, plus plenty of migratory birds. In February the elephants take to the marula trees, and October to March sees beautiful grasses and flowers.

HLUHLUWE-IMFOLOZI PARK

Why Go This is an incredibly scenic park, very mountainous, and the viewing opportunities allow for excellent wildlife-spotting. This is one park in KwaZulu-Natal that should not be missed. Crawling along open mountain ridges spotting wildlife is a wonderful African experience.

When to Go Any time of year is good. May to August is best for wildlife-spotting on the open savannah.

Practicalities Gates are open 5am to 7pm November to February, and 6am to 6pm between March and October. Petrol is available at Mpila Camp in iMfolozi and at Hilltop Camp in Hluhluwe, where you can also get diesel.

Budget Tips Stay outside the park! Try **Hluhluwe Backpackers** or **Isinkwe**. If you want to try a wilderness trail, stick with the **Primitive Trail** (p264) for good value.

Sights & Activities

Centenary Centre MUSEUM
(⏲8am-4pm) The Centenary Centre, a wildlife-holding centre with an attached museum, information centre and excellent craft market, is in the eastern section of iMfolozi. It incorporates rhino enclosures and antelope pens, and was established to allow visitors to view animals in transit to their new homes. To see the animals, ask at the Centenary Centre kiosk; you must be accompanied by a guide (around R20 per person).

Wildlife Drives

Wildlife drives here are very popular. Hilltop Camp (p264) offers morning and evening drives, while Mpila Camp (p264) does evening drives only. The camp-run drives are open to resort residents only and cost R300 per person. Most visitors to the area self-drive.

Hiking

One of iMfolozi's main attractions is its extraordinary trail system, in a special 240-sq-km wilderness area (note: these trails are seasonal; there's a four-person minimum) where there are no roads, only walking tracks. The trail walks are guided and last from two to five days. They are run by KZN Wildlife and all food, water, cooking equipment etc is provided. Accommodation is in tented camps and you can certainly expect to see wildlife. These walks are truly once-in-a-lifetime experiences and thus extremely popular, so book ahead.

Hluhluwe-iMfolozi Park

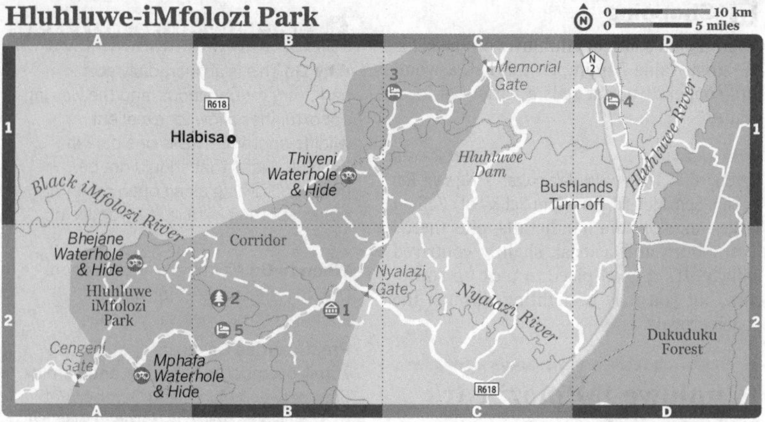

Hluhluwe-iMfolozi Park

Sights

1 Centenary Centre B2
2 Hluhluwe-iMfolozi Park B2

Sleeping

3 Hilltop Camp C1
4 Isinkwe Backpackers Bushcamp D1
5 Mpila Camp B2

The **Base Trail** (R3900, three nights) is, as the name suggests, at a base camp. Hikers carry day packs on the daily outings. The **Short Wilderness Trail** (R2350, two nights) is at satellite camps with no amenities (bucket shower) but are fully catered. Similar is the **Extended Wilderness Trail** (R3450, three nights), but guests must carry their gear for 7km into camp. On the **Primitive Trail** (R2900, four nights) you carry equipment, help prepare the food (provided) and sleep under the stars. Some consider this trail to be more fun than the others because you are able to participate more (for example, hikers must sit up in 1½-hour watches during the night).

Sleeping & Eating

You must book accommodation in advance through Ezemvelo KZN Wildlife (p277) in Pietermaritzburg. Last-minute bookings – those made up to 48 hours ahead – should be made direct with the camps. Note: all accommodation options are billed per person but are subject to a minimum charge. Additionally, if you are self-catering, remember to bring your own food!

As well as Hilltop Camp and Mpila Camp, there's a range of fabulous lodges (some even come with chefs, but you provide the food), but minimum charges apply; they cater for six to eight guests. See www.kznwildlife.com for more, but we recommend **Gqoyeni Bush Camp** (8-bed bush lodges per person R595, minimum charge R4200), **Hlathikhulu Bush Lodge** (8-bed bush lodges per person R595, minimum charge R3780), **Masinda Lodge** (6-bed lodge incl wildlife drives & walks per person R550), **Mthwazi Lodge** (minimum charge R4500), **Muntulu Bush Lodge** (8-bed bush lodges per person R595, minimum charge R4320) and **Munyaweni Bush Lodge** (8-bed bush lodges per person R595, minimum charge R4320).

★ **Hilltop Camp** CABIN $$
(035-562 0848; 2-person rondavels/chalets R575/1100; ❄) The signature resort on the Hluhluwe side: a cold drink followed by dinner on the patio with mountains silhouetted into the distance is a memorable experience. Unfortunately, KZN Wildlife has let standards slip: we couldn't get a key to our *rondavel* because, apparently, the locks have rusted over. We suggest you lock your valuables out of sight in your car.

If you want peace and quiet, try one of the private and sedate accommodation options. Although described as 'bush lodges', they are out of this world: fully equipped and reasonably upmarket. Some come with their own chef – although you supply the food.

Mpila Camp CABIN $$
(2-bed safari camp d R820, chalet d R820) The main accommodation centre on the iMfolozi

side, spectacular and peaceful Mpila Camp is perched on top of a hill in the centre of the reserve. The safari tents are the most fun, but self-contained cabins (called 'chalets') are available, too. Note: there's an electric fence, but wildlife (lions, hyenas, wild dogs) can still wander through.

Getting There & Away

You can access the park via three gates. The main entrance, Memorial gate, is about 15km west of the N2, about 50km north of Mtubatuba. The second entrance, Nyalazi gate, is accessed by turning left off the N2 onto R618 just after Mtubatuba on the way to Nongoma. The third, Cengeni gate, on iMfolozi's western side, is accessible by road (tarred for 30km) from Ulundi.

iSimangaliso Wetland Park

The **iSimangaliso Wetland Park**, a Unesco World Heritage Site, stretches for 220 glorious kilometres from the Mozambique border to Maphelane, at the southern end of Lake St Lucia. With the Indian Ocean on one side and a series of lakes (including Lake St Lucia) on the other, the 3280-sq-km park protects five distinct ecosystems, offering everything from offshore reefs and beaches to lakes, wetlands, woodlands and coastal forests. Loggerhead and leatherback turtles nest along the park's shores; whales and dolphins appear offshore and the park is occupied by numerous animals, including antelopes, hippos and zebras. The ocean beaches pull big crowds during the holiday season for everything from diving to fishing.

Lake St Lucia is Africa's largest estuary. After dipping to its lowest level for around 55 years due to a former environmental-management policy that kept the Lake St Lucia Estuary separate from the iMfolozi River, the two water bodies were naturally linked in 2012. This, along with more consistent rainfall, saw the water return to its former level in 2014 and the reappearance of fish and prawns. A new management strategy is also in place to ensure water levels remain stable and the ecosystem healthy.

iSimangaliso Wetland Park (formerly Greater St Lucia Wetland Park) relaunched its eco-destination image in 2007, part of which was the park's new name: iSimangaliso means 'Miracle' or 'Wonder' and, given its extraordinary beauty, it's an appropriate title.

ISIMANGALISO WETLAND PARK

Why Go This park is unique in South Africa and indeed on the continent. It contains most of South Africa's remaining swamp forests and is Africa's largest estuarine system.

When to Go Year-round.

Practicalities The park is a huge area spreading over 220km, much of it sand dunes and forest. There are four main regions: the south (easily accessed via St Lucia, from where you can enter the Eastern and Western Shores); the centre (Sodwana Bay, accessed from Rte 22); and the least accessible but very beautiful north (Kosi Bay, located at the end of Rte 22). A road west off Rte 22 allows for fairly easy access to uMkuze Game Reserve.

Budget Tips There are a couple of good hostels in St Lucia that can advise on cheap tour options. Self-drive safaris split between three or four people are the cheapest way to see the park.

There's a wonderful range of accommodation, from camping to private lodges to excellent options managed by Ezemvelo KZN Wildlife (p277). It's a good idea to book at least 48 hours ahead.

St Lucia is the main settlement and a good accommodation and supply base; the Eastern and Western Shores take you into the heart of the wetlands; Sodwana Bay is a separate access point to the park and is popular with divers; Lake Sibaya and Kosi Bay in the park's northern reaches are both remote and beautiful; and uMkhuze Game Reserve is further inland.

Activities

As part of the iSimangaliso Wetland Park Authority's responsible-tourism practices, every few years an ecotour operator must officially reapply for a permit – known as a concession – to operate activity tours. Go to www.isimangaliso.com for a list of current companies and organisations.

Birdwatching

Birdwatching is a delight in St Lucia (p267) and beyond. Check out the **Zululand Birding Route** (www.zululandbirdingroute.co.za) website for heaps of info plus guide services.

iSimangaliso Wetland Park

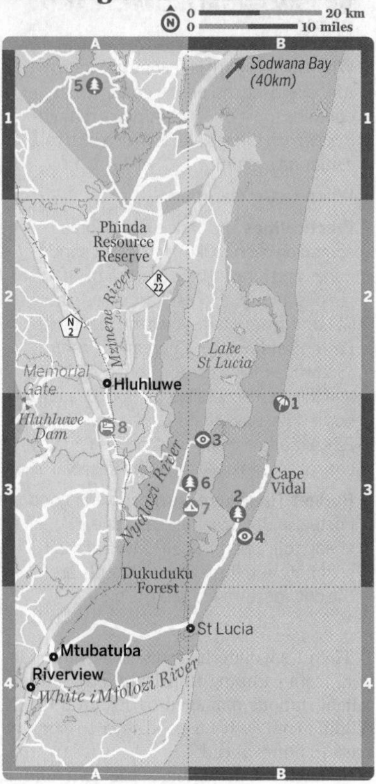

iSimangaliso Wetland Park

Sights

	Bats Cave	(see 4)
1	Cape Vidal	B3
2	Eastern Shores	B3
3	Fani's Island	B3
4	Mission Rocks	B3
	Mt Tabor Lookout	(see 4)
5	uMkhuze Game Reserve	A1
6	Western Shores	B3

Sleeping

7	Charters Creek	B3
8	Isinkwe Backpackers Bushcamp	A3

Themba's Birding & Eco Tours BIRDWATCHING
(☎071 413 3243; stluciabirdsnbirding@gmail.com; St Lucia; per person from R200, minimum 2 people) Themba is a recommended guide who gets great reports from travellers for his birding and local-area knowledge.

Boat Tours & Whale-Watching

Whatever you do, keep aside some money for a whale-watching experience. In season, there's a high chance of spotting whales here, as well as dolphins and other sea creatures. Trips cost around R200 per person. You can also head upriver on boat tours to view hippos and crocodiles. Most trips operate from St Lucia, though Sodwana Bay Lodge (p271) offers whale-watching out of Sodwana Bay.

Advantage Tours CRUISE
(St Lucia Tours; ☎035-590 1259; www.advantagetours.co.za; 1 McKenzie St, Dolphin Centre) Runs daily whale-watching boat tours between June and September, weather permitting. You can also head upriver on boat tours to view hippos and crocodiles.

Ocean Experience CRUISE
(☎035-590 1555; www.stlucia.co.za) Runs a two-hour hippo and croc cruise up the St Lucia Estuary. Also offers the opportunity to disembark from the boat and continue with a walking tour into the bush and the opportunity to see zebras and antelopes.

Diving & Deep-Sea Fishing

Sodwana Bay (p270) is a hotbed for scuba diving and deep-sea fishing.

Horse Riding

Hluhluwe Horse Safaris HORSE RIDING
(☎035-562 1039; www.hluhluwehorsesafaris.co.za; 1½/2½hr ride R395/550) Horse riding is a wonderful way to see wildlife; these rides are in the False Bay region. You may spot antelope species, as well as other animals. A second option heads to Falaza Game reserve, where you can see rhinos, buffaloes and giraffes. It operates out of Hluhluwe River Lodge (p262).

Kayak Safaris

St Lucia Kayak Safaris KAYAKING
(☎035-590 1233; www.kayaksafaris.co.za; per person R295) St Lucia Kayak Safaris offers novel ways to enjoy the wetland, including a 2½-hour trip starting from Honeymoon Bend in the estuary with a wildlife guide. This outfit also offers snorkelling at Cape Vidal.

Turtle Watching

Fascinating night turtle tours operate from Cape Vidal. Sodwana Bay Lodge (p271) runs trips at Sodwana Bay, as does **Kosi Bay Lodge** (☎035-592 9561; www.kosibaylodge.co.za) at Kosi Bay.

HEALTH & SAFETY WARNING

In 2004, the World Health Organization declared KwaZulu-Natal – as far northeast as St Lucia – malaria free. Note: a low-risk area extends from Sodwana Bay (iSimangaliso Wetland Park) northwards. The risk may be higher north and northeast near the borders of Swaziland and Mozambique. There is the risk of bilharzia in some waterways and dams, especially those less than 1200m above sea level. Also beware of crocs and hippos: both can be deadly. Be careful at night (including in the town of St Lucia), as this is when hippos roam. In more remote areas hippos might be encountered on shore during the day – maintain your distance and retreat quietly. Do not enter any inland water (St Lucia Estuary) – there are crocodiles, sharks, hippos and bilharzia. Swimming is possible (in good conditions and at low tide) at Cape Vidal beach.

St Lucia Turtle Tours WALKING TOUR
(☎082 2575 612; www.extremenaturetours.co.za; ⏲per person R900) Run by Extreme Nature Tours, this environmentally focused outfit runs very good turtle-watching tours as part of a local community-development project. For example, they walk - they do not drive vehicles - along the beach, to ensure nesting turtles are not disturbed.

Euro Zulu Safaris ECOTOUR
(☎035-590 1635; www.eurozulu.com; per person incl dinner & drinks R900) Fascinating night turtle-watching tours operate (from November to March) from Cape Vidal and Kosi Bay.

Wildlife-Watching

uMkhuze Game Reserve (p270) has some of the best wildlife-viewing in the country, and there are a number of operators offering excellent day and night trips on the Eastern (p269) and Western Shores (p269). Operators are listed on www.isimangaliso.com. Self-guided drives are also rewarding ways to seek out wildlife.

Shakabarker Tours TOUR
(☎035-590 1162; www.shakabarker.co.za; 43 Hornbill St) Shakabarker Tours operates out of St Lucia and conducts a range of excellent wildlife trips, including tours of local wildlife parks and a guided bike ride (R225 per person) around St Lucia with a real Zulu guide.

St Lucia

POP 1104

Although not officially within the iSimangaliso Wetland Park, the pleasant village of St Lucia is a useful base from which to explore the park's southern sections. In high season St Lucia is a hotbed of activity as the population swells with visitor numbers. The main drag, McKenzie St (a former hippo pathway), is packed with restaurants, lively hostels and bars, but the quieter avenues behind it offer a touch more hush and a good selection of B&Bs. Hippos sometimes amble down the town's quieter streets (beware: these are not cute, just dangerous).

Sleeping

There's rarely a shortage of places to stay, but it's worth booking ahead during the summer months.

BiB's International Backpackers BACKPACKERS $
(☎035-590 1056; www.bibs.co.za; 310 McKenzie St; dm R100, d with/without bathroom R275/200, safari tent d R375; P@≋) Although the compound inside looks a bit scrappy, this is an excellent budget option. Doubles have fridge, cupboard, en suite bathroom, and African art on the walls. Rooms are well kept and you can stay inside the main building or in the outbuilding to the rear, where you have more privacy. Reception is just outside the entry, in a small office.

Dave's Place BACKPACKERS $
(☎072 0275 384; McKenzie St; camping R80, beds R120) This big old place doesn't look much from outside, and inside it doesn't get a lot better. Beds in a temporary set-up upstairs are likely to be noisy due to the flimsy partitions separating them. Outside is where this place shines, with a large outdoor area where you can spark a fire and cook a braai. Bar and restaurant also on-site.

St Lucia Wilds APARTMENT $
(☎035-590 1033; www.stluciawilds.co.za; 174 McKenzie St; apt & flatlet from R600) An excellent budget/midrange alternative with three apartments and one flatlet for those allergic to backpackers; no meals provided.

Sugarloaf Campsite CAMPGROUND $
(☎033-845 1000; www.kznwildlife.com; Pelican St; camping R180) This pretty campground on the estuary is within snorting distance of hippos, monkeys and crocodiles.

Hornbill House B&B $$
(☎035-590 1162; www.hornbillhouse.com; 43 Hornbill St; s/d incl breakfast R550/900; ❄@≋) A very pleasant place to nest, with lovely rooms (some with private balconies overlooking the tropical vegetation in the garden), friendly dogs and a small pool for a dip. That is, if you're not flitting about on one of the many ecofriendly trips or activities offered by the knowledgable owner, Kian, who runs a tour company.

Sunset Lodge CABIN $$
(☎035-590 1197; www.sunsetstlucia.co.za; 154 McKenzie St; cabins R675-1550; ❄📶≋) Seven well-maintained, self-catering log cabins, lined in dark wood and with a safari theme. Affords a lovely view overlooking the estuary from your private patio – you can watch the hippos, mongoose and monkeys wander onto the lawn. Rates significantly lower outside high season.

Santa Lucia Guesthouse GUESTHOUSE $$
(☎035-590 1151; www.santalucia.co.za; 30 Pelikaan St; s/d incl breakfast R600/900; ❄📶≋) At the back of town, and opposite a lovely park, the guesthouse has affable hosts who ensure a very comfortable stay. Relax over a hearty breakfast enjoying the tropical garden from a lower or upper deck.

Lodge Afrique LODGE $$
(☎071 592 0366; www.lodgeafrique.com; 71 Hornbill St; d R1380; ≋) Smart 'African chic'-style chalets crammed into a suburban block but with lush surrounds. It's a safe bet, if not booked out by groups; reservations required.

Umlilo Lodge LODGE $$
(☎035-590 1717; www.umlilolodge.co.za; 9 Dolphin Ave; s/d R900/1400; ❄📶≋) Centrally located with a lovely lush garden, 10 separate rooms and a lovely indoor-outdoor lounge in which to kick back after a day's activities. Delightful owner.

Serene Estate Guesthouse GUESTHOUSE $$$
(☎072 365 2450; www.serene-estate.co.za; 119 Hornbill St; s/d incl breakfast from R1250/1800; ❄📶≋) A world away from St Lucia, minimalist Dutch meets lush African forest and creates a stylish experience in Serene Estate's six rooms and beyond. The breakfasts, served with one of Olga's daily surprises, are memorable.

Eating

Gourmet isn't a word that has yet hit St Lucia. Nearly all eating options are along McKenzie St.

Rich's Cafe CAFE $
(McKenzie St; mains R40-50; ⏲7.30am-4pm Mon-Fri, 8am-2pm Sun) Serves up wraps, sandwiches, real coffee and all-day breakfasts in a nice little courtyard garden.

Barraca INTERNATIONAL $$
(McKenzie St; mains R60-110; ⏲9am-10pm) A large, open verandah onto the main street makes this place easy to spot. It's friendly, the food's tasty and it's great for people-watching and grabbing a bite any time of the day. For lunch there are open sandwiches, while for dinner seafood options include the prawn curry or seafood paella.

Braza FUSION $$
(McKenzie St; mains R40-120; ⏲lunch & dinner) Cuisine with a touch of Portugal, Brazil, Mozambique and Angola – at least that's what this lively place promotes. It translates as good meaty dishes and grills, although a

MARINE TURTLES

Five species of turtle live off the South African coast, but only two actually nest on the coast: the leatherback turtle *(Dermochelys coriacea)* and the loggerhead turtle *(Caretta caretta)*. The nesting areas of both species extend from the St Lucia mouth, north into Mozambique.

Both species nest at night in summer. The female moves above the high-tide mark, finds a suitable site and lays her eggs. The loggerheads' breeding area is more varied, as they clamber over rocks in the intertidal zone; leatherbacks will only nest on sandy beaches.

About 70 days later, the hatchlings scramble out of the nest at night and make a dash for the sea. Only one or two of each 1000 hatchlings will survive until maturity. The females return 12 to 15 years later to the very same beach to nest.

decent vegetarian platter is on offer (but not on the menu).

ℹ Information

The main banks (Standard Chartered Bank, Nedbank and FNB) have an ATM in the main street. Note that the tourist information office was being renovated when we were in town, and there was no clear timetable for when it would be reopening.

Internet Cafe (☑035-590 1056; 310 McKenzie St; per 30min R15; ☺8am-6pm) By far the best service; at BiB's International Backpackers.

ℹ Getting There & Away

Avis (☑035-590 1634; www.avis.co.za; McKenzie St; ☺8am-4pm Mon-Fri, to noon Sat) Avis is a reliable hire-car operator.

Minibus shared taxis connect Durban and Mtubatuba (R120); the latter is 25km from St Lucia, and it's from where you must catch a connecting minibus taxi to St Lucia. Alternatively, buses run between St Lucia, Richards Bay and Mtubatuba; you must change at each point. If you're not doing tours out of St Lucia Estuary, the only way of getting around is to have your own wheels.

A private transfer shuttle, **Mthuyi's** (☑079 026 3660; mthuyis@gmail.com) runs between St Lucia and Durban (airport and accommodations). The service costs R750 per person for two people, plus R500 for every person after that in your group.

Eastern Shores

The **Eastern Shores** (☑035-590 1633; www.isimangaliso.com; adult/child/vehicle R40/25/45; ☺5am-7pm Nov-Mar, 6am-6pm Apr-Oct), in the southern part of iSimangaliso Wetland Park, is among the most accessible from St Lucia Estuary. It affords opportunities for self-guided drives through the wonderful network of wildlife-viewing roads (there's everything from hippos to antelope, and prolific birdlife). Part of a rehabilitation scheme with Western Shores, this area is where hundreds of thousands of square metres of plantation land has been returned to its former state (yes, that's why there are all those tree stumps).

◉ Sights & Activities

The four scenic routes in the Eastern Shores – pan, *vlei* (marshland), coastal dune and grassland – each reflect their different features and ecosystems. Hides, decks and viewpoints provide vistas and wildlife-viewing opportunities.

Mission Rocks WATERFRONT
About 14km north of the entrance, Mission Rocks is a rugged and rock-covered shoreline. At low tide you can view a fabulous array of sea life in the rock pools (note: you cannot swim here).

Bats Cave CAVE
At low tide you can walk the 5km from Mission Rocks to this bat-filled cave.

Mt Tabor Lookout VIEWPOINT
About 4km before Mission Rocks is the Mt Tabor lookout (signed), which provides a wonderful view of Lake St Lucia and the Indian Ocean.

Cape Vidal BEACH
Twenty kilometres north of Mission Rocks (30km from St Lucia Estuary), taking in the land between Lake Bhangazi and the ocean, is Cape Vidal. Some of the forested sand dunes are 150m high and the beaches are excellent for swimming.

🛏 Sleeping

Cape Vidal Camp CAMPGROUND, CABIN
(☑033-845 1000; www.kznwildlife.com; campsites for up to 4 people R420, 5-bed log cabins minimum R1020) The Eastern Shores' excellent accommodation option, pretty Cape Vidal Camp is set near the shores of Lake Bhangazi. It's managed by Ezemvelo KZN Wildlife; minimum charges apply.

ℹ Getting There & Away

The Eastern Shores' gate lies 2km north of the town of St Lucia, adjacent to the St Lucia Crocodile Centre.

Western Shores

The region northwest of St Lucia Estuary is called the **Western Shores** (☑035-590 1633; www.isimangaliso.com; adult/child/vehicle R40/25/45; ☺5am-7pm Nov-Mar, 6am-6pm Apr-Oct). It comprises two stunning lakeside spots known as **Fani's Island** and **Charters Creek**. Fani's was closed to visitors at the time of writing, but a new road provides access to the dense coastal forest and grasslands of Charters Creek (entrance is off the N2, 18km north of Mtubatuba and 32km south of Hluhluwe). The route offers excellent leisurely wildlife-drive opportunities up the western side of Lake St Lucia (it had just opened at the time of writing), and the drive up the western shore reveals antelope (waterbuck and kukdu in particular) plus the possibility of hippo sightings.

To access the Western Shores from the town of St Lucia, leave town on the road to Mtubatuba, and after 2km turn right at the Dukuduku gate.

uMkhuze Game Reserve & Around

The **uMkhuze Game Reserve** (☎031-845 1000, 035-573 9004; www.kznwildlife.com; adult/child/vehicle R42/25/47; ⏲5am-7pm Nov-Mar, 6am-6pm Apr-Oct) is, in a phrase, a trip highlight. Established in 1912 to protect the nyala antelope, and now part of iSimangaliso Wetland Park, this reserve of dense scrub and open acacia plains covers some spectacular 360 sq km. It successfully re-introduced lions in 2014, and just about every other sought-after animal is represented, as well as more than 400 bird species, including the rare Pel's fishing owl *(Scotopelia peli)*. The reserve has fabulous hides, some at waterholes; the pans, surrounded by fever trees, offer some of the best wildlife-viewing in the country. It's 15km from Mkuze town (18km from Bayla if heading north).

Activities

Excellent evening drives (R220) are offered by Mantuma.

Fig Forest Walk WALKING TOUR
(per person R200) Don't miss the wonderful Fig Forest Walk, an escorted walk across multi-level walkways. It's offered by Mantuma.

> **UMKHUZE GAME RESERVE**
>
> **Why Go** uMkhuze has all the Big Five and is a very beautiful park. Nyala and other antelope are often seen around the rest camp. Guides here are very knowledgable and a wildlife drive is a highlight.
>
> **When to Go** The best time for viewing is October and November, when the grass has been burnt so its easier to see the wildlife and it's not too hot.
>
> **Practicalities** Park gates are open 5am to 7pm November to March, and 6am to 6pm between April and October. The nearest town is Mkhuze.
>
> **Budget Tips** Rest huts are a bargain; self-cater, as there are plenty of braais.

Sleeping

Mantuma CHALET $$
(☎033-845 1000; www.kznwildlife.com; huts R410, d chalets R800) Mantuma is in a lovely setting and is unfenced, so there's often wandering wildlife, especially nyala. It's an old camp – the accommodation has seen better days – but it's clean, well positioned and good value. You're better off self-catering than relying on the restaurant.

Nhlonhlela Bush Lodge LODGE $$$
(☎033-845 1000; www.kznwildlife.com; 8-bed lodges R2400) Nhlonhlela bush lodge features a communal area overlooking a pan, and four comfortable units linked by boardwalks. You have your own ranger and chef (you bring your own food).

Ghost Mountain Inn INN $$$
(☎035-573 1025; www.ghostmountaininn.co.za; Fish Eagle Rd; s/d incl breakfast from R1015/1430; ❄📶🏊) Outside of the park, Ghost Mountain Inn is an old-school colonial place with a modern (and luxurious) touch, indoor-outdoor lounge areas and blooming gardens. It's an excellent base for exploring the reserves. There are fascinating cultural tours in the scenic surrounds; recommended tours include trips to uMkhuze Game Reserve and Dingaan's Grave.

Getting There & Away

Access from the north is via Mkhuze town (from the south, you turn off the N2 around 35km north of Hluhluwe village, but it's on a dirt road). On the eastern side there's access about 40km south of Sodwana Bay, off Rte 22. It's a mix of dirt roads and badly potholed bitumen that's OK for 2WDs, but drive carefully as it can get treacherous. There's also a road from Sodwana Bay.

Sodwana Bay

Get past the approach to the park – a mishmash of lodges, signs and temporary-looking constructions – and you're in for a pleasant surprise. **Sodwana Bay** (http://isimangaliso.com; adult/child R30/20; ⏲24hr) is bordered by lush forest on one side and glittering sands on another. The area is best known for its **scuba diving** – the diversity of underwater seascapes and marine flora and fauna makes it one of South Africa's diving capitals. Serious **deep-sea fishing** occurs here too; you can be inundated with huntin', shootin', fishin' types who head out in their water machines. On that note: avoid the silly

GHOST MOUNTAIN

The town of Mkuze is southwest of the Lebombo Range on the N2. Ghost Mountain, south of the town, was an important burial place for the Ndwandwe tribe and has a reputation for eerie occurrences, usually confined to strange lights and noises. Occasionally human bones, which date from a big battle between rival Zulu factions in 1884, are still found near Ghost Mountain.

season (summer holidays) when thousands throng here to take the plunge – literally. At all other times it's a beautifully peaceful place. That said, most people come here for the diving or fishing; outside of that, there's not much to do here but walk along the beach and admire this beautiful area.

Services, including accommodation options, dive operators, a couple of cafes and tour operators, sprawl along the road leading to the park entrance. Facilities inside this section of the park include a campsite plus a couple of diving operator–lodges.

There is an ATM in the **general store** (open 8.30am to 4.30pm Monday to Friday, to 11.30am Saturday) at the park's entrance. Otherwise you'll need to head to Mbazwana, 14km west.

Sleeping & Eating

Natural Moments Bush Camp & Diving BACKPACKERS $
(☎083 256 1756; www.divesodwana.com; huts R155, r R195) This rustic backpackers of the laid-back, hippie variety has small huts crammed into a lush garden setting. It also runs a campsite and Zulu-hut accommodation nearby.

Ezemvelo KZN Wildlife CAMPGROUND $$
(☎033-845 1000; www.kznwildlife.com; campsites for up to 4 people from R440, 4-bed cabins R1320) Has hundreds of well-organised campsites and cabins set within the park's coastal forest. Minimum charges apply.

Sodwana Bay Lodge LODGE $$
(☎035-571 6000; www.sodwanabaylodge.co.za; s/d with half board R835/1540) This resort has neat boardwalks, banana palms and pine-filled, slightly dated rooms. The chalets here are very comfortable, with huge decks. It caters to divers and offers various dive and accommodation packages, which can be great value. It's on the main road on the approach to the park. **Sodwana Bay Lodge Scuba Centre** (☎035-571 0117; www.sodwanadiving.co.za; Sodwana Bay Lodge) is on the premises.

Coral Divers LODGE $$
(☎033-345 6531; www.coraldivers.co.za; Sodwana Bay; d tent R460, d cabin with/without bathroom from R930/770; @≋) Inside the park proper, this factory-style operation continues to 'net the shoals' with its diving packages and other activities. There's a large dining area–bar, and a tadpole-size pool. There's something for all budgets, from tents and small dollhouse-style cabins to nicer, upmarket cabins with their own patch of lawn and bathrooms.

It can look a bit overused depending on whether or not maintenance has been done after the hordes have gone.

Leatherbacks SEAFOOD
(☎035-571 6000; Sodwana Bay Lodge; mains R70-130; ⌚7am-10pm) This lovely eating area is open to the breeze, has a range of simple dishes and is a quiet respite from the main road. It's open all day and evening, making it ideal for a bite of pizza, pasta or well-prepared seafood any time.

Getting There & Away

Turn off the N2 at Hluhluwe village heading to Mbazwana, and continue about 20km to the park. Minibus shared taxis ply this route.

Lake Sibaya & Coastal Forest

Remote grassland plains, lush forests and pristine beaches are the main features of the magical Coastal Forest. Its beauty can, in part, be explained by its location – this area is one of the most remote sections of iSimangaliso – and it is accessed either along the coastal sandy track between Kosi Bay and Sodwana Bay or from KwaNgwanase, in both instances by 4WD. Highlights include Black Rock (a rugged rocky peninsula easily reached by climbing over sand dunes) and Lala Nek, a beautiful and seemingly never-ending stretch of sand.

Further south sits Lake Sibaya, the largest freshwater lake in South Africa. It covers between 60 and 70 sq km, depending on the water level. Hippos, crocs and a large range of birdlife (more than 280 species) occupy the lake. Canoeing trips can be arranged through Thonga Beach Lodge (p272).

But beauty doesn't always come cheap. Accommodation in this region is made up mainly (but not entirely) of luxury lodges. All offer excellent snorkelling, diving and other activities. The lodges transfer guests from the main road; you leave your car in a secure parking area.

Day-visitor permits (per person/child/vehicle R30/15/20) are required for this section of the park; go to the Manzengwenya and Kosi Bay offices of Ezemvelo KZN Wildlife.

Sleeping

Mabibi Camp
CAMPGROUND $

(☑035-474 1504; www.mabibicampsite.co.za; camping R100) If you can get here, you'll have heaven to yourself – almost. This rustic community-owned camp is right next to upmarket Thonga Beach Lodge, but this is luxury of a different kind – nestled in a swath of forest and only a hop, skip and 137 steps (via a stairway) from the beach. Bring your own tent, food and gear.

Thonga Beach Lodge
LODGE $$$

(☑035-474 1473; www.isibindiafrica.co.za; d with full board R7180-9350; ✸☒) Popular with European visitors, this isolated and luxurious beach resort offers spacious huts scattered through coastal forest. Spectacular ocean views – whales sometimes pass by – and activities provide the entertainment, while the wide, white beach and spa treatments (at extra cost) are a welcome relief after the rigours of a safari. The cuisine is excellent, especially the buffet lunches.

Rocktail Beach Camp
LODGE $$$

(☑in Johannesburg 011-807 1800; www.wildernesssafaris.com; s/d with full board R2870/5740; ☒) New York Soho meets Durban chic at Rocktail Beach Camp. Twelve safari tents (with pine floors and tasteful wood-sided bathrooms) and three family units are nestled in dune forest in a tropical environment, with a choice of forest-canopy or sea views. The light and breezy, spacious communal area is an enjoyable place to relax. Offers seasonal specials.

Kosi Bay

The jewel of iSimangaliso Wetland Park, Kosi Bay (☑035-845 1000; adult/child/vehicle R30/15/20; ☺6am-6pm) features a string of four lakes, starting from an estuary lined with some of the most beautiful and quiet beaches in South Africa. Fig, mangrove and raffia-palm forests provide the greenery (it's the only place in South Africa with five mangrove species in one place). Within the estuary mouth is excellent snorkelling. Note: stonefish are present here, so protect your feet if walking in the estuary.

Hippos, Zambezi sharks and some crocs live within the lake system. More than 250 bird species have been identified here, including rare palmnut vultures.

You'll need a 4WD and permit to visit. KwaNgwanase is the nearest service centre, some 10km west of the reserve, and you will find shops and an ATM here.

Sleeping & Eating

Most lodge accommodation is dispersed around the region's sandy dunes, several kilometres from KwaNgwanase. In many cases 4WDs are needed to negotiate the sandy tracks.

Utshwayelo Lodge
CAMPGROUND, CHALET $

(☑074 587 1574; www.kosimouth.co.za; camping R350, sahara tents R490, chalets R740; ☒) This lovely community-run camp offers basic but neat bamboo-lined chalets with a communal kitchen. It also has permanent tents with wooden decks and communal ablutions. It's right by the entrance to the park at the Kosi Bay Mouth access road. Issues car-entry permits to Kosi Bay Mouth.

Ezemvelo KZN Wildlife
CAMPGROUND, CABIN $$

(☑033-845 1000; www.kznwildlife.com; campsites for up to 4 people R440, 2-/5-/6-bed cabins R510/1360/1700) Offers camping and fully equipped, pleasant cabin accommodation within lush forest surrounds on the western shore of Lake Nhlange; minimum charges apply. Popular with fishers.

Maputaland Lodge
CHALET $$

(☑035-592 0654; www.maputalandlodge.co.za; KwaNgwanase; s/d R530/740; ✸☒) These 23 simple, yet pleasant, self-catering chalets in KwaNgwanase have all mod cons including DSTV, a bar and a restaurant. A good option in a creature-free zone.

★ Kosi Forest Lodge
LODGE $$$

(☑035-474 1473; www.isibindi.co.za; per person with full board R2160; ☒) The only private lodge in iSimangaliso's Kosi Bay region, and surrounded by the sand forest's Umdoni trees, this intimate 16-bed lodge offers a dreamy, luxurious – given the remote circumstances and lack of electricity – experience. Accommodation is in romantic safari tents. They're a blend of *Out of Africa* (wooden decor and muted furnishings) and natural (the ultimate in ingenious outdoor bathrooms).

There are activities (some included in the nightly rate) on tap, and guest transfers are available.

Getting There & Away

A 4WD and permit are required to access Kosi Bay, but don't let this deter you. There are two entrances to the park: at Kosi Bay Camp (7km north of KwaNgwanase) and Kosi Bay Mouth (19km north of KwaNgwanase). Only 4WDs can enter the access roads, and numbers are limited; permits are required to enter **Kosi Bay Mouth** (adult/child/vehicle R40/20/40). These must be arranged a day in advance by calling ☎ 035-592 0236, or through some lodgings.

Kosi Forest Lodge organises pick-ups from KwaNgwanase, and some lodges in other areas organise trips to Kosi Bay. There is no public transport to the area.

If you are driving – approaching from any direction – the best access is via N2; at Hluhluwe turn onto Rte 22. If heading from Sodwana Bay, continue north up Rte 22. If you have a 4WD, the sandy coastal route is not to be missed.

Tembe Elephant Park

Heading west along a dirt road to the N2 from Kosi Bay, South Africa's last free-ranging elephants are protected in the sandveld (dry, sandy coastal belt) forests of **Tembe Elephant Park** (☎ 031-267 0144; www.tembe.co.za; adult/child/vehicle R30/15/35; ⏲ 6am-6pm). This transfrontier park on the Mozambique border is owned by the Tembe tribe and managed by Ezemvelo KZN Wildlife. Around 230 elephants live in its 300 sq km; these are the only indigenous elephants in KZN, and the largest elephants in the world, weighing up to 7000kg. The park boasts the Big Five (lion, leopard, buffalo, elephant and rhino), plus more than 300 bird species.

Tembe Lodge LODGE $$$

(☎ 082 651 2868; www.tembe.co.za; with full board & activities per person R950-1450;) Tembe Lodge offers accommodation in delightful, secluded, upmarket safari tents built on wooden platforms (the tents have bathrooms).

TEMBE ELEPHANT PARK

Why Go Not only does this park contain the legendary big tuskers – the largest elephants in the world – it also has the Big Five. Staying in a safari tent is a delightful way to experience the park, and this accommodatiom, which includes meals and activities, is very good value.

When to Go The drier months (May to September) offer the best wildlife-viewing. Using the hide at the waterhole normally produces excellent results at this time. Day visitors are advised to arrive early, as the park only allows 10 vehicles in per day.

Practicalities There's a sealed road all the way to the park entrance, but only 4WD vehicles are allowed to drive through the park itself; secure parking is available and visitors are collected in open safari vehicles.

Budget Tips Forget the budget! If you made it this far it's worth shelling out for the excellent accommmodation in the park. Budget in advance.

Ndumo Game Reserve

Just west of Tembe Elephant Park, **Ndumo Game Reserve** (☎ 035-591 0004, 035-845 1000; www.kznwildlife.com; adult/child/vehicle R40/20/40; ⏲ 5am-7pm Oct-Mar, 6am-6pm Apr-Sep) is beside the Mozambique border and close to the Swaziland border, about 100km north of Mkhuze. On some 100 sq km, there are black and white rhinos, hippos, crocodiles and antelope species, but it's the birdlife on the Phongolo and Usutu Rivers, and their flood plains and pans, that attracts visitors. The reserve is known locally as a 'mini Okavango'.

Wildlife-viewing and birdwatching guided walks (R120) and vehicle tours (R240) are available. This is the southernmost limit of the range of many bird species and the reserve is a favourite with birdwatchers, with more than 400 bird species recorded.

Fuel and limited supplies are usually available 2km outside the park gate. Camping and rest huts are offered by **Ezemvelo KZN Wildlife Accommodation** (☎ 033-845 1000; www.kznwildlife.com; camping R120, 2-bed rest huts R700); minimum charges apply.

THE MIDLANDS

The Midlands run northwest from Pietermaritzburg (KwaZulu-Natal's capital) to Estcourt, skirting the Battlefields to the northeast. West of Pietermaritzburg is picturesque, hilly country, with horse studs and plenty of European trees. It was originally settled by English farmers.

Today, the region appeals more to art and craft lovers; it promotes itself heavily as the Midlands Meander, a slightly contrived concoction of craft shops, artistic endeavours, tea shops and B&Bs, winding along and around Rte 103 west of the N3, northwest of Pietermaritzburg.

Pietermaritzburg

POP 223,500

Billed as the heritage city, and KZN's administrative and legislative capital, Pietermaritzburg and its grand historic buildings hark back to an age of pith helmets and midday martinis. While many buildings have been converted into museums, much of the CBD has, sadly, lost its gloss, especially in the past few years. This is partly due to the dire state of the local-government coffers. Elsewhere, the inner suburbs – plus Hilton, a suburb 9km northwest of the city centre – are green, leafy and pretty.

Pietermaritzburg comprises a very contemporary mix: the city's numerous private schools are home to many students; a large Zulu community sets a colourful tone; and the Indian community brings echoes of the subcontinent to the city's busy streets. Pietermaritzburg is a reasonable base from which to tackle the Midlands Meander (p276).

History

After defeating the Zulu at the decisive Battle of Blood River, the Voortrekkers began to establish their republic of Natal. Pietermaritzburg (usually known as PMB) was named in honour of leader Pieter Mauritz Retief, and was founded in 1838 as the capital (later the 'u' was dropped and, in 1938, it was decreed that Voortrekker leader Gert Maritz be remembered in the title). In 1841 the Boers built their Church of the Vow here to honour the Blood River promise. The British annexed Natal in 1843, but they retained Pietermaritzburg – well positioned and less humid than Durban, and already a neat little town – as the capital. In 2004 it became the provincial capital, and in 2005 street names were altered to reflect a more local flavour.

Alan Paton, author of *Cry, the Beloved Country,* was born in Pietermaritzburg in 1903.

Sights & Activities

Tatham Art Gallery GALLERY
(033-392 2800; www.tatham.org.za; Chief Albert Luthuli St (Commercial Rd); 10am-5pm Tue-Sun) FREE In keeping with Pietermaritzburg's self-styled role as the 'heritage city', one of its finest sights, the art gallery, was started in 1903 by Mrs Ada Tatham. Housed in the beautiful Old Supreme Court, it contains a fine collection of French and English 19th- and early-20th-century works.

The ground floor has abstract depictions of South Africa's people and street scenes. It's as if the country's history is either too painful or too complex to be shown through realism. Upstairs is more formal, with portraits and landscapes sharing the wall space along with sculptures and colourful displays of ceramics and lithographs.

KwaZulu-Natal National Botanical Garden GARDENS
(033-344 3585; www.sanbi.org; 2 Swartkops Rd, Prestbury; adult/child R20/free; 8am-6pm Oct-Apr, to 5.30pm May-Sep) Located 2km west of the train station on the continuation of Hoosen Haffejee St and spread over 4200 sq metres, these gardens have exotic species and indigenous mist-belt flora.

KwaZulu-Natal Museum MUSEUM
(033-345 1404; www.nmsa.org.za; 237 Jabu Ndlovu St; adult/child R10/3; 8.15am-4.30pm Mon-Fri, 9am-4pm Sat, 10am-3pm Sun) Has a range of displays reflecting a diversity of cultures, including settler history, war records, stuffed birds, marine life and African mammals.

Macrorie House Museum MUSEUM
(033-394 2161; 11 Jabu Ndlovu St; adult/child R10/5; 10am-4pm Mon, 9am-1pm Tue-Fri) Built in 1860, this old family residence is furnished in Victorian style. Here you'll find furniture and items of the early British settlers, and plenty of documented ghosts!

Msunduzi Museum MUSEUM
(033-394 6834; www.voortrekkermuseum.co.za; 351 Langalibalele St (Longmarket St); adult/student R10/5; 9am-4pm Mon-Fri, to 1pm Sat) Formerly known as Voortrekker Museum, Msunduzi Museum comprises a complex that incorporates the Church of the Vow, the home of Andries Pretorius, a Voortrekker house and a girls' school (the museum's administrative building). The **Church of the Vow** was built in 1841 to fulfil the Voortrekkers' promise to God at the Battle of Blood River. The words of the vow are in the **Modern Memorial Church**.

Pietermaritzburg

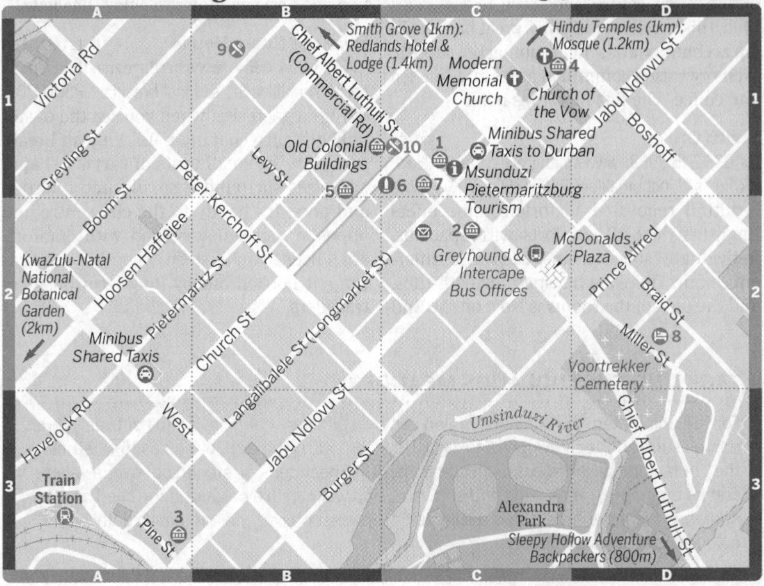

More recently the museum has had a name change and now describes itself as a multicultural institution, incorporating Zulu and Indian displays.

City Hall HISTORIC BUILDING
(cnr Langalibalele St (Longmarket St) & Chief Albert Luthuli St (Commercial Rd)) The colonial-era City Hall is the largest load-bearing red-brick building in the southern hemisphere.

Standard Chartered Bank HISTORIC BUILDING
(Church St Mall) Architect Phillip Dudgeon modelled the Standard Bank on the Bank of Ireland in Belfast.

Hindu Temples HINDU
(Langalibalele St (Longmarket St)) Three Hindu temples grace the northern end of Langalibalele St.

Mosque MOSQUE
(Masukwane St (East St)) Pietermaritzburg's main mosque.

Statue of Gandhi MONUMENT
(Church St) A statue of Gandhi, who was famously ejected from a 1st-class carriage at Pietermaritzburg station, stands defiant opposite some old colonial buildings on Church St.

Pietermaritzburg

Sights

1	City Hall	C1
2	KwaZulu-Natal Museum	C2
3	Macrorie House Museum	A3
4	Msunduzi Museum	C1
5	Standard Chartered Bank	B1
6	Statue of Gandhi	C1
7	Tatham Art Gallery	C1

Sleeping

8	Heritage Guest House	D2

Eating

9	Rosehurst	B1
10	Tatham Art Gallery Cafe	C1
	Traffords	(see 8)

Sleeping

Most B&Bs cater to the business crowds who stay in town tending to council and other matters of commerce. Pietermaritzburg Tourism can help with bookings, or try the **Pietermaritzburg B&B Network** (☎073-154 4444; www.pmbnetwork.co.za), a group of B&Bs that help promote each other.

Sleepy Hollow Adventure Backpackers BACKPACKERS $
(☎033-347 3015; www.sleepyhollowbackpackers.com; 489 Town Bush Rd, Montrose; dm/d/f

R150/350/500;) Within walking distance of the town centre and close to Cascades Mall, this excellent place has great backpackers accommodation in an upmarket suburb. Well-organised communal areas and free tea and coffee. The Baz Bus stops here.

Smith Grove B&B $$
(033-345 3963; www.smithgrove.co.za; 37 Howick Rd; s/d incl breakfast R595/850;) This beautiful renovated Victorian home offers English-style B&B comforts with spacious, individually styled rooms, each in a different colour. There are freestanding bath-tubs, and the pick of the rooms is No 5 on the 2nd floor, facing away from the main road with two good-size windows to enjoy the views.

Heritage Guest House GUESTHOUSE $$
(033-394 4364; www.heritageguesthousepmb.co.za; 45 Miller St; s/d incl breakfast R500/700;) It's a good sign when you see the owner in chef's garb cooking a full English breakfast. Here six small units of varying shapes and sizes surround a small, pretty garden and pool. It's handy to the city centre and opposite the cemetery, and with comfortable beds, you'll sleep like the dead. It can get booked out by long-term business travellers.

TACKLING THE MIDLANDS MEANDER

For the uninitiated, the Midlands region can be a bit overwhelming. It's full of twee venue names such as 'Piggly Wiggly' and 'Ugly Duckling', with little explanation as to whether they're tasteful galleries or kitsch gift shops. The meander – stretched out over a valley and its offshoots – is relaxing and enjoyable and well worth a detour off the N3. The *Midlands Meander* brochure is available from tourist offices and contains a detailed colour-coded map of the area.

Ardmore Ceramic Studio (033-940 0034; www.ardmoreceramics.co.za; Caversham Rd, Lidgetton; 8.30am-4.30pm) This extraordinary gallery was started by artist Fée Halset-Berning in 1985. She trained Bonnie Ntshalintsahli, the daughter of a farm employee. Sadly, Bonnie has since passed away, but the studio flourished, firstly in the Drakensberg with a group of highly gifted artists. In 2009, the studio moved to its current site, set among greenery and stunning trees.

The studio's artists create the most extraordinary pieces of ceramic art, some functional, others ornamental. So renowned are the pieces that Christie's holds an annual auction of selected items. You can see the artists at work in the studio and visit the gallery; works are for sale, too.

Dargle Valley Pottery (082 420 7729; D66; 9am-5pm) Started by famous South African potter Ian Glenny, this old-school, '70s-style pottery place is at the earthy and rural end of Ardmore's range of arts centres but no less captivating for that. You can wander through the barnlike gallery and watch the current local potter as he turns the pots. The pieces are noted for their stunning glazing; the tagines are popular.

Granny Mouse Country House (033-234 4071; www.grannymouse.co.za; Old Main Rd, Balgowan; d incl breakfast from R2045) This deceptively named place near the village of Balgowan, south of Mooi River, is not one abode but more a resort-style range of neat, thatched, luxurious cottages, complete with a chapel and spa. Specials are often available.

Sycamore Avenue Tree Houses (033-263 5009; www.treehouse-acc.co.za; 11 Hidcote Rd, Mooi River; d R1700) These extraordinary tree houses are functional art at its best: recycled materials, unique carvings, wooden hinges and ingenious artistic touches have been incorporated into comfortable the surroundings. One house even has a 'Jacuzzi in the sky', connected by a walkway. Near Hidcote, Sycamore is located 50km from Giant's Castle, Drakensberg; see the website for directions.

Cafe Bloom (033-266 6118; Nottingham Rd, Country Courtyard; mains R40-70; 7.30am-4.30pm, closed Tue) One of the nicest cafes in the area. Located in a small complex with a garden, this homely, funky cafe is decked out in a melange of retro decor. You'll find great coffee, snacks and all-day breakfasts, and all products are made on the premises, from bread and cakes to the daily seasonal special (the likes of vegie curries and quiches).

Ceramics and artworks are for sale.

Elbow's Rest CHALET $$
(☎082 963 7523; www.elbowsrest.co.za; 15 Azalea Dr, Hilton; s/d R500/700) These three self-catering units have a pretty, cottagelike feel in a secure environment. The decor is slightly old-world, with lots of pine trimmings, and a delightful English cottage–style courtyard and garden borders each one. It would suit couples or older tourists. It's only 10km away in Hilton.

Redlands Hotel & Lodge HOTEL $$$
(☎033-394 3333; www.redlandshotel.co.za; cnr Howick Rd & George MacFarlane Lane; s R1280-1670, d R1680-2020; ❄📶🏊) Swish and stately, this elegant place offers contrived but tasteful colonial-style surrounds. It's a favourite among government dignitaries. The spacious grounds add to the escape-from-it-all ambience. It's north of the centre off Howick Rd, past the Royal Agricultural Showgrounds.

Eating

Tatham Art Gallery Cafe CAFE $
(Chief Albert Luthuli St (Commercial Rd); mains R50-70; ⏰10am-4pm Mon-Sat) Dip into quiche, beef curry or lasagne at the Tatham Gallery, upstairs in a quiet room with tables and chairs or on the outside balcony. Also on offer are sweet treats like muffins and brownies.

Traffords INTERNATIONAL $$
(☎033-394 4364; http://traffords.co.za; 43 Miller St; lunch mains R55-90, dinner mains R95-150; ⏰noon-3pm Tue-Fri, 6.30-10.30pm Tue-Sat; 🖉) This place serves up quality international cuisine in appealingly quaint surrounds: the rooms of a converted heritage home. Choose from the likes of cherry tobacco duck or smoked, black-pepper-rubbed entrecôte. Lunches include more salad-based offerings. Vegetarians are well catered for. Decor is of the preloved linen tablecloth variety… it's like having an elegant meal in the home you'd love to have.

★ **Rosehurst** INTERNATIONAL $$
(☎033-394 3833; 239 Boom St; mains R75; ⏰8.30am-4.30pm Mon-Fri, to 2pm Sat) This delightful oasis, in a lovely Victorian house behind a rather chintzy gift shop, is a quintessential English garden in the middle of 'Maritzburg – complete with topiary trees and quaint chairs and tables. Relax under blossoms and pink bougainvillea while enjoying fresh and very tasty salads, sandwiches and pastries. There are excellent breakfasts, too.

Drinking & Nightlife

Franki Bananaz BAR
(9 Armitage Rd, Bird Sanctuary; ⏰11am-late) This upmarket cocktail bar is a great spot to mix with a cross-section of locals. It's particularly popular with students and young professionals, especially on Friday night. It also does tasty burgers and other quality pre-prepared offerings. Local bands play here monthly. Note: only ever take a taxi to and fro.

Information

EMERGENCY

Police Station (☎033-845 2400, 10111; Jabu Ndlovu St)

INTERNET ACCESS

Cyber World (Shop 5, Victoria Mall, Langalibalele St (Longmarket St); per hour R10; ⏰9am-5pm Mon-Fri, to 1pm Sat) Reliable public internet access.

MEDICAL SERVICES

Medi-Clinic (☎033-845 3700, 24hr emergency 033-845 3911; www.mediclinic.co.za; 90 Payn St) Well-equipped hospital with emergency department on the banks of the Umsinduzi River.

MONEY

There are several banks located across town and in major shopping malls.

ABSA (cnr Langalibalele St (Longmarket St) & Buchanan St) Has an ATM and change facilities.

First National Bank (Church St) In a handy location in the city centre.

POST

Main Post Office (Langalibalele St)

TOURIST INFORMATION

Ezemvelo KZN Wildlife Headquarters (☎033-845 1000; www.kznwildlife.com; Peter Brown Dr, Queen Elizabeth Park; ⏰reception 8am-4.30pm Mon-Fri, reservations 8am-5.30pm Mon-Thu, to 4.30pm Fri, to 12.30pm Sat) Provides information and accommodation bookings for all Ezemvelo KZN Wildlife parks and reserves. To get to the office, head out to Howick Rd (an extension of Chief Albert Luthuli St) and after several kilometres you'll come to a roundabout. Veer right and head over the N3. This road has a very small sign directing you to 'Country Club', which is 2km further. It's hard to get to without your own transport, although some minibus shared taxis pass the roundabout on their way to Hilton. Note that at least 48 hours' notice is required for bookings.

Msunduzi Pietermaritzburg Tourism (☎033-345 1348; www.pmbtourism.co.za; Publicity

House, 117 Chief Albert Luthuli St; ⏲8am-5pm Mon-Fri, to 1pm Sat) The tourist office has brand spanking new premises just behind the current office – although when it officially moves is anybody's guess.

Getting There & Away

BUS

The head offices of most bus companies are in Berger St, or directly opposite in McDonalds Plaza. **Translux** (☎0861 589 282; www.translux.co.za) and its no-frills affiliate, City to City, are based at the train station.

Destinations offered from Pietermaritzburg include Jo'burg (R340 to R420, six to seven hours), Pretoria (R340 to R400, seven to eight hours) and Durban (R200 to R280, 1½ hours). Offices are generally open 7am or 8am until 11pm. Tickets for all major services can be purchased at Checkers/Shoprite or online at www.computicket.com.

NUD Express (☎033-701 2750, 079 696 7108; www.underbergexpress.co.za) NUD Express offers a daily service to Durban's King Shaka International Airport (R500) and Durban Central (R600). You must book these services; note that the buses are not known for their reliability in sticking to times.

Baz Bus (☎0861 229 287; www.bazbus.com) The Baz Bus travels between Durban and Pietermaritzburg three times a week.

SHARED TAXI

Minibus taxis to Durban leave from behind City Hall (R70, one hour), while those to Underberg depart from the corner of West and Pietermaritz Sts. Destinations from this stop also include Ladysmith (R90, 2½ hours), Underberg (R80, 2½ hours), and Jo'burg (R200, eight hours).

TRAIN

Shosholoza Meyl (☎0860 008 888; www.shosholozameyl.co.za) Pietermaritzburg is serviced by the Shosholoza Meyl.

Getting Around

Metro Cabs (☎033-397 1912; www.metrotaxis.co.za) Reliable taxi service.

DRAKENSBERG & UKHAHLAMBA-DRAKENSBERG PARK

If any landscape lives up to its airbrushed, publicity-shot alter ego, it is the jagged, green sweep of the Drakensberg range's tabletop peaks. This forms the boundary between South Africa and the mountain kingdom of Lesotho, and offers some of the country's most awe-inspiring landscapes. It provided the backdrop for the films *Zulu* (1964) and *Yesterday* (2004) and the setting for Alan Paton's novel *Cry, the Beloved Country,* and is the inspiration for a million picture postcards.

Within the area is a 2430-sq-km sweep of basalt summits and buttresses; this section was granted World Heritage status in November 2000, and was renamed uKhahlamba-Drakensberg Park. The park is part of the wider Drakensberg region, extending from Royal Natal National Park in the north to Kokstad in the south, the region and battlefields around Estcourt and Ladysmith, and the southern Midlands. Today, some of the vistas are recognisably South African, particularly the unforgettable curve of the Amphitheatre in Royal Natal National Park. Prominent peaks include Mont-aux-Sources, the Sentinel, Eastern Buttress and Devil's Tooth.

Drakensberg means 'Dragon Mountains'; the Zulu named it Quathlamba, meaning 'Battlement of Spears'. The Zulu word is a more accurate description of the sheer escarpment, but the Afrikaans name captures something of the Drakensberg's otherworldly atmosphere. People have lived here for thousands of years – this is evidenced by the many San rock-art sites (visit Didima, Cathedral Peak, Kamberg and Injisuthi).

The San, already under pressure from the tribes that had moved into the Drakensberg foothills, were finally destroyed with the coming of white settlers. Some moved to Lesotho, where they were absorbed into the Basotho population, but many were killed or simply starved when their hunting grounds were occupied by others. Khoe-San cattle raids annoyed the white settlers to the extent that the settlers forced several black tribes to relocate into the Drakensberg foothills to act as a buffer between the whites and the Khoe-San. These early 'Bantu locations' meant there was little development in the area, which later allowed the creation of a chain of parks and reserves.

Climate

The frosts come in winter, but the rain falls in summer, and snow has been recorded on the summit every month of the year. The summer weather forecasts, posted in each of the Ezemvelo KZN Wildlife park offices, can often make bleak reading for those hoping for blue skies and sunshine. Whenever you visit, always carry wet-weather gear, and be prepared for icy conditions and snowfalls.

UKHAHLAMBA-DRAKENSBERG PARK

Why Go This is one of South Africa's greatest sights. The sheer majesty of the mountains is worth travelling here to see; add to this brilliant hiking opportunities and San rock art. Be aware, though, that this is not a traditional South African wildlife park where you can drive around and see the animals. The parks inside Ukhahlamba-Drakensberg have few or no roads – instead they are specifically set up for walking and hiking.

When to Go Summer gets the best weather for hiking – you can often bet on clear, dry mornings, with the thunderheads only rolling in during the afternoon.

Practicalities There is no single road linking all the main areas of interest – you have to enter and exit and re-enter each region of the park from the N3, Rte 103 and Rte 74 or, if road conditions permit, from secondary roads.

Budget Tips Stick to camping and the few budget accommodation places in the area. If there's a group of you it's worth hiring a car and splitting the costs.

Hiking

The Drakensberg range is one of the best hiking destinations in Africa. Valleys, waterfalls, rivers, caves and the escarpment, which rises to an impressive 3000m, provide spectacular wilderness experiences for walkers of all levels. Climbing is popular throughout the Drakensberg; only experienced climbers should attempt peaks in this region.

Broadly speaking, there are three main degrees of difficulty: gentle day walks, moderate half-day hikes and strenuous 10- to 12-hour hikes. Overnight treks and multi-day hikes are for more serious and experienced hikers.

The trails are accessed through any of the park's entrances – Royal Natal National Park (renowned for its excellent day walks), Cathedral Peak, Monk's Cowl, Injisuthi and Giant's Castle, and the remote wilderness areas in the Southern Drakensberg.

To plan any walk, hike or trek, make sure you obtain the relevant 1:50,000-scale maps that show trails and have essential information for hikers. You should always seek advice on the current status of any trail – consult with experienced hikers, accommodation owners and Ezemvelo KZN Wildlife officers. You must always fill in a register, and permits are needed on all hikes within the park; organise them with Ezemvelo KZN Wildlife offices at the various trailheads. The only trail accommodation is at Giant's Castle; in some areas hikers can use caves, but always carry a tent.

Registered guides can be organised for short walks (R150 per person) or longer hikes (R250 per person). Guides for overnight hikes are around R600 per person per night. This depends on numbers and should be established at each point. Hikers are not allowed to light fires, so you'll need to bring a stove.

April to July are good months for hiking. Summer hiking can be made frustrating, and even dangerous, by rain and flooding rivers; in winter, frost is the main hazard, and snow occurs occasionally. Snakes inhabit the area.

Wildlife

With plentiful water, a range of up to 3000m in altitude and distinct areas such as plateaus, cliffs and valleys, it isn't surprising that the uKhahlamba-Drakensberg has extremely varied flora. The park is mainly grassland, wooded gorges and high basalt cliffs with small forests in the valleys. There's also some protea savannah and, during spring, swaths of wildflowers. At higher altitudes grass yields to heath and scrub. At lower levels, but confined to valleys (especially around Royal Natal National Park), are small yellowwood forests.

The park is home to numerous and varied animals and hundreds of bird species. Altogether there are thought to be about 60 mammal species. There are several species of antelope, with relatively large numbers of elands (more in the Southern Berg). The rarest antelope is the klipspringer, which is sometimes spotted on the higher slopes. There are otter, African wildcats, porcupine and even the odd leopard. Baboons forage for food on some of the steepest mountains. The rarest species is a small, short-tailed rodent called the ice rat, which lives in the boulders near the mountain summits. The bearded vulture (a rare bird of prey), black eagles and other vultures are found around the cliffs, capitalising on the peaks' thermals. Various hides throughout the park allow for closer viewing.

Drakensberg

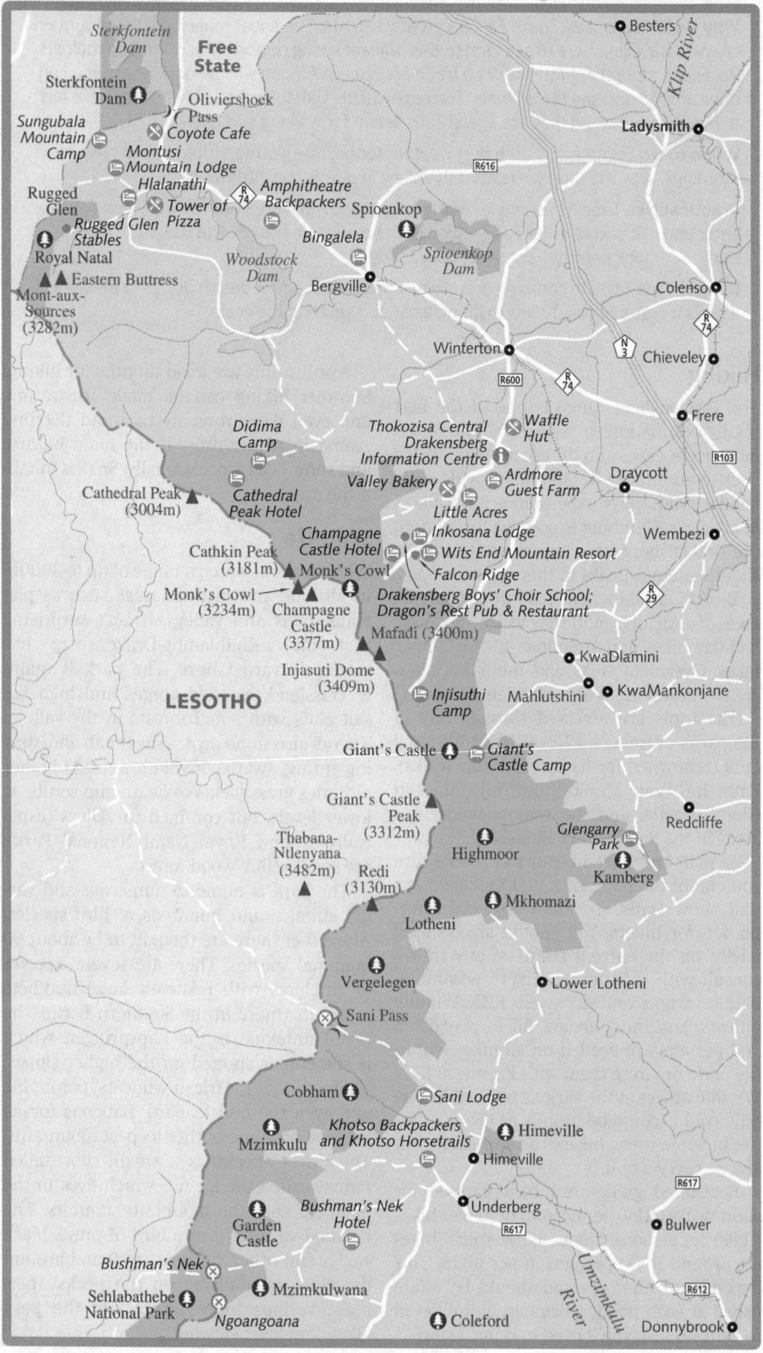
0 20 km
0 10 miles
Sterkfontein Dam
Free State
Sterkfontein Dam
Olivershoek Pass
Sungubala Mountain Camp
Coyote Cafe
Montusi Mountain Lodge
Hlalanathi
Amphitheatre Backpackers
Rugged Glen
Tower of Pizza
Rugged Glen Stables
Royal Natal
Eastern Buttress
Mont-aux-Sources (3282m)
Spioenkop
Bingalela
Spioenkop Dam
Woodstock Dam
Bergville
Besters
Klip River
Ladysmith
R616
Colenso
R74
N3
Chieveley
Winterton
R600
R74
Frere
Didima Camp
Thokozisa Central Drakensberg Information Centre
Waffle Hut
R103
Ardmore Guest Farm
Draycott
Valley Bakery
Cathedral Peak (3004m)
Cathedral Peak Hotel
Little Acres
Champagne Castle Hotel
Inkosana Lodge
Wembezi
Wits End Mountain Resort
Cathkin Peak (3181m)
Monk's Cowl
Falcon Ridge
Monk's Cowl (3234m)
Champagne Castle (3377m)
Drakensberg Boys' Choir School; Dragon's Rest Pub & Restaurant
R29
Mafadi (3400m)
KwaDlamini
Injasuti Dome (3409m)
LESOTHO
Injisuthi Camp
Mahlutshini
KwaMankonjane
Giant's Castle
Giant's Castle Camp
Giant's Castle Peak (3312m)
Redcliffe
Glengarry Park
Thabana-Ntlenyana (3482m)
Highmoor
Kamberg
Redi (3130m)
Mkhomazi
Lotheni
Vergelegen
Lower Lotheni
Sani Pass
Cobham
Sani Lodge
Khotso Backpackers and Khotso Horsetrails
Himeville
Mzimkulu
Himeville
R617
Bushman's Nek Hotel
Underberg
Garden Castle
R617
Bulwer
Bushman's Nek
Umzimkulu River
Sehlabathebe National Park
Mzimkulwana
R612
Ngoangoana
Coleford
Donnybrook

Accommodation

The perfect way to see uKhahlamba-Drakensberg Park is to stay at one of Ezemvelo KZN Wildlife's excellent accommodation options: campgrounds, upmarket safari tents, equipped cabins and chalets. Note that a minimum charge may apply. Other more upmarket options include private resorts, which dot the foothills along the range. If you're hiking, caves and camping are the only options, with a few huts on the mountains (these are mainly in the Southern Berg).

Information

Ezemvelo KZN Wildlife (p277) in Pietermaritzburg can provide information on the various parks and accommodation options. In general, you must book all Ezemvelo KZN Wildlife accommodation in advance, through Ezemvelo KZN.

Central Drakensberg Information Centre (036-488 1207; Info Centre Bldg; 8am-4.30pm) Based in the Thokozisa complex, 13km outside Winterton on Rte 600, this private enterprise stocks tree-loads of promotional literature.

Southern Berg Tourism (033-701 1471; www.drakensberg.org; Old Main Rd, Clocktower Centre, Underberg; 8am-4pm Mon-Fri, 9am-1pm Sat & Sun) Friendly, helpful office. Has the useful *Southern Drakensberg Pocket Guide*.

Getting There & Around

There is little public transport to and within the Drakensberg, although there is a lot of tourist traffic and the occasional minibus shared taxi ferrying resort staff. The main jumping-off points are on or near the N3. The Baz Bus (p278) drops off and picks up at a couple of hostels in the area. Through hostels in Durban you can arrange a shuttle to the hostels near Sani Pass and Himeville.

Sani Pass is the best-known Drakensberg route into Lesotho, but note that you can only go in a 4WD. Further south there are other passes over the escarpment, but most don't connect with anything larger than a walking track (if that) in Lesotho.

Many back roads in the Drakensberg area are unsealed, and after rain some are impassable – stick to the main routes.

Southern Berg

Best accessed from the pleasant towns of Himeville and Underberg, the Southern Berg boasts one of the region's highlights: the journey up to Lesotho over Sani Pass. It is also renowned as a serious hiking area. As well as some great walks (including the fabulous Giant's Cup Trail), the region also offers a smorgasbord of wilderness areas.

Southern Drakensberg Wilderness Areas

The areas of Highmoor, Kamberg, Lotheni and Cobham are south of Giant's Castle and are administered by Ezemvelo KZN Wildlife. These areas are more isolated, although they're accessible for those with time. The region is good for hiking (the rates for overnight-hiking permits are dependent on what you do.)

Sights

Highmoor Nature Reserve NATURE RESERVE
(033-845 1000; www.kznwildlife.com; adult/child R35/20, camping R120; 6am-6pm) Although more exposed and less dramatic than some of the Drakensberg region, the undulating hills of the reserve make for pleasant walks. It's also one of the few places where you're driving 'on top of' the foothills. There are two caves – Aasvoel Cave and Caracal Cave – both 2.5km from the main office, and Fultons Rock, which has rock paintings (a 4km easy walk), plus caves for overnight hikers. Access is via the towns of Nottingham Road or Rosetta (it's well signed).

There are no chalets here, but campsites are available.

Kamberg Nature Reserve NATURE RESERVE
(033-267 7251; www.kznwildlife.com; adult/child R35/20, chalets R600; 5am-7pm Oct-Mar, 6am-6pm Apr-Sep) Southeast of Giant's Castle, Kamberg Nature Reserve has a number of antelope species and a rock-art walk (the art is in a cave three hours' walk from reception). You can get here from Nottingham Road or Rosetta, off the N3 south of Mooi River.

Sleeping & Eating

Ezemvelo KZN Wildlife CHALET $
(033-267 7251; www.kznwildlife.com; 2-bed chalets from R460) For accommodation within the park, Ezemvelo KZN Wildlife has well-equipped chalets that are in beautiful natural settings and tastefully decorated with small kitchens and floor-to-ceiling glass overlooking lawns and mountains. Bring your own supplies. There are other sleeping options outside the park.

Glengarry Park LODGE $$

(☎033-267 7225; www.glengarry.co.za; camping R100, self-catering chalets per person R350) Perfect for families, Glengarry Park has pleasant, unpretentious chalets with a lovely green outlook, facing a small lake. Although in need of a renovation, the chalets are sturdy and homely and have fireplaces. It's near the Glengarry–Highmoor road, just off the Kamberg Rd, 11km from the park entrance at Kamberg.

There's a bowling green, a small golf course and great walks, and the owner is happy to lead the way on a mountain-bike trail.

Cleopatra Mountain Farmhouse RESORT $$$

(☎033-267 7243; www.cleomountain.com; Balgowan; per person from R1895) If God were to top off the beauty of the Drakensberg with a gourmet treat, Cleopatra Mountain Farmhouse would be it. Guests enjoy a nightly six-course menu of quality produce prepared innovatively and accompanied by rich, creamy sauces. Each of the 11 rooms is decked out in a theme and features quirky touches, such as a picket-fence bedhead and Boer memorabilia.

This luxury retreat is owned by renowned South African chef Richard Poynton.

Underberg, Himeville & Around

POP 4400

Clustered in the foothills of the southern Drakensberg, the small farming town of Underberg fills up in summer, when Durbanites head to the peaks for a breath of the fresh stuff. It has good infrastructure, and is the place to go for money and shopping and to organise activities in the region. Only a few kilometres from Underberg, Himeville is a pretty, if sedate, jumping-off point for the southern Drakensberg. Except for an excellent museum, a characteristic old pub and a cluster of reasonable B&Bs, there's not much else here. Minibus shared taxis run between Himeville and Underberg (R10, 10 minutes).

Sights & Activities

Himeville Museum MUSEUM

(☎033-702 1184; Main Rd; admission by donation; 9am-3pm Tue-Sat, to 12.30pm Sun) One of the best rural museums in the country. Housed in the last *laager* built in South Africa (c 1896), the museum now contains an incredible array of bric-a-brac, from the Union Jack flown at the siege of Ladysmith to a map of El Alamein signed by Montgomery. Mike, the man at the desk, is the man in the know.

Khotso Horsetrails HORSE RIDING

(☎033-701 1502; www.khotsotrails.co.za; horse rides 1hr/day R160/600) Offers rides and treks (plus tubing and fishing) in the area and into Lesotho – owner Steve is described by readers as 'South Africa's Crocodile Dundee'. It's about 7km northwest of Underberg on Drakensberg Gardens Rd.

Tours

Several companies offer day tours up Sani Pass (from around R600, excluding lunch), as well as tailored special-interest packages.

Drakensberg Adventures TOUR

(☎033-702 0330; www.drakensbergadventures.co.za; Sani Lodge, Sani Pass) Started by the owners of Sani Lodge. Practises responsible tourism through involvement with local communities.

Major Adventures TOUR

(☎033-701 1628; www.majoradventures.com; Old Main Rd, Underberg) Major Adventures' Sani Pass day tour focuses on the history of the pass, local plants and animals, and the Basotho people.

CAUGHT MIDWAY IN KWAZULU-NATAL – KOKSTAD & VRYHEID

Kokstad, 182km southwest of Pietermaritzburg, serves as a stopover point for many people who underestimate the trip from Mpumalanga Province to KwaZulu-Natal's South Coast, or who are taking public transport to/from Underberg. A convenient place to drop your head is **Mount Currie Inn** (☎039-727 1178; Kokstad; s/d from R380/600;), 2.5km from the town centre on the main road leading to the N2. It has pleasant rooms – budget, standard, executive and deluxe – a good bar and Cassandra's restaurant (mains R30 to R70, open for lunch and dinner Monday to Friday).

Another useful overnight stop is **Vryheid**, 62km south of Piet Retief (Mpumalanga Province), especially if you're making a late run from Swaziland or Kruger National Park. Here, you can't go past the ultrafriendly, clean and well-signed **Siesta B&B** (☎034-980 8023; 182 Emmet St; s/d R400/500).

Sani Pass Tours TOUR
(☎033-701 1064; www.sanipasstours.com; Shop 22, Trout Walk Centre, Underberg) Good mix of tours involving Sani Pass.

Thaba Tours TOUR
(☎033-701 2333; www.thabatours.co.za; Clocktower Centre, Underberg) Runs mountain-biking tours along with trips up Sani Pass and into Lesotho.

Sleeping

There are several good accommodation options in and near Underberg and Himeville.

Khotso Backpackers BACKPACKERS $
(☎033-701 1502; www.khotso.co.za; Treetower Farm, Underberg; dm/d from R130/380; wi-fi) A good budget accommodation, located in a rural environment. The owners lead horse rides into Lesotho and surrounds, and you can get your adrenalin fix by rafting and tubing. It's about 7km northwest of Underberg on Drakensberg Gardens Rd.

Tumble In B&B $
(☎033-701 1556; www.tumbleinunderberg.co.za; 60 Sani Rd, Underberg; r incl breakfast per person R320, self-catering per person R280) This unpretentious place offers spacious, homely, old-style rooms. The rooms overlook a delightful garden of pear and apple blossoms, with birds galore. It's 2.5km from Underberg on Himeville Rd. No credit cards. Great budget option.

★**Himeville Arms** HISTORIC HOTEL $$
(☎033-702 1305; www.himevillehotel.co.za; Main Rd, Himeville; dm/s/d R185/500/960) Quaint Middle England comes to Himeville at this old-fashioned inn. It offers a choice of accommodation and eating options, and an atmospheric old-fashioned bar. The dorms here are particularly great value: essentially old stone rooms with either twin beds or a double and single.

Yellowwood Cottage B&B B&B $$
(☎033-702 1065; 8 Mackenzie St, Himeville; s/d incl breakfast R500/720; P wi-fi) An enjoyable, homey experience: four cosy, frilly rooms in a pretty house with a lovely garden outlook, views of Hodgson's Peaks, and delightful owners.

Albizia House B&B B&B $$
(☎033-702 1837; www.africaalbizia.co.za/bnb; 62 Arbuckle St, Himeville; s/d incl breakfast R500/750; P wi-fi) Neat, clean and carpeted, with trimmed-lawn views. Family room available with cot and high chair. The friendly owners ensure an enjoyable stay.

Eating

★**Pucketty Farm** DELI $
(☎033-701 1035; www.puckettyfarm.co.za; Main Rd, Underberg; ⏲8am-5pm) Beatrix Potter meets Jamie Oliver: there's more to this extraordinarily cute place than meets the eye. There's a huge selection of great-value gourmet products, plus an art gallery and a small cafe. (Surprisingly, there's no Mrs Tiggywinkle here, but other named animals enjoy the attention). Perfect for self-caterers. The farm is 1.5km east of the Himeville turn-off.

The enterprise started 18 years ago, and it's been organic in every sense. The epicurean corner has a range of delights (try the sweet berry relish and soused prunes), and the carrot cake is legendary.

Lemon Tree Bistro INTERNATIONAL $$
(☎033-701 1589; www.lemontreeb.co.za; Clocktower Centre, Main Rd, Underberg; mains R60-130; ⏲8am-5pm, dinner Tue-Sat) This friendly place serves up zesty pastas, burgers, wraps and pancakes at lunchtime. In the evenings dine out on trout, kudu fillet and springbok carpaccio.

Grind Cafe CAFE $$
(Underberg Village Mall, Underberg; mains R60-80; ⏲8am-9pm Mon-Sat, to 5pm Sun; wi-fi) One of the most popular eateries in Underberg, this big barn of a place in the Village Mall has great coffee, good cakes and a wide selection of pasta, burgers and pizzas. There's also wi-fi.

Information

First National Bank (Old Main Rd, Underberg) Has an ATM.

Southern Berg Escape (☎033-701 1471; www.drakensberg.org; Clocktower Centre, Old Main Rd, Underberg; ⏲8am-4pm Mon-Fri, 9am-1pm Sat & Sun) Friendly and helpful office. Has the useful *Southern Drakensberg Pocket Guide*.

Standard Chartered Bank (Underberg Village Mall, Underberg) Has an ATM.

Getting There & Away

If you're arriving at Kokstad from the KZN south coast, or are heading to the Wild Coast/Port Elizabeth, one daily minibus shared taxi runs between central Kokstad and Underberg, departing Underberg (Spa car park) at 9am and Kokstad at 2pm (Baz Bus and bus arrivals are at Mount Currie Inn, 2.5km from the centre; you will have to ask the minibus to take you there, for an extra cost).

Minibus taxis run between Himeville and Underberg (R12, 10 minutes) and from Underberg to Pietermaritzburg (R70, 1½ hours).

NUD Express (☎079 696 7108; www.underbergexpress.co.za) NUD Express operates shuttle-bus services between Underberg (and Sani Lodge) and central Durban (R500), Durban's King Shaka International Airport (R600) and Pietermaritzburg (R300). You must book these services; note that they are not known for their reliability in sticking to times.

Underberg Metered Taxi Association (☎072 016 5809, 076 199 5823, 076 719 2451) Can take up to four passengers to Durban (R1500), Pietermaritzburg (R800), and Kokstad (R600).

Sani Pass

The drive up Sani Pass is a trip to the roof of South Africa: a spectacular ride around hairpin bends up into the clouds to the kingdom of Lesotho. At 2865m, this is the highest pass in the country and the vistas (on a clear day!) are magical, offering stunning views out across the Umkhomazana River to the north and looming cliffs, almost directly above, to the south. There are hikes in almost every direction, and inexpensive horse rides are available. Amazingly, this is also the only road link between Lesotho and KwaZulu-Natal.

At the top of the pass, just beyond the Lesotho border crossing, is Sani Top Chalet; various operators run 4WD trips up to the chalet.

Daily minibus shared taxis bring people from Mokhotlong (Lesotho) to South Africa for shopping; if there's a spare seat going back, this is the cheapest way to head over the pass to Lesotho, and you are taken to a town, not just the isolated lodge at the top of the pass. Ask at the tourist office. You need a passport to cross into Lesotho. The border is open from 6am to 6pm daily, but check beforehand; times alter. Make sure you allow sufficient time to arrive at either end. Also be aware that coming back into South Africa will require another visa.

Sani Lodge BACKPACKERS $

(☎033-702 0330; www.sanilodge.co.za; camping R75, dm/d without bathroom R125/370, 2-bed rondavels R460) At the bottom of the pass and on a tarred road, Sani Lodge tops the pops in the local-knowledge stakes, offering a range of fabulous tours and activities and insider tips about the region through its company, Drakensberg Adventures. Some of the rooms are basic (the *rondavels* are nicer), but it makes up for this with its communal, ski-lodge-style atmosphere.

A kitchen is available for general use, or pre-arranged dinners cost R85. It's about 10km from Himeville on the Sani Pass road.

Bushman's Nek

This is a South Africa–Lesotho border post (although with no vehicles!). From here there are hiking trails up into the escarpment, including to Lesotho's Sehlabathebe

GIANT'S CUP TRAIL

If you are planning to stretch your legs anywhere in South Africa, this is the place to do it. Without doubt, the Giant's Cup Trail (68km, five days and five nights), running from Sani Pass to Bushman's Nek, is one of the nation's great walks. Any reasonably fit person can walk it, so it's very popular. Early booking, through **Ezemvelo KZN Wildlife** (p281), is advisable in local holiday seasons. Weatherwise, the usual precautions for the Drakensberg apply – expect severe cold snaps at any time of the year. Fees are based on the composition of the hiking party.

The stages are: day one, 14km; day two, 9km; day three, 12km; day four, 13km; and day five, 12km (note that it's not a circuit walk). An unofficial sixth day can take you from Bushman's Nek up into Lesotho to Sehlabathebe National Park (passports required). Highlights include the Bathplug Cave, with San rock paintings, and the breathtaking mountain scenery on day four. You can make the trail more challenging by doing two days in one, and you can do side trips from the huts if the weather is fine. Maps are sold at Sani Lodge for R45.

Camping is not permitted on this trail, so accommodation is in limited shared **huts** (adult/child per trail R65/50), hence the need to book ahead. No firewood is available, so you'll need a stove and fuel. Sani Lodge is almost at the head of the trail; arrange for the lodge to pick you up from Himeville or Underberg.

National Park. You can trot through the border and into Lesotho on horseback with Khotso Horsetrails (p282).

Silverstreams Caravan Park CAMPGROUND $
(☎ 082 331 6670; www.silverstreams.co.za; camping R200-500, cottages R600-1200) At the foot of the Drakensberg in a beautiful natural setting, the Silverstreams Caravan Park has campsites and cottages next to the Lesotho border. Rates are at their cheapest during the week.

Bushman's Nek Hotel RESORT $$
(☎ 033-701 1460; www.bushmansnek.co.za; r from R1200;) Bushman's Nek Hotel is a full-on resort about 2km east of the Lesotho border post.

Central Berg

Crowned with some of the Drakensberg's most formidable peaks, including Giant's Castle peak (3312m), Monk's Cowl (3234m) and Champagne Castle (3377m), the Central Berg is a big hit with hikers and climbers. But with dramatic scenery aplenty, this beautiful region is just as popular with those who prefer to admire their mountains from a safe distance. Champagne Valley, leading into Monk's Cowl, is full of cafes and accommodation options for all budgets.

The sedate little town of **Winterton** is the gateway to the Central Drakensberg. The tiny, parochial **Winterton Museum** (☎ 036-488 1885; Kerk St; admission by donation; 8am-4pm Mon-Fri, 9am-noon Sat) offers an insight into San rock art (there are some excellent photos with notes) and the history of local peoples, and there are photos relating to the Spioenkop battle. Winterton's best place to stay is **Bridge Lodge** (☎ 036-488 1554; 18 Springfield Rd; s/d from R310/570), a friendly pub on the main street with great-value, renovated rooms.

Minibus shared taxis head to Cathedral Peak (30 minutes), Bergville (15 minutes) and Estcourt (45 minutes).

Cathedral Peak Nature Reserve

In the shadow of the ramparts of Cathedral Peak, **Cathedral Peak Nature Reserve** (☎ 036-488 8000; www.kznwildlife.com; adult/child R30/15; 6am-6pm) backs up against a colossal escarpment of peaks between Royal Natal National Park and Giant's Castle, west of Winterton. With the Bell (2930m), the Horns (3005m) and Cleft Peak (3281m) on the horizon, this is a beautifully photogenic park.

The **Didima San Art Centre** (☎ 036-488 1332; adult/child R55/25; 8am-4pm), at Didima Camp 1km into the park, offers an excellent multimedia insight into San rock art. The entrance price includes entry to the park; you must tell staff at the gate that you intend to visit the centre.

Didima Camp CAMPGROUND, CHALET $$
(☎ 033-845 1000; www.kznwildlife.com; camping R160, 2-person chalets R955;) One of Ezemvelo KZN Wildlife's swankiest offerings, this upmarket thatched lodge, constructed to resemble San rock shelters, boasts huge views, a restaurant, tennis courts and a range of two- and four-bed self-catering chalets (full-board options are also available, on request). Minimum charges apply.

Cathedral Peak Hotel HOTEL $$$
(☎ 036-488 1888; www.cathedralpeak.co.za; r per person R1200) Upmarket rooms at this private hotel 4km into the park have stupendous views and all the mod cons you would expect from a swish hotel. It is also, unfortunately, very ugly from the outside! But if it's comforts you're after, it's comforts you'll get.

Monk's Cowl & Champagne Valley

Within uKhahlamba-Drakensberg Park, **Monk's Cowl** (☎ 036-468 1103; www.kznwildlife.com; adult/child R35/20; 6am-6pm), another stunning slice of the Drakensberg range, offers superb hiking and rock climbing. Within the reserve are the three peaks Monk's Cowl, Champagne Castle and Cathkin Peak.

TAKING CARE IN THE MOUNTAINS

Ezemvelo KZN Wildlife warns that walkers should not go alone – even on day walks. Usually, guides are available for hire. For any walk, including short walks, you must always sign the rescue register. Be sure to obtain instructions and times regarding the hikes. For overnight treks, Ezemvelo KZN Wildlife recommends a minimum of four people. Note: attempting peaks in a day – as opposed to the more leisurely 'day walks' – is only for the very fit and experienced.

The area en route to the park is known as **Champagne Valley**. This is full of cafes, pleasant accommodation options, bakeries, and enough (non-hiking) tourist activities to keep you busy for days.

The **Thokozisa** complex, 13km out of Winterton on R600 and at the crossroads to Cathedral Peak, Monk's Cowl and Giant's Castle (via Estcourt), is a useful spot to orientate yourself. It has a clutch of craft shops.

Sights & Activities

Overnight hiking (adult/child R55/25) is possible but the shelter caves must be booked in advance through Ezemvelo KZN Wildlife (p277).

Drakensberg Boys' Choir School CHOIR
(☎036-468 1012; http://web.dbchoir.co.za) Just off Dragon Peaks Rd are South Africa's singing ambassadors the Drakensberg Boys' Choir School. There are public performances at 3.30pm on Wednesday during school terms.

Falcon Ridge WILDLIFE RESERVE
(☎082 774 6398; adult/child R60/25; ⏲displays 10.30am Tue-Sun) Seven kilometres from the Drakensberg Sun turn-off is Falcon Ridge, with awesome raptor-flying demonstrations and talks.

Ushaka Horse Trails HORSE RIDING
(☎072 664 2993; www.monkscowl.com; 4 Bell Park Dam Rd; 2hr/day R180/550) One-hour to full-day horse trails are available through Ushaka Horse Trails. Ring for directions.

Drakensberg Canopy Tour ADVENTURE SPORTS
(☎036-468 1981; www.drakensbergcanopytour.co.za; per person R495; ⏲7.30am-2.30pm) Drakensberg Canopy Tour boasts superlatives – 12 slides, of which seven are over 100m; the highest point is 65m and the longest is 179m. You 'fly' above a beautiful canopy of an ancient indigenous forest, with a stream and waterfalls. It's an extreme sport – don't attempt it if you have vertigo. Book ahead.

Sleeping

Inkosana Lodge BACKPACKERS $
(☎036-468 1202; www.inkosana.co.za; camping R125, dm/d without bathroom R175/550; P ≋) Travellers rave about this lodge. Its indigenous garden, ecofriendly swimming pool, clean rooms and lovely *rondavels* make it one of the best spots around. Although promoted as a 'backpacker lodge', it's more than this; its range of rooms would suit any discerning traveller. Centrally located for activities in and around the area, it's on Rte 600, en route to Champagne Castle.

Excellent cuisine and heaps of activities and walks are on offer. Former mountaineer and welcoming owner Ed can give expert advice on hikes.

★ **Wits End Mountain Resort** CHALET $$
(☎036-468 1133; www.witsend.co.za; R600; chalets per person R380) Although the resort promotes itself as a wedding and function centre, the excellent chalets here are available on a walk-in basis. Four-/six-/eight-sleeper chalets have a braai area, a large kitchen and wonderful views. Cheaper rates on weekdays.

Ardmore Guest Farm LODGE $$
(☎036-468 1314; www.ardmore.co.za; rondavels per person with half board R545-695) A refreshing change from the area's resorts, this pleasant place, situated on a working farm, has a range of comfortable options. There are cottages and thatched *rondavels* (some with log fires), and meals are served in the original farmhouse. Also here are the Steve Bull Gallery, housing ceramics and paintings, and African Loom, featuring handwoven textiles spun on-site by local Zulu women.

Little Acres B&B $$
(☎082 305 3387; www.littleacres.co.za; Rte 600; r incl breakfast R640, self-catering R780) The new owners at this little gem were installing flat-screen TVs as part of a room upgrade when we visited. The two separate bungalows have their own entrance (and kitchenettes), while others are within the main house. The facilities are great, the views of the Drakensberg lovely and the hosts friendly. But the highlight is undoubtedly the two black labradors.

Champagne Castle Hotel RESORT $$$
(☎036-468 1063; www.champagnecastle.co.za; s/d with full board from R1085/2170) The ever-reliable and predictably 'nice' Champagne Castle is one of the area's best-known resorts, conveniently in the mountains at the end of Rte 600 to Monk's Cowl.

Eating

Valley Bakery BAKERY, CAFE $
(☎036-468 1257; R600; mains R35-60; ⏲8am-5pm Mon-Fri, to 2pm Sat) Baguettes, croissants and a range of sticky treats are baked on the premises (the owners even grow and grind their wheat). A quaint wrought-iron veran-

dah is the place for a wonderful selection of breakfasts, including eggs benedict or muesli with fresh fruit. Wraps, sandwiches and homemade pies feature later in the day.

Waffle Hut CAFE $
(mains R40-70; 8am-4.30pm) After you've stuffed yourself with savoury and sweet waffles, get your fill of handmade rugs (some locally made, others imported) at this cafe located at KwaZulu Weavers. It's on Rte 600 south of Winterton.

Dragon's Rest Pub & Restaurant PUB $$
(036-468 1218; mains R70-100; 10.30am-2.30pm & 6-8.30pm) Sit outside at this delightful place and drink in the damside and mountain views while enjoying some fine Berg cooking and a cold drink. Inside is a log fire. Sublime. It's near the auditorium of the boys' choir.

Information

The **park office** (036-468 1103; camping R190-210) is 3km beyond Champagne Castle Hotel, which is at the end of Rte 600 running southwest from Winterton. The Central Drakensberg Information Centre (p281) is also helpful.

Injisuthi

Injisuthi, on the northern side of Giant's Castle, is another 'wow' spot of the Drakensberg. It's a secluded and extraordinarily beautiful place with a terrific view of the Monk's Cowl peak. This reserve, originally a private farm (Farm Solitude) was purchased by KZN Wildlife in the late 1970s. Injisuthi features the Drakensberg's highest points, Mafadi (3400m) and Injisuthi (3300m). Please note: these peaks cannot be done in a day. The many day walks include Marble Baths (four to five hours), where you can swim.

Injisuthi is the departure point for the guided hike to the extraordinary **Battle Cave**, a massive rock overhang featuring remarkable San paintings. The extraordinary scenes – depicting figures and animals – were believed to represent a battle, but this has been disproven, with experts now proposing that they represent hallucinatory dreams or a spiritual trance. This is a six-hour round-trip hike, both exposed and shady (at times it passes under leafy canopies); the guides will point out medicinal plants and other interesting snippets. Walks must be reserved in advance (036-431 9000; around R80 per person, minimum three people; rates can depend on numbers).

Injisuthi Camp CAMPGROUND, CHALET $
(033-845 1000; camping R80; 2-person safari camps R315, 4-person chalets R870) There are self-contained cabins and campsites here. The area has caves for overnight hikers (however, check on their state before setting out).

Giant's Castle

Established in 1904, mainly to protect the eland, **Giant's Castle** (033-845 1000, 036-353 3718; www.kznwildlife.com; adult/child R30/15; 5am-10pm Oct-Mar, 6am-10pm Apr-Sep, reception 8am-4.30pm) is a rugged, remote and popular destination, with varying dramatic landscapes. The Giant's Castle ridge itself is one of the most prominent features of the Berg. (If coming from the south on the N3, use the off-ramp exit 175, not marked on all maps.)

As is the case elsewhere, there are many excellent day walks and longer trails here. The office at Giant's Castle Camp (p288) gives out a basic map of the trails (distances not stated). Here, too, is a shop selling basic provisions, and fuel is available.

Sights

Lammergeier Hide VIEWPOINT
(036-353 3718; giants@kznwildlife.com; per person R230, minimum R690) The rare lammergeier, also known as the bearded vulture (*Gypaetus barbatus*), which is found only in the Drakensberg, nests in the reserve. Reserve staff sometimes give guests bones to put out to encourage the birds to feed here. The Lammergeyer Hide is the best place to see these raptors. The hide is extremely popular, so it's necessary to book in advance.

Main Cave HISTORIC SITE
(adult/child R35/20; 9am-3pm) The Giant's Castle area is rich in San rock art. It's thought that the last San lived here at the beginning of the 20th century. To see some of these paintings, you can visit Main Cave, 2.3km south of Giant's Camp. A guide waits at the cave's entrance where, every hour, he conducts an explanatory tour.

The walk from Giant's Camp to the cave takes 45 minutes; there's a shorter return of 1.5km.

Sleeping

There are several excellent accommodation options inside the reserve, as well as caves and trail huts for hikers.

Giant's Castle Camp CHALET $$
(☎033-845 1000, 036-353 3718; www.kznwildlife.com; trail huts per person R55, 2-person chalets from R765) The main camp here is an impressive and remote set-up 8km from the main gate. Two-, four- and six-bed chalets have fireplace, kitchenette, floor-to-ceiling windows, TV and thatched verandah. Eight-bed mountain huts are also available. The restaurant has a lovely deck with superb mountain views (but when the summer mists descend visibility gets down to a few metres).

Getting There & Away

If coming from the north or south along the N3, take Rte 29 to Giant's Castle (it links with Estcourt, to the east). From Winterton or Champagne Valley you can get here on Rte 10 and then south via Draycott (from Draycott there's 25km of good gravel road meandering through pine plantation, which joins the tar at White Mountain Lodge; from here it's 23km on tarred roads to Giant's Castle, hooking up with Rte 29).

Infrequent minibus shared taxis do the run from Estcourt to villages near the main entrance (KwaDlamini, Mahlutshini and KwaMankonjane), but these are still several kilometres from Giant's Camp.

Northern Berg

An ideal stopover on the journey between Durban and Jo'burg, the Northern Berg is crowned with the beautiful Royal Natal National Park, with some excellent day walks and wonderfully empty spaces.

Bergville

The nearest town, Bergville, is small and rough around the edges but is nevertheless a useful stocking-up and jumping-off point for the Northern Drakensberg. The minibus-taxi park is behind the tourist office.

BUSES

None of the long-distance bus lines run very close to Bergville. You'll have to get to Ladysmith and take a minibus shared taxi from there (45 minutes). A daily Greyhound bus stops at Estcourt and Ladysmith. Taxis run into the Royal Natal National Park area for about R20, but few run all the way to the park entrance.

Bingalela CHALET $
(☎082 390 3133, 036-448 1336; bingelela@mweb.co.za; s/d incl breakfast R370/560;) If you've timed your arrival a bit late, Bingalela is one of the few places worth laying your head, 3km from Bergville on R74. Attractive double and family-size *rondavels* are set in dusty, slightly car-park-like surrounds, under lovely eucalypts. Note that it holds its own beerfest in October, so the action might not be for everyone.

There's a lively restaurant and bar that attracts the locals.

Information

Okhahlamba Drakensberg Tourism (☎036-448 1296; www.drakensberg.org.za; Bergville; ⏲7.30am-5.30pm Mon-Fri, 8.30am-12.30pm Sat) The privately owned Okhahlamba Drakensberg Tourism has plenty of brochures, but the help stops there.

Royal Natal National Park

Fanning out from some of the range's loftiest summits, the 80-sq-km **Royal Natal National Park** (☎036-438 6310; www.kznwildlife.com; adult/child R35/20; ⏲5am-7pm summer, 6am-6pm winter) has a presence that far outstrips its relatively meagre size: many of the surrounding peaks rise as high into the air as the park stretches across. With some of the Drakensberg's most dramatic and accessible scenery, the park is crowned by the sublime Amphitheatre, an 8km wall of cliff and canyon that's spectacular from below and even more so from up on high. Here, the Tugela Falls drop 850m in five stages (the top one often freezes in winter). Looming up behind is Mont-aux-Sources (3282m), so called because the Tugela, Elands and Western Khubedu Rivers rise here; the latter eventually becomes the Senqu (Orange) River and flows all the way to the Atlantic. The park is renowned for its excellent day walks and hiking opportunities.

Other notable peaks in the area are the Devil's Tooth, the Eastern Buttress and the Sentinel. Rugged Glen Nature Reserve adjoins the park on the northeastern side.

The park's **visitors centre** (☎036-438 6310; ⏲8am-4.30pm) is 3km in from the main gate. It doubles as a shop selling basic provisions. Day walks are explained in a simple map provided by the centre.

PROTECTING THE SAN PAINTINGS

There are thousands of San paintings in caves and rockscapes around KwaZulu-Natal. Sadly, many of these have suffered through the actions of ignorant visitors, and many have been defaced with graffiti, or completely destroyed. Travellers should be aware of taking appropriate measures to ensure the ongoing preservation of these cultural treasures. For example, never splash paintings with water.

KwaZulu-Natal currently has an agreement with Amafa (the provincial cultural and heritage conservation body) to have preservation practices in its management plans. This includes ensuring that guides accompany visitors to sites, and educating visitors not to touch or harm the sites.

⊙ Sights & Activities

San Rock Art HISTORIC SITE
(guided walk adult/child R30/20; ⊙9am-4pm) Of several San rock-art sites within the park, this is the only one open to tourists. You can organise a guided walk with community guides. The return trip takes about an hour, including time to rest and chat. Look for the 'San Rock Art' sign near the first bridge after entry.

Rugged Glen Stables HORSE RIDING
(☑036-438 6422; 1/2hr rides R170/220) Just outside the Royal Natal National Park gates, Rugged Glen Stables organises a wide range of horse-riding activities, including two-day trails.

🛏 Sleeping & Eating

INSIDE THE PARK

Rustic camping is available at Mahai (camping R90), which is a beautiful campground approximately 1km from the visitors centre, and at Rugged Glen Nature Reserve (camping R90), a more basic experience.

Thendele CHALET $$
(☑033-845 1000; www.kznwildlife.com; chalet s/d from R680/1360) The park's fabulous main camp has two- and four-bed chalets as well as cottages and a lodge for larger groups. The chalets are set around lawns and driveways; all have in-your-face views of the peaks opposite. Those at the top are slightly more expensive because of their wondrous views, but all are good. It's a great walking base.

OUTSIDE THE PARK

Amphitheatre Backpackers BACKPACKERS $
(☑082 855 9767; www.amphibackpackers.co.za; camping from R85, dm R140, d R400-600; 🛜🏊) This place gets mixed reviews from travel-lers – some report feeling pressured to do the backpackers' organised trips (when there are other options around), while others enjoy the rolled-out convenience. The level of service also seems to be erratic. Facing out over the Amphitheatre, the backpackers has a selection of sleeping options from dorms to comfortable four-person 'luxury' rooms.

There's a busy bar, a pool and activities galore. Found 21km north of Bergville on Rte 74.

★Hlalanathi RESORT $$
(☑036-438 6308; www.hlalanathi.co.za; camping R160, 2-/4-bed chalets R800/1500; 🏊) With a location lifted straight from an African chocolate-box lid and next to the local golf course, this pretty, unpretentious resort offers camping and excellent accommodation in thatched chalets on a finger of land overlooking the Tugela River. Go for a site facing the river and mountains. Prices are substantially cheaper outside high seasons.

Sungubala Mountain Camp BUNGALOW, CHALET $$
(☑036-438 6000; www.sungubala.com; tents without bathroom per person R300, 6-bed bungalows R1300) Six safari tents (with thatched gazebos and beds) or three A-frame units with shared bathrooms are available here, along with *rondavels*, chalets and a mountain bungalow. There's budget accommodation, too, if you have your own bedding; rates for this are even cheaper if you walk in on your own.

Montusi Mountain Lodge LODGE $$$
(☑036-438 6243; www.montusi.co.za; s/d with half board R1800/3200; 🛜🏊) With oodles of bushlodge exclusivity, this opulent place blends a thatch-and-fireplace homeliness with plenty of luxury comforts in very swish chalets. There's guided hiking, including a daily morning walk on the property, and horse riding can be arranged. The turn-off is just after the Tower of Pizza; follow the signs.

Tower of Pizza ITALIAN $

(☎036-438 6480; www.towerofpizza.co.za; pizzas R65; ⊙noon-8.30pm Tue-Thu, to 9pm Fri & Sat, 10am-9pm Sun) Yep, there really is a tower, where very good wood-fire pizza is prepared. Grab a table on the outside decking and enjoy the clean air and mountain views at this excellent place near the Drakensberg mountains. Be warned: it doesn't accept cash – credit cards only! It also offers quaint *rondavels* and cottages (doubles per person, including breakfast, are R430).

Coyote Cafe CAFE $$

(mains R50-100; ⊙7am-8.30pm) Catering to visiting interstaters, this modern, sleek place serves up some almost-gourmet snacks and excellent cakes. Try the jambalya or seafood pasta. It's on Rte 74 at the entrance to Little Switzerland; on a clear day the views are lovely.

Getting There & Away

The road into Royal Natal runs off R74, about 30km northwest of Bergville and about 5km from Oliviershoek Pass.

BATTLEFIELDS

Big wildlife, big mountains and big waves may top the agenda for many visitors to the province, but the history of KwaZulu-Natal is intrinsically linked to its battlefields, the stage on which many of the country's bloodiest chapters were played out. The province's northwestern region is where fewer than 600 Voortrekkers avenged the murder of their leader, Piet Retief, by defeating a force of 12,000 Zulu at Blood River, and where the British Empire was crushed by a Zulu army at Isandlwana. Here they subsequently staged the heroic defence of Rorke's Drift, where the Boers and the Brits slogged it out at Ladysmith and Spioenkop. These days, the region offers some luxurious accommodation options, and for keen punters it can be most rewarding.

Many towns look as though they've been in more recent wars – and, in a way, they have. With the construction (in the 1980s and '90s) of the N3, which bypassed many towns, and the subsequent closure of their factories, many local people left for the cities. See www.battlefields.kzn.org.za or pick up KZN Tourism's *Battlefields Route* brochure from KZN Tourism.

Spioenkop Nature Reserve

The 60-sq-km **Spioenkop Nature Reserve** (☎036-488 1578; www.kznwildlife.com; admission R25; ⊙5am-7pm Oct-Mar, 6am-6pm Apr-Sep) is based on the Spioenkop Dam, on the Tugela River. The reserve is handy for most of the area's battlefield sites and not too far from the Drakensberg for day trips into the range. Animals include zebras, white rhinos, giraffes, various antelope species and over 270 bird species.

There are two driving tracks, both quite short – the dam is huge but you only access a small part of the shoreline as a visitor. The roads inside the reserve are just OK for 2WDs – drive slowly, and keep your eyes open for eroded parts of the track. You can even head out among the wildlife at a vulture hide, or on horse-riding trips and guided walks. There's a lovely stroll through aloe plants and woodlands.

The Spioenkop Nature Reserve is northeast of Bergville, but the entrance is on the eastern side, 13km from Winterton off Rte 600. If you're coming from the south on the N3, take exit 194 for Rte 74 towards Winterton. The Spioenkop battlefield is accessed from Rte 616 (not Rte 600; follow the signs). You will need a car to access both places.

iPika CAMPGROUND $

(www.kznwildlife.com; camping/bush camp per person R75/220) iPika, inside the reserve in a valley, offers campsites and one four-bed tented bush camp in very pretty surrounds, overlooking a reservoir. It's peaceful and offers plentiful birdlife, plus the odd specimen of hoofed wildlife. Book accommodation directly through the reserve.

Three Trees at Spioenkop LODGE $$$

(☎036-448 1171; http://threetreehill.co.za; s/d with full board R2790/4230) This upmarket eco-friendly house with plush contemporary-meets-colonial creature comforts is a treat for those who want to explore the Spioenkop area. Beautiful setting and views, a delightful open-plan living area and an eco focus make for a fabulous stay. Horse riding and battlefield tours are made to order. It's conveniently located near Spioenkop, between Ladysmith and Bergville off Rte 616.

Ladysmith

POP 65,000

Ladysmith is a large, bustling town. Apart from its historical aspect – several very good

Battlefields

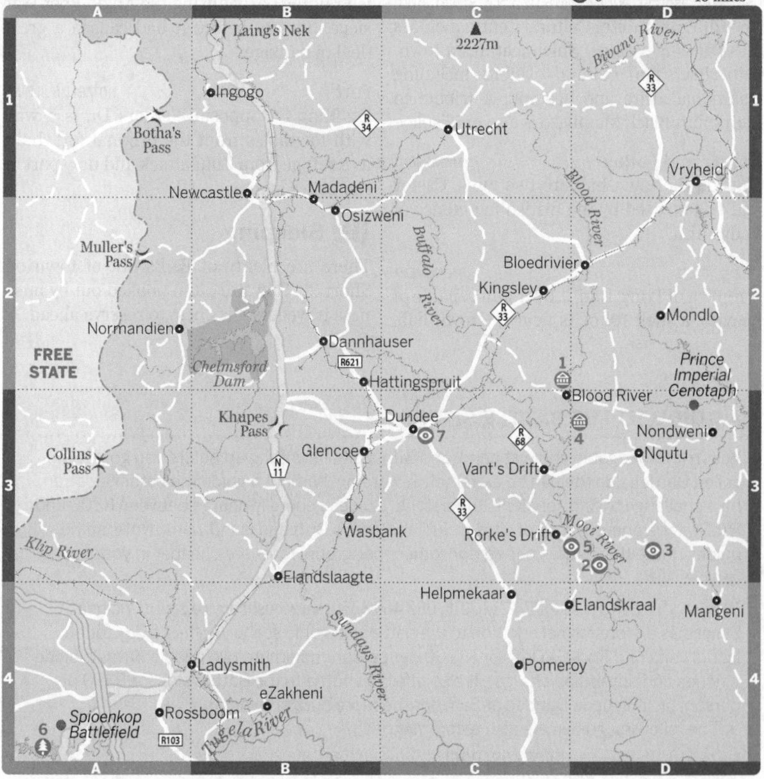

museums and buildings were here during the Anglo-Boer War siege – it's a reasonable base for the area's battlefield tours.

Ladysmith was named after the wife of Cape governor Sir Harry Smith. The town achieved fame during the 1899–1902 Anglo-Boer War, when it was besieged by Boer forces for 118 days. Musical group Ladysmith Black Mambazo has its roots here, but the town's pretty colonial vestiges are looking a little tired these days.

Sights & Activities

Siege Museum MUSEUM

(Murchison St; adult/child R11/5; 9am-4pm Mon-Fri, to 1pm Sat) The excellent museum, next to the town hall in the old Market House (built 1884), was used to store rations during the Anglo-Boer War siege. It has displays about the war, stocks information about the town and surrounds, and can provide a list of battlefield tour guides.

Battlefields

Sights

	Blood River Monument	(see 1)
1	Blood River Museum	C2
	Evangelical Lutheran Church Art & Craft Centre	(see 5)
2	Fugitive's Drift	D3
3	Isandlwana	D3
	Isandlwana Visitors Centre	(see 3)
4	Ncome Museum	D3
5	Rorke's Drift	D3
	Rorke's Drift Orientation Centre	(see 5)
6	Spioenkop Nature Reserve	A4
7	Talana Heritage Park & Battlefield	C3

Sleeping

	Isandalwana Lodge	(see 3)
	Rorke's Drift Hotel	(see 5)

Emnambithi Cultural Centre MUSEUM
(316 Murchison St; adult/child R11/5.50; ⏲9am-4pm Mon-Fri) Emnambithi Cultural Centre includes a **Cultural Museum**, which features a township shack and cultural exhibits including traditional attire and beading. A tribute to Ladysmith Black Mambazo is also on display.

Castor and Pollux MONUMENT
Outside the town hall are two guns, Castor and Pollux, used by the British in defence of Ladysmith.

Long Tom MONUMENT
A replica of Long Tom, a Boer gun capable of heaving a shell 10km, is near the town hall. Long Tom was put out of action by a British raiding party during the Anglo-Boer War siege, but not before it had caused a great deal of damage.

Fort NOTABLE BUILDING
On King St, opposite Settlers Dr, is a wall with loopholes from the original fort, built as a refuge from Zulu attack and now part of the police station.

Sleeping

There are plenty of B&Bs out of town off Short St. They are often booked out by business travellers – it's best to reserve ahead.

A GUIDE TO THE BATTLE SITES

With a knowledgable guide at hand, and with a bit of swotting up before you go, the so-called Battlefields Rte can be extremely rewarding. Without a guide the battlefields can be a challenge to find, let alone understand. Guides generally charge between R800 and R1500 for a one-day tour of sites including Rorke's Drift and Isandlwana. Note: some guides quote these rates per person, others per group; rates are cheaper in your own vehicle.

BushBaby Safaris (☎034-212 3216, 082 466 8350; www.bushbaby.co.za; 110 Victoria St, Dundee) is a more formal addition to the battlefield guide scene. It offers a day tour to Isandlwana and Rorke's Drift for R1800 per person (minimum two people; rates exclude lunches and admission charge). It also offers a shuttle to the Battlefields for R390 per person, picking up in Dundee at 8am, for the more budget minded.

The following guides are also recommended:

Bethuel Manyathi (☎083 531 0061; Nquthu)

Elisabeth Durham (☎072 779 5949; cheznous@dundeekzn.co.za; Dundee)

Ken Gillings (☎083 654 5880; ken.gillings@mweb.co.za; Durban)

Thulani Khuzwayo (☎072 872 9782; thulani.khuzwayo@gmail.com; Rorke's Drift)

Liz Spiret (☎072 262 9669; lizs@telkomsa.net; Ladysmith)

Paul Garner (☎082 472 3912; garner@xsinet.co.za; Dundee)

Lists of further battlefield guides are available from Talana Heritage Park & Battlefield, plus tourism offices in Dundee and Ladysmith. Be sure to pick up a Battlefields brochure or to consult www.battlefields.kzn.org.au.

Main Battles

Battle of Blood River Voortrekker–Zulu conflict (1838).

Battle of Isandlwana, Battle of Rorke's Drift Anglo-Zulu War (1879).

Battles of Laing's Nek, Schuinshoogte and Majuba First Anglo-Boer War (Transvaal War of Independence; 1880–81).

Battle of Talana, Battle of Elandlaagte Second Anglo-Boer War (1899–1902), which led to the Siege of Ladysmith.

Battle of Spioenkop Occurred on 23 and 24 January 1900, when the British fought to relieve the besieged town of Ladysmith from the surrounding Boer forces.

Battle of Colenso One of the largest battles (15 December 1899) in the southern hemisphere, between Boers and Brits.

THE BATTLE OF SPIOENKOP

On 23 January 1900 the British, led by General Buller, made a second attempt to relieve Ladysmith, which had been under siege by the Boers since late October 1899. At Trichardt's Drift, 500 Boers prevented 15,000 of General Buller's men from crossing the Tugela River, and he decided that he needed to take Spioenkop – the flat-topped hill would make a good gun emplacement from which to clear the Boers from their trenches.

During the night, 1700 British troops climbed the hill and chased off the few Boers guarding it. They dug a trench and waited for morning. Meanwhile the Boer commander, Louis Botha, heard of the raid. He ordered his field guns to be pointed towards Spioenkop, and he positioned some of his men on nearby hills. A further 400 soldiers began to climb Spioenkop as the misty dawn broke.

The British might have beaten off the 400, but the mist finally lifted, and was immediately replaced by a hail of bullets and shells. The British retreated to their trench and, by mid-afternoon, continuous shellfire caused many to surrender. By now, reinforcements were on hand and the Boers could not overrun the trench. A bloody stalemate was developing.

After sunset, the British evacuated the hill; so did the Boers. Both retreats were accomplished so smoothly that neither side was aware that the other had left. That night Spioenkop was held by the dead.

It was not until the next morning that the Boers again climbed Spioenkop and found that it was theirs. The Boers had killed or wounded 1340 British – Mahatma Gandhi's stretcher-bearer unit performed with distinction at this battle. Buller relieved Ladysmith a month later on 28 February.

★ **Budleigh Guesthouse** B&B $$
(☎036-635 7700; 12 Berea Rd; s/d incl breakfast R550/750; 📶❄) Just like something out of a BBC TV production with its verandahs, trimmed lawns and stunning garden, this mansion has a range of neat, sophisticated rooms with wooden bedsteads and faux antiques. It's in the heart of Ladysmith.

Buller's Rest Lodge B&B $$
(☎036-637 6154; www.bullersrestlodge.co.za; 59 Cove Cres; s/d incl breakfast from R575/790; 📶❄) It's worth digging in at this smart thatched abode. There's the snug 'Boer War' pub, scrumptious home cooking (R160 for three courses), and views from the attractive sundeck–bar area. Turn right at Francis Rd off Harrismith (Poort) Rd, and follow the signs.

Eating

Office Cafe ITALIAN $
(San Marco Centre, cnr Harrismith & Francis Rds; mains R50-75; ⌚8am-4pm Mon-Fri, to 2pm Sat) This informal place dabbles in a few homemade dishes – the pizza is probably the best, although foccacias and burgers are good at lunchtime.

Guinea Fowl INTERNATIONAL $$
(☎036-637 8163; San Marco Centre, cnr Harrismith & Francis Rds; mains R90-140; ⌚lunch & dinner Mon-Sat) One of the only reasonable restaurants in Ladysmith, this eatery does curries along with steak, chicken and seafood dishes at a shopping centre. Burgers available too.

Information

ABSA (cnr Queen & Murchison Sts) Has two branches on the same crossroads, one with an ATM.

Emnambithi Cultural Centre (316 Murchison St; ⌚9am-4pm Mon-Fri) Ask here about guided tours of the Battlefields or to nearby townships.

Police Station (☎036-638 3309; King St) By the NG Church.

Getting There & Away

BUS

Bus tickets can be purchased from Shoprite/Checkers in the Oval Shopping Centre. Buses depart from the Guinea Fowl petrol station (not to be confused with the restaurant) on Murchison Rd, and they connect Ladysmith with Durban (R330, four hours), Pretoria (R360, seven hours) and Cape Town (R600, 19 hours).

SHARED TAXI

The main minibus taxi rank is east of the town centre near the corner of Queen and Lyell Sts. Taxis bound for Jo'burg are nearby on Alexandra St. Destinations include Pietermaritzburg (1½ hours), Durban (2½ hours) and Jo'burg (five hours).

Dundee

POP 35,000

If you can look past the gritty main street (Victoria St), Dundee is a leafy and quite pretty spot. The reason to come here is to explore the Battlefields and regional history sites.

◉ Sights

**Talana Heritage Park
& Battlefield** HISTORIC SITE
(☑034-212 2654; www.talana.co.za; adult/child R25/2; ☺8am-4.30pm Mon-Fri, 9am-4.30pm Sat & Sun) Talana means 'the shelf where precious items are stored' – strangely appropriate for this excellent battlefield site turned heritage park. There are memorials, cairns and 27 historic buildings relating to the 1899 Anglo-Boer Battle of Talana (the first Anglo-Boer battle was fought on the site). Spread around these buildings are comprehensive displays on the Anglo-Zulu and Anglo-Boer Wars, including a photograph of Mahatma Gandhi during his stretcher-bearing days; local history; exquisite Zulu beading; and a glassworks display. Curator Pam McFadden is Talana's knowledge guru.

Located on the Vryheid road, 1.5km out of town.

⌕ Sleeping & Eating

Some accommodations charge extra during winter months to cover the cost of heating. Eating choices are ridiculously limited in Dundee, unless you run the gauntlet of fast-food outlets.

**Battlefields Backpackers
International** BACKPACKERS $
(☑034-212 4040; www.bbibackpackers.co.za; 90 Victoria St; dm/s/d R170/190/390; @) Run by registered Battlefields guide Evan Jones and his wife, this is the town's simple budget option. There's a fire pit and braai, along with plenty of information on the Battlefields.

NQUTU & BEYOND

East of Dundee, 52km away via Rte 33 and Rte 66, is the regional centre of Nqutu, an important trading hub for the surrounding Zulu community. A further 30km north of Nqutu, near Nondweni, is the Prince Imperial cenotaph. Prince Imperial Louis Napoleon, the last of the Bonaparte dynasty, was killed here on 1 June 1879.

Chez Nous B&B $$
(☑034-212 1014; www.cheznousbb.com; 39 Tatham St; s/d incl breakfast from R530/840, self-catering units R2000; ❊@☎) This centrally located, comfortable place, run by Elisabeth Durham, efficient French *madame* and tour guide (with a special interest in Prince Imperial Louis Napoleon, who died near Dundee in 1879), comes recommended. Half-board options are also available. Chez Nous also offers half- and full-day tours of the Battlefields with a guide, using your car.

Sneezewood B&B $$
(☑034-212 1260; www.sneezewood.co.za; s/d incl breakfast R695/1100; ❊☎) Located 5km from the tourist-information centre on Wasbank Rd (south of town), this delightful spot, on a working farm, oozes city-meets-country style: chic designer fabrics and lots of trimmings, plus a delightful lounge and outdoor area. The hospitable, knowledgable owners ensure a relaxing stay.

Royal Country Inn HOTEL $$
(☑034-212 2147; www.royalcountryinn.com; 61 Victoria St; backpacker s/d R340/480, s/d incl breakfast R620/870) This old dame exudes a slightly faded, late-19th-century charm, and its English-style flavour is perfect for a spot of post–Rorke's Drift R&R. Rooms are decent (though backpackers' ones are less than appealing) and the hotel's restaurant serves up a good feed (dinner R190).

**Penny Farthing
Country House** GUESTHOUSE $$
(☑034-642 1925; www.pennyf.co.za; s/d incl breakfast R700/1200; ❊❊) Located 30km south of Dundee on Rte 33 towards Greytown, this is well placed for visits to Rorke's Drift and Isandlwana. Owner Foy Vermaak is a renowned tour guide. Half-board option and tours to the Battlefields available.

ⓘ Information

Tourism Dundee (☑034-212 2121; www.tourdundee.co.za; Victoria St; ☺9am-4.30pm Mon-Fri) Tourism Dundee, by the gardens in the centre, can put you in touch with Battlefields guides and accommodation options.

ⓘ Getting There & Away

There is very little transport to Dundee; this is a location where your own vehicle is ideal. Minibus shared taxis head to and from Ladysmith to the southwest and Vryheid to the northeast.

Isandlwana & Rorke's Drift

If you've seen *Zulu* (1964), the film that made Michael Caine a star, you will doubtless have heard of Rorke's Drift, a victory of the misty-eyed variety, where on 22 and 23 January 1879, around 150 British soldiers successfully defended a small mission station from around 4000 Zulu warriors. Queen Victoria lavished 11 Victoria Crosses on the survivors and the battle was assured its dramatic place in British military history.

However, for the full picture you must travel 15km across the plain to Isandlwana, the precursor to Rorke's Drift. It's here that, only hours earlier, the Zulus dealt the Empire one of its great Battlefields disasters by annihilating the main body of the British force in devastating style. Tellingly, *Zulu Dawn* (1979), the film made about Isandlwana, never became the cult classic *Zulu* is now. Victories sell better than defeats.

Sights & Activities

Ideally, the battlefields of Isandlwana and Rorke's Drift should be visited together.

Isandlwana Visitors Centre HISTORIC SITE

(adult/child R30/15; 8am-4pm Mon-Fri, 9am-4pm Sat & Sun) The Isandlwana Visitors Centre has a small museum; the entrance fee includes the battlefield. The battlefield itself is extremely evocative. White cairns and memorials mark the spots where British soldiers fell.

Rorke's Drift Orientation Centre HISTORIC SITE

(034-642 1687; adult/child R30/15; 8am-4pm Mon-Fri, 9am-4pm Sat & Sun) Rorke's Drift Orientation Centre, on the site of the original mission station, is excellent. The Zulu know this site as Shiyane, their name for the hill at the back of the village. The *Rorke's Drift–Shiyane Self-Guided Trail* brochure (R3) is a helpful reference. *Zulu* was actually filmed in the Drakensberg, so the scenery around Rorke's Drift may come as a bit of a disappointment to those familiar with the film. The landscape is still beautifully rugged, however.

Evangelical Lutheran Church Art & Craft Centre ARTS & CRAFTS

(034-642 1627; www.centre-rorkesdrift.com) Behind the Rorke's Drift Orientation Centre, this operation was one of the few places to offer artistic training to black artists during apartheid. As well as the beautiful craft shop, several workshops – for weaving, printmaking and pottery – are in separate buildings in the vicinity; you are welcome to visit these, with the artists' permission.

Fugitive's Drift HISTORIC SITE

About 10km from Rorke's Drift is Fugitive's Drift. Two British soldiers were killed here while attempting to rescue the Queen's Colours.

Sleeping

Several lodges – of varying degrees of luxury – are in the surrounding area; all organise tours of the Battlefields.

THE BATTLE OF ISANDLWANA

It hardly bears thinking about. When a soldier from one of the five British armies sent to invade Zululand peered over a ridge on 22 January 1879, he was confronted not with an empty stretch of savannah but with 25,000 Zulu warriors crouching to attack. They had intended to delay their attack until the following day, the day after the full moon, but once discovered they moved into battle formation – two enclosing horns on the flanks and the main force in the centre – and fell on the British, catching them off guard and unprepared. (General Chelmsford had made a fatal decision to divide the column, taking half of it away from the camp after they were lured in another direction by the Zulus.) By the end of the day, the remaining British column had been annihilated and the Anglo-Zulu War, for the invaders at least, had got off to a very bad start.

Meanwhile, the small British contingent that had remained at Rorke's Drift (where the army had crossed into Zululand) to guard supplies, heard of the disaster and fortified their camp. They were attacked by about 4000 Zulus, but the defenders, numbering fewer than 150 fit soldiers, held on through the night until a relief column arrived. Victoria Crosses – 11 in all – were lavished on the defenders, and another couple went to the two officers who died defending the Queen's Colours at Fugitive's Drift, about 10km south of Rorke's Drift.

Isandalwana Lodge LODGE **$$$**
(☎034-271 8301; www.isandlwana.co.za; r per person with full board R1860-2315;) Top marks for location: the lodge's stunning rooms have expansive views over Mt Isandlwana, the Anglo-Zulu battle site. For such a modern construction, the lodge ingeniously blends into the landscape. Specials are offered throughout the year.

Rorke's Drift Hotel LODGE **$$$**
(☎034-642 1760; www.rorkesdrifthotel.com; s/d with half board R1300/1940) The common areas and restaurant of this giant rotunda – a wide expanse with massive sofas and an enormous central fireplace – promise big things. The rooms are less appealing, with not-quite-there but pleasant enough decor. The nearest place to Rorke's Drift, the restaurant is a popular snack spot for day trippers.

Getting There & Away

The battle sites are southeast of Dundee. Isandlwana is about 70km from Dundee, off Rte 68; Rorke's Drift is 42km from Dundee, accessible from Rte 68 or Rte 33 (the Rte 33 turn-off is 13km south of Dundee). The roads to both battlefields can be dusty and rough. A dirt road connects Isandlwana and Rorke's Drift.

Blood River & Ncome Monuments

On 16 December 1838 a small force of Voortrekkers avenged the massacre of Piet Retief's diplomatic party by crushing an army of 12,000 Zulus. More than 3000 Zulus died – the river ran red with their blood – while the Voortrekkers sustained barely a few casualties. The battle became a seminal event in Afrikaner history. The victory came to be seen as the fulfilment of God's side of the bargain and seemed to prove that the Boers had a divine mandate to conquer and 'civilise' Southern Africa, and that they were, in fact, a chosen people.

However, Afrikaner nationalism and the significance attached to Blood River grew in strength simultaneously and it has been argued (by Graham Leach in *The Afrikaners – Their Last Great Trek* and others) that the importance of Blood River was deliberately heightened and manipulated for political ends. The standard interpretation of the victory meshed with the former apartheid regime's world view: hordes of untrustworthy black savages were beaten by Boers who were on an Old Testament–style mission from God. Afrikaners still visit the site on 16 December, but the former 'Day of the Vow' is now the 'Day of Reconciliation'.

The battle site is marked by a full-scale bronze re-creation of the 64-wagon *laager*. The cairn of stones was built by the Boers after the battle to mark the centre of their *laager*. The monument and the nearby **Blood River Museum** (☎034-632 1695; adult/child R30/15, car R10; 8am-4.30pm Mon-Fri, to 4pm Sat & Sun) are 20km southeast of R33; the turn-off is 27km from Dundee and 45km from Vryheid.

The interesting **Ncome Museum** (☎034-271 8121; www.ncomemuseum.co.za; admission by donation; 8am-4.30pm), on the other side of the river, is accessible by a dirt road that links the two. It offers the Zulu perspective on events. The museum takes the shape of buffalo horns, the traditional method of attack. A symbolic display of Zulu shields (in metal) represents the Zulu regiments that fought in the battle.

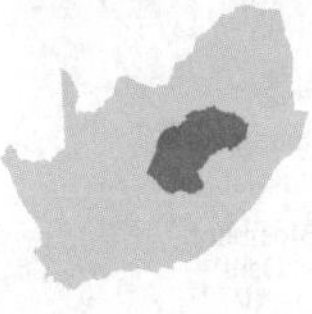

Free State

Includes ➡

Best Places to Eat

- Picnic (p302)
- Seven on Kellner (p303)
- Bella Casa Trattoria (p303)
- Vitos Restaurant & Bar (p311)
- O's Restaurant (p306)

Best Places to Stay

- Hobbit Boutique Hotel (p301)
- Cranberry Cottage (p314)
- Karma Backpackers (p310)
- Courtyard B&B (p311)
- Fisant Bokmakierie & Hoephoep Guest House (p312)

Why Go?

A place of big skies and open pastureland, the Free State is ideal for a road trip. Broad horizons are interrupted only briefly by a smattering of towns and villages and, apart from Bloemfontein, the urban centres are small and manageable.

The Eastern Highlands, around the Drakensberg and the Lesotho border, is a vast area of rocky mountains, steep valleys and summer electrical storms. It's spectacular country, well known for its fruit farms, especially cherries. There are some excellent accommodation options in this part of the country, along with the stunning and walkable Golden Gate Highlands National Park.

The Free State tends to be a place travellers pass through rather than a destination in its own right. However it's well worth exploring for its natural beauty, adventure sports and history – especially Bloemfontein, which, although historically an Afrikaner city, is also the birthplace of the African National Congress (ANC).

When to Go

Bloemfontein

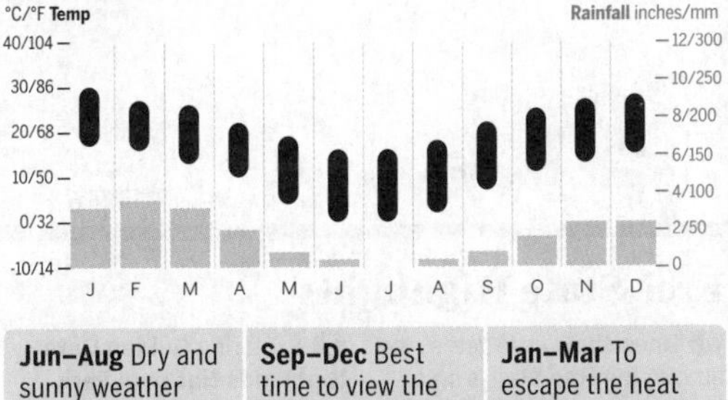

Jun–Aug Dry and sunny weather makes a road trip under big blue skies perfect.

Sep–Dec Best time to view the cherry trees in full bloom and go wild at Ficksburg's cherry festival.

Jan–Mar To escape the heat head for the snow at the foothills of the Maluti Mountains.

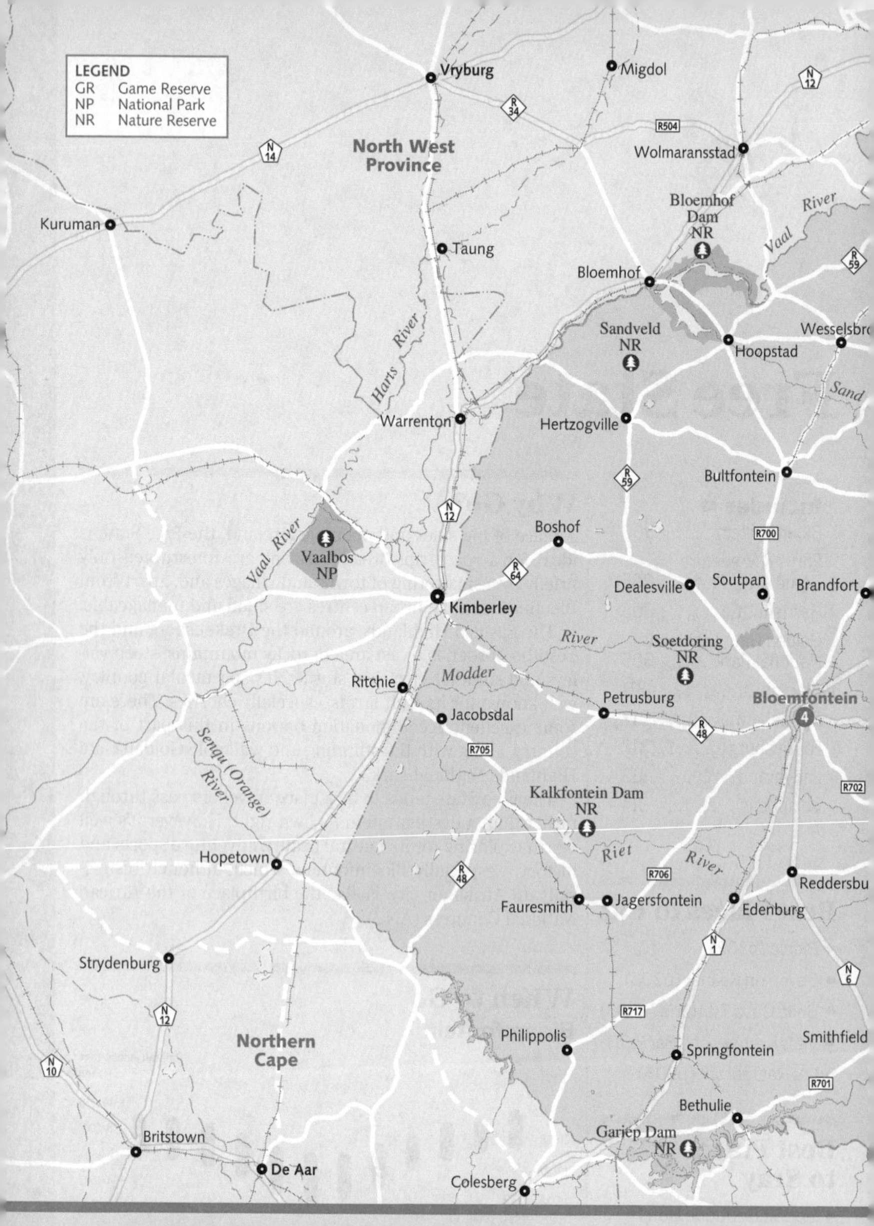

Free State Highlights

1 Unearthing little gems among the Free State's small towns and big skies, such as **Clarens** (p311), a nugget of sophistication that's perfect for people-watching.

2 Exploring **Golden Gate Highlands National Park** (p309) on foot and spotting the wildlife that inhabits the grasslands and spectacular sandstone formations.

3 Following the **Sentinel Hiking Trail** (p310) up over the dizzying heights of the Drakensberg plateau.

4 Enjoying excellent museums documenting South African history, and the province's best accommodation and eating options in **Bloemfontein** (p300), one of the country's most relaxed cities.

5 Getting intimate with the outdoors around **Parys** (p305), the Free State's adventure capital.

History

The Free State's borders reflect the prominent role it has played in the power struggles of South Africa's history. To the east is Lesotho, where forbidding mountains, combined with the strategic warfare of the Sotho king Moshoeshoe the Great, halted the tide of Boer expansion. To the southeast, however, the Free State spills across the river as the mountains dwindle into flat grassland - an area that proved harder for Moshoeshoe to defend.

The Voortrekkers established their first settlement near Bloemfontein, and various embryonic republics then came and went. In addition, there was a period of British sovereignty after the 1899–1902 Anglo-Boer War.

The 'Orange Free State' was created in 1854, with Bloemfontein as the capital. The 'Orange' part of the province's title was dropped in 1994, following South Africa's first democratic elections.

The ANC celebrated its centenary anniversary in Bloemfontein, where it started, in January 2012.

Language

Sotho (64.4%) is the dominant tongue in the Free State, followed by Afrikaans (11.9%) and Xhosa (9.1%). Only about 2% of the Free State's inhabitants speak English as a first language.

Getting There & Around

Trains and buses stop in Bloemfontein on their way to and from Johannesburg (Jo'burg), Pretoria and southern parts of the country. Likewise, it's easy to get to and from Lesotho – shared taxis and buses leave Bloemfontein daily for the border. Elsewhere, you'll need to take your own vehicle or rely on the sporadic minibus shared taxis.

BLOEMFONTEIN

POP 256,500

With the feel of a small country village, despite its double-capital status – it's the Free State's capital and the judicial capital of the country – Bloemfontein is one of South Africa's most pleasant cities. Although it doesn't possess the type of big-name attractions that make it worth a visit in its own right, you'll likely pass through 'Bloem' at some point on your way across South Africa's heartland.

Note that some areas of downtown are not considered safe, so seek local advice before going for a wander around the central business district. Apart from this the city has a relaxed, welcoming feel and some excellent eating and accommodation options.

Sights & Activities

Oliewenhuis Art Museum GALLERY
(051-447 9609; 16 Harry Smith St; 8am-5pm Mon-Fri, 9am-4pm Sat & Sun) FREE One of South Africa's most striking art galleries, the Oliewenhuis Art Museum occupies an exquisite 1935 mansion set in beautiful gardens. An imaginative and poignant contemporary photographic exhibition gives a good insight into modern South Africa. The museum also holds a collection of works by South African artists, including Thomas Baines.

National Women's Memorial MEMORIAL
(Monument Rd) Commemorating the 26,000 women and children who died in British concentration camps during the 1899–1902 Anglo-Boer War, the National Women's Memorial depicts a bearded Afrikaner setting off on his pony to fight the British, bidding a last farewell to his wife and baby, who are to perish in one of the camps. It's a powerful image and one still buried in the psyche of many Afrikaners.

Anglo-Boer War Museum MUSEUM
(051-447 3447; www.anglo-boer.co.za; Monument Rd; adult/child R10/5; 8am-4.30pm Mon-Fri, 10am-5pm Sat, 2-5pm Sun) Behind the National Women's Memorial, the Anglo-Boer War Museum has some interesting displays, including photos from concentration camps set up not only in South Africa but also in Bermuda, India and Portugal. Apart from a few modern touches, this museum remains unchanged since its inception. The large paintings depicting battle scenes are striking. If you're interested in this chapter of South African history you could easily spend a couple of hours here.

Naval Hill PARK
(051-412 7016; Franklin Game Reserve 8am-5pm) FREE This was the site of the British naval-gun emplacements during the Anglo-Boer War. Carved on the eastern side of the hill is a large white horse (akin to a Wiltshire horse) that served as a landmark for British cavalry during the war.

There are good views from the top of the hill, which is also home to the **Franklin Game Reserve**. Walking is permitted, and you may see ostriches wandering about. Entry is from Union Ave.

Orchid House
GARDENS

(☑ 051-412 7000; Union Ave; ☻10am-4pm Mon-Fri, to 5pm Sat & Sun) **FREE** This glasshouse has a beautiful collection of flowers and some dazzling orchids. The park outside is an ideal place to take the kids for a picnic.

National Museum
MUSEUM

(☑ 051-447 9609; www.nasmus.co.za; 36 Aliwal St; adult/child R5/3; ☻8am-5pm Mon-Fri, 10am-5pm Sat, noon-5pm Sun) A great re-creation of a 19th-century street, complete with sound effects, is the most interesting display at this museum. It also has a shop and a cafe.

☞ Tours

Manguang Township
CULTURAL TOUR

The African National Congress (ANC) was born in the shantytown of Manguang, 5km outside Bloemfontein, in 1912. Today, you can experience township life, and learn some important history, on a guided tour.

Tours are informal and cost about R500. The operators change, so it's best to ask at the tourist office for an up-to-date list of guides.

Manguang, and other black townships around the Bloem area, played an integral role in the fight to end apartheid. Tours visit culturally important sights such as Mapikela House, now a national monument, where Thomas Mapikela, a founder of the ANC, once resided.

🛏 Sleeping

Odessa Guesthouse
GUESTHOUSE $

(☑ 084 966 0200; 4 Gannie Viljoen St; s/d from R350/470; @🏊) For Ukrainian hospitality in the Free State, check out Odessa. The multilingual (Russian and Ukrainian are spoken along with English) guesthouse has a good rep for its home-away-from-home vibe and friendly hosts. Set in a quiet suburb, just off the N1 (take the Nelson Mandela turn-off, towards the city), its rooms are simple but spotless. Breakfast in bed can be arranged.

Reyneke Caravan Park
CARAVAN $

(☑ 051-523 3888; www.reynekepark.co.za; Brendar Rd; camping up to 4 people R230, r & chalets R400-750; 🏊) Two kilometres out of town (take the N8 towards Kimberley), this well-organised park has a swimming pool, a trampoline and a kids' play area. It's a good place for families. Basic rooms and modern brick chalets sleep up to four.

★ Matanja
GUESTHOUSE $$

(☑ 079 494 9740; www.matanja.co.za; 74A Albrecht St, Dan Pienaar; s/d incl breakfast R520/680; ✴) Small luxuries, such as pure goose-down duvets, and a stylish, rustic ambience set this little B&B apart. There are honesty fridges in the bedrooms. With only four rooms there is attention to detail, and your comfort seems a priority to the owners, who will even arrange breakfast in bed. Prebooking recommended.

Hobbit Boutique Hotel
BOUTIQUE HOTEL $$

(☑ 051-447 0663; www.hobbit.co.za; 19 President Steyn Ave, Westdene; r incl breakfast from R950; ✴@🏊) This charming Victorian guesthouse, comprising two 1921 houses, is popular with visiting dignitaries but also perfect for literati and romantic types. The cottage-style bedrooms have painted bathtubs, plus a couple of teddy bears apiece. The reading room has a chess table, and the local Tolkien society meets here to talk about all things JRR. Check out the pub and lovely outdoor patio.

At night there's a turndown service with sherry and chocolate.

Urban Hotel
HOTEL $$

(☑ 051-444 3142; www.urbanhotel.co.za; cnr Parfitt Ave & Henry St; r R850; ✴🏊) This hotel fills an important niche in Bloem's accommodation market. It's at the cheaper end of midrange, and service reflects this. Very modern rooms, however, are quite decadent, with lovely bathrooms and great beds. Try to get an upstairs room near the back. It's in an excellent location, too, close to all the Westdene and Waterfront action.

De Akker Guest House
GUESTHOUSE $$

(☑ 051-444 2010; www.de-akker.co.za; 25 Parfitt Ave; r R530-700; 🏊) This stylish offering in a central location has eight rooms, including some with sink-in-and-smile king beds, and both bath and shower in attached en suites. It's very friendly and is popular with visiting cricket teams, so book ahead in summer. Breakfast is R60.

Protea Hotel Willow Lake
HOTEL $$

(☑ 051-412 5400; www.proteahotels.com/protea-hotel-willow-lake.html; 101 Henry St; r from R1200; ✴@🏊) A big move up from the city's other midrange choices, the Protea offers very stylish rooms. Plump bedding and a shower cubicle that looks like it belongs at NASA complete the experience. A genuine touch of luxury close to the Waterfront, and overlooking the zoo.

Bloemfontein

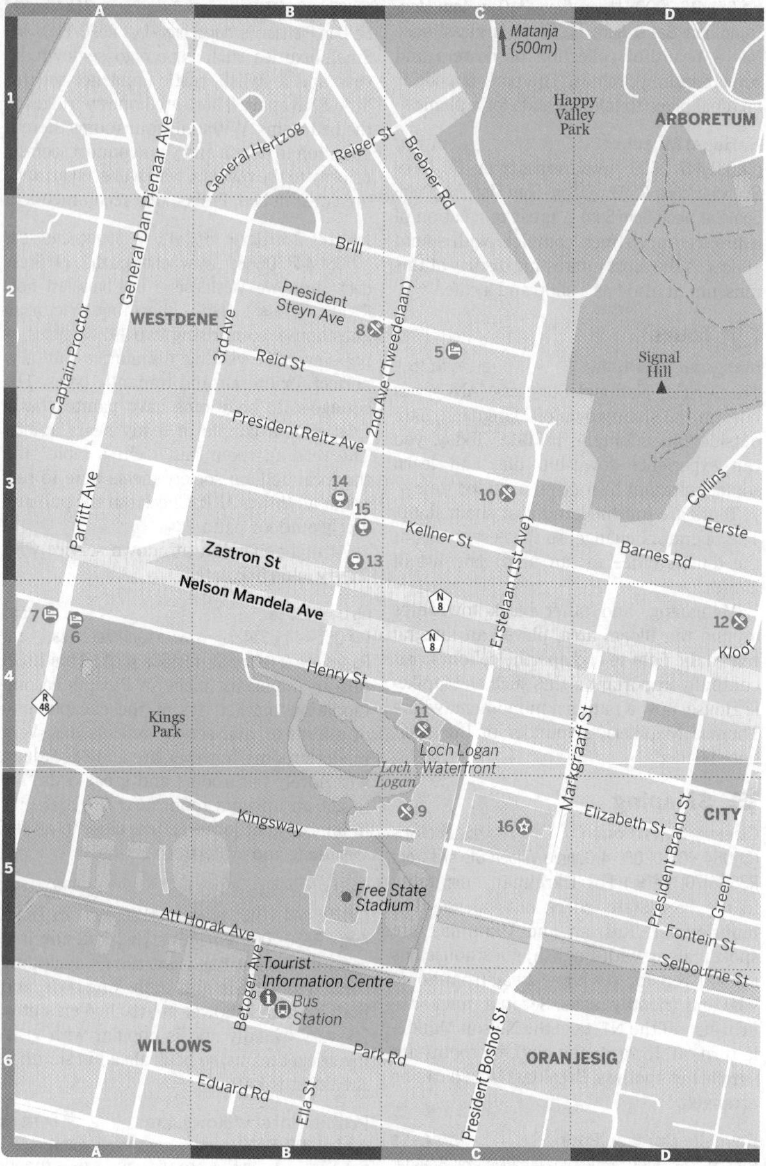

Eating

Modelled after Cape Town's waterfront, the Loch Logan waterfront isn't nearly as impressive, but it's a good, safe spot for dinner, drinks or a movie on a rainy day. You'll find the usual South African chains in the Waterfront and Mimosa Mall shopping centres. The main eating street is 2nd Ave.

Picnic CAFE $

(Loch Logan Waterfront; mains R50-70; ⏱8am-5pm) A cool place with a great outlook over the water, perfect for a long, lazy chill. The

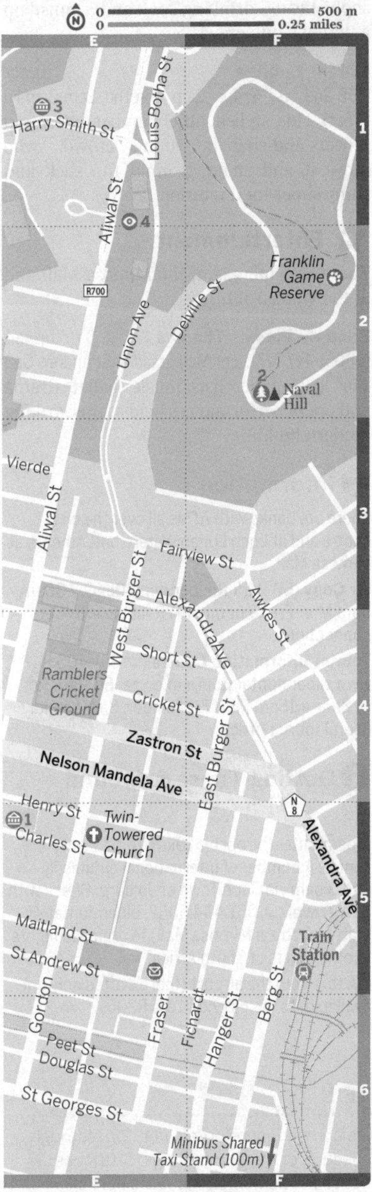

food is excellent – especially the salads and sandwiches – as is the service. Enjoy the fresh bread, quality ingredients and homemade touches such as tomato chutney (recommended on rye with ham and camembert).

Bloemfontein

Sights
1 National Museum......E5
2 Naval Hill......F2
3 Oliewenhuis Art Museum......E1
4 Orchid House......E1

Sleeping
De Akker Guest House......(see 7)
5 Hobbit Boutique Hotel......C2
6 Protea Hotel Willow Lake......A4
7 Urban Hotel......A4

Eating
8 Bella Casa Trattoria......B2
9 Braza......C5
10 Moerby Gallery-Restaurant......C3
11 Picnic......C4
12 Seven on Kellner......D4

Drinking & Nightlife
13 Barba's Café......B3
14 Mystic Boer......B3
15 Oolong Lounge......B3

Entertainment
16 Sand du Plessis Theatre......C5

Moerby Gallery-Restaurant CAFE **$**
(051-430 1142; 67 President Reitz Ave, Westdene; mains R45-70; 7.30am-5pm Mon-Fri, to 2pm Sat) For a snack or full-blown breakfast or lunch, try this quiet cafe at the serene end of President Reitz Ave. Out the front are comfy chairs and tables, while inside it supports various local arts and cultural pursuits such as live music.

★ **Seven on Kellner** INTERNATIONAL **$$**
(051-447 7928; www.sevenonkellner.co.za; 7 Kellner St, Westdene; mains R80-135; noon-2pm Mon-Fri, from 6.30pm Mon-Sat) Set in an old house with inside and outside dining options, Seven on Kellner offers an informal, intimate atmosphere. Poultry, meat and seafood dishes are delicately prepared with expert hands along a Middle Eastern– and Indian-inspired theme. Excellent wine list.

When we had dinner at this place there was a power failure and the flickering candlelight made it all the more alluring. Although what really impressed was the chef's ability to cook without electricity!

Bella Casa Trattoria ITALIAN **$$**
(051-448 9573; 31 President Steyn Ave; mains R70-100; Mon-Sat;) This efficient Italian trattoria serves lots of pasta choices along with pizzas and salads. It's a cheerful,

family-friendly place with a cosy indoors and ample courtyard seating at tables covered with blue chequered cloths. The thin-crust Naples-style pizzas are recommended. Extensive wine list.

Braza MEDITERRANEAN $$
(051-447 2821; www.braza.co.za; Loch Logan Waterfront; mains R80-150; 11am-10pm Mon-Sat, to 9pm Sun) The Portuguese-inspired cuisine here will appeal to both meat lovers and seafood aficionados. If you just want a taster, try the starter platter (R129), which gives a small sample of four dishes. Outside tables are right on the water's edge.

Drinking & Nightlife

As a university town, Bloem has a good range of places to drink, party and listen to live music. The corners of 2nd Ave and Kellner St, and Zastron St and Nelson Mandela Ave bustle with revellers in the evening and compete for the nightlife scene with the Waterfront.

Mystic Boer PUB
(www.diemysticboer.co.za; 84 Kellner St;) Bloem's most popular long-standing pub and live-music venue provides an eccentric twist on Afrikaner culture – check out the psychedelic pictures of long-bearded Boers on the walls. There are regular gigs by unsigned rock and hip-hop outfits. The bar specialises in tequila, while pizza and burgers provide the fuel.

Barba's Café BAR
(051-430 2542; www.barbas.co.za; 16 2nd Ave; 7.30am-2am Mon-Thu, to 4am Fri & Sat) A self-professed party house, Barba's is open late, has DJs and occasional bands, and the wildest, most insane party nights this side of the Drakensberg. Earlier in the evening an extensive cocktail list makes it more of a sophisticated drinking spot, and a 'must' on a 2nd Ave pub crawl.

Oolong Lounge LOUNGE
(16B 2nd Ave; 4pm-2am Mon-Thu, 2pm-2am Fri & Sat) This stylish little number attracts a movers-and-shakers young crowd, who move it and shake it amid the slick and shiny super-mod interior.

Entertainment

There are cinemas in the Mimosa Mall and at the Waterfront.

Sand du Plessis Theatre THEATRE
(051-447 7771; cnr Markgraaff & St Andrew Sts) The local paper lists music, ballet, drama and opera performances held at this striking modern building.

Information

There are banks with ATMs all over the city centre and at Loch Logan Waterfront. Amex is at Mimosa Mall.

Mr Copy (60 Park Rd; per min 40c; 7.30am-5pm Mon-Fri, to noon Sat) Reliable internet connections.

Tourist Information Centre (051-405 8489; www.bloemfonteintourism.co.za; 60 Park Rd; 8am-4.15pm Mon-Fri, to noon Sat) A mildly useful tourist office.

Getting There & Around

AIR

Bloemfontein airport is 10km from the city centre. A number of international airlines fly into Bloem via Cape Town or Jo'burg. Check with **STA Travel** (051-444 6062; bloemfontein@statravel.co.za; Mimosa Mall) to organise flights to other parts of South Africa.

A taxi from the airport (there's often only one available) to the city centre is R200.

JRR TOLKIEN: LORD OF BLOEMFONTEIN

JRR Tolkien, author of *The Lord of the Rings*, was born in Bloemfontein in 1892. Although he moved to England when he was five, his recollection of the Bloemfontein district as 'hot, dry and barren' is considered a sign by Bloem's residents that his years here inspired him to create the legendary kingdom of Mordor. Or perhaps, as some graffiti in a Cape Town pub once said, 'Tolkien was just another Bloemfontein boy on acid'...

Regardless, if you're interested in learning more about the local Tolkien scene, head over to the **Hobbit Boutique Hotel** (p301), home of the Tolkien literary society. Staff there can direct you to the house where Tolkien was born, the cathedral in which he was baptised and the grave where his father is buried. If you're in the area, and fascinated with all things Tolkien, it's definitely worth strolling over to the Hobbit for a cosy fireside chat.

BUS & SHARED TAXI

Long-distance buses leave from the tourist centre on Park Rd. Translux (Greyhound and Interstate have similar services) runs daily buses to:

Cape Town (R520, 10 hours)
Durban (R310, nine hours)
East London (R360, seven hours)
Jo'burg/Pretoria (R260, five hours)
Port Elizabeth (R360, nine hours)

Most minibus shared taxis leave from opposite the train station and head to Maseru, Lesotho (R80, three hours), Kimberley (R100, four hours) and Jo'burg (R160, six hours). There's usually at least one bus daily, but times vary.

TRAIN

The Algoa runs three times weekly via Bloemfontein between Jo'burg (tourist/economy R190/120, about seven hours) and Port Elizabeth (R290/200). The Amatola runs three times weekly via Bloemfontein on the run between Jo'burg (economy R130) and East London (R180). Contact **Shosholoza Meyl** (☎011-774 4555, 0860 008 888; www.shosholozameyl.co.za) for more details.

NORTHERN FREE STATE

Pretty country of rolling hills, northern Free State offers a growing number of hiking, mountain-biking and fishing opportunities. Near Parys in the far north, at Vredefort Dome, is the world's largest visible meteor crater, one of South Africa's seven Unesco World Heritage Sites.

Further south is a golden region of maize farms and sunflowers. The small towns around here are rural enclaves where people live and work, and they see few tourists.

Parys & Vredefort Dome Area

POP 8100

Parys is a small, vibrant town that sits beside the Vaal River just 120km south of Jo'burg. It is home to a few impressive buildings, including the 1915 **Anglican Church**, built from blue-granite blocks. The immediate area is quite beautiful, with its valleys, ravines and cliffs, its covering of lush flora, and the many resident plants, animals and birds. But it's the adventure-sport options and the art and craft outlets lining the main street that draw most of the town's visitors, particularly Jo'burgers on the weekend.

Parys is also handy for visiting **Vredefort Dome**, an enigmatic area of hills created by the impact of a gigantic meteorite two billion years ago.

Sights

Vredefort is the oldest and largest meteorite-impact site on earth, measuring about 200km in diameter. In 2005, the dome, which actually refers to the bowl (or upside-down dome) shape that characterises the central part of the crater, was named a Unesco World Heritage Site, South Africa's sixth. It's well worth taking a drive across the site – or better yet, a hike – to experience this unique landscape.

At Venterskroon is an **information centre** (☎018-291 1580; ⏲8am-6pm Mon-Fri, 9am-5pm Sat & Sun) where you can watch a brief video on the dome (ask for the English version unless you understand Afrikaans) and organise guided walks (from R340 per person) around the nearby crater.

Activities

Parys has numerous activities on offer, including abseiling, sky diving, mountain biking, quad biking, rafting, hiking and birding. Otters' Haunt runs white-water rafting excursions (half/full day R345/575) down the Vaal River below Parys. The Class I to III rapids are not wild by world standards, but they can be quite exciting, especially in high water. The Gatsien Rapid is the best paddle on the 6km stretch – it can be walked up to and ridden down numerous times. Otters' Haunt also guides mountain bikers and leads hikes around the Vredefort Dome.

Stone Adventures OUTDOORS
(☎056-811 4664; www.stoneadventures.co.za; Kopjeskraal Rd) Stone Adventures, based at the Stonehenge in Africa lodge, can arrange tandem skydives (from R1800), an 8km rafting trip to Rocky Ridge (R250), abseiling with 13m (R195) and 44m drops (R230), and other activities.

Sleeping & Eating

Tourism around Parys is growing fast, with hotels and holiday resorts opening each year.

Otters' Haunt GUESTHOUSE $
(☎084 245 2490, 056-818 1814; www.otters.co.za; Kopjeskraal Rd; r from R320, cottages per person from R375; @ 📶 🐾) Some of the

accommodation at this cheerfully overgrown place is getting a bit tatty, but the secluded location right on the Vaal River is unbeatable. Options include bungalows, thatched-roof cabins set around a swimming pool, and a three-bedroom cottage with its own pool. Turn left after you cross the bridge out of town and go for 2km along the river.

All sleeping options come with kitchenettes and/or access to braais. Grab a canoe and go for a paddle downstream, or tackle something else from the long list of activities on offer.

Waterfront Guest House
GUESTHOUSE $$

(☑ 056-811 3149; www.waterfrontguesthouseparys.co.za; 22 Grewar Ave; s/d R500/600; ❈ @ 🛜 ⛲) This rambling mansion occupies a peaceful riverside plot where the only thing that interrupts the quiet is bird noise. It has nine individually styled rooms to choose from; ask to see a few if you can. Breakfast costs an extra R90 per person.

Suikerbos
CHALET $$

(☑ 018-294 3867; www.suikerbos.co.za; camping R160, hikers' huts R360, chalets R750-900) Herds of impala graze peacefully between the buildings at this very popular farm-reserve. The chalets are airy and modern, with giant bathtubs and loads of light. A caravan, and basic hikers' huts sleeping four, are also on site.

From Parys head to Potch, take the gravel road to Venterskroon and after 20km it's a left turn to Suikerbos.

O's Restaurant
INTERNATIONAL $$

(☑ 056-811 3683; www.osrestaurant.co.za; 1 de Villiers St; mains R70-120; ⊗ 11am-10pm Wed-Sat, to 3pm Sun) In this stylish, thoroughly satisfying restaurant down by the river, have some garlic mussels followed by peri peri–topped steak, or fillet flambé prepared at your table. The pizza menu is also worth a browse, and there are some kids' meals too. Dine in the elegant interior, out on the deck or amidst the foliage in the gorgeous garden.

Feast
CAFE $$

(☑ 056-811 2397; 83 Bree St; mains R70-120; ⊗ 8am-4.30pm Mon-Fri, 7.30am-4.30pm Sat & Sun; ▱) The aptly named Feast is a warm, spacious cafe that's great for a morning omelette or French toast, or a more filling lunchtime spread. Vegetarians will be pleased by the numerous non-meat choices, from haloumi wraps and chickpea salad to a grilled veggie curry. There's also a good range of South African wines, including an unpretentious chardonnay called Fat Bastard.

Drinking

Pickled Pig
PUB

(☑ 056-817 7814; Bree St) This dark, cosy pub, more like an alcove than a full-blown bar, is accessed via a small courtyard off Bree St. A local favourite, it's good for a refreshing ale after an afternoon's browsing in the local shops or a dusty drive around Vredefort.

The owners also run the Plum Tree restaurant across the road, whose menu is made available for breakfast and lunch; at

SADDLE UP: MOUNTAIN BIKING THE FREE STATE

There's a lot of activity around Parys these days, but cycling wild veld single-track is our pick for an adrenaline-pumping adventure. Otters' Haunt (p305) maintains a dozen mountain-bike trails, catering to all skill levels, that snake out from its property 2km outside town. Some trails are open to day visitors (R80), but many require an Otters guide (half/full day R450/850 for one to six people) – not all of them are well marked and it's easy to get lost. Bike rental costs an extra R195 per day. Experienced cyclists can challenge themselves on steep and stony single-track, boasting wicked-fast descents and lung-busting climbs, while beginners can take an easy gravel-road pedal along the Vaal River.

Tweezer Rocks (about 18km, two hours) is one of the most popular options, and can be done alone or on a guided trip – locals call it the 'breakfast run' because it's a fast-wakeup ride. Beginners should be OK on this trail (take a guide), but note that the ride includes a few steep climbs and a rocky descent into a dry riverbed (it can be walked if necessary). Taking you in a giant loop past scenic kopjes and featuring stunning mountain vistas, the route gets its name from the two giant boulders holding a third between them (like a tweezer) visible during the first hill climb.

For more trail details, as well as rules and restrictions, visit www.otters.co.za.

WORTH A TRIP

WILLEM PRETORIUS GAME RESERVE

Willem Pretorius Game Reserve (☎057-651 4003; admission R60; ⏱7am-6.30pm) Off the N1, about 70km south of Kroonstad, is the Willem Pretorius Game Reserve, one of the Free State's biggest recreation areas. Divided by the Sand River and Allemanskraal Dam, the reserve encompasses two ecosystems: grassy plains with large herds of elands, blesboks, springboks, black wildebeests and zebras, and, further north, a bushy mountain region with baboons, mountain reedbucks and duikers.

White rhinos and buffalos are equally at home on either side of the reserve, but elephants and predators such as lions are not found here. If you enter via the West Gate, head up to the nearby lookout for great views of the area.

Aldam Resort (☎057-652 2200; www.aldamestate.co.za; campsites from R210, chalets from R630) Adjacent to Willem Pretorius Game Reserve, this resort offers rustic but well-appointed chalets, many of them with magnificent views over Allemanskraal Dam. Fishing is popular here and there are hiking trails. The bar-restaurant (mains R60 to R90; open from 8am daily) serves grilled meats and burgers; enjoy the expansive view from the outside patio while having a drink.

The resort is well signposted in the reserve.

night, the pub serves delicious homemade pies, including oxtail and pepper steak.

ℹ Information

Parys Info Centre (☎056-811 4000; www.parys.info; 30 Water St; ⏱8am-5pm Mon-Fri, 9am-1pm Sat & Sun) Parys Info Centre can provide a map of the town and detailed information on accommodation options and activity providers.

ℹ Getting There & Away

The R59 leads into Parys, which is just west of the N1 heading north from Jo'burg. You'll need a vehicle to get here.

Kroonstad & Around

POP 25,000

The province's third-largest town, Kroonstad, on the N1, is an orderly place with wide central streets. It makes a good base for exploring nearby Koppies Dam Nature Reserve.

Koppies Dam Nature Reserve NATURE RESERVE
(☎056-777 2034; per car R60; ⏱5am-9pm Sep-Apr, 7am-6pm May-Aug) The 40-sq-km Koppies Dam Nature Reserve, about 70km northeast of Kroonstad on the Rhenoster River, is popular with anglers. Yellowfish, barbell, mudfish and carp are all abundant. Windsurfing, sailing and water-skiing are also very popular here. Camping is available (R100 per car).

Arcadia Guesthouse GUESTHOUSE $$
(☎082 9400 715; www.arcadiakroonstad.co.za; s/d incl breakfast R600/700) This smart, four-star guesthouse with classically elegant rooms is in the middle of a large garden scattered with faux-Greek statues. It's in a peaceful spot on the edge of town, and you'll need a car to get here (it's near the entrance to the N1 – follow the signs in town).

Alfredo's ITALIAN $
(☎056-215 2886; 58 Orange St; mains cafe R30, restaurant R50) This Italian restaurant and cafe is in the Plumbago Garden Centre, a block off the main street. It has a lovely outdoorsy ambience.

ℹ Getting There & Away

Translux (☎058-408 4888; www.translux.co.za) is one of several bus companies doing daily runs to Jo'burg (R210, three hours) from the Shell Ultra petrol station.

EASTERN HIGHLANDS & SOUTHERN FREE STATE

With the Kingdom of Lesotho tucked into its crook, the mighty Eastern Highlands are the Free State's star attraction. The wild, rugged border winds its way past snow-shrouded mountains in winter and amber foliage in autumn – the views are spectacular, particularly in the northwest around Clarens.

Encompassing an area roughly from Rte 26 and Rte 49 east of Bethlehem to Harrismith,

Eastern Highlands

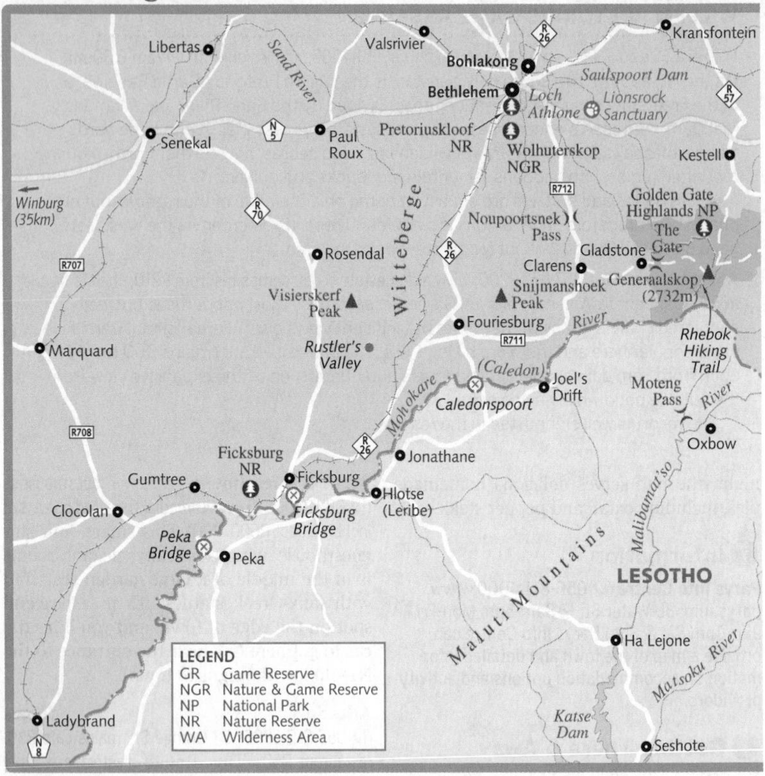

the region boasts sandstone monoliths towering above undulating golden fields, fantastic Golden Gate Highlands National Park and South Africa's coolest country village art destination, trendy Clarens.

Harrismith

POP 96,000

Harrismith is a useful junction town where the N3 to Jo'burg or Durban and the N5 towards Bloemfontein intersect. It's also a jumping-off point for exploring the Drakensberg range just inside the border of KwaZulu-Natal. It's a ramshackle country town with wide streets, picturesque old buildings around a grassy square, and distant Drakensberg views.

Sleeping & Eating

The Bergview complex is your best bet for eating, where you'll find the usual chains (Debonairs, Nando's and Ocean Basket) along with a couple of classier cafes.

Book House Cottage COTTAGE $
(☎082 411 8838; bookhouse@mweb.co.za; 24 Milner St; s/d from R300/450; ❄) Lovely, spacious self-catering units in a peaceful suburb good for families and couples. The kitchens are well kitted out and the cottages have lovely views of Platberg Mountain. There's also good privacy from the owner's residence. The place is signposted from town.

Platberg Harrismith Backpackers BACKPACKERS $
(☎058-622 3737; www.platbergbackpackers.co.za; 55 Biddulph St; dm or d per person R150; @ 📶) This well-run place with safe parking has three dorm rooms and a double, all in good shape. You can use the braai outside, and there are great views of Platberg Mountain. If you want to explore your spectacular surrounds you can also hire a mountain bike or grab a hiking map.

Lala Nathi CHALET $$

(☎058-623 0282; www.lalanathi.co.za; s/d from R450/650; ❄📶) Just off the N3, 3km from Harrismith (towards Durban), and offering convenience, great value and traditional *rondavels*, this is a sure bet – especially if you intend to hit the highway in the morning.

Information

N3 Help Centre (☎0800 634 357; ⏰8am-4.30pm Mon-Fri) The very helpful N3 Help Centre is in the Bergview complex (a cluster of restaurants and retail near the entrance to the N3). It's overflowing with brochures and printed material on the wider region. Staff are knowledgeable and eager to assist with queries.

Getting There & Away

Intercape runs daily bus services to Durban (R360, four hours) and Jo'burg (R370, four hours). The bus station is on McKechnie St.

Sterkfontein Dam Nature Reserve

Sterkfontein Dam Nature Reserve NATURE RESERVE

(☎058-622 3520; admission R60; ⏰6am-10pm) The small Sterkfontein Dam Nature Reserve is in a beautiful area of the Drakensberg foothills, 23km south of Harrismith on the Oliviershoek Pass road into KwaZulu-Natal. Looking out over this expansive dam with its backdrop of rugged peaks feels like gazing across an inland sea. There are many viewpoints, and watersports such as windsurfing and fishing are popular.

Camping (camping R60) and rustic four-bed **chalets** (chalets R450) are available.

Golden Gate Highlands National Park

Right before the darkness erases the remaining flecks of colour from the sky, something magical happens in **Golden Gate Highlands National Park** (☎058-255 1000; www.sanparks.org/parks/golden_gate; adult/child R152/76). The jagged sandstone outcrops fronting the foothills of the wild, maroon-hued Maluti Mountains glow golden in the dying light; lemon-yellow rays silhouette a lone kudu standing still in a sea of mint-green grasses before the sky explodes in a fiery collision of purple and red. The park might not boast any of the Big Five, but it does feature fantastic nightly sunsets.

There are quite a few animals in the park, though, including grey rheboks, blesboks, elands, oribis, Burchell's zebras, jackals, baboons and numerous bird species, including the rare bearded and Cape vultures as well as the endangered bald ibis. The park is popular with hikers on long treks, but there are also shorter walking trails. You buy entry permits at the park reception.

Activities

Rhebok Hiking Trail HIKING

(per person R100) This well-maintained, circular, 33km trail is a two-day trek and offers a great way to see the park. On the second day the track climbs up to a viewpoint on the side of Generaalskop (2732m), the highest point in the park, from where Mont-aux-Sources and the Maluti Mountains can be seen. The return trail to Glen Reenen passes Langtoon Dam.

GOLDEN GATE HIGHLANDS NATIONAL PARK

Why Go The opportunity to hike in national parks in South Africa is rare. Not only can you walk without a guide here but also the landscape is mesmerising and you have a great chance of seeing wildlife including various antelope.

When to Go The park can get very cold in winter, when temperatures can plummet to -15°C (June to August) and snow is common. September to April is the best time for travel to the park, although in summer afternoon thunderstorms do occur.

Practicalities Carry sufficient water if you're hiking and remember that the weather can change unpredictably up here. With your own vehicle you can approach from Harrismith on Rte 74 and then Rte 712.

Budget Tips Bring your own food. Minibus shared taxis run between Bethlehem and Harrismith, via Clarens and Phuthaditjhaba, and go right through the park.

The trail starts at the Glen Reenen Rest Camp, located next to the park reception. It has some steep sections, so hikers need to be reasonably fit. The trail is limited to 18 people and must be booked through the park board in advance – check the park's website.

Tours

There are two easy drives close to park headquarters.

Blesbok Loop DRIVING TOUR
This 6.7km scenic route traverses low-cut, stony grasslands. The mountain views and sense of isolation make it well worth the drive.

Oribi Loop DRIVING TOUR
The 4.2km Oribi Loop offers magnificent scenery. You may spot its namesake antelope wandering about, but the highlight is the view of the Drakensberg.

Sleeping

Glen Reenen Rest Camp CAMPGROUND $
(058-255 1000; camping R220, 2-person rondavels from R870) This place is conveniently located on the main road, buried among the craggy limestone, and has well-maintained chalets and campsites by the river. A shop sells basic supplies.

Getting There & Away

Rte 712 is a sealed road that runs into the park from Clarens, south of Bethlehem.

Phuthaditjhaba

POP 55,000

Phuthaditjhaba, about 50km southwest of Harrismith, was the capital of the apartheid homeland of QwaQwa. Today, the town shows the signs of its neglect, although the highlands around Phuthaditjhaba are great hiking country.

Sentinel Hiking Trail HIKING
(bookings & information 058-713 6361/2; car park/hike R30/60) The most famous of the hiking trails in the area is the 10km Sentinel Hiking Trail, which commences in the Free State and ends in KwaZulu-Natal. The trail starts at the Sentinel car park, at an altitude of 2540m, and runs for 4km to the top of the Drakensberg plateau, where the average height is 3000m.

It's about a two-hour ascent for those of medium fitness. At one point you have to use a chain ladder that runs up over a set of sheer rocks. Those who find the ladder frightening can take the route up The Gully, which emerges at Beacon Buttress (although some hikers argue that this route is even more hair-raising!). The reward for the steep ascent is majestic mountain scenery and the opportunity to climb Mont-aux-Sources (3282m).

Karma Backpackers BACKPACKERS $
(058-563 1433; www.karmalodge.co.za; 2 Piet Retief St; camping/dm/d R70/140/330; @) Located in Kestell, a small maize-farming village on Rte 57 about 22km north of Phuthaditjhaba, Karma Backpackers is a peaceful, cosy place. The friendly hosts have lots of firsthand knowledge on regional hikes, and there are views of Sentinel Peak and the Maluti Mountains from the gorgeous garden. The hostel sells yummy homemade jams, cheese and yoghurt.

Excellent day trips to Lesotho are also offered. Basotho guide Zee takes you over mountain passes to San rock paintings and a remote village, where you sample local sorghum brew in a shebeen and eat lunch in a home.

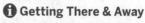

Clarens

POP 800

The jewel of the Free State, Clarens is one of those places you stumble upon and find yourself talking about long after you depart. With a backdrop of craggy limestone rocks, verdant green hills, spun-gold fields and the magnificent Maluti Mountains, Clarens is a picture-perfect village of whitewashed buildings and quiet, shady streets. It makes a bucolic country retreat.

It's also an art destination, with many galleries focusing on quality works by well-known South African artists. Charming guesthouses (ranging from very simple to extraordinarily posh), gourmet restaurants, eclectic cafes and myriad adventure activities round out the appeal.

Activities

Clarens Xtreme ADVENTURE SPORTS
(☎082 563 6242; www.clarensxtreme.co.za; Sias Oosthuizen St) Head over to this one-stop shop for all things outdoors. Popular activities include quad biking (from R200), white-water rafting (R450/650 half/full day) on the dam-fed Ash River (some rapids rate as high as Class IV), mountain biking (R200/300 half/full day) in the mountains behind Clarens with views over the town and valley, and zip lining (from R80) through an adventure park.

Sleeping

Clarens Inn & Backpackers BACKPACKERS $
(☎082 377 3621; www.clarensinn.com; 93 Van Reenan St; camping R100, dm R150, self-catering cottages per person from R200, d from R200) The town's best budget option offers single-sex dorms and basic doubles built around a central courtyard with a big open fire pit and outdoor bar. The locale is rustic and tranquil, pushed up against the mountain at the bottom of Van Reenen St (look for it after the Le Roux turn-off).

★**Courtyard B&B** B&B $$
(☎082 650 1503; Swart St; s/d incl breakfast R450/700; @ 📶) An excellent option in a quiet location at the bottom of town (especially at weekends, when Clarens can get very busy). Rooms are upstairs (No 3 has a balcony) and are very spacious, with a kitchen and sitting area including couch and armchairs. The downstairs cafe has all manner of yummy treats.

Patcham Place B&B $$
(☎058-256 1017; www.patchamplace.co.za; 262 Church St; s/d incl breakfast from R560/920) A good central option often offering better value in this range than competitors around town – a recent makeover included the addition of satellite TV in its five airy rooms, which have fab views from the balconies. The bathrooms are spotless and the beds firm, and there's even a small kitchen for guests' use.

Lake Clarens Guesthouse GUESTHOUSE $$
(☎058-256 1436; Lake Clarens Dr; r per person incl breakfast from R500) This impeccably maintained, four-star guesthouse offers buckets of intimate country charm. Fresh flowers, giant bathtubs, heated floors and silky-soft linens are all highlights of the luxuriously appointed bedrooms. Slightly more expensive rooms in the main house with enormous king beds are worth the extra.

Eating

Vitos Restaurant & Bar ITALIAN $$
(☎058-256 1328; 325 Market St; mains R70-110; ⏲8am-late) Offering an array of well-prepared meals all day, traditional Italian Vitos dabbles in pork, lamb, chicken, steak and seafood dishes and, of course, pizza and pasta. Don't miss the chocolate volcano for dessert. Service is excellent and the setting unpretentious.

Clementines Restaurant INTERNATIONAL $$
(☎058-256 1616; cnr Van Zyl & Church Sts; mains R70-120; ⏲noon-3pm & 6pm-late Tue-Sun; 🖉) The food at this souped-up country kitchen tastes just as good as it looks on the gourmet international menu, featuring everything from rainbow trout with almond butter to tender ostrich fillets. Professional service, intimate ambience, a lengthy wine list and vegie options are more perks. Make sure to check out the daily specials on the wall.

Drinking

Clarens Brewery BREWERY
(☎058-256 1193; www.clarensbrewery.co.za; 326 Main St; ⏲10am-6pm Mon-Thu, to 7pm Fri & Sat, to 5pm Sun) Finely crafted local brews such as English ale, stout and IPA go down very well at this exposed-brick bar across from Clarens Sq. Try the Weiss, a German-style unfiltered beer with a spicy, fruity aroma of banana and clove – it's very refreshing on a sunny day while sitting on the outdoor bench seating.

QWAQWA

QwaQwa (meaning 'Whiter than White') was named after the sandstone hill that dominates the area. It was created in the early 1980s as a homeland for southern Sotho people. The dumping of 200,000 people on a tiny patch of agriculturally unviable land, remote from employment centres, was one of the more obscene acts of apartheid.

Masupatsela Adventure Tourism (☎079 551 8356; 5hr tours for up to 4 people R490) is a local company that runs insightful township tours in QwaQwa that are both diverse and sensitively conducted. You'll visit a shepherd's village, the oldest Dutch church in the area, Jerusalem – a Rastafarian village – and a shebeen (an unlicensed drinking establishment). There's a minimum of only one person.

Shopping

With tidy, tree-lined streets and myriad boutiques and galleries to peruse, Clarens is made for aimless wandering. In the galleries, keep an eye out for pieces by Pieter van der Westhuizen or Hannetjie de Clercq, two well-respected South African artists.

Clarens Gallery & Woven Arts ARTS & CRAFTS
(☎058-256 1909; www.clarensgallery.co.za; 323 Main St; ⏲9am-4.30pm Tue-Sun) There are some lovely works of art in here that combine bright watercolours to accentuate the earth, sky and trees. It also sells imported rugs and woven mats from Pakistan, Afghanistan and Iran.

Art & Wine Gallery on Main GALLERY
(☎058-256 1298; 279 Main St; ⏲9am-4pm) Offering a fantastic selection of regional wines and paintings.

Bibliophile BOOKS
(☎058-256 1692; 313 Church St; ⏲9am-5pm Mon-Sat, to 3pm Sun) A quaint bookshop with a huge range of titles and jazz CDs.

Getting There & Away

Clarens is best reached by private transport.

Bethlehem

POP 16,500

The main commercial centre of the eastern Free State, Bethlehem has a nice, wide-open feel and, although it's of little interest to travellers beyond a night's rest, the buzzing township makes a good spot to lay your head.

Sights

Lionsrock WILDLIFE RESERVE
(☎058-304 1691; www.lionsrock.org; wildlife safaris from R140) Eighteen kilometres from town, Lionsrock is a 1200-sq-metre sanctuary and wildlife park for big cats rescued from all over the world and includes lions, cheetahs and leopards. There are also many species of antelope and wild dog, and guided game drives are offered. Accommodation is available from R450 per person.

Sleeping

★ **Fisant Bokmakierie & Hoephoep Guest House** GUESTHOUSE $$
(☎058-303 7144; www.fisant.co.za; 8-10 Thoi Oosthuyse St; s/d incl breakfast from R550/850; @📶) Amid magnificent bird-attracting gardens are rooms and some luxurious self-catering chalets in two combined guesthouses. The rooms are beautifully appointed and very spacious, some with small kitchens and private patios. They combine modern facilities such as power showers with classic polished-wood furniture and sumptuous bedding. It's very friendly, has good security and is well signposted.

La Croché GUESTHOUSE $$
(☎058-303 9229; cnr Kerk & Theron Sts; s/d with breakfast from R580/900; 📶) The owners' love of the Mediterranean is obvious at classy La Croché, which marries African architecture, including a soaring thatched roof, with Italian and French themes beautifully. Rooms are a good size and the architect's fine touches are everywhere.

Getting There & Away

Translux buses run to Durban (R300, five hours) and Cape Town (R600, 16 hours) and stop in Church St. The minibus-taxi ranks are on the corner of Cambridge and Gholf Sts, north of the town centre on the way to the train station.

Fouriesburg

POP 700

Surrounded by wild, craggy mountains, Fouriesburg occupies a magnificent spot just 12km north of the Caledonspoort border post to Lesotho. Two nearby peaks, Snijmanshoek and Visierskerf, are the highest in the

DON'T MISS

RUSTLER'S VALLEY

Dreaming about a journey into the wildly beautiful heart of nowhere? Ditch the pavement and let your subconscious guide you down rich, brown, dusty byways in this remote valley, to random oases scattered amid the rough-and-ready countryside.

Off Rte 26 between Fouriesburg and Ficksburg, Rustler's Valley is home to the enchanting **Franshoek Mountain Lodge** (☎051-933 2828; www.franshoek.co.za; r per person with half board R580; @ ≋). A working farm with comfortable sandstone cottages in its garden, and great views of the valley, it exudes a lovely country charm. Note that it was closed for renovations when we passed through but should be open by the time you read this.

The main turn-off for Rustler's Valley is about 25km south of Fouriesburg on Rte 26 to Ficksburg – follow the signposts down a dirt road that crosses a train line. From the turn-off it is 13km to Franshoek.

Free State; you'll also find the largest sandstone overhang in the southern hemisphere, **Salpeterkrans**, around here – look for the signs off Rte 26; it's just northwest of town. An eerie example of wind erosion, the area is considered sacred and is used by local tribes for ancestral worship.

Camelroc Guest Farm CAMPGROUND, CHALET **$$**
(☎058-223 0368; www.camelroc.co.za; camping R190, s/d incl breakfast R400/600, chalets from R660) About 11km outside Fouriesburg, and just 800m from the Lesotho border, Camelroc sits in a spectacular location against a camel-shaped sandstone outcrop with fine views over the Maluti Mountains. It's a great rustic retreat, offering dorms in a simple hikers hut and fully equipped chalets that range in size and style. Good hiking and 4WD trails are nearby.

Windmill Pub & Grill PUB **$**
(Robertson St; mains R50-90; ⏲from 11.30am) If your thirst needs quenching or if steak is on your wishlist, try Windmill Pub & Grill in town, with bench seating in a lush, shady setting.

Ficksburg

POP 5500

Ficksburg is a lovely little mountain village on the banks of the Mohokare (Caledon) River that's home to some fine **sandstone buildings**; keep an eye out for the town hall and the post office. Nestled into the purple-hued Maluti range, Ficksburg is particularly fetching in winter when dollops of snow cover the craggy peaks.

Mild summers and cold winters make this area perfect for growing stone fruits, and Ficksburg is the centre of the Free State's cherry industry. There's a **Cherry Festival** (☎051 933 6486; www.cherryfestival.co.za) in November, but September and October are the best times to see the trees in full bloom.

Highlands Hotel Hoogland HOTEL **$**
(☎051-933 2214; highlandshotel@isat.co.za; 37 Voortrekker St; s/d R300/600) The African-themed rooms at the Highlands Hotel Hoogland are the best budget option – backpacker rooms share bathrooms, while those with en suites are still basic but are spacious and have more creature comforts. It's a genuine old-style hotel with loads of character and a great lived-in feel. You'll find it next to the town hall.

Imperani Guest House & Coffee Shop GUESTHOUSE **$$**
(☎051-933 3606; www.imperaniguesthouse.co.za; 53 McCabe Rd; s/d incl breakfast from R460/650; ≋) In a quiet spot, the Imperani has an African-flavoured, country-cottage vibe. The 11 spotless, modern rooms have wooden floors and big windows and are in thatched-roof buildings. In a big airy *boma* (large open-air, thatched-roof hut) nearby, the on-site restaurant is a good lunch stop if you're passing through Ficksburg.

Along with strong coffee, the restaurant does excellent wraps for lunch. It also offers salads and other light meals at breakfast and lunch. There's a very good kids' menu too.

Ladybrand

POP 18,000

In a valley surrounded by jagged peaks, 16km from Lesotho's capital, Maseru, Ladybrand is an attractive small town loaded with sandstone buildings, dramatic scenery and ancient history. It's also a handy place to overnight on your way to and from Southern Africa's mountain kingdom.

Catharina Brand Museum MUSEUM
(17 Church St) FREE The most impressive exhibit here explains how ashes taken from an ancient hearth in the **Rose Cottage Cave**, not far from Ladybrand, prove that humans first inhabited the area more than 55,000 years ago. To really delve into the region's history, ask here about visiting the Khoe-San rock-art sites (more than 300 in caves around Ladybrand).

Note that the museum was closed when we passed through. It usually keeps fairly erratic opening hours, but there were rumours of a renovation.

Modderpoort Cave Church CHURCH
Nestled under a huge boulder in scenic surroundings about 12km north of Ladybrand, Modderpoort Cave Church is one of the quaintest churches (c 1869) around.

★Cranberry Cottage GUESTHOUSE $$
(☎051-924 2290; www.cranberry.co.za; 37 Beeton St; s/d incl breakfast from R590/960;) The best place to sleep in Ladybrand (and one of the best in the Free State) is this rambling stone guesthouse. Spacious rooms have a touch of luxury and the feel of nature. A foliage-decked garden, a grapevine-covered patio and lovely swimming pool, a cosy dining room with crackling log fire and an old-time polished-wood bar all await.

Cranberry also offers cheaper self-catering options down the road.

Getting There & Away

Ladybrand is 4km off the N8 on Rte 26 – the road to Ficksburg – and about 130km south of Bloemfontein. Minibus shared taxis can be found near the church on Piet Retief St and run to Ficksburg (R45, one hour). For a wider choice of destinations, take a minibus taxi to Maseru Bridge (R20), at the Lesotho border, and find a long-distance taxi in the big minibus-taxi rank there.

Gariep Dam Nature Reserve

Gariep Dam Nature Reserve NATURE RESERVE
(☎051-754 0026; per vehicle R60) The Free State's largest nature reserve is a combination of the 365-sq-km Gariep Dam (which holds back a vast 6 billion cubic litres of water) on the Senqu (Orange) River and a 112-sq-km wildlife sanctuary on its northern shore.

During February the world's longest **inland rubber-duck race** takes place on the dam. The event runs over 500km and is completed in a single day. Well-laid-out **Forever Resorts Gariep** (☎051-754 0045; www.forevergariep.co.za; camping/chalets from R180/1130) offers loads of watersport activities.

In the reserve you can choose from seven chalets (from R550) or campsites (from R100); there are more options in the town of Gariep Dam, near the dam wall at the reserve's western edge.

Philippolis

POP 1000

Founded in 1823 as a mission station, Philippolis, on Rte 717, is a beautiful place, and the oldest town in the Free State. Seventy-five of its buildings have been declared national monuments, including the library, and many places are built in Karoo style (made with thick walls to keep the heat at bay).

Old Jail HOTEL $
(☎082 550 4421; cells from R300) If you've ever fancied spending a night behind bars, here's your big chance. The town's jail has been converted into basic but comfortable self-catering accommodation – well, if you consider a 2m by 3m cell with 60cm-thick outer walls and 45cm-thick inner walls comfortable (the place does stay cool in summer and warm in winter, and the cells are virtually soundproof).

Rooms come with two authentic single prison beds, and a mat on the floor accommodates a third person.

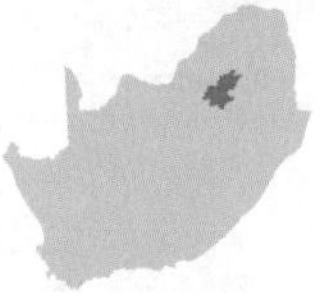

Johannesburg & Gauteng

Includes ➡

Best Places to Eat

- Service Station (p334)
- LeSel@The Cradle (p350)
- Grillhouse (p339)
- Lucky Bean (p335)
- Boer'geoisie (p359)

Best Places to Stay

- Residence (p330)
- Oasis Signature Hotel (p329)
- Motel Mipichi (p328)
- Satyagraha House (p330)
- Foreigners Friends Guesthouse (p354)

Why Go?

If you're in search of urban vibes, Gauteng will enthrall you. This small province is the throbbing heart of the South African nation and the economic engine of Africa. Its epicentre is Johannesburg (Jo'burg), the country's largest city. And what a city! Its centre is undergoing an astonishing rebirth and its cultural life has never been so dynamic. Once considered a place to avoid, Jo'burg is now one of the most inspiring and happening metropolises in the world.

For a change of scene, head to Pretoria, a short drive north. The country's administrative capital is decidedly less urbane but is somewhat grander with its stately buildings, attractive museums and jacaranda-lined streets.

Gauteng also has a unique geological history that's evident at the World Heritage–listed Cradle of Humankind. This vast valley full of caves and fossils is one of the African continent's most important archaeological sites.

When to Go

Johannesburg

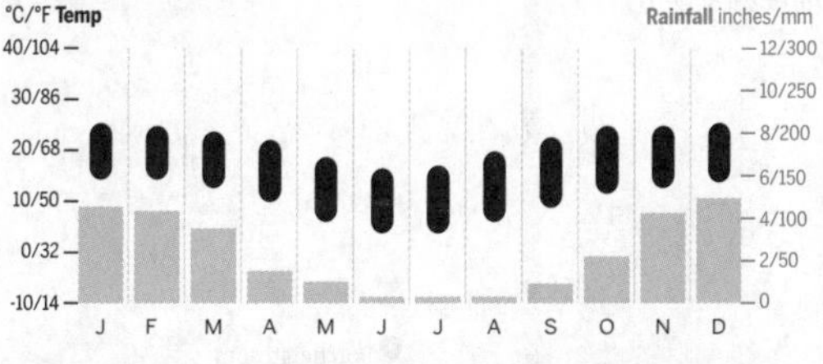

Mar School's back, so Jo'burg's Melville, Maboneng and Braamfontein hop. High fashion is out in Sandton.

Aug Festival season led by Joy of Jazz, the Dance Umbrella and a hectic calendar of theatre.

Late Nov–Mar Spectacular near-daily lightning strikes. Enjoy less traffic and a great NYE carnival.

Johannesburg & Gauteng Highlights

1. Hooking up with Southern Africa's cultural hub in the revamped Johannesburg neighbourhoods of **Newtown** (p319), **Braamfontein** (p323) and **Maboneng** (p324).
2. Revisiting South Africa's chilling history at Jo'burg's **Apartheid Museum** (p325) and **Constitution Hill** (p324).
3. Leaping off the **Orlando Towers** (p348) in Soweto.
4. Cruising the cafes and bars in the leafy streets of Jo'burg's **Melville** (p341).
5. Going deep underground in the caves and fossil sites at the **Cradle of Humankind** (p349).
6. Paying respects to the fallen at **Freedom Park** (p354) in Pretoria.
7. Taking a tour of **Jo'burg's Inner City** (p331) and marvelling at its architectural gems.

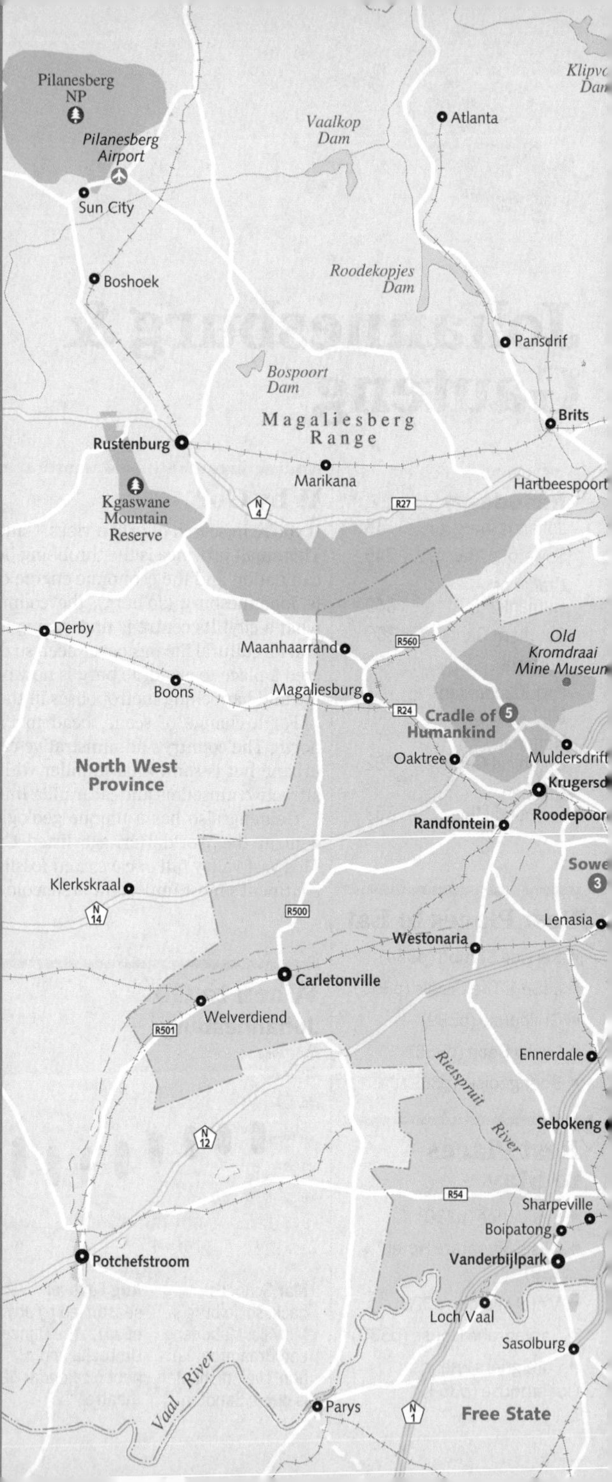

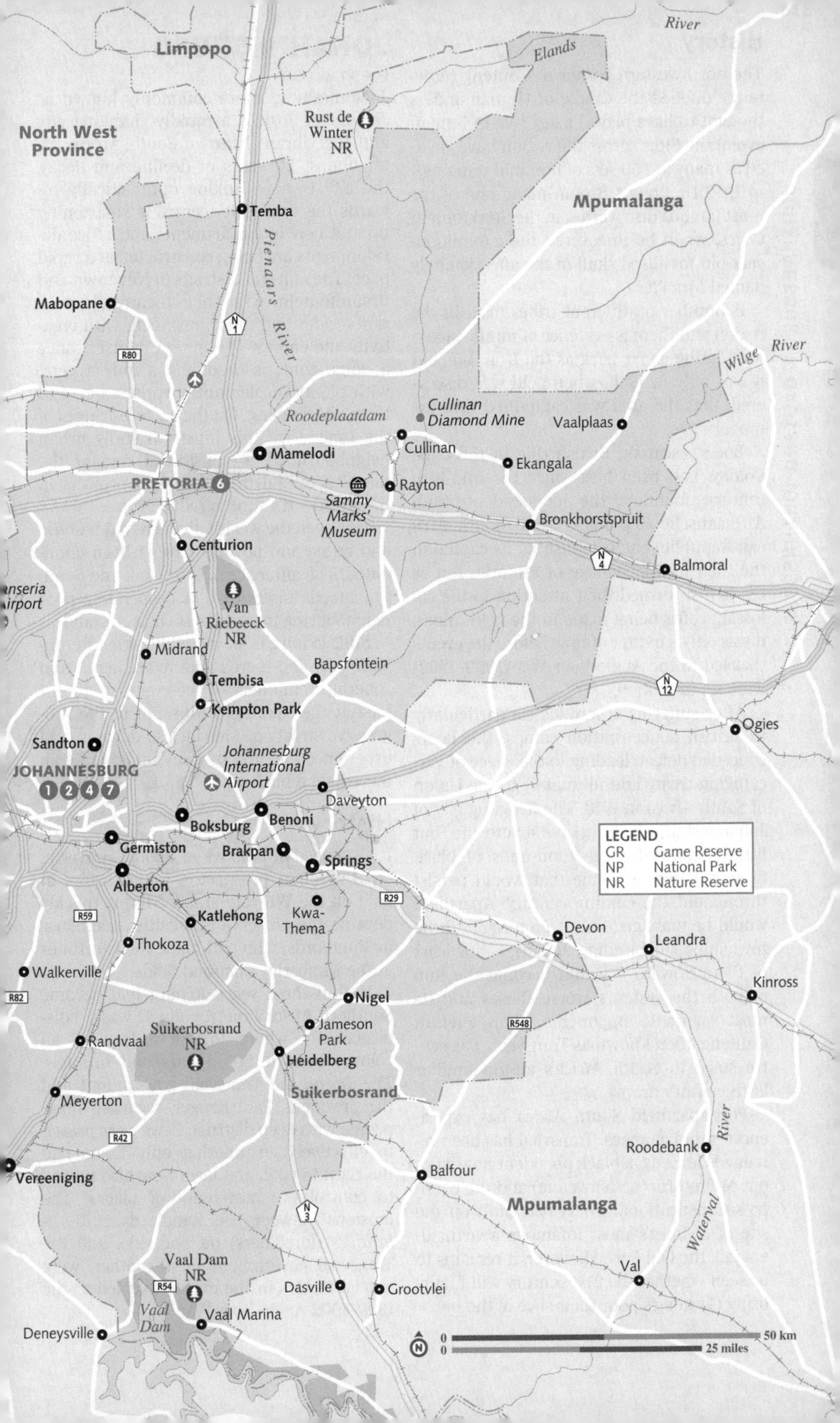

Limpopo
North West Province
Rust de Winter NR
Elands
River
Mpumalanga
Temba
Pienaars River
Mabopane
N1
R80
Wilge River
Roodeplaatdam
Cullinan Diamond Mine
Vaalplaas
Cullinan
Mamelodi
Ekangala
PRETORIA 6
Rayton
Sammy Marks' Museum
Bronkhorstspruit
Centurion
N4
Balmoral
Van Riebeeck NR
Midrand
Bapsfontein
Tembisa
N12
Kempton Park
Ogies
Sandton
Johannesburg International Airport
JOHANNESBURG 1 2 4 7
Daveyton
Benoni
Boksburg
Germiston
Brakpan
Springs
LEGEND
GR Game Reserve
NP National Park
NR Nature Reserve
Alberton
R29
R59
Kwa-Thema
Katlehong
Devon
Leandra
Thokoza
Walkerville
Kinross
R82
Nigel
Suikerbosrand NR
Jameson Park
R548
Randvaal
Heidelberg
Suikerbosrand
Meyerton
Waterval River
R42
Roodebank
Vereeniging
Balfour
N3
Mpumalanga
Vaal Dam NR
Val
R54
Dasville
Grootvlei
Vaal Dam
Vaal Marina
Deneysville
0 50 km
0 25 miles

History

The northwestern corner of Gauteng (*how-teng*), dubbed the Cradle of Humankind, is thought to have played a key role in human evolution. Sites across the region have yielded as many as 850 sets of hominid remains – in 1947 Dr Robert Broom made one of the most famous discoveries, in the Sterkfontein Caves, when he uncovered the 2.5-million-year-old fossilised skull of the affectionately named Mrs Ples.

A number of different tribes lived in the region and there is evidence of mining activities dating as far back as the Iron Age, but it was only in 1886, when gold was discovered, that the area was catapulted into the modern age.

Boers, escaping British rule in the Cape Colony, had been here since the mid-19th century, founding the independent Zuid-Afrikaansche Republiek (ZAR; South African Republic) and establishing its capital in the then frontier village of Pretoria. But as the British turned their attention to the colossal profits being made in the gold mines, it was only a matter of time before the events that led to the Anglo-Boer War (1899–1902) were set in motion.

After suffering severe losses, particularly in British concentration camps, the Boers conceded defeat, leading to the Peace of Vereeniging treaty and ultimately to the Union of South Africa in 1910. The fledgling city of Johannesburg (Jo'burg) burst into life, but little changed for the thousands of black miners. It was a theme that would persist throughout the coming century. Apartheid would be managed out of Pretoria, and the townships surrounding Jo'burg – not least of them Soweto – would become the hub of both the system's worst abuses and its most energetic opponents. Consequently, Gauteng, then known as Transvaal, was centre stage in South Africa's all-too-familiar 20th-century drama.

Post-apartheid South Africa has experienced rapid changes. Transvaal has been renamed Gauteng, a black president now rules out of Pretoria (or Tshwaane) and the country's Constitutional Court was built on the site of Jo'burg's most infamous apartheid-era jail, the Old Fort. However, it remains to be seen whether the 21st century will finally bring Gauteng's poor their slice of the pie.

JOHANNESBURG

POP 5.7 MILLION

Johannesburg, more commonly known as Jo'burg or Jozi, is a rapidly changing city and the vibrant heart of South Africa. After almost 20 years of decline and decay, the city is now looking optimistically towards the future. Its centre is smartening up and new loft apartments and office developments are being constructed at a rapid pace. The cultural districts of Newtown and Braamfontein, with their theatres, restaurants, cafes and museums, teem with creativity and energy. The Inner City itself, once a no-go zone, is becoming a tourist gem, with plenty of pleasant surprises. Oh, and there's Maboneng. On the eastern fringes of the Inner City, this hipster-friendly urban neighbourhood is considered one of the most successful urban-renewal projects in the world – it's sure to seduce you.

However, the wealth divide remains stark, and crime and poverty haven't been eliminated. The affluence of Rosebank and Sandton breeds discontent in desperately poor neighbouring townships such as Alexandra.

Still, Jo'burg is an incredibly friendly, unstuffy city and there's a lot to see here, from sobering reminders of the country's recent past at the Apartheid Museum to the progressive streets of Melville. So delve in and experience the buzz of a city undergoing an incredible rebirth.

History

It all started in 1886 when George Harrison, an Australian prospector, found traces of gold on the Witwatersrand. Mining quickly became the preserve of wealthy magnates, or Randlords, who had made their fortunes at the Kimberley diamond fields.

Within three years Jo'burg had become Southern Africa's metropolis. It was a boisterous city where fortune-seekers of all colours lived it up in bars and brothels. The Boers, the Transvaal government and the president, Paul Kruger, regarded these people with deep distrust. Laws were passed to effectively ensure that only Boers had the right to vote, and laws were also passed to control the movement of blacks. The tensions between the Randlords and *uitlanders* (foreigners) on one side, and the Transvaal government on the other, were crucial factors in the events that led to the 1899–1902 Anglo-Boer War.

JOHANNESBURG IN...

Two Days

Wander through the rejuvenated civic spaces of **Newtown** and **Constitution Hill** (p324), and check out the creative hub around **Braamfontein** (p323) before experiencing the magical energy of hip **Maboneng** (p324).

On day two gain some perspective at the **Apartheid Museum** (p325), then take a half-day tour of **Soweto** (p345) before heading to **Melville** (p334) for dinner in a trendy restaurant.

Four Days

Head west to the **Cradle of Humankind** (p349), where you can visit the **Sterkfontein Caves** (p350), chill out at the **Nirox sculpture park** (p350) and have a divine lunch at the **Cradle** (p350). Spend the night at **Maropeng Hotel** (p350).

On day four visit **Freedom Park** (p354) and the **Voortrekker Monument** (p351) on the outskirts of Pretoria. Head back to the leafy northern suburbs for retail therapy at **Sandton** (p342) and dinner in **Parkmore** (p339).

Under increasing pressure in the countryside, thousands of blacks moved to the city in search of jobs. Racial segregation had become entrenched during the interwar years, and from the 1930s onwards, vast squatter camps had developed around the outskirts of Jo'burg. Under black leadership these camps became well-organised cities.

Apartheid officially took hold during the 1960s, but this didn't prevent the arrival of black squatters in their thousands, and the city expanded further. Large-scale violence finally broke out in 1976, when the Soweto Students' Representative Council organised protests against the use of Afrikaans in black schools.

The most important change in the city's history came with the removal of apartheid and the country's first democratic elections in 1994. Since then, the black townships have been integrated into the municipal government system, the city centre is alive with hawkers and street stalls, and the suburbs are becoming increasingly multiracial.

Sights & Activities

Since the mass exodus of white-owned businesses in the 1990s, a steady recovery has been led by both the creative sector and far-sighted property developers. Public art is prettying up the streets and old warehouses, and art deco buildings have been snapped up by those who consider themselves to have good taste.

Whatever your inclination, the many historic spaces and places in Jo'burg will leave you speechless.

Inner City & Newtown

Ask South Africans what they think about downtown Johannesburg and the chances are they'll say 'unsafe' and 'rundown'. Not many are aware of the tremendous progress that is under way. Large areas of the Inner City are being revitalised, upgraded and modernised. Sure, there remain a number of dodgy enclaves, but what was before a no-go zone is regaining attractiveness.

One of the most appealing (and safest) areas is Marshalltown, Jo'burg's old financial and corporate district, where you'll find many mining-company and bank head offices. Amid the imposing skyscrapers you'll find some excellent cafes, plenty of small-scale sights and even a few inspiring parks where you can hone your people-watching skills.

Further north, the district called Newtown is also experiencing a massive revival.

During the day, you can walk pretty safely around the area west of the Carlton Centre and south of Jeppe St, but it pays to keep your wits about you, especially around Park Station. Don't flash around valuables such as cameras and watches, and avoid carrying bags.

Gandhi Square SQUARE

(Map p326; Inner City) Mohandas (Mahatma) Gandhi came to South Africa in 1893 and lived in Johannesburg, where he worked as a lawyer, from 1903 to 1914. The square was renamed Gandhi Sq in his honour and a bronze statue representing him as a young lawyer was erected in the middle.

Rissik Street Post Office HISTORIC BUILDING

(Map p326; Rissik St, Inner City) One of Jozi's most noteworthy heritage buildings is this grand post office dating from 1897. Sadly, the superb colonial-era building has been vacant and dilapidated since the 1990s, but there are plans to restore it to its former glory.

Johannesburg

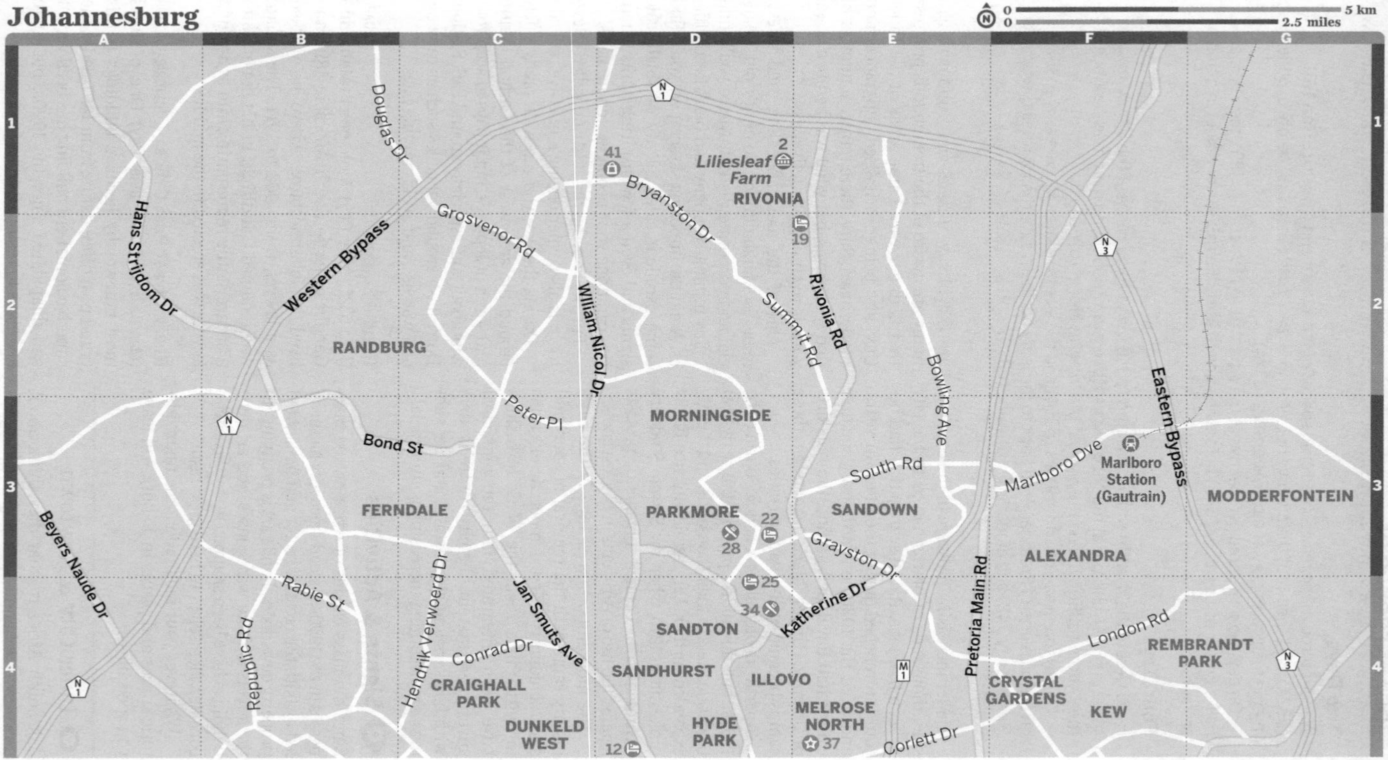

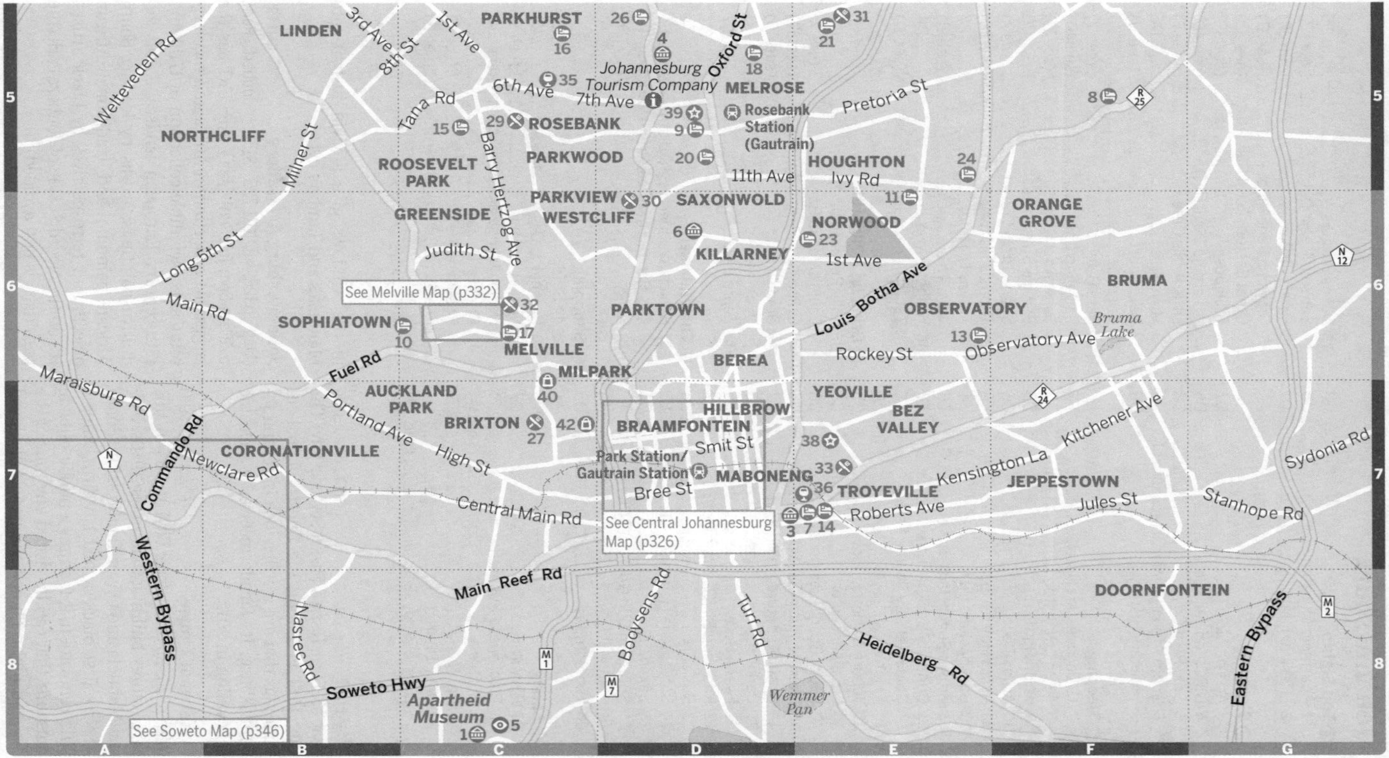
LINDEN
PARKHURST
NORTHCLIFF
ROOSEVELT PARK
GREENSIDE
PARKWOOD
ROSEBANK
PARKVIEW
WESTCLIFF
SAXONWOLD
MELROSE
HOUGHTON
NORWOOD
KILLARNEY
ORANGE GROVE
BRUMA
OBSERVATORY
PARKTOWN
SOPHIATOWN
MELVILLE
MILPARK
AUCKLAND PARK
BRIXTON
BEREA
HILLBROW
BRAAMFONTEIN
YEOVILLE
BEZ VALLEY
MABONENG
TROYEVILLE
JEPPESTOWN
CORONATIONVILLE
DOORNFONTEIN
Welteveden Rd
3rd Ave
8th St
1st Ave
Tana Rd
6th Ave
7th Ave
Milner St
Barry Hertzog Ave
Judith St
Long 5th St
Main Rd
Fuel Rd
Maraisburg Rd
Portland Ave
High St
Commando Rd
Newclare Rd
Central Main Rd
Western Bypass
Main Reef Rd
Nasrec Rd
Soweto Hwy
Apartheid Museum
Booysens Rd
Turf Rd
Wemmer Pan
Heidelberg Rd
Eastern Bypass
Oxford St
Pretoria St
Johannesburg Tourism Company
Rosebank Station (Gautrain)
11th Ave
Ivy Rd
1st Ave
Louis Botha Ave
Rockey St
Observatory Ave
Bruma Lake
Kitchener Ave
Kensington La
Sydonia Rd
Jules St
Stanhope Rd
Roberts Ave
Smit St
Park Station/ Gautrain Station
Bree St
See Melville Map (p332)
See Central Johannesburg Map (p326)
See Soweto Map (p346)
N1
N12
M1
M2
M7
R24
R25
A
B
C
D
E
F
G
5
6
7
8

Johannesburg

Top Sights
1 Apartheid Museum ... C8
2 Liliesleaf Farm ... D1

Sights
3 Arts on Main ... D7
4 CIRCA on Jellicoe ... D5
5 Gold Reef City ... C8
6 South African National Museum of Military History ... D6

Sleeping
7 12 Decades Art Hotel ... E7
8 44 on Livingston ... F5
9 54 on Bath ... D5
10 Arum Place ... C6
11 Ascot Hotel ... E6
12 Backpackers Ritz ... D4
13 Brown Sugar Backpackers ... E6
14 Curiocity Backpackers ... E7
Gold Reef City Theme Park Hotel ... (see 5)
15 Joburg Backpackers ... C5
16 Liz at Lancaster ... C5
17 Lucky Bean Guesthouse ... C6
18 Melrose Place Guest Lodge ... D5
19 Oasis Signature Hotel ... E2
20 Parkwood ... D5
21 Peech Hotel ... E5
22 Radisson Blu Gautrain Hotel ... D3
23 Residence ... E6
24 Satyagraha House ... E5
25 Saxon ... D4
Southern Sun Gold Reef City Hotel ... (see 5)
26 Ten Bompas ... D5

Eating
27 Bismillah ... C7
Blackanese Sushi ... (see 7)
Bukhara ... (see 34)
Canteen ... (see 3)
28 Delhi Dharbar ... D3
Doppio Zero ... (see 29)
29 Dukes Burgers ... C5
Eat Your Heart Out ... (see 7)
Eatery JHB ... (see 28)
Giovanni Pane Vino ... (see 11)
Great Eastern Food Bar ... (see 32)
Grillhouse ... (see 39)
Il Giardino Degli Ulivi ... (see 40)
Little Addis Café ... (see 7)
30 Moyo's ... D6
Next Door ... (see 11)
31 Orient ... E5
Pata Pata ... (see 7)
Salvation Cafe ... (see 40)
Schwarma Co ... (see 11)
32 Service Station ... C6
Sharp! Braai Corner ... (see 7)
Thomas Maxwell Bistro ... (see 28)
33 Troyeville Hotel ... E7
Vovo Telo ... (see 11)
34 Walnut Grove ... D4
Zahava's ... (see 11)

Drinking & Nightlife
35 Jolly Roger Pub ... C5
Lenin's Vodka Bar ... (see 7)
Office ... (see 29)
Stanley Beer Yard ... (see 40)
Uncle Merv's ... (see 7)
36 Zebra Inn ... E7

Entertainment
37 Bidvest Wanderers Stadium ... E4
38 Ellis Park – Emirates Airline Park ... E7
39 Katzy's ... D5

Shopping
40 44 Stanley ... C7
41 Bryanston Organic Market ... D1
Market on Main ... (see 3)
Nelson Mandela Square ... (see 34)
42 Oriental Plaza ... C7
Rosebank Mall ... (see 9)
Rosebank Sunday Market ... (see 9)

City Hall HISTORIC BUILDING
(Map p326; cnr Rissik & Market Sts, Inner City) The City Hall is among the finest colonial-era buildings that are worth a look in central Johannesburg. Its facade received a welcome renovation in 2012.

Chancellor House BUILDING, MUSEUM
(Map p326; 25 Fox St, Inner City) It was in this three-storey building that, in the 1950s, Nelson Mandela and Oliver Tambo set up South Africa's first black-owned law firm. After a 2012 renovation, it features a public 'outside museum' that can be visited any time of the day and night. Photos and panels displayed in the windows give a vivid insight into Mandela's and Tambo's lives.

Johannesburg Art Gallery GALLERY
(Map p326; 011-725 3130; Joubert Park; 10am-5pm Tue-Sun) FREE The JAG has the largest art collection in Africa and regularly rotates its incredible collection of 17th- and 18th-century European landscape and figurative paintings; works by leading South African painters; and traditional African objects and retrospectives by black artists. It's on the Noord St side of Joubert Park (the park itself is best avoided).

Standard Bank Art Gallery GALLERY
(Map p326; ☎011-631 1889; www.standardbankarts.com/gallery/; cnr Simmonds & Frederick Sts, Inner City; ⏰8am-4.30pm Mon-Fri, 9am-1pm Sat) FREE A wonderfully light-filled building featuring regularly changing exhibitions by important South African artists. It also has a permanent African art collection, some of which is on display at Wits University.

Top of Africa VIEWPOINT
(Map p326; 50th fl, Carlton Centre, 152 Commissioner St, Inner City; adult/child R15/10; ⏰9am-6pm Mon-Wed, to 2am Thu & Fri) The iconic Carlton Centre (223m) has been Africa's tallest building for more than 40 years now. The basement shelters a buzzing shopping mall. For awesome city vistas, head to the observation deck at the top (entrance is via a special lift one floor below street level).

Mary Fitzgerald Square SQUARE
(Map p326; Jeppe St, Inner City) Named after South Africa's first female trade unionist, this square is the best place to start a visit to central Jo'burg. The square is lined with an array of heads, carved from old railway sleepers by Newtown artists, and is bordered by the Jazz Walk of Fame, a Hollywood Blvd–style walkway that pays tribute to South Africa's most influential jazz musicians. There's also a bronze sculpture honouring Brenda Fassie, one of the country's most popular musicians, who died in 2004.

Museum Africa MUSEUM
(Map p326; ☎011-833 5624; www.gauteng.net/attractions/entry/museum_africa; Old Market Bldg, 121 Bree St, Newtown; ⏰9am-5pm Tue-Sun) FREE This museum is housed in the impressive old Bree St fruit market. The thoughtful curatorship features exhibitions on the Treason Trials of 1956–61, the development of South African music and the history of housing in the city. The satirical 'Cartoons in Context' are worth a look, as is the Sophiatown display, which contains a mock-up of a shebeen (unlicensed bar).

Market Theatre LANDMARK
(Map p326; www.markettheatre.co.za; cnr Bree & Miriam Makeba Sts, Newtown) This lively complex puts on regular shows and has a couple of restaurants and some craft stalls.

Nelson Mandela Bridge BRIDGE
(Map p326) Built two days after Mandela's 85th birthday in 2003, this cable-stayed bridge is the longest of its kind in Southern Africa and an icon of the rejuvenated city centre.

SAB World of Beer MUSEUM
(Map p326; ☎011-836 4900; www.worldofbeer.co.za; 15 President St, Newtown; admission & tour adult/child R75/20; ⏰10am-6pm Tue-Sat) Take a 1½-hour jaunt through the history of beer. Taste *chibuku* in a mock African village, sample a cheeky half-pint at a re-created Victorian pub, then nail two free pints in the bar afterwards. You even get a World of Beer glass keepsake.

Turbine Hall BUILDING
(Map p326; cnr Jeppe & Miriam Makeba Sts, Inner City) An icon of the city's rebirth, this massive power station was refurbished in 2007 and now houses the impressive new headquarters of AngloGold Ashanti.

Sci-Bono Discovery Centre MUSEUM
(Map p326; ☎011-639 8400; www.sci-bono.co.za; cnr Miriam Makeba & President Sts, Newtown; adult/child R35/20; ⏰9am-4.30pm Mon-Fri, to 4pm Sat & Sun) Testament to the remarkable reawakening of downtown Jo'burg, this well-organised science museum full of interactive exhibitions occupies a former power station.

Workers' Museum MUSEUM
(Map p326; ☎011-832 2447; 52 Jeppe St, Newtown; ⏰8am-4.30pm Mon-Sat) FREE This important museum is in the restored Electricity Department's compound, which was built in 1910 for 300-plus municipal workers and has been declared a national monument. There is a workers' library, a resource centre and a display of the living conditions of migrant workers.

Braamfontein

A resounding triumph of urban renewal, Braamfontein is one of Jo'burg's proudest exemplars of the continuous effort to transform once-neglected neighbourhoods into vibrant, modernised areas. Braamfontein is also the city's student capital – it's home to the University of Witwatersrand campus.

★ **Wits Art Museum** MUSEUM
(WAM; Map p326; ☎011-717 1365; www.witsfoundation.co.za; cnr Jorissen & Bertha Sts, Braamfontein; ⏰10am-4pm Wed-Sun) FREE Completed in May 2012, this modern museum is the leading museum of African art on the continent, with an extraordinary collection of 10,000 works and a dynamic program of events and exhibitions. With its clean, modern lines, it will also appeal to architecture buffs.

Planetarium MUSEUM
(Map p326; ☎011-717 1390; www.planetarium.co.za; Yale Rd, WITS University, Braamfontein; shows adult/concession R40/27; ⊙8.30am-4pm) If you're serious about astronomy, consider visiting the Planetarium. You can look around for free, or attend shows on Friday, Saturday and Sunday – check the website for exact times. There's an extra 'space travel' show on Saturday morning at 10.30am.

Origins Centre MUSEUM
(Map p326; ☎011-717 4700; www.origins.org.za; cnr Yale Rd & Enoch Sontonga Ave; adult/child incl audio guide R80/40; ⊙10am-5pm Mon-Sun) This stunning museum explores the African origins of humankind through interactive exhibits. The centre is brilliant for school-age children and holds the most formidable collection of rock art in the world, led by the work of the San tribe. An extra-cool offering is a DNA test that traces your ancestral heritage.

Hillbrow, Berea & Constitution Hill

Dominated by two iconic buildings – the 269m **Telkom Tower** and the cylindrical **Ponte City** – Hillbrow and neighbouring Berea were once the liveliest and most interesting suburbs in the city and were the nation's first 'Grey Areas' – zones where blacks and whites could live side by side.

These days, however, these densely populated neighbourhoods have a reputation for crime. Your best bet is to visit them with a savvy guide from Dlala Nje (p331).

Constitution Hill MUSEUM
(Map p326; ☎011-381 3100; www.constitutionhill.org.za; Kotze St; tours adult/child R50/20; ⊙9am-5pm Mon, Tue, Thu & Fri, to 2pm Wed, 10am-3pm Sat & Sun) Inspiring Constitution Hill is one of the city's most important attractions. It offers travellers interested in the modern South African story an integral understanding of the legal and historical ramifications of the struggle. The development focuses on South Africa's new Constitutional Court, built within the ramparts of the Old Fort, which dates from 1892 and was once a notorious prison, where many of the country's high-profile political activists, including Nelson Mandela and Mohandas (Mahatma) Gandhi, were held.

The modern structure incorporates sections of the old prison walls, plus large windows that allow visitors to watch the proceedings.

Maboneng

On a stretch of the eastern fringe of downtown Jo'burg, this once-gritty enclave is the darling of the many architectural and creative hubs springing up across the city. A breeding ground of creativity and innovation packed full of galleries, artist and

JO'BURG FESTIVAL CALENDAR

Chinese New Year At Wemmer Pan, south of the centre. Celebrated in January or February.

Dance Umbrella (www.danceforumsouthafrica.co.za) The premier showcase of South African dance performance takes place in February and March.

Rand Easter Show (www.randshow.co.za) Held during April at the Johannesburg Expo Centre.

Joy of Jazz Festival (www.joyofjazz.co.za) Staged in venues across Newtown in late August and September.

Arts Alive Festival (www.arts-alive.co.za) Held in September. The festival provides a particularly good opportunity to hear excellent music, on or off the official program. Most events are staged in Newtown.

City of Gold (www.cityofgoldfestival.co.za) Showcases the finest in both international and local graffiti and street artists. Includes street-art tours, an exhibition and large-scale mural projects. It's held in early October at various venues around the Inner City.

Gay Pride March (www.johannesburgpride.co.za) Held on the last Saturday every October.

Johannesburg Carnival Held on New Year's Eve. This event, which started on the last night of 2010, sees a parade of choirs, troupes, floats and bands from Hillbrow to Newtown, finishing with a party in Mary Fitzgerald Sq.

cultural spaces, cool bars, coffee shops, restaurants, fashion shops and startups, Maboneng is an exemplar of Jo'burg's vision for future and is a hipster paradise. Be sure to explore its dynamic streets and soak up its unique atmosphere.

Arts on Main GALLERY
(Map p320; www.artsonmain.info; 264 Fox St, Maboneng; ⌚10am-4pm Tue, Wed & Fri-Sun, to 8pm Thu) FREE This multifaceted arts centre, occupying a former warehouse with a superb courtyard, has a mission to generate some cultural vibrancy in the Maboneng precinct. The once-dilapidated building has been transformed into a creative haven with cultural spaces, artists' studios, galleries, various retail areas and a restaurant, offering visitors regular performances and events. It's also home to an incredibly popular Sunday market.

Northern Suburbs

CIRCA on Jellicoe GALLERY
(Map p320; ☎011-788 4805; www.circaonjellicoe.co.za; 2 Jellicoe Ave, Rosebank; ⌚9am-6pm Tue-Fri, to 1pm Sat) An essential part of the Jo'burg cultural landscape, CIRCA on Jellicoe is both an architectural landmark and a superb gallery hosting contemporary works of art. Overlooking the northern suburbs, the spiral structure houses unusual sculptures, sketches and contemporary work from across South Africa. It is surrounded by 400 10m-tall variegated aluminum 'fins' that reference a protective Zulu *kraal* (livestock enclosure).

★ **Liliesleaf Farm** MUSEUM
(Map p320; ☎011-803 7882; www.liliesleaf.co.za; 7 George Ave, Rivonia; adult/child R60/35; ⌚8.30am-5pm Mon-Fri, 9am-4pm Sat & Sun) Possibly the city's most underrated museum, Liliesleaf Farm was the secret headquarters of the ANC (African National Congress) during the 1960s and reopened as a museum in June 2008. This well-organised complex tells the story of South Africa's liberation struggle through a series of high-tech, interactive exhibits.

South African National Museum of Military History MUSEUM
(Map p320; ☎010-001 3515; www.ditsong.org.za; 22 Erlswold Way, Saxonwold; adult/child R30/25; ⌚9am-4.30pm) If you're fascinated by guns, tanks and aircraft, you can see artefacts and implements of destruction from the 1899–1902 Anglo-Boer War through to WWII at one of Jo'burg's most popular museums. It's at the eastern end of the zoo's grounds.

Southern Suburbs

★ **Apartheid Museum** MUSEUM
(Map p320; ☎011-309 4700; www.apartheidmuseum.org; cnr Gold Reef Rd & Northern Parkway, Ormonde; adult/child R70/55; ⌚9am-5pm) The Apartheid Museum illustrates the rise and fall of South Africa's era of segregation and oppression, and is an absolute must-see. It uses film, text, audio and live accounts to provide a chilling insight into the architecture and implementation of the apartheid system, as well as inspiring stories of the struggle towards democracy. It's invaluable in understanding the inequalities and tensions that still exist today. Located 8km south of the city centre, just off the M1 freeway.

Visiting the museum is an overwhelming experience; particularly distressing is a small chamber in which hang 131 nooses, representative of the 131 government opponents who were executed under antiterrorism laws.

Gold Reef City AMUSEMENT PARK
(Map p320; ☎011-248 6800; www.goldreefcity.co.za; cnr Northern Parkway & Data Cres, Ormonde; admission R175, child under 130cm R110; ⌚9.30am-5pm Wed-Sun) Offers a vaudevillian ride through Johannesburg's gold-rush period. Ninety per cent Disneyland clone, this theme park only offers a token nod to historical authenticity but provides ample means for filling a spare afternoon, especially if you have kids in tow.

Sleeping

There are tons of sleeping options in Jo'burg, with most of the tourist accommodation concentrated in the northern suburbs.

Melville and Norwood provide the best options if you like to walk to bars and restaurants. Places in the northern suburbs tend to be quite spread out, with no entertainment or shopping options on their doorstep.

The city centre is slowly improving its tourist infrastructure, but there is still only a handful of decent options. If you want to be close to the Inner City, your best bet is to stay in Braamfontein or Maboneng.

Most hostels offer free pick-up from the airport or the Gautrain stations at Sandton and Rosebank. Nearly all hostels are on the route of the Baz Bus. Guesthouses and hotels will also arrange for an airport pick-up, but you'll be charged around R600. Most hotels organise tours to Soweto, Kruger National Park and elsewhere.

Central Johannesburg

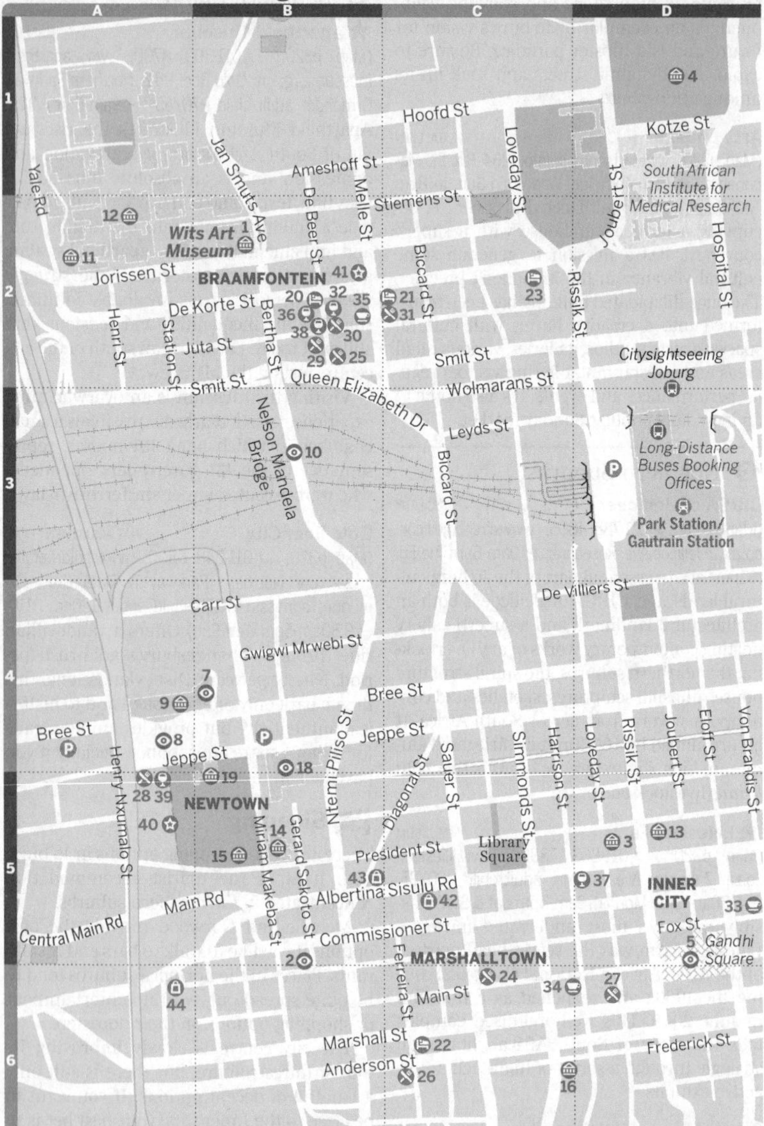

🛏 Inner City

Faircity Mapungubwe Hotel Apartments APARTMENT $$
(Map p326; ☎011-429 2600; www.mapungubwehotel.co.za; 50-54 Marshall St, Marshalltown; d R1215-1515; P) Popular with the nearby mining and banking businesses, this renovated office building is a safe choice in downtown Jo'burg, despite the fact it feels a tad impersonal. Staff can be a little aloof, but the facilities include a small pool

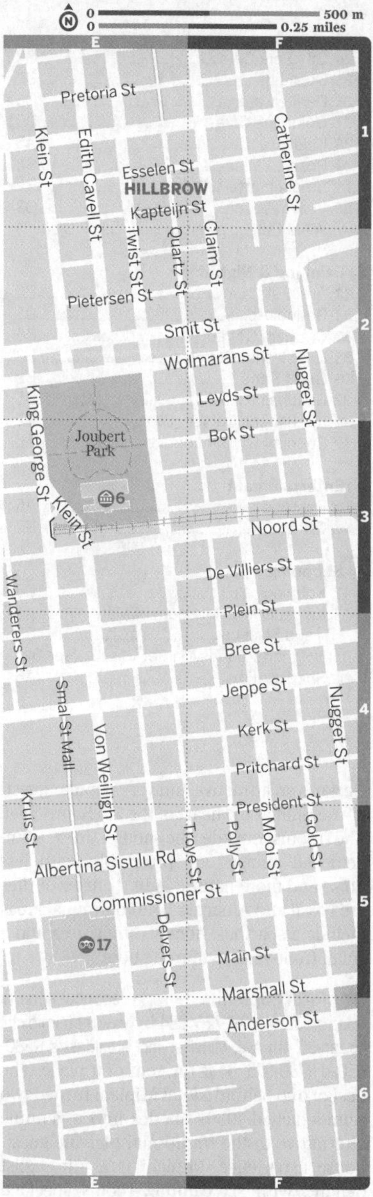

deck, restaurant and converted vault bar. The open-plan apartments are spacious and well equipped. Ask about special rates on weekends.

Braamfontein

Bannister Hotel HOTEL $

(Map p326; 011-403 6888; www.bannisterhotel.co.za; 9 De Beer St, Braamfontein; d R545-695;) If you're after stumbling access to Braamfontein's bars and restaurants then this recently modernised establishment is a no-brainer. Its rooms are discreetly decorated, functional and comfortable, with quality mattresses and prim bathrooms. Double-glazing keeps out the traffic hum from busy De Beer St. Another draw is the on-site restaurant. Covered parking is available about 100m away and costs R40.

easyHotel HOTEL $$

(Map p326; 011-242 8600; www.easyhotel.com; 90 De Korte St, Braamfontein; d R600-850;) No fuss, no luxury. In the heart of Braamfontein, this 60-room hotel with a bold orange and brown colour scheme is functional, quirky and stylish at the same time. It's also convenient if you want to be close to the action. If you're a light sleeper, ask for a room on the upper floors. Wi-fi costs R25 per hour and breakfast is R100.

Protea Hotel Parktonian HOTEL $$

(Map p326; 011-403 5741; www.parktonian.co.za; 120 De Korte St, Braamfontein; s/d incl breakfast R1000/1300;) As far as looks go, this tall, modern building is a real plain Jane, but it offers great facilities, rates are good and it's handily set if you want to be close to Park Station (complimentary shuttle to/from the hotel) or Braamfontein's bars and restaurants. There's a fabulous rooftop terrace (with small pool) on which to have an evening drink.

Maboneng

Curiocity Backpackers BACKPACKERS $

(Map p320; 072 880 9583, 011-592 0515; www.curiocitybackpackers.com; 302 Fox St, Maboneng; dm R160-200, s/d without bathroom R260/360, rooftop r R500;) This is a superlative place to stay thanks to the dedication of young proprietor Bheki Dube. Occupying a converted printing house in the desirable Maboneng precinct, this quirky, offbeat backpackers features clean dorms, unadorned yet neat rooms and a rooftop suite. It also has a buzzing bar, kitchen facilities and a small restaurant. The congenial atmosphere is hard to beat.

Central Johannesburg

Top Sights
1 Wits Art Museum ... B2

Sights
2 Chancellor House ... B5
3 City Hall ... D5
4 Constitution Hill ... D1
5 Gandhi Square ... D5
6 Johannesburg Art Gallery ... E3
7 Market Theatre ... B4
8 Mary Fitzgerald Square ... A4
9 Museum Africa ... A4
10 Nelson Mandela Bridge ... B3
11 Origins Centre ... A2
12 Planetarium ... A2
13 Rissik Street Post Office ... D5
14 SAB World of Beer ... B5
15 Sci-Bono Discovery Centre ... B5
16 Standard Bank Art Gallery ... C6
17 Top of Africa ... E5
18 Turbine Hall ... B4
19 Workers' Museum ... B5

Sleeping
20 Bannister Hotel ... B2
21 easyHotel ... C2
22 Faircity Mapungubwe Hotel Apartments ... C6
23 Protea Hotel Parktonian ... C2

Eating
86 Public ... (see 31)
24 City Perk Café ... C6
25 Dahleahs ... B2
26 Darkie Cafe ... C6
27 Goldmine Cafe ... D6
28 Kaldi's ... A5
29 Post ... B2
30 Smokehouse & Grill ... B2
31 Velo ... C2
WAM Cafe ... (see 1)

Drinking & Nightlife
32 Anti-Est ... B2
33 Boundless ... D5
34 Cramers Coffee ... C6
35 Doubleshot Coffee & Tea ... B2
36 Great Dane ... B2
37 Guildhall ... D5
38 Kitchener's Carvery Bar ... B2
39 Sophiatown Bar Lounge ... A5

Entertainment
40 Bassline ... A5
41 Orbit ... B2

Shopping
42 Kohinoor ... C5
43 KwaZulu Muti Museum of Man and Science ... B5
Neighbourgoods Market ... (see 30)
44 Sheds@1Fox ... A6

Mainstreetwalks (p331), which offers great walking tours of various suburbs, is based here.

12 Decades Art Hotel BOUTIQUE HOTEL **$$**
(Map p320; ☎011-026 5601; www.urbanhiphotels.com; 7th fl, Main Street Life Bldg, 286 Fox St, Maboneng; d R900; P❄📶) This terrific concept hotel in the heart of the Maboneng precinct has 12 7th-floor rooms (the rest are residential), each one designed by a different international pairing and inspired by a particular era in the city's history. The Sir Abe Bailey Suite takes on a late-19th-century Chinese gold rush aesthetic, while 'Perpetual Liberty' is decidedly more contemporary. A special experience.

No breakfast is served, but there's no shortage of eateries nearby.

Melville

Sleepy Gecko GUESTHOUSE **$**
(Map p332; ☎082 745 0434, 011-482 5224; www.sleepygecko.co.za; 84 3rd Ave, Melville; s/d incl breakfast from R450/600; P❄@🏊) The laid-back Gecko is an attractive and very popular guesthouse right at the heart of the 7th St mischief. The rooms outside the house, in a semi-detached annexe, are preferable, with less noise and more natural light – our favourites are Fossil and Amarula. The communal areas include a spacious, homey dining area and a small front-yard swimming pool.

★**Motel Mipichi** BOUTIQUE HOTEL **$$**
(Map p332; ☎011-726 8844; www.motelmipichi.co.za; 35 4th Ave, Melville; incl breakfast s R580-650, d R780-975; P@) A gem of a place. The design duo behind Motel Mipichi turned two semidetached 1930s abodes into a genuine alternative to the traditional Melville guesthouse experience. Mipichi is a minimalist delight, with six calming rooms speckled with pastel splotches and walk-through showers. The open-plan kitchen and living area, with original Portuguese tiles, is an ideal place to decompress. Book ahead.

Lucky Bean Guesthouse GUESTHOUSE **$$**
(Map p320; ☎082 902 4514; www.luckybeantree.co.za; 129 1st Ave, Melville; incl breakfast s R600-

700, d R850-900; P wifi ac) Owner Conway has turned this villa into a peaceful, welcoming B&B with stylish, large and well-equipped rooms (with private entrances) and great amenities, like flat-screen TVs, quality bedding, a swimming pool and insider tips on the best Melville has to offer. The property is an easy walk to 7th St, Melville's most vibrant strip. Book early, as it fills fast.

Arum Place GUESTHOUSE **$$**
(Map p320; ☎011-482 5247; www.arumplace.co.za; cnr 1st & Motor Sts, Melville; s/d incl breakfast R675/900; P wifi pool) This stately 1935 villa on the outskirts of Melville is just the ticket for those seeking a stylish 'home away from home' experience. The eight rooms are different in design and are comfortably spread out on two floors; our choice is 'Touch of Grey', with its own terrace and entrance. In the garden you'll find a highly enticing pool area.

It's located on a pleasant street, though a decent walk to 7th St; luckily, the helpful owners will happily drive you to the restaurant of your choice.

Ginnegaap Guest House GUESTHOUSE **$$**
(Map p332; ☎011-482 3507; www.ginnegaap.co.za; 54 4th Ave, Melville; incl breakfast s R690-750, d R850-950; P wifi) Ginnegaap is a contemporary inner-city townhouse attached to an old-world Melville beauty. Guests come for the established garden that runs right up to the front gate, or to slump blissfully on the wraparound verandah. Service is prompt, yet discreet, while the rooms are excellent value for the quality of bedding, the warmth of design and the overall size.

Saffron Guesthouse & Johannesburg Suites GUESTHOUSE **$$**
(Map p332; ☎011-726 6646; www.saffronguesthouse.co.za; cnr 5th Ave & 7th St, Melville; s/d incl breakfast R790/990; P ac wifi) Just a hop, skip and jump from the bustle of 7th Ave, Saffron is quite a find, with seven modern, elegant and comfortable rooms with sparkling bathrooms and fancy decorative touches. The only downside: there's no pool. For breakfast, Saffron has arrangements with a nearby cafe.

84 on 4th Guesthouse GUESTHOUSE **$$**
(Map p332; ☎011-482 2725; www.84onfourth.co.za; 84 4th Ave, Melville; incl breakfast s R750-900, d R850-1100; P wifi) A coin's toss from the 7th St hoo-ha, this rambling home is a reliable choice if you want to be in the thick of things. Rooms vary widely – some are small and unpretentious, while others are grand and stylish – and are arranged around a garden.

Northern Suburbs

Brown Sugar Backpackers BACKPACKERS **$**
(Map p320; ☎011-648 7397; www.brownsugarbackpackers.com; 75 Observatory Ave, Observatory; incl breakfast camping per person R130, dm/s/d without bathroom from R180/340/240, s/d R340/400; P @ wifi pool) A bonanza for budget-conscious visitors, this venture is set in a large mansion that looks like a miniature castle. The wide assortment of options includes dorms with bathroom, a female-only dorm, log cabins and a few quirkily decorated private rooms, as well as TV lounge, pool, and kitchen and laundry facilities. Bonus: free pick-up from the airport or Park Station.

Dinners (R65) are available on request. Note that credit cards are accepted but there's an additional 5% commission.

Backpackers Ritz BACKPACKERS **$**
(Map p320; ☎011-325 7125; www.backpackers-ritz.co.za; 1A North Rd, Dunkeld West; dm/s/d without bathroom R165/330/495; P wifi pool) A longstanding institution, the Ritz scores high on its excellent shared facilities, prime location and beautiful views. It's owned by three brothers, who ensure a family atmosphere is maintained on its sprawling, leafy grounds. The 12- to 14-bed dorms are spacious, and there are plans to renovate the shared bathrooms. A touch-up in some private rooms wouldn't do any harm either.

Joburg Backpackers BACKPACKERS **$**
(Map p320; ☎011-888 4742; www.joburgbackpackers.com; 14 Umgwezi Rd, Emmarentia; dm R150, r with/without bathroom R480/380; P wifi pool) This discreet hostel in the leafy streets of Emmarentia is clean, safe and well run. It has a range of well-appointed rooms and a relaxed country feel. The en-suite rooms are terrific value and open onto big grassy lawns, while the eight- and 10-bed dorms are spacious and spotless. No meals are served, but Greenside's eateries are a 10-minute stroll away.

★ **Oasis Signature Hotel** HOTEL **$$**
(Map p320; ☎082 857 0707, 011-807 4351; www.oasisguesthouse.co.za; 29 Homestead Rd, Rivonia; incl breakfast s R1100-1500, d R1400-1800; P ac pool) This is a delightful suburban hideaway, presided over by an astute couple who cater for businesspeople and holidaymakers with

equal aplomb. The lush garden surrounds feature a kidney-shaped pool and a spacious *lapa* (South African thatched gazebo). The 14 rooms vary in size and price, but all are stylish and thoughtfully furnished. The breakfast smorgasbord is worthy of special mention.

If you're feeling peckish and don't fancy venturing out, there's an on-site restaurant (from Monday to Thursday).

★Satyagraha House GUESTHOUSE $$
(Map p320; ☎011-485 5928; www.satyagrahahouse.com; 15 Pine Rd, Orchards; d incl breakfast from R1800; P 📶) A wonderful urban sanctuary, Satyagraha is the former home of Mohandas (Mahatma) Gandhi, who lived here between 1907 and 1908. This heritage building has been restored into an innovative guesthouse and museum. The seven rooms are organised into a *kraal*, and the intimate history of the great pacifist's time here is on display to reward guests in unexpected ways. Meals are vegetarian.

★Parkwood BOUTIQUE HOTEL $$
(Map p320; ☎011-880 1748; www.theparkwood.com; 72 Worcester Rd, Parkwood; d incl breakfast R1700-2000; P ❄ @ 📶 🏊) Comfort, charm and atmosphere: this superb venture has it all. It offers the chance to unplug in a series of separate, narrow, self-contained buildings that ensure discretion during your stay. The rooms are all class, thanks to the interior-designer owner, with contemporary art facing stone walls, day beds facing fountains, two lap pools, a library and a gym. Dinners on request.

It's within walking distance of the Gautrain station.

44 on Livingston GUESTHOUSE $$
(Map p320; ☎011-485 1156; www.44onlivingston.com; 5 Sandler Rd, Linksfield; s/d incl breakfast from R780/950; P @ 🏊) This lovely, small guesthouse in the heart of Jewish Johannesburg has all the hallmarks of a great deal; seven tasteful, immaculate rooms complete with swish bathrooms, quality bedding and luxurious linens as well as a large pool. In-house massage is available and dinner costs R140. One downside: there's no air-con. Brilliant value.

Liz at Lancaster B&B $$
(Map p320; ☎011-442 8083; www.lizatlancaster.co.za; 79 Lancaster Ave, Craighall Park; incl breakfast s R800-1090, d R950-1310; P @ 📶 🏊) It's pure pleasure to walk into this modern oasis after a day's sightseeing. The bathrooms are beautifully kept, the rooms are well appointed and comfortable, the breakfasts are generous and the welcome is more than friendly. All units – two rooms, three flatlets and two family-friendly cottages – have their own entrances and courtyards. A safe choice.

Melrose Place Guest Lodge HOTEL $$
(Map p320; ☎083 457 4021, 011-442 5231; www.melroseplace.co.za; 12A North St, Melrose; s/d incl breakfast R1375/1700; P 📶 🏊) Life feels less hurried in this oasis of calm, between Rosebank and Sandton. This secluded country-style home harbours 30 rooms and is perfect for those who crave space – the expansive garden is a good place to mooch around and soak up the tranquil charm, or you can relax in the large swimming pool. Evening meals are available on request.

Radisson Blu Gautrain Hotel HOTEL $$
(Map p320; ☎011-245 8000; www.radissonblu.com; cnr West St & Rivonia Rd, Sandton; d from R2360; P ❄ 📶 🏊) A brisk jaywalk from Sandton's Gautrain station exit, this mammoth hotel is a great place to stay if you have a plane to catch in the morning. The rooms are cleverly designed with showers facing into the bedroom. The restaurant is excellent and the splash pool outside the lobby is a real scene.

Ascot Hotel HOTEL $$
(Map p320; ☎011-483 3371; www.ascothotel.co.za; 59 Grant Ave, Norwood; d incl breakfast R980-1450; P @ 📶) The Ascot is a stylish business hotel with a red-roped lobby entrance and adjacent day spa. The sense of affordable prestige suits the suburb's easygoing attitude. Rooms are smallish but well presented and comfortable. The prime selling point here is the location, within hollering distance of some of the neighbourhoods's best bars and restaurants.

★Residence BOUTIQUE HOTEL $$$
(Map p320; ☎011-853 2480; www.theresidence.co.za; 17 4th Ave, Houghton; d incl breakfast R2900-4500; P ❄ @ 📶 🏊) If you could smell charm, this super-smooth boutique hotel set in a former embassy would reek of it to high heaven. This quiet little paradise is the epitome of a refined cocoon, with 17 opulent, individually designed suites and swish communal areas. After a day of turf pounding, take a dip in the stress-melting pool or relax in the spa.

54 on Bath BOUTIQUE HOTEL $$$
(Map p320; ☎011-344 8500; www.tsogosunhotels.com; 54 Bath Ave, Rosebank; d incl breakfast from

DON'T MISS

BEST TOURS OF JO'BURG

Despite the positive changes that are underway, Jo'burg may still feel a bit intimidating for a number of travellers. The best (and safest) way to get your bearings and gain confidence is in the company of a knowledgeable tour guide. Whether it's a focus on history, architecture, urban regeneration, cultural life or street art that you're after, you'll find an experienced guide to lead the way.

Mainstreetwalks (☎072 880 9583; www.mainstreetwalks.co.za) Led by young entrepreneur Bheki Dube, who also manages Curiocity Backpackers, Mainstreetwalks specialises in tours of Maboneng, where it is based, but it also offers excellent tours of the Inner City, Troyeville and the utterly fascinating Little Addis Ethiopian district. And if you want to get a taste of Jo'burg nightlife, the Underground Pub Crawl is a must.

JoburgPlaces (☎082 894 5216; www.joburgplaces.com) Gerald Garner's inner-city tours are sure to change your perceptions about downtown Jo'burg. A hot favourite is the six-hour Regenerated Inner City Walk, which explores the way central Johannesburg has changed over recent years. Other walking tours include Western Edge to Gandhi Sq (three hours), Inner City Swimming Pools (six hours) and Fashion District & Little Addis (five hours).

Past Experiences (☎083 701 3046, 011-678 3905; www.pastexperiences.co.za) Run by Jo Buitendach and her team of hip guides, Past Experiences offers something different, with a range of fascinating tours that have a special focus on graffiti, street art and shopping. Participants have the opportunity to learn about artists' history and the local graffiti culture. Tours take in Braamfontein, Newtown and the Fashion District. Warmly recommended.

Mulaudzi Alexandra Tours (☎071 279 3654, 061 365 7695; www.alexandratours.co.za) Explore Alexandra, one of South Africa's oldest townships, in the company of friendly Jeff Mulaudzi. Born and raised in Alexandra, this young entrepreneur offers a two- to four-hour bicycle tour where you'll venture into the heart of this lesser-known township. It's a truly enlightening experience. Jeff meets visitors at the Marlboro Gautrain station, where secure parking is available.

Dlala Nje (☎072 397 2269, 082 550 8615; www.dlalanje.org) Run by Nickolaus Bauer and Mike Luptak, this pioneering company offers unique tours to three of Jo'burg's most impoverished and misunderstood areas: Hillbrow, Berea and the West African immigrant community of Yeoville. This is a great opportunity to change negative perceptions about these districts and learn more about the diverse communities that live there.

Tours start from the iconic Ponte City, where Dlala Nje operates a community centre. A visit of Ponte City is also included in the Hillbrow tour.

Cashan Tours (☎082 491 9370; www.cashanafrica.com) Run by Jo'burg native and wildlife guide Chris Green, these tailor-made tours are recommended for their passion, deep knowledge and informality. Accommodation is also available.

R3700; P❄📶🏊) Best described as 'urban chic', this sexy number is a short amble from Rosebank's shopping malls. The 75 rooms are spacious and elegantly restrained, and the uber-cool 4th-floor garden terrace and pool deck is a great place to decompress. Extra in-house perks include a top-notch restaurant, two bars and a fitness center.

If you want a room with city views, snaffle one of the poolside rooms on the upper floors. There's a free shuttle service to the Gautrain station.

Ten Bompas BOUTIQUE HOTEL **$$$**
(Map p320; ☎011-341 0282; www.tenbompas.com; 10 Bompas Rd, Dunkeld West; ste incl breakfast R3500; P❄📶🏊) More centrally located than some other top Johannesburg hotels – it's in the upmarket neighbourhood of Dunkeld West – 'Ten Rooms' is also a pioneer of the boutique tag. Dark wood and savannah hues colour an exquisite private collection of African art. The restaurant is a destination in its own right.

Melville

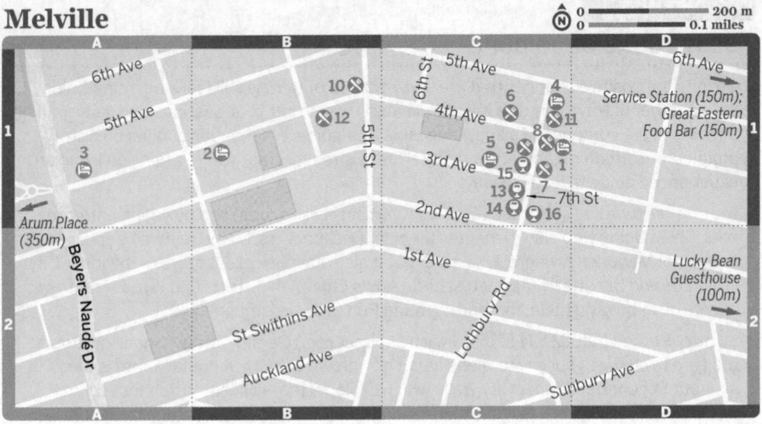

Melville

Sleeping

1 84 on 4th Guesthouse........C1
2 Ginnegaap Guest House........B1
3 Motel Mipichi........A1
4 Saffron Guesthouse & Johannesburg Suites........C1
5 Sleepy Gecko........C1

Eating

6 Bambanani........C1
7 Brauhaus........C1
8 Café de la Creme........C1
9 La Luna of Melville........C1
10 Leopard........B1
11 Lucky Bean........C1
12 Picobella........B1

Drinking & Nightlife

13 Jo'Anna Melt Bar........C1
14 Liberation Cafe........C1
15 Ratz Bar........C1
16 Six Cocktail Bar & Restaurant........C1

Peech Hotel BOUTIQUE HOTEL $$$
(Map p320; ☎011-537 9797; www.thepeech.co.za; 61 North St, Melrose; d incl breakfast R2400-2800; P ❄ ☰ ≋) Your money goes far with these four converted duplex apartment blocks scattered amid a beautifully landscaped garden. The 16 rooms are amply sized and feature subtle trendy design details, but it's the setting that's the pull here. Another plus is the pool.

Saxon HOTEL $$$
(Map p320; ☎011-292 6000; www.thesaxon.com; 36 Saxon Rd, Sandhurst; d incl breakfast from R7000; P ❄ @ ☰ ≋) The pride of Sandhurst is a palatial suite hotel where Mandela completed his famed memoir. If you're not bowled over by features such as private elevators, personal attendants and the finest day spa in the country, you certainly will be by the nifty pool, the high-quality restaurant and the exclusively designed suites. Pure bliss if you're after some serious cosseting and privacy.

Southern Suburbs

Gold Reef City Theme Park Hotel HOTEL $$
(Map p320; ☎011-248 5700; www.tsogosunhotels.com; 14 Shaft St, Ormonde; d incl breakfast R1600; P ❄ ☰) This recently renovated venture strategically located inside the theme-park gates is easy on the eye, with its decor reminiscent of a turn-of-the-century mining town. It scores high on amenities and its 75 rooms are spacious and lavishly appointed.

Southern Sun Gold Reef City Hotel HOTEL $$
(Map p320; ☎011-248 5000; www.tsogosunhotels.com; cnr Northern Parkway & Data Cres, Ormonde; s/d incl breakfast from R1750/1850; P ❄ ☰) If you're sleepless in the southern suburbs, these colourful and plush rooms are great-value, four-star affairs. They contain faux-riche furniture, comfy beds and salubrious bathrooms. Guests receive free entry to the Gold Reef City Theme Park. The hitch? It's a bit noisy. There are only 38 rooms, so be sure to reserve.

Airport Area

Africa Footprints GUESTHOUSE $
(☎011-391 8448; www.airportaccommodation.co.za; 1 Crestwood Rd, Kempton Park; incl break-

fast s R540-650, d R650-750; P ❄ 📶 🏊) A good pick if you need to stay near the airport (it's 7km from OR Tambo), Africa Footprints offers a good combination of business facilities and home comforts. The 14 rooms are nothing exceptional but are well priced and the breakfast is substantial. Note that the cheaper rooms are not air-conditioned. Free one-way transport from the airport.

Dinners are available on request.

Eating

Jo'burg is a fabulous city for foodies, with restaurants to suit all persuasions. Melville, Greenside, Braamfontein, Maboneng and increasingly the Inner City have lots of fun, lively places to feast.

Inner City & Newtown

Kaldi's VEGETARIAN, CAFE $

(Map p326; ☎083 757 0277; 30 Jeppe St, Newtown; mains R30-50; ⏰7.30am-5pm Mon-Fri, to 3.30pm Sat; 🥗) Opposite Museum Africa, this agreeable little vegan and vegetarian spot sells baked goods (including highly popular muffins and cinnamon buns) as well as an array of sandwiches, wraps and salads. The reasonable prices and all-day breakfasts keep things busy. There's also first-rate coffee and vitamin-packed fruit juices.

Darkie Cafe CAFE $$

(Map p326; ☎011-492 1556; cnr Anderson & Ferreira Sts, Marshalltown, Inner City; mains R60-130; ⏰6am-9pm Mon-Thu & Sat, to 11pm Fri) The king of cafes in central Jo'burg, snazzy Darkie Cafe is never short of a discriminating mob. That's all thanks to four winning details: its location in the heart of Jo'burg's banking and mining district; the uplifting ambience; the design-led decor; and, of course, the excellent something-for-everyone menu.

City Perk Café CAFE $$

(Map p326; ☎011-838 4993; www.cityperkcafe.co.za; 70 Fox St, Marshalltown, Inner City; mains R70-140; ⏰7.30am-4.30pm Mon-Fri) Good luck at securing a seat at this super-popular cafe that makes splendid breakfasts, sandwiches, wraps, grills and salads as well as serving decent coffee at affordable prices. Lunch for under R80? Count us in! Ample outdoor seating on warm days.

Goldmine Cafe SOUTH AFRICAN $$

(Map p326; ☎011-689 1000; 58 Anderson St, Marshalltown, Inner City; mains R45-110, buffets R140-160; ⏰6am-10pm) This favourite cafe on the ground floor of the Reef Hotel has a relaxed vibe and pleasingly kooky industrial interior. The visibly busy kitchen generates traditional meals without fanfare: stir-fried beef, pork ribs, burgers and sandwiches.

Braamfontein

Post CAFE $

(Map p326; ☎072 248 2078; 70 Juta St, Braamfontein; mains R35-60; ⏰6.30am-4pm Mon-Fri, 8.30am-2pm Sat; 📶) Fill up at this great little cafe before (or after) delving into Braamfontein. Come for delicious breakfasts, gourmet sandwiches, frondy salads and changing lunch specials. The chalkboard menu adds to the casual atmosphere. Oh, and it serves delectable coffee.

Velo CAFETERIA $

(Map p326; ☎011-403 0695; www.lovevelo.co.za; Grove Corner, cnr Juta & Melle Sts, Braamfontein; mains R35-70; ⏰7am-4pm Mon-Wed, to 10pm Thu & Fri, 9am-10pm Sat, to 6pm Sun) This sweet little spot just off the street has gained a die-hard following for its tasty ciabattas, appetising sandwiches, creative salads, excellent coffee and friendly baristas – not to mention excellent breakfasts.

Dahleahs CAFETERIA $

(Map p326; ☎011-403 0243; 6 De Beer St, Braamfontein; mains R30-80; ⏰8.30am-5pm Tue-Fri, 9am-5.30pm Sat; 📶) Despite an influx of fashionable eateries in Braamfontein, there's a reason Dahleahs remains a favourite with discerning foodies. The menu is straightforward but scrummy and features tasty dishes such as pita bread filled with haloumi cheese, prego rolls and Greek salad. Something sweet to finish? Try a muffin or a scone.

WAM Cafe CAFE $

(Map p326; ☎011-717 1000; cnr Jorissen St & Jan Smuts Ave, Braamfontein; mains R20-60; ⏰7am-4pm Mon-Fri, 10am-2pm Sat; 📶) What was once a petrol station is now one of the most popular cafes in Braamfontein – a slick, modern, design-led eatery with large picture windows looking onto the street. Actually, the real reason most are here is for the lunch buffet – at R60, it's awesome value.

Smokehouse & Grill STEAK $$

(Map p326; ☎011-403 1395; cnr Juta & De Beer Sts, Braamfontein; mains R70-170; ⏰noon-9.30pm Mon-Thu, to 10.30pm Fri & Sat) Students, hipsters, moms and pops: everyone dives into this busy steakhouse for a rockin' feed.

Get messy with slow-pit-smoked ribs, slabs of juicy steak and succulent burgers, or watch the waist with the lightly seasoned grilled-chicken options or frondy salads. Good wines and beers, too.

86 Public PIZZA **$$**
(Map p326; ☎011-403 1155; www.86public.co.za; cnr Melle & Juta Sts, Braamfontein; mains R55-95; ⏲11.30am-10pm, to midnight Sat; 📶) Right in the heart of Braamfontein, 86 Public does brisk business with students and office workers – always a sign that you've found a good bargain. The pie ain't gourmet and doesn't claim to be, but if you're craving a decent slice to go, this is your baby. There's a huge variety of toppings.

Maboneng

★Eat Your Heart Out DELI **$**
(Map p320; ☎082 485 9393; www.eatyourheartout.co.za; cnr Kruger & Fox Sts, Maboneng; mains R30-70; ⏲7.30am-4pm Tue-Sun; 📶) The best spot in Maboneng to start the day. The Israeli breakfast – omelette, toasted pita, diced salad, pickled cabbage and cottage cheese – is the highlight, while the bagels and cheesecakes will leave your taste buds reeling. Healthy fruit juices, great coffee and sweet treats are also on offer, and there's outdoor seating.

Sharp! Braai Corner SOUTH AFRICAN **$**
(Map p320; ☎072 810 3109; 20 Kruger St, Maboneng; mains R20-60; ⏲11.30am-9pm) This cooler-than-cool little braai stand probably has the cheapest food in trendy Maboneng, attracting both penny-pinching locals and thrifty visitors. Top marks go to the quirky setting – a converted shipping container and up-cycled beer crates – and the excellent *shisa nyama* (barbecued meat served with traditional sides). Amazing value.

Blackanese Sushi SUSHI **$$**
(Map p320; ☎011-024 9455; 20 Kruger St, Maboneng; mains R50-140; ⏲9am-10pm Tue-Sun) Sushi with an African twist? Yes, it's possible at Blackanese. A highly original concept in Jo'burg, it fuses African flavour with Japanese cuisine. The result: spectacular. On top of the classics – sashimi, nigiri – tuck into seductive offerings like biltong California rolls or strawberry and cream cheese sushi. 'Industrial-chic' is an accurate description of the decor.

Canteen INTERNATIONAL **$$**
(Map p320; ☎011-334 5947; Arts on Main, 264 Fox St, Maboneng; mains R70-140; ⏲noon-2.30pm & 6-9pm Tue & Wed, 9am-9pm Thu-Sun) One of the best spots to chill in the 'hood, this lively eatery inside hip Arts on Main boasts a lovely setting, with a large, festive 'garden-party' courtyard shaded by olive trees and a rooftop bar. Foodwise, the emphasis is on burgers, salads, pasta and meat dishes.

Little Addis Café ETHIOPIAN **$$**
(Map p320; ☎082 683 8675; 280 Fox St, Maboneng; mains R60-85; ⏲12.30-9pm Tue-Sat, to 6pm Sun) A great experience for gastronauts, this eatery is all about spicy *doro wot* (chicken stew), *kitfo* (mince meat) and *tibs* (fried meat and vegetables), served traditionally on plate-sized *injera* (sourdough pancakes), which you rip up and use to eat with instead of cutlery.

Pata Pata INTERNATIONAL **$$**
(Map p320; ☎073 036 9031; 286 Fox St, Maboneng; mains R80-130; ⏲7am-10.30pm) Though it might not be as 'hip' as it once was, this Maboneng classic still delivers the same winning formula of rustic-chic decor, beautifully presented cuisine and attitude-loaded staff. The eclectic menu runs the gamut from pizzas and burgers to grilled meats and seafood. In the warmer months tables spill out onto the pavement. There's live music most evenings.

Melville

Melville has a wide selection of restaurants and cafes, almost all of which have outdoor seating.

★Service Station BISTRO **$**
(Map p320; ☎011-726 1701; Bamboo Centre, cnr 9th St & Rustenburg Rd, Melville; mains R50-80; ⏲7.30am-5pm Mon-Fri, 8am-5pm Sat, 8.30am-3pm Sun) In a far corner of Melville, Service Station is that easy-to-miss 'secret spot' that locals like to recommend. Bountiful breakfasts featuring flapjacks and brioches are reeling 'em in. As is the kaleidoscope of freshly prepared goodies – think grilled vegetables with cheese, gourmet burgers and grilled beef with caramelised onions. It also has irresistible ice creams and superb coffee.

Picobella ITALIAN **$**
(Map p332; ☎011-482 4309; 66 4th Ave; mains R30-100; ⏲8am-10pm) Picobella is the best Italian in the neighbourhood. Nothing too fancy here, just good, honest wood-fire pizza, delicious pasta – try the oglio with pecorino cheese – and reliable salads and starters on a faux-Roman terrace. Breakfast

is also highly recommended and very popular with coupled-up travellers.

Café de la Creme CAFE $
(Map p332; ☎011-726 7716; cnr 7th St & 4th Ave, Melville; mains R50-80; ⏰7am-4.30pm Mon, to 6.30pm Tue-Sat) This bakery-cafe does a roaring lunchtime trade in sandwiches, burgers and cakes, but it's the morning bread run that really gets up your nose, in a good way. Grab a coffee and a magazine and watch the world go by through the huge open windows.

Great Eastern Food Bar ASIAN $$
(Map p320; ☎011-482 2910; Bamboo Centre, cnr 9th St & Rustenburg Rd, Melville; mains R60-160; ⏰noon-11pm Tue-Fri, 1-11pm Sat, 1-8pm Sun) If you think Jozi is a dud at creative Asian food, prepare to eat your words (and everything in sight) at this exciting, well-priced, obscenely delicious eatery located on the roof of the trendy Bamboo Centre. Owner-chef Nick Scott turns out succulent concoctions prepared with top-of the-line ingredients. Musts include kimchi dumplings, sashimi tacos and smoked trout.

Book ahead, especially if you want a table with a view of Melville Koppies nature reserve.

★ **Lucky Bean** MODERN AFRICAN $$
(Map p332; ☎011-482 5572; www.luckybeantree.co.za; 16 7th St, Melville; mains R65-130; ⏰11am-9.30pm Tue-Thu, to 11pm Fri & Sat; 📶) Low lighting, slick tunes, a decked-out cocktail bar and waiters who happily skip down a flight of stairs to serve – Lucky Bean is easily the most atmospheric place in Melville. The food is spot on, too – light any-time meals, a few vegetarian options, gamey stews, creative starters and scrumptious steaks (teriyaki ostrich fillet, anyone?).

Leopard INTERNATIONAL $$
(Map p332; ☎011-482 9356; www.leopardfoodcompany.com; 63A 4th Ave, Melville; mains R50-140; ⏰6am-10pm Mon-Thu, 11am-11pm Fri & Sat) At this unpretentious yet top-notch restaurant, Chef Andrea Burgener cooks up a changing rainbow of eclectic dishes such as taro-leaf masala, and quail stuffed with cashews and coriander, all prepared with the best ingredients available. There's a small but perfectly formed wine list, and the desserts are a treat.

Brauhaus GERMAN $$
(Map p332; ☎011-482 4219; www.brauhaus-melville.co.za; cnr 7th St & 3rd Ave, Melville; mains R70-130; ⏰4-10pm Tue-Sat, 11am-10pm Sun) The Brauhaus' highly deserved reputation comes from its well-prepared German specialities with a South African twist – where else could you tuck into wildebeest ragout with homemade *spätzle* (pasta)? Other typical dishes include Vienna sausages and beef goulash.

Bambanani INTERNATIONAL $$
(Map p332; ☎011-482 2900; www.bambanani.biz; 85 4th Ave, Melville; mains R50-110; ⏰9am-8pm Tue-Fri, from 8am Sat & Sun; 📶👪) Not your average eatery, Bambanani is a concept restaurant that caters for families. Picture this: at the back is a huge deck and garden area with a massive, multilevelled children's play den. Foodwise, it cooks up a wide array of dishes, including pizzas, pasta, salads and various nibbles that will put a smile on everybody's face.

La Luna of Melville ITALIAN $$$
(Map p332; ☎011-482 7451; www.laluna-melville.co.za; 9 7th St, Melville; mains R80-195; ⏰4-9.30pm Mon, 11.30am-9.30pm Tue-Sat) Enter this snazzy restaurant and be comforted by the elegant design, airy spaces and genteel ambience. Begin with fabulous starters, then delve into the pumpkin ravioli, grilled monkfish and calamaretti and the amazing homemade pastas with grilled prawns. Don't miss the luscious tiramisu for dessert.

Milpark

Salvation Cafe CAFE $$
(Map p320; ☎011-482 7795; www.salvationcafe.co.za; 44 Stanley Ave, Milpark; mains R60-100; ⏰8am-3pm Tue-Sun) Organic deliciousness awaits at this casual cafe (bonus points for the covered verandah and inviting courtyard). All bases are covered, from baked treats and vibrant salads to made-from-scratch burgers, delicious wraps and scrumptious breakfasts (served until 11.45am). Local gourmands rave about the eggs Benedict and carrot cake.

Il Giardino Degli Ulivi ITALIAN $$
(Map p320; ☎011-482 4978; www.ilgiardino.co.za; 44 Stanley Ave, Milpark; mains R60-185; ⏰11.30am-10pm Tue-Sat, to 4pm Sun) Inside the hip 44 Stanley precinct, Il Giardino feels like a charming old-world trattoria, its leafy courtyard the backdrop to nourishing dishes at reasonable prices. Top selections: gorgonzola gnocchi, beef carpaccio with Parmesan cheese and bubbling thin-crust pizzas. There's a small but respectable wine list, with equally fair prices.

1

RICHARD I'ANSON / GETTY IMAGES ©

DOELAN YANN / GETTY IMAGES ©

1. Sterkfontein Caves (p350)
These caves form one of the world's most significant archaeological sites.

2. African mask
Intricate beadwork decorates this artistic piece.

3. Orlando Towers (p348), Soweto
Colourful murals cover these towers, which have become a popular spot for bungee jumping.

4. Illustrating the past
An installation about migration at the must-see Apartheid Museum (p325), Johannesburg.

DAVE HAMMAN / GETTY IMAGES ©

Greenside

Not far from Melville, the suburb of Greenside has a couple of excellent restaurants and trendy bars, although the crowd isn't as young as in Melville. The restaurants are in a little cluster on Gleneagles Rd and Greenway, just off Barry Hertzog Ave, and along adjacent 4th Ave.

Dukes Burgers BURGERS **$$**
(Map p320; ☎011-486 0824; www.dukesburgers.co.za; 14 Gleneagles Rd, Greenside; mains R70-110; ⏰11.30am-9pm Sun-Thu, to 10pm Fri & Sat) Elevating the humble burger to high art, this inviting and warmly lit eatery on a restaurant-lined stretch of Gleneagles Rd serves up lusty burgers that come in many variations. The vegetarion option is tops, especially when paired with sweet-potato wedges and a rich, creamy milkshake. There's a sheltered courtyard out back.

Doppio Zero ITALIAN **$$**
(Map p320; ☎011-646 8740; www.doppio.co.za; cnr Barry Hertzog Ave & Gleneagles Rd, Greenside; mains R60-120; ⏰7am-9pm Sun-Thu, to 10pm Fri & Sat) Gauteng's edition of this low-scale Italian cafe franchise is hugely popular, with good reason. The corner terrace is packed on weekends with the breakfast crowd, who linger for goodies baked on site, and the excellent pasta and pizza.

Orient ASIAN **$$**
(Map p320; ☎011-684 1616; www.thai-africa.co.za; 4 High St, Melrose Arch; mains R50-170; ⏰noon-2.30pm & 6-9.30pm Mon-Thu, noon-10pm Fri-Sun) Orient is the best of a number of Asian-themed restaurants imagined into existence by the same clever company. The A-list crowd laps it up, partly for the fusion food and fresh sushi, and partly for the future-metro decor.

Parkview

Moyo's SOUTH AFRICAN **$$**
(Map p320; ☎011-646 0058; www.moyo.co.za; Zoo Lake, Parkview; mains R60-160; ⏰8.30am-10pm Mon-Thu & Sun, to 11pm Fri & Sat) South Africa's 'chic-est' chain restaurant is feeling a little tired but still draws the family crowd thanks to its great location, atmospheric decor and extensive menu.

Norwood

A large portion of Grant Ave is lined with cafes and restaurants, most of which are open every day, and provide a cross-section of street life.

Zahava's MIDDLE EASTERN **$**
(Map p320; ☎011-728 6511; www.zahavas.co.za; 47A Grant Ave, Norwood; mains R50-80; ⏰7.30am-4pm Mon-Fri, 8.30am-4.30pm Sat & Sun; 📶) With its colourful paintings enlivening the walls and its relaxed atmosphere, Zahava's can do no wrong. It's known for its freshly prepared Middle Eastern specialities, including snack-size *zivas* (flatbread), *latkes* (potato fritters) and toothsome Morrocan lamb *tajine*. You'll also find a great courtyard patio for warm days, plus breakfast offerings.

Schwarma Co MIDDLE EASTERN **$$**
(Map p320; ☎011-483 1776; www.schwarmacompany.co.za; 71 Grant Ave, Norwood; mains R50-150; ⏰11am-10pm) This Jo'burg institution is renowned for delicious platters of *shwarma* (meat sliced off a spit, served in pitas with chopped tomatoes), yummy kebabs and copious salads. For dessert, try the belt-bustingly good *baklavas* (layered filo pastries with honey and nuts). Grab an upstairs table on the breezy terrace and observe Grant Ave's gentle mayhem down below as you dig in.

Vovo Telo CAFE, BAKERY **$$**
(Map p320; ☎011-483 1398; www.vovotelo.co.za; cnr Grant Ave & Nellie Rd, Norwood; mains R50-90; ⏰7am-8pm; 📶) This sassy cafe–bakery is worth visiting for its wholesome dishes. Stop in briefly for a gourmet sandwich and fresh juice, or stay longer and nosh on freshly prepared pastas, pizzas or salads served in snug surrounds. Nab an outdoor table on a sunny afternoon.

Next Door JEWISH **$$**
(Map p320; ☎011-728 2577; 80 Grant Ave; mains R90-170; ⏰11am-10pm Sun-Thu, 11am-2.30pm Fri, 7-11pm Sat; ❄) Rub shoulders with rabbis and Jewish families in this welcoming kosher restaurant, which fills up quickly most evenings. Bagels and wood-fire pizzas will titillate your tastebuds.

Giovanni Pane Vino ITALIAN **$$**
(Map p320; ☎011-483 1515; 66 Grant Ave, Norwood; mains R60-120; ⏰noon-9pm Mon-Thu & Sun, to 10pm Sat) This classic Italian joint has the requisite red-and-white tablecloths and bowls of pasta big enough to feed a small soccer team, as well as pizzas dense enough to drown grandpa's dentures.

Rosebank & Sandton

The many eating options in these affluent suburbs are centred on the huge shopping malls that form the core of northern-suburb society.

Walnut Grove CAFE $$

(Map p320; ☎011-783 6111; www.walnutgrove.co.za; Shop B38, Sandton City Mall, cnr 5th St & Rivonia Rd, Sandton; mains R50-160; ⏲9am-6pm) Located inside Sandton City Mall, the Walnut Grove is a handy spot for an affordable, uncomplicated, walk-in bite. Choose from *tramezzini* (small sandwiches on white or wholewheat bread), bagels, cakes, gourmet sandwiches, meat dishes and salads, all delicious and moderately priced. It also has excellent coffee drinks.

★**Grillhouse** STEAK $$$

(Map p320; ☎011-880 3945; www.thegrillhouse.co.za; The Firs Shopping Centre, cnr Oxford Rd & Bierman Ave, Rosebank; mains R100-300; ⏲noon-2.30pm & 6.30-9.30pm Sun-Fri, 6.30-9.30pm Sat) Get an honest-to-goodness Jozi steakhouse experience at this New York–style institution inside The Firs. Rub elbows with red-meat lovers of all stripes and choose your cut: prime sirloin, T-bone, spare ribs or fillet. Thick chops of veal, ostrich medallions and various seafood options are also on tap, as are heaping portions of character thanks to the skilled waiters and cosy decor.

There's also an incredible selection of single malts and fabulous local wines.

Bukhara INDIAN $$$

(Map p320; ☎011-883 5555; www.bukhara.com; Nelson Mandela Square mall, cnr West & Maude Sts, Sandton; mains R130-210; ⏲noon-3pm & 6-11pm Mon-Sat, to 10pm Sun) One of the best Indian restaurants in town, Bukhara manages to be atmospheric despite its location in the sanitised Nelson Mandela Square mall. It serves authentic, richly flavoured tikka masala, korma, curry and tandoori dishes. It's a classy place complete with marble floor, teak furniture and ochre walls. Needless to say, service is excellent.

Parkmore

Delhi Dharbar INDIAN $

(Map p320; ☎011-883 4407; 136A 11th St, Parkmore; mains R40-95; ⏲11am-10.30pm) This is not the fanciest Indian restaurant in Jo'burg, but the setting is cosy and the North Indian cuisine gets rave reviews. Those wishing to stretch their entree experience beyond samosas should try tandoori mushrooms or onion *bhaji* (spicy fried onions). Fave mains include lamb vindaloo and chicken tikka masala. Also does takeaway.

Eatery JHB BISTRO $$

(Map p320; ☎011-783 1570; www.eateryjhb.co.za; cnr 11th St & Victoria Ave, Parkmore; mains R60-120; ⏲noon-3pm & 6-9pm Mon-Fri, 6-9pm Sat) You really need to know this place is here, but luckily now you do. Just off 11th St, this easy-to-miss restaurant is a surprise, with its hip setting that combines exposed beams and industrial touches, superb bistro food and convivial ambience. It cooks up just a few starters, three or four mains and a handful of desserts – and none disappoint.

★**Thomas Maxwell Bistro** BISTRO $$$

(Map p320; ☎011-784 1575; www.thomasmaxwell.co.za; 140 11th St, Parkmore; mains R120-200; ⏲12.30-2.30pm & 6.30-9.30pm Mon-Fri, 6.30-9.30pm Sat, 12.30-2.30pm Sun) The king of bistros in Parkmore, bustling Thomas Maxwell is never short of a discriminating mob. That's all thanks to three winning details: its rustic-chic decor; the uplifting Jozi-meets-NYC mood; and, of course, the stellar crowd-pleasing menu. Highlights include the outstanding rabbit risotto, steak tartare and sirloin wasabi.

Fordsburg

You'll find dozens of Indian restaurants in Fordsburg. Note that most venues do not serve alcohol and shops are closed on Friday during prayer times.

Bismillah INDIAN $

(Map p320; ☎011-838 8050; www.bismillahrestaurant.co.za; 78 Mint Rd, Fordsburg; mains R30-110; ⏲8am-10.30pm) Over in Fordsburg you'll find the best Indian food in Jo'burg, and Bismillah is, we reckon, the pick of the lot. The menu is classic North Indian – tandooris, tikkas, biryanis and masalas are all here, plus a few surprises – while the service is refreshingly earnest. Best of all, it's super cheap.

Eastern Suburbs

Near Bruma Lake is Derrick Ave, Cyrildene, off Observatory Rd, and there's an established Chinatown with a number of cheap restaurants.

Troyeville Hotel PORTUGUESE $$

(Map p320; ☎011-402 7709; www.troyevillehotel.co.za; 1403 Albert Sisulu St, Troyeville; mains

R80-140; ⏲11am-10pm) Located in an old part of town, the Troyeville is a memorable place for a long meal. This character-filled hotel has been frequented by the Portuguese community since well before the paint began to peel. The Iberian influence is found in the delicious Mozambican prawns, the tasty *feijoada* (bean stew) and the chilled red wine. Its Sunday braai is deservedly popular.

Drinking & Nightlife

Jo'burg has an ever-revolving bar scene and you'll find everything from crusty bohemian haunts to chic cocktail lounges to conservative wine bars here. Maboneng and Braamfontein have some great lively places, but much of the nightlife is in the northern suburbs, particularly around Melville, Greenside and Rosebank.

Inner City & Newtown

Guildhall PUB

(Map p326; ☎011-833 1770; cnr Albertina Sisulu Rd & Harrison St, Marshalltown; ⏲9am-7pm Mon-Wed, to 2am Thu & Fri, to 6pm Sat) City of Gold fortunes have been squandered in Jo'burg's oldest bar (established c 1888). This is one of the Inner City's best meeting places and it's completely unpretentious. Nab a seat on the breezy balcony upstairs for some serious people-watching. DJs perform most weekends; if not, you can often bust out the karaoke. Good Portuguese-style pub food is also available.

Sophiatown Bar Lounge BAR

(Map p326; ☎011-836 5999; www.sophiatownbarlounge.co.za; cnr Jeppe & Henry Nxumalo Sts, Newtown; ⏲8.30am-10pm Sun-Thu, to midnight Fri & Sat) Sophiatown was once the heart of African cultural resistance, and the township's spirit is celebrated in one of Newtown's most enjoyable venues. Grainy photographs add a touch of whimsy to the jazzy sounds – there's live music on Friday and Saturday nights – while the food is hearty and gamey.

Boundless CAFE

(Map p326; www.boundlesscity.com; 1st fl, cnr Fox & Von Brandis Sts, Inner City; ⏲9am-7pm Mon-Thu, 9am-2am Fri & Sat, 10am-10pm Sun; 📶) Opened in 2014 and run by an American expat, this offbeat cafe enjoys an ace location, a stone's throw from the Carlton Centre. Freshly squeezed fruit juices, mouth-watering sandwiches and snacks, excellent coffee, free wi-fi, colourful paintings on the walls and chilled seating make it a great place to recharge the batteries.

Cramers Coffee CAFE

(Map p326; www.cramerscoffee.com; 17 Harrison St, Inner City; ⏲6am-5.30pm Mon-Fri, 7am-1.30pm Sat; 📶) Superb coffee is served at this always-bustling joint west of Gandhi Sq. Some say this is the best cup of joe in town. There's also an array of sweet temptations, including croissants and muffins.

Braamfontein

Doubleshot Coffee & Tea CAFE

(Map p326; www.doubleshot.co.za; cnr Juta & Melle Sts, Braamfontein; ⏲8am-6pm Mon-Sat) Coffee, tea and a few baked treats is all you'll get at this roaster but, man, are they good. The espresso is dark and intense, brewed by competent baristas and swilled by a bevy of cool kids and clued-in corporate people.

Kitchener's Carvery Bar PUB

(Map p326; ☎011-403 3646; cnr Juta & De Beer Sts, Braamfontein; ⏲11am-midnight, to 4am Fri & Sat) What used to be a grand colonial hotel is now hipster central and epitomises the new swagger of Braamfontein. By day it's a popular pub, known for its knockout burgers, fish 'n' chips and vast choice of drinks served in vintage surrounds; by night DJs spin soul, funk and electro. Cover charges usually apply on Friday and Saturday nights.

Anti-Est BAR

(Map p326; De Beer St, Braamfontein; ⏲11am-midnight Wed-Fri, to 2am Sat) Anti-Est ticks all the cool boxes: a great terrace for people-watching, an enticing industrial interior and an enviable medley of craft beers, tequilas and whiskies.

Great Dane BAR

(Map p326; 5 De Beer St, Braamfontein; ⏲noon-2am Thu-Sat) Fun and friendly Great Dane is one of the mainstays of the ever-changing Braamfontein bar strip. The music is a danceable mix of 1980s pop, rock, electro and disco and staff make you feel like friends. Early on it's a good place for warm-up drinks, especially in the appealing courtyard; come midnight the tables are cleared and the dancing commences.

Maboneng

Uncle Merv's CAFE

(Map p320; ☎073 211 5127; cnr Fox & Kruger Sts, Maboneng; ⏲7am-4pm) This hole-in-the-wall is famous for its perfectly brewed coffee, decadent banana bread, yummy croissants and killer milkshakes. Our favourite is the Macci Porter, a rich blend of tahini, banana, soy milk, cashews and dates. Stackable chairs and nearby pavement benches provide places to sit. Very Maboneng.

Zebra Inn BAR
(Map p320; cnr Albertina Sisulu Rd & Kruger St, Maboneng; noon-1am) This one-of-a-kind Maboneng institution will stun you with its mind-blowing decor and old-world atmosphere. It feels like a taxidermist shop, with an onslaught of hunting trophies and African masks adorning the lime-green walls. Also serves pub grub. Ring for entrance.

Lenin's Vodka Bar COCKTAIL BAR
(Map p320; www.lenins.co.za; 300 Commissioner St, Maboneng; 4pm-midnight Wed-Sat, noon-midnight Sun) This Maboneng gem is famous for one thing and one thing only: vodka. With more than 50 varieties, you're sure to find something that will tickle your fancy. For non-vodka drinkers, there's a good choice of other drinks on the menu. Bag a table in the moodily lit interior or on the shady terrace. In between drinks, snack on salads and sandwiches.

Melville

Jo'Anna Melt Bar BAR
(Map p332; 7th St, Melville; 2-10pm Mon-Fri, noon-11pm Sat) A lively bar awash with people getting jolly on the abundant cocktails and craft beers. The decor – exposed brickwork and a massive, rectangular bar – is easy on the eye.

Six Cocktail Bar & Restaurant COCKTAIL BAR
(Map p332; 011-482 8306; 7th St, Melville; noon-2am) Six has single-handedly shifted the 7th St dress code, thanks to its so-far-above-average cocktails and so-better-looking-than-you clientele. This is a wonderful place for a drink. Fabulous artwork, soft orange and red colour scheme, iconic reggae, and soul and house music at a level conducive to hearing key questions: want another one?

Ratz Bar COCKTAIL BAR
(Map p332; www.ratzbar.co.za; 9 7th St, Melville; 4pm-2am) Ratz is a tiny cocktail bar that cranks the '80s rock and cheesy pop. There's always a crowd for the cheap cocktails.

Liberation Cafe BAR
(Map p332; 7 7th St, Melville; 4pm-2am Wed-Sun) Liberation is not a huge space, but it offers a full cocktail menu of contemporary and classic drinks in colourful surrounds.

GAY & LESBIAN GAUTENG

Gauteng has a thriving gay scene and, since the liberalisation of the constitution in 1994, the twin metropolises of Jo'burg and Pretoria have become centres for gays and lesbians from across Africa. Gays are well organised and increasingly accepted – things are a far cry from the puritanical attitudes of the past.

The annual Gay Pride March, held in Johannesburg on the last weekend of September, is the focal point but by no means the only organised activity. In fact, one of the highlights is taking a **Queer Johannesburg Tour** (011-717 4239; www.gala.co.za; per person R200-350).

A number of websites provide information on the province's gay scene: www.gaysouthafrica.net and out.org.za are packed with useful material. Also check out the monthly *Gay Times* magazine.

Milpark

Stanley Beer Yard BEER GARDEN
(Map p320; 011-481 5791; www.44stanley.co.za; 44 Stanley Ave, Milpark; noon-11pm Tue-Sun) The cognoscenti of Jo'burg's beer world pack this attractive haven inside the 44 Stanley precinct. It serves unique craft beers as well as delectable pub grub and hosts live bands on Saturday (from 2pm). The eye-catching interior is complete with armchairs and a huge log fire; outside there are long wooden tables under olive trees.

Greenside

Office BAR
(Map p320; 011-023 9863; Gleneagles Rd, Greenside; 4pm-1.30am Tue-Sat, 2-10pm Sun) Sharp-looking joint that appeals to fans of cocktails, craft beer, cool design and good music. The menu and vibe are upmarket and quite sophisticated, making this a more grown up, but not less diverse, alternative to Greenside's grungier, student-oriented bars.

Parkhurst

Jolly Roger Pub PUB
(Map p320; 011-327 5883; cnr 4th Ave & 6th St, Parkhurst; 4pm-2am Mon, noon-2am Tue-Sun) This two-storey, English-style pub on the edge of burgeoning 4th Ave is very good. Upstairs it serves good pub grub and offers

fabulous views of the busy street below. Downstairs is a more traditional sports pub with tap beer aplenty. Across the road is its newer sports bar.

Entertainment

The best entertainment guide appears in Friday's *Mail & Guardian*. 'Tonight' in the daily *Star* is also good. For entertainment bookings by credit card, contact **Computicket** (☎011-915 8000; www.computicket.com). For parties and get-togethers, check out www.jhblive.co.za or www.joburg.org.za.

Live Music

Jo'burg is an excellent place to see live music, especially across the jazz-tipped and electronic spectrum.

Many bars in Braamfontein, Melville, Greenside and Sandton host live bands.

Bassline LIVE MUSIC
(Map p326; ☎011-838 9145; www.bassline.co.za; 10 Henry Nxumalo St, Newtown; ⌚hours vary) This is still the most respected live-music venue in Jo'burg, gaining prominence as a Melville jazz haunt in the late '90s before getting on the world-music tip and relocating to Newtown in 2004. Today it covers the full range of international musicianship and more popular reggae, rock and hip-hop styles.

Orbit JAZZ
(Map p326; ☎011-339 6645; www.theorbit.co.za; 81 De Korte St, Braamfontein; ⌚11.30am-2am Tue-Sun) This is by far the most famous of the city's jazz clubs. Plenty of freedom is given to young producers and artists, and its convivial atmosphere attracts a mix of jazz fans, students and in-the-know tourists. An upmarket bistro greets you downstairs, while you'll find the highly impressive concert venue upstairs. Its complete monthly agenda is available online.

Katzy's JAZZ
(Map p320; ☎011-880 3945; www.katzys.co.za; The Firs Shopping Centre, cnr Oxford Rd & Bierman Ave, Rosebank; ⌚noon-midnight Mon-Wed, noon-2am Thu-Fri, 6.30pm-2am Sat) One of the loveliest hangouts in the neighbourhood, this swanky den recalls the atmosphere of an old NYC jazz club. You'll find mellow, live jazz five nights a week, as well as the tasty carnivore menu of the restaurant next door, The Grillhouse. A cover charge (from R100) applies on Thursday, Friday and Saturday nights.

It also boasts an exceptional menu of whiskies, cognacs and bourbons.

Sport

Jo'burg is a great place to catch a cricket, rugby or football (soccer) match, with world-class facilities and dedicated fans.

Bidvest Wanderers Stadium CRICKET
(Map p320; ☎011-340 1500; www.wanderers.co.za; Corlett Dr, Illovo) This impressive stadium, just off the M1 freeway to Pretoria, is the city's most important cricketing venue. Watch from the stands or head to the grassy banks near the Western Pavilion and braai yourself a steak while you watch a local limited-overs match or see South Africa's best take on an international team.

Ellis Park – Emirates Airline Park RUGBY
(Map p320; www.lionsrugby.co.za; Doornfontein) The spiritual home of Jo'burg rugby, just east of the city centre, was the scene of one of the new nation's proudest moments – victory in the 1995 World Cup. Rugby supporters are fanatical: a Saturday afternoon at the rugby can be an almost religious experience. Renamed Emirates Airline Park in January 2015, it's still widely known as Ellis Park.

Shopping

Rosebank Sunday Market CRAFTS
(Map p320; www.rosebanksundaymarket.co.za; Cradock Ave, Rosebank; ⌚9am-4pm Sun) This is one of the most convenient places to shop for traditional carvings, beadwork, jewellery, books and fertility dolls. It's held in Rosebank Mall's multilevel car park, on the rooftop.

Bryanston Organic Market MARKET
(Map p320; www.bryanstonorganicmarket.co.za; Culross Rd, Bryanston; ⌚9am-3pm Thu & Sat) Arts and crafts are on offer here, but the main attraction is the splendid organic produce.

KwaZulu Muti Museum of Man & Science TRADITIONAL MEDICINE
(Map p326; ☎011-836 4470; 14 Diagonal St, Newtown; ⌚7.30am-5pm Mon-Fri, to 1.30pm Sat) This quirky, highly photogenic venture – ask permission first – is the most accessible of the downtown *muti* (traditional medicine) stores. Amid incredible bric-a-brac, it sells walking sticks, drums, beads, animal parts and roots.

Oriental Plaza MALL
(Map p320; www.orientalplaza.co.za; Bree St, Fordsburg; ⌚9am-5pm Mon-Fri, to 3pm Sat) A bustling collection of mostly Indian-owned stores

DON'T MISS

JO'BURG'S BEST MARKETS

Mall culture is alive and well in Johannesburg, but there are also several delightfully atmospheric markets.

Market on Main (Map p320; www.marketonmain.co.za; Arts on Main, 264 Fox St, Maboneng; ⏲10am-3pm Sun, 7-11pm 1st Thu of month) This beloved market is housed in a refurbished industrial building packed with food stands selling freshly baked goods, gourmet edibles and other temptations. You'll also find local fashion designers and artists' studios.

Sheds@1Fox (Map p326; www1fox.co.za; 1 Fox St, Newtown; ⏲11am-6pm Thu-Sun) Opened in late 2014, this venue occupying a former industrial warehouse on the western edge of downtown Jo'burg is a shining example of redevelopment and preservation. It's now a thriving marketplace with gourmet outlets as well as a collection of food stands, bars and craft stalls.

44 Stanley (Map p320; www.44stanley.co.za; 44 Stanley Ave, Milpark) 44 Stanley is the antithesis of consumer tack and is a blueprint for future mall development. It's in a previously disused building with shady courtyards and features an eclectic collection of local designers, speciality boutiques and interesting restaurants.

Neighbourgoods Market (Map p326; www.neighbourgoodsmarket.co.za; cnr Juta & de Beer Sts, Braamfontein; ⏲9am-3pm Sat) Cape Town's wondrous community market has come to Braamfontein to continually 'reinvent the public market as civic institution'. The two-storey brick warehouse fills with artisan purveyors and their foodie fans, who hoover up healthy brunches, 'slow' beer and stiff coffee. Upstairs you can grab a bench and watch the sun shine off city buildings.

selling everything from spices to cheap watches to cookware. If you need your mobile phone fixed, this is the place to come, and if you get peckish, there are plenty of stalls selling samosas, sweets and other goodies.

Rosebank Mall MALL
(Map p320; www.themallofrosebank.co.za; Baker St, Rosebank; ⏲9am-7pm Mon-Thu, to 8pm Fri, to 6pm Sat, to 5pm Sun) If you're after serious retail therapy, head to this interlocking series of malls, with central parking on the corner of Cradock Ave and Baker St.

Nelson Mandela Square MALL
(Map p320; www.nelsonmandelasquare.co.za; cnr West & Maude Sts, Sandton; ⏲9am-7pm Mon-Thu, to 8pm Fri, to 6pm Sat & Sun) Adjoining, and similar to, Sandton City Mall, this large mall is built around an Italian-style piazza full of restaurants. There's also a 6m-high bronze statue of Nelson Mandela that's a favourite spot for selfies.

Kohinoor MUSIC
(Map p326; ☎011-834 1361; 54 Market St, Newtown; ⏲9am-5pm Mon-Sat) In a basement underneath a furniture store, Kohinoor is one of the best sources of ethnic/African music, and sells everything from kwaito to jazz.

ℹ Information

EMERGENCY

Fire (☎10111)

Police (☎10111; Main Rd)

MEDICAL SERVICES

Jo'burg's medical services are good, but they can be pricey, so make sure you get insurance before you leave home.

Charlotte Maxeke Johannesburg Hospital (☎011-488 4911; M1/Jubilee Rd, Parktown) Jo'burg's main public hospital.

Netcare Rosebank Hospital (☎011-328 0500; 14 Sturdee Ave, Rosebank; ⏲7am-10pm) A private hospital in the northern suburbs, with casualty, GP and specialist services.

MONEY

There are banks with ATMs and exchange facilities at every commercial centre.

TOURIST INFORMATION

Guesthouses or hostels as well as tour guides are your best sources of tourist information.

Johannesburg Tourism Company (Map p320; ☎011-214 0700; www.joburgtourism.com; ground fl, Grosvenor Corner, 195 Jan Smuts Ave, Parktown North; ⏲8am-5pm Mon-Fri) A private endeavour; covers the city of Jo'burg.

Getting There & Away

AIR

South Africa's major international and domestic airport is **OR Tambo International Airport** (Ortia; 011-921 6262; www.johannesburg-airport.com).

Make sure you only deal with official Airports Company employees. A friendly 'No, thanks' should dissuade any potential crooks.

If you're in a hurry, some domestic flights are definitely worth considering. Smaller budget airlines **Kulula** (0861-585 852; www.kulula.com), **1time** (0861-878 278; www.1time.co.za) and **Mango** (086-100 1234; www.flymango.com) link Jo'burg with major destinations.

For regular flights to national and regional destinations try **South African Airways** (SAA; 0861 359 722; www.flysaa.com), **South African Airlink** (SAAirlink; 0861 606 606; www.flyairlink.com) and **South African Express** (0861 729 227; www.flyexpress.aero). All flights can be booked through SAA, which also has offices in the domestic and international terminals of Ortia.

BUS

There are a number of international bus services that leave Jo'burg from the Park Station complex and head for Mozambique, Lesotho, Botswana, Namibia, Swaziland and Zimbabwe.

The main long-distance bus lines (national and international) also depart from and arrive at the Park Station transit centre, in the northwestern corner of the site, where you'll also find their booking offices.

The nearest large town to Kruger National Park is Nelspruit. Phalaborwa is a good option if you're staying at a more northerly Kruger National Park camp such as Olifants.

Baz Bus (0861 229 287; www.bazbus.com) Connects Jo'burg with the most popular parts of the region (including Durban, the Garden Route and Cape Town) and picks up at hostels in Jo'burg and Pretoria, saving you the hassle of going into the city to arrange transport. Note that Baz Bus no longer services Swaziland. All hostels have current timetables and prices. A seven-day travel pass costs R2180.

Citybug (0861 334 433; www.citybug.co.za) Runs a shuttle service between Jo'burg and Nelspruit, stopping in Pretoria and a few smaller towns along the way.

City to City (0861 589 282; www.citytocity.co.za) National and international bus services.

Greyhound (083 915 9000; www.greyhound.co.za) National and international bus services.

Intercape (021-380 4400; www.intercape.co.za) National and international bus services.

Lowveld Link (083 918 8075, 013-750 1174; www.lowveldlink.com) Runs a shuttle between the airport and Nelspruit, via Pretoria.

Translux (0861 589 282; www.translux.co.za) National and international bus services.

CAR

All the major car-rental operators have counters at OR Tambo and at various locations around the city, and many offer deals with unlimited mileage.

HITCHING

We say don't hitch. If you're strapped for cash, you could ask about share-drives. These are often advertised in the weekly newspaper *Junk Mail* (junkmail.co.za), and most hostels have noticeboards with details of free or shared-cost lifts.

GAUTRAIN

Jo'burg's pride and joy, the rapid-transit Gautrain (p614) offers a direct service between the airport, Sandton, Rosebank, Park Station, Pretoria and Hatfield. Trains depart every 12 minutes at peak times (5.30am to 8.30am and 3pm to 6pm Monday to Friday), and every 20 to 30 minutes outside peak times. A one-way ticket between Pretoria and Park Station costs R64. If you're travelling in peak periods, or staying near a station, it's a fast, state-of-the-art and cost-effective way to enter/exit the city.

TRAIN

Long-distance train services link Jo'burg with a number of destinations including Pretoria, Cape Town, Bloemfontein, Kimberley, Port Elizabeth, Durban, Komatipoort and Nelspruit. A number of these services have sleeper compartments. Tickets can be booked through **Shosholoza Meyl** (011-774 4555, 0860 008 888; www.shosholozameyl.co.za) or at Jo'burg's Park Station.

Getting Around

TO/FROM THE AIRPORT

OR Tambo International Airport (Ortia) is about 25km east of central Johannesburg in Kempton Park.

The rapid-transit Gautrain offers a direct service between the airport and Jo'burg. There are Gautrain stations at Sandton, Rosebank and Park Station. A one-way ticket to Park Station costs R145 (R135 to Sandton).

Airport Shuttle (0861 397 488; www.airportshuttle.co.za) charges R530 for most destinations in Jo'burg and will pick up 24 hours a day, although it should be booked a day in advance if possible. **Magic Bus** (011-394 6902; www.magicbus.co.za) offers a similar service and charges R615 for most destinations.

By car, the airport is easily accessible (via the R24 and the N12), but if you need to get there during the weekday rush hour (5pm to 7pm) allow up to an extra hour's travelling time.

Most hostels will collect you from the airport for free. Guesthouses and hotels will also arrange pick-ups but usually for about the same charge as a taxi.

BUS

Rea Vaya (☎0860 562 874; www.reavaya.org.za) These buses were introduced in the build-up to the 2010 World Cup as a way of addressing the lack of safe, reliable public transport between Soweto (and other townships) and downtown Johannesburg. The network has rapidly expanded since then and includes the Inner City, Newtown, Braamfontein and Auckland Park. The fleet is colourful and comfortable, and timetables are more strictly adhered to than metro lines. An inner-city circular route costs R5.50, while a full trip from the feeder routes to the Inner City costs R12.50.

Citysightseeing Joburg (Map p326; ☎0861 733 287; www.citysightseeing.co.za; Park Station) Starting from Park Station, these hop-on, hop-off red buses run to 11 major tourist sites around central Johannesburg, including Gandhi Sq, Constitutional Hill and Carlton Centre, as well as the Apartheid Museum, Gold Reef CIty, Newtown and Braamfontein. They run from roughly 9am to 6pm. A ticket valid for one day costs R170. Check the website for details.

SHARED TAXI

R6 will get you around the inner suburbs and the city centre and R10 will get you almost anywhere.

If you take a minibus shared taxi into central Jo'burg, be sure to get off before it reaches the end of the route, and avoid the taxi rank – it's a mugging zone. Getting a minibus taxi home from the city is a more difficult proposition.

There's a complex system of hand/finger signals to tell a passing taxi where you want to go, so it's best to look as though you know where you're going and raise a confident index finger (drivers will stop if they're going the same way).

TAXI

There are taxis, but they are relatively expensive. They all operate meters, but it's wise to ask a local the likely price and agree on a fare from the outset. **Maxi Taxi Cabs** (☎011-648 1212; www.maxitaxicabs.co.za) and **Rose Taxis** (☎011-403 9625; www.rosetaxis.com) are two reputable firms. These days, most Jo'burgers prefer to use **Uber** (www.uber.com/cities/johannesburg).

AROUND JOHANNESBURG

The biggest attraction in the Jo'burg surrounds is the pulsating township of Soweto. Dig a little deeper and you'll also discover a World Heritage Site spanning three million years of human history.

Soweto

POP 2.3 MILLION

The 'South West Townships' have evolved from an area of forced habitation to an address of pride and social prestige and a destination in their own right. Though it's devoid of spectacular sights, Soweto is now well on the tourist trail. Travellers come to be part of the welcoming township life and to visit places of tremendous historical significance, including the former homes of Desmond Tutu and Nelson Mandela, and the Hector Pieterson Museum. A stroll down laid-back Vilakazi St offers an insight into modern African sensibilities, while the addition of Soccer City and the Soweto Bungee provide quality, concrete experiences in a place of great political abstraction. And while it was considered foolhardy to get there on your own a decade ago, it's now safe to visit the main sights independently.

Mirroring much of South Africa, the rising middle class lives here alongside shack dwellers and the mass unemployed, yet all are equally buoyed by the history of Soweto as an icon of the struggle. Many who break the cycle decide to stay and reinvest, and most laud their Sowetan upbringing. The townships are the heart of the nation and none beats louder than Soweto.

History

As ANC stalwart and long-time Soweto resident Walter Sisulu once said, the history of South Africa cannot be understood outside the history of Soweto.

Using the outbreak of bubonic plague in 1904 as an excuse, the Jo'burg City Council (JCC) moved 1358 Indians and 600 Africans from a Jo'burg slum to Klipspruit, 18km by road from the city centre. It wasn't until the late 1930s, after the suburb of Orlando had been built and cynically marketed by the JCC as 'somewhat of a paradise', that the population began its astonishing growth.

By the end of WWII, Jo'burg's black population had risen by more than 400,000, and by 1958 more than 20 new suburbs had appeared around Orlando, each filled with row upon row of identical houses.

During the 1950s, organisations such as the ANC took a bigger role in opposing apartheid, and before long Soweto (as it was officially named in 1961) would be recognised as the centre of resistance. Confirmation of this came in 1955 when 3000 delegates from

Soweto

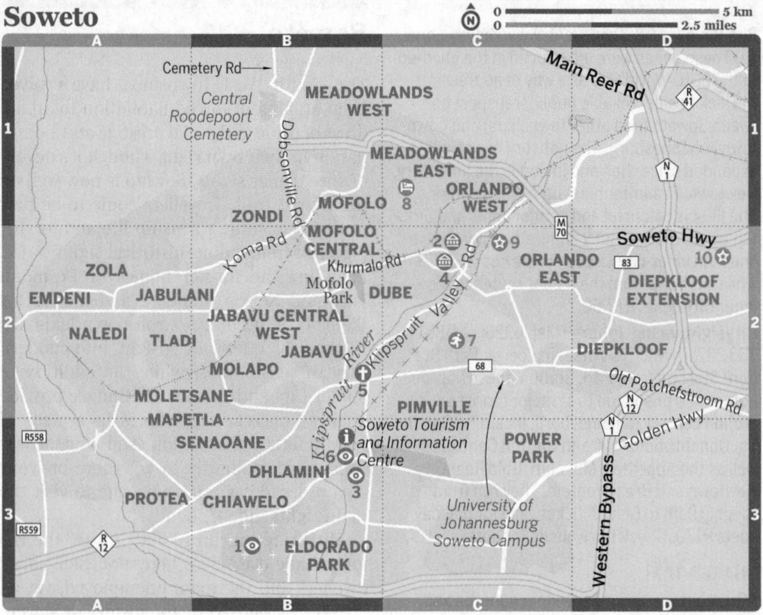

Soweto

Sights
1 Avalon Cemetery B3
Freedom Charter Monument .... (see 6)
Hector Pieterson Memorial .... (see 2)
2 Hector Pieterson Museum C2
Home of Archbishop Desmond Tutu .... (see 4)
3 Kliptown B3
4 Mandela House Museum C2
5 Regina Mundi Church B2
6 Walter Sisulu Square of Dedication B3

Activities, Courses & Tours
7 Orlando Towers C2

Sleeping
Dakalo B&B .... (see 4)
8 Lebo's Soweto Backpackers C1
Nthateng's B&B .... (see 4)
Soweto Hotel .... (see 6)
Vhavenda Hills B&B .... (see 4)

Eating
Nambitha .... (see 2)
Restaurant Vilakazi .... (see 2)
Sakhumzi Restaurant .... (see 4)
Thrive Café .... (see 4)

Entertainment
9 Orlando Stadium C2
10 Soccer City D2

around the country gathered in Kliptown Sq (known today as Freedom Sq) at the Congress of the People. The result was the Freedom Charter, which is the pillar of ANC philosophy and integral to the new constitution.

The movement was forced underground in 1960 after the Sharpeville Massacre (p520). While the struggle continued at a slower pace, it was not the only change taking place here. The demographics of the townships were changing, and as second-generation Sowetans matured, so did Soweto style. New forms of music emerged and the youth led development of a unique urban culture. Football also offered an escape, and massive support for teams such as the Moroka Swallows, Orlando Pirates and (after they split from the Pirates) Kaizer Chiefs reflected the development of an urban black identity.

The development of this new identity only served to strengthen the desire to be treated as equals. Resistance eventually spilled over on 16 June 1976, when a student protest became the precursor to the Soweto uprising.

Within days of the fighting, world opinion had turned irreversibly against the apartheid regime and Soweto became the most potent symbol of resistance to a racist South Africa.

Scenes of burning cars, 'necklaced' people and mass funerals flowed out of Soweto throughout the 1980s, while the death throes of apartheid could be felt. Mandela was released in 1990 and returned to live in his tiny home in Vilakazi St, just 200m from Archbishop Desmond Tutu.

However, Mandela's release was no panacea. Encouraged by the government, supporters of rival political parties murdered each other by the hundreds in the run-up to the 1994 free elections.

More recently life has been stable, and since 1994 Sowetans have had ownership rights over their properties. The relative calm has been further promoted by a number of redevelopment projects. The 2010 World Cup also brought great positive press for the township and the glittering Soccer City as its prime legacy, as well as improved street lighting, parks and paved roads.

Indeed, many parts of Soweto are safer and more laid-back than Johannesburg's wealthy, high-security northern suburbs.

Sights & Activities

Mandela House Museum MUSEUM

(☎011-936 7754; www.mandelahouse.com; cnr Vilakazi & Ngakane Sts, Orlando West; adult/child R60/20; ⌚9am-4.45pm) Nelson Mandela lived with his first wife, Evelyn, and later with his second wife, Winnie, in this four-room house, just off Vilakazi St. The museum, which was renovated in 2009, includes interactive exhibits on the history of the house and some interesting family photos. Just down Vilakazi St, by Sakhumzi Restaurant, is the **home of Archbishop Desmond Tutu**.

Hector Pieterson Memorial MEMORIAL

(Kumalo St, Orlando West) North of Vilakazi St is Hector Pieterson Sq. It's named after the 13-year-old who was shot dead in the run-up to the Soweto uprising in 1976, and it features this poignant memorial.

Hector Pieterson Museum MUSEUM

(☎011-536 0611; cnr Pela & Kumalot Sts, Orlando West; adult/child R30/10; ⌚10am-5pm Mon-Sat, to 4.30pm Sun) This powerful museum illuminates the role of Sowetan life in the history of the independence struggle. It follows the tragic incidents of 16 June 1976, when a peaceful student protest against the introduction of Afrikaans as a language of instruction in black secondary schools was violently quelled by police. In the resulting chaos police opened fire and a 13-year-old boy, Hector Pieterson, was shot dead.

The ensuing hours and days saw students fight running battles with the security forces in what would become known as the Soweto uprising. On the first day alone, close to 200 teenage protesters were killed.

Regina Mundi Church CHURCH

(Mkize St, Rockville; admission by donation) This church – the largest Catholic church in South Africa, with a capacity of 5000 – was an important meeting point during the apartheid years and was central to the struggle. During the 16 June 1976 student uprisings, students sought refuge inside the church, but the police followed them inside and opened fired. Bullet holes and gun-butt cracks are still visible.

Avalon Cemetery CEMETERY

(Tshabuse St; ⌚8am-4pm) Here you'll find the graves of Joe Slovo (plot B35311; the former leader of the South African Communist Party) and Hector Pieterson (plot EC462).

Kliptown NEIGHBOURHOOD

Established in 1904 and found southwest of Orlando West, Kliptown is the oldest settlement in Jo'burg to accommodate all races. It is also where the Freedom Charter was adopted on 26 June 1955. The site of the adoption, once a football field, has become the **Walter Sisulu Square of Dedication** (cnr Union Ave &

SOWETO FESTIVAL CALENDAR

Soweto Wine Festival (www.sowetowinefestival.co.za) Meet South Africa's best winemakers at this festival in early September. It takes place at the University of Johannesburg's Soweto campus.

Soweto Festival Expo (www.sowetofestivalexpo.co.za) Enjoy music, poetry, food stalls and a lifestyle expo on the last weekend of September at the Johannesburg Expo Centre.

Soweto Beer Festival (www.sowetobeerfestival.co.za) This festival is held in the last weekend of October at SHAP stadium, opposite Mofolo Park.

Soweto Marathon (www.sowetomarathon.com) Takes place in early November.

Main Rd), which includes an information centre, a hotel, banks, curio shops and the conical brick Freedom Charter Monument.

★ **Orlando Towers** ADVENTURE SPORTS
(☑ 071-674 4343; www.orlandotowers.co.za; cnr Chris Hani Rd & Dynamo St; viewing platform/bungee jumping R60/480; ☉ 10am-6pm Thu-Sun) Built originally for Orlando's Power Station, the towers host one of the world's more incongruous bungee jumps. Once painted a drab white, one tower is now decorated with a colourful mural depicting, among others, Nelson Mandela, singer Yvonne Chaka Chaka and a football stadium. The other tower displays the FNB logo (the bank commissioned the murals in 2002).

Abseiling and rap jumping (forward abseiling) are also available (R360). There's a bar and hang-out area.

 ## Tours

Dozens of companies offer tours of Soweto; your accommodation should be able to put you in touch with them or offer an in-house service.

Lebo's Soweto Bicycle Tours BICYCLE TOUR
(☑ 011-936 3444; www.sowetobicycletours.com; 2hr/day R350/550) Soweto's clay paths and grassy nooks make for fabulous cycling terrain. The company also owns Lebo's Soweto Backpackers, which offers R50 tour discounts for guests.

Africa My Beginning Tours CULTURAL TOUR
(☑ 082 634 4841, 011-075 2201; www.sowetovisits.co.za) Runs various tours of Soweto, including minibus-taxi tours (R400, four hours), bicycle tours (R500, four hours) and full-day Johannesburg and Soweto tours (R700).

Taste of Africa TOUR
(☑ 082 565 2520, 011-482 8114; www.tasteofafrica.co.za) Offers an excellent 24-hour tour (R780 per person) where you can explore Soweto with locals, far off the beaten track.

Vhupo Tours CULTURAL TOUR
(☑ 076-601 3204; www.vhupo-tours.com) Run by Soweto resident Bruce Luthanga, this place offers a range of tours around Soweto, including an evening out at a shebeen.

Sleeping

There are many B&Bs in the township, most in the immediate vicinity of Vilakazi St.

Lebo's Soweto Backpackers BACKPACKERS $
(☑ 084 851 8681, 011-936 3444; www.soweto-backpackers.com; 10823A Pooe St, Orlando West;

dm/s/d without bathroom R160/270/390; P 🛜) For the real township experience, this well-established hostel set by lovely parklands is your answer. It's a healthy walk from the Vilakazi St action, but guests love the shaded beer garden, restaurant (meals from R60) and pool table. Dorms are neat and clean and the double rooms are excellent value. The friendly staff encourages interactivity, while all kinds of tours are available.

Free Baz Bus shuttles to Johannesburg can be arranged.

Nthateng's B&B GUESTHOUSE $$
(☑ 082 335 7956, 011-051 9362; nthatengmd@gmail.com; 6991 Inhlwathi St, Orlando West; s/d incl breakfast R535/695; P 🛜) Dark woods, tan linens, sandy-coloured walls and a few kitschy touches give this spacious guesthouse an air of early '80s post-disco chill. However, Nthateng is an animated host who insists on top-shelf personal tours, delicious breakfasts and a *mi casa es su casa* state of mind. It's in an ideal location near the museum and restaurants.

Soweto Hotel HOTEL $$
(☑ 011-527 7300; www.sowetohotel.co.za; Walter Sisulu Sq of Dedication, Kliptown; s/d incl breakfast from R1200/1400; P @ 🛜) You wouldn't guess from the outside, but this muscular concrete building overlooking a square shelters snug, clean-as-a-pin rooms, all in beiges and maroons, that offer tranquil havens for businesspeople and travellers. There's a jazz design that continues in the restaurant and bar. Prices drop to R940 on weekends.

Vhavenda Hills B&B GUESTHOUSE $$
(☑ 082 213 1630, 011-936 4275; www.sowetobnb.co.za; 11749 Mampuru St, Orlando West; s/d incl breakfast R500/750; P 🛜) It's pure pleasure to walk into Vhavenda Hills' cool interior after a long day's sightseeing, and to savour the double rewards of a friendly welcome from the owner, Soweto-born-and-bred Kate Luthaga, and a comfy room. It's a five-minute stroll from the Mandela House Museum.

Dakalo B&B GUESTHOUSE $$
(☑ 082 723 0585, 011-936 9328; www.dakalobedandbreakfast.co.za; 6963 Inhlwathi St, Orlando West; s/d incl breakfast R450/800; P 🛜) Spitting distance from Vilakazi St (but on a quiet lane), this friendly family home is full of funky decor, from the psychedelic blue-spotted tiles in the bathroom to animal-print curtains and rococo collectibles. There are four rooms; try for the one that opens onto the flower-filled garden at the back.

Eating

There are tons of places to go out for a drink in Soweto, from informal shebeens to more upmarket bars and restaurants. The most tourist-friendly eateries are on Vilakazi St.

Restaurant Vilakazi SOUTH AFRICAN **$$**
(☎011-057 1290; www.restaurantvilakazi.co.za; Vilakazi St, Orlando West; mains R70-150; ⊙10am-10pm) A seductive setting complete with a breezy terrace is the draw at this well-regarded joint up Vilakazi St. The chef prepares a colourful assortment of palate pleasers, such as salads, fish dishes, burgers and pastas as well as local-style carnivorous options, including oxtail, *boerewors* (sausage) and *mogodu* (tripe).

Nambitha SOUTH AFRICAN **$$**
(☎011-936 9128; www.nambitharestaurant.co.za; Vilakazi St, Orlando West; mains R80-170; ⊙10am-10pm) Vilakazi St's most stylish option, this open-fronted bar and restaurant is popular with Soweto's bright young 20-somethings. It's a great place to try out African staples, such as *mogodu* with spinach, but you'll also find a large selection of more conventional dishes if your tummy and palate are timid. Live dinnertime jazz certain days cranks the hip atmosphere a notch.

Thrive Café INTERNATIONAL **$$**
(☎011-536 1838; www.thrivecafe.co.za; 8038 Vilakazi St, Orlando West; mains R50-130; ⊙7am-6pm Tue & Wed, 10am-10pm Thu, 10am-11pm Fri-Sun; 📶) A surprisingly hip restaurant with a sleek, design-led interior, this cool culinary outpost opened in 2013 and is a sign of the township's changing sensibilities. It serves up snack options, light meals, crunchy salads and a few meaty mains. It's also a good place to hang out and just soak up the atmosphere while nursing a beer on the upstairs terrace.

Sakhumzi Restaurant SOUTH AFRICAN **$$**
(☎011-536 1379; www.sakhumzi.co.za; 6980 Vilakazi St, Orlando West; lunch buffet R140, mains R70-190; ⊙11am-10pm daily) Brimming with good cheer, Sakhumzi is firmly on the tourist trail and bus parties regularly pass through for the excellent-value daily lunch buffets. Patrons spill onto the street tables and mingle joyfully with passers-by. Expect African staples such as mutton stew, *umleqwa* (traditional-style steamed chicken) and mealie pap as well as more conventional burgers and steaks.

SOCCER CITY

Soccer City (Baragwanath Rd, Diepkloof) The headquarters of the 2010 FIFA World Cup, Soccer City stadium is shaped like a calabash and dominates the abandoned mining tracts on the outskirts of Soweto. It's an architectural treat, courtesy of Bobby van Bebber, that reminds hazy locals that they did indeed host the famous sporting event. If you want to walk through the players' race and imagine forgotten glory, take an excellent **guided tour** (☎011-247 5300; per person R80; ⊙9am, 10.30am, noon & 3pm).

Entertainment

Soccer City, also known as FNB Stadium, is the new headquarters of South African football. It's a destination in its own right due to its architectural brilliance. **Orlando Stadium** (Mooki St & Valley Rd, Orlando East) is also worth a visit, especially when the Orlando Pirates meet their sworn enemy, the Kaizer Chiefs.

Information

There are banks with ATMs in Walter Sisulu Square of Dedication. Foreign exchange is available at the Soweto Hotel, also in the square.

Soweto Tourism and Information Centre (☎011-342 4316; www.joburgtourism.com; Walter Sisulu Sq of Dedication, Kliptown; ⊙8am-5pm Mon-Fri) Has a few brochures and can help with tours.

Getting There & Away

Many tourists take a half- or full-day guided tour of Soweto, but you can choose to travel independently using the safe Rea Vaya bus system. It's also pretty straightforward (and safe) to drive to Soweto with your own wheels.

Cradle of Humankind

The area to the west of Jo'burg is one of the world's most important palaeontological zones, focused on the Sterkfontein hominid fossil fields. The area is part of the 470-sq-km **Cradle of Humankind** (www.cradleofhumankind.co.za), which is listed for preservation by Unesco. Most Jo'burg-based tour operators offer full- and half-day tours of the area, but it's also an easy drive if you have your own wheels.

WORTH A TRIP

NIROX FOUNDATION

Nirox Foundation (www.niroxarts.com; Rte 540, Kromdraai Rd) Located in the heart of the Cradle of Humankind, the Nirox Foundation is an evolutionary advancement for the creative arts and a gorgeous place to visit. Leading South African and international sculptors, painters and conceptual artists take up secluded residencies or display their work for public perusal in the 1500-sq-m private property. The goal is no less than to 'advance Africa's place in the global contemporary arts'.

Sights & Activities

Maropeng MUSEUM
(☎014-577 9000; www.maropeng.co.za; Rte 400, off Rte 563, Hekpoort Rd; adult/child R160/90, with Sterkfontein Caves R215/143; ⊙9am-5pm) Maropeng is well worth a visit. Housed in a building that looks like a giant grassy mound on one side and shiny modern steel on the other, it's an all-in-one information centre, visitor attraction and entertainment complex. The exhibits here show how the human race has progressed since its very beginnings. There are active fossil sites, restaurants, a curio shop and a 5000-seat amphitheatre for outdoor events.

There's also a pretty cool boat ride back in time that takes visitors through the ice age and even to a simulated black hole. Even better are the series of interactive exhibits on the evolvement of the species, including the use of fire and the development of language.

Sterkfontein Caves CAVE
(☎011-577 9000; www.maropeng.co.za; Sterkfontein Caves Rd; adult/child R195/97, with Maropeng R215/143; ⊙9am-5pm) About 10km away from Maropeng (it's signposted), this place includes a permanent hominid exhibit and a walkway past the excavation site. Tours down into the caves, one of the most significant archaeological sites in the world, leave every 30 minutes. The last tour is at 4pm. A discount ticket that covers the caves and Maropeng must be purchased by 1pm.

Old Kromdraai Mine Museum MUSEUM
(☎082 259 2162, 073 147 8417; Ibis Ridge Farm, Rte 540, Kromdraai Rd; adult/child R150/80; ⊙by appointment Tue-Fri, 9am-5pm Sat & Sun, last tour 4pm) Here is the first goldmine on the Witwatersrand – operations started in 1881. Guided tours leave the converted shed every hour.

Sleeping & Eating

Maropeng Hotel HOTEL $$$
(☎014-577 9000; www.maropeng.co.za; Rte 400, off Rte 563, Hekpoort Rd; s/d incl breakfast R1500/2200; P❄@☜≋) Inside the Maropeng complex, this low-slung pad offers 24 rooms that are fancily decorated and blessed with breathtaking views of the Witwatersberg and Magaliesberg ranges.

LeSel@The Cradle INTERNATIONAL $$
(☎011-659 1622; www.thecradle.co.za; Rte 540, Kromdraai Rd; mains R120-160, menu R245; ⊙noon-4pm Thu, noon-4pm & 6-10pm Fri, 8-11am, noon-4pm & 6-10pm Sat, 8-11am & noon-4pm Sun) Set in a sprawling 30-sq-km wildlife reserve, this restaurant has won accolades for its brilliant-value set menu (Sunday only) and tasty mains, but the real appeal is the open-air terrace with panoramic views of the undulating hills.

Southern Gauteng

Bisected by the Vaal River, this area is home to the cities of Vereeniging, Sebokeng and Vanderbijlpark, and has an eventful past. The Vaal River – the *gij!garib* (tawny) to the San, *lekoa* (erratic) to the Sotho and *vaal* (dirty) to the Afrikaners – played an important role in Southern African history, serving as a natural dividing line between the 'Transvaal' and the south.

It was near the Vaal that the Treaty of Vereeniging, which led to the end of the 1899–1902 Anglo-Boer War, was negotiated. And more recently, at Sharpeville and Evaton, on 21 March 1960, black civilians protested against the pass laws by publicly burning their passbooks. Police opened fire on the protestors at Sharpeville, killing 69 and wounding about 180; most were shot in the back. Today, 21 March is commemorated in South Africa as Human Rights Day (a public holiday).

In 1984 in Sebokeng, security forces violently reacted to a black boycott of rent and service tariffs. About 95 people were killed. These slaughters galvanised the black population into a more unified force, and ultimately hastened the fall of apartheid.

PRETORIA

POP 1.65 MILLION

South Africa's administrative centre is a handsome city, with a number of gracious old houses in the city centre, large, leafy suburbs, and wide streets that are lined with a purple haze of jacarandas in October and November.

It's more of an Afrikaner city than Jo'burg, and its bars and restaurants are less cosmopolitan – sedate Pretoria was once at the heart of the apartheid regime and its very name a symbol of oppression. Today it's home to a growing number of black civil servants and foreign embassy workers, who are infusing the city with a new sense of multiculturalism.

History

The fertile Apies River, on which the city of Pretoria sits today, was the support system for a large population of Nguni-speaking cattle farmers for hundreds of years.

However, the Zulu wars caused massive destruction and dislocation. Much of the black population was slaughtered and most of the remaining people fled north into present-day Zimbabwe. In 1841 the first Boers trekked into a temporary vacuum. With no one around, they laid claim to the land that would become their capital.

By the time the British granted independence to the Zuid-Afrikaansche Republiek (ZAR) in the early 1850s, there were estimated to be 15,000 whites and 100,000 blacks living between the Vaal and Limpopo Rivers. The whites were widely scattered, and in 1853 two farms on the Apies River were bought as the site for the republic's capital.

Pretoria, which was named after Andries Pretorius, was nothing more than a tiny frontier village with a grandiose title, but the servants of the British Empire were watching it with growing misgivings. They acted in 1877, annexing the republic; the Boers went to war (Pretoria came under siege at the beginning of 1881) and won back their independence.

The discovery of gold on the Witwatersrand in the late 1880s changed everything, and within 20 years the Boers would again be at war with the British.

With the British making efforts towards reconciliation, self-government was again granted to the Transvaal in 1906, and through an unwieldy compromise Pretoria was made the administrative capital. The Union of South Africa came into being in 1910, but Pretoria was not to regain its status until 1961, when the Republic of South Africa came into existence under the leadership of Hendrik Verwoerd.

WORTH A TRIP

VAAL DAM

With over 600km of coastline and a 5km-long island, South Africa's largest dam is hugely popular with the boating fraternity. There are nine yacht clubs and seven marinas, hosting a number of nautical events that are worth checking out, including the Round the Island **yacht race** in April, the Keelboat Week Regatta in September and the Bayshore Marina Treasure Hunt in spring.

It's about a two-hour drive from Johannesburg and there are plenty of places to stay and eat in towns like **Vaal Marina** in Gauteng, and Deneysville, Villiers and Franfort across the border in Free State.

Sights

Voortrekker Monument MONUMENT

(Map p362; ☎012-326 6770; www.vtm.org.za; Eeufees Rd; adult/child R55/30; ⌚8am-6pm Sep-Apr, to 5pm May-Aug) The imposing Voortrekker Monument was constructed between 1938 and 1949 to honour the journey of the Voortrekkers, who trekked north over the coastal mountains of the Cape into the heart of the African veld. The monument is 3km south of the city and is clearly signposted from the N1 freeway. It is surrounded by a 3.40-sq-km nature reserve.

The edifice is ringed by a stone wall carved with 64 wagons in a traditional defensive *laager* (circle). The building itself is a huge stone cube and each corner bears the face of an Afrikaner hero. A staircase and elevator lead to the roof and a great panoramic view of Pretoria.

Church Square SQUARE

(Map p352) At the heart of Pretoria, **Church Square** is surrounded by imposing public buildings. These include the **Palace of Justice**, where the Rivonia Trial that sentenced Nelson Mandela to life imprisonment was held, on the northern side; the **OuRaadsaal (Old Government) building** on the southern side; the **Old Capitol Theatre** in the northwestern corner; **First National Bank** in the northeast; the **Old Nederlandsche Bank building**, which adjoins Café Riche and houses the tourist information centre; and the **main post office** on the western side.

Old Lion (Paul Kruger) takes pride of place in the centre, surveying his miniature kingdom.

Melrose House HISTORIC BUILDING
(Map p352; ☎012-322 2805; 275 Jeff Masemola St (Jacob Maré St); adult/child R20/5; ⏲10am-5pm Tue-Sun) This stately mansion built in 1886 is of strong historical significance. On 31 May 1902 the Treaty of Vereeniging, which marked the end of the Anglo-Boer War (1899–1902), was signed in the dining room. Highlights of the house include a grand billiard room with a vibrant stained-glass smoking nook and a conservatory containing a collection of political cartoons from the Anglo-Boer War.

Central Pretoria

0 — 400 m
0 — 0.2 miles

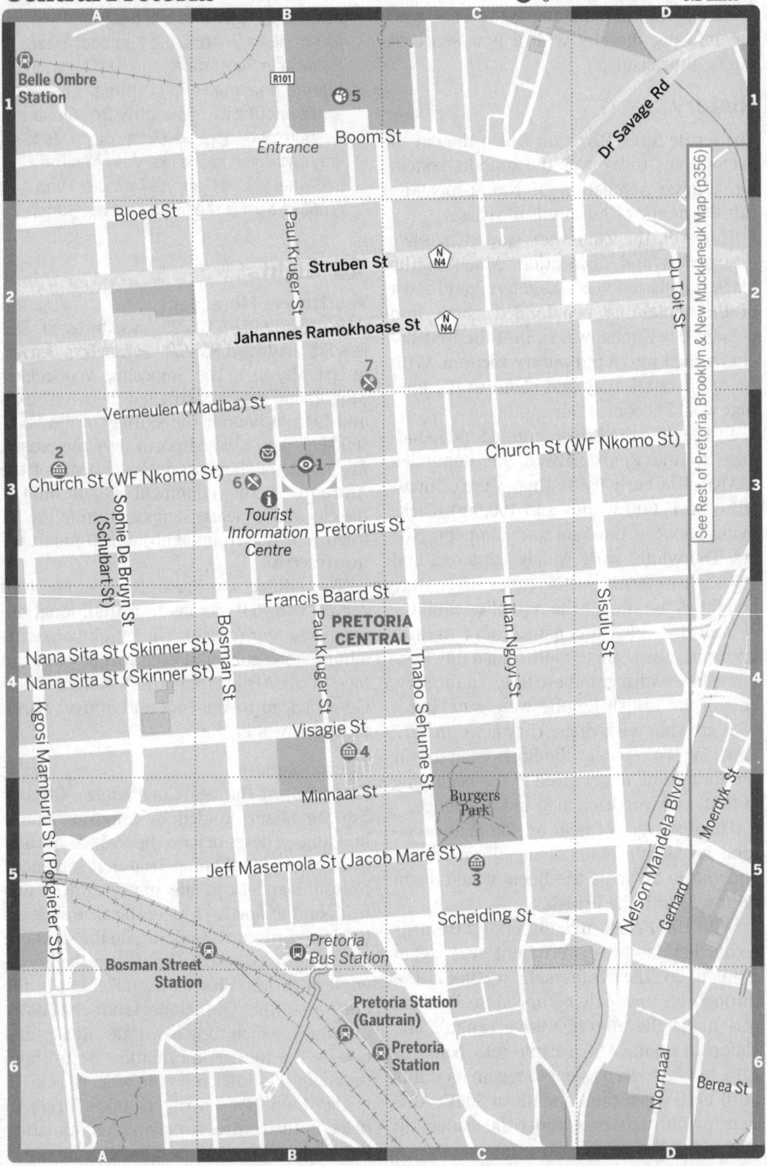

Central Pretoria

Sights

1 Church Square B3
2 Kruger Museum A3
3 Melrose House C5
4 National Cultural History
 Museum .. B4
5 Pretoria National Zoological
 Gardens.. B1

Eating

6 Café Riche.. B3
7 Tribeca .. B2

Pretoria National Zoological Gardens ZOO
(Map p352; ☑012-328 3265; www.nzg.ac.za; cnr Paul Kruger & Boom Sts; adult/child R85/55, cable car R10/8; ◷8.30am-4.30pm) There's a reptile park and an aquarium here, as well as a vast collection of exotic trees and plenty of picnic spots. The highlight, though, is the **cable car**, which runs up to the top of a hill that overlooks the city. It's about 1km out of the city centre.

Union Buildings BUILDING
(Map p356; Government Ave) **FREE** These sweeping sandstone buildings are the headquarters of government and home to the presidential offices. The gardens are often used for public celebrations, and Nelson Mandela's inauguration took place here back in 1994. Statues of a few former prime ministers inhabit the grounds, including an impressive General Louis Botha on horseback. There's also a WWI memorial here, and a memorial to the South African police.

The buildings themselves aren't open to the public, but the grounds are open seven days a week.

Kruger Museum MUSEUM
(Map p352; ☑012-000 0010; www.ditsong.org. za; 60 Church St; adult/child R35/15; ◷8.30am-4.30pm) A short walk west from Church Sq is the former residence of Paul Kruger, now the Paul Kruger house museum. The house, built in 1884, would have been grand at the time but today seems lost on the busy street. Guarded by two stone lions, the house contains period furniture and a random collection of personal knick-knacks belonging to Kruger and his wife.

National Cultural History Museum MUSEUM
(Map p352; ☑012-324 6082; www.ditsong.org.za; cnr Visagie & Schubert Sts; adult/child R35/20; ◷8am-4pm) Concentrating on the cultural

history of South Africa, this museum features exhibitions on San rock art, Iron Age figurines from Limpopo and a small gallery of contemporary South African works, among others.

Pretoria Art Museum GALLERY
(Map p356; ☑021-358 6750; www.pretoriaartmuseum.co.za; cnr Francis Baard & Wessels St, Arcadia Park; adult/child R20/5; ◷10am-5pm Tue-Sun) This art museum specialises in South African art from throughout the country's history. It also features regularly changing exhibitions.

⚜ Festivals & Events

Oppikoppi Music Festival MUSIC
(www.oppikoppi.co.za) A Woodstock-type bash where local and international rock bands congregate in a celebration of peace, love and music. It's usually staged in August – visit the website for the latest.

Pretoria Show FAIR
This immensely popular agricultural show and flea market is held during the third week of August at the Tshwane Events Centre.

🛏 Sleeping

🛏 Arcadia & Hatfield

1322 Backpackers International BACKPACKERS $
(Map p362; ☑012-362 3905; www.1322backpackers.com; 1322 Arcadia St, Hatfield; dm R150-170, without bathroom & incl breakfast s R250-300, d R350-380; P@🛰🗲) This hostel is a welcoming retreat, where travellers congregate around a backyard pool and a buzzing little anteroom bar. You can stay in neat three-to eight-bed dorms, or smallish, converted wood and brick sheds at the bottom of the garden (a bit stifling in summer). The shared bathrooms are clean and all guests have kitchen access. Cash only.

Pumbas Backpackers BACKPACKERS $
(Map p356; ☑012-362 5343; www.pumbas.co.za; 1232 Arcadia St, Hatfield; incl breakfast dm R150, d without bathroom R450; P🛰🗲) Although this budget-friendly hostel won't knock your socks off, it features an assortment of tidy and serviceable private rooms and dorms and is optimally placed in Hatfield, a short stroll from the Gauteng station. There's a kitchen for guests' use and a pocket-sized pool.

FREEDOM PARK: A HOLISTIC APPROACH TO HISTORY

Freedom Park (Map p362; ☎012-336 4000; www.freedompark.co.za; cnr Koch St & 7th Ave; adult/child park R45/25, museum R60/45; ⏲8am-4.30pm, tours 9am, noon & 3pm) This stunning memorial adopts an integrated approach to South Africa's war history and is a place of architectural imagination and collective healing. Located across the *kopjie* (rocky hill) from the austere Voortrekker Monument, Freedom Park honours fallen South Africans in all major conflicts. Highlights include the Isivivane Garden of Remembrance; Sikhimbuto, the wall of inscribed names of fallen heroes; //hapo, a museum and interpretative centre focussing on Southern African history; and Mveledzo, a spiral path that cuts into the natural landscape.

Bed & Breakfast in Hatfield GUESTHOUSE $$
(Map p356; ☎083 447 2066, 012-362 5392; www.bandbhatfield.co.za; 1265 Arcadia St, Hatfield; s/d incl breakfast R680/840; P❄📶🏊) A short amble from the Hatfield Gauteng station, this B&B is the epitome of a refined cocoon, revelling quietly in minimalist lines, soothing colour accents and well-thought-out decorative touches – it helps that the owner is a retired architect. The pool at the back is a bonus. Note that only three rooms come equipped with air-con.

East View Guest House GUESTHOUSE $$
(Map p356; ☎082 451 6516, 012-343 7180; eastview1@mweb.co.za; 175 East Ave, Arcadia; s/d incl breakfast R650/780; P📶🏊) At this calm haven in a backstreet few know, Lynette Blignaut offers the perfect small B&B experience, with six fresh rooms done out in taupe and grey shades, and modern bathrooms. It occupies an imposing villa in the embassy district, close to the Union Buildings. Breakfasts are copious – mmm, the homemade muffins! – and evening meals can be arranged.

Village in Hatfield GUESTHOUSE $$
(Map p356; ☎012-362 5370; www.hatfieldvillage.co.za; 324 Glyn St, Hatfield; incl breakfast s R400-680, d R600-890; P@🏊) On the corner of Arcadia St is this delightful property that offers well-presented private rooms and helpful service. There's a swimming pool and a shaded courtyard. Excellent value.

Courtyard Arcadia Hotel HOTEL $$
(Map p356; ☎012-342 4940; www.clhg.com; cnr Park & Hill Sts, Arcadia; d R1400-1500; P❄📶🏊) At the upper end of the City Lodge chain spectrum is this Cape Dutch manor house in the heart of the embassy district. The 69 rooms, which occupy several residences, are a little pedestrian for the grandeur of the setting, but service is assured and the evening happy hours are a nice touch. Booking online gets you the best deal.

Protea Hotel Hatfield HOTEL $$
(Map p356; ☎012-364 0300; www.proteahotels.com; 1141 Burnett St, Hatfield; d R955-1130; P❄📶🏊) If you're after stumbling access to Hatfield's shops and bars, then this is the only place to consider. Luckily, it's pretty good, too. The tall, modern building has sparkling three-star rooms with decent-size bathrooms. If you plan to stay here, aim high – the views get better the higher you go. Look out for internet deals at weekends.

Khayalethu Guest House GUESTHOUSE $$
(Map p362; ☎082 440 4325, 012-362 5403; www.ghk.co.za; 1322 Arcadia St, Hatfield; s/d incl breakfast R500/700; P📶🏊) Colourful and quirky, this discreet number is a reliable bet if you're counting the pennies. The bedrooms are small and simple but well tended. Local curios and kitsch adorn the kitchen walls, and there's a small pool.

🛏 Brooklyn, Lynnwood & Menlo Park

★Foreigners Friend Guesthouse GUESTHOUSE $$
(☎082 676 2585, 011-975 8524; www.foreignersfriend.co.za; 409A Om die Berg St, Lynnwood; incl breakfast s R750-1000, d R1000-1250; P❄📶🏊) Character and charm. Somewhere between a boutique hotel and a B&B, this enchanting abode is an oasis of tranquillity in a wonderfully quiet neighbourhood. It has 10 spacious, well-organised rooms, a well-furnished ground-floor living area, a lush garden and a spiffing swimming pool. A beautifully presented breakfast is served on a breezy terrace.

Brooks Cottages GUESTHOUSE $$
(Map p356; ☎082 448 3902, 012-362 3150; www.brookscottages.co.za; 283 Brooks St, Brooklyn; s/d incl breakfast R670/920; P📶🏊) About

the only thing wrong with this attractive address is that it's in high demand, meaning you need to book well in advance to snag one of its cosy, excellent-value rooms with sparkling bathrooms. With its pressed ceilings, wooden floors and soberly elegant living room, this lovingly restored house has charm in spades. Dinner is available on request.

Richtershuyz GUESTHOUSE **$$**
(Map p362; ☎012-346 2025; www.richtershuyz.co.za; 375 Mackenzie St, Brooklyn; incl breakfast s R770-800, d R990; P ❄ 📶 🏊) In a residential neighbourhood, this venture in a low-slung building feels like a warm, soft nest. It conceals seven rooms that come with private entrances, attractive tiled bathrooms, crisp linen, excellent bedding and complimentary snacks, while the swimming pool in the garden is a little beauty. Evening meals are available (weekdays only).

Ambiance Guesthouse GUESTHOUSE **$$**
(Map p362; ☎083 280 0981; www.ambianceguesthouse.com; 28 3rd St, Menlo Park; s/d R640/890; P 📶 🏊) This elegant villa in the leafy suburb of Menlo Park is just the ticket for those seeking a stylish home-away-from-home experience in Pretoria. The four rooms are different in design and colour scheme and open onto a delightful garden complete with a nifty pool; our choice is 'Petit Paris', with a claw-footed bath. Breakfast costs R55.

314 on Clark GUESTHOUSE **$$**
(Map p356; ☎012-346 2760; www.314onclark.com; 314 Clark St, Brooklyn; incl breakfast s R600-780, d R960; P ❄ 📶) A true find for peace seekers, this well-run establishment shelters 13 immaculate rooms of varying sizes and shapes, including a couple of self-catering units. The manicured garden is another highlight. What's missing? A pool.

Bwelani GUESTHOUSE **$$**
(Map p356; ☎083 200 5939, 012-362 1148; www.bwelani.co.za; 210 Roper St, Brooklyn; s incl breakfast R470-770, d incl breakfast R750-1100, apt s R900-1000, d R1400-1600; P ❄ 📶 🏊) Concealed behind high walls down near the university, this bright, contemporary B&B has lots of personality. The seven rooms, including two self-catering apartments, are imaginatively designed and embellished with various African art pieces collected by the owner. Our fave is Jozi, with its funky decor and supersized bedroom. Dinner available on request.

WORTH A TRIP

MULDERSDRIFT

Kloofzicht Lodge & Spa (☎0861 148 866; www.kloofzicht.co.za; Rte 374, Muldersdrift; incl breakfast s R1950-2245, d R2660-4500, lunch buffet R165-175, dinner R225; ⏲noon-2.30pm) Kloofzicht is on a small nature reserve featuring elands, warthogs, blue wildebeests, red hartebeests, gemsbok and zebras. There's also a fly-fishing academy where visitors can rent a rod and cast off. On Sunday it hosts a stupendous buffet lunch with 'cliff views', which books out every week. The day spa is equally impressive. You'll feel a long way from downtown Johannesburg.

The lodge is found north of Krugersdorp, alongside the N14, in the pretty hamlet of Muldersdrift. It's particularly popular for weddings and with weekenders.

Alpine Attitude BOUTIQUE HOTEL **$$$**
(☎082 579 1628, 012-348 6504; www.alpineattiude.co.za; 522 Atterbury Rd, Menlo Park; incl breakfast s R1200-1500, d R1500-2200; P ❄ 📶 🏊) Looking for a night somewhere extra special? Make a beeline for this unique boutique hotel. The seven rooms have been creatively designed – each one has its own theme and decor. The Transparent room, where, as the name suggests, everything (except the bedding) is transparent, has to be seen to be believed. Amenities include restaurant, bar and pool.

It also features five self-catering apartments. It's on a busy thoroughfare, but most units overlook a quiet garden at the back.

Groenkloof

131 Herbert Baker BOUTIQUE HOTEL **$$$**
(Map p362; ☎012-751 2070; www.131.co.za; 131 Herbert Baker St, Groenkloof; d incl breakfast from R7200; P ❄ 📶 🏊) A hotel with style, this venture strikes a perfect balance between sophistication, seclusion and privacy (there are only eight rooms), on a hillside south of the centre – the location is one of the best in Pretoria. Shame that only rooms 1, 2 and 3 come with city views. One quibble: for the price, you'd expect a bigger pool.

There's an on-site restaurant.

Eating

There are plenty of good places to eat in Pretoria and prices are a little lower than

Rest of Pretoria, Brooklyn & New Muckleneuk

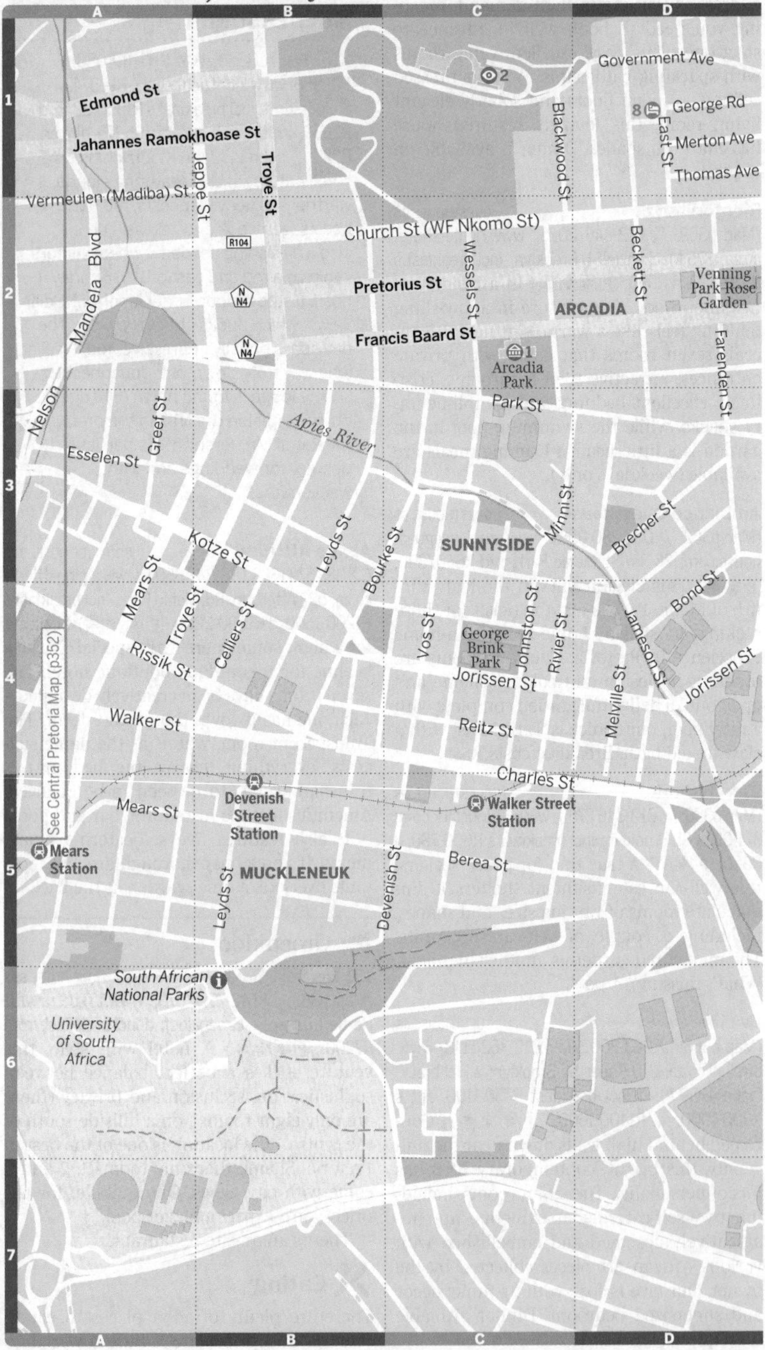
A
B
C
D
1
2
3
4
5
6
7
Government Ave
George Rd
Merton Ave
Thomas Ave
East St
Blackwood St
Edmond St
Jahannes Ramokhoase St
Vermeulen (Madiba) St
Jeppe St
Troye St
Church St (WF Nkomo St)
R104
Mandela Blvd
Pretorius St
Wessels St
Beckett St
Venning Park Rose Garden
ARCADIA
N4
Francis Baard St
Arcadia Park
Farenden St
Nelson
Park St
Greef St
Apies River
Esselen St
Minni St
Brecher St
Kotze St
Leyds St
Bourke St
SUNNYSIDE
Mears St
Bond St
Troye St
Celliers St
Vos St
George Brink Park
Johnston St
Rivier St
Jameson St
Rissik St
Jorissen St
Melville St
Jorissen St
See Central Pretoria Map (p352)
Walker St
Reitz St
Charles St
Devenish Street Station
Walker Street Station
Mears St
Mears Station
Berea St
Leyds St
MUCKLENEUK
Devenish St
South African National Parks
University of South Africa

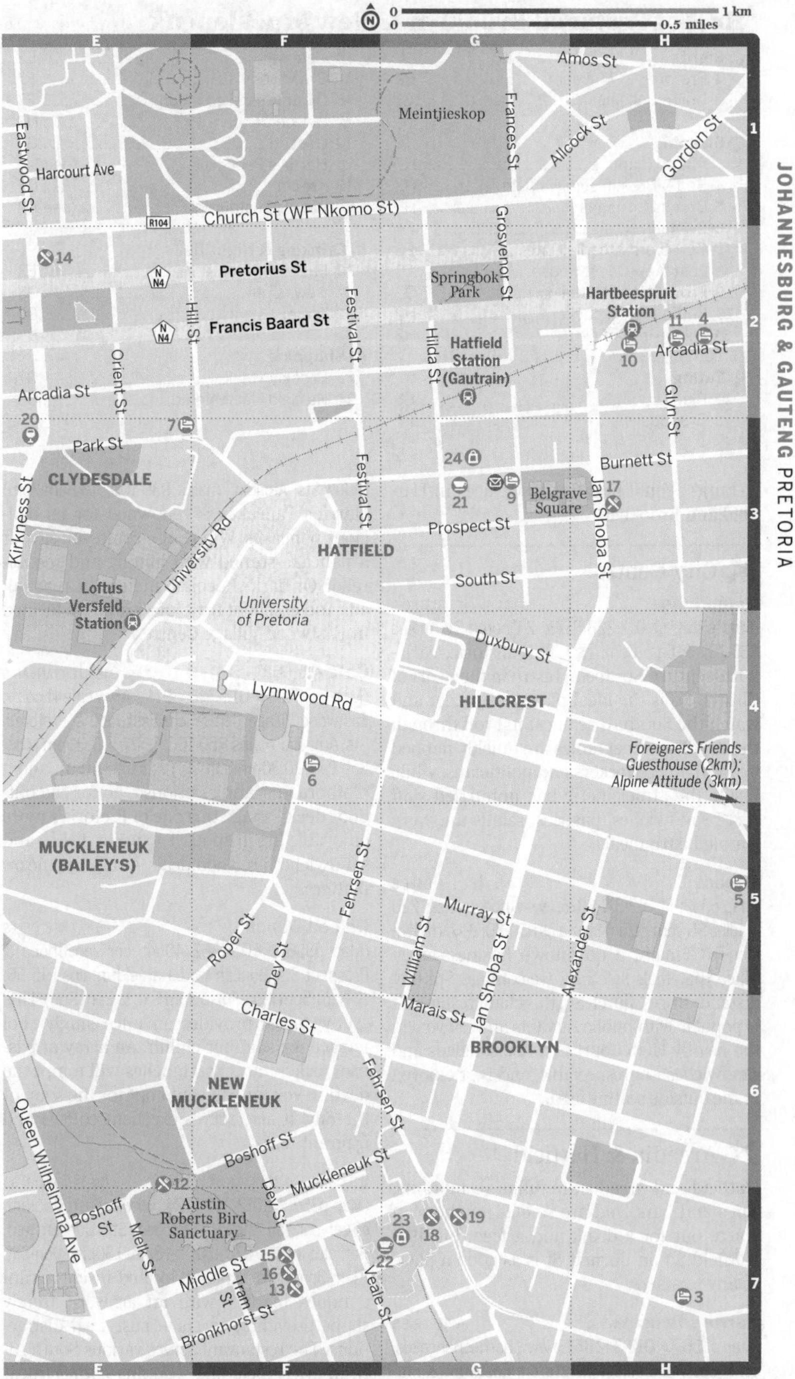
0 1 km
0 0.5 miles
E
F
G
H
1
2
3
4
5
6
7
Amos St
Meintjieskop
Frances St
Allcock St
Gordon St
Eastwood St
Harcourt Ave
Church St (WF Nkomo St)
R104
Grosvenor St
Pretorius St
N4
Springbok Park
Hill St
Francis Baard St
Festival St
Hilda St
Hartbeespruit Station
11
4
10
Arcadia St
Orient St
Hatfield Station (Gautrain)
Glyn St
Arcadia St
20
7
Park St
24
Burnett St
CLYDESDALE
21
9
Belgrave Square
Jan Shoba St
17
Kirkness St
University Rd
Festival St
Prospect St
HATFIELD
South St
Loftus Versfeld Station
University of Pretoria
Duxbury St
Lynnwood Rd
HILLCREST
Foreigners Friends Guesthouse (2km); Alpine Attitude (3km)
6
MUCKLENEUK (BAILEY'S)
Fehrsen St
5
Murray St
Roper St
Dey St
William St
Jan Shoba St
Alexander St
Marais St
Charles St
BROOKLYN
NEW MUCKLENEUK
Fehrsen St
Queen Wilhelmina Ave
Boshoff St
Muckleneuk St
12
Dey St
Boshoff St
Melk St
Austin Roberts Bird Sanctuary
23
18
19
15
16
13
22
Middle St
Tram St
Veale St
Bronkhorst St
3
JOHANNESBURG & GAUTENG PRETORIA

Rest of Pretoria, Brooklyn & New Muckleneuk

Jo'burg's. You'll find the best places in Hatfield and Brooklyn.

City Centre

Café Riche BISTRO $
(Map p352; ☎012-328 3173; 2 Church St; mains R35-70; ⊙6am-6pm; ☜) This historic, early-20th-century European bistro in the heart of Church Sq is the ideal place to sip beer and watch the South African capital roll through the day. The street tables are quickly nabbed by local office workers and politicians, while inside the atmospheric bar, unhurried staff serve sandwiches, pastries, salads and very simple bistro meals.

Tribeca CAFE $
(Map p352; ☎012-321 8876; www.tribeca.co.za; 220 Madiba St (Vermeulen) St; mains R50-80; ⊙7am-5pm Mon-Fri) Finally, a downtown business-lunch place that feels safe and welcoming. Spitting distance from Church Sq, this chain restaurant is popular with public servants and lawyers in the nearby High Court Chambers. Salads and sandwiches are respectable, and best enjoyed in the outside seating area.

Arcadia & Hatfield

Hatfield and Arcadia are full of restaurants, cafes and bars, and are safe at any hour. If you're out for a drink and a feed, bustling Hatfield Sq on Burnett St is as good a place as any to start.

Harrie's Pancakes CREPERIE $
(Map p356; ☎012-342 3613; www.harriespancakes.com; Eastwood Village Centre, cnr Eastwood & Pretorius Sts, Arcadia; mains R30-100; ⊙8am-7pm) Harrie's Pancakes is renowned for its delicious pancakes. Where else could you savour a pancake stuffed with biltong and mozzarella? Or dark-chocolate mousse? Great salads and excellent fruit juices, too. It's located in Eastwood Village Centre.

Café 41 MEDITERRANEAN $
(Map p356; ☎012-342 8914; www.cafe41.co.za; Eastwood Village Centre, cnr Eastwood & Pretorius Sts, Arcadia; mains R50-105; ⊙7am-11.30pm Mon-Sat, 9am-10.30pm Sun; ☜) A huge menu and a plethora of seating options – go for the outdoor deck – make this one of Pretoria's more enjoyable lunch spots. The pasta dishes and sandwiches are good deals, as are the mezze platters.

Deli on Duncan CAFE, DELI $
(Map p356; ☎012-362 4054; cnr Jan Shoba & Prospect Sts, Duncan Yard, Hatfield; mains R15-50; ⊙8am-5pm Mon-Fri, to 3pm Sat, to 2pm Sun) This groovy place provides an unceasingly cool terrace for summer chillin'. An array of pastries, cakes, tarts and quiches will tempt the devil in you, or you could opt for the soup of the day. It also serves excellent coffees and fragrant teas.

Papa's Restaurant SOUTH AFRICAN $$
(Map p356; ☎012-362 2224; www.papasrestaurant.co.za; cnr Jan Shoba & Prospect Sts, Duncan Yard, Hatfield; mains R70-150; ⊙8am-9.30pm Mon-Sat, 10am-3pm Sun) Papa's is located inside a mini antiques market, with an array of trendy shops providing welcome post-meal distractions. The restaurant serves various South African faves, including steaming *potjies* (meat

and vegetables cooked in a cast-iron pot over an open fire) as well as delicious grilled meats, pizzas and pastas. The lovely courtyard gives you a good excuse to take your time.

★La Pentola FUSION $$$
(Map p362; ☎012-329 4028; www.lapentola.co.za; 5 Well St, Arcadia; mains R80-190; ⏰noon-3pm & 5-10pm Mon-Sat) This well-established eatery is still going strong, with locals and well-informed tourists enjoying its old-fashioned decor and excellent menu of items that transgress all culinary boundaries. Warthog with honey mustard, Cajun seafood salad and snails wrapped in bacon are just a few examples of the dishes on offer. There are vegetarian options, too. Warning: service can be painfully slow.

Brooklyn & New Muckleneuk

The area around Middle and Fehrsen Sts has some good restaurants, amid the shopping-mall staples.

Broodhuijs BAKERY, CAFE $
(Map p356; ☎012-346 5753; www.broodhuijs.com; cnr Bronkhorst & Dey Sts, Brooklyn; mains R20-40; ⏰7am-5pm Mon-Fri, 8am-2pm Sat; 📶) On a peaceful stretch of Bronkhorst St, this neighborhood charmer makes a great setting for a meet-up with a friend or a fine spot to linger over a light meal (sandwiches, pizzas, salads) when you're solo. It also sells baked goods (including highly popular croissants and muffins) and has good coffee.

★Boer'geoisie SOUTH AFRICAN $$
(Map p362; ☎012-460 0264; 13th St, Greenlyn Village, Menlo Park; mains R70-170; ⏰11am-3pm & 6-9pm Mon-Fri, 10am-10pm Sat, 10am-3pm Sun) This venue has a tantalising menu showcasing all the classics of traditional South African cuisine, served in snug surrounds complete with corrugated iron, wooden floors, metal pillars and South African memorabilia. If the *skilpadjie* (lamb liver wrapped in caul fat) doesn't grab you, try out some of the other hearty meat dishes. The *souskluitjies* (cinnamon dumplings) will finish you off sweetly.

Crawdaddy's BRASSERIE $$
(Map p356; ☎012-460 0889; www.crawdaddys.co.za; cnr Middle & Dey Sts, Brooklyn Plaza, Brooklyn; mains R80-170; ⏰11.30am-11pm Mon-Sat, to 9pm Sun) An old favourite with hungry locals, this brasserie never fails to satisfy the requirements of its loyal punters. The key to its success is an eclectic menu that ranges from curries and stir-fries to grilled meats and seafood. It has several dining rooms and an open-air terrace that overlooks a busy intersection (noise!).

Geet INDIAN $$
(Map p356; ☎012-460 3199; www.geetindianrestaurant.com; 541 Fehrsen St, Brooklyn; mains R50-100; ⏰11am-3pm & 5-10pm Mon-Sat, 11am-8pm Sun; 🖉) You wouldn't guess it from the humble surrounds here, but chef Gita Jivan concocts first-class Indian dishes, fusing Indian flavours with European presentation. The huge menu emphasises North Indian delights, and vegetarians can feast. The whisky lounge, where you can dine sitting on cushions, is a treat.

Cynthia's Indigo Moon INTERNATIONAL $$
(Map p356; ☎012-346 8926; www.cynthiasindigomoon.co.za; 283 Dey St, Brooklyn; mains R70-170; ⏰11.30am-10pm Mon-Fri, 6am-11.30pm Sat; 📶) You'll enjoy this place almost as much for the decor as the food, with nods to Paris and New York, dimly lit corner tables and plenty of mirrors adorning the walls. Signature dishes include Norwegian salmon, Cynthia's fillet and venison (usually springbok, kudu or ostrich). The chicken couscous salad is a hit, too.

Blue Crane SOUTH AFRICAN $$
(Map p356; ☎012-460 7615; www.bluecranerestaurant.co.za; 156 Melk St, New Muckleneuk; mains R60-170; ⏰7.30am-3pm Mon, 7.30am-10pm Tue-Fri, 9am-10pm Sat; 📶) As part of the Austin Roberts Bird Sanctuary, Blue Crane is famous to ornithologists worldwide (and anyone else who enjoys a Castle at sunset), with a menu that begins with breakfast and moves on to steaks, salads, burgers and sandwiches. There are various dining rooms, including an atmospheric *boma* and a splendid deck overlooking a pond.

Kream INTERNATIONAL $$$
(Map p356; ☎012-346 4642; www.kream.co.za; 570 Fehrsen St, Brooklyn Bridge; mains R120-200; ⏰noon-10pm Mon-Sat, to 2.30pm Sun) A bold concept in a conservative city, Kream, in many ways, *is* the cream of the crop. The uber-trendy menu features exotic starters and the usual grilled suspects for main course. The white-chocolate and passion-fruit cheesecake with a dash of the long whisky list is a fine way to finish a night.

Pacha's SOUTH AFRICAN $$$
(Map p362; 012-460 3220; www.pachas.co.za; 27 Maroelana St; mains R90-200; noon-2.30pm & 6-9.30pm Mon-Fri, 6-9.30pm Sat, noon-2.30pm Sun) Fashionable Pacha's is the address of choice for those looking for both style and substance. It's a pleasant modern restaurant with large picture windows, an aquarium and quality furniture, but high-quality meat dishes, especially venison, are the main attraction here. Non-carnivores, fear not: it also offers a good selection of seafood dishes.

Drinking & Nightlife

Hatfield is the best place for a night out, with bars, restaurants and clubs catering for all types. Hatfield Sq is a university-student stronghold after dark.

News Café CAFE
(Map p356; www.newscafe.co.za; Hatfield Sq, Burnett St, Hatfield; 8am-midnight;) The pick of the Burnett St coffee houses is this popular yet noisy chain cafe, which does dependable burgers and salads and serves a wide selection of cocktails. The TV screens, fast wi-fi and laissez-faire feel make this a hit with the student fraternity.

Tings an' Times BAR
(Map p362; www.tings.co.za; Waterglen Shopping Centre, cnr Garsfontein & Jan Masilela Rds; noon-1.30am) This bohemian bar attracts an eclectic crowd to chill out to a reggae soundtrack punctuated by regular live performances. Late on weekend nights it pulls in up-for-it students and the dancing goes on till the small hours. If you get the munchies, the speciality is pitas, which come toasted with toppings or stuffed with all kinds of tasty treats.

TriBeCa Lounge CAFE
(Map p356; www.tribeca.co.za; Brooklyn Sq, Veale St, Brooklyn; 7am-10pm) Laid-back and stylish, this cafe is the perfect place to chill out with a latte and browse the magazines for a few hours, or join the beautiful people in sipping exquisite cocktails on weekend nights. It serves pub grub as well.

Eastwoods PUB
(Map p356; 012-344 0243; www.eastwoods.co.za; 391 Eastwood St, Arcadia; 10am-11pm Mon-Fri, 10am-1am Sat, 10am-9pm Sun) This hugely popular pub is often packed, especially at lunchtime and after work hours. There's a large outdoor deck, and banquette seating and a big bar inside. It has won the 'best pub in Pretoria' award several times and serves up good meals throughout the day, excellent craft beers and a large selection of cocktails and spirits.

Shopping

Brooklyn Mall MALL
(Map p356; www.brooklynmall.co.za; Bronkhorst St, Brooklyn; 9am-7pm Mon-Fri, to 5pm Sat & Sun) A mega-mall where you'll find anything from fashion to kids' toys, homewares and clothing.

Boeremark MARKET
(Map p362; Pioneer Park, Silverton; 6-9am Sat) Held by the Pioneer Park Museum in Silverton, this market is full of stalls selling all kinds of organic food, from cheeses to cakes to preserves. Come early because it's all sold out by 9am.

Hatfield Flea Market MARKET
(Map p356; Hatfield Plaza car park, Burnett St, Hatfield; 9am-5pm Sun) This place peddles the usual flea-market paraphernalia, and has some handmade African crafts.

Information

EMERGENCY

Fire (10111)

Police (10111)

INTERNET ACCESS

Most places to stay offer free internet facilities.

MEDICAL SERVICES

Hatfield Clinic (012-362 7180; www.hatmed.co.za; 454 Hilda St; 8am-7pm Mon-Thu, to 6pm Fri, to 1pm Sat, to noon Sun) A well-known suburban clinic.

Tshwane District Hospital (012-354 5958; Dr Savage Rd) The place to head in a medical emergency.

MONEY

There are banks with ATMs and change facilities across town.

POST

Hatfield Post Office (Map p356; Hatfield Sq; 8am-4.30pm Mon-Fri, to noon Sat) The most commonly used post office.

Main Post Office (Map p352; Church Sq; 8.30am-4.30pm Mon-Fri, 8am-noon Sat) In a historic building on the main square.

TOURIST INFORMATION

South African National Parks (SANParks; Map p356; 012-428 9111; www.sanparks.org; 643 Leyds St, Muckleneuk; office 7.30am-3.45pm Mon-Fri, call centre to 5pm Mon-Fri,

8am-1pm Sat) Your best bet for all wildlife-reserve bookings and enquiries.

Tourist Information Centre (Map p352; ☎012-358 1430; www.tshwanetourism.com; Old Nederlandsche Bank Bldg, Church Sq; ⏲7.30am-4pm Mon-Fri) Fairly unhelpful for most travellers; you're better off asking your hotel or locals for advice.

Getting There & Away

AIR

OR Tambo International Airport (p344; Ortia) is South Africa's international hub, accepting flights from across the globe.

BUS

Most national and international bus services commence in Pretoria before picking up in Jo'burg, unless the general direction is north. The **Pretoria Bus Station** (Map p352; Railway St) is next to Pretoria's train station. You will also find the major companies' booking and information offices here, as well as a good cafe and an ATM.

Most Translux (p344), City to City (p344), Intercape (p344) and Greyhound (p344) services running from Jo'burg to Durban, the South Coast and Cape Town originate in Pretoria. Services running north up the N1 also stop here.

Translux, Greyhound and Intercape fares from Pretoria are identical to those from Jo'burg, regardless of the one-hour difference in time. If you only want to go between the two cities, it will cost about R90.

Baz Bus (p344) will pick up and drop off at Pretoria hostels.

CAR

Many larger local and international companies are represented in Pretoria.

GAUTRAIN

The Gautrain (p614) service offers regular high-speed connections with Hatfield, Johannesburg (Park Station, Rosebank and Sandton) and the airport.

TRAIN

The historic Pretoria train station is an attractive location to commence or complete a journey.

For long distances, Shosholoza Meyl (p344) trains running through Pretoria are the Trans Karoo (daily from Pretoria to Cape Town) and the Komati (daily from Jo'burg to Komatipoort via Nelspruit). The luxury Blue Train, which links Pretoria, Jo'burg and Cape Town, originates here.

METRO

Because of a high incidence of crime, we don't recommend travelling between Pretoria and Jo'burg by Metro.

Getting Around

TO/FROM THE AIRPORT

If you call ahead, most hostels, and many hotels, offer free pick-up.

Get You There Transfers (☎011-791 6331; www.getyoutheretransfers.co.za) operates shuttle buses between Ortia and Pretoria. They can pick you up from the airport and deposit you in Pretoria for about R600 (the same price as a taxi). Airport Shuttle (p344) offers the same service for about R550.

SHARED TAXI

Minibus taxis run pretty much everywhere and the standard fare is about R5, but they're not very convenient for travellers who prefer to use taxis.

TAXI

If you don't have your own transport, the easiest and safest way to get around is by taxi. You can get a metered taxi from **Rixi Taxis** (☎086 100 7494; www.rixitaxi.co.za; per kilometre around R10).

AROUND PRETORIA

Think of Gauteng and you think of big cities, but there is some beautiful countryside out there, as well as a few interesting museums and other attractions.

Smuts House Museum

Smuts House Museum MUSEUM

(Map p362; ☎012-667 1176; www.smutshouse.co.za; Nellmapius Rd, Irene; adult/child R20/10, picnic garden per car R5; ⏲8am-4pm Mon-Fri, 8.30am-4.30pm Sat & Sun) JC Smuts' home for over 40 years has been turned into an interesting museum. Surrounded by a wide verandah and shaded by trees, it has a family atmosphere and gives a vivid insight into Smuts' life. If you're travelling to/from Pretoria by car, it's worth dropping in for a look. The house is signposted from both the N14 freeway (Rte 28) and Rte 21.

Scholar, Boer general, politician and international statesman JC Smuts was instrumental in creating the Union of South Africa, and served as prime minister from 1919 to 1924 and from 1939 to 1948.

Fort Klapperkop Military Museum

Fort Klapperkop FORT

(Map p362; ☎012-346 7703; Johann Rissik Dr; adult/child R20/5; ⏲10am-5pm Tue-Sun) This fort was

Around Pretoria

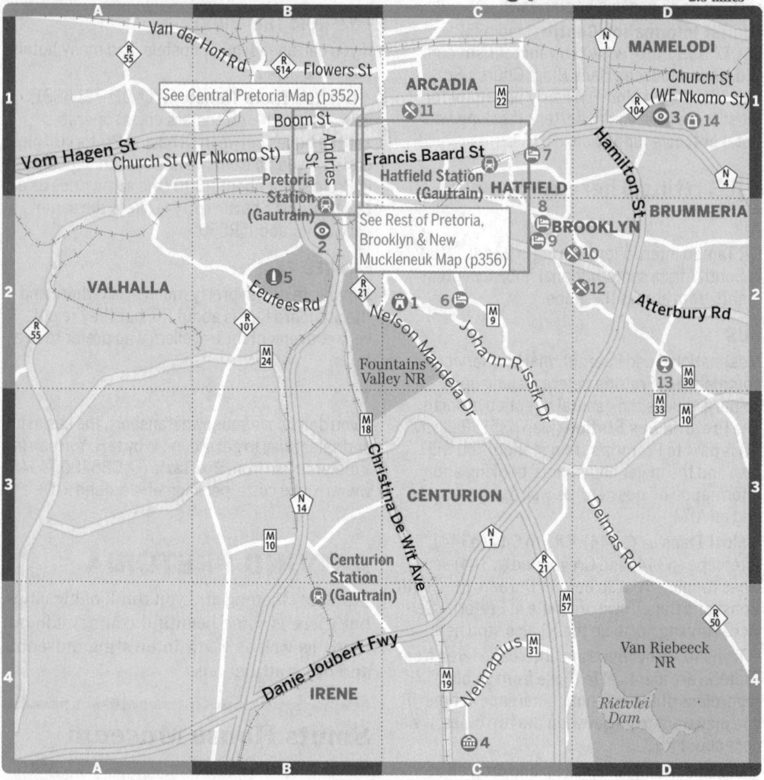

Around Pretoria

Sights

1 Fort Klapperkop C2
2 Freedom Park B2
3 National Botanical Garden D1
4 Smuts House Museum C4
5 Voortrekker Monument B2

Sleeping

6 131 Herbert Baker C2
7 1322 Backpackers International C1
8 Ambiance Guesthouse C2
Khayalethu Guest House .... (see 7)
9 Richtershuyz C2

Eating

10 Boer'geoisie D2
11 La Pentola C1
12 Pacha's D2

Drinking & Nightlife

13 Tings an' Times D2

Shopping

14 Boeremark D1

one of four built to defend Pretoria, although in the end it was never used for that purpose. Located 6km south of the city, it's one of the best-preserved forts in South Africa, and its **museum** tells the story of the country's military history from 1852 to the end of the 1899–1902 Anglo-Boer War. There are panoramic views across the city and the region.

National Botanical Garden

National Botanical Garden GARDENS
(Map p362; ☎012-843 5071; 2 Cussonia Ave, Brummeria; adult/child R26/12; ⏲6am-6pm) Around 9km east of the city centre, these gardens cover 7700 sq m and are planted with indigenous flora from around the country. The 20,000-odd plant species are labelled and grouped according to their region of origin, so a visit is a must for keen botanists. Garden picnic concerts are held from May to September.

By car, head east along Church St (Rte 104) for about 8km, then turn right into Cussonia Rd; the gardens are on the left-hand side.

Sammy Marks Museum

Sammy Marks Museum MUSEUM
(☎012-755 9541; www.ditsong.org.za; R104, Old Bronkhorstspruit Rd; adult/child R45/15; ⏲10am-4pm Tue-Sun) This handsome Victorian mansion was built in 1884 for English industrial, mining and agricultural magnate Sammy Marks. Now it's a museum. There are five daily tours of the mansion and its outbuildings, an atmospheric Victorian tea garden, and beautiful gardens in which you can picnic and imagine the old days of croquet and sandwiches on the lawn. To get to the museum, follow signposting off Rte 104, 20km east of Pretoria.

Cullinan Diamond Mine

Historic Cullinan is a pretty 100-year-old village full of quaint Herbert Baker architecture. The village is home to one of the biggest and most productive diamond-bearing kimberlite pipes in the world. It has produced three of the largest diamonds ever found.

Cullinan is little more than a handful of picturesque streets clustering around the mine, but the last years have seen a proliferation of accommodation options, restaurants, bistros, antique shops and art galleries. Its addictive relaxed atmosphere, charming architecture and good infrastructures draw lots of weekending families from both Pretoria and Jo'burg.

For more information on the village, check the website www.cullinan24.co.za.

To get here from Pretoria, take the N4 east and the Hans Strijdom off-ramp, then turn left and follow the signs.

Tours

Premier Diamond Tours TOUR
(☎012-734 2170; www.tourcullinan.co.za; Oak Ave; 1½hr tour R120-150, 4hr tour R500-550; ⏲8am-2pm, 1½hr tour 11am & 1.30pm, 4hr tour 10.30am Mon & Fri, 9.30am Tue-Thu, 8am Sat) This reputable operator runs excellent tours of the mine. The 1½-hour tour takes in the massive hole and the headgear of the skips that transport the ore from underground, and also includes the processing plant and the huge dump of waste material. The four-hour Underground Tour will get you into the workings of the mine – a fascinating experience.

Sleeping & Eating

Gastehys JanHarmsgat B&B $$
(☎074 322 5225; www.gastehys.co.za; 7 Hospital St; incl breakfast s R680, d R760-980; P ᯤ) Not your average B&B, this highly original – make it zany – four-room venture in a renovated farmhouse is more like something from an interior-design magazine. It's all recycled knick-knacks, from old hospital tables to bicycle taps and iron work. All up it's something of a work of art. The lush garden is another asset.

Cockpit Brewhouse PUB FOOD $
(☎012-734 0656; www.thecockpitbrewhouse.co.za; 80 Oak Ave; mains R50-85; ⏲noon-9pm Thu, 11am-9pm Fri & Sat, 11am-4pm Sun; ᯤ) The aviation-themed Cockpit Brewhouse serves deliciously hoppy pale ales and decent beer food, including a tasty lamb and beef burger. It's in the middle of town.

Harrie's Pancakes CREPERIE $$
(☎012-734 1054; www.harriespancakes.com; 112 Oak Lane; mains R20-100; ⏲8am-7pm) This enticing crêperie has a bumper selection of gourmet crêpes and substantial salads. The outdoor tables occupy a prime location alongside picturesque Oak Lane.

Mpumalanga

Includes ➡

Best Places to Eat

- Wild Fig Tree (p371)
- Summerfields Kitchen (p376)
- Kruger's Gold (p373)
- Saffron (p379)
- Food Fundi (p379)

Best Places to Stay

- Woodsman (p370)
- Royal Hotel (p372)
- Graskop Hotel (p373)
- Trees Too (p381)
- River House Lodge (p380)

Why Go?

Mpumalanga is one of South Africa's smallest provinces and one of its most exciting. Visually it is a simply beautiful region with vistas of mountains, lush green valleys and a collection of cool-climate towns. Its natural assets make it a prime target for outdoor enthusiasts, who head here to abseil down waterfalls, throw themselves off cliffs, negotiate rivers by raft, inner tube or canoe, and hike or bike numerous wilderness trails.

Mpumalanga's major draw, though, is the massive Blyde River Canyon, which carves its way spectacularly through the Drakensberg Escarpment. It is one of South Africa's iconic sights and on a clear day one of the many vantage points can leave you breathless.

And, of course, the province provides access to the southern half of Kruger National Park (p384), with an excellent selection of lodges and wilderness activities right on the mighty park's doorstep.

When to Go

Nelspruit

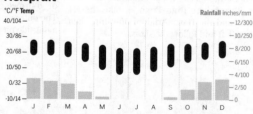

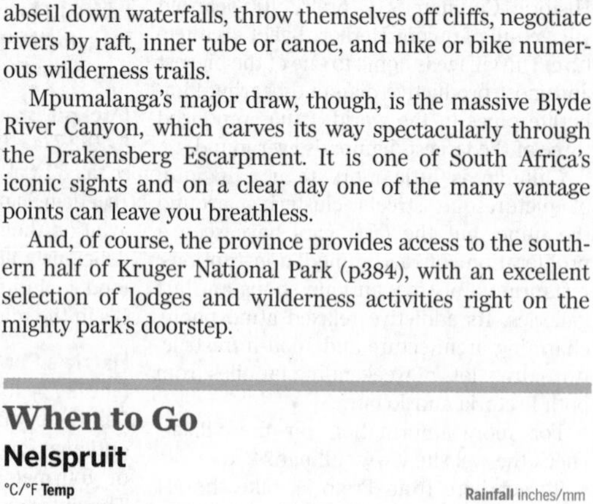

Jan–Mar Head onto the escarpment to escape the steamy lowveld during summer.

Jun–Aug The capital goes off during InniBos with artists and theatre groups packing venues.

Sep–Dec Visit alpine Dullstroom in mid-December to catch its Arts & Cultural Festival.

Mpumalanga Highlights

1 Throwing a line in the water for trout around sophisticated **Dullstroom** (p366) and enjoying the cool alpine climate.

2 Picking up fine African arts and crafts in **Graskop** (p372) before hurling yourself into a gorge on the Big Swing outside town.

3 Gazing in awe from the Three Rondavels at **Blyde River Canyon** (p374), the world's third-largest canyon.

4 Hitting the bike trails around **Sabie** (p369), or simply taking in the misty mountain views.

5 Discovering the heritage of **Barberton** (p381) with a stroll around the province's most enjoyable town.

History

During the *difaqane* (forced migration) of the early 19th century, groups of Shangaan, Swazi and Ndebele entered the area, escaping turbulent times in Zululand. Voortrekkers first arrived on the scene in the late 1830s and had established the Transvaal (the province's previous name) as a republic within 10 years. The Transvaal was the scene for the first Anglo-Boer War; the Boers were victorious, claiming back their territory and making Paul Kruger their first president. This independence lasted only a few years, until the end of the war, when the Transvaal (and the Orange Free State) was returned to British hands.

National Parks & Reserves

The Blyde River Canyon Nature Reserve is the most spectacular of the bunch. The wildlife riches of southern Kruger National Park (p384), and many private wildlife reserves on its southwestern edge, also call Mpumalanga home.

Language

Swati, Zulu and Ndebele are the main languages spoken in Mpumalanga, but it's easy to get by with English. In and around Nelspruit, you'll also hear a lot of Afrikaans.

Getting There & Around

Mpumalanga Kruger International Airport (MKIA), about 28km northeast of Nelspruit, off Rte 40, has regular connections to major South African cities as well as a service to Livingstone in Zambia.

The roads in Mpumalanga are generally good-quality tarmac and there are excellent connections between towns. Around the transport hub of Nelspruit, there are good bus and minibus services, but away from the main routes public transport is virtually nonexistent and to get around easily you'll certainly need a hire car.

A passenger train line cuts through the middle of the province, connecting Johannesburg (Jo'burg) with Komatipoort via Nelspruit.

DRAKENSBERG ESCARPMENT

Home to some of South Africa's most striking landscapes, the Drakensberg Escarpment was, until a couple of centuries ago, untamed rainforest roamed by elephants, buffaloes and even lions. Today it's holidaying South Africans who wander the highlands, enjoying the beautiful landscape in their droves. The escarpment marks the point where the highveld plateau plunges down over 1000m, before spilling out onto the eastern lowveld, forming a dramatic knot of soaring cliffs, canyons, sweeping hillsides and cool valleys thick with pine trees – an apt backdrop for the myriad adventure activities that are on offer here.

Dullstroom

POP 600 / ELEV 2053M

This little oasis is all about good food, old-fashioned English pubs, piles of accommodation, fresh country air and fishing in the surrounding cool waters. When you arrive you would be forgiven for thinking you had taken a wrong turn and ended up in Canada. Replete with pine trees and lined with pretty clapboard buildings, Dullstroom is one of the coldest towns in the country. It's famous for one thing: trout, but there's lots more to do here, including hiking and horse riding.

Sights & Activities

Dullstroom Bird of Prey & Rehabilitation Centre BIRD SANCTUARY
(☎079 502 1519; www.birdsofprey.co.za; adult/child R50/20; ⏲9am-4pm, flying displays 10.30am & 2.30pm, closed Tue) This centre, just outside town off Rte 540, teaches visitors about raptor species and the dangers facing them – you can even learn the art of falconry for a day. There are regular flying displays involving peregrine falcons, kestrels, buzzards and black eagles among others.

Dullstroom Riding Centre HORSE RIDING
(☎082 442 9766; www.dullstroomhorseriding.co.za; 2hr countryside ride adult & child R250, town ride R500) This place offers horseback tours through the surrounding countryside or, for more experienced riders, through the town itself (including a tour of the local pubs!). It's at the Owl & Oak Trading Post, 9km from Dullstroom on Rte 540 to Lydenburg.

Festivals & Events

Dullstroom Arts & Cultural Festival CULTURE
Try catching this platform for showcasing local talent in mid-December. Expect photography, art, sculpture, music and food.

Sleeping & Eating

Old Transvaal Inn INN $
(☎013-254 0222; Naledi St; r R200-350) Set in a beautiful old building, this inn is a decent

Drakensberg Escarpment & Eastern Lowveld

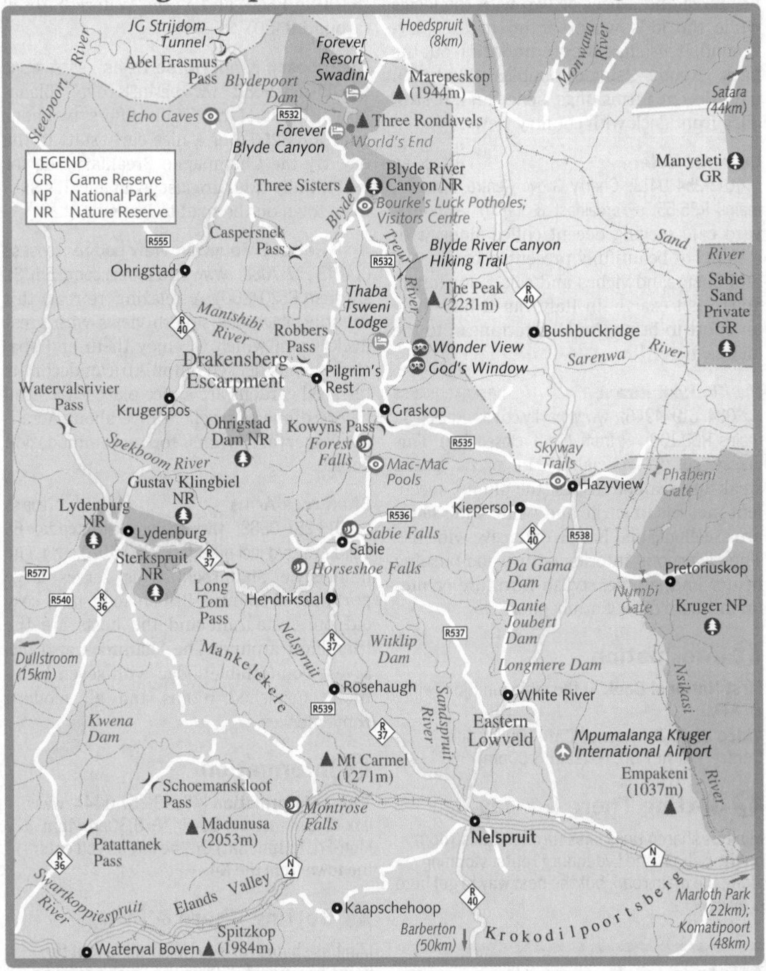

cheapie option in a pinch. The very rudimentary but clean rooms have low-slung roofs and tiny bathrooms. It's also home to the town's best **sweet shop**, which sells homemade fudge, truffles and other treats.

Cherry Grove GUESTHOUSE $$
(☎013-254 0421; www.cherry-grove.co.za; Cherry Grove Centre, Main Rd; s/d R600/1200; ❄) These luxury Mediterranean villas are stylishly constructed in stone and wood and have upstairs 'piazza-view' balconies. They've been intelligently built to capture the light and working fireplaces keep the suites warm and cosy on cold evenings.

Critchley Hackle BUNGALOW $$$
(☎0861 226 787; Teding van Berkhout St; s/d incl breakfast from R1400/2100; @ ≋) This is the best place to stay in town. Accommodation is in stone cottages dotted around grassy, flower-filled lawns. Rooms have vaulted ceilings, a sitting area, an open fireplace and a terrace overlooking a small lake. The great restaurant is glass-fronted and has views over the gardens. It's at the northeastern edge of town, signposted from the main road.

Duck & Trout INN $
(☎013-254 0047; www.duckandtrout.co.za; light meals from R30; ⏲11am-10pm Sun-Thu,

10am-10pm Fri & Sat) A good place for a wood-fire pizza and a beer or two with the locals while the kids whoop it up in the playground. It also has **accommodation** out the back. Rooms (singles/doubles R300/500) have decent furnishings, space and, best of all, a front deck with country views.

Legendz Cafe CAFE $
(☎013-254 0413; Cherry Grove Centre, Main Rd; mains R35-55; ⏰breakfast & lunch) A courtyard cafe serving decent coffee along with a range of beautifully presented breakfasts, and open sandwiches and salads for lunch. You're not exactly in Italy, but it has made an effort to bring the Mediterranean to the 'piazza' here.

Mayfly Restaurant INTERNATIONAL $$
(☎084 619 4946; www.mayfly.co.za; Naledi St; mains R60-100; ⏰from 10am, closed Tue) This classy set-up specialises in pizza, pasta, steak and seafood dishes (the plump, succulent mussels in garlic and white wine sauce are excellent) and has an extensive wine list. The cavernous interior with wood-burning heater and simple, stylish furniture creates an intimate dining atmosphere.

Information

First National Bank At the main junction, with an ATM.

Video Shop & Internet Cafe (Dullstroom Centre; per hr R60; ⏰11am-6.30pm)

Getting There & Away

Minibus shared taxis pass through Dullstroom on the Belfast and Lydenburg route, stopping along the main road, but the best way to get here is by car.

Waterval Boven

POP 2500

Rock climbers, mountain bikers and other adrenaline junkies flock to this minute town, just off the N4, for serious adventure-sport action. Nestled into the Drakensberg Mountains, the town has a spectacular natural setting.

Roc 'n Rope Adventures ROCK CLIMBING
(☎013-257 0363; www.rocrope.com; 53 Third Ave) The cliffs around Waterval Boven are one of South Africa's premier climbing destinations. Roc 'n Rope Adventures organises a range of excursions in the area, including a two-day Introduction to Rockclimbing (R1600), a half-day Adventure Climb (R400 to R550) and a 60m Waterfall Abseil (around R430).

Blaaubosch Kraal Horse Trails HORSE RIDING
(☎013-256 9081; www.bbktrails.co.za) Blaaubosch Kraal Horse Trails offers two-hour trips for R250. For a nice early start to the day, try the Champagne Breakfast ride for R450. Daily rides are also available. It's 8km from town on the road to Lydenburg.

Acra Retreat Mountain View Lodge LODGE $$
(☎013-257 7088; www.acra-retreat.com; 5th St; s/d from R520/800) A relaxing retreat, this friendly place has superb views with great decks from which to enjoy them and spacious rooms decked out in African decor. Its terraced gardens are a nice place for a stroll before dinner. Travellers rave about Acra – it's Waterval Boven's top accommodation choice.

Shamrock Arms PUB $$
(☎013-257 0888; www.shamrockarms.co.za; 68 Third Ave; s/d incl breakfast R720/1070; 📶) The home-style Shamrock Arms serves large portions of country British food in a cosy old pub-restaurant and the hosts are the friendliest around. The Shamrock also has a very comfortable lodge with seven beautifully furnished rooms and all modern conveniences.

Information

Tourist Information (☎013-257 0444; www.linx.co.za/waterval-boven; ⏰8.30am-4pm Mon-Fri, to 1pm Sat) On the left as you enter the town from the N4.

Getting There & Away

Minibus shared taxis to Nelspruit (about two hours away) cost R50; you can pick one up on Third Ave.

Lydenburg

POP 900

Lydenburg has wide streets, open spaces and the feel of history in its worn streets and landmark buildings. It makes a pleasant stopover on the way to Jo'burg or Kruger.

Lydenburg Museum MUSEUM
(Long Tom Pass Rd; ⏰8am-4pm) FREE On a rainy day, Lydenburg Museum is worth poking your nose into. It's located at the en-

trance to Gustav Klingbiel Nature Reserve about 3km east of town along Rte 37.

Gustav Klingbiel Nature Reserve NATURE RESERVE
(☎013-235 2213; admission R10; ⏰8am-4pm Mon-Fri, to 5pm Sat & Sun) Gustav Klingbiel Nature Reserve is 20 sq km of prime birdwatching territory, but those not into our feathered friends can look out for zebras, impalas and kudus. It's 3km east of town along Rte 37.

De Ark Guest House GUESTHOUSE $$
(☎013-235 1125; www.dearkguesthouse.co.za; 37 Kantoor St; s/d from R600/850, deluxe s/d R680/950;) It's worth paying the extra for a deluxe room at De Ark Guest House, a four-star B&B housed in one of the town's oldest buildings. Each room drips with 19th-century touches.

Lodge Laske Nakke LODGE $$
(☎013-235 2886; www.laskenakke.co.za; unit s/d from R380/680, budget d R300) This Afrikaner-run place has a range of good-value accommodation including rooms for backpackers and even camping options.

Getting There & Away

The minibus-taxi stop is in the town centre on the corner of Voortrekker and Clerq Sts, with daily vehicles to Sabie (R40, one hour) and Belfast (R50, 1½ hours).

Sabie

POP 9200 / ELEV 1100M

Sabie is a lovely little town, and one of Mpumalanga's best places to base yourself. There are some excellent eating options and a good range of accommodation, and the lush, mountainous countryside makes a delightful backdrop. Once you venture out of town you'll quickly discover hidden waterfalls, streams and walking trails. It's a favourite with outdoorsy types who can enjoy the heart-pumping opportunities – including rafting, canyoning (known as kloofing around these parts) and hiking – that abound in the area.

Sights & Activities

Waterfall fanatics will be in their element here – the area around Sabie positively gushes with falls (admission to each R5 to R10). They include **Sabie Falls**, just north of town on Rte 532 to Graskop; the 70m **Bridal Veil Falls**, northwest of Sabie, off Old Lydenburg Rd; the 68m **Lone Creek Falls**, also off Old Lydenburg Rd, and with wheelchair access on the right-hand path; and the nearby **Horseshoe Falls**, about 5km southwest of Lone Creek Falls. The popular **Mac-Mac Falls**, about 12km north of Sabie, off Rte 532 to Graskop, take their name from the many Scots on the local mining register. About 3km southeast of the falls are the **Mac-Mac Pools**, where you can swim.

> **ALL THE SMALL TREES YOU SEE...**
>
> The plantation forest around Sabie is pine and eucalyptus – one of the largest human-made forests in the world. Decimated by fires seven or eight years ago, it will be over 20 years before the forests are fully recovered.

Komatiland Forestry Museum MUSEUM
(cnr Ford St & Tenth Ave; adult/child R5/2; ⏰8am-4.30pm Mon-Fri, to noon Sat) This museum has displays on local forests and the history of the South African timber industry. There's a historical examination of the use of timber and the introduction of plantations to protect indigenous forests that were disappearing fast. Upstairs has information on day/overnight forest hiking trails. The museum has wheelchair access.

Sabie Xtreme Adventures ADVENTURE SPORTS
(☎013-764 2118; www.sabiextreme.co.za; Main St) If you're into adventure activities this outfit, based in the Sabie Backpackers Lodge, can organise kloofing, candlelight caving, rafting, tours of Blyde River Canyon and more.

Sleeping

Sabie Backpackers Lodge BACKPACKERS $
(☎013-764 2118; www.sabiextreme.co.za; Main St; camping R80, dm R130, d without bathroom R300, d R350; @) A pretty rustic backpackers with a decent location in town. Dorms are small and the double with en suite is poky but well furnished and clean. There are regular barbecues and parties, but there's plenty of space to chill out as well. Sabie Xtreme Adventures is based here. The lodge owners will pick you up from Nelspruit.

Billy Bongo Backpackers BACKPACKERS $
(☎072 370 7219; Old Lydenburg Rd; camping R70, dm/s/d R125/150/300) This place has a

Sabie

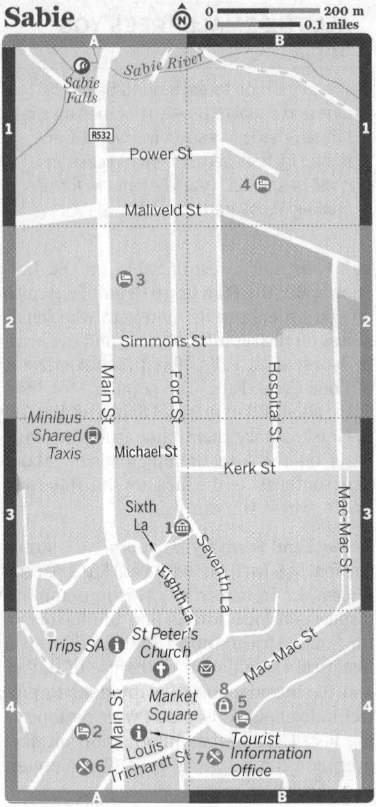

Sabie

Sights
1 Komatiland Forestry Museum A3

Activities, Courses & Tours
Sabie Xtreme Adventures .... (see 3)

Sleeping
2 Country Kitchen A4
3 Sabie Backpackers Lodge A2
4 Sabie Townhouse B1
5 Woodsman B4

Eating
6 Petena's Pancakes A4
7 Wild Fig Tree B4
Woodsman .... (see 5)

Shopping
Bookman's Corner .... (see 5)
8 Mphozeni Crafts B4

definite party atmosphere with nights full of drinking, bongo drumming and bonfires. It's about 1km down Old Lydenburg Rd, off Main St.

★ Woodsman INN $$
(☎013-764 2015; www.thewoodsman.co.za; 94 Main St; s/d incl breakfast R485/700) A landmark pub, the Woodsman offers accommodation next door in an uninspiring brick building. They're not all that flash, but rooms are spacious with powerful showers, and there are small balconies upstairs. But, best of all, it's stumbling distance to Sabie's best two eating and drinking options: the Woodsman itself and Wild Fig Tree.

Sabie Townhouse B&B $$
(☎013-764 2292; www.sabietownhouse.co.za; Power St; s/d incl breakfast R545/1000; @ 🛜 🏊) This pretty river-stone house has a pool and terrace, and fabulous views over the hills. Travellers rave about the warm hospitality from Greg and family. The Zebra suite is the pinnacle of luxury here, with king-size bed, private patio and hot tub – best of all is the breakfast-in-bed service when you book this room. A family unit and budget rooms are also available.

Country Kitchen PUB $$
(☎013-764 2091; Main St; s/d R500/700) At the back of this pub-restaurant are some pretty slick rooms in a slightly soulless setting around a conference room. Tastefully furnished, the rooms are excellent value, and you can easily walk to Wild Fig Tree or the Woodsman for meals.

Artists' Café & Guest House GUESTHOUSE $$
(☎078 876 9293; r per person R340) Wonderfully quirky place in Hendriksdal, about 15km south of Sabie along Rte 37. Accommodation is in old train-station buildings that have been converted into rooms, retaining lots of the original signs and quirks. Our fave is the '1st class waiting room' which has a ginormous bathroom and comfy couch.

Lone Creek River Lodge LODGE $$$
(☎013-764 2611; www.lonecreek.co.za; Old Lydenburg Rd; s/d incl breakfast R1075/1720, ste s/d incl breakfast R1380/2360; ❄ @ 🛜 🏊) Lone Creek offers luxurious rooms in the main house as well as individual suites right by the river, self-catering timber lodges and two freshwater pools. Rooms overlooking the river are recommended.

Eating & Drinking

Petena's Pancakes CREPERIE $

(Main St; pancakes R50-70; ⏲9am-5pm) Petena's has a delicious selection of savoury and sweet pancakes – and we can't go past the ice cream, choc sauce and nuts (scrummy). There are great views to drink in while you wolf it all down. It's a few hundred metres down Main St heading south out of town.

★ **Wild Fig Tree** SOUTH AFRICAN $$

(☎013-764 2239; cnr Main & Louis Trichardt Sts; light meals R40-60, mains R90-130; ⏲8am-9pm Mon-Sat, to 8pm Sun) There's a meat-driven menu and a warm atmosphere here, with candles and African-print wall hangings. Try the SA mezze for dinner, which includes ostrich medallions, warthog carpaccio and crocodile kebabs. The ploughman's or trout platter makes a terrific lunch. With seating on a breezy balcony, it's a very pleasant place to while away a Sabie afternoon.

Woodsman GREEK $$

(☎013-764 2015; 94 Main St; mains R80-110; ⏲7am-late) Half pub, half restaurant, the Woodsman offers great food with a Greek twist. Souvlaki, grilled calamari, mezedhes and other offerings are mixed with more local dishes: pan-fried trout and ostrich in red wine and oregon also feature. Most folk will find their spot, be it raucous beer drinking at the bar or fine dining by candelit table on the balcony.

Shopping

Mphozeni Crafts ARTS & CRAFTS

(☎013-764 2074; thewoodsman.co.za; 94 Main St; ⏲8.30am-5.30pm) Lots of African arts and crafts and some quality textiles.

Bookman's Corner BOOKS

(cnr Main & Mac-Mac Sts; ⏲9am-4.30pm Mon-Fri, 8.30am-4pm Sat, 8am-4.30pm Sun) This place sells secondhand books; the chat comes for free.

Information

First National Bank (Market Sq) Has an ATM.

Tourist Information Office (☎083 763 7353; Market Sq, Main St; ⏲9am-4pm Mon-Fri, to noon Sat, to 2pm Sun) Helpful office with accommodation recommendations and plenty of information on the local area.

Trips SA (☎013-764 1177; www.sabie.co.za; Main St) Information centre and booking agent for tours and accommodation.

Sabie Internet Cafe (☎013-764 2875; Main St; per 30min R15; ⏲8am-6pm Mon-Fri, 9am-4pm Sat) Reliable internet access.

Getting There & Away

There are daily buses from Jo'burg to Nelspruit, from where you can get minibus shared taxis to Sabie (R40, one hour between Nelspruit and Sabie). Minibus shared taxis also run frequently to and from Hazyview (R40, one hour). Minibus taxis stop next to the Engen petrol station.

Pilgrim's Rest

POP 1730

Tiny little Pilgrim's Rest appears frozen in time – a perfectly preserved gold-rush town with wooden and corrugated-iron houses lining a pretty, manicured main street. Tourists come here by the coachload and the town can feel swamped and a little Disney-fied during the height of the day. Best to come early in the morning, or even stay the night – when you'll be better able to soak up the ghosts of the past.

Beware the competitive ferociousness of the informal carpark attendants waving cars into parks on the side of the road.

Sights & Activities

At the information centre you can buy a ticket (R12) for four of the town's museums: the Printing Museum, the House Museum, Dresden Store and the Central Garage Transport Museum.

Printing Museum MUSEUM

(admission R12; ⏲9am-12.45pm & 1.45-4pm) The Printing Museum explores the history of printing in the town and has a collection of old presses. Admission includes entry to the House and Central Garage Transport Museums and Dresden Store.

House Museum MUSEUM

(admission R12; ⏲9am-12.45pm & 1.45-4pm) The House Museum is a restored Victorian home full of black-and-white photos, old dolls and furniture, including a wooden carved commode in the main bedroom. Admission includes entry to the Printing and Central Garage Transport Museums and Dresden Store.

Dresden Store MUSEUM

(admission R12; ⏲9am-12.45pm & 1.45-4pm) The Dresden Store is a general store re-created as it would have been in 1930s, complete with flying ceramic ducks on the wall. Admission includes entry to the Printing, House and Central Garage Transport Museums.

Central Garage Transport Museum MUSEUM
(admission R12; ⊙9am-12.45pm & 1.45-4pm)
Illustrates the development of transport in
the town from the 1870s to the 1950s. For
classic-car enthusiasts. Admission includes
entry to the House and Printing Museums
and Dresden Store.

Alanglade MUSEUM
(☑013-768 1060; admission R20; ⊙tours 11am &
2pm Mon-Sun) A former mine-manager's residence at the northern edge of town, beautifully decked out in 1920s style with original
artefacts. Tours need to be booked 30 minutes in advance.

Diggings Museum MUSEUM
(guided tours adult/child R12/6; ⊙tours 10am,
11am, noon, 2pm & 3pm) Just east of town along
the Graskop road is the open-air Diggings
Museum, where you can see how gold was
panned. You need to visit on a tour, arranged
through the information centre.

🛏 Sleeping & Eating

Pilgrim's Rest Caravan Park CARAVAN PARK $
(☑072 820 4033, 013-768 1309; camping R70,
guesthouse r per person R400; ☒) This is a
beautiful camping spot right alongside the
Blyde River, with large grounds and barbecue facilities. There's also guesthouse
accommodation.

Royal Hotel HOTEL $$
(☑013-768 1044; www.royal-hotel.co.za; s/d incl
breakfast from R600/900; ☒) An elegant, his-
torical building at the centre of Uptown, it's
definitely worth spending the night here if
you can. Rooms have Victorian baths, brass
beds and other period features. Most are not
in the main building but scattered about in
houses on the main street, many with porch-
es and great views. The Church Bar, adjoin-
ing, is a good spot for a drink.

Stables Deli & Cafe CAFE $
(meals R20-40; ⊙8.30am-5pm) Cute little
place in Uptown with a corrugated-tin roof
and wooden tables and benches outside. It
serves light meals, sandwiches, salads, sa-
voury and sweet pancakes and good-value
wines by the glass. Limited menu but food
is well prepared.

ⓘ Information

Visitor Information Centre (☑013-768 1060;
Main St; ⊙9am-12.45pm & 1.15-4.30pm)

There's a helpful visitor information centre in
town where you buy tickets for the museums.

ⓘ Getting There & Away

Sporadic minibus shared taxis run between Pil-
grim's Rest and Graskop, but most traffic along
this treacherous road is in private vehicles.

Graskop

POP 4000 / ELEV 1450M

While it's a popular stop with the tour
buses, little Graskop somehow seems to
swallow them quite well, leaving plenty of
room around town for everyone else. The
compact town is one of the most appealing
in the area, with a sunny disposition, sleepy
backstreets and gently sloping hills in every
direction. There are good guesthouses, res-
taurants and craft shops to keep visitors
happy. On summer afternoons, restaurant
terraces are full and there's a friendly buzz.
It's also a useful base for exploring the Blyde
River Canyon, and the nearby views over the
edge of the Drakensberg Escarpment are
magnificent.

◉ Sights & Activities

There's good hiking and mountain biking
in the area. Trips SA (p374) can point you
in the right direction, or you can hire bikes
(R300 per day) from Graskop Valley View
Backpackers.

Big Swing ADVENTURE SPORTS
(☑013-737 8191; single/tandem jump R320/R600,
zip line only R100) One of the highest cable
gorge swings in the world, Big Swing has
a freefall of 68m (that's like falling 19 sto-
reys in less than three seconds) into Gras-
kop Gorge. You then swing like a pendulum
across the width of the gorge, from where
you get an outstanding view. It's 1km out of
town on the Hazyview road.

You can work up the courage with a drink
at the lodge next door. There's also a 135m
highwire 'foefie slide' (zip line).

🛏 Sleeping

★**Graskop Valley View
Backpackers** BACKPACKERS $
(☑013-767 1112; www.valley-view.co.za; 47 De
Lange St; camping R90, dm R130, tw & d R280-
360; ☒☎☒) This friendly Dutch-run back-
packers has a variety of rooms in excellent
condition, plus *rondavels* (round huts) and
a self-catering flat. The owners can organ-

ise adventure tours and rent out mountain bikes for private use (R200 per day). Take the road to Sabie, turn left at the first four-way stop and take another left on De Lange St. Highly recommended.

Autumn Breath B&B **$**
(082 877 2811; Louis Trichardt St; r per person incl breakfast R250-275) This quaint B&B has three modern rooms. Room No 1 is big, blue, huge and the best. Room No 2, with a balcony, is also good.

★ **Graskop Hotel** HOTEL **$$**
(013-767 1244; www.graskophotel.co.za; cnr Hoof & Louis Trichardt Sts; s/d incl breakfast R700/1000;) This classy hotel is one of our favourites in the province. Rooms here are slick, stylish and individual, several featuring art and design by contemporary South African artists. Rooms out the back are little country cottages with dollhouse-like furniture (but are extremely comfortable), an impression exemplified by the glass doors opening onto the lush garden at the rear. Book ahead.

Le Gallerie GUESTHOUSE **$$**
(013-767 1093; www.legallerie.co.za; cnr Louis Trichardt & Oorwinning Sts; s/d incl breakfast R520/920; @) A luxury guesthouse and art gallery with three rooms, each with sumptuous furnishings and private access; bathrooms are also very spacious and well presented. It's in a good location, just on the fringe of the action in town.

Blyde Chalets BUNGALOW **$$**
(013-767 1316; www.blydechalets.co.za; Louis Trichardt St; cottages R700-900;) Simple self-catering cottages, each with a kitchen, lounge and braai (barbecue), in a central location.

Eating

Harrie's Pancakes CREPERIE **$**
(Louis Trichardt St; pancakes R50-70; 8am-7pm) The chic white minimalist interior, full of modern art and quirky touches, is somewhat at odds with the cuisine. You won't find breakfast-style pancakes here but mostly savoury and exotic fillings, as well as some sweet offerings. Its reputation perhaps outdoes what it delivers, but Harrie's is a nice spot for a breakfast croissant and fresh-brewed coffee.

Kruger's Gold INTERNATIONAL **$$**
(071 361 0715; www.krugersgold.co.za; Eagle's View Eco Estate, Rte 533; mains R100-135; lunch & dinner) At last fine dining has come

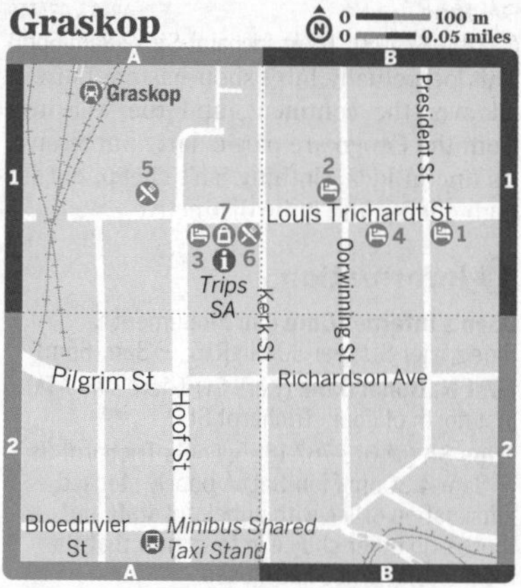

Graskop

Sleeping
1 Autumn Breath B1
2 Blyde Chalets B1
3 Graskop Hotel A1
4 Le Gallerie B1

Eating
5 Canimambo A1
6 Harrie's Pancakes A1

Shopping
7 Delagoa A1

to Graskop! Situated on an estate currently under development and overlooking the God's Window Escarpment, just outside town, this restaurant does wonderful things with beef, pork, lamb and seafood. Simple dishes such as slow-braised lamb are beautifully prepared. There are also wood-fire pizzas.

Canimambo PORTUGUESE **$$**
(013-767 1868; cnr Hoof & Louis Trichardt Sts; dishes R80-140; breakfast, lunch & dinner;) A Portuguese and Mozambican joint serving up spicy stews and grills as well as some excellent seafood dishes. Try the bean stew with chorizo or smoked chicken. Alternatively, Canimambo does some wonderfully scrumptious things with prawns.

Shopping

There are several good craft shops in town, concentrated around Louis Trichardt St. Although there's a lot of dross, there's quality to be found too.

Delagoa ARTS & CRAFTS

(☎013-767 1081; Louis Trichardt St; ⏰8am-6pm) This perpetually busy shop has crafts from all over the continent, and the weavings from the Congo are particularly impressive. Its line in kids' clothing isn't cheap, but it's high quality and quite distinctive.

ℹ Information

Daan's Internet Cafe (cnr Monument & Bloedrivier Sts; per 30min R15; ⏰8am-6pm)

First National Bank (Kerk St) There's an ATM just north of Louis Trichardt St.

Trips SA (☎013-767 1886; Louis Trichardt St; ⏰8am-4.30pm Mon-Sat) A poorly stocked information office with unhelpful staff, but there's no other choice in town now that the local tourist office has closed.

ℹ Getting There & Away

Minibus Shared Taxi Stand (Hoof St) The minibus-taxi stand is at the southern end of town, with daily morning departures to Pilgrim's Rest (R10, 30 minutes), Sabie (R25, 40 minutes) and Hazyview (R30, one hour).

Blyde River Canyon

Increasingly popular with international visitors, Blyde River Canyon is the third largest canyon in the world and one of South Africa's most outstanding natural sights. The canyon's scale and beauty make a trip here a memorable experience – especially if you're lucky enough to visit on a fine day.

Much of the canyon is bordered by the 260-sq-km **Blyde River Canyon Nature Reserve** (☎021-424 1037; www.mtpa.co.za; per person/car R30/10), which winds its way north from Graskop, following the Drakensberg Escarpment and meeting the Blyde River as it snakes down to the lowveld. The majority of visitors drive along the canyon's edge, and there are plenty of viewpoints along the way where you can stop and gaze in awe. If you have enough time, however, it's even better explored on foot.

Activities

The Forever Blyde Canyon resort has information on six hiking routes in the area.

Belvedere Day Walk WALKING

This short but reasonably strenuous walk takes you in a circular route to the Belvedere hydroelectric power station at Bourke's Luck Potholes. Bookings should be made at Potholes; the walk takes approximately five hours. When walking here, don't go to the river; instead turn left at the guesthouse and down a path to some beautiful waterfalls and rock pools.

WORTH A TRIP

TOURING AROUND BLYDE RIVER CANYON

Heading north from Graskop, look first for the **Pinnacle**, a striking skyscraper-like rock formation (lock up your vehicle here). Just to the north along Rte 534 (a loop off Rte 532) are **God's Window** and **Wonder View** – two viewpoints with amazing vistas and an even more amazing number of craft stalls. At God's Window take the trail up to the rainforest (300 steps), where you might spot rare birds, including the elusive loeire.

When you return to Rte 532, take a short detour 2km south to the impressive **Lisbon Falls** (or if you are coming back to Graskop, catch it in the afternoon).

The Blyde River Canyon starts north of here, near **Bourke's Luck Potholes**. These bizarre cylindrical holes were carved into the rock by whirlpools near the confluence of the Blyde and Treuer Rivers. There's a **visitors centre** where you can pay the reserve entry fee and get information on the canyon's geology, flora and fauna.

Continuing north past Bourke's Luck Potholes and into the heart of the nature reserve, you'll reach a viewpoint overlooking the **Three Rondavels** – enormous rounds of rock with pointed, grassy tops that look like giant huts carved into the side of the canyon. There are a number of short walks in the surrounding area to points where you can look down to the Blydepoort Dam at the reserve's far north.

West of here, outside the reserve and off Rte 36, are the **Echo Caves** (☎013-238 0015; www.echocaves.co.za; admission & guided tour adult/child R60/30), where Stone Age relics have been found. The caves get their name from dripstone formations that echo when tapped.

The power station was built in 1911 and was once the largest of its kind in the southern hemisphere.

Sleeping

It's easy to explore the canyon by vehicle as a day jaunt from Graskop, Sabie or Pilgrim's Rest. If you're continuing further north, a good alternative is to stay in or around the nature reserve, or in Hoedspruit.

Forever Blyde Canyon RESORT **$$**
(☎0861 226 966; www.foreverblydecanyon.co.za; camping R280, chalets from R940;) This rambling resort has a wide choice of accommodation. The solid brick chalets are very well set up, and the pricier ones are worth it for the views and extra space. (For jaw-dropping views of the Three Rondavels ask for Nos 89 to 96.)

Watch out for the cheeky baboons – a couple of years ago this author had one jump in the window and pinch a loaf of bread from the kitchen!

Thaba Tsweni Lodge LODGE **$$**
(☎013-767 1380; www.blyderivercanyonaccommodation.com; d from R800, breakfast R100) Beautifully located just a short walk from Berlin Falls in the heart of the panorama route are several self-catering chalets with stone walls, African-print bedspreads, kitchens, private garden areas with braai facilities, wood-burning fireplaces and beautiful views. It's just off Rte 352 in the direction of Berlin Falls.

Forever Resort Swadini RESORT **$$**
(☎015-795 5141; www.foreverswadini.co.za; campsites R128, plus per person R67, chalets from R1454;) These basic chalets are improved greatly by the good location and impressive views. In addition to hiking, the resort can organise white-water rafting, abseiling and more. It's at the northern end of the reserve along the Blyde River, and about 5km from Blydepoort Dam. There's a supermarket, liquor store and laundry facilities. It's a lot cheaper in low season.

EASTERN LOWVELD

The hot and dry Eastern Lowveld is mostly used as a staging post on the way into and out of Kruger National Park. You can learn about the history of the gold rush in the feel-good town of Barberton or get your big-city fix in Nelspruit, and there are plenty of country lodges to whet your appetite for mighty Kruger National Park.

Hazyview

POP 4300

Spread out along Rte 40 and with no real centre, Hazyview has developed purely because of its proximity to Kruger National Park. There are good facilities, a couple of decent restaurants and even some activities to keep you busy if you feel the need to stop here for a day or two. It is close to the Phabeni (12km), Numbi (15km) and Paul Kruger (47km) gates.

Sights & Activities

Shangana Cultural Village VILLAGE
(☎013-737 5804; www.shangana.co.za; tours R136; 9am-4pm) About 5km north of town, along Rte 535, is a very touristy re-creation of a traditional Shangaan community. At various times of the day it features a market, farming activity and house building. There are also displays of *masocho* (warrior) uniforms and weaponry, the relating of customs and history by a *sangoma* (traditional healer), cooking, dancing and the imbibing of *byala* (traditional beer). The Marula Crafts Market is also located here.

Midday visits with a traditional meal cost from R295 and the evening program with a good dinner costs R480.

Skyway Trails ADVENTURE SPORTS
(☎013-737 6747; www.skywaytrails.com; Perry's Bridge Trading Post; Cable Trail R500, Tree Top Challenge R200) This is 'Mpumalanga's longest Aerial Cable Trail' – fly through the forest while clipped to a wire! It takes up to 2½ hours to complete the 10 platforms and various 70m to 230m cable sections (1.2km in total). The Tree Top Challenge – a family-friendly elevated obstacle course – is the latest adventure.

Sleeping & Eating

Gecko Lodge & Backpackers LODGE, BACKPACKERS **$$**
(☎071 292 5616, 013-590 1020; www.geckolodge.co.za; camping R70, dm R110-160, s/d incl breakfast R695/1100;) The en-suite rooms in this sprawling, well-equipped lodge have vaulted ceilings, wrought-iron bedsteads and very comfy beds. The backpackers is a separate property next door and has recently been

renovated. It offers a variety of room configurations and is good value. Gecko is located 3km from Hazyview, just off the R536 (the Sabie Rd).

The lodge is set in expansive gardens and you can walk through the forest to the Sabie River.

Perry's Bridge Hollow Hotel　　HOTEL **$$**
(☑ 013-737 7752; www.seasonsinafrica.com; Rte 40; s/d incl breakfast R850/1100; ✸) Worth it for the sheer convenience of being in a retail centre, and pretty stylish to boot, Perry's Bridge Hollow offers large rooms decorated in muted tones, with dark wood and grey plaster floors. All rooms have patios overlooking the gardens or the pretty pool area.

Idle & Wild　　BUNGALOW **$$**
(☑ 013-737 8173; www.idleandwild.com; s/d rondavels incl breakfast R625/920; ℗) In a wonderful tropical garden that will make your heart sing (no, really!) are these excellent *rondavels*. Standard ones are very roomy and include kitchenette; the honeymoon *rondavel* (add R100) has slightly nicer linen and a large spa bath. All have beautiful garden outlooks and outside table and chairs to enjoy them. It's 5km from Hazyview on Rte 536 to Sabie.

Summerfields Kitchen　　FUSION **$$**
(☑ 013-737 6500; mains R125-160; ⊗ lunch & dinner) For something romantic, head to Summerfields, some 5km out of town on Rte 536. The food is beautifully presented and generally on the rich side, including meats with creamy sauces, buttery trout and sinful desserts (we recommend the vanilla pannacotta). On a hot afternoon you can enjoy the cooling breeze from a corner table on the sweeping deck.

Pioneer Restaurant　　STEAKHOUSE **$$**
(☑ 013-737 7397; Rendezvous Tourism Centre, Rte 40; mains R90-160; ⊗ noon-3pm & 6-9pm) Denee Fick is a well-known South African chef and brings her considerable talents to this modern restaurant. She specialises in fine cuts of beef cooked to perfection: try the sirloin with mushroom sauce. There's also seafood on offer as well as local game such as ostrich.

ⓘ Information

Big 5 Country Tourist Office (☑ 013-737 7414; ⊗ 8am-5pm Mon-Sat, 9am-1pm Sun) This helpful office is in the Rendezvous Centre, as you are coming into Hazyview from the south.

PostNet (Blue Haze Mall, cnr Rtes 536 & 40; per 15min R10) Reliable internet access in the largest shopping centre in town.

ⓘ Getting There & Away

Minibus shared taxis go daily to Nelspruit (R40, one hour) and Sabie (R40, one hour).

White River

POP 16,700 / ELEV 950M

White River (Witrivier) is a large, messy town dating back to the days of the Anglo-Boer War. Less humid than Nelspruit, it makes an alternative base for a trip into Kruger. There are also two useful shopping centres here: the countrified Casterbridge Farm has restaurants and shops, art galleries and a cinema; and the Bagdad Centre has faux–Cape Dutch, Moroccan and Zanzibar architecture and good restaurants. The centres are opposite each other, just 2km north of town on Rte 40 to Hazyview.

Gypsies Travellers Inn　　BACKPACKERS **$**
(☑ 079 6049 675; Plot 119, Jatinga Rd; per person R120, 8-person self-catering cottages R1200; ✸) This friendly, rustic spot just outside White River has a range of dorms and rooms in cabins. It is the closest backpackers to Kruger Mpumalanga International Airport.

Karula Hotel　　HOTEL **$$**
(☑ 013-751 2277; www.karulahotel.co.za; Old Plaston Rd; incl breakfast s/d R690/1100, luxury s/d R800/1300; ✸ 🛜 ✸) Situated in a little green oasis just 2km outside town on Rte 538, this peaceful retreat makes for a relaxing night's kip amongst the jacaranda and bougainvillea. Standard rooms are a little dated, but the luxury rooms are well worth the extra, as they're larger and come with couch and bushy outlooks. Rates include dinner.

Fez at Baghdad　　MIDDLE EASTERN **$$**
(☑ 013-750 1250; Bagdad Centre; mains from R90; ⊗ closed Sun evening & Mon) White-robed and fez-clad waiters serve up a mix of North African and Middle Eastern favourites, including large sharing plates of mezze, *tajines* and grills. The restaurant also houses, somewhat incongruously, a sushi bar.

ⓘ Information

First National Bank (Tom Lawrence St) Has an ATM.

Lowveld Tourism (☑ 013-755 1988; Casterbridge Centre, Rte 40; ⊗ 9am-4pm Mon-Sat, 10am-2pm

Sun) Quite bizarrely in the Antiques & Artifacts Car Museum, at the Casterbridge Centre.

Getting There & Away

Minibus shared taxis go throughout the day to/from Nelspruit (R15, 20 minutes) and Hazyview (R35, one hour).

Nelspruit

POP 58,700

Nelspruit (also known as Mbombela) is Mpumalanga's largest town and the provincial capital. While not unpleasant, it's more a place to get things done than a worthwhile destination for tourists. There are, however, good accommodation options and a couple of excellent restaurants, so it makes a good-enough stopover on the way elsewhere.

Sights & Activities

Lowveld National Botanical Garden GARDENS
(☎013-752 5531; www.sanbi.org; adult/child R25/14; ⏰8am-6pm) Out of town, the 15,000-sq-m Botanical Garden (established 1969) is home to tropical African rainforest and is a nice place for a stroll among the flowers and trees. Over 240 bird species have been recorded here. It's on Rte 40 about 2km north of the junction with the N4.

Chimpanzee Eden ZOO
(☎013-737 8191; www.janegoodall.co.za; Rte 40; adult/child R160/80) This chimp centre, 12km south of Nelspruit on Rte 40, acts as a sanctuary for rescued chimpanzees. Here you can see chimps in a semi-wild environment and learn about the primates' behaviour and plight. The entry fee includes a guided tour (10am, noon and 2pm).

Hiking

There are also some good (and strenuous) hikes in the area. For information and bookings, contact Komatiland Forests Eco-Tourism (p380).

Kaapschehoop Trail HIKING
(per night R105) There is a variety of trail options around Kaapschehoop in the historic goldfields area between Nelspruit and Barberton. Birdwatching is a highlight of the trails and you could also see wild horses, vervet monkeys, bushbucks, jackals, klipspringers, mountain reedbucks, and even leopards. Hikes last two, three or four days.

Uitsoek Trail HIKING
(per night R105) This trail begins 80km north-west of Nelspruit. Cape clawless otters, grey rhebucks, mountain reedbucks, duikers, bushbucks and plenty of bird life can be seen. Hikes last one or two days.

Tours

African Safari Adventures TOUR, SAFARIS
(☎013-737 6218; www.tourist.co.za) Very experienced outfit running a plethora of day and overnight tours to Kruger and Blyde River Canyon, as well as specialist activity safaris such as birdwatching and river rafting. Also runs tours to Swaziland and Mozambique.

Funky Safaris (Discover Kruger) TOUR, SAFARIS
(☎013-744 1310; www.discoverkruger.com) Based at Funky Monkey Backpackers, this operator does one- to three-day safaris to Kruger, where it has its own tented camp, as well as day trips to Blyde River Canyon.

Kruger and More TOUR, SAFARIS
(☎013-744 0993; www.krugerandmore.co.za) A well-organised company leading multiday tours to Kruger, Blyde River Canyon and Mozambique.

Festivals & Events

InniBos CULTURE, MUSIC
(www.innibos.co.za) Held every June or July, this is Nelspruit's biggest festival, bringing together artists, musicians and theatre groups for five days of fun. Entry is around R50 per day.

Sleeping

Old Vic Travellers Inn BACKPACKERS $
(Crazy Kangaroo Backpackers; ☎013-744 0993; www.krugerandmore.co.za; 12 Impala St; dm R145, d R520, d without bathroom R400, 4-person self-catering houses R800; @ 📶 🏊) A friendly, somewhat upscale backpackers, with self-catering facilities and lots of information on the area. Double rooms are a bit dark but clean and well kept, and shared bathrooms are in good order. A big, rambling garden leads down to the river. It's about 3km south of the centre and is a Baz Bus stop.

Funky Monkey Backpackers BACKPACKERS $
(☎013-744 1310; www.funkymonkeys.co.za; 102 Van Wijk St; camping R90, dm R150, s/d without bathroom R250/400; @ 🏊) Although it gets mixed reviews from readers, and it's a little out of town, this is a good option for

Nelspruit

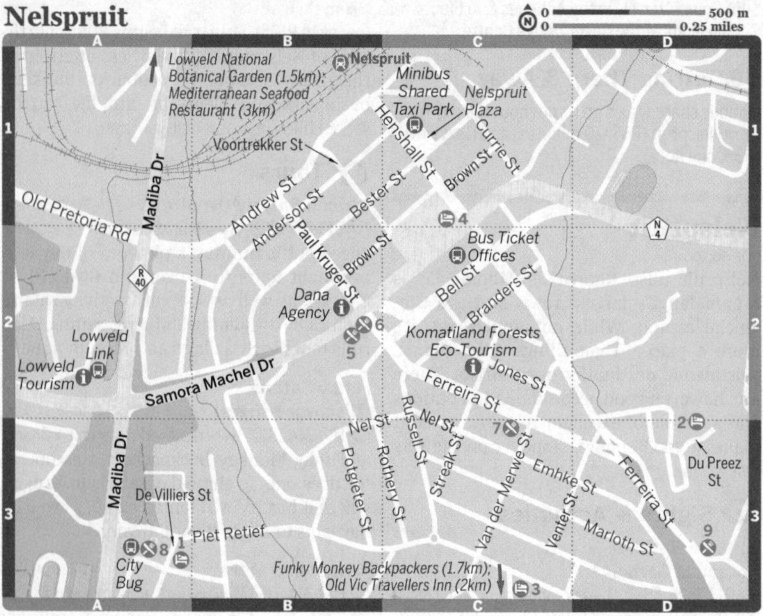

Nelspruit

Sleeping

1 Auberge Guest Lodge A3
2 Francolin Lodge & Boutique Hotel D3
3 Haden's B&B C3
4 Orion Promenade Hotel C1

Eating

5 Costa do Sol B2
6 Food Fundi B2
7 Jock Pub & Grill C3
Orange Restaurant .... (see 2)
8 Puzzle A3
9 Saffron D3

backpackers, with clean dorms and doubles in a rambling house with spacious garden. To get here take Ferreira St east, then turn right onto Van der Merwe St, which turns into Van Wijk St.

The pool and braai area sees some great parties, and meals are available.

★Utopia in Africa GUESTHOUSE **$$**
(☎013-745 7714; www.utopiainafrica.co.za; 6 Daleen St; s/d incl breakfast from R750/1200; ❄📶🏊) Simplicity, elegance and a masterly design that keeps the premises cool using the afternoon breeze mark this exceptional accommodation. Rooms are beautifully furnished and have balconies overlooking a nearby nature reserve. Head south on Madiba Dr, turn left onto Dr Enos Mabuza Dr, then left onto Halssnoer St (which becomes Augusta) and keep following it – Utopia is well signposted from here.

It's very much like staying with friends – the warmth and inclusiveness are really appealing.

Haden's B&B GUESTHOUSE **$$**
(☎013-752 3259; www.hadensrest.com; cnr Van Wijk St & Mostert Rd; s/d incl breakfast R550/750; ❄📶🏊) Rooms at this friendly B&B are lent a dash of colour from the bright African art on the walls. Some rooms are better (ie larger) than others, so ask to see a few: No 4 is a good one. It's well located for access to the city. To get here take Ferreira St east and turn right onto Van der Merwe St, which turns into Van Wijk St.

Auberge Guest Lodge B&B **$$**
(☎013-741 2866; www.aubergeguestlodge.com; 3 De Villiers St; s/d incl breakfast R550/750; @📶🏊) A quiet, well-maintained and sunny guesthouse with a plant-filled courtyard and a pool. Motel-like rooms are straight-up-and-down, some with ceiling fans. It's in a good location behind the Sonpark Centre, with cafes and restaurants just across the road.

Orion Promenade Hotel HOTEL $$
(☎011-718 6452; www.oriongroup.co.za; cnr Samora Machel Dr & Henshall St; r incl breakfast R1600;) Right in the town centre, across from the bus offices, this bastion is a warren of hallways. Some rooms, like No 204, have been renovated and now boast funky fixtures and improved beds and linen. Other rooms have not had the touch of the magic wand but have acres of space. All are the same price. Weekend specials available.

Francolin Lodge & Boutique Hotel GUESTHOUSE $$$
(☎013-744 1251; www.francolinlodge.co.za; 4 Du Preez St; s/d incl breakfast R1110/1700;) This is a top Nelspruit guesthouse. The rooms have double-height ceilings, private patios and corner bathrooms with views. The easiest way to approach it is off the N4 coming into town from the east – it's well signposted.

It also owns the equally lovely Loerie's Call next door, with plush rooms set apart from the main house along decked walkways, each with their own entrance.

Eating

★**Food Fundi** SANDWICHES $
(☎013-755 1091; ABSA Sq; mains R40-60; 7am-4pm Mon-Fri, 8am-1pm Sat) Using fresh lowveld ingredients, this outstanding cafe is an excellent choice for breakfast or lunch. Wraps, sandwiches (try the rooibos-smoked chicken, toasted cashew nuts, pineapple chutney and feta), salads and burgers all decorate the menu. Craft beer, wine and sweet treats also available.

Puzzle CAFE $
(Sonpark Shopping Centre, Rte 40; mains R30-60; 7am-4.30pm Mon-Fri, to 1pm Sat) This bright, reliable place is a very pleasant spot and serves good-value, no-frills breakfast and lunch, including sandwiches, wraps and quiche. It's friendly and homely, and a convivial meeting point for locals.

★**Saffron** TAPAS $$
(☎013-744 0324; www.saffronnelspruit.co.za; 54/56 Ferreira St; tapas R20-40; noon-2pm Tue-Fri, 6-9pm Mon-Sat) Serving quality tapas dishes such as house-smoked pork loin with honey-mustard cream, and onion marmalade tartlets topped with goat cheese, Saffron is the latest exciting addition to Nelspruit's growing culinary scene. Dine in the intimate interior or outside on the lovely deck. Book ahead as it's popular with locals and visitors alike.

Jock Pub & Grill PUB $$
(☎013-755 4969; www.jockpubandgrill.co.za; Ferreira St; mains R80-140; kitchen 8am-9.30pm) This rambling 'outback-style' pub is very pleasant, set amid large lawns. The food is up a notch in quality from many other Nelspruit offerings: great salads, wood-fire pizzas, burgers, Mozambique-style seafood and a decent vegetarian selection. The playground helps to make it family friendly. Very popular with locals.

Mediterranean Seafood Restaurant MEDITERRANEAN $$
(Hub, Riverside Mall, Rte 40; mains R90-150; 10.30am-9.30pm) Cane chairs, a large outdoor seating area, floor-to-ceiling wine racks and pretty sun-drenched pastels adorn this restaurant. Doing delightful things with seafood (including sushi), this open-air place may overlook a carpark, but it remains one of Nelspruit's best eateries. Seafood platters and curries are highlights.

Turn to the back of the menu for the chef's specials and note that there are some great deals on Tuesday and Thursday.

Costa do Sol PORTUGUESE, ITALIAN $$
(☎013-752 6382; Paul Kruger St, ABSA Sq; meals R60-100; 11am-10pm Mon-Fri, 6.30-10pm Sat) An old-fashioned favourite, where the darkish dining room serves Italian or Portuguese food including fish, pasta dishes and prawns. A good city-centre option – the cool interior is a nice break from the frenetic streets outside.

Orange Restaurant FUSION $$$
(☎013-744 9507; www.eatatorange.co.za; 4 Du Preez St; mains lunch R60-100, dinner R80-160; lunch & dinner) Put on your finest and treat yourself to some beautifully prepared cuisine, such as artful servings of ostrich carpaccio, at this classy restaurant at the Francolin Lodge. The terrific views are the icing on the cake.

Information

The Mozambique Consulate (p585) does visa processing.

EMERGENCY

Police Station (☎013-759 1000; 15 Bester St) Opposite Nelspruit Plaza.

INTERNET ACCESS

PostNet (Nelspruit Crossing Mall; per 15min R10; 8am-5pm Mon-Fri, 9am-1pm Sat) Reliable internet access.

MEDICAL SERVICES

Nelmed Forum (☎013-755 1541; www.nelmed.co.za; cnr Nel & Rothery Sts) Offers 24-hour emergency medical care.

Nelspruit Mediclinic (☎013-759 0500; www.mediclinic.co.za; 1 Louise St) Private hospital offering 24-hour emergency medical care.

MONEY

First National Bank (Bester St) Does foreign exchange.

Nelspruit Crossing Mall (cnr Samora Machel & Madiba Drs) Has an ATM.

Standard Bank (Brown St) Has an ATM.

TOURIST INFORMATION

Dana Agency (☎013-753 3571; www.danaagency.co.za; Shop 12, Nelspruit Crossing Mall; ⏰8am-4.30pm Mon-Fri, 9am-noon Sat) This long-standing agent can help with air tickets and other travel arrangements.

Lowveld Tourism (☎013-755 1988; www.lowveldtourism.com; cnr Madiba & Samora Machel Drs; ⏰7am-6pm Mon-Fri, 8am-1.30pm Sat) This helpful office at Nelspruit Crossing Mall (behind News Cafe) takes bookings for all national parks, including Kruger, and can help arrange accommodation and tours.

Komatiland Forests Eco-Tourism (☎013-754 2724; www.komatiecotourism.co.za; 10 Streak St) Provides information and takes bookings for hikes in the area.

ℹ Getting There & Around

AIR

Kruger Mpumalanga International Airport (MKIA; ☎013-753 7500; www.kmiairport.co.za) Mpumalanga Kruger International Airport is the closest commercial airport to Nelspruit.

Airlink (☎013-750 2531, 0861-606 606; www.flyairlink.com) There are daily flights with Airlink to Jo'burg (R1200 to R1400, one hour), Cape Town (R2800 to R3200, two hours 40 minutes) and Durban (R2200 to R2700, 1½ hours).

BUS

The major bus companies all go daily between Jo'burg (and Pretoria) and Maputo (Mozambique) via Nelspruit.

Greyhound (☎013-753 2100; www.greyhound.co.za) Routes include Pretoria to Nelspruit (R315, five hours, three daily) and Nelspruit to Maputo (R320, four hours, one daily).

Translux (☎0861-589 282; www.translux.co.za)

CAR RENTAL

Avis (☎013-750 1015; www.avis.co.za) At the airport.

Europcar (☎013-751 1855; www.europcar.co.za) At the airport.

First (☎013-750 2538; www.firstcarrental.co.za) At the airport.

SHARED TAXI

The local bus and minibus-taxi park is behind Nelspruit Plaza near the corner of Bester and Henshall Sts. Minibus-taxi destinations and fares include White River (R15, 20 minutes), Barberton (R30, 40 minutes), Hazyview (R40, one hour), Graskop (R45, 1½ hours) and Jo'burg (R140, five hours).

City Bug (☎086-133 4433; www.citybug.co.za) City Bug operates a twice-weekly shuttle to Durban (R630 per person one way, nine hours), a daily shuttle to Pretoria (R410, 3½ to five hours), and several per day to OR Tambo International Airport (R410 per person one way, four to 5½ hours, four or five daily). All services depart from the Sonpark BP petrol station.

Lowveld Link (☎013-750 1174; www.lowveldlink.com) Lowveld Link operates a convenient daily shuttle from Nelspruit to Pretoria (R390 one way, 3½ hours), OR Tambo International Airport (R390 one way, 4¼ hours) and Sandton (R390 one way, 4¾ hours). It leaves from the Lowveld Tourism office.

TRAIN

Shosholoza Meyl (☎0860-008 888; www.shosholozameyl.co.za) Operates the seat-only Komati run, which travels twice weekly between Jo'burg (eight hours) and Komatipoort (2½ hours) via Nelspruit.

Malelane

POP 3500

Malelane is essentially a stopover point and service centre for Kruger National Park. There are some good lodges here, however, most with views of Crocodile River and close enough to the wildlife to whet your appetite for the main event.

Malelane is on the N4, and Malelane Gate, 3km northeast of town, will take you into Kruger's southern regions.

★ **River House Lodge** GUESTHOUSE $$
(☎013-790 1333; www.riverhouse.co.za; 27 Visarend St; s/d R700/1400) Perched right on the park boundary, this cracking lodge is a great place to relax and unwind pre- or post-Kruger. All rooms have their own balconies, from which you can see all the way into the park. The service is very friendly and the eclectic design has many elements of yesteryear. It's west of town and signposted from the main road.

Masungulo River Camp LODGE $$
(☎013-744 1310; half-board per person R350; 🏊) Run by the good folk at Funky Monkey in

Nelspruit, this new bush camp is in a wildlife reserve overlooking Crocodile River. It's a great base for safaris into Kruger, which can be booked on site. Accommodation is in safari tents. Between the Malelane and Crocodile Bridge Kruger entrance gates, it's also only 25km from the Mozambique border gate.

Serenity Lodge LODGE $$$
(☎013-790 2000; www.serenitylodge.co.za; s/d incl breakfast R1800/2400, dinner R200;) Serenity's gorgeous thatched suites, all with terraces, are tucked away in the forest and linked by elevated walkways. It's a perfect place to get away from it all and the grounds have walking trails, small waterfalls and trees full of birds, butterflies and monkeys.

Komatipoort

POP 4700

Cradled by the Lebombo Mountains, Komatipoort sits near the confluence of the Komati and Crocodile Rivers, only 10km from Kruger National Park's Crocodile Bridge gate. If you're travelling to/from Mozambique or Swaziland it makes for a good stopover. There's a Spar supermarket, a petrol station and an ABSA bank with exchange facilities.

If you happen to be in Komatipoort in late June, ask around for the **Prawn Festival**, which celebrates the modest crayfish in all its glory.

Sleeping & Eating

Kruger View Backpackers BACKPACKERS $
(☎013-793 7373; www.krugerview.com; 61 Bosbok St; dm/d R150/465; @) This is an upmarket backpackers just five minutes from Crocodile Bridge gate where you can see wildlife from the balcony. With gorgeous views into Kruger, there are spacious dorms and doubles sleeping two to five people.

★**Trees Too** GUESTHOUSE $$
(☎013-793 8262; www.treestoo.com; s/d R765/980;) This place is a standout, with great thatch-and-brick rooms, an honesty bar, a pool and very friendly service. Staff have heaps of info about Kruger and serve breakfast and dinner. Wildlife artworks decorate rooms along with quality furniture. It's on a leafy side street about 500m in from Rissik St and signposted.

Stoep Café B&B $$
(☎083 457 3909; www.stoepcafeguesthouse.co.za; 74 Rissik St; s/d incl breakfast R400/700;) Stoep is a very pretty, green and white colonial-style house with a small garden and pool in the heart of town. There are three tidy rooms with small kitchenettes and an onsite coffee shop with a large, shady verandah serving tasty meals, snacks and pancakes.

Restaurante Tambarina PORTUGUESE $$
(☎013-790 7057; Rissik St; mains R80-120; ⌚lunch & dinner, closed Sun) Seafood platters and paella are standouts here, where the fish and prawns draw locals and there are also interesting selections such as crab curry. Choose between the large dining area and the outside terrace. Flaky service lets things down: put your hand up, wiggle your bum, do what you have to in order to get their attention.

Getting There & Away

Minibus shared taxis leave from just off Rissik St near the Score supermarket and regularly do the run between Komatipoort and Maputo (Mozambique; R90, 1½ to two hours). If you're driving, there are two tolls along the N4 on the Mozambique side. Exit procedures are fairly swift.

The Komati train travels daily except Saturday between Jo'burg and Komatipoort (R120, 11 hours) via Malelane and Nelspruit.

Barberton

POP 12,000

Barberton is a friendly, walkable little town with quiet, leafy streets set against a striking backdrop of green and purple mountains. It has a great feel to it, no doubt enhanced by its beautifully preserved historical buildings, the laidback nonchalance of its inhabitants and its compact centre. It makes an excellent alternative base to Nelspruit.

Dating back to the gold-rush days, the town boomed in the late 19th century and was home to South Africa's first stock exchange.

Sights & Activities

Barberton boasts several restored houses dating back to the late 19th and early 20th centuries. All are open for touring (contact the Barberton Museum for more details) and give a glimpse into the town's early history. They include **Belhaven House** (Lee St; adult/child R15/8; ⌚tours on the hour 10am-3pm Mon-Fri); **Stopforth House** (Bowness St; adult/child R15/8; ⌚tours on the hour 10am-3pm Mon-Fri) at the top of the town, with incredible views and a wonderful front deck; and **Fernlea House** (Lee St; ⌚9am-4pm Mon-Fri) FREE, which is in a beautiful wooded location.

Barberton

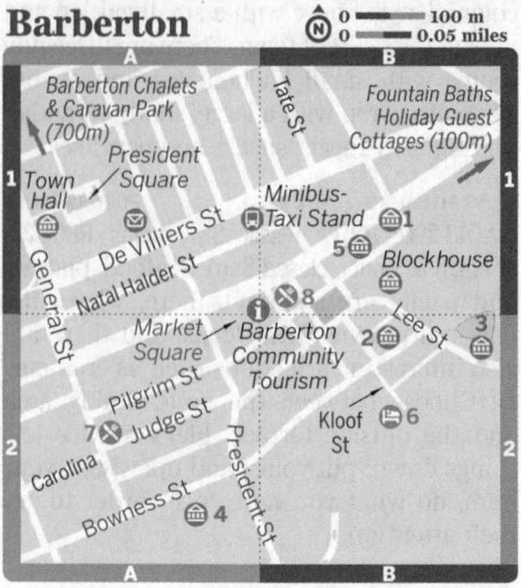

Barberton

⊙ Sights
1	Barberton Museum	B1
2	Belhaven House	B2
3	Fernlea House	B2
4	Stopforth House	A2
5	Umjindi Gallery	B1

🛏 Sleeping
6	Kloof House	B2

✕ Eating
7	Papa's	A2
8	Victorian Tea Garden & Restaurant	B1

You can pick up a **Heritage Walk** map and leaflet at the tourist information centre. It's a self-guided tour that takes in the restored houses as well as other sights.

On the southwestern edge of town is an abandoned 20.3km **aerial cableway**, once the longest operating industrial cableway in the world. It brought asbestos down from a mine in Swaziland and coal was carried in the other direction to provide counterweight.

Barberton Museum MUSEUM
(☑ 013-712 4208; 36 Pilgrim St; ⊙ 10am-4pm) **FREE** Barberton Museum is looking a bit worse for wear these days, but it has interesting exhibits on local history and geology, including a great black-and-white photo display of the town through the years.

Umjindi Gallery GALLERY
(☑ 013-712 5807; www.umjindijewellery.co.za; Pilgrim St; ⊙ 8am-5pm Mon-Fri) **FREE** Umjindi sells a range of crafts and has a workshop where you can watch the artists at work. The jewellery is stunning, especially the silver: you can pick up an earrings-and-pendant set decorated with delightful animal carvings for R600. Note that the gallery was undergoing a major renovation when we passed through.

Lone Tree Hill PARAGLIDING
(admission R20, plus key deposit R50) Just southwest of town is an excellent paragliding location at Lone Tree Hill. To get here, follow De Villiers St west from town and turn left about 500m past the prison. Contact **Hi Tech Security** (☑ 013-712 3256; McPherson St) off Kruger St for keys and access.

🛏 Sleeping

Bushwhacked LODGE $
(☑ 073 691 5646; Plot 370 Brommersplaas, Kruger St; s/d R130/250) Bushwacked is a terrific self-catering addition to Barberton's budget-accommodation scene. This rustic place has a basic setup with clean, comfortable rooms and great views. It welcomes wildlife enthusiasts in particular, although anyone can stay here. There are mountain bikes for hire.

Barberton Chalets & Caravan Park CARAVAN $
(☑ 013-712 3323; www.barbertonchalets.co.za; General St; camping R70, cottage s/d/tr R350/500/600; 🐾) This caravan park, in large grassy, shady grounds, is conveniently close to the town centre. 1970s-style chalets sleep four, but two would be more comfortable in the poky but clean and tidy interiors.

Kloof House GUESTHOUSE $$
(☑ 013-712 4268; www.kloofhuis.co.za; 1 Kloof St; s/d incl breakfast R450/700; @🛜) Kloof is a lovely old hillside Victorian house with simple but appealingly large rooms offering homey comforts. Rooms open out onto a wraparound verandah with great views. There's also a self-catering chalet.

Fountain Baths Holiday Guest Cottages GUESTHOUSE $$
(☑ 013-712 2707; 48 Pilgrim St; cottages per person R325) These spotless, good-size cottages, in a beautiful and historical location just on the northeastern edge of town, are well kitted out and full of character. The lovely quiet garden ensures you wake up to the sound of birdsong.

Eating & Drinking

Victorian Tea Garden & Restaurant CAFE $
(Crown St, Market Sq; light meals R30-40; ⏲8am-5pm Mon-Fri, to 1pm Sat; 📶) Here you can enjoy sandwiches, cakes and more substantial offerings while sitting in a gazebo and watching the world go by. It's between Pilgrim and Crown Sts, next to the tourist information office, and it's also a wi-fi hot spot.

Papa's MEDITERRANEAN $
(☎013-712 4645; 18 Judge St; mains R30-60; ⏲breakfast, lunch & dinner; 👪) Family friendly and with a nice, large garden courtyard, this pseudo-Mediterranean establishment is the best place in town for dinner or a hot lunch. Offering pizzas, pastas, the odd burger and even shwarmas, it's also an exceedingly pleasant place for a beer and an afternoon read of the newspaper.

Information

Standard Bank (Crown St) Has an ATM.

Barberton Community Tourism (☎013-712 2880; www.barberton.co.za; Crown St, Market Sq; ⏲7.30am-4.30pm Mon-Fri, 9am-3pm Sat) This helpful office in the town centre can assist with accommodation, tours of historic sites and day hikes in the area.

Umjindi Resource Centre (Barberton Library, Pilgrim St; per hr R20)

Getting There & Away

A few minibus shared taxis stop in town near Shoprite, but you'll be waiting forever unless you go to the minibus-taxi park near Emjindini (3km from town on the Nelspruit road). The fare to Nelspruit is R30 (40 minutes). Most departures are in the early morning.

Songimvelo Game Reserve

Songimvelo Game Reserve WILDLIFE RESERVE
(☎017-883 7943; adult/child R30/15, wildlife drive R140; ⏲5am-6pm) This beautiful 560-sq-km reserve sits in lowveld country south of Barberton, with high-altitude grassland areas on its eastern edge along the mountainous Swaziland border. There are no lions, but there are numerous other introduced species, including elephants, zebras, giraffes and various antelopes, and both walking and horse riding are popular. Note that walking is limited to certain areas, and walkers must be accompanied by a guide.

Songimvelo is also home to some of the earth's oldest rocks – perhaps dating to four billion years ago – and some interesting archaeological sites.

You can stay overnight at **Kromdraai Camp** (cabins R425), with simple, self-catering, six-person wooden cabins. There are also campsites in the reserve.

Piet Retief

POP 57,500

This dull farming backwater is not the kind of place you'd make a special visit to, but it's the largest town in southern Mpumalanga and a good spot to break your journey if you're headed for Swaziland or KwaZulu-Natal. The area south of Piet Retief is known for its many Anglo-Boer War battlefields.

Greendoor B&B $
(☎017-826 3208; www.thegreendoor.co.za; Market St; s/d incl breakfast R395/560) Greendoor has simple, good-value en-suite rooms, some with African decor, in the centre of town. There are braai facilities and evening meals are available. It also runs a restaurant and coffee shop nearby.

Holme Lea Manor GUESTHOUSE $$
(☎017-826 2767; 10 Hansen St; s/d R550/800) A good accommodation choice if you're overnighting in town, Holme Lea has comfortable and snug rooms, some with private entrances, set in a palm-filled garden around a pool. A self-catering unit is also available.

Getting There & Away

Greyhound buses stop in town on their daily Pretoria–Durban run. The fare from Piet Retief to Pretoria is R300; to Durban it's R340.

The minibus-taxi stand is at the back of SuperMac. From here to the Swaziland border post at Mahamba costs R30 (30 minutes).

Kruger National Park

Includes ➡

Best Rest Camps

- Lower Sabie (p391)
- Olifants (p395)
- Skukuza (p391)
- Letaba (p397)
- Satara (p396)

Best Private Lodges

- Singita Boulders (p400)
- Londolozi Varty Camp (p401)
- Outpost (p394)
- Rhino Post Safari Lodge (p395)
- Singita Lebombo (p396)

Why Go?

In terms of wildlife alone, Kruger is one of the world's greatest national parks. The diversity, density and sheer number of animals is almost unparalleled, and all of Africa's iconic safari species – elephant, lion, leopard, cheetah, rhino, buffalo, giraffe, hippo and zebra – live out their dramatic days here, along with a supporting cast of 137 other mammals and over 500 varieties of bird.

The landscape is on a grand scale, stretching over 19,485 sq km, and although less in your face than the wildlife, it certainly has the power to charm. Beautiful granite kopjes (hills) pepper the bushveld in the south, the Lebombo Mountains rise from the savannah in the east, and the tropical forests cut across the far north.

But what makes Kruger truly special is the access and opportunities it provides the visitors. A vast network of roads are there to explore on your own (incredibly), guided wildlife activities are everywhere and accommodation is both plentiful and great value.

When to Go

Skukuza

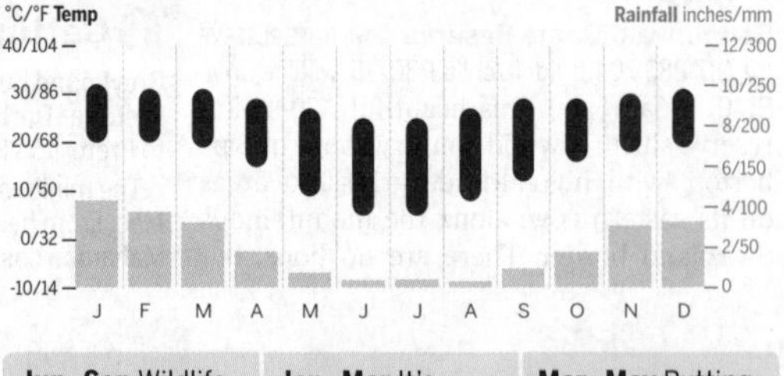

Jun–Sep Wildlife viewing is best in winter when the park is driest and animals meet at waterholes.

Jan–Mar It's hot but quiet as school holidays are over; accommodation's easy to find.

Mar–May Rutting-season spectaculars see impala, wildebeest and other species go head to head.

History

The area that is now Kruger National Park first came under government protection in 1898, when Paul Kruger (president of the Transvaal Republic) established the Sabie Game Reserve, between the Sabie and Crocodile Rivers, as a controlled hunting area. In 1902, following the second Anglo-Boer War, James Stevenson Hamilton became the reserve's first warden. Hamilton was also the first to see the tourism potential of wildlife watching and conservation. In 1926, Sabie Game Reserve was joined with neighbouring Shingwedzi Game Reserve and various private farms to become Kruger National Park. The park was opened to the public in 1927.

In 2002, together with Zimbabwe's Gonarezhou National Park and Limpopo National Park in Mozambique, Kruger became part of the Great Limpopo Transfrontier Park.

Significant portions of the park continue to remain subject to pending land claims. A large claim in the greater Kruger was upheld in late 2013, which saw the government buy the ownership of MalaMala Game Reserve (for a figure thought to be R1 billion) and transfer it to the N'wandlamharhi Community Property Association (CPA).

KRUGER NATIONAL PARK

Why Go Astounding wildlife, ease of self-drive access and incredible-value safaris. Perhaps Africa's best-run national park.

When to Go Year-round; avoid school holidays.

Practicalities Entry costs R280 per adult, R140 per child. Gate times (p398) for the park and camps are strictly adhered to. Speed limits (50km/h on sealed routes, 40km/h on dirt roads) are also stringently enforced. Don't lose your exit receipt (given to you on entry). And detailed park maps (R60) are worth their weight in gold.

Budget Tips Save 5% on SANParks camping and accommodation by booking online. Book tours at backpackers in Hazyview, Nelspruit or Graskop, or group together to share accommodation and car hire. Buy a Wild Card (p584).

Sights

Kruger encompasses a variety of landscapes and ecosystems, with each favouring particular species. That said, elephants, impalas, buffaloes, Burchell's zebras, wildebeest, kudus, waterbucks, baboons, vervet monkeys, leopards and smaller predators are widespread, and birdlife is incredible, especially along waterways. Rivers are hubs of activity and the major ones flow from west to east, including the Limpopo, Luvuvhu, Shingwedzi, Letaba, Olifants, Timbavati, Sand and Sabie. All of them are lined with riverine forest (often with enormous fig trees), which supports a wealth of wildlife.

While your drives along the extensive road network will throw up the majority of your animal sightings, there are numerous lookouts that offer great opportunities to see wildlife, or simply enjoy a stunning view.

Southern Kruger

Southern Kruger is perhaps the most physically beautiful section of the park, with numerous granite kopjes climbing above the undulating grasslands and the thick stands of acacias, bushwillows, sycamore figs and flowering species such as the red-and-orange coral tree. The changes in elevation in the west offer you some staggering views over the wilderness that at times can look like a never-ending sea of green. Its flora is fed by the park's highest amount of rainfall, some 50% more than in the north. This has in turn led to Kruger's highest proportion of wildlife calling the area home. The terrain is particularly favoured by white rhinos, buffaloes and zebras, but the thickness of the bush in some areas can make it harder to spot predators. Lions, hyenas and leopards are still spotted regularly, however, and wild dogs and cheetahs make occasional appearances.

This is the most visited section of Kruger.

Mathekenyane VIEWPOINT

(Granokop; Map p400) The top of this granite kopje south of Skukuza has an uninterrupted panorama of the surrounding wilderness (best at sunset).

Steilberg Loop VIEWPOINT

(Map p388) Located near Berg-en-dal, the steep S120 loop drive offers great views of the Malelane Mountain bushveld.

Sunset Dam VIEWPOINT

(Map p388) On the doorstep of Lower Sabie, the dam is often alive with birdlife, hippos, crocs and more.

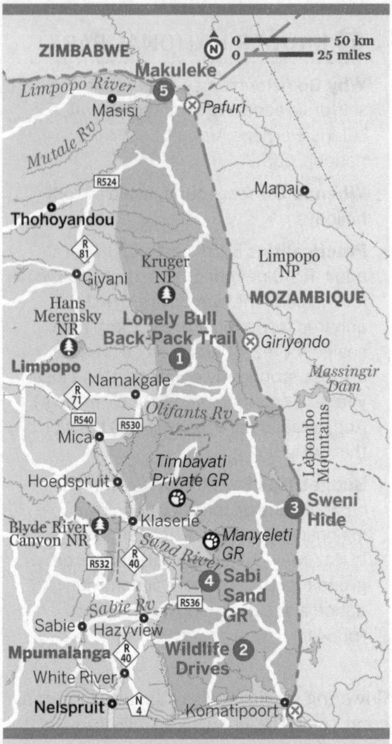

Kruger National Park Highlights

1. Waking to the sweet sounds of nature's alarm clock when camping wild on the **Lonely Bull Back-Pack Trail** (p389).
2. Getting yourself stuck behind unforgettable traffic – elephants, rhinos, giraffes – on **wildlife drives** (p387).
3. Discovering that birdwatching has its benefits at **Sweni Hide** (p389).
4. Tracking leopards through the wildlife riches of the **Sabi Sand Game Reserve** (p400).
5. Journeying into the tropics and exploring the fever tree forests and gorges of **Makuleke** (p394) in northern Kruger.

Renosterpan VIEWPOINT

(Map p388) This waterhole north of Berg-endal usually lives up to its name (*renoster* is rhino in Afrikaans).

Transport Dam VIEWPOINT

(Map p388) Large waterhole where the famous YouTube video 'Battle of Kruger' (lions versus buffaloes versus croc) was filmed.

Central Kruger

With the exception of the Lebombo Mountains that flank the Mozambique border to the east, the landscape between the Sabie and Olifants Rivers is less varied than in the south, with large swaths of open savannah, particularly west and southeast of Satara. The buffalo grass and red grass in these areas is interspersed with knobthorn, leadwood and marula trees, and hosts large populations of impalas, zebras, wildebeest, kudus, giraffes and elephants. Joining them are predators, especially lions. Leopards are commonly sighted, and the road between Satara and Orpen is one of the most likely places in Kruger to spot cheetahs.

Orpen Dam VIEWPOINT

(Map p388) A thatched viewing pavilion on an elevated hillside has great views of the dam.

Nkumbe VIEWPOINT

(Map p388) Set atop a rare ridge, Nkumbe offers a vast view over the western savannah.

Nsemani Dam VIEWPOINT

(Map p388) Nsemani is always worth a stop between Satara and Orpen. Hippos, birdlife and elephants are often present.

Bobbejaankrans VIEWPOINT

This overlooks a section of the Timbavati River that animals often visit to slake their thirst.

Northern Kruger

North of the Olifants River the rolling landscape becomes more and more dominated by the elephant's favourite dish: the mopane tree. So it's no surprise that huge herds roam this region. Towards the Lebombo Mountains in the east the trees are so stunted by the clay soils on the basalt plains that the elephants' backs rise above the canopy. The mopaneveld also attracts large herds of buffalo and numerous tsessebes, elands, roans and sables. Leopards, lions and rhinos are less numerous.

Kruger's far north, around Punda Maria and Pafuri, lies completely in the tropics and supports a wider variety of plants (baobabs are particularly noticeable), high wildlife concentrations and an exceptional array of birds not found further south. Between the Luvuvhu and Limpopo Rivers is a gorgeous tropical riverine forest with figs, fever trees and jackalberries. The far north is a winter grazing ground for elephants, and lions and leopards are also regularly encountered.

Red Rocks VIEWPOINT
(Map p388) Lions, giraffes, rhinos and elephants are often sighted at this spot on the Shingwedzi River. It's off the H1-6 on the S52.

Crooks Corner VIEWPOINT
(Map p388) On the outskirts of a beautiful fever-tree forest, Crooks Corner marks not only the confluence of the Luvuvhu and Limpopo Rivers but also the historic meeting place of Zimbabwe, Mozambique, South Africa and smugglers (it's all in the name).

Engelhard Dam VIEWPOINT
(Map p388) This dam on the Letaba River along the S62 is worth a visit. Waterbucks and lions are regularly sighted here, and en route you may pass elephants, buffaloes and steenboks.

Activities

Despite its mammoth size, Kruger is exceptionally well organised and there are numerous opportunities to enrich your wildlife watching throughout.

Wildlife Drives

Self-driving is fantastic for so many reasons, but do strongly consider joining some guided drives – they are a great way to maximise your safari experience. For starters, all the SANParks options roam the park when you can't (ie before camps open and after they've closed), and guides will often shed light on species and behaviours that you weren't aware of. Guides at lodges in private concessions can also take you closer to the wildlife as off-road driving is permitted in most.

SANParks operates three-hour **sunrise drives** and **sunset drives** at almost all rest camps, bushveld camps and many park gates. Costs vary between R300 and R260 depending on whether a 10- or 20-seat vehicle is used (R380 at Crocodile Bridge). Two-hour **night drives** (R200), which are great for nocturnal animals such as bush babies, hippos and big cats, are common too. Book in advance or upon arrival. Children under the age of six are not permitted.

Wildlife Walks

The bush becomes so much more alive when you step out on foot and leave the security blanket of your vehicle behind. And it's often not the large wildlife that captures your imagination – the smallest of creatures, whether insects, reptiles or birds, take on a new light of importance and you truly start to understand how the environment works.

Most SANParks rest camps offer three-hour **morning bush walks** (R450) with knowledgeable armed guides, as do all of the lodges in the private concessions. Berg-en-dal, Letaba, Olifants, Satara and Skukuza currently also offer **afternoon walks** (R375). Olifants adds **river walks** (R260) too. SANParks options can be booked in advance or arranged at the relevant camp upon arrival.

If you truly want to embrace the wilderness, book one of the park's **wilderness trails** or **backpack trails** well in advance of your trip. Lasting four days (departing Wednesday and Sunday), these guided walks provide some of the park's most memorable experiences. The catered wilderness trails are based out of a remote camp with basic huts or safari tents, and are not overly strenuous, covering around 20km per day. Backpack trails are more rugged, with the group camping wild each evening (minimum of four people required).

All walking groups limit numbers to eight participants, and no children under 12 are permitted.

Wolhuter Wilderness Trail WILDLIFE WATCHING
(Map p388; ☎012-428 9111; www.sanparks.org; 4 days incl meals R4300) Wolhuter is the original wilderness trail, and is based in southern Kruger in an area inhabited by lions and white rhinos. The trail has great history, as does the ground it covers – Stone and Iron Age relics abound. Take it all in from high atop a granite kopje. Meet prior at Berg-en-dal Rest Camp.

Napi Wilderness Trail WILDLIFE WATCHING
(Map p388; ☎012-428 9111; www.sanparks.org; 4 days incl meals R4300) Following the Mbyamithi and Napi Rivers between Pretoriuskop and Skukuza, Napi is known for its black and white rhino sightings at seasonal pans (waterholes). Camp consists of four safari tents. Trips commence at Pretoriuskop Rest Camp.

Sweni Wilderness Trail WILDLIFE WATCHING
(Map p388; ☎012-428 9111; www.sanparks.org; 4 days incl meals R4300) A highly rewarding trail, Sweni is known for herds of wildebeest, zebras and buffaloes (and the lions that stalk them). It's an evocative environment with vast grassy plains. Sweni starts and finishes at Satara Rest Camp.

Kruger National Park

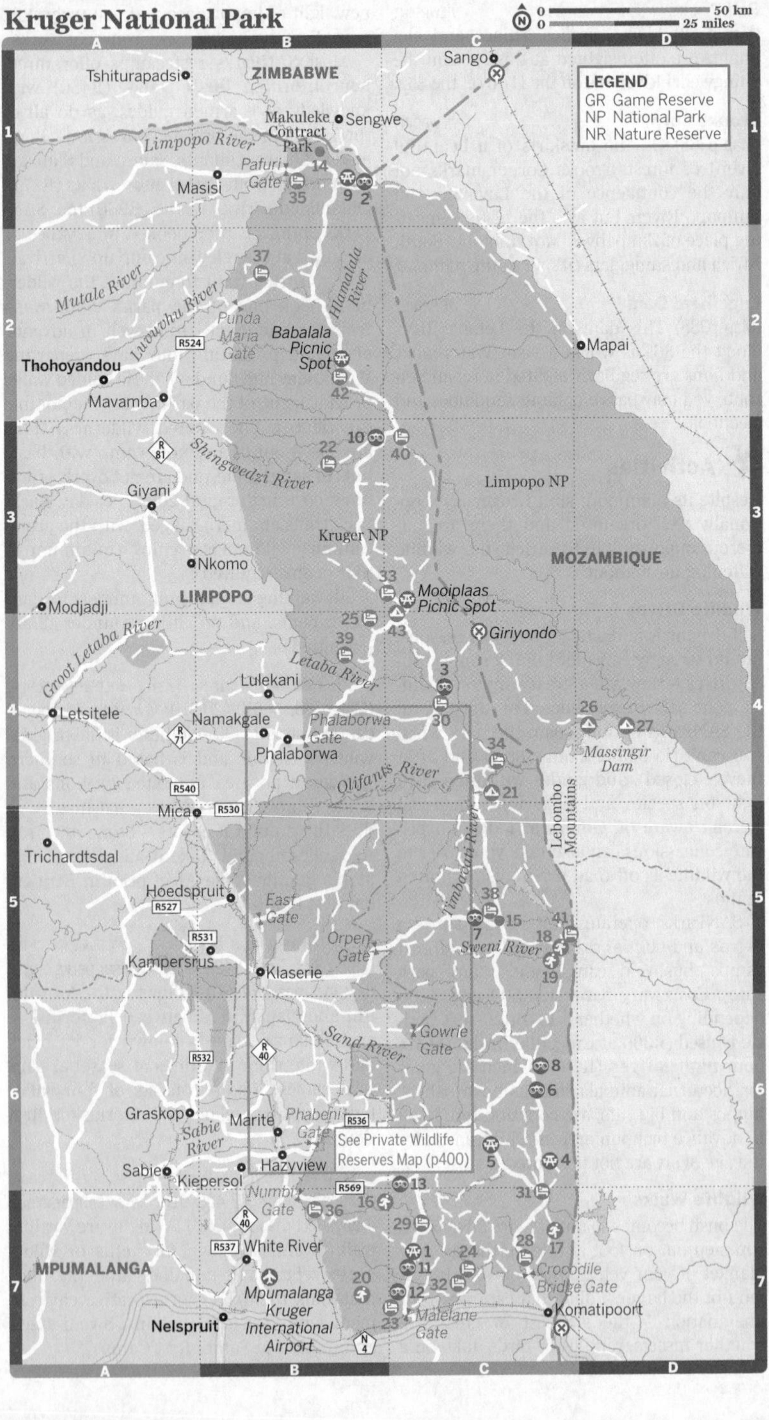
0 50 km
0 25 miles
LEGEND
GR Game Reserve
NP National Park
NR Nature Reserve
ZIMBABWE
Tshiturapadsi
Sango
Makuleke Contract Park
Sengwe
Limpopo River
Pafuri Gate
Masisi
Mutale River
Luvuvhu River
Hlamalala River
Punda Maria Gate
Babalala Picnic Spot
R524
Thohoyandou
Mavamba
Mapai
R81
Shingwedzi River
Giyani
Limpopo NP
Kruger NP
Nkomo
MOZAMBIQUE
LIMPOPO
Modjadji
Mooiplaas Picnic Spot
Giriyondo
Groot Letaba River
Letaba River
Lulekani
Letsitele
Namakgale
Phalaborwa Gate
Phalaborwa
R71
Massingir Dam
Olifants River
R540
Mica
R530
Timbavati River
Lebombo Mountains
Trichardtsdal
Hoedspruit
R527
East Gate
R531
Sweni River
Kampersrus
Orpen Gate
Klaserie
Sand River
Gowrie Gate
R40
R532
Graskop
Marite
Phabeni Gate
R536
Sabie River
See Private Wildlife Reserves Map (p400)
Sabie
Hazyview
Kiepersol
Numbi Gate
R569
R40
R537
White River
MPUMALANGA
Crocodile Bridge Gate
Mpumalanga Kruger International Airport
Nelspruit
Malelane Gate
Komatipoort
N4
KRUGER NATIONAL PARK

Kruger National Park

Olifants River Back-Pack Trail WILDLIFE WATCHING
(Map p388; ☎012-428 9111; www.sanparks.org; 4 days R2500; ⊙Apr-Oct) The trail's superb riverine setting offers the chance to get close to elephants, hippos, crocs and more. It's also known for birds, including the African fish eagle and the rare Pel's fishing owl. You must provide your own camping and cooking kit, as well as food and drink. Water can be collected en route. Walks commence from Olifants Rest Camp.

Lonely Bull Back-Pack Trail WILDLIFE WATCHING
(Map p388; ☎012-428 9111; www.sanparks.org; 4 days R2500; ⊙Feb-Oct) Following along the Letaba River and crossing various dry riverbeds, this trail throws up some great sightings of buffaloes, elephants and even leopards. You must be self-sufficient, with your own tent, cooking equipment and food. Water is available. Based from Shimuwini Bushveld Camp.

Birdwatching

Kruger offers excellent birdwatching everywhere, but the very far north is arguably one of the best birding regions on the continent. There are many great hides found in prime viewing areas.

Sweni Hide BIRDWATCHING
(Map p388) One of the most stunning hide locations, this L-shaped hide overlooks a bend in the Sweni River. The blue-cheeked bee-eater, cinnamon-breasted bunting and black-chested snake eagle are species of note. We also enjoyed watching elephants frolicking in the water here.

Pioneer Hide BIRDWATCHING
(Map p388) Opposite Mopani on Pioneer Dam. There's a good chance of spying rufous-crowned rollers, great egrets and white-breasted cormorants.

Lake Panic Hide BIRDWATCHING
(Map p400) Set on a section of the Sabie River, Lake Panic hide is a relaxing place to ogle African pygmy kingfishers, black-crowned night herons, African rails and southern red bishops.

> **PICNIC SPOTS**
>
> There are almost a dozen picnic spots for you to take a break during your wildlife drives. Besides giving you the chance to alight from your vehicle, they have toilets, and several serve food and drinks. Skukuza's and Letaba's day-visitor sites even include pools.

Nthandanyathi Hide BIRDWATCHING

(Map p388) Beautiful spot looking over a broad expanse of the Nhlowa River. Species to look for here include the black coucal, woolly-necked stork, magpie shrike and eastern nicator.

Shipandani Overnight Hide BIRDWATCHING

(Map p388; ☎013-735 6535) Overlooks a narrow, gullied section of the Tsendze River. Green-backed herons, Burchell's coucals, Diederick cuckoos and African openbills are regular visitors (and so are elephant and hippo, as we found out).

There are six beds that can be hired exclusively for the night (R630 for the first two people, plus R290 for each extra person). You'll need to bring wood/fuel, cooking kit, food and water (there is a braai (barbeque) area and a toilet) – book at Mopani Rest Camp.

Sable Overnight Hide BIRDWATCHING

(Map p400; ☎013-735 6509) On the edge of the large Sable Dam, this hide provides a good chance to spy on the iconic African fish eagle, as well as black-winged stilts and African cuckoos.

Sable can be hired exclusively for the night (R630 for the first two people, plus R290 for each extra person). There are nine fold-down beds, a toilet and a braai area. You'll need to bring the rest – book at Phalaborwa gate.

4WD Trails

If you're travelling by 4WD, these trails are an incredible way to experience the remote bush and its wildlife.

Lebombo Motorised Eco Trail DRIVING TOUR

(Map p388; ☎012-426 5117, 012-428 9111; www.sanparks.org; per vehicle (max 4 people) R8600; ⊙Apr-Oct) Covering a rugged 500km over five days (Sunday to Thursday), the Lebombo Motorised Eco Trail is Kruger's premier 4WD trail. Departing from Crocodile Bridge, the route skirts the park's entire eastern boundary before finishing at **Pafuri picnic spot** (Map p388) near Crooks Corner. Besides providing your own 4WD and camping kit, you must bring all your food, drink and cooking equipment.

Only five vehicles are permitted on the trail (joined by an expert ranger's 4WD). Book well in advance.

Mananga Adventure Trail DRIVING TOUR

(Map p388; ☎013-735 6306; www.sanparks.org; per vehicle R460 plus refundable deposit R100) Covering 48km (four hours), you'll drive through knobthorn and marula savannah likely dotted with herds of buffalos, zebras and wildebeest. Keep an eye out for cheetahs. Book upon arrival at Satara Rest Camp. Maximum of six 4WD per day. GPS is handy.

WILDLIFE-WATCHING

Some call it a game of chance, but wildlife-watching is actually a skill in its own right. There is never a guaranteed outcome, of course, but play your cards right and you'll increase your chances of unforgettable encounters. And no matter when you visit Kruger, you do have the odds stacked in your favour.

- Purchase a detailed map (R60) from a rest-camp shop that denotes pans (waterholes), dams, rivers and other key lookouts.
- View sighting boards at camps each evening; these map out the notable sightings from the day, and some animals may not have moved far.
- Wake early and get out of camp when the gates open; many species are most active at this time, particularly big cats (look around waterholes). Activity will pick up again before sunset.
- Drive slowly; going any faster than 25km/h will reduce your chance of noticing game stoppers like leopard and cheetah.
- Be patient, stop frequently and turn the engine off; you'll be amazed how many more species you'll spot coming out of the woodwork while you're at rest.
- If you see a herd of herbivores all staring in the same direction, follow their gaze.
- Watch for big cats enjoying the breezes from rocky knolls; leopards will often rest high off the ground in tree branches.
- Join a guided drive and learn some animal-behaviour patterns to use on your own.

Mountain Biking

SANParks currently runs morning (R636, four hours) and afternoon (R353, three hours) guided mountain-bike trails at Olifants (p395). Must be booked in advance.

Tours

At the budget level, the best places to contact for tours into Kruger are the backpacker lodges in Hazyview (p375), Nelspruit (p377) and Graskop (p372), most of which organise tours from about R1750 per day, including entry fees and meals. There are also some hotels in Hoedspruit (p424) and Phalaborwa (p422) that offer central and/or northern Kruger tours.

At the upper end of the price spectrum, or if you're on a tight schedule and want to connect directly from Johannesburg (Jo'burg) or Cape Town, you have several good options.

Signature Tours (p613) has tailored self-drive and guided packages with a focus on wildlife.

Wildlife Safaris (☎011-791 4238; www.wildlfesaf.co.za) offers four-day panorama tours of Blyde River and Kruger for R8800 per person.

Upscale, conservation-focused **Wilderness Safaris** (☎011-807 1800; www.wilderness-safaris.com) offer high-end safaris and special-interest trips.

Sleeping & Eating

Kruger has various types of accommodation, ranging from SANParks' numerous budget and midrange options in rest camps, bushveld camps and satellite camps to five-star luxury lodges within the park's private concessions. The latter include exclusive on- and off-road access to some of Kruger's richest wildlife areas. Regardless of your choice, all accommodation should be booked in advance during the high season (October to mid-January) and over school holidays.

The majority of visitors stay in Kruger's 12 large rest camps, most of which offer serviced caravan and camping sites, plus a range of comfortable accommodations. Furnished safari tents and huts are usually the most basic, though they still typically have fans and fridges – like the campground, they share ablutions (hot showers) and have access to communal cooking facilities consisting of sinks, hotplates and braais. The roomier bungalows and cottages are almost always en suite and often come complete with fans/air-con, kitchen, cutlery, pans and plates, while others share the camps' communal cooking facilities, consisting of sinks, hotplates and braais. Bedding and towels are provided for all non-camping options (including safari tents). All rest camps are fenced and have petrol stations, laundry facilities and reasonably well-stocked shops, and 10 of them have restaurants.

Bushveld camps are a recommended option if you want more of a wilderness experience than is possible at the rest camps. The cottages are equipped for self-catering, but only ice and firewood are available on site. Satellite camps are similar, but most only have communal kitchens and ablutions blocks – they are usually set within 3km of a rest camp, however.

Southern Kruger

★ Lower Sabie Rest Camp BUNGALOW, CAMPGROUND **$$**

(Map p388; ☎013-735 6056, reservations 012-428 9111; www.sanparks.org; camping per site R285, hut d without bathroom R550, safari tent/bungalow d with kitchen R885/1215; ❄ ≋) The most popular rest camp, Lower Sabie is set on a gorgeous bend of the Sabie River that attracts elephants, hippos, buffaloes and other animals. LST2U-class safari tents and BD2U/BD3U bungalows have river views. The riverside dining area of the **Mugg & Bean** (www.themugg.com; mains R55-140) is one of Kruger's most scenic, though the pool area is less so.

★ Skukuza Rest Camp BUNGALOW, CAMPGROUND **$$**

(Map p400; ☎013-735 4152, reservations 012-428 9111; www.sanparks.org; camping per site R275, safari tent d/q without bathroom R550/850, bungalow d with/without kitchen R1220/1120; ❄ ≋) Although more town than camp, Kruger's largest camp is unobtrusive and has a great location on the Sabie River. There's an extensive range of accommodation, including four-/six-person cottages (from R2150). The attractive pool areas will lead you to linger. Additional services include bank, ATM, post office, doctor, library, museum and information centre.

The riverside **Cattle Baron** (www.cattlebaron.co.za; mains R60-190) restaurant has free wi-fi, great food (the fillet steak is divine) and a lovely setting. The takeaway stand is less appetising. A second restaurant on the opposite side of camp is due to reopen in late 2015.

1

2

4

MOODBOARD / GETTY IMAGES ©

FRANK SLACK / GETTY IMAGES ©

WAYNE PARSONS / GETTY IMAGES ©

1. Vervet monkeys
These adaptable monkeys live throughout Kruger National Park.

2. Leopards
While on safari, look up – leopards often rest high up in tree branches.

3. European bee-eater
Kruger National Park offers plenty of birdwatching opportunities.

4. Plains zebras
Southern Kruger is particularly favoured by buffaloes and zebras.

WORTH A TRIP

MAKULEKE CONTRACT PARK

The heart of Kruger's far north is Makuleke Contract Park – a beautiful and geologically unique area consisting of a 240-sq-km wedge of land rimmed by the Limpopo and Luvuvhu Rivers. In 1969, South Africa's apartheid government forcibly removed the Makuleke people from the area in order to incorporate their traditional lands into Kruger National Park.

In the late 1990s, the land was returned to the Makuleke, who in turn agreed not to resettle it but to use it for ecotourism purposes. A 'contract park' was created in which the land is administered and managed environmentally as part of Kruger, with tourism developments owned by the Makuleke, who have since granted concessions to a select few companies.

Elephants favour the area during the winter months, while buffaloes, hippos, lions, leopards and nyalas are plentiful year-round. Birdlife is prolific.

Outpost (Map p388; ☎011-327 3920; www.theoutpostcamp.com; s/d all-inclusive from R5100/10,200;) Sleep inside or out, with the press of a button. Set high above the Luvuvhu River at the northern extreme of Kruger, the outward-facing walls of these 12 super-contemporary 'living spaces' can be raised by remote, allowing you to wake to a breathtaking panorama. Walks through local gorges and the fever-tree forest are highly recommended, as are wildlife drives.

The lodge – which employs local staff almost exclusively – operates under a community-partnership arrangement where a portion of profits is paid to the Makuleke community. After the expiry of its lease, the lodge will be turned over in its entirety to the community.

EcoTraining (Map p388; ☎013-752 2532; www.ecotraining.co.za) Various one-week to one-month field-guide training courses for budding professionals and enthusiastic amateurs. Go Bear Grylls wild in the bush for a week on the Wilderness Trails Skills option.

Berg-en-dal Rest Camp BUNGALOW, CAMPGROUND **$$**

(Map p388; ☎013-735 6106, reservations 012-428 9111; www.sanparks.org; camping per site R275, bungalow d with kitchen R1150;) This modern brick-built camp 12km from Malelane gate lacks the old-school bush feel, but its location in the Malelane Mountains' shadow makes up for it. Camp has views over Berg-en-dal Dam and its associated wildlife. Options include six-person family cottages (from R2150). There's a visitors' centre, evening nature movies (except Sunday), and a short walking path (Rhino Walking Trail) on the camp edge.

The **Tindlovu** (mains R55-150) restaurant and cafe serve average food.

Biyamiti Bushveld Camp COTTAGE **$$**

(Map p388; ☎013-735 6171, reservations 012-428 9111; www.sanparks.org; 4-/5-person cottages from R1275/2350) This small self-catering camp's 15 cottages are set along the bank of the ephemeral Biyamiti River (Nos 1 to 9 have the best views). There is a great bird hide. The shop sells firewood and ice, but no food. The drive to get here is stunning.

Pretoriuskop Rest Camp BUNGALOW, CAMPGROUND **$$**

(Map p388; ☎013-735 5128, reservations 012-428 9111; www.sanparks.org; camping per site R275, hut d without bathroom R550, bungalow d with/without kitchen R1235/1085;) Kruger's oldest and highest (thus coolest) camp is next to Numbi gate. Located within an attractive region dotted with granite outcrops and frequented by rhinos, the camp is pretty too, with bougainvillea, flowering trees and a natural rock swimming pool. There's a wide choice of accommodation, ranging up to nine-person guesthouses (from R3750). Food is limited to a Wimpy fast-food outlet (free wi-fi).

Crocodile Bridge Rest Camp BUNGALOW, CAMPGROUND **$$**

(Map p388; ☎013-735 6012, reservations 012-428 9111; www.sanparks.org; camping per site R275, safari tent/bungalow d with kitchen R550/1250;) Next to Crocodile Bridge gate, this small camp has croc and hippo pools nearby. Despite zebras, buffaloes and wildebeest in the immediate area, too, the wilderness ambience is somewhat diluted by the views of industry outside the park. The shop sells sandwiches and pies, and there's a coffee hut.

★Rhino Post Safari Lodge
LODGE $$$

(Map p400; ☎035-474 1473; www.isibindi.co.za; s/d all inclusive R5382/8280; ❄📶🏊) The most authentic private bush lodge in southern Kruger, Rhino Post has eight suites constructed from wood, canvas, glass and gabion baskets. Each oozes safari appeal, and you feel part of the tree canopy. Sit on the deck and watch wildlife come and go from the Mutlumuvi riverbed.

The lodge is within the only private concession that is a declared wilderness area, so there are no off-road drives. However, SANParks has allowed them access to 130km of park roads after closing. Inquire about the Rhino Walking Safaris.

★Lion Sands Narina Lodge
LODGE $$$

(Map p400; ☎011-880 9992; www.lionsands.com; s/d all-inclusive from R12,420/16,560; ❄📶🏊) Hovering over the bank of the Sabie River in a private concession, Narina's nine bright suites live beneath stepped thatched roofs. They are full of natural woods and modern furnishings, much like the open-plan common areas. Views are everywhere. Bathrooms have warm stone floors and massive eggshell-shaped tubs that radiate light. All decks include plunge pools and private showers.

Exclusive activities take place not only in the concession but also in the renowned Sabi Sand Game Reserve.

Lion Sands Tinga Lodge
LODGE $$$

(Map p400; ☎011-880 9992; www.lionsands.com; s/d all-inclusive from R12,420/16,560; ❄📶🏊) Tinga's nine luxury suites enjoy beautiful views of the Sabie River. The colonial-feeling rooms feature polished dark-wood floors and furniture, formal leather loungers, huge windows, outdoor showers and private plunge pools. The massive open-plan common areas are more contemporary and drop down onto a huge riverside deck surrounding a majestic jackalberry tree.

Activities are within both the concession and the Sabi Sand Game Reserve.

Lukimbi Safari Lodge
LODGE $$$

(Map p388; ☎011-792 6165; www.lukimbi.com; s/d all-inclusive from R7900/11,700; ❄🏊) Within Kruger's 150-sq-km Lukimbi private concession, this attractive lodge and its 16 thatched-roof suites are all perched on the bank of the Lwakhale. The rooms and common areas all flow out onto a series of riverside decks. The large suites are open plan, with sunken living rooms and outdoor showers. Guests have access to the highly ranked Leopard Creek Golf Course.

Jock Safari Lodge
LODGE $$$

(Map p388; ☎041-509 3000; www.jocksafarilodge.com; s/d all-inclusive from R8175/10,900; ❄📶🏊) The first private lodge in the park, Jock rests at the confluence of the Biyamiti and Mitomeni Rivers within an exclusive 60-sq-km conservancy. The 12 rooms (some adjoining for families) all have plunge pools and river views.

🛏 Central Kruger

Balule Satellite Camp
HUT, CAMPGROUND $

(Map p388; ☎012-428 9111; www.sanparks.org; camping per site R275, hut tr without bathroom from R415) Just south of Olifants, this atmospheric camp has just six huts and 15 campsites. There's no electricity, but lanterns are provided for huts (a torch is still wise). A communal freezer and stove are available. Sunset and night drives are possible on request. Check in at Olifants, Satara, Orpen or Letaba.

Maroela Satellite Camp
CAMPGROUND $

(Map p400; ☎012-428 9111; www.sanparks.org; camping per site R275) A few kilometres from Orpen Rest Camp (where check-in is), this campsite is fairly open, without much bush or privacy. There are braai racks, and hotplates and freezers in the communal kitchen.

★Olifants Rest Camp
BUNGALOW, COTTAGE $$

(Map p388; ☎013-735 6606, reservations 012-428 9111; www.sanparks.org; bungalow d with/without kitchenette R1125/1045; 🏊) High atop a bluff,

KRUGER FOR CHILDREN

Kruger is very family friendly, and is ideally set up for taking children with you on safari. The rest camps are all fenced, almost all have swimming pools and restaurants offering special children's meals, and several have play areas. Berg-en-dal, Letaba, Skukuza, Satara and Shingwedzi also have regular evening wildlife movies that are good for all ages, and Letaba has an interesting elephant museum. Camp shops, however, generally don't stock nappies (diapers), processed baby food or formula, so bring these items with you.

Children under the age of 12 are not allowed on SANParks wildlife walks, and those under six are prohibited from the park's wildlife drives. Age of acceptance varies for both activities and accommodation at private lodges.

this camp offers fantastic views down to the Olifants River, where elephants, hippos and numerous other animals roam. Bungalow Nos 1 and 9 (of BBD2V class) have the best views, as do the eight-person Nshawu and Lebombo self-catering guesthouses (from R4000). There's also a new camp pool.

Mugg & Bean (www.themugg.com; mains R55 to R140) has a wide variety of food, good coffee and a delightful deck beneath a knobbly fig tree – bring binoculars. At sunset look for the bat colony departing.

★ **Satara Rest Camp** BUNGALOW, CAMPGROUND **$$**
(Map p388; ☎013-735 6306, reservations 012-428 9111; www.sanparks.org; camping per site from R245, bungalow d with/without kitchen R1255/1130; ❄) Satara – the second-largest option after Skukuza – may lack the riverside views of other camps, but it's optimally situated in the heart of 'big cat' territory, with open plains making viewing easier. An incongruous Debonairs Pizza (www.debonairspizza.co.za; pizzas R25 to R80) outlet joins Mugg & Bean (www.themugg.com; mains R55 to R140) here.

Tamboti Satellite Tented Camp BUNGALOW **$$**
(Map p400; ☎012-428 9111; www.sanparks.org; safari tent d without bathroom R580, d with kitchen R1345) Tamboti has 40 safari tents spread along a curve in the Timbavati River, including 10 very comfy options with kitchens and en suite bathrooms. All have fridges, fans and views, and dense bush makes most rather private affairs. There's plenty of wildlife, a hide, and residents can use Orpen's nearby pool.

Orpen Rest Camp BUNGALOW, COTTAGE **$$**
(Map p400; ☎013-735 6355, reservations 012-428 9111; www.sanparks.org; bungalow d with kitchen R1175, 6-person cottages from R2150; ❄) Located by Orpen gate, this small camp is convenient for late arrivals. There's no restaurant, but there is a small shop (with coffee bar) and all bungalows have self-catering facilities.

Talamati Bushveld Camp COTTAGE **$$**
(Map p400; ☎012-428 9111; www.sanparks.org; 4-/6-person cottages from R1275/2350) On the bank of the N'waswitsontso riverbed in an exceptionally wildlife-rich area, Talamati has 15 self-catering cottages, two bird hides and a nearby waterhole. Firewood and ice are available.

Roodewal Bush Lodge LODGE **$$**
(Map p400; ☎012-428 9111; www.sanparks.org; up to 8 people R6500, per additional adult R640) This 18-person bush lodge on the Timbavati River must be booked in advance and on an exclusive basis. There are no facilities other than equipped kitchens, braai areas and bedding. Solar provides power for just lights and fans.

★ **Singita Lebombo Lodge** LODGE **$$$**
(Map p388; ☎021-683 3424; www.singita.com; s/d all-inclusive R17,300/34,600; ❄) This 15-room flagship ultra-luxury lodge on Singita's private concession in Kruger's Lebombo Mountains is themed around a bird's nest, with each open-plan suite built amongst trees high atop a bluff and clad in oversized twigs. All have views down to the Sweni River (Nos 4 and 5 are the best), and you can choose to bed down on your private deck.

Already with a light footprint, Lebombo (and the staff village) now run on solar power. Mega-prides of lions frequent the area.

★ **Imbali Safari Lodge** LODGE **$$$**
(Map p400; ☎011-516 4367; www.extraordinary.co.za; d all-inclusive from R4285; ❄) The largest lodge in the Mluwati concession, Imbali is fenced and welcomes children of all ages. There are 12 large suites (each with private plunge pool or hot tub) nestled in riverine forest, nine of which overlook the N'waswitsontso riverbed and its associated wildlife.

Hoyo Hoyo Safari Lodge LODGE **$$$**
(Map p400; ☎011-516 4367; www.extraordinary.co.za; d all-inclusive R3290; ❄) Partly owned by a local community, the small six-suite lodge in the Mluwati concession embraces Tsonga culture and you'll be welcomed with the Shangaan greeting of 'hoyo hoyo'. The orange-coloured beehive rooms resemble traditional dwellings in style but are full of luxury. It's the most affordable option in Kruger's exclusive private concessions.

SOCIAL MEDIA & RHINO POACHING

Poaching of rhino is an escalating problem (p558), and increasingly Facebook, Instagram and Twitter posts of safari images have been used by criminals to track down the exact location of rhinos in Africa, with accounts even hacked to retrieve GPS coordinates embedded in the image file. To help combat the problem, turn off the geo-tagging facility on your phone and don't mention the exact location of these animals in social-media posts.

Hamiltons Tented Camp LODGE $$$
(Map p400; ☎011-516 4367; www.extraordinary.co.za; d all-inclusive R4490; ❄≋) The highest-end option within the private 100-sq-km Mluwati concession, Hamiltons has six sumptuous safari tents that are built on stilts next to the dry riverbed of the N'waswitsontso.

Northern Kruger

In addition to the many standard SANParks accommodation options available in this area, Shipandani (p390) and Sable (p390) overnight hides can be hired on an exclusive basis for the night.

Tsendze Rustic Camping Site CAMPGROUND $
(Map p388; ☎012-428 9111; www.sanparks.org; camping R275) A basic campground 8km south of Mopani. There are communal gas cookers and fridges, but no electricity.

★**Letaba Rest Camp** BUNGALOW, CAMPGROUND $$
(Map p388; ☎013-735 6636, reservations 012-428 9111; www.sanparks.org; camping per site R275, hut/safari tent d without bathroom R685/550, bungalow tr with/without kitchen from R1125/1045; ❄≋) One of Kruger's best rest camps, this leafy haven on the Letaba River has shady lawns, resident bushbucks, SANParks' most attractive pools and a wide variety of accommodation. There are great views from various bungalows (No 32, of BD3U class is best), six-person guest cottages (ask for newly refurbished No 101, class FQ6) and a **Mugg & Bean** (www.themugg.com; mains R55-140).

Although elephants are a common sight in the river here, be sure to visit the Elephant Hall museum. Each evening (except Sunday) wildlife films are shown. There's also an ATM.

★**Shimuwini Bushveld Camp** COTTAGE $$
(Map p388; ☎013-735 6683, reservations 012-428 9111; www.sanparks.org; 4-/5-/6-person cottages from R1230/2040/2200) This beautiful small camp and bird hide have a picturesque riverine setting, with 15 self-catering cottages staggered on lawns overlooking a wide stretch of the Letaba River. Ask for No 8 (GC5 class), as it was rebuilt after flooding and is the most comfortable and modern.

Bateleur Bushveld Camp COTTAGE $$
(Map p388; ☎013-735 6843, reservations 012-428 9111; www.sanparks.org; 6-person cottages from R2040; ❄) The oldest and smallest of the bushveld camps, Bateleur has loads of wilderness ambience. The seven thatched-roof self-catering cottages with their 1930s steel-frame windows have a rustic feel, and they are set along the Mashokwe (ask for Nos 1 or 7, of GA6 class). The hide has a light for night viewing. Firewood and ice are available.

Shingwedzi Rest Camp BUNGALOW, CAMPGROUND $$
(Map p388; ☎013-735 6806, reservations 012-428 9111; www.sanparks.org; camping per site from R245, hut d without bathroom R535, bungalow d with/without kitchen R1045/950; ❄≋) Tall mopane trees and palms shade this relaxed camp, which now has a mix of old-style bungalows in circle A and some large, new modern options in circle B (Nos 32 to 35 and 69 to 79 of BD2 class, and Nos 38 to 41 of the BG2 class). Although it's on the Shingwedzi River, only the Tindlovu restaurant (mains R55 to R150) offers views.

Punda Maria Rest Camp BUNGALOW, CAMPGROUND $$
(Map p388; ☎013-735 6873, reservations 012-428 9111; www.sanparks.org; camping per site from R245, bungalow d with/without kitchen R1120/950, safari tents with kitchen R1070; ❄≋) Quaintly residing up a forested slope in far northern Kruger, this petite camp has plenty of old-world charm, with picturesque thatched-roof bungalows dating back to the 1930s. While those options are a little cramped, seven new 'luxury' safari tents provide more comfort and space (Nos 2 and 3 of ST2 class are the most private).

Sirheni Bushveld Camp COTTAGE $$
(Map p388; ☎013-735 6860, reservations 012-428 9111; www.sanparks.org; 2-/6-person cottages from R1230/2040) At this pretty camp in a lightly wooded area, all but one of the 15 self-catering cottages overlook the Sirheni Dam (avoid No

KRUGER FOR TRAVELLERS WITH DISABILITIES

Facilities for travellers with disabilities are now available at all rest camps except Orpen. Tamboti Satellite Camp, near Orpen, has two safari tents with disabled access. The SANParks website (www.sanparks.org) has an excellent overview of facilities at each camp, and is worth investigating. Note that all disabled options have 'Z' in the room-class code, and bookings can only be made one month in advance.

13, of CO4 class). It's an excellent spot for birding, with a good hide. There is a deep freeze, and ice and firewood are available.

Mopani Rest Camp BUNGALOW, COTTAGE **$$**
(Map p388; ☎013-735 6536, reservations 012-428 9111; www.sanparks.org; bungalow q with kitchen from R1105, 6-person cottages from R2000; ❄☒) A modern rest camp with an overly manufactured feel, Mopani lacks the traditional bush atmosphere of other rest camps. And although the view over Pioneer Dam is rather impressive, the size of the deck to take it in at the **Tindlovu** (mains R55-150) restaurant and Memorable Waterhold bar certainly isn't. As compensation, it's quite serene, and the pool is rather pretty.

Boulders Bush Lodge LODGE **$$$**
(Map p388; ☎012-428 9111; www.sanparks.org; up to 4 people R3240, per additional person R640) Set high among large granite boulders 23km south of Mopani, this five-bungalow self-catering lodge has views over the plains. The lodge must be booked in advance by one party on an exclusive basis. Solar provides power for fans and lights only.

ℹ Information

BOOKINGS

Bookings for SANParks (p360) accommodation and most activities can be done up to a year in advance (but only one month prior for disabled facilities) online, by phone or in person. Except for school holidays and weekends, bookings are advisable but not essential. Between October and mid-January, book as far in advance as possible. Nelspruit's Lowveld Tourism (p380) office can also make arrangements, as can the Cape Town branch.

EMERGENCY

Kruger National Park 24hr Emergency Call Centre (☎013-735 4325, 076 801 9679)

ENTRY

Park entry for international visitors costs R280/140 per adult/child per day or for an overnight stay (SANParks' Wild Card (p584) applies). During school holidays park stays are limited to 10 days, and five days at any one rest camp (10 days if you're camping). Throughout the year authorities restrict the total number of visitors, so in the high season arrive early if you don't have a booking. Bicycles and motorcycles are not permitted.

INTERNET ACCESS

Free wi-fi is limited to the restaurants at Skukuza and Pretoriuskop. You can buy limited access at Mopani (R30 per 30 minutes) and Skukuza's conference centre (R50 per 30 minutes).

MONEY

Only Skukuza and Letaba have ATMs that take international cards, but cards are accepted almost everywhere. There are 'mini-ATMs' at rest-camp stores, but they only accept local cards, and withdrawls are limited to R800 (or less, depending on cash availability in the store till).

TELEPHONE

You can buy mobile air-time at all park shops; use is only permitted at gates, in camps or in the event of an emergency.

ℹ Getting There & Around

There are nine South African entry gates with unified hours of operation, which vary slightly by season (opening times range from 5.30am to 6am; closing times from 5.30pm to 6.30pm). Camp gate times are almost in complete unison with the park gates, and fines are issued for late arrival. It's also possible to enter Kruger from Mozambique at the Giriyondo and Pafuri border crossings (p600).

KRUGER ENTRY TIMES (GATES & CAMPS)

MONTH	GATES/CAMPS OPEN (AM)	GATES & CAMPS CLOSE (PM)
Jan	5.30/4.30	6.30
Feb	5.30/5.30	6.30
Mar	5.30/5.30	6
Apr	6/6	6
May-Jul	6/6	5.30
Aug & Sep	6/6	6
Oct	5.30/5.30	6
Nov & Dec	5.30/4.30	6.30

OFF THE BEATEN TRACK

GREAT LIMPOPO TRANSFRONTIER PARK

Together with Mozambique's **Limpopo National Park** (Parque Nacional do Limpopo; ☎21-713000; www.limpopopn.gov.mz; adult/vehicle Mtc400/400, payable in meticais or South African rand) and Zimbabwe's Gonarezhou National Park, Kruger forms part of the Great Limpopo Transfrontier Park, a vast area that will ultimately encompass 35,000 sq km. Gonarezhou links continue to be a work in progress, but Kruger and Limpopo are linked via two border posts: **Giriyondo** and **Pafuri** (p600).

However, for those interested in exploring the core of Limpopo, the only real option is Giriyondo, which is reached via the H15 gravel road that branches off the tarmac route 19km north of Letaba. You won't find concentrations of wildlife comparable to Kruger's, but the journey makes for a satisfyingly adventurous bush experience.

Once you've finished with the border paperwork for your 4WD (p602), pass through immigration, where Mozambique visas are available (R884/Mtc2136/US$90). You'll also need to pay Limpopo park fees and show proof of overnight accommodation in Limpopo. There are three accommodation options: campgrounds and basic self-catering chalets at both **Campismo Aguia Pesqueira** (Map p388; camping Mtc20 (R80), 2-bed chalets Mtc1500 (R550)), near Massingir Dam, and **Campismo Albufeira** (Map p388; camping Mtc20 (R80), 2-/4-bed chalets Mtc1200/1500 (R450/550)), near Massingir gate, and the upmarket **Machampane Wilderness Camp** (www.dolimpopo.com; s/d all-inclusive R2860/4400).

Machampane has five spacious, well-appointed safari tents in a tranquil setting directly overlooking a section of the Machampane River, where you're likely to see hippos plus a variety of smaller wildlife and many birds. Morning and evening guided walks are included. Machampane is 20km from Giriyondo, and pick-ups can be arranged from Letaba (where you can leave your car).

AIR

SAAirlink (www.flyairlink.com) and **South African Airways** (www.flysaa.com) now team up to provide a direct daily flight to **Skukuza Airport** (Map p400; www.skukuzaairport.com/) in Kruger from both Cape Town (from R3027, 2¼ hours) and Johannesburg (R1720, 50 minutes). The airlines provide more abundant options to **Mpumalanga Kruger International Airport** (MKIA; Map p388; www.kmiairport.co.za) near Nelspruit from Jo'burg (from R1240, 45 minutes), Durban (from R2220, one hour) and Cape Town (from R2520, 2¼ hours). They also fly from Jo'burg to Hoedspruit's **Eastgate Airport** (Map p400; from R1506, one hour) for Orpen gate, and to **Kruger Park Gateway Airport** (Map p400; from R2036, one hour), near Phalaborwa gate.

CAR & 4WD

Kruger's southern gates are all within 475km (five hours) of Jo'burg; Orpen and Phalaborwa gates are around 525km (six hours) away, and Punda Mara and Pafuri gates are over 600km (seven hours) away.

Once in the park most visitors drive themselves as it's very straightforward. Kruger's road system is excellent, with a network of great sealed routes and many well-maintained gravel side roads. However, keep an eye out for other vehicles stopping suddenly, distracted drivers and darting animals. You won't need a 4WD for most secondary gravel roads, though check with rangers if it has been raining heavily. There are petrol stations at all the rest camps.

Avis (☎013-735 5651; www.avis.co.za) has a rental branch at Skukuza Rest Camp, and there are numerous agencies at MKIA (28km from Nelspruit). Eastgate Airport (Hoedspruit) and Kruger Gateway Airport (Phalaborwa) have more options.

PRIVATE WILDLIFE RESERVES

Spreading over a vast area just west of Kruger is a string of private reserves that offer some of Africa's most compelling safari viewing. The Big Five-plus populations roaming these protected areas are no different from those in the park – in fact, there is no fence or physical boundary separating the main reserves – Sabi Sand, Manyeleti and Timbavati – from Kruger itself.

Much like in the private concessions within Kruger, what makes the biggest difference to the wildlife-viewing experience is the level of guiding, the ability of safari vehicles to go off road, and the exclusivity of walking and driving activities. Animals don't deal with

Private Wildlife Reserves

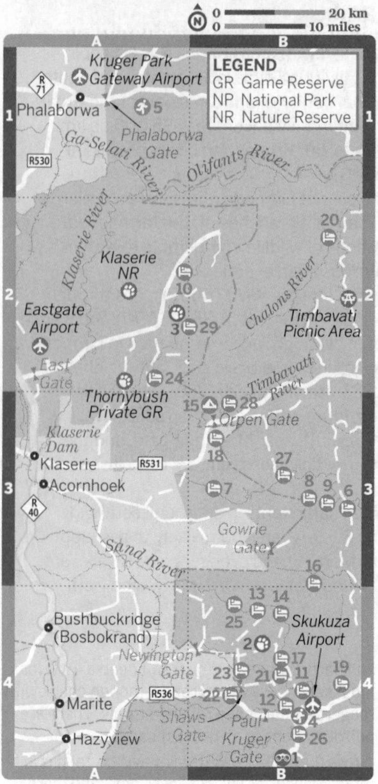

Private Wildlife Reserves

Sights

1 Mathekenyane B4
2 Sabi Sand Game Reserve B4
3 Timbavati Private Nature Reserve A2

Activities, Courses & Tours

4 Lake Panic Hide B4
5 Sable Overnight Hide A1

Sleeping

6 Hamiltons Tented Camp B3
Honeyguide Khoka Moya .... (see 7)
7 Honeyguide Mantobeni B3
8 Hoyo Hoyo Safari Lodge B3
9 Imbali Safari Lodge B3
10 Jaydee Bush Camp A2
11 Kirkman's Camp B4
12 Lion Sands Narina Lodge B4
Lion Sands Tinga Lodge .... (see 12)
Londolozi Tree Camp .... (see 13)
13 Londolozi Varty Camp B4
14 MalaMala Main Camp B4
15 Maroela Satellite Camp B3
16 Nkorho Bush Lodge B3
17 Nottens Bush Camp B4
18 Orpen Rest Camp B3
19 Rhino Post Safari Lodge B4
20 Roodewal Bush Lodge B2
21 Sabi Sabi Bush Lodge B4
22 Sabi Sabi Earth Lodge B4
23 Sabi Sabi Little Bush Lodge B4
24 Shindzela A2
25 Singita Boulders B4
26 Skukuza Rest Camp B4
27 Talamati Bushveld Camp B3
28 Tamboti Satellite Tented Camp B3
29 Umlani Bushcamp B2

crowds or self-drivers here, just experienced guides who always pay them the respect they deserve. And, in turn, the animals tend to offer up incredible close-quarters sightings.

This all comes at a price, of course, as you must stay in one of the exclusive lodges to gain access, but if your budget permits, consider a night or two at the end of your stay in Kruger.

Sabi Sand Game Reserve

Bound by the Sabi River and containing much of the Sand River, this large **reserve** (Map p400; www.sabisand.co.za; vehicle fee R190, per passenger R50) straddles what might be the richest wedge of wilderness on the continent. Particularly famous for leopards, it is routinely the choice of wealthy safari cognoscenti. Sabi Sand is actually a conglomeration of smaller private reserves, with each one traditionally hosting only its own vehicles within its unfenced boundaries (some now share traversing rights).

Sleeping & Eating

★ **Singita Boulders** LODGE $$$

(Map p400; ☎021-683 3424; www.singita.com; s/d all-inclusive R17,300/34,600; ❄@✱) Singita has been distinguished by the top-end travel industry as having among the best lodges in Africa. Its Boulders lodge on the bank of the Sand River is our favourite. The dining areas, lounge, library, wine cellar and cavernous suites are all framed by Great Zimbabwe–esque stacks of large dark stones that contrast beautifully with contemporary furnishings and African artwork.

Amenities and service are impeccable.

★Londolozi Varty Camp LODGE $$$

(Map p400; ☎011-280 6655; www.londolozi.com; s/d all-inclusive from R13,425/17,900; ❄📶🏊) Built on the site of the Varty family's original 1920s Sparta Hunting Camp, Varty Camp was Londolozi's first photographic safari lodge and has metamorphosed into a contemporary safari marvel. The original 1920s huts are still on show behind the modern grand lounge, which stares out over the Sand River and frames a gorgeous jackalberry tree (the very tree that inspired the site of Sparta).

It's more down to earth than Londolozi's other options, and children over six are welcome (there are interconnecting rooms). Varty's eight chalets and two suites exude luxury and comfort, and guiding at Londolozi is always first class.

★MalaMala Main Camp LODGE $$$

(Map p400; ☎011-442 2267; www.malamala.com; s/d all-inclusive from US$1110/1480; ❄📶🏊) While very comfortable, Main Camp doesn't offer plunge pools, perfectly chopped throw pillows or chic interiors. And it doesn't care – everything here is about providing ultimate wildlife experiences. Key is the relationship its guides have fostered with the animals over decades (MalaMala was the first photographic safari reserve in the country). At 135-sq-km, it also dwarfs the other reserves.

Guests are encouraged to dine with their safari guides at each meal, which promotes even more understanding of the environment, wildlife and South Africa – it also makes activities feel much more personal. The reserve is now owned by the N'wandlamhari CPA, with the original MalaMala owners continuing to operate on a lease basis.

★Sabi Sabi Earth Lodge LODGE $$$

(Map p400; ☎013-735 5261; www.sabisabi.com; s/d all-inclusive R12,700/25,400; ❄📶🏊) Subterranean bliss, Earth Lodge is unlike any other lodge in Africa – where else can you look up though a skylight to an elephant looking down at you? Using sloping topography brilliantly, its ultra-modern rooms, open communal areas and private plunge pools are flooded with light. The super-thick walls and polished-cement floors are dotted with artwork and natural materials.

★Nottens Bush Camp LODGE $$$

(Map p400; ☎013-735 5105; www.nottens.com; s/d all-inclusive R6292/8390) This comfortable, family-run six-room camp offers great value. The open dining area and two rooms (Nos 3 and 4) overlook the waterhole, though the beautiful pool does not. Lighting is limited to candles and paraffin lamps, which is romantic (but not everyone's cup of tea). There is power for fans/plugs in the rooms, but not the common areas.

There are two family suites (kids over six are welcome). Wildlife is common, with rhinos and elephants patrolling at times (a lion left its print in cement during the pool's construction). Traversing rights are shared with Sabi Sabi, which ensures great wildlife viewing.

Londolozi Tree Camp LODGE $$$

(Map p400; ☎011-280 6655; www.londolozi.com; s/d all-inclusive R21,525/28,700; ❄📶🏊) Londolozi's flagship lodge reopened in 2015 after extensive renovations and it is stunning. The towering thatch roofs, dark wood, white walls, chocolate accents and local art in the common areas and six suites are a mere backdrop for the Sand River views. Private decks and plunge pools throughout. Despite its grand scale, it still feels intimate. No kids under 16.

The theme for Tree Camp is leopards, lanterns and leadwood trees (you'll likely see plenty of all three while on safari here).

Kirkman's Camp LODGE $$$

(Map p400; ☎011-809 4300; www.andbeyondafrica.com; s/d all-inclusive R9000/12,000; ❄📶🏊) Full of charm and 1920s ambience, this is the original homestead of Kruger's legendary Harry Kirkman (there is plenty of his paraphernalia about). The 18 corrugated-iron-roof cottages are very comfortable and mimic the original house (Nos 11 to 14 have the best views down over the distant Sand River). Kids of all ages are welcome.

Traversing rights are shared with Lion Sands, which uniquely gives access to both the Sand and Sabie Rivers.

Nkorho Bush Lodge LODGE $$$

(Map p400; ☎013-735 5367; www.nkorho.com; s/d all-inclusive R4380/6740; ❄📶🏊) This very friendly former farmstead has seven green-brick, thatched-roof chalets, a petite deck and an infinity pool, most of which overlook lawns and wildlife congregating at a somewhat distant waterhole. Avoid chalet Nos 1 and 2 as they are behind the communal areas (ask for No 5). In northern Sabi Sand, Nkorho is accessed by Gowrie gate. The price is pleasant (for Sabi Sand).

Sabi Sabi Bush Lodge LODGE $$$

(Map p400; ☎013-735 5656; www.sabisabi.com; s/d all-inclusive R9700/19,400; ❄📶🏊) This large 25-suite traditional bush lodge is perfect for families, with the Elefun Centre providing endless entertainment for kids of all ages. The common areas are big and breezy and overlook a large waterhole. Rooms are large, with huge daybeds converting to beds for young ones.

Sabi Sabi Little Bush Lodge LODGE $$$
(Map p400; ☎013-735 5080; www.sabisabi.com; s/d all-inclusive R9700/19,400;) Small but perfectly formed, this luxury six-suite lodge overlooks the Msuthlu River and is perfect for couples. Dine on the lantern-lit riverbed, chill by the rock pool or soak in your private hot tub.

Getting There & Away

Most visitors fly into Kruger's Skukuza Airport (p399) or directly into Sabi Sand with **Federal Airlines** (www.fedair.com), which serves Londolozi, Mala Mala, Sabi Sabi and Singita airstrips from Jo'burg and MKIA.

Manyeleti Game Reserve

During the apartheid era, the 230-sq-km **Manyeleti** (www.manyeleti.com; vehicle fee R50, per passenger R105 (incl community levy R75)) was the only wildlife reserve that blacks were permitted to visit. Due to its unfenced boundary with Kruger there is no shortage of animals here (including the Big Five), but you may have to look a littler harder than in Sabi Sand. The upside is that prices are much lower here. Access is via Orpen Gate Rd.

Sleeping & Eating

★ **Honeyguide Mantobeni** LODGE $$$
(Map p400; ☎021-424 3122; www.manyeleti.com; s/d all-inclusive R4725/8600;) Aimed at couples, this small camp has 12 East African–style safari tents dotted amongst trees (No 4 overlooks a waterhole; No 1 is the most private). Elevated on platforms, the petite tents are very comfortable and have bathrooms that are partly open to the bush. The lounge and pool area also embraces nature but is very modern in look and feel.

Honeyguide Khoka Moya LODGE $$$
(Map p400; ☎021-424 3122; www.honeyguidecamp.com; s/d all-inclusive R4725/8600;) Khoka Moya has 15 permanent safari tents spread out along an elevated boardwalk in the bush. Each has a sitting area, covered deck, polished-cement floors and enough room to accommodate beds for kids (all ages OK). The sizeable bathrooms are a little dark. The open quad-shaped lounge surrounds a fire pit – the corrugated-iron roof gives it an old homestead feel.

Timbavati Private Game Reserve

It was the discovery of white lions in the mid-1970s that put this **reserve** (Map p400; www.timbavati.co.za; vehicle fee R150, per passenger R180) on the map. Due to the incredible rarity and recessive nature of the leucism genetic mutation, there are only two of these bright beasts in the reserve currently. But the reserve, which has open boundaries to Kruger, is still one of the region's best for overall wildlife.

★ **Shindzela** LODGE $$$
(Map p400; ☎087 806 2068; www.shindzela.co.za; s/d all-inclusive R2440/3780) A great entry-level option for those wanting a taste of Timbavati without breaking the bank, Shindzela has eight small safari tents, each with attached loos under thatched roofs. Most tents overlook the busy waterhole (Nos 7 and 8 are more private and view the riverbed).

Umlani Bushcamp LODGE $$$
(Map p400; ☎021-785 5547; www.umlani.com; s/d all-inclusive R4578/6870;) This rustic, compact camp has lost none of its charm, despite some of its eight reed and thatch *rondavels* being replaced with modern versions, complete with solid walls and glass windows. There's limited electricity and lighting is still provided by candles, lanterns and fires, which gives the place an ethereal atmosphere in the evenings. The pool and lounge overlook the active riverbed.

Ask about staying a night in the remote treehouse.

Jaydee Bush Camp LODGE $$$
(Map p400; ☎083 283 8237; www.jaydeecamp.co.za; 10-person camp R10,000;) A great option for groups or large families, this very comfortable five-suite self-catering lodge is rented on an exclusive basis. There is a large braai area and a full kitchen (with private chef on request, R450 per day). Elevated decks allow wildlife viewing, and there's a pool and playground for kids. Wildlife drives are included.

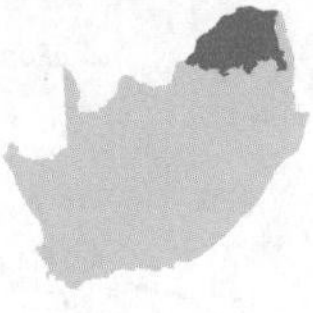

Limpopo

Includes ➡

Best Places to Eat

- Red Plate (p420)
- Iron Crown (p420)
- Market Cafe (p421)
- Buffalo Pub & Grill (p424)
- Sleepers Railway Station Restaurant (p425)

Best Places to Stay

- Plumtree Lodge (p407)
- 139 on Munnik (p413)
- Ilala Country Lodge (p414)
- Kings Walden (p421)
- Kaia Tani (p423)

Why Go?

Limpopo is a huge and diverse province characterised by culture, history, vast open spaces and wildlife. In just a single visit to Mapungubwe National Park visitors can walk through the country's most significant Iron Age site, gaze from a rocky bluff over the stunning riverine landscape where South Africa, Botswana and Zimbabwe meet, and observe iconic animals in the wild such as meerkats and rhinos. Culture and traditional art shine in the enigmatic region of Venda, an area dotted with hilltops, lakes and forests of great spiritual significance. Nature takes centre stage in the Waterberg, where the eponymous Unesco biosphere reserve has endless skies, a landscape of distinctly South African beauty and great safari wildlife, particularly in Marakele National Park.

It's easy to rush through Limpopo, either en route to Kruger National Park on its eastern edge, or to Zimbabwe via Musina, but investing in a detour or two will pay rather lovely dividends.

When to Go

Polokwane (Pietersburg)

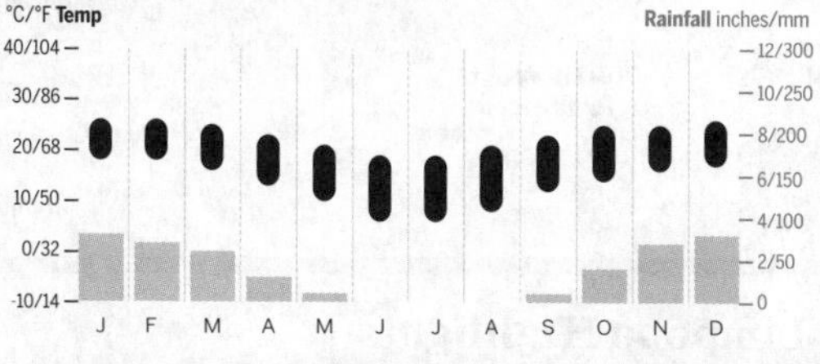

Jun–Aug Normally steamy conditions cool down, making this a great time to visit Mapungubwe National Park.

Sep–Dec The Rain Queen near Modjadjiskloof presides over a festival for the coming of the rains.

Jan–Mar Summer is hot and dry so head for the cooler hills and the berry festival in Haenertsburg.

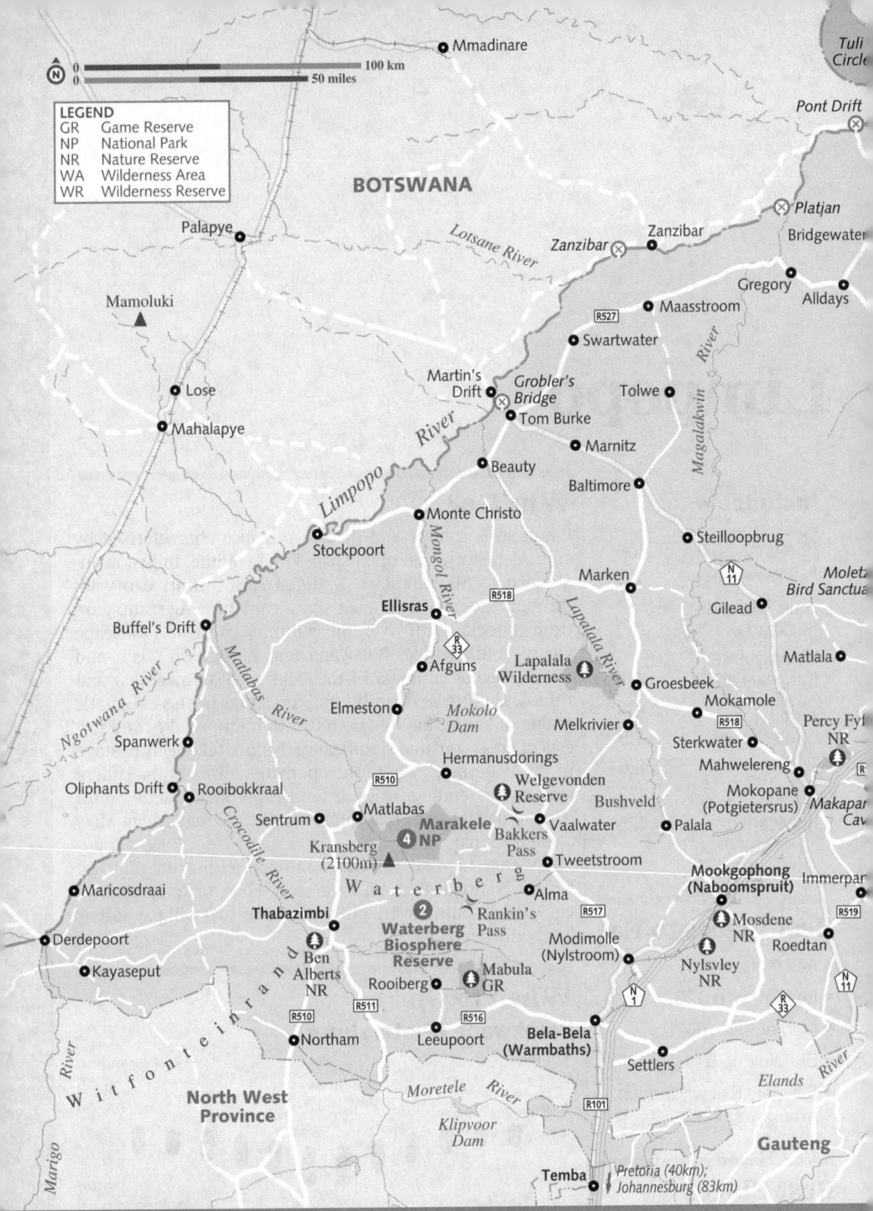

Limpopo Highlights

1. Exploring ancient civilisation and stunning landscapes in **Mapungubwe National Park** (p415).

2. Discovering solitude and space among the reserves of the vast and wild **Waterberg Biosphere Reserve** (p411).

3. Searching out traditional crafts in the **Venda** (p416) region or the intricate and colourful weavings at **Kaross** (p422).

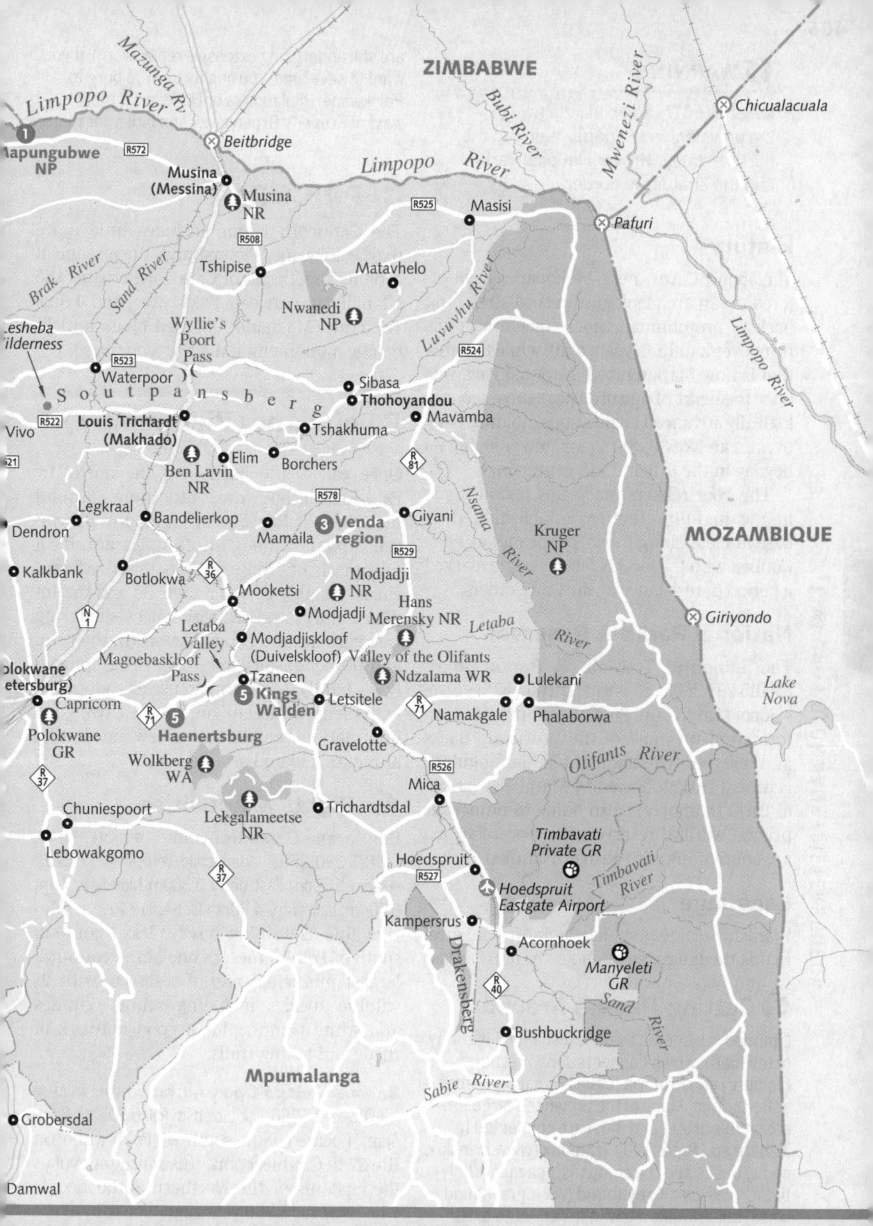

4 Watching the sun slide behind blue bluffs from the vulture-viewing point at **Marakele National Park** (p412).

5 Revelling in the cool climate, misty forests and relaxed living in **Haenertsburg** (p419) and **Kings Walden** (p420).

WARNING

Malaria (p617) and bilharzia (p618) are prevalent in Limpopo, mainly in the northeast near Kruger National Park and the Zimbabwe border.

History

Makapan's Caves, near Mokopane, have offered up an archaeological record stretching back to protohuman times (including tools from over a million years ago), while the area that is now Mapungubwe National Park was once the heart of one of Africa's most technologically advanced civilisations, holding sway over an area of 30,000 sq km and enjoying its heyday in the 8th and 9th centuries.

The Voortrekkers made this region home in the mid-19th century, establishing their base in Pietersburg (now Polokwane) in 1886. Conflict with the local Ndebele people marked a period of resistance against the settlers.

National Parks & Reserves

The **Limpopo Tourism & Parks Board** (015-293 3600; Southern Gateway, N1; 8am-4.30pm Mon-Fri), in Polokwane, provides information on most of the province's parks and reserves. The highlight is Mapungubwe National Park, followed by Marakele National Park. Limpopo is also home to numerous private wildlife reserves, the best of which are contiguous with Kruger National Park.

Language

English is widely spoken but Afrikaans remains the language of choice in most areas.

Getting There & Around

Limpopo is bisected by the excellent N1 highway (a toll road), which connects Johannesburg (Jo'burg) and Pretoria to the Zimbabwe border at Beitbridge. Many of the province's large towns are on this artery and most are connected to Jo'burg and Pretoria by **Translux** (www.translux.co.za) buses and the company's cheaper City to City services. **Greyhound** (www.greyhound.co.za) buses make a few stops en route to Harare and Bulawayo (but you can't get off before the border).

Translux also runs along Rte 71 to locations including Tzaneen and Phalaborwa (for Kruger's Phalaborwa gate). Some destinations can be hard to access without a car, but minibus shared taxis trundle to most parts of the province.

Hiring a vehicle is by far the best way to see Limpopo (most roads are good although many are still undergoing extensive repair work); if you want to save time, you can fly from Jo'burg to Polokwane, Phalaborwa or Hoedspruit (northwest of Kruger's Orpen gate) and hire a car there.

CAPRICORN

The Capricorn region includes little more than Polokwane (Pietersburg), the provincial capital. The Tropic of Capricorn crosses the N1 halfway between Polokwane and Louis Trichardt (Makhado), marked by an anticlimactic monument and a few aloe trees.

Polokwane (Pietersburg)

POP 130,000

Once called 'the bastion of the north' by Paul Kruger, but now a little rough around the edges, Polokwane is Limpopo's provincial capital. Although not unpleasant, it's a mishmash of lively, semiorganised African chaos (roughly between Civic Sq and the Indian Centre) and security fences sheltering vast gardens and clipped lawns (in the prim and proper eastern suburbs). Geographically, it's handy for visitors to use as a stopover, with plenty of decent guesthouses, two good information centres and a few interesting attractions in and around town.

Sights & Activities

Polokwane Game Reserve WILDLIFE RESERVE

(015-290 2508; adult/child/vehicle R20/16/31; 7am-5.30pm, last entry 3.30pm May-Sep, 7am-6.30pm, last entry 4.30pm Oct-Apr) Go on safari at this 32.5-sq-km reserve less than 5km south of Polokwane. It's one of the country's largest municipal nature reserves, with 21 wildlife species including zebras, giraffes and white rhinos, plus a good network of roads and hiking trails.

Bakone Malapa Open-Air Museum MUSEUM

(015-290 2180; adult/child R9/8.50; 8am-4pm) Located 9km south of Polokwane on Rte 37 to Chuniespoort, this museum evokes the customs of the Northern Sotho people who lived here 300 years ago. The tour of the recreated village shows pots being made and demonstrations of tools such as the antelope-horn trumpet and marula-root matches.

Hugh Exton Photographic Museum MUSEUM

(015-290 2186; Civic Sq; 9am-3.30pm Mon-Fri) FREE Set in a restored 19th-century church, this museum covers Polokwane's first half-century and the second Anglo-Boer War through the work of the prolific photographer Hugh Exton, who left 23,000 glass negatives.

Polokwane Art Museum MUSEUM
(☎015-290 2177; cnr Grobler & Hans van Ransburgh Sts, Library Gardens; ⊙9am-4pm Mon-Fri, 10am-noon Sat) FREE This museum is worth ducking into for its modern take on colonialism, many depictions of Nelson Mandela and interesting display on women and art in South Africa. It features artists from Limpopo and across the country.

Tours

Vuwa Safari & Tours TOUR
(☎015-291 1384; www.vuwasafaritours.co.za; 88 Grobler St) For cultural, heritage and wildlife tours around Limpopo.

Sleeping

As is the case throughout Limpopo, accommodation options are concentrated in the midrange bracket.

★**Plumtree Lodge** GUESTHOUSE $$
(☎015-295 6153; www.plumtree.co.za; 138 Marshall St; s/d incl breakfast R650/820; ❄📶🏊) This German-run guesthouse's bungalow rooms are some of the most spacious and appealing in town. Standard features are high ceilings, lounge areas, minibars, DSTV and desks where you can tap into the free wi-fi. A poolside *lapa* (circular building with low walls and a thatched roof) bar and generous breakfast complete the package.

African Roots GUESTHOUSE $$
(☎015-297 0113; www.africanroots.info; 58a Devenish St; s/d incl breakfast R700/880; ❄📶🏊) Built from a 1920s farmhouse, the rooms here have original steel pressed ceilings and pine floors that blend comfortably with the modern facilities. Each one has its own entrance into either the garden or pool area. It's popular with businesspeople and tourists, and you'll find both lazing around the pool.

Rustic Rest GUESTHOUSE $$
(☎015-295 7402; www.rusticrest.co.za; 36 Rabe St; s/d incl breakfast R660/950; ❄) Occupying a 1940s house and a purpose-built building, the family-run Rustic Rest has gorgeous, modern rooms that espouse luxury with soft furnishings and bedding. If you're here in October you'll see the massive jacaranda tree that shades the rooms in its full glory.

Victoria Place GUESTHOUSE $$
(☎015-295 7599; www.victoriaplace.co.za; 32 Burger St; s/d incl breakfast R650/850; ❄) Victoria Place is graced with elegance and plenty of smiles. It has spacious rooms with beautiful linen and basic bathrooms, and you can eat breakfast among pot plants on the verandah. Self-catering units, incorporating a kitchenette, are also available.

Cycad Guest House GUESTHOUSE $$
(☎015-291 2181; www.cycadguesthouse.co.za; cnr Suid & Schoeman Sts; s/d R800/1000; ❄@) A 'motel-style' option, Cycad makes the most of its brutal brick shell with modern, glossy rooms and slick service. There's an all-weather balcony good for lounging in the evening and a laundry service.

Polokwane (Pietersburg)

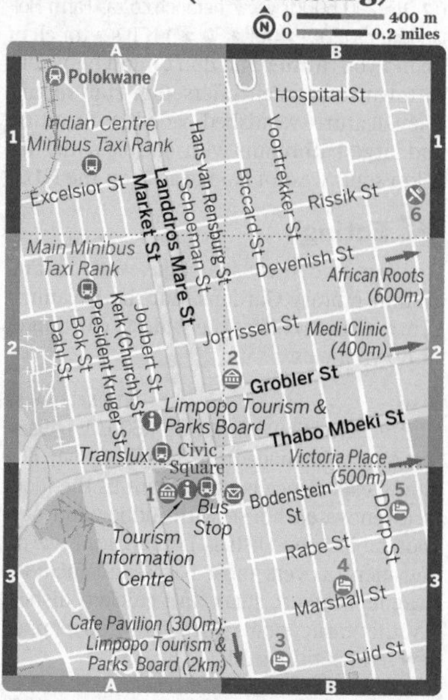

Polokwane (Pietersburg)

Sights
1 Hugh Exton Photographic Museum A3
2 Polokwane Art Museum B2

Sleeping
3 Cycad Guest House B3
4 Plumtree Lodge B3
5 Rustic Rest B3

Eating
6 Dish B1

Protea Hotel – Ranch Resort HOTEL **$$$**
(☑ 015-290 5000; www.theranch.co.za; Farm Hollandrift; r R1200-3400; 🌐 @ 🏊) If it's a touch of luxury you're after and don't mind being out of town, the ranch offers four-star rooms. They feature varnished wooden furniture and large bathrooms with marble sinks. It's 25km southwest of Polokwane (on the N1).

 Eating

You can find the usual takeaways in and around Library Gardens, but the Savannah Centre (Rte 71) offers the widest selection of sit-down meals.

Dish INTERNATIONAL **$$**
(☑ 079 553 3790; 96 Burger St; R60-110; ⊙ 9am-5pm Mon, to 10pm Tue-Fri, to 3pm Sat & Sun) The dining experience is as pleasant as the food. In a renovated house with indoor and outdoor tables, the Dish is homely and warm. The menu covers most bases and includes lasagne, seafood, steak and chicken dishes. Try the garlic snails with feta and pepper dew to kick things off.

Cafe Pavilion CAFE **$$**
(☑ 015-291 5359; Church St, Sterkloop Garden Pavilion; mains R60-120; ⊙ 8am-5pm Mon-Sat, to 2pm Sun) Overlooking a garden centre, and boasting its own water feature in the covered outdoor area, the Pavilion is a great spot for breakfast or lunch. The food has the usual focus on meat feasts (think biltong and avocado T-bone) prepared in a variety of styles, with a couple of salads thrown in for good measure.

Cofi INTERNATIONAL **$$**
(☑ 015-296 2538; Grobler St, Savannah Centre; mains R60-120; ⊙ 8am-late) Sit back and 'chillate' at this friendly bar-restaurant. With an enormous round bar and a postmodern dining room, it's as trendy as fine dining gets in the city. Meat-driven mains dominate the menu, with the Afro Fusion platter featuring Russian flowers and pap (a traditional African food made from ground maize) the most interesting dish on the menu.

ℹ Information

EMERGENCY
Police Station (☑ 015-290 6000; cnr Schoeman & Bodenstein Sts)

INTERNET
There are cafes with wi-fi in the Savannah Centre (Rte 71) and the Mall of the North (N1).

PostNet (☑ 015-265 1341; Mall of the North; per half hour R20; ⊙ 8am-4.30pm Mon-Fri, to 1pm Sat) Reliable internet connections.

MEDICAL SERVICES
Medi-Clinic (☑ 015-290 3600, 24hr emergency 015-290 3747; www.mediclinic.co.za; 53 Plein St) Private hospital with 24-hour emergency centre.

Polokwane Hospital (☑ 015-287 5000; cnr Hospital & Dorp St) Public hospital.

MONEY
There are plenty of banks throughout the centre.
ABSA (70 Hans van Rensburg St) Has an ATM and exchange facilities.

POST
Main Post Office (Landdros Mare St; ⊙ 8am-5.30pm Mon-Fri, 8am-1pm Sat)

TOURIST INFORMATION
Limpopo Tourism & Parks Board (☑ 015-293 3600; www.golimpopo.com; N1; ⊙ 8am-4.30pm Mon-Fri) Covers the whole province and offers the useful *Limpopo Explorer* map and the *Know Limpopo* guide. On the N1, approaching town from the south.

Tourism Information Centre (☑ 015-290 2010; cnr Thabo Mbeki & Church Sts, Civic Sq; ⊙ 8am-5pm Mon-Fri) The best source for Polokwane information; has brochures and a list of accommodation.

ℹ Getting There & Away

AIR
Polokwane airport is 5km north of town.
Airlink (☑ 015-288 0166; www.flyairlink.com) Subsidiary of South African Airways with offices at the airport; flies daily to/from Jo'burg (from R1500 one way).

BUS
Translux (☑ 0861 589 282; www.translux.co.za; cnr Joubert & Thabo Mbeki Sts) Runs services to Jo'burg (R210, four hours) via Pretoria (R210, 3½ hours) at 10.30am, 11.15am and 2.30pm. Two cheaper City to City buses (R170) leave in the mornings.

CAR
Major car-rental agencies are located at the airport.

SHARED TAXI
Minibus taxis run to destinations including Louis Trichardt (R60, 1½ hours) and Thohoyandou (R70, 2½ hours) from the rank at the Indian Centre, on the corner of Church and Excelsior Sts.

BUSHVELD

The main reason to head southwest of Polokwane is to visit the Waterberg, a Unesco biosphere reserve the size of the Okavango Delta. The source of four of Limpopo's perennial rivers, its biodiversity is reflected in the San rock paintings of large mammals on the area's sandstone cliffs. Elsewhere, the Bushveld region is typical African savannah. If you want to break your journey up the N1, there is a string of roadside towns with some pit-stop potential.

Mokopane (Potgietersrus)

POP 30,000

Mokopane is a sizeable Bushveld town that makes a good place to break a trip up the N1. The main attraction for visitors is Makapan's Caves.

◉ Sights

Makapan's Caves CAVE

(☑082 496 1800, 079 515 6491; adult/student R25/15) Declared a Unesco World Heritage Site for their palaeontological significance, these caves yielded the famous 3.3-million-year-old Taung skull, which belonged to a humanoid known as *Australopithecus africanus*. In the Historic Cave, chief Makapan and 1000-plus followers were besieged for a month in 1854 by Paul Kruger and the Voortrekkers. You must prebook visits to the site, 23km northeast of town; the guide also speaks French.

The fossilised remains of long-extinct animals such as the sivatherium, an offshoot of the giraffe clan, have been discovered in the caves, which are littered with fossils and bones.

Game Breeding Centre WILDLIFE RESERVE

(☑015-491 4314; Thabo Mbeki Dr; adult/child R20/10, feeding tours R40; ☺8am-4.30pm Mon-Fri, to 6pm Sat & Sun) This 13-sq-km reserve on Rte 101 is a breeding centre for the National Zoo in Pretoria and has a wide variety of native and exotic animals, including gibbons, wild dogs, giraffes and lions. You can drive through the reserve; go in the morning when its inhabitants are animated.

Arend Dieperink Museum MUSEUM

(97 Thabo Mbeki Dr; adult R22; ☺8am-4pm Mon-Fri) At the back of the tourism association, this museum recounts local history, with a focus on the town's development after Voortrekkers founded it in 1852.

WORTH A TRIP

NATURE A STONE'S THROW FROM THE N1

Nylsvley Nature Reserve (☑014-743 6925; www.nylsvley.co.za; adult/child/vehicle R15/10/25; ☺6am-6pm) This 40-sq-km reserve, on the Nyl River floodplain, is one of the country's best places to see birds (380 species are listed). The reserve, 20km south of Mookgophong, is signposted from Rte 101 to Modimolle.

Bundox Bush Camp (☑072 523 2796; www.bundox.co.za; tent/chalet per person R400/450) Three kilometres north of Mookgophong off Rte 101, this camp has gorgeous open-plan chalets and East African tents in a reserve that hosts a conservation centre with cheetahs, 129 bird species and a thatched library.

🍴 Sleeping & Eating

Game Breeding Centre GUESTHOUSE $

(☑015-491 4314; Thabo Mbeki Dr; s/d R240/300, camping R40; ❄) Certainly the most novel choice in Mokopane. The rooms are all a bit different – some with interior or exterior kitchens and bathrooms. But all are a good size with a lovely outlook onto the reserve. Room No 1 is our fave – you can see the gibbons at play from your window.

Thabaphaswa HUT $

(☑082 389 6631, 015-491 4882; www.thabaphaswa; camping R90, hut per person R130-200; ❄) If you don't mind roughing it a little, this unique property offers accommodation in climbers' huts beneath rocky escarpments. The glass-walled huts have bunk beds and patios with braai (barbecue) pits and open-air showers. There are biking and walking trails on the property.

Follow the Percy Fyfe Rd (signposted from Rte 101 after it crosses the bridge just north of Mokopane) for 13km, then turn at the brown 'Thabaphaswa Hiking and Mountain Bike Trail' sign. It's 2km to the gate, then straight on for another 1.3km to the homestead.

Platinum GUESTHOUSE $$

(☑015-491 3510; theplatinum@connectit.co.za; 4 Totius St; s/d incl breakfast R450/720; ❄@🛜) This suburban house belies the luxury accommodation on offer. Rooms are beautifully presented with touches of elegance and comfort everywhere. The friendly owner is happy to show her rooms so have a look at a few because layout and size differ – all are first class. It's signposted off Rte 101 as you enter town from Modimolle.

La Bamba Restaurant & Sports Bar PUB $
(☎083 368 6846; Hoog St; mains R40-80; ⏲11am-late Mon-Sat) This plain, tiled-floor pub – with rugby or cricket usually on the box – is a good place to fuel up on burgers, schnitzels and steaks. It also has a salad bar.

Information

Mokopane Tourism Association (☎015-491 8458; www.mogalakwena.gov.za; 97 Thabo Mbeki Dr; ⏲8am-4.30pm Mon-Fri, 9am-noon Sat) On Rte 101; has plenty of local information.

PostNet (Thabo Mbeki Dr, Crossing Mall; per hour R40; ⏲8am-5pm Mon-Fri, to 1pm Sat) For internet access.

Getting There & Away

Translux and City to City have daily buses to Jo'burg (R200 and R150, 3¾ hours) via Pretoria; to Phalaborwa (R200, 3¾ hours) via Tzaneen; and to Sibasa (R200 and R160, four hours) via Polokwane and Louis Trichardt.

Minibus shared taxis leave from outside Shoprite on Nelson Mandela Dr; from Mokopane to Polokwane it's about R40.

Modimolle (Nylstroom)

POP 12,500

Some towns just have that feel-good factor – Modimolle (Place of the Spirits) is one of them. Perhaps the heat just makes the place languid and easygoing. It's a good stopover on the way to/from Vaalwater in the Waterberg, or when heading north.

Boshoffstraat Gastehuis GUESTHOUSE $
(☎014-717 4432; www.boshoffstguesthouse.co.za; 15 Boshoff (Gowan Mbeki) St; r per person incl breakfast R320) Signposted from Rte 101 on the southern side of town, this guesthouse has good-size, simple rooms on a large suburban property, which are basic but clean, well located, and come with a genial owner. The largest room, with three single beds, is the pick if you can forgive the dated bathroom decor.

Lekkerbly B&B, CHALET $$
(☎014-717 3702; lekkerblygh@telkomsa.net; 10 Rupert St; s/d R450/750; ❄) Provides cramped self-catering chalets or B&B rooms. There's also a bar on-site. It's signposted on the way to/from Vaalwater.

Oudewerf CAFE $
(☎014-717 2104; Van Rhyneveldt St; snacks R15-24; ⏲9am-4pm Mon-Fri, to 1pm Sat) Sit among the antiques while you have a coffee, tea or light snack.

Bela-Bela (Warmbaths)

POP 37,200

Bela-Bela is a hot, chaotic, seemingly perpetually busy place, but works as a spot to break a journey, especially if you like to indulge in 'warm baths'. Bela-Bela takes its name from the town's hot springs (which bubble out of the earth at a rate of 22,000L per hour), discovered by the Tswana in the early 19th century. Bathing in the soporific pools is a popular treatment for rheumatic ailments.

Sights & Activities

Thaba Kwena Crocodile Farm FARM
(☎014-736 5059; www.tkwena.co.za; adult/child R35/17; ⏲9am-4pm daily, feeding 2pm Sat) This farm is home to more than 10,000 crocodiles, each reaching up to 5.5m in length. The beasts are bred for their skin and meat, which is exported worldwide. It's just north of De Draai Gastehuis, 4km from Rte 101.

Hydro SPA
(☎014-736 8500; www.foreverwarmbaths.co.za; Chris Hani Dr; day/evening R100/120; ⏲7am-4pm & 5-10pm) At Warmbaths (a Forever Resort), the Hydro spa has a series of interlinked indoor and outdoor pools. Children head to the cold pools with twisty slides, while those who prefer a relaxing experience can wallow in 38°C to 42°C baths or peruse the many other enhancers and therapies involving the cleansing waters.

Sleeping & Eating

Flamboyant Guesthouse B&B $
(☎014-736 3433; www.flamboyantguesthouse.com; 5 Flamboyant St; r per person incl breakfast R300; ❄) Among the jacaranda trees on the northern edge of town, the Flamboyant has flowery patios aplenty, decor that may take you back a few years and a personable owner. Rooms and flats sleeping up to five are available and it's wheelchair friendly.

Elephant Springs Hotel HOTEL $$
(☎014-736 2101; www.elephantsprings.co.za; 31 Sutter Rd; s/d R500/1200; ❄📶🏊) Primarily (but not exclusively) used for conferences, this old-fashioned little beauty provides spacious lodging. Although underneath its smiling

veneer there are some rough edges, it's very friendly, the beds are comfy and it makes a good change from staying at guesthouses.

Greenfields CAFE $
(Old Pretoria Rd, The Waterfront; mains R35-70; ⏲7am-10pm) A '70s wood-cabana feel makes this place homely and, importantly, it gets the food right. There are croissants, muffins and pancakes from the bakery for breakfast. Lunch is a mix of dishes including burgers, salads and steaks.

Information

Bela-Bela Community Tourism Association (☎014-736 3694; www.belabelatourism.co.za; Old Pretoria Rd, Waterfront; ⏲8am-5pm Mon-Fri, 9am-1pm Sat) In the Waterfront development, over the bridge from the town centre.

Getting There & Away

Minibus shared taxis run from Ritchie St, between the Forever Resort and Elephant Springs Hotel, to destinations including Polokwane (R70, 2½ hours) and Jo'burg (R90, two hours).

The Waterberg

Paul Kruger used to damn troublesome politicos with the phrase 'Give him a farm in the Waterberg', but that fate may not strike you as such a hardship. The 150km-long range, which stretches northeast from Thabazimbi past Vaalwater, is protected by the 15,000-sq-km Waterberg Biosphere Reserve, one of Africa's two savannah biospheres. Rising to 2100m, it has a mild climate and some wild terrain for spotting the Big Five (lion, leopard, buffalo, elephant and rhino), with rivers and distinctive mountains scything through bushveld and *sourveld* (a type of grassland).

WATERBERG MEANDER

The **Waterberg Meander** (www.waterbergmeander.co.za), a 350km signposted tourist route around the Waterberg, links 13 community projects, and sites of interest such as those significant in the Anglo-Boer War, along with viewpoints of some stunning landscapes, and arts and crafts outlets. Look out for the excellent *Waterberg Meander* booklet in tourist offices.

Vaalwater & Around

POP 4000

Strung out along the highway, Vaalwater (faalvater) is a jumble of tourist and local facilities. It makes a top base for exploring the many attractions of the Waterberg and is by far the most pleasant town between Polokwane and Limpopo's southwestern border.

Sights & Activities

St John's Church CHURCH
About 10km from Vaalwater on the Melkrivier road, turn right onto the Vierentwintigriviere road and, after 8.7km, turn left towards Naauwpoort – St John's will be on your left. The 'church of thatch and stone... whose quiet charm doth strike a lovely note' (in the words of the poem by the door) dates to 1914. It is said to have been designed by Sir Herbert Baker but is often overlooked in studies of the great colonial architect.

Horizon Horseback Adventures HORSE RIDING
(www.ridinginafrica.com) Inspiring fervent loyalty in returning riders, this operation near Waterberg Cottages offers adventurous options including cattle mustering and an eight-day horse safari that includes wildlife-watching in Botswana.

Waterberg Welfare Society VOLUNTEERING
(☎014-755 3594; www.waterbergwelfaresociety.org.za; Timothy House, 208-209 Waterberg St; ⏲8.30am-5pm) Founded to assist individuals and their families affected by HIV/AIDS, the Waterberg Welfare Society operates a visitor centre, Timothy House, giving the public an opportunity to interact with the orphans and to learn about its programs and work with HIV/AIDS sufferers. Please call before visiting.

Sleeping & Eating

Zeederberg Cottage & Backpackers BACKPACKERS $
(☎082 332 7088; www.zeederbergs.co.za; camping R65, dm R170, cottage s/d R380-550;) Behind the centre of the same name, Zeederberg has a thatched cottage and a Zulu-style *rondavel* as well as backpacker dorms and doubles. The only drawback is that some beds aren't the greatest. The lawn is dotted with jacaranda and tipuana trees and the main building is well set up for backpackers' lounging needs.

Waterberg Cottages CABIN $
(☎014-755 4425; www.waterbergcottages.co.za; r per person R260-460;) These cottages, 33km

north of Vaalwater off the Melkrivier road, range from the dual-level 'Bushwillow', with its free-standing bath and modern kitchen, to simpler offerings; it's all lent some charm by furniture belonging to the family's ancestors. Activities include astrology with the resident star buff, wildlife-watching and farm tours.

La Fleur ITALIAN $$
(014-755 3975; Voortrekker St; mains R40-100; 8am-10pm Mon-Sat) With a pretty classy setup inside and an outdoor terrace where you can keep an eye on the comings and goings in town, this is Vaalwater's only restaurant. It dabbles in pizza, pasta, salads, pancakes and steaks, and the chatty kitchen staff do everything well.

Shopping

There are two craft shops in Zeederberg's Centre. Kamotsogo sells handmade products by local Sotho women living with HIV/AIDS and Black Mamba sells craftwork from across the continent.

Beadle ARTS & CRAFTS
(014-755 4002; Sterkstroom Rd; 7.30am-5pm Mon-Fri, to 1pm Sat & Sun) Next to an essential oils factory in the Waterberg Cottages area, Beadle is a community project that sells attractive leather and beaded crafts, handmade in the workshop by local villagers.

MARAKELE NATIONAL PARK

Why Go The park contains all the larger African species including the big cats, and has the largest colony of endangered cape vultures in the world. The Waterberg massif affords spectacular views of the area.

When to Go Year-round but heavy rains can occur in February and March.

Practicalities Entry fee is R152 per adult. Day visitors can enter the park between 7am and 4pm. The Marakele 4x4 Eco Trail is sometimes closed due to rain damage. The park entrance booking office is on the Thabazimbi–Alma road, 3km northeast of the intersection with the Matlabas–Rooiberg road.

Budget Tip Stay in Thabazimbi, a few kilometres away – it's much cheaper than the park unless you're camping.

Getting There & Away

A newly laid road along Rte 33 between Modimolle and Vaalwater has made the journey out to Vaalwater quick and easy. Private transport is your best bet.

Marakele National Park

This mountainous **national park** (014-777 6928; www.sanparks.co.za/parks/marakele) is at the southwest end of the Waterberg Biosphere Reserve. The animals grazing beneath the red cliffs include elephants, black and white rhinos, giraffes, zebras, leopards and cheetahs. A great place to eyeball the landscape from is the vulture-viewing point (be warned, the road up is precipitous), where you can also see one of the world's largest colonies of the endangered Cape vulture (800-plus breeding pairs).

The park is divided into two sections, with the second section (you press a buzzer to open the gate) wilder and richer in wildlife (the Big Five are present). However, the gravel roads are in much better shape in the first section, so if it's been raining that may be as far as you want to go.

Sleeping & Eating

Bontle Camping Site CAMPGROUND $
(camping per 2-person site R205, extra adult/child R68/34) The park has tent sites at Bontle.

Tlopi Tent Camp CAMPGROUND $$
(tents R1065) This two-bed tented accommodation is 15km from reception. The furnished tents, overlooking a dam where antelope and wildebeest come to drink, have a bathroom and open-air kitchen, with refrigerator, and braai. Note, you'll have to bring your own food.

Getting There & Away

The easiest route to the park is on Rte 510 from Thabazimbi. An alternative is the hard-dirt Bakkerspas Rd, which runs alongside the mountains, with spectacular views. Turn left 6km west of Vaalwater and, after 60km, right at the T-junction; the park entrance is 45km further, a few kilometres after the tar begins.

SOUTPANSBERG

The Soutpansberg region incorporates the most northern part of South Africa, scraping southern Zimbabwe. The forested slopes of the Soutpansberg mountains are strikingly lush compared with the lowveld to the north, where baobab trees rise from the dry plains. The highlights here are the mountains, the Venda region and Mapungubwe National Park, which is well worth the 260km drive from Polokwane.

Louis Trichardt (Makhado)

POP 25,500

Leafy Louis Trichardt has a very busy centre with streets of booming retail chain outlets and hordes of shoppers. The outlying streets reveal verdant parkland, wide roads and shady jacarandas, giving the place a very pleasant feel. There's not much to do here but it makes a great northern base.

The nearby spectacular Soutpansberg mountains boast an extraordinary diversity of flora and fauna, with one of the continent's highest concentrations of the African leopard and more tree species than there are in the whole of Canada.

Sights & Activities

There are a couple of great hikes in the Soutpansberg mountains, both of which start from the Soutpansberg Hut on the outskirts of town. One is a 2½-hour walk; the other is the two-day, 20.5km **Hanglip Trail**, which climbs through indigenous forest to a 1719m peak with views across the Bushveld. Take precautions against malaria (p617), bilharzia (p618) and ticks. Overnight accommodation is in huts (per person R105) with bunk beds, showers and braais. Contact Komatiland Forests Eco-Tourism (p380) in Nelspruit for more information and details of how to make reservations.

Sleeping & Eating

There are several options in Louis Trichardt, or soak up the Soutpansberg and stay in the hills outside town.

Louis Trichardt Lodge MOTEL $
(015-516 2222; Hlanganani St; s/d R480/580) You'll receive curt service at this red-brick motel on the main road. It has basic, serviceable rooms with kitchenettes and braai areas. Breakfast is R60.

139 on Munnik GUESTHOUSE $$
(083 407 0124; www.139onmunnik.co.za; 139 Munnik St; r incl breakfast per person from R650;) Without doubt Louis Trichardt's most luxurious accommodation. Modern fittings, stylish touches, great beds and facilities such as a bar and coffee shop make this place a standout. According to the owner it even has the best wi-fi in town. Book ahead, it's popular.

Ultimate Guest House GUESTHOUSE $$
(015-517 7005; www.ultimategh.co.za; s/d incl breakfast R575/750;) After a long day on the N1, this quirky, colourful, mist-shrouded guesthouse's name seems a fair description. It has a bar-restaurant (mains R90) with a verandah (ideal for a gin and tonic in the evening) overlooking a lush valley. It's 10km from the centre; turn left 100m after Mountain Inn, head 1.6km along the dirt track and it'll be on your right.

Madi a Thavha LODGE $$
(015-516 0220; www.madiathavha.com; camping R100, s/d incl breakfast R700/1200;) A cleansing Soutpansberg hideaway, this farm lodge is very involved with local community. Accommodation is in colourful little cottages with Venda bedspreads and cushions, tealight candles aplenty and kitchenettes. The Dutch owners organise tours of local craft studios, and hiking, birding and village tours are also available. It's some 10km west of Louis Trichardt, off Rte 522.

Purple Olive INTERNATIONAL $
(015-516 5946; 129 Krogh St; mains R60-90; 8am-5pm Mon-Sat) Presenting seafood dishes, grills, loads of burger variations, salads and pastas, this place is a great stop any

OFF THE BEATEN TRACK

LESHIBA WILDERNESS

Leshiba Wilderness (015-593 0076; www.leshiba.co.za; 2-person chalets R840, s/d incl full board & activity R1920/3200;) Perched in the clouds of the Soutpansberg mountains, this Fair Trade–accredited resort is based on a Venda village, created with the help of acclaimed Venda artist Noria Mabasa. It's signposted 36km west of Louis Trichardt on Rte 522.

Surrounded by wildlife, including rare brown hyenas and leopards, and with greenery supplied by 350-plus tree species, the hideaway offers self-catering and full-board accommodation in *rondavels* (round huts with conical roofs) with features such as private plunge pools and views of Botswana.

time of day. A formal atmosphere pervades but it gets more casual at the outside seating area which opens onto a garden.

Information

ABSA (Krogh St, cnr Songozwi Rd) Has ATMs and exchange facilities.

PC Worx (015-516 5988; Shop 34, Makhado Crossing, cnr N1 & Sebasa St; per 30 min R15; 9am-5pm Mon-Fri, to 1pm Sat) Internet access.

Police Station (015-519 4300; Krogh St) Police station.

Soutpansberg Tourist Office (015-516 3415; www.soutpansberg-tourism.co.za; Songozwi Rd; 8am-4.30pm Mon-Sat) Helpful office. Ask about tours around the Venda region.

Getting There & Away

Most buses to Jo'burg (R260, six hours) and Harare, Zimbabwe (R380, 11 hours) stop by the Caltex petrol station on the corner of the N1 and Baobab St.

The minibus shared taxi rank is in the Shoprite supermarket car park off Burger St. Destinations from Louis Trichardt include Musina (R50, 1½ hours) and Polokwane (R50, 1½ hours).

Ben Lavin Nature Reserve

Ben Lavin Nature Reserve NATURE RESERVE
(073 535 0466; adult/child R30/10; 6am-9.30pm) This reserve is worth visiting for its walking and mountain-bike trails. It contains 200-plus bird species, as well as giraffes, zebras and jackals.

Take the N1 south from Louis Trichardt for about 10km, then follow the signpost on the left. After about 3km you'll see the entrance gate on your left.

A range of excellent renovated accommodation (camping per person R155, chalet/safari unit R455/510) is available, including chalets with huge outdoor areas and lovely vistas. No kitchens but there are hotplates and a braai. Safari units are innovative, being half chalet and half safari tent. There are even family cottages with separate areas for the kids.

Musina (Messina)

POP 43,000

Some 18km south of the Beitbridge border crossing, Musina hums with typical border-town tension. It's busy, there are traffic snarls, and you should keep your wits about you when walking the streets.

You will probably pass through the town en route to the spectacular Mapungubwe National Park; the drive passes through a starkly beautiful landscape on empty, baobab-lined roads.

Sights

Giant baobab trees *(Adansonia digitata)*, which look like they have been planted upside down with their roots in the air, characterise this region. You don't have to drive far from Musina to spot some impressive examples. Whoppers such as the largest in the country, known as 'the Big Tree' (located near Sagole in northeast Limpopo) are more than 3000 years old.

Musina Nature Reserve NATURE RESERVE
(015-534 3235; 8am-6.30pm) FREE With South Africa's highest concentration of baobabs, the reserve is 5km south of the town off the N1, and has animals such as impalas and blue wildebeest.

Sleeping & Eating

Backpackers Lodge BACKPACKERS $
(082 401 2939; 12 Harper Rd; dm/r R70/200) This excellent budget option set up in a suburban home is great value. Beds are firm, the place is clean, rooms have TVs and the cooking facilities are well equipped. The four rooms each sleep two or three people. Located off Rte 508.

★ **Ilala Country Lodge** LODGE $$
(076 138 0699; www.ilalacountrylodge.co.za; Rte 572; s/d incl breakfast R550/700;) The sweeping views of the Limpopo River Valley into Zimbabwe at this old country lodge are something special. And there are few better places in Limpopo for a cold drink in the evening. The accommodation is outstanding, with rooms sleeping four in the main homestead, and huge chalets with lounge area, braai facilities and separate kitchen. It's 8km northwest of town, on the way to Mapungubwe.

Old Mine Guest House GUESTHOUSE $$
(0825 683 215; www.oldmineguesthouse.com; 1 Woodburn Ave; r R300-600;) In a residence built in 1919 by the first manager of Musina's copper mine, this guesthouse reeks of class and olde-world charm (it is seemingly out of place in Musina!). A verandah overlooks the leafy grounds, and there are stylish rooms and self-catering units with private outdoor patio areas.

Information

ABSA (6 National Rd) Has change facilities and an ATM. It is on the N1 as it passes through the centre of town.

Musina Tourism (015-534 3500; www.golimpopo.com; National Rd; 7am-4pm Mon-Fri) In a thatched hut on the way into town on the N1 from Polokwane. Very helpful office.

PostNet (National Rd; per hour R60; 8.30am-4.30pm Mon-Fri, 8-11am Sat) Internet access.

Getting There & Away

The Zimbabwe border at Beitbridge, 15km north of Musina, is open 24 hours. There is a large taxi rank on the South African side of the border; taxis between the border and Musina cost R40 (20 minutes). If you want to take a minibus shared taxi further south than Musina, catch one here – there are many more than in Musina.

Greyhound buses between Johannesburg (seven hours) and Harare (nine hours) stop in Musina and across the border in Beitbridge at the Ultra City.

Mapungubwe National Park

Stunningly stark, arid, rocky landscapes reverberate with cultural intrigue and wandering wildlife at **Mapungubwe National Park** (015-534 7923; www.sanparks.org/parks/mapungubwe; adult/child R152/76; 6am-6.30pm). A Unesco World Heritage Site, Mapungubwe contains South Africa's most significant Iron Age site, as well as animals ranging from black and white rhinos to the rare Pel's fishing owl and meerkats.

The park will realise its full potential when plans to incorporate it into an 8000-sq-km transfrontier conservation area stretching into Botswana and Zimbabwe are implemented by the respective governments. In 2014, not much progress had been made towards this goal.

The park is as much about history as wildlife. In 1933 archaeologists unearthed a 13th-century grave site on Mapungubwe Hill, containing ornaments, jewellery, bowls and amulets, much of it covered in gold foil. The most spectacular of these pieces was a small, gold-covered rhinoceros. Apartheid kept this discovery under wraps, as the regime attempted to suppress any historical information that proved black cultural sophistication.

MAPUNGUBWE NATIONAL PARK

Why Go One of South Africa's best national parks but rarely busy as it's new and quite remote. Wonderful combination of history, culture and wildlife. Stunningly beautiful landscapes.

When to Go Year-round, given the diversity of attractions, but June to October is high season and the best weather for a visit.

Practicalities The only way to get here is to drive, most commonly from Musina, the border town to the east. Gates are open 6am to 6.30pm September to March, and 6.30am to 6pm April to August. The roads heading south through the Waterberg are in a horrendous state, more potholes than tar – plan extra time if heading this way.

Budget Tips Bring your own food – do your shopping at a supermarket on your way through Musina.

Sights & Activities

The park is divided into eastern and western sections (with private land in between). The main gate is on the eastern side along with the interpretative centre, Mapungubwe Hill, a Treetop Walk, Leokwe (the main camp), and a magnificent viewpoint of the confluence of South Africa, Botswana and Zimbabwe. The four viewing decks on a bluff come complete with scurrying rock dassies (little guinea pig–like creatures) and are well positioned for sweeping views of the landscape, and the Limpopo and Shashe Rivers.

Interpretative Centre MUSEUM
(adult/child R40/20) The impressive centre, one of the country's finest modern buildings, was designed in sympathetic resemblance to the landscape. Inside it is contemporary, air-conditioned and has tastefully curated exhibits. There's plenty of information on the Mapungubwe cultural landscape, including finds from archaeological digs. Keep an eye out for the exquisite beadwork and the replica of the famous gold rhino.

Sleeping & Eating

There is a very simple restaurant but no petrol and no food supplies for self-catering, so stock up before you enter the park.

Limpopo Forest Camp CAMPGROUND $$
(camping per site from R250, luxury tent R1075) This lovely forest location has well-equipped

safari tents with kitchen area containing fridge/freezer and a separate bedroom area with twin beds and a fan.

Leokwe Camp CHALET **$$**
(chalets from R1200; ❄☒) These chalets are the best we've seen in any South African national park. They include a huge living space, fully equipped kitchen, outside braai area and a traditional *rondavel*-thatch-roof design. There are also outdoor showers.

Getting There & Around

A 2WD will get you around but the tracks are pretty rough and you'll see more with a 4WD. The western side of the park is rougher again and you'll need a 4WD to really see it. The park is a 60km drive from Musina on Rte 572 to Pont Drift.

Venda

With perhaps the most enigmatic ambience of the Soutpansberg region, this is the traditional homeland of the Venda people, who moved to the area in the early 18th century. Even a short diversion from the freeway takes you through an Africa of mist-clad hilltops, dusty streets and mud huts. A land where myth and legend continue to play a major role in everyday life, Venda is peppered with lakes and forests that are of great spiritual significance, and its distinctive artwork is famous nationwide.

Thohoyandou

POP 70,000

Created as the capital of the apartheid-era Venda homeland, Thohoyandou (Elephant Head) is a scrappy and chaotic town in a lush region of beautiful Venda scenery. It's useful as a base for exploring the Venda region or to overnight on the way to/from Kruger's Punda Maria gate, a 60km drive. The adjacent town of **Sibasa** is 5km north of Thohoyandou.

Sights

Dozens of **art and craft studios** dotted around the lush countryside are open to the public. The region is best known for its raw

THE VENDA & NDEBELE PEOPLES

Limpopo has a rich ethnic tapestry. The main ethnic group, the Venda people, have obscure origins although it's believed that they migrated across the Limpopo River in the early 18th century and settled in the Soutpansberg area. When they arrived they called their new home 'Venda' or 'Pleasant Land'.

The Boers came into contact with the Venda at the end of the 18th century and noted their extensive use of stone to build walls. The Venda were skilled in leatherwork and beadwork, and made distinctive grain vessels that doubled as artwork hung from their huts.

Traditional Venda society shows respect for the very young and the very old – the young having recently been with their ancestors and the old about to join them. The Venda *kgosi* (king) is considered a living ancestor and must be approached on hands and knees.

Women enjoy high status within Venda society and can inherit property from their father if there is no male heir. Rituals cannot be performed unless the oldest daughter of a family is present. One of the most important Venda ceremonies is the *domba* (snake) dance, which serves as a coming-of-age ritual for young women.

A subgroup, the Lemba, regard themselves as the nobility of the Venda. The Lemba have long perplexed scholars as they seem to have had contact with Islam. They themselves claim to be one of the lost tribes of Israel, and DNA testing has shown they have a genetic quality similar to Jewish people elsewhere. Traditionally, they keep kosher, wear head coverings and observe the Sabbath.

Another ethnic group, the Ndebele, entered the region from KwaZulu-Natal at least 100 years before the Venda. The structure of their authority was similar to the Zulu, with several tiers of governance. An *ikozi* (headman) oversaw each community.

Ndebele, who today number around 700,000, are renowned for their beadwork, which goes into making rich tapestries, toys, wall decorations, baskets, bags and clothing. You can see examples of their work at www.thebeadsite.com. Traditionally, women wear copper and brass rings around their arms and necks, symbolising faithfulness to their husbands.

During apartheid, the Venda and Ndebele peoples were forced onto 'homelands' that were given nominal self-rule.

Venda

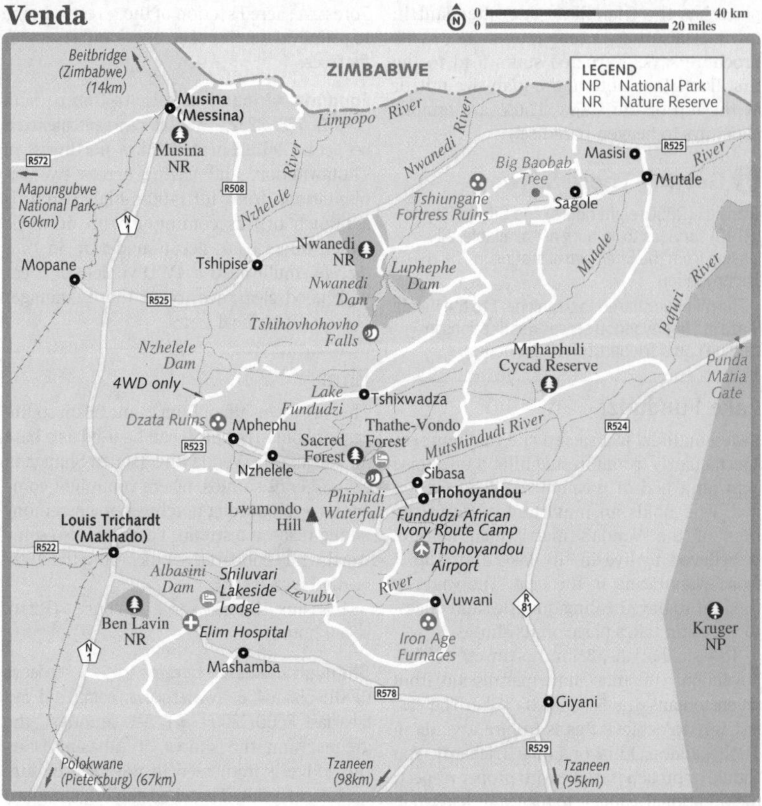

woodcarvings (exemplified by the Venda doyenne Noria Mabasa, whose work adorns Pretoria's Union Buildings); its pottery (often painted silver and maroon using graphite and ochre); and bright, stripy batiks and textiles. Hiring a guide makes finding the studios easy (some can be hidden down dusty backroads) and provides great insight into local culture – a full-day trip costs approximately R1000. Thohoyandou/Sibasa-based guides include **Avhashoni Mainganye** (☎084 725 9613; a.mainganye@yahoo.com) who has a great knowledge of different media and the artists in the area.

The **Ribolla Route** is a self-drive itinerary which allows you to discover the artistic traditions of the Venda and its people in your own time. Check out www.openafrica.org/experiences/route/96-ribolla-open-africa-route and look for Open Africa brochures and maps in tourist offices.

Thohoyandou Arts & Culture Centre ARTS CENTRE
(Punda Maria Rd, Thohoyandou; ⏲8am-4pm) One starting point for cultural explorations is this centre which displays craftwork including carved wood animals, prints, local pottery and traditional drums. A lot of it is for sale. If you get chatting to the artists then you'll be in for a real treat.

Sleeping

Muofhe Graceland Lodge HOTEL $$
(☎015-962 4926; www.muofhegraceland.co.za; Mphephu St; d incl breakfast R900) Overlooking the main drag, Thohoyandou's own Graceland is popular with businesspeople. The white complex's small rooms are a little bland but clean and secure.

Avkhom Hotel HOTEL $$
(☎015-962 1929; www.avkhomhotel.co.za; Main St; s/d R490/690) In a central Thohoyandou location and with bucketloads of rooms, this

place has the friendliest gate attendant in town. It also has decent rooms and, as its brochure says, 'Carpeted stairs lead to the first floor. Take note of the man-size mirror at the top of the stairs. These are famous stairways to heaven-paradise'.

Getting There & Away

Translux (R250, eight hours) and City to City (R190) services to Jo'burg are available, all leaving from the Shell petrol station in Thohoyandou.

The minibus shared taxi rank next to the Venda Plaza in Thohoyandou serves destinations including Louis Trichardt (R40, 1½ hours).

Lake Fundudzi

Lake Fundudzi is a sacred site that emerges spectacularly from forested hills, a turquoise gem on a bed of green velvet. The python god, who holds an important place in the rites of the Venda's matriarchal culture, is believed to live in the lake and stop it from evaporating in the heat. The water is thought to have healing qualities and ancestor worship takes place on its shores.

To visit the lake, 35km northwest of Thohoyandou, you must have permission from its custodians, the Netshiavha tribe. The easiest way to achieve this is to hire a guide in Thohoyandou, Elim or Louis Trichardt. You should approach the lake with proper respect; the traditional salute is to turn your back to it, bend over, and view it from between your legs.

You need 4WD transport to reach the lake, but a car can manage the dirt tracks in the surrounding hills, where there are panoramic viewpoints and the Thathe-Vondo Forest. A sacred section of the forest is home to primeval tangles of creepers and strangler fig trees.

Fundudzi African Ivory Route Camp HUT $
(☎072 778 3252; www.africanivoryroute.co.za; per person R475) Located 25km northwest of Thohoyandou, and gazing across two tea plantations from its 1400m-high perch, is a branch of this community-run network, which offers basic accommodation in *rondavels*. You'll need a 4WD vehicle or a car with good clearance to get there. Manager Nelson offers local tours.

Elim

The tiny township of Elim, some 25km southeast of Louis Trichardt, can be used as a base for touring the Venda and Tsonga-Shangaan art and craft studios, where you might come across a zebra-dung notebook or a ceremony taking place at a studio. There are also some worthwhile cooperatives including the **Twananani weavers**.

Translux buses serve Jo'burg (R240, seven hours).

Shiluvari Lakeside Lodge LODGE $$
(☎015-556 3406; www.shiluvari.com; s/d incl breakfast R600/1200; ❄) Set amongst the greenery on the shores of Albasini Dam, this lodge is immersed in the local culture and countryside. Thatched chalets, standard rooms and a family suite, reached on walkways lined with sculptures, are adorned with local craftwork which can be purchased in the on-site shop. There's also a country restaurant and pub.

SAVING LAKE FUNDUDZI

The importance of Lake Fundudzi cannot be underestimated. The traditional custodians of the lake, the Netshiavha (People of the Pool), consider it a holy place for the burial of their dead.

For scientists, the lake is also special because it's one of South Africa's few natural freshwater lakes. It is believed to have been created 20,000 years ago when a rock slide blocked the path of a river, causing the lake to rise behind it.

Recent decades, however, have seen severe degradation of the lake, including loss of surrounding forest and grassland to plantations. Access has long been a privilege granted by the Netshiavha but this was undermined in the mid-1990s when a road was constructed to the lake's edge, giving open access to the site.

The chief launched a campaign to protect the lake. The Netshiavha, along with neighbouring tribes, implemented laws to limit land use around the lake and mitigate the effects of tourism. Long-term management strategies are being developed by the Mondi Wetlands Project – a joint project of the World Wide Fund for Nature (WWF) and a fellow NGO, the Wildlife & Environmental Society of South Africa.

Mukondeni Pottery ARTS & CRAFTS
(☎076 873 5771; Mukondeni, Hamulima) A group of 15 women producing traditional and contemporary design pottery, including pots, bowls and beads.

VALLEY OF THE OLIFANTS

These days the Valley of the Olifants may be largely devoid of pachyderms, but the subtropical area feels exotic in places. The region is culturally rich, being the traditional home of the Tsonga-Shangaan and Lobedu peoples. Phalaborwa, a popular entry point to the Kruger National Park, is the start of the 'Kruger to Beach' trail to the Mozambican coast. The main town of Tzaneen and the pretty village of Haenertsburg make pleasant bases for trips to the scenic Modjadji and Magoebaskloof areas.

Letaba Valley

The Letaba Valley, east of Polokwane, is subtropical and lush, with tea plantations and fruit farms overlooked by forested hills. At Haenertsburg, known locally as 'the Mountain', Rte 71 climbs northeast over the steep Magoebaskloof Pass. There are plenty of places where you can stop for short hikes that are signposted from the road. A less scenic route to Tzaneen is via Rte 528, which runs along the gentler George's Valley.

Haenertsburg

POP 300

A small mountain hideaway with a great pub and a couple of upmarket restaurants, Haenertsburg is well worth a stop to breathe in the fresh, crisp mountain air. When the mist rolls in over the surrounding pine plantations, it's easy to imagine yourself far away from Africa – in the Pacific Northwest or the Scottish Highlands, perhaps. It makes an excellent alternative base to Tzaneen.

Sights & Activities

There are several good hiking trails near Haenertsburg, including the 11km **Louis Changuion Trail**, which has spectacular views.

With 10-plus dams and four rivers teeming with trout, Haenertsburg is a good place for a spot of fly-fishing. Ask around town, try Pennefather or get in touch with **Mountain Flyfishing** (☎083 255 7817; pirie@mweb.co.za).

War Memorial & Long Tom Monument MEMORIAL
(Mare St) The last Long Tom gun was destroyed here during the second Anglo-Boer War, which became symbolic of the Boer defeat.

Magoebaskloof Adventures ADVENTURE SPORTS
(☎083 866 1546; http://magoebaskloofadventures.co.za) Off Rte 71, this outfit runs adventure trips in the area, including kloofing (canyoning), tubing, fly-fishing, mountain biking, horse riding and canopy tours.

Sleeping

Bali Will Will CAMPGROUND, GUESTHOUSE $
(☎015-276 2212; camping per person R70, s/d incl breakfast R355/620) About 4km out of town and off a dirt road, this farm has a beautiful, scenic forest location and great camping possibilities, along with bed and breakfast and self-catering options.

Black Forest Mountain Lodge LODGE $
(☎082 572 9781; www.wheretostay.co.za/blackforestlodge; Black Forest; camping/cabins R100/500) You want privacy? You can have privacy. Set among a gorgeous forested landscape, this lodge is 4km from town along a dirt road of varying quality, and is well signposted.

Pennefather CABIN $$
(☎015-276 4885; www.thepennefather.co.za; Rissik St; s/d R450/650) Part of a complex containing antiques, junk, a museum and secondhand books, this olde-worlde place run by charming older women is hot property, especially at weekends. One of its major assets is its short walking distance to the Iron Crown and Red Plate. The red-roofed cottages have comfortable interiors featuring fireplaces and kitchenettes.

Eating & Drinking

Minki's CAFE $
(☎015-276 4781; breakfast R35-55, mains R60; ⌚8.30am-4pm Mon-Sat, to 3pm Sun; 📶) Combining an old-fashioned gift shop with gourmet treats, this little operation also has an excellent coffee shop. Try the *tramezzini* (small Italian sandwiches) for breakfast or the springbok carpaccio for lunch. Best coffee in town.

DON'T MISS

A POTTERY STOP

Afrikania (☎015-781 1139; www.afrikania.co.za) For a coffee stop and a browse through some wonderful locally made pottery at a little, landscaped, grass-roots initiative, stop at Afrikania on your way to/from Tzaneen. The pottery reflects traditional patterns found among the Tsonga and Pedi people. It's about 90km south of Tzaneen.

Pot 'n Plow PUB $
(☎082 691 5790; pizzas R60-75; ⏲11am-late) A mountain pub well worth ducking into, which attracts every expat and eccentric in the mountains. The Pot 'n Plow is an essential stop for pizza, pool and plenty of chat. It also has a beer garden and a legendary Sunday roast. It's about 10km northeast of Haenertsburg on Rte 71.

Red Plate INTERNATIONAL $
(☎083 305 2851; 161 Rissik St; mains R50-80; ⏲9am-9pm Wed-Sat, to 4pm Sun-Tue;) A classy set-up in the middle of the village, the Red Plate offers dishes using fresh ingredients, including crisp salads, a selection of wraps, homemade burgers and deboned whole trout. Vegetarians also catered for.

Iron Crown PUB $$
(☎015-276 4755; Rissik St; mains R70-85; ⏲10.30am-9pm Tue-Sat, to 4pm Sun) The village pub has a warm country atmosphere made even better by a new beer garden. Decent pub menu and braai options are available; venison pie recommended.

Getting There & Away

A car is definitely your best option for accessing the town and for getting around – the attractions and accommodation are quite spread out.

Magoebaskloof Pass

Magoebaskloof is the escarpment on the edge of the highveld, and the road from here careers down to Tzaneen and the lowveld, winding through plantations and tracts of thick indigenous forest.

There are a number of waterfalls in the area, including the glorious **Debengeni Falls** (De Hoek State Forest; adult R20; ⏲8am-5pm), where a suspension bridge leads between pools. Take Rte 36 from Tzaneen and then look for a sign on the Magoebaskloof Rd to Polokwane.

Of the 10 walking trails in the area, lasting between two and five days, a recommended option is the three-night, 40km **Dokolewa Waterfall Trail**. There are six huts, including some above Debengeni Falls; to book them, contact Komatiland Forests Eco-Tourism (p380) in Nelspruit.

Off Rte 71, near the junction of Rte 36, **Pekoe View Tea Garden** (☎015-305 4999; ⏲10am-5pm) is on the estate where Magoebaskloof tea is grown.

Tzaneen

POP 26,000

An affluent town with a chaotic street layout, Tzaneen makes a very pleasant place to base yourself for a few days on your way to Kruger, down to the Blyde River Canyon or deeper into Limpopo's arts and crafts territory further north. The Letaba Valley's largest town has personality, although when we passed through, the town centre was looking worse for wear, with especially terrible litter. However, there are a few attractions and the cool mountainous retreat of Haenerstsburg is well worth a visit if not an overnight stop. It's often hot around here but sudden downpours cool things off.

Sights & Activities

Tzaneen Museum MUSEUM
(Agatha St; donation welcome; ⏲9am-4pm Mon-Fri, to noon Sat) The town museum has an impressive collection of artefacts, ranging from a 'house guard' totem used by the Rain Queens to some pretty spine-chilling Congolese masks. It's particularly interesting if you're visiting Modjadji or the Venda region.

Kings Walden GARDENS
If steamy Tzaneen is making you droop, climb to this spectacular 300-sq-metre English garden at 1050m in the African bush. The views of the Drakensberg Mountains from the sweeping lawn are interrupted only by a lightning-struck tree, and leafy walkways wind away from the refreshing swimming pool. From town, take Joubert St south then turn right onto Claude Wheatley St. There's no charge for the gardens but it's good form to buy a drink or even a slice of cake from the restaurant.

Sleeping

Satvik Backpackers Village BACKPACKERS $
(015-307 3920; satvik@pixie.co.za; George's Valley Rd; camping per person R60, dm/d/cottages R100/280/540) These cottages, on a slope above a dam, have a kitchen and a braai along with views of wooded hills. Activities such as fishing are offered, but watch out for the crocs and hippos. Head out of town south on Agatha St; it's about 4km away.

Avispark Lodge GUESTHOUSE $$
(015-307 5460; www.avisparklodge.co.za; 2 Aqua Ave; r incl breakfast R450-700;) This place has a bunch of rooms at varying prices; best bet is to see a few. Nos 1 and 2 in the main house are great value and No 2 even has a balcony. The cheaper rooms can be a little dark and dingy. With friendly service, it's a good option for most folk, especially families. There's a handy pub and supermarket across the road.

Silver Palms Lodge HOTEL $$
(015-307 9032; Monument St; r incl breakfast from R650;) This good-value hotel has some pleasant touches such as marula-based shower gel in the smart rooms. Cheaper on the weekends (but with no breakfast included), the luxury rooms are in better shape. The big plus to staying here is the gorgeous, sunken swimming pool, which backs onto a bar…

★**Kings Walden** HOTEL $$$
(015-307 3262; www.kingswalden.co.za; Old Coach Rd, Agatha; s/d incl breakfast R1000/1750;) The sizeable rooms are as dreamy as the gardens and mountains they overlook, with fireplaces, antiquated prints everywhere and bathrooms you could get lost in. Picnic hampers can be provided; four-course dinners are R320 per person.

Eating

★**Market Cafe** CAFE $
(Tzaneen Lifestyle Centre; mains R35-60; 8am-6pm) The new 'lifestyle' centre is sanitised (yes, you overlook a carpark) but the Market Cafe – a small operation that's part of a larger food market here – delivers quality breakfasts, light lunches (salads and wraps) and more substantial meals such as steaks and pizza. Try the brie, bacon and cranberry-sauce croissant. Excellent coffee.

Tzaneen

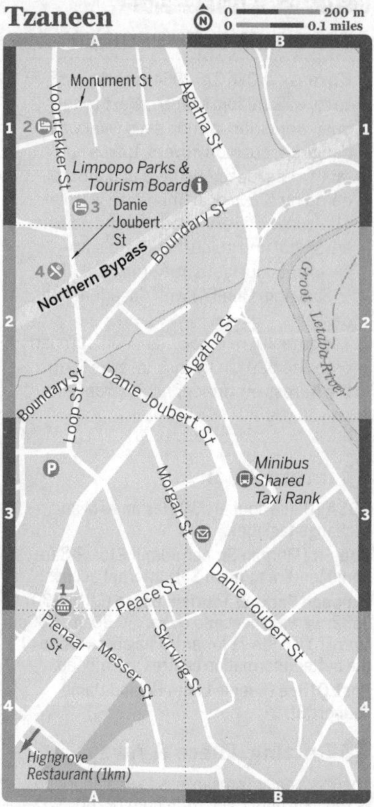

Tzaneen

Sights
1 Tzaneen Museum A3

Sleeping
2 Avispark Lodge A1
3 Silver Palms Lodge A1

Eating
4 Market Cafe A2

Highgrove Restaurant INTERNATIONAL $$
(015-307 7242; Agatha St; mains R70-90; 7am-8.30pm) One of Tzaneen's most reliable restaurants, Highgrove serves dishes including steaks with a choice of eight sauces, pasta, burgers and hearty breakfasts. With a lovely poolside setting, it's the best spot in town for dinner.

OFF THE BEATEN TRACK

TRADITIONAL EMBROIDERY

Kaross (☎086 276 2964; www.kaross.co.za; ⏰8am-4pm Mon-Fri) Next to the busy workshop, a shop sells vivid wall hangings, cushion covers, tunics and table mats, designed here and embroidered by 1200 local Shangaan women. The quality is very good and the designs are skilful and colourful. There's an excellent courtyard **cafe** (mains R50; ⏰8am-4pm Mon-Fri) with decadent desserts.

Some 30km east of Tzaneen, turn left onto Rte 529 to Giyani and, after 9km, the Kaross embroidery cooperative is on your right.

Information

ABSA (Danie Joubert St) Has an ATM and exchange facilities.

Copy-it (Morgan St; per 30min R15; ⏰8am-5pm Mon-Fri, to noon Sat) Internet access.

Limpopo Parks & Tourism Board (☎015-307 3582; www.tzaneeninfo.co.za; ⏰7.30am-4.30pm Mon-Fri) On Rte 71 towards Phalaborwa; one of the better information centres in Limpopo.

Post Office (Lannie Lane) Behind Danie Joubert St.

Getting There & Away

There is a daily Translux bus to Phalaborwa (R150, one hour), and to Jo'burg (R260, 5½ hours) and Polokwane (R150, 1¾ hours).

Most minibus shared taxis depart from the rank behind the Tzaneng Mall; destinations include Polokwane (R70, two hours).

Modjadjiskloof (Duivelskloof)

POP 1850

Modjadjiskloof, named Duivelskloof by European settlers after the devilish time they had getting their caravans up and down the surrounding hills, is a gateway to some worthwhile stops.

Modjadji Nature Reserve NATURE RESERVE
(adult/vehicle R10/20; ⏰7am-4.30pm) Covering 30,000 sq metres, this reserve protects forests of the ancient Modjadji cycad. In the summer mists, the reserve and surrounding Bolobedu Mountains take on an ethereal atmosphere. Take the Modjadji turn-off from Rte 36 about 10km north of Modjadjiskloof (Duivelskloof); after 10km, turn left at the signpost to the reserve, then right at the signpost 12km further, and continue for 5km.

Sunland Big Baobab GARDENS
(☎082 413 2228; www.bigbaobab.co.za; Sunland Nursery; adult/child R15/free; ⏰9am-4pm) On the road to Modjadji, look out for signs to this 22m-high boabab, with a 47m circumference. According to carbon dating it's 6000 years old. A bar occupies the two cavities inside the tree, which 60 drinkers have squeezed into.

Modjadji African Ivory Route Camp CAMPGROUND $
(☎015-781 0690; www.africanivoryroute.co.za; rondavels per person R460) This camp is 5km into the Modjadji Nature Reserve, accessible by car if it hasn't rained recently. Part of a community-run network, the camp offers basic *rondavels* and hiking trails among the 800-year-old cycads. A *rondavel* with meals and activities is R1080.

Ndzalama Private Wildlife Reserve

Ndzalama Private Wildlife Reserve WILDLIFE RESERVE
(☎083 627 8175; www.ndzalamalodge.co.za; Letsitele) With animals including four of the Big Five (everything but buffalo is represented) and klipspringer antelopes roaming its 80-plus sq km, Ndzalama Wildlife Reserve is named after a locally revered rock formation, which couldn't be more phallic. No day visitors are allowed into the reserve (you have to stay at least one night); book ahead to stay in a self-catering stone-and-thatch chalet (per person R1500). Meals are available on request.

To get to Ndzalama from Tzaneen, follow Rte 71 for 35km and turn left onto the tarred road to Eiland. After 16km, turn right onto the dirt road and you'll see the reserve entrance after 4km.

Phalaborwa

POP 13,500

Phalaborwa makes an ideal starting point if you're intending to explore central and northern Kruger. For people with limited time in South Africa, it is possible to visit Kruger by flying from Jo'burg to Phalaborwa and hiring a car at the airport (with its thatched terminal building). Phalaborwa rocks between suburban tidiness and the bush, with a green belt in the centre and the occasional warthog grazing on a lawn.

The town is also a gateway to Mozambique – it's possible to drive across Kruger and into Mozambique via the Giriyondo Gate in a vehicle with good clearance.

🏃 Activities

Leka Gape CULTURAL TOUR
(☑ 076 986 9281; www.lekagape.de; R650) A half-day township tour with an NGO in Lulekani, 13km northwest of Phalaborwa, includes a visit to a handicrafts workshop. Call Danielle to book; if she is not running a tour on the day you want to go, she may be able to pass you onto other local operators.

Hans Merensky Estate GOLF
(☑ 015-781 3931; www.hansmerensky.com; 3 Copper Rd; 9-/18-hole round R260/455) Just south of Phalaborwa is an 18-hole championship golf course with a difference: here you have to hold your shot while wildlife, elephants included, crosses the fairways. Be careful – the wildlife is 'wild'.

Africa Unlimited TOURS
(☑ 015-781 7466; www.africaunltd.co.za) Offers activities including culture tours, river cruises, bush walks, visits to animal rehabilitation centres and trips through Kruger to Mozambique.

🛏 Sleeping

There are scores of places to stay in Phalaborwa, many of them just out of town in the bush.

Elephant Walk BACKPACKERS $
(☑ 082 495 0575, 015-781 5860; elephant.walk@nix.co.za; 30 Anna Scheepers Ave; camping R100, dm/s/tw without bathroom R120/220/340, B&B s/d R340/550; ❄) Close enough to Kruger to hear the lions roar, this is a great spot to plan your foray into the park. The owners have quite a few rules that they ask guests to stick to, such as no noise after 10pm. It also has an excellent range of reasonably priced tours and activities. The rooms with en suite are more like a guesthouse.

Daan & Zena's APARTMENT $
(☑ 015-781 6049; www.daanzena.co.za; 15 Birkenhead St; r/flats R450/R900; ❄ @ ☷) Though looking a bit worn around the edges these days, Daan & Zena's is brought to life by lashings of colour and a friendly atmosphere, and it still presents good value. The two-room flats across the road from the main establishment are spacious, well equipped, and No 1 has a door leading onto a lovely grassed area.

★ Kaia Tani GUESTHOUSE $$
(☑ 015-781 1358; www.kaiatani.com; 29 Boekenhout St; r per person incl breakfast R720; ❄ ☷ ☷) This 'exclusive guesthouse' delivers a lot of style for your money. The six rooms with traditional African furniture have flourishes such

LIMPOPO PHALABORWA

MODJADJI, THE RAIN QUEEN

In Africa it is unusual for a woman to be sovereign of a tribe, but the Rain Queen is an exception. The queen resides in the town of GaModjadji in the Bolobedu district near Modjadjiskloof. Every year, around November, she traditionally presides over a festival held to celebrate the coming of the rains. The *indunas* (tribal headmen) select people to dance, to call for rain, and to perform traditional rituals, including male and female initiation ceremonies. After the ceremony, the rain falls. The absence of rain is usually attributed to some event such as the destruction of a sacred place – a situation resolved only with further ritual.

Henry Rider Haggard's novel *She* is based on the story of the original Modjadji, a 16th-century refugee princess. Successive queens have lived a secluded lifestyle, confined to the royal kraal, and following the custom of never marrying, but bearing children by members of the royal family. However, the currrent millennium has been a time of crisis for the matrilineal line.

In June 2001 Rain Queen Modjadji V died in Polokwane. In an unfortunate turn of events, her immediate heir, Princess Makheala, had died three days earlier, and it wasn't until April 2003 that the 25-year-old Princess Mmakobo Modjadji was crowned Modjadji VI. It was raining on the day of the ceremony, which was taken to be a good omen. Sadly, Modjadji VI passed away two years later, leaving a baby daughter, Princess Masalanabo. The princess may accede when she reaches the age of 16, but traditionalists point out that her father is not a member of the royal family, and the clan has lost a lot of respect.

NETWORKED NAPS

A provincewide tourism network to look out for is **African Ivory Route** (015-781 0690; www.africanivoryroute.co.za; Bollanoto Tourism Centre, Phalaborwa). Its 10 community-run camps offer accommodation in *rondavels* or safari tents, costing from R125 per twin unit. Meals, tribal dances and activities are on offer; when reserving, call the camp (see website for details) as well as the head office.

as rope-lined wooden walls, and a thatch restaurant-bar overlooks the rock swimming pool. It's off Essenhout St.

Cajori Hotel HOTEL $$
(015-781 3156; http://cajori.wozaonline.co.za; 39 Palm Ave; r incl breakfast R680;) The only hotel in town does a pretty decent job of providing comfortable accommodation. It's located in a central spot and rooms are a good size, although bathrooms are on the smallish side. The one great feature are the enormous, sink-in-and-smile beds.

Sefapane LODGE $$$
(015-780 6700; www.sefapane.co.za; Copper Rd; s/d standard rondavel from R950/1500;) With a whiff of exclusivity, this 1000-sq-metre resort has a restaurant and sunken bar, a long list of safaris for guests and mushroom-shaped *rondavels*. There are spacious self-catering 'safari houses' overlooking a dam, and donations are made to projects for local children. Lots of packages available, from two to seven nights.

Eating

★**Buffalo Pub & Grill** PUB $$
(015-781 0829; 1 Lekkerbreek St; mains R80-150; 11am-late;) If you've emerged from Kruger feeling like a hungry lion, stop here for some pub grub. It's a very meat-driven menu – for a lean steak alternative try the ostrich or impala fillet. Excellent service and there's a terrace for alfresco dining.

Villa Luso PORTUGUESE $$
(Molengraaf St; mains R65-100; 8am-late;) The influence of the Portuguese owner can be seen on the Villa's menu: seafood, buffalo wings, surf and turf and Portuguese steaks are a few of the dishes on offer. With a garden bar (and long cocktail list), it's a pleasant place to dine. Also has a kids playground.

Information

Bollanoto Tourism Centre (072 216 7802; www.phalaborwa.co.za; cnr Hendrick van Eck & Pres Steyn Sts; 7am-5pm Mon-Fri, to 1pm Sat) Helpful information office.

Cyber World (Tambotie St, Tambotie Park; wi-fi per hour R40, internet per hour R50) Good, reliable internet connections.

Getting There & Away

AIR

The regional carrier **Airlink** (015-781 5823; www.flyairlink.com) has an office at the airport, and flies daily to Jo'burg (from R2050). The airport is 2km north of town.

BUS

Sure Turn Key Travel (015-781 7760; Sealene St) is the local agent for Translux and City to City buses; it's right behind the Shoprite supermarket. Sure Turn Key also has an office (015-781 2498) at the airport.

Translux connects Phalaborwa with Jo'burg (R270, seven hours) via Tzaneen (R150, one hour), Polokwane (R190, 2½ hours) and Pretoria (R270, six hours); City to City buses travel to Jo'burg (R220, 9½ hours) via Middelburg.

CAR

Hiring a car is often the cheapest way of seeing Kruger National Park, starting at about R280 per day. Major car-rental companies have offices at the airport, generally open 8am to 5pm Monday to Friday and to meet flights or by appointment at weekends.

First Car Rental (015-781 1500; Phalaborwa airport)

Hoedspruit

POP 3500

Just 70km northwest of Kruger's Orpen gate, Hoedspruit makes a convenient launch pad for exploring the park's central and southern sections.

Sleeping & Eating

Loerie Guesthouse GUESTHOUSE $
(015-793 3990; www.loerieguesthouse.com; 85 Jakkals St; s/d R370/550;) This guesthouse specialises in warm welcomes. The best rooms are upstairs in the separate accommodation wing out the back. All rooms are a decent size and well set up. Breakfast is available (R65).

Pangolin Bush Camp CAMPGROUND $$
(073 049 7494; www.shikwari.co.za; Lydenburg Rd (Rte 36); rondavels R600;) This utterly

THE MIGHTY MARULA

The silhouette of a marula tree at dusk is one of the more evocative images of the African bush, but the real value of this mighty tree is what comes out of it.

In summer the female marula sags under the weight of its pale yellow fruit. Chacna baboons love the stuff and you can see them by the road chomping on the golden delicacy, which has four times as much vitamin C as an orange. Elephants, also big marula fans, spend their days ramming into tree trunks to knock the fruit to the ground. Their somewhat obsessive behaviour has led to the marula being dubbed the 'elephant tree'.

Local people have long valued the marula fruit's medicinal qualities, particularly its aphrodisiac nature, and it is now used in a popular cream liqueur. Limpopo's answer to Baileys, Amarula debuted in 1989 and is now available in more than 70 countries.

The best way to enjoy a glass of creamy Amarula is to visit the **Amarula Lapa** (015-781 7766; www.amarula.com; Rte 40; 8am-5pm Mon-Fri, 9am-4pm Sat) FREE, located next to the production plant, 10km west of Phalaborwa. Groups of at least five can visit the plant during harvest season; at other times, exhibits and a seven-minute DVD explain all.

charming self-catering option has delightful *rondavels* set around a pool in a beautiful bush setting. Facilities are communal, including kitchen, bathroom and outdoor shower. There is also a boma with a fire pit and braai facilities. It's a great set-up and would suit families in particular. Pangolin is on the property of luxury Shikwari Bush Lodge, about 35km from Hoedspruit.

Maruleng Lodge HOTEL $$
(015-793 0910; www.marulenglodge.co.za; s/d incl breakfast R470/600;) This lodge has enormous rooms. So big in fact that they're kinda spartan – if you like your space you'll love this place. A recent spruce up, including additional water features, together with the lodge's convenient location – right next to all the services and eating options at the Kamagelo Centre – make it a good bet.

Sleepers Railway Station Restaurant INTERNATIONAL $$
(015-793 1014; Rte 40, Train Station, Hoedspruit Crossings; mains R70-110; breakfast, lunch & dinner Mon-Sat) This old station house is a fantastic venue for devouring quality dishes and has a very extensive menu with local game a speciality (try the organic ostrich medallions). Dine on the outside deck under the branches of two enormous trees.

Cala la Pasta ITALIAN $$
(015-793 0452; Kamagelo Centre; mains R70-100; 8am-4.30pm Mon-Tue, to late Wed-Sat) How a slice of Italiana found its way to Hoedspruit we're not sure, but this place serves up authentic and quality dishes from the motherland. Try the pasta al forno (cream, mushrooms and ham baked in the oven with mozzarella cheese). The food takes a while to prepare but it's well worth the wait.

Getting There & Away

SA Express (0861 729 227; www.flyexpress.aero) flies daily out of **Hoedspruit Eastgate Airport** (Rte 40), 7km south of town, to Jo'burg (from R2100).

City to City runs a daily bus to Jo'burg (R220, 8½ hours).

Acornhoek

Located on the outskirts of this township is the **Mapusha Weavers Cooperative** (072 469 7060; www.mapusha.org; 10am-4pm Mon-Fri); it was established in 1973 to give unemployed women a craft and an income. You can visit the loom-filled workshop next to the Catholic Mission, and take home some of the excellent quality carpets and tapestries.

To get there, continue south on Rte 40 for 5km after the turning for Mafunyani Cultural Village and the Orpen Gate, then turn left towards Acornhoek. After 4.3km, turn right onto a dirt road marked 'Dingleydale' and, after 1.8km, you will see the Catholic Mission on your right.

North West Province

Includes ➡

Best Places to Eat

- ➡ Cape Town Fish Market (p429)
- ➡ Deck (p429)
- ➡ Upper Deck (p437)

Best Places to Stay

- ➡ Palace of the Lost City (p429)
- ➡ Mosetlha Bush Camp (p434)
- ➡ Tau Game Lodge (p434)
- ➡ Bakubung (p433)
- ➡ Kwa Maritane (p433)
- ➡ Masibambane (p427)
- ➡ Sparkling Waters Hotel & Spa (p437)

Why Go?

This stretch of bushveld between Pretoria and the Kalahari is famous for Sun City, the southern hemisphere's answer to Las Vegas. Though its slot machines and kitsch edifices are grotesquely fascinating, you may prefer a different kind of gambling in nearby Pilanesberg National Park. Wager that lions and rhinos will wander to the waterhole you have staked out – sightings on self-drive safaris come with a serendipitous thrill.

Alternatively, improve your odds of spotting elusive predators in Pilanesberg and Madikwe Game Reserve by joining a guided drive or walk. And for that once-in-a-lifetime, romantic *Out of Africa*–style experience, a night in the bush at Madikwe's exclusive lodges can't be beaten.

Conveniently, these opportunities to encounter both big cats and one-armed bandits are all within four hours' drive of Johannesburg (Jo'burg). En route, the Magaliesberg area offers detours from the N4, ranging from zip lining to rural accommodation near Rustenburg.

When to Go

Rustenburg

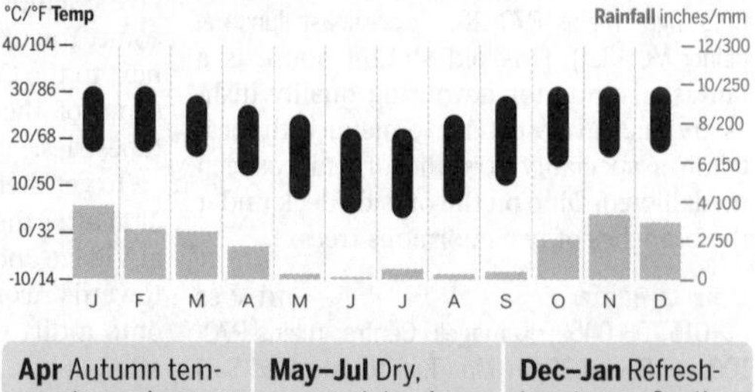

Apr Autumn temperatures drop; wildlife-watching conditions are optimum through to the winter.

May–Jul Dry, sunny winter days, and (bar mid-June to early July) school terms mean thinner crowds.

Dec–Jan Refreshing storms; South Africans head to the coast, leaving more room here for foreign travellers.

History

The North West Province takes in much of the area once covered by the fragmented apartheid homeland of Bophuthatswana (Bop), a dumping ground for thousands of 'relocated' Tswana people. The nominally independent homeland became famous for the excesses of the white South African men who visited its casinos and pleasure resorts for interracial encounters with prostitutes – an illegal practice elsewhere in South Africa.

The area was the site of a complex and sophisticated Iron Age civilisation, centred on the 'lost city' of Kaditshwene, about 30km north of modern-day Zeerust. The people who lived here had an economy so developed they traded copper and iron jewellery with China. By 1820, when European missionaries first visited the city, they found it to be bigger than Cape Town. In the end, Kaditshwene's peace-loving inhabitants proved no match for the Sotho, displaced by Zulu incursions into the Free State. The city was sacked by a horde of 40,000 people in the 1830s and fell into ruins.

Getting There & Around

Convenient for Rustenburg and the Magaliesberg, **Lanseria International Airport** (011-367 0300; www.lanseria.co.za; off Rte 512) is 30km south of Hartbeespoort Dam en route to Jo'burg. Kulula.com has daily flights from Lanseria to Cape Town and Durban; **Mango** (www.flymango.com) flies daily to Cape Town. Car-hire companies operate from the airport.

Hiring a car is the easiest way to travel around the province. Secure parking is readily available at accommodation, restaurants and sights.

Rustenburg

POP 105,000

Sitting on the edge of the Magaliesberg range, Rustenburg is a big country town with an urban grittiness to its crowded central business district. Pedestrians weave between honking cars on Nelson Mandela Dr (the main drag through the long downtown area), and sidewalks heave with vendors selling mobile-phone cases and the like in front of takeaway chicken shops and undertakers.

It's Rustenburg's location, however, just 40km southeast of Sun City and Pilanesberg National Park, that is its main selling point – it's an option for travellers wishing to visit these major attractions without paying high accommodation rates.

Sights & Activities

Royal Bafokeng Stadium STADIUM
(off Rte 565) Northwest of town 15km, en route to Sun City, is this stadium, which hosted first- and second-round 2010 FIFA World Cup football matches. Built in 1999, it seats more than 40,000 spectators and its major shareholders are members of the Bafokeng tribe.

Sleeping

Bushwillows B&B B&B $
(082 680 5890; wjmcgill@lantic.net; r per person incl breakfast R250;) This country retreat is owned by local wildlife artist Bill McGill, whose paintings decorate the breakfast room. Birdwatching tours to areas such as Pilanesberg are offered. Coming from the Waterfall Mall, look for the white sign on the right after 5km. From there, it's 2km up the hill.

The rooms are basic and the decor frozen in time, but this matters little in light of the warm welcome you'll get, and the wonderful view of the Magaliesberg from the terrace.

Hodge Podge Backpacker Lodge HOSTEL $
(084 698 0417; www.hodgepodgebackpackers.co.za; Plot 66, Kommiesdrift; camping/dm R70/180, s/d from R350/500;) Set below some impressive cliffs, Hodge Podge gives a taste of slow-paced country life up a rocky red track. The outdoor pool is refreshing in the heat and the verandah bar is ideal for sundowners. Colourful bedspreads and bushveld scenes brighten the dinky en suite cabins; airport shuttles and activities including Sun City and Pilanesberg tours are offered. It's signposted about 10km south of the Waterfall Mall.

★ **Masibambane** GUESTHOUSE $$
(083 310 0583; www.masibambaneguesthouse.co.za; Kroondal; s/d incl breakfast R540/820;) This thatched property is a peaceful, relaxing place, its flowerbeds, mature trees and water features attracting a variety of birdlife, from hoopoes to sunbirds. A three-course dinner (R135) can be organised on weeknights. It's signposted 5km south of Waterfall Mall; the guesthouse is on the right at the end of the paved side-road, just beyond the 'Private Road' sign.

It has a pint-size bar that opens onto a lawn-fronted terrace, and a poolside *lapa* (circular building with low walls and a thatched roof) for braais.

Eating

Most restaurants in Rustenburg are found in the Waterfall Mall (p429), which is sterile but safe and reliable. Options range from standalone restaurants to chains – Woolworths for self-catering plus Spur, Wimpy, Steers, Mugg & Bean and Debonairs Pizza. The mall is surprisingly atmospheric on weekend evenings, when local couples and families eat out.

Steakout Grill STEAKHOUSE **$**
(014-592 0766; Waterfall Mall; mains R75; 10am-10pm) This busy eatery has a small seafood menu but it's the sizeable meat dishes that are the reason it gets crowded most evenings. Try the hunter's steak (with chicken livers in piri piri sauce) or treat yourself to the *eisbein* – a kilo of roasted pork knuckle. Various platters and specials are available.

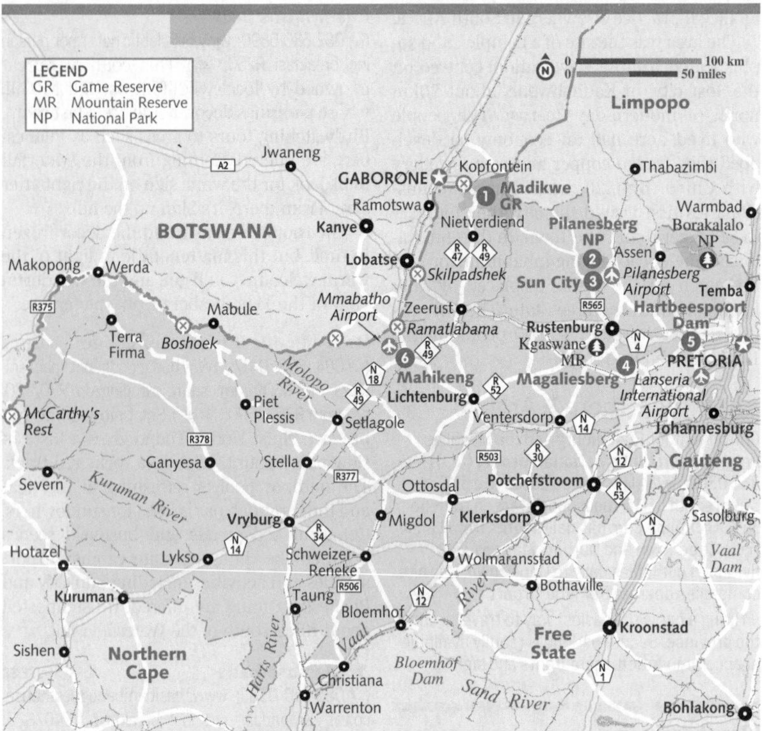

North West Province Highlights

1 Stopping within metres of a pride of lions resting under a thorn tree, on a safari in **Madikwe Game Reserve** (p433).

2 Chilling on the deck of your lodge at **Pilanesberg National Park** (p431), keeping an eye on the bush for Big Five sightings.

3 Body surfing the Valley of the Waves and soaking up **Sun City's** (p429) deliciously gaudy ambience.

4 Riding the scenic aerial cableway to the top of the **Magaliesberg** (p436) range.

5 Circling **Hartbeespoort Dam** (p436) and shopping at Welwitischia Country Market.

6 Touring the exhibits at **Mahikeng Museum** (p435), such as a shredded corrugated iron roof that was struck by the Boers' Long Tom artillery gun.

★Deck STEAKHOUSE $$

(☎014-537 2042; Rte 24; mains R80; ⏰10am-10pm Mon-Sat, 9am-3pm Sun) The menu at this local favourite is hearty even by South African standards. There are combos, baskets, platters, sauces, sides and specials galore, including the double-decker chicken breast. Steaks come in a range of cuts and weights, and lasagne and burgers are classed as light meals. Deck is located a few kilometres south of the Waterfall Mall.

Sit in the smart dining room or slide onto a banquette at a stone-topped table on the centrepiece deck. Children can occupy themselves on a small climbing frame, but note that there are no kids' meals as such.

Cape Town Fish Market SEAFOOD, ASIAN $$

(☎083 400 2005; www.ctfm.co.za; Waterfall Mall; mains R85; ⏰11am-11pm) The dark interior and blue neon lighting of the Waterfall Mall's most stylish restaurant are probably meant to hint at oceanic depths, but what they conjure is more like a nightclub feel. Still, it's a spacious place, the service is efficient, and there's lots of seafood to sample, from salmon and crayfish to kingklip and dorado.

Shopping

Waterfall Mall SHOPPING CENTRE

(Augrabies Ave) Rustenburg's main shopping mall, off Rte 24 around 3km south of the centre, is a safe and relaxing place for shopping.

Information

Tourist Information Centre (☎014-590 3321; www.tourismnorthwest.co.za; Main Rd; ⏰8am-4.30pm Mon-Fri, 8am-noon Sat) Rustenburg's helpful, well-stocked tourist information centre is located in the municipal offices that sprawl between Nelson Mandela Dr and Fatima Bhayat St just west of the Rte 24 turn-off. It provides sundry brochures and a local map.

Getting There & Away

Rustenburg is just off the N4, about 120km northwest of Jo'burg and 110km west of Pretoria. Hiring a car is the only option for getting here and for travelling around the region.

Sun City

At **Sun City** (☎014-557 1544; www.suninternational.com/sun-city; day visitors R60, hotel guests free; ⏰24hr), the legendary creation of entrepreneur Sol Kerzer, Disneyland collides with ancient Egypt in Africa's version of Vegas. Filled with gilded statues of lions and monkeys, acres of artificial beaches, 1200 hotel rooms and line upon line of clinking slot machines, it serves no other purpose than to entertain. Yet even though there's no question this gambling-centric resort is almost grotesquely gaudy, a visit can be pretty damn fun.

Sun City opened in 1979 as an apartheid-era exclusive haven for wealthy whites. These days, one of its most prominent features is the mix of black, white and Asian people who flock here at weekends.

The complex is dominated by the Lost City, an extraordinary piece of kitsch claiming to symbolise African heritage. In fact, it has even less to do with African culture than Disneyland Paris has to do with French, but it's still entertaining.

If you're travelling with children or on a budget, Sun City is a pretty good bargain. The admission fee covers the main attractions, and there are countless activities on offer for an extra outlay. The complex also boasts one of the world's most luxurious hotels, a shrine to all things glittery and golden.

Should the gambling weigh on your conscience, you can rest easy in regards to at least one area – the resort is green. Yes, despite the show of lavishness, Sun City has received awards for practising sustainable, environmentally friendly tourism.

REGAL LUXURY

The **Palace of the Lost City** (www.suninternational.com/sun-city/palace/Pages/default.aspx; Sun City Resort; r incl breakfast from R4600; ❄📶🏊), its turquoise domes overlooking the Valley of the Waves, is a hallucinatory dazzle of glamour in the bushveld. Frequently rated one of the world's top hotels by travel media, it does a good job of exceeding guests' fantasies of luxury.

The 330-plus rooms and suites have flourishes such as butler service and marble bathrooms, but it's the awesome public spaces that hog the limelight. Confronted by the frescos, mosaics and painted ceilings in the grand atriums and halls, restaurants and bars, you almost begin to believe this is the kingly residence of an ancient ruler. In the surrounding pleasure garden, fountains, pools and waterfalls sparkle among the thick foliage.

DON'T MISS

LOST CITY

Sun City's kitsch heart is the Lost City, a sort of mega amusement park in high-glitz style, teeming with attractions that range from botanic gardens to simulated volcanic eruptions. It's reached from the Entertainment Centre via the Bridge of Time, which is flanked by life-size fake elephants.

Most of the fun takes place in the **Valley of the Waves** (www.suninternational.com/sun-city/activities/valleyofwaves; Sun City; adult/child from R120/70, hotel guests free; ⏲9am-6pm Sep-Apr, 10am-5pm May-Aug) water park, overlooked by the towers of the **Palace of the Lost City** (p429) hotel. The water park is gaudy and outlandish even by Sun City's standards – and children love it. Its centrepiece is the **Roaring Lagoon**, a 6500-sq-metre wave pool with a palm-fringed beach. Slides, flumes and chutes such as the 70m-long **Temple of Courage** get the adrenaline flowing; tubing on the **Lazy River** and swimming in the **Royal Bath** pool are two of the slower activities. Another Lost City attraction is its **Maze** (www.suninternational.com/sun-city/activities/maze; adult/child R100/60; ⏲9am-10pm), an enormous labyrinth in the form of an archaeological site.

Sights & Activities

Visit the Welcome Centre for the lowdown on the mind-boggling range of activities available. These include golfing at two courses, jet skiing, parasailing, a crocodile park and zip lining.

Entertainment Centre CASINO

As well as housing smoking and nonsmoking casinos, this two-storey centre has food courts, shops, cinemas and the Superbowl performance venue. Its style might best be described as 'nouveau Flintstone', embellished by a jungle theme.

Mankwe Gametrackers TOUR, OUTDOORS

(☎014-552 5020; www.mankwegametrackers.co.za; Welcome Centre, Entertainment Complex; ⏲5am-7pm) From Sun City, this tour and outdoor activity company runs two three-hour **wildlife drives** (adult/child R460/225) to Pilanesberg National Park each day, usually departing at 5.30am and 5pm (times vary depending on the time of year). It also runs four-hour, early-morning **wildlife walks** (per person R550) in the park for people aged 16 or older.

The company also offers **hot-air balloon flights** (per person R3950) and has an outdoor adventure centre where you can try quad biking, clay-pigeon shooting, archery, paintballing and djembe drumming.

Sleeping & Eating

Sun International (☎011-780 7800; www.suninternational.com/sun-city/accommodation; Sun City) operates the four hotels at the resort, and direct bookings must be made through its reservation centre. Rates can fluctuate significantly depending on occupancy levels; you can usually find a good rate using an online booking engine. All the hotels have a selection of restaurants and there are plenty of fast-food joints in the Entertainment Centre.

If you have your own transport, consider staying in Pilanesberg and visiting Sun City on a day trip. Rustenburg is also close enough to use as a base.

Cascades LUXURY HOTEL $$$

(r incl breakfast from R3300;) In this azure, Mediterranean-inspired environment, waterfalls cascade into a lake and cocktails go down nicely in the beach bar. There are multiple pools, alfresco island dining at Santorini restaurant, and luxuries such as dressing rooms in the palatial bedrooms.

Sun City Hotel CASINO HOTEL $$$

(r incl breakfast from R2800;) Sun City's liveliest hotel (and its first) packs in casinos, slot machines and an entertainment centre, as well as multiple restaurants and bars. With foliage hanging in the jungle-themed foyer, and oversize roulette chips stacked outside the Raj Indian restaurant, it's a good choice for anyone looking for a little hedonism with their gambling.

Sun City Cabanas RESORT $$$

(r incl breakfast from R1800;) Sun City's most informal and affordable option is the best one for families, with facilities and activities for children. The modern rooms have retro stylings and upmarket conveniences, and the atmosphere is laid-back from the balconied foyer onwards. Family rooms with a fold-out sofa and up to eight beds are available.

Information

Welcome Centre (014-557 1544; 8am-7pm Mon-Fri, 8am-10pm Sat & Sun) At the entrance to the Entertainment Centre, this place has maps and just about any information you could possibly need. Also here are lockers and a branch of Hertz.

Getting There & Away

The car park for nonguests is at the entrance, about 2km from the Entertainment Centre. Buses and an elevated monorail Sky Train (the latter offering good views of the complex and Pilanesberg) shuttle people from the car park to the Entertainment Centre and Cascades, passing Sun City Cabanas and Sun City Hotel.

Sun City is less than three hours' drive northwest of Jo'burg, signposted from the N4. Coming from Gauteng on the N4, the most straightforward route is to stay on the freeway past Rustenburg and take Rte 565 via Phokeng and Boshoek.

Tours from Gauteng combine Sun City and Pilanesberg.

Pilanesberg National Park

Occupying an eroded alkaline crater north of Sun City, in a transition zone between the Kalahari and wet lowveld vegetation, the 550-sq-km **Pilanesberg National Park** (014-555 1600; www.parksnorthwest.co.za/pilanesberg; adult/child R65/20, vehicle R20, map R20; 5.30am-7pm Nov-Feb, 6am-6.30pm Mar, Apr, Sep & Oct, 6.30am-6pm May-Aug) is a wonderfully scenic place to see a variety of South African wildlife.

Conceptualised as a back-to-nature weekend escape for nearby city dwellers at the end of the 1970s, Pilanesberg remains a haven where lions, buffaloes and day-trippers still roam. But although the park may appear developed in comparison with some South African wildernesses, don't mistake it for a zoo. The animals roaming the extinct volcano crater are 100% wild.

In 1979, Operation Genesis reclaimed this area of land from agriculture and released 6000 animals into the new park. Today, all the Big Five are here, as are cheetahs, caracals, African wild dogs, jackals, hyenas, giraffes, hippos, zebras, a wide variety of antelope (including sables, elands and kudus) and 300-plus bird species.

Activities

Most lodges in the park offer sunrise and sunset wildlife drives but, with nearly 200km of excellent gravel roads, Pilanesberg was designed with self-drive safaris in mind. Although you have a better chance of spotting cats on one of the ranger-led wildlife drives, steering yourself is cheaper, and more rewarding when you do see an animal. You'll never forget the first time you brake to let a lumbering elephant cross your path, or the size of these animals, and how tough and dirty and wrinkly a pachyderm's rump looks up close.

Driving yourself around the park also means you can move at your own pace. And in Pilanesberg, this means slowly. Devote at least a few hours to sitting with a cooler full of beverages and a pair of binoculars in one of the many public hides around Pilanesberg and wait for the action to come to you. Basically big, raised, covered decks with chairs that have been camouflaged so the wildlife doesn't notice you, these hides have been purposefully constructed next to water sources that attract thirsty animals.

Keep in mind that no matter which way you choose to explore the park, Pilanesberg is still an urban reserve. It's very popular, and the number of folks driving around, combined with the guided-tour vehicles, means there's usually a lot of traffic. Pilanesberg has strict regulations about driving off-road – you can't do it. If your vision of the perfect safari includes a remote bush location, few roads and even fewer cars, drive three hours further northwest and shell out the extra cash to stay in Madikwe Game Reserve instead.

PILANESBERG NATIONAL PARK

Why Go The park is South Africa's most accessible Big Five reserve. Wild dogs can also be sighted as can rarer antelope such as roan and sable. This malaria-free park is less than a three-hour drive from Jo'burg.

When to Go Dry season is best (June to September), when the grass is short and the animals congregate around water holes. January to April the bush is very dense making wildlife-spotting more difficult.

Practicalities The two southern gates are within about 10km of Sun City.

Budget Tips Bring a tent and your own food.

Pilanesberg National Park

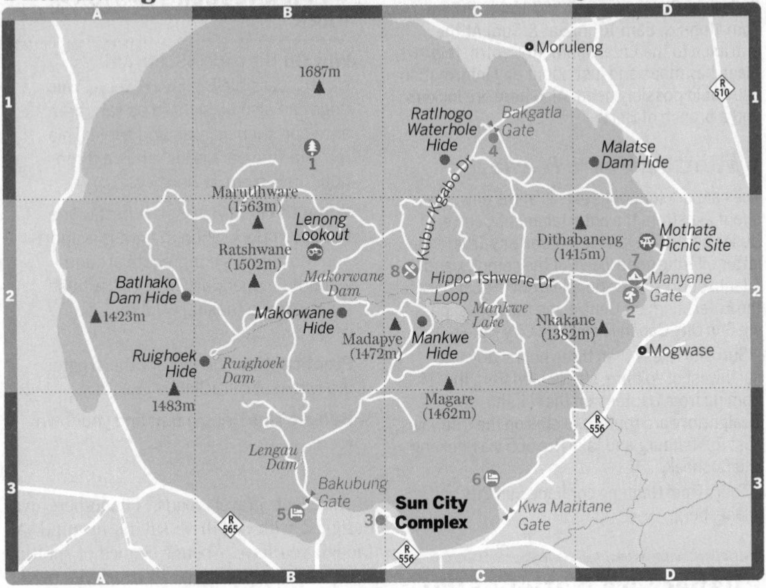

Pilanesberg National Park

Sights
1 Pilanesberg National Park B1

Activities, Courses & Tours
2 Mankwe Gametrackers D2
3 Mankwe Gametrackers B3
4 Mankwe Gametrackers C1

Sleeping
Bakgatla .... (see 4)
5 Bakubung B3
6 Kwa Maritane C3
7 Manyane D2

Eating
8 Pilanesberg Centre C2
Zebra Crossing .... (see 8)

Mankwe Gametrackers SAFARIS
(☎ 014-556 2710; www.mankwegametrackers.co.za; Bakgatla; ⏰ 5am-7pm) This outdoor adventure company runs a variety of organised activities within the park. The three-hour **wildlife drives** (adult/child R395/195; ⏰ 5.30am, 9.30am & 5pm) provide a good introduction to wildlife-watching, and you have a better chance of spotting animals when driven around by a knowledgeable ranger. Another option is a four-hour **wildlife walk** (per person R450); you must be aged 16 or older to take part.

Also on offer are birdwatching excursions, bush braais and breakfasts, and four-hour **hot-air balloon safaris** (R3950 incl 1-hour flight time, breakfast, sparkling wine & transfers). There is a second **office** (☎ 014-555 5469; Manyane) at Manyane.

Sleeping & Eating

There are eight lodges in the park. Manyane, Bakgatla, Bakubung and Kwa Maritane serve lunch to day-trippers and offer bush braais and full-/half-board packages. They also have activities and facilities for children, such as pools, playgrounds and minigolf, and offer discounts to families. There are more-exclusive lodges to the west of Kudu/Kgabo Dr.

Manyane CAMPGROUND, RESORT $$
(☎ 014-555 1000; www.goldenleopardresorts.co.za; camping R180, safari tent s/d incl breakfast from R980/1100, chalet s/d incl breakfast R1470/1590; ❄ 🏊 👪) Manyane's thatched African chalets are comfortable and the safari tents feature a fridge and tea-making facilities. The restaurant borders an enticing pool, with a number of its tables sitting on a patio under thatched awnings. Baboons regularly scamper through the dry and dusty camping area.

Bakgatla CAMPGROUND, RESORT **$$$**
(☎ 014-555 1000; www.goldenleopardresorts.co.za; camping R180, safari tent s/d/tr incl breakfast from R1715/1815/1915, chalet s/d/tr incl breakfast from R2015/2115/2215;) This resort is nestled among some hills and has as its centrepiece a massive U-shaped pool. The restaurant was being extensively renovated when we visited; there's also a superette with basic supplies at the conference centre. The colonial-style chalets and 'executive' safari tents have private patios.

Bakubung LODGE **$$$**
(☎ 014-552 6314; www.legacyhotels.co.za/en/hotels/bakubung; s/d with half board R3140/4430, chalets from R1350;) Bakubung is a sizeable enterprise that has hotel rooms and more than 60 self-catering chalets, all overlooking a waterhole framed by the hills of Pilanesberg; a spa facility was recently added. The smart Marula Grill restaurant serves grilled meat, seafood and pasta.

Kwa Maritane LODGE **$$$**
(☎ 014-552 5100; www.legacyhotels.co.za/en/hotels/kwamaritane; s/d with half board R3000/4200, chalets from R2300;) A sister property to Bakubung, Kwa Maritane's smart thatched rooms encircle its pool, and the restaurant verandah has a bird's-eye view of bush-covered hills and rocky cliffs. The Kwa Lefakeng restaurant puts on various buffets and carveries, or order a la carte out on the terrace.

Pilanesberg Centre SELF-CATERING **$**
(Kgabo Dr; ⏲ 6.30am-5.30pm) In the centre of the park, this place has a gift shop and a store with a reasonable range of basic supplies.

Zebra Crossing CAFE **$**
(mains R40-90; ⏲ 7.30am-4pm Mon-Fri, 7.30am-4.30pm Sat & Sun) A cafe with a large terrace that provides good views of the surrounding terrain. It serves pizza, burgers, wraps and salads, plus some kids' meals.

ℹ Getting There & Away

Tours from Gauteng combine Pilanesberg and Sun City. Bakubung and Kwa Maritane gates are convenient if you're driving from Sun City. If you're driving down from Limpopo on Rte 510 (between Rustenburg and Thabazimbi), Manyane and Bakgatla gates are your closest entry point.

ℹ Getting Around

Kubu/Kgabo Dr, crossing the park between Bakubung and Bakgatla gates, is tarred; as are Tau Link and Tshwene Dr, which link Kubu/Kgabo Dr and Manyane gate. The gravel roads are in good condition and passable in cars.

There is a 40km/h speed limit in the park and you can't go much faster on the roads skirting Pilanesberg. Cattle and donkeys wander onto the road; locals may wave to warn you of a herd ahead.

Madikwe Game Reserve

Madikwe (☎ 018-350 9931; www.parksnorthwest.co.za/madikwe; adult/child R160/65) is the country's fourth-largest reserve, covering 760 sq km of bushveld, savannah grassland and riverine forest on the edge of the Kalahari. It offers Big Five wildlife-watching and dreamy lodging among striking (and malaria-free) red sand and clay thorn bushveld.

Madikwe does not allow self-drive safaris or day visitors, which means you must stay at one of its 16 lodges to explore the reserve. Experiencing Madikwe isn't cheap, but you get what you pay for at these exclusive bush hideaways. The animals have become used to the sturdy open-sided jeeps and don't view them as a threat. So when your guide pulls up to a herd of buffalo and cuts the engine, you usually have time to snap some good shots without your subjects tearing off. Rangers also communicate via radio with the other drivers in the reserve, so if a family of lions napping in the shade of a thorn tree, or a bull elephant in musk, pursuing a female, is spotted nearby, your driver will hear about it. Restrictions on driving off-road are minimal and the jeeps are tough enough to tackle most terrain, getting you close to the animals.

Madikwe was formed in 1991 with a dual mandate to protect endangered wildlife and to use sustainable tourism initiatives to create jobs for the poor, remotely located local people. A massive translocation operation reintroduced more than 10,000 once-indigenous animals, whose numbers had been depleted by hunting and farming. The operation took more than seven years to complete, with animals (including entire herds of elephants) being flown or driven in from other Southern African reserves. Madikwe, run as a joint venture between the North West Parks & Tourism Board, the private sector and local communities, has ultimately provided the promised jobs, as well as a home for healthy numbers of all the Big Five, a flourishing population of endangered African wild dogs and 350-plus bird species.

MADIKWE GAME RESERVE

Why Go Because only the lodges' trained rangers are allowed to run tours in the reserve, the chances of seeing wildlife are better here than at Pilanesberg or even Kruger. The reserve is well known for its large lion population, and wild dog sightings are possible.

When to Go A year-round destination but May to September is the best time for wildlife-watching as animals concentrate around waterholes and the vegetation thins out.

Practicalities Gates are open from 6am to 6pm, but organised night drives do run later in the evening. It is about 3½ hours by car from Johannesburg and Pretoria.

Budget Tips The best time to look for discounts is the low season – this varies between lodges, but May to August is generally quiet. Staying for a few nights also reduces the daily rate. Check the following websites for discounts and reviews of lodges:

- www.madikwegamereserve.net
- www.safarinow.com
- www.uyaphi.com
- madikwe.safari.co.za

Sleeping & Eating

Most lodges include two wildlife drives in their full-board rates. Advance booking is mandatory: you will not be allowed through the gates without a reservation (the guard will telephone your lodge to check you have a booking). Visits to Madikwe normally run from lunchtime until late the following morning.

★Mosetlha Bush Camp & Eco Lodge — LODGE $$$

(☎011-444 9345; www.thebushcamp.com; Abjaterskop gate; s/d per person full board R2495/3990) Madikwe's second-oldest lodge is also the reserve's only non-five-star option, but Mosetlha's relatively low rates are not its only attraction. With nine open-fronted cabins around the camp fire, Mosetlha is truly off the grid – it has no electricity or running water. Staying in the unfenced camp, which animals wander into at night, is romantic rather than rough.

The ecolodge features in Hitesh Mehta's authoritative book on the subject, *Authentic Ecolodges*. It made it into Mehta's 'innovative technology' category for its donkey boilers, bucket shower and VIP toilet (ventilation-improved pit). Paraffin lamps stand in for bedside lamps, conversation for TV, and the meals are as delicious as the bushveld air.

Tau Game Lodge — LODGE $$$

(☎011-466 8715; www.taugamelodge.com; Tau gate; chalet per person full board R3600;) When it comes to value for money, Tau is one of the park's best bets. The 30 cosy thatched chalets have giant bathtubs, massive outdoor bush showers, huge beds, and private decks for watching the waterhole action – improved a few years ago by the introduction of a croc family of five. Also on-site are a spa and curio shop.

The Tau Foundation seeks to benefit the local people, and guests can visit schools and community schemes.

Buffalo Ridge Safari Lodge — LODGE $$$

(☎011-234 6500; www.buffaloridgesafari.com; Wonderboom gate; chalet per person full board R4250;) This swish lodge exemplifies the sustainable community-based tourism envisioned by Madikwe's founders – owned by the Balete people from the local village of Lekgophung, it was the first of its kind in South Africa. Designed by a well-known local architect, Buffalo Ridge has eight ultraprivate thatched chalet suites that blend seamlessly into the bushveld.

Done up in neutral colours, the rooms have huge sliding-glass doors that lead onto private decks and offer lots of natural light. A ravine bridge connects the chalets to the main lodge, which is an impressive place to eat dinner.

Jaci's Lodges — LODGE $$$

(☎083 700 2071; www.madikwe.com; Molatedi gate; r per person full board from R2995;) For panache and design flair, Jaci's contiguous lodges – Safari Lodge and Tree Lodge – are excellent places to indulge. Safari Lodge's eight rooms are constructed to feel like tents, with canvas siding and outdoor showers made from natural stone. Handmade ceramic fireplaces and private decks with waterhole views complete the elegantly natural picture. There are discounts for children under 12, child minders and wildlife drives geared towards families.

Even more exclusive, Tree Lodge brushes the canopy, with elevated rooms built around trees and connected by walkways. Constructed from rosewood and thatch, the eight abodes are luxurious but also built to let nature flow in – while mostly pleasant, this can mean unwanted visitors such as (in rare cases) snakes.

Getting There & Away

Madikwe is next to the Kopfontein gate/Tlokweng gate border crossing with Botswana, about 400km northwest of Johannesburg and Pretoria via the N4 and Rte 47/49 (the road is referred to by both numbers).

Madikwe's main gates are Abjaterskop and Wonderboom, adjoining Rte 47/49 on the reserve's western side; Tau and Deerdepoort on the northern side; and Molatedi on the eastern side. All the lodges can be reached from Rte 47/49; when you make a reservation, your lodge will give you directions.

There is one charter flight per day between OR Tambo International Airport in Jo'burg and the landing strip in Madikwe. Tickets cost around R4000 return, and are arranged through your lodge at the time of booking.

If driving yourself from Madikwe to Sun City and Pilanesberg, ask your lodge for directions and take the back roads. This route is quicker and bypasses the R75 charge at the Swartruggens toll gate on the N4. This shortcut is not recommended en route to Madikwe as it's trickier in that direction and getting lost is more likely.

Without your own transport, the best option is to organise a transfer through your lodge. Alternatively, take a Gaborone (Botswana) bus and arrange for your lodge to pick you up from the Kopfontein border crossing, where the bus will stop.

Mahikeng (Mafikeng)

POP 16,000

The capital of North West Province is a friendly place with a sizeable middle-class black population. It's quite rundown and not worth a special visit, but if you're passing, Mahikeng Museum makes an interesting pit stop.

Some locals still refer to the town as 'Mafikeng', which it was called until the name change was approved in 2010.

History

Mafeking (as the Europeans called it) was the administrative capital of the British Protectorate of Bechuanaland (present-day Botswana). The small frontier town, led by British colonel Lord Baden-Powell, was besieged by Boer forces from October 1899 to May 1900. The siege was in some ways a civilised affair, with the Boers coming into town on Sundays to attend church. The Baralong and Mfengu peoples, however, sustained casualties in the service of the colonialists and saw their herds of cattle raided by the Boers for food. During the siege, Baden-Powell created a cadet corps for the town's boys, which was the forerunner to his Boy Scout movement.

Mahikeng and Mmabatho were once twin towns about 3km apart but were combined under one name. Mmabatho, built as the capital of the 'independent' homeland of Bophuthatswana, became famous for the monumental and absurd buildings erected by controversial Bophuthatswana president Lucas Mangope.

Sights

Mahikeng Museum MUSEUM
(018-381 0773; Martin St, cnr Carrington St; admission by donation; 8am-4pm Mon-Fri, 10am-12.30pm Sat) Among the many displays in this excellent regional museum are an exhibit charting the rise of the Boy Scout Movement and a presentation on the famous 217-day siege, with original photographs and documents, and information about the role played by the town's black population. It occupies the former town hall, which was built in 1904.

When we visited the museum, it was closed for lengthy renovations. While it was expected that the exhibits would remain basically unchanged, the telephone number, opening hours and entry fee are likely to change; check these with the town's information centre.

Sleeping & Eating

There are numerous guesthouses on the suburban streets east of the centre, signposted from Shippard St. The **Crossing Mall** (Sekame Rd, cnr Nelson Mandela Dr) has chain restaurants including News Cafe, Ocean Basket and Spur.

Ferns Country House GUESTHOUSE $$
(018-381 5971; 12 Cooke St; s/d from R600/700;) Set in the residential area east of the centre, Ferns is a quiet haven in the city. Ask to see a selection of rooms before you take one – each has a different aesthetic, and

some are much larger than others and include a small lounge setting. There's a good on-site **bar-restaurant** (mains R80) if you don't feel like venturing too far for lunch, dinner or a drink.

Protea Hotel Mafikeng HOTEL $$
(018-381 0400; www.proteahotels.com/mahikeng; 80 Nelson Mandela Dr; s/d from R835/1050;) The Protea is a stylish accommodation option, and one of the more pleasant places in town to loiter, with its pillars and the vintage photos of old Mahikeng decorating reception. Rooms feature white fluffy duvets with lots of pillows, heavy curtains, mood lighting and international TV channels. Facilities include a bar and restaurant.

Purple Peppa Cafe CAFE $
(071 845 4204; 58 Proctor Ave; mains R50; 8am-6pm) Formerly called Lewoni's, this modest cafe is tucked inside a small suburban complex surrounded by curio shops and nail salons. It has a tiny courtyard and is a cool retreat from Mahikeng's hectic streets. The simple menu offers the usual omelettes, toasties and burgers, along with daily specials.

Information

North West Parks & Tourism Board (018-397 1500; www.tourismnorthwest.co.za; Heritage House; 7.30am-4.30pm Mon-Fri) It doesn't have much printed material, but the staff are helpful and can provide a map of town. When heading south on Nelson Mandela Dr, turn right on Molopo St (a block past Shippard St), then take the second left and head through the underpass on the left (it's next to Cooke's Lake).

Getting There & Away

Mahikeng is 25km southeast of the Ramatlabama border crossing with Botswana. The best way to get there is by car. From Pretoria or Rustenburg take the N4 to Zeerust and then veer off on Rte 27 to Mahikeng. The town is also on the N18, which heads south towards Northern Cape and Free State.

Magaliesberg

If you've had your fill of South African urbanity, treat yourself to a peaceful day, or night, in the mountains. An hour's drive from Pretoria and less than two from Jo'burg, but worlds apart in looks and attitude, is the 120km-long Magaliesberg range. A favourite weekend escape for Gautengers, these mountains form a half-moon arc from Hartbeespoort Dam in the east to Rustenburg in the west. Hit the back roads leading off Rtes 104 and 24 to appreciate this region of scrub-covered hills, streams, forests and lots of fresh, clean air.

Hartbeespoort Dam, less than an hour's drive from both Jo'burg and Pretoria, has been marked by commercialisation seeping out of the cities. Billboards and building projects line the 55km shoreline and cars zip along en route to the nearby N4. Nonetheless, the area's rolling hills, winding country roads and green-blue dam waters make for a pleasant stop for lunch and shopping en route to Gauteng. An added attraction is the recently resurrected cableway that hoists visitors to the roof of the Magaliesberg.

Sights & Activities

East of the four-way stop in Damdoryn, the road leads through an Arc de Triomphe-style gate, across **Hartbeespoort Dam** and through a tunnel. Art galleries and upscale eateries then line the road as it passes through Schoemansville on the dam's north-eastern shore, on its way to a meeting with the N4 to Pretoria.

Magaliesberg Canopy Tour OUTDOORS
(014-535 0150; www.magaliescanopytour.co.za; Sparkling Waters Hotel & Spa, Rietfontein Farm; tours incl light meal R495; 6.30am-4.30pm Sep-Apr, 7.30am-3pm May-Aug) Skim treetops and whizz between cliffs on steel zip lines up to 140m long, suspended 30m above a stream. This brilliant eco-adventure takes you on an exhilarating 2½-hour descent through Ysterhout Kloof. Along the way you stop at 11 platforms, built into the cliff's face, for the views and the scoop on local ecology from a guide.

A minimum of two participants is required and advance booking is recommended; Sparkling Waters guests receive a 20% discount.

Aerial Cableway CABLE CAR
(072 241 2654; www.hartiescableway.co.za; off Rte 104; adult/child R175/95; ticket office 8.30am-4pm) Just east of Schoemansville is this cable-car ride that thrived for two decades before closing in 2005, only to reopen after an extensive refitting in 2010. It deposits you atop the Magaliesberg, where you can take in magnificent views of the surrounding region. There's a restaurant at the base station; at the top is another eatery plus a pizza shack-cum-bar and a kids' playground.

Welwitischia Country Market MARKET
(☎083 302 8085; www.countrymarket.co.za; Damdoryn; ⏰9am-5pm Tue-Sun) FREE Stock up on 'Boks tops and biltong, leather goods and wirework. Located just west of the four-way stop in Damdoryn, near the northwest corner of Hartbeespoort Dam, this market is more authentic than the nearby Chameleon Village tourist complex, with several dozen stalls housed in wooden cabins. There's a small playground and aviary to keep children occupied, plus three restaurants, and craftwork and classic South African gifts for sale.

Sleeping & Eating

Sparkling Waters Hotel & Spa HOTEL $$
(☎014-535 0000; www.sparklingwaters.co.za; Reitfontein Farm; s/d incl breakfast R780/1350;) The large grounds of this low-key, Tudor-style hotel contain pools, minigolf, tennis courts, a health spa, a games room and a playground – plenty to keep families occupied – while the Magaliesberg bush lies beyond the sweeping lawns. The rooms, arrayed around the landscaped grounds, sport oddly rendered exteriors and plain furnishings, but they're well maintained, and some standard rooms are huge.

The hotel is 32km southeast of Rustenburg, accessible from Rte 104 near Buffelspoort or Rte 24 via the Oorsaak turn-off in Rex.

Upper Deck PUB $$
(☎012-253 2586; www.theupperdeck.co.za; Welwitischia Country Market, Damdoryn; mains R80; ⏰8.30am-5pm Mon, 8.30am-10pm Tue-Sat, 8.30am-8pm Sun) The large beer garden of this pub-style restaurant is a good place in which to take a break from Welwitschia curio browsing. Grilled meats and burgers dominate the menu, which also offers some salads and a couple of kids' meals. There's live music from Friday to Sunday nights.

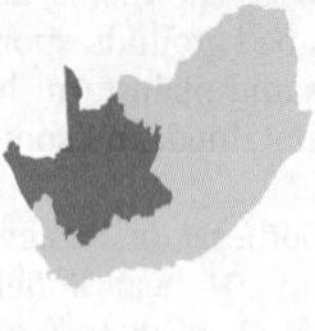

Northern Cape

Includes ➡

Best Places to Stay

- Kalahari Tented Camp (p453)
- 75 on Milner (p443)
- Kimberley Club (p443)
- Le Must River Residence (p449)
- Tatasberg Wilderness Camp (p459)

Best Places off the Beaten Track

- Witsand Nature Reserve (p448)
- Wildebeest Kuil Rock Art Centre (p445)
- Tankwa Karoo National Park (p460)
- Wonderwerk Cave (p448)
- Kokerboom Food & Wine Route (p454)

Why Go?

With just a million people inhabiting its 373,000 sq km, the Northern Cape is South Africa's last great frontier. Its scattered towns are hundreds of kilometres apart, connected by empty roads across the wildernesses of Namakwa, the Kalahari and Upper Karoo. In these sublime, surreal expanses, reality disappears faster than a meerkat into its burrow. Under the remorseless sun, vehicles share park roads with lions, dune boards swish down roaring sands, and Kimberley's pubs have been serving since the 19th-century diamond rush.

It's a raw, elemental land, where gnarly camel-thorn, quiver and Halfmens trees break the boundless horizons. Yet some of nature's greatest tricks here are instances of rejuvenating beauty. The Gariep (Orange) River waters the dry region, creating the Green Kalahari with its vineyards and epic Augrabies Falls. Following the rains, red Kalahari sands shimmer with grasses, and Namakwa's spring blooming carpets rocky hills and plains with wildflowers.

When to Go

Kimberley

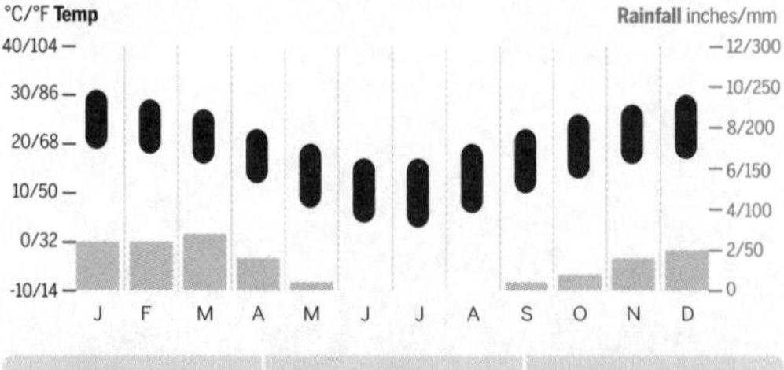

Jan–Mar Augrabies Falls most impressive; weather scorching but Kgalagadi wildlife-watching excellent.

May–Jul Winter is cooler, night skies are brighter and dry conditions bring animals to waterholes.

Aug–Sep Namakwa's barren expanses explode with colour during the spring wildflower bloom.

Language & People

English is widely spoken in the Northern Cape but Afrikaans is the dominant language, with about 54% of the province speaking it. Tswana (33%) and Xhosa (6%) are the other main languages. The population includes Afrikaners, Tswana and descendants of the region's earliest inhabitants, the Khoe-San, who can still be seen around the Kalahari.

KIMBERLEY

POP 97,000

Kimberley, the provincial capital, is the centre of the region known as the Diamond Fields. The city that gave birth to De Beers and 'a diamond is forever' remains a captivating place, with a Wild West vibe.

Whether you are drinking in raucous saloons dating back to the diamond rush, surveying the world's largest hand-dug hole, or taking a ghost tour and learning about the folk who lived, mined and died here, Kimberley is an excellent place to get stuck into South Africa's eventful history.

The last earth was shovelled at the landmark Big Hole back in 1914, but the Northern Cape's capital remains synonymous with diamonds. Step inside an atmospheric old pub, with dark interiors, scarred wooden tables and last century's liquor ads, and you'll feel you've been transported back to Kimberley's rough-and-ready mining heyday. Wander the period-perfect Victorian mining settlement at the Big Hole Complex, and you'll leave imagining Cecil Rhodes is alive and well and pointing his horse towards Rhodesia.

The Northern Cape's only real city is also home to fantastic museums, some wonderful accommodation and Galeshewe, a township with plenty of its own history.

ARCHITECTURE

Thanks to its fascinating history, Kimberley holds a lot for the architecture enthusiast. Check out **Rudd House** (053-839 2722; 5 Loch Rd; adult/child R25/12; by appointment), a fine example of the residences constructed for rich Kimberlites in the 19th century, and **Dunluce** (053-839 2722; 10 Lodge Rd; adult/child R25/12; by appointment), an elaborate Victorian residence.

For something more modern, head to the striking **Northern Cape Legislature Building** (053-839 8024; www.ncpleg.gov.za; off Green St, Galeshewe; 8am-4pm Mon-Thu, to noon Fri) FREE in Galeshewe, designed to reflect the culture, nature and history of Kimberley and the Northern Cape. The building is signposted from the city centre, but it is best visited on a guided Galeshewe tour.

Sights

★Big Hole MUSEUM
(053-830 4417; www.thebighole.co.za; West Circular Rd; adult/child R90/50; 8am-5pm, tours on the hour) Although the R50 million that turned the Big Hole into a world-class tourist destination came from De Beers, touring the world's largest hand-dug hole gives an honest impression of the mining industry's chequered past in Kimberley. Visits start with a 20-minute film about mining conditions and characters in late-19th-century Kimberley, and a walk along the Big Hole viewing platform. The open-air steel contraption, jutting over the 1.6km-round, 215m-deep chasm, enhances the vertigo-inducing view of the 40m-deep turquoise water.

A lift takes you down a shaft for the simulated mine experience, where audio and visual effects give an idea of how bad life was for the early diamond miners. Sounds of tumbling rubble and explosions add to the claustrophobia.

After exiting the mine, spend some time in the exhibition centre, which covers South African history and diamonds in general, as well as Kimberley's story. Also here is the guarded diamond vault, holding more than 3500 diamonds and replicas of the Eureka and 616 (the world's largest uncut eight-sided diamond, weighing 616 carats), which were unearthed here.

Outside, and entered for free, is a partial reconstruction of Kimberley's 1880s mining settlement, constructed using original relocated buildings, including a corrugated-iron church, funeral parlour, sweet shop and bank, as well as a functioning pub-restaurant and guesthouse. Try your luck panning for diamonds and hitting skittles in the bowling alley.

If you just want to see the hole itself, a reduced rate is offered (though not generally advertised).

McGregor Museum MUSEUM
(053-839 2700; Atlas St; adult/child R25/15; 9am-5pm Mon-Sat, 2-5pm Sun) This

Northern Cape Highlights

1. Watching a black-maned lion nap under a thorn tree in the wild crimson Kalahari wonderland of **Kgalagadi Transfrontier Park** (p451).
2. Taking a spring hike through a sea of brilliant blue, purple and golden wildflowers in **Namakwa** (p456).
3. Stepping into the diamond-dealing past of **Kimberley** (p439) on a ghost tour or historic pub crawl.
4. Gasping at the water surging between vertiginous cliffs in **Augrabies Falls National Park** (p454).
5. Meeting eccentric locals and poking around the museum in **Calvinia** (p461).
6. Embarking on an adventure across surreal mountainous desert in ultra-remote **|Ai-|Ais/Richtersveld Transfrontier Park** (p459).
7. Taking in the astonishingly starry night skies across the province, particularly in **Sutherland** (p460).

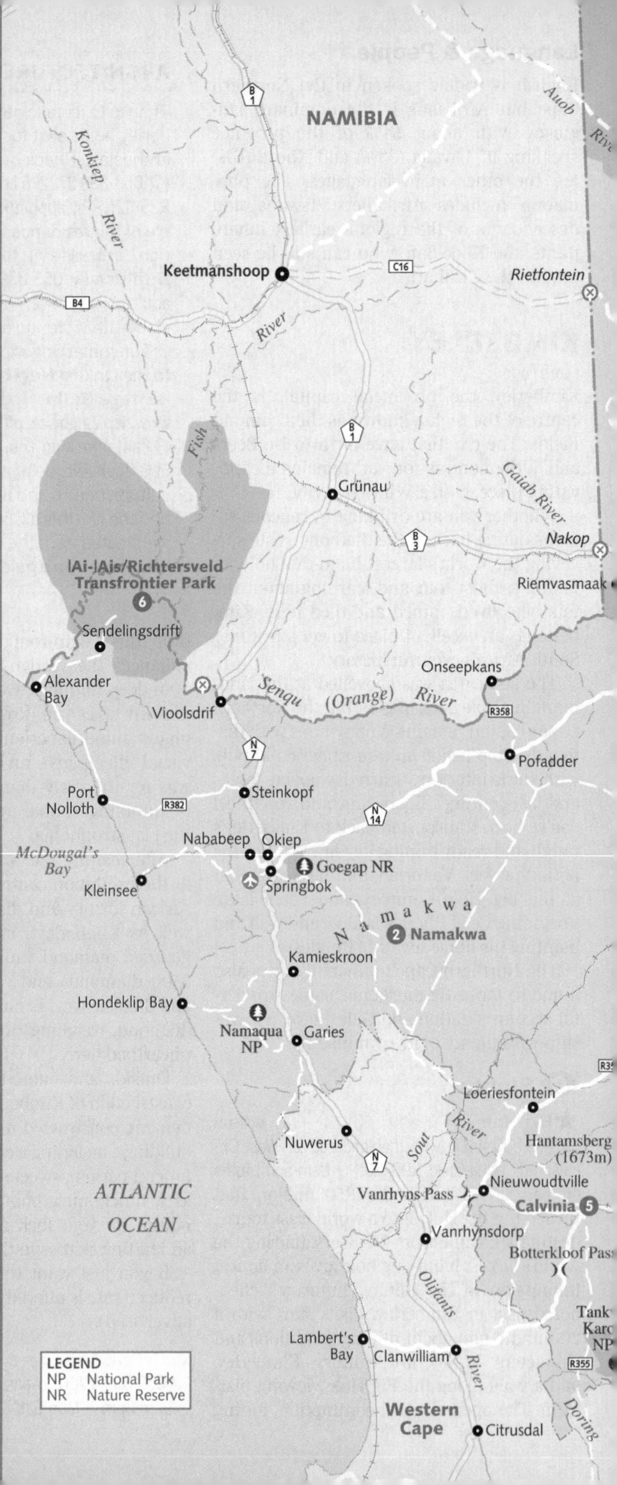

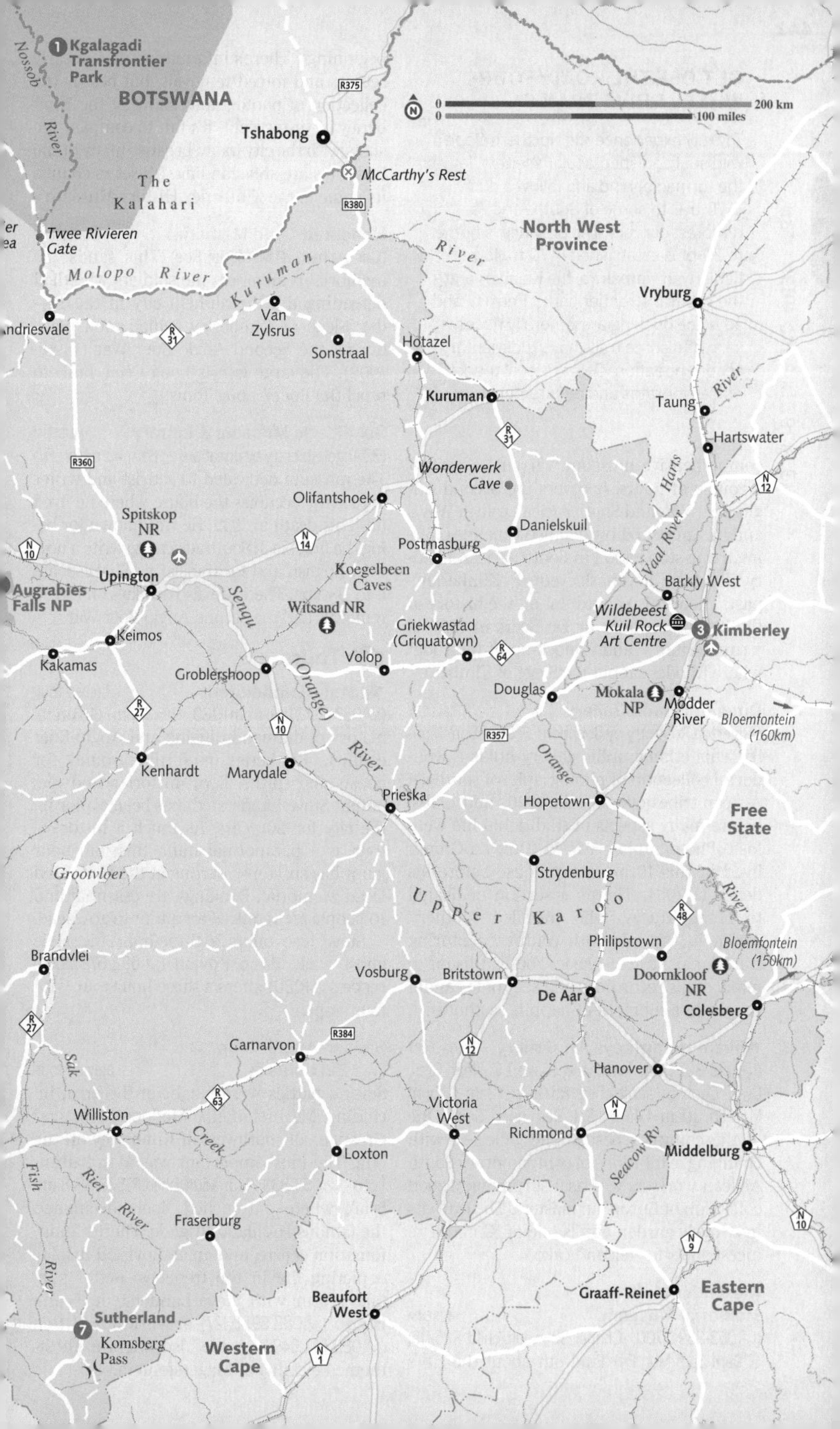

1 Kgalagadi Transfrontier Park
BOTSWANA
Nossob River
R375
Tshabong
McCarthy's Rest
R380
0 200 km
0 100 miles
The Kalahari
Twee Rivieren Gate
Molopo River
Kuruman River
North West Province
Vryburg
Andriesvale
R31
Van Zylsrus
Sonstraal
Hotazel
Kuruman
Taung
Harts River
Hartswater
R360
Wonderwerk Cave
Olifantshoek
N12
Spitskop NR
Danielskuil
N10
N14
Postmasburg
Vaal River
Upington
Koegelbeen Caves
Augrabies Falls NP
Sengu (Orange) River
Witsand NR
Barkly West
Wildebeest Kuil Rock Art Centre
3 Kimberley
Keimos
Griekwastad (Griquatown)
R64
Kakamas
Volop
Groblershoop
Douglas
Mokala NP
Modder River
Bloemfontein (160km)
R27
R357
Orange
Kenhardt
Marydale
Prieska
Hopetown
Free State
Grootvloer
Strydenburg
Upper Karoo
River
R48
Philipstown
Bloemfontein (150km)
Brandvlei
Vosburg
Britstown
Doornkloof NR
De Aar
Colesberg
R384
Carnarvon
Sak River
Hanover
R63
N1
Victoria West
Williston
Richmond
Creek
Seacow Rv
Middelburg
Loxton
Fish River
Riet River
N9
Fraserburg
Graaff-Reinet
Eastern Cape
Beaufort West
7 Sutherland
Komsberg Pass
Western Cape

GET OFF THE ROAD: FOUR-WHEEL DRIVE TRAILS

To truly experience the Northern Cape's wild soul and spectacular scenery, leave the tarmac behind and follow a dusty 4WD trail to some of South Africa's remotest corners. The province is home to 20-plus established 4WD trails, particularly in Namakwa, the Kalahari and the two transfrontier parks. Permits and advance booking are generally necessary, and some trails have rudimentary accommodation. Contact local tourist offices for rates and requirements.

comprehensive museum warrants a visit of a couple of hours. It covers the Second Anglo-Boer War and South Africa's role in WWI, and has an incredibly detailed timeline offering a one-stop lesson in South African history, alongside landmark events in Kimberley's past. There's also an exhibit on the history of the building – built by De Beers in 1897 as a sanatorium – and a mock-up of the room where Rhodes sat out the Siege of Kimberley.

Duggan-Cronin Gallery GALLERY
(Edgerton Rd; entry by donation; ⏲ 9am-5pm Mon-Fri) This ethnographic gallery holds a wonderful collection of photographs of southern African tribes taken in the 1920s and 1930s, before many aspects of traditional life were lost. Photographer Alfred Duggan-Cronin lived in this 19th-century house before his death in 1954. There's a section dedicated to Hugh Tracey, who travelled southern Africa in the mid-20th century, capturing traditional African music. You can listen to many of his recordings and see some candid caught-in-a-moment-of-happiness photos.

William Humphreys Art Gallery GALLERY
(☎ 053-831 1724; www.whag.co.za; 1 Cullinan Cres, Civic Centre; adult/child R5/2; ⏲ 8am-4.45pm Mon-Fri, 10am-4.45pm Sat, 9am-noon Sun) One of the country's best public galleries, with changing exhibitions of contemporary South African work, as well as a surprisingly good collection of European masters. The cafe sits in a lovely garden and is one of Kimberley's nicest spots for tea and cake.

Alexander McGregor Memorial Museum MUSEUM
(☎ 053-839 2700; Chapel St; adult/child R25/15; ⏲ 9am-5pm Mon-Fri) Find out about the city's beginnings. There's information on the early settlers and forced removals, but best is the collection of photographs showing the Kimberley of yesteryear – it's fun to compare the shots with the city today, because many of the buildings are still standing. It's set to change its name to the Kimberley History Museum

Honoured Dead Memorial MONUMENT
(Cnr Dalham & Memorial Rds) This sandstone memorial remembers the soldiers who died defending the British-held city in the 124-day Siege of Kimberley, which took place during the Second Anglo-Boer War (1899–1902). The large gun is Long Cecil, built to repel the Boers' Long Toms.

Sol Plaatje Museum & Library MUSEUM
(32 Angel St; entry by donation; ⏲ 8am-4pm Mon-Fri) The museum dedicated to activist and writer Sol Plaatje occupies the house where he lived until his death in 1932. He was known for being the first black South African to write a novel in English and for translating Shakespeare into Tswana. There are also displays on forced removals and the Second Anglo-Boer War.

Tours

★ **Steve Lunderstedt** GUIDED TOUR
(☎ 083 732 3189; from R180; ⏲ 6.30pm) Given its history of diamond digging and Anglo-Boer conflict, Kimberley is fertile ground for ghosts and spirits. Local historian and raconteur Steve Lunderstedt has been exploring the city for 20 years. As much a historical tour as a paranormal hunt, this four-hour jaunt has six stops, starting at the Honoured Dead Memorial. Bookings are essential and 10 people are required for a tour to go ahead.

Steve also offers a three-hour Big Hole ghost walk; **Jaco Powell** (☎ 082 572 0065; per person R180) offers a three-hour tour with four stops.

Second Anglo-Boer War Battlefields DRIVING TOUR
Several battles were fought in the area, including Magersfontein, Modder River and Graspan, all southwest of Kimberley off the N12. The most important was **Magersfontein** (☎ 053-833 7115; adult/child R15/8; ⏲ 8am-5pm), where entrenched Boers decimated the famous Highland Brigade. There's an infomation centre, and an audiovisual display depicting life in the trenches. Better still, take a tour with Steve Lunderstedt, **Frank Higgo** (☎ 082 591 5327) or **Veronica Bruce** (☎ 083 611 6497); Steve also offers a ghost-themed evening at Magersfontein.

Galeshewe Township GUIDED TOUR
(☎078 069 5104; bphirisi@yahoo.com; half-day R340) Joy Phirisi leads tours of this friendly township, an integral player in the anti-apartheid struggle. Stops include the Mayibuye Uprising Memorial, where anti-apartheid protests took place in 1952; Robert Sobukwe's practice, where the Pan African Congress (PAC) founder worked while under house arrest; and the Northern Cape Legislature Building. To visit a home or artist's studio, ask in advance.

Sleeping

Southwest of the Diamond Visitors Centre, Bishops Ave and the adjoining streets are a good area for budget and midrange accommodation.

Gum Tree Lodge HOSTEL $
(☎053-832 8577; www.gumtreelodge.com; Hull St; dm R150, r without bathroom R200, s/d R350/500; ❄≋) As close as Kimberley gets to a backpackers, this former convict station occupies leafy grounds off Rte 64, 5km east of the centre. Rooms are uninspiring but it's a pleasant environment, with greenery overhanging the corrugated roofs.

Heerengracht Guest House GUESTHOUSE $
(☎053-831 1531; www.heerengracht.co.za; 42 Heerengracht Ave, Royldene; s without bathroom R400, d from R550; ❄📶≋) This bare brick set-up on a leafy suburban street has rooms and spacious self-catering units (R850). It's walking distance from two malls with fast-food eateries. Clientele is largely made up of business travellers so rates are cheaper on weekends. Breakfast R75.

★**75 on Milner** GUESTHOUSE $$
(☎082 686 5994; www.75onmilnerlodge.co.za; 75 Milner St; s/d from R610/770; ❄📶≋) Highly recommended by travellers, this very friendly guesthouse has spacious, well-equipped rooms with fridge, microwave and cable TV. Rooms are set around a small patio and there's a good-size pool. Little touches set it apart, including a welcome drink, snacks in the room and superb information on local attractions.

★**Kimberley Club** BOUTIQUE HOTEL $$
(☎053-832 4224; www.kimberleyclub.co.za; 72 Du Toitspan Rd; s/d from R995/1230; ❄📶) Founded by Rhodes and his diamond cronies as a private club in 1881, and rebuilt following a fire in 1896, this reputedly haunted building became a hotel in 2004. The 21 bedrooms are period elegant, and offer the chance to pad in the slipper-steps of illustrious visitors such as Queen Elizabeth II. The entrance is on Currey St. Breakfast R110.

Edgerton House GUESTHOUSE $$
(☎053-831 1150; www.halfwayhousehotel.co.za; 5 Edgerton Rd; r R695; ❄≋) Edgerton has bright rooms with modern decor and gigantic TVs and showers. The bedrooms at the front can pick up noise from the nearby Halfway House pub; rooms at the back, entered from a pleasant courtyard, are quieter. The Madiba Room has hosted dignitaries including Nelson Mandela. Reception is based at Halfway House (p444).

Australian Arms Guesthouse GUESTHOUSE $$
(☎053-832 1526; www.australianarms.co.za; Big Hole Complex; s/d incl breakfast from R800/880; ❄) It's based in the reconstructed mining settlement, and the highlight of a stay is walking around the largely deserted mining village at night, imagining diamond dealers of yore drinking in the taverns after a long day's digging. The comfortable but unspectacular rooms have black-and-white photos of Kimberley, a free-standing bath and shower, DSTV and a fridge.

The bar-restaurant (mains R75) is evocative of the era, with an old piano and vintage Castle Lager posters, though the plasma-screen TV somewhat ruins the effect. Dishes include steaks, ribs and salads. You do not have to pay the Big Hole admission to access the Australian Arms.

Protea Hotel Kimberley HOTEL $$$
(☎053-802 8200; www.proteahotels.com/kimberley; West Circular Rd; s/d from R1340/1515; ❄📶≋) The swanky, four-star Protea is the only hotel with Big Hole views – enjoyed from the viewing deck outside the lobby, with its magnificent crystal chandeliers and historical photos of the mine. The 120 compact rooms are scattered with faux antiques, but the Victorian-style elegance really shines in the lobby and bar-restaurant (open to nonguests). Weekend specials are normally offered. Breakfast is R175.

Eating & Drinking

The most atmospheric places to eat and drink are the historic pubs, many of which have been around since the diamond rush.

Lemon Tree CAFE $
(www.nclemontree.co.za; Angel St; mains R50-90; ⏲8am-5pm Mon-Fri, to 1.30pm Sat) A

Kimberley

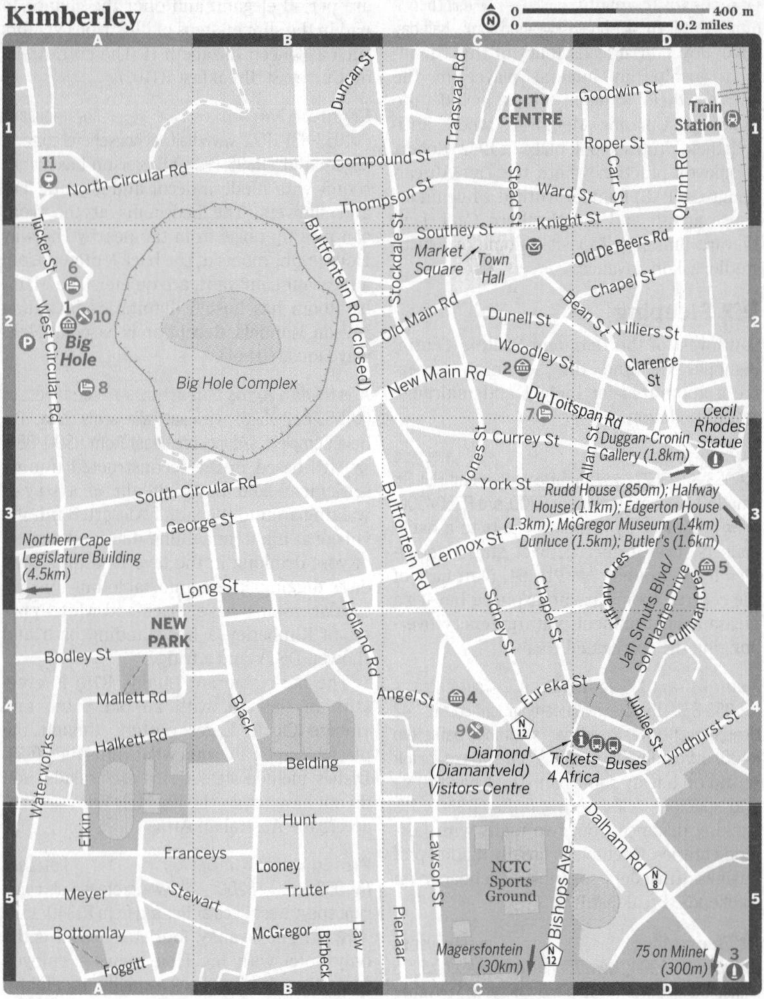

long-established cafe offering light lunches, a range of cakes and a hangover breakfast, in case you've overdone it in Kimberley's historic pubs.

★ **Halfway House** PUB $$

(✆053-831 6324; www.halfwayhousehotel.co.za; Du Toitspan Rd, cnr Carrington Rd; mains R60-140; ⏲11am-11pm; 📶) Soak up Kimberley's diamonds-and-drink history, quite literally, in this watering hole dating to 1872. It might be the world's only 'drive-in' bar, stemming from Rhodes' insistence on being served beer without dismounting his horse. The interiors are beautifully historic, with spittoons along the base of the scarred, wood-backed bar, old liquor ads, and frosted windows etched with Rhodes quotes.

It's worth asking staff about stories and legends from the pub's past. These days, locals flock in to shoot pool, watch bands in the courtyard, and chomp pub grub such as burgers, steaks and pizzas. Monday to Saturday, dinner is served in more refined surrounds in adjoining Annabell's. There are surprisingly modern rooms (double from R400) available upstairs, though the noise from the pub makes getting an early night unlikely.

Kimberley

Top Sights
1 Big Hole A2

Sights
2 Alexander McGregor Memorial Museum C2
3 Honoured Dead Memorial D5
4 Sol Plaatje Museum & Library C4
5 William Humphreys Art Gallery D3

Sleeping
6 Australian Arms Guesthouse A2
7 Kimberley Club C2
8 Protea Hotel Kimberley A2

Eating
Kimberley Club .... (see 7)
9 Lemon Tree C4
10 Occidental Grill Bar A2

Drinking & Nightlife
11 Star of the West A1

Occidental Grill Bar PUB $$
(053-830 4418; Big Hole Complex; mains R70-150; 9am-7pm Mon-Thu, to 11pm Fri & Sat, to 5pm Sun;) With a long bar and black-and-white photos of old-time prospectors, this Victorian-era saloon is a fun place to pause on a Big Hole tour. Dishes include bunny chow (a hollow bread loaf filled with curry), chops, ribs and a couple of token salads. You do not have to pay the Big Hole admission to access the Occidental.

Kimberley Club INTERNATIONAL $$
(72 Du Toitspan Rd; mains R50-130; lunch & dinner) Wear closed shoes and smart-casual dress to eat among Rhodes memorabilia in the one-time gentlemen's club he founded, now a boutique hotel. There's also Café Vitello, an Italian restaurant serving light lunches on the terrace.

Butler's FUSION $$$
(053-832 2668; www.theestate.co.za; 7 Lodge St; mains R90-195; dinner Mon-Sat) Kimberley's fanciest dining option has a fairly small menu featuring venison steaks, lamb loin and a popular pork-belly dish. For dessert try the frozen peanut-butter cheesecake. It's based in the Estate guesthouse, once Ernest Oppenheimer's home.

Star of the West PUB
(North Circular Rd) The vintage beer ads, worn floorboards and wooden tables at this 'old time' hostelry, established in 1870, tell of many raucous nights, though the place could do with a bit of an overhaul. There's standard pub grub (mains R50 to R110) on offer.

Information

Diamond (Diamantveld) Visitors Centre (053-832 7298; www.northerncape.org.za; 121 Bultfontein Rd; 8am-5pm Mon-Fri, to noon Sat) Pick up the *Kimberley Meander* brochure, with suggested self-guided walking and driving tours.

Getting There & Around

AIR

Taxis connect the city centre with the airport, 6km south.

Hamba Nathi (053-831 3982; www.hambanathi.co.za; 121 Bultfontein Rd, Diamond Visitors Centre) Sells airline tickets.

SA Express (053-838 3337; www.flyexpress.aero) Flies to/from Johannesburg and Cape Town.

BUS

Tickets 4 Africa (053-832 6040; tickets4africa@hotmail.com; 121 Bultfontein Rd, Diamond Visitors Centre) sells tickets for **Greyhound** (www.greyhound.co.za), **Intercape** (www.intercape.co.za) and **City to City** (www.citytocity.co.za). There are direct services to Cape Town (R550, 12 hours, daily) and Jo'burg (R400, six hours, daily). Intercape runs services to Upington (R420, six hours) on Sunday and to Bloemfontein (R430, two hours) on Thursday and Saturday, returning on Friday and Sunday.

Translux (www.translux.co.za) also services Kimberley.

WORTH A TRIP

WILDEBEEST KUIL ROCK ART CENTRE

Wildebeest Kuil Rock Art Centre (053-833 7069; www.wildebeestkuil.itgo.com; Rte 31; adult/child R25/15; 9am-4pm Mon-Fri, by appointment Sat & Sun) On a site owned by the !Xun and Khwe San people, who were relocated from Angola and Namibia in 1990, this small sacred hill has 400-plus rock engravings dating back millennia. Visits start with a video detailing the troubled history of the !Xun and Khwe, followed by an excellent, interpretative guided tour.

The centre is 16km northwest of town, en route to Barkly West. A minibus shared taxi costs R35; a private taxi costs R360 return, including waiting time.

CAR

Avis, Budget, Europcar, First, Hertz, Sixt and Tempest have desks at Kimberley airport.

TAXI

Rikki's Taxis (☎053-842 1764)

TRAIN

Blue Train (www.bluetrain.co.za) Stops for a tour of the Big Hole Complex en route from Pretoria to Cape Town.

Shosholoza Meyl (www.shosholozameyl.co.za) Trans-Karoo trains stop in Kimberley en route between Jo'burg and Cape Town.

THE UPPER KAROO

Heading southwest from Kimberley, you'll find the sparsely populated plains of the Upper Karoo. Part of the Great Karoo, which extends into the Eastern and Western Capes, this is a desolate land of big skies and empty spaces. Its inhabitants are predominantly sheep farmers, who live as they have for generations on giant tracts of barren land. Towns are few and far between, and are mostly of interest as stopovers offering spectacular stargazing and a taste of Karoo lamb.

Mokala National Park

Named after the Tswana for camel thorn, the dominant tree found in South Africa's newest national park, **Mokala** (☎053-204 8000; www.sanparks.org; adult/child R128/64; ⏲6.30am-6pm late-Mar, Apr, Aug & Sep, 7am-5.30pm May-Jul, 6am-7pm Oct–mid-Mar) encompasses grassy plains studded with rocky hills and the trademark trees. Indigenous to Southern Africa, camel thorns can range from small, spiny shrubs standing barely 2m to 16m-tall trees with wide, spreading crowns. The species is an important resource for both the people and wildlife living in this harsh region – the local tribes use the gum and bark to treat coughs, colds and nosebleeds. Some even roast the seeds as a coffee substitute. Mammals in the 200-sq-km park include black and white rhinos, roan antelope, Cape buffaloes, giraffes and zebras.

Organised activities include sunset wildlife drives, fly-fishing and bush braais (barbeques). All activities should be booked ahead.

> WORTH A TRIP
>
> **TRANSKAROO COUNTRY LODGE**
>
> **Transkaroo Country Lodge** (☎053-672 0027; www.transkaroocountrylodge.co.za; r without bathroom per person R250, s/d from R590/690; ❄≋) The quaintly furnished rooms are fine for a stopover, but it's the attached restaurant (mains R60 to R110) that sets Britstown apart from other unremarkable Karoo *dorps* (villages). Chequered tablecloths in the leafy courtyard give a provincial French feel, yet the food is Northern Cape through and through – go for the superlative dinner buffet (R160), with Karoo lamb cooked every possible way.

Sleeping & Eating

Motswedi Campsite CAMPGROUND $
(camping from R310) A superb campground with just six sites, all overlooking a waterhole. Each site has its own ablutions and kitchen.

Stofdam Bird Hide HUT $
(☎053-204 0158; 1-4 people R440) A much sought after and very rustic sleeping option. It cannot be booked online and only one-night stays are possible. Bring all your own bedding and cooking utensils.

Mosu Lodge LODGE $$
(bungalows from R600; ❄≋) Mokala's most upmarket accommodation, with facilities such as electric blankets, fireplaces and DSTV in the self-catering luxury executive suites. The smart poolside bar-restaurant is open all day, serving dishes from vegetable stir-fry to venison pie (mains R60 to R120).

Kameeldoorn Tree House CABIN $$
(☎053-204 0158; 2 people R1100) A delightful self-catering cabin nestled in a tree in the centre of the park. Book well in advance.

Haak-en-Steek Camp CHALET $$
(1-4 ppl from R895) This rustic cottage tucked away in the west of the park sleeps four. There is a well-equipped kitchen and a braai area, but no restaurant, bar or pool.

Lilydale Rest Camp CHALET $$
(r from R735; ❄≋) Lilydale is on the banks of the Riet River, which has good fly-fishing. Its self-catering units are perfect for getting back to nature, especially the thatched chalets. There's a swimming pool and a restaurant open for breakfast and lunch.

Getting There & Away

In the rainy season, the roads might not be passable with a 2WD – always call in advance to check.

To enter the park, head about 60km southwest of Kimberley on the N12, then turn right at the 'Mokala Mosu' sign and follow the dirt road for 21km. It's possible to cross the park and exit by the Lilydale gate, then follow a dirt road for 16km and meet the N12 about 40km southwest of Kimberley.

Victoria West

POP 8300

Located roughly halfway between Jo'burg and Cape Town, Victoria West is a gracefully fading old railway town. It offers little more than an overnight stop on the way across the Karoo but if you want to sleep in farm-fresh country air and get a feel for small-town life, Victoria West has a certain stuck-in-time allure.

On Church St are the **Victoria West Regional Museum** (Church St; ⊘ 7.45am-1pm & 2-4.45pm Mon-Fri) **FREE**, covering local natural and social history; the quaint whitewashed **St John's Church** (1869); **Apollo Theatre**, an art deco cinema with its original interior intact; and the late-19th-century Victoria West Hotel, dominating the street like a colonial dinosaur. Ask at the museum if you'd like to see inside the theatre.

🛏 Sleeping & Eating

Kingwill's B&B GUESTHOUSE $
(☑ 053-621 0453; 5 Victoria St; r R500; ❄ ≋)
There are lovely rooms in the main building as well as spacious garden units with flatscreen TV, modern decor, microwave and fridge. Dinner is available.

De Oude Scholen GUESTHOUSE $
(☑ 053-621 1043; deoudescholen@telkomsa.net; 1 Auret St; s/d from R450/550; ❄ ≋) These simple units are based in the old classrooms of the town's first school. They're well equipped with attractive bedspreads, fridges, microwaves and large bathrooms. Lunches and evening braais (R120) are available but must be booked in advance. Breakfast R75.

Karoo Deli CAFE $
(mains R45-60; ⊘ 7am-5pm Mon-Fri, to 1pm Sat)
Has a light menu including buffet lunches, cooked breakfasts and traditional meals such as *bobotie* (curry topped with an egg crust) and offal. It's behind the Victoria West Hotel.

ℹ Information

Victoria West has ATMs and a garage. The town is at the junction of the N12 and Rte 63, which leads west to Calvinia via the towns of Loxton, Carnarvon and Williston.

THE KALAHARI

A voyage to the Kalahari is akin to being catapulted into a parallel universe. It's a surreal *Alice in Wonderland* experience, where everything looms larger than life in the scorching desert heat. A collage of fiery sunsets and shifting crimson sands, lush green fields and gushing waterfalls, magnificent parks and tidy vineyards, this region will continue to enchant long after you have departed. Get a feel for it before you leave home in the works of Laurens Van der Post, who brought the Kalahari alive in books including *The Lost World of the Kalahari* and *A Far-Off Place*.

The Kalahari also covers much of Botswana and extends as far as Namibia and Angola. In South Africa, it's divided into two distinct areas: the arid semidesert and desert regions; and the 'Green Kalahari', an irrigated, fertile belt along the banks of the Gariep (Orange) River. In this agricultural area, dunes give way to fruit and wine farms producing goodies such as delicious sultana grapes and vast amounts of table wine. Nonetheless, the Green Kalahari retains a frontier feel, with dazzling night skies and plenty of wide-open spaces.

Kuruman

POP 13,000

A mining town set deep in wild country, rough little Kuruman is not a place to linger, but its remote location makes this a natural stopping point on trans-Kalahari trips.

The helpful **tourist office** (☑ 053-712 8819; Main Rd; ⊘ 8am-5pm Mon-Fri) has Kalahari brochures and maps.

◉ Sights

Moffat Mission RELIGIOUS
(adult/child R10/5; ⊘ 8am-5pm) The London Missionary Society established the Moffat Mission in 1816. It was named after long-serving Scottish missionaries Robert and Mary Moffat. They converted the local Batlhaping people to Christianity, started a school and translated the Bible into Tswana. The mission became a famous staging point for explorers and missionaries heading further into Africa. The Moffats' daughter married David Livingstone in the mission church, a stone-and-thatch building with 800 seats.

It's a quiet and atmospheric spot shaded by large trees that provide a perfect escape from the desert heat. These days it's a little neglected but you do get a real sense of history. It is

OFF THE BEATEN TRACK

WONDERWERK CAVE

Wonderwerk Cave (☎087 310 4356; adult/child R25/15; ⏲8am-5pm) There have been important archaeological finds in this dolomite cave, including evidence of hominids using fire. It has a longer record of human occupation than any other known cave. Archaeological digs are still in progress and there's a small information centre with some details on the cave's former inhabitants, including early Stone Age people. Unfortunately the guided tour is low on details – visit the McGregor Museum in Kimberley first to get some background. It's 45km south of Kuruman on Rte 31.

5km north of Kuruman on Rte 31 to Hotazel, signposted from town. The side gate is often closed, so use the conference centre entrance, and if there's no one around, drop your entrance fee into the donations box.

Eye of Kuruman PARK
(Main Rd; adult/child R10/5; ⏲7am-6pm) The town's famed natural spring is in the park between the tourist office and Palmgate Centre. Discovered in 1801, the prolific spring produces about 20 million litres of water a day – without fail. The park is a pleasant enough spot for a picnic, with trees ringing the clear pond, where some sizeable fish dart beneath the lily pads

Sleeping & Eating

The local mining staff fill accommodation between Monday and Thursday, so book ahead.

Kuru-Kuru Guesthouse GUESTHOUSE $$
(☎053-712 0319; www.kurukuru.co.za; cnr Albutt & Buckle Sts; s/d from R500/640) A friendly guesthouse with simple rooms, some with self-catering facilities and all with a small terrace. There's no swimming pool but there is a bar, library and pool table. It's in the suburbs 2km north of town, just off Rte 31. Breakfast R50.

Palmgate Centre SUPERMARKET
(22 Main Rd) There's a supermarket in this shopping centre, as well as a bar-restaurant serving pizza, pasta, burgers and steaks.

Caffe Palermo INTERNATIONAL $$
(☎053-712 3951; 7 Main Rd; mains R65-135) In a small mall on the western side of town, this makes a reviving pit stop, with shaded outside seating. The long menu includes burgers, quiches, pastas, salads and heavier options.

Getting There & Away

Intercape (www.intercape.co.za) stops daily en route between Jo'burg (R620, 7½ hours) and Upington (R530, 3½ hours).

Witsand Nature Reserve

As if a reserve based on a 9km-by-5km and 70m-high white-sand dune system, standing in stark contrast to the surrounding red Kalahari sands, wasn't enough, **Witsand** (☎083 234 7573; www.witsandkalahari.co.za; adult/child R50/30; ⏲8am-6pm) also comes with a soundtrack. When conditions are hot and dry, the sand sings. The 'roaring sands' effect is created by air escaping from the tightly packed grains; the bass, organ-like sound is sometimes audible in the reserve office, 5km away.

Activities include hiking, sandboarding (boards per day R120), mountain biking (bicycles per day R100) and a 40km 4WD route through the dunes. Although it's not a major wildlife-watching spot, you can expect to see various antelopes and a host of birdlife. There are no organised activities but you can roam at your will.

Sleeping

The thatch-roofed, self-catering **chalets** (per adult/child R480/240, minimum 3 people; ❄✉) sleep up to six in three comfortable, compact rooms with shared bathroom, and there is a swimming pool shared between the chalets. Two- and four-person **bungalows** (adult/child R200/100) – more accurately, huts with bedding, shared ablutions and field kitchen – and **camping** (camping per adult/child R110/60) are also available nearby. There's a second swimming pool between the huts and camping ground.

Getting There & Away

From the N14, the turn-off to the reserve is about 5km southwest of Olifantshoek, 105km from Kuruman. From there, the gravel road leads 75km southwest to the reserve. From Rte 62, the turn-off is about 60km east of Groblershoop and 5km east of Volop; the reserve is then 45km north on the gravel road. You shouldn't need a 4WD, but always phone the reserve first to check the condition of the roads. Witsand does not have a petrol station and the shop sells only the very basics, so fill up before you set off, and come equipped with food and water.

Upington

POP 57,000

Home to lush gardens and hundreds of date palm trees, Upington is a prosperous, orderly town on the banks of the Gariep (Orange) River. The central hub for the Green Kalahari, it's a good place to recoup after a long desert slog – although it gets blazing hot in summer. If you yearn to see the Northern Cape's most remote parts but don't have the means to do so on your own, this is also a good place to organise a guided tour. Wide boulevards, slightly cluttered with supermarkets and chain stores, fill the town centre. Step onto a side street near the river, however, and you'll enter a peaceful world where refreshing, watery views and rows of palms hold quiet court.

Sights & Activities

Kalahari-Orange Museum MUSEUM
(4 Schröder St; adult/child R10/2; ⏲9am-12.30pm & 2-5pm Mon-Fri) Occupying the mission station established by Reverend Schröder in 1875, the museum focuses on local social history, with domestic and agricultural artefacts. Displays cover the Upington 26, who were wrongly jailed under apartheid.

Orange River Cellars WINERY
(☎054-337 8800; www.orangeriverwines.com; 32 Industria St; tastings from R10) There's a vast range of well-priced wines to taste, including dessert and sparkling wines, as well as a juice tasting for kids and nondrinkers. It's in an industrial area 6km northeast of town, not the most atmospheric place to sip (a new tasting room in central Upington is planned).

★**Sakkie se Arkie** CRUISE
(☎082 564 5447; www.arkie.co.za; Park St; adult/child R90/50; ⏲6pm Fri-Sun, daily during holidays) Soak up the last rays of the Kalahari sun cruising the Gariep (Orange) River on the top deck of Sakkie's barge. Dire Straits, Afrikaans pop and other classics keep everyone entertained on the two-hour sunset cruise as the water turns silvery and the bartender lines up cold beers.

Tours

Upington is the best place to organise a Kalahari adventure.

Kalahari Safaris ADVENTURE TOUR
(☎054-332 5653; www.kalaharisafaris.co.za) Runs small-group (two to five people) trips to locations including the Kgalagadi and Augrabies Falls parks, Witsand Nature Reserve and Namakwa. Tours last from one to seven days and cater to all budgets.

Kalahari Tours & Travel ADVENTURE TOUR
(☎054-338 0375; www.kalahari-tours.co.za) Offers itineraries around the province, including three- to nine-day Kgalagadi 4WD adventures.

Sakkie's Adventures ADVENTURE TOUR
(☎082 564 5447; www.arkie.co.za; Park St) Organises rafting on the Gariep (Orange) River, Kgalagadi tours by 4WD and bus, and quad-bike and camping safaris to Riemvasmaak, |Ai-|Ais/Richtersveld Transfrontier Park and Namakwa.

Sleeping

Guesthouses on Budler St and Murray Ave overlook the river, their lawns leading to the water.

★**Le Must River Residence** GUESTHOUSE $$
(☎054-332 3971; www.lemustupington.com; 14 Budler St; s/d incl breakfast from R890/1180; ❄📶🏊) This elegant riverside getaway has 11 African-themed rooms with antique furnishings and crisp linen. Sitting rooms and terraces open onto the artful garden with its Italianate pool. Under the same ownership is nearby **Le Must River Manor** (☎054-332 3971; www.lemustupington.com; 12 Murray Ave; s/d incl breakfast from R680/930; ❄🏊); opt for room 4, whose balcony overlooks the river.

Aqua Viva GUESTHOUSE $$
(☎054-331 2524; www.aquaviva.co.za; 26A Schröder St; s/d R550/650; ❄) Tucked behind the Protea Hotel, this is a peaceful place with spacious rooms that are sparsely but stylishly decorated. They come with large bathrooms, comically small TVs and a shared verandah leading on to a lawn overlooking the river.

Affinity Guesthouse GUESTHOUSE $$
(☎054-331 2101; www.affinityguesthouse.co.za; 4 Budler St; s/d incl breakfast from R720/850; ❄📶🏊) There's a slightly institutional feel in the common areas, but staff are helpful and the rooms pleasant. Facilities include fridges, flat-screen TVs and shared balcony. Ask for a river-view room.

Die Eiland Holiday Resort CAMPGROUND, CHALETS $$
(☎054-334 0287; resort@kharahais.gov.za; camping from R125, huts without bathroom from R300, chalets from R770; 🏊) A palm-lined avenue

Upington

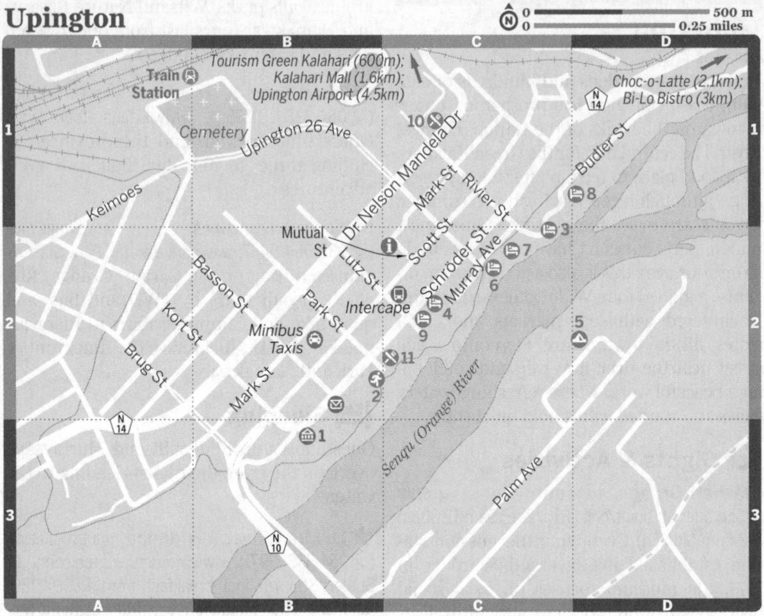

Upington

Sights

1 Kalahari-Orange Museum B3

Activities, Courses & Tours

2 Sakkie se Arkie B2
Sakkie's Adventures ....(see 2)

Sleeping

3 Affinity Guesthouse C2
4 Aqua Viva C2
5 Die Eiland Holiday Resort D2
6 Island View House C2
7 Le Must River Manor C2
8 Le Must River Residence D1
9 Protea Hotel Oasis C2

Eating

10 Dros C1
11 Irish Pub & Grill C2

leads to 'the Island', in a wonderful natural setting on the river's southeastern bank. The basic self-catering chalets have kitchenettes with hob and microwave, and tiny bathrooms with shower.

Island View House B&B $$
(☎054-331 1328; www.islandviewhouse.co.za; 10 Murray Ave; s/d incl breakfast R700/900; ❄📶🏊) The Mocké family offers a friendly welcome and modern rooms with showers and a shared lounge, kitchen and balcony.

Protea Hotel Oasis HOTEL $$$
(☎054-337 8500; www.proteahotels.com; 26 Schröder St; r from R1600; ❄📶) The Oasis offers some of Upington's most stylish accommodation. The swimming pool and restaurant are at the Protea Upington, across the road. Breakfast R165.

Eating & Drinking

You'll find a range of fast-food eateries and chain restaurants at the huge Kalahari Mall, east of the town centre.

Choc-o-Latte CAFE $
(13 Du Toit St; mains R50-80; ⏲8am-4pm Mon-Fri, 8.30am-2pm Sat; 📶) Enjoy a decent cup of coffee on the terrace or inside this suburban cafe whose walls are lined with art. Sandwiches and salads are on offer, as well as large slabs of cake. There's a B&B here too. Follow signs for the Medi-Clinic.

Bi-Lo Bistro INTERNATIONAL, SUSHI $$
(www.bilobistro.co.za; 9 Green Point Rd; mains R60-120; ⏲breakfast, lunch & dinner; 📶👪) Birds hop between palm trees and kids play on the swings at this popular spot in the suburbs. The vast menu features everything from steak to sushi – the latter surprisingly decent.

Irish Pub & Grill PUB $$
(☎054-331 2005; 20 Schröder St; mains R70-150) For sundowners or an early evening meal, you can't beat this Irish bar's patio overlooking the river. The menu features pizza, a few salads and plenty of meat.

Dros INTERNATIONAL $$
(☎054-331 3331; www.dros.co.za; Pick 'n' Pay Centre; mains R70-160) A chain bar-restaurant focusing on meat, with a few salads, seafood dishes and pizzas. It's a pleasantly cool spot after a hot drive.

Information

Tourism Green Kalahari (☎054-337 2800; off Rte 360; ⏲7.30am-4.30pm Mon-Fri) Call ahead as opening times aren't always followed.

Upington Tourist Office (☎054-338 7152; www.northerncape.org.za; Mutual St, Municipal Bldg; ⏲7.30am-4.30pm Mon-Fri) This office's location in the municipal building is temporary; there are plans to move it back to the library.

Getting There & Away

AIR

South African Airways (www.flysaa.com) flies to/from Jo'burg and Cape Town.

BUS

Intercape (☎0861 287 287; www.intercape.co.za; Lutz St) buses go to Bloemfontein (R390, eight hours, Thursday and Saturday); Cape Town (R600, 14 hours, Sunday to Friday nights); Jo'burg (R700, 11 hours, daily); and Windhoek, Namibia (R630, 12 hours, Tuesday, Thursday, Friday and Sunday nights).

CAR

Agencies including Avis and Europcar have offices at Upington airport. Budget and Tempest have offices in town.

SHARED TAXI

Destinations of minibus taxis include Springbok (R240, four hours) and Windhoek, Namibia (R650, 13 hours).

Kgalagadi Transfrontier Park

A long, hot road leads between crimson dunes from Upington to Africa's first transfrontier **park** (☎054-561 2000; www.sanparks.org; adult/child R264/132), one of the world's last great, unspoilt ecosystems. Once you enter the magical park, tucked away alongside Namibia in the Northern Cape and southwest Botswana, you'll soon see why the journey was well worth the effort.

The Kgalagadi is a wild land of harsh extremes and frequent droughts, where shifting red and white sands meet thorn trees and dry riverbeds. Yet despite the desolate landscape, it's teeming with wildlife. From prides of black-maned lions to packs of howling spotted hyenas, there are some 1775 predators here. It's one of the best places in the world to spot big cats, especially cheetahs. Add in giant, orange-ball sunsets and black-velvet night skies studded with twinkling stars, and you'll feel like you've entered the Africa of storybooks.

We found the section between Urikaruus and Mata-Mata to be particularly good for predator sightings, while the east–west routes linking the two rivers are rich in scenery and birdlife. The semiarid countryside also supports large populations of reptiles, rodents, small mammals and antelopes. Most of the animals are remarkably tolerant of vehicles, allowing you to get extraordinarily close.

KGALAGADI TRANSFRONTIER PARK

Why Go Superlative big cat sightings; beautiful 4WD routes; endlessly photogenic skies; a wilder feel than many South African parks.

When to Go May to August, when the weather is coolest (below freezing at night) and the animals are drawn to the bores along the dry river beds. The extreme heat from December to February entices animal to waterholes, making wildlife-spotting easier.

Practicalities Gates open between 5.30am and 7.30am and shut between 6pm and 7.30pm. Times vary from month to month, but generally follow the rising and setting sun. Petrol and diesel are available at rest camps. Carry drinking water at all times. Kgalagadi tours can be organised in Upington. Visitors must remain in their cars, except at the six designated picnic sites and accommodation.

Budget Tips If you arrive late in the afternoon, consider spending the night outside the park to avoid paying that day's fees.

The landscape is hauntingly beautiful. Between the Nossob and Auob Rivers (usually dry), the Kalahari dunes are characteristically red due to iron oxide. Elsewhere the sand varies from pink and yellowish to grey; following the rains, shimmering pioneer grasses give the land a green tint.

Activities

The park operates sunrise, sunset, night and full-morning **wildlife drives** (adult/child from R180/90) and three-hour **walking safaris** (adult from R315, no one under 12 years). Both depart from Twee Rivieren, Nossob, Mata-Mata and Kalahari Tented Camp. We recommend trying at least one guided activity; you have a better chance of spotting predators when accompanied by a trained ranger. At least two people are needed for safaris to depart.

For an extra fee, there are 4WD trails to tackle (R2500 per vehicle).

Kgalagadi Transfrontier Park

0 — 40 km
0 — 20 miles

Sleeping & Eating

Accommodation can be booked on the **South African National Parks** (SANParks; ☎012-428 9111; www.sanparks.org/parks/kgalagadi) website or at Twee Rivieren Gate (!Xaus Lodge excepted). Advance bookings are recommended.

The rest camps have shops selling basic groceries, soft drinks and alcohol, and are open from 7.30am until 15 minutes after the gates close (Nossob and Mata-Mata's close between 12.30pm and 1.30pm).

Twee Rivieren Rest Camp has the park's only **restaurant** (mains from R70; ⏰7.30-10am, 6-9pm).

Park Rest Camps

The camps have a range of campsites, chalets, bungalows and cottages, with bedding, towels, fully equipped kitchens, braais and bathrooms. Twee Rivieren has 24-hour electricity; at the others, power is cut overnight.

Twee Rivieren CHALET $$
(camping from R190, cottages/chalets from R910/1220; ❄🏊) The largest camp is also the most convenient, located next to the park entrance and with the most facilities. The cottages have between two and four single beds; the chalet has six. Also has cheaper campsites without power.

Mata-Mata CHALET $$
(camping from R220, 2-/4-person chalets from R720/1220; ❄🏊) Surrounded by thorny Kal-

Kgalagadi Transfrontier Park

Sights
1 Kgalagadi Transfrontier Park ... A2

Sleeping
2 !Xaus Lodge ... A4
3 Bitterpan ... A3
4 Gharagab ... A1
5 Grootkolk ... A1
6 Kalahari Tented Camp ... A3
7 Kielekranke Wilderness Camp ... B4
8 Mata-Mata ... A3
9 Nossob ... B2
10 Twee Rivieren ... B4
11 Urikaruus ... A3

Eating
Twee Rivieren Rest Camp Restaurant ... (see 10)

ahari dune bushveld, over three hours from Twee Rivieren Gate, Mata-Mata is a good place to spot giraffes. The riverfront chalets (from R1310) are worth the extra splurge – you stand a good chance of spotting wildlife in the dry riverbed from your patio.

Nossob CHALET **$$**
(camping from R220, chalets/cottages/guesthouses from R750/1325/1485;) Situated within the dry Nossob riverbed and surrounded by tree savannah, this camp is a good place to spot predators. The chalets, guesthouses and cottage vary in size but all have similar amenities and a somewhat spartan, institutional feel. It's over four hours from Twee Rivieren Gate.

Park Wilderness Camps

These remote camps offer the opportunity to immerse yourself in nature and are highly recommended. The camps are unfenced, which means animals can wander in; a ranger is on duty at all times. Stock up on petrol/diesel, drinking water and wood/charcoal before visiting, and book ahead. Children under 12 are only allowed at Kalahari Tented Camp.

★**Kalahari Tented Camp** CAMPGROUND **$$**
(2-4 person tents from R1250;) Kgalagadi's most luxurious wilderness camp has 14 stilted desert tents with rustic furnishings and views of a waterhole in the Auob riverbed – a popular hang-out for herds of wildebeest. It provides a remote, rustic feel while being only 3km from the conveniences of Mata-Mata (and over three hours from Twee Rivieren Gate).

Kielekranke Wilderness Camp CABIN **$$**
(cabins from R1270) Sunk into a sand dune and with decks gazing over the vast desert, these gorgeous tented cabins feel like they're in the middle of nowhere, though it's only 90 minutes from Twee Rivieren.

Bitterpan CABIN **$$**
(cabins from R1140) These stilted cabins perch in a very remote section of the park, with excellent sunset vistas across a pan. Access is via a rough, one-way, 4WD-only route over three hours from Nossob. Cabins have private bathrooms but share a kitchen.

Gharagab CABIN **$$**
(cabins from R1120) Among camel-thorn trees and grass savannah, Gharagab's elevated log cabins survey the red dunes. Perks at the remote spot, accessed on a one-way, 4WD-only trail from Union's End, include decks overlooking a waterhole popular with brown hyenas. Over three hours from Nossob.

Grootkolk CABIN **$$**
(cabins from R1270) Nestled amid red sand dunes at a remote spot in the far north of the park, Grootkolk's desert cabins are made from sandbags and canvas. As if the stars and silence weren't enough, predators are often spotted at the waterhole.

Urikaruus CABIN **$$**
(cabins from R1270) Perched on the banks of the Auob River, these four stilted cabins are connected by raised walkways between the camel-thorn trees. Urikaruus is the second-closest wilderness camp to Twee Rivieren (over two hours from Twee Rivieren Gate).

!Xaus Lodge LODGE **$$$**
(021-701 7860; www.xauslodge.co.za; s/d full board R4290/6600;) Kgalagadi's most upmarket option is owned and operated by the local San community. The lodge is a dreamy fantasy in ochre, overlooking a circular pan so perfect it almost looks artificially constructed. Cultural activities and excellent wildlife drives round out a wonderful package.

CROSSING INTO NAMIBIA OR BOTSWANA

You'll find SANParks reception, South African immigration (open 7.30am to 4pm) and border police at Twee Rivieren Gate.

The Botswana side of the park is only accessible by 4WD and there must be at least two vehicles travelling together. Accommodation is in unfenced camps and campsites. Book in advance through **Botswana Wildlife** (267 318 0774; www.mewt.gov.bw/DWNP; Gabarone), which has an office at Twee Rivieren. If you want to exit the park into the rest of Botswana, you must carry out border-crossing formalities at Twee Rivieren and spend at least two nights in the park.

If you want to enter Namibia through Kgalagadi's Mata-Mata gate, there's also a two-night minimum stay. Present your passport to South African immigration at Twee Rivieren, and to Namibian immigration at Mata-Mata. There's a levy of R240 per vehicle at Namibian immigration.

LOCAL KNOWLEDGE

KOKERBOOM FOOD & WINE ROUTE

With grapes galore (this area is now producing 10% of the country's wines) and rustic farm stalls selling biltong, dried fruit and other local goodies dotting the lonely highways, the area between Upington and Kakamas offers some offbeat culinary experiences. The Kokerboom Food and Wine Route aims to bring small, local producers together. It's in its infancy but there are already a few stops worth a visit.

Bezalel (☎054-491 1325; www.bezalel.co.za; tastings R60, restaurant mains R60; ⏲9am-5pm Mon-Fri, to 1pm Sat) Possibly the most varied tasting of any estate in the country, with samples of wine, port, brandy, various cream-based liqueurs and the challenge of swigging *mampoer* (moonshine) without grimacing. There's a restaurant and a leafy courtyard where you can enjoy your chosen tipple. It's 25km southwest of Upington on the N14.

Die Mas Van Kakamas (☎054-431 0245; www.diemasvankakamas.co.za; ⏲entry by appointment) The winemakers here experiment with a wider range of grape varieties than most other vineyards in the region, though the *jerepigo* and *hanepoot* wines that the Gariep (Orange) River is known for are still the best. Activities include farm tours, hiking trails, donkey cart trips and quad biking, and there's self-catering accommodation and campsites. It's well signposted from the N14 as you enter Kakamas.

Kalahari Gateway Hotel Bar-Restaurant (☎054-431 0838; www.kalaharigateway.co.za; Kakamas; mains R75, sushi platters from R150; ⏲7am-10pm) The first but no longer the only sushi bar in the Northern Cape sees Kalahari additions such as springbok sashimi appearing alongside the more familiar fishy options (fresh fish is flown in from Cape Town every two days). There's also a typically meat-oriented menu with children's offerings. Accommodation and adventure activities are available.

Outside the Park

There are dozens of places to stay on Rte 360 from Upington to Twee Rivieren Gate.

Kalahari Trails LODGE $
(☎054-511 0900; www.kalahari-trails.co.za; Rte 360; camping R80, s/d R300/500) This private reserve, 35km south of Twee Rivieren, offers a Kalahari experience on foot. Guests can walk the dunes by themselves, while guided walks and drives explore the surrounds by day and night. Safari tents, a self-catering chalet and cheaper rooms with shared bathrooms also available.

Molopo Kalahari Lodge LODGE $$
(☎054-511 0008; www.ncfamouslodges.co.za; Rte 360; camping per site R300, s/d incl breakfast R550/700; ❄@≋) About 60km south of Twee Rivieren, Molopo is a traditional safari lodge. The *rondavels* (huts) are a reasonable way to visit Kgalagadi on a budget, though the chalets (R800) are more pleasant, decorated with Khomani San artwork. The restaurant (mains from R90) serves meaty dishes and toasted sandwiches. Sister properties include Vischgat Game Lodge and Elandspoor Bush Camp, some 60km further south.

Getting There & Around

Twee Rivieren Gate is 270km northwest of Upington on the tarred Rte 360.

A 4WD vehicle is useful but not essential: the park's four main routes are gravel/sand roads but they're in decent condition and can be driven in a 2WD if you take care. Beware of patches of deep sand and loose gravel on the park's roads, which can make corners treacherous. The speed limit is 50km/h. Allow plenty of time to get to the camps as no driving is permitted after dark.

Augrabies Falls National Park

The Khoe-San people called it 'Aukoerbis', meaning place of great noise, and when the waterfall for which this **park** (☎054-452 9200; www.sanparks.org; adult/child R152/76; ⏲7am-6.30pm) is named is fat with rainy-season run-off, its thunderous roar is nothing short of spectacular. You can easily spend an hour hopping from one vertiginous lookout to another, accompanied by fluffy dassies (rodentlike mammals) scrambling across giant boulders.

The falls is the world's sixth tallest, formed where the Gariep (Orange) River crashes into an 18km-long ravine with 200m-high cliffs. The main falls drop 56m, while the adjoining Bridal Veil Falls plunge 75m. It's a short walk from the visitor centre to the viewing platforms. The park has a harsh climate, with an average rainfall of only 107mm and daytime summer temperatures that reach 46°C.

Most people visit the falls and perhaps meander to the other viewpoints along the ravine. These are undeniably impressive but if you care to linger a while you will have some great – and largely deserted – opportunities to watch wildlife. The 500-sq-km park is home to 52 mammal species including giraffes, several types of antelope, African clawless otters and endangered Hartmann's mountain zebras. You're less likely to spot the predators but caracals, black-backed jackals, African wild cats and rarely glimpsed leopards all roam here.

Aim to spend at least one full day in the park, grabbing a picnic to enjoy at one of the lookout points and charging your camera batteries for some wildlife encounters that you'll likely have all to yourself.

AUGRABIES FALLS NATIONAL PARK

Why Go Thundering waterfalls; hikes into rugged, otherworldly scenery; uncrowded wildlife drives; gentle river rafting outside the park.

When to Go Spring (March to May) is perfect: the falls are at their most impressive from January but high temperatures make hiking uncomfortable until March; winter (June to August) nights can be freezing.

Practicalities Your own transport is best; alternatively, get a tour from Upington or Kakamas. Gates are open from 7am to 6.30pm, but late check-ins can be arranged. A well-stocked shop sells groceries, alcoholic drinks and firewood.

Budget Tips Park highlights can be seen in a day, so consider staying outside to save on a second day's entrance fees.

Activities

The road to the rest camp and the main lookout over the falls is tarred and you can easily reach the viewpoints at Ararat and Oranjekom in a 2WD. If you take it slowly, you can explore further without a 4WD, though you'll need one to complete the 94km-long Wilderness Road. Call in advance to check the state of the roads as heavy rains can cause havoc. There are also two-hour guided night drives available; book ahead directly with the park.

Kalahari Outventures RAFTING, CANOEING
(☎082 476 8213; www.kalahari-adventures.co.za; Augrabies; per person R350) The flagship rafting trip, Augrabies Rush, is a half-day tour taking in Grade II and Grade III rapids on a 9km section of the Gariep (Orange) River, finishing 300m above the main falls. Overnight and multiday river expeditions are also offered, as is a five-day tour incorporating Riemvasmaak and Kgalagadi Transfrontier Park (R7000).

Dassie Trail HIKING
This three-hour, 9km trail is well worth doing, particularly if your time is fairly short. The hike involves clambering over rocks through some magical landscapes.

Klipspringer Trail HIKING
(per person R470; ⏲Apr–mid-Oct) The three-day, 36km Klipspringer Trail leads along the southern banks of the Gariep River. You'll spend two nights in rustic huts with bunk beds, toilets, firewood and rudimentary cooking utensils, but no electricity or showers and you need to bring drinking water. There's a minimum requirement of two hikers; advance booking is essential.

Sleeping & Eating

Augrabies Rest Camp CHALET, CAMPGROUND $$
(www.sanparks.org; camping R195, chalets/cottages from R1050/1585; ❄🏊) Within the park and close enough to the falls to hear them after rains, the rest camp has self-catering chalets, two-bedroom cottages and a campsite with ablutions. The restaurant offers a decent selection of dishes; it's open 7am to 8pm.

Augrabies Falls Lodge & Camp HOTEL $$
(☎054-451 7203; www.augfallslodge.co.za; Rte 359; camping per site R225, s/d R420/620; ❄) One of a number of sleeping options on the road to the park (8.5km from the park gate), this 1950s building has a modernised interior that is adorned with African art. The spacious rooms have pleasant furnishings and balconies with views across the countryside. There's a restaurant (mains R70, breakfast R35), bar and a four-person self-catering room (R750).

Getting There & Away

The park is 39km northwest of Kakamas; head west on the N14 for 8km, then northwest on Rte 359.

OFF THE BEATEN TRACK

RIEMVASMAAK

If you're looking for real off-the-beaten-track adventure, Riemvasmaak will deliver. The remote village is located in 74 sq km of harsh lunar landscape. In this mountain desert wilderness, donkey carts remain a crucial mode of transport across the cracked expanse of frosted orange rock and sand.

In 1973 the apartheid government removed the local Xhosa and Nama communities, relocating them to the Eastern Cape and Namibia, respectively, in order to turn this land into a military training camp. Following South Africa's transition to democracy in 1994, the government began a massive effort to return the local population to Riemvasmaak. In 2002 the formerly displaced residents were given plots of land.

Riemvasmaak remains a poor village, relying on self-sustainable farming. Unemployment rates are astronomical and community tourism projects offer an important, if sporadic, means of income. The region has much to offer off-the-grid explorers: three challenging 4WD trails (41km, 49km and 79km), and activities including hiking and mountain biking, birdwatching and Riemvasmaak's crowning glory, its hot springs. Just beyond the village is the rough and rocky Molopo River gorge.

There are designated campsites (R85 for two people) on the trails, and chalets (from R375) in the canyon next to the springs. Contact Clarissa Damara at the **Riemvasmaak Community Centre** (☎083 873 7715) to book activities, accommodation and guides. Don't just rock up in Riemvasmaak on a whim – everything must be booked in advance.

There are two routes to Riemvasmaak from the south. Although the western route, which follows the Augrabies road, is largely tarred, past the national park the road condition becomes terrible and a 4WD is required. If you're in a 2WD, opt for the turn-off 5km east of Kakamas. The first 3km is tarred and while the next 45km is gravel, it's a good road that's doable in a 2WD in all but the wettest of weather. The last 5km into the village is tarred, providing a sort of red carpet as you approach this movie-set-like place.

NAMAKWA

A land of immense skies and stark countryside, rugged Namakwa is truly South Africa's Wild West. The roads seemingly stretch forever through vast, empty spaces, and scorching days lead to dramatically quiet and still nights, when the stars appear bigger and brighter than anywhere else. From exploring the misty shipwrecked diamond coastline on the country's far western edge to four-wheel driving through the Mars-like landscape of remote |Ai-|Ais/Richtersveld Transfrontier Park, its pleasures are simple yet flabbergasting.

Namakwa is also a proficient magician, who performs its favourite trick each spring, shaking off winter's bite with an explosion of colour, covering the sun-baked desert in a spectacular multihued wildflower blanket.

The region takes its name from the Nama (also known as Namkwa or Namaqua, which means 'Nama people'), a Khoekhoen tribe from northwest Namakwa (previously known as Namaqualand).

Springbok

POP 12,800

Springbok sits in a valley surrounded by harsh rocky hills that turn into a rainbow tapestry during the spring wildflower season. When the flowers aren't blooming there's little to see or do, although the town's remoteness, desolate landscape and 300-plus days of sunshine make it a pleasant enough stopover. Springbok is 120km south of the Vioolsdrif crossing to Namibia, from where it is about 800km to Windhoek (Namibia).

From an edgy frontier town, Springbok has grown into a busy service centre for Namakwa's copper and diamond mines. Farmers from remote outlying areas also point their *bakkies* (pick-up trucks) to the main drag, Voortrekker St, for their weekly shopping trips; Springbok is a good place to rest up and do jobs before continuing into the wilderness.

Sights & Activities

The route to Nababeep, 16km northwest of Springbok via the N7, passes through prime flower-viewing territory in season. If you want to stretch your legs, the **Nababeep**

Mining Museum (Nababeep; admission R10; ⏲9am-1pm Mon-Fri) is worth a quick look. For info on heading further into the wilds, pick up a leaflet covering the multiday Namakwa 4x4 Trail from Springbok tourist office. Permits are required and camping is possible. Richtersveld Challenge, based at Cat Nap Accommodation, hires out 4WD vehicles.

Goegap Nature Reserve NATURE RESERVE
(☎027-718 9906; admission R30; ⏲7.30am-4pm) This 150-sq-km semidesert reserve, 15km east of Springbok past the airport, supports some 600 indigenous plant species, 45 mammal species and 94 types of bird. It is one of the best places in the region to take a walk during flower season, with circular 4km and 7km hiking trails. There is a 13km circuit for cars, and trails for 4WD vehicles, and accommodation is available in basic four-bed huts (R160) and campsites (R90).

Namakwaland Museum MUSEUM
(☎027-718 8100; Monument St; ⏲8am-1pm Mon-Fri, 2-5pm Mon-Thu, 2-4pm Fri) FREE Springbok's former synagogue, built in 1929, has been converted into the town's small museum. It's mostly a ramshackle collection of bric-a-brac, though the matchstick model of the immense church in the dusty *dorp* of Pella is impressive. Next door, the town's first Dutch Reformed church sits empty, though there are plans to convert it into a gallery showcasing local artists' work.

Sleeping

During the flower season, accommodation in Springbok fills up and rates rise.

Cat Nap Accommodation HOSTEL $
(☎027-718 1905; richtersveld.challen@kingsley.co.za; 99 Voortrekker St; dm R165, s R200-310, d R460; ❄) The walls of this spacious old house are adorned with nature photos, and rooms are cosy African-themed affairs. There's a self-catering kitchen and dorm beds in the barn, although they're incredibly close together and it gets hot in summer.

★**Kliprand Guesthouse** GUESTHOUSE $$
(☎027-7122 604; www.kliprandguesthouse.co.za; 2 King St; s/d R400/700; 🏊) A friendly and extremely well-priced option, with smart, well-appointed rooms and a large swimming pool in the garden. Breakfast R80.

Annie's Cottage GUESTHOUSE $$
(☎027-712 1451; www.springbokinfo.com; 4 King St; s/d incl breakfast R900/1200; ❄📶🏊) The ornate bedrooms are cutesy in places, but the Afro-themed rooms are fun, or request the honeymoon suite at no extra cost. Afternoon tea and cake are served and there is a self-catering room in the garden.

Old Mill Lodge GUESTHOUSE $$
(☎027-718 1705; www.oldmilllodge.com; 69 Van Riebeeck St; s/d incl breakfast R700/850; ❄@🏊) In a peaceful garden on a quiet side street, this place has pleasant rooms that are decorated with modern art and have large bathrooms. Flower-season tours can be arranged.

Mountain View GUESTHOUSE $$
(☎027-712 1438; www.mountview.co.za; 2 Overberg Ave; s/d incl breakfast from R800/900; ❄📶🏊) Perched in a tranquil location up against the hills, some of the four-star rooms open onto a garden leading to the pool, which has wonderful views.

Eating

Caffe Bella CAFE $
(50 Voortrekker St; mains R50; ⏲8am-5pm Mon-Fri, to 1pm Sat) The coffee is average but there's

WILDFLOWERS OF NAMAKWA

For most of the year Namakwa appears an inhospitable desert, where nothing but the hardiest shrubs can survive. But winter rains transform the dry landscape into a kaleidoscope of colours, as daisies, herbs, aloes, lilies and numerous other indigenous flower species blanket the ground. About 4000 species of plant grow in the region, drawing visitors from around the world to this often-forgotten corner of South Africa each spring.

The quality of the bloom and the optimum time to visit are dependent on the rains and vary from year to year. Generally, you have the best chance of catching the flowers at their peak between mid-August and mid-September (sometimes the season can begin early in August and extend to mid-October). The best flower areas also change from year to year, so be sure to get local advice on where to go.

Most varieties of wildflower are protected by law, and you can incur heavy fines if you pick them.

a nice brunch menu, with some slightly snazzier options such as brie and rocket panini sneaking in alongside more expected dishes such as *vetkoek* (deep-fried doughy bread) and mince. It's 1km south of the tourist-information office.

★**Tauren Steak Ranch** STEAKHOUSE **$$**
(☎027-712 2717; 2 Hospital St; mains R60-150; ⏲11.30am-late Mon-Sat) Meat lovers rejoice, Tauren serves steaks weighing up to a kilogram with a host of delectable sauces. The menu also features burgers, a few vegetarian choices and pizzas with toppings including biltong and *boerewors* (farm sausage). The ambience is country-relaxed, with *boeremusiek* on the stereo.

Melkboschkuil Plaaskombuis SOUTH AFRICAN **$$**
(☎083 242 4779; 75 Voortrekker St; mains R60-150; ⏲8am-late Mon-Sat, to 3pm Sun) Hearty food, including lamb curry, spare ribs and tripe, is on the menu. The deck overlooking Voortrekker St is a nice spot for lunch and some people-watching. If you're looking for nightlife, this is the place to come on Friday or Saturday.

Information

Tourist Office (☎027-712 8035; www.experiencenortherncape.com; Voortrekker St; ⏲7.30am-4.15pm Mon-Thu, to 3pm Fri) Has some maps and info on southern Namibia as well as Namakwa.

Getting There & Away

Buses, including **Intercape** (www.intercape.co.za), serve Cape Town (R500, 9½ hours, Sunday to Friday) and Windhoek, Namibia (R570, 13 hours, Tuesday, Thursday, Friday and Sunday).

Minibus shared taxis serve Upington (R270, four hours), Port Nolloth (R120, two hours) and Cape Town (R450, 8½ hours). Contact the **Namakwaland Taxi Association** (☎027-718 2840; Cnr Van der Stel & Namaqua Sts) for bookings.

Port Nolloth

POP 6100

The drive alone justifies a visit to this remote seaside town. One minute you're engulfed in nothingness, covered in a layer of red Kalahari sand; the next, you're cresting a hill, watching the icy blue vastness of the Atlantic appear on the horizon. Way off the beaten path near South Africa's northwest corner, the exposed and sandy little nowhere town of Port Nolloth exudes raw, final-frontier vitality. The bracing air smells of fish and salt, and the town is home to a motley, multicultural group of runaways, holidaymakers and fortune seekers.

Established as the shipping point for the region's copper, Port Nolloth is now dependent on the diamond dredgers and crayfish trawlers that gather at its small commercial pier. The dredgers are fitted with pumps, which vacuum diamond-bearing gravel from the ocean floor. Despite the De Beers complex standing guard, glittery catches do sometimes go astray. However, buying a diamond on the black market is not recommended – pitfalls include slenters (fake diamonds cut from lead crystal) and undercover police officers.

There are ATMs on Beach Rd and a tourist office in the harbour. The small **museum** (Beach Rd; admission R10; ⏲10am-4pm) is worth a look – it covers the region's diamond industry.

Sleeping & Eating

★**Scotia Inn Hotel & Restaurant** HOTEL **$$**
(☎027-851 8353; www.scotiainnhotel.co.za; Beach Rd; s/d from R350/650; 📶❄) There are standard rooms on the ground floor and bright, modern deluxe rooms (single/double R450/800) upstairs, some with sea-facing balconies. Request an ocean view – there's no extra fee. Also has a bar-restaurant.

Bedrock Lodge GUESTHOUSE **$$**
(☎027-851 8865; www.bedrocklodge.co.za; Beach Rd; s/d incl breakfast from R580/850, cottages R500-900; @📶❄) A funky place crammed with all sorts of eccentric knick-knacks and antique collectables. It's right on the seafront, with ocean views through the windows in the corrugated iron facade, and six nautical-chic self-catering cottages nearby.

Anita's Tavern SEAFOOD **$$**
(☎027-851 7039; Beach Rd; mains R70-130; ⏲dinner) A rustic, ramshackle beach shack, full of fishing junk. The menu is seafood oriented (of course) and the oysters are recommended.

Vespetti ITALIAN **$$**
(☎027-851 7843; 2099 Beach Rd; mains R60-120; ⏲lunch & dinner) This Italian restaurant, its awning twined with fishing rope, serves seafood as well as pizza and pasta.

Getting There & Away

Namakwaland Taxi Association (☎027-718 2840) runs minibus shared taxis to/from Springbok (R120, two hours, Monday to Saturday).

|Ai-|Ais/Richtersveld Transfrontier Park

Sculpted by millions of years of harsh elemental exposure, South Africa's most remote **transfrontier park** (027-831 1506; www.sanparks.org; adult/child R180/90; 7am-7pm Oct-Apr, to 6pm May-Sep) is a seemingly barren wilderness of lava rocks, humanlike trees and sandy moonscapes studded with semiprecious stones. The 6000 sq km of surreal mountain desert joins South Africa's Richtersveld National Park with Namibia's |Ai-|Ais Hot Springs Game Park.

Accessible only by 4WD, the Richtersveld is South Africa's final wild frontier. The South African section of the park covers 1630 sq km, and is most beautiful during the spring wildflower season, when, like elsewhere in Namakwa, it turns into a technicolour wonderland. Hiking here is demanding but spectacular; trails traverse jagged peaks, grotesque rock formations, deep ravines and gorges.

This is a place for those who seek to wander way off the beaten track and even those who crave a little survivalist action. There are almost no facilities so you need to be completely self-sufficient and it's highly recommended that you travel in convoy as the harsh terrain is challenging even for experienced 4WD drivers. Day visits are impractical considering the park's remoteness; you need at least three days, and preferably closer to a week.

|AI-|AIS/RICHTERSVELD TRANSFRONTIER PARK

Why Go Challenging 4WD terrain; remote, offbeat adventure; wilderness hiking; craggy desert landscapes; far-flung birdwatching; endless photography opportunities.

When to Go August to October, when temperatures are cooler and the flowers are in bloom. November to February is excruciatingly hot.

Practicalities Drive in from Alexander Bay. Basic facilities include a petrol station (open 7.30am to 4pm, no unleaded petrol available), small general store (open weekdays) and public phone at Sendelingsdrift. Bring all food and drinking water and ideally drive in convoy. Book all tours and accommodation in advance.

Budget Tips Due to its remoteness, the park isn't ideal for budget travellers. Renting a 4WD and camping is the cheapest option.

Activities

There are three hiking trails on the South African side, open from April to September. **Ventersval** (four days, three nights) encompasses the southwestern wilderness; **Lelieshoek-Oemsberg** (three days, two nights) takes in a huge amphitheatre and waterfall; and **Kodaspiek** (two days, one night) allows the average walker to view mountain desert scenery. On our most recent research trip the park did not have any guides available: you were still allowed to hike but you must come with a qualified local guide, contact Richtersveld Tours, Springbok Tourism or Cat Nap Accommodation (p457) to arrange this.

Tours

The easiest way to visit the park is on a tour. Accommodation is normally camping, with equipment provided. Tours can be organised in Port Nolloth, Springbok and Upington. Richtersveld Challenge, based at Cat Nap Accommodation (p457) in Springbok, offers group 4WD tours (about R1400 per person per day).

Richtersveld Tours GUIDED TOURS
(082 335 1399; www.richtersveldtours.com; per day R1850) 4WD tours including all meals and equipment.

Sleeping & Eating

There are four campsites (one to two people R195) on the South African side of the park; Potjiespram is near Sendelingsdrift Gate. Showers (cold water only) are available in all but Kokerboomkloof, which has no water at all.

★ **Tatasberg** CABIN $$
(cabins from R710) The delightful cabins at this camp each have a covered deck with magnificent views over the Gariep River. Made from corrugated tin, reed and canvas, they have a striking, rustic feel that blends perfectly with the park's scenery. Each has two single beds, a fridge, gas stove and shower.

Gannakouriep CABIN $$
(cabins from R710) Staying in these stone and canvas cabins is like upmarket camping.

Great efforts have been made to showcase the camp's magnificent setting in a rocky valley. Each cabin comes with two beds, gas stove and solar-powered fridge.

Sendelingsdrift CAMPGROUND, CHALET **$$**
(camping from R195, chalets from R715;) The two- to four-bed self-catering chalets at the park entrance are surprisingly comfortable, with porches overlooking the river.

Getting There & Around

A tar road leads 82km from Port Nolloth to Alexander Bay, from where a 90km gravel road leads to Sendelingsdrift Gate. This section is passable in a car but you need a 4WD vehicle in the park – sedans are not permitted. Richtersveld Challenge hires out 4WD vehicles and sells maps.

You can cross the Gariep (Orange) River into Namibia on a pontoon at Sendelingsdrift; it operates from 8am to 4.15pm, weather permitting.

WORTH A TRIP

SUTHERLAND

Surrounded by the Roggeveld Mountains, Sutherland (population 4000) is an attractive Karoo *dorpie* (town) with sandstone houses, a 19th-century church and gravel side streets. Perched at about 1500m above sea level, it's the coldest place in South Africa and snow carpets the ground every year. The clear skies combined with the minimal light pollution found in Sutherland's remote position make the area perfect for stargazing. The boffins agree: the Southern African Large Telescope (SALT), the southern hemisphere's largest optical telescope, is 14km east of town.

Other than stargazing, there's a 145km self-drive botanical tour, covering both the Roggeveld and lower Tankwa Karoo. The area enjoys an annual wildflower bloom similar to the one that carpets nearby Namakwa. Tourist information is available at the caravan park, 1km south of town on the Matjiesfontein road.

There is no public transport to Sutherland and the only tarred road is Rte 354 from Matjiesfontein, 110km south. There are gravel roads from Calvinia and Loxton (via Fraserburg). Contact your accommodation for an update on the state of the gravel roads, which deteriorate in the rain. The town's petrol station keeps short hours – fill up before you set off.

South African Astronomical Observatory (023-571 2436; www.saao.ac.za; Rte 356; night tour adult/child R80/40, day tour per person R60; night tour Mon, Wed, Fri, Sat, day tour 10.30am & 2.30pm Mon-Sat) During the day you can take a guided tour of the huge research telescopes, including the SALT, but it's the two-hour night tours that are the real draw. After a short video, you head outside to take a sky safari, thanks to two 16in telescopes. Times vary depending on the time of year and bookings are essential. Dress *very* warmly, even in summer.

Tankwa Karoo National Park (027-341 1927; www.sanparks.org; adult/child R128/64; 6.30am-6pm) With a car with good clearance, you can access this 1430-sq-km park, where Tankwa desert moonscapes meet sheer Roggeveld cliffs. There's great birdwatching and accommodation is available in the form of campsites or self-catering cottages.

Jurg Wagener (023-571 1481; www.sutherlandinfo.co.za; 19 Piet Retief St; stargazing R90; 8pm) Jurg's nightly stargazing evenings, on which he reveals the secrets of the Milky Way and beyond with the help of a laser pointer and five powerful telescopes, are highly recommended. Once a month on a Saturday night, Stars to Midnight (R290) begins with a hearty *boerekos* (literally, farmer's food) dinner, with the stargazing continuing until midnight.

Kambro-Kind (www.sutherlandinfo.co.za; camping R90, s/d incl breakfast R520/840) Offers a variety of guesthouses, a caravan park and some self-catering accommodation – the cute 'honeymoon suite' in a cottage on the edge of town is recommended. There's also a farm cottage 2km from Sutherland with no electricity and an open fire.

Perlman House (023-571 1445; Piet Retief St; mains R80-150; dinner Tue-Sat) A long-running resturant with a mostly meaty menu. Go for the Karoo lamb chops. The Roggeveld vegetation chomped by the sheep gives the meat a distinctive taste.

Namaqua National Park

For much of the year, **Namaqua National Park** (☎027-672 1948; www.sanparks.org; adult/child R64/32; ⏰8am-5pm) is largely forgotten. Until the spring, that is, when the park's coastal hills catch rain from the Atlantic, making its 1030 sq km a dependable place to see and photograph the spectacle that is the wildflower bloom. There are short nature trails and drives with viewpoints.

Accommodation largely consists of coastal campsites (from R115) with no facilities at all – not even ablutions. The **Skilpad Rest Camp** (chalets from R525) has pleasant and well-equipped chalets sleeping up to three people. Each year from mid-August to mid-September the **Namaqua Flowers Beach Camp** (per person incl breakfast, picnic lunch & dinner from R2775) opens, offering preerected dome tents with single beds, electricity and private bathrooms. Book well in advance.

In flower season, park accommodation fills rapidly. Search as well in the nearby towns of **Kamieskroon** and **Garies**, desolate places sitting amid the tumbleweed and scrub brush that characterises the Namakwa region. The park is 22km west of Kamieskroon along a poor gravel road. A longer but better route is the 73km gravel road from Garies. Some roads within the park are accessible with a 2WD, but a 4WD is recommended, and is essential for reaching some of the camps.

Intercape buses stop in Kamieskroon en route to/from Springbok, 67km north on the N7.

Calvinia

POP 9700

At the base of the dolerite-covered Hantam Mountains, hundreds of kilometres from anywhere, is this remote outback town with laid-back charm. Home to blazing bright light during the day, clear skies at night, quaint white-stone buildings and tree-lined streets, Calvinia is the principal town in this sheep-farming region. It's quiet for most of the year but when the rocky countryside blooms in spring, nearly all of the year's tourists arrive in one frenetic burst.

Sights

Calvinia Museum MUSEUM
(☎027-341 8500; 44 Kerk St; adult/child R10/5; ⏰8am-1pm & 2-5pm Mon-Fri) Housed in a former synagogue, this museum is surprisingly large and interesting for a small town. It concentrates on the white settlement of the region, with a section devoted to sheep farming, and has exhibits ranging from Victorian garb to the local telephone exchange switchboard, used until 1991.

Junkyard Blues GALLERY
(☎027-341 1423; 37 Stigling St) Stop at this 'rustic art' emporium to marvel at owner Dirk's collection of found objects, vintage gear and general junk. Road signs, sheep skulls, tin cups, watering cans, bed pans, old shoes, bicycles and farm implements decorate the exterior. Funky accommodation is available (R300 per person).

Flower Post Box MONUMENT
(Hoop St) A water tower has been converted into this giant post box. Letters and postcards posted here receive a special flower postmark.

Akkerendam Nature Reserve NATURE RESERVE
(☎027-341 8500; off Voortrekker St) North of town, this 275-sq-km reserve has one- and two-day hiking trails. The spring wildflower bloom carpets the mountainous terrain. Head to the **municipal office** (20 Hoop St) for hiking permits.

Activities

There are some fantastic 4WD routes around the surrounding countryside. One of the prettiest is the unpaved Rte 364, which leads southwest to Clanwilliam and the Cederberg via several stunning passes, including the Pakhuis Pass. Ask at the tourist office for access to the Hantam Flower 4x4 Route, which traverses an escarpment north of town. The trail follows a dry riverbed where huge fig trees cling to rocky cliffs.

Festivals & Events

AfrikaBurn CULTURE
(www.afrikaburn.com) The subcultural survivalist blowout happens about 100km south of Calvinia, off Rte 355 (untarred) to Ceres, near Tweefontein and the Tankwa Karoo National Park. It's a weeklong event, usually taking place in late April.

Hantam Meat Festival FOOD
(www.hantamvleisfees.co.za) The local love of meat is celebrated on the last weekend of August. Expect to taste everything from lamb chops to 'smileys' (sheep's head), along with live music and plenty of beer.

Sleeping & Eating

During the wildflower season, hotels and restaurants are often fully booked.

Die Blou Nartjie GUESTHOUSE $
(☎027-341 1263; www.nartjie.co.za; 35 Water St; s/d incl breakfast R390/520;) The Blue Orange's garden bungalow rooms are relaxing after a long drive, with sofa, shower and hot drinks. The restaurant (mains R65 to R120, dinner Monday to Saturday) serves traditional tucker such as *bobotie* and Karoo lamb chops.

African Dawn B&B $
(☎027-341 1482; www.calviniaretreat.co.za; 17 Strauss Ave; s/d incl breakfast R500/580;) In the leafy surrounds of a nursery, with a weaving cooperative nearby, these three tasteful rooms have flower paintings on their grey walls. Breakfast is served in a *lapa* (an 'African gazebo'), and the coffee shop (mains R50 to R75; open 9am to 5pm Monday to Friday and 9am to 2pm Saturday) serves toasted sandwiches, burgers and light meals.

★ **Hantam Huis** GUESTHOUSE $$
(☎027-341 1606; www.calvinia.co.za; 42 Hoop St; s/d incl breakfast from R495/790, r per person from R300;) Occupying a series of beautifully restored townhouses, Hantam is the perfect place to soak up Calvinia's country quiet and old-world charm. Die Dorphuis, a Victorian national monument, has luxury rooms packed with antiques. At the rear of the townhouse are cosy standard options in former servants' quarters and rooms once used by visiting church congregation members; Knegtekamer is particularly cute.

Lunch (mains R70 to R140) and three-course dinners (R290) are offered in the 19th-century Hantam Huis itself – Calvinia's oldest house.

Getting There & Away

The fastest and easiest route from Cape Town is via the N7 and Rte 27, which climbs the scenic Vanrhyns Pass to Calvinia, then runs northeast to Keimos and Upington. Rte 63 leads east from Calvinia to Victoria West via the quirky Karoo towns of Williston, Carnarvon and Loxton. There is no public transport to Calvinia.

Information

Calvinia has ATMs, a post office, petrol station and **tourist office** (☎027-341 8100; Stigling St; 7.30am-1pm & 1.45-4.15pm Mon-Fri).

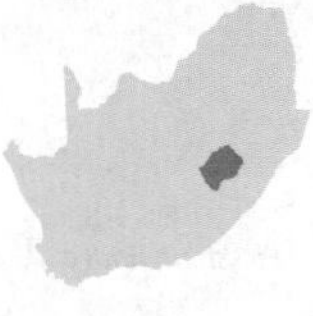

Lesotho

Includes ➡

Best Places to Eat

- No.7 Restaurant (p469)
- Sky Restaurant (p479)
- Semonkong Lodge (p483)
- Maliba Mountain Lodge (p477)

Best Places to Stay

- Malealea Lodge (p484)
- Maliba Mountain Lodge (p477)
- Semonkong Lodge (p483)
- Sani Mountain Lodge (p480)
- Ramabanta Trading Post (p474)
- Morija Guest Houses (p474)

Why Go?

Beautiful, culturally rich, safe, affordable and easily accessible from Durban and Johannesburg, mountainous Lesotho (le-*soo*-too) is a vastly underrated travel destination. The contrast with South Africa could not be more striking, with the Basotho people's distinct personality and the altitudinous terrain's topographical extremes. Even a few days in Lesotho's hospitable mountain lodges and trading posts will give you a fresh perspective on Southern Africa.

This is essentially an alpine country, where villagers on horseback in multicoloured balaclavas and blankets greet you round precipitous bends. The hiking and trekking – often on a famed Basotho pony – is world class and the infrastructure of the three stunning national parks continues to improve.

The 1000m-high 'lowlands' offer craft shopping and sights, but don't miss a trip to the southern, central or northeastern highlands, where streams traverse an ancient dinosaur playground. This is genuine adventure travel.

When to Go

Maseru

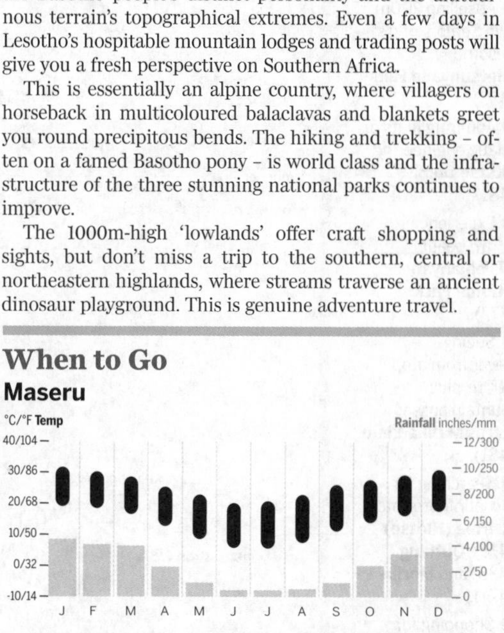

Mar–Apr Purple Cosmos flowers in the green meadows and cool autumn temperatures.

Jun–Aug See snow frosting the mountaintops and hit the slopes at Afriski Mountain Resort.

Sep Morija Arts Festival celebrates Sotho culture and peach blossoms colour the landscape.

Lesotho Highlights

1. Staying in a former trading post such as **Malealea Lodge** (p484) for mountain views and authentic village life.
2. **Pony trekking** (p468) or hiking through the highlands, staying in traditional Basotho huts.
3. Raising a glass in Southern Africa's highest pub, perched atop the Sani Pass in **Sani Top** (p480).
4. Finding rugged isolation in **Sehlabathebe National Park** (p486).
5. Abseiling 200m down Semonkong's awesome **Maletsunyane Falls** (p483).
6. Admiring feats of aquatic engineering at **Katse Dam** (p481).
7. Experiencing the raw beauty of **Ts'ehlanyane National Park** (p477).
8. Seeing forever from atop 3000m-plus mountain passes such as **Mafika-Lisiu** (p481).
9. Searching for dinosaur footprints in **Leribe (Hlotse)** (p476), **Quthing** (p485) and **Morija** (p474).
10. Shopping for tapestries in craft capital **Teyateyaneng** (p475).

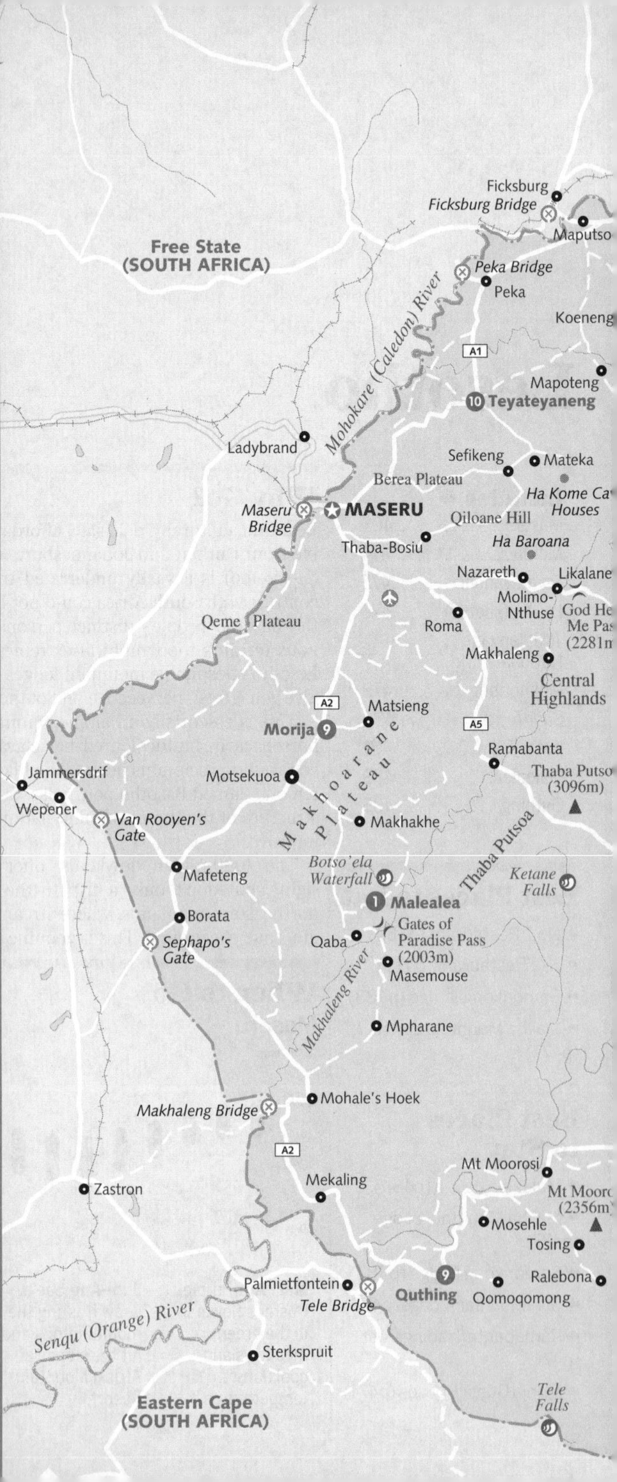

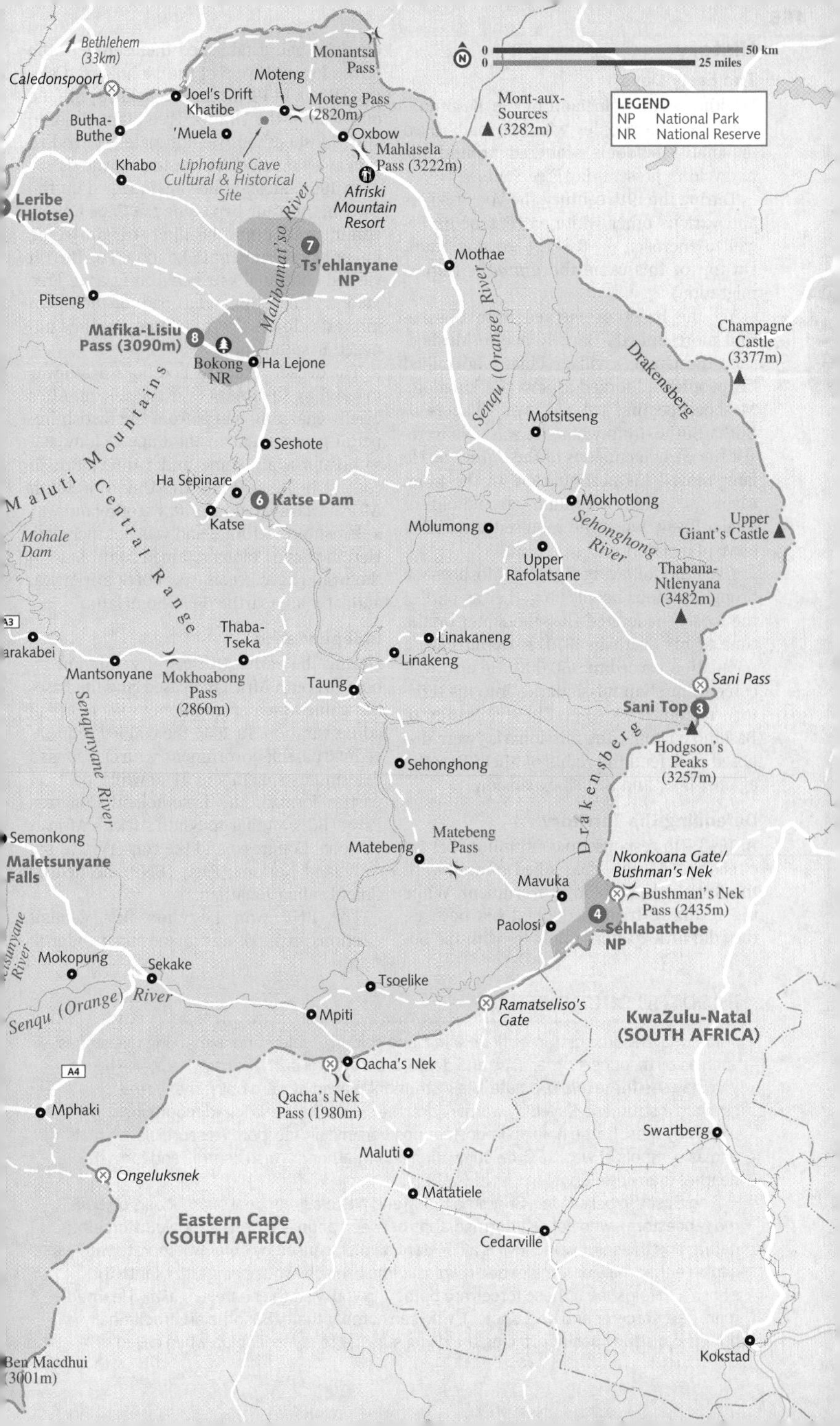

0 — 50 km
0 — 25 miles
LEGEND
NP National Park
NR National Reserve
Bethlehem (33km)
Caledonspoort
Joel's Drift
Khatibe
Moteng
Monantsa Pass
Moteng Pass (2820m)
Butha-Buthe
'Muela
Oxbow
Mahlasela Pass (3222m)
Mont-aux-Sources (3282m)
Khabo
Liphofung Cave Cultural & Historical Site
Afriski Mountain Resort
Leribe (Hlotse)
Malibamat'so River
Ts'ehlanyane NP
Mothae
Pitseng
Mafika-Lisiu Pass (3090m)
Bokong NR
Ha Lejone
Senqu (Orange) River
Champagne Castle (3377m)
Drakensberg
Maluti Mountains
Motsitseng
Seshote
Central Range
Ha Sepinare
Katse Dam
Katse
Mokhotlong
Molumong
Sehonghong River
Upper Giant's Castle
Mohale Dam
Upper Rafolatsane
Thabana-Ntlenyana (3482m)
A3
Thaba-Tseka
Linakaneng
Linakeng
Mantsonyane
Mokhoabong Pass (2860m)
Taung
Sani Pass
Sani Top
Hodgson's Peaks (3257m)
Senqunyane River
Sehonghong
Drakensberg
Semonkong
Maletsunyane Falls
Matebeng Pass
Matebeng
Nkonkoana Gate/ Bushman's Nek
Bushman's Nek Pass (2435m)
Mavuka
Paolosi
Sehlabathebe NP
Mokopung
Sekake
Tsoelike
Senqu (Orange) River
Ramatseliso's Gate
Mpiti
KwaZulu-Natal (SOUTH AFRICA)
Qacha's Nek
A4
Qacha's Nek Pass (1980m)
Mphaki
Swartberg
Maluti
Ongeluksnek
Matatiele
Eastern Cape (SOUTH AFRICA)
Cedarville
Kokstad
Ben Macdhui (3001m)

History

The Early Days

Lesotho is the homeland of the Basotho – Sotho-Tswana peoples who originally lived in small chiefdoms scattered around the highveld in present-day Free State.

During the 19th century, the Voortrekkers and various other white entrepreneurs began to encroach on Basotho grazing lands. On top of this came the *difaqane* (forced migration).

Yet the Basotho emerged from this period more united – largely due to Moshoeshoe the Great, a village chief who rallied his people and forged a powerful kingdom. Moshoeshoe first led his own villagers to Butha-Buthe, from where he was able to resist the early incursions of the *difaqane*. He later moved his headquarters to the more easily defended mountain stronghold of Thaba-Bosiu, where he repulsed wave after wave of invaders.

Over the following decades, Moshoeshoe brought various peoples together as part of the loosely federated Basotho state; by the time of his death in 1870, it would have a population exceeding 150,000. He also welcomed Christian missionaries into his territory. In return for some Christianisation of Basotho customs, the missionaries were disposed to defend the rights of 'their' Basotho against Boer and British expansion.

Defending the Territory

In 1843 – in response to continuing Boer incursions – Moshoeshoe allied himself with the British Cape Colony government. While the resulting treaties defined his borders, they did little to stop squabbles with the Boers, who had established themselves in the fertile lowveld west of the Mohokare (Caledon) River. In 1858, tensions peaked with the outbreak of the Orange Free State–Basotho War. Moshoeshoe was ultimately forced to sign away much of his western lowlands.

In 1868, Moshoeshoe again called on the British, this time bypassing the Cape Colony administration and heading straight to the imperial government in London. The British viewed continual war between Orange Free State and Basotholand as bad for their own interests. To resolve the situation, they annexed Basotholand.

The decade after Moshoeshoe's death was marked by squabbles over succession. After briefly changing hands from the British imperial government to the Cape Colony, Basotholand again came under direct British control in 1884. When the Union of South Africa was created in 1910, Basotholand was a British protectorate and was not included. Had the Cape Colony retained control, Lesotho would have become part of South Africa, and later an apartheid-era homeland.

Independence

During the early 20th century, migrant labour to South Africa increased, and the Basotho gained greater autonomy under British administration. In 1955 the council requested internal self-government, with elections to determine its members. Meanwhile, political parties formed: the Basotholand Congress Party (BCP; similar to South Africa's African National Congress) and the conservative Basotholand National Party (BNP), headed by Chief Leabua Jonathan.

The BNP won Lesotho's first general elections in 1965, and made independence

BASOTHO CULTURE

Traditional Basotho culture is flourishing, and colourful celebrations marking milestones, such as birth, puberty, marriage and death, are a central part of village life. While hiking you may see the *lekolulo*, a flute-like instrument played by herd boys; the *thomo*, a stringed instrument played by women; and the *setolo-tolo*, a stringed mouth instrument played by men. Cattle hold an important position in daily life, both as sacrificial animals and as symbols of wealth. Crop cultivation and weather are also central, and form the heart of many traditions.

The Basotho believe in a Supreme Being and place a great deal of emphasis on *balimo* (ancestors), who act as intermediaries between people and the capricious forces of nature and the spirit world. Evil is a constant danger, caused by *boloi* (witchcraft; witches can be either male or female) and *thkolosi* (small, mischievous beings, similar to the Xhosa's *tokoloshe*). If these forces are bothering you, visit the nearest *ngaka* (a learned man, part sorcerer and part doctor), who can combat them. Basotho are traditionally buried in a sitting position, facing the rising sun and ready to leap up when called.

from Britain the first item on its agenda. The following year, the Kingdom of Lesotho attained full independence, with Chief Jonathan as prime minister and King Moshoeshoe II as nominal head of state.

Chief Jonathan's rule was unpopular, and the opposition BCP won the 1970 election. Jonathan suspended the constitution, arrested and expelled the king, and banned opposition parties. Lesotho effectively became a one-party state.

Coup Decades

A military coup deposed Chief Jonathan in 1986, and restored Moshoeshoe II as head of state. Yet, following ongoing power disputes between the king and coup leader Justin Lekhanya, Moshoeshoe II was deposed and exiled in 1990. His son, Letsie III, assumed the throne, with only ceremonial powers, in 1992.

The '90s were a decade of unrest. A BCP split led prime minister Ntsu Mokhehle to form the breakaway Lesotho Congress for Democracy (LCD) and continue to govern, with the BCP now in opposition. Mokhehle died in 1998, and Pakalitha Mosisili took over the leadership of the LCD. The party subsequently won a landslide victory in elections that were declared reasonably fair by international observers but were widely protested against within Lesotho.

In September 1998, the government called on its Southern African Development Community (SADC) treaty partners – Botswana, South Africa and Zimbabwe – to help it restore order. Rebel elements of the Lesotho army resisted, resulting in heavy fighting and widespread looting in Maseru. The LCD won again in the 2002 elections, but opposition parties gained a significant number of seats.

In 2006, 17 LCD members led by Thomas Thabane formed the breakaway All Basotho Convention (ABC) party. In the controversial 2007 elections, the LCD retained its majority, and national strikes against the government ensued. A two-week curfew was imposed, there was an assassination attempt on Thabane, and many people were detained and tortured. In 2009, there was an assassination attempt on Mosisili.

In the hotly contested 2012 elections, Thabane became prime minister after the ABC formed a coalition with other parties including the LCD. Lesotho teetered on the verge of another coup in 2014, when Thabane fled to South Africa, accusing the military of trying to overthrow him. Following SADC mediation, general elections took place in February 2015. Thabane's ABC lost narrowly, and a coalition government of seven parties was headed by Pakalitha Mosisili's new party, the Democratic Congress. Mosisili is once again prime minister, with Mothetjoa Metsing of the LCD remaining deputy prime minister.

MALOTI OR RAND?

The South African rand is universally accepted in Lesotho, but even though it's tied to its neighbour's currency, the maloti is not accepted in South Africa. Most ATMs dispense maloti, so don't get caught with a pocketful. If you are spending a short time here before returning to South Africa, stocking up on rand will eliminate the worry of having to spend all your maloti before leaving Lesotho.

Climate

Clear, cold winters, with frosts and snow in the highlands, await you in Lesotho, so pack warm clothing. In summer (late November to early March), dramatic thunderstorms are common, as are all-enveloping clouds of thick mist. Summer temperatures can exceed 30°C in the valleys, though it's usually much cooler in the mountains, even dropping below freezing. Nearly all Lesotho's rain falls between October and April. Throughout the year, the weather is notoriously changeable.

Visits are possible at any time; autumn (especially March to April) and spring (especially September) are optimal.

Language

The official languages are Southern Sotho (Sesotho) and English. For more on Sesotho language and culture, visit www.sesotho.web.za.

Dangers & Annoyances

Travellers should not flaunt valuables anywhere. Be especially vigilant in Maseru; do not walk around at night, as muggings have occurred. Bag-snatching and pickpocketing are the main risks during the day. Occasional political unrest generally affects only the capital; stay off the streets and avoid large crowds.

PONY TREKKING

Pony trekking is one of Lesotho's top drawcards. It's done on sure-footed Basotho ponies, the result of crossbreeding between short Javanese horses and European full mounts. Good places to organise treks include **Malealea Lodge** (p484), **Semonkong Lodge** (p483), **Ts'ehlanyane National Park** (p477) and **Bokong Nature Reserve** (p481).

Advance booking is recommended, and no prior riding experience is necessary. Whatever your experience level, expect to be sore after a day in the saddle. For overnight treks, you'll normally need to bring food (stock up in Maseru), a sleeping bag, a torch (flashlight), water-purification tablets and warm, waterproof clothing. Check Malealea's website for more on the provisions and preparation required.

If you're hiking without a guide, you might be hassled for money or 'gifts' by shepherds in remote areas, and there's a very slight risk of robbery. Children sometimes beg and throw stones at cars, especially 4WD vehicles, on remote roads.

There are numerous police roadblocks; halt at the first stop sign and wait to be waved forward. Most policemen will quickly check your papers or just wave you on. Some may suggestively tell you how thirsty they are if they see you have drinks.

Lives are lost each year from lightning strikes; keep off high ground during electrical storms and avoid camping in the open. Waterproof clothing is essential for hiking and pony trekking.

Getting There & Around

Airlink flies a few times weekly between Jo'burg and Moshoeshoe I International Airport, 21km south of Maseru (from R1810, one hour). Flying to Bloemfontein airport (130km west of Maseru) is cheaper, as is hiring a car in South Africa, and most travellers enter Lesotho by road. Maseru Bridge border post is the busiest crossing; weekend traffic can cause queues on Friday and Sunday evenings.

You can now access most of Lesotho in a 2WD car, but it is still not possible to do a complete circuit without a 4WD, due to rough gravel roads in the east between Mokhotlong and Qacha's Nek. Bus and shared-taxi networks cover the country; taxis do not normally operate to a schedule but leave only when full.

MASERU

POP 430,000 / ELEV 1600M

Maseru is one of the world's more low-key capital cities. It sprawls across Lesotho's lower-lying western edge, rimmed by the Berea and Qeme Plateaus. Founded by the British in 1869 as an administrative post, over the past few decades Maseru has rapidly expanded and today there's a modicum of traffic congestion. A major city-rebuilding program has hidden many of the once-visible scars of the 1998 political unrest.

The city boasts a temperate climate, well-stocked shops and a decent selection of restaurants and accommodation. While it has few sights, Maseru is where you can get your bearings, sort out logistics and stock up on supplies before heading into the highlands and beyond.

Activities

Kick4Life FOOTBALL

(2832 0707; www.kick4life.org; Lesotho Football for Hope Centre, Nightingale Rd; per person M20; 6-8pm Tue & Thu) Join a game of five-a-side football at this soccer-focused NGO, which runs the world's first football club exclusively dedicated to social change. Alternatively, spectate with a glass of wine from the adjoining No.7 Restaurant. The planned stadium here will be the world's only sports stadium purpose-built for mass HIV/AIDS testing.

Sleeping

Maseru's B&B scene is fairly modest, but there is no shortage of options. Most people kick on to stay at Roma or Thaba-Bosiu, both of which are easy drives from the capital and have a few good sleeping options.

Foothills Guesthouse GUESTHOUSE $

(5870 6566; melvin@xsinet.co.za; 121 Maluti Rd; s/d M400/500, breakfast M40; P) This comfortable and friendly suburban guesthouse is good value by Maseru standards. The eight garden rooms are plain and their bathrooms old, but two have a kitchenette, in addition to the self-catering kitchen and thatched *lapa* (semiopen entertainment area) with braai (barbecue).

Maseru Backpackers & Conference Centre BACKPACKERS $

(2232 5166; www.lesothodurhamlink.org; Airport Rd; camping/dm/r M70/140/400; P) Linked to a British Anglican NGO and run by locals, this hostel has sparse, clean four- to eight-bed dorms and private rooms. A Basotho-style self-catering *rondavel* (round hut with a conical roof; M500), with a double, twin and lounge, is right on Maqalika Reservoir. It's 3km from the city centre; look out for the 'Lesotho Durham Link' sign.

The main reason to stay here is for outdoor activities, including canoeing and kayaking on the reservoir, rock climbing, abseiling and archery. Meals are available with notice.

★Kick4Life Hotel & Conference Centre HOTEL $$
(☎2832 0707; www.kick4life.org; Lesotho Football for Hope Centre, Nightingale Rd; r incl breakfast M580-650; P 📶) Attached to the football-focused NGO Kick4Life, this smart, soccer-themed hotel funds the charity's work, and its staff includes Kick4Life protégées. In reception is a picture of two lucky Lesothan lads meeting the England squad, while soccer strips decorate the 12 attractive rooms, all named after famous footballers.

The terrace's city view is second only to that of the nearby Lesotho Sun; it also overlooks the 11-a-side pitch.

Maseru Sun HOTEL $$
(☎2231 2434; www.suninternational.com; 12 Orpen Rd; s/d incl breakfast M1280/1450; P ❄ 📶 ≋) Part of the Sun International chain, this pleasant city-centre retreat has spacious rooms and suites. Facilities include a restaurant, bar, craft shops, a small casino, ATM and basic gym. Rates are cheaper for walk-ins.

Lancer's Inn HOTEL $$
(☎2231 2114; www.lancersinn.co.ls; cnr Kingsway & Pioneer Rd; s/d from M825/925; P ❄ 📶 ≋) Owned by the Dutch ambassador, this popular central business hotel has renovated rooms with satellite TV and open bathroom, while garden paths meander to pleasant stone *rondavels* and self-catering chalets. The restaurant, **Rendezvous** (lunch/dinner mains M60/70), bar and adjoining travel agency make this a good package.

Mohokare Guest House GUESTHOUSE $$
(☎2231 4442; www.mohokare.co.ls; 260 Pioneer Rd; incl breakfast s/d from M515/685, luxury s/d/tw M685/800/1000; P ❄ 📶) By a busy road near Pioneer Mall, Mohokare has a good reputation locally and a cute little bar. The self-catering **chalets** (M855, excl breakfast) have plenty of space; luxury rooms have kitchenette and free-standing bath, although they are not vastly better than the standard options. Shuttles and activities can be organised.

Black Swan B&B GUESTHOUSE $$
(☎2231 7700; www.blackswan.co.ls; 28 Manong Rd, New Europa; s/d incl breakfast M490/900; P ❄ 📶 ≋) With its gazebo, braai, resident rooster and bird pond, the Black Swan is a calm suburban refuge. The spartan but spacious rooms have satellite TV and all amenities. For a little extra you can have a room or *rondavel* with kitchenette (singles/doubles including breakfast from M650/1000) and rates are lower at weekends.

Lesotho Sun HOTEL $$$
(☎2224 3000; www.suninternational.com; Hilton Rd; s/tw/d incl breakfast from M1905/2060/2240; P ❄ @ 📶 ≋) Surveying Maseru from its hilltop perch since 1979, the capital's landmark hotel has a range of rooms and facilities including two restaurants, two bars, a casino, a travel agent and shops.

Eating

Maseru's restaurant scene is limited, but most of the following offer reasonable cuisine.

Pioneer Mall (p471) has chain restaurants Spur, Wimpy and Ocean Basket, a Pick 'n' Pay supermarket and the **Renaissance Café** (mains M70; ⏰7am-9pm Mon-Sat, to 6pm Sun). The **LNDC Centre** (cnr Kingsway & Pioneer Rd) has a Shoprite supermarket and cafes.

Ouh La La CAFE $
(☎2832 3330; cnr Kingsway & Pioneer Rd; mains M35; ⏰7.30am-9pm Mon-Fri, 8am-7pm Sat, 9.30am-4pm Sun; 📶) Locals and expats mix easily in this streetside garden cafe, which takes its Gallic theme from the adjoining Alliance Française cultural centre. The light menu is mostly sandwiches, crepes, pastries and salads, but the coffee is decent and wine is available by the glass.

★No.7 Restaurant INTERNATIONAL $$
(☎2832 0707; www.kick4life.org; Lesotho Football for Hope Centre, Nightingale Rd; lunch/dinner mains M50/95; ⏰7am-10pm Mon-Sat; 🖉) Attached to the football-focused NGO Kick4Life and its hotel, No.7 pumps its profits back into Kick4Life's charitable work, and the team includes young locals training for a career in hospitality. The restaurant is a stylish spot with city views and a menu fusing European sophistication with Basotho touches, offering dishes such as fillet steak and bouillabaisse.

Maseru

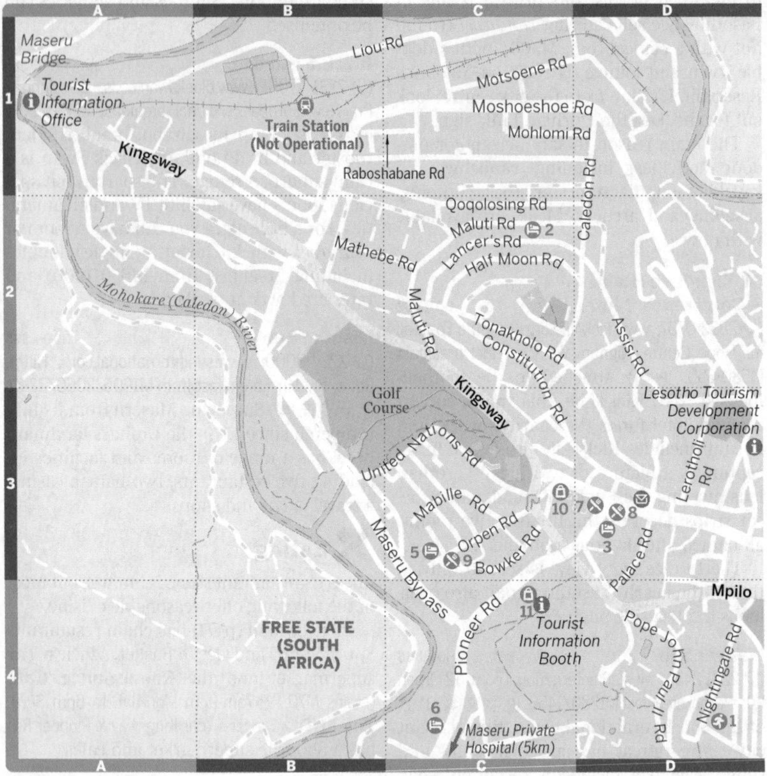

Maseru

Activities, Courses & Tours
1 Kick4Life D4

Sleeping
2 Foothills Guesthouse C2
Kick4Life Hotel & Conference Centre .... (see 1)
3 Lancer's Inn D3
4 Lesotho Sun E4
5 Maseru Sun C3
6 Mohokare Guest House C4

Eating
7 LNDC Centre D3
No.7 Restaurant .... (see 1)
8 Ouh La La D3
9 Piri Piri C3
Regal Restaurant .... (see 10)
Renaissance Café .... (see 11)
Rendezvous .... (see 3)

Drinking & Nightlife
Lancer's Inn .... (see 3)
Lesotho Sun .... (see 4)
Times Caffe .... (see 7)

Shopping
10 Basotho Hat C3
Collectables .... (see 11)
11 Pioneer Mall C4

On the way in, you might pass Kick4Life program members playing football.

Piri Piri INTERNATIONAL **$$**
(Orpen Rd; mains M100; ⏲9am-9pm Mon-Sat) This restaurant near the Maseru Sun does Portuguese, Mozambican and South African dishes, including steaks, seafood, *feijoada* (a traditional Portuguese stew) and piri piri chicken. Choose between romantic, low-lit rooms and gazebos.

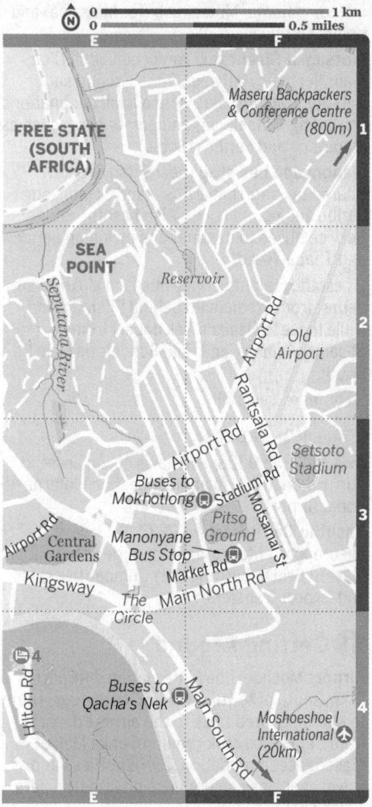

Regal Restaurant INDIAN $$

(☎2231 3930; off Kingsway; mains M50-120;) Occupying a Basotho-hat-style building, this 1st-floor Indian restaurant is a favourite among businessmen and politicians. Lesotho's only Indian eatery, it serves classics such as korma, madras, rogan josh and vegetable curries, and also offers steaks and noodle dishes. The service is professional, the Hindi music is unobtrusive and you can almost imagine you're in a British curry house.

Drinking

Lesotho Sun BAR

(www.suninternational.com; Hilton Rd;) Maseru's expat community and local players climb the hill for sundowners with a view. Cocktails at the pool bar are a popular way to kick off the weekend on Friday.

Lancer's Inn BAR

(www.lancersinn.co.ls; cnr Kingsway & Pioneer Rd) This modern hotel bar is a comfortable city-centre retreat.

Times Caffe BAR, CAFE

(Level 1, LNDC Centre, cnr Kingsway & Pioneer Rd) All funky leather sofas, stylish lights, plastic chairs, colourful stools and tiled surfaces, Times is popular with the local cool crowd. An outdoor terrace overlooks the main drag.

Shopping

Basotho Hat CRAFTS

(www.golesotho.co.za/Other Pages/Maseru.html; Kingsway; ⊙8am-5pm Mon-Fri, to 4.30pm Sat) More expensive than elsewhere, but convenient and well stocked, with two floors of quality crafts from across the country. Credit cards are accepted and it's a low-pressure shopping environment.

Collectables CRAFTS

(Pioneer Mall, cnr Pioneer & Mpilo Rds; ⊙9am-8pm) Souvenirs, sandals, and items including bags by the local Seihati Weavers.

Pioneer Mall MALL

(www.pioneer.co.ls; cnr Pioneer & Mpilo Rds; ⊙9am-6pm Mon-Fri, to 4pm Sat, to 2pm Sun) A modern mall with a Pick 'n' Pay supermarket, chain restaurants, numerous services and retailers. Pick 'n' Pay and some of the restaurants have longer hours than the mall in general.

Information

Pioneer Mall has banks, internet cafes, a currency-exchange bureau, a Western Union branch and a pharmacy.

EMERGENCY

Fire Department (☎112)

Police (☎112)

MEDICAL SERVICES

In an emergency, try contacting your embassy, as most keep lists of recommended practitioners. For anything serious, you'll need to go to South Africa.

Maseru Private Hospital (☎2231 2276, 2231 3260; off Pioneer Rd, Ha Thetsane) In the suburb of Ha Thetsane, about 7km south of central Maseru.

MONEY

There are several banks with ATMs on Kingsway. The top-end hotels will do foreign-exchange transactions (at poor rates).

TOURIST INFORMATION

Tourist Information Booth (☎2833 2238; visitlesotho.travel; Pioneer Mall, cnr Pioneer & Mpilo Rds; ⊙10am-6pm Mon-Fri, to 3pm Sat, to 2pm Sun) This helpful booth gives out a good AA map of Lesotho, Maseru maps and brochures. The staff also offer advice on public transport and tours.

Tourist offices can also be found at Maseru Bridge Border Post (☎2231 2427; ⊙8am-5pm Mon-Fri, 9am-1pm Sat & Sun), Moshoeshoe I International Airport (☎2835 0479; ⊙8am-5pm) and the headquarters of the Lesotho Tourism Development Corporation (LTDC; ☎2231 2238; cnr Linare Rd & Parliament St; ⊙8am-5pm Mon-Fri).

TRAVEL AGENCIES

There are travel agencies at Pioneer Mall, the LNDC Centre and Lancer's Inn hotel.

Leloli Travel Agency (☎5885 1513; Pioneer Mall, cnr Pioneer & Mpilo Rds; ⊙8am-5pm Mon-Fri, 9am-noon Sat) Books flights and Budget hire cars.

Maseru Travel (☎2231 4536; gracem.maserutravel@galileosa.co.za; Maseru Book Centre, Kingsway; ⊙8.30am-5pm Mon-Fri, 9-11am Sat) Represents Budget hire cars, Intercape buses and airlines including South African Airways.

Getting There & Away

BUS & SHARED TAXI

There are three main transport stands to the northeast of the main roundabout:

Sefika taxi rank (behind Sefika Mall) A major stand with services to nationwide destinations, including Roma, Motsekuoa (for Malealea) and points south.

Motsamai Street taxi rank (behind KFC on Main North Rd, between Pitso Ground and Setsoto Stadium) Services to local destinations (including Motsekuoa) and points north such as Maputsoe and Leribe (Hlotse).

Manonyane bus stop (near Pitso Ground) Shared taxis to Thaba-Bosiu and Semonkong, Leribe and points north. Also Lesotho Freight Service buses to destinations including Leribe and Thaba-Tseka.

Lesotho Freight Service buses to Mokhotlong depart from Stadium Rd behind Pitso Ground, while those to Qacha's Nek depart from next to St James Primary and High Schools on Main Rd South.

For more, see p598.

CAR & MORORCYLE

Avis (☎2235 0328; www.avis.co.za; Lesotho Sun, Hilton Rd) Also at Moshoeshoe I International Airport.

Basotho Car Rental (☎2232 4123; www.basothocarrental.com; Camara de Lobos Bldg, Maseru Bridge border post) Competitive rates and airport transfers.

Getting Around

Airport Moshoeshoe I International Airport is 21km south of town, off Main South Rd en route to Morija. Shared taxis to the airport depart from Sefika taxi rank (behind Sefika Mall). Maseru accommodation, tourist offices and travel agencies can organise private transfers, which cost around M100.

Taxi The standard shared-taxi fare around town is M6.50; M50 for a nonshared taxi.

BLANKET COVERAGE

The Basotho blanket is an important part of public, social and private life, not only as a practical article of clothing but also as a symbol of wealth. In 1860, when European traders presented King Moshoeshoe I with a blanket, the Basotho people were so taken with it that blankets superseded animal hides. By the 1880s, traders were overwhelmed with demand for blankets, which were manufactured from high-quality woven cloth in England.

Today's woollen blanket provides insulation in the heat and the cold, is fireproof and a status symbol (each costs a hefty M500). Look out for a maize cob (a symbol of fertility), a crown or military markings (a legacy of British imperialism) and a cabbage leaf (meaning prosperity). Young married women wear a blanket around their hips until their first child is conceived; and young boys are presented with a blanket upon circumcision, symbolising their emergence into manhood.

The solid lines on a blanket's edges are worn vertically; the Basotho believe that worn horizontally the blanket can stunt growth, wealth and development.

Less common, but still used in rural areas, is the Basotho hat *(mokorotlo* or *molianyeo),* with its distinctive conical shape and curious top adornment. The hat is supposedly modelled on the shape of Qiloane Hill, near Thaba-Bosiu.

AROUND MASERU

Maseru's surrounding areas hold several attractions, which make easy day or overnight excursions from the capital.

Thaba-Bosiu

About 25km east of Maseru is the famed and flat-topped Thaba-Bosiu (Mountain at Night), where King Moshoeshoe the Great established his mountain stronghold in 1824. It's regarded as the birthplace of the Basotho nation and, although an unassuming spot, is Lesotho's most important historical site.

The origins of Thaba-Bosiu's name are unclear and numerous versions exist. The most interesting is that, to intimidate enemies, magic herbs were placed on a rope, which was wrapped around the mountain. When intruders crossed the rope at night, they were overcome with the drugged-like sensation that Thaba-Bosiu was 'growing' and thus an unconquerable mountain.

At the mountain's base is a **visitor information centre** (☎2835 7207; ⏲8am-5pm Mon-Fri, from 9am Sat, 9am-1pm Sun) where you can organise a guide to walk with you to the top (M40, two hours). Horse riding is also available (M90; book ahead).

From the summit, there are good views over the surrounding area, including to **Qiloane Hill**, which allegedly provided the inspiration for the Basotho hat. Also fascinating to see are the remains of fortifications, Moshoeshoe's grave and parts of his original settlement.

The **cultural village** (admission M20; ⏲8am-sunset; P) adjoining the visitor information centre has a traditional Basotho village, museum and amphitheatre.

Sleeping & Eating

Thaba-Bosiu's accommodation options are within walking distance of each other on the main road.

Mmelesi Lodge LODGE $
(☎5250 0006; www.mmelesilodge.co.ls; s/d M420/510, breakfast M65; P) Mmelesi Lodge has sandstone chalets in the style of thatched *mokhoro* (traditional Basotho huts), reached along flower-lined paths. It often fills with with government workshoppers, and the bar-restaurant can get jumping when musicians are in town.

OFF THE BEATEN TRACK

MATSIENG

Royal Archives & Museum (☎2700 6984; www.royalarchives.org.ls; admission M15; ⏲9am-4.30pm Mon-Fri, to 1pm Sat; P) Morija's unremarkable neighbouring village, Matsieng, is the unlikely site of a royal compound. A new palace was built in Maseru in the '60s, but the royals still weekend here. The adjoining archives and small museum display items from the royal collection and information and documents about the monarchy.

Staff can give you a **tour** (M40) of the village and point out notable elements of the compound.

Nokaneng Backpacker BACKPACKERS $
(☎5896 2461; www.nokanengbackpacker.com; dm/r M140/M300; P) Basotho-American couple Kennedy and Rose offer rustic accommodation with solar electricity, a self-catering kitchen and showers.

Cultural Village RESORT $$
(☎6286 1361; www.thababosiuculvil.co.ls; r incl breakfast M900; P) The tourist complex has comfortable chalets and an appealing restaurant (mains M90).

Getting There & Away

Shared taxis to Thaba-Bosiu (M18, 30 minutes) depart from the Manonyane transport stand in Maseru. If you're driving, take the Mafeteng Rd for about 13km and turn left at the Roma turn-off; after about 6km take the signposted road left. Thaba-Bosiu is 10km further along.

Ha Baroana

Ha Baroana is one of Lesotho's more important and publicised rock-art sites. It's worth a visit if you have extra time, although neglect and vandalism have taken their toll.

Just before the village of Nazareth, there's a signposted gravel track to the paintings. Follow this 3km to Ha Khotso village, turn right at a football field and continue 2.5km to a hilltop overlooking a gorge. A footpath zigzags down the hillside to the rock shelter with the paintings.

To get to Nazareth, take the Roma turn-off from the Mafeteng Rd; continue for about 8km to the Thaba-Tseka junction. Turn left (towards Thaba-Tseka) and continue about 12km to Nazareth. Shared taxis

WORTH A TRIP

RAMABANTA TRADING POST

Ramabanta Trading Post (☎2234 0202; s/d M300/600, breakfast/meals M75/150, half board per person M525; P) About 40km southeast of Roma, off the tar road to Semonkong and the south, is this sister property to the Roma Trading Post guesthouse. Set in neat grounds with mountain views, the smart and spacious *rondavels* have lounge and dining room, three have kitchenette, and the main building features a lounge, bar and restaurant.

Activities including pony trekking, hiking and village visits are offered. Staying here provides the chance to link up Roma, Ramabanta, Semonkong and other places in the area on overnight hikes and pony treks. Shared taxis serve Ramabanta from Maseru (M50, two hours), continuing to Semonkong.

between Maseru and Thaba-Tseka can drop you at the Ha Baroana turn-off.

Roma

Nestled amid sandstone cliffs about 35km southeast of Maseru, Roma was established as a mission town in the 1860s. Today it's Lesotho's centre of learning, with the country's only university, as well as several seminaries and secondary schools. The beautiful National University of Lesotho **campus** is worth a wander and boots hanging from phone lines confirm Roma's student credentials. The southern entry/exit to town takes you through a striking gorge landscape, and is best travelled during the morning or late afternoon when the lower sun lights the cliffs to full advantage.

Shared taxis run throughout the day to/from Maseru (M25, 45 minutes).

★**Roma Trading Post** GUESTHOUSE $
(☎2234 0202; www.tradingpost.co.za; s/d M250/500, without bathroom M175/350, camping M85, breakfast/dinner M55/100; P) Roma Trading Post is a charming fourth-generation trading post operated since 1903 by the Thorn family. The attached guesthouse includes garden rooms, *rondavels* and the original sandstone homestead, with shared kitchen, set in a lush garden. The accommodating and personable staff can organise adventures including pony trekking, hiking, visits to nearby *minwane* (dinosaur footprints) and local attractions.

It is clearly signposted on the north (Maseru) side of town.

Kaycees FAST FOOD $
(mains M25) Kaycees, off Roma's main drag, is a popular hangout serving fast food and cans of Maluti lager to happy students.

Morija

Tiny Morija is the site of the first European mission in Lesotho. It's an important and attractive town with a rich cultural heritage that makes a pleasant stopover or day trip from Maseru. The Morija Museum is the unofficial national one, and if you're here in late September or early October, don't miss the Morija Festival.

Sights & Activities

Morija Museum & Archives MUSEUM
(☎2236 0308; www.morija.co.ls; admission M10; ⌚8am-5pm Mon-Sat, from noon Sun; P) This small, considered museum contains ethnographical exhibits, archives from the early mission and scientific artefacts. There's an excellent collection of books for sale, including those by curator Stephen Gill. Staff will guide you to **dinosaur footprints** (M50 per person) in the nearby Makhoarane Mountains, a 1½-hour return walk.

Maeder House Crafts Centre ARTS CENTRE
(☎5991 1853; ⌚by appointment; P) Crafts centre in a missionary house near the museum.

If you're staying overnight, the ladies in the adjoining shop can make you a *shweshwe* (printed dyed cotton fabric) shirt for M350. Lesotho's first printing press is in the neighbouring printing works.

Pony Trekking & Hiking

Pony trekking (per person per hour/half-day/day M190/500/750), guided hikes to dinosaur footprints and **village sleepovers** (incl full board per hiker/rider M370/890) can be organised through Morija Guest Houses. Reserve a day in advance. An optional packhorse for luggage is M400 extra.

Sleeping & Eating

★**Morija Guest Houses** GUESTHOUSE $
(☎6306 5093; www.morijaguesthouses.com; r per person without bathroom M220-300, camping M110, breakfast/lunch/dinner M66/110/134; P) At

this sterling stone-and-thatch house perched high above the village, guests can choose between cosy rooms in the main building and cottages below. Entertainment from mountain biking to traditional choir and dance performances is offered, making this a top spot to experience the area. Backpackers who arrive by public transport receive a discounted rate of M175 per person.

Lindy's B&B GUESTHOUSE $
(☎5885 5309; www.lindysbnb.co.ls; s/d M380/550, without bathroom M280/460, breakfast/dinner M65/120; P 📶) Lindy offers a large, modern stone duplex with two en suite rooms, and a century-old cottage with two more rooms, both ringed by the Makhoarane Mountains.

Morija Museum Tearoom CAFE $
(mains M40; ⏲8am-5pm Mon-Sat, from noon Sun) The small courtyard tearoom at Morija Museum serves dishes such as pizzas and chicken and chips. It comes to life on weekends and during the Morija Festival.

Getting There & Away

Shared taxis run throughout the day to/from Maseru (M25, 45 minutes) and Matsieng (M7, 10 minutes).

NORTHWESTERN LESOTHO

The lowlands of northwestern Lesotho comprise a number of busy little commercial towns. Only the craftwork-selling towns of Teyateyaneng and Leribe (Hlotse) draw travellers, along with the stunning Ts'ehlanyane National Park, but the area gives way to the majestic northeastern highlands and features a few major border crossings.

Teyateyaneng

Teyateyaneng (Place of Quick Sands; usually known simply as 'TY') is the craft centre of Lesotho, and is worth a stop to buy tapestries or watch them being made.

Sleeping & Eating

Blue Mountain Inn HOTEL $$
(☎2250 0362; www.bmilesotho.com; s/d incl breakfast M700/800, mains M70; P ❄ 📶 🏊) Its plain motel-style rooms enlivened by scattered paintings, Blue Mountain really comes into its own at the rear, where the bar-restaurant overlooks a garden and small pool. The restaurant serves salads, steaks, burgers, good pizzas and more elaborate dishes, such as chicken with peppers in white-wine sauce.

Ka-Pitseng Guest House GUESTHOUSE $$
(☎2250 1638; s/d incl breakfast M500/650; P ❄ 📶) Ka-Pitseng is set in scrubby gardens by the main road on the south (Maseru) side of town. The cool and comfy rooms have satellite TV, plastic flowers, lilac pillars and conference charisma. There is also a bar-restaurant.

Shopping

Lesotho Mountain Crafts CRAFTS
(actionlesotho.ie; ⏲9am-5pm Mon-Fri, to 4pm Sat & Sun) You can buy the work of 10 local co-operatives at this showroom and workshop, by the main road about 2km before Teyateyaneng (coming from Maseru). Items include jewellery, shawls, slippers, tapestries, bags and *seshoeshoe* (Basotho dress made of traditional cotton print), incorporating materials such as cow horn, felt, rose leather, sheepskin and wool.

Setsoto Design CRAFTS
(www.setsotodesign.com; ⏲8am-5pm) Next to a primary school near the Blue Mountain Inn, you can see the painstaking tapestry-making process at Setsoto Design. A dozen women weave away in the workshop, and the shop sells a beautiful selection of tapestries

DON'T MISS

MORIJA ARTS FESTIVAL

This highlight of Lesotho's cultural calendar continues to grow in prestige; an increasing number of attendees make the trip from South Africa each year. The five-day event, held annually in late September or early October, showcases the diversity of Sotho culture through dance, electronic and jazz music, poetry and theatre. Past highlights have included horse racing, *moraba-raba* (the African equivalent of chess) competitions, and performances by the likes of South Africa's Hugh Masekela and Zimbabwe's Oliver Mtukudzi. For more information, visit www.morija.co.ls or contact the Morija Museum.

OFF THE BEATEN TRACK

HA KOME CAVE HOUSES

Ha Kome Cave Houses (www.golesotho.co.za/Other Pages/Kome caves.html; admission M20; ⌚8am-5pm Mon-Fri, from 9am Sat, 9am-1pm Sun; P) The Ha Kome cave houses are an anomaly in this area, 21km from Teyateyaneng and several kilometres from the village of Mateka. These extraordinary inhabited mud dwellings are nestled under a rock overhang, hidden within the pink-and-orange cliffs. There's a small information centre with toilets and a few basic maps. In a 2WD, you should be able to reach the caves from TY or from Maseru or Thaba-Bosiu via Sefikeng, but do check on road conditions. Shared taxis go there from TY and Maseru. A music and beer **festival** (www.komecavesfestival.com) takes place here in November.

(M250 to M6500) and other crafts. Credit cards are accepted.

Elelloang Basali Weavers CRAFTS
(www.africancraft.com; ⌚8am-5pm Mon-Fri, to 2pm Sat) Elelloang Basali (Be Aware Women) makes hand-spun mohair rugs with geometric patterns, as well as tapestries and other items. Find it in a building made of recycled cans by the main road on the northern (Maputsoe) side of town.

Getting There & Away

Shared taxis run throughout the day to/from Maseru (M25, one hour) and Maputsoe (for Leribe (M20, one hour). Chartering a taxi from Maseru costs about M200 one way (rates can change depending on fuel prices).

Leribe (Hlotse)

Leribe (also known as Hlotse) is a busy regional market hub. It served as an administrative centre under the British, as attested to by a few old buildings slowly decaying in the leafy streets.

Sights

Major Bell's Tower LANDMARK
Leribe's main sight is this crumbling tower near the market. It was built in 1879, and spent most of its career as a storehouse for government records. The tower is not open to visitors.

Subeng River Dinosaur Footprints HISTORIC SITE
(⌚24hr) FREE Dinosaur footprints abound near Leribe. About 7km north of town (en route to Butha-Buthe) are the Subeng River footprints. At the signpost, just before the road crosses the river, walk down about 500m to a concrete causeway. The worn footprints of at least three species of dinosaur are about 15m downstream on the right bank. Local children will likely offer to guide you.

Tsikoane Village Dinosaur Footprints HISTORIC SITE
(⌚24hr) FREE This set of footprints is a few kilometres south of Leribe at Tsikoane village. Immediately after the Tsikoane Primary School, take the small dirt road to the right towards some rocky outcrops. Follow it up to the church. Children will vie to lead you the 1km slog up the mountainside to the *minwane,* in a series of caves, and a guide can be helpful here. The prints are clearly visible on the rock ceiling.

Sleeping & Eating

If you're heading into the highlands, Leribe is the last good place to stock up – there's a Shoprite supermarket in town.

Mahlakapese Guest House GUESTHOUSE $
(☎6207 8633; mahlakapese@gmail.com; s/d incl breakfast from M500/600; P) Mahlakapese picks up a little noise from the nearby mosque and main road, but it's a reasonable deal overall with comfortable and spacious rooms. Find it on the Butha-Buthe side of town.

Mountain View Hotel HOTEL $$
(☎2240 0559; www.mvhlesotho.com; Main St; s/d incl breakfast M650/750, mains M70; P ❄ 📶 🏊) This reliable hotel is adjacent to both the highway and Leribe's main drag. Rooms are bland but spacious and functional, and they outdo most places in town; those upstairs have a shower, while downstairs you get a bath with hand-held shower. The restaurant serves pizzas, burgers, grills and sandwiches.

Shopping

Leribe Craft Centre CRAFTS, CLOTHING
(⌚8am-4.30pm Mon-Fri, to 1pm Sat) Sells a range of high-quality mohair goods from ponchos to stoles, plus craftwork and books on Lesotho, at good prices. Find it on the main road, downhill from the Mountain View Hotel and opposite the hospital.

Getting There & Away

Shared taxis run throughout the day between Leribe and Maseru (M50, two hours), usually with a change of vehicles at Maputsoe. There are also several vehicles daily to/from Katse (M100, three hours) and Butha-Buthe (M15, 40 minutes).

Butha-Buthe

Lesotho's second-largest town, Butha-Buthe (Place of Lying Down), was so named by King Moshoeshoe the Great because it was here that his people first retreated during the chaos of the *difaqane*. Its frontier-town scrappiness is redeemed by an attractive setting alongside the Hlotse River, with the beautiful Maluti Mountains as a backdrop.

There are ATMs and petrol stations here. A few accommodation options are signposted from the main road on the northeastern (Oxbow) side of town.

Crocodile Inn HOTEL **$$**
(☎2246 0223; crocodileinn@yahoo.com; s/d/tr incl breakfast M480/602/888, rondavel s/d incl breakfast M530/700; P ❄) Butha-Buthe's main hotel is overpriced and dated, with a busy bar and a smell of bleach in the institutional corridors, leading to the rooms' sweaty odours. Rooms only have bath (no shower) and the kitchy restaurant takes 30 minutes to produce chops, one hour for pizza. Nonetheless, it's safe and secure, with TV, tea and coffee in the rooms and *rondavels*.

Getting There & Away

Many shared taxis travel to/from Maseru via Maputsoe (M25, 20 minutes), where you'll usually need to change vehicles. Shared taxis (M110, three hours) and buses also serve Mokhotlong. Butha-Buthe is the last reliable place to buy petrol if you're heading to Mokhotlong.

Ts'ehlanyane National Park

This Lesotho Northern Parks–administered **national park** (☎in Leribe 2246 0723; reception@datacom.co.ls; per person/vehicle M40/10; ⏲gate 8am-4.30pm; P) protects a beautiful, 56-sq-km patch of rugged wilderness, including one of Lesotho's only stands of indigenous forest, at a high altitude of 2000m to 3000m. This underrated and underused place is about as far away from it all as you can get and is perfect for hiking.

In addition to day walks, there's a 39km day hike or pony trek to/from Bokong Nature Reserve, covering some of Lesotho's most dramatic terrain. Heading north from Bokong to Ts'ehlanyane is easier, as Bokong is higher; the challenging route is also better tackled by pony or horse. Hiking guides can be arranged at Ts'ehlanyane gate (M30 within the park, M410 to Bokong) or Maliba Mountain Lodge.

Community-run **pony trekking** (1-3hr/3-5hr/day per person M320/420/470) and horse riding can be arranged through Maliba or the park gate. Book at least 24 hours ahead.

Maliba also offers community-run **tours** (half-day per car M160) of the villages bordering Ts'ehlanyane.

Sleeping & Eating

Maliba Mountain Lodge's excellent **restaurant** (breakfast M150, lunch main/3-course set menu M120/180, dinner main/3-course set menu M150/270; ⏲7am-10pm) serves dishes such as honey-soy pork chops, three-bean curry and malva pudding in the park. Advance booking is advised.

★**Maliba Mountain Lodge** LODGE **$$$**
(☎6351 5367, in South Africa 031-702 8791; www.maliba-lodge.com; chalet s/d incl full board M2635/3518; P 📶) Maliba (Madiba) offers a range of accommodation in Ts'ehlanyane National Park, but its signature offering is six lavish chalets. Each features a four-poster bed, antique furniture, terrace and hot tub facing the mountain range, heated towel racks and sherry by the door. Go for the secluded room 6, the honeymooners' choice.

Walking trails lead to waterfalls, and the swish new main lodge has restaurant, bar, VIP section, verandah and fireplaces, all with sweeping mountain views.

Accommodation also includes well-equipped self-catering **cottages** (M1530 plus M100 per person), with terraces overlooking the river and gazing up a mountain valley; quaint stone and thatch riverside **huts** (s/d incl full board M1250/1960), near swimming holes and hiking trails (hut 3 offers privacy for romantic couples); and comfortable **rooms** (s/d incl breakfast M693/990) with adjoining bar in the block above the main lodge, known as the mountainside retreat.

Getting There & Away

If you're driving, take the signposted turn-off from the main road about 6km southwest of Butha-Buthe, from where the park gate is 30km on a tar road. Maliba is 2km further on.

Shared taxis from Butha-Buthe marked 'Ts'ehlanyane' serve the villages en route to the park. If you ask before departure, they can take you to the gate or Maliba for about M30. Take the driver's number to organise transport back.

NORTHEASTERN HIGHLANDS

East of Butha-Buthe, the road weaves up dramatically through spectacular mountains – part of the Drakensberg range – with rocky cliffs and rolling hills. South Africa does a good job of marketing its portion of the Drakensberg escarpment, but the raw beauty of the Lesotho section is hard to beat, with stunning highland panoramas, low population density and winter snow.

All the areas covered in this section are excellent for hiking, but you'll need to be fully equipped with a four-season sleeping bag, waterproof gear, topographical maps and a compass. Trout fishing is reputed to be top notch.

This area has many of the country's worst stretches of main road. In places, the asphalt has actually made the road more pot-holey, making for a wild and slow ride in a regular vehicle. Lesotho's mass, Chinese-run roadwork program is another complication, as the work can further slow traffic.

Liphofung Cave Cultural & Historical Site

Just beyond the village of Muela is the signposted turn-off for this small Lesotho Northern Parks–administered **site** (☎6718 5155, 2246 0723; adult/child M30/15; ⏰8.30am-4.30pm Mon-Fri, from 9am Sat & Sun; P), which includes a cave with some San paintings and Stone Age artefacts. King Moshoeshoe the Great is rumoured to have stopped here on his travels around Lesotho.

There is a cultural centre and a small shop selling local crafts. Day walks are possible and with notice you can arrange guided hikes and and pony treks.

Accommodation is available in simple, but comfortable, stone, four-person *rondavels* with kitchen facilities and sweeping views. It is also possible to camp in the cave – a novel and atmospheric experience. Either way, you'll need to bring your own food. Staying in Oxbow or Ts'ehlanyane National Park is a better option.

Getting There & Away

To get here by public transport, take a shared taxi heading from Butha-Buthe towards Moteng, and get out at the turn-off to Mamohase or Liphofung (M18, 25 minutes). Liphofung is then an easy 1.5km walk down from the main road along a tarmac access ramp. Daily (except Sunday) buses to Mokhotlong and Maseru pass the turn-offs in the morning (ask around for times); shared taxis to Butha-Buthe pass in the morning and those to Mokhotlong pass all day.

Oxbow

Reached after crossing the dramatic Moteng Pass (2820m), Oxbow consists of a few huts and a couple of lodges nestled amid some wonderful mountain scenery, and is an ideal place to get away from the bustle while still enjoying amenities. The area regularly receives snow in winter, and boasts a ski resort. It's also popular with South African trout anglers and birdwatchers.

Activities

Afriski Mountain Resort SKIING, HIKING
(☎086 123 747 54; www.afriski.net; half-/full-day pass M290/400, half-/full-day equipment rental M230/340; ⏰slopes 9am-4pm May-Aug) Skiers and snowboarders should make tracks to Afriski Mountain Resort, about 10km from Oxbow via the Mahlasela Pass (3222m), one of Southern Africa's highest road passes. The world-class resort has 3km of slopes, with lessons and packages available. In summer, activities including hiking, fly fishing, mountain biking and abseiling are offered.

Sleeping & Eating

New Oxbow Lodge LODGE $
(☎in South Africa 051-933 2247; www.oxbow.co.za; s/d M295/500, breakfast M55-110, mains M20-98; P) On the banks of the Malibamat'so River, this incongruous alpine chalet would look more at home in the Alps. It fills during winter with South African skiers and snow oglers; at other times, its eerie isolation and intermittent electricity, compounded by golfball-size hailstones clattering on the deserted games room and bar, bring to mind *The Shining*.

The dated rooms and *rondavels* have bath (no shower), tea and coffee, gas fire and bedside candles for the black mountain nights. You can dine in the restaurant or bar; room-only accommodation and *à la carte* meals will likely work out cheaper than half board. A small shop here supplies the basics.

Afriski Mountain Resort RESORT $$
(☎086 123 747 54; www.afriski.net; r from M1550, backpacker dm/r from M240/436, self-catering chalets from M4650) The ski resort offers myriad accommodation options, all comfortable and modern. Book ahead from May to July, especially over the weekend. Prices peak in July, and drop outside the May-to-August ski season.

★ **Sky Restaurant** PIZZA, INTERNATIONAL $$
(mains M90; ⏰7am-9pm; 📶) Africa's highest restaurant (3010m) overlooks the slopes at Afriski Mountain Resort, and reflects the resort's international sheen with its stylish wood finish and big red pizza oven. Lunch choices include pizzas, burgers and steaks, with pasta dishes and Lesotho trout on the dinner menu.

There is also a small shop here and, during winter, a cafe-bar at the foot of the gondola.

Getting There & Away

The daily (except Sunday) bus between Maseru and Mokhotlong will drop you at Oxbow (M120, 4½ hours), passing in both directions in the morning. Shared taxi is a better option for Mokhotlong, as the bus is packed by the time it reaches Oxbow. Taxis run in the morning to Butha-Buthe from Oxbow (M65, 1½ hours) and Afriski Mountain Resort (M80, two hours), with services to Mokhotlong throughout the day. The road follows a series of hairpin turns up the Moteng and Mahlasela Passes, and can be treacherous in snow and ice.

Mokhotlong

From Oxbow, a tarmac road winds its way over a series of 3200m-plus passes and through some superb high-altitude scenery before dropping down to Mokhotlong (Place of the Bald Ibis). The route was the original **Roof of Africa Rally** (www.roofofafrica.org.ls) course.

Mokhotlong is the main town in eastern Lesotho, albeit a remote outpost with a Wild West feel. There's not much to do other than watch life go by, with locals sporting Basotho blankets passing by on their horses. However, the Senqu (Orange) River – Lesotho's main waterway – has its source near Mokhotlong, and the town makes a good base for walks. There are also accommodation options out in the mountain wilds en route to Thaba-Tseka and Oxbow.

Sleeping & Eating

In Town

Shops in town sell the basics.

Senqu Hotel HOTEL $
(☎6302 1645, 2292 0330; senquhotel@gmail.com; s/d incl breakfast M420/480, mains M45) Signposted from the main road at the western end of town, the comfortable and spacious rooms in Senqu's new wing have balconies with sweeping views of the village and mountains. The restaurant serves spaghetti bolognese, Basotho beef or lamb stew, steaks and burgers.

Grow HOSTEL $
(☎5989 8949; s/d without bathroom M90/180; P) This NGO has an office just off the main road into Mokhotlong; look for it on the left about 2km after the Senqu Hotel. It offers two clean twin rooms, a kitchen and a lounge with intermittent electricity in the neighbouring building. It's happy to accept travellers if volunteers and training groups aren't staying.

Outside Town

St James Lodge LODGE $
(☎in South Africa 071 672 6801; www.stjameslodge.co.za; r/q from M300/400, camping M70; P) This working mission is a humble yet quietly stylish place to stay. The rooms and *rondavels* offer an electricity-free, self-catering experience, so bring your own food. Pony trekking, scenic walks and Sehonghong River tubing are available, as are guided tours of the church, mission, village and St James' projects. It's 12km southwest of Mokhotlong on the road to Thaba-Tseka.

Molumong Lodge & Pony Trekking Centre BACKPACKERS $
(☎in South Africa 083 254 3323; molumong.wordpress.com; per person M170, camping M80; P) About 15km southwest of Mokhotlong, off the road to Thaba-Tseka, is this former colonial trading post, offering basic

(electricity-free) self-catering rooms and *rondavels* with shared kitchen and bathrooms. Bring whatever food you'll need from Mokhotlong. Pony treks lasting a few hours or overnight are offered.

Chalets in the Sky LODGE $$
(Maloraneng Lodge; ☎6301 6982, 2832 6982; www.chaletsinthesky.co.ls; 1-4 people M960; P) Signposted from the main road near the Letseng Diamond Mine, roughly halfway between Mokhotlong and Oxbow, is this wilderness getaway in the pristine Khubelu Valley. The six riverside self-catering *rondavels* nestle in a verdant landscape, with gas standing in for electricity and no cellphone signal. Only accessible by 4WD.

Pony trekking and activities are offered and, in summer, accommodation rates fall to M240 per person.

Getting There & Away

Mokhotlong's shared-taxi rank is above the main road near the Pep store. There are a few shared taxis daily to/from Butha-Buthe (M110, three hours), with occasional direct services to Maseru (M150, six hours). A bus runs daily except Sunday to/from Maseru (M130), departing in each direction by about 6am. Shared taxis to Linakaneng (M40) will drop you by St James Lodge or Molumong Lodge & Pony Trekking Centre; change in Linakaneng for Thaba-Tseka, although there are infrequent services on this rough and little-travelled route. There was a daily shared taxi to Sani Top (M80, two hours), departing Mokhotlong early in the morning, but it was not running when we visited due to roadworks.

Petrol and diesel are normally available in Mokhotlong. You need a 4WD vehicle to tackle the road to Thaba-Tseka. At the time of writing, the road to/from Sani Top was in bad condition due to upgrading and not suitable for cars; check for updates, as the road will be accessible again when the work is completed.

Sani Top

Sani Top sits atop the steep Sani Pass, the famous road into Lesotho through the Drakensberg range in KwaZulu-Natal. South Africa's highest mountain pass, it offers stupendous views on clear days and unlimited hiking possibilities.

Activities

Besides local hikes, a rugged three- to four-day hike south to Sehlabathebe National Park (p486) is possible. The route follows a remote Drakensberg escarpment edge and should only be attempted if you're well prepared, experienced and in a group of at least four people.

Thabana-Ntlenyana HIKING
Africa's highest peak south of Mt Kilimanjaro, Thabana-Ntlenyana (3482m) is a popular but long and arduous hike (12km, nine hours). There's a path, but a guide (from M350) would be handy; arrange one the night before through Sani Mountain Lodge. It's also possible to do the ascent on horseback.

Hodgson's Peaks HIKING
Hodgson's Peaks (3257m) is a 6km, five-hour hike up a valley. There are views of KwaZulu-Natal from the summit.

Sleeping & Eating

There are also good hostels on the KwaZulu-Natal side (p284) of the pass.

★ **Sani Mountain Lodge** LODGE $$
(☎in South Africa 073 541 8620, in South Africa 078 634 7496; www.sanitopchalet.co.za; s/d/tr/q with half board M1250/1840/2100/2800, dm/camping M215/95, mains from M55; P) At 2874m, this lodge atop the Sani Pass stakes a claim to highest drinking hole in Southern Africa. Pub trivia aside, cosy *rondavels* and excellent meals reward those who make the steep ascent from KwaZulu-Natal. Backpackers doss down the road in modern rooms that hold between two and six people.

In winter, the snow is sometimes deep enough for skiing; pony trekking and village visits can be arranged with notice. A 4WD shuttle (M250) to/from the South African border post is offered to guests.

Getting There & Away

At the time of writing, the road to/from Sani Top was in bad condition due to upgrading and not suitable for cars; check for updates, as the road will be accessible again when the work is completed. There was a daily shared taxi to Sani Top (M80, two hours), departing Mokhotlong early in the morning, but it was not running when we visited due to roadworks.

Tour operators (p282) run day trips and expeditions up the pass from KwaZulu-Natal. Driving, you'll need a 4WD to get up the pass, but confident drivers can descend it in a car.

CENTRAL HIGHLANDS

Lesotho's rugged interior boasts the country's two trademark sights: the breathtaking Maletsunyane Falls (204m), which are almost twice the height of the Victoria Falls and offer the world's longest commercially operated, single-drop abseil; and the humanmade spectacle of Katse Dam, an engineering feat holding a shimmering lake surrounded by rippling mountain slopes. The area offers an incredible mix of scenery, activities and engineering marvels, accessed from the lowlands up tortuous but stunning passes such as the God Help Me Pass (2281m).

In a 2WD vehicle, the Central Highlands are cut off from the Northeastern Highlands, as a 4WD is needed to tackle the rough gravel road between Mokhotlong and Thaba-Tseka. Shared taxis are also unreliable on this remote stretch of road. To travel between Mokhotlong and Thaba-Tseka, you must therefore take the long way round via Leribe (Hlotse). Fortunately, this is an extremely scenic detour, taking in one of Lesotho's most beautiful roads up the Mafika-Lisiu Pass (3090m).

Bokong Nature Reserve

Bokong (5950 2291; adult/child M10/5, camping M40, basic 4-person huts M250; 8am-4pm) has perhaps the most dramatic setting of the three Lesotho northern parks, with stunning vistas over the Lepaqoa Valley from the roadside **visitors centre** (5950 2291; adult/child M10/5; 8am-4pm), various short walks and a good, rugged eight-hour hike to Ts'ehlanyane National Park. Bearded vultures, rock shelters, waterfalls and valleyhead fens (wetland areas) are features here. **Hiking guides** (within the park M30, to Ts'ehlanyane M410) are available, and **pony trekking** (per day M180) can be booked ahead through the visitors centre.

★ **Aloes Guest House** GUESTHOUSE $
(2700 5626; dm M180, s/d/f incl breakfast M395/600/810, camping M60, mains M65; P) Situated in front of an old sandstone trading post, the bungalows have high thatch ceilings, tiled floors, mod cons and an old-fashioned feel. The grounds are like an English cottage garden with mountain views, and it's a pleasant spot to catch up on writing postcards. Activities including horse riding and guided hikes are offered.

The restaurant serves light dishes such as *shwarmas*, burgers and sandwiches, as well as heavier fare including beef stew, mutton chops and chicken or fish curry. Aloes is signposted from the main road in Pitseng village, about 30km from Bokong towards Leribe (Hlotse).

Bokong Chalets CHALET $
(per person M250) Basic, four-person chalets with shared kitchen and ablutions. Bookings must be made through **Lesotho Northern Parks** (in Butha-Buthe 2246 0723). When we visited, new chalets were being built and the restaurant upgraded. The reserve sits at just over 3000m and gets cold at night, so come prepared.

Getting There & Away

Bokong lies roughly midway between Leribe (Hlotse) and Katse. Shared taxis from Leribe (M50, two hours) and Katse (M65, 1½ hours) will drop you at the visitors centre, about 2km south of the viewpoint atop the stunning Mafika-Lisiu Pass (3090m). When leaving, you may have to wait a while before a taxi with space passes.

Katse Dam

This engineering marvel stores 1950 million cu metres of water bound for thirsty Gauteng, South Africa's most populous province. The high-altitude, 35.8-sq-km body of blue also generates hydroelectric power for Lesotho. Ringed by steep, green hillsides, the dam is a serene if surreal spot; the usual Basotho names on signposts give way to 'Mohale Tunnel Outlet' and the like. Even if you're not impressed by engineering feats, the area makes for a relaxing pause.

Sights

Katse Dam Visitors Centre VIEWPOINT, MUSEUM
(2291 0377; www.lhda.org.ls; 8am-5pm; P) On the main road is Katse Dam's visitors centre, with information, displays and a dam-viewing deck. Look for the bright blue roof a few kilometres east of Katse village. Guided tours of the dam wall (M10, one hour) depart at 9am and 2pm (weekdays) and 9am and 11am (weekends).

Katse Botanical Garden GARDENS
(www.lhda.org.ls; Katse village; adult/child M5/3; 9am-5pm; P) Katse Botanical Garden was originally established to protect the spiral

aloes displaced from the dam's construction. It has flourished to include gravel, hillside trails passing via a rock garden; indigenous flowers; a medicinal section; and a dam viewpoint. A plant-propagation project takes place in the greenhouse.

Sleeping & Eating

You can camp for free at the Katse Dam visitors centre, which has ablutions and security.

Orion Katse Lodge HOTEL $$
(☎2291 0202; www.katselodge.co.za; Katse village; incl half board s/d M989/1378, without bathroom from M839/1078; P 📶) In a suburban estate-like gated village, this Orion property initially looks rather bland, but it improves when you see the terrace's stunning dam view. Accommodation is comfortable, including the so-called 'dormitory' rooms (private rooms with shared bathroom; solo travellers may find it galling to pay M839 and share a changing-room-style bathroom with several other guests).

For couples, combining a self-catering house (for four/six people M996/1494) with *à la carte* restaurant meals works out cheaper. The restaurant serves light lunches (mains M50), and dinner mains (M100) including curries, steaks, poached trout and delicious trout *almondine* (trout garnished with almonds). Activities including dam cruises, village tours, guided hikes and pony rides are offered.

Getting There & Away

The 122km road between Leribe (Hlotse) and Katse is excellent but steep and winding, and slick in the rain. Allow at least two hours for driving, longer if going by public transport.

Shared taxis run all day to Leribe (M85, three hours) and Thaba-Tseka (M46, two hours). The quickest and easiest way to travel to Maseru is by taxi via Leribe and Maputsoe (total M130, seven hours).

Daily buses also run to/from Maseru (M110, nine hours) via Thaba-Tseka (M25, 2½ hours), leaving Katse at 5am and Maseru at 9am. In Katse, public transport stops near the Katse village junction.

Thaba-Tseka

Thaba-Tseka is a remote town on the eastern edge of the Central Range, over Mokhoabong Pass (2860m) from Mohale Dam and the west. The town was established in 1980 as a centre for the mountainous district, and is a scrappy place serving mostly as a convenient transport junction for travel north to Katse or west to Maseru.

Motherland Guest House GUESTHOUSE $$
(☎2890 0404; motherlandguesthouse@gmail.com; s/d incl breakfast from M500/700, mains M50-70; P 📶) Motherland Guest House is an excellent option in the heart of the town that peeks at the mountains and bubbles with village life. The modern rooms are decorated with photos of Katse Dam and flowery bedspreads, there are numerous facilities and power points, and the bar-restaurant serves curries, steaks and lighter dishes. There are plenty of signs to guide you.

Getting There & Away

The daily bus to/from Maseru (M90, six hours) leaves Thaba-Tseka at 8.30am and Maseru at 9am; shared taxis (M110, 4½ hours) leave from around 7.30am. Several daily taxis also serve Katse (M46, two hours); Mokhotlong is trickier, as you must change at Linakaneng and services are infrequent on this rough and little-travelled route.

Driving, the road is tarred from Maseru and from Katse there's a good-condition gravel road suitable for 2WD cars.

Mohale Dam

Built across the Senqunyane River, this impressive 145m-high, rock-filled dam is the second phase of the Lesotho Highlands Water Project, following Katse Dam. There are commanding views of the lake and mountains beyond. Water can flow for 32km along the Mohale Tunnel between here and Katse.

The **visitors centre** (☎2293 6217; ⏰8am-5.30pm Mon-Fri, 10am-4pm Sat & Sun; P) is 15km from the main road, signposted west of Mohale village. It offers dam views, a guided tour (M10) and boat cruises (per person from M100; book ahead).

Orion Mohale Lodge HOTEL $$
(☎2293 6134; www.mohalelodge.co.za; s/d incl breakfast M829/1039, mains M75; P ❄ 📶) The pleasant interiors at Orion Mohale Lodge make up for its distant dam view. The comfortable rooms are replete with modern furnishings and trimmed with Afro-decor, and the restaurant is a pleasant spot to break a journey.

Molimo-Nthuse INTERNATIONAL $
(☎6224 7365; mains M65; ⏰7am-11pm; 📶) This pleasant roadside lunch stop, 62km

east of Maseru at the foot of the God Help Me Pass (2281m), is a restaurant in the round overlooking a mountain valley. Dishes include New York sirloin, jerk chicken, trout fillet and daily specials. When we visited, midrange rooms and a campsite were opening.

Semonkong

Semonkong (Place of Smoke), a one-pony town in the rugged Thaba Putsoa range, gets its name from the nearby **Maletsunyane Falls** (204m), which are at their loudest in summer. The town is the starting point for many fine hiking and pony-trekking trails, including the two-day ride via the peaks of the Thaba Putsoa to **Ketane Falls** (122m).

★ **Semonkong Lodge** LODGE $$
(☎2700 6037; www.placeofsmoke.co.ls; dm/s/d from M160/435/730, rondavel s/d M465/720, camping M90) Near the Maletsunyane River, this is a model of community tourism and a great place for everyone from families to adventure seekers. If the inviting accommodation, including cosy *rondavels* with fireplaces, doesn't make you extend your stay in the mountains, fireside feasts in the lodge's **Duck & Donkey Tavern** (lunch/dinner mains M75/100) surely will.

There's also a kitchen for those who want to self-cater. Staff can arrange all kinds of tours and hikes, employing locals to navigate the villages and steep trails – including extreme fishing expeditions, pony trekking and even pub crawls by donkey. Then there's the world's longest commercially operated, single-drop abseil (204m) down the Maletsunyane Falls. The lodge is signposted from the town centre, 2km down a gravel road.

Getting There & Away

Semonkong is about 130km southeast of Maseru on the tar road to Qacha's Nek; both are a three-hour drive. Shared taxis run all day to/from Maseru (M70). At the time of writing, there were no regular shared taxis to/from Qacha's Nek, but services are expected to start, charging around M70. A nonshared taxi to/from Qacha's Nek costs around M250.

When we visited, a shuttle was being set up between Coffee Bay on the Wild Coast and Qacha's Nek, with a possible onward service to Semonkong. Enquire at Semonkong Lodge or Ocean View Hotel in Coffee Bay for updates.

SOUTHERN LESOTHO

The region south of Morija, across to Sehlabathebe National Park in the southeast, is less developed than the northwest but lingers in the memory banks of all who pass through. The mountain ranges eat up the sky out here, where a velvety orange-pink light pours over rocky peaks and yawning valleys. If you like hiking and pony trekking in rugged isolation, head south.

The road from Quthing to Qacha's Nek is one of Lesotho's most stunning drives, taking you along the winding Senqu (Orange) River gorge and through some striking canyon scenery before climbing up onto the escarpment. Another stunner is the road through the interior from Semonkong down to Qacha's Nek. Despite what some maps show, both are tarred all the way to Qacha's Nek.

Malealea

This remote village has three travel trump cards: its breathtaking mountain scenery, its trading-post lodge and its successful community-based tourism. Many visitors to Lesotho head straight here to sample traditional Basotho life or, as the sign outside town says, to just 'pause and look upon a gateway of paradise'. The area has been occupied for centuries, as shown by the many **San rock paintings** in the vicinity.

Sights & Activities

Organise activities through Malealea Lodge.

Pony Trekking

Options range from easy **two-hour rides** (1/2/3 people M370/520/720) to San rock art or a gorge viewpoint, to **overnight expeditions** (per day M700/950/1275) with accommodation in **Basotho village huts** (per hut for 1-3 people M100). Multiday routes include Ribaneng Waterfall (two days, one night); Ribaneng and Ketane Waterfalls (four days, three nights); and Ribaneng, Ketane and Semonkong (six days, five nights).

Hiking

You can hike to spots including **Pitseng Gorge** (three or six hours return) with its gnarly cliffs and swimming holes, and **Botsoela Waterfall** (four hours; five including San rock art). Hiring a **guide** (per hour M15) is recommended. Guided **overnight hikes** (with/without packhorse per day M510/150) are also possible, with accommodation in huts.

Village Visits

Village visits provide a stimulating insight into the local people and their customs. Down the slope from Malealea Lodge are the tiny museum and craft shop, housed in traditional Basotho huts, from where you can wander through the village – solo or with a guide. You can pay **guided visits** (per hour M15) to the *sangoma* (traditional medicine practitioner; only for the genuinely interested), the village school and the late Mr Musi's reclaimed *donga* (eroded ravine used for small-scale agriculture).

Mountain Biking & Scenic Drives

The six-day, 300km-plus **Lesotho Sky** (lesothosky.com; late Sep) race passes through this rugged area, while the **Malealea Monster Weekend** (lesothosky.com/monster; late May) features rides and trail runs up to 80km. Year-round you can **hire bikes** (half/full day incl guide per person M150/300). Malealea Lodge can also recommend scenic drives for 4WD and high-clearance 2WD vehicles.

Sleeping & Eating

★ **Malealea Lodge** LODGE $

(in South Africa 082 552 4215; www.malealea.co.ls; s/d from M435/580, without bathroom from M262.50/350, camping M100; P) Offering Lesotho in a nutshell, Malealea is a deserving poster child for the mountain kingdom. Every sunset, village choirs and bands perform at the mountaintop lodge; activities are community run, and a proportion of tourist revenues and donations goes directly to supporting local projects. The views, meanwhile, are stupendous.

Accommodation ranges from campsites and twin 'forest' (backpacker) huts in a pretty wooded setting away from the lodge to simple, cosy en-suite rooms and *rondavels*. A sense of history pervades the site, which began life in 1905 as a trading post, established by teacher, diamond miner and soldier Mervyn Smith. From 1986 the Jones family ran the store before transforming it into accommodation and integrating it with the surrounding community.

Malealea also offers a bar, hearty **meals** (breakfast/lunch/dinner M80/100/135), self-catering facilities and a shop with basic goods. There are now intermittent wi-fi and mobile-phone signals at the lodge. September to December are the busy months.

Getting There & Away

Early-morning shared taxis connect Maseru and Malealea (M50, 2½ hours). Later in the day, catch a shared taxi to the junction town of Motsekuoa (M30, 1½ hours), from where there are connections to Malealea (M22, one hour). Services from Mafeteng and the south also stop in Motsekuoa.

Driving, head south from Maseru on the Mafeteng road (Main Rd South) for 60km to Motsekuoa. Opposite the shared-taxi corner, turn left (east) at the sign for Matelile, Qaba and Malealea Lodge. Ten kilometres further on, take the right fork and continue another 15km. When you reach the signposted turn-off to Malealea, travel about 7km along an unsealed road over the Gates of Paradise Pass (2003m) to the village and lodge.

It's also possible to approach Malealea from the south, via Mpharane and Masemouse, but this gravel road is rough and not suitable for a 2WD car.

Mafeteng

On the scenic main road south of Motsekuoa (the turn-off for Malealea) is Mafeteng, a scruffy town with a busy main drag. Although not worth a stop, it's the best place to stock up before heading south, and there are a few places to sleep and eat if the need arises. Shared taxis, sprinters (Mercedes minibuses; faster and more expensive than shared taxis) and buses stop in Mafeteng (near Van Rooyen's Gate border crossing) en route between Maseru and Quthing.

Mafeteng Hotel HOTEL $

(2270 0236; www.hotelmafeteng.co.ls; s/d from M380/500, breakfast/mains M58/70; P) In leafy grounds on the edge of town, Mafeteng Hotel offers worn rooms in a peachy-pink hexagonal building that looks like a displaced air-traffic-control tower. There's a bar and meat-oriented restaurant. From the main road, follow the sign to the National AIDS and HIV Commission, between the roundabout and FNB bank on the south (Mohale's Hoek) side of town.

Mohale's Hoek

Like Mafeteng, this shabby town has little to offer other than a place to overnight. Shared taxis, sprinters and buses running between Maseru and Quthing stop in Mohale's Hoek (near Makhaleng Bridge border crossing).

Hotel Mount Maluti
HOTEL $$

(☑ 2278 5224; www.hmmlesotho.com; s/d incl breakfast M650/750, mains M70; P 🤖 🔊) Offers dated rooms in cool blocks, opening onto pleasant gardens. Its restaurant is a decent lunch stop, serving sandwiches, burgers, pizza and pasta, and the whole shebang is signposted off the main road.

Quthing

Quthing, the southernmost major town in Lesotho, is also known as Moyeni (Place of the Wind). It was established in 1877, abandoned during the Gun War of 1880 and then rebuilt at the present site. Activity centres on the new part of town, Lower Quthing, with its bustling main road.

⊙ Sights & Activities

Upper Quthing
AREA

On the hill above Lower Quthing, overlooking the Senqu (Orange) River gorge, this former colonial administrative centre has good views and gently dilapidated buildings. Walk or catch a shared taxi up from Lower Quthing to escape the hustle and bustle and have a quiet stroll.

Masitise Cave House Museum
MUSEUM

(☑ 2700 3259; adult/child M10/3; ⊙ 8.30am-5pm Mon-Fri, to 2pm Sat & Sun; P) Five kilometres west of Quthing is this intriguing section of an old mission, built directly into a San rock shelter in 1866 by Reverend David-Frédéric Ellenberger, a Swiss missionary who was among the first to Lesotho. There's a cast of a dinosaur footprint in the ceiling, a museum with displays on local culture and history, and San paintings nearby.

To get here, take the signposted turn-off near the Masitise Primary School and follow the road about 1km back past the small red church. At the neighbouring house you can ask for the key from the caretaker, the church pastor. From here, the museum is five minutes further on foot.

Dinosaur Footprints
ARCHAEOLOGICAL SITE

(admission M10; ⊙ 8am-5pm; P) One of Quthing's main claims to fame is the proliferation of dinosaur footprints in the surrounding area. The most easily accessible are signposted on the left as you leave town heading northeast towards Qacha's Nek. In this building are 230-million-year-old footprints and a craft shop. Children will offer to guide you to more footprints for a small tip.

🛏 Sleeping & Eating

Fuleng Guest House
GUESTHOUSE $

(☑ 2275 0260; info.fulengguesthouse@gmail.com; s/d from M399/513, breakfast/meals M50/70; P) This hillside guesthouse offers *rondavels* with a view, a restaurant, cheeky garden gnomes, a rock feature and a friendly local atmosphere. Find it by the main road on the way up to Upper Quthing.

ⓘ Getting There & Away

The transport stand is in Lower Quthing. Shared taxis serve Maseru (M70, 2½ hours) and Qacha's Nek (M80, 2½ hours), as do faster, more expensive sprinters and slower, cheaper buses. Services to/from the capital are more frequent. Shared taxis run to/from Tele Bridge border post, which is linked by shared taxi to Sterkspruit (South Africa) for onward transport. The gravel road connecting Tele Bridge and the main Quthing–Mohale's Hoek road is passable in a 2WD car.

Qacha's Nek

Originally a mission station, Qacha's Nek was founded in 1888 near the pass (1980m) of the same name. The sleepy border town has an attractive church and a variety of colonial-era sandstone buildings, plus nearby stands of California redwood trees, some over 25m high. There is a **tourist office** (☑ 5886 0452; ⊙ 8am-12.30pm & 2-4pm Mon-Fri) next to the New Central Hotel.

Letloepe Guesthouse
GUESTHOUSE $

(☑ 2295 0383; s/d M300/500, breakfast M50; P 🤖) On the edge of town opposite the main police station, Letloepe offers rustic self-catering *rondavels* and bungalows with mountain views. Cheaper rooms with shared bathroom are also available.

New Central Hotel
BUSINESS HOTEL $

(☑ 2295 0482; r incl breakfast from M500; P ❄) Rooms have mountains of pillows and facilities in this smart hotel at the northern entrance to town. Lunch and dinner (two courses M90) should be ordered in advance.

ⓘ Getting There & Away

The daily bus to Maseru (M120, 6½ hours) leaves at 8.30am, while the shared taxi (M140, five hours) goes at 11am, with a faster Mercedes minibus (M140, four hours) departing around 7am. Most services take the Quthing route, but a few go via Semonkong and shared taxis are expected to launch on that route.

Small shared taxis link the main transport stand with the border (M5.50), from where shared *bakkies* (pick-up trucks) and vans run to Matatiele (South Africa), where you can pick up onward transport.

Sehlabathebe National Park

Lesotho's most undervisited national **park** (per person/vehicle M40/10; ⏲gate 8am-4.30pm) is remote, rugged and beautiful. The rolling grasslands, wildflowers and silence provide complete isolation, with only the prolific birdlife (including the bearded vulture) and the odd rhebok for company. Hiking (and horse riding from Sani Top or the Drakensbergs) is the main way to explore the waterfalls and surrounds, and angling is possible in the park's dams and rivers.

Come well prepared for the changing elements: this is a summer-rainfall area, and thick mist, potentially hazardous to hikers, is common. The winters are clear but it gets cold at night, with occasional light snowfalls.

Sehlabathebe is under the jurisdiction of the **Ministry of Tourism, Environment and Culture** (☎in Maseru 2231 6574, in park 6253 7565; Post Office Bldg, 7th fl, Kingsway, Maseru).

Sleeping & Eating

Camping is permitted in the park, though there are no facilities besides plenty of water. You'll need to bring all your own food.

Thamathu Rural Homestay HOMESTAY $
(☎2231 1767, 2232 6075; per person incl breakfast M100; P) If you're travelling by public transport, the bus reaches Mavuka village, near Sehlabathebe gate, around 7pm, so you'll need to overnight here. In a program supported by the Ministry of Tourism, Environment and Culture, local homestead owners have been officially trained to host and guide park visitors. **Mabotle Lodge** is a popular option, with basic *rondavels*.

Sehlabathebe National Park Lodge LODGE $$
(☎6347 2851; r M990-2400, camping M80; P) At this privately run lodge, a prefabricated building houses a self-catering kitchen, dining room, lounge with central fireplace and several bedrooms, some with sumptuous king-size beds. Breakfast and dinner are available but should be booked before arrival – as should accommodation. It is 12km into the park, and 4WD vehicles are required if driving.

The original 1970s Jonathan's Lodge, built for the trout-loving prime minister of the same name, is set to open with improvements in 2015.

Getting There & Away

A daily bus connects Mavuka village, near the park gate, and Qacha's Nek (M100, five hours), leaving Mavuka around 5am and returning at 2pm.

The gravel road from Qacha's Nek is not recommended in a 2WD car, but check locally for updates on its condition. The road from the north is extremely rough and challenging even by 4WD; the 150km from Thaba-Tseka takes several hours. Both roads can be affected by storms and landslides, so consult locals before setting out. You can arrange to leave your vehicle at the police station in Paolosi village, about 3km south of Mavuka, while you're in the park. The nearest petrol stations are in Qacha's Nek and Thaba-Tseka.

On foot, the simplest way into Sehlabathebe is to hike 10km up the escarpment from KwaZulu-Natal. Packhorses can be arranged through Sehlabathebe National Park Lodge. From Bushman's Nek border crossing up the pass to Nkonkoana gate takes about six hours. To trot up the pass on horseback, **Khotso Trails** (☎in South Africa 033 701 1502; www.khotsotrails.co.za) offers a two- or three-day expedition from Underberg (Southern Drakensberg).

For those coming on charter flights, there's an airstrip at Paolosi.

Swaziland

Includes ➡

Best Places to Eat

- Ramblas Restaurant (p492)
- Sambane Coffee Shoppe (p498)
- Malandela's Restaurant (p499)
- Lihawu Restaurant (p495)

Best Places to Stay

- Stone Camp (p505)
- Sondzela Backpackers (p498)
- Brackenhill Lodge (p491)
- Lidwala Backpacker Lodge (p493)
- Phophonyane Falls Ecolodge & Nature Reserve (p502)

Why Go?

In short: big things come in small packages. The intriguing kingdom of Swaziland is diminutive but boasts a huge checklist for any visitor. Rewarding wildlife-watching? Tick. Adrenaline-boosting activities such as rafting and mountain biking? Tick. Lively and colourful local culture, with celebrations and ceremonies still common practice? Tick. Plus there are superb walking trails, stunning mountain and flatland scenery, varied accommodation options and excellent, high-quality handicrafts.

Unlike South Africa, Swaziland has managed to hold on to that slow-down-this-is-Africa feeling, and that's why it's gaining in popularity. Everything remains small and personable, and the atmosphere is remarkably relaxed. Instead of making a flying visit here on your way to Kruger National Park, KwaZulu-Natal or Mozambique, consider staying at least a week to do the country justice. If you plan a visit during the winter months, try to make it coincide with the Umhlanga festival, one of Africa's biggest cultural events.

When to Go

Mbabane

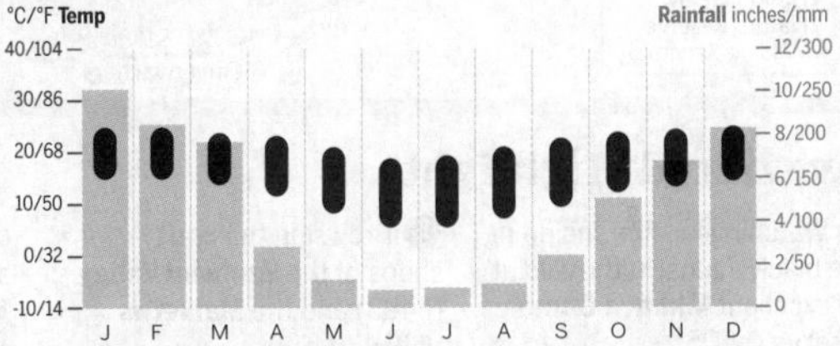

Dec–Apr Full rivers and lush vegetation are the backdrops for photography and adventuring.

Feb–Mar Buganu season – enjoy home-brew marula wine in rural Swaziland.

May–Sep Cooler days make for wonderful wildlife viewing in the lowveld.

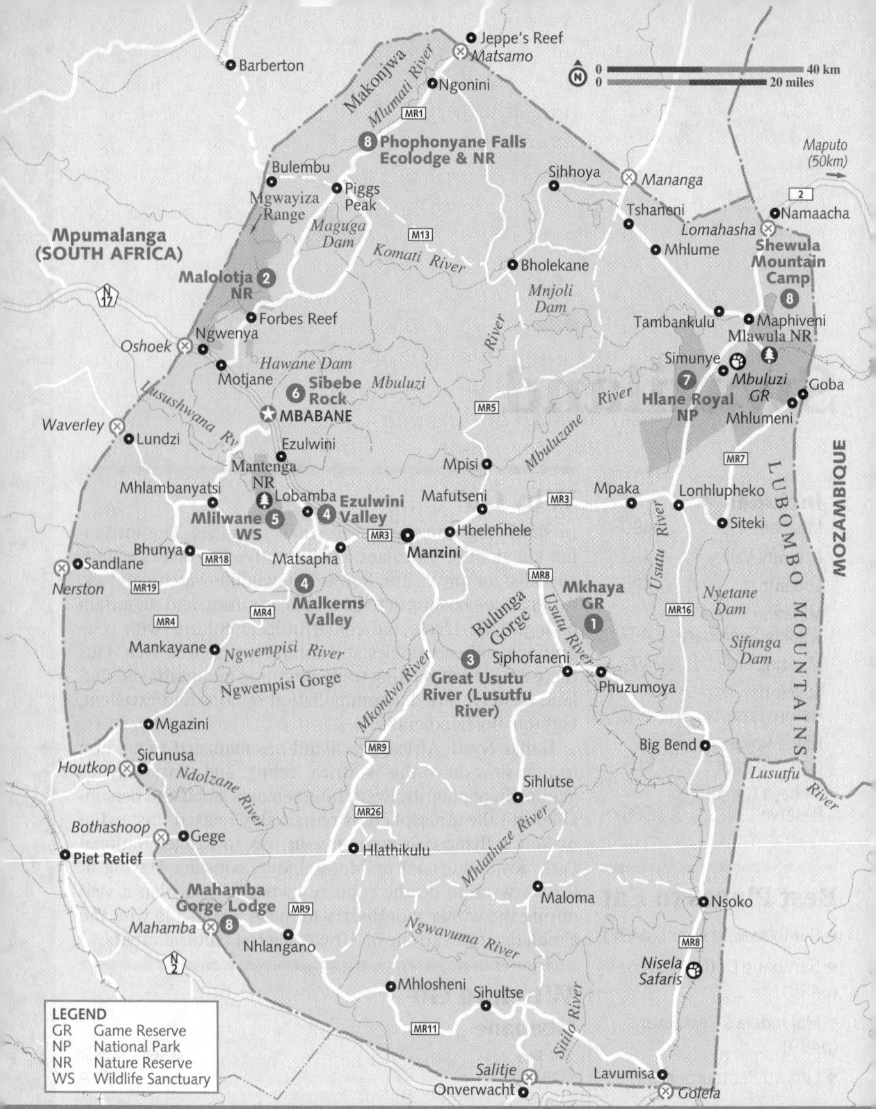

Swaziland Highlights

1 Watching wildlife, including rare black rhinos, in the wild at the excellent **Mkhaya Game Reserve** (p505).

2 Walking or hiking in the **Malolotja Nature Reserve** (p501), an enchanting wilderness area.

3 Shooting over white-water rapids on the **Great Usutu River (Lusutfu River)** (p493).

4 Browsing the craft shops of the **Ezulwini Valley** (p493) and the **Malkerns Valley** (p498).

5 Cycling or meandering around **Mlilwane Wildlife Sanctuary** (p497) and relaxing in its comfortable, lovely lodges.

6 Climbing **Sibebe Rock** (p490), a massive granite dome just outside the capital, and soaking up the lovely views.

7 Coming face to face with a pride of lions at **Hlane Royal National Park** (p503).

8 Getting away from it all at **Mahamba Gorge Lodge** (p506), **Phophonyane Falls Ecolodge & Nature Reserve** (p502) or **Shewula Mountain Camp** (p504).

History

Beginnings of a Nation

The area that is now Swaziland has been inhabited for millennia, and humanlike remains possibly dating back as far as 100,000 years have been discovered around the Lubombo Mountains in eastern Swaziland. However, today's Swazis trace their ancestors to much more recent arrivals. By around AD 500, various Nguni groups had made their way to the region as part of the great Bantu migrations. One of these groups settled in the area around present-day Maputo (Mozambique), eventually founding the Dlamini dynasty. In the mid-18th century, in response to increasing pressure from other clans in the area, the Dlamini king, Ngwane III, led his people southwest to the Pongola River, in present-day southern Swaziland and northern KwaZulu-Natal. This became the first Swazi heartland.

Ngwane's successor, Sobhuza I, established a base in the Ezulwini Valley, which still remains the centre of Swazi royalty and ritual. Next came King Mswazi (or Mswati), after whom the Swazi take their name. Despite pressure from the neighbouring Zulu, Mswazi succeeded in unifying the whole kingdom.

From the mid-19th century, Swaziland attracted increasing numbers of European farmers in search of land for cattle, as well as hunters, traders and missionaries.

Over the next decades, the Swazis saw their territory whittled away as the British and Boers jostled for power in the area. In 1902, following the second Anglo-Boer War, the Boers withdrew and the British took control of Swaziland as a protectorate.

Struggle for Independence

Swazi history in the early 20th century centred on the ongoing struggle for independence. Under the leadership of King Sobhuza II (guided by the capable hands of his mother, who acted as regent while Sobhuza was a child), the Swazis succeeded in regaining much of their original territory. This was done in part by direct purchase and in part by British government decree. This was a major development, as Swazi kings are considered to hold the kingdom in trust for their subjects, and land ownership is thus more than just a political and economic issue.

Independence was finally achieved – the culmination of a long and remarkably nonviolent path – on 6 September 1968, 66 years after the start of the British Protectorate.

The first Swazi constitution was largely a British creation, and in 1973 the king suspended it on the grounds that it did not accord with Swazi culture. Four years later parliament reconvened under a new constitution vesting all power in the king.

Sobhuza II died in 1982, at that time the world's longest-reigning monarch. In 1986 the young Mswati III ascended the throne, where he continues today to represent and maintain the traditional Swazi way of life, and to assert his pre-eminence as absolute monarch. Despite an undercurrent of political dissent, political parties are still unable to participate in elections.

Current Events

King Mswati III regularly comes under attack, especially in the foreign press, for his autocratic status, lax spending habits and polygamous practices. Critics say this hinders economic progress and the fight against HIV/AIDS, by which around 26% of the population is believed to be affected. But even his harshest Swazi critics don't seem to want to do away with him altogether, calling for a constitutional, not absolute, monarch.

In December 2014, Swaziland was removed from the list of countries eligible for benefits from the USA's AGOA (African Growth and Opportunity Act) free trade agreement because it didn't meet some essential criteria – namely respect for workers' rights and freedom of association. While most of the benefits from AGOA were limited to low-paying jobs in the textile sector, the loss of any job in a country where the unemployment rate hovers around 50% is problematic. Economic growth is expected to slow from 2.5% to 1% in 2015 and thereafter.

Climate

Most of Swaziland enjoys a climate similar to that of South Africa's eastern lowveld, with rainy, steamy summers and agreeably cooler winters. Between December and February, temperatures occasionally exceed 40°C and torrential thunderstorms are common. May to August are the coolest months. In the higher-lying areas of the west, winters bring cool, crisp nights and sometimes even frost.

Language

The official languages are Swati and English, and English is the official written language.

Dangers & Annoyances

Petty crime such as pickpocketing and phone- and bag-snatching can happen in urban areas. Always take common-sense precautions and be

SWAZI CEREMONIES & FESTIVALS

Incwala

Incwala (also known as Ncwala) is the most sacred ceremony of the Swazi people. It is a 'first fruits' ceremony, where the king gives permission for his people to eat the first crops of the new year. It takes place around 21 December and lasts a week, but preparation for the ceremony begins some weeks in advance, according to the cycle of the moon.

Umhlanga Dance

The *umhlanga* (reed) dance is Swaziland's best-known cultural event. Though not as sacred as the Incwala, it serves a similar function in drawing the nation together and reminding the people of their relationship to the king. It is something like a week-long debutante ball for marriageable young Swazi women, who journey from all over the kingdom to help repair the queen mother's home at Lobamba. It takes place in late August or early September.

Buganu Festival

Another 'first fruits' festival, this takes place in February and celebrates the marula fruit. The women gather the fruit and ferment a brew (known as *buganu;* it packs a punch). Locals – mainly males – gather to drink and celebrate. The festival is becoming one of the country's most popular traditional ceremonies, and is attended by King Mswati III and other royalty.

MTN Bushfire Festival

Held annually for three days over the last weekend of May, this increasingly popular festival features music, poetry and theatre among other performances. It takes place at House on Fire in Malkerns. Check the website (www.bush-fire.com) for more information about the program.

vigilant at all times. Never walk around unescorted at night or flaunt valuables.

Schistosomiasis (bilharzia) and malaria are both present in Swaziland, although Swaziland is taking serious steps to be the first country in sub-Saharan Africa to move to malaria-free status.

Getting There & Around

There are flights into Swaziland (King Mswati III International Airport) from Johannesburg (Jo'burg).

Most travellers enter Swaziland overland. Car rental is available from **Avis** (☎2518 6226, 2518 6222; www.avis.co.za; Airport; ⊙7am-5.30pm Mon-Thu, 10.30am-5.30pm Sat & Sun) and **Europcar** (☎2518 4393; www.europcar.com/car-swaziland.html; Airport; ⊙8am-5pm Mon-Fri, 10am-5pm Sat & Sun), but it's usually cheaper to rent a car in South Africa.

There is a good network of minibus shared taxis covering Swaziland.

MBABANE

Mbabane's main draw? Its lovely setting in the craggy Dlangeni Hills. Swaziland's capital and second-largest city, Mbabane is a relaxed and functional place perched in the cool highveld (it sits at an altitude of about 1200m).

There's a handful of good restaurants and places to stay, but for the traveller the nearby Ezulwini and Malkerns Valleys have most of the attractions and, on the whole, a better choice of accommodation.

During the colonial era, the British originally had their base in Manzini but moved it in 1902 to Mbabane to take advantage of the cooler climate in the hills.

Sights & Activities

Sibebe Rock LANDMARK

(Pine Valley; admission E30) About 8km north-east of Mbabane is Sibebe Rock, a massive granite dome hulking over the surrounding countryside. Much of the rock is completely sheer, and dangerous if you should fall, but it's a good adrenaline charge if you're reasonably fit and relish looking down steep rock faces. Your best bet is to contact Swazi Trails (p493) in Ezulwini Valley, which takes half-day nontechnical climbs up the rock (E780 per person, including transport).

Sleeping

Bombaso's Backpackers BACKPACKERS $

(☎7681 9191, 2404 5465; www.swazilandhappenings.co.za/photos_bombasos.htm; Lukhalo St; camping

E80, dm E145, d without bathroom E300;) Bombaso's offers a buzzy vibe and has a variety of accommodation options, from campsites (on grassy lawns) and a seven-bed dorm to clean private rooms, a swimming pool, a bar, a TV room and relaxing gardens. No meals are served, but there are excellent kitchen facilities. Jason and Lwazi, who run the place, are well clued up about the country.

It's about 2km north of the centre, with easy public transport.

★ Brackenhill Lodge GUESTHOUSE $$
(2404 2887; www.brackenhillswazi.com; Mountain Dr; s/d incl breakfast from E640/870;) With its wonderfully relaxing atmosphere and bucolic setting, this little cracker located 4.5km north of Mbabane is sure to win your heart. It offers eight comfortable, well-equipped and airy rooms, and its 162 hectares have several walking trails, great birdlife and splendid panoramas. Facilities include gym, sauna, swimming pool and even tennis courts. Lovely owners; evening meals on request.

There's a 10% discount if you pay cash.

The Place BUNGALOW $$
(7828 6040, 7828 5090; www.theplaceswaziland.com; Mantsholo St; s/d incl breakfast E700/1000;) Opposite the golf course, this recent venture has modern, functional facilities, and attracts visitors looking for impeccable, well-equipped rooms with sparkling bathrooms. The free-standing units open onto a manicured garden and a pool, and there's a reputable restaurant next door. A great find.

Mountain Inn INN $$
(2404 2781; www.mountaininn.sz; Sihawu Cres, Highland View; incl breakfast s E880-950, d E1040-1220;) This sprawling inn is a bit bland and its decor feels dated, but it's friendly, unpretentious and a safe bet. It comprises three wings linked by a covered walkway; be sure to ask for a room in the South Wing, which proffers stupendous views over the valley. There's a pool, a library, lawns and a well-regarded restaurant.

It's about 4km south of the city centre, in a tranquil neighbourhood.

Eating

There are supermarkets, chain restaurants and fast-food outlets at Swazi Plaza, which is the main shopping mall in the city centre.

Indingilizi Gallery & Restaurant CAFE $
(2404 6213; www.africanoriginal.com; 112 Dzeliwe St; mains E40-70; 8am-5pm Mon-Fri, 8.30am-1pm Sat) Indingilizi is that easy-to-miss 'secret spot' that locals like to recommend. This small outdoor cafe is at the back of an art gallery and offers breakfasts, snacks and light lunches. Also does takeaway.

Riverside Café CAFETERIA $
(2404 9547; Swazi Plaza, Plaza Mall Dr; mains E20-100; 8am-4.30pm Mon-Fri, to 3pm Sat) This cheerful cafeteria is no place to escape the crowds, but the food is tasty and great value. Pastries are the reason to come, with a tempting choice of homemade treats such as muffins and scones. It's also a good spot for a light meal at lunchtime.

Mbabane

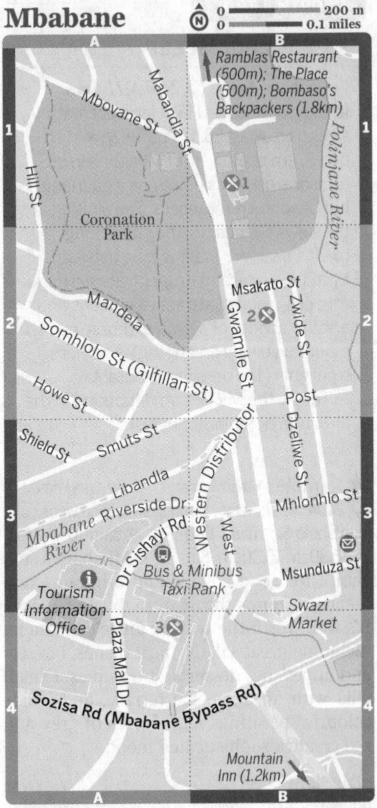

Mbabane

Eating

1 Albert Millin B1
2 Indingilizi Gallery & Restaurant B2
3 Riverside Café A4

WORTH A TRIP

A PEACEFUL SLEEP

Foresters Arms (2467 4177; www.forestersarms.co.za; MR19, Mhlambanyatsi; s/d incl breakfast E620/960; P) Hidden 27km southwest of Mbabane in picturesque hills, this place has a haunting but beautiful remoteness. The air is clean, the views suggestive, the peace tangible. It's a superb staging post between KwaZulu-Natal and Kruger National Park, with cosy rooms, attractive gardens and a smorgasbord of activities (horse riding, mountain biking and hiking). Another highlight is the on-site restaurant.

Follow the MR19 from Mbabane in the direction of Mhlambanyatsi.

★**Ramblas Restaurant** INTERNATIONAL **$$**
(2404 4147; www.ramblasswaziland.webs.com; Mantsholo St; mains E80-160; 8am-10pm Mon-Fri, 8.30am-10.30pm Sat;) Mbabane's top choice for good cuisine and a buzzing ambience, a stone's throw from the golf course. It's well worth the trip for an eclectic menu including great salads, meat dishes, burgers and appetising desserts. It occupies a small villa with an agreeable terrace, and inside colourful paintings and shades of grey and red create a sophisticated mood.

eDladleni FUSION **$$**
(7841 4110, 2402 5743; http://edladleni.100webspace.net/index.html; Manzini/Mbabane Hwy, Mvubu Falls; mains E50-110; noon-3pm & 6-10pm Tue-Sun;) Delicious food, a serene setting and cracking views – if you're after an authentic Swazi experience, eDladleni's hard to beat. Here you can tuck into specialities that are hard to find elsewhere, and it's got excellent vegetarian options. It's about 6km from Mbabane, off the main highway (follow the sign 'Mvubu Falls'); check the website for directions.

The charismatic owner, Dolores Godde-froy, is committed to reviving traditional recipes based on local produce. It's a pity, then, that service is so slow and not all dishes on the menu are available. Opening hours are unreliable – it's wise to call ahead.

Albert Millin CAFETERIA, PUB **$$**
(2404 9942; Gwamile St; mains E50-120; 10am-10pm Tue & Wed, to midnight Thu-Sat;) This eatery-pub on the grounds of the Mbabane Club is very popular with expats and has a modern feel. From pizzas and salads to burgers and satisfying grilled meats, the menu covers enough territory to please most palates. It's also a good place to just enjoy the cool atmosphere with a cold beer in hand.

Information

EMERGENCY

Police (999, 2404 2221)

MEDICAL SERVICES

Mbabane Clinic (2404 2423; www.theclinicgroup.com; Mkhonubovu St; 24h) For emergencies try this well-equipped clinic in the southwestern corner of town just off the bypass road.

MONEY

Banks with ATMs include First National Bank, Nedbank and Standard Bank; these are located in Swazi Plaza.

TOURIST INFORMATION

Tourism Information Office (2404 2531; www.thekingdomofswaziland.com; Swazi Mall, Dr Sishayi Rd; 8am-5pm Mon-Fri, 9am-5pm Sat) Inside Swazi Mall. Has maps and brochures.

Getting There & Around

The main bus and shared-taxi park is just behind Swazi Plaza. Minibus shared taxis leave for Jo'burg (E210, four hours) throughout the day; another option is to catch one from Manzini.

There are several sharted taxis daily to Ngwenya and the Oshoek border post (E15, 50 minutes), and Malkerns Valley (E15, 45 minutes). All vehicles heading towards Manzini (E15, 35 minutes) and points east pass through the Ezulwini Valley, although most take the highways, bypassing the valley itself.

Nonshared taxis congregate just outside the transport park behind Swazi Plaza. Nonshared taxis to the Ezulwini Valley cost from E120, more to the far end of the valley (from E200). Expect to pay from E150 to get to King Mswati III International Airport.

TransMagnific (2404 9977; www.goswaziland.co.sz) and **Sky World** (7664 0001, 2404 9921; www.skyworld.co.sz) offer a daily luxury shuttle service between Johannesburg (OR Tambo International Airport and Sandton) and Mbabane for R500.

CENTRAL SWAZILAND

The country's tourist hub, central Swaziland is a heady mix of culture, nature and epicurean indulgences, and has plenty to keep you occupied for a few days. There are wildlife reserves to explore, museums to visit, great restaurants to sample and quality handicrafts to bring home.

WHITE-WATER RAFTING & CAVING

One of the highlights of Swaziland is rafting the Great Usutu River (Lusutfu River). The river varies radically from steep creeks to sluggish flats, but in the vicinity of Mkhaya Game Reserve it passes through a gorge, where a perfect mix of rapids can be encountered all year round.

Swazi Trails is the best contact to organise a rafting trip – it offers full- and half-day trips (E1200/950 per person, including lunch and transport, minimum two people). Abseiling and cliff jumps are added for extra adrenaline in the winter months.

For an off-the-scale challenge rating, the company's adventure-caving trips offer a rare window into the elite world of cave exploration. A few kilometres from Mbabane, the vast Gobholo Cave is 98% unexplored. You can choose between the 8.30am departure (E700) and the 4.30pm dinner trip (E850; it includes a hot-spring soak, pizza and beer).

Ezulwini Valley

What a difference a few kilometres can make! Swaziland's tourism centre, the Ezulwini Valley begins just outside Mbabane but feels a world away from the hullabaloo of the capital. With an excellent selection of places to stay and wonderful craft shopping, it's a convenient base for many visitors.

Sights & Activities

Mantenga Cultural Village & Nature Reserve NATURE RESERVE
(☎2416 1151; www.sntc.org.sz/reserves/mantenga.asp; Ezulwini Valley; admission E100; ⏰8am-6pm) The entrance fee to this tranquil, thickly forested reserve covers a guided tour of the reserve's Swazi Cultural Village, a 'living' cultural village with authentic beehive huts and cultural displays, plus a *sibhaca* dance (performed daily at 11.15am and 3.15pm) and a visit to the impressive Mantenga Falls. The reserve is also great for hiking; day hikers pay only E50. Although it's not a big wildlife park, it offers a chance to see vervet monkeys, baboons, warthogs, nyalas and duikers.

Birdlife abounds, including the endangered southern bald ibis. It's located 1km from Mantenga Lodge and is well signposted from the MR103.

Swazi Trails ADVENTURE SPORTS
(☎7602 0261, 2416 2180; www.swazitrails.co.sz; Mantenga Craft Centre, Ezulwini Valley; ⏰8am-5pm) Based in the Mantenga Craft Centre in Ezulwini Valley, this is one of the country's major activity companies, and the place to go to for caving, rafting, hikes and general cultural and highlights tours. Also houses the Ezulwini Tourist Office.

Cuddle Puddle HOT SPRINGS
(☎2416 1164; MR103, Ezulwini Valley; adult/child E30/15; ⏰7am-11pm Thu-Tue, to 8pm Wed) For personal pampering, head to the Royal Valley's own hot mineral springs. The magnesium-rich waters are a constant 32°C. There's also a spa, complete with sauna, gym and massage.

Tours

All Out Africa ADVENTURE TOUR
(☎2416 2260; www.alloutafrica.com; MR103, Ezulwini Valley; ⏰8am-5pm) Runs a range of adventure trips and activities throughout Swaziland, plus to Kruger National Park. Highly recommended is the half-day cultural tour through Lobamba (per person R345; minimum two people). It's housed in Lidwala Backpacker Lodge.

Mandla Masuku/ Ekhaya Cultural Tours CULTURAL TOUR
(☎7644 3257; www.ekhayatours.com; company vehicle/own car per person R1200/600, minimum 2 people; ⏰daily by reservation) For a taste of rural Swazi life – including a visit to Lobamba, a school and a family – a good contact is local Mandla Masuku of Ekhaya Cultural Tours. He also speaks French.

Sleeping

★**Lidwala Backpacker Lodge** BACKPACKERS $
(☎7690 5865, 2550 4951; www.lidwala.co.sz; MR103, Ezulwini Valley; camping per tent R120, dm & safari tents per person E160, d E380-440; P 🛜 🏊) What a magical setting! This comfortable, well-run spot is nestled in a splendid garden with a pool among big boulders and a chuckling stream. Rooms are a typical dorm-style, backpacker set-up, with a laid-back, friendly feel. The separate safari tents are popular, while the private rooms are smallish but neat.

Ezulwini & Malkerns Valleys

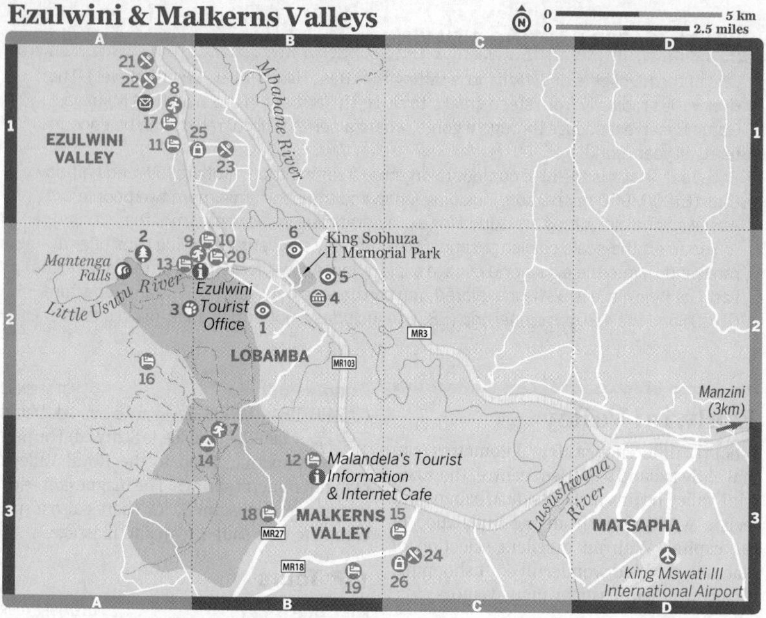

Ezulwini & Malkerns Valleys

Sights
1 Eludzidzini Royal Residence.................B2
King Sobhuza II Memorial Park..(see 4)
2 Mantenga Cultural Village & Nature Reserve A2
3 Mlilwane Wildlife Sanctuary A2
4 National Museum.................................. B2
5 Parliament B2
6 Somhlolo National Stadium................. B2

Activities, Courses & Tours
7 Chubeka Trails....................................... B3
8 Cuddle Puddle..A1
9 Swazi Trails.. B2

Sleeping
Legends Backpackers Lodge....... (see 13)
10 Lidwala Backpacker Lodge.................. B2
11 Lugogo Sun Hotel A1
12 Malandela's B&B.................................. B3
Mantenga Cultural Village & Nature Reserve ....(see 2)
13 Mantenga Lodge & Restaurant............ A2
14 Mlilwane Wildlife Sanctuary Main Camp B3
15 Rainbird Chalets....................................C3
16 Reilly's Rock Hilltop Lodge...................A2
17 Royal Swazi Spa A1
18 Sondzela Backpackers..........................B3
19 Umdoni B3
20 Victory Guesthouse B2

Eating
21 Boma Restaurant A1
22 Calabash... A1
23 Lihawu Restaurant B1
Malandela's Restaurant................(see 12)
Mantenga Restaurant...................(see 13)
24 Sambane Coffee Shoppe C3

Entertainment
House on Fire.................................(see 12)

Shopping
Baobab Batik..................................(see 26)
25 Ezulwini Craft Market B1
Gone Rural......................................(see 12)
Mantenga Craft Centre.................(see 13)
26 Swazi Candles..C3
Yebo Art & Design ....(see 13)

There are kitchen and laundry facilities and meals are available. Fancy hiking? Lidwala has its own trail that starts behind the lodge and leads to a summit where you get a panoramic view of the Ezulwini Valley. Lidwala is run by All Out Africa, which organises trips and activities.

Legends Backpackers Lodge BACKPACKERS $
(☎7602 0261, 2416 1870; www.legends.co.sz; Mantenga Falls Rd, Ezulwini Valley; camping E80, dm E150, d without bathroom E400; P 📶 🏊) It's far from flash, but this mellow place is the most obvious choice if funds are short, with an assortment of 10- to 12-bed dorms, a self-catering kitchen, a chill-out lounge with TV and a small pool in the garden. Those needing privacy can opt for the plain but restful private rooms in a separate building. Breakfast costs E45.

Swazi Trails, the lodge's sister company and local adventure-activity operator, is just across the road, and the nearest supermarket is a 10-minute stroll away.

Victory Guesthouse GUESTHOUSE $
(☎2416 3309; Mantenga Estate, Ezulwini Valley; d incl breakfast E450; P) In a quiet neighbourhood close to the main road, this family-run venture is an acceptable plan B. The eight rooms are unmemorable but get the job done.

Mantenga Cultural Village & Nature Reserve BUNGALOW $$
(☎2416 1151, 2416 1178; www.sntc.org.sz; Ezulwini Valley; d incl breakfast E720; P) These digs within the Mantenga Nature Reserve offer something different, with a cluster of offbeat bungalows set in lush bushland, many of which overlook a river. Very 'Me Tarzan, you Jane'. With wooden furnishings and modern amenities (but no air-con), they represent a nicely judged balance between comfort, rustic charm and seclusion. Visitors don't pay entry to the nature reserve.

A pleasant restaurant is nearby, set in a luxuriant rainforest.

Mantenga Lodge & Restaurant HOTEL $$
(☎2416 1049; www.mantengalodge.com; Mantenga Falls Rd, Ezulwini Valley; incl breakfast s E530-730, d E710-910; P ❄ 📶 🏊) We're suckers for the relaxing atmosphere that prevails in this oasis of calm. The 38 rooms of varying standards (and different prices) are nothing too out of the ordinary but are set in a lush wooded area where you can mooch around, and the pool is an instant elixir when it's swelteringly hot. Another plus is the attached restaurant.

Lugogo Sun Hotel HOTEL $$
(☎2416 4500; www.suninternational.com; MR103, Ezulwini Valley; s/d incl breakfast from E1000/1200; P ❄ 📶 🏊) The rooms in this undistinguished motel-like building seriously lack character, but it will do for a night's kip, especially if you nab a room with a pool view – the other ones look onto the parking lot. It's popular with tour groups.

Royal Swazi Spa HOTEL $$$
(☎2416 5000; www.suninternational.com; MR103, Ezulwini Valley; incl breakfast s E2400-2800, d E2600-2900; P ❄ @ 📶 🏊) Distinctly unimpressive for the price, the Royal Swazi is not quite the five-star heavyweight it thinks it is, but the rooms have the requisite comforts and it features a host of facilities and amenities, including two restaurants, three bars, a large pool, a spa, a casino and a golf course.

Eating & Drinking

★ Lihawu Restaurant FUSION $$
(☎2416 7035; www.lihawu.co.sz; Royal Villas, Ezulwini Valley; mains E85-180; ⏰noon-2pm & 6-10.30pm) Within the swish Royal Villas resort nestles Swaziland's most elegant restaurant, with a tastefully decorated dining room and an outdoor eating area that overlooks a swimming pool. The menu is Afro-fusion, with meaty signature dishes such as lamb stew and beef fillet, but there are also vegetarian options. Needless to say the accompanying wine list is top class.

Mantenga Restaurant INTERNATIONAL $$
(☎2416 1049; Mantenga Lodge & Restaurant, Mantenga Falls Rd, Ezulwini Valley; mains E70-140; ⏰6.30am-9.30pm) Inside Mantenga Lodge (but open to nonguests), this restaurant with a raised wooden deck has a fabulous outlook over the trees. The pasta dishes and grilled meats are good deals, as are the sandwiches.

Boma Restaurant INTERNATIONAL $$
(☎2416 2632; off MR103, Ezulwini Valley; mains E70-150; ⏰11am-10.30pm) This atmospheric, boma-shaped restaurant with thatched roof has a massive menu with all the favourites – grills to pastas – and is within the grounds of Timbali Lodge. You can't really go wrong – everything is pretty good – but if you want a recommendation, go for the wood-fire pizzas.

Calabash GERMAN, FRENCH $$$
(off MR103, Ezulwini Valley; mains E90-220; ⏰12.30-2.30pm & 6-10pm) Grilled *eisbein* (pig knuckle) and *escargots bourguignons* (Burgundy snails) in Swaziland? Yes, it's possible. German and French cuisine are the incongruous highlights at this long-standing and dated, but smart, place located at the upper end of the Ezulwini Valley. It also has an impressive wine cellar.

Shopping

The Ezulwini Valley, together with the nearby Malkerns Valley, offers some of the best craft shopping in the region, with a wide selection, high quality and reasonable prices.

Yebo Art & Design ARTS & CRAFTS
(☎2416 2984; www.yeboswaziland.com; Mantenga Falls Rd, Ezulwini Valley; ⏰9am-5pm Wed-Sat, 10am-3pm Sun) This modern art gallery hosts regular exhibitions and showcases the work of both established and up-and-coming artists, artisans and designers from around Swaziland. The shop within the gallery has a good selection of handmade gifts and textiles.

Ezulwini Craft Market ARTS & CRAFTS
(MR103, Ezulwini Valley; ⏰8am-5pm) Don't miss this well-stocked market that's opposite the Zeemans Filling Station on the corner of MR103 and Mpumalanga Loop Rd. Look for the blue tin roofs. The stalls sell a vast array of local carvings, weavings and handicrafts.

Mantenga Craft Centre ARTS & CRAFTS
(☎2416 1136; Mantenga Falls Rd, Ezulwini Valley; ⏰8am-5pm) This colourful, compact craft centre has several shops featuring everything from weaving and tapestries to candles, woodcarvings and T-shirts.

Information

There are ATMs at the Gables Shopping Centre.

Big Game Parks (☎2528 3943/4; www.biggameparks.org; Malkerns; ⏰8am-5pm Mon-Fri) The central reservations office is accessed through the Mlilwane Wildlife Sanctuary. Contact it for accommodation in Mlilwane Wildlife Sanctuary, Mkhaya Game Reserve and Hlane Royal National Park, although you can also book direct with the reserves.

Ezulwini Tourist Office (☎7602 0261, 2416 2180; www.swazitrails.co.sz; Mantenga Craft Centre, Ezulwini Valley; ⏰8am-5pm) Inside Swazi Trails you'll find the Ezulwini Tourist Office with information and bookings services for all the reserves, community tourism facilities, tour operators, activities and general accommodation.

Getting There & Away

Nonshared taxis from Mbabane cost E120 to E200, depending on how far down the valley you go.

During the day you could get on a minibus bound for Manzini, but make sure the driver knows that you want to alight in the valley, as many aren't keen on stopping.

Lobamba

Welcome to Swaziland's spiritual, cultural and political heart. Just east of Ezulwini Valley lies Lobamba, an area that's been playing host to Swaziland's monarchy for over two centuries. It's home to some of the most notable buildings in the country. Despite its importance, Lobamba feels surprisingly quiet – except during the spectacular Incwala and Umhlanga ceremonies, when the nation gathers on the surrounding plains for several days of intense revelry.

Sights

Eludzidzini Royal Residence NOTABLE BUILDING
At the end of a palm-lined avenue south of Lobamba lies Eludzidzini, the queen mother's royal residence. It's not open to the public except during festivities, notably the Incwala ceremony or the *umhlanga* (reed) dance.

National Museum MUSEUM
(☎2416 1179; Lobamba; adult/child E80/30; ⏰8am-4.30pm Mon-Fri, 10am-4pm Sat & Sun) This museum has some interesting displays of Swazi culture, as well as a traditional beehive village and cattle enclosure and several of King Sobhuza I's 1940s cars.

King Sobhuza II Memorial Park MEMORIAL
(☎2416 2131; Lobamba; adult/child E80/30; ⏰8am-4.30pm Mon-Fri, 10am-4pm Sat & Sun) Adjacent to the parliament, this memorial was established as a tribute to King Sobhuza II, who led Swaziland to independence from British rule in 1968. Its main highlight is a 3m-tall bronze statue of the late, revered king. There's a small museum with various pictures and documents about his life. The king's mausoleum is also within the park.

Parliament NOTABLE BUILDING
(Lobamba) Opened in 1969 as a postindependence gift from the departing British, this hexagonal building topped with a brass dome is a major landmark in Lobamba. It is sometimes open to visitors; if you want to visit, wear neat clothes and use the side entrance.

Somhlolo National Stadium NOTABLE BUILDING
(Lobamba) Built for Swaziland's independence in 1968, the 20,000-capacity national stadium hosts important state occasions, such as coronations (including that of Mswati III, which took place on 25 April 1986), and

soccer matches. It is named after Swaziland's King Sobhuza I, also known as Somhlolo, the founding father of the Swazi nation.

Mlilwane Wildlife Sanctuary

While it doesn't have the drama or vastness of some of the bigger South African parks, the tranquil **Mlilwane Wildlife Sanctuary** (☎2528 3943; www.biggameparks.org/mlilwane/; admission E40; ⏲6am-6pm) near Lobamba is well worth a visit: it's beautiful, tranquil and easily accessible. The landscape is another highlight; its terrain is dominated by the Nyonyane Mountain, whose exposed granite peak is known as Execution Rock (1110m). Small wonder that the reserve is an outdoor-lover's paradise, with a wide range of activities available.

Situated in a transitional zone between highveld and middleveld, it supports a large diversity of fauna (mostly large herbivores and birds) and flora, and it has no dangerous wildlife to worry about (except hippos). Tip: the best wildlife and birdwatching areas are the waterhole at the main camp and the main dam to the north. The enclosed area near Reilly's Rock shelters some rare species of antelope and is accessible only on a guided drive.

This private reserve was Swaziland's first protected area, created by conservationist Ted Reilly on his family farm in the 1950s. Mlilwane now covers an area of 4560 hectares ranging from 680m to 1474m above sea level.

MLILWANE WILDLIFE SANCTUARY

Why Go Easy access from Mbabane and Ezulwini Valley; rewarding year-round wildlife-watching and birding; zebras, warthogs, wildebeest, numerous species of antelope (including the rare blue duiker), crocodiles, hippos and rare bird species; wide range of activities available; no dangerous animals; excellent accommodation options.

When to Go Year-round.

Practicalities From Mbabane or Ezulwini Valley, take the MR103 to the south. Drive past Lobamba; the turn-off to the reserve is well signposted on the right. After initial check-in at Sangweni main gate, visitors enjoy 24-hour park access.

Budget Tips For sleeping, the reserve's beehive huts are cheap and pleasant, and there's also a top-notch backpackers.

Activities

All activities can be booked through reception at Mlilwane Wildlife Sanctuary Main Camp (p498).

Horse Riding

Wildlife viewing on horseback gives you a fantastic opportunity to explore areas that are otherwise inaccessible to the public and get up close and personal with a number of species that are usually shy.

Chubeka Trails HORSE RIDING
(☎2528 3943; www.biggameparks.org/chubeka/; Mlilwane Wildlife Sanctuary; per hour E180; ⏲daily by reservation) This well-run outfit offers various horse-riding programs for all ability levels. The one-hour jaunt is a lovely ramble amid the plains that surround the main camp. The ultimate is the 'Rock of Execution Challenge', which will take you to the top of Nyonyane peak (about four hours; E650). All excursions depart from the sanctuary's main camp.

Mountain Biking

With its excellent network of roads and trails, the sanctuary is a top two-wheel destination. Bikes are available for hire at the main camp (E135 per hour).

Walking

The sanctuary offers a rare opportunity to wander unguided in pristine African bushveld and to explore for yourself the many trails and roads that lead around the reserve. Hiking up the Nyonyane Mountain is a firm favourite. A map is available at the reception. Fear not: there are no predators.

Guided birding walks (E190) can also be arranged at the main camp.

Wildlife Drives

The sanctuary's guided wildlife drives come recommended. They last 1½ hours and cost E235 (minimum two people). Sunrise and sunset drives are also available (two hours, E295).

Tours

Want a break from the wildlife? Consider taking a cultural tour (two hours; per person

E105), during which you'll visit the homestead of a local chief (a female at the time of research) and get a taste of rural Swazi culture. Bookings (minimum four people) are made at the main camp.

Sleeping & Eating

All accommodation in the sanctuary can be booked in advance via telephone or email at **Big Game Parks** (☎2528 3943/4; www.biggameparks.org).

★ Sondzela Backpackers BACKPACKERS $
(☎2528 3117; www.biggameparks.org/sondzela; Mlilwane Wildlife Sanctuary; camping E80, dm E105, s/d without bathroom E210/300, rondavel s/d without bathroom E210/330; P ≋) A top choice for budgeteers, in the southern part of the Mlilwane Wildlife Sanctuary, Sondzela boasts fine, breezy dorms, clean private doubles and a clutch of lovely *rondavels* with wraparound views. And it doesn't end there. The delightful gardens, kitchen, swimming pool and a hilltop perch provide one of the best backpackers' settings in Southern Africa.

Breakfast and hearty traditional dinners (cooked on the outside braai) are available for a song. If you're driving, you'll need to use the main Mlilwane Wildlife Sanctuary entrance, pay the entry fee and drive through the park to reach Sondzela. Alternatively, Sondzela's own shuttle bus departs the lodge at 8am and 5pm, and from Malandela's B&B in Malkerns Valley 30 minutes later.

Mlilwane Wildlife Sanctuary Main Camp CAMPGROUND, HUT $$
(☎2528 3943/4; www.biggameparks.org/mlilwane; Mlilwane Wildlife Sanctuary; camping E95, hut s/d E520/780, rondavel s/d E550/830; P ᯤ ≋) This homey camp is set in a scenic wooded location about 3.5km from the entry gate, complete with well-appointed *rondavels* and simple huts – including traditional beehive huts – and the occasional warthog snuffling around. The Hippo Haunt Restaurant serves excellent grilled meat and overlooks a waterhole. There are often dance performances in the evening. The pool is another drawcard.

Reilly's Rock Hilltop Lodge LODGE $$$
(☎2528 3943/4; www.biggameparks.org/reilly; Mlilwane Wildlife Sanctuary; with half board s E1160-1245, d E1780-1910; P) Promoted as 'quaintly colonial', this is an oh-so delightfully tranquil, old-world, nonfussy luxury experience at its best. In an incredible setting – a Royal Botanic Garden with aloes, cycads and an enormous jacaranda – the main house, which shelters four rooms, has striking views of the valley and Mdzimba Mountains. Entry to the reserve is included.

Generous dinners are served in the dining room and full breakfasts are enjoyed on the verandah in sight of beautiful birds and even small antelope.

Malkerns Valley

About 7km south of Lobamba/Ezulwini Valley on the MR103 is the turn-off to the fertile Malkerns Valley, known for its arts and crafts outlets, and, together with the Ezulwini Valley, offering a scenic and fun drive.

Sleeping & Eating

Malandela's B&B B&B $$
(☎2528 3339, 2528 3448; www.malandelas.com; MR27, Malkerns Valley; s/d incl breakfast E500/700; P @ ᯤ ≋) This is a wonderfully relaxing option with six tastefully designed rooms, a pool and a terrific sculpture garden. Each room has a theme and is decorated differently; our fave is the supersized Purple. There's an excellent restaurant if you're feeling too lazy to travel elsewhere. Wi-fi costs extra. Book ahead. Malandela's is along the MR27, about 1km from the junction with the MR103.

Umdoni B&B $$
(☎7602 0791, 2528 3009; www.umdoni.com; Malkerns Valley; s/d incl breakfast E615/970; P ❄ ᯤ ≋) An upmarket experience in the heart of the Malkerns Valley. The manicured garden – there's not a leaf out of place – gives a good indication of this abode: chic and stylish rooms in two colonial-style cottages. There are crisp white sheets, DSTV and a breakfast on the patio overlooking flower beds. Wonderful staff is a bonus. It's off the MR18.

Rainbird Chalets CHALET $$
(☎7603 7273; www.rainbird.com; Malkerns Valley; s/d incl breakfast E700/1200; P ❄ ᯤ ≋) It's the bucolic setting that's the pull here. Eight chalets – three log, and five brick A-frames – are set in a manicured private garden near the owners' house and overlook a small dam. All are fully equipped and feature smart bathrooms. Breakfast is served on a verandah blessed with soul-stirring views of the surrounding hills.

★ Sambane Coffee Shoppe CAFE $
(☎7604 2035; Swazi Candles Craft Centre, Malkerns Valley; mains E40-80; ⏲8.15am-5pm) If you

need to re-energise after a bout of shopping in the adjoining handicrafts outlets, there's no better place than this delightful cafe. It has a fine selection of pastries, sandwiches, burgers and salads – all homemade. Mmm: the warm chocolate brownie with ice cream. Tip: arrive early, as it's usually packed to the rafters with hungry tourists at lunchtime.

Malandela's Restaurant INTERNATIONAL $$$
(☎2528 3115; www.malandelas.com; MR27, Malkerns Valley; mains E80-140; ⊙9-11am, noon-3pm & 6-9.30pm;) Part of the Malandela's complex, this is a reliable option, with an eclectic menu featuring grilled meats, seafood dishes, frondy salads and scrumptious house desserts – don't miss out on the chocolate cake. There's pleasant outdoor seating; indoors there's a fire for when it's chilly and it's candlelit at night.

Entertainment

House on Fire LIVE MUSIC
(☎2528 2001; www.house-on-fire.com; MR27, Malkerns Valley) People visit this especially for the ever-mutating cultural site–living gallery and experimental-performance space. Part of the Malandela's complex, the well-known venue hosts everything from African theatre, music and films to raves and other forms of entertainment. Since 2007 it has hosted the annual MTN Bushfire Festival (p490).

Shopping

There's some excellent shopping on the Malkerns Valley loop, well marked on tourist maps and well signed.

★ **Swazi Candles** HANDICRAFTS
(☎2528 3219; www.swazicandles.com; Malkerns Valley; ⊙8am-5pm) A mandatory stop for the souvenir hunter, Swazi Candles is one of the most famous handicrafts outlets in Southern Africa. Here you can wax lyrical about these creative pigment-coloured candles – in every African-animal shape and hue; it's fun to watch the workers hand-mould the designs. It's 7km south of the MR103 turn-off for Malkerns.

Gone Rural ARTS & CRAFTS
(☎2550 4936; www.goneruralswazi.com; Malkerns Valley; ⊙8am-5pm Mon-Sat, 9am-5pm Sun) The place to go for good-quality produce – baskets, mats and traditional clay pots – made by groups of local women. It's based at Malandela's B&B.

Baobab Batik HANDICRAFTS
(☎2528 3242; www.baobab-batik.com; Malkerns Valley; ⊙8am-5pm) This is the place to head if you're dye-ing for a wall hanging or a cushion cover.

> **WORTH A TRIP**
>
> **OVERNIGHT CULTURAL EXPERIENCE**
>
> **Woza Nawe Tours** (☎7642 6780; www.swaziculturaltours.com) Headed by local Swazi Myxo Mdluli, this outfit runs highly recommended village visits (day tour R1250) and overnight stays (adult/child E1450/725) to Kaphunga, 55km southeast of Manzini. The fee includes transport, meals and a guide. Guests join in on whatever activities are going on in the village – including cooking, planting and harvesting.

Information

Malandela's Tourist Information & Internet Cafe (MR17, Malkerns Valley; per hour E45; ⊙8am-5pm) Internet access and tourist information.

Getting There & Away

Minibus shared taxis run between here and the Ezulwini Valley for around E5. As the craft shops and sleeping places are spread out, you'll really need a car to get around.

Manzini

Swaziland's largest town, Manzini is a chaotic commercial and industrial hub whose small centre is dominated by office blocks and a couple of shopping malls that run down two main streets. With the exception of the market, Manzini itself has limited appeal for the tourist. That said, it's a main transport hub, so you're likely to pass through here if you're getting around on public transport.

Accommodation is limited; you're best to head to the Malkerns or Ezulwini Valleys, only 12km away.

Sights

Market MARKET
(cnr Mhlakuvane & Mancishane Sts; ⊙7am-5pm Mon-Sat) Manzini's main drawcard is its colourful market, whose upper section is packed with handicrafts from Swaziland and elsewhere in Africa. Thursday morning is a good time to see the rural vendors and Mozambican traders bringing in their handicrafts and textiles to sell to the retailers.

Manzini

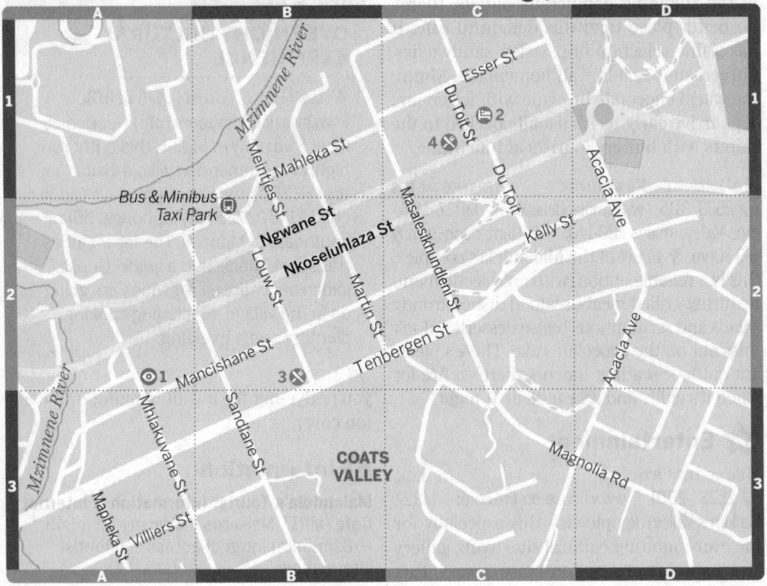

Manzini

Sights

1 Market A2

Sleeping

2 George Hotel C1

Eating

3 Baker's Delight B2

4 Gil Vincente Restaurant C1

Sleeping & Eating

George Hotel BUSINESS HOTEL **$$**

(☎2505 2260; www.tgh.co.sz; cnr Ngwane & Du Toit Sts; incl breakfast s E665-870, d E940-1100; P ❄ 📶 🏊) Don't be discouraged by the modest exterior and the unspectacular location up the main road. Manzini's fanciest hotel attempts an international atmosphere and features a respectable collection of various-size comfy rooms (tip: ask for a poolside one), two stylish restaurants, a lovely garden with a pool, a small spa and conference facilities.

Baker's Delight BAKERY **$**

(☎2505 9181; cnr Tenbergen & Louw Sts; snacks E20-75; ⏲7am-4.30pm Mon-Fri, to 2pm Sat) If, like us, you think life is unbearable without a chocolate eclair or a scone, bookmark this snazzy bakery. Also serves up snack options, including salads and burgers, at lunchtime. Good breakfasts, too.

Gil Vincente Restaurant INTERNATIONAL **$$$**

(☎2505 3874; Ngwane St; mains R80-140; ⏲9am-10pm Tue-Sun) Gourmands saunter here for well-prepped Portuguese-inspired dishes with a twist, a respectable wine list, efficient service and smart decor. Sink your teeth into a juicy *bitoque* (beefsteak with fried egg) or a succulent *bacalhau* (cod). Enough proteins? Pastas and salads are also available.

Getting There & Away

The main **bus and shared-taxi park** is at the northern end of Louw St, where you can also find some nonshared taxis. A minibus shared-taxi trip up the Ezulwini Valley to Mbabane costs E15 (35 minutes). Shared taxis to Mozambique (E90) also depart from here.

NORTHWESTERN SWAZILAND

Lush hills undulating off towards the horizon, green velvet mountains cloaked in layers of wispy cloud, majestic plantations and woodlands, streams and waterfalls, and plunging ravines are the main features of Swaziland's beautiful northwest. As well as boasting the best scenery in Swaziland, this area offers some excellent hiking and accommodation options.

Ngwenya

Tiny Ngwenya, 5km east of the border with Mpumalanga, is the first town you'll reach if you're arriving in Swaziland via Oshoek. If you can't wait until you reach the Ezulwini Valley to do your shopping, there are several excellent craft outlets here. For history buffs, the Ngwenya iron-ore mine is well worth a detour.

◉ Sights

Ngwenya Iron Ore Mine HISTORIC SITE
(Ngwenya; admission E28; ⊙8am-4pm) Ngwenya is one of the world's oldest known mines. The **Visitors Centre** has an interesting display of photographs and information, including the original excavation tools. To visit the mine, even if you are travelling by vehicle, you'll need to be accompanied by a ranger, who will explain the mine's history (note: tips appreciated). The entrance is signposted off the MR3.

Although the mine is part of Malolotja Nature Reserve, you can't continue on into the rest of Malolotja from here.

🛏 Sleeping & Eating

Hawane Resort RESORT **$$**
(☑2444 1744; www.hawane.co.sz; Hawane; dm E120, chalet s/d incl breakfast E600/890; P 🐾 🏊) Framed by the Malolotja peaks, these quirky chalets are a blend of traditional Swazi materials (wattle and grass) and glass, with ethnic African interiors. Backpackers are stabled in a converted barn. The resort restaurant serves African cuisine (dinner buffet E155). It's a convenient base for visiting Malolotja Nature Reserve, though some visitors say it's overpriced and service is lackadaisical.

Horse riding and mountain biking are available on the premises. It's about 5km up the Piggs Peak road from the junction of the MR1 and MR3, and 1.5km off the main road.

🛍 Shopping

Ngwenya Glass Complex is a hub of boutiques selling all kinds of quality arts and crafts. It's well signposted off the MR3 on a road that leads to the Ngwenya iron-ore mine.

★Ngwenya Glass ARTS & CRAFTS
(☑2442 4142; www.ngwenyaglass.co.sz; Ngwenya Glass Complex, Ngwenya; ⊙8am-4pm) One of

Swaziland's major tourist attractions, this superb glass-blowing factory and boutique showcases a fantastic selection of animal figurines, vases, decorative-art glass and tableware made from recycled glass. On weekdays you can watch the glass-blowers at work from an overhead balcony. Magical!

Quazi Design Process ARTS & CRAFTS
(☑2422 0193; www.quazidesign.com; Ngwenya Glass Complex, Ngwenya; ⊙8am-4pm) Run by a group of women, this outlet sells modern accessories of cutting-edge design, made from recycled paper.

Rosecraft ARTS & CRAFTS
(☑2442 4047; www.rosecraft.net; Ngwenya Glass Complex, Ngwenya; ⊙8am-4pm) A lovely boutique selling top-quality handwoven shawls, cushion covers, bags, blankets and other colourful items.

Malolotja Nature Reserve

One of Swaziland's premier natural attractions, the beautiful **Malolotja Nature Reserve** (☑2442 3048, 7660 6755; www.sntc.org.sz/reserves/malolotja.asp; adult/child E30/15; ⊙6am-6pm) is a true wilderness area that's rugged and, in the most part, unspoiled. The terrain ranges from mountainous and high-altitude grassland to forest and lower-lying bushveld. The reserve is laced by streams and cut by three rivers, including the Komati River, which flows east through a gorge in a series of falls and rapids until it meets the lowveld. No prize for guessing that this spectacular

ⓘ MALOLOTJA NATURE RESERVE

Why Go Breathtaking mountain scenery; excellent playground for hikers and mountain bikers; abundant birdlife and diverse flora; no dangerous animals; the sole canopy tour in the country.

When to Go Year-round, but expect heavy mist between October and March.

Practicalities The entrance gate for Malolotja is about 35km northwest of Mbabane, along the Piggs Peak road (MR1). It's well signposted. Some stretches of road that are heavily eroded require a 4WD in wet weather.

Budget Tips The reserve has camping facilities.

WORTH A TRIP

HIDEAWAY

Phophonyane Falls Ecolodge & Nature Reserve (☎2431 3429; www.phophonyane.co.sz; incl breakfast d safari tent/beehive/cottage from E1360/2040/1780;) This little morsel of paradise about 14km north of Piggs Peak is a dream come true for those seeking to get well and truly off the beaten track. It lies on a river in its own nature reserve of lush indigenous forest. Accommodation is in comfortable cottages, stylish beehives or luxury safari tents overlooking cascades.

There's a network of walking trails around the river and waterfall. Excellent meals are available in the stylish dining area. Day visitors to the reserve are charged E40/30 per adult/child. Turn at signs indicating Phophonyane Falls; then it's 4.5km on dirt road.

area is a fantastic playground for nature-lovers and an ornithologist's paradise, with more than 280 species of bird.

Fans of flora will also get their kicks here; wildflowers and rare plants are added attractions, with several (including the Woolly, Barberton and Kaapschehoop cycads) found only in this region of Africa. As if this weren't enough, Malolotja is home to the country's first and only canopy tour.

Don't expect to see plenty of large mammals, though. It's the scenery that's the pull here, rather than the wildlife. That said, you'll certainly come across various antelope species as well as small groups of zebras and wildebeest.

Activities

Malolotja offers some of the most inspirational **hiking** trails in Swaziland, so pack your sturdy shoes. Options range from short walks to multiday hikes. Well-known and much enjoyed walks include the Malolotja Falls Walk, with superb views of the Malolotja Valley, and the Komati River Trail.

Printouts of hiking trails are available for free at reception inside the park. Also check the well-organised SNTC website (www.sntc.org.sz/tourism/malolotjawalks.asp) for descriptions of walks and trails.

Malolotja Canopy Tour OUTDOORS
(☎7660 6755; www.malolotjacanopytour.com; Malolotja Nature Reserve; per person R595; ⏲8am-2pm) This tour is a definite must-do for those who want to experience the reserve from a different perspective. Here you will make your way across Malolotja's stunning, lush tree canopy on 10 slides (11 wooden platforms) and via a 50m-long suspension bridge. It's very safe, and no previous experience is required.

From the restaurant inside the park you're driven to a base point, from where it's a 15-minute walk to the canopy starting point. Tours leave every 30 minutes.

Sleeping & Eating

Malolotja Camping CAMPGROUND $
(Malolotja Nature Reserve; camping at main camp/on trails E70/50) Camping is available at the well-equipped main site near reception, with ablutions (hot shower) and braai area, or along the overnight trails (no facilities).

Malolotja Cabins CABIN $
(☎2444 3048; www.sntc.org.sz/tourism/malolotja.asp; Malolotja Nature Reserve; per adult/child E250/125; P) These cosy, fully equipped, self-catering wooden cabins, each sleeping a maximum of five, are located near reception and afford lovely mountain views. If cooking's not your thing, there's a restaurant near reception. Wi-fi is available at reception and costs E25 per hour.

Komati Valley

East of Malolotja Nature Reserve, the Komati River valley is a delight, with its majestic mountainscape, rural atmosphere and impressive Maguga Dam. It's hard to believe that Mbabane is only a short drive away.

Maguga Dam LANDMARK
This very scenic dam is on the Komati River, and was constructed to provide irrigation and energy to local communities. With its glittering waters surrounded by the muscular hills of the highveld, it fits the picture-postcard ideal.

Nsangwini Rock Art Shelter ARCHAEOLOGICAL SITE
(adult/child E30/20; ⏲8am-4pm) Culture buffs will love this community-run archaeological site. The well-preserved paintings are under a small but impressive rock shelter, which is perched over the Komati River and affords lovely views across the mountains. The

cave was believed to be that of the Nsangwini Bushmen and features the only known paintings of winged humans. Nsangwini is signed from the main Piggs Peak road and the Maguga Dam loop road. Follow a dirt road for 7.5km.

Note that conditions can get a bit rough after rain. A local guide will take you on the slightly steep and rocky walk (15 minutes down; 20 minutes up) and will give a brief explanation.

Maguga Dam Lodge LODGE $$
(☎2437 3975; www.magugalodge.com; Maguga Dam; camping per adult/child E135/70, s/d incl breakfast E650/980; P ❄ 📶 🏊) Scenically positioned on the southern shore of Maguga Dam, this laid-back venture is blessed with commanding views of the dam and surrounding hills. It comprises two well-equipped camping grounds, a clutch of spacious and light-filled *rondavels* and an excellent restaurant with a deck overlooking the dam. Various activities are on offer, including fishing, cultural tours, hiking and boat cruises.

NORTHEASTERN SWAZILAND

The northeastern Swaziland lowveld nestles in the shadow of the Lubombo Mountains, within an easy drive to the Mozambique border. This remote corner of the country is the country's top wildlife-watching region. Here you'll find a duo of excellent wildlife parks – Hlane Royal National Park and Mkhaya Game Reserve – as well as a couple of lesser-known nature reserves that also beg exploration. If it's action you're after, the superb rapids of the Great Usutu River (Lusutfu River) provide an incredible playground.

Hlane Royal National Park

Hlane Royal National Park (☎2528 3943; www.biggameparks.org/hlane; admission E40; ⏰6am-6pm) belongs in the elite of Swaziland's wildlife parks, and it's easy to see why. Here you can expect to see most safari A-listers, with the exception of buffaloes. The country's largest protected area, this well-organised reserve is home to elephants, lions, leopards, white rhinos and many antelope species, and offers wonderfully low-key wildlife- and birdlife-watching. And it's so easy to enjoy it: hippos and elephants are found around Ndlovu Camp just metres from your cottage. There's plenty to keep you occupied, including bush walking, wildlife drives, mountain biking and cultural tours.

There's a good network of roads that can be tackled in a 2WD, but note that you'll need to book a guided wildlife drive to explore the lion enclosure.

> **HLANE ROYAL NATIONAL PARK**
>
> **Why Go** Has four of the Big Five; the only reserve in Swaziland where you can encounter lions; dedicated rhino wildlife drive; excellent accommodation; good birdwatching; various activities on offer.
>
> **When to Go** Year-round.
>
> **Practicalities** The gate is about 7km south of Simunye (it's signposted). Once at the park, you can explore most of it with a 2WD, with the notable exception of the special lion compound, which can be visited on the wildlife drives only.
>
> **Budget Tips** Ndlovu Camp has camping facilities.

Activities

All activities can be booked at Ndlovu Camp (p504).

Mountain Biking

Mountain biking is a fun and ecofriendly way to commune with the bushveld. Guided mountain-bike outings led by expert rangers cost E230 and last two hours. Tours start from Ndlovu Camp.

Bush Walks

There are guided walking trails and **birding trips** (per person E190), which afford the opportunity to see elephants and rhinos. Serious walkers or bush fanatics can book the one- or two-night fully catered **Ehlatsini bush trails** (from E1280), which take in some lesser-known areas of the park. Contact reception at Ndlovu Camp.

Wildlife Drives

Hlane's major attraction is its large mammals and predators and the easiest way to spot them is on a wildlife drive in an open vehicle. The 2½-hour **sunrise and sunset drives** (per person E325), which are for those overnighting

A TASTE OF RURAL SWAZILAND

Shewula Mountain Camp (☑ 7621 8058, 7603 1931; www.shewulacamp.org; Shewula; camping per person E70, r E350) This sweet little place 37km northeast of Simunye in the Lubombo Mountains (21km on tarred road and 16km on dirt road; turn at signs indicating Shewula) is a marvellous 'stop the world and get off' place. Accommodation is pretty basic – you can camp or there are stone and thatch *rondavels* (no electricity) with shared ablutions (three have bathrooms).

But it's wonderful to be able to enjoy the jaw-dropping views and get a taste of rural life. Activities include guided cultural walks to nearby villages. Local meals can also be arranged.

at Ndlovu Camp, are best for wildlife and photography; they include the lion enclosure, where you have good chances to see the big cats. A dedicated 1½ hour **white-rhino drive** (E235) will allow you to get up close and personal with these behemoths.

 Tours

Growing weary of antelope, rhinos and lions? Bookmark the Ndlovu Camp's two-hour **Umphakatsi Experience cultural tour** (per person E105, minimum 4 people), during which you'll visit a chief's village and learn about traditional Swazi culture.

Sleeping & Eating

Ndlovu Camp CAMPGROUND, COTTAGE **$$**
(☑ 2528 3943; www.biggameparks.org/hlane; Hlane Royal National Park; camping E95, rondavel s/d from E520/940, cottage s/d from E550/830; **P**) Ndlovu Camp is a delightfully mellow spot, with spacious grounds and an atmospheric restaurant that serves outstanding food. Accommodation is in *rondavels* and self-catering cottages with no electricity (paraffin lanterns are provided). You can also pitch your tent on a grassy plot. Ndlovu is just inside the main gate, and near a waterhole that draws hippos and rhinos.

In the evening, don't miss the traditional dance performance around the campfire.

Bhubesi Camp BUNGALOW **$$**
(☑ 2528 3943; www.biggameparks/hlane; Hlane Royal National Park; s/d E530/800; **P**) Set in a

pristine setting about 14km from Ndlovu Camp, Bhubesi Camp features tasteful, stone, four-person, self-catering bungalows that overlook a river and green lawns and are surrounded by lush growth. Electricity is available, but there's no restaurant.

Mlawula Nature Reserve

The low-key **Mlawula Nature Reserve** (☑ 2383 8885; www.sntc.org.sz/reserves/mlawula. asp; adult/child E25/12; ☉ 6am-6pm), where the lowveld plains meet the Lubombo Mountains, boasts antelope species and a few spotted hyenas, among others, plus rewarding birdwatching. Keep your expectations in check, though; wildlife is more elusive here than anywhere else in the country and visitor infastructure is fairly limited. The park's real highlight is its network of walking trails amid beautifully scenic landscapes. There are 10 self-guided walks ranging from a one-hour stroll to a full-day hike. Ask for the *Trails and Day Walks* flier at the gate.

The turn-off for the entrance gates to the reserve is about 10km north of Simunye, from where it's another 4km from the main road.

Sleeping & Eating

The reserve has a campsite where you can pitch your tent and a self-catering cottage, but neither are of a good standard.

Magadzavane Lodge CHALET **$$**
(☑ 2383 8885; magadzavane@sntc.org.sz; Mlawula Nature Reseve; s/d incl breakfast E470/800; **P** 🛜 ⚟) This great option offers 20 enticing chalets in the southern part of the reserve, on the edge of the Lubombo escarpment, with magnificent views of the valley below. There's a restaurant and a small infinity pool. From the northern gate, it's a 17km drive on a gravel road; the last kilometres are very steep (but manageable in a standard vehicle in dry weather).

It's also possible to use the southern gate.

Mbuluzi Game Reserve

The small and privately owned **Mbuluzi Game Reserve** (☑ 2383 8861; mbuluzireception@gmail.com; admission E35; ☉ 6am-6pm) boasts a range of animals, including giraffes, zebras, warthogs, antelope species and wildebeest. Twitchers are sure to get a buzz: more than 300 bird species have been recorded here, including some rare and uncommon species. The reserve is split into two sections, divided by the public road. The southern section has a more dense wildlife population, while the northern sector offers outstanding mountain views. Most areas can be explored in a standard vehicle along well-maintained gravel roads, and no guides are necessary. There's a good network of clearly marked walking trails, which make for a fun activity.

The turn-off for Mbuluzi is the same as for Mlawula; the reserve entrance is about 300m from the turn-off and on the left.

Mbuluzi Camping CAMPGROUND $
(☎2383 8861; mbuluzireception@gmail.com; Mbuluzi Game Reserve; camping E100) Campsites are available near the Mbuluzi River on the reserve's northern side. Facilities include ablution blocks with hot showers.

★ **Mbuluzi Lodges** LODGE $$
(☎2383 8861; mbuluzireception@gmail.com; s E520-550, d E800-1100; P ❄) What a pleasant surprise! The reserve offers a choice of superb five- or eight-person fully equipped, beautifully furnished self-catering lodges and luxury tented camps. Each unit is unique in design and character. Most have spacious verandahs and wooden viewing decks and are scenically set on the Mlawula River in the reserve's southern sector.

Mkhaya Game Reserve

The crowning glory of Swaziland's parks, the top-notch and stunning **Mkhaya Game Reserve** (☎2528 3943; www.mkhaya.org) is famous for its black and white rhino populations (it boasts that you're more likely to meet rhinos here than anywhere else in Africa and, judging from our experience, this is true). Its other animals include roan and sable antelope, giraffes, tsessebe, buffaloes and elephants, along with a rich diversity of birds. If you're lucky, you might spot the elusive narina trogon and other rare species.

Activities

Wildlife Drives

Wildlife drives in an open vehicle are included in Stone Camp's accommodation rates. For overnight guests, they take place in the early morning and late afternoon. For day trippers, they start at 10am and last two hours.

Bush Walks

Mkhaya's signature activity, guided bush walks are an ideal way to approach wildlife, especially white rhinos. You periodically disembark from the open vehicle and track rhinos on foot under the guidance of an experienced ranger. You'll learn plenty about rhino behaviour. Unforgettable!

Bush walks take place at 11am. Note that they're offered to Stone Camp's overnight guests only.

Sleeping & Eating

★ **Stone Camp** LODGE $$$
(☎2528 3943; www.mkhaya.org; Mkhaya Game Reserve; s/d with full board & activities from E2295/3350) A dream come true for nature-lovers, Stone Camp consists of a series of rustic and luxurious semiopen stone and thatch cottages (a proper loo with a view!), located in secluded bush zones. The price includes wildlife drives, walking safaris and meals, and is excellent value compared with many of the private reserves in Southern Africa. Simply arrive, absorb and wonder.

No electricity, but paraffin lanterns are provided.

MKHAYA GAME RESERVE

Why Go Swaziland's most exclusive safari retreat; a real sense of wilderness; *really* close encounters with rhinos; atmospheric accommodation; excellent wildlife drives and sensational bush walks run by expert guides.

When to Go Year-round.

Practicalities The reserve is near the hamlet of Phuzumoya, off the Manzini–Big Bend road (it's signposted off the MR8). You can't visit the reserve without booking in advance, and even then you can't drive in alone; you'll be met at Phuzumoya at a specified pick-up time – either 10am or 4pm – and escorted to the ranger base station where you'll leave your vehicle.

Budget Tips While day tours can be arranged, it's ideal (and better value) to stay for at least one night.

SOUTHERN SWAZILAND

Southern Swaziland is usually glimpsed in passing by most tourists on the route down to (or up from) KwaZulu-Natal, which is a shame because there are charming pockets in the area that beg discovery, including the picturesque Lubombo Mountains and the dramatic Mahamba Gorge. Sure, tourism here remains on a humble scale, but this less-visited part of the country is where you can experience Swaziland from a different perspective.

Nsoko

Nsoko, halfway between Big Bend and the border post of Lavumisa, lies in the heart of sugar-cane country, with the Lubombo Mountains as a backdrop. This line of rugged volcanic hills rises abruptly from the lowveld to about 600m and forms a scenic natural barrier between Swaziland and Mozambique.

Nisela Safaris WILDLIFE RESERVE
(☎2303 0318; www.niselasafaris.com; Nsoko; activities from E130) Nisela is a small private reserve nestled at the foot of the Lubombo Mountains. Wildebeest, giraffes, zebras, warthogs and numerous species of antelope are widespread throughout the reserve, but there's no big stuff. It's also famed for its abundant birdlife, especially raptors. Various activities can be arranged, including wildlife drives (E150 to E180), guided walks (E150) and horse rides (E130). If you want to explore the reserve with your own vehicle, a 4WD is recommended.

Nisela Safaris CAMPGROUND, LODGE $$
(☎2303 0318; www.niselasafaris.com; MR8, Nsoko; camping E110, incl breakfast beehive hut s/d E140/280, guesthouse s/d E430/780, rondavel s/d E540/880; P Wi-Fi) Conveniently located along the MR8, this privately managed reserve has ample choice of accommodation options, including a campsite, fully-equipped *rondavels* in a shady area deep inside the reserve and simple village-style beehive huts behind reception. The guesthouse is a few kilometres away on the main road. There's also a traditional restaurant with a wooden deck overlooking a waterhole.

It's an ideal stopover point en route to Kruger National Park or Mozambique.

Nhlangano & Around

Nhlangano is the closest town to the border post at Mahamba, useful if you get stuck here.

Mahamba Gorge Lodge LODGE $
(☎2237 0100, 7617 9880; www.mahambagorgelodge.com; Mahamba; camping E60, d incl breakfast E580; P) In search of an authentic rural experience in a wonderfully scenic location? Beeline for this community-run lodge perched high on the edge of a gorge in Mahamba, about 25km west of Nhlangano. Three lovely stone chalets provide simple but clean and comfortable rooms with hot showers; all have decks from which you can look over the Mkhondvo River.

Electricity is available 24 hours and the chalets are self catering; if you don't fancy cooking, meals can be arranged. Hiking opportunities abound within the gorge; you can hire local guides for around E50 per day.

From the Mahamba border post, turn left immediately after the post onto a dirt road (follow the sign 'Mahamba High School'); continue for around 2.5km to Mahamba Church. The lodge is another 3km. It's accessible in a normal vehicle in dry weather.

Phumula Farm Guest House GUESTHOUSE $$
(☎2207 9099; www.phumulaguesthouse.co.za; Nhlangano; s E440, d E715-825; P Wi-Fi Pool) A good pick in a picturesque, secluded property surrounded by gum-tree plantations. Many pleasant rooms of all shapes and sizes are around manicured lawns and gardens with a pool and braai area. Breakfast costs from E70; lunch and dinner are also available. It's 3km from town (around 10km from the border) and 1km off MR9 along a forestry track.

Getting There & Away

Several minibus shared taxis run daily between Nhlangano and Manzini (E60, 1½ hours). There are also frequent connections to the Mahamba border post (E10), where you must change for Piet Retief in South Africa (E30, one hour).

Understand South Africa, Lesotho & Swaziland

South Africa, Lesotho & Swaziland Today

More than two decades after Nelson Mandela came to power, life in South Africa remains dominated by social inequality. Central Cape Town's mountain and beach communities contrast with the townships sprawling across the Cape Flats, lining the N2 with shacks and portaloos. Seeing First-World wealth alongside African poverty is confronting for first-time visitors. Yet every day, millions of South Africans embrace progress by trying to understand and respect the vastly different outlooks of people from other economic and racial groups.

Race Relations

What makes South Africa an uplifting place to visit is the dissolution of racial divisions. Projects are in place that aim to empower inhabitants of the townships and former homelands, and to provide work in a country with 25% unemployment. Finding common ground can be challenging, but race relations are informed by the miracle that Mandela et al performed.

However, given the decades of segregation under apartheid, relations are never straightforward. South African society still lacks the cohesion enjoyed by many Western countries; different racial groups work together, but infrequently socialise or intermarry. There are periodic black-white flare-ups in the media and politics, and the ruling African National Congress (ANC) party often links current woes to apartheid, perhaps seeking to lessen its own culpability and reinforce its image as South Africa's liberator.

Relations between black ethnic groups are equally as sensitive as those between black and white groups – from the Xhosa and Zulus to foreign immigrants. Economic refugees flock to the townships from neighbouring countries, intensifying pressure on infrastructure and competition for jobs. Xenophobic violence swept the country in 2008, and periodic attacks on immigrants and looting of foreign-owned shops continue to be features of township life.

AIDS & Gender

South Africa has the world's largest population of people with HIV/AIDS (more than six million). Swaziland has the world's highest percentage of people living with HIV/AIDS, and Lesotho the second highest. Educational efforts face numerous taboos, *sangomas* (traditional healers) preach superstitious lore and, every day, funerals commemorate supposed 'tuberculosis' victims.

South Africa's record on gender issues exemplifies the country's contradictions. Its constitution, adopted in 1996, is the world's most progressive, promoting the rights of women and gay people (same-sex marriage is

Best in Print

The Housemaid's Daughter (Barbara Mutch) Apartheid-era drama set in the Karoo.

Cobra (Deon Meyer) Captain Benny Griessel returns in the Cape Town crime king's latest.

Reports Before Daybreak (Brent Meersman) Moving novel set in '80s Cape Town.

50 People Who Stuffed Up South Africa (Alexander Parker) Pacey look at history's great villains.

Zoo City (Lauren Beukes) Crime thriller set in Jo'burg's underbelly.

Khayelitsha (Steven Otter) A white journalist living in Cape Town.

Best on Film

Invictus (Clint Eastwood) Covers the historic 1995 Rugby World Cup; stars Morgan Freeman and Matt Damon.

District 9 (Neill Blomkamp) Peter Jackson–produced sci-fi gem about giant alien 'prawns' overrunning Jo'burg.

Mandela: Long Walk to Freedom (Justin Chadwick) Condensed but enjoyable biography, covering Madiba's journey to presidency.

Chappie (Neill Blomkamp) In the director's *Elysium* follow-up, gangsters played by band Die Antwoord kidnap a robot in Jo'burg.

legal) among others. Yet the street-level reality is far harsher, with one of the world's highest reported incidences of rape, including 'corrective' rape of lesbians.

Political Scene

When Mandela died, in 2013, South Africa came together in a way not seen since the 2010 World Cup. Madiba's death was, though, a reminder that the ANC is losing its apartheid-busting glow, as it presides over a country where crime, corruption and institutional incompetence are rife. As the hope surrounding 1994's election recedes, millions of South Africans still live in shacks and struggle to find work. The Limpopo textbooks scandal summarised local worries for future generations – in 2012, despite its budget of R22 billion (US$2.2 billion), the northern province's education department failed to supply textbooks to schools, having run out of money.

President Jacob Zuma's tenure will be remembered for the Marikana massacre, in which police killed 34 people after opening fire on striking miners; and Nkandlagate, in which Zuma was accused of spending R246 million (US$24.6 million) of public funds to upgrade Nkandla, his sprawling homestead in Zululand.

The 2016 municipal elections and 2019 general election will again pit the ANC against opposition parties the Democratic Alliance (DA), which already governs the Western Cape, and Julius Malema's Economic Freedom Fighters (EFF). With policies of land reform and nationalisation, the EFF targets the critical mass of poor black voters with Afro-socialist policies; its members wear red boiler suits and berets in parliament.

Lesotho & Swaziland

A bloodless coup attempt rocked Lesotho in August 2014, harking back to 1998, when South African Development Community (SADC) forces had to restore order. Prime Minister Thomas Thabane fled the country and accused the military of trying to overthrow him; following SADC mediation, peaceful general elections took place in February 2015. Thabane's All Basotho Convention lost narrowly, and a coalition government was formed by seven other parties. The Basotho-dominated country did not experience apartheid and, with life revolving around subsistence farming, levels of social inequality and crime are lower than in South Africa. The kingdom does face serious issues though, including unemployment, food shortages, a 23% HIV/AIDS rate and a life expectancy of 53 years.

Democratic freedom is an issue in Swaziland, where absolute monarch King Mswati III has been accused of silencing opponents. Despite calls for greater democracy, pride in the monarchy lingers, and some propose a constitutional monarchy. The rural, homogenous country has many challenges, including widespread poverty, a declining economy reliant on South Africa and an average life expectancy of 51 years. In 2014 the UN reported that Swaziland was curbing its 26.5% HIV/AIDS rate.

POPULATION:
SOUTH AFRICA: 53 MILLION; LESOTHO: 1.9 MILLION ; SWAZILAND: 1.4 MILLION

AREA:
SOUTH AFRICA: 1,219,090 SQ KM ; LESOTHO: 30,355 SQ KM ; SWAZILAND: 17,363 SQ KM

if South Africa were 100 people

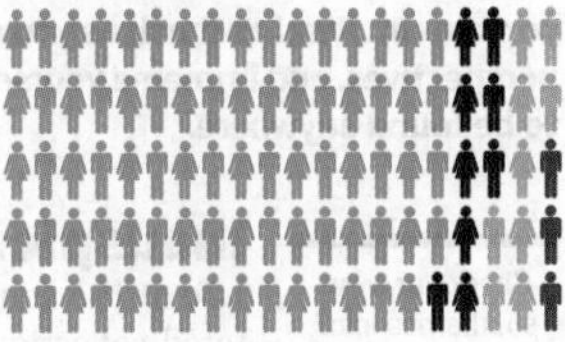

79 would be Black
9 would be White
9 would be Coloured
3 would be Indian/Asian

belief systems

(% of population)

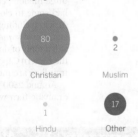

population per sq km

History

Visit South Africa and you'll see reminders of its past at every turn. The country's human drama is reflected in the faces and body language of millions of its citizens. It's seen in where and how they live. It's on display in centuries-old rock paintings and modern-day urban graffiti, in isolated battlefields and sober apartheid-era memorials. It permeates every corner with its pain and injustice but also with its hope. As South Africa continues the struggle to remake itself into a truly rainbow nation, its history plays out daily in all corners of the country – from dusty, isolated *dorps* (villages) to crowded township *shebeens* (unlicensed bars); from staid and fortified middle-class neighbourhoods to the carpeted chambers of parliament. Read as much as you can before you arrive, talk to people of all persuasions and perspectives, and immerse yourself in one of the most anguished yet most inspiring stories to be found anywhere.

Check out www.southafrica.info/about/history/history.htm for a comprehensive but easily readable overview of South African history.

Inauspicious Beginnings

Life at the southern tip of Africa began inauspiciously enough. A scattered collection of striking rock-art paintings provides evidence that as early as 25,000 years ago, and possibly as early as 40,000 years ago, nomadic San hunter-gatherers were living in the area that is now South Africa. Small numbers of San still live in South Africa today, making theirs one of the world's oldest continuous cultures.

Before this, the picture is murkier. But a wealth of fossil finds at Sterkfontein near Johannesburg show that the Gauteng area may have been almost as much of a population centre in prehistoric times as it is today, with humanlike creatures (hominids) roaming across the highveld at least three million years ago. By about one million years ago, these creatures had come to closely resemble modern humans, and ranged well beyond Africa, including in Europe and Asia. Somewhere around 100,000 years ago, *Homo sapiens* (modern humans) came onto the scene. Although it's still a topic of debate, fossils found near the mouth of the Klasies River in the Eastern Cape indicate that our *Homo sapiens* ancestors may have been travelling around South Africa as early as 90,000 years ago.

Around 2500 years ago the shaping of modern-day South Africa took a dramatic turn with descendants of the early San hunter-gatherer groups

TIMELINE

40,000–25,000 BC

The San – southern Africa's first residents and one of the world's oldest traditional cultures – leave rock paintings documenting their nomadic lifestyle and hunter-gatherer traditions.

AD 500

A centuries-long series of migrations from West Africa's Niger Delta culminates when Bantu speakers reach what is now KwaZulu-Natal. These people are the ancestors of most modern-day South Africans.

1200–1270

The thriving trade centre of Mapungubwe – in today's Limpopo province – rises to become centre of the largest kingdom in sub-Saharan Africa, with trade links as far afield as Egypt, India and China.

acquiring livestock and becoming pastoralists. This introduced concepts of personal wealth and property ownership. The pastoralist San – who became known as Khoekhoen ('men of men') – began to build more established communities and develop chieftaincies. They also began to move from inland areas south towards the coast, while smaller groups of more traditionalist hunter-gatherer San continued to inhabit the interior.

New Arrivals

Around AD 500, a new group of peoples – Bantu speakers originally from the Niger Delta in West Africa – began settling in what is now South Africa. Their arrival marked the end of a migration that had begun about 1000 BC, culminating when the first groups reached present-day KwaZulu-Natal.

The contrasts between the Bantu speakers and the early San hunter-gatherers couldn't have been greater. The Bantu speakers lived in settled villages where they tended their livestock. They were also skilled iron workers and farmers, growing maize and other crops.

While it's certain that Bantu speakers mixed with the Khoe-San, the type of contact isn't known. Rock paintings show the groups interacting, several Bantu languages (notably Xhosa and Zulu) have incorporated Khoe-San clicks, and Khoe-San artefacts have been found at early Bantu settlements.

Before long, the Bantu speakers – from whom most modern-day South Africans are descended – had entrenched themselves. Some groups – the ancestors of today's Nguni peoples (Zulu, Xhosa, Swazi and Ndebele) – settled near the coast. Others, now known as the Sotho-Tswana peoples (Tswana, Pedi, Basotho), settled in the highveld, while the Venda, Lemba and Shangaan-Tsonga peoples made their home in what is now northeastern South Africa.

As the pastoralist Khoekhoen mixed with the hunter-gatherer San, it soon became impossible to distinguish between the two groups – hence the oft-used term 'Khoe-San'.

Early Kingdoms

The hills and savannahs in South Africa's northeastern corner are dotted with ruins and artefacts left by a series of highly organised Iron Age kingdoms that flourished between about AD 1200 and the mid-17th century.

The first major one, Mapungubwe, was in present-day Limpopo province at the confluence of the Limpopo and Shashe Rivers, where Botswana, Zimbabwe and South Africa meet. Although its residents – ancestors of today's Shona people – were farmers, it was trade in gold and other goods that was the source of the kingdom's power. Pottery pieces, beads, seashells and other artefacts have been found at the site, showing that Mapungubwe was one of the major inland trading hubs in the Southern Africa region from about 1220 until 1300. Its trading network extended eastwards to the coast, and from there to places as far afield as Egypt, India and China. Mapungubwe is also notable in that the kingdom's inhabitants believed in a mystical relationship between their ruler and the land, similar to that

1487

Portuguese explorer Bartholomeu Dias successfully navigates the Cape of Good Hope. Although he doesn't linger, his journey marks the start of a long history of European involvement in Southern Africa.

1497

Natal is named by Vasco da Gama, who, sighting its coast on Christmas Day 1497, names it for the natal day of Christ.

1647

The marooned crew of a Dutch vessel build a fort in current-day Cape Town; a year passes before they are rescued.

1652

The Dutch East India Company, seeking a secure way-station en route eastwards, establishes the first permanent European settlement at Table Bay, Cape Town, under Jan van Riebeeck's leadership.

which is part of Shona and Venda traditions today. In the 14th century, Mapungubwe declined. The reason is uncertain, with theories ranging from climate change to shifting trade routes.

Mapungubwe's decline coincided with the rise of a similarly structured but larger Shona kingdom nearby in what was known as Great Zimbabwe (now Zimbabwe), suggesting that the focus of trade shifted northwards.

A Short History of Lesotho from the Late Stone Age to the 1993 Elections, by Stephen J Gill, is a concise and readable history of the mountain kingdom.

With the abandonment of Great Zimbabwe in the mid-15th century, several of the early Shona groups made their way back to the area just south of the Limpopo River that is now part of northern Kruger National Park. There they established numerous settlements in the Pafuri region. These included the walled kingdom of Thulamela, the last of the great Iron Age kingdoms, which flourished from about the mid-16th to the mid-17th centuries. Like Mapungubwe and Great Zimbabwe, Thulamela – which means 'place of giving birth' in the local Venda language – owed its prominence to far-flung trading networks for gold and other goods. Shells, glass beads and Chinese porcelain fragments found at the site show that Thulamela was linked by these trade networks with the coast and beyond.

Thulamela is also significant because several of its artefacts, most notably an iron gong of the type also found in Ghana, show that its trading links stretched as far as West Africa.

First Europeans

Apart from Portuguese explorer Bartholomeu Dias naming the Cabo da Boa Esperança (Cape of Good Hope) in 1487, the Portuguese showed little interest in South Africa – the Mozambican coast was more to their taste.

By the late 16th century, the Portuguese were being significantly challenged along their trade routes by the English and the Dutch.

In 1647 a Dutch vessel was wrecked in what is now Cape Town's Table Bay. The marooned crew built a fort and stayed for a year until they were rescued, becoming the first Europeans to attempt settlement in the area.

A CHOSEN PEOPLE

Boer lifestyle and culture – both real and idealised – have had a major influence on South Africa's history. While many of the early members of the Dutch VOC expedition planned to ultimately return to Europe, the Boers soon began to develop a view of themselves as a distinct community that was permanently settled in South Africa.

According to their Calvinist beliefs, the Boers were God's chosen people, who had the duty to civilise their black neighbours and thereby ensure their salvation. Some scholars also say that it was Calvinism, and especially its doctrine of predestination, that spawned the Afrikaner idea of racial superiority: the separation of the races had been divinely ordained and thus justified all efforts to preserve the purity of the white race.

1657

The Dutch East India Company releases employees to establish their own farms and supply the settlement with produce. These farmers – known as free burghers – soon expand into the lands of the Khoekhoen.

1658

Slaves from Madagascar and Indonesia – the first to be imported into South Africa – are brought into the country by the Dutch.

1660

Jan van Riebeeck plants a bitter-almond hedge separating the Dutch from the neighbouring Khoekhoen – in retrospect, an early step towards apartheid.

1786

Moshoeshoe, founder of the Basotho nation, later to become Lesotho, is born; Shaka, future king of the Zulu, is born the following year.

Shortly thereafter, the Dutch East India Company (Vereenigde Oost-Indische Compagnie; VOC) – one of the major European trading houses sailing the spice route to the East – decided to establish a permanent settlement. A small VOC expedition, under the command of Jan van Riebeeck, was launched, reaching Table Bay in April 1652.

No sooner were they off their boats than the Dutch expedition found itself in the midst of the, by then, well-established Khoekhoen peoples. Yet, while the new settlers traded with the neighbouring Khoekhoen out of necessity, there were deliberate attempts on the part of the Dutch to restrict contact. To alleviate a labour shortage, the VOC released a small group of Dutch employees to establish their own farms, from which they would supply the VOC settlement. The arrangement proved highly successful.

While the majority of these free burghers (as these farmers were called) were of Dutch descent, and members of the Calvinist Reformed Church of the Netherlands, there were also numerous Germans. In 1688 they were joined by French Huguenots, also Calvinists, who were fleeing religious persecution under Louis XIV.

Europeans Leave Their Mark

The VOC also began to import large numbers of slaves, primarily from Madagascar and Indonesia. With this additional labour, not only was South Africa's population mix broadened but the areas occupied by the VOC were expanded further north and east, where clashes with the Khoekhoen were inevitable. The beleaguered Khoekhoen were driven from their traditional lands, decimated by introduced diseases and destroyed by superior weapons when they fought back – which they did in a number of major wars and with guerrilla resistance that continued into the 19th century. Most survivors were left with no option but to work for the Europeans in an arrangement that hardly differed from slavery. Over time, the Khoe-San, their European overseers and the imported slaves mixed, with the offspring of these unions forming the basis for modern South Africa's coloured population.

As the burghers continued to expand into the rugged hinterlands of the north and east, many began to take up a semi-nomadic pastoralist lifestyle, in some ways not so far removed from that of the Khoekhoen whom they were displacing. In addition to their herds, a family might have had a wagon, a tent, a Bible and a couple of guns. As they became more settled, a mud-walled cottage would be built – frequently located, by choice, days of hard travel away from the nearest European. These were the first of the Trekboers (Wandering Farmers; later shortened to Boers) – completely independent of official control, extraordinarily self-sufficient and isolated. Their harsh lifestyle produced courageous individualists but also a people with a narrow view of the world, whose only source of written knowledge was often the Bible.

For an overview of rock art in Southern Africa and other parts of the continent, see University of the Witwatersrand's Rock Art Research Institute page at www.wits.ac.za/academic/science/geography/research/5616/rock_art_research_institute.html.

1814
The British, keen to outmanoeuvre the French, gain sovereignty over the Cape as Dutch mercantile power fades.

1816
Shaka becomes chief of the Zulu, triggering the rise of a militaristic state and setting off the *difaqane* (forced migration) – a wave of disruption and terror throughout Southern Africa.

1820
The British try to mediate between the Boers and the Xhosa in Cape Colony by encouraging British immigration. The plan fails, but the new settlers solidify Britain's presence.

1828
Shaka is killed by his half-brothers; as the *difaqane* continues for another decade, Dingaan seeks to establish relations with British traders.

Arrival of the British

As the 18th century drew to a close, Dutch power began to fade, and the British moved in to fill the vacuum. They seized the Cape to prevent it from falling into rival French hands, then briefly relinquished it to the Dutch, before finally garnering recognition of their sovereignty of the area in 1814.

Awaiting the British at the Cape was a colony with 25,000 slaves, 20,000 white colonists, 15,000 Khoe-San and 1000 freed black slaves. Power was restricted to a white elite in Cape Town, and differentiation on the basis of race was already entrenched. Outside Cape Town and the immediate hinterland, the country was populated by isolated black and white pastoralists.

One of the first tasks for the British was trying to resolve a troublesome border dispute between the Boers and the Xhosa on the colony's eastern frontier. In 1820 about 5000 middle-class British immigrants – mostly traders and business people – were persuaded to leave England and settle on tracts of land between the feuding groups with the idea, at least officially, of providing a buffer zone (they were known as the '1820 Settlers'; see p190). The plan was singularly unsuccessful. By 1823 almost half of the settlers had retreated to the towns – notably Grahamstown and Port Elizabeth – to pursue the jobs they had held in Britain.

While doing nothing to resolve the border dispute, this influx of settlers solidified the British presence in the area, igniting another flame under the now-simmering cauldron. Where the Boers and their ideas had once been largely unchallenged, there were now two language groups and two cultures. A pattern soon emerged whereby English speakers were highly urbanised and dominated politics, trade, finance, mining and manufacturing, while the largely uneducated Boers were relegated to their farms.

The gap between the British settlers and the Boers further widened with the abolition of slavery in 1833 – a move that was generally regarded by Boers as being against the God-given ordering of the races. Meanwhile, British numbers rapidly increased in Cape Town, in the area east of the Cape Colony (present-day Eastern Cape), in Natal (present-day KwaZulu-Natal) and, after the discovery of gold and diamonds, in parts of the Transvaal (mainly around present-day Gauteng).

Difaqane

The first half of the 19th century was a time of immense upheaval and suffering among the African peoples of the region. This period is known as the *difaqane* (forced migration) in Sotho and as *mfeqane* (the crushing) in Zulu.

While the roots of the *difaqane* are disputed, certain events stand out. One of the most significant was the rise of the powerful Zulu kingdom. In the early 19th century, Nguni tribes in what is now KwaZulu-Natal began to shift from loosely organised collections of kingdoms into a centralised,

1838
Several thousand Zulus are killed in the Battle of Blood River. Until 1994, the anniversary was celebrated by whites as the Day of the Vow, before it was renamed the Day of Reconciliation.

1843
Boer hopes for a Natal republic are dashed when the British annex the area and set up a colony in modern-day Durban.

1852
The Boer Republic of Transvaal is created. The first president is Marthinus Wessel Pretorius, elected in 1857, son of Andries Pretorius – the famous Voortrekker leader.

1860
MS *Truro* arrives in Durban with over 300 Indians for indentured service, signalling the beginning of an influx of Indians into South Africa.

MAHATMA GANDHI

In 1893 a young and then completely unknown Indian solicitor named Mohandas Gandhi set sail for Durban, South Africa, to take on a one-year legal contract. Little did he know it, but his experiences in the country were to shape the course of his entire life.

At the time Gandhi arrived, anti-Indian sentiment in Natal was running high, and upon his arrival he was thrown out of a 1st-class train wagon at Pietermaritzburg because of his race. The incident, together with other discrimination that he experienced in the early months after his arrival, had a profound effect on Gandhi. He began schooling himself in methods of nonviolent resistance, and became increasingly involved with the local Indian community, working with them to safeguard their political rights. Within a short period, Gandhi had established himself as not only a successful attorney but also the leading spokesperson for Indian interests in South Africa.

In 1896, and again in 1901, Gandhi returned briefly to India, where he lobbied extensively to bring attention to the plight of Indians in South Africa. Back in South Africa, Gandhi gave up the trappings of a successful attorney, began washing his own clothes, committed himself to a life of celibacy and nonpossession, and devoted himself fully to service. He also developed his defining philosophy of *satyagraha* (meaning, very loosely, truth through nonviolence).

In 1907 the Transvaal government passed the Asiatic Registration Act requiring all Indians to register with the Registrar of Asiatics and to carry a certificate of registration. Gandhi called on the Indian community to defy the act and to offer no resistance if they should be arrested. Over the next seven years, numerous similar discriminatory incidents followed, including a court decision nullifying all Hindu and Muslim marriages, which Gandhi and his followers also peacefully defied. In response, Gandhi – along with thousands of other Indians who had joined him in his *satyagraha* struggle – was repeatedly arrested. He garnered various victories, and became convinced of the importance and effectiveness of nonviolent resistance.

Gandhi finally returned to India in 1914 to begin another chapter of his life.

militaristic state under Shaka, son of the chief of the small Zulu clan. After building large armies, Shaka sent them out on a massive program of conquest and terror. Those who stood in his way were enslaved or decimated.

Tribes in the path of Shaka's armies fled, becoming aggressors against their neighbours. This wave of disruption and terror spread throughout Southern Africa and beyond, leaving death and destruction in its wake.

In 1828 Shaka met his untimely end when he was killed by his half-brothers Dingaan and Umhlanga. The weaker and less-skilled Dingaan became king and attempted to establish relations with British traders on the Natal coast, but events were unfolding that were to see the demise of Zulu independence.

1869

The first diamond is found near Kimberley in the walls of a house. This spells trouble for the Boers as the British quickly move to annex the area.

1879

The Zulus inflict one of the most humiliating defeats on the British army at the Battle of Isandlwana in 1879, but Zululand eventually comes under British control.

1881

First Anglo-Boer War ends with a decisive victory for the Boers at the Battle of Majuba Hill; Transvaal becomes the South African Republic.

1886

Gold is discovered on the Witwatersrand, setting off rapid population growth and development in Johannesburg. The Witwatersrand contains the world's largest gold deposit.

Great Trek & Battle of Blood River

The Boers were growing increasingly dissatisfied with British rule in the Cape Colony. The British proclamation of equality of the races was a particularly sharp thorn in their side. Beginning in 1836, several groups of Boers, together with large numbers of Khoekhoen and black servants, decided to trek off into the interior in search of greater independence. North and east of the Senqu (Orange) River (which formed the Cape Colony's frontier), these Boers, or Voortrekkers (Pioneers), found vast tracts of apparently uninhabited grazing lands. They had entered, so it seemed, their promised land, with space enough for their cattle to graze, and for their culture of anti-urban independence to flourish. Little did they know that what they found – deserted pasture lands, disorganised bands of refugees and tales of brutality – were the result of the *difaqane*.

With the exception of the relatively powerful Ndebele, the Voortrekkers encountered little resistance among the scattered peoples of the plains. Dispersed by the *difaqane* and lacking horses and firearms, the locals' weakened condition also solidified the Boers' belief that European occupation heralded the coming of civilisation to a savage land.

The *difaqane* (forced migration) caused huge suffering and accelerated the formation of several states, notably those of the Sotho (present-day Lesotho) and Swazi (now Swaziland).

However, the mountains (where King Moshoeshoe I was forging the Basotho nation later to become Lesotho) and the wooded valleys of Zululand were a more difficult proposition. Resistance here was strong, and the Boer incursions set off a series of skirmishes, squabbles and flimsy treaties that were to punctuate the next 50 years of increasing white domination.

The Great Trek's first halt was at Thaba 'Nchu, near present-day Bloemfontein, where a republic was established. Following disagreements among their leadership, the various Voortrekker groups split, with most crossing the Drakensberg into Natal to establish a republic there. As this was Zulu territory, Voortrekker leader Piet Retief paid a visit to King Dingaan and was promptly massacred by the suspicious Zulu. This massacre triggered others, as well as a revenge attack by the Boers. The culmination came on 16 December 1838 at the Ncome River in Natal. Several Boers were injured and several thousand Zulus were killed.

After this victory (the result of superior weapons) in what came to be known as the Battle of Blood River, the Boers felt that their expansion really did have that long-suspected stamp of divine approval. Yet their hopes for establishing a Natal republic were short-lived. The British annexed the area in 1843 and founded their new Natal colony at present-day Durban. Most of the Boers headed north, with yet another grievance against the British.

The British set about establishing large sugar plantations in Natal, and looked to India to resolve their labour shortage. From 1860 into the early 20th century, more than 150,000 indentured Indians arrived, as well as numerous free 'passenger Indians'.

1893

Mohandas (Mahatma) Gandhi sets sail for South Africa. His early days in the country mark the beginning of his doctrine of nonviolent protest and influence his entire life's work.

1897

Enoch Mankayi Sontonga, a choir leader from the Eastern Cape, composes 'Nkosi Sikelel' i Afrika'. It is first recorded in 1923 and made the national anthem in 1994.

1902

The brutality of the second Anglo-Boer War is shocking and causes the death of 26,000 people from disease and neglect.

1902

The Treaty of Vereeniging ends the second Anglo-Boer War, although the peace it brings is fragile and challenged by all sides.

Diamonds & Anglo-Boer Wars

The Boers meanwhile pressed on with their search for land and freedom, ultimately establishing themselves at Transvaal (encompassing parts of present-day Gauteng, Limpopo, North West and Mpumalanga provinces) and the Orange Free State. Then the Boers' world was turned on its head in 1869 with the discovery of diamonds near Kimberley. The diamonds were found on land belonging to the Griqua but to which both the Transvaal and Orange Free State laid claim. Among the best-known Khoekhoen groups, the Griqua had originally lived on the western coast between St Helena Bay and the Cederberg Range. In the late 18th century, they managed to acquire guns and horses and began trekking northeastwards. En route, they were joined by other groups of Khoe-San, coloureds and even white adventurers, and rapidly gained a reputation as a formidable military force.

Britain quickly stepped in and resolved the issue of who had rights to the diamonds by annexing the area for itself.

The establishment of the Kimberley diamond mines prompted a flood of European and black labourers to the area. Towns sprang up in which the 'proper' separation of whites and blacks was ignored, and the Boers were angry that their impoverished republics were missing out on the economic benefits of the mines.

Long-standing Boer resentment became a full-blown rebellion in the Transvaal, and in 1880 the first Anglo-Boer War broke out. (Afrikaners – as the descendants of the early Boers became known – called it the War of Independence.) The war was over almost as soon as it began, with a crushing Boer victory at the Battle of Majuba Hill in early 1881. The republic regained its independence as the Zuid-Afrikaansche Republiek (ZAR; South African Republic). Paul Kruger, one of the leaders of the uprising, became president in 1883. Despite the setbacks, the British forged ahead with their desire to federate the Southern African colonies and republics.

In 1879 Zululand came under British control. Then in 1886, gold was discovered on the Witwatersrand (the area around Johannesburg). This accelerated the federation process and dealt the Boers yet another blow. Johannesburg's population exploded to about 100,000 by the mid-1890s, and the ZAR suddenly found itself hosting thousands of *uitlanders* (foreigners), both black and white, with the Boers squeezed to the sidelines. The influx of black labour was particularly disturbing for the Boers, many of whom were going through hard times and resented the black wage-earners.

The situation peaked in 1899, when the British demanded voting rights for the 60,000 foreign whites on the Witwatersrand. (Until this point, Kruger's government had excluded all foreigners from the franchise.) Kruger refused, calling for British troops to be withdrawn from the ZAR's borders. When the British resisted, Kruger declared war. This

For an overview of the famous figures who have shaped South African history, check out www.sahistory.org.za for a well-presented list of biographies.

1910
The Union of South Africa is created. English and Dutch are made the official languages, and there are no voting rights for blacks. Lesotho and Swaziland remain British protectorates.

1912
Pixley ka Isaka Seme, a Columbia University–educated lawyer, calls a conference of chiefs. A union of all tribes is proposed, resulting in formation of what will become the ANC.

1914
Following demonstrations and strikes, the Indian Relief Bill is passed, restoring recognition of Hindu and Muslim marriages and convincing Gandhi of the power of nonviolent resistance.

1925
Afrikaans is made an official language with the rise of Afrikaner nationalism. Its proposed introduction into township schools is one of the triggers of the 1976 Soweto uprising.

second Anglo-Boer War was more protracted and the British were better prepared than at Majuba Hill. By mid-1900, Pretoria, the last of the major Boer towns, had surrendered. Yet resistance by Boer *bittereinders* (bitter enders) continued for two more years with guerrilla-style battles, which in turn were met by scorched-earth tactics by the British. In May 1902 the Treaty of Vereeniging brought a superficial peace. Under its terms, the Boer republics acknowledged British sovereignty.

A Fragile Peace

During the immediate postwar years, the British focused their attention on rebuilding the country, in particular the mining industry. By 1907 the mines of the Witwatersrand were producing almost one-third of the world's gold. But the peace brought by the treaty was fragile, and challenged on all sides. The Afrikaners found themselves in the position of being poor farmers in a country where big mining ventures and foreign capital rendered them irrelevant. They were particularly incensed by Britain's unsuccessful attempts to anglicise them, and to impose English as the official language in schools and the workplace. Partly as a backlash to this, Afrikaans came to be seen as the *volkstaal* (people's language) and a symbol of Afrikaner nationhood, and several nationalistic organisations sprang up.

All the building blocks for the modern South African pariah state of the mid 20th-century were now in place. Blacks and coloureds were marginalised. Harsh taxes were imposed, wages reduced and the British caretaker administrator encouraged the immigration of thousands of Chinese to undercut any resistance. Resentment was given full vent in the 1906 Bambatha Rebellion, in which 4000 Zulu died after protesting tax legislation.

The British moved ahead with their plans for union. After several years of negotiation, the 1910 Act of Union was signed, bringing the republics of Cape Colony, Natal, Transvaal and Orange Free State together as the Union of South Africa. Under the provisions of the act, the Union was still a British territory, with home rule for Afrikaners. The British High Commission Territories of Basotholand (now Lesotho), Bechuanaland (now Botswana), Swaziland and Rhodesia (now Zimbabwe) continued to be ruled by Britain.

English and Dutch were made the official languages. Despite a campaign by blacks and coloureds, only whites could be elected to parliament.

The first government of the new Union was headed by General Louis Botha, with General Jan Smuts as his deputy. Their South African National Party (later known as the South African Party or SAP) followed a generally pro-British, white-unity line. More radical Boers split away under the leadership of General Barry Hertzog, forming the National Party (NP) in 1914. The NP championed Afrikaner interests, advocating separate development for the two white groups and independence from Britain.

1927

Kruger National Park opens to the public, although its proud history is tainted during apartheid when the government removes people from their traditional lands to allow for the park's expansion.

1932

World-famous singer Miriam Makeba (Mama Africa) is born in Johannesburg – she spends 30 years outside South Africa in exile for criticism of the apartheid government.

1948

The darkness descends – the National Party under the leadership of DF Malan gains control of the government after campaigning on a policy of segregation, and apartheid is institutionalised.

1955

At a congress held at Kliptown near Johannesburg, a number of organisations, including the Indian Congress and the ANC, adopt a Freedom Charter, still central to the ANC's vision of South Africa.

Racism Entrenched & Birth of the ANC

There was no place in the new Union for blacks, even though they constituted over 75% of the population. Under the Act of Union, they were denied voting rights in the Transvaal and Orange Free State areas, and in the Cape Colony they were granted the vote only if they met a property-ownership qualification. Following British wartime propaganda promising freedom from 'Boer slavery', the failure to grant the franchise was regarded by blacks as a blatant betrayal. It wasn't long before a barrage of oppressive legislation was passed, making it illegal for black workers to strike, reserving skilled jobs for whites, barring blacks from military service and instituting restrictive pass laws. In 1913 the Natives Land Act was enacted, setting aside 8% of South Africa's land for black occupancy. Whites, who made up 20% of the population, were given over 90% of the land. Black Africans were not allowed to buy, rent or even be sharecroppers outside their designated area. Thousands of squatters were evicted from farms and forced into increasingly overcrowded and impoverished reserves or into the cities. Those who remained were reduced to the status of landless labourers.

Against this turbulent background, black and coloured opposition began to coalesce, and leading figures such as John Jabavu, Walter Rubusana and Abdullah Abdurahman laid the foundations for new nontribal black political groups. Most significantly, a Columbia University–educated attorney, Pixley ka Isaka Seme, called together representatives of the various African tribes to form a unified national organisation to represent the interests of blacks and ensure that they had an effective voice in the new Union. Thus was born the South African Native National Congress, known from 1923 onwards as the African National Congress (ANC).

Almost parallel to this, Mohandas (Mahatma) Gandhi had been working with the Indian populations of Natal and the Transvaal to fight against the ever-increasing encroachments on their rights.

The Elders (www.theelders.org) is a group of world leaders founded by Nelson Mandela and convened by Desmond Tutu and Graça Machel to bring voices of integrity and wisdom to resolution of global issues.

Rise of Afrikaner Nationalism

In 1924 the NP, under Hertzog, came to power in a coalition government, and Afrikaner nationalism gained a greater hold. Dutch was replaced by Afrikaans (previously only regarded as a low-class dialect of Dutch) as an official language of the Union, and the so-called *swart gevaar* (black threat) was made the dominant issue of the 1929 election. Hertzog joined briefly in a coalition with the more moderate Jan Smuts in the mid-1930s, after which Smuts took the reins. However, any hopes of turning the tide of Afrikaner nationalism were dashed when Daniel François (DF) Malan led a radical breakaway movement, the Purified National Party, to the central position in Afrikaner political life. The Afrikaner Broederbond, a secret Afrikaner brotherhood that had been formed in 1918 to protect

1960

Sharpeville massacre; ANC and Pan African Congress (PAC) banned; Miriam Makeba is denied entry to South Africa after trying to return for her mother's funeral.

1961

Soon after the Sharpeville massacre Prime Minister Hendrik Verwoerd, the 'architect of apartheid' announces a referendum – in May South Africa leaves the Commonwealth and becomes a republic.

1961

On 16 December, Umkhonto we Sizwe, the military wing of the ANC, carries out its first attacks, marking the start of the armed struggle against apartheid.

1963

Miriam Makeba's citizenship is revoked after she speaks out against apartheid before the UN as part of her ongoing criticism of the policy.

Afrikaner culture, soon became an extraordinarily influential force behind both the NP and other organisations designed to promote the *volk* (people; the Afrikaners).

Due to the booming wartime economy, black labour became increasingly important to the mining and manufacturing industries, and the black urban population nearly doubled. Enormous squatter camps grew up on the outskirts of Johannesburg and, to a lesser extent, outside the other major cities. Conditions in the townships were appalling, but poverty was not only the province of blacks; wartime surveys found that 40% of white schoolchildren were malnourished.

Across Boundaries: The Journey of a South African Woman Leader, by Mamphela Ramphele, traces the life of an extraordinary woman who was internally 'exiled' to the town of Tzaneen for seven years but later rose to become the University of Cape Town's vice-chancellor.

Walls of Apartheid Go Up

In the months leading up to the 1948 elections, the NP campaigned on its policy of segregation, or 'apartheid' (an Afrikaans term for the state of being apart). It was voted in, in coalition with the Afrikaner Party (AP), and under the leadership of DF Malan.

Thus it was that apartheid, long a reality of life, became institutionalised under Malan. Within short order, legislation was passed prohibiting mixed marriages, making interracial sex illegal, classifying individuals by race and establishing a classification board to rule in questionable cases. The noxious Group Areas Act of 1950 set aside desirable city properties for whites

HOMELANDS

In 1962 the Transkei was born. It was the first of 10 so-called 'bantustans' or 'homelands' that were intended to provide a home for all black South Africans. On these lands – so went the white South African propaganda – blacks would be self-sufficient, self-governing citizens, living together with others of their own ethnic group.

The realities were much different. The homeland areas had no infrastructure or industry, and were incapable of producing sufficient food for the growing black population. All the homelands together constituted only 14% of South Africa's land, while blacks made up close to 80% of the country's population. Tribal divisions were made arbitrarily, and once a person had been assigned to a homeland, they could not leave without a pass and permission. The resulting suffering was intense and widespread.

Following creation of the homelands, blacks flooded the cities seeking work: while life in urban squatter camps was bad, life in the homelands was worse. The government responded by banning blacks from being employed as shop assistants, receptionists, typists and clerks. The construction of housing in the black 'locations' (dormitory suburbs for black workers) was halted, and enormous single-sex hostels were built instead.

Although the homelands concept came to an end with the demise of apartheid, its legacy – including completely insufficient infrastructure and distorted population concentrations in the homeland areas – continues to scar South Africa today.

1964
Nelson Mandela is sentenced to life imprisonment – a sentence that will span 27 years and include 18 years at the notorious Robben Island prison.

1966
As a part of the post-WWII independence wind blowing through Africa, Lesotho gains independence from Britain; Swaziland achieves this two years later.

1966
Verwoerd is stabbed to death by Dimitri Tsafendas, a parliamentary messenger, who suffers from schizophrenia and is resentful of being shunned for being dark-skinned, though he is classified as 'white'.

1976
On 16 June the Soweto uprisings begin, setting off a chain of violence around the country, and marking the first major internal challenge to the apartheid government.

and banished nonwhites into the townships. The Separate Amenities Act created separate beaches, buses, hospitals, schools and even park benches.

The existing pass laws were further strengthened: blacks and coloureds were compelled to carry identity documents at all times and were prohibited from remaining in towns, or even visiting them, without permission.

In 1960 tensions came to a head: on 21 March 1960, Robert Sobukwe, who founded ANC splinter group the Pan African Congress (PAC), and many thousands of followers protested against the hated pass laws at police stations in Gauteng and the Western Cape. Police opened fire on the demonstrators surrounding a police station in Sharpeville, a township near Vereeniging. In what became known as the Sharpeville massacre, at least 67 people were killed and 186 wounded; most were shot in the back.

Soon thereafter, Prime Minister Hendrik Verwoerd, credited with the unofficial title of 'architect of apartheid', announced a referendum on whether the country should become a republic. The change was passed by a slim majority of voters. Verwoerd withdrew South Africa from the Commonwealth, and in May 1961 the Republic of South Africa came into existence.

See www.anc.org.za for the official view of everything past and present on the African National Congress, including detail on anniversary celebrations.

ANC Begins the Long Walk

The further entrenchment of apartheid pushed the hitherto relatively conservative ANC into action. In 1949 it had developed an agenda that for the first time advocated open resistance in the form of strikes, acts of public disobedience and protest marches. Resistance continued throughout the 1950s and resulted in occasional violent clashes. In 1959 a group of disenchanted ANC members, seeking to sever all links with the white government, broke away to form the more militant PAC.

To many onlookers, the struggle had crossed a crucial line at Sharpeville, and there could no longer be any lingering doubts about the nature of the white regime. In the wake of the shooting, a massive stay away from work was organised, and demonstrations continued. Prime Minister Verwoerd declared a state of emergency, giving security forces the right to detain people without trial. More than 18,000 demonstrators were arrested, including much of the ANC and PAC leadership, and both organisations were banned.

In response, the ANC and PAC began a campaign of sabotage through their organisations, Umkhonto we Sizwe (Spear of the Nation, MK) and Poqo ('Pure' or 'Alone'), respectively. In July 1963, 17 members of the ANC underground movement were arrested and tried for treason at the Rivonia Trial. Among them was Nelson Mandela, an ANC leader and founder of Umkhonto we Sizwe, who had already been arrested on other charges. In June 1964, Mandela and seven others were sentenced to life imprisonment. Oliver Tambo, a member of the ANC leadership, managed to escape South Africa and lead the ANC in exile. On 20 April 1964, during the Rivonia Trial, Nelson Mandela said, 'I have fought against White domination and I have

1977
Steve Biko is murdered. News of his death draws increased international attention to the brutality of the apartheid regime.

1978–88
The South African Defence Force (SADF; now the South African National Defence Force, or SANDF) launches a number of major attacks inside Angola, Mozambique, Zimbabwe, Botswana and Lesotho.

1982
The first AIDS death is recorded in South Africa, marking the start of an ongoing scourge spreading to, and devastating, communities across the country.

1989
Mandela pleads to Botha from prison for negotiations to avert a civil war in South Africa. His appeal falls on deaf ears.

PROFILE: NELSON MANDELA

Nelson Rolihlahla Mandela, one of the millennium's greatest leaders, was once vilified by South Africa's ruling whites and sentenced to life imprisonment. Twenty-seven years later, he emerged from incarceration calling for reconciliation and forgiveness.

Mandela, son of a Xhosa chief, was born on 18 July 1918 in the village of Mveso on the Mbashe River. After attending the University of Fort Hare, Mandela headed to Johannesburg, where he soon became immersed in politics. He finished his law degree and, together with Oliver Tambo, opened South Africa's first black law firm. Meanwhile, in 1944, together with Tambo and Walter Sisulu, Mandela formed the Youth League of the African National Congress (ANC). During the 1950s, Mandela was at the forefront of the ANC's civil disobedience campaigns, for which he was arrested in 1952, tried and acquitted. After the ANC was banned in the wake of the Sharpeville massacre, Mandela led the establishment of its underground military wing, Umkhonto we Sizwe. In 1964 Mandela was brought to stand trial for sabotage and fomenting revolution in the widely publicised Rivonia Trial. After brilliantly arguing his own defence, he was sentenced to life imprisonment, and spent the next 18 years in the infamous Robben Island prison before being moved to the mainland.

Throughout his incarceration, Mandela repeatedly refused to compromise his political beliefs in exchange for freedom, saying that only free men can negotiate.

In February 1990, Mandela was released and in 1991 he was elected president of the ANC. In 1993 Mandela shared the Nobel Peace Prize with FW de Klerk and, in the first free elections the following year, was elected president of South Africa. In his speech 'Free at Last!', made after winning the 1994 elections, he focused the nation's attention firmly on the future, declaring, 'This is the time to heal the old wounds and build a new South Africa'.

In 1997 Mandela – or Madiba, his traditional Xhosa name – stepped down as ANC president, although he continued to be revered as an elder statesman. On 5 December 2013 Nelson Mandela, aged 95 years, died from an ongoing respiratory infection. South Africans grieved openly for the man who had given so much of himself to his country. South African president Jacob Zuma said, 'Our nation has lost its greatest son. Nothing can diminish our sense of a profound and enduring loss'. The world also grieved for the man who had inspired so many with his moral authority. One of the largest gatherings of world leaders came together for the memorial service.

The legacy of Nelson Mandela is what he achieved with unswerving determination, generosity of spirit and lack of vengeance. And his gift to South Africans was the major role he played in bringing peace and reconciliation to a country torn by racial discrimination. It is a legacy that reverberates far beyond his country's borders.

fought against Black domination. I have cherished the ideal of a democratic and free society in which all persons live together in harmony and with equal opportunities. It is an ideal which I hope to live for and to achieve. But if needs be, it is an ideal for which I am prepared to die.'

1989

FW de Klerk replaces Botha as president after the latter has a stroke. De Klerk lifts the ban on the ANC.

1990

In what becomes a historic moment in South African history, Nelson Mandela is freed after 27 years in prison, preaching not hatred but forgiveness and reconciliation.

1993

Nelson Mandela and FW de Klerk, the two men shaping the future of South Africa through tough negotiation, are awarded the Nobel Peace Prize.

1994

In a triumph for democracy and Mandela's path of reconciliation and freedom for all, the first democratic elections are held; Nelson Mandela is elected president.

PROFILE: MIRIAM MAKEBA

Singer Miriam Makeba (known as 'Mama Africa'), who died in 2008 at the age of 76, was long a larger-than-life figure on international stages. Combining her music with criticism of apartheid, she starred in the 1960 anti-apartheid documentary *Come Back, Africa* and gave an address before the UN in 1963. As a result of her outspokenness, Makeba's passport was revoked and she was stripped of her citizenship. She spent over 30 years in exile before returning to South Africa in 1990 at the urging of Nelson Mandela. In 2005 she said, 'We have only had 11 years of democracy but we are moving, we are moving forward faster than many countries who have been independent a long, long time before. We all have to do it together, all of us...black, white or whatever.'

Decades of Darkness

With the ANC banned, and Mandela and most of its leadership in jail or exile, South Africa moved into some of its darkest times. Apartheid legislation was enforced with increasing gusto, and the walls between races were built higher. Most odious was the creation of separate 'homelands' for blacks.

During the 1970s, resistance again gained momentum, first channelled through trade unions and strikes, and then spearheaded by the South African Students' Organisation under the charismatic Steve Biko. Biko, a medical student, was the main force behind the growth of South Africa's Black Consciousness Movement, which stressed the need for psychological liberation, black pride and nonviolent opposition to apartheid.

Things culminated in 1976, when the Soweto Students' Representative Council organised protests against the use of Afrikaans (regarded as the language of the oppressor) in black schools. On 16 June, police opened fire on a march led by Tsietsi Mashinini, a central figure in the book *A Burning Hunger: One Family's Struggle Against Apartheid* and now immortalised by a monument in Soweto. This began demonstrations, strikes, mass arrests, riots and violence that, over 12 months, took more than 1000 lives.

In September 1977, Steve Biko was killed by security police. South Africa would never be the same. A generation of young blacks committed themselves to a revolutionary struggle against apartheid ('Liberation before Education' was the catch-cry) and black communities were politicised.

The Soft Vengeance of a Freedom Fighter by Albie Sachs is an extraordinary and moving tale of an influential ANC member who lost an arm and an eye in the struggle for freedom.

South Africa Under Siege

As international opinion turned decisively against the white regime, the government (and most of the white population) increasingly saw the country as a bastion besieged by communism, atheism and black anarchy. Considerable effort was put into circumventing international sanctions, and the government even developed nuclear weapons (since destroyed).

1995

A vital tool in the country's healing process, the Truth and Reconciliation Commission is established, chaired by Archbishop Desmond Tutu.

1996

After much negotiation and debate, South Africa's parliament approves a revised version of the 1993 constitution that establishes the structure of the country's new, democratic government.

1997

In an almost unheard-of move by an African head of state, Nelson Mandela retires as ANC president and is succeeded by Thabo Mbeki.

1999

The ANC wins a landslide victory in the second democratic elections held in South Africa, falling just short of the 66.7% required to change the constitution.

PROFILE: STEVE BIKO

Steve Biko, born in 1946 in the Eastern Cape, was one of the most prominent and influential anti-apartheid activists. His Black Consciousness Movement mobilised urban youth and was a major force behind the 1976 Soweto uprisings. As a result of his activities, Biko was high on the list of those targeted by the apartheid regime. In 1973 he was restricted to his birthplace of King William's Town and prohibited from speaking in public. Despite these restrictions, he continued his activism and community work, including establishing literacy programs and a health clinic.

On 18 August 1977, Biko was detained under the Terrorism Act. Less than a month later, he was dead – from a hunger strike, according to the police. In 1997 the Truth and Reconciliation Commission reported that five former members of the South African security forces had admitted to killing Biko, although they were never prosecuted. Biko had been beaten until he fell into a coma, went without medical treatment for three days, and died in Pretoria. At the inquest, the magistrate found that no one was to blame, although the South African Medical Association eventually took action against the doctors who failed to treat him.

Biko's death prompted a huge public outcry and drew international attention to the brutality of the apartheid system. Biko's funeral service, celebrated by the Reverend Desmond Tutu, was attended by thousands, including representatives from various Western countries. Thousands more were barred from attending by security forces. Biko's story was the centrepiece of the 1987 film *Cry Freedom*.

Negotiating majority rule with the ANC was not considered an option (publicly, at least), which left the government reverting to the use of sheer military might. A siege mentality developed among most whites, and although many realised that a civil war against the black majority could not be won, they preferred this to 'giving in' to political reform. To them, brutal police and military actions seemed entirely justifiable.

From 1978 to 1988 the South African Defence Force (SADF; now the South African National Defence Force, or SANDF) made a number of attacks inside Angola, Mozambique, Zimbabwe, Botswana and Lesotho. All white males were liable for national service, and thousands fled into exile to avoid conscription. Many more were scarred mentally and physically.

Paradoxically, the international sanctions that cut whites off from the rest of the world enabled black leaders to develop sophisticated political skills, as those in exile forged ties with regional and world leaders.

Winds of Change

In the early 1980s, a fresh wind began to blow across South Africa. Whites constituted only 16% of the total population, in comparison with 20% 50 years earlier, and the percentage was continuing to fall. Recognising the

2004

Mbeki guides the ANC to a decisive victory in the 2004 national elections. In accordance with his vision of an 'African renaissance', South Africa increases regional engagement.

2003

JM Coetzee is announced the winner of the Nobel Prize for Literature.

2005

President Thabo Mbeki dismisses Jacob Zuma from his position as deputy president following corruption charges, igniting a political war between the two men that Mbeki ultimately loses.

2006

Over five million South Africans are living with HIV/AIDS; the devastation wrought by the disease is a reflection on many years of neglect by the government.

inevitability of change, President PW Botha told white South Africans to 'adapt or die'. Numerous reforms were instituted, including repeal of the pass laws. But Botha stopped well short of full reform, and many blacks (as well as the international community) felt the changes were only cosmetic. Protests and resistance continued at full force as South Africa became increasingly polarised and fragmented, and unrest was widespread. A white backlash gave rise to a number of neo-Nazi paramilitary groups, notably the Afrikaner Weerstandsbeweging (AWB), led by Eugène Terre'Blanche. The opposition United Democratic Front (UDF) was also formed at this time. With a broad coalition of members, led by Archbishop Desmond Tutu and the Reverend Allan Boesak, it called for the government to abolish apartheid and eliminate the homelands.

International pressure also increased, as economic sanctions began to dig in harder, and the value of the rand collapsed. In 1985 the government declared a state of emergency, which was to stay in effect for five years. The media were censored and by 1988, according to ANC estimates, backed up by those of human-rights groups, 30,000 people had been detained without trial and thousands had been tortured.

The Wild Almond Line, by Larry Schwartz, is a memoir of growing up in a segregated country and being a conscript in the apartheid-era army.

Mandela Is Freed

In 1986 President Botha announced to parliament that South Africa had 'outgrown' apartheid. The government started making a series of minor reforms in the direction of racial equality while maintaining an iron grip on the media and on all anti-apartheid demonstrations.

In late 1989, a physically ailing Botha was succeeded by FW de Klerk. At his opening address to parliament in February 1990, De Klerk

PROFILE: MAX DU PREEZ & VRYE WEEKBLAD

In 1988 renegade Afrikaner journalist Max du Preez, together with a handful of other white anti-apartheid activists, founded *Vrye Weekblad,* South Africa's first Afrikaans-language anti-apartheid newspaper. From the start, the newspaper drew the wrath of the state. Its offices were bombed, du Preez received numerous threats and the newspaper was sued for defamation by then-president PW Botha. Yet, during its short life, it was ground-breaking for its commitment to free speech, its tireless campaigning against oppression and its exposés of corruption and brutality on all sides of the political spectrum. After just over five years of cutting-edge investigative reporting, *Vrye Weekblad* was forced to close down shortly before the 1994 elections. Du Preez went on to work as producer for the South African Broadcasting Corporation's (SABC) TV coverage of the Truth and Reconciliation Commission hearings and today he continues to work as a journalist.

For an account of the paper's history, look for a copy of du Preez' book, *Oranje Blanje Blues*.

2007

The HIV/AIDS tragedy affects the country's most vulnerable. According to Unaids, there are approximately 280,000 South African children living with HIV and 1.4 million orphaned by AIDS.

2007

In December, Thabo Mbeki is defeated by Jacob Zuma as chairman of the ANC. New corruption charges – following the dropping of earlier charges in 2006 – are brought against Zuma.

2008

Long-simmering social discontent boils over and xenophobic rioting wracks townships around the country, causing more than 60 deaths and forcing many workers from neighbouring countries to return home.

2008

The Shikota movement, headed by former Gauteng premier Mbhazima Shilowa and Mosiuoa Lekota, form a new ANC-breakaway political party called the Congress of the People (COPE).

announced that he would repeal discriminatory laws and legalise the ANC, the PAC and the Communist Party. Media restrictions were lifted, and De Klerk released political prisoners not guilty of common-law crimes. On 11 February 1990, 27 years after he had first been incarcerated, Nelson Mandela walked out of the grounds of Victor Verster prison a free man.

From 1990 to 1991 the legal apparatus of apartheid was abolished. A referendum – the last of the whites-only vote held in South Africa – overwhelmingly gave the government authority to negotiate a new constitution with the ANC and other groups.

Nelson Mandela's autobiographical *Long Walk to Freedom* is essential reading and the ultimate recounting of the early days of resistance and the years that followed.

Elections & South Africa's Constitution

In December 1991 the Convention for a Democratic South Africa (Codesa) began negotiations on the formation of a multiracial transitional government and a new constitution extending political rights to all groups.

In 1993 a draft constitution was published guaranteeing freedom of speech and religion, access to adequate housing and numerous other benefits, and explicitly prohibiting discrimination on almost any grounds. Finally, at midnight on 26/27 April 1994, the old national anthem 'Die Stem' (The Call) was sung and the old flag was lowered, followed by the raising of the new rainbow flag and the singing of the new anthem 'Nkosi Sikelel i Afrika' (God Bless Africa). The election went off peacefully, amid a palpable feeling of goodwill throughout the country.

The ANC won 62.7% of the vote, less than the 66.7% that would have enabled it to rewrite the constitution. As well as deciding the national government, the election decided the provincial governments, and the ANC won in all but two provinces. The NP captured most of the white and coloured vote and became the official opposition party.

Thabo Mbeki: The Dream Deferred, by Mark Gevisser, is an intriguing examination of both the man who stood at the forefront of South African politics for over a decade, and of South Africa itself.

In 1996, after much negotiation and debate, South Africa's parliament approved a revised version of the 1993 constitution that established the structure of the country's new, democratic government. The national government consists of a 400-member National Assembly, a 90-member National Council of Provinces and a head of state (the president), who is elected by the National Assembly.

A South African president has more in common with a Westminster-style prime minister than a US president, although as head of state the South African president has some executive powers denied to most prime ministers. The constitution is most notable for its expansive Bill of Rights.

In 1999 South Africa held its second democratic elections. Two years earlier Mandela had handed over ANC leadership to his deputy, Thabo Mbeki, and the ANC's share of the vote increased to put the party within one seat of the two-thirds majority that would allow it to alter the constitution.

The Democratic Party (DP) – traditionally a stronghold of liberal whites, with new support from conservatives disenchanted with the NP, and from some middle-class blacks – won official opposition status.

2009

The ANC wins the country's fourth general election in a landslide. Just before the election charges that have dogged Jacob Zuma are dropped.

2010

The FIFA World Cup of football is held in South Africa and, despite fears that visitors would become victims of crime, goes without a hitch.

2011

With two billion rand 'lost' from its national accounts, Limpopo province is declared bankrupt by the national treasury and the federal ANC government seizes direct control of the province.

2011

South Africa becomes a member of BRICS (Brazil, Russia, India, China and South Africa) – an association of the most economically powerful developing nations in the world.

PROFILE: DESMOND TUTU

Few figures in South Africa's anti-apartheid struggle are as recognisable as Desmond Mpilo Tutu, the retired Anglican Archbishop of Cape Town. Tutu, born in 1931 in Klerksdorp, Transvaal (now in North West Province), rose from humble beginnings to become an internationally recognised activist. During the apartheid era Tutu was a vigorous proponent of economic boycotts and international sanctions against South Africa. Following the fall of the apartheid government, Tutu headed South Africa's Truth and Reconciliation Commission, an experience that he chronicles in his book *No Future Without Forgiveness*.

Today Tutu continues to be a tireless moral advocate. He has been a particularly outspoken critic of the ANC government, lashing out against corruption, HIV/AIDS and poverty, and taking the government to task for failing to adequately tackle poverty. Tutu has been awarded the Nobel Peace Prize, the Gandhi Peace Prize and numerous other distinctions. It is Tutu who is generally credited with coining the phrase 'rainbow nation' as a description for post-apartheid South Africa.

By any account, Mbeki had huge shoes to fill as president, although how close he came is the subject of sharply divided debate, and his years in office can only be characterised as a roller-coaster ride. In the early days of his presidency, Mbeki's effective denial of the HIV/AIDS crisis invited global criticism, and his conspicuous failure to condemn the forced reclamation of white-owned farms in neighbouring Zimbabwe and to speak out publicly against his long-time comrade, Zimbabwean president Robert Mugabe, unnerved both South African landowners and foreign investors.

Rabble-Rouser for Peace: The Authorised Biography of Desmond Tutu, by John Allen, is a fascinating and inspirational look at the life of one of South Africa's most influential figures.

Truth & Reconciliation

Following the first elections, focus turned to the Truth and Reconciliation Commission (1994–99), which worked to expose crimes of the apartheid era. The dictum of its chairman Archbishop Desmond Tutu was: 'Without forgiveness there is no future, but without confession there can be no forgiveness'. Stories of horrific brutality and injustice were heard, offering some catharsis to people and communities shattered by their past.

The commission operated by allowing victims to tell their stories and perpetrators to confess their guilt, with amnesty on offer to those who made a clean breast of it. Those who chose not to appear before the commission would face criminal prosecution if their guilt could be proven. Yet, while some soldiers, police and 'ordinary' citizens confessed their crimes, many of the human-rights criminals who gave the orders and dictated the policies failed to present themselves (PW Botha is one famous no-show).

2012

Wildcat strikes sweep the nation as 12,000 mine workers are fired for striking. The appalling conditions endured by many mine workers are brought to national prominence.

2012

The ANC celebrates its 100-year anniversary with major celebrations in Bloemfontein, where it was founded; and events commemorating its centennial continue throughout the year all over the country.

2012

Three years after charges of corruption, racketeering, tax-evasion and money-laundering against president Jacob Zuma are dropped, the country's supreme court rules to allow a review of the decision.

2013

Nelson Mandela dies from respiratory failure. His death causes an outpouring of grief in South Africa and beyond. Leaders from around the world attend his memorial service.

South Africa Recently

In 2005 Mbeki dismissed his deputy president Jacob Zuma in the wake of corruption charges against him, setting off a ruthless internal ANC power struggle, which Zuma won. In September 2008, in an unprecedented move by the party, Mbeki was asked to step down as president.

After the Party, by former ANC MP Andrew Feinstein, is a detailed and highly critical look at the ANC behind the scenes during the post-Mandela years.

Corruption charges against Zuma were dropped and, as widely expected, the ANC won the 2009 election, with Jacob Zuma declared president. Zuma managed to balance out considerable domestic and international criticism with his approachable personality and strong grassroots popularity. There is a widely held view, however, that he has demonstrated weak leadership and failed to fulfill promises to create jobs and alleviate poverty. The opposition has also brought charges of corruption against him.

In the 2014 elections, the country's media excitedly talked up the chances of the Democratic Alliance (DA) – the official opposition that is an amalgamation of the old Democratic Party and numerous smaller parties. Disenchantment with perceived corruption, crime and slow progress on providing critical services to poor communities fed a growing desire for change. In the end, though, the ANC won comfortably with 62.1% of the vote (down from 65.9% in 2009), and the Democratic Alliance won 22.2%, highlighting the mammoth task it faces in wresting government from the ANC.

More people have HIV/AIDS in South Africa than any other country – for more on the history of HIV/AIDS in South Africa and on what's being done today, see www.avert.org/aidssouthafrica.htm.

Perhaps the most surprising result was from the Economic Freedom Fighters – a new political party headed by Julius Malema, a former ANC youth leader kicked out of his former party for corruption and bringing the ANC into disrepute. Though he enjoys grassroots popularity for his talk of economic equality and fighting poverty, his radical views against 'white monopoly power' and on the need for faster land redistribution has worried many. Once one of Zuma's greatest supporters, he now rails against his former mentor and the corrupt practices that he accuses the ANC of perpetrating.

The ability of opposition parties to pressure the government to tackle the country's problems continues to be an important test of South Africa's political maturity. Corruption, crime, economic inequality and HIV/AIDS all loom as major challenges.

Given the country's turbulent recent history, ongoing crime problems and issues of corruption – the latter two are always talking points among the populace – it's not surprising that there is a range of views among South Africans about the future of the 'rainbow nation'. Most of them would agree, however, that the country today is an immeasurably more optimistic and relaxed place than it was in 1990, despite the massive problems that it still confronts.

2013

President Jacob Zuma is criticised by the anti-corruption ombudsman for a R20-million refurbishment of his private home.

2014

The opposition accuse President Jacob Zuma of corruption relating to upgrades to the president's private Nkandla homestead in KwaZulu-Natal. The police begin investigating, but no formal charges are laid.

2014

The country holds its fifth general election since the end of apartheid. The ANC wins (with a reduced majority), with 62.1% of the vote, and Jacob Zuma begins a second term as president.

2014

The country's newest political party, Economic Freedom Fighters, led by former disgraced ANC youth leader Julius Malema, captures 6.4% of the vote in national elections.

Music

Just as music fuelled the resistance to apartheid, it continues to sing out for freedom and justice, while providing a soundtrack to everyday lives. Music is everywhere in South Africa, coming through every available medium, communicating in every imaginable style. Want a 'typical' South African sound? Forget it: South Africa has perhaps the greatest range of musical styles on the continent, and more than any country of similar size anywhere in the world.

It is a nation of record collectors who get down to rock, jazz, classical, gospel, rap, reggae, Afro-house, maskanda, mbaqanga, kwaito, and much more. Centuries-old traditions jostle with new genres, and Western styles are given an idiosyncratic stamp. The country's gargantuan recording industry (with its small but determined crop of independent black-owned labels) watches, ready to pounce. No one sound will ever pigeonhole South Africa, which can only be a good thing – the annual South African Music Awards is multicategory, multitextured and, consequently, a very long ceremony.

Two decades of freedom have proved that a recovering country can produce sophisticated talent to the highest international standards. So get humming, swing your hips and dive in.

The first known musicians in South Africa were the San people, some 4000 years ago. They sang in a uniquely African click language, played rattles, drums and simple flutes and even their hunting bows.

Musical History

The Zulu, Xhosa and Sotho people have been singing and dancing for thousands of years – this is the music that attracted Paul Simon and fed into his 1986 masterpiece, *Graceland* – just as the Venda (and in Lesotho, the Basotho) have been playing their *mbiras* (thumb pianos) and reed pipes. There are eight distinct 'tribal' traditions in South Africa, and the democratic era has seen a resurgence in traditional musicians making very traditional music. But from the earliest colonial times to the present day, South Africa's music has created and reinvented itself from a mixture of older local and imported styles. Most of the popular styles use either Zulu a-capella singing or harmonic mbaqanga as a vocal base, ensuring that whatever the instrument – and the banjo, violin, concertina and electric guitar have all had a profound influence – the sound stays proudly, resolutely African.

European Influence

Ever wondered why the chord sequences of many South African songs seem familiar? Blame the church: the Protestant missionaries of the 19th century developed a choral tradition that, in tandem with the country's first formal music education, South African composers would blend with traditional harmonic patterns. Enoch Sontonga's 1897 hymn 'Nkosi Sikelel' iAfrika' (God Bless Africa), originally written in Xhosa, is now part of the country's national anthem.

Zulu music's veteran exponents Ladysmith Black Mambazo – wrongly considered 'typical' South African music by many Westerners, thanks to their rapid-fire album releases and relentless international touring schedule – exemplify the way indigenous harmonies were neatly mixed with the sounds of European and African church choirs (a vocal style known as mbube). In the same way that much contemporary South African art was born from oppression, Ladysmith's 'tiptoe' *isicathamiya* music, with its high-kicking, soft-stepping dance, has its origins in all-male miners' hostels in Natal province in the 1930s, where workers were at pains not to wake their bosses. *Isicathamiya* choirs still appear in weekly competitions in Johannesburg and Durban; such choirs, or versions thereof, often busk South African city streets.

Apartheid Sounds

Kwela music, like most modern South African styles, came out of the townships. Meaning 'get up' in Zulu, in township slang 'kwela' was both an invitation to dance and a warning that police vans (known as the *kwela-kwela*) were coming. Once-infamous areas such as Soweto, Sharpeville, District Six and Sophiatown gave rise to urban, pan-tribal genres, mostly inspired by music coming in (or back) from America, such as jazz, swing, jive and soul. Black South Africans added an urban spin: kwela, with its penny whistles (an instrument evolved from the reed flutes of indigenous cattle herders) and one-string bass became sax-jive, also known as mbaqanga. Marabi soul took off in the 1970s and 'bubblegum' pop dominated the 1980s.

America and Europe were the inspiration for white South African artists. Sixties phenomenon Four Jacks and a Jill were pure Western pop. British punk inspired 1970s working-class outfits such as Wild Youth, whose sound recalls the Buzzcocks and the Stooges. The 1980s saw a crossover of black and white musicians: Johnny Clegg and his former bands Juluka and Savuka used a fusion of white rock and pop with traditional Zulu music to challenge racist restrictions and set a precedent for others.

Modern Era

Kwaito, South Africa's very own hip hop, exploded in the 1990s and remains, apart from gospel, rap and a burgeoning R&B scene, the country's most popular genre. Grunge helped shape the likes of Scooters Un-

MELODIC MOVIES

- *Searching for Sugar Man* (2012) is a brilliant documentary about Rodriguez, the Dylanesque singer-songwriter from Detroit who was bigger than Elvis in South Africa – but didn't find out until 30 years later. The Oscar-winning film shows how Rodriguez' early '70s compositions, such as 'Sugar Man', were anthems for liberal white South Africans during apartheid.
- Featuring music by and interviews with Abdullah Ibrahim, Hugh Masekela and Miriam Makeba among others, Lee Hirsch's *Amandla! A Revolution in Four-Part Harmony* (2003) explores the role of music in the fight against apartheid. Made over nine years, this is a deeply affecting film.
- Pascale Lamche's *Sophiatown* (2003) looks at Jo'burg's bustling Sophiatown, the Harlem of South Africa. Home to many artists and musicians, it was flattened for redevelopment in the 1950s. The film's archival footage and interviews make for compulsive viewing.
- The 2005 Oscar-winning township drama *Tsotsi* features a soundtrack composed by kwaito star Zola (who also plays local gang boss Fela), as well as haunting tracks by singer-songwriter Vusi Mahlasela.
- *Fokofpolisiekar: Forgive Them for They Know Not What They Do* (2009), a documentary about Afrikaner rockers Fokofpolisiekar (Fuckoffpolicecar), is a fascinating glimpse of contemporary Afrikanerdom. The seminal band voiced the frustrations of young Afrikaners, tired of the conservatism and Christianity of Afrikaner society, and ruffled establishment feathers.

ion, the Springbok Nude Girls and other 1990s guitar bands, while acts including Seether, Prime Circle and former Springbok frontman Arno Carstens ensure that rock continues to flourish. Afrikaans rock continues to build on the legacy of the Voëlvry movement and Fokofpolisiekar, who developed the genre and its following from the '80s onwards.

Acts such as Die Heuwels Fantasties (watch their song 'Noorderlig' on YouTube), Van Coke Cartel, Chris Chameleon and aKING entertain the alternative crowd, while singer-songwriter David Kramer's musicals have received critical acclaim. And then there's the huge cutting-edge dance scene: house, techno, acid jazz, R&B, dancehall and all grooves in between, often with live elements thrown in. South Africa's trance scene is second only to Israel's, and parties regularly happen near Cape Town. The tie-dye crowd converges on the AfrikaBurn festival (www.afrikaburn.com), held every April/May in the Tankwa Karoo.

The effects of apartheid on lives and culture are still sorely felt; musicians such as jazz legend and former exile Hugh Masekela stress the need for continued sensitivity. Award-winning protest singer Vusi 'the Voice' Mahlasela, who performed at Mandela's inauguration in 1994, continues to spread Mandela's message as an official ambassador to Mandela's HIV/AIDS initiative, 46664.

The creation of a black-owned, black-run music industry and distribution network has been a long battle (resistance by moguls from the old-school white biz was fierce). However, South African music is becoming more Africanised, with a healthy selection of Westernised English- and Afrikaans-language indie and electronic acts in the mix. The passionate music of the anti-apartheid resistance, meanwhile, has maintained its fire by changing its focus: other scourges – such as HIV/AIDS, poverty, the abuse of women and children – are being written and sung about. Many of these issues, especially the HIV/AIDS epidemic, remain taboo despite their devastating effects on township communities; music is a good way to get people listening and talking about these topics.

Opportunities abound in the current climate of cultural and artistic expression. Boundaries are down and styles are cross-pollinating; many genres, especially jazz and Afro-house, are booming and venues are following suit. Democracy, so bitterly won, has never sounded so sweet.

Music Websites

South African Music (www.music.org.za): Definitive reference on Southern African musicians.

One World (www.oneworld.co.za): Independent music cyberstore selling South African CDs and DVDs.

South African Musical Styles

Marabi

In the early 20th century, travelling African American minstrel shows, vaudeville acts, ragtime piano players and gospel groups impressed local audiences in the growing cities of Cape Town and Jo'burg. Urbanisation had a domino effect on musical styles: visiting American jazz artists and records by the likes of Louis Armstrong and Duke Ellington kick-started what would later become the South African jazz scene. By the 1920s and '30s the urban ghettos were singing and swinging to *marabi,* a defining, dangerous (in Sotho it means 'gangster') small-band sound.

Played on cheap pedal organs and keyboards with accompaniment from pebble-filled cans, *marabi* flooded illegal township shebeens and dance-halls. Its siren call got people in and drinking, but it also offered some dignity and consolation to the oppressed working-class areas where it was played. *Marabi's* trancelike rhythms and cyclical harmonies had links to American Dixieland and ragtime; subsequent decades saw the addition of penny whistle, drums, banjo, elements of big-band swing and even bebop.

Marabi made its way into the jazz-dance bands that produced the first generation of professional black musicians: the Jazz Maniacs, Merry Blackbirds and Jazz Revellers. Often referred to simply (and not always correctly) as 'African jazz' or 'jive', *marabi* went on to spawn other styles. One of these was kwela.

Kwela

Kwela was the first popular South African style to make the world sit up and take notice. Initially played on acoustic guitar, banjo, one-string bass and, most importantly, the penny whistle, kwela was taken up by kids with no access to horns and pianos but keen to put their own spin on American swing. Groups of tin-flautists would gather to play on street corners in white areas, with the danger of arrest (for creating a 'public disturbance') upping the music's appeal and attracting rebellious white kids known as 'ducktails'. Many such groups were also lookouts for the shebeens.

Kwela combos gained a live following but little recording took place until 1954, when Spokes Mashinyane's 'Ace Blues' became the smash African hit of the year and sent white producers scurrying into the black market. Artists such as Sparks Nyembe and Jerry Mlotshwa became popular; the hit 'Tom Lark' by Elias and His Zig Zag Jive Flutes crossed over to Britain, where it stayed in the charts for 14 weeks.

In the early 1960s Mashinyane introduced the saxophone to kwela with his song 'Big Joe Special', ending the penny-whistle boom and creating sax-jive. Sax-jive quickly became mbaqanga.

The Voëlvry (Free as a Bird) movement united Afrikaner musicians opposed to apartheid in the 1980s, culminating in a nationwide tour. For local musicians, it was a watershed akin to the cultural revolution that swept the West in the '60s.

Mbaqanga

The saxophone became vital to South African jazz, which, much to the dismay of white kwela fans, was now limited to performances in the townships. Mbaqanga ('daily bread' in Zulu) had its innovators: Joseph Makwela and Marks Mankwane of celebrated session players the Makhona Tshole Band added electric guitars to the cascading rhythms – notably a funky, muscular bass – while sax player and producer West Nkosi set the pace. This hugely popular electric sound backed singers whose vocal style was later named *mqashiyo* (after a dance style), even though it was really no different from mbaqanga.

Mbaqanga's idiosyncratic vocals echoed 1950s groups such as the Manhattan Brothers and Miriam Makeba's Skylarks, who copied African American doo-wop outfits but used Africanised five-part harmonies instead of four. In the 1960s, Aaron 'Jack' Lerole (of Elias and His Zig Zag Jive Flutes fame) added his groaning vocals to the mix, but it was the growling bass of Simon 'Mahlathini' Nkabinde and his sweet-voiced Mahotella Queens (backed by the Makhona Tshole Band) that would inspire a generation, including Izintombi Zeze Manje Manje and the Boyoyo Boys. More recently, Lerole founded the band Mango Groove and toured with the USA's Dave Matthews Band before his death in 2003; the Mahotella Queens are still going strong – sans Mahlathini – and British producer/chancer Malcolm McLaren sampled the Boyoyo Boys on his 1983 British hit, 'Double Dutch'.

Mbaqanga remains an important force in South African music, its influence apparent in everything from soul and reggae to R&B, kwaito and, of course, jazz.

Jazz

Structurally, harmonically and melodically distinctive, the force that is South African jazz started as an underground movement and became a statement of protest and identity. In the hands of such talented exiled stars as singer Miriam 'Mama Africa' Makeba, pianist Abdullah Ibrahim (formerly Dollar Brand) and trumpeter Hugh Masekela, it was famously an expatriate music style that represented the suffering of a people. Legendary outfit the Blue Notes – led by Chris McGregor and featuring saxophonist Dudu Pukwana – helped change the face of European jazz after relocating to the UK. Jazzers who stayed behind kept a low profile while developing new sounds and followings with, variously, jazz-rock fusion, Latin and even Malay crossovers.

World-renowned exiles, who returned home after the end of the anti-apartheid cultural boycott, had to work hard to win back local audiences. Most now enjoy healthy followings – Makeba passed away aged 76 in 2008, making Masekela his country's most enduring musical ambassador – in what is now a mainstream scene. Frequent festivals, often featuring top overseas acts (Erykah Badu and Level 42 appeared at the 15th Cape Town International Jazz Festival in 2014), are providing platforms and the South African media is lending its support.

Well-known locals are moving jazz forward, working with DJs, artists, poets and dance companies. The late Coltrane-esque saxophonist Zim Ngqawana, who led a group of 100 drummers, singers and dancers at Nelson Mandela's inauguration, drew on folk and rural traditions as well as Indian, avant garde and classical music. Before his death, in 2011, he founded the Zimology Institute, mentoring young jazz musicians and offering an alternative to formal music education on a farm outside Jo'burg.

Late jazz icon Miriam Makeba sings her most famous song, 'Qongqothwane' (or 'The Click Song'), in the clicking Xhosa language.

Ngqawana's former sideman, pianist Andile Yenana, combines the traditional and experimental with Monk-ish flair. Renowned guitarist Jimmy Dludlu, a sort of African George Benson, takes time out to work with music-school graduates. Lesotho has produced Tsopo Tshola, known for his early work with the Maseru band Sankomota and more recent solo albums such as *The Village Pope*. High-profile South African chanteuses include Afro-jazz queen Pinise Saul, Sibongile Khumalo, Judith Sephumo, and Xhosa vocalist Simphiwe Dana; the latter has been proclaimed the 'new Miriam Makeba' for her fusion of jazz, Afro-soul, rap and traditional music. Many such singers are enjoying success in another genre sharing common roots with jazz: gospel.

Gospel

The music industry's biggest market – bolstered by the country's 80% Christian black population – South Africa's gospel is an amalgam of European choral music, American influences, Zulu a-cappella singing and other African traditions incorporated within the church (Zionist, Ethiopian, Pentecostal and Apostolic). All joy, colour and exuberance, rhythm, passion and soul, gospel choirs perform throughout South Africa, lifting the roofs off big, formal venues and community halls alike. Like many big choirs, the 30-piece ensemble and overseas success story, Soweto Gospel Choir, which won Grammy awards in 2007 and 2008 for its albums *Blessed* and *African Spirit,* features a band with drummers and dancers.

This vast genre is divided into traditional gospel – personified by the International Pentecostal Church Choir (IPCC), Solly Moholo, Hlengiwe Mhlaba and Jabu Hlongwane – and contemporary gospel. Beacons of the

ESSENTIAL LISTENING

marabi – *From Marabi to Disco,* various artists

kwela – *King Kwela,* Spokes Mashiyane

mbaqanga – *Kuze Kuse,* Soul Brothers

jazz – *African Marketplace,* Abdullah Ibrahim

gospel – *Tales of Gospel SA*

neotraditional music – *Amakhansela,* Phuzekhemisi

soul, reggae and R&B – *Respect,* Lucky Dube

bubblegum and kwaito – *New Construction,* Bongo Maffin

zef and current trends – *Father Creeper,* Spoek Mathambo

TOP 10 SOUTH AFRICAN ALBUMS

- *The Indestructible Beat of Soweto* – various artists
- *Jazz in Africa, Volume 1* – Jazz Epistles
- *Her Essential Recordings* – Miriam Makeba
- *Hope* – Hugh Masekela
- *The Best of Mahlathini and the Mahotella Queens*
- *Shaka Zulu* – Ladysmith Black Mambazo
- *Ibokwe* – Thandiswa Mazwai
- *Acceptance Speech* – Hip Hop Pantsula
- *Naledi Ya Tsela (Guiding Star)* – Vusi Mahlasela
- *The One Love Movement on Banto Biko Street* – Simphiwe Dana

latter include veteran superstar Rebecca 'Ribs' Malope, also a TV host; the multiplatinum-selling Zulu diva Deborah Fraser; Reverend Benjamin Dube (known as 'the Gospel Maestro'); and the pastor and former Durban street kid Andile Ka Majola. Besthusile Mcinga, whose 'Uzundithwale' won best gospel song at the Crown Gospel Music Awards 2014, is a name to watch. Popular Swazi acts include France Dlamini, the 'father of Swazi gospel', Shongwe & Khuphuka and the Ncandweni Christ Ambassadors, fronted by former parliamentarian Timothy Myeni.

Gospel also comprises much of the oeuvre of Ladysmith Black Mambazo (whose album *Ilembe: Honoring Shaka Zulu* scooped the 2009 Grammy for Best Traditional World Music Album). Their Zulu *isicathamiya* style is a prime example of the way traditional South African music has appropriated Western sounds to produce unique musical styles. Gloria Bosman, Sibongile Khumalo, Pinise Saul and other top black South African artists are now working across a range of genres (gospel, jazz, classical, opera), having started singing in mission-school choirs or in church. Others, such as Rebecca Malope, crossed to gospel from the shiny world of pop.

Neotraditional Music

Away from the urban life of the townships and the cities' recording studios, traditional musicians from the Sotho, Zulu, Pedi and Tsonga regions have developed dynamic social music. Since the 1930s, many have mixed call-and-response singing with the dreamy 10-button concertina, an instrument that has made a comeback in Zulu pop. The Sotho took up the accordion (accordion players and groups still abound in Lesotho); the Pedi the German autoharp; and the Zulu embraced the guitar.

Maskanda (or *maskandi*) is a form of rhythmic and repetitive guitar picking born through the Zulu experience of labour migration. Many migrants made do with an *igogogo,* an instrument fashioned from an oil can; late *maskanda* stalwart Shiyani Ngcobo used the *igogogo* in his live sets. Other top-selling *maskanda* acts include virtuoso guitarist Phuzekhemisi, whose shows often include dozens of singers, dancers and instrumentalists; the popular duo Shwi No Mtkehala; and the poetic Bhekumuzi Luthuli, who died in 2010.

The upbeat and vaguely Latin-sounding Tsonga music tends to feature a male leader backed by, variously, a female chorus, guitars, synths, percussion and an unabashed disco beat. Best-known acts include Doctor Sithole, George Maluleke, Conny Chauke and Fanie Rhingani.

In her traditional/urban crossovers, young Xhosa artist Lungiswa is one of the few female South African musicians to play the *mbira.* The late veteran Zulu chanteuse Busi Mhlongo fused traditional Zulu sounds with hip hop and kwaito.

In Lesotho, a group of shepherds known as Sotho Sounds play instruments made from discarded objects: one-string fiddle *(qwadinyana),* guitars *(katara),* drums fashioned out of disused oil cans, car tyres, twigs and a kitchen sink. A triumph at Britain's Womad Festival, they are based in Malealea, where they continue to compose and rehearse (and still perform for guests of Malealea Lodge).

But, again, it's in South Africa that musical roots are being mixed with every sound imaginable, from country, blues, rap (check out Hip Hop Pantsula and Molemi) and house (see DJs Black Coffee, Mbuso and Vinny da Vinci) to rock, Afro-house, reggae and soul.

Soul, Reggae & R&B

The American-led soul music of the 1960s had a huge impact on township teenagers. The local industry tried various cheap imitations; the few South African 'soul' groups that made it did so on the back of a blend of soul and *marabi,* such as the Movers, or soul and electric bass mbaqanga, such as the Soul Brothers, a band who spawned dozens of imitators. Contemporary South African soul is often filed under mbaqanga: the genre from which evergreen reggae star Lucky Dube – shot dead in a car-jacking in Johannesburg in 2007 – grew to the status of Africa's Bob Marley. Over 25 years, he recorded two-dozen albums in Zulu, English and Afrikaans; his CDs still have pride of place in shops and market stalls throughout sub-Saharan Africa.

Dube's legacy aside, in South Africa reggae is often subsumed into other genres such as ragga and kwaito: Bongo Maffin throws kwaito, house, reggae, ragga, gospel and hip hop into the pot. Homegrown R&B, meanwhile, has surged, with huge stars such as Loyiso Bala. The wonderful Thandiswa Mazwai (Bongo Maffin's erstwhile frontwoman) nods in the R&B direction on her second solo album, *Ibokhwe*. The soulful sounds of DJ, singer and media player Unathi Nkayi seem to be everywhere, while in Cape Town, you will likely hear the upbeat local outfits Goldfish and Freshlyground; their breezy Capetonian sounds fall somewhere between soul, pop and electro.

Paul Simon's *Graceland* album has sold more than 14 million copies worldwide and, despite the controversy over breaking the global musicians' boycott of apartheid South Africa, was vital in alerting the rest of the world to South African music.

Bubblegum & Kwaito

The disco that surfaced during the 1970s came back – slick, poppy and Africanised – in the 1980s as 'bubblegum'. Vocally led and aimed squarely at the young, this electronic dance style owed a debt to mbaqanga as well as America. What the Soul Brothers started, superstars such as the late Brenda Fassie, Sello 'Chicco' Twala and Yvonne 'princess of Africa' Chaka Chaka refined; Chaka Chaka's track 'Umqombothi', named after Xhosa homebrew, soundtracks the opening of the film *Hotel Rwanda* (2005). Bubblegum's popularity waned in the 1990s, and in its place exploded kwaito (meaning 'cool' in Isicamtho, the Gauteng township slang; a bastardisation of the Afrikaans word *kwaai,* which means strict or angry).

The music of young, black, urban South Africa, kwaito is a rowdy mix of everything from bubblegum, hip hop, R&B and ragga to mbaqanga, traditional, jazz, and British and American house music. It is also a fashion statement, a state of mind and a lifestyle. Chanted or sung in a mixture of English, Zulu, Sesotho and Isicamtho (usually over programmed beats and backing tapes), kwaito's lyrics range from the anodyne to the fiercely political. A unique fusion, kwaito has caught the imagination of post-apartheid South Africa and is evolving even as the 'Is kwaito dead?' debate rages. Acts such as Zola, Boom Shaka, Mapaputsi, Spikiri and Trompies were trailblazers; the current crop includes Mandoza, Thokozani 'L'vovo Derrango' Ndlovu, Big Nuz and Howza.

Zef & Current Trends

Two acts that have created their own genres, and achieved international success in the process, are Die Antwoord and Spoek Mathambo – both have proved adept at repackaging South Africa's unique and little-known subcultures for an international audience. Die Antwoord ('the answer' in Afrikaans), featuring Ninja (Watkin Tudor Jones) and cyberpunk pixie Yolandi Visser (Anri du Toit), have created a harsh, futuristic sound and image under the banner of 'zef'. The term was long used to describe the culture of low-income white South Africans (without the negative connotations of 'bogan' in Australia or 'chav' in the UK), and Die Antwoord appropriated the word for their frenetic rap-rave and tongue-in-cheek white-trash look. Another zef artist is rapper Jack Parow, who is like an Afrikaner version of Britain's the Streets; describing himself as 'the pirate of the caravan park', he sings about suburban life in Cape Town. Die Antwoord, however, are currently in a league of their own in South Africa, having toured internationally with the likes of Aphex Twin and created unsettling visions in their music videos. Check out 'Enter the Ninja', 'I Fink U Freeky' and 'Ugly Boy' on YouTube.

At Kirstenbosch Summer Sunset Concerts, the likes of Hugh Masekela perform in the blissful setting of Cape Town's botanic gardens.

Spoek Mathambo calls his sound, which merges electronic beats, lo-fi guitars and African influences, 'township tech'. His second album, *Father Creeper*, released in 2012 on Amerian label Sub Pop, encapsulates the linguistic mash of the townships, switching between black African languages, English, Afrikaans, Western references and South African subjects. He has enjoyed some success abroad, gaining attention by covering British post-punk band Joy Division's 'She's Lost Control' and appearing on Damon Albarn's Africa Express tour in 2012.

In South Africa, freedom of expression for everyone, from black youth to white middle-class rockers, is no longer the luxury it was under apartheid. The first place this freedom became visible was the music scene – a scene that is still thriving, creating and reinventing itself in ever-increasing and exciting ways.

Lesotho & Swaziland

In Swaziland, where thousands of bare-breasted virgins dance about for polygamous absolute monarch King Mswati III in the ancient but controversial *umhlanga* (reed) dance ceremony, things aren't quite so liberal as they are in South Africa. Nonetheless, music pulses strongly here; Mswati himself has long hosted fundraising concerts that feature international stars (such as Eric Clapton) and local performers. Music, he has said, 'is a healing weapon for a depressed soul as well as an expression of joy'.

Swaziland's traditional music is used as an accompaniment to harvests, weddings, births and other events. But the sounds of South Africa have an inevitable influence on its smaller neighbours, and Swaziland also has local choral music, jazz, Afropop, rock, a hip-hop scene and, above all else, gospel. Swazi acts to look out for range from African house DJ Simza and female rapper Pashu – aka Princess Sikhanyiso, King Mswati's eldest daughter – to Franco-Swazi jazzers Lilanga, sweet-voiced soul singer Bholoja and gospel act the Ncandweni Christ Ambassadors.

Up in Lesotho, the hills and valleys are alive with the sound of music. Choirs are popular, as are reggae and *famo* (singing, often with ululations, accompanied by an accordion, oil-can drum and sometimes a bass), followed by Afropop, jazz and kwaito. The Basotho people love their songs and instruments: children in villages harmonise their hearts out in choirs; shepherd boys play their *lekolulo* flutes and sing in pure, pitch-perfect voices; women play the stringed *thomo;* and men the *setolo-tolo*, a sort of extended Jew's harp that's played using the mouth.

Food & Drink

Take a bit of black magic, a dash of Dutch heartiness, a pinch of Indian spice and a smidgin of Malay mystery and what you get is an amazing array of cultures all simmering away in the *potjie* (pot) of culinary influences that is South African cuisine.

The earliest inhabitants survived on animals hunted for meat, seafood gathered from the beaches and sea, and myriad vegetables and tubers. When it became necessary to have fresh vegetables and fruit available for passing ships, the Dutch arrived and planted their famous vegetable garden (now Cape Town's Company's Garden). Their rich cuisine was infused with nutmeg, cinnamon and cassia, as well as rice from their colonies in the east. Malay slaves from Madagascar, Java and Indonesia added to the mix, providing spicier accompaniments to the bland fare on offer.

The Cape was the birthplace of South African cuisine, but KwaZulu-Natal was important too: there were blacks who migrated from other African countries, British settlers, and Mauritians who planted exotic fruits and introduced their spicy tomato sauces. And when the Indian indentured labourers arrived in the mid-19th century, they brought their spices with them. It's exciting to be aware of the cultural influences that abound in South African cuisine and explore all the options.

While chefs are looking to their inherited culinary roots with renewed energy, there's a back-to-basics move, too. The most innovative chefs, such as Shaun Schoeman at Fyndraai Restaurant (p109) on the Solms-Delta wine estate in Franschhoek, are becoming market gardeners, planting vegetables and herbs to have instant access to perfect produce to enhance the flavours of their creations. And it's not just the chefs: the public is also seeking out artisanal foods and drinks at neighbourhood markets, craft breweries and boutique cheese makers, all the while conscious of green ethics and sustainability.

There's a happy marriage here: today's chefs and their public are respectful of the intoxicating flavours South Africa is famous for, and enthusiastic about making those flavours surprising, colourful and mouth-wateringly modern.

Need some *padkos* (literally 'road food') for a long journey? The classic South African choice would be a box or two of natural fruit juices along with biltong, *droëwors* (dried sausage), a hard-boiled egg or two and dried guava.

Homages to Food

- *Olive Festival, Riebeek Kasteel (May)*
- *Oyster Festival, Knysna (July)*
- *Meat Festival, Calvinia (August)*
- *Cherry Festival, Ficksburg (November)*
- *Crayfish Festival, Paternoster (November)*

Cultural Staples & Specialities

Trout in Mpumalanga, mealies (or mielies; cobs of corn) in Gauteng, *umngqusho* (maize and bean stew) in the Eastern Cape, Free State venison and cherries, maize or sorghum porridge in Swaziland and Lesotho, Durban curries, crayfish on the West Coast and succulent Karoo lamb – the variety is boundless.

The Afrikaner history of trekking led to their developing portable food, hence the traditional biltong (dried strips of salted, spiced meat, called *umncweba* in Swaziland); rusks (hard biscuits) for dunking; dried fruit; and *boerewors* (sausages), where meat is preserved with spices and vinegar, also found dried.

FOOD MARKETS

South Africa's love affair with the artisanal is best embodied at the weekly food markets that take place across the country. You'll find organic veggies, freshly baked breads, handmade cheeses and a range of sauces, jams and pickles to take home, but the markets are as much about eating in as taking away. Vendors sell everything from chickpea pancakes to paella; from delicate dim sum to hearty sandwiches filled with free-range meat. There's always lots of boutique booze available and sometimes little extras such as live music, crafts for sale or a children's play area. Most markets take place on weekends and, while the bulk of them are in Cape Town and the Winelands, you'll find the odd market everywhere from small Garden Route towns to larger cities such as Bloemfontein and, of course, Johannesburg.

Cape cuisine is a fusion of Malay influence on Dutch staples, and so you'll find dishes such as *bobotie* (sweet and spicy mince with rice), chicken pie and *bredies* (lamb and vegetable stew). Desserts can be the rich *malva* pudding (sticky sponge pudding) or *melktert* (custard-like tart), usually brightened up with a sprinkling of cinnamon.

Black cuisine is founded on the staples of maize, sorghum and beans, enhanced with *morogo* (leafy greens) or *imifino* (maize meal and vegetables), cooked with onions, peanuts and chilli.

South African Indian cooking brings delicious curries and *breyanis* (similar to biryanis) and also fuses with Malay cooking, so that you'll get hotter curries in Durban and milder ones in Cape Town.

What brings everyone together is the cross-cultural South African institution of braaing (barbecuing). A social occasion, the braai usually features meat and vegetables – lamb chops or *sosaties* (spiced meat skewers), *boerewors*, corn cobs and sweet potatoes – and can be found everywhere from the townships to the farmlands to the cities.

The Karoo is renowned for its superlative lamb and many meats are falsely claimed to be from the semi-desert region. A new 'meat of origin' certification has been developed to ensure that your Karoo lamb meets strict standards. See www.karoomeatoforigin.com for more information.

Staples

Mealie pap (maize porridge) is the most widely eaten food in South Africa, as well as in Swaziland and Lesotho. It's thinner or stiffer depending on where you eat it, and is completely bland. However, it's ideal if you want something filling and economical, and can be quite satisfying served with a good sauce or stew. *Samp* (dried and crushed maize kernels) and beans fulfil the same role, making an ideal base for vegetable or meat stews.

Rice and potatoes are widely available and you might even be served both on the same plate. From *roosterkoek* (bread traditionally cooked on the braai) to panini, bread in South Africa is good and comes in infinite varieties.

Cookbooks are big business in South Africa. Look out for those by South African celebrity chefs including Pete Goffe-Wood, Justin Bonello, Reuben Riffel and Jenny Morris.

Meat

In certain areas of South Africa meat is considered a 'staple'. Afrikaners will eat *boerewors* (sausages) or beef mince for breakfast and you often hear people joking that chicken is a vegetable. Alongside the more traditional beef and lamb, you'll find game meats such as ostrich, springbok and kudu. Steaks in particular are excellent.

Seafood

Considering the fact that South Africa is lapped by two oceans, it has a remarkably modest reputation as a seafood-lover's destination. Yet Cape Town, the West Coast and the Garden Route have some delicious fish dishes. Among the highlights: lightly spiced fish stews, *snoekbraai* (grilled snoek), mussels, oysters and seawater crayfish. Pickled fish is popular in Cape cuisine, while in Swaziland prawns are a common feature on restaurant menus, courtesy of nearby Mozambique. On the West Coast, look out for *bokkoms* (salty, sun-dried mullet that can best be described as 'fish biltong').

In Lesotho, look for *motoho* (a fermented sorghum porridge). Swazi variants include *sishwala* (maize and bean porridge, usually eaten with meat or vegetables) and *incwancwa* (slightly fermented maize porridge).

Drinks

Water

Tap water is generally safe in South Africa's cities. However, in rural areas (or anywhere that local conditions indicate that water sources may be contaminated), as well as throughout Swaziland and Lesotho, it's best to purify it or use bottled water.

Beer

Beer is the national beverage. The world's second-largest brewer, SAB Miller, originates in South Africa, and has vast breweries in all of the major cities. The country has long been a lager-drinking nation, with Castle and Black Label the best-sellers and Castle Lite a new favourite. In recent years, though, ales have started to gain popularity and a 'craft-beer revolution' has swept across the country. Today there are upwards of 150 breweries in every province bar in the Northern Cape. Larger brands such as Boston Breweries, Cape Brewing Company, Darling Brew, Jack Black and Mitchell's are found everywhere, while nano-breweries tend to only produce enough to supply their own village or town. Look out for unusual brews using local plants such as rooibos or buchu (a medicinal herb with a strong minty flavour) to add a unique South African tang.

Craft ciders, too, are in vogue, mainly in the Western Cape's Elgin Valley. Check out Windermere and Everson's.

Beer comes in bottles (or cans) from around R20, and bars serve draught from around R25. Craft beers are a little more expensive.

Best Craft Breweries

- *Devil's Peak*
- *Cape Brewing Company*
- *Standeaven*
- *Brauhaus am Damm*
- *Copperlake*

Wine

South African wine debuted in 1659. Since then, it's had time to age to perfection, and is both of a high standard and reasonably priced. Dry

SOUTHERN AFRICAN SUSTAINABLE SEAFOOD INITIATIVE

With more and more people turning to fish as a healthy alternative source of protein, there are fears that stocks around South Africa's coastlines (and beyond) are not sustainable. Overfishing and the use of inappropriate fishing methods are taking their toll on the populations of many fish.

With innovative foresight, South Africa's branch of the World Wide Fund for Nature (WWF) set up the Southern African Sustainable Seafood Initiative (SASSI) in 2004 to educate people about which fish are sustainable (Green List), which should be eaten with caution (Orange List) and which are so endangered that catching them is against the law (Red List).

You'll be pleased to know that most of the fish that you're likely to find on a South African restaurant menu is on the Green List: snoek, yellowtail, tuna, dorado, angelfish and hake. Species unlikely to be able to sustain heavy fishing, and therefore found on the Orange List, include west coast crayfish, perlemoen (abalone), haarders, prawns, red roman, white stumpnose, geelbek, kingklip, kob and swordfish. While restaurateurs are allowed to sell them, you might want to consider your actions. Absolute no-nos are galjoen, white musselcracker, steenbras, stumpnose and blue-fin tuna.

Fortunately, you don't need to remember every fish on the lists to make an informed, pro-environment choice. Simply send an SMS with the name of the fish to ☎079 499 8795 and you'll be told right away whether it's a good choice or not.

For more information, see www.wwfsassi.co.za.

whites are particularly good – try sauvignon blanc, riesling, colombard and chenin blanc – while popular reds include cabernet sauvignon, pinotage (a local cross of pinot and cinsaut, which was known as hermitage), shiraz and pinot noir. Wines are all certified and labels reflect their estate, vintage and origin. Although South African sparkling wine may not be called champagne, a number of producers use chardonnay and pinot noir blends and the *méthode champenoise* – the local name is MCC *(methode Cap classique)*. Likewise, port-style wines cannot use 'port' in their title – look out for Cape Ruby and Cape Tawny. Calitzdorp in the Klein Karoo is particularly known for its fortified wines.

Published annually, the *John Platter Wine Guide* is the quintessential guide to South African wines. See also www.wineonaplatter.com, where there's a host of information on Cape wine routes.

Wine prices average from around R60 in a bottle store, twice that in a restaurant. Wine by the glass is often available from around R35.

Spirits

If you prefer your grapes distilled, there are some world-class brandies in the Cape Winelands – try KWV or Van Ryn's. Brandy and cola is a particularly popular drink in much of the country.

Mampoer (moonshine) and *witblits* (a grape-based spirit similar to grappa) are found throughout South Africa, but with alcohol percentages upwards of 50, these tipples can be a little rough around the edges.

Better are the hand-crafted spirits coming out of the emerging boutique-distillery scene; try Jorgensen's and Inveroche in the Western Cape – the latter uses *fynbos* plants to flavour its range of gins.

Where to Eat & Drink

If you're after fine dining in magnificent surroundings, head to the Winelands. Along the Western Cape coast, open-air beachside eateries serve multi-course fish braais, with everything cooked before your eyes. A highlight of visiting a township is experiencing some family-style cooking in a B&B. In addition to speciality restaurants, every larger town has several places offering homogenised Western fare at homogenised prices (from about R75). Many restaurants are licensed, but there's still a BYO wine option pretty much everywhere – corkage charges almost always apply.

In Lesotho, watch for coloured flags hung in villages to advertise home-brewed beer or available food – white is for sorghum beer, yellow for ginger sorghum beer, green for vegetables and red signifies that meat is for sale.

All towns have cafes where you can enjoy a cappuccino and a sandwich or other light fare. In rural areas, 'cafe' *(kaffie)* usually refers to a small corner shop selling soft drinks, chips, basic groceries and braai wood. Most cafes are open from about 8am to 5pm.

Large towns have a good selection of pubs and more upmarket cocktail lounges. Franchised bars proliferate in urban areas, and most smaller towns have at least one hotel with a bar. In townships, things centre on shebeens (informal drinking establishments that were once illegal but are now merely unlicensed). Throughout South Africa, and in major towns in Lesotho and Swaziland, you can buy all alcoholic drinks

A LEKKER BRAAI

The national pastime and the main food-centred social event is the braai (barbecue). Even the public holiday officially known as Heritage Day (24 September) has been rebranded National Braai Day.

If you're invited to a braai, it's customary to take a bottle of your favourite tipple. Sometimes the host will provide the meat, but more often than not guests bring meat, side dishes or dessert. Dress is casual and the atmosphere relaxed. Typically, men do the cooking while women make the salads.

Jan Scannell, better known as Jan Braai, is the poster child for the national pastime and the driving force behind Braai Day. His book *Fireworks* is a good place to learn the fine art of cooking over coals.

COOKING COURSES

Cape Town, a gourmet's paradise, is the best place for cooking courses.

Andulela (☎021-418 3020; www.andulela.com) Packages include a half-day Cape Malay cookery course in the Bo-Kaap (R795), bread baking in the Winelands (R1395) and an African cooking class (R795) in a family home in the township of Guguletu, where you can learn to prepare traditional Xhosa foods.

Bo-Kaap Cooking Tour (☎074 1308 124; www.bokaapcookingtour.co.za; per person R600) After a short walking tour of the Bo-Kaap and a bit of spice shopping, join Zainie in her home for a hands-on Cape Malay cooking class.

at bottle stores and wine at supermarkets, though there are few options for take-out booze on Sunday.

Vegetarians & Vegans

South Africa is a meat-loving society, but most restaurants have at least one vegetarian option on the menu. In larger towns you might find a vegetarian restaurant. Cafes are good bets, as many will make vegetarian food to order. Indian and Italian restaurants are also useful, although many pasta sauces contain animal fat. Larger towns have health-food stores selling tofu, soy milk and other staples, and can point you towards vegetarian-friendly venues.

Eating vegan is more difficult: most nonmeat dishes contain cheese, and eggs and milk are common ingredients. Health-food shops are your best bet, though most are closed in the evening and on Sunday. Larger supermarkets also stock soy products, and nuts and fruit are widely available. Look out for vendors selling seasonal fruit and vegetables along the roadside throughout the country.

In Lesotho and Swaziland, you'll find plenty of bean, peanut and other legume dishes, usually offered with vegetables.

Ukutya Kwasekhaya: Tastes from Nelson Mandela's Kitchen, by Xoliswa Ndoyiya, includes the traditional recipes enjoyed by Madiba. Xoliswa, Mandela's personal chef, includes African recipes such as *umqusho* (maize and beans) and *umsila wenkomo* (oxtail stew) alongside international dishes.

Eat Your Words

Want to know *potjie* from *umphokoqo?* Know your *skilpadjies* from your *sosaties*? Get behind the cuisine scene by getting to know the language.

Menu Decoder

It's unlikely that you'll see all of these items on the same menu, but they provide an insight into the diversity of South African cuisine.

Food

Meat Dishes

bobotie – curried-mince pie topped with savoury egg custard, served on a bed of yellow rice with chutney
boerewors – spicy sausages, traditionally made of beef and pork plus seasonings and plenty of fat; an essential ingredient at any braai and often sold like hot dogs by street vendors
bredie – hearty Afrikaner pot stew, traditionally made with lamb and vegetables
breyani – fusion of Hindu and Cape Malay influences, this is a spicy, layered rice-and-lentil dish with meat, similar to the Indian biryani
eisbein – pork knuckles
frikkadel – fried meatball
mashonzha – name for mopane worms in Venda, where they're served with *dhofi* (peanut sauce)
mopane worms – caterpillars found on mopane trees; legs are removed, and the caterpillar is dried and served as a crunchy snack; see also *mashonzha*

potjiekos – meat and vegetables layered in a three-legged pot and slowly simmered over a fire, often served with *potjiebrood* (bread cooked in another pot)
skilpadjies – (literally, 'little tortoises') lamb's liver wrapped in caul fat and braaied
smileys – slang term for boiled and roasted sheep heads; often sold in rural areas
sosatie – lamb cubes, marinated with garlic, tamarind juice and curry powder, then skewered with onions and apricots, and grilled; originally Malay; also made with chicken
venison – often springbok, but could be kudu, eland, blesbok or any other game meat
vienna – hot-dog sausage, usually pork
waterblommetjie bredie – Cape Malay stew of lamb with Cape Pondweed *(Aponogeton distachyos)* flowers, lemon juice and sorrel

Curries, Condiments & Spices

atchar – Cape Malay pickle of fruit and vegetables, flavoured with garlic, onion and curry
chakalaka sauce – spicy tomato-based sauce seasoned with onions, *peri peri*, green peppers and curry, and used to liven up *pap* and other dishes
curry – just as good as in India; head to Durban if you like your curry spicy, and to Cape Town (Bo-Kaap) for a milder, Malay version
peri peri/piri piri – hot chilli
samoosa – spicy Indian pastry filled with potatoes and peas; sometimes with mince or chicken

Hungry for a quick bite? Try a roasted mealie (cob of corn) or Durban's filling *bunny chow* (curry-to-go: half a loaf of bread, scooped out and filled with curry).

Bread & Sweets

koeksister – plaited doughnut dripping in syrup (very gooey and figure enhancing); the Cape Malay version is fluffier, spicier and dusted with coconut
konfyt – fruit preserve
malva pudding – delicious sponge dessert; sometimes called vinegar pudding, since it's traditionally made with apricot jam and vinegar
melktert – rich, custardlike tart made with milk, eggs, flour and cinnamon
roosterkoek – bread traditionally cooked on the braai
rusk – twice-cooked and particularly hard biscuit, best dipped in coffee
vetkoek – deep-fried dough ball sometimes stuffed with mince; called *amagwinya* in Xhosa

Grains, Legumes & Vegetables

amadumbe – yam-like potato; a favourite staple in KwaZulu-Natal
imbasha – Swazi fried delicacy of roasted maize and nuts
imifino – Xhosa dish of mealie meal and vegetables
mealie/mielie – cob of corn, popular when braaied
mealie meal – finely ground maize
mealie pap – maize porridge; a Southern African staple, best eaten with sauce or stew
morogo – leafy greens, usually wild spinach, boiled, seasoned and served with *pap*
pap and sous – maize porridge with a tomato and onion sauce or meat gravy
phutu – Zulu dish of crumbly maize porridge, often eaten with soured milk; called *umphokoqo* in Xhosa
samp – mix of maize and beans; see *umngqusho*
tincheki – boiled pumpkin cubes with sugar; common in Swaziland
ting – sorghum porridge; popular among the Tswana
umngqusho – *samp* (dried and crushed maize kernels) boiled, then mixed with beans, salt and oil, and simmered; a Xhosa delicacy (called *nyekoe* in Sotho)
umvubo – sour milk and *mealie meal*

Fish

kingklip – excellent firm-fleshed fish, usually pan-fried; South Africa's favourite fish
linefish – fresh fish caught on a line
snoek – firm-fleshed migratory fish that appears off the Cape in June and July; served smoked, salted or curried, and good braaied

Drinks

mampoer – moonshine made from just about any fruit but often with peaches, citrus fruits or apricots
rooibos – literally 'red bush' (Afrikaans); herbal tea that has therapeutic qualities. Look out for the 'red cappuccino', a caffeine-free equivalent using rooibos instead of coffee
springbok – cocktail featuring crème de menthe topped with Amarula Cream liqueur
steen – chenin blanc; most common variety of white wine
sundowner – any drink, but typically alcohol, drunk at sunset
umqombothi – sorghum beer, a low-alcohol and slightly sour traditional beer that is pinkish in colour and opaque
witblits – a white spirit distilled from grapes, mostly produced in the Western Cape

Rooibos (*Aspalathus linearis*) grows only in the Cederberg region of the Western Cape and has been used as a tea since the San inhabited the area. There's a renewed pride in this strictly South African beverage, sought after for its health benefits. Check out the dedicated rooibos route in Clanwilliiam.

People & Culture

Dubbed the 'rainbow nation' by Archbishop Desmond Tutu, South Africa has become more integrated in the two decades since its first democratic elections. There's still a long way to go, perhaps a generation or two, but people tend to live and work more harmoniously these days, and the nation is divided less by colour than by class. Lesotho and Swaziland have recently experienced political and economic problems, but their biggest issue is having the world's highest HIV/AIDS infection rates.

The numerous issues that stir racial tension and shake international confidence in South Africa include government corruption and the disparity between rich and poor; land reform and farm attacks; the controversial Black Economic Empowerment and affirmative action; and inflammatory tirades from the likes of Economic Freedom Fighters (EFF) leader Julius Malema. All have contributed to the weakening rand; between 2011 and 2015 its value dropped from roughly seven to the US dollar to 12 to the dollar.

Below the Poverty Line

South Africa: 31%

Lesotho: 49%

Swaziland: 69%

The country's reputation for crime continues to dent its considerable appeal as a tourism destination. It is important to keep things in perspective so as not to miss out on three inspiring and hope-filled countries at the tip of Africa. Visiting South Africa provides a rare chance to experience a nation that is rebuilding itself after profound change. A backdrop to all this change is magnificent natural scenery, and the remarkably deep bond – perhaps best expressed in the country's literature – that most South Africans feel for their land.

People & Economy

South Africa, Lesotho and Swaziland together form a beautiful and rich tapestry of cultures and ethnic groups. In addition to their cultural roots, the three countries also have fascinatingly complex and interlocking socio-economic compositions.

South Africa

South Africa's Gauteng province, which includes Johannesburg and Pretoria, is the economic engine of the country, generating over a third of South Africa's GDP – and 10% of Africa's. It's also the most densely populated and urbanised province. At the other end of the scale is the rural and underdeveloped Eastern Cape, where around 25% of adults are illiterate.

Unemployment

South Africa: 25%

Lesotho: 25%

Swaziland: 40%

Millions of immigrants from across the continent make their way to South Africa to take advantage of the country's powerhouse economy. While some arrive legally, many illegal immigrants live in the townships of Jo'burg and other cities, causing resentment among some locals, who accuse the outsiders of taking jobs, committing crime and increasing pressure on service delivery.

Beyond economics, different racial groups have complicated relationships. While much of the focus in South Africa has been on black–white relations, there is also friction and distrust between black people, coloured people and South Africans of Indian descent. Yet, locals are often surprisingly open when they talk about the stereotypes and prejudices that exist across racial lines. Relations within racial groups are also complex; ask a Zulu what he or she thinks about Xhosas or quiz English-speaking white people about their views on Afrikaners.

Lesotho

Lesotho's main link with South Africa has been the mining industry. For most of the 20th century, Lesotho's main export was labour, with about 60% of males working in South Africa, primarily in mining. In the early 1990s, at least 120,000 Basotho men were employed by South African mines, and up to one-third of Lesotho's household income was from wages earned by the miners. When the mining industry was restructured, the number of Lesotho miners was halved and many have returned home to Lesotho to join the ranks of the unemployed.

Chinese-owned textile factories subsequently became the country's major employers and exporters. In recent years, the US economic slowdown and increased competition from countries such as Vietnam and Bangladesh have taken their toll.

Economic immigrants from South Africa's neighbouring countries and beyond are widely employed in tourism and hospitality nationwide. During your stay, you will likely meet waiters, hotel porters and car guards from countries including Zimbabwe, Mozambique, Malawi and the Democratic Republic of the Congo.

Swaziland

Swaziland's socio-economic scene is almost completely wrapped up in that of its larger neighbour. About two-thirds of Swazi exports go to South Africa and more than 90% of goods and services are imported. Some 70% of Swazis live in rural areas and rely on subsistence farming for survival. Swazi culture is very strong and quite distinct from that of South Africa. The monarchy influences many aspects of life, from cultural ceremonies to politics. While some Swazis are proud of the royal traditions and suspicious of those who call for greater democracy, a growing number of human-rights and opposition activists believe power should be transferred from the king to the people.

Racial Groups

Black

The vast majority of South Africans – about 80% – are black Africans. Although subdivided into dozens of smaller groups, all ultimately trace their ancestry to the Bantu speakers who migrated to Southern Africa in the early part of the 1st millennium AD. Due to the destruction and dispersal caused by the *difaqane* (forced migration) in the 19th century, and to the forced removals and separations of the apartheid era, tribal affiliation tends to be much weaker in South Africa than in other areas of the continent.

In South Africa's uniquely multicultural but racially conscious society, people are not shy about referring to themselves and others as black, coloured or white. This can come as a bit of a shock for visitors from countries where such referrals are considered politically incorrect.

Today, discussions generally focus on ethno-linguistic groupings. With the constitution's elevation of 11 languages to the status of 'official' language, the concept of ethnicity is also gaining a second wind. The largest ethno-linguistic group is the Nguni, which includes Zulu, Swazi, Xhosa and Ndebele peoples. Other major groups are the Sotho-Tswana, the Tsonga-Shangaan and the Venda.

The Zulu maintain the highest-profile ethnic identity, and 23% of South Africans speak Zulu as a first language – including President Zuma. The second-largest group is the Xhosa, who have been extremely influential in politics. Nelson Mandela was Xhosa, as were many figures in the apartheid struggle, and Xhosa have traditionally formed the heart of the black professional class. About 16% of South Africa's population uses Xhosa as a first language.

Internet Users

South Africa: 48.9%

Lesotho: 5%

Swaziland: 24.7%

Other major groups include the Basotho (found primarily in and around Lesotho and South Africa's Free State), the Swazi (most of whom are in Swaziland) and the Tswana (who live primarily in the North West Province and Northern Cape, as well as neighbouring Botswana). The Ndebele and Venda peoples, found mostly in Mpumalanga and Limpopo respectively, are fewer in number, but have maintained very distinct cultures.

Coloured

During apartheid, 'coloured' was generally used as a catch-all term for anyone who didn't fit into one of the other racial categories. Despite this, a distinct coloured cultural identity has developed over the years – forged, at least in part, by white people's refusal to accept coloureds as equals, and coloureds' own refusal to be grouped socially with blacks.

Among the diverse ancestors of today's coloured population are Afrikaners and others of European descent, West African slaves, political prisoners and exiles from the Dutch East Indies, and some of South Africa's original Khoe-San peoples. One of the largest subgroups of coloureds is the Griqua.

For an insight into coloured society and culture, Chris van Wyk's *Shirley, Goodness and Mercy* and *Eggs to Lay, Chickens to Hatch* are entertaining memoirs about growing up in a coloured Jo'burg suburb.

Another major subgroup is the Cape Muslims, also know as the Cape Malays, with roots in places as widely dispersed as India, Indonesia and parts of East Africa. They have preserved their Asian-influenced culture and cuisine, which you can experience on a walking tour of Cape Town's Bo-Kaap neighbourhood.

Today, most coloured people live in the Western and Northern Capes, with a significant population also in the Eastern Cape. About 20% speak English as their first language, while about 80% are Afrikaans speakers; one of the oldest Afrikaans documents is a Quran transcribed using Arabic script. South Africa's roughly 4.6 million coloured people comprise about 9% of the total population.

White

Most of South Africa's approximately 4.6 million white people (about 9% of South Africans) are either Afrikaans-speaking descendents of the early European settlers or English speakers. The Afrikaners, who constitute about 5% of the country's total population, have had a disproportionate influence on South Africa's history. Rural areas of the country, with the exception of the Eastern Cape, KwaZulu-Natal and the former homelands, continue to be dominated by Afrikaners, who are united by language and by membership in the Dutch Reformed Church – the focal point of life in country towns.

The typical Afrikaner's genealogy includes about a third Dutch blood, with smaller percentages of French (mostly Huguenot), German, coloured and British blood.

While a few Afrikaners still dream of a *volkstaat* (an independent, racially pure Boer state), the urbanised middle class has become considerably more moderate. Happily, the further the distance between the apartheid era and the 'new South Africa', the more room there is for all Afrikaners to be proud of their heritage. Two reflections of this are the growing popularity of Oudtshoorn's Absa Klein Karoo National Arts Festival and the blossoming Afrikaans indie music scene.

About two-thirds of South Africa's white English speakers trace their roots to the British immigrants who began arriving in South Africa in the 1820s. Other white South Africans include about 70,000 Jews, a Greek community numbering 50,000-plus people and a similar amount of Portuguese.

Asian

The majority of South Africa's almost 1.3 million Asians are Indians. Many are descended from the indentured labourers brought to KwaZulu-Natal in the 19th century, while others trace their ancestry to the free 'passenger Indians' who came to South Africa during the same period as merchants and businesspeople. During apartheid, Indians were both discriminated against by whites and seen as white collaborators by some blacks.

Today's South African Indian population is primarily Hindu, with about 20% Muslims and small numbers of Christians. Close to 90% live in Durban and other urban areas of KwaZulu-Natal. Most speak English as a first language; Tamil or Hindi and Afrikaans are also spoken.

There are more than 300,000 Chinese people in South Africa, concentrated primarily in Johannesburg but running shops nationwide, and small numbers of other East Asians.

SOUTHERN AFRICA'S MELTING POPULATION POT

There are few countries where racial and ethnic conflicts have been as turbulent and high profile as in South Africa. The country's heart pulses with the blood of diverse groups including the ancient San, 17th-century Dutch settlers, 19th-century British traders, Bantu-speaking African peoples, Indians, Indonesians, Chinese, Jews and Portuguese. Yet it is only since 1994 that there has been any significant degree of collaboration and peace between the various groups.

During the apartheid era, the government attempted to categorise everyone into one of four major groups. The classifications – black (at various times also called African, 'native' and 'Bantu'), coloured, Asian or white – were often arbitrary and highly contentious. They were used to regulate where and how people could live and work, and became the basis for institutionalised inequality and intolerance. To get a feel for this, visit Jo'burg's Apartheid Museum, entered through chillingly evocative racial classification gates.

Today, discrimination based on wealth is threatening to replace racial discrimination. While the apartheid-era classification terms continue to be used, they work only to a certain extent, and within each of the four major categories are dozens of subgroups that are even more subjective and less clearly defined.

Lesotho and Swaziland were never subject to racial categorisation. This, plus the fact that both countries were for the most part formed around a single tribal group (the Basotho in Lesotho and the Swazi in Swaziland), means that the constant racial awareness that you'll experience while travelling in South Africa is largely absent from these societies.

Women

South Africa

Women have enjoyed a uniquely high profile during South Africa's turbulent history: they were at the centre of the anti-pass law demonstrations and bus boycotts of the 1950s, protesting under the slogan 'You strike the woman and you strike the rock'. Women are also well represented in South Africa's current parliament, the constitution guarantees women's rights, and the ruling African National Congress (ANC) party has a 50% women quota system.

However, the daily reality for many South African women is very different, with poverty, sexual violence and HIV/AIDS overshadowing other gains. South Africa has one of the world's highest rape rates, with more than 65,000 offences reported to the police annually. In one study, one in four men admitted to having raped a woman. A woman is raped every four minutes and gang rape is common. The brutal gang rape and mutilation of teenager Anene Boysen in the Overberg town of Bredasdorp in 2013 was a 'Delhi moment' for South Africa, sparking protests about the horrific epidemic and echoing the previous year's outcry in India.

Women are statistically more likely than men to be infected with HIV, and many women become infected at an early age. Worsening the situation is the threat of sexual violence, which often undermines the ability of young women to ensure their partner is wearing a condom.

> The Zulu word for grandmother is *gogo*. The *gogo* plays a vital role in many families and her monthly pension is often the only regular source of income for the extended family.

Lesotho

Basotho women shouldered a big share of economic, social and family responsibilities while their husbands and male relatives went to work in the mines in South Africa. As mining jobs disappeared, the textile industry became an important part of Lesotho's economy, and about 90% of the new jobs went to women.

Contrary to the trend elsewhere in the region, Basotho women are often better educated than their male counterparts, because many boys in rural areas are forced to tend cattle (or head off to South Africa to work), instead of spending time in the classroom. Lesotho has a high rape rate, due partly to entrenched beliefs in men's sexual entitlement.

> *Basali: Stories by and about Women in Lesotho*, edited by K Limakatso Kendall, provides good insights into Lesotho's rural life as seen through the eyes of local women.

Swaziland

Swazi women's rights have recently improved dramatically. The 2005 constitution guarantees women equal political, economic and social rights and reserves one-third of parliamentary seats for women, but this is not always instituted, and discriminatory practices continue. Traditional social systems discriminate against women, and one survey conducted by Unicef found that one-third of Swazi females had experienced sexual violence before they turned 18. But it is estimated that over 70% of small businesses in Swaziland are operated by women, who tend to be more entrepreneurial than the men.

Women in Parliament

South Africa: 41.5% (11th in world)

Lesotho: 26.7% (43rd)

Swaziland: 6.2% (134th)

Media

Having experienced decades of repression during apartheid, South Africa's media is coming into its own, despite threats to press freedom from the ANC's proposed Protection of State Information (or Secrecy) Bill. The national broadcaster, SABC, is an important source of news for South Africans, and is adjusting to its role as an independent voice. SABC currently has 20 radio stations and five TV channels; private channels are e.tv and M-Net.

South Africa's most popular English-language dailies include the *Daily Sun* (www.dailysun.co.za), *Star* (www.iol.co.za/the-star) and *Sowetan* (www.sowetanlive.co.za). All three primarily cater to English-literate black readers; the *Sowetan* began as an anti-apartheid publication and has a left-leaning editorial tone. The *Sunday Times* (www.timeslive.co.za) and *City Press* (www.citypress.co.za) are the nation's favourite Sunday papers, while the *Mail & Guardian* (mg.co.za) is a popular Friday paper among middle-class readers. In other languages, Afrikaans Sunday broadsheet *Rapport* and Zulu daily tabloid *Isolezwe* are the most popular reads.

South Africa's press freedom ranking, according to Reporters Without Borders, rose to 42nd in the world in 2014 (the US was 46th). Lesotho rose to 74th and Swaziland dropped to 156th (out of 180).

Lesotho's media is in a decent state, although the government still exercises considerable power. The *Lesotho Times* (lestimes.com), *Sunday Express* (sundayexpress.co.ls) and *Public Eye* are English-language weeklies. TV is state-run, as is the only national radio station, Radio Lesotho, but four private stations are available in Maseru.

Swaziland's media is mostly government-controlled, and includes the dailies the *Swazi Observer* (www.observer.org.sz) and privately owned *Times of Swaziland* (www.times.co.sz). TV channels are Swazi TV (www.swazitv.co.sz), operated by the Swaziland Television Authority, and privately owned Channel S. The Swaziland Broadcasting and Information Services delivers 18 hours daily of English radio programming.

Religion

Religion plays a central role in the lives of most people in South Africa, Lesotho and Swaziland and church attendance is generally high. Christianity is dominant in all three countries, with almost 80% of South Africans, a similar amount of Lesotho's population, and more than 60% of Swazis identifying themselves as Christians. Major South African denominations include the Dutch Reformed Church, which has more than a million members and more than 1000 churches across the country, and the considerably more flamboyant Zion Christian Church (ZCC), with up to six million followers in South Africa, plus more in neighbouring countries including Swaziland.

About 15% of South Africans are atheist and agnostic, while Muslims, Hindus and Jews combined make up less than 5% of the population. Up to two-thirds of South Africa's Indians have retained their Hindu faith. Islam has a small but growing following, particularly in the Cape. There is a declining Jewish community of about 70,000 people, mostly in Jo'burg and the Cape.

African traditional believers make up around 1% of South Africa's population, compared with 20% in Lesotho. However, their traditions and practices have a significant influence on the cultural fabric and life of the region. Visting the *sangoma* (traditional healer) for some *muti* (traditional medicine) is widespread, even among those who practise Christianity.

Arts

Cinema

South African cinema has seen a turnaround since 1994 and the film industry is bursting with new talent. The first major feature film directed by a black South African was *Fools* (1997) by Ramadan Suleman, who later directed *Zulu Love Letter* (2004). Other directors and films to look out for include Zola Maseko *(Drum)*, Zulfah Otto-Sallies *(Raya)*, Teboho Mahlatsi, Simon Wood *(Forerunners)*, Timothy Green *(Skeem)*, Khalo Matabane *(State of Violence)*, Gavin Hood *(Tsotsi)*, Oliver Hermanus *(Skoonheid)* and Sara Blecher *(Otelo Burning)*.

The most internationally acclaimed South African filmmaker is *Elysium* (2013) director Neill Blomkamp, who presents a dystopian vision of Jo'burg in *District 9* (2009) and *Chappie* (2015), both featuring the South African actor Sharlto Copley. Named one of Africa's most powerful celebrities by Forbes, Blomkamp was slated to direct Sigourney Weaver in *Alien 5* after *Chappie*.

The Forgotten Kingdom (2014), the first Sotho feature film, narrates a Basotho man's journey home to Lesotho. *Wah-Wah* (2006) recounts director Richard E Grant's childhood in Swaziland.

Literature

South Africa

South Africa has an extraordinarily rich literary history, and there's no better way to get a sense of the country than by delving into local literature.

Many of the first black South African writers were missionary-educated, including Sol Plaatje. In 1930 his epic romance, *Mhudi*, became one of the first books published in English by a black South African. The first major South African novel published internationally was Olive Schreiner's *Story of an African Farm* (1883), which depicts colonial life in the Karoo.

In 1948 South Africa made an impression on the international literary scene with Alan Paton's global bestseller, *Cry, the Beloved Country*. Today, this beautifully crafted tale is still one of the country's most widely recognised titles.

Nadine Gordimer's acclaimed *A Guest of Honour* was published in 1970. The country's first Nobel laureate in literature (1991), her most famous novel, *July's People* (1981), depicts the collapse of white rule.

In the 1960s and '70s Afrikaner writers gained prominence as powerful voices for the opposition. Poet and novelist Breyten Breytenbach was jailed for becoming involved with the liberation movement, while André Brink's novel *Looking on Darkness* was the first Afrikaans book to be banned by the apartheid government. His autobiography, *A Fork in the Road* (2009), gives a fascinating account of anti-apartheid activities by Afrikaners.

Afrikaner poet Ingrid Jonker is often compared with Sylvia Plath. Nelson Mandela read Jonker's poem 'The Child Who Was Shot Dead by Soldiers at Nyanga', inspired by protests against the pass laws, at his inauguration in 1994.

The 1970s also gave rise to several influential black poets, including Mongane Wally Serote, a veteran of the liberation struggle. His work gives insights into the lives of black South Africans during the worst years of oppression.

JM Coetzee gained international acclaim with his novel *Disgrace* (1999), which won him his second Booker Prize. Coetzee was awarded the Nobel Prize for Literature in 2003.

One of the most prominent contemporary authors is Zakes Mda. With the publication of *Ways of Dying* in 1995, Mda became an acclaimed novelist. His memoir, *Sometimes There is a Void* (2011), is a transfixing account of his exile in Lesotho and eventual return to South Africa.

Lesotho & Swaziland

Little Lesothan literature is available in English. However, Thomas Mofolo's *Chaka* (1925), one of the greatest 20th-century African novels, and *Traveller to the East* (1907), the first Sesotho novel, have been translated into English. Other authors to look out for include Mpho 'M'atsepo Nthunya, who writes about female experiences in the autobiographical *Singing Away the Hunger* (1996).

Most of the books available about Swaziland were written during the colonial era by Brits. Noted indigenous writers include James Shadrack Mkhulunyelwa Matsebula, who pioneered the use of Swati as a written language. Stanley Musa N Matsebula's novels, including *Siyisike Yinye Nje* (We Are in the Same Boat; 1989), opened up the debate about gender inequality in Swaziland.

Although he often portrays South African society negatively, JM Coetzee's writing is exquisite and gives a sense of the violence and isolation under apartheid. Look out for *Disgrace* and *Age of Iron*.

Architecture

Among the highlights of Southern African indigenous architecture are the 'beehive huts' that you'll see dotted throughout the region, including in Swaziland and rural parts of KwaZulu-Natal. A typical homestead, or *umuzi* as it's known in Zulu, consists of a group of these dwellings arranged in a circle around a cattle kraal (enclosure), and surrounded by a fence made of stones or bush. Traditionally the huts were set on an eastward-facing slope, with the chief's residence at the highest point.

In the Xhosa areas of the rural Eastern Cape, you'll see thatched, round, straight-walled huts scattered over the hillsides, often painted turquoise or pink.

Elaborately painted Ndebele houses – a relatively recent tradition – are another highlight. Their exteriors sport brightly coloured geometric motifs or more elaborate artwork, which may depict cars, street lamps, aeroplanes and other symbols of the modern world.

Basotho homes often feature geometric and sometimes highly symbolic mural art known as *litema*. During the anti-apartheid struggles, some Basotho women used *litema* as a political statement, painting their houses in the gold, black and green colours of the ANC. Today, *litema* is used for special celebrations and holidays, such as births, weddings and religious feasts.

South Africa's national football (soccer) team is called Bafana Bafana ('the boys', in Zulu). The women's team is called Banyana Banyana (the Girls).

The colonial era left a rich architectural legacy. One of its most attractive building styles is the graceful, gabled Cape Dutch house so typical of the Western Cape. Pretoria also showpieces colonial-era architecture, with an impressive collection of conservative and stately creations including the famous Union Buildings, designed by English architect Sir Herbert Baker.

Jo'burg grew quickly after the discovery of gold in 1886 and mining magnates were eager to display their wealth with palatial homes and

SPORT: ALMOST A RELIGION

South Africans are sports fanatics, with club sports generating passionate loyalties. Football (soccer) is the most popular spectator sport, followed by rugby and cricket. Traditionally, the majority of football fans were black, while cricket and rugby attracted predominately white crowds, but this is changing.

Hosting the 2010 World Cup was a historic event for South Africa. The action took place at 10 venues from Cape Town to Polokwane (Pietersburg), and the country spent more than US$1 billion on building new stadiums and renovating existing ones.

The second most popular sport, South African rugby has benefited from development programs across the colour divides. The beloved national team, the Springboks (or 'Boks'), is one of the world's best, having won the 2007 and historic 1995 World Cups. South Africa's cricket team, nicknamed the Proteas, is also one of the world's best-performing, and fans enjoy a friendly rivalry with fellow members of the Commonwealth.

grand offices. In Durban, the designs show more art deco influences, giving the city its own style. Cape Town's building boom in the 1930s also left a wealth of impressive art deco designs, especially around Greenmarket Sq. A highlight is the colourful houses in the Bo-Kaap area.

One of the most noteworthy examples of new South African architecture is the Constitutional Court in Jo'burg. Another is the new Northern Cape Legislature Building in Kimberley, notable for its lack of columns and the minimisation of hard right angles and lines. In Pretoria, Freedom Park, an inspiring monument to people who died in the name of freedom, faces the modernist celebration of Afrikaner nationalism, the Voortrekker Monument.

Visual Arts

South African art had its beginnings with the San, who left their distinctive designs on rock faces and cave walls throughout the region. When European painters arrived, many of their early works centred on depictions of Africa for colonial enthusiasts back home, although with time, a more South Africa–centred focus developed.

Black artists were sidelined for many decades. Gerard Sekoto was one of the first to break through the barriers of racism, becoming a major figure in South African modern art. Throughout the apartheid era, racism, oppression and violence were common themes. Many black artists who were unable to afford materials adopted cheaper alternatives, such as lino prints.

A recent lack of public funds for the arts sector has meant that it has become more reliant on corporate collectors and the tourism industry. Contemporary art ranges from the vibrant crafts sold in the Venda region, or on the side of the road in cities and tourist areas, to high-priced paintings hanging in galleries. Innovative township artists are using 'found' materials such as telephone wire, safety pins, beads, plastic bags and tin cans. Local sculpture is also diverse; artists working in various media include the Venda woodcarvers and bronze sculptor Dylan Lewis.

See www.artthrob.co.za for news, features and listings on South Africa's contemporary visual arts scene.

Lesotho is more renowned for its craftwork than its fine art. The colourful Basotho blankets and conical hats are national trademarks, and craft centres in Maseru and northern Lesotho sell works ranging from tapestries to horsehair fly whisks.

Swaziland has, similarly, realised the value of local crafts as a tourist drawcard, and galleries throughout the country sell work from carvings and artefacts to handmade candles and glass.

Individual works by major 20th-century and contemporary South African artists, including Irma Stern, Pierneef, William Kentridge and Tretchikoff, have fetched over US$1 million at auction.

Theatre & Dance

After the colonial era, home-grown playwrights, performers and directors gradually emerged. Writer and director Athol Fugard was a major influence in the 1960s in developing black talent, and more recently wrote *Tsotsi*. Other big names include actor and playwright John Kani, a veteran (like Fugard) of Jo'burg's Market Theatre; try to catch a performance here or at Cape Town's Fugard Theatre, Baxter Theatre Centre or Artscape.

Jo'burg's Dance Umbrella (www.danceforumsouthafrica.co.za) festival of contemporary dance and choreography, held in February and March, brings together local and international artists and provides a stage for new work.

Lesotho and Swaziland both have a strong tradition of dance, famously seen at Swaziland's *umhlanga* (reed) dance performed by traditionally dressed maidens. The country's altogether more manly *sibhaca* dance, a vigorous display of foot-stomping, is performed by men and sometimes takes the form of a competition. Traditional dance and music feature at Lesotho's Morija Festival (late September or early October), and Malealea Lodge offers nightly performances by local bands and choirs.

The first all-race theatre venue was the Market Theatre, which opened in 1976. The run-down buildings at Jo'burg's old 'Indian' fruit market were converted and patrons and performers defied the apartheid government's notorious Group Areas Act.

Environment

South Africa has incredible biological diversity, and for Africa in particular is highly urbanised. Lesotho is far more rural while Swaziland is somewhere between the two. The wildlife in this region is Africa at its best: South Africa boasts some of the most accessible wildlife-viewing on the entire continent. Probably your best chance of seeing the Big Five – rhino, buffalo, elephant, leopard and lion – is in that country.

The Land & Sea

A windswept and beautiful coast is the face that South Africa turns to the rest of the world – tempestuous and tamed, stormy and sublime. It spans two oceans as it winds its way down the Atlantic seaboard in the west and up into the warmer Indian Ocean waters to the east. In all, the country has more than 2500km of coastline. Two major ocean currents shape the country's climate and provide for a rich marine life. The chilly Benguela current surges up from Antarctica along the country's Atlantic Coast and is laden with plankton. The north-to-south Mozambique/Agulhas current gives the east coast its warmer waters.

South Africa measures around 1,219,090 sq km, or five times the size of the UK. It's Africa's ninth-largest and fifth-most-populous country.

And this is just the start of the region's topographical wealth. Head further inland, and you'll find yourself climbing from the eastern lowlands (lowveld) to the cool heights of the Drakensberg Escarpment and onto the vast plateau (highveld) that forms the heart of the country. This plateau, which averages about 1500m in height, drops off again in the northwestern part of the country to the low-lying Kalahari basin.

The Drakensberg range is at its most rugged in tiny Lesotho – a 30,355-sq-km patch of mountain peaks and highland plateau that is completely surrounded by South Africa. It has the highest lowest point of any country in the world – 1380m, in southern Lesotho's Senqu (Orange) River valley.

Swaziland is the smallest of the Southern African trio at only 17,363 sq km in area, but with a remarkable diversity of landscapes, climates and ecological zones for its size. These range from low-lying savannah to the east, rolling hills towards the centre, and rainforest and perpetually fog-draped peaks in the northwest.

Wildlife

South Africa

South Africa is home to the world's three largest land mammals (the African elephant, white rhino and hippopotamus), its tallest (giraffe), fastest (cheetah) and smallest (pygmy shrew).

The country's 800-plus bird species include the world's largest (ostrich), the heaviest flying bird (Kori bustard) and the smallest raptor (pygmy falcon).

Off its long coastline is a rich diversity of marine life – 11,000 species have been recorded. Eight whale species are found in South African waters including the largest mammal in the world, the blue whale. Although it's the great white shark that snares most of the headlines, turtles, seabirds and penguins are also popular sightings.

THE GREAT IVORY DEBATE

In 1990, following a massive campaign by various conservation organisations, the UN Convention on International Trade in Endangered Species (CITES) banned ivory trading in an effort to protect Africa's then-declining elephant populations. This promoted recovery of elephant populations in areas where they had previously been ravaged. Yet in South Africa – where elephants had long been protected – the elephant populations continued to grow, leading to widespread habitat destruction.

Solutions to the problem of elephant overpopulation have included creating transfrontier parks to allow animals to migrate over larger areas, relocating animals, small-scale elephant contraception efforts, and – most controversially – culling.

In 2002, after much pressure, CITES relaxed its worldwide ivory trading ban to allow ivory from legally culled elephants to be sold. The decision has been strongly disputed by several governments on the grounds that resuming trade will increase demand for ivory and, thus, encourage poaching. The idea behind the move was that earnings would benefit elephant conservation efforts and communities living around elephant areas, and that CITES would monitor whether poaching increased after the ban was relaxed.

The most recently approved major one-off ivory sale was in mid-2008, when 108 tonnes of ivory from South Africa (51 tonnes), Namibia, Botswana and Zimbabwe was exported to China in a CITES-authorised transaction. Following such a sale, CITES mandates a nine-year resting period during which no additional ivory sales from these countries are permitted. In China – long one of the main markets for the illegal ivory trade – ivory is used for everything from jewellery and artwork to mobile-phone ornamentation.

Endangered species include black rhinos (sometimes spotted in uMkhuze Game Reserve, and Hluhluwe-iMfolozi Park); riverine rabbits (found only near rivers in the central Karoo); wild dogs (Hluhluwe-iMfolozi Park and Kruger National Park); and roan antelope.

Endangered bird species include the wattled crane and the blue swallow. The African penguin and the Cape vulture are threatened.

Lesotho

Due primarily to its altitude, Lesotho is home to fewer animals than much of the rest of the region. Those you may encounter include rheboks, jackals, mongooses, meerkats, elands and rock hyraxes. However, Lesotho's montane areas are of particular interest for their rare smaller species. Many are found only in the Drakensberg, including the highly threatened Maloti minnow, the African ice rat, several species of lizards and geckos, and the Lesotho river frog.

The country's almost 300 recorded bird species include the lammergeier (bearded vulture) and the southern bald ibis.

Among Lesotho's earliest wild inhabitants were dinosaurs: the small, fast-running Lesothosaurus was named after the country.

Swaziland

Swaziland has about 120 mammal species, representing one-third of Southern Africa's nonmarine mammal species. Many (including elephants, rhinos and lions) have been introduced, and larger animals are restricted to nature reserves and private wildlife farms. Mongoose and large-spotted genets are common, and hyenas and jackals are found in the reserves. Leopards are rarely seen.

Swaziland's varied terrain supports abundant birdlife, including the blue crane, ground woodpecker and lappet-faced vulture, and more species have been spotted in the country than in the larger Kruger National Park.

Safari & Birding Guides

Field Guide to Mammals of Southern Africa, by Chris and Tilde Stuart

A Field Guide to the Tracks and Signs of Southern and East African Wildlife, by Chris and Tilde Stuart

The Safari Companion: A Guide to Watching African Mammals, by Richard Estes

Birds of Southern Africa, by Ber Van Perlo

Newman's Birds of Southern Africa, by Kenneth Newman

Birds of Southern Africa, by Ian Sinclair et al

Watching Wildlife

The most straightforward and cheapest way to visit the parks (especially if you're in a group) is usually with a hired car. A 2WD is adequate in most parks, but during winter when the grass is high, you'll be able to see more with a 4WD or other high-clearance vehicle. Organised safaris are readily arranged with major tour operators and with backpacker-oriented outfits.

Several major parks (including Kruger, Hluhluwe-iMfolozi and Pilanesberg) offer guided wilderness walks accompanied by armed rangers. These are highly recommended, as the subtleties of the bush can be much better experienced on foot than in a vehicle. Book well in advance with the relevant park authority. Shorter morning and afternoon walks are also possible at many wildlife parks, and can generally be booked the same day.

Sasol eBirds of Southern Africa features images, distribution maps and descriptions of birds. This great app is essentially a digital version of the Sasol field guidebook. Compare birds, store a list of sightings and verify an identity by matching it to one of 630 recorded birdcalls.

Throughout South Africa, park infrastructure is of high quality. You can often get by without a guide, although you'll almost certainly see and learn more with one. All national parks have rest camps offering good-value accommodation, ranging from campsites to self-catering cottages. Many have restaurants, shops and petrol pumps. Advance bookings for accommodation are essential during holiday periods; at other times it's available at short notice.

Safari Safety

One of South Africa's major attractions is the chance to go on safari and get 'up close and personal' with the wildlife. Remember, however, that the animals aren't tame and their actions are often unpredictable. Some tips for staying safe:

- Never get between a mother and her young.
- Never get between a hippo and the water.
- Watch out for black rhinos (although they are rare), which will charge just about anything.
- Be careful around buffalo herds – they charge without warning and the whole herd will charge together.
- Although elephants often appear docile, never take them for granted – be especially careful around females with young and agitated young males.
- Remember that a fake charge from an elephant is probably a precursor to the real thing.

ENJOYING SOUTH AFRICA'S MARINE ENVIRONMENT

There are many ways to enjoy South Africa's unique and plentiful marine life. Spending time on top of, or under, the water could prove to be a highlight of your trip. In the Western Cape, Hermanus is regarded as the best land-based whale-watching destination in the world: southern right whales cruise past from June to December.

A unique opportunity exists to come face to face with a great white shark in KwaZulu-Natal and the Western Cape. Despite its detractors, shark-cage diving remains a popular adventure sport. And scuba diving is all the rage off the coast of KwaZulu-Natal, with Aliwal Shoal considered one of the best dive sites in the world. Colourful coral, turtles, rays and many species of sharks can be seen.

The Greatest Shoal on Earth is the sardine run that occurs between May and July, when a seething mass of sardines appears off the coasts of the Eastern Cape and KwaZulu-Natal, stretching for up to 15km. Predators, such as sharks, dolphins and seabirds, come from far and wide to gorge themselves, and snorkelling or diving around the shoal is an incredible experience.

THE CAPE FLORAL KINGDOM

The Cape Floral Kingdom – parts of which are now a Unesco World Heritage Site – is the smallest of the world's six floral kingdoms, but the most diverse, with 1300 species per 10,000 sq km. This is some 900 more species than are found in the South American rainforests. The main vegetation type is *fynbos* (fine bush), characterised by small, narrow leaves and stems. The *fynbos* environment hosts nearly 8500 plant species, most of which are unique to the area. Some members of the main *fynbos* families – heaths, proteas and reeds – have been domesticated elsewhere and are relatively widespread, but many species have a remarkably small range.

The Cape Floral Kingdom extends roughly from Cape Point east almost to Grahamstown and north to the Olifants River, and includes the Kogelberg and parts of several biosphere reserves. However, most of the remaining indigenous vegetation is found only in protected areas, such as Table Mountain and the Cape Peninsula.

When to Watch

Wildlife-watching is rewarding at any time of year, although spotting tends to be easier in the cooler, dry winter months (June to September) when foliage is less dense and animals congregate at waterholes. The summer (late November to March) is rainy, warmer and scenic, with greener landscapes, although animals are more widely dispersed and may be difficult to see.

Birding is good year-round, with spring (September to November) and summer generally the best times.

Plants

South Africa's more than 20,000 plant species represent 10% of the world's total, although the country constitutes only 1% of the earth's land surface. Dozens of flowers that are domesticated elsewhere grow wild here, including gladioli, proteas, birds of paradise and African lilies. South Africa is also the only country with one of the world's six floral kingdoms entirely within its borders. In the drier northwest are succulents (dominated by euphorbias and aloes) and annuals, which flower brilliantly after the spring rains.

South Africa has few natural forests. They were never extensive, and today there are only remnants. Temperate forests occur on the southern coastal strip between George and Humansdorp, in the KwaZulu-Natal Drakensberg and in Mpumalanga. Subtropical forests are found northeast of Port Elizabeth in areas just inland from the Wild Coast, and in KwaZulu-Natal.

In the north are savannah areas, dotted with acacias and thorn trees.

Lesotho is notable for its high-altitude flora, including Cape alpine flowers and the spiral aloe *(Aloe polyphylla)*, the national flower, which is found on the slopes of the Maluti Mountains and occurs naturally only in Lesotho.

Swaziland's grasslands, forests, savannahs and wetlands host about 3500 plant species, or about 14% of Southern Africa's recorded plant life.

The Wildlife & Environmental Society of South Africa (www.wessa.org.za) is a leading environmental advocacy organisation that runs a high-profile Rhino Initiative to stop the illegal trade in rhino horn.

National Parks & Protected Areas

South Africa

South Africa has close to 600 national parks and reserves, many featuring wildlife, while others are primarily wilderness sanctuaries or hiking areas.

All national parks charge a daily conservation fee, discounted for South African residents and nationals of Southern African Development Community (SADC) countries.

In addition to its national parks, South Africa is party to several transfrontier conservation areas. These include the still-in-process Greater

TOP PARKS & RESERVES

Location	Park/Reserve	Features	Activities	Best time to visit
Cape Peninsula	Table Mountain National Park	rocky headlands, seascapes, African penguins, elands, water birds, bonteboks	hiking, mountain biking	year-round
Western Cape	Cederberg Wilderness Area	mountainous and rugged; San rock paintings, sandstone formations, plant life	hiking	year-round
Mpumalanga/ Limpopo	Kruger National Park	savannah, woodlands, thornveld; the Big Five	vehicle safaris, wildlife walks	year-round
	Blyde River Canyon Nature Reserve	canyon, caves, river; stunning vistas	hiking, kloofing (canyoning)	year-round
Northern Cape	Augrabies Falls National Park	desert, river, waterfalls; klipspringers, rock dassies; striking scenery	hiking, canoeing, rafting	Apr-Sep
	|Ai-|Ais/ Richtersveld Transfrontier Park	mountainous desert; haunting beauty; klipspringers, jackals, zebras, plants, birds	hiking	Apr-Sep
Eastern Cape	Addo Elephant National Park	dense bush, grasslands, forested kloofs; elephants, black rhinos, buffaloes	vehicle safaris, walking trails, horse riding	year-round
	Tsitsikamma National Park	coast, cliffs, rivers, ravines, forests; Cape clawless otters, baboons, monkeys, birdlife	hiking	year-round

Mapungubwe Transfrontier Conservation Area linking South Africa, Zimbabwe and Botswana; Kgalagadi Transfrontier Park, combining the Northern Cape's former Kalahari Gemsbok National Park with Botswana's Gemsbok National Park; the Maloti-Drakensberg Peace Park, which links Sehlabathebe National Park and other areas of the Lesotho Drakensberg with their South African counterparts in uKhahlamba-Drakensberg; and the Great Limpopo Transfrontier Park, which spans the borders of South Africa, Mozambique and Zimbabwe. Private wildlife reserves also abound.

In total, just under 3% of South African land has national park status, with an estimated 4% to 5% more enjoying other types of protective status. The government has started teaming up with private landowners to bring private conservation land under government protection, with the goal of increasing the total amount of conservation land to over 10%.

In addition to this, South Africa has 21 Marine Protected Areas (MPAs) designed to protect and stabilise fish and other marine-life populations

Location	Park/Reserve	Features	Activities	Best time to visit
KwaZulu-Natal	Hluhluwe-iMfolozi Park	lush, subtropical vegetation, savannah; rhinos, giraffes, lions, elephants, birds	wilderness walks, wildlife-watching	May-Oct
	iSimangaliso Wetland Park	wetlands, coastal grasslands; elephants, birds, hippos	wilderness walks, vehicle/boat safaris	Mar-Nov
	uMkhuze Game Reserve	savannah, woodlands, swamp; rhinos and almost everything else; hundreds of bird species	guided walks, bird walks, vehicle safaris	year-round
	uKhahlamba-Drakensberg Park	awe-inspiring Drakensberg escarpment; fantastic scenery and wilderness areas	hiking	year-round
Free State	Golden Gate Highlands National Park	spectacular sandstone cliffs and outcrops; zebras, jackals, rheboks, elands, birds	hiking	year-round
Lesotho	Sehlabathebe National Park	mountain wilderness; wonderful isolation; rheboks, baboons; bearded vultures	hiking	Mar-Nov
Swaziland	Malolotja Nature Reserve	mountains, streams, waterfalls, grasslands, forests; rich bird and plant life, impalas, klipspringers	hiking	year-round

against overfishing, pollution, uncontrolled tourism and mining. The world's seventh-largest MPA was declared in 2013 and lies 2000km southeast of the country's coastline around Prince Edward and Marion Islands. Marine life falling under the protection of the new MPA includes albatrosses, penguins, fur seals, killer whales and Patagonian toothfish.

CapeNature (☎021-483 0190; www.capenature.org.za) Promotes nature conservation in the Western Cape, and is responsible for permits and bookings for Western Cape reserves.

Ezemvelo KZN Wildlife (☎033-845 1000; www.kznwildlife.com) Responsible for wildlife parks in KwaZulu-Natal.

Komatiland Forests Eco-Tourism (☎013-754 2724; www.komatiecotourism.co.za) Oversees forest areas, promotes ecotourism and manages hiking trails around Mpumalanga.

South African National Parks (SANParks; ☎012-426 5000; www.sanparks.org) The best place to start your safari.

Lesotho

In part because land tenure allows communal access to natural resources, less than 1% of Lesotho is protected – the lowest protected-area coverage of any nation in Africa. Sehlabathebe National Park is the main conservation area, known for its isolated wilderness. Other protected areas include Ts'ehlanyane National Park and Bokong Nature Reserve.

Swaziland

About 4% of Swaziland's area is protected. Its conservation areas tend to be low-key, with fewer visitors than their South African counterparts, and good value for money. They include Mlilwane Wildlife Sanctuary, Mkhaya Game Reserve, Malolotja Nature Reserve, which is mainly for hiking, and Hlane Royal National Park. Mlilwane, Mkhaya and Hlane are included in the Wild Card program (www.sanparks.org/wild).

Rhinos aren't named for their colour, but for their lip shape: 'white' comes from *wijde* (wide) – the Boers' term for the fatter-lipped white rhino.

Environmental Issues

South Africa

South Africa is the world's third most biologically diverse country. It's also one of Africa's most urbanised, with over 50% of the population living in towns and cities. Major challenges for the government include managing increasing urbanisation while protecting the environment.

Land degradation is one of the country's most serious problems, with about one-quarter of South Africa's land considered to be severely degraded. In former homeland areas, years of overgrazing and overcropping have resulted in massive soil depletion. This, plus poor overall conditions, is pushing people to the cities, further increasing urban pres-

RHINO POACHING IN SOUTH AFRICA

Rhino horn has long been a sought-after commodity in some Asian countries. It is a status symbol and is believed to be a healing agent. A single rhino horn can fetch a lot of money on the black market in countries such as Vietnam and China.

This market has provided plenty of motivation for the illegal trade in rhino horn. From the late 1970s to mid-1990s, rhino populations were periodically decimated in Africa by poaching.

In recent years rhino poaching has again escalated sharply. In 2003, 22 rhinos were poached in South Africa; in 2012 this figure rose to 668; and by the end of 2014, a staggering 1020 rhinos had been poached that year. Of that figure almost 700 were slaughtered in Kruger National Park, a place that is home to 60% of the world's remaining rhino population.

Kruger National Park is officially part of the Great Limpopo Transfrontier Park, which combines Kruger with Limpopo in Mozambique. Many poachers come from Mozambique through the long, porous border between the two parks. In Mozambique, Limpopo's underresourced and undercapacity anti-poaching unit does battle with poaching syndicates that have unlimited resources.

Overwhelmed by the challenge of monitoring the park's huge and largely unattended border with Mozambique, the South African government is embarking upon a massive relocation program. It earmarked at least 500 rhinos for transport to safer areas within Kruger and other parks in South Africa and neighbouring countries, with the vast majority moved in 2015.

In the meantime, innovative ways of tracking down poachers are being deployed. These include Shotspotter, a technology usually rolled out in crime-ridden cities in the USA. When a shot is fired, hidden microphones in the bush pick up the sound, triangulate it and feed location information to rangers and police who can respond in real time.

For more information on the ongoing battle to save the African rhino from extinction, check out www.savetherhino.org and www.stoprhinopoaching.com.

sures. The distorted rural–urban settlement pattern is a legacy of the apartheid era, with huge population concentrations in townships that generally lack adequate utilities and infrastructure.

South Africa receives an average of only 500mm of rainfall annually, and droughts are common. To meet demand for water, all major South African rivers have been dammed or modified. While this has improved water supply to many areas, it has also disrupted local ecosystems and caused increased silting.

South Africa has long been at the forefront among African countries in conservation of its fauna. However, funding is tight and will likely remain so as long as many South Africans still lack access to basic amenities. Rhino poaching across the country, and particularly in Kruger National Park, is exacerbated by underfunding. Potential solutions include public-private-sector conservation partnerships, and increased contributions from private donors and international conservation bodies such as World Wide Fund for Nature (WWF).

Estimates have put South Africa's potential shale gas deposits at 485 trillion cubic feet of gas. That's gained a lot of interest from oil companies, and according to Econometrix (in a report commissioned by Shell) the shale gas industry could be worth R200 billion annually to GDP and lead to the creation of 700,000 jobs. But hydraulic fracturing (fracking) to extract the gas is either banned or under a moratorium in many countries including South Africa. There are serious environmental concerns about the safety of the technology used in fracking, which uses large amounts of clean water mixed with sand and a 'chemical cocktail' to crack underground rocks and release the shale gas. The debate over fracking in South Africa's Northern Cape (in the Karoo) continues to rage with these serious environmental concerns pitted against vested economic interests – in particular large oil companies. By the end of 2014 it appeared that the South African government was determined to proceed with the controversial mining technique, drafting new regulations with exploratory licences due to be granted in mid-2015.

Scorched: South Africa's Changing Climate, by Leonie Joubert, is a thought-provoking journey through South Africa. It transforms climate change and other environmental issues from dry discourse into sobering, near-at-hand realities.

Going Green

More than 90% of South Africa's electricity is coal-generated – more than double the international average. Yet on a local level, there are many commendable projects showcasing the country's slow but sure progress towards going green.

Lynedoch EcoVillage (Map p106; www.sustainabilityinstitute.net) South Africa's first ecologically designed and socially mixed community is slowly taking form, with the design of energy-efficient houses and community buildings, and a focus on the establishment of a self-sufficient community.

Monwabisi Park Eco-Cottages Project Under the auspices of the Shaster Foundation, the Monwabisi Park squatters' settlement of Khayelitsha is gradually being transformed into an ecovillage: informal shacks are being replaced by community-built eco-cottages.

The Kuyasa Project More than 2000 low-income houses in Cape Town's Khayelitsha township have been retrofitted with renewable energy technologies such as solar water heaters, energy-efficient lighting and insulated ceilings. In addition to promoting energy savings (averaging about 40% per household), the project has also created jobs and offered other sustainable development benefits.

SAN Parks (p557) Facilities at parks in the SANParks network are being upgraded with installation of solar water heaters and other energy-saving devices to be more energy efficient.

Tree planting More than 200,000 indigenous trees were planted as part of the Greening Soweto Project, which sought to beautify the massive township as a legacy of the 2010 FIFA World Cup. The project incorporates ongoing environmental awareness programs.

Wind farms Two wind farm projects are under way near Cape Town, with the Darling Wind Farm – a national demonstration project – already linked to the national power grid.

Lesotho

Environmental discussion in Lesotho centres on the controversial Highlands Water Project. Among the concerns are disruption of traditional communities, flooding of agricultural lands and possible adverse ecological impacts on the Senqu (Orange) River.

Other issues include animal population pressure (resulting in overgrazing) and soil erosion. About 40 million tonnes of topsoil are lost annually, with sobering predictions that there may well be no cultivatable land left by 2040.

On a brighter note, Lesotho and South Africa are working together within the framework of the Maluti-Drakensberg Transfrontier Conservation and Development Project to protect these two alpine areas.

Swaziland

Three of Swaziland's major waterways (the Komati, Lomati and Usutu Rivers) arise in South Africa, and Swaziland has been closely involved in South Africa's river control efforts. Drought is a recurring problem in eastern lowveld areas. Other concerns include lack of community participation in conservation efforts, low levels of environmental awareness and lack of government support.

Responsible Travel

Tourism is big in Southern Africa, and making environmentally and culturally sensitive choices can have a significant impact. Following are a few guidelines for visitors:

- Travel involves a responsibility to local cultures and people – consider giving back to local communities through a donation of money to a reputable NGO working in the field, or through volunteering some of your time.
- Always ask permission before photographing people.
- Avoid indiscriminate gift giving. Donations to recognised projects are more sustainable, less destructive to local cultural values and have a better chance of reaching those who need them most.
- Support local enterprises, buy locally whenever possible, and buy souvenirs directly from those who make them.
- Seek entities that promote sustainable, community-oriented tourism. The list on the website of Fair Trade in Tourism South Africa (www.fairtrade.travel) is a good place to start.
- Avoid buying items made from ivory, skin, shells etc.
- Carry a Sassi wallet card (downloadable from www.wwfsassi.co.za) if you enjoy dining at seafood restaurants.
- For cultural attractions, try to pay fees directly to the locals involved, rather than to tour company guides or other middlepeople.
- Respect local culture and customs.
- Don't litter. On treks, in parks or when camping, carry out all your litter (most parks give you a bag for this purpose), and leave trails, parks and campsites cleaner than you found them.
- Maximise your 'real' time with locals, choosing itineraries that are well integrated with the communities in the areas where you will be travelling.

Wildlife & Habitat

South Africa encompasses one of the most diverse landscapes on the entire continent. There are habitats ranging from verdant forests, stony deserts and soaring mountains to lush bushveld and classic African savannahs. It is home to penguins and flamingos, caracals and sables, wild dogs, dwarf mongooses and hulking African elephants. The number and variation of species is astounding and a deep immersion into wildlife-watching is a pure joy of travel here. Showcasing this diversity are more than 700 publicly owned reserves (including 19 national parks) and about 200 private reserves, with world-renowned Kruger National Park and Kgalagadi Transfrontier Park being the largest.

Zebras (p568)

GODEEPBLUE/GETTY IMAGES ©

Cats

The three big cats provide the high point for many South African safaris. The presence of these apex predators, even the mere suggestion that they may be nearby, is enough to draw the savannah taut with attention.

Leopard

1 Weight 30-60kg (female), 40-90kg (male); length 170-300cm. The leopard relies on expert camouflage to stay hidden. At night there is no mistaking the bone-chilling groans that sound like wood being sawn at high volume.

Lion

2 Weight 120-150kg (female), 150-225kg (male); length 210-275cm (female), 240-350cm (male). Those lions sprawled out in the shade are actually Africa's most feared predators. Equipped with teeth that tear effortlessly through bone and tendon, they can take down an animal as large as a bull giraffe. Females do all the hunting; swaggering males fight among themselves and eat what the females catch.

Caracal

3 Weight 8-19kg; length 80-120cm. The caracal is a tawny cat with extremely long, pointy ears. It is able to make vertical leaps of 3m and swat birds out of the air.

Wildcat

4 Weight 3-6.5kg; length 65-100cm. If you see what looks like a tabby wandering along fields and forest edges, you may be seeing a wildcat, the direct ancestor of our domesticated house cats.

Cheetah

5 Weight 40-60kg; length 200-220cm. Less cat than greyhound, the cheetah is a world-class sprinter. Although it reaches 112km/h, the cheetah runs out of steam after 300m and must cool down for 30 minutes before hunting again.

1

4

2

KARL LEHMANN/GETTY IMAGES ©

3

DAVID WALL/GETTY IMAGES ©

Primates

While East Africa is the evolutionary cradle of primate diversity, South Africa is a relative newcomer on the scene and home to just five species of monkeys, apes and prosimians (the primitive ancestors of modern primates). Some of these, however, are common and widespread, meaning that you are likely to see a lot of fascinating primate behaviour.

Vervet Monkey

1 Weight 4-8kg; length 90-140cm. If any monkey epitomises South Africa it is the adaptable vervet monkey. If you think its appearance too drab, check out the bright blue and scarlet colours of the male sexual organs when it gets excited.

Greater Bushbaby

2 Weight up to 1.5kg; length 80cm, including 45cm tail. Named for their plaintive call, bushbabies are actually primitive primates. They have small heads, large rounded ears, thick bushy tails, dark-brown fur and enormous eyes.

Chacma Baboon

3 Weight 12-30kg (female), 25-45kg (male); length 100-200cm. Chacma baboons are worth watching for their complex social dynamics. Look for signs of friendship, deception or deal-making.

Samango Monkey

4 Weight 3.5-5.5kg (female), 5.5-12kg (male); length 100-160cm. Samango monkeys are part of a vast group of African primates called gentle, or blue, monkeys. They are found exclusively in forests.

Greater Galago

5 Weight 550g-2kg; length 55-100cm. A cat-sized, nocturnal creature with a doglike face, the greater galago belongs to a group of prosimians that have changed little in 60 million years.

KELLEY MILLER/GETTY IMAGES ©

MITCH REARDON/GETTY IMAGES ©

1

3

CHRIS DU PLESSIS/GETTY IMAGES ©

2

ECOPIC/GETTY IMAGES ©

Cud-Chewing Mammals

Africa is most famous for its astounding variety of ungulates – hoofed mammals that include everything from buffaloes and rhinos to giraffes. The subgroup of ungulates that ruminate (chew their cud) and have horns are bovines. Among this family, antelopes are particularly numerous, with more than 20 species in South Africa.

Wildebeest

1 Weight 140-290kg; length 230-340cm. Look for the black-shouldered blue wildebeest and the white-tailed black wildebeest (a South African speciality).

Sable

2 Weight 200-270kg; length 230-330cm. Looking like a colourful horse with huge soaring horns, the sable ranks as one of Africa's most visually stunning mammals.

Impala

3 Weight 40-80kg; length 150-200cm. Gregarious and having a prodigious capacity to reproduce, impalas can reach great numbers.

Springbok

4 Weight 20-40kg (female), 30-60kg (male); length 135-175cm. Lacking the vast grasslands of East Africa, South Africa is home to only one gazellelike antelope – the lithe, little springbok.

Gemsbok

5 Weight 180-240kg; length 230cm. With straight, towering, 1m-long horns and a boldly patterned face, this elegant desert antelope can survive for months on the scant water it derives from the plants it eats.

Hoofed Mammals

A full stable of Africa's mega-charismatic animals can be found in this group of ungulates. Other than the giraffe, these ungulates are not ruminants. They have been at home in Africa for millions of years and are among the most successful mammals to have ever wandered the continent.

Mountain Zebra

1 Weight 230-380kg; length 260-300cm. South Africa's endemic mountain zebra differs from its savannah relative in having an unstriped belly and rusty muzzle.

Giraffe

2 Weight 450-1200kg (female), 1800-2000kg (male); height 3.5m-5.2m. Though they stroll along casually, giraffes can outrun most predators.

African Elephant

3 Weight 2200-3500kg (female), 4000-6300kg (male); height 2.4m-3.4m (female), 3-4m (male). Commonly referred to as 'the king of beasts', elephant society is actually ruled by a lineage of elder females.

Hippopotamus

4 Weight 510-3200kg; length 320-400cm. Designed like a floating beanbag with tiny legs, the 3000kg hippo spends its time in or very near water chowing down on aquatic plants.

White Rhinoceros

5 Weight 1400-2000kg (female), 2000-3600kg (male); length 440-520cm. Brought to the brink of extinction in the early 1990s, this majestic creature was largely saved by the efforts of South African wildlife managers. Poaching has once again become a major problem though, particularly in Kruger National Park.

2

EDWIN REMSBERG/GETTY IMAGES ©

3

URGEN & CHRISTINE SOHNS/GETTY IMAGES ©

Other Carnivores

In addition to seven types of cats, South Africa is home to 25 other carnivores ranging from slinky mongooses to highly social hunting dogs. All are linked in having 'carnassial' (slicing) teeth. A highlight for visitors is witnessing the prowess of these highly efficient hunters.

Honey Badger

1 Weight 7-16kg; length 75-100cm. Africans say they would rather face a lion than a honey badger, and even lions relinquish their kill when one shows up. It finds its favourite food by following honey guide birds to bee hives. It's also known as a 'ratel'.

Spotted Hyena

2 Weight 40-90kg; length 125-215cm. Living in groups that are ruled by females (who grow penis-like sexual organs), hyenas use bone-crushing jaws to disembowel terrified prey on the run.

Aardwolf

3 Weight 8-12kg; length 75-110cm. This animal is actually the smallest hyena, but its carnivorous tendencies are limited to lapping up soft-bodied termites.

African Wild Dog

4 Weight 20-35kg; length 100-150cm. Uniquely patterned hunting dogs run in packs of 20 to 60 that ruthlessly chase down antelopes and other animals. Organised in complex hierarchies maintained by rules of conduct, these highly social canids are incredibly efficient hunters.

Meerkat

5 Weight 0.5kg-1kg; length 50cm. South Africa's nine species of mongoose may be best represented by the delightfully named meerkat. Energetic and highly social meerkats spend much of their time standing up with looks of perpetual surprise.

1

3

ANGELIKA STERN/GETTY IMAGES ©

ARNO MEINTJES WILDLIFE/GETTY IMAGES ©

1

WINFRIED WISNIEWSKI/ MINDEN PICTURES/GETTY IMAGES ©

4

NIGEL DENNIS/GETTY IMAGES ©

2

NICO SMIT/GETTY IMAGES ©

3

ROBERT MUCKLEY/GETTY IMAGES ©

Birds of Prey

South Africa is home to about 60 species of hawks, eagles, vultures and owls. Look for them perching on trees, soaring high overhead or gathered around a carcass. Your first clue to their presence, however, may be the scolding cries of small birds harassing one of these feared hunters.

African Fish Eagle

1 Length 75cm. Given its name, it's not surprising that you'll see the African fish eagle hunting for fish around water. It is most familiar for the loud ringing vocalisations that have become known as 'the voice of Africa'.

Bateleur

2 Length 60cm. The bateleur is an attractive serpent-eagle. In flight, look for this eagle's white wings and odd tail-less appearance; close up, look for the bold colour pattern and scarlet face.

Secretary Bird

3 Length 100cm. In a country full of unique birds, the secretary bird stands head and shoulders above the masses. With the body of an eagle and the legs of a crane, this idiosyncratic, grey-bodied raptor is commonly seen striding across the savannah.

Lappet-Faced Vulture

4 Length 115cm. Seven of South Africa's eight vultures can be seen mingling with lions, hyenas and jackals around carcasses. Here, through sheer numbers, they often compete successfully for scraps of flesh and bone. The monstrous lappet-faced vulture, a giant among vultures, gets its fill before other vultures move in.

Bearded Vulture

5 Length 110cm. Around the soaring cliffs of the Drakensberg you may be lucky enough to spot one of the world's most eagerly sought-after birds of prey – the massive bearded vulture, also known as the lammergeyer.

1

3

NIGEL DENNIS/GETTY IMAGES ©

2

MITCH REARDON/GETTY IMAGES ©

Other Birds

Come to South Africa prepared to see an astounding number of birds in every shape and colour imaginable. If you're not already paying attention to every bird you see, you may find them an energising and pleasant diversion after a couple of days staring at impalas and snoring lions.

Lesser Flamingo

1 Length 100cm. Coloured deep rose-pink and gathering by the thousands on salt lakes, lesser flamingos create some of the most dramatic wildlife spectacles in Africa, especially when they all fly at once or perform synchronised courtship displays.

Ground Hornbill

2 Length 90cm. Looking somewhat like a turkey, the ground hornbill spends its time on the ground stalking insects, frogs, reptiles and small mammals, which it kills with fierce stabs of its large powerful bill.

Lilac-Breasted Roller

3 Length 40cm. Nearly everyone on safari gets to know the gorgeously coloured lilac-breasted roller. Related to kingfishers, rollers get their name from the tendency to 'roll' from side to side in flight to show off their iridescent blues, purples and greens.

Ostrich

4 Length 200-270cm. If you think the ostrich looks prehistoric, you aren't far off. Standing 2.7m tall and weighing upwards of 130kg, these ancient flightless birds escape predators by running away at 70km/h or lying flat on the ground.

African (Jackass) Penguin

5 Length 60cm. Yes, they are silly looking, but jackass penguins are actually named for their donkeylike calls, part of the ecstatic courtship displays given by the males. Found along the coast and on offshore islands, some penguin colonies are ridiculously tame.

Habitats

Nearly all of South Africa's wildlife occupies a specific type of habitat, and you will hear rangers and fellow travellers refer to these habitats repeatedly. Your wildlife-viewing experience will be greatly enhanced if you learn how to recognise these habitats, and the animals you might expect in each one.

Karoo

1 Much of western South Africa sees so little rain that shrubs and hardy grasses are the dominant vegetation. Known locally as the Karoo, this semiarid desert merges with true desert in Namibia. Lack of water keeps larger animals such as zebras and antelopes close to waterholes, but when it rains this habitat explodes with plant and animal life. During the dry season many plants shed their leaves to conserve water.

Fynbos

2 The dense, low shrub cover that can be found around Cape Town is so utterly unique that it is considered one of the six major plant biomes in the world. Of the 8578 plant species found here, 68% occur nowhere else in the world. Many of the plants are unsuitable for grazing animals, but this is a region of remarkable insect and bird diversity.

Bushveld

3 The classic African landscape is broad, rolling savannah grasslands dotted with acacia trees. In South Africa it is known as bushveld. This open landscape is home to large herds of zebras and antelopes, in addition to fast-sprinting predators such as cheetahs. Bushveld lacks woody plants, and on the central plateau it is known as highveld.

1

2

Right
1. Little Karoo (p150) 2. Fynbos, Table Mountain National Park (p64)

Survival Guide

Directory A-Z

Accommodation

South Africa offers a range of good-value accommodation. You'll generally find high standards, often for significantly less than you would pay in Europe or North America.

Seasons Rates rise steeply during the summer school break (mid-December to early January) and the Easter break (late March to mid-April). Room prices sometimes double and minimum stays are imposed; advance bookings are essential. The other school holidays (late June to mid-July and late September to early October) are classified as either high or shoulder season. You can get excellent deals during the winter low season, which is also the best time for wildlife-watching.

Discounts Discounted midweek and multi-night rates are common, so always ask. Occasionally, in towns geared towards business travellers rather than tourists, such as mining centres, rates can be more expensive during the week. Discounted rates for children are common.

Budget accommodation The main budget options are campsites, backpacker hostels, self-catering cottages and community-run offerings including homestays. Campsites are fairly ubiquitous, but other budget options are often scarce outside tourist areas.

Midrange This category is particularly good value, and includes guesthouses, B&Bs and many self-catering options in national parks.

Top end South Africa boasts some of Africa's best wildlife lodges, as well as superb guesthouses and hotels, including historic properties and accommodation on wine estates. Prices at this level are similar to, or slightly less than, those in Europe or North America. There are also some not-so-superb hotels and guesthouses, which can be expensive disappointments, so be selective.

Townships In Soweto, Khayelitsha and several other areas, you can sleep in township B&Bs, backpackers and homestays, excellent ways to get an insight into township life. Many owners offer township tours, and unparalleled African hospitality.

Lesotho Rates are comparable to South Africa's, and you usually get excellent value for money in tourist lodges. Standards and value for money in business- and government-oriented hotels in Maseru and lowland towns are decidedly worse, so plan your trip to stay at good accommodation. Top-end accommodation is scarce – exceptions are a few hotels in Maseru and wilderness lodges, notably Maliba Mountain Lodge. Camping opportunities abound away from major towns.

Swaziland Rates are similar to those in South Africa. There is a handful of backpacker hostels, and camping is possible on the grounds of many accommodation options.

SLEEPING PRICE RANGES

Rates quoted are for high season (November to March), with a private bathroom. Exceptions are noted in listings. Reviews are ordered by budget and, within those categories, by preference. Price ranges are based on the cost of a double room.

$ less than R600

$$ R600 to R1500

$$$ more than R1500

In Cape Town, Johannesburg and the Garden Route, price ranges rise:

$ less than R800

$$ R800 to R2500

$$$ more than R2500

Online Booking

A few of the centralised online booking services that

BOOK YOUR STAY ONLINE

For more accommodation reviews by Lonely Planet authors, check out http://lonelyplanet.com/hotels/. You'll find independent reviews, as well as recommendations on the best places to stay. Best of all, you can book online.

cover South Africa are listed below. Because most booking services charge listing fees, the cheapest places sometimes aren't included. Many regions also have B&B organisations and tourist offices or associations that take bookings; they're good places to find local gems such as farmstays.

www.bedandbreakfast.co.za B&Bs in all provinces.

www.fairtrade.travel Fair Trade Tourism–certified accommodation, tours and itineraries. Fourteen- to 35-day travel passes are available; see www.fairtradetravelpass.com.

www.farmstay.co.za Farmstays and rural activities.

www.hostelworld.com Hostels, guesthouses, lodges and hotels throughout Africa.

www.portfoliocollection.com Upscale guesthouses, boutique hotels, lodges and self-catering from Cape Town to Lesotho and Swaziland.

www.roomsforafrica.com Accommodation including B&Bs and self-catering nationwide, plus travel tips.

www.safarinow.com Thousands of properties nationwide, from tented camps to Cape Dutch villas.

www.seastay.yolasite.com Coastal farmstays.

www.wheretostay.co.za Covers a range of accommodation, activities and restaurants in South Africa, Swaziland and the neighbouring countries.

Backpackers

South Africa is backpacker friendly, with a profusion of hostels in popular areas such as Cape Town and the Garden Route. Visit **Backpacking South Africa** (www.backpackingsouthafrica.co.za) for more ideas.

Accommodation In addition to dorm beds (from about R120 per night), hostels often offer private rooms (singles/doubles from about R200/400). Many will also allow you to pitch a tent on their grounds.

Facilities Hostels are often of a high standard, with wi-fi, self-catering facilities, a bar and a travellers' bulletin board. Some offer meals. Staff can provide information on the area and local transport, and organise pick-ups if the hostel is not on the Baz Bus route.

Hostelling International South Africa has hostels nationwide affiliated with **HI** (www.hihostels.com), so it's worth taking an HI card.

Lesotho and Swaziland Backpacker accommodation is found in areas including Malealea, Semonkong, Morija, Roma, Ramabanta and Sani Top in Lesotho; and Mbabane and the Ezulwini Valley in Swaziland. Prices and facilities are similar to those in South Africa.

B&Bs & Guesthouses

B&Bs and guesthouses are two of South Africa's accommodation treats. They're found throughout the country, from cities to villages, while in rural areas you can stay on farms. Some of the cheapest places are unexciting, but in general standards are high and rooms are good value.

Facilities Unlike B&Bs in some other countries, most South African establishments offer much more than someone's spare room; unlike motels, their bedrooms are individual and often luxurious. Antique furniture, a private bathroom and verandah, big gardens and a pool are common. In scenic areas such as the Cape Winelands, wonderful settings are part of the deal. Breakfasts are usually large and delectable.

Rates Prices start around R400/600 per single/double, including breakfast and private bathroom. With the odd exception, starting prices tend to be higher in Cape Town, Johannesburg (Jo'burg) and the Garden Route.

Camping

Camping grounds and caravan parks have long been the accommodation of choice for many South African families. Grounds in popular areas are often booked out during school holidays. Free-camping isn't recommended in South Africa, but you can often pitch your tent at backpackers for R60 or so.

Municipal Most towns have an inexpensive municipal campsite and caravan park, ranging from pleasant to unappealing. Those near larger towns are often unsafe.

Private Altogether better are privately run campsites, and those in national parks. These are invariably well equipped and appealing, with ablution blocks, power points, cooking areas and water supply. Tourist areas often have fancy resorts, complete with swimming pool, restaurant and minimarket.

Prices Rates are either per person (from about R100) or per site (from about R150). Except where noted, we have quoted camping prices per person.

Rules Some caravan parks ban nonporous groundsheets (which are sewn in to most small tents) to protect the grass. If you're only staying a night or two, you can usually convince the manager that your tent won't do any harm. Some parks may not allow tents at all, though if you explain that you're a foreigner without a caravan, it may be possible to get a site.

Lesotho and Swaziland Apart from in national parks, nature reserves and lodges, there are few official campsites. It's usually possible to free-camp, but

ACCOMMODATION LINGO

If a hotel touts rooms costing, say, R300, this often means R300 *per person* in a twin or double room. Furthermore, the price is based on two people sharing, and a single supplement is normally charged; a solo traveller might pay R450 in this example, or even have to pay the same as two people.

Half board includes breakfast and another meal (usually dinner); full board includes all meals. All-inclusive accommodation prices are also found: in game lodges, they generally cover all meals, wildlife drives and sometimes also park entry fees; in coastal resorts, they include all meals, access to resort facilities and some activities.

get permission from elders in the nearest village before setting up, both out of respect for the local community and to minimise security risks. You may be offered a hut for the night; expect to pay a token fee of about R20 for this.

Hotels

These cover the full spectrum, from spartan set-ups to exclusive boutique properties.

Budget Most budget hotels are rundown and inadequate. There are a few reasonable old-style country hotels, where you can get a single/double from about R300/500, have a meal and catch up on gossip in the pub.

Midrange These options are more dependable than their budget counterparts, offering good value and atmospheric surroundings.

Top end Rates are high in local terms, and generally in line with international prices, but the appealing properties include boutique, historic and design hotels.

HOTEL CHAINS

Chain hotels are common, found in cities and tourist areas.

City Lodge (Map p234; ☎0861 563 437, 011-557 2600; www.citylodge.co.za) Decent value, with Road Lodges (slightly superior standards to the rival SUN1 chain, for about R550 for a room accommodating one to three); Town Lodges (around R850/1000 per single/double); City Lodges (about R1200/1400 per single/double); and Courtyard Hotels (from around R770/1450 per room/apartment). Lower rates are offered for online bookings.

InterContinental Hotels Group (IHG; ☎0861 444 435; www.ichotelsgroup.com) Offers a range of accommodation across its Holiday Inn, Holiday Inn Express, Crowne Plaza and InterContinental hotels in the major cities.

Protea (☎0861 119 000, 021-430 5300; www.protea hotels.com) A South Africa–wide network of three- to five-star hotels. Protea's Prokard loyalty club offers discounts of up to 10% and VIP privileges. Owned by Marriott International.

Sun International (☎011-780 7810; www.sun international.com) Runs top-end, resort-style hotels in the former homelands, plus Lesotho and Swaziland, usually with casinos attached. Standards are generally high and package deals are available.

Tsogo Sun (☎0861 447 744, 011-461 9744; www.tsogosun hotels.com) Operates various chains and properties in South Africa, including Southern Sun Hotels, the midrange Garden Court brand, and SUN1. Previously known as Formule1, SUN1 offers South Africa's cheapest chain hotels, with functional but cramped rooms accommodating one to three from about R400.

Lodges

In and around the national parks, you can relax comfortably in bush settings. Staying at a wildlife lodge is an unmissable experience; you also have to stay at one to gain access to parks such as Madikwe Game Reserve (North West Province).

Facilities Accommodation is usually in a luxurious lodge or a safari tent. Expect many of the amenities that you would find in a top-end hotel – including en suites with running hot and cold water, comfortable bedding, delicious cuisine, and even a pool at the top end. However, many lodges don't have landlines, wi-fi, TVs or, in especially rustic cases, electricity. Most luxury lodges charge all-inclusive rates, which include wildlife drives and meals.

Reservations It's important to phone ahead if you plan to stay at a lodge or self-catering option in the wilderness. Not only can they be tricky to find without directions, and the staff may need to pick you up if your vehicle doesn't have good clearance, but if you turn up unannounced you might find there's no one home.

Lesotho The country's mountain lodges, in places such as Ts'ehlanyane National Park, Semonkong and Malealea, are its finest accommodation options.

Self-Catering Accommodation

This can be excellent value, from around R400 per two-person cottage – also called chalets, cabins, huts and *rondavels* (round huts with conical roofs). Options range from farm cottages and campsite accommodation to community-run camps and holiday resorts.

Facilities Apart from the occasional run-down place, most self-catering accommodation comes with bedding, towels and a fully equipped kitchen, though confirm what is included in advance. In some farm cottages you'll have to do without lights and electricity.

Locations Small-town tourist information centres and their websites are the best places to find out about self-catering accommodation. Self-catering chalets, often available in campsites and caravan parks, are common in tourist areas such as the coast and around parks and reserves. Many are located in scenic but remote locations, more suited to travellers with a car, although cottages are also found in towns and villages.

Parks and reserves South African National (SAN) Parks offers well-maintained, fully equipped options, ranging from bungalows and cottages to safari tents and *rondavels*. You pay a premium for the privilege of staying in the park or reserve, but the units are usually appealing, with larger options for families. Some parks and reserves also have simpler huts, with shared bathrooms.

Reservations Booking ahead is essential. You normally have to pay 50% (occasionally 100%) in advance by bank deposit or transfer. In a small community, there's a chance you'll get a ride to the cottage if you don't have a car.

Activities

Thanks to South Africa's diverse terrain and favourable climate, almost anything is possible – from abseiling to zip lining. Good facilities and instruction mean that most activities are accessible to anyone, whatever their experience level.

Aerial Pursuits

Favourable weather conditions year round and an abundance of high points to launch yourself from make South Africa a fine destination for aerial pursuits. Taking to the South African skies is fairly inexpensive; a helpful contact for getting started is the **Aero Club of South Africa** (☎011-082 1100; www.aeroclub.org.za).

Paragliding South Africa is one of the world's top paragliding destinations, especially Lion's Head and Table Mountain in Cape Town, with further opportunities throughout the Western Cape and nationwide. The strongest thermals are from November to April. For experienced pilots, airspace restrictions are minimal and there's great potential for long-distance, cross-country flying. **South African Hang Gliding & Paragliding Association** (SAHPA; ☎074 152 2505; www.sahpa.co.za) can provide information on flying sites, schools and clubs.

Microlighting A useful resource with forums and a list of airfields is microlighters.co.za.

Birdwatching

With its enormous diversity of habitats, South Africa is a paradise for birdwatchers. There are birdwatching clubs nationwide, and most parks and reserves can provide birding lists, with some information from SANParks (www.sanparks.org). Many parks, reserves and accommodation also have field guides, but it's still worth bringing your own.

BirdLife South Africa (www.birdlife.org.za) Useful information and links. Promotes avitourism (birding ecotourism) routes.

Birding Africa (www.birdingafrica.com) Day trips from Cape Town and tours further afield, covering birds and flowers.

Bird-Watch Cape (www.birdwatch.co.za) Small, Cape Town–based outfit for twitchers, with tours including 17- and 27-day, nationwide packages.

Cape Birding Route (www.capebirdingroute.org) Information relating to western South Africa, from Cape Point to the Kalahari.

Greater Limpopo Birding Routes (www.limpopobirding.com) Lists guides and four routes, including one taking in the Soutpansberg mountains and Limpopo River Valley.

Indicator Birding (www.birding.co.za) Information, articles and tours. Based in Gauteng.

Southern African Birding (www.sabirding.co.za) Multimedia guides and information, also covering Lesotho and Swaziland.

Zululand Birding Route (www.zbr.co.za) Avitourism project in an area of northern KwaZulu-Natal featuring over 600 bird species.

Canoeing, Kayaking, Rafting & Tubing

South Africa has few major rivers, but the ones that do flow year round offer rewarding rafting and canoeing. Rafting is highly rain dependent, with the best months in most areas from December/January to April.

Felix Unite (www.felixunite.com) Runs trips on the Breede, Cunene and Senqu (Orange) Rivers.

Induna Adventures (indunaadventures.wozaonline.co.za) White-water rafting and tubing ('geckoing') on the Sabie River.

Intrapid (www.raftsa.co.za) Rafting trips on rivers including the Senqu (Orange), Doring and Palmiet.

PaddleYak (www.seakayak.co.za) Sea-kayak shop, news and tours.

Swazi Trails (www.swazitrails.co.sz) Trips on Swaziland's Great Usutu River and around the country.

Diving

Take the plunge off the southern end of Africa into the Indian and Atlantic Oceans. Strong currents and often windy conditions mean advanced divers can find challenges all along the coast. Sodwana Bay on KwaZulu-Natal's Elephant Coast is a good all-round choice for beginners, while Aliwal Shoal and Port Elizabeth are also popular.

Conditions These vary widely. The best time to dive the KwaZulu-Natal shoreline is from May to September, when visibility tends to be highest. In the west, along the Atlantic seaboard, the water is cold year-round, but is at its most diveable,

SAFE DIVING

In popular diving areas such as Sodwana Bay, there is a range of diving companies – including slipshod operations. When choosing an operator, make quality, rather than cost, the priority. Factors to consider include an operator's experience and qualifications; knowledge and seriousness of staff; whether it's a fly-by-night operation or well established with a good reputation locally; and the type and condition of equipment and frequency of maintenance. Assess whether the overall attitude is professional, and ask about safety considerations – radios, oxygen, emergency evacuation procedures, boat reliability and back-up engines, first-aid kits, safety flares and life jackets. On longer dives, do you get an energising meal, or just tea and biscuits?

Using operators offering courses certified by the **Professional Association of Diving Instructors** (PADI; www.padi.com) gives you the flexibility to go elsewhere in the world and have your certification recognised at other PADI dive centres.

with many days of high visibility, between November and January/February.

Costs Prices are generally lower in South Africa than elsewhere in the region. Expect to pay from R3000 for a three- or four-day open-water certification course, and from R300 for a dive.

Equipment Coastal towns where diving is possible have dive outfitters. With the exception of Sodwana Bay during the warmer months (when a 3mm wetsuit will suffice), you'll need at least a 5mm wetsuit for many sites, and a dry suit for some sites to the south and west.

Fishing

Sea fishing is popular, with a wide range of species in the warm and cold currents that flow past the east and west coasts, respectively.

River fishing, especially for introduced trout, is popular in parks and reserves, with some particularly good highland streams in the Drakensberg, for example in the Rhodes area.

Licences are available for a few rand at park offices, and some shops and accommodation rent equipment.

Lesotho is an insider's tip among trout anglers. As in South Africa, the season runs from September to May. There is a small licence fee of M5, and a bag limit of 12 trout over 25cm in length. Only rod and line and artificial non-spinning flies may be used.

The nearest fishing area to Maseru is the Makhaleng River, 2km downstream from Molimo-Nthuse restaurant, about 60km east of Maseru at the foot of God Help Me Pass. You can also access the river from Ramabanta and Malealea.

Bass Fishing South Africa (BFSA; www.bassfishing.co.za) Forum and details of fishing sites.

Sealine (www.sealine.co.za) Angling and boating community.

Southern African Trout and Flyfishing Directory (www.flyfisher.co.za) Inspiration for a flyfishing safari.

Wild Trout Association (www.wildtrout.co.za) Rhodes-based repository of fishing lore.

Hiking

SOUTH AFRICA

South Africa is a wonderful destination for hiking, with an excellent system of well-marked trails varied enough to suit every ability.

Accommodation Some trails offer accommodation, from camping and simple huts with electricity and running water, to hotels on slackpacking trails in the Eastern Cape and elsewhere. Book well in advance.

Guided walks These are possible, accompanied by armed rangers, in many national parks. You won't cover much distance, but they offer the chance to experience the wild with nothing between you and nature. Parks, including Kruger, offer hikes ranging from two- to three-hour bush walks to overnight or multi-day wilderness trails. Numerous tour operators also offer guided hikes in areas such as the Wild Coast and Drakensberg – excellent ways to get off the beaten track and experience African village life.

Off-trail hiking Some designated wilderness areas offer this. Routes are suggested, but it's basically up to you to survive on your own.

Regulations Many trails have limits as to how many hikers can be on them at any one time, so book ahead. Most longer routes and wilderness areas require hikers to be in a group of at least three or four, although solo hikers may be able to join a group.

Safety This is not a major issue on most trails, but longer trails have seen muggings and burglaries of accommodation, while robberies and attacks occur on the contour paths on Table Mountain, neighbouring Lion's Head, Signal Hill and especially Devil's Peak. Check with the local hiking club or park office. On longer and quieter trails, hike in a group, and limit the valuables you carry; in Cape Town, do not walk alone, and avoid early mornings, evenings and other quiet times. The Table Mountain plateau is usually safe.

Seasons Hiking is possible year-round, although you'll need to be prepared in summer for extremes of heat and wet. The best time is March to October.

RESOURCES

Recommended books:

➡ *Best Walks of the Drakensberg* by David Bristow.

➡ *Easy Walks in the Cape Peninsula* by Mike Lundy.

➡ *Hiking Trails of South Africa* by Willie and Sandra Olivier.

Online resources:

CapeNature (www.capenature.co.za) Administers numerous trails in the Western Cape.

Ezemvelo KZN Wildlife (www.kznwildlife.com) Controls various trails in the KwaZulu-Natal Drakensberg and Elephant Coast.

Hiking Organisation of Southern Africa (HOSA; www.hosavosa.co.za) Information, forum and links to hiking clubs.

SANParks (www.sanparks.org) SANParks and the various forestry authorities administer most trails. Lots of information on its website.

LESOTHO

➡ The entire country is ideal for hiking, away from major towns.

➡ The eastern highlands and the Drakensberg crown attract serious hikers.

➡ There are few organised hiking trails – mostly footpaths.

➡ You can walk almost everywhere, accompanied by a compass and the relevant topographical maps.

➡ In all areas, especially the remote eastern highlands, rugged conditions can make walking dangerous if you aren't experienced and prepared. Temperatures can plummet to zero even in summer, and thunderstorms and thick fog are common.

➡ Waterproof gear and warm clothes are essential.

➡ In summer, rivers flood and fords can become dangerous; be prepared to change your route or wait until the river subsides.

➡ By the end of the dry season, good water can be scarce, especially in higher areas.

SWAZILAND

➡ Some of the nature reserves are particularly good for hiking.

➡ In most rural areas, you can follow the generations-old tracks that criss-cross the countryside.

➡ If you're hiking during the summer, be prepared for torrential downpours and hailstorms.

Horse Riding & Pony Trekking

➡ In South Africa, Lesotho and Swaziland it's easy to find rides ranging from hours to days, and for all experience levels.

➡ Riding is offered in several South African national parks.

➡ Pony trekking on tough Basotho ponies is a popular way of seeing the Lesotho highlands.

OPERATORS

Equus Horse Safaris (www.equus.co.za) In the Waterberg, Limpopo.

Fynbos Trails (www.fynbostrails.com) In the Western Cape.

Haven Horse Safaris (www.havenhotel.co.za) One of many operators offering rides on the beaches of the Wild Coast and Eastern Cape.

Horizon Horseback Adventures (www.ridinginafrica.com) In the Waterberg, Limpopo.

Khotso Trails (www.khotsotrails.co.za) In the Southern Drakensberg, including Lesotho.

Nyanza Farm (www.nyanza.co.sz) In Swaziland.

Kloofing (Canyoning)

Kloofing (called canyoning elsewhere), a mix of climbing, hiking, swimming and some serious jumping, has a small but rapidly growing following in South Africa.

There's an element of risk in the sport, so when hunting for operators, check their credentials carefully before signing up.

Mountain Biking

There are trails almost everywhere in South Africa, from the Garden Route to the Kalahari. Cape Town is an unofficial national hub for the activity.

Linx Africa (www.linx.co.za/trails/lists/bikelist.html) Province by province listings of trails.

Mountain Bike South Africa (www.mtbsa.co.za) Mountain-biking information, community and e-zine.

Ride (www.ride.co.za) South African mountain-biking magazine.

Rock Climbing

Climb ZA (www.climbing.co.za) News, articles, directory and forum.

Mountain Club of South Africa (www.mcsa.org.za) Information and links to regional clubs.

SA Climbing Info Network (www.saclimb.co.za) Has listings and photos of climbing and bouldering routes.

Surfing

The best time of the year for surfing South Africa's southern and eastern coasts is autumn and early winter (from about April to July). Boards and gear can be bought in most of the big coastal cities. New boards typically cost about R3500.

Wavescape (www.wavescape.co.za) Surf forecasting and coastal lifestyle website.

Zig Zag (www.zigzag.co.za) South Africa's main surf magazine.

Whale-Watching

➡ South Africa is considered one of the world's best spots to sight whales from land.

➡ Southern right and humpback whales are regularly seen offshore between June/July and November, with occasional spottings of Bryde's and killer whales.

➡ Whale-watching spots dot the southern and eastern coastlines, from False Bay to iSimangaliso Wetland Park.

➡ Hermanus, where southern right whales come to calve, is the unofficial whale-watching capital.

Wildlife-Watching

South Africa's populations of large animals are one of

the country's biggest attractions. In comparison with other countries in the region (Botswana and Zambia, for example), wildlife-watching in South Africa tends to be very accessible, with good roads and accommodation for all categories of traveller. It is also comparatively inexpensive, although there are plenty of pricier choices for those seeking a luxury experience in the bush.

Swaziland also offers excellent wildlife-watching.

Customs Regulations

- You're permitted to bring 2L of wine, 1L of spirits and other alcoholic beverages, 200 cigarettes and up to R5000 worth of goods into South Africa without paying duties.
- Imported and exported protected-animal products such as ivory must be declared.
- Visit www.southafrica.info/travel/advice/redtape.htm for more information.

Discount Cards

- A valid student ID will get you discounts on bus tickets, museum admission and so on.
- **UR Card** (www.urcard.co.za), sold online and by backpackers and tourist businesses, offers discounts on accommodation, transport, tours and activities.
- If you're planning to spend more than eight days in national parks, seriously consider buying a **Wild Card** (www.sanparks.org/wild). A year pass for foreigners is R1770 (R2770 per couple, R3310 per family), which gives free access to more than 80 parks and reserves run by SANParks, Ezemvelo KZN Wildlife, Cape Nature, Msinsi and Swazi organisations.
- The **Fair Trade Travel Pass** (www.fairtradetravelpass.com) gives you 14 to 35 days' access to Fair Trade–accredited accommodation, tours and activities in areas including the Wild Coast.

Electricity

There are frequent power cuts nationwide.

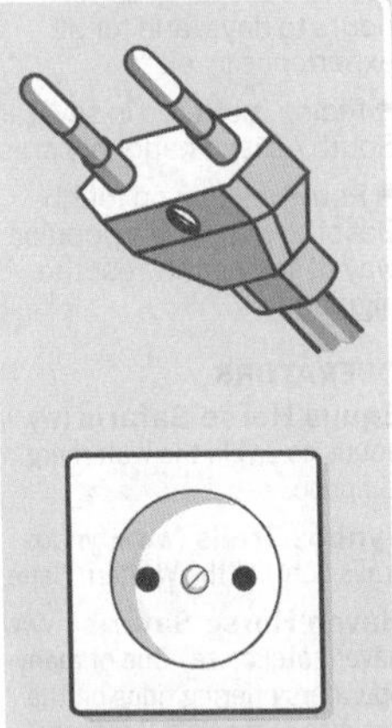

220-230V/50Hz

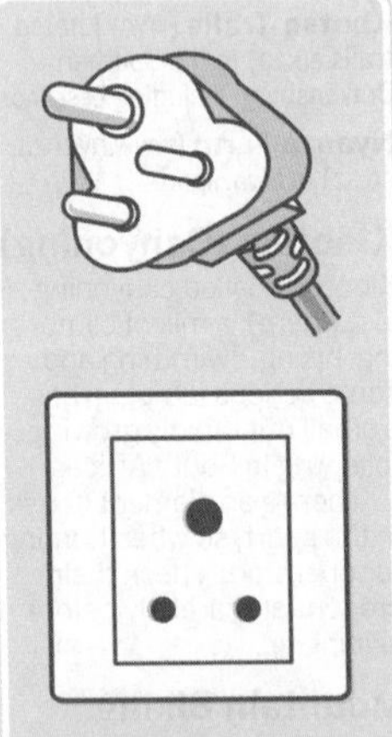

220-230V/50Hz

Embassies & Consulates

Embassies & Consulates in South Africa

Most countries have their main embassy in Pretoria, with an office or consulate in Cape Town (which may become the embassy during Cape Town's parliamentary sessions).

Most open for visa services and consular matters on weekday mornings, between about 9am and noon. For more information, see www.dfa.gov.za/foreign/forrep/index.htm.

Australian High Commission (☎012-423 6000; www.southafrica.embassy.gov.au; 292 Orient St, Arcadia, Pretoria)

Botswanan High Commission (☎012-430 9640; www.mofaic.gov.bw; 24 Amos St, Colbyn, Pretoria) Also has a consulate in Jo'burg.

Canadian High Commission (☎012-422 3000; southafrica.gc.ca; 1103 Arcadia St, Hatfield, Pretoria) Also has consulates in Cape Town (☎021-421 1818; 1502 Metlife Centre, Walter Sisulu Ave, Foreshore) and Durban.

French Embassy (☎012-425 1600; www.ambafrance-rsa.org; 250 Melk St, New Muckleneuk, Pretoria) Also has consulates in Cape Town (☎021-423 1575; www.consulfrance-lecap.org; 78 Queen Victoria St, Gardens; 🚌Upper Long/Upper Loop) and Jo'burg.

German Embassy (☎012-427 8900; www.southafrica.diplo.de; 180 Blackwood St, Arcadia, Pretoria) Also has a consulate in Cape Town (☎021-405 3052; 19th fl, Triangle House, 22 Riebeeck St, City Bowl).

Irish Embassy (☎012-452 1000; www.embassyofireland.org.za; 2nd fl, Parkdev Bldg, Brooklyn Bridge Office Park, 570 Fehrsen St, Brooklyn, Pretoria) Also has a liaison office in Cape Town.

Lesothan High Commission (☎012-460 7648; www.foreign.gov.ls; 391 Anderson St, Menlo Park, Pretoria)

Mozambican High Commission (☎012-401 0300; www.embamoc.co.za; 529 Edmond St, Arcadia, Pretoria) Also has consulates in Cape Town (☎021-426 2944; 11th fl, Pinnacle Bldg, 8 Burg St, City Bowl), Nelspruit (☎013-753 2089; mozconns@mweb.co.za; 32 Bell St; ⊙8am-3pm Mon-Fri), Durban and Jo'burg.

Namibian High Commission (☎012-481 9100; www.namibia.org.za; 197 Blackwood St, Arcadia, Pretoria)

Netherlands Embassy (☎012-425 4500; southafrica.nlembassy.org; 210 Florence Ribeiro/Queen Wilhelmina Ave, cnr Muckleneuk St, New Muckleneuk, Pretoria) Also has missions in Cape Town (☎021-421 5660; http://southafrica.nlembassy.org; 100 Strand St, City Bowl; 🚉Strand) and Durban.

New Zealand High Commission (☎012-435 9000; www.nzembassy.com/south-africa; 125 Middle St, New Muckleneuk, Pretoria) Also has an honorary consul in Cape Town (☎021-683 5762; www.nzembassy.com/south-africa; Eastry Rd, Claremont).

Swazi High Commission (☎012-344 1910; www.swazihighcom.co.za; 715 Government Ave, Arcadia, Pretoria) Also has an office in Jo'burg.

UK High Commission (☎012-421 7500; ukinsouthafrica.fco.gov.uk; 255 Hill St, Arcadia, Pretoria) Also has a consulate in Cape Town (☎021-405 2400; www.gov.uk/government/world/organisations/british-consulate-general-cape-town; 15th fl, Norton Rose House, 8 Riebeeck St, Foreshore; 🚉Adderley).

US Embassy (☎012-431 4000; southafrica.usembassy.gov; 877 Pretorius St, Arcadia, Pretoria) Also has consulates in Cape Town (☎021-702 7300; http://southafrica.usembassy.gov/; 2 Reddam Ave, Westlake), Durban and Jo'burg.

Zimbabwean Embassy (☎011-615 5879, 012-342 5125; www.zimfa.gov.zw; 798 Merton Ave, Arcadia, Pretoria) Also has a consulate in Jo'burg.

Embassies & Consulates in Lesotho

Embassies and consulates are found in Maseru. Missions in South Africa generally have responsibility for Lesotho. For more listings, visit www.foreign.gov.ls.

German Honorary Consul (☎2233 2292, 2233 2983; www.southafrica.diplo.de)

Netherlands Honorary Consul (☎2231 2114; www.dutchembassy.co.za; Lancer's Inn, cnr Kingsway & Pioneer Rd)

South African High Commission (☎2222 5800; www.dfa.gov.za; cnr Kingsway & Old School Rd)

US Embassy (☎2231 2666; maseru.usembassy.gov; 254 Kingsway)

Embassies & Consulates in Swaziland

Embassies and consulates are found in Mbabane. Missions in South Africa generally have responsibility for Swaziland. For more listings, visit www.gov.sz.

German Liaison Office (☎2404 3174; www.southafrica.diplo.de; 3rd fl, Lilunga House, Samhlolo St)

Mozambican High Commission (☎2404 1296; www.minec.gov.mz; Princess Drive Rd, Highlands View)

Netherlands Honorary Consul (☎2404 3547; southafrica.nlembassy.org)

South African High Commission (☎2404 4651; www.dfa.gov.za; 2nd fl, the New Mall, Dr Sishayi Rd)

US Embassy (☎2404 6441; swaziland.usembassy.gov; 7th fl, Central Bank Bldg, Mahlokohla St)

EATING PRICE RANGES

The following price ranges refer to a standard main course.

$ less than R75

$$ R75 to R150

$$$ more than R150

Food

See our Food chapter (p537) for more information.

Gay & Lesbian Travellers

South Africa's constitution is one of the few in the world that explicitly prohibits discrimination on the grounds of sexual orientation. Gay sexual relationships are legal and gay marriages are recognised. There are active gay and lesbian communities and scenes in Cape Town and Jo'burg, and to a lesser degree in Pretoria and Durban. Cape Town is the focal point, and is the most openly gay city on the continent.

Please see the boxed texts on gay and lesbian travel in Cape Town (p88) and Gauteng (p341) for more information.

Attitudes Despite the liberality of the new constitution, it will be a while before the more conservative sections of society begin to accept it. Particularly in rural areas, and in both black and white communities, homosexuality remains frowned upon, if not taboo.

Lesotho Male homosexual relations are illegal, through prosecutions for consenting adult relationships are unheard of. The country's law does not protect against discrimination based on sexual orientation or gender identity, and gay sexual relationships are taboo, with open displays of affection frowned upon.

Swaziland One of the most conservative countries in Southern Africa. Male homosexual activities are illegal, and gay relationships are culturally taboo, with homosexuals subjected to discrimination and harassment.

Resources

Check chain bookstores such as CNA and gay venues for newspapers and magazines.

Behind the Mask (@BehindTheMask99) Jo'burg-based media and activist organisation, supplying information and a platform for dialogue about LGBTI issues in Africa.

Exit (www.exit.co.za) LGBTI monthly newspaper.

Gay Johannesburg (http://gayjohannesburg.blogspot.com) News and links.

Gay Pages (www.gaypagessa.co.za) Bimonthly glossy magazine, available nationwide.

South African Tourism (www.southafrica.net) Information on gay Jo'burg, Cape Town, Durban and beyond.

Triangle Project (thetriangleproject.org) The Cape Town–based organisation campaigns for LGBT rights and supports the community through various programs.

Events

Jo'burg Pride (johannesburgpride.co.za) Dating to 1990, Africa's first ever gay and lesbian pride parade takes place every September/October.

Mother City Queer Project (www.mcqp.co.za) One of Cape Town's main gay events, this fabulous fancy-dress dance party is held every December.

Out in Africa (www.oia.co.za) Gay and lesbian film festival, held in Jo'burg and Cape Town in November.

Insurance

➡ Travel insurance covering theft, loss and medical problems is highly recommended.

➡ Before choosing a policy, shop around; policies designed for short European package tours may not be suitable for the South African veld.

➡ Read the fine print – some policies specifically exclude 'dangerous activities', which can mean scuba diving, motorcycling, bungee jumping and more.

➡ Some policies ask you to call (reverse charges) a centre in your home country, where an immediate assessment of your problem is made.

➡ Worldwide travel insurance is available at www.lonelyplanet.com/travel-insurance. You can buy, extend and claim online any time – even if you're already on the road.

Internet Access

➡ Internet access is widely available in South Africa.

➡ Connections may be slower than you're used to.

➡ Accommodation options usually offer wi-fi or, less commonly, a computer with internet access for guest use.

➡ We have used the 📶 icon where an establishment has a wi-fi network.

➡ The @ icon is used in sleeping reviews where an accommodation option offers a computer with internet access for guest use.

➡ Many malls, cafes, bars and restaurants (including chains) have wi-fi, often for free. Alternatively, it may be through a provider such as **Skyrove** (www.skyrove.com) or **Red Button** (www.redbutton.co.za), for which you will need to buy credit online using a credit card, or from the hot-spot owner.

➡ If you are staying some time, a USB modem or smart-phone data package may be useful, as wi-fi can be temperamental.

➡ Local mobile-phone companies such as **MTN** (www.mtn.co.za) sell USB modems and data packages.

➡ There are internet cafes in major towns and, sometimes, smaller locations. Charges are about R30 per hour.

➡ In Lesotho, web access is available in Maseru, and a few accommodation options elsewhere have wi-fi.

➡ In Swaziland, you can log on in spots including Mbabane, Manzini and the Malkerns Valley.

Language Courses

There are numerous language schools for learning Xhosa, Zulu, Afrikaans and English. You can also do Teaching English as a Foreign Language (TEFL) teacher training here.

Inlingua (www.inlingua.co.za; Green Point, Cape Town) Afrikaans, English.

Interlink (www.interlink.co.za; Sea Point, Cape Town) English.

International English School (www.english.za.net; Somerset West, Western Cape) English.

Jeffrey's Bay Language School (www.learnenglishlanguage.co.za; Jeffrey's Bay, Eastern Cape) One of a few English schools in the surf town.

Language Teaching Centre (www.languageteachingcentre.co.za; Foreshore, Cape Town) Xhosa, Zulu, Afrikaans, English.

Phaphama Initiatives (www.phaphama.org; Soweto, Gauteng) Teaches most of the African languages. Immersive tours and homestays in Gauteng townships and rural villages provide opportunities to learn outside the classroom.

Ubuntu Bridge (www.learnxhosa.co.za; Newlands, Cape Town) Xhosa.

Wits Language School (www.witslanguageschool.com; Braamfontein, Johannesburg) Zulu, Sesotho, Tswana, Afrikaans, English. Part of the University of the Witwatersrand.

Legal Matters

➡ Key areas to watch out for are traffic offences such as speeding and drink driving, and drug use and possession.

➡ Despite a relatively open drug culture, use and possession are illegal: arrests happen and penalties are stiff.

➡ South Africans may complain about police corruption and claim to have bribed police officers, but offering bribes is not recommended, as it could easily backfire.

➡ If you get arrested in South Africa, you have the following rights: to remain silent; to be released on bail or warning, unless there's a good reason to keep you in jail; to a lawyer; and to food and decent conditions.

Money

Visit www.southafrica.info/travel/advice/currency.htm for more information on money in South Africa.

Cards Because South Africa has a reputation for scams, many banks abroad automatically prevent transactions in the country. Particularly if you plan to use a credit card in South Africa, contact your bank before leaving home and inform it of your travel plans.

Foreign currencies The best currencies to bring are US dollars, euros or British pounds. A debit or credit card will be more useful, as many businesses only accept rand.

Major banks South Africa's major banks are Absa (owned by Barclays), FNB (First National Bank), Nedbank and Standard Bank.

South Africa South Africa's currency is the rand (R), which is divided into 100 cents. The notes are R10, R20, R50, R100 and R200; the coins are R1, R2 and R5, and five, 10, 20 and 50 cents. Transactions are often rounded up or down by a few cents. The rand is weak against Western currencies, making travelling in South Africa less expensive than in Europe and North America.

Swaziland and Lesotho Swaziland's currency is the lilangeni (plural emalangeni, E), divided into 100 cents; Lesotho's is the loti (plural maloti, M), divided into 100 lisente. Both are fixed at a value equal to the rand. Rand are accepted everywhere in both Lesotho and Swaziland, though you will invariably be given maloti or emalangeni in change.

ATMs

➡ ATMs are widespread in South Africa, both in the cities and beyond.

➡ Stash some cash if visiting rural areas such as Kruger National Park.

➡ In Lesotho, there are bank ATMs that accept international cards in Maseru and the main lowland towns.

➡ In Swaziland, there are ATMs that accept international cards in Mbabane, the Ezulwini Valley and a few other locations around the country.

Cards

➡ MasterCard and Visa are widely accepted in South Africa; Diners Club and American Express are less commonly accepted.

➡ Credit and debit cards can be used at many ATMs to withdraw cash.

➡ Despite bank charges for international use, paying and withdrawing money with a foreign card generally works out cheaply, due to the weak rand.

➡ In both Lesotho and Swaziland, credit cards are only accepted at major tourist establishments.

➡ If you get a failed transaction or anything irregular happens while making a payment with a credit or debit card, retrieve your card as quickly as possible and do not try the procedure again.

Moneychangers

SOUTH AFRICA

➡ Cash is readily exchanged at banks and foreign-exchange bureaux in the major cities.

➡ Thomas Cook and American Express travellers'

TIPPING

Wages are low, and tipping is expected. The main exceptions are in rural parts of Lesotho and Swaziland, where it's generally the custom to simply round up the bill.

Service	Tip
Restaurant	10% to 15%
Cafe	10%
Car guard	R2 (R5 for longer periods)
Petrol station attendant	R5
Taxi	Round up fare
Hotel porter	R10
Guide/tracker at private game reserve	R200/100 per group per day

cheques in major currencies can be cashed at banks, foreign-exchange bureaux and some hotels – with varying commissions.

➡ Buying cheques in a stronger currency such as US dollars will work out better than buying them in rand.

➡ If you buy rand or rand cheques, watch the market, as the currency is extremely volatile; failing that, buying them just before departure will minimise the effects of devaluation.

➡ There are **American Express** (www.americanexpressforex.co.za) foreign-exchange offices in major cities.

➡ Keep at least some of your exchange receipts, as you'll need them to reconvert leftover rand when you leave.

LESOTHO

➡ Maseru is the only place where you can reliably exchange foreign cash and travellers cheques.

➡ Rand notes are usually available on request.

SWAZILAND

➡ FNB and Nedbank change cash and travellers cheques – their rates are similar, but commissions vary.

➡ Most banks ask to see the purchase receipt when cashing travellers cheques.

➡ Nedbank, FNB and Standard Bank have branches in Mbabane, Manzini, Matsapha and around the country.

Taxes & Refunds

SOUTH AFRICA

➡ South Africa has a value-added tax (VAT) of 14%, but departing foreign visitors can reclaim most of it on goods being taken out of the country.

➡ To make a claim, the goods must have been bought at a VAT-registered vendor, their total value must exceed R250, and you need a tax invoice for each item.

➡ Your receipt usually covers the requirements for a tax invoice. It must include the following: the words 'tax invoice', the seller's name, address and 10-digit VAT registration number (starting with a 4); a description of the goods purchased; the cost of the goods in rand; the amount of VAT charged, or a statement that VAT is included in the total cost; a tax invoice number; the date of the transaction; and for purchases of more than R5000, the buyer's name and physical address and the quantity or volume of the goods.

➡ All invoices must be originals – no photocopies.

➡ A commission of 1.3% of the reclaimed sum is charged for the service (minimum R10, maximum R250).

➡ At your point of departure, you'll need to fill in a form or two and show the goods to a customs inspector.

➡ At airports, if your purchases are too large for hand luggage, make sure you have them checked by the inspector before you check in your bags.

➡ After going through immigration, make the claim and pick up your refund, issued as either a rand cheque (which, at Cape Town and Jo'burg OR Tambo International Airports, can then be cashed at a bank); or a MasterCard or Visa electron card, which will be loaded with your home (or another foreign) currency, and can be used to make purchases or withdraw money within a few days.

➡ If your claim comes to more than R3000, the refund will not be given on the spot; it will be loaded onto the card you are given, or a cheque will be posted, up to six weeks later.

➡ You can claim at Jo'burg, Cape Town and Durban's major international airports, and in the smaller airports at Lanseria (Jo'burg), Bloemfontein, Polokwane (Pietersburg), Nelspruit, Pilansberg, Port Elizabeth and Upington.

➡ It's also possible to claim at major harbours, and at some posts on the borders with Botswana, Mozambique, Namibia, Swaziland and Zimbabwe.

➡ You can claim the refund by post within three months of leaving South Africa, but it is much easier to do it in person.

➡ Visit www.taxrefunds.co.za for more information.

LESOTHO & SWAZILAND

➡ Both Lesotho and Swaziland have a VAT of 14%, applied similarly to that in South Africa, although there are not yet any systems for refunds in place.

➡ In both, many hotels omit the tax when quoting rates.

Opening Hours

➡ **Banks** 9am to 3.30pm Monday to Friday, till 11am Saturday.

➡ **Post offices** 8.30am to 4.30pm Monday to Friday, till noon Saturday.

➡ **Government offices** 8am to 3pm Monday to Friday, till noon Saturday (Lesotho 8am to 12.45pm and 2pm to 4.30pm Monday to Friday; Swaziland 8am to 4pm Monday to Friday).

➡ **Cafes** 7am to 5pm.

➡ **Restaurants** 11.30am to 3pm and 7pm to 10pm (last orders); many open 3pm to 7pm.

➡ **Bars** 4pm to 2am.

➡ **Businesses and shopping** 8.30am to 5pm Monday to Friday, till 1pm Saturday; many supermarkets also 9am to noon Sunday; major shopping centres till 9pm daily.

Photography

➡ In South Africa, cameras, memory cards, film and

accessories are readily available in large towns.

➡ Camera and equipment selection is more limited in Lesotho and Swaziland, with a modest selection available in Maseru and Mbabane.

➡ In all three countries, don't photograph or film soldiers, police, airports, defence installations, border posts and government buildings.

➡ You should always ask permission before taking a photo of anyone, but particularly so if you're in a tribal village.

➡ In Cape Town, a recommended camera and equipment shop is **Orms** (www.ormsdirect.co.za).

➡ Pick up Lonely Planet's *Travel Photography* for inspiration and advice.

Post

➡ In South Africa and Swaziland, both domestic and international deliveries are generally reliable but can be slow.

➡ In Lesotho, delivery is slow and unreliable.

➡ There are periodic postal strikes in South Africa, which delay delivery times.

➡ For mailing anything valuable or important, use a private mail service such as **PostNet** (www.postnet.co.za).

➡ Do not receive anything of value from overseas, as parcels are often impounded by customs.

Public Holidays

South Africa

New Year's Day 1 January

Human Rights Day 21 March

Good Friday March/April

Family Day March/April

Freedom Day 27 April

Workers' Day 1 May

Youth Day 16 June

National Women's Day 9 August

Heritage Day 24 September

Day of Reconciliation 16 December

Christmas Day 25 December

Day of Goodwill 26 December

Lesotho

New Year's Day 1 January

Moshoeshoe's Day 11 March

Good Friday March/April

Easter Monday March/April

Workers' Day 1 May

Africa or Heroes' Day 25 May

Ascension Day May/June

King's Birthday 17 July

Independence Day 4 October

Christmas Day 25 December

Boxing Day 26 December

Swaziland

New Year's Day 1 January

Good Friday March/April

Easter Monday March/April

King Mswati III's Birthday 19 April

National Flag Day 25 April

Workers' Day 1 May

Ascension Day May

King Sobhuza II's Birthday 22 July

Umhlanga (Reed) Dance August/September

Somhlolo (Independence) Day 6 September

Christmas Day 25 December

Boxing Day 26 December

Incwala Ceremony December/January

School Holidays

➡ Late March to mid-April (varying, depending on

PRACTICALITIES

➡ All three countries use the metric system for weights and measures.

➡ *Mail & Guardian* (www.mg.co.za) is a national weekly newspaper.

➡ *The Sowetan* (www.sowetanlive.co.za) is a national daily.

➡ Other nationals include the *Sunday Independent* (www.iol.co.za/sundayindependent), the *Sunday Times* (www.timeslive.co.za) and *Business Day* (www.businessday.co.za).

➡ *News24* (www.news24.com) is publisher Media 24's portal, with news and features.

➡ *Times of Swaziland* (www.times.co.sz) and *Swazi Observer* (www.observer.org.sz) carry Swazi news.

➡ The *Sunday Express* (sundayexpress.co.ls) and *Lesotho Times* (www.lestimes.com) carry Lesothan news.

➡ *Getaway* (www.getaway.co.za), *Go!* (Weg!; www.gomag.co.za) and *Country Life* (www.countrylife.co.za) are South African travel magazines.

➡ SABC (www.sabc.co.za) broadcasts local TV programs from soap operas to news.

➡ M-Net (mnet.dstv.com) offers US films and series.

➡ e.tv (www.etv.co.za) offers local programs and international favourites.

➡ SAfm (www.sabc.co.za) broadcasts news and chat online and on 104-107FM.

when Easter is); late June to mid-July; late September to early October; and early December to mid-January.

➡ For exact dates, see the calendars at www.saschools.co.za.

➡ The main school-holiday periods in Lesotho and Swaziland parallel those in South Africa.

Telephone

South Africa

➡ South Africa has good telephone facilities, operated by **Telkom** (www.telkom.co.za).

➡ Telkom WorldCall prepaid calling cards are widely available, in denominations from R10 to R200.

➡ Charges are similar to a landline, but they enable you to pay for making calls from other people's phones.

➡ WorldCall charges per minute from landlines are R0.77 for local calls, R0.46 for long-distance calls and R1.30 for calling a mobile phone.

➡ International WorldCall charges per minute from landlines include R0.72 to an Australian landline, R0.50 to Canada and R0.53 to the UK.

➡ Rates drop between 7pm and 7am Monday to Friday, and over the weekend.

➡ International calls are cheaper between 8pm and 8am Monday to Friday, and over the weekend.

➡ Coin-operated public phones are blue; card-operated phones are green.

➡ A good way to avoid high charges when calling home, or to make reverse-charge calls, is to dial a 'Home Direct' number, which puts you through to an operator in your country. Call Telkom's 24-hour international call centre to find out the number for your country.

➡ For more information on making calls in South Africa, visit www.southafrica.info/travel/advice/telecoms.htm.

IMPORTANT NUMBERS

South Africa

Ambulance ☎10177

Cape Town emergencies ☎107

Cape Town emergencies (from mobiles) ☎021-480 7700

Cape Town Rape Crisis ☎021-447 9762

Collect/reverse-charge calls ☎0900

Directory services ☎1023

Emergencies (from mobiles) ☎112

International call centre ☎10900, 10903

Lifeline Johannesburg (crisis/rape counselling) ☎011-728 1347

Mobile Yellow Pages ☎34310

Netcare 911 medical emergencies (private service) ☎082 911

Police ☎10111

Talking Yellow Pages ☎10118

Lesotho

Ambulance ☎2231 3260, 2231 2276, 112

Fire ☎112

Police ☎2231 2934, 2232 2099, 112

Swaziland

Ambulance ☎2404 2423, 977

Fire ☎933

Police ☎2404 2221, 999

PHONE CODES

Telephone numbers in South Africa are 10 digits, including the local area code, which must always be dialled.

In South Africa, there are several four-digit nationwide prefixes, followed by six-digit numbers. These include:

➡ ☎080 (usually ☎0800; toll free)

➡ ☎0860 (charged as a local call)

➡ ☎0861 (flat-rate calls)

MOBILE PHONES

➡ Mobile-phone networks cover most of South Africa, and mobile-phone ownership is widespread.

➡ There are GSM and 3G digital networks.

➡ GSM phones on roaming should work here, apart from older dual-band phones from North America and tri-band phones from Central and South America.

➡ The major mobile networks: **Cell C** (www.cellc.co.za), **MTN** (www.mtn.co.za), **Virgin Mobile** (www.virginmobile.co.za) and the Vodafone-owned **Vodacom** (www.vodacom.co.za).

- South Africa's 10-digit mobile numbers begin with 06, 07 or 08.
- You can hire a mobile phone through your car-rental provider.
- A cheaper alternative is to use a local prepaid SIM card in your own phone, provided it's unlocked and on roaming.
- SIM cards and credit are available almost everywhere in shops and malls throughout the cities and larger towns.
- A new SIM should cost about R20; they tend to be more expensive in airport shops.
- You need some form of ID and proof of South African address to buy and 'RICA' (register) a SIM card.
- The proof of address can be a signed statement from your host or accommodation that you are residing with them, or an accommodation receipt.
- Various prepaid plans and airtime or data bundles are available.
- On Vodacom's Anytime Per Second plan, for example, calls cost R1.20 per minute, SMSes R0.50 and international SMSes R1.74.

Lesotho

- Lesotho's telephone system works reasonably well in the lowlands, but even landlines are temperamental in the highlands.
- There are no area codes.
- Lesotho's eight-digit landline and mobile-phone numbers respectively begin with 2 and 5 or 6.
- International calls are expensive.
- For international reverse-charge calls dial ☎109.
- Mobile-phone signals are rare in the highlands, and can only be picked up on a few mountain passes.
- The main mobile-phone service providers are **Vodacom Lesotho** (www.vodacom.co.ls) and **Econet Telecom** (www.etl.co.ls).
- Most villages have a Vodacom or Econet booth, selling credit and SIM cards (about M30; bring your passport).
- The booths generally have a landline, offering calls to Lesotho and South Africa for about M7 per minute.
- Mobile credit comes in R5 vouchers; international bundles are available.
- South African SIMs work on roaming.

Swaziland

- Swaziland has a reasonably good telephone network, operated by **SwaziTelecom** (www.sptc.co.sz/swazitelecom).
- There are no area codes.
- Swaziland's eight-digit landline and mobile-phone numbers respectively begin with 2 and 7.
- Dial ☎94 to make a reverse-charge call.
- International calls are most easily made using MTN phonecards.
- Outside the major towns, dial ☎94 to book international calls.
- **MTN Swaziland** (www.mtn.co.sz) provides the mobile-phone network.
- You can buy SIM cards for a nominal fee and South African SIMs work on roaming.

Time

- SAST (South Africa Standard Time) is two hours ahead of GMT/UTC.
- There is no daylight-saving period.
- Lesotho and Swaziland are in the same time zone as South Africa.
- This is a wide region to be covered by one time zone; the sun can rise and set an hour earlier in Durban than in Cape Town.
- Most timetables and businesses use the 24-hour clock.

Toilets

- Finding a clean, sit-down toilet in South Africa is usually not a problem.
- There are few public toilets, but malls generally have them.
- Tourist offices and restaurants are normally happy to let you use their facilities.

DIFFERENCES FROM STANDARD SOUTH AFRICA TIME

COUNTRY	CAPITAL CITY	DIFFERENCE FROM SOUTH AFRICA
Australia	Canberra	+8hr
Canada	Ottawa	-7hr
France	Paris	-1hr
Germany	Berlin	-1hr
Japan	Tokyo	+7hr
Netherlands	Amsterdam	-1hr
New Zealand	Wellington	+10hr
Spain	Madrid	-1hr
UK	London	-2hr
USA	Washington, DC	-7hr

Tourist Information

South Africa

Almost every town in the country has a tourist office.

These are often private entities, which will only recommend member organisations and may add commissions to bookings they make on your behalf. They are worth visiting, but you may have to push to find out about all the possible options.

In state-run offices, staff are often badly informed and lethargic; asking for assistance at your accommodation may prove more useful. **South African Tourism** (www.southafrica.net) has a helpful website, with practical information and inspirational features.

PROVINCIAL TOURIST BOARDS

Eastern Cape Parks & Tourism Agency (www.ectourism.co.za)

Free State Tourism Authority (www.freestatetourism.org)

Gauteng Tourism Authority (www.gauteng.net)

Limpopo Tourism Agency (www.golimpopo.com)

Mpumalanga Tourism & Parks Agency (www.mpumalanga.com)

North West Parks & Tourism Board (www.tourismnorthwest.co.za)

Northern Cape Tourism (www.northerncape.org.za)

Tourism KwaZulu-Natal (www.zulu.org.za)

Western Cape Tourism (www.thewesterncape.co.za)

TOURIST OFFICES ABROAD

Visit www.southafrica.net for details of South African Tourism's offices and call centres in Amsterdam, Beijing, Frankfurt, London, Milan, Mumbai, New York, Paris, Tokyo and Sydney.

Lesotho & Swaziland

There are tourist offices in Maseru, Mbabane and the Ezulwini and Malkerns Valleys; elsewhere they are thin on the ground.

- **Lesotho Tourism Development Corporation** (visitlesotho.travel)
- **See Lesotho** (www.seelesotho.com)
- **Swaziland National Trust Commission** (www.sntc.org.sz)
- **Swaziland Tourism** (www.thekingdomofswaziland.com)
- **Swazi.travel** (www.swazi.travel)

Travellers with Disabilities

- South Africa is one of the best destinations on the continent for travellers with disabilities, with an ever-expanding network of facilities catering to those who are mobility impaired or blind.
- Establishments and destinations with facilities and access for travellers with disabilities have been noted in the book.
- Several gardens and nature reserves have Braille or trails for the visually impaired.
- Boardwalks for wheelchair access are found at many parks and attractions, and some can organise activities for travellers with disabilities.
- Hand-controlled vehicles can be hired at major car-rental agencies.

Resources

Accessible Cape Town (www.accessiblecapetown.com) Tours, transport, accommodation, sights, shopping and more in the Mother City.

Access-Able Travel Source (www.access-able.com) Lists tour operators, accommodation, sights and activities.

Disabled Travel (www.disabledtravel.co.za) Country-wide recommendations of accommodation, restaurants and services from an occupational therapist.

Epic-Enabled (www.epic-enabled.com) Offers accommodation and tours, including Kruger safaris.

Flamingo Tours (www.flamingotours.co.za) Tours around Cape Town, along the Garden Route and elsewhere.

Linx Africa (www.linx.co.za/trails/lists/disalist.html) Lists accessible nature trails.

QuadPara Association of South Africa (QASA; www.qasa.co.za) Has wheelchairs for beach use in Durban and the KwaZulu-Natal south coast.

Rolling SA (www.rollingsa.co.za) Tours including a nine-day safari covering Kruger.

SANParks (www.sanparks.org/groups/disabilities/general.php) Has a detailed and inspirational overview of accommodation and accessibility for blind, deaf and mobility-impaired travellers at its parks, including Kruger.

SouthAfrica.info (http://www.southafrica.info/travel/advice/disabled.htm) Has an overview of facilities and links to tour operators and local organisations.

Sponge Project (thespongeproject.yolasite.com) SMS information service for people with disabilities.

Visas

If you have recently travelled in a yellow-fever area, or even transited for over 12 hours en route to South Africa, you need to show a vaccination certificate to enter South Africa, Lesotho and Swaziland.

South Africa

- Travellers from most Commonwealth countries (including Australia, New Zealand, Canada and the UK), most Western European countries, Japan and the USA are issued with a free, 90-day visitor's permit on arrival.

➡ Your passport should be valid for at least 30 days after the end of your intended visit, and should have at least two blank pages.

➡ From June 2015, **new immigration regulations** (p37) require that all children aged under 18 show an unabridged birth certificate, with additional paperwork needed in some cases. Your airline will likely alert you to these new immigration regulations when you buy your flight.

➡ Immigration officers rarely ask to see it, but you should technically be able to present evidence of a return flight, or onward travel, from South Africa.

➡ If you have an onward flight, print a copy of your e-ticket, or ask your airline's help desk at the departing airport to print a copy of your itinerary.

➡ If you aren't entitled to a visitor's permit, you'll need to obtain a visa at a South African diplomatic mission in your home country, or one nearby.

➡ Visas are not issued at the borders.

➡ If you do need a visa, get a multiple-entry visa if you plan to visit Lesotho, Swaziland or any other neighbouring country. This avoids the hassle of applying for another South African visa.

➡ For any entry – whether you require a visa or not – you need to have at least two completely blank pages in your passport, excluding the last two pages.

➡ For more information, visit the websites of the **Department of Home Affairs** (www.dha.gov.za) and **Brand South Africa** (http://www.southafrica.info/travel/advice/disabled.htm).

VISA EXTENSIONS

➡ It is possible to extend your visitor's permit for an additional 90 days.

➡ Apply soon after arrival through **VFS Global** (www.vfsglobal.com/dha/southafrica/index.html).

➡ VFS Global also processes applications for temporary residence permits, which typically last for up to two years. It has offices in 11 cities including Cape Town, Durban, Jo'burg and Port Elizabeth.

➡ Immigration consultants include **TIES** (www.english.za.net; Somerset West, Western Cape).

➡ Extension applications cost R1775 and take two to eight weeks to process. They must be submitted in person, and required documents include an onward flight ticket, three months' bank statements and proof of South African address.

➡ Changes made to the immigration regulations in 2014 preclude 'visa runs'. If you reenter South Africa with a still-valid visa, you will not be given a new one unless you are coming from your country of residence; if your visa has expired, you will be given a visa allowing entry for up to seven days, unless you are coming from your country of residence, in which case you will be granted your full entitlement.

Lesotho

➡ Citizens of most Western European countries, the USA and most Commonwealth countries are granted a free entry permit at the border or airport.

➡ The standard permitted stay is 30 days.

➡ To stay for an extra 14 days, apply at the **Ministry of Home Affairs immigration department** (www.gov.ls; Maseru).

➡ If you ask for longer at the border (or the ministry), it may be granted.

➡ Another option is a 'visa run' to South Africa, reentering Lesotho when your visa has expired.

➡ Travellers who require a visa can get one at diplomatic missions in Pretoria and elsewhere.

➡ If you arrive at the Maseru Bridge border crossing without a visa, with some luck you'll be issued a temporary entry permit to allow you to get to Maseru, where you can apply for a visa at the Ministry of Home Affairs. However, don't count on this, as it depends on border officials' whim.

Swaziland

➡ Visitors from most Western countries don't need a visa to enter Swaziland for up to 30 days.

➡ To stay for longer than 30 days, apply at the **Ministry of Home Affairs immigration department** (www.gov.sz; Mbabane).

➡ People who need visas can get them at diplomatic missions in Pretoria and elsewhere.

➡ Visa applications must be accompanied by documents including a letter of invitation.

➡ Visas cost E80 for single entry, from E300 for multiple entry.

Volunteering

Volunteering is a growing area, with opportunities across South Africa, and in Lesotho and Swaziland. There are some rip-off operators, often around animal-related projects. Book through local rather than foreign organisations, get previous volunteers' opinions, and check that most of your payment will go to the schemes involved rather than middlemen.

To work on an unpaid, voluntary basis for a short period, a visitor's permit or visa suffices. If you want to take a lengthy placement (in South Africa, for example, longer than the 90 days afforded by a visitor's permit), the organisation facilitating your placement should help you apply for the correct visa.

Shorter experiences of a few hours, days or weeks are available through accommodation options and tourist businesses, which often give ongoing support to one or two local schemes. But keep in mind that while short visits are interesting for the visitor, they may be of limited use to the project, beyond any fee paid for the trip. Some prominent volunteer organisations have actually suggested that short-term volunteers may do more harm than good.

African Conservation Experience (www.conservationafrica.net; UK) Conservation projects and courses in Southern Africa.

African Impact (www.africanimpact.com; Cape Town) Volunteering and internship opportunities in areas including healthcare and conservation.

Backpacking South Africa (www.backpackingsouthafrica.co.za; Cape Town) Province-by-province listings of opportunities.

Eco-Access (www.eco-access.org; Jo'burg) A charity championing the rights of people with disabilities, and promoting better access to nature.

GoAbroad.com (www.volunteerabroad.com; USA) Listings of opportunities in South Africa, Lesotho and Swaziland.

Greater Good SA (www.myggsa.co.za; Cape Town) Has details on many local charities and development projects.

Grow (www.facebook.com/GROWMokhotlong/timeline; Mokhotlong) There are opportunities with this NGO implementing community-development programs in eastern Lesotho.

How 2 Help (www.h2h.info; Cape Town) Publishes a guide focusing on smaller, grassroots development projects.

i-to-i (www.i-to-i.com; UK) Conservation opportunities in South Africa, Swaziland and beyond, including monitoring great white sharks.

Kick4Life (www.kick4life.org; Maseru) Opportunities in Lesotho including the annual football tour, which mixes HIV education and soccer matches.

Life Skills (www.lifeskillsinsa.com; The Crags) Reforestation and other green projects on the Garden Route.

One World 365 (www.oneworld365.org; UK) Opportunities in areas including human rights, conservation, English teaching and healthcare.

Streetfootballworld (www.streetfootballworld.org; Germany) A starting point for football-related volunteering opportunities.

Uthando South Africa (www.uthandosa.org/projects; Cape Town) A tour company that supports a range of charitable projects.

VolunTourism (www.voluntourism.org; USA) General information and advice.

Wilderness Foundation (www.wildernessfoundation.org; Port Elizabeth) Conservation NGO running projects throughout Southern Africa.

World Wide Opportunities on Organic Farms (WWOOF; www.wwoofsa.co.za; Durban) Opportunities to stay and work on organic farms across South Africa; **Fynbos Estate** (www.fynbosestate.co.za) near Cape Town is recommended.

Women Travellers

Attitudes Towards Women

Old-fashioned attitudes to women are still common among South African men, regardless of colour. However, you should not tolerate sexist behaviour.

There's a high level of sexual assault and other violence against women in South Africa, the majority of which occurs in townships and poor rural areas. Given the HIV/AIDS epidemic, the problem is compounded by the transfer of infection. Rape victims have escaped infection by persuading the attacker to wear a condom.

For most female visitors, patriarchal attitudes and mildly sleazy behaviour are the main issues. However, there have been incidents of travellers being raped, and women should always take precautions.

Safety Precautions

- Single female travellers have a curiosity value that makes them conspicuous, but it may also bring forth generous offers of assistance and hospitality. Despite the risk of assault, many women travel alone safely in South Africa.
- The risk depends on where you go and what you do: riskiest (and not recommended) are hiking alone, hitching and picking up hitchers.
- Risks are reduced if two women travel together or, better, if a woman travels as part of a mixed-sex couple or group.
- Inland and in the more traditional black communities, it's best to behave conservatively. On the coast, casual dress is the norm, but elsewhere dress modestly (full-length clothes that aren't too tight) if you do not wish to draw attention to yourself.
- Always keep common sense and caution at the front of your mind, particularly at night.
- Don't go out alone in the evenings on foot; always take a taxi, preferably with others.
- Even during the day, avoid isolated areas, roadsides and quiet beaches.
- Carry a mobile phone if you'll be driving by yourself.
- If you are spending a long period in a more dangerous place such as Jo'burg, consider buying a can of pepper spray or similar to keep with you.

Safe Travel

CRIME

Caused by South Africa's poverty and social inequality, crime is the national obsession. Apart from car accidents, it's the major risk that you'll face here. However, try to keep things in perspective: despite the statistics and newspaper headlines, the majority of travellers visit without incident.

The risks are highest in Jo'burg, followed by some townships and other urban centres.

You can minimise risks by following basic safety precautions, including the following:

- Store your travel documents and valuables in your room if it's secure, in a safe or at least out of sight.
- If your room does not have a safe or is not secure, inquire if there is a safe in reception.
- Don't flash around valuables such as cameras, watches and jewellery.
- Don't look like you might be carrying valuables; avoid wearing expensive-looking clothes.
- Completely avoid external money pouches.
- Divide your cash into a few separate stashes, with some 'decoy' money or a 'decoy' wallet ready to hand over if you are mugged.
- Keep a small amount of cash handy and separate from your other money, so that you don't need to pull out a large wad of bills for making purchases.
- Don't keep money in your back pocket.
- Avoid groups of young men; trust older mixed-sex groups.
- Listen to local advice on unsafe areas.
- Avoid deserted areas day and night, including isolated beaches and parts of Cape Town's mountains.
- Avoid the downtown and central business district (CBD) areas of larger towns and cities at night and weekends.
- If you're visiting a township, join a tour or hire a trusted guide.
- Try not to look apprehensive or lost.
- If you get a local phone number, bear in mind that 419-style telephone and SMS scams are rife.

GOVERNMENT TRAVEL ADVICE

For the latest information, check the following websites:

www.auswaertiges-amt.de German Federal Foreign Office.

www.gov.uk/government/organisations/foreign-commonwealth-office UK Foreign & Commonwealth Office.

www.minbuza.nl Netherlands Ministry of Foreign Affairs.

www.mofa.go.jp Japanese Ministry of Foreign Affairs.

www.safetravel.govt.nz New Zealand Ministry of Foreign Affairs and Trade.

www.smartraveller.gov.au Australian Department of Foreign Affairs and Trade.

www.travel.gc.ca Canadian Ministry of Foreign Affairs, Trade and Development.

www.travel.state.gov US Department of State's Bureau of Consular Affairs.

In Transit

- On the flight over, keep your valuables in your hand luggage.

BEATING THE ATM SCAMS

There are dozens of ATM scams that involve stealing your cash, your card or your personal identification number (PIN) – usually all three. Thieves are just as likely to operate in Stellenbosch as in downtown Jo'burg, and they are almost always well-dressed and well-mannered men.

In the most common scam, the thief tampers with the ATM so your card becomes jammed. By the time you realise this you've entered your PIN. The thief will have seen this, and when you go inside to report that your card has been swallowed, he will take the card – along with several thousand rand. In a less common but equally surreptitious scam, a wireless device that records PINs is attached to the ATM. Always bearing the following rules in mind will help you avoid mishaps.

- Avoid ATMs at night and in secluded places. Rows of machines in shopping malls are usually safest.
- Most ATMs have security guards. If there's no guard around when you're withdrawing cash, watch your back, or get someone else to watch it.
- Watch the people using the ATM ahead of you carefully. If they look suspicious, go to another machine.
- Use ATMs during banking hours, and if possible, take a friend. If your card jams in a machine, one person can stay at the ATM while the other seeks assistance from the bank.
- Do not use an ATM if it appears to have been tampered with.
- When you put your card into the ATM, press cancel immediately. If the card is returned, you know there is no blockage in the machine and it should be safe to proceed.
- Refuse any offers of help to complete your transaction – or requests of help to complete someone else's.
- If someone does offer assistance, end your transaction immediately and find another machine.
- Carry your bank's emergency phone number, and report card loss immediately.
- Avoid using ATMs that inform you at the beginning of the transaction that they will not issue a receipt.
- If there are complications or the withdrawal fails, don't try again; retrieve your card.

- If arriving or changing planes at OR Tambo International Airport (Jo'burg), vacuum-wrap your baggage. Items are sometimes pilfered from bags before they reach the carousel.
- To travel around towns and cities after dark, take a taxi or, if your destination is very close, drive or walk with others.
- As a general rule, avoid walking by yourself or driving at night.
- Keep your car doors locked and windows up.
- Especially if you'll be driving alone, put your home mobile phone on roaming, buy a local SIM card or hire a phone.
- Leave your car in secure parking at night and avoid parking in secluded areas during the day.
- Don't leave anything valuable in your car, or give the impression that you are on a road trip with bags in the boot (trunk).
- One of the greatest dangers during muggings or carjackings (most common in Jo'burg) is that your assailants will assume that you are armed and will kill them if you get a chance. Stay calm, and don't resist or give them any reason to think you will fight back.

Lesotho & Swaziland

Crime rates are nowhere near as high as they are in South Africa. As long as you follow the basic precautions, you should be fine.

- Maseru, Lesotho, has seen an increase in armed robberies, break-ins and carjackings targeting expats (though it's small-scale compared with South Africa).
- Street crime is rising in Mbabane and Manzini, Swaziland.
- Elsewhere in Lesotho and Swaziland, crime is negligible.

DRUGS

➡ The legal system does not distinguish between soft and hard drugs.

➡ *Dagga* or *zol* (marijuana) is illegal but widely used.

➡ People often use marijuana openly, as you may discover in some backpacker hostels and bars. This is not recommended; there are heavy penalties for use and possession.

➡ Ecstasy is as much a part of club culture and the rave scene in South Africa as it is elsewhere.

➡ South Africa is a major market for the barbiturate Mandrax (known locally as 'buttons'), which is banned there and in many other countries because of its devastating effects.

➡ Drugs such as cocaine and heroin are becoming widely available and their use accounts for much crime.

➡ Local drugs, including *tik* (crystal meth) in Cape Town, compound social problems in the townships. Users are irrational and aggressive.

SOLO TRAVEL

➡ Solo travel in South Africa, Lesotho and Swaziland is straightforward.

➡ While you may be a minor curiosity in rural areas – and this is especially so for solo women travellers – in most places it's likely that nobody will even bat an eyelid.

➡ Times when you should join a tour or group include at night and on hiking trails.

➡ Particularly for women, going it alone on hiking trails is not recommended. There is normally a three-person minimum on trails for safety reasons – incidents have occurred.

➡ Especially in urban areas and at night, lone women travelling should use caution, and avoid isolating situations.

Transport

GETTING THERE & AWAY

Entering South Africa, Lesotho & Swaziland

Passports

As long as you have complied with visa and entry-permit requirements, there are no restrictions on any nationalities for entering South Africa, Lesotho or Swaziland.

South Africa

➡ South Africa is straightforward and hassle-free to enter, although airport customs officers often check bags for expensive gifts and items purchased overseas.

➡ Immigration officials rarely ask to see it, but travellers should technically be able to show an onward ticket; preferably an air ticket, although an overland ticket is also acceptable.

➡ The same applies to proof that you have sufficient funds for your stay; it pays to be neat, clean and polite.

➡ Immigration rules have been changing with regards to **travelling with children** (p37), which involve unabridged birth certificates etc, so check the latest details well before departure.

➡ For more information see www.southafrica.info.

Lesotho

➡ Entry permits are easy to get at Lesotho's land borders and Maseru's Moshoeshoe I International Airport.

➡ If you are a citizen of a country for which a visa is required, it's best to arrange this in advance.

Swaziland

➡ Entry via Swaziland's land borders and Manzini's King Mswati III International Airport is usually hassle-free.

➡ People who need visas can get them at Swazi diplomatic missions in Jo'burg, Pretoria and elsewhere.

Air

Airports & Airlines

South African Airways (☎0860 003 146; www.flysaa.com) is South Africa's national airline, with an excellent route network and safety record. In addition to its long-haul flights, it operates regional and domestic routes together with its partners **Airlink** (☎0861 606 606; www.flyairlink.com) and **SA Express** (☎0861 729 227; www.flyexpress.aero).

OR Tambo International Airport (JIA | JNB | ORTIA; ☎011-921 6262; www.airports.co.za), east of Jo'burg, is the major hub for Southern Africa.

CLIMATE CHANGE & TRAVEL

Every form of transport that relies on carbon-based fuel generates CO_2, the main cause of human-induced climate change. Modern travel is dependent on aeroplanes, which might use less fuel per kilometre per person than most cars but travel much greater distances. The altitude at which aircraft emit gases (including CO_2) and particles also contributes to their climate change impact. Many websites offer 'carbon calculators' that allow people to estimate the carbon emissions generated by their journey and, for those who wish to do so, to offset the impact of the greenhouse gases emitted with contributions to portfolios of climate-friendly initiatives throughout the world. Lonely Planet offsets the carbon footprint of all staff and author travel.

DEPARTURE TAX

South Africa Airport departure tax is included in ticket prices.

Lesotho Departure tax is M20.

Swaziland Departure tax is E20.

The other principal international airports are:

Cape Town International Airport (CPT; ☎021-937 1200; www.airports.co.za)

King Shaka International Airport (DUR; ☎032-436 6585; kingshakainternational.co.za) Durban.

Moshoeshoe I International Airport (MSU) Maseru, Lesotho.

King Mswati III International Airport (SHO; Map p494; ☎2518 4390; www.swacaa.co.sz) Manzini, Swaziland.

INTERNATIONAL AIRLINES

South Africa Numerous airlines fly to South Africa, mostly Jo'burg, from all over the world.

Lesotho Airlink connects Moshoeshoe I and OR Tambo.

Swaziland Airlink subsidiary **Swaziland Airlink** (☎2335 0100; www.flyswaziland.com) connects King Mswati III and OR Tambo.

Tickets

International fares to South Africa are usually at their highest during December and January, and between July and September. They are at their lowest in April and May (except for during the Easter holiday period) and in November. The rest of the year falls into the shoulder-season category.

It's normally cheaper to fly via Jo'burg than directly to Cape Town. If an airline serves both, an 'open jaw' ticket may be available, allowing you to fly into one city and out of another; more commonly, you may be able to fly to Jo'burg and return from Cape Town via Jo'burg (or vice versa).

London is a hub for airlines offering discounted fares.

INTERCONTINENTAL (ROUND-THE-WORLD) TICKETS

Some standard RTW itineraries include South Africa.

It's possible to include both Jo'burg and Cape Town, allowing you to fly into one city and out of the other, and make your own way between the two.

The easiest and cheapest option may be to fly in and out of Jo'burg on a RTW ticket, and make separate arrangements from there for Southern African travel.

From Africa

There are good connections between Jo'burg and most major African cities.

South African Airways, Airlink, SA Express, the other countries' national carriers and **British Airways** (☎011-441 8600; www.britishairways.com) are good starting points.

Most transcontinental flights have set pricing, with little of the competition-driven discounting that you'll find in other parts of the world. Flying via Europe or the Middle East is often cheaper.

SOUTHERN AFRICA

Jo'burg is well connected, including to secondary Southern African airports. For example, **Air Botswana** (☎011-390 3070; www.airbotswana.co.bw) offers direct flights from Jo'burg to Francistown, Kasane and Maun as well as the Botswanan capital, Gaborone.

Four budget South African airlines serve other destinations in the region:

Kulula (☎0861 585 852; www.kulula.com) Offers online discounts on British Airways flights from Jo'burg to Harare (Zimbabwe), Victoria Falls (Zimbabwe), Livingstone (Zambia), Mauritius, and Windhoek (Namibia), and on Kenya Airways flights from Jo'burg to Nairobi (Kenya).

Mango (☎0861 001 234; www.flymango.com) Jo'burg to Zanzibar (Tanzania).

Fastjet (☎011 289 8090; www.fastjet.com) Jo'burg to Dar es Salaam (Tanzania), with onward connections from the latter.

Flyafrica.com (☎010 100 3540; www.flyafrica.com) Jo'burg to Harare, Victoria Falls, Bulawayo (all Zimbabwe), Lusaka (Zambia) and Windhoek (Namibia), and Cape Town to Windhoek.

From Asia

Most of the major hubs have direct connections to Jo'burg.

South African Airways (www.fly-saa.com) From Bangkok, Beijing (with Air China), Hong Kong, Singapore, and several Indian airports (via Abu Dhabi).

Cathay Pacific (www.cathaypacific.com) From Hong Kong, with connections to Cape Town, Port Elizabeth and Durban.

Singapore Airlines (www.singaporeair.com) From Singapore, with connections to Cape Town and Durban.

Air Mauritius (www.airmauritius.com) Hong Kong, Beijing, Shanghai, Kuala Lumpur, Singapore, Delhi, Mumbai, Bengaluru and Chennai via Mauritius to Jo'burg, Cape Town and Durban.

From Australia & New Zealand

It often works out cheaper to travel via Asia, the Middle East or London.

Air Mauritius Perth via Mauritius to Jo'burg, Cape Town and Durban.

Singapore Airlines Perth, Adelaide, Melbourne, Sydney, Brisbane, Darwin, Auckland and Christchurch via Singapore to Jo'burg.

South African Airways Perth to Jo'burg.

Emirates (www.emirates.com) Most major cities in Australia and New Zealand via Dubai to Jo'burg, Cape Town and Durban.

Qantas (www.qantas.com.au)

From Canada & the USA

The cheapest route is often via London, continental Europe or even the Middle East. A discounted transatlantic ticket and separate onward ticket to Jo'burg or Cape Town may work out cheaper than a through-fare.

Some airlines fly via West African airports such as Accra (Ghana) and Dakar (Senegal).

From the US west coast, you can sometimes get good deals via Asia.

South African Airways flies to Jo'burg from New York and Washington, DC, via Dakar.

From Continental Europe

- You can fly to South Africa from most European capitals.
- Paris, Amsterdam, Frankfurt, Munich and Zurich are hubs; all are within about nine hours of Jo'burg.
- Several airlines fly direct to both Jo'burg and Cape Town, including KLM from Amsterdam and South African Airways from Munich.
- South African Airways also flies direct from Frankfurt and Zurich to Jo'burg.
- It can work out cheaper to fly via the Middle East.
- Turkish Airlines offers competitive fares to Jo'burg and Cape Town via Istanbul.

From South America

Travelling via London or continental Europe opens up more choice.

South African Airways São Paulo to Jo'burg.

From the Middle East

Emirates Dubai to Jo'burg, Cape Town and Durban.

South African Airways Abu Dhabi and Cairo to Jo'burg; Dubai to Jo'burg, Cape Town and Durban.

Turkish Airlines Istanbul to Jo'burg and Cape Town.

Egypt Air (www.egyptair.com) Cairo to Jo'burg, with connections to Cape Town and Durban.

Qatar Airways (www.qatarairways.com) Doha to Jo'burg and Cape Town.

From the UK & Ireland

Virgin Atlantic and British Airways fly direct from London to Jo'burg and Cape Town, with onward connections.

South African Airways flies direct from London to Jo'burg.

Cheap fares are also available via the Middle East, with airlines such as Turkish Airlines, Emirates and Qatar Airways, and via continental Europe.

From Ireland, you'll need to fly via London or continental Europe.

As well as travel agents, preferably those registered with the Association of British Travel Agents (www.abta.com), check ads in the travel sections of weekend newspapers; and in such publications as *TNT*, the *South African*, *Time Out* and the *Evening Standard*.

Land

Bicycle

There are no restrictions on bringing your own bicycle into South Africa, Lesotho or Swaziland. Sources of information:

Cycling South Africa (www.cyclingsa.com)

International Bicycle Fund (www.ibike.org)

Border Crossings

BOTSWANA

There are 15 official South Africa–Botswana border posts, open between at least 8am and 3pm.

Some of the more remote crossings are impassable to 2WD vehicles and may be closed during periods of high water. Otherwise, the crossings are hassle-free.

Citizens of most Western nations do not require a visa to enter Botswana. People who do require a visa should apply in advance through a Botswanan mission (or a British mission in countries without Botswanan representation).

Grobler's Bridge/Martin's Drift (8am-6pm) Northwest of Polokwane (Pietersburg).

Kopfontein Gate/Tlokweng Gate (6am-midnight) Next to Madikwe Game Reserve; a main border post.

Pont Drift (8am-4pm) Convenient for Mapungubwe National Park (Limpopo) and Tuli Block (Botswana).

Ramatlabama (6am-10pm) North of Mahikeng; a main border post.

Skilpadshek/Pioneer Gate (6am-midnight) Northwest of Zeerust; a main border post.

Swartkopfontein Gate/Ramotswa (6am-10pm) Northwest of Zeerust.

Twee Rivieren (7.30am-4pm) At the South African entrance to Kgalagadi Transfrontier Park.

LESOTHO

All of Lesotho's borders are with South Africa and are straightforward to cross.

The main crossing is at Maseru Bridge, east of Bloemfontein. Queues here are sometimes very long exiting and, on some weekend evenings, entering Lesotho; use other posts if possible.

MOZAMBIQUE

Citizens of Western countries should apply in advance for tourist visas at a Mozambican mission. Border visas may be issued to people coming from countries where there is no Mozambican consular representation, but travellers in this situation should check with the Mozambican high commission in Pretoria (or Mbabane).

The following are the Mozambique–South Africa border posts.

Giriyondo (8am-4pm Oct-Mar, 8am-3pm Apr-Sep) Between Kruger National Park's Phalaborwa Gate and Massingir (Mozambique).

Kosi Bay/Ponta d'Ouro (8am-4pm) On the coast, well north of Durban.

Lebombo/Ressano Garcia (6am-midnight) The main crossing, east of Nelspruit; also known as Komatipoort.

Pafuri (8am-4pm) In Kruger National Park's northeastern corner.

NAMIBIA

Citizens of most Western nations do not require a visa to enter Namibia for up to three months. People who do require a visa should apply in advance through a Namibian mission.

South Africa–Namibia border posts include the following.

Alexander Bay/Oranjemund (6am-10pm) On the Atlantic coast; access is reliant on the ferry.

Nakop/Ariamsvlei (24 hours) West of Upington.

Rietfontein/Aroab (8am-4.30pm) Just south of Kgalagadi Transfrontier Park.

Vioolsdrif/Noordoewer (24 hours) North of Springbok, en route to/from Cape Town.

SWAZILAND

There are 11 South Africa–Swaziland border posts, all of which are hassle-free, including the following. Note that small posts close at 4pm.

Goba/Mhlumeni (24hr) To/from Mozambique.

Golela/Lavumisa (7am-10pm) En route between Durban and Swaziland's Ezulwini Valley.

Josefdal/Bulembu (8am-4pm) Between Piggs Peak and Barberton (Mpumalanga); can be tricky in wet weather.

Lomahasha/Namaacha (7am-8pm) The busy post in extreme northeast Swaziland is the main crossing to/from Mozambique.

Mahamba (8am-8pm) The best crossing to use from Piet Retief in Mpumalanga. Casinos nearby attract traffic, especially on weekends – good places to look for lifts into and out of the country.

Mananga (8am-6pm) Southwest of Komatipoort.

Matsamo/Jeppe's Reef (8am-8pm) Southwest of Malelane and a possible route to Kruger National Park. Casinos nearby attract traffic, especially on weekends – good places to look for lifts into and out of the country.

Onverwacht/Salitje (8am-6pm) North of Pongola in KwaZulu-Natal.

Oshoek/Ngwenya (7am-10pm) The busiest crossing (and a good place to pick up lifts), about 360km southeast of Pretoria.

ZIMBABWE

- Citizens of most Western nations need a visa to enter Zimbabwe, and these should be purchased at the border.
- **Beitbridge** (24hr), on the Limpopo River, is the only border post between Zimbabwe and South Africa.
- There's lots of smuggling, so searches are thorough and queues often long.
- The closest South African town to the border is Musina (15km south), where you can change money.
- Ignore touts on the Zimbabwe side trying to 'help' you through Zimbabwe immigration and customs;

LESOTHO BORDERS

BORDER	OPENING HOURS	NEAREST LESOTHO CROSSING/SOUTH AFRICAN TOWN
Caledonspoort	6am-10pm	Butha-Buthe/Fouriesburg
Makhaleng Bridge	8am-6pm	Mohale's Hoek/Zastron
Maputsoe Bridge	24hr	Maputsoe/Ficksburg
Maseru Bridge	24hr	Maseru/Ladybrand
Nkonkoana Gate	8am-4pm	Sehlabathebe NP/Bushman's Nek
Ongeluksnek	7am-7pm	Mphaki/Matatiele
Peka Bridge	6am-4pm	Peka/Clocolan
Qacha's Nek	8am-10pm	Qacha's Nek/Matatiele
Ramatseliso's Gate	8am-6pm	Tsoelike/Matatiele
Sani Pass	8am-4pm	Mokhotlong/Himeville
Sephapo's Gate	8am-4pm	Mafeteng/Boesmanskop
Tele Bridge	8am-10pm	Quthing/Sterkspruit
Van Rooyen's Gate	8am-10pm	Mafeteng/Wepener

there's no charge for the government forms needed for immigration.

Bus

- Numerous bus lines cross between South Africa and its neighbours.
- It's the most efficient way to travel overland, unless you have your own vehicle.
- Sometimes-lengthy queues are usually the only major hassle.
- You'll have to disembark to take care of visa formalities, then reboard and carry on.
- Visa prices are not included in ticket prices.

SHARED TAXI

- You can travel to/from South Africa's neighbours by local shared taxi.
- A few routes go direct.
- It's normally necessary to walk across the border and pick up a new taxi on the other side.
- Long-distance services generally leave early in the morning.

BOTSWANA

Intercape (☎021-380 4400; www.intercape.co.za) runs daily between Gaborone (Botswana) and Jo'burg (R210 to R310, seven hours) via Pretoria.

Less safe and comfortable than buses, shared taxis run from Jo'burg to Gaborone (6½ hours) and Lobatse (Botswana) with a change in Mahikeng (North West Province). Another route from Jo'burg is via Grobler's Bridge/Martin's Drift to Palapye (Botswana; eight hours).

LESOTHO

Shared taxis connect Jo'burg and Maseru.

It's quicker and easier to catch a bus to Bloemfontein, then continue by shared taxi to Maseru (three hours).

South African bus lines including Intercape also link Bloemfontein with Ladybrand (2½ hours), a few kilometres from the Maseru Bridge crossing.

Leaving Maseru, long-distance shared taxis leave from the rank at Maseru Bridge.

Other possible shared-taxi routes:

- Butha-Buthe to/from Fouriesburg (Free State).
- Leribe (Hlotse) to/from Ficksburg (Free State).
- Quthing to/from Sterkspruit (Eastern Cape).
- Qacha's Nek to/from Matatiele (Eastern Cape).

MOZAMBIQUE

Bus companies including **Greyhound** (☎011-611 8000; www.greyhound.co.za), **Intercape** (☎021-380 4400; www.intercape.co.za) and **Translux** (☎0861 589 282; www.translux.co.za) run daily 'luxury' coaches between Jo'burg/Pretoria and Maputo (Mozambique) via Nelspruit and Ressano Garcia (Komatipoort; R350, eight hours). Passengers must have a valid Mozambique visa before boarding the bus.

The above route can be tackled in shared taxis.

Mozambique-based **Cheetah Express** (☎in South Africa 013-755-1988; Lowveld Tourism, Nelspruit Crossing Mall, cnr Madiba & Samora Machel Drs, Nelspruit) runs shuttles between Nelspruit and Maputo.

Taxis run between Maputo and the Namaacha/Lomahasha post on the Swazi border (1¾ hours); some continue to Manzini (3¼ hours).

NAMIBIA

Intercape (☎021-380 4400; www.intercape.co.za) runs buses from Windhoek (Namibia) to Cape Town (R680 to R950, 21½ hours) on Monday, Wednesday, Friday and Sunday, returning Tuesday, Thursday, Friday and Sunday.

SWAZILAND

Daily shuttles run between Jo'burg and Mbabane.

Shared taxi routes:

- Jo'burg to/from Mbabane (four hours); some continue to Manzini.
- Durban to/from Manzini (eight hours).
- Manzini to/from Maputo (3¼ hours).

ZIMBABWE

Greyhound (☎011-611 8000; www.greyhound.co.za) and **Intercape** (☎021-380 4400; www.intercape.co.za) operate daily buses between Jo'burg and Harare (Zimbabwe; R500, 17 hours), and between Jo'burg and Bulawayo (Zimbabwe; R475, 14 hours) both via Pretoria.

Shared taxis run south from Beitbridge to Musina and beyond.

Car & Motorcycle

- If you rent a car in South Africa and plan to take it across an international border, you'll need a permission letter from the rental company.
- Most companies permit entry to most neighbouring counties, including Lesotho and Swaziland; some may be reluctant regarding Mozambique.
- Check that the right information is on the permission letter; companies often get it wrong.
- South African car-rental companies typically charge the following cross-border fees, including the permission letter: Botswana R1500, Lesotho R500, Mozambique R2000, Namibia R1500, Swaziland R300, Zimbabwe R1500.
- Taking a car across a border also raises the insurance excess.

BRINGING YOUR OWN VEHICLE

- You'll need the vehicle's registration papers, liability

insurance and your driving licence.

- You'll also need a *carnet de passage en douane*, the international customs document, which allows the temporary admission of motor vehicles.
- Obtain a carnet through your local automobile association (from about US$300).
- Drivers of vehicles from outside Africa must typically pay a 50% refundable security deposit of 25% of the vehicle's value.
- Cars registered in South Africa, Lesotho, Swaziland, Botswana and Namibia, and driven by citizens or permanent residents of these countries, don't need a carnet to visit the other countries in this group.

BOTSWANA

The following crossings are passable in 2WD cars:

- Grobler's Bridge/Martin's Drift
- Kopfontein Gate/Tlokweng Gate
- Ramatlabama
- Skilpadshek/Pioneer Gate

LESOTHO

Road tax of M30 (or R30) is payable on entering Lesotho. The easiest entry points for cars and motorcycles are on the northern and western sides of the country.

Most of the entry points to the south and east are unpaved, though many are passable in a 2WD, depending on weather conditions. A sealed road runs around the perimeter of the country from Qacha's Nek clockwise to Mokhotlong.

It's more economical to rent a car in South Africa than in Lesotho. You must have two red hazard triangles in your car in case of a breakdown.

MOZAMBIQUE

You must have two red hazard triangles in your car in case of a breakdown.

Kosi Bay/Ponta d'Ouro Travelling to/from Mozambique via this border post, you'll need your own 4WD vehicle. Accommodation options in Ponta d'Ouro (Mozambique) offer transfers.

Lebombo/Ressano Garcia (Komatipoort) The N4 highway connects Pretoria with this post, joined by the N12 from Jo'burg. the EN4 highway runs southeast from here to Maputo. There are tolls on both sides of the border.

Namaacha/Lomahasha The roads leading to this border post with Swaziland are sealed, and negotiable with 2WD.

Giriyondo It's 95km from Kruger's Phalaborwa gate to Giriyondo, and 75km further to Massingir, the first major town on the Mozambique side. A 4WD and proof of overnight accommodation in the relevant park are required.

Pafuri Just 29km from Kruger's Pafuri gate, but on the Mozambique side there is an unbridged crossing of the Limpopo River near Mapai (makeshift ferry during rains) and a rough bush track thereafter via Mabote and Mapinhane to Vilankulo (4WD required). Allow two full days for the journey. Proof of accommodation in Kruger or Limpopo park is required.

NAMIBIA

2WD Highways lead to the Vioolsdrif/Noordoewer and Nakop/Ariamsvlei crossings.

4WD A 4WD opens up more options for crossing the border, including through the Kgalagadi and |Ai-|Ais/Richtersveld transfrontier parks.

SWAZILAND

- Swaziland's borders can be crossed in a 2WD.
- Road tax of E50 is payable on entering the country.
- It's more economical to rent a car in South Africa than in Swaziland.

ZIMBABWE

Entering or leaving South Africa, vehicles pay a toll at the border to use the Limpopo Bridge.

Train

The Man in Seat Sixty-One (www.seat61.com) has ideas for train travel throughout Southern Africa.

MOZAMBIQUE

Caminhos de Ferro de Moçambique (CFM; www.cfm.co.mz) Daily train between Maputo and the Lebombo/Ressano Garcia (Komatipoort) border post (US$1 3¾ hours), where you can cross the border on foot and continue by bus or shared taxi.

NAMIBIA

TransNamib StarLine (www.transnamib.com.na) Connects Walvis Bay, Swakopmund and Windhoek with Keetmanshoop and Karasburg in southern Namibia. From the latter, you can catch an Intercape bus across the border to Upington (Northern Cape).

Sea

South Africa is an important stop on world shipping routes. Cape Town is a major port of call for cruise ships, and many also stop at Durban. Both are good places to look for crew berths on private yachts sailing up the East African coast.

It's possible to find cruise and freighter lines linking South Africa with Mozambique, Madagascar and Mauritius. Many freighters have comfortable passenger cabins.

Even on freighter lines, the thrill of approaching the tip of the continent by sea certainly doesn't come cheap. Fares from South Africa tend to be lower than those to the country.

Helpful contacts:

Cruise People (www.cruisepeople.co.uk) Based in London.

Cruiser Log (www.cruiserlog.com) Forum and crew positions.

Cunard (www.cunard.co.uk) Luxury cruises to Cape Town. Has a list of cruise travel agents around the world.

LBH Africa (www.tallships.co.za) South Africa.

Maris Freighter Cruises (www.freightercruises.com) USA.

Perpetual Travel (http://perpetualtravel.com/rtw/rtwfreighters.html) Suggests reference books and further links.

Royal Mail Ship St Helena (www.rms-st-helena.com) Cape Town to St Helena and Ascension Island.

Safmarine (www.safmarine.com) Denmark. Cargo ships.

Tours

Dozens of tour and safari companies organise package tours to South Africa, Lesotho, Swaziland and their neighbouring countries.

If you prefer a more independent approach, you can book flights and accommodation for the first few nights, then join tours locally.

Itineraries typically include Kruger National Park and Cape Town and the peninsula.

For particular interests such as birdwatching and botany, check the advertisements in specialist magazines.

Australia

Adventure World (www.adventureworld.com.au) A range of tours and safaris in South Africa and the region.

African Wildlife Safaris (www.africanwildlifesafaris.com.au) Customised tours and safaris in South Africa and neighbouring countries.

Peregrine Travel (www.peregrineadventures.com) Guided and independent tours and safaris in South Africa, Swaziland and beyond, including family adventures.

France

Makila Voyages (www.makila.fr) Upper-end tailored tours and safaris in South Africa and its neighbours.

UK

Dragoman (www.dragoman.co.uk) Overland tours.

Exodus Travels (www.exodus.co.uk) A variety of tours, including overland trips, walking, cycling, wildlife and conservation itineraries, covering South Africa and surrounds.

Face Africa (www.faceafrica.com) Tailor-made ethical tours, self-drive trips, safaris, honeymoons and family holidays around South Africa and beyond, incorporating cultural tourism.

Intrepid Travel (www.intrepidtravel.com) Tours espousing the philosophy of independent travel; numerous itineraries cover South Africa, Swaziland and the region.

In the Saddle (www.inthesaddle.com) Strictly for horse aficionados, with various rides in South Africa (including the Wild Coast and the Witteberg mountains near Lesotho) and its northern neighbours.

Naturetrek (www.naturetrek.co.uk) Specialist nature tours, visiting parts of South Africa (including the Drakensberg and Kruger National Park) and its northern neighbours.

Temple World (www.templeworld.co.uk) Upper-end 'educational' tours in South Africa, Swaziland and elsewhere in the region, focusing on themes such as history, culture and wildlife.

USA

Adventure.com (adventure.com) Formerly known as Adventure Center, it offers activity-focused adventures with a local slant throughout Africa.

Africa Adventure Company (www.africa-adventure.com) Upper-end wildlife safaris, including the private reserves around Kruger National Park, plus itineraries in and around Cape Town.

Born Free Safaris & Tours (www.safaris2africa.com) Itineraries covering areas from the Cape to Swaziland and further north in Southern Africa.

Bushtracks Expeditions (www.bushtracks.com) Luxury safaris and private air charters.

GETTING AROUND

Air

Airlines in South Africa, Lesotho & Swaziland

Domestic fares are affordable depending on the route. A budget flight from Jo'burg to Cape Town, a popular route served by numerous airlines, costs from R500, but Cape Town to East London, a less competitive route, costs from R1800.

It can save money, or offer convenience at no extra cost, to tie domestic flights into an international ticket; eg fly from London to Jo'burg and on to Cape Town with South African Airways.

Computicket Travel (☎0861 915 4000; www.computickettravel.com) is a good first port of call, as it covers several airlines, as is South African Airways' website, which covers Airlink, SA Express and Mango as well as SAA flights.

Keep costs down by booking online months before travelling.

Airlink (☎0861 606 606; www.flyairlink.com) South African Airways' partner has a good network, including smaller destinations such as Upington, Mthatha and Maseru.

Comair (☎0860 435 922; www.comair.co.za) Operates British Airways flights in Southern Africa, and has flights linking Jo'burg with Cape Town, Durban, Port Elizabeth and Southern Africa.

SA Express (☎0861 729 227; www.flyexpress.aero) This South African Airways partner has a good network, including direct flights between Cape Town and

Hoedspruit (for Kruger National Park).

South African Airways (☎0860 003 146; www.flysaa.com) The national airline, with an extensive domestic and regional network.

Swaziland Airlink (☎in South Africa 0861 606 606, in Swaziland 2335 0100; www.flyswaziland.com) Flies between Jo'burg and Manzini.

BUDGET AIRLINES

South Africa's budget airlines also offer hotel bookings, car rentals and holiday packages.

FlySafair (☎0871 351 351; www.flysafair.co.za) A new airline offering rock-bottom fares between Jo'burg, Cape Town, Port Elizabeth and George.

Kulula (☎0861 585 852; www.kulula.com) Comair's budget airline connects Jo'burg, Cape Town, Durban, George and East London. It also offers discounts on British Airways flights.

Mango (☎0861 001 234; www.flymango.com) The South African Airways subsidiary flies between Jo'burg, Cape Town, Durban, Port Elizabeth, George and Bloemfontein.

Skywise.co.za (☎0861 989 895; www.skywise.co.za) A new airline connecting Jo'burg and Cape Town from R500, with Durban set to join its network.

Bicycle

South Africa

As long as you're fit enough to handle the hills, South Africa offers some rewarding cycling. It has scenic and diverse terrain, abundant campsites, and numerous quiet secondary roads. The major drawback is sharing the tarmac with South Africa's erratic and aggressive drivers.

Good areas The roads around the Cape peninsula and Winelands are popular, although busy; the Wild Coast is beautiful and challenging; the northern lowveld offers wide plains.

Public transport Trains can carry bicycles, but most bus lines don't want bicycles in their luggage holds, and shared taxis don't carry luggage on the roof. Cape Town's Cape Metro Rail trains and MyCiTi buses accept bikes.

Purchase Larger South African cities, especially Cape Town, have a good selection of mountain bikes for sale. Jo'burg and Cape Town are the best places to look for touring bikes. To resell your bicycle at the end of your trip, try hostel notice boards, bike shops and clubs, and www.gumtree.co.za.

Rental For day rides, some hostels offers short-term mountain-bike rental. Rentals can also sometimes be arranged through bike shops in the cities, though you'll usually be required to leave a credit-card deposit.

Safety Distances between major towns are often long, although, except in isolated areas such as the Karoo, you're rarely far from a village or farmhouse. Many roads don't have a hard shoulder; on those that do, motorists use the shoulder as an unofficial slow lane. It's illegal to cycle on highways, and roads near urban areas are too busy and hazardous. Before heading off anywhere, contact other cyclists, through local cycling clubs or bicycle shops, to get recent information on the routes you're considering. Bring a good lock to counter the ever-present risk of theft, store the bike inside your accommodation (preferably inside your room) and chain it to something solid.

Spare parts Mountain bikes and parts are widely available in the cities. It's often difficult to find specialised parts for touring bikes, especially outside Cape Town and Jo'burg. Establish a relationship with a good bike shop in a city before you head off into the veld, in case you need something couriered to you.

Weather Much of the country (except for the Western Cape and west coast) gets most of its rain in summer (late November to March), often in the form of violent thunderstorms. When it isn't raining, summer days can be unpleasantly hot, especially in the steamy lowveld.

Lesotho & Swaziland

Both are excellent cycling destinations, for which you need a mountain bike. Stock up on spare parts in South Africa. Summer thunderstorms and flooding are an issue. Transporting bicycles on public transport is uncommon, but you can often arrange something with the driver.

Lesotho The mountainous terrain means Lesotho is only for the physically fit. You can rent bikes from accommodation such as **Malealea Lodge** (www.malealea.co.ls), where two annual mountain-biking events take place. There are countless options, but for experienced cyclists, the Sani Pass is Lesotho's classic mountain-bike route. It's sometimes possible to hire bicycles through lodges on the South Africa side of the pass. Beware of icy roads in winter.

Swaziland Avoid the main towns and the heavily travelled Ezulwini Valley. Short pedals are available on the mountain-bike trails of Hlane Royal National Park and Mlilwane Wildlife Sanctuary, which respectively offer guided rides and bike rental.

Boat

There are few opportunities to travel by boat. The most likely possibilities are between Cape Town, Port Elizabeth and Durban.

Local yacht clubs are good starting points.

Bus

South Africa

A good network of buses, of varying reliability and comfort, links the major cities.

Classes There are no class tiers on the bus lines, although major companies generally offer a 'luxury' service, with features such as air-con, a toilet and films.

BAZ BUS

A convenient alternative to standard bus lines, **Baz Bus** (☎0861 229 287; www.bazbus.com) caters almost exclusively to backpackers and travellers. It offers hop-on, hop-off fares and door-to-door service between Cape Town and Jo'burg via the Garden Route, Port Elizabeth, Mthatha, Durban and the Northern Drakensberg.

Baz Bus drops off and picks up at hostels, and has transfer arrangements with those off its route in areas such as the Wild Coast. You can book directly with Baz Bus or at most hostels.

Point-to-point fares are more expensive than on the major bus lines, but it can work out economically if you take advantage of the hop-on/hop-off feature.

Sample one-way hop-on, hop-off fares from Cape Town: Jo'burg R4500, Durban R3750, Port Elizabeth R1940.

One-/two-/three-week travel passes cost R2100/R3400/4200.

Discounts The major bus lines offer student, backpacker and senior-citizen discounts, as well as specials – check their websites for details. Inquire about travel passes if you'll be taking several bus journeys.

Fares Roughly calculated by distance, although short runs are disproportionately expensive. Your fare may also be based on the bus's whole journey (so travelling from Jo'burg to Bloemfontein costs the same as from Pretoria). Prices rise during school holidays.

Safety Lines are generally safe. Note, however, that many long-distance services run through the night. On overnight journeys, travellers should take care of their valuables and women might feel more comfortable sitting near the front of the bus.

Ticket purchase For the main lines, purchase tickets at least 24 hours in advance, and as far in advance as possible for travel during peak periods. Tickets can be bought through bus offices, **Computicket** (☎0861 915 8000; www.computicket.co.za) and Shoprite/Checkers supermarkets.

BUS LINES

Greyhound and Translux are considered the premium lines.

City to City (☎0861 589 282; www.citytocity.co.za) In partnership with Translux, it operates the routes that once carried people between the homelands and the cities under apartheid. The no-frills service is less expensive than the other lines, and serves many off-the-beaten-track places, including townships and mining towns. Destinations include Mthatha (for the Wild Coast), Nelspruit (for Kruger National park), Beitbridge (for Zimbabwe), Cape Town and Durban.

Greyhound (☎011-611 8000; www.greyhound.co.za) An extensive nationwide network of comfortable buses, including Jo'burg to Durban via Richards Bay. Also operates other lines including the cheaper Citiliner buses.

Intercape (☎021-380 4400; www.intercape.co.za) An extensive network stretching from Cape Town to Limpopo and beyond. For longer hauls (including Cape Town to Windhoek, Namibia, and Mossel Bay to Jo'burg), it's worth paying extra for a reclining seat on an overnight Sleepliner bus.

Translux (☎0861 589 282; www.translux.co.za) The main long-distance operator, serving destinations including Cape Town, Durban, Bloemfontein, Port Elizabeth, East London, Mthatha, Nelspruit and the Garden Route.

Lesotho

Buses and shared taxis A good network of buses, minibus shared taxis (known locally as just 'taxis'), sprinters and private or shared car taxis (known as 'four plus ones') covers most of the country. Minibus taxis serve the major towns and many smaller spots. Buses (cheaper and slower) and sprinters (faster and more expensive) serve the major towns. There are no classes, and service is decidedly no-frills.

Departures Most departures are in the morning (generally, the longer the journey, the earlier the departure).

Northern Lesotho Heading northeast from Maseru by shared taxi, you usually have to change at Maputsoe. The transfer sometimes happens en route into Maputsoe if your vehicle meets another taxi.

Tickets On larger local buses, although you'll be quoted long-distance fares, it's best to just buy a ticket to the next major town. Most passengers will likely get off there, leaving you stuck waiting for the vehicle to fill up again while other buses and shared taxis leave. Buying tickets in stages is only slightly more expensive than buying a direct ticket. It's not necessary (or possible) to reserve a seat in advance.

Swaziland

➡ Minibus shared taxis are the main form of public transport.

➡ They run almost everywhere, with frequent stops en route.

➡ Shared taxis leave when full; no reservations are necessary.

➡ Only a few domestic buses.

➡ Most start and terminate at the main stop in central Mbabane.

➡ Buses are slightly cheaper than minibuses.

Car & Motorcycle

- South Africa is one of the world's great countries for a road trip.
- Away from the main bus and train routes, having your own wheels is the best way to get around.
- If you're in a group, hiring a car is often the most economical option.
- Road maps, a worthwhile investment, are readily available in South Africa.

Automobile Associations

Automobile Association of South Africa (AASA; ☎011-799 1001, emergencies 0861 000 234; www.aasa.co.za) offers a vehicle breakdown service, which can be useful if you'll be driving in the areas it covers.

Its fleet of emergency response vehicles operates out of Johannesburg, Pretoria, Durban, Cape Town, Pietermaritzburg, Port Elizabeth, Nelspruit, Polokwane (Pietersburg), Bloemfontein, Rustenburg, Somerset West, Stellenbosch and East London, with AA-approved operatives available elsewhere.

Membership costs from R42 per month.

Members of foreign clubs in the **Fédération Internationale de l'Automobile** (FIA; www.fia.com) group have free access to AASA services for three months, including roadside repairs in Jo'burg, Pretoria, Cape Town, Durban and Port Elizabeth.

In Lesotho and Swaziland, you'll need to rely on local repair facilities in the major towns.

Driving Licence

- You can use your driving licence from your home country, provided it is in English (or you have a certified translation).
- In South Africa, it should also carry your photo.
- Otherwise you'll need an international driving permit.
- Police generally ask to see foreign drivers' passports, so keep a photocopy in your car.

Fuel & Spare Parts

- Unleaded petrol costs about R12 per litre in all three countries.
- An attendant will fill your tank and clean your windows.
- Tip R2.
- If they check your oil, water or tyres, tip R5.
- Along the main roads in South Africa and Swaziland, there are plenty of petrol stations.
- Many stay open 24 hours.
- There are petrol stations in all major South African towns.
- In rural areas, and throughout Lesotho, fill up whenever you can.

LESOTHO

- The main petrol stations are in Maseru.
- Other major towns have limited facilities and unreliable fuel availability.
- Carry a jerry can, as fuel is not readily available in remote areas.

SWAZILAND

- Mbabane and Manzini have the best facilities.
- Manzini is the best place for sourcing spare parts.

Hire

- Car rental is inexpensive in South Africa compared with Europe and North America, starting well below R200 per day.
- Many companies levy a surcharge for drivers aged below 21 (23 in Swaziland).
- Most companies ask for a credit card, and will not accept a debit card. Most use a chip-and-pin machine, so you need to know your credit card's pin number.
- For low rates, book online months in advance.
- Most companies stipulate a daily mileage limit, with an extra fee payable for any mileage over this limit. This can be a drawback if you're planning a long road trip. Four hundred kilometres a day is generally sufficient. If you plan one- or two-day stops along the way, 200km a day might be sufficient.
- A few local companies offer unlimited mileage. If you rent through an international company, and book through an overseas branch, you may get unlimited mileage for no extra cost, except at peak times such as December to January.

PARKING & CAR GUARDS

Parking is readily available at sights, eateries and accommodation throughout South Africa, Lesotho and Swaziland. Particularly in Jo'burg and other locations where crime is a problem, secure parking is often offered.

If you are parking in the street or even a car park in larger South African towns and cities, you will often be approached by a 'car guard'. They will keep an eye on your motor in exchange for a tip: R2 for a short period, R5 to R10 for long stays. They may also offer to wash your car for an extra R20. Do not pay them until you are leaving, or if they did not approach you when you arrived. Ensure you give the money to the right person; in Cape Town, for example, approved car guards often wear high-visibility vests.

- Make sure that quoted prices include the 14% value-added tax (VAT).
- One-way rental is charged according to the distance of the relocation.
- If loaded up with people or luggage, small cars may struggle on hills. Even on major highways, hills can be steep in areas such as the Wild Coast.
- Steep hills may also make automatics unpleasant to drive.
- South Africa has rental operations in cities, major towns and airports.
- It's generally cheapest to hire in a hub such as Jo'burg or Cape Town.

LESOTHO & SWAZILAND

- It usually works out cheaper to rent a vehicle in South Africa and drive it over the border (you'll need a permission letter from the rental company to cross the border; this costs about R500 for Lesotho, R300 for Swaziland).
- Lesotho has rental operations in Maseru and Moshoeshoe I International Airport.
- Swaziland has rental operations in Mbabane and King Mswati III International Airport.

RENTAL COMPANIES

Also check with backpacker hostels and travel agents, as many offer good deals. Local companies are usually less expensive, though they tend to come and go, and their vehicles are often older.

Abba (www.abbacarrentals.co.za) Covers South Africa.

Argus (www.arguscarhire.co.za) Online consolidator, covering South Africa, Lesotho and Swaziland.

Around About Cars (www.aroundaboutcars.com) Covering South Africa and Swaziland, this recommended budget agent gets low rates with other operators, including Budget, Tempest and First. One of the few companies offering unlimited mileage.

Avis (www.avis.co.za) Covers South Africa, Lesotho and Swaziland.

Budget (www.budget.co.za) Covers South Africa and Lesotho.

Europcar (www.europcar.co.za) Covers South Africa, Lesotho and Swaziland.

First (www.firstcarrental.co.za) Covers South Africa.

Hertz (www.hertz.co.za) Covers South Africa.

Sixt (www.sixt.com) Covers South Africa.

Tempest (www.tempestcarhire.co.za) Covers South Africa.

Thrifty (www.thrifty.co.za) Covers South Africa.

CAMPERVANS, 4WD & MOTORCYCLES

- Some campervan/motorhome rentals include camping gear.
- One-way rental is not always possible.
- 'Bakkie' campers, sleeping two in the back of a canopied pick-up, are cheaper.
- Mopeds and scooters are available for hire in Cape Town and other tourist areas.
- For Lesotho and provinces such as the Northern and Eastern Capes with many gravel roads and national parks, consider a 4WD.
- Besides standard rental-car companies, check: **African Leisure Travel** (www.africanleisure.co.za) Jo'burg, 4WD and campervans; **Britz 4x4 Rentals** (www.britz.co.za) Cape Town and Jo'burg, 4WD; **Drive South Africa** (www.drivesouthafrica.co.za) Cape Town, 4WD and campervans; **Maui** (www.maui.co.za) Cape Town and Jo'burg, motorhomes; and **Motozulu** (www.motozu.lu.ms) Port Shepstone (KwaZulu-Natal), motorcycles.

Insurance

Insurance for third-party damage and damage to or loss of your vehicle is highly recommended, though it's not legally required for private-vehicle owners.

Generally it is only available on an annual basis.

If you're renting a vehicle, insurance with an excess should be included, with an excess waiver or reduction available for extra.

Check that hire-car insurance or the rental agreement covers hail damage, a costly possibility during the summer in the highveld and lowveld regions.

Insurance providers include:

Automobile Association of South Africa (AASA; ☎011-799 1001, emergencies 0861 000 234; www.aasa.co.za)

Old Mutual iWyze (www.oldmutual.co.za/personal/insurance/car-insurance.aspx)

Outsurance (www.outsurance.co.za)

Sansure (www.sansure.co.za)

Purchase

South Africa is the best place in the region to purchase a vehicle for a Southern African, or larger sub-Saharan, journey. It's worth buying a vehicle if you plan to stay longer than about three months.

Jo'burg is the best place to buy; prices are often lower and cars tend to build up rust in Cape Town and coastal towns. Cape Town is the best place to resell; the market is smaller and prices tend to be higher.

In Jo'burg, you'll find a good congregation of used-car dealers on Great North Rd, Benoni; in Cape Town, on Voortrekker Rd between Maitland and Bellville metro train stations.

Buying privately, prices are considerably lower, although you won't have any dealer warranties and shopping around is likely to take longer. Dealers can advise on the arduous process of registering the car, and may have some of the forms you need. You may find one willing to agree to a buy-back deal, although the terms are likely to be unfavourable.

Prices are high. Lonely Planet readers and authors have paid R124,000, at a Benoni dealership, for a four-year-old Nissan 2.4 4WD bakkie with a canopy and 135,000km on the clock; and R70,000 to a private seller in Cape Town for a seven-year-old Toyota Corolla with 95,000km on the clock.

PAPERWORK

Make sure that the car details correspond accurately with the ownership (registration) papers, that there is a current licence disc on the windscreen, and that the service-history book is up to date. Check the owner's name against their identity document, and check the car's engine and chassis numbers.

Privately bought cars normally come without an up-to-date roadworthy certificate – required when you submit the change-of-ownership form and pay tax for a licence disc. Roadworthy test centres issue certificates for a few hundred rand, and will generally overlook minor faults. In Cape Town, many test centres are found on Oswald Pirow St (also known as Christiaan Barnard St), near the Civic Centre.

REGISTRATION

Registering your car is a bureaucratic headache and will likely take a couple of weeks. Officials have told travellers they cannot register a car without South African citizenship, but this is untrue.

The forms you need to complete should be available at vehicle registration offices, dealers or through the websites listed. They include the following:

- ANR8 (application and notice in respect of traffic register number)
- RLV/NCO5 (notification of change of ownership/sale of motor vehicle)

Submit your ANR8 as soon as possible, as this registers individuals to drive on South African roads. Without this piece of paperwork, you cannot register a car in your name; it takes several weeks to process.

To submit your RLV/NCO5, present yourself at a vehicle registration office along with the following:

- your passport and a photocopy of it
- a copy of the seller's ID
- the registration certificate (in the seller's name)
- a roadworthy certificate
- proof of purchase
- proof of address (a letter from your accommodation should suffice)
- a valid licence
- your fee (in cash).

The seller should accompany you and bring their ID.

Charges rise annually, and typically start at around R400 to register and license a car.

If the licence has expired, you will have to pay a penalty.

CONTACTS & RESOURCES

Auto Trader (www.autotrader.co.za) Car ads nationwide.

Cape Ads (www.capeads.com) Car ads around Cape Town.

Capetown.gov.za (http://tinyurl.com/72c42nw) Details of vehicle registration offices in and around the city.

eNaTIS (www.enatis.com) Forms and information on registering vehicles.

Gumtree South Africa (www.gumtree.co.za) Car ads nationwide.

Mahindra Benoni (www.msmdealer.co.za) Jo'burg dealer offering car and bakkie sales and trade-ins; has experience of selling to foreigners and helping them register vehicles.

South African Government Services (www.gov.za/services/services-foreigners/driving) Information on applying for a traffic register number and driving licence.

South African Forums (southafricanforum.co.za) Vehicle purchase is among the topics discussed.

Suedafrika-forum.net (suedafrika-forum.net) A forum in German.

Western Cape Government (www.westerncape.gov.za/service/vehicle-registration) Forms and advice on registering a vehicle in the Western Cape.

Road Conditions

SOUTH AFRICA

- A good network of highways covers the country.
- Major roads are generally in good condition.
- Outside large towns and cities, you may encounter gravel (dirt) roads, most of which are graded and reasonably smooth.
- Check locally on tertiary and gravel roads' condition, which can deteriorate when it rains.
- In the former homeland areas, beware of hazards such as dangerous potholes, washed-out roads, unannounced hairpin bends, and livestock, children and dogs on the road.
- The N2 highway through the Wild Coast region is in bad condition.

LESOTHO

- Driving in Lesotho can be challenging, with steep terrain, hairpin turns and inclement weather.
- Roads are being built and upgraded, many financed by Chinese mining corporations and the Highlands Water Project.
- During roadworks, previously passable gravel and tar roads become impassable to 2WD cars.
- At the time of writing, roadworks made travel slow in the Northeastern Highlands.

- A tarred road, passable in a 2WD, runs clockwise from Qacha's Nek to Mokhotlong, with possible onward access to Sani Top.
- Stretches of tar and good gravel also give 2WD access to Semonkong (from both the north and south), Thaba-Tseka (from the north and west) and Ts'ehlanyane National Park.
- Apart from issues caused by roadworks, sealed roads in the highlands are generally good, but very steep in places.
- Rain will slow you down and ice and snow in winter can make driving dangerous.
- If you're driving an automatic, you'll rely heavily on your brakes to negotiate steep downhill corners.
- Away from main roads, there are places where even a 4WD will struggle, such as the road north from Sehlabathebe National Park.
- Rough roads and river floodings after summer storms are the biggest problems.
- People and animals on the road can also be a hazard.
- There are sometimes police or army roadblocks.

SWAZILAND

- Swaziland's road network is good.
- Most major routes are tarred.
- The MR3, which crosses Swaziland roughly from west to east, is a major highway as far east as Manzini.
- Good tarmac roads connect other major towns.
- Elsewhere are mostly unpaved roads, most in reasonably good condition, except after heavy rains.
- There are some rough back roads through the bush.
- Malagwane Hill, from Mbabane into the Ezulwini Valley, was once listed in *Guinness World Records* as the world's most dangerous road.
- Driving down the Ezulwini Valley in heavy traffic and bad conditions can be dangerous.
- Away from the population centres and border-crossing areas there is little traffic.

Road Hazards

- South Africa's roads are among the world's most treacherous, with a horrific accident rate, and well over 10,000 deaths annually.
- Notably dangerous stretches of highway: N1 between Cape Town and Beaufort West, and between Polokwane (Pietersburg) and Louis Trichardt (Makhado); N2 between Cape Town and Caledon, along the Garden Route, between East London and Kokstad, and Durban and Tongaat; N12 between Springs and Witbank; N4 between Middelburg and Belfast.
- The main hazards are your fellow drivers. Motorists from all sections of society drive sloppily and aggressively. Be particularly wary of minibus-taxi drivers, who operate under pressure on little sleep in shoddy vehicles.
- Overtaking blind and/or with insufficient passing room is common.
- On major roads, drivers coming up behind you will expect you to move into the hard shoulder to let them pass, even if you are approaching a corner and regardless of what is happening in the hard shoulder. Motorists often remain hard on your tail until you move over.
- Oncoming motorists will sometimes flash their lights at you and expect you to move into the hard shoulder so they can overtake.
- Drivers on little-used rural roads often speed and assume that there is no other traffic.
- Watch out especially for oncoming cars at blind corners on secondary roads.
- Despite roadblocks and alcohol breath-testing in South Africa and Swaziland, particularly in urban areas, drink driving is widespread.
- Do not be seduced by the relaxed local attitude to drink driving; you can end up in a cell, so nominate a designated driver.
- Farm animals, wildlife (particularly baboons) and pedestrians stray onto the roads, especially in rural areas. If you hit an animal in an area where you're uncertain of your safety, continue to the nearest police station and report it there.
- In roads through townships (such as the N2 from Cape Town International Airport to the city), foreign objects

CARJACKING

In Jo'burg, and to a lesser extent in the other big cities and elsewhere in the northeastern provinces, carjacking is a danger. It's more likely if you're driving something flash rather than a standard rental car. Stay alert, keep your taste in cars modest, and avoid driving in urban areas at night; if you have to do so, keep windows wound up and doors locked. If you're waiting at a red light and notice anything suspicious, it's standard practice to check that the junction is clear, and jump the light. If you do get carjacked, don't resist; just hand over the keys immediately. The carjackers are almost always armed, and people have been killed for their cars.

are occasionally placed on the road and motorists robbed when they pull over after driving over the object. Continue to a garage and police station to inspect your car and report the incident.

➡ During the rainy season, thick fog can slow you to a crawl, especially in the higher areas of KwaZulu-Natal.

➡ In the highveld and lowveld, summer hail storms can damage your car.

➡ Lesotho's mountainous terrain and road conditions are its principal dangers.

➡ Children sometimes beg and throw stones at cars, especially 4WD vehicles, on remote roads in Lesotho.

➡ In Swaziland, look out for drunk drivers, wandering cattle and speeding minibuses, especially on gravel roads.

Road Rules

➡ In South Africa, Lesotho and Swaziland, driving is on the left-hand side of the road.

➡ Seatbelts are mandatory for the driver and front-seat passengers.

➡ The main local idiosyncrasy is the 'four-way stop' (crossroad), found even on major roads. All vehicles are required to stop, with those arriving first the first to go (even if they're on a minor cross street).

➡ If you're driving a car hired in South Africa and get stopped in Lesotho or Swaziland, you will likely have to show the letter from the rental agency giving you permission to take the car across the border.

➡ In Lesotho, there are numerous police roadblocks; halt at the first stop sign and wait to be waved forward. Most police officers will quickly check your papers or just wave you on.

➡ In Swaziland, if an official or royal motorcade approaches, you're required to pull over and stop.

SPEED LIMITS

Stick to speed limits, as speed traps (cameras and guns) are increasingly common in South Africa, although limits remain widely ignored by locals.

South Africa 100km/h on open roads; 120km/h on most major highways; 60km/h in built-up areas; and 40km/h in wildlife parks and reserves.

Lesotho 80km/h on main roads; 50km/h in villages.

Swaziland 80km/h on open roads; 120km/h on most major highways; and 60km/h in towns.

Signage

Signage is good in South Africa. As in Western countries, signposts are sparser on secondary and tertiary roads, sometimes only giving route numbers or directing you to nearby towns, rather than the next large town or city.

Roads are normally numbered (eg R44, shown in this book as Rte 44). When you ask directions, most people will refer to these numbers.

In Lesotho, main routes are numbered, beginning with A1 (Main North Rd). Side roads branching off from these have 'B' route numbers.

Tolls

On some South African highways a toll is payable, based on distance. You can usually pay with cash or card.

There's always plenty of warning that you're about to enter a toll section (marked by a black 'T' in a yellow circle), and normally an alternative route (marked by a black 'A' in a yellow circle).

Calculate journey tolls at **Drive South Africa** (www.drivesouthafrica.co.za).

Hitching

Hitchhiking and picking up hitchers are inadvisable in all three countries, especially South Africa.

If you're strapped for cash, you could look into drive-shares. Hostel noticeboards often have details of free or shared-cost lifts. Also check out **Junk Mail** (junkmail.co.za).

Local Transport

See p613 for information on metro commuter trains.

Bus

➡ Several urban areas, including Cape Town, Durban, Pretoria and Jo'burg, have city bus networks.

➡ Fares are cheap.

➡ Routes, which are signboarded, are extensive.

➡ Services often stop running early in the evening, and there aren't many on weekends.

➡ In terms of safety and convenience, only Cape Town's MyCiTi buses and Durban People Mover are recommended.

Shared Taxi

Minibus shared taxis run almost everywhere – around cities, to the suburbs and to neighbouring towns.

➡ They leave when full.

➡ 'Full' in South Africa isn't as packed as in many African countries.

➡ Most accommodate 14 to 16 people.

➡ Slightly larger 'sprinters' accommodate about 20.

➡ Away from train and bus routes, shared taxis may be the only choice of public transport.

➡ They offer an insight into local life.

➡ At weekends they generally have reduced services or no departures.

➡ Car taxis are sometimes shared, for example in Lesotho.

➡ In some towns, and on some longer routes, a shared car taxi may be the only transport option.

SHARED TAXI ETIQUETTE

➡ Passengers with lots of luggage should sit in the first row behind the driver.

➡ Move along the seat to the window to give others easy access.

➡ Pay the fare with coins, not notes.

➡ Pass the money forward (your fare and those of the people around you) when the taxi is full. Hand the money to a front-seat passenger, rather than the driver. If you're sitting in the front seat, you might have to collect fares and dole out change from the driver's stash.

➡ If you sit on the folding seat by the sliding door, it's your job to open and close the door when passengers get out. You'll have to get out of the taxi each time.

➡ Some shared taxis, for example in Cape Town, have a conductor who calls out to potential passengers and handles the minibus door.

➡ Say 'Thank you, driver!' when you want to get out, rather than just 'Stop!'

➡ Shared car taxis are more expensive than minibus taxis, and comparable in safety.

SECURITY

Money saved by taking minibus shared taxis is far outweighed by safety considerations.

➡ Overall, taking shared taxis is not recommended.

➡ Driving standards and vehicle conditions are poor.

➡ There are frequent accidents.

➡ There are occasional gangster-style clashes between rival companies.

➡ Shared taxi stations and their immediate surroundings are often unsafe.

➡ Muggings, pickpocketing, sexual harassment and other incidents are common.

➡ If you want to try riding in a shared taxi, don't travel at night, read the newspapers and seek local advice on lines and areas to avoid.

➡ In a few areas, shared taxis are relatively safe during daylight hours. This is notably the case in central Cape Town, where locals from different social and racial backgrounds use shared taxis.

➡ Do not travel with luggage, partly because most shared taxis don't carry bags on the roof, and stowing backpacks can be a hassle.

LESOTHO & SWAZILAND

Minibus shared taxis don't have stellar road-safety records but have none of the violence associated with their South African counterparts. They are widely used for short and long routes. See also p606.

Private Taxi

➡ Larger cities in all three countries have private taxi services.

➡ There are taxi stands in popular areas.

➡ Phoning for a cab is often safer; you will have to wait for the taxi to arrive, but the vehicle will likely be better quality than those at the stands.

➡ Rates vary between cities; in Cape Town, they average R10 per kilometre, often with a minimum charge of R20 or more.

➡ In Lesotho, taxis (known as 'four by ones') can be chartered or shared for long-distance journeys to other parts of the country.

➡ Local variations on private and shared taxis are found in places such as Durban, which has rickshaws.

Tours

There are dozens of tours by local companies, ranging from budget overland truck journeys to exclusive luxury safaris, 4WD adventures to half-day overviews.

Backpacker hostels around the country are good sources of information on tours geared towards budget travellers. Many are affiliated with budget tour operators, and have travel desks and bulletin boards.

Try to book day or overnight trips as close to the destination as possible. For example, if you're in Durban and want to visit a reserve in northern KwaZulu-Natal, it's usually cheaper to travel to a hostel near the reserve and take a day-trip from there, rather than booking a longer excursion from Durban. You usually also get to spend more time at the reserve.

Acacia Africa (www.acacia-africa.com) Adventure tours, eg from Cape Town to Kgalagadi Transfrontier Park. Also overland trips and voluntourism.

Ashworth Africa (www.ashworthafrica.com) Luxury tailored tours and safaris in South Africa and the region.

Bok Bus (www.bokbus.com) Budget-oriented tours along the Garden Route and around.

Cape Gourmet Adventure Tours (gourmet.cape-town.info) Mouth-watering tours of Cape Town and the Western Cape, ranging from catching your own seafood to a gourmet treasure hunt.

Drifters (www.drifters.co.za) Southern Africa adventures and Wild Coast accommodation.

Go 2 Africa (www.go2africa.com) African safari specialist, offering experiences from beach holidays to luxury train travel.

Malealea Lodge (www.malealea.co.ls) Pony trekking and hiking in the Lesotho highlands.

Oasis Overland (www.oasisoverland.co.uk) UK-based overland specialist covering South Africa and the region.

Signature Tours (www.signaturetours.co.za) General interest tours with a focus on nature and wildlife; tailored self-drive and guided packages available.

Springbok-Atlas (www.springbokatlas.com) Coach tours and safaris nationwide and around the region.

Swazi Trails (www.swazitrails.co.sz) Trips on Swaziland's Great Usutu River and around the country.

Thaba Tours (www.thabatours.co.za) Mountain-bike, 4WD, horseriding, hiking and bird-watching tours of Lesotho and the Drakensberg.

Thompsons Africa (www.thompsonsafrica.com) Mid-range and top-end package tours and safaris.

Ukholo (www.ukholotravelandtours.co.za) Western Cape itineraries, from Cape Town city tours to the Garden Route.

Wilderness Safaris (www.wilderness-safaris.com) Upscale, conservation-focused operator offering high-end safaris and special-interest trips; also operates several luxury bush camps.

Wilderness Travel (www.wildernesstravel.com) Various small-group tours of Southern Africa, covering locations from Cape Town to the Drakensberg and focused mainly on wildlife and walking.

Wildlife Safaris (www.wildlifesaf.co.za) Midrange safaris from Jo'burg to Kruger and Pilanesberg National Parks, Madikwe Game Reserve and Blyde River Canyon for individuals and small groups.

Train

South Africa's **Shosholoza Meyl** (☎011-774 4555, 0860 008 888; www.shosholozameyl.co.za) offers regular services connecting major cities.

For an overview of services, descriptions of trains and valuable advice, visit The Man in Seat Sixty-One (www.seat61.com).

Classes

Both of the following are affordable options. Unlike on long-distance buses, fares on short sectors are not inflated.

Tourist class Recommended: scenic, authentic but safe, and more comfortable than taking the bus, albeit sometimes slower. The overnight journey from Jo'burg to Cape Town is a wonderful way to get a sense of the country's vastness: entering the Karoo as night falls and eating a celebratory lunch as the train swishes through the Winelands (read a description at http://tinyurl.com/6v2rs93). There's a dining car and showers, and the fare includes accommodation in a two-berth coupé or four-berth compartment. Depending on what's available, couples are given coupés and single travellers and groups are put in compartments. If you are travelling alone and you want a coupé to yourself, you could buy two tickets. There's an additional R40 charge for bedding hire. Cars can be transported on the Jo'burg–Cape Town and Jo'burg–Durban routes.

Economy class Does not have sleeping carriages and is not a comfortable or secure option for overnight travel.

Tickets & Fares

- At the time of writing, Jo'burg to Cape Town in tourist/economy class cost R630/400.
- As Shosholoza Meyl does not sell tickets online (it only takes bookings in this way), the easiest way to purchase tickets is through travel agent **African Sun Travel** (☎0878 026 674; africansuntravel.com).
- African Sun charges a commission (about R90 for Cape Town–Jo'burg tickets and R60 for Jo'burg–Durban tickets).
- Tickets can be purchased up to three months in advance, and at least 48 hours before departure.
- Tourist-class sleepers can get fully booked a month or two ahead, especially on popular routes such as Jo'burg–Cape Town.
- Bookings can be made at train stations, by phone or through Shosholoza Meyl's website.
- You must then collect and pay for your tickets at a station within two days.
- A more complicated and lengthy option is to deposit the money in Shosholoza Meyl's bank account and send the company proof of payment; it takes four days for funds to clear in Shosholoza Meyl's account.

Routes

Jo'burg–Cape Town Via Kimberley and Beaufort West; 27 hours; tourist (Tuesday to Friday and Sunday) and economy (Wednesday, Friday and Sunday).

Jo'burg–Durban Via Ladysmith and Pietermaritzburg; 13 hours; tourist and economy (Friday and Sunday).

Jo'burg–East London Via Bloemfontein; 21 hours; tourist and economy (Wednesday, Friday and Sunday).

Jo'burg–Port Elizabeth Via Bloemfontein; 20 hours; tourist and economy (Friday and Sunday).

Queenstown–Cape Town Via Worcester and Beaufort West; 24 hours; economy (Thursday and Friday).

Metro Trains

Cape Metro Rail (☎0800 656 463; www.capemetrorail.co.za) Services from Cape Town to either Simon's Town or the Winelands are considered

RIDING THE RAILS

In addition to the Shosholoza Meyl services, there are numerous special lines. Travel agent **New Fusion** (☎021-557 7047; www.newfusion.co.za) offers bookings on the Blue Train, Premier Classe and Rovos Rail.

Blue Train

(www.bluetrain.co.za) South Africa's famous train travels between Pretoria and Cape Town, stopping en route in Matjiesfontein or Kimberley. For 27 hours of luxury, one-way fares (per person sharing) are R17,030/19,245 for deluxe/luxury during high season (September to mid-November), including all meals, drinks, off-train excursions and en-suite bathroom. Fares drop by about R3500 during low season. You can book directly or through travel agents, both in South Africa and overseas. Inquire about packages including accommodation and one-way flights between Pretoria/Jo'burg and Cape Town. The train also occasionally travels from Pretoria to Durban.

Premier Classe

(www.premierclasse.co.za) Shosholoza Meyl's luxury offering is an affordable alternative to the Blue Train et al. Trains run from Cape Town to Jo'burg on Tuesday, returning on Thursday. The fare (R2840 per person) includes meals in the deluxe air-conditioned dining car; single travellers occupy two-berth coupés, couples occupy four-berth compartments. There's a lounge-bar and shared bathrooms, and vehicles can be transported.

Rovos Rail

(www.rovos.co.za) Rovos rivals the Blue Train as Africa's most luxurious and expensive service. Regular cruises include Pretoria–Cape Town over two nights/three days, with stops at Kimberley and Matjiesfontein; Pretoria–Durban over three days; Pretoria–Swakopmund (Namibia) over nine days, via Etosha National Park and other Namibian highlights; and Pretoria–Victoria Falls (Zimbabwe) over four days.

Shongololo Express

(www.shongololo.com) Not as sumptuous as the other special lines, Shongololo offers four train tours, including between Jo'burg/Pretoria and Victoria Falls, and a 12-night, 13-day cruise between Jo'burg/Pretoria and Cape Town via Swaziland and Durban. You travel by night and disembark during the days.

JB Train Tours

(www.jbtours.co.za) Train tours, mostly from Jo'burg, to locations including Cape Town, Kruger National Park, the Garden Route, Namakwa and Mozambique.

Umgeni Steam Railway

(www.umgenisteamrailway.co.za) Steam-train trips in KwaZulu-Natal.

Atlantic Rail

(www.atlanticrail.co.za) Steam-train excursions from Cape Town to Simon's Town and the Winelands.

reasonably safe during peak daylight hours.

Gautrain (☎0800 428 87246; www.gautrain.co.za) The rapid-transit Gautrain is a safe and slick link between OR Tambo International Airport, Sandton, Rosebank, Park Station (downtown Jo'burg), Pretoria and Hatfield. Trains depart every 12 minutes at peak times (5.30am to 8.30am and 3pm to 6pm Monday to Friday), and every 20 to 30 minutes outside peak times. A one-way ticket between Pretoria and Park Station costs R64.

If you're travelling in peak periods, or staying near a station, it's a fast, state-of-the-art and cost-effective way to enter/exit Jo'burg.

Health

As long as you stay up to date with vaccinations and take basic preventative measures, you're unlikely to succumb to any hazards.

While South Africa, Lesotho and Swaziland have an impressive selection of tropical diseases, suffering from diarrhoea or a cold is more likely than contracting an exotic malady.

The main exception to this is malaria, which is a real risk in lower-lying areas of Swaziland, and in northeastern South Africa.

BEFORE YOU GO

- Visit a doctor or travel clinic at least four weeks before departure for vaccinations; some don't ensure immunity for two weeks.
- Get a check-up from your doctor if you have any regular medication or chronic illness.
- Assemble a medical and first-aid kit, especially if you will be hiking or staying in parks and reserves.
- Become a member of the **International Association for Medical Assistance to Travellers** (IAMAT; www.iamat.org), which lists trusted English-speaking doctors.
- If you'll be spending much time in remote rural areas, such as parts of Lesotho and the Eastern Cape, consider doing a first-aid course, for example one offered by the **American Red Cross** (www.redcross.org) or **St John Ambulance** (www.sja.org.uk; UK).
- Particularly if you're going hiking, you could take a wilderness medical training course, such as those offered in the UK by **Wilderness Medical Training** (WMT; wildernessmedicaltraining.co.uk) and the **Royal Geographical Society** (www.rgs.org).
- Bring medications in their original, clearly labelled containers.
- A signed and dated letter from your physician describing your medical conditions and medications, including generic names, is helpful.
- If carrying syringes or needles, ensure you have a physician's letter documenting their medical necessity.
- See your dentist before a long trip.

Insurance

- Find out in advance whether your insurer will make payments directly to providers or reimburse you later for overseas health expenditures.
- If your policy requires you to pay first and claim later for medical treatment, be sure to keep all documentation.
- Ensure that your travel insurance will cover any emergency transport required to get you to a hospital in a major city, or all the way home, by air and with a medical attendant if necessary.
- If you'll be in Lesotho and Swaziland, check whether the evacuation plan extends to these countries.

Recommended Vaccinations

America's **Centers for Disease Control and Prevention** (CDC; www.cdc.gov/travel; USA) suggests immunisations including the following as routine for adults.

- Diphtheria
- Influenza
- Measles
- Mumps
- Pertussis (whooping cough)
- Polio
- Rubella
- Tetanus
- Varicella (chicken pox)

The CDC also suggests the following for South Africa, Lesotho and Swaziland:

- Hepatitis A
- Typhoid

The CDC suggests the following for some travellers to the region, depending on the areas to be visited:

- Hepatitis B
- Malaria
- Rabies

Ask your doctor for an International Certificate of Vaccination or Prophylaxis (ICVP or 'yellow card'), listing all the vaccinations you've received.

Medical Checklist

Consider packing the following in your medical kit:

- antibacterial ointment (eg Bactroban) for cuts and abrasions
- antibiotics (if travelling off the beaten track)
- antidiarrhoeal drugs (eg loperamide)
- antihistamines (for hay fever and allergic reactions)
- anti-inflammatory drugs (eg ibuprofen)
- antimalaria pills (if you'll be in malarial areas)
- bandages, gauze
- DEET-containing insect repellent
- insect spray for clothing, tents and bed nets
- iodine or other water-purification tablets
- oral rehydration salts (eg Dioralyte)
- paracetamol or aspirin
- scissors, safety pins, tweezers, pocket knife
- sterile needles and syringes (if travelling to remote areas)
- sun block
- thermometer

Websites

In addition to the information on their websites, the World Health Organization (WHO) and CDC publish annual handbooks.

Centers for Disease Control and Prevention (CDC; www.cdc.gov/travel; USA)

Health Canada (www.hc-sc.gc.ca; Canada)

Immunization Action Coalition (IAC; www.immunize.org; USA)

International Association for Medical Assistance to Travellers (IAMAT; www.iamat.org)

Lonely Planet (www.lonelyplanet.com)

MD Travel Health (www.mdtravelhealth.com; USA)

National Health Service (NHS; www.fitfortravel.nhs.uk; UK)

Netdoctor (www.netdoctor.co.uk/travel; UK)

Smarttraveller (www.smartraveller.gov.au; Australia)

World Health Organization (WHO; www.who.int/ith)

Further Reading

In addition to the following, the WHO and CDC publish annual handbooks.

- *The Essential Guide to Travel Health* by Jane Wilson-Howarth
- *Travel Health Guide* by Mark Wise
- *Travels with Baby* by Shelly Rivoli
- *Traveller's Good Health Guide* by Ted Lankester
- *Travellers' Health* by Dr Richard Dawood
- *Wilderness and Travel Medicine* by Eric Weiss

IN SOUTH AFRICA, LESOTHO & SWAZILAND

Availability & Cost of Health Care

- Good-quality health care is available in all of South Africa's major urban areas.
- Private hospitals are generally of an excellent standard.
- Public hospitals are often underfunded and overcrowded.
- In off-the-beaten-track areas, such as the former homelands and in Lesotho and Swaziland, reliable medical facilities are rare.
- Your accommodation should be able to recommend the nearest source of medical help.
- Western embassy websites often list doctors and clinics, and your travel insurer might also be able to help.
- In an emergency, contact your embassy or consulate.
- Most doctors expect payment immediately after the consultation.
- Bring drugs for chronic diseases from home.
- Blood-transfusion services test donated blood for hepatitis B and C, syphilis and HIV, but there is nonetheless a tiny risk of contracting HIV from infected transfusions.
- The **Blood Care Foundation** (www.bloodcare.org.uk; UK) is a useful source of safe, screened blood, which can be transported to any part of the world; join before you need its services.

Infectious Diseases

Cholera

Spread through Contaminated drinking water. The risk is low, and mostly confined to occasional outbreaks in rural parts of Limpopo, Mpumalanga, KwaZulu-Natal, the Eastern Cape and Swaziland.

Symptoms and effects Profuse watery diarrhoea, which causes debilitation if fluids are not replaced quickly.

Prevention and treatment In rural parts of eastern South Africa, pay close attention to drinking water, don't drink tap water, and avoid potentially contaminated food such as unpeeled or uncooked fruits and vegetables. Treatment is by fluid replacement (orally or via a drip); sometimes antibiotics are needed. Self-treatment is not advised.

Dengue Fever

Spread through Mosquito bites; in the north of KwaZulu-Natal's Elephant Coast and eastern Swaziland, and from there up South Africa's northeastern border to the top of Kruger National Park.

Symptoms and effects Feverish illness with headache and muscle pains, similar to those experienced during severe, prolonged influenza attacks. There might be a rash.

Prevention and treatment Avoid mosquito bites. Self-treatment: paracetamol (not asprin or non-steroidal anti-inflammatory drugs such as ibuprofen), hydration and rest. Dengue hemorrhagic fever, which mostly affects children, is more serious and requires medical attention.

Hepatitis A

Spread through Contaminated food (particularly shellfish) and water. Very occasionally, close physical contact with an infected person.

Symptoms and effects Jaundice, dark urine, a yellow colour to the whites of the eyes, fever and abdominal pain. Although rarely fatal, it can cause prolonged lethargy – recovery can be slow.

Prevention and treatment Vaccine (eg Avaxim, Vaqta, Havrix or Epaxal) is given as an injection, with a booster extending the protection offered. Can also be given as a combined single-dose vaccine with Hepatitis B (Twinrix) or typhoid (Hepatyrix or Viatim). If you've had hepatitis A, you shouldn't drink alcohol for up to six months afterwards.

Hepatitis B

Spread through Infected blood, contaminated needles and sexual intercourse.

Symptoms and effects Jaundice and liver problems (occasionally failure).

Prevention Those visiting high-risk areas for long periods or those with increased social or occupational risk should be immunised. Regular travellers in sub-Saharan Africa should consider having hepatitis B as a routine vaccination.

HIV

Spread through Infected blood and blood products; sexual intercourse with an infected partner; 'blood to blood' contacts, such as through contaminated instruments during medical, dental, acupuncture and other body-piercing procedures, or sharing intravenous needles. HIV and AIDS are widespread in South Africa, Lesotho and Swaziland.

Symptoms and effects Progressive failure of the immune system, leading to death.

Prevention and treatment Be cautious about relationships with locals, regardless of their background, and don't have one-night stands. Travellers and aid workers have been infected by locals. If you think you might have been infected, a blood test is necessary; a three-month gap after exposure is required to allow antibodies to appear in the blood. There is no cure, but medication to keep the disease under control is available.

Lymphatic Filariasis (Elephantiasis)

Spread through The bite of an infected mosquito. Larvae are deposited on the skin and migrate to the lymphatic vessels, where they turn into worms.

Symptoms and effects Localised itching and abnormal enlargement of body parts, commonly the legs and/or genitalia, causing pain and disability. In severe cases, the kidneys and lymphatic and immune systems are damaged.

Prevention and treatment Avoid mosquito bites. If infected, seek treatment, preferably by a specialist in infectious diseases or tropical medicine. Diethylcarbamazine (DEC) is commonly used to treat travellers.

Malaria

Spread through A parasite in the bloodstream, spread via the bite of the female Anopheles mosquito. Malaria is mainly confined to northeastern South Africa (northern KwaZulu-Natal, Mpumalanga, Limpopo and Kruger National Park) and Swaziland.

Symtoms and effects Falciparum malaria, the most dangerous type of malaria, is the predominant form in South Africa. The early, flu-like symptoms of malaria include headaches, fevers, aches and pains, and malaise. Abdominal

ANTIMALARIAL A TO D

A Awareness of the risk. No medication is totally effective, but protection of over 90% is achievable with most drugs, as long as other measures are taken.

B Bites, to be avoided at all costs. Sleep in a screened room, use a mosquito spray or coils, and sleep under a permethrin-impregnated net. Cover up at night with light-coloured long trousers and long sleeves – preferably permethrin-treated clothing. Apply repellent (preferably DEET-based) to all areas of exposed skin in the evenings.

C Chemical prevention (ie antimalarial drugs) is usually needed in malarial areas. Get medical advice, as resistance patterns can change, and new drugs are in development. Not all antimalarial drugs are suitable for everyone. Most antimalarial drugs need to be started at least a week beforehand, and continued for four weeks after the last possible exposure to malaria.

D Diagnosis. If you have a fever or flu-like illness within a year of travel to a malarial area, malaria is a possibility, and immediate medical attention is necessary.

pain, diarrhoea and a cough can also occur. If not treated, the next stage can develop within 24 hours, particularly if falciparum malaria is the parasite: jaundice, then reduced consciousness and coma (also known as cerebral malaria) followed by death. Malaria in pregnancy frequently results in miscarriage or premature labour; the risks to both mother and foetus are considerable.

Prevention Infection rates vary with the season and climate, so check out the situation before departure. During the summer months, prophylaxis is essential. Several drugs are available and up-to-date advice from a travel clinic or similar is essential; some medication is more suitable than others (eg people with epilepsy should avoid mefloquine, and doxycycline should not be taken by pregnant women or children aged under 12). There is no conclusive evidence that antimalarial homeopathic preparations are effective, and many homeopaths do not recommend their use. It's a dangerous misconception that malaria is a mild illness, and that taking antimalarial drugs causes more illness through side effects than actually getting malaria. Immunity, developed by surviving a bout of malaria, wanes after 18 months of nonexposure; even if you have had malaria or lived in a malaria-prone area, you might no longer be immune. If you decide against taking antimalarial prophylaxis, you must understand the risks and be obsessive about avoiding mosquito bites.

Treatment If you develop a fever in a malarial area, assume malarial infection until a blood test proves negative, even if you are or have been taking antimalarial medication. Report any fever or flu-like symptoms to a doctor as soon as possible. Treatment in hospital is essential; even in the best intensive-care facilities, there is still a chance of fatality in the worst cases.

Rabies

Spread through Bites or licks on broken skin from an infected animal. Few human cases are reported in South Africa, with the risks highest in rural areas.

Symptoms and effects Initial symptoms are pain or tingling at the site of the bite with fever, loss of appetite and headache. With 'furious' rabies, there is a growing sense of anxiety, jumpiness, disorientation, neck stiffness, sometimes seizures or convulsions, and hydrophobia (fear of water). 'Dumb' rabies (less common) affects the spinal cord, causing muscle paralysis then heart and lung failure. If untreated, both forms are fatal.

Prevention and treatment People travelling to remote areas, where a reliable source of post-bite vaccine is not available within 24 hours, should be vaccinated. Any bite, scratch or lick from a warm-blooded, furry animal should immediately be thoroughly cleaned. If you have not been vaccinated and you get bitten, you will need a course of injections starting as soon as possible after the injury. Vaccination does not provide immunity, it merely buys you more time to seek medical help.

Schistosomiasis (Bilharzia)

Spread through Flukes (minute worms) are carried by a species of freshwater snail, which sheds them into slow-moving or still water. The parasites penetrate human skin during swimming and migrate to the bladder or bowel. They are excreted via stool or urine and could contaminate fresh water, beginning the cycle again. Bilharzia is found in northeastern South Africa and Swaziland, reaching as far south as the Wild Coast and (very occasionally) as far west as the Northern Cape section of the Senqu (Orange) River.

Symptoms and effects Early symptoms may include fever, loss of appetite, weight loss, abdominal pain, weakness, headaches, joint and muscle pains, diarrhea, nausea and cough, but most infections are asymptomatic at first. Untreated, bilharzia can cause problems including kidney failure and permanent bowel damage.

Prevention and treatment Avoid swimming in stagnant or slow-running water, for example in a dam, lake or river. Heat baths and showers and vigorously towel yourself after swimming. A blood test can detect the parasite, and treatment is available – usually taking the drug praziquantel (Biltricide).

Tuberculosis

Spread through Close respiratory contact and, occasionally, infected unpasteurised milk or milk products. Tuberculosis (TB) is highly endemic in South Africa, Lesotho and Swaziland. People mixing closely with the local population, for example working as a teacher or health-care worker, or planning a long stay are most at risk.

Symptoms and effects Can be asymptomatic, although symptoms can include a cough, loss of appetite or weight, fatigue, fever or night sweats months or even years after exposure. An X-ray is the best way to confirm if you have TB.

Prevention and treatment Avoid overcrowded and unventilated environments where TB carriers might be found, such as hospitals and homeless shelters. Bacillus Calmette–Guérin (BCG) vaccine is recommended for those likely to be mixing closely with the local population; as it's a live vaccine, it should not be given to pregnant women or immunocompromised individuals. Travellers at risk should have a pre-departure skin test and be re-tested after leaving the country. Treatment is a multiple-drug regimen for six to nine months.

Typhoid

Spread through Food or water that has been contaminated by infected human faeces.

Symptoms and effects Initially, fever, a pink rash on the abdomen, appetite loss and listlessness. Septicaemia (blood poisoning) may also occur.

Prevention Vaccination given by injection. In some countries, an oral vaccine is available. Antibiotics are usually given as treatment.

TAP WATER

High-quality water is widely available in South Africa and drinking from taps is fine, except in rural areas.

In Lesotho and Swaziland, stick to bottled water, and purify stream water before drinking it.

Environmental Hazards

Heat Exhaustion

Causes Occurs following heavy sweating and excessive fluid loss with inadequate replacement of fluids and salt. This is common in hot climates when taking unaccustomed exercise before full acclimatisation.

Symptoms and effects Headache, dizziness and tiredness.

Prevention Dehydration is already happening by the time you feel thirsty – drink sufficient water such that you produce pale, diluted urine. The African sun can be fierce, so bring a hat.

Treatment Fluid replacement with water and/or fruit juice, and cooling by cold water and fans. Treat the salt loss by consuming salty fluids such as soup or broth, and adding a little more table salt to foods than usual.

Heatstroke

Causes Extreme heat, high humidity, physical exertion or use of drugs or alcohol in the sun and dehydration. Occurs when the body's heat-regulating mechanism breaks down.

Symptoms and effects An excessive rise in body temperature, accompanied by sweating ceasing, irrational and hyperactive behaviour, and eventually loss of consciousness and death.

Treatment Rapid cooling by spraying the body with water and fanning. Emergency fluid and electrolyte replacement by intravenous drip is usually also required.

Insect Bites & Stings

Causes Mosquitoes, scorpions (found in arid areas), ticks (a risk outside urban areas), bees and wasps.

Symptoms and effects Bites can cause irritation and get infected. The scorpion's painful bite can be life-threatening. If you're stung, take a painkiller and seek medical treatment if your condition worsens. Tick-bite fever (rickettsia), a bacterial infection transmitted by ticks that can cause malaria-like symptoms, is a risk in the lowveld, including Swaziland.

Prevention and treatment Take the same precautions as for avoiding malaria. If you pick up a tick, press down around its head with tweezers, grab the head and gently pull upwards. Avoid pulling the rear of the body, as this may squeeze the tick's gut contents through its mouth into your body, or leave its head inside you; both outcomes increase the risk of infection and disease. Smearing chemicals on the tick will not make it let go and is not recommended. If you suspect tick-bite fever, visit a doctor; treatment is a strong dose of antibiotics.

Snake Bites

Causes Venomous snakes found in South Africa include the black mamba, puff adder and Cape cobra. Snakes like to bask on rocks and sand, retreating during the heat of the day.

Prevention Do not walk barefoot or stick your hand into holes or cracks.

Treatment If bitten, do not panic. Half of those bitten by venomous snakes are not actually injected with poison (envenomed). Immobilise the bitten limb with a splint (eg a stick) and apply a bandage over the site with firm pressure, similar to bandaging a sprain. Do not apply a tourniquet, or cut or suck the bite. Note the snake's appearance for identification purposes, and get medical help as soon as possible so that antivenene can be given.

Traditional Medicine

If you are ill, some locals may recommend you see a *sangoma* (traditional healer, usually a woman) or *inyanga* (traditional healer and herbalist, usually a man). These practitioners hold revered positions in many communities and are often interesting characters to meet on a tour. However, if you are ill, recourse to tried-and-tested Western medicine is a wiser option. Likewise, treat the traditional medicinal products found in local markets with circumspection.

Language

South Africa has 11 official languages – English, Afrikaans and nine indigenous languages (Ndebele, Northern Sotho, Southern Sotho, Swati, Tsonga, Tswana, Venda, Xhosa and Zulu). Forms, brochures and timetables are usually in English and Afrikaans, but road signs alternate. Most Afrikaans speakers also speak English, but this is not always the case in small rural towns and among older people. In and around Cape Town three languages are prominent: Afrikaans, English and Xhosa.

The official languages of Lesotho are Southern Sotho and English. In Swaziland, Swati and English are both official.

AFRIKAANS

Afrikaans developed from the dialect spoken by the Dutch settlers in South Africa from the 17th century. Until the late 19th century it was considered a Dutch dialect (known as 'Cape Dutch'), and in 1925 it became one of the official languages of South Africa. Today, it has about six million speakers.

If you read our coloured pronunciation guides as if they were English, you should be understood. The stressed syllables are in italics. Note that aw is pronounced as in 'law', eu as the 'u' in 'nurse', ew as the 'ee' in 'see' with rounded lips, oh as the 'o' in 'cold', uh as the 'a' in 'ago', kh as the 'ch' in the Scottish *loch*, zh as the 's' in 'pleasure', and r is trilled.

Basics

Hello.	*Hallo.*	ha·*loh*
Goodbye.	*Totsiens.*	tot·*seens*
Yes.	*Ja.*	yaa
No.	*Nee.*	ney
Please.	*Asseblief.*	a·si·*bleef*
Thank you.	*Dankie.*	*dang*·kee
Sorry.	*Jammer.*	*ya*·min

How are you?
Hoe gaan dit? hu khaan dit

Fine, and you?
Goed dankie, en jy? khut *dang*·kee en yay

What's your name?
Wat's jou naam? vats yoh naam

My name is ...
My naam is ... may naam is ...

Do you speak English?
Praat jy Engels? praat yay *eng*·ils

I don't understand.
Ek verstaan nie. ek vir·*staan* nee

WANT MORE?

For in-depth language information and handy phrases, check out Lonely Planet's *Africa Phrasebook*. You'll find it at **shop.lonelyplanet.com**, or you can buy Lonely Planet's iPhone phrasebooks at the Apple App Store.

Accommodation

Where's a ...?	*Waar's 'n ...?*	vaars i ...
campsite	*kampeerplek*	kam·*peyr*·plek
guesthouse	*gastehuis*	*khas*·ti·hays
hotel	*hotel*	hu·*tel*

Do you have a single/double room?
Het jy 'n enkel/ dubbel kamer? het yay i *eng*·kil/ *di*·bil *kaa*·mir

How much is it per night/person?
Hoeveel kos dit per nag/ persoon? *hu*·fil kos dit pir nakh/ pir·*soon*

Eating & Drinking

Can you recommend a ...?	*Kan jy 'n ... aanbeveel?*	kan yay i ... *aan*·bi·feyl
bar	*kroeg*	krukh
dish	*gereg*	khi·*rekh*

SOUTH AFRICAN ENGLISH

English has undergone some changes during its use in South Africa. Quite a few words have changed meaning, new words have been appropriated and, thanks to the influence of Afrikaans, a distinctive accent has developed. Vocabulary tends to lean more towards British rather than US English (eg 'lift', not 'elevator'; 'petrol', not 'gas'), as do grammar and spelling, and there are influences from other indigenous languages such as Zulu and Xhosa as well. Repetition for emphasis is common: something that burns you is 'hot hot', fields after the rains are 'green green', a crowded minibus with no more room is 'full full' and so on. Here's just a smattering of the local lingo you're likely to hear:

babalaas (from Zulu) – a monster hangover

bakkie – pick-up truck (US); ute/utility (Aus)

bonnet – car hood (US)

boot – car trunk (US)

cool drink – soda (US)

Howzit? – Hello/Greetings; How are you?

Izzit? – Is that so? Really?

just now – soon

lekker – nice, delicious

naartjie – tangerine

petrol – gasoline (US)

robot – traffic light

rubbish – garbage (US)

(Og) Shame! – Ohh, how cute! (in response to something like a new baby or a little puppy); Really! Oh no! (with a sympathetic tone)

soda – soda water; club soda (US)

sweeties – lollies; candy

tekkies – runners; joggers

place to eat	*eetplek*	*eyt*·plek
I'd like ..., please.	*Ek wil asseblief ... hê.*	ek vil a·si·*bleef* ... he
a table for two	*'n tafel vir twee*	i *taa*·fil fir twey
that dish	*daardie gereg*	*daar*·dee khi·*rekh*
the bill	*die rekening*	dee *rey*·ki·ning
the menu	*die spyskaart*	dee *spays*·kaart

Emergencies

Help!	*Help!*	help
Call a doctor!	*Kry 'n dokter!*	kray i *dok*·tir
Call the police!	*Kry die polisie!*	kray dee pu·*lee*·see

I'm lost.
Ek is verdwaal. — ek is fir·*dwaal*

Where are the toilets?
Waar is die toilette? — vaar is dee toy·*le*·ti

I need a doctor.
Ek het 'n dokter nodig. — ek het i *dok*·tir *noo*·dikh

Numbers

1	*een*	eyn
2	*twee*	twey
3	*drie*	dree
4	*vier*	feer
5	*vyf*	fayf
6	*ses*	ses
7	*sewe*	*see*·vi
8	*agt*	akht
9	*nege*	*ney*·khi
10	*tien*	teen

Shopping & Services

I'm looking for ...
Ek soek na ... — ek suk naa ...

How much is it?
Hoeveel kos dit? — *hu*·fil kos dit

What's your lowest price?
Wat is jou laagste prys? — vat is yoh *laakh*·sti prays

I want to buy a phonecard.
Ek wil asseblief 'n foonkaart koop. — ek vil a·si·*bleef* i *foon*·kaart koop

I'd like to change money.
Ek wil asseblief geld ruil. — ek vil a·si·*bleef* khelt rayl

I want to use the internet.
Ek wil asseblief die Internet gebruik. — ek vil a·si·*bleef* dee *in*·tir·net khi·*brayk*

Transport & Directions

A ... ticket, please.	*Een ... kaartjie, asseblief.*	eyn ... *kaar*·kee a·si·*bleef*
one-way	*eenrigting*	*eyn*·rikh·ting
return	*retoer*	ri·*tur*

How much is it to ...?
Hoeveel kos dit na ...? — *hu*·fil kos dit naa ...

Please take me to (this address).
Neem my asseblief na (hierdie adres). — neym may a·si·*bleef* naa (*heer*·dee a·*dres*)

Where's the (nearest) ...?
Waar's die (naaste) ...? — vaars dee (*naas*·ti) ...

Can you show me (on the map)?
Kan jy my (op die kaart) wys? — kan yay may (op dee kaart) vays

What's the address?
Wat is die adres? — vat is dee a·*dres*

NDEBELE

Ndebele is spoken as a first language in relatively small numbers in South Africa's northern provinces.

Hello.	*Lotsha.*
Goodbye.	*Khamaba kuhle./ Sala kuhle.*
Yes.	*I-ye.*
No.	*Awa.*
Please.	*Ngibawa.*
Thank you.	*Ngiyathokaza.*
What's your name?	*Ungubani ibizo lakho?*
My name is ...	*Ibizo lami ngu ...*
I come from ...	*Ngibuya e ...*

NORTHERN SOTO

Most mother-tongue speakers of Northern Sotho (also known as Sepedi) inhabit South Africa's northeastern provinces, with the vast majority to be found in Limpopo.

Hello.	*Thobela.*
Goodbye.	*Sala gabotse.*
Yes.	*Ee.*
No.	*Aowa.*
Please.	*Ke kgopela.*
Thank you.	*Ke ya leboga.*
What's your name?	*Ke mang lebitso la gago?*
My name is ...	*Lebitso laka ke ...*
I come from ...	*Ke bowa kwa ...*

SOUTHERN SOTO

Southern Sotho is the official language of Lesotho, alongside English. It is also spoken by the Basotho people in the Free State, North-West Province and Gauteng in South Africa. It's useful to learn some phrases if you're planning to visit Lesotho, especially if you want to trek in remote areas.

Hello.	*Dumela.*
Greetings father.	*Lumela ntate.*
Peace father.	*Khotso ntate.*
Greetings mother.	*Lumela 'me.*
Peace mother.	*Khotso 'me.*
Greetings brother.	*Lumela abuti.*
Peace brother.	*Khotso abuti.*
Greetings sister.	*Lumela ausi.*
Peace sister.	*Khotso ausi.*

There are three common ways of saying 'How are you?', each one with a standard response. Note, however, that these questions and answers are interchangeable.

How are you?	*O kae?* (sg)
	Le kae? (pl)
I'm here.	*Ke teng.*
We're here.	*Re teng.*
How do you live?	*O phela joang?* (sg)
	Le phela joang? (pl)
I live well.	*Ke phela hantle.*
We live well.	*Re phela hantle.*
How did you get up?	*O tsohele joang?* (sg)
	Le tsohele joang? (pl)
I got up well.	*Ke tsohile hantle.*
We got up well.	*Re tsohile hantle.*

When trekking, people always ask *Lea kae?* (Where are you going?) and *O tsoa kae?* or the plural *Le tsoa kae?* (Where have you come from?). When parting, use the following expressions:

Stay well.	*Sala hantle.* (sg)
	Salang hantle. (pl)
Go well.	*Tsamaea hantle.* (sg)
	Tsamaeang hantle. (pl)

'Thank you' is *kea leboha* (pronounced 'ke·ya le·bo·wa'). The herd boys may ask for *chelete* (money) or *lipompong* (sweets), pronounced 'dee·pom·pong'. If you want to reply 'I don't have any', just say *ha dio* (pronounced 'ha dee·o').

SWATI

Swati is the official language of Swaziland, along with English. It's also widely spoken as a first language in South Africa's Mpumalanga province. It's very similar to Zulu, and the two languages are mutually intelligible.

Hello. (to one person)	*Sawubona.*
Hello. (to a group)	*Sanibonani.*
How are you?	*Kunjani?*
I'm fine.	*Kulungile.*
We're very well.	*Natsi sikhona.*
Goodbye. (if leaving)	*Salakahle.*
Goodbye. (if staying)	*Hambakahle.*
Yes.	*Yebo.* (also a common all-purpose greeting)
No.	*Cha.* (pronounced as a click)
Please.	*Ngicela.*
I thank you.	*Ngiyabonga.*
We thank you.	*Siyabonga.*
Sorry.	*Lucolo.*
What's your name?	*Ngubani libito lakho?*
My name is ...	*Libitolami ngingu ...*
I'm from ...	*Ngingewekubuya e ...*

Do you have ...?	*Une yini ...?*
How much?	*Malini?*
Is there a bus to ...?	*Kukhona ibhasi yini leya ...?*
When does it leave?	*Isuka nini?*
Where is the tourist office?	*Likuphi lihovisi leti vakashi?*

morning	*ekuseni*
afternoon	*entsambaba*
evening	*kusihlwa*
night	*ebusuku*
yesterday	*itolo*
today	*lamuhla*
tomorrow	*kusasa*

TSONGA

Tsonga is spoken as a first language in South Africa's north, predominantly in the provinces of Limpopo and Gauteng, and to a lesser extent in Mpumalanga and North-West Province.

Hello. (morning)	*Avusheni.*
Hello. (afternoon)	*Inhelekani.*
Hello. (evening)	*Riperile.*
Goodbye.	*Salani kahle.*
Yes.	*Hi swona.*
No.	*A hi swona.*
Please.	*Nakombela.*
Thank you.	*I nkomu.*
What's your name?	*U mani vito ra wena?*
My name is ...	*Vito ra mina i ...*
I come from ...	*Ndzihuma e ...*

TSWANA

Tswana is spoken in South Africa as a first language mainly in Gauteng and North-West Province, with lesser numbers of first-language speakers in the eastern areas of Northern Cape and the western parts of the Free State.

Hello.	*Dumela.*
Goodbye.	*Sala sentle.*
Yes.	*Ee.*
No.	*Nnya.*
Please.	*Ke a kopa.*
Thank you.	*Ke a leboga.*
What's your name?	*Leina la gago ke mang?*
My name is ...	*Leina la me ke ...*
I come from ...	*Ke tswa ...*

VENDA

Venda is spoken mainly in the northeastern border region of South Africa's Limpopo province.

Hello. (morning)	*Ndi matseloni.*
Hello. (afternoon)	*Ndi masiari.*
Hello. (evening)	*Ndi madekwana.*
Goodbye.	*Kha vha sale zwavhudi.*
Yes.	*Ndi zwone.*
No.	*A si zwone.*
Please.	*Ndikho u humbela.*
Thank you.	*Ndo livhuwa.*
What's your name?	*Zina lavho ndi nnyi?*
My name is ...	*Zina langa ndi ...*
I come from ...	*Ndi bva ...*

XHOSA

Xhosa belongs to the Bantu language family, along with Zulu, Swati and Ndebele. It is the most widely distributed indigenous language in South Africa, and is also spoken in the Cape Town area. About six and a half million people speak Xhosa.

Numbers – Xhosa

English numbers are commonly used.

1	*wani*	*waa*·nee
2	*thu*	tu
3	*thri*	tree
4	*fo*	faw
5	*fayifu*	*faa*·yee·fu
6	*siksi*	*seek'*·see
7	*seveni*	se·*ve*·nee
8	*eyithi*	e·*yee*·tee
9	*nayini*	*naa*·yee·nee
10	*teni*	*t'e*·nee

In our pronunciation guides, the symbols b', ch', k', p', t' and ts' represent sounds that are 'spat out' (only in case of b' the air is sucked in), a bit like combining them with the sound in the middle of 'uh-oh'. Note also that hl is pronounced as in the Welsh *llewellyn* and dl is like hl but with the vocal cords vibrating. Xhosa has a series of 'click' sounds as well; they are not distinguished in this chapter.

Hello.	*Molo.*	*maw*·law
Goodbye.	*Usale ngoxolo.*	u·*saa*·le ngaw·*kaw*·law
Yes.	*Ewe.*	e·*we*
No.	*Hayi.*	haa·*yee*
Please.	*Cela.*	*ke*·laa
Thank you.	*Enkosi.*	e·*nk'aw*·see
Sorry.	*Uxolo.*	u·*aw*·law
How are you?	*Kunjani?*	k'u·*njaa*·nee

Fine, and you?
Ndiyaphila, unjani wena? — ndee·yaa·*pee*·laa u·*njaa*·nee *we*·naa

What's your name?
Ngubani igama lakho? — ngu·*b'aa*·nee ee·*gaa*·maa laa·*kaw*

My name is ...
Igama lam ngu ... — ee·*gaa*·maa laam ngu ...

Do you speak English?
Uyasithetha isingesi? — u·yaa·see·*te*·taa ee·see·*nge*·see

I don't understand.
Andiqondi. — aa·ndee·*kaw*·ndee

ZULU

Zulu is a language from the Bantu group, and it's closely related to the other Bantu languages in southern Africa, particularly Xhosa. About 10 million Africans speak Zulu as a first language, with the vast majority (more than 95 per cent) in South Africa. It is also spoken in Lesotho and Swaziland.

In our pronunciation guides, the symbols b', ch', k', p', t' and ts' represent sounds that are 'spat out' (only in case of b' the air is sucked in), a bit like combining them with the sound in the middle of 'uh-oh'. Note also that hl is pronounced as in the Welsh *llewellyn* and dl is like hl but with the vocal cords vibrating. Xhosa has a series of 'click' sounds as well; they are not distinguished in this chapter.

Hello.
Sawubona. (sg) — saa·wu·*b'aw*·naa
Sanibonani. (pl) — saa·nee·b'aw·*naa*·nee

Goodbye. (if leaving)
Sala kahle. (sg) — saa·laa *gaa*·hle
Salani kahle. (pl) — saa·laa·nee *gaa*·hle

Goodbye. (if staying)
Hamba kahle. (sg) — haa·mbaa *gaa*·hle
Hambani kahle. (pl) — haa·mbaa·nee *gaa*·hle

Yes.
Yebo. — *ye*·b'aw

No.
Cha. — kaa

Thank you.
Ngiyabonga. — ngee·yaa·*b'aw*·ngaa

Sorry.
Uxolo. — u·*kaw*·law

How are you?
Unjani?/Ninjani? (sg/pl) — u·njaa·nee/nee·njaa·nee

Fine. And you?
Sikhona. — see·*kaw*·naa
Nawe?/Nani? (sg/pl) — naa·we/naa·nee

What's your name?
Ngubani igama lakho? — ngu·b'aa·nee ee·gaa·maa laa·kaw

My name is ...
Igama lami ngu-... — ee·gaa·maa *laa*·mee ngu·...

Do you speak English?
Uyasikhuluma isiNgisi? — u·yaa·see·ku·lu·maa ee·see·ngee·see

I don't understand.
Angizwa. — aa·*ngee*·zwaa

Numbers – Zulu

English numbers are commonly used.

1	*uwani*	u·*waa*·nee
2	*uthu*	u·*tu*
3	*uthri*	u·*three*
4	*ufo*	u·*faw*
5	*ufayifi*	u·*faa*·yee·fee
6	*usiksi*	u·*seek*·see
7	*usevene*	u·se·*ve*·nee
8	*u-eyithi*	u·*e*·*yeet*
9	*unayini*	u·*naa*·yee·nee
10	*utheni*	u·*the*·nee

GLOSSARY

For more food and drink terms, see the Menu Decoder (p541).

Afrikaans – the language spoken by Afrikaners, derived from Cape Dutch
Afrikaner – Afrikaans-speaking white person
amahiya – traditional Swazi robe
ANC – African National Congress; national democratic organisation formed in 1912 to represent blacks
AWB – Afrikaner Weerstandsbeweging, Afrikaner Resistance Movement; an Afrikaner extremist right-wing group

bakkie – pick-up truck
balimo – ancestors (Sotho)
Bantu – literally 'people'; during the apartheid era, used derogatorily to refer to blacks; today, used only in reference to ethnolinguistics ie Bantu languages, Bantu-speaking peoples
Bantustans – see homelands
BCP – Basotholand Congress Party
Big Five (the) – lion, leopard, elephant, buffalo and black rhino
bilharzia – another name for schistosomiasis, a disease caused by blood flukes, passed on by freshwater snails
biltong – dried meat
bittereinders – 'bitter enders' in Afrikaans; Boer resistors in the 1899–1902 South African War who fought until the 'bitter end'
BNP – Basotholand National Party
bobotie – curried mince with a topping of savoury egg custard
Boers – see *Trekboers*
braai – short for *braaivleis*, a barbecue at which meat is cooked over an open fire
Broederbond – secret society open only to Protestant Afrikaner men; was highly influential under National Party rule
bubblegum – a form of township music influenced by Western pop
byala – traditional beer

coloureds – apartheid-era term used to refer to those of mixed-race descent

dagga – marijuana, also known as *zol*
Democratic Alliance – the official opposition party to the ANC
diamantveld – diamond fields
difaqane – 'forced migration' of many of Southern Africa's Nguni peoples; known as *mfecane* in Zulu
dorp – small village or rural settlement
drostdy – residence of a Landdrost

free-camp – camping where you want, away from a formal campsite; permission should be sought and money offered
fynbos – literally 'fine-leafed bush', primarily proteas, heaths and ericas

gogo – grandmother

highveld – high-altitude grassland region
homelands – areas established for blacks under apartheid and considered independent countries by South Africa (never accepted by the UN); reabsorbed into South Africa after 1994

IFP – Inkatha Freedom Party; black political movement, founded around 1975 and lead by Chief Mangosouthu Buthelezi
igogogo – musical instrument made from an oil can
igqirha – Xhosa spiritual healer
impi – Zulu warriors; also any group of soldiers
indunas – tribal headmen
inyanga – traditional medicine man and herbalist who also studies patterns of thrown bones
isicathamiya – a soft-shoe-shuffle style of vocal music from KwaZulu-Natal
ixhwele – Xhosa herbalist

jol – party, good time

karamat – tomb of a Muslim saint
Khoekhoen – pastoralist San
Khoe-San – collective term referring to the closely related San and Khoekhoen peoples
kloof – ravine
kloofing – canyoning
knobkerry – traditional African weapon; a stick with a round knob at the end, used as a club or missile
kommando – Boer militia unit
kopje – small hill
kraal – a hut village, often with an enclosure for livestock; also a Zulu fortified village
kroeg – bar
kwaito – form of township music; a mix of *mbaqanga*, jive, hip hop, house, ragga and other dance styles
kwela – township interpretation of American swing music

landdrost – an official acting as local administrator, tax collector and magistrate
lapa – a circular building with low walls and a thatched roof, used for cooking, partying etc
LCD – Lesotho Congress for Democracy
lekgotla – place of gathering
lekker – very good, enjoyable or tasty
lekolulo – a flutelike instrument played by herd boys
lesokoana – wooden stick or spoon, traditionally used for stirring mealie pap
liqhaga – 'bottles' that are so tightly woven that they are used for carrying water
lowveld – low-altitude area, having scrub vegetation

maskanda – Zulu form of guitar playing
matjieshuis – Afrikaans term for traditional woven Nama 'mat' huts
mbaqanga – form of township music; literally 'dumpling' in Zulu, combining church choirs, doo-wop and sax-jive
mdube – vocal style mixing European and African church choirs
mfeqane – see *difaqane*
minwane – dinosaur footprints
Mkhulumnchanti – Swazi deity

mokorotlo – conical hat worn by the Basotho
molianyeoe – see *mokorotlo*
moraba-raba – popular board game played with wooden beads and four rows of hollows; known elsewhere in Africa as *mancala* and *bao*
moroka-pula – rainmaker
mqashiyo – similar vocal style to mbaqanga
muti – traditional medicine

Ncwala – Swazi first-fruits ceremony
ndlovukazi – she-elephant, and traditional title of the Swazi royal mother
ngaca – (also *ngaka*) learned man
ngwenyama – lion, and traditional title of the Swazi king

PAC – Pan African Congress; political organisation of blacks founded in 1959 to work for majority rule and equal rights
peri peri – hot pepper
pinotage – a type of wine, a cross between Pinot noir and Hermitage or shiraz
pont – river ferry
Poqo – armed wing of the PAC

Rikki – an open, small van used as public transport in Cape Town
robot – traffic light
rondavel – a round hut with a conical roof

San – nomadic hunter-gatherers who were South Africa's earliest inhabitants
sangoma – traditional healer
sandveld – dry, sandy belt
setolo-tolo – stringed instrument played with the mouth by men
shebeen – drinking establishment in black township; once illegal, now merely unlicensed
slaghuis – butchery
slenter – fake diamond
snoek – firm-fleshed migratory fish that appears off the Cape in June and July; served smoked, salted or curried
sourveld – a type of grassland
swart gevaar – 'black threat'; term coined by Afrikaner nationalists during the 1920s

Telkom – government telecommunications company
thkolosi – small, maliciously playful beings
thomo – stringed instrument played by women
thornveld – a vegetation belt dominated by acacia thorn trees and related species
tokoloshe – malevolent spirit or short manlike animal, similar to the Sotho *thkolosi*
township – planned urban settlement of blacks and coloureds, legacy of the apartheid era
Trekboers – the first Dutch who trekked off into the interior of what is now largely Western Cape; later shortened to Boers
trokkie – truck stop
tronk – jail
tuk-tuk – motorised tricycle

uitlanders – 'foreigners'; originally the name given by Afrikaners to the immigrants who poured into the Transvaal after the discovery of gold
Umkhonto we Sizwe – the ANC's armed wing during the years of the struggle; now defunct

veld – elevated open grassland (pronounced 'felt')
velskoene – handmade leather shoes
VOC – Vereenigde Oost-Indische Compagnie (Dutch East India Company)
volk – collective Afrikaans term for Afrikaners
volkstaal – people's language
volkstaat – an independent, racially pure Boer state
Voortrekkers – original Afrikaner settlers of Orange Free State and Transvaal who migrated from the Cape Colony in the 1830s in search of greater independence

Behind the Scenes

SEND US YOUR FEEDBACK

We love to hear from travellers – your comments keep us on our toes and help make our books better. Our well-travelled team reads every word on what you loved or loathed about this book. Although we cannot reply individually to your submissions, we always guarantee that your feedback goes straight to the appropriate authors, in time for the next edition. Each person who sends us information is thanked in the next edition – the most useful submissions are rewarded with a selection of digital PDF chapters.

Visit **lonelyplanet.com/contact** to submit your updates and suggestions or to ask for help. Our award-winning website also features inspirational travel stories, news and discussions.

Note: We may edit, reproduce and incorporate your comments in Lonely Planet products such as guidebooks, websites and digital products, so let us know if you don't want your comments reproduced or your name acknowledged. For a copy of our privacy policy visit lonelyplanet.com/privacy.

OUR READERS

Many thanks to the travellers who used the last edition and wrote to us with helpful hints, useful advice and interesting anecdotes: Adam Asghar, Melanie Beschler, David Espinosa, Gary Millar, Tristan Mostert, Joe Neustadt, Geoffrey Oddie, Stuart Rison, Diane Trillwood, Bertaud Vincent, Michael Walti, Andrew Welch, Eloise Whitaker, Wilda Wong

AUTHOR THANKS

James Bainbridge

Thanks, *dankie, enkosi* and cheers to the fine people of the Eastern Cape and Lesotho, who cheerfully helped with my research queries and car problems. Offering assistance, chat, good humour and a cold beer from the Karoo to the Drakensberg, they are too innumerable to list – although Brad from Dijembe deserves a mention for riding a horse into a bar. From Wild Coast hangouts such as Buccs to mountaintop trading posts like Malealea, I was constantly reminded that South Africans are some of the warmest and friendliest folk worldwide.

Jean-Bernard Carillet

Heaps of thanks to the editorial and cartography teams at Lonely Planet for their great job. Coordinating author James Bainsbridge deserves a *grand merci* for his support, as does DE Matt for his understanding and support when I fell ill in South Africa. In Swaziland, special thanks to Darron. In South Africa, I'm grateful to Mbeki, Jo, Jeff, Nicolas and Gerald. In Pretoria, special thanks to my friend André and his family for their friendly welcome. And finally, once again a *gros bisou* to Christine and Eva.

Lucy Corne

Thanks to Matt and James for all the help and support. For tips and help on the road, a big enkosi to Terri-Lee Adendorff, Cathy Marston, Aliwiya Mac Minn, Laura Freeman, Steve Lunderstedt and Jurg Wagener, plus the staff at tourist offices, especially in Stellenbosch, Hermanus, Tulbagh, Montagu, Mossel Bay, Knysna, Oudtshoorn and Springbok. Massive thanks to Elisah for helping take care of Kai and of course to Shawn, for coping wonderfully as a single dad while I was on the road!

Alan Murphy

I would like to dedicate my work on this book to my late father, Alan Edward Murphy. There were so many people who helped with research on this update, a huge thanks to all I met on the road. A special thanks goes to Smitzy, travelling companion extraordinaire. Lastly, thanks to my wife Alison, who is my strength and my home.

Matt Phillips

A huge thanks to my lovely travel companion (and birdwatcher extraordinaire) Kat, who joined me on the second leg of my journey, as well to my family in the UK and back in Canada. Thanks to David Carroll and Nóirín Hegarty for giving me the chance head back to South Africa, and for all the animals that left me starstruck while there.

Simon Richmond

Many thanks to all the people who made my time in Cape Town such a pleasure and continuing education, including: fellow author Lucy and Shawn, Brent Meersman, Iain Harris, Lee Harris, Toni Shina, Nicole Biondi, Alison Foat, Sally Grierson, Patrick Craig, Cathy Marston, Tony Elvin, Rashiq Fataar, Zayd Minty, Daniel Sullivan, Sheryl Ozinsky, Bulelwa Makalima-Ngewana, Juma Mkwela, Gamidah Jacobs, Cindy Taylor, Iain Manley, Marco Morgan and Caroline Jordan.

ACKNOWLEDGMENTS

Climate map data adapted from Peel MC, Finlayson BL & McMahon TA (2007) 'Updated World Map of the Köppen-Geiger Climate Classification', *Hydrology and Earth System Sciences*, 11, 163344.

Cover photograph: Lion and lioness, Timbavati Private Game Reserve, Kruger National Park, Thomas Retterath / Getty Images ©.

THIS BOOK

This 10th edition of Lonely Planet's *South Africa, Lesotho & Swaziland* guidebook was researched and written by James Bainbridge, Jean-Bernard Carillet, Lucy Corne, Alan Murphy, Matt Phillips and Simon Richmond. The previous edition was written by James Bainbridge, Kate Armstrong, Lucy Corne, Michael Grosberg, Alan Murphy, Helen Ranger, Simon Richmond and Tom Spurling. This guidebook was produced by the following:

Destination Editor Matt Phillips

Product Editors Elizabeth Jones, Luna Soo, Amanda Williamson

Senior Cartographer Corey Hutchison

Book Designer Virginia Moreno

Assisting Editors Sarah Bailey, Imogen Bannister, Katie O'Connell, Kirsten Rawlings, Kathryn Rowan

Assisting Cartographer Diana von Holdt

Cover Researcher Campbell McKenzie

Thanks to Sasha Baskett, Brendan Dempsey, Ryan Evans, Victoria Harrison, Kate James, Kate Mathews, Claire Naylor, Karyn Noble, Martine Power, Wibowo Rusli, Diana Saengkham, Tony Wheeler, Tracy Whitmey

Index

Map Pages **000**
Photo Pages **000**

Map Pages **000**
Photo Pages **000**

Map Pages **000**
Photo Pages **000**

Map Pages **000**
Photo Pages **000**

Map Pages **000**
Photo Pages **000**

X

Z

Map Legend

Sights
- Beach
- Bird Sanctuary
- Buddhist
- Castle/Palace
- Christian
- Confucian
- Hindu
- Islamic
- Jain
- Jewish
- Monument
- Museum/Gallery/Historic Building
- Ruin
- Shinto
- Sikh
- Taoist
- Winery/Vineyard
- Zoo/Wildlife Sanctuary
- Other Sight

Activities, Courses & Tours
- Bodysurfing
- Diving
- Canoeing/Kayaking
- Course/Tour
- Sento Hot Baths/Onsen
- Skiing
- Snorkelling
- Surfing
- Swimming/Pool
- Walking
- Windsurfing
- Other Activity

Sleeping
- Sleeping
- Camping

Eating
- Eating

Drinking & Nightlife
- Drinking & Nightlife
- Cafe

Entertainment
- Entertainment

Shopping
- Shopping

Information
- Bank
- Embassy/Consulate
- Hospital/Medical
- Internet
- Police
- Post Office
- Telephone
- Toilet
- Tourist Information
- Other Information

Geographic
- Beach
- Gate
- Hut/Shelter
- Lighthouse
- Lookout
- Mountain/Volcano
- Oasis
- Park
- Pass
- Picnic Area
- Waterfall

Population
- Capital (National)
- Capital (State/Province)
- City/Large Town
- Town/Village

Transport
- Airport
- Border crossing
- Bus
- Cable car/Funicular
- Cycling
- Ferry
- Metro station
- Monorail
- Parking
- Petrol station
- Subway station
- Taxi
- Train station/Railway
- Tram
- Underground station
- Other Transport

Note: Not all symbols displayed above appear on the maps in this book

Routes
- Tollway
- Freeway
- Primary
- Secondary
- Tertiary
- Lane
- Unsealed road
- Road under construction
- Plaza/Mall
- Steps
- Tunnel
- Pedestrian overpass
- Walking Tour
- Walking Tour detour
- Path/Walking Trail

Boundaries
- International
- State/Province
- Disputed
- Regional/Suburb
- Marine Park
- Cliff
- Wall

Hydrography
- River, Creek
- Intermittent River
- Canal
- Water
- Dry/Salt/Intermittent Lake
- Reef

Areas
- Airport/Runway
- Beach/Desert
- Cemetery (Christian)
- Cemetery (Other)
- Glacier
- Mudflat
- Park/Forest
- Sight (Building)
- Sportsground
- Swamp/Mangrove

Alan Murphy

Kwazulu-Natal, Free State, Mpumalanga, Limpopo, North West Province, History, Environment, Wildlife & Habitat Alan has travelled extensively across Southern Africa, and has been coming to South Africa for Lonely Planet for the past 15 years. From the first time he bounced around in the rear of a bakkie on the way from Jo'burg airport to the current day, he simply loves to travel in this country. Wildlife is a passion and he was lucky enough to be taught the nuances of wildlife-watching by expert Algy Vaisutis. Alan also passionately believes in travellers giving back to local communitites that they spend time in.

Matt Phillips

Kruger National Park Matt first visited South Africa in 2001 as part of a year-long solo overland journey to Morocco. It was a trip that would change his life – soon his rock hammer and geological career were replaced by a laptop and a job writing for Lonely Planet. He's subsequently written about 26 African nations for Lonely Planet and various other publications, including *Travel Africa*, the magazine he was editor of for seven years. Now back at Lonely Planet as Destination Editor in charge of sub-Saharan Africa, he jumped at the opportunity to explore a place he truly loves, Kruger National Park.

Simon Richmond

Cape Town Simon has been hooked on Cape Town since first visiting in 2001 to research Lonely Planet's *South Africa, Lesotho & Swaziland* guide and the *Cape Town* guide. He's returned for every edition since, exploring practically every corner of the Cape and surrounding area, taking full advantage of a travel writer's license to meet a cast of inspirational locals and indulge in the fruits of the land – not least of which are its delicious wines! An award-winning journalist and photographer, Simon has written scores of titles for Lonely Planet and other publishers, as well as contributing features to many magazines and newspapers around the world. Follow him on Twitter, Instagram and at www.simonrichmond.com.

OUR STORY

A beat-up old car, a few dollars in the pocket and a sense of adventure. In 1972 that's all Tony and Maureen Wheeler needed for the trip of a lifetime – across Europe and Asia overland to Australia. It took several months, and at the end – broke but inspired – they sat at their kitchen table writing and stapling together their first travel guide, *Across Asia on the Cheap*. Within a week they'd sold 1500 copies. Lonely Planet was born.

Today, Lonely Planet has offices in Franklin, London, Melbourne, Oakland, Beijing and Delhi, with more than 600 staff and writers. We share Tony's belief that 'a great guidebook should do three things: inform, educate and amuse'.

OUR WRITERS

James Bainbridge

Coordinating Author, Plan section, Eastern Cape, Lesotho, South Africa, Lesotho & Swaziland Today, Music, People & Culture, Survival Guide James is a British travel writer and tour guide based among the Western Cape's mountains and vineyards, where he lives in a rustic little town with his wife and son. He regularly explores South Africa on family jaunts and media assignments; his writing appears in publications including the UK *Guardian*, *Condé Nast Traveller*, *BBC Travel*, *Safari Bookings* and *AFK Travel*. Coordinating this book for the third time, he is never happier than when hiking, photographing and wine tasting in South Africa's beautiful landscapes and charming towns. He has been contributing to Lonely Planet guides and coffee-table books for a decade, including several editions of *Turkey* and *Morocco*. You can read James's articles on Southern Africa at james bainbridge.net.

Read more about James at:
auth.lonelyplanet.com/profiles/james_bains

Jean-Bernard Carillet

Johannesburg & Gauteng, Swaziland A Paris-based journalist and photographer, Jean-Bernard has travelled the breadth and length of Africa for more two decades. He first visited Swaziland, Jo'burg and Pretoria in the early 1990s. Highlights researching for this edition included coming face to face with rhinos and lions in Swaziland, exploring the up-and-coming neighbourhoods of Jozi (now one of his favourite cities) and searching for the best-value B&Bs in Pretoria. Jean-Bernard's wanderlust has taken him to six continents, inspiring numerous articles and some 50 guidebooks.

Lucy Corne

Western Cape, Northern Cape, Food & Drink Lucy fell in love with South Africa in 2002 and eventually moved to Cape Town in 2010. She is constantly exploring the Western Cape but was thrilled to travel extensively again in the Northern Cape. Highlights of this trip included not getting eaten by a lion when changing a wheel in the Karoo National Park, seeing Saturn through a Sutherland telescope and getting sandblasted atop a dune on her first trip to the Witsand Nature Reserve. Lucy also blogs about the South African beer scene at www.brewmistress.co.za.

Read more about Lucy at:
http://www.lonelyplanet.com/members/lucycorne

OVER PAGE MORE WRITERS

Published by Lonely Planet Publications Pty Ltd
ABN 36 005 607 983
10th edition – November 2015
ISBN 978 1 74321 010 9

10 9 8 7 6 5 4 3 2 1
Printed in China